THE
GLADSTONE
DIARIES

Gladstone photographed by Eveleen Myers, 25 April 1890

THE
GLADSTONE
DIARIES

WITH
CABINET MINUTES
AND
PRIME-MINISTERIAL
CORRESPONDENCE

VOLUME XII
1887–1891

Edited by

H. C. G. MATTHEW

CLARENDON PRESS · OXFORD
1994

Oxford University Press, Walton Street, Oxford OX2 6DP

Oxford New York Toronto
Delhi Bombay Calcutta Madras Karachi
Kuala Lumpur Singapore Hong Kong Tokyo
Nairobi Dar es Salaam Cape Town
Melbourne Auckland Madrid
· and associated companies in
Berlin Ibadan

Oxford is a trade mark of Oxford University Press

Published in the United States
by Oxford University Press Inc. New York

British Library Cataloguing in Publication Data
Data available
ISBN 0-19-820463-9

Library of Congress Cataloging in Publication Data
Data applied for

1 3 5 7 9 10 8 6 4 2

Set by Joshua Associates Limited, Oxford
Printed in Great Britain
on acid-free paper by
Biddles Ltd., Guildford and King's Lynn

PREFACE

Volumes XII and XIII (together with the index, Volume XIV) bring to a close this edition of Gladstone's diaries. In addition to the daily diary text, Volumes XII and XIII include, as with the other volumes covering the years from 1868 onwards, all Gladstone's cabinet minutes, many of his memoranda, and a generous selection of his letters written while Prime Minister (over 500 letters for 1892–4).

Her Majesty the Queen is gratefully to be thanked for permission to include material from the Royal Archives, as is the Archbishop of Canterbury—owner of the diaries—for permission to publish them. Sir William Gladstone has given permission to publish material written by his great-grandfather and preserved in the British Library, St. Deiniol's Library at Hawarden, and in many other collections. He has been a generous and helpful friend to this edition. The Gladstone family have followed their illustrious ancestor in setting an excellent example in their scrupulous and historical attitude to the Gladstone papers. The editor is also very grateful to the Earl of Rosebery, the late Lord Harcourt, and Mr. A. F. Thomson for permission to quote from papers in their possession.

The following have generously given permission for their illustrations to be used in these volumes: Sir William Gladstone, the Governing Body of Newnham College, Cambridge, Clwyd Record Office, the Trustees of the National Portrait Gallery, the Trustees of the Scottish National Portrait Gallery, and the Curators of the Bodleian Library. Illustrations not attributed to an owner in the lists of illustrations are the property of the editor.

The editor continues to be much indebted to the *ad hoc* committee which superintends the publication of the edition. Lord Blake has been its chairman since I was appointed editor in 1972; other members of the committee presently are Lord Bullock, Dr. Richard Palmer, Mr. William Thomas, Mr. A. F. Thompson, Dr. Jonathan Wright, with Dr. Ivon Asquith of the Oxford University Press as its secretary, and Dr. Fram Dinshaw of St. Catherine's College (the edition's academic sponsor) as its treasurer. Like Lord Blake, Lord Bullock and Mr. A. F. Thompson have been members of the committee throughout my editorship. No editor could wish for a better committee to which to be responsible.

The research for these volumes has been financed by the Archbishop of Canterbury and the Gladstone Memorial Trust, and especially by the Rhodes Trust which has carried the chief burden of the research costs since the mid-1970s. The Rhodes Trust has been both generous and non-bureaucratic. It has required the edition to be edited and it has not slowed that process by requesting elaborate documentation. In today's world that is an unusual and very welcome abstinence.

Equally important in the progress of the edition to its conclusion has been Gladstone's own College of Christ Church, Oxford. Since 1970, it has provided rooms for the project, use of its magnificent library, and a Lectureship in

Gladstone Studies for the editor. Just as valuable has been my membership of the rare academic community which is the University of Oxford. Editing Gladstone's diaries has been for me really a re-education—classical, linguistic and theological as much as historical—and my two Colleges of Christ Church and, more recently, St. Hugh's, have provided the context for much of it. My time on the Governing Body of Christ Church taught me better than any book to understand the working of nineteenth-century government as practised by Gladstone and his circle. Of that community, past and present, I would especially mention Dr. Ross McKibbin, Dr. Boyd Hilton, Dr. John Robertson, Professor Peter Parsons, Mr. A. F. Thompson, Mr. Charles Stuart, Dr. José Harris, Dr. Mark Curthoys, Mr. Peter Ghosh, Dr. Michael Freeden, Dr. Colin Crouch, and Dr. John Walsh.

The day-to-day burden of the preparation of these last two volumes of text has continued to be borne by Mrs. Francis Phillips and Mrs. Jean Gilliland, the first responsible for bibliographical research and the second for transcription. The difficulties involved in both these tasks have greatly increased in Gladstone's final decade with the decline in his handwriting—by the 1890s often very hard to decipher. Despite this, and despite their reluctance to find fascinating work finally ending, Mrs. Phillips and Mrs. Gilliland maintained their flow of text at their usual expeditious rate. No editor could wish for more effective and less fussy helpers.

Many others have assisted in various ways with the preparation of the two final volumes of text. Mrs. Ria Audley-Miller and Mrs. Katherine Manville typed (and re-typed) the Introduction accurately and patiently. Mr. John Wing of Christ Church Library, Mr. Geoffrey Bill and Dr. Richard Palmer of Lambeth Palace Library, Mrs. Helen Rogers and her staff in 'Upper' and Mr. Colin Harris in '132' in the Bodleian Library have all been most helpful. Mr. Christopher Williams at the Clwyd Record Office has been an unflagging respondent with respect to any questions to do with the Gladstone family, Hawarden matters and the family papers which he knows so well. I am also grateful for the help given by Ms. Anne Gelling of Oxford University Press.

Professor H. W. Lawton's transcription of the diaries—the starting point of our preparations for publication—maintains its high accuracy despite the increasing problem of Gladstone's legibility. The Lawton transcript made manageable a task which would otherwise have seemed endless.

Gladstone's declining eyesight means that the MS both of the diary and of memoranda and letters contains many oddities. I have used '[*sic*]' only sparingly so as not to clog the text and I have not corrected Gladstone's slips. If the printed text consequently gives an impression of oddities, it is faithfully reflecting the character of the original.

Presenting the daily diary text, the cabinet minutes, the memoranda, the letters and the notes in an attractive form on the printed page has been a task demanding a very high quality of expertise and much common-sense. Mrs. Vera Keep has set all the years from 1868 to the end in 1896 and the edition has very greatly benefited from her skill.

Oxford University Press has over the years maintained its support for the publication of this edition, in times that have not always been easy. C. H.

Roberts, D. M. Davin, and Ivon Asquith have been successive Secretaries to the Gladstone Diaries Committee and have also provided an informal but highly effective link with the publishers as well as being an encouragement and a prop to the editor.

This Introduction, as with all the others I have written, has had the advantage of the comments of Lord Blake, Mr. A. F. Thompson, Dr. Ross McKibbin, Dr. Boyd Hilton, and Mrs. Sue Matthew, a team formidable in its variety of personality and historical knowledge and understanding. I have tried—in my early fifties—to do justice in this Introduction to Gladstone's *dénouement*, as—in his eighties—he 'wound down the coil of life'. Its shortcomings are mine.

Working on these last two volumes of text has certainly demonstrated the extraordinary energy and resilience of their author. Despite his failing physical powers—his poor eyesight, his deafness, his slightly failing memory, his problems with 'the lower department' (as he called it)—Gladstone maintained until mid-1894 his regular supply of copy for editing. The standard components of the diary entries—the lists of correspondents to be identified, the lists of books and articles read and written, the details of Church and Commons' attendance and of travel—are just as copious as when he was in his prime. But they are less legible.

Still, we have at last reached the end, and the final entry was worth reaching and is worth reading. The rock face has taken nearly a quarter of a century of my life to climb. There have been many stops and starts and some changes of route. Achieving the summit of a climb is always exhilarating even when the view is not altogether clear. Gladstone has been a happy companion on this always fascinating if sometimes bizarre journey through his century. The record of his life made in his journal is sometimes exasperating to one trained as a political historian. The addition of minutes, memoranda and letters has to an extent reshaped that record and I have tried to do that justly. There cannot be many historical figures of primarily political significance for whom respect and interest grow on extended acquaintance. But Gladstone is certainly among their number.

My family have been my closest living companions on this journey; they have sometimes also acted as bearers. We have talked so often of 'life after Gladstone' that its imminent arrival seems almost unreal. My children, David, Lucy and Oliver, and my wife, Sue, have succeeded both in being constantly encouraging and in reminding me that life is more than text, footnotes and Introductions. Happy the editor whose family enables editing and prevents obsession! It is worth repeating Goethe's lines:

> Grau, teurer Freund, ist alle Theorie,
> Und grün des Lebens goldner Baum

COLIN MATTHEW

Oxford
September 1993

CONTENTS

LIST OF ILLUSTRATIONS

Frontispiece

Gladstone photographed by Eveleen Myers, 25 April 1890
  Reproduced by courtesy of the Trustees of the National Portrait Gallery

between pp. 298 and 299

The Gladstones planting a tree at Newnham College, Cambridge,
  31 January 1887.
  Reproduced by courtesy of the Principal and Fellows of Newnham College, Cambridge

The Gladstones at Hawarden, *ca.* 1895
  Reproduced by courtesy of Clwyd Record Office

Gladstone photographed by Eveleen Myers, 25 April 1890
  Reproduced by courtesy of the Scottish National Portrait Gallery

Facsimile of 15–20 August 1888
  Lambeth 1452, f. 89

Facsimile of 3–4 July 1891 (death of W. H. Gladstone)
  Lambeth 1454, f. 23

Millais's portrait of W. E. and W. G. C. Gladstone
  Reproduced by courtesy of Sir William Gladstone

ABBREVIATED CHRISTIAN AND SURNAMES

in text of Volumes XII and XIII

(*prefixed or suffixed to a name in a footnote indicates an article in the
Dictionary of National Biography)

A.	Agnes Wickham, *daughter, or* the duke of Argyll
A., D. of	duke of Argyll
Agnes	Agnes Wickham, *daughter*
A.K.	A. Kinnaird
A.L.	Alfred *or* Arthur Lyttelton
A.M.	A. Morley
Arthur	A. Gordon
Arthur, Lord	Clinton
B., Lord	Lord Beaconsfield
B., Mr.	A. J. Balfour *or* Mr. Barker, *solicitor*
B., Mrs.	Mrs. Bennett, *cousin*, or Mrs. Birks, *neighbour*
B.C., Mr.	Bertram Currie
C.	Catherine Gladstone, *née* Glynne, *wife*
C., Lord F.	Lord Frederick Cavendish
C., Lucy	Lady Frederick Cavendish, *née* Lucy Lyttelton
C., Mr.	Bertram Currie
C., Sir J.	Sir J. M. Carmichael, *secretary*
C.G.	Catherine Gladstone
C.N.G., Lady	Lady Charlotte Neville Grenville
D.	B. Disraeli *or* Sir C. W. Dilke
D., Lord	Lord Derby
D. of D.	Duke of Devonshire
Dossie	Dorothy Drew, *grand-daughter*
E.	Elizabeth Honoria Gladstone, *née* Bateson, *sister-in-law*
E.C.	Edward Cardwell *or* Elizabeth Collins *or* Emma Clifton
E.M.P., Lady	Lady Elizabeth M. Pringle
E.T.	Edward Stuart Talbot
E.W.	Edward C. Wickham, *son-in-law*
E.W.H.	E. W. Hamilton, *secretary*
F., Mr.	W. E. Forster
F.C., Lord	Lord Frederick Cavendish
F.E., Lord or Lady	Lord *or* Lady F. Egerton
Ff., Archd.	Archdeacon Ffoulkes

F.H.D.	Sir F. H. Doyle
F.L.	Frank Lawley *or* F. Leveson [Gower]
Frank	Frank Lawley
G.	George Lyttelton, *wife's brother-in-law, or* Lord Granville *or* Lord Richard Grosvenor
G., Mr.	J. A. Godley, *secretary*
Gertrude/Gertie	Gertrude Pennant, *née* Glynne, *or* Gertrude Gladstone, *née* Stuart
G.L.	George Lyttelton
G.L.G.	George Leveson-Gower, *secretary*
H.	(Bishop) W. K. Hamilton
H., Lord	Lord Hartington
H., Lady	Lady Herbert of Lea
H., Mr.	E. W. Hamilton, *secretary*
H., Mr. and Mrs.	Mr. and Mrs. Hampton, *the butler and his wife*
Harry	Henry Neville Gladstone, *son*
Helen	Helen Gladstone, *daughter*
Herbert	Herbert John Gladstone, *son*
H.J.G.	*the same*
H.N.G.	Henry Neville Gladstone, *son*
H.P., Sir	Sir Henry Ponsonby, *the Queen's secretary*
H.S.	Horace Seymour, *secretary*
Hs., the two	Harry and Herbert, *sons*
I., Mr.	Henry Irving
J.	John Neilson Gladstone, *brother, or* Johnnie Gladstone, *nephew*
J.L. & co.	Johnson, Longden & Co., *stockbrokers*
J.M., Lord	Lord John Manners
J.M.	John Morley
J.M.G.	James Milnes Gaskell, *or* John Murray Gladstone, *cousin*
J.M.G.(R.)	J. M. G. Robertson, *cousin*
Johnnie	John Gladstone, *nephew*
J.R.	J. M. G. Robertson, *cousin*
J.S.W.	James Stuart-Wortley
K.	A. Kinnaird *or* Lord Kimberley
Kate *or* Katie	Catherine Glynne, *wife's niece, or* Katherine Gladstone, *niece*
L.	Lyttelton *or, occasionally,* Marquis of Lorne
L., Lady	Lady Lonsdale
L., Lord	Lord Lansdowne
Lavinia	Lavinia Glynne, *née* Lyttelton, *wife's sister-in-law*

Lena	Helen Gladstone, *daughter*
L.L.	Lucy Lyttelton
Ln	Lord Lyttelton *or, occasionally*, W. H. Lyttelton
Louey	Louisa Gladstone, *niece*
Louisa	Louisa Gladstone, *née* Fellowes, *sister-in-law*
Lucy	Lady Frederick Cavendish
M.	Meriel Sarah Lyttelton, *wife's niece*
M., Dr.	Dr. Moffatt
M., Mr.	A. *or* J. Morley
Marj.	E. Marjoribanks, *chief whip*
Mary	Mary Gladstone, *daughter*
Mary Ellen	Mrs. Robertson Gladstone, *née* Jones, *sister-in-law*
May	Mary Lyttelton, *wife's niece*
Mazie *or* Mary	Mary Gladstone, *daughter, or* Mary Lyttelton, *wife's niece*
M.E.	Mrs. Robertson Gladstone, *sister-in-law*
Meriel	Meriel S. Lyttelton, *wife's niece*
M.G.	Mary Gladstone, *daughter*
Molly	Mary Glynne, *wife's niece*
N., D. of	duke of Newcastle
N.	N. G. Lyttelton, *wife's nephew, or* Sir S. H. Northcote
Neville *or* Nevy	*the same* (N. G. Lyttelton)
Nina	Helen Gladstone, *daughter*
Nora	Honora Glynne, *wife's niece*
P., Col.	Col. Ponsonby
P., Mr.	H. Primrose, *secretary*
R.	Robertson Gladstone, *brother*
R., Lord	Lord Ripon *or* Lord Richard Grosvenor, *chief whip, or* Lord Rosebery ·
R.G.	Robertson Gladstone, *brother*
Rn (G.)	*the same*
Robn	*the same*
Ronald	Ronald Leveson-Gower
R.P.	Robert Phillimore
R.W., Sir	Sir R. Welby
S.	Lord Spencer
S., Mr.	Horace Seymour, *secretary*
S. of A.	Lord Stanley of Alderley
S.E.G.	Stephen Gladstone, *son*
S.G.	*the same*
Stephy	*the same*
Sybilla	Sybella Lyttelton

T.	(Sir) Thomas Gladstone, *brother*
T., Mrs. *or* Th., Mrs.	Laura Thistlethwayte
T. & B.	Townshend & Barker, *solicitors*
T.G.	Sir Thomas Gladstone, *brother*
Tom	*the same*
V., Mr.	J. S. Vickers, *Hawarden agent*
W.	William Henry Gladstone, *son*
W., Lady	Lady Wolverton
W., Lord	Lord Wolverton
W.H., Sir	Sir William Harcourt
W.H.L.	William Lyttelton
William of Wickham	William Wickham, *grandson*
Willy	William Henry Gladstone, *son*
Winny	Lavinia Lyttelton, *wife's niece*
W.L.	William Lyttelton
W.W., Sir	Sir Watkin Williams Wynn
Xt	Christ

ABBREVIATED BOOK TITLES, MSS COLLECTIONS, ETC.

Used in Volumes XII and XIII

Acland	*Memoir and letters of. . . Sir Thomas Dyke Acland* (privately printed, 1902)
Acland MSS	Papers of Sir T. D. and Sir H. W. Acland in the Bodleian Library
Add MS(S)	*Additional Manuscript(s), British Library*
Africa and the Victorians	R. Robinson and J. A. Gallagher, with A. Denny, *Africa and the Victorians. The official mind of imperialism* (1961)
After thirty years	*After thirty years by the Rt. Hon. the Viscount Gladstone* (1928)
Argyll	Eighth Duke of Argyll, *Autobiography and memoirs*, 2v. (1906)
Armytage	W. H. G. Armytage, *A. J. Mundella* (1951)
Autobiographica	J. Brooke and M. Sorensen, eds., *The prime minister's papers: W. E. Gladstone*. I–IV (1971–81)
Bannerman	J. A. Spender, *The life of. . . Sir Henry Campbell-Bannerman, G.C.B.*, 2v. (n.d., [1923])
Bassett	A. Tilney Bassett, ed., *Gladstone to his wife* (1936)
Bassett, *Speeches*	A. Tilney Bassett, ed., *Gladstone's speeches: descriptive index and bibliography* (1916)
BFSP	*British and Foreign State Papers*
Blunt, *Secret History*	W. S. Blunt, *Secret history of the English occupation of Egypt* (1907)
Boase, *M. E. B.*	F. Boase, *Modern English Biography*, 6v. (1892–1921)
B.Q.R.	*British Quarterly Review*
Bradlaugh MSS	Papers of Charles Bradlaugh on film in the Bodleian Library
Bryce MSS	Papers of James Bryce in the Bodleian Library
Buxton, *Finance and Politics*	Sydney Buxton, *Finance and politics: an historical study, 1783–1885*, 2v. (1888)
CAB	Prime Minister's letters to the Queen, on film in the Bodleian Library
Cambridge University Library	Papers of Sir J. D. Acton, first Baron Acton, in the Cambridge University Library
Carnegie	B. J. Hendrick, *The life of Andrew Carnegie*, 2v. (1932)
Cecil, *Salisbury*	Lady Gwendolen Cecil, *Life of Robert Marquis of Salisbury*, 4v. (1921–32)
Chadwick, *Acton and Gladstone*	[W.] Owen Chadwick, *Acton and Gladstone* (1976)

Chamberlain MSS	Papers of Joseph Chamberlain in Birmingham University Library
Chamberlain, *Political memoir*	*A political memoir 1880–92*, edited by C. H. D. Howard (1953)
Checkland	S. G. Checkland, *The Gladstones: a family biography, 1764–1851* (1971)
Childers	S. Childers, *The life and correspondence of Hugh C. E. Childers*, 2v. (1901)
Conzemius	*Ignaz von Döllinger: Lord Acton. Briefwechsel 1850–1890*, edited by Victor Conzemius, 3v. (1963–71)
C.R	*Contemporary Review*
Crewe, *Rosebery*	Marquess of Crewe, *Lord Rosebery*, 2v. (1931)
Cromer	*Modern Egypt by the Earl of Cromer*, 2v. (1908)
Cromer, *Abbas II*	*Abbas II by the Earl of Cromer* (1915)
Dalmeny MSS	Papers and diary of 5th Earl of Rosebery in Dalmeny House
Derby MSS	Papers of the 15th Earl of Derby in the Liverpool Record Office
Derby	J. Vincent, ed., *The later Derby diaries* (1981)
DLFC	J. Bailey, ed., *Diary of Lady Frederick Cavendish*, 2v. (1927)
D.N.	*Daily News*
D.N.B.	*Dictionary of National Biography*, 71v. (1885–1957)
D.T.	*Daily Telegraph*
E.H.D.	Unpublished diary of E. W. Hamilton in the British Library
E.H.R.	*English Historical Review* (from 1886)
Elliot	A. R. D. Elliot, *Life of G. J. Goschen*, 2v. (1911)
E.R.	*Edinburgh Review*
Fitzmaurice	Lord E. Fitzmaurice, *Life of Earl Granville*, 2v. (1905)
F.J.	*Freeman's Journal*
F.O.C.P.	Foreign Office Confidential Prints, P.R.O.
F.R.	*Fortnightly Review*
Gardiner	A. G. Gardiner, *Life of Sir William Harcourt*, 2v. (1923)
Garvin	J. L. Garvin, *Life of Joseph Chamberlain*, 4v. (1932–1951)
Gleanings	W. E. Gladstone, *Gleanings of past years*, 7v. (1879)
Guedalla, *Q*	P. Guedalla, ed., *The Queen and Mr Gladstone*, 2v. (1933)
Gwynn	S. L. Gwynn and G. M. Tuckwell, *Life of Sir Charles Dilke, Bart.*, 2v. (1917)
H	*Hansard's Parliamentary Debates*, third series (1830–91)
4H	Ibid., fourth series, from 1892
H.V.B.	Hawarden Visitors' Book
Hammond	J. L. Hammond, *Gladstone and the Irish Nation* (1938)

Hawn P	Hawarden Papers (deposited in St Deiniol's Library, Hawarden)
Holland	B. Holland, *Life of Spencer Compton, eighth Duke of Devonshire*, 2v. (1911)
Hutton and Cohen, *Speeches*	*The Speeches and Public Addresses of the Right Hon. W. E. Gladstone M.P.*, edited by A. W. Hutton and H. J. Cohen (vol. X, 1892, vol. XI, 1894)
I.H.S.	*Irish Historical Studies*
Kimberley MSS	Papers and diaries of 1st Earl of Kimberley in the Bodleian Library
Knaplund, *Imperial Policy*	P. Knaplund, *Gladstone and Britain's imperial policy* (1927)
Later gleanings	W. E. Gladstone, *Later Gleanings. A new series of Gleanings of Past Years* (2nd ed. 1898)
Lathbury	D. C. Lathbury, *Correspondence on church and religion of W. E. Gladstone*, 2v. (1910)
LQV	A. C. Benson, Viscount Esher, and G. E. Buckle, *Letters of Queen Victoria*, 9v. (1907–32) in three series: 1st series: 1837–61; 2nd series 1862–85; 3rd series 1886–1901
Loughlin	J. Loughlin, *Gladstone, Home Rule and the Ulster Question 1882–93* (1986)
Lucy, *Salisbury Parliament*	H. W. Lucy, *A diary of the Salisbury Parliaments, 1886–1892* (1892)
Lyall, *Dufferin*	Sir A. Lyall, *The Life of the Marquis of Dufferin and Ava*, 2v. (1905)
Lyons, *Parnell*	F. S. L. Lyons, *Charles Stewart Parnell* (1977)
Lyons, *Fall of Parnell*	F. S. L. Lyons, *The Fall of Parnell 1890–91* (1960)
MacColl	G. W. E. Russell, *Malcolm MacColl* (1914)
Magnus	Sir Philip Magnus, *Gladstone* (1954)
Magnus, *Edward VII*	Ibid., *King Edward the Seventh* (1964)
Mallet, *Northbrook*	B. Mallet, *Thomas George Earl of Northbrook* (1908)
Mary Gladstone	*Mary Gladstone (Mrs. Drew). Her diaries and letters*, ed. Lucy Masterman (1930)
Masterman	C. F. G. Masterman, ed. and abridged J. Morley, *Life of Gladstone* (1927)
Matthew, *Gladstone*	H. C. G. Matthew, *Gladstone* * *1809–1874* (1986)
Matthew, 'Vaticanism'	H. C. G. Matthew, 'Gladstone, Vaticanism and the Question of the East' in D. Baker, ed., *Studies in Church History*, xv (1978)
Morgan, *Wales in British Politics*	K. O. Morgan, *Wales in British Politics 1868–1922* (1963)
Morley	J. Morley, *Life of William Ewart Gladstone*, 3v. (1903)

Morley's diary and MSS	Diary and Papers of John Morley in Wadham College, Oxford
Morley, *Recollections*	John Viscount Morley, *Recollections*, 2v. (1917)
Morrell	W. P. Morrell, *Britain in the Pacific Islands* (1960)
Mundella MSS	Papers of A. J. Mundella in Sheffield University Library
N.A.R.	*North American Review*
National Library of Wales	Miscellaneous letters in the National Library of Wales
Newman	*The Letters and Diaries of John Henry Newman*, edited by C. S. Dessain and T. Gornall (1961 ff.)
N.L.S.	National Library of Scotland
N.C.	*Nineteenth Century*
O'Brien, *Parnell*	R. Barry O'Brien, *The Life of Charles Stewart Parnell, 1846–1891*, 2v. (1898)
Ornsby	R. Ornsby, *Memoirs of J. R. Hope-Scott*, 2v. (1884)
O'Shea, *Parnell*	Katharine O'Shea, *Charles Stewart Parnell. His love story and political life*, 2v. (1914)
Perham, *Lugard*	Margery Perham, *Lugard. The years of adventure. 1858–1898* (1956)
P.M.G.	*Pall Mall Gazette*
Ponsonby	A. Ponsonby, *Henry Ponsonby* (1943)
PP	*Parliamentary Papers*
Purcell	E. S. Purcell, *Life of Cardinal Manning*, 2v. (1962)
Q.R.	*Quarterly Review*
R.A.	Royal Archives, Windsor Castle
Redlich	J. Redlich, *The procedure of the House of Commons*, 3v. (1908)
Reid, *F*	(Sir) T. Wemyss Reid, *Life of ... William Edward Forster*, 2v. (1888)
Reid, *G*	Sir T. Wemyss Reid, ed., *Life of W. E. Gladstone* (1899)
Rendel	*The Personal Papers of Lord Rendel* (1931)
Richmond Papers, The	A. M. W. Stirling, *The Richmond Papers from the correspondence and manuscripts of George Richmond, R.A., and his son Sir William Richmond, R.A., K.C.B.* (1926)
Rosebery MSS	Papers of 5th Earl of Rosebery, in the National Library of Scotland
Rosebery's diary	Diary of 5th Earl of Rosebery, in Dalmeny House
Selborne MSS	Papers of 1st Earl of Selborne in Lambeth Palace Library
Selborne, II	Earl of Selborne, *Memorials Personal and Political 1865–1895*, 2v. (1898)

Speeches on the Irish question	W. E. Gladstone, *Speeches on the Irish question in 1886* (1886)
Spencer	*The Red Earl. The papers of the fifth Earl Spencer 1835– 1910*, ed. P. Gordon, 2v. (1981–6)
Special aspects	*W. E. Gladstone, Special aspects of the Irish question. A series of reflections in and since 1886* (1892)
Stead, *M.P. for Russia*	W. T. Stead, *The 'M.P. for Russia'. Reminiscences and Correspondence of . . . Olga Novikoff*, 2v. (1909)
T.A.P.S.	*Transactions of the American Philosophical Society*
Tennyson	*Alfred Lord Tennyson. A memoir, by his son*, 2v. (1897)
Thomas, *Gladstone of Hawarden*	I. Thomas, *Gladstone of Hawarden* (1936)
T.T.	*The Times*
Thorold	A. L. Thorold, *The life of Henry Labouchere* (1913)
Tollemache, *Talks*	L. A. Tollemache, *Talks with Mr. Gladstone* (3rd ed. 1903)
Walling, *Diaries of Bright*	R. A. J. Walling, *The Diaries of John Bright* (1930)
Ward, *Victorian Oxford*	W. R. Ward, *Victorian Oxford* (1965)
West, *P.D.*	H. G. Hutchinson, ed., *Private Diaries of Sir Algernon West* (1922)
West, *Recollections*	Sir Algernon West, *Recollections 1832 to 1886*, 2v. (1899)
Wolf, *Ripon*	L. Wolf, *Life of the first Marquess of Ripon*, 2v. (1921)
W.R.	*Westminster Review*

OTHER ABBREVIATIONS

ab	about
abp.	archbishop
acct.	account
aft(n).	afternoon
agst. or agt	against
amdt.	amendment
appt.	appointment
apptd.	appointed
arr.	arrived
aut.	autograph
b.	book *or* born *or* brother
bart.	baronet
Bd.	board of trade
B.I.R.	board of inland revenue
Bkfst.	breakfast
B.M.	British Museum
B.N.A.	British North America
B. of T.	board of trade
bp.	bishop
B.P.	Book Post *or* Book Parcel
br.	brother
B.S.	Bedford *or* Berkeley Square
B.T.	board of trade
ca.	*circa*
C.G.	Carlton Gardens
Ch.	church *or* Chester
Ch. of Exchr.	Chancellor of the Exchequer
C.H.T.	Carlton House Terrace
C.L.	Civil List
C.N.	Central News
C.O.	colonial office
commee.	committee
commn.	commission
cons.	conservative
cr.	created
ctd.	continued
cttee.	committee
cum	with
d.	died
da.	daughter

deb.	debate
deptn. or dpn.	deputation
dft.	draft
div.	division
do.	ditto
Dowr.	Dowager
Dr.	doctor *or* dowager
E.	Earl
eccl.	ecclesiastical
ed.	edited *or* edition *or* editor *or* educational
E.I.	East Indies *or* East Indian
Ep.	epistle
evg.	evening
f.	father *or* folio
fa.	father
ff.	folios *or* following
fiveocloquai	five o'clock tea
F.O.	foreign office
1°R	first reading
G. & co.	Gladstone and company
gd.	granddaughter
gf.	grandfather
G.I. Bill	Government of Ireland Bill
Gk.	Greek
gm.	grandmother
govt.	government
gs.	grandson
G.S.	Grosvenor Square (Mrs. Thistlethwayte, usually)
H.C.	holy communion
H. Hall	Hawarden Hall
Hn.	Hawarden
Ho.	house of commons
H.O.	home office
H. of C.	house of commons
H. of L.	house of lords
H.S.	holy scripture *or* Harley Street
I.	Ireland
Ibid.	*ibidem*, in the same place
I.O.	India office
K.	killed

l.	letter
Ld.	lord
lect.	lecture
L.G.B.	Local Government Board *or* Bill
lib.	liberal
L.L.	Lord Lieutenant
Ln.	London
Lord C.J.	Lord Chief Justice
Lpool	Liverpool
Ly.	lady
m.	married *or* mother *or, with figures*, mille (a thousand)
ma	*ma* ('but' in Italian)
Mad./Made	Madame
Maharajah, The	Duleep Singh
M.D.R.	Metropolitan and District Railway
mem.	memorandum
mg.	morning
m	a million
Nk.	Newark
N.S.	National Society
N.S.W.	New South Wales
nt.	night
n.y.n.	not yet numbered
N.Z.	New Zealand
No. 11	11 Carlton House Terrace
No. 15	15 Grosvenor Square (Mrs. Thistlethwayte)
No. 42 P.P.	42 Portland Place (Lytteltons)
No. 73 H.S.	73 Harley Street
O.G.	Ogilvy, Gillanders & Co.
O.R.	Olympic Religion
P.A.	Press Association
p., pp	page(s)
Par./Para.	paragraph
P.O.	post office
p.p.c.	*pour prendre congé* (to take leave)
pr. or priv.	private
pt.	part
re	concerning
rec(d).	receive(d)
Rector, The	Stephen Gladstone
resp.	respecting
Rev(d)	reverend

R.R.	railway
R.T.	Richmond Terrace
2°R	second reading
s.	son *or* series *or* sister
Sact.	sacrament
Sec. Euch.	Secreta Eucharistica
sd. or shd.	should
S.K.M.	South Kensington Museum
soc.	society
Sol. Gen.	solicitor-general
sp.	speech
S.P.G.	Society for the Propagation of the Gospel
succ.	succeeded
3°R	third reading
T.	Treasury
tel.	telegram
T.P.	Temple of Peace
tr.	translated or translation
Univ.	university
U.P.	United presbyterian
v.	verso *or* very *or* volume
V.C.	vice-chancellor
vol.	volume
vss.	verses
v.v.	*vice versa*
vy.	very
w.	wife
wd.	would
wh.	which
W.I.	West Indies
W.L.	Wine Licences
Xtn	Christian
yesty.	yesterday

Signs used by the diarist

X	rescue work done this day
+	prayer, usually when on a charitable visit *or* plus
ᛗ	million
ma	'but'
(B.P.)	Book Post or Package

Signs inserted into the text editorially

[R]	follows names of subjects of diarist's rescue work
⟨ ⟩	words written by diarist and then deleted

INTRODUCTION

On this great [Easter] day what are my special prayers? They are three.
1. For the speedy concession to Ireland of what she most justly desires.
2. That the concession may be so timed and shaped as to be entirely severed from all temptation to self-glorifying so far as I am concerned.
3. That thereafter the tie between me and the contentious life may at once be snapped. But now one prayer absorbs all others: Ireland, Ireland, Ireland.[1]

This has been a period of inner education, and disclosure of special wants: the spirit of faith: the spirit of prayer: the spirit of dependence: the spirit of manhood: the spirit of love. The weight on me is great and presses at many points: but how trifling when compared with the trials of great Christians.[2]

Eighty three birthdays! What responsibilities have old men as such for prolonged and multiplied opportunity. And what have I, as among old men. What openings, what cares, what blessings, and what sins.[3]

I

The seventh decade of Gladstone's public life was dominated, as had been most of the others, by Ireland. In the age of industrialism, the British had expected that class—whether the middle or the working class—would disrupt the political system. But it was the national question, not the class question, which the British political establishment failed to solve. In 1886, Gladstone had offered a bold answer, an answer which recognized national distinctiveness and at the same time pacified it within the Union. His answer was rejected by the Commons in 1886—a decision on the whole confirmed by the electorate later that year—and by the Lords in 1893. None the less, it was an answer so compelling that it was eventually adopted by the Unionists—too little, too late—in 1921, and it provided the framework within which all subsequent legislative attempts at modification of the constitution of the United Kingdom at the Parliamentary level have been made. Over a century later, and with six governmental Home Rule initiatives having failed (with the ironic exception of their implementation by the Unionists in Ulster), Gladstone's proposals of 1886 still hold the field as the means of constitutional reorganization of the United Kingdom. If there was to be constitutional change, it would be by some form of devolved Home Rule: Chamberlain's federal alternative has never, as yet, received serious consideration by a British Cabinet.

Gladstone sensed in 1886 that he had taken the first step down what was to

---

[1] 10 Apr. 87; references to the diary text are in this form.   [2] 9 Aug. 92.   [3] 29 Dec. 92.

be a long trail. He had linked the Liberal Party and the Home Rule party in Ireland in the boldest way. He had done so not as a crude political bargain, but as a recognition of a just demand fairly stated and as a conservative means of maintaining for its most important purposes the unity of the state.[1] Gladstone termed 'the measure Conservative in exactly the same sense as he would term the repeal of the Corn Laws conservative, through its promoting the union of classes and giving a just contentment to the people'.[2] Failure to so act would eventually endanger the state: 'There is but one end to that matter', he wrote after the defeat of the first attempt to give Ireland 'Home Rule'; 'if what we ask is refused, more will have to be given'.[3]

The failure of the plan of 1886 in the context of the disruption of the Liberal Party and an exceptional level of political vituperation encouraged in Gladstone and in some of his followers a Mosaic view of political life, with Gladstone leading a purged party through the wilderness. Biblical comparisons in the political language of the day—a sharp shift from the coolness of traditional classicism—reflected the intensity of political feeling, especially at the Westminster level. As the quotations at the start of this Introduction show, Gladstone was aware of the comparisons. Yet they also show his sense of balance and of obligation: his mention of the 'trials of great Christians' reflects the level of comparison commonly made at the time in Liberal circles, but he mentions it in order to present his role as, relatively speaking, 'trifling'. 'Self-glorifying' was to be avoided; but, of course, the mention of it acknowledged at least the danger and perhaps the fact.

Gladstone was 82 when he became Prime Minister for the fourth time on 15 August 1892. His age is, consequently, a dominating theme of these volumes, both for him and for others. It is significant in several different respects.

First, it gave him a totemic role in progressive politics. To see a man in his eighties successfully addressing full-scale speeches to large meetings without any mechanical means of amplification was to see what was clearly a remarkable phenomenon. These were often extraordinary occasions. The physical and mental power required from the orator seemed to emphasize the heroic individualism which was so central a feature of late-Victorian politics, and especially liberal politics. The leader's speech was both a rationalistic transfer of opinion and the focal moment of an emotional rally. In so being, it captured the essence of liberal political consciousness in an extended electorate, by being both rationalistic and popular. It had to contain content interesting to the readers of its report in the next day's newspapers and it had to move the audience actually present. This mode of political communication fitted Gladstone perfectly. His physical qualities, even in advanced age, enabled him to control the largest of audiences; the content of his speeches retained to the end the element of unpredictability which had made him throughout his long oratorical career so mesmeric a figure. After addressing the N.L.F. in Birmingham in 1888 he noted: 'To the great meeting at Bingley Hall, 18,000 to 20,000 persons. I believe all heard me. I was at once conscious of a great strain

---

[1] See above, x. cxff.   [2] Memorandum for the Queen, 28 Oct. 92.
[3] To Laura Thistlethwayte, 21 August 1886, Appendix in this volume, p. 516.

upon the chest: yet strength & voice were given me for a speech of $1\frac{3}{4}$ hours. . . .'[1]

Despite his age, Gladstone maintained the breadth of his appeal. He retained his curiosity and his enthusiasm, and the range of his speeches reflected this. He addressed vast meetings in—amongst numerous others—Swansea and Cardiff in 1887,[2] at the Eisteddfod in 1888,[3] in Plymouth in 1889,[4] in Midlothian and in Dundee in 1890,[5] on Clapham Common in 1892, in London, Glasgow and Midlothian in his last but demanding election campaign in 1892.[6] After a short tour of the West Country in 1889, he noted: '18 sp[eeches] in all'.[7] He led a great crowd up the slopes of Snowdon and spoke to them from what became known as 'Gladstone's Rock'.[8] He addressed the annual meetings of the National Liberal Federation in 1887 (Nottingham), 1888 (Birmingham), 1889 (Manchester), and 1891 (Newcastle),[9] large and important meetings, vital for the maintenance of party enthusiasm. He was the first party leader regularly to attend and address an annual conference.[10] He could turn his hand apparently to any topic, from an attractive little speech at the Port Sunlight gallery[11] to addressing a 'labourers' conference' in the Holborn Restaurant in London a few days later.[12]

Gladstone also remained able to lecture extensively and successfully to academic audiences, in French—'after doubting to the last moment'—to the Paris Society of Political Economy (one of several speeches during the celebrations of the centenary of the Revolution),[13] on Homeric subjects at Eton[14] and at the Oxford Union,[15] and in the Sheldonian Theatre in Oxford on medieval universities—the first Romanes Lecture and a major academic occasion.[16]

In the House of Commons, Gladstone was still in the 1890s a compelling figure, pushing the Government of Ireland Bill through its various stages over 82 days in the face of intense Unionist hostility: any slip or momentary absence of concentration would have been immediately and viciously exposed. Gladstone's energy held out to the end: the muddles over the Bill—as we shall see—were in its planning and drafting, not in its defence.

Gladstone was not only known through his words, but directly by his voice (or a rendering of it). He was the first European politician whose voice was heard across the English-speaking world, through the new medium of the phonograph. Colonel Gourand, Thomas Edison's European agent, made several phonographic recordings of Gladstone which were played at public meetings in Britain and America.[17] Gladstone's recording for Lord Carrington, Governor

---

[1] 7 Nov. 88. [2] 4, 7 June 87. [3] 4 Aug. 88.
[4] 14 June 89. [5] 27–9 Oct. 90. [6] 18 June–11 July 92.
[7] See 8–18 June 89. [8] 13 Sept. 92.
[9] 18 Oct. 87, 6 Nov. 88, 2 Dec. 89, 2 Oct. 91.
[10] He avoided the 1890 Conference, held in the midst of the Parnell divorce hearings.
[11] 28 Nov. 90. [12] 11 Dec. 90. [13] 7 Sept. 89.
[14] 14 Mar. 91. [15] 5 Feb. 90. [16] 24 Oct. 92.
[17] See 22 Nov. 88, 7 Mar. 90, 24 July 90. Gladstone had attended an early demonstration of the phonograph, see 18 Mar. 78. For an example of a public playing of the recording in the U.S.A., see Colonel Gouraud's letter in *Scottish Leader*, 5 April 1890, 6e: 'the golden words you spoke have been communicated in your matchless voice to delegates representing over 5000 associations . . .'. Recordings of his voice were played at fair-ground stalls, e.g. at Witney in Oxfordshire (a small town

General of New South Wales, was the first ever sent from England to Australia.[1]
What appears to be the original Edison recording is in the possession of the
B.B.C.[2] Gladstone made a note of the occasion:

> I dined with Mr. Knowles & afterwards witnessed the astonishing performance of Mr
> Eddison's [*sic*] phonograph, and by desire made a brief address to him which is to pass
> vocally across the Atlantic.[3]

Its powerful harmonics, strong vocal range and slight North Welsh accent
attest to its authenticity,[4] as does the confidence and vitality of the voice: the
hearer can readily imagine it filling the Manchester Free Trade Hall. As Gladstone had in the 1860s grasped so quickly the opportunities of the extra-
parliamentary speech nationally reported, so in the 1880s he quickly associated
himself with what was to be the political weapon of the future: the politician's
recorded voice. It awaited only broadcasting to make the full transition to the
modern age.[5]

Gladstone paralleled this persistence of oratorical energy with a remarkable
demonstration of literary productivity. In the years covered by these volumes,
he wrote six books, sixty-eight articles and book reviews—many of them
substantial—and edited a further volume of collected articles in *Later Gleanings*.[6]
In 1890 he was still able to earn £1915 8*s*. 7*d*. from articles and reviews.[7] An
attempt at his collected speeches was begun, edited by A. W. Hutton and H. J.
Cohen. Only two volumes were published: if Gladstone had been his own
editor, the series would doubtless have been completed![8] He finished his long-
planned edition of Bishop Butler, with a volume of commentary. Of his major

with a nonconformist tradition in a Tory county); at the 1893 fair, 'Mr. Gladstone's Speech' was
played in repertoire with 'The Charge of the Light Brigade' and 'Daddy wouldn't buy me a bow-
wow'; *Witney Gazette*, 16 September 1893.

[1] See 8 Mar. 90.

[2] B.B.C. Sound Archives. As the wax cylinders on which the voice was preserved could not be
duplicated, actors made copies by rendering the original voice as accurately as they could. The
B.B.C. recording certainly has an authentic quality.

[3] 22 Nov. 88. The B.B.C. recording's content is quite different from the *verbatim* report of another
recording (also dated 1888) in the Edison archives, printed in F. A. Jones, *Thomas Alva Edison. Sixty
years of an inventor's life* (1908), 161. As both versions address the absent Edison, they may have been
recorded at the same time. This is the more likely given Rowland Prothero's story, that the listeners
were so absorbed by Gladstone's voice that they failed to notice that space on the cylinder had
expired! This would account for the rather inconclusive end of the B.B.C. recording and the more
finished version in Jones's book. However, it is not clear to which recording session Prothero's
account refers; for it, see 24 July 90n.

[4] It is sometimes said that Gladstone retained a slight Liverpudlian accent. This is probably not
incompatible with the accent on the recording, though today that would be regarded as North
Welsh rather than Liverpudlian; the two cultures are of course closely intertwined. Gladstone
cemented his links with Liverpool by purchasing the advowson of the city for £7200 in 1889 (see 23,
31 Dec. 89); he thus appointed its clergymen.

[5] His is the earliest recording of a statesman that survives. The earliest surviving recordings of a
President are, surprisingly, those of Taft (1908) and Roosevelt (1912); earlier recordings were made
but were lost; see A. Koenigsberg, *Edison Cylinder Records, 1889–1912* (1969), xxiv.

[6] See below, Vol. XIII Appendix II.

[7] See 20 Mar. 91.

[8] Gladstone checked the list of speeches proposed for the volumes which were published (covering 1886–91); see 23–4 Oct. 91.

projects only his work on 'Olympian Religion' was left partially finished. His sole half-hearted effort was his autobiography, spasmodically started under pressure from friends and publishers and never gaining his full involvement.

In addition to this, he planned what he saw as his memorial, the future St. Deiniol's Library at Hawarden (briefly named 'Monad' (the first number, ultimate unity) but named 'St. Deiniol's'—a Welsh saint—in December 1889).[1] He drew up a detailed memorandum on its purposes,[2] and spent much energy surveying and pegging out various possible sites, moving books from the Castle into a temporary iron building, spending hours humping the books out of boxes and onto shelves.[3] When at Hawarden, work in the library at St. Deiniol's took the place of treefelling—or 'axe-work' as he described it with characteristic precision when he ceased to be able to topple a tree—which from December 1891 he could no longer physically undertake.[4]

Even in his eighties, Gladstone retained undiminished the restless drive for self-improvement, the *leit motif* of these diaries and of the epoch they chronicled. The struggle for self-knowledge, the urge not only to understand but to act on that understanding, the need to justify through a demonstration of time well-spent, and the sense that he could do better, drove Gladstone forward. A true representative of his age, he sought repose through achievement but knew that he had not found it: 'May God at the length give me a true self-knowledge. I have it not yet.'[5]

All this represented the reality, not merely the appearance, of an exceptionally energetic octogenarian,[6] able to maintain his position as the dominant political personality of his time. Gladstone himself sensed the extent to which work towards an achievable end sustained his constitution: the Irish crusade, and confidence in its accomplishment, retarded the natural process of bodily decline. He noted on his eightieth birthday:

My physical conservation is indeed noteworthy. In the senses of sight and hearing and in power of locomotion there is decline, and memory is not quite consistent. But the trunk of the body is in all its ordinary vital operations, as far as I can see, what it was ten years back: it seems to be sustained and upheld for the accomplishment of a work.[7]

This vigour, carefully guarded, underpinned the continued projection of Gladstone's public personality and the constant promotion of his Irish policy. Public prominence, maintained by speeches and periodical articles was, as ever, vital to his success.

[1] 31 Oct. 89, 5 Dec. 89. It is not quite clear in which precise sense Gladstone used the term 'Monad'; in Pythagoras it means an arithmetical unit; *O.E.D.* gives several definitions, including its use as a definition of the Supreme Being, quoting Newman's *Grammar of Assent*, i, iv. 49 (which Gladstone had read and annotated): 'But of the Supreme Being it is safer to use the word 'monad' than unit.'

[2] Printed 12 Nov. 88.

[3] See 15 Sept. 87, 31 May 88. The first books were transferred on 21 Dec. 89 and from then sorting books there was a constant occupation. The Trust Deed was planned from 12 Nov. 88; see also 29 Sept. 90, 11 Jan. 91, 8 Apr. 93, 2 Nov. 95, 29 Dec. 96.

[4] For the last recorded tree-felling, see 2 Dec. 91.   [5] 29 Dec. 92.

[6] He was fit enough, when knocked down by a cab at the age of 79, to pursue it, though badly shaken, to apprehend the driver, and to stay with him until the arrival of the police, without revealing his identity; 24 May 89.   [7] 29 Dec. 89

The press, predominantly Liberal before 1885, swung to Unionism more decisively than the electorate. From 1886 and for at least a century, the press was to be Unionist and hostile to the parties of progress. For the Liberals, this was the reversal of a quarter-century of Liberal press-predominance and with their rationalist approach to politics this was a clear disadvantage. Gladstone's position in politics and his capacity to mesmerise Unionists even while they hated him was a powerful countervailing force to the Liberals' loss of press control. His speeches were reported *verbatim* in the Unionist press—the only Liberal leader thus consistently reported in these years—and he therefore constituted in effect a regular free page of advertisement for liberalism in the Unionist press.[1] His centrality to the Liberal campaign thus intensified in his later years, and his vigour became the focus of constant interest on both sides. A fall, a cold, even his insomnia, received detailed coverage in the newspapers.

This ability to convey a genuine sense of vigour was sustained on less public occasions also. Charles Oman, a strong tory, recalled of Gladstone's visit to All Souls in 1890, when he spent eight days in the College:

> I was beginning to regard him as past mischief.... Rather a pathetic picture of fallen greatness was the way in which I summed him up.... I was far from suspecting, till I had seen him close, what vigour there still was in the old man.[2]

Gladstone charmed the Fellows with his vigorous conversation, skilfully avoiding recent political controversy. What Oman and C. R. L. Fletcher—both of whom left memoirs of the visit—failed to realize was that they were seeing only one side of Gladstone's Oxford visit. In addition to cultivating the Fellows of All Souls with classical and literary high-table chat and giving them the impression of his single-minded attention, he was also conducting a complex series of political negotiations with the Oxford Liberals, who wanted a more obvious political presence in the city from their leader. On this occasion, Gladstone worked to exclude politics as much as possible from his visit;[3] he could do so because he still had the capacity to work several different interests simultaneously.

The vigorous literary *persona* which he presented in All Souls reflected an important aspect of his character, especially in his last years. Gladstone was the oratorical equivalent of the Victorian literary sage. Victorian sages were defined as being writers who talked; Gladstone was a talker who wrote. His conversation was recorded by diarists and memorialists, who were not necessarily political admirers. His age linked the generation of the 1890s to an epoch by now almost mythical: the epoch of the 1830s, a golden age of whiggery; of the start of Tractarianism; of the pre-railway, localized political system with its Eatanswill hustings; of Scott, Wordsworth and Coleridge. Yet the Prime

---

[1] See H. C. G. Matthew, 'Rhetoric and politics in Great Britain, 1860–1950', in P. J. Waller, ed., *Politics and social change in modern Britain: essays presented to A. F. Thompson* (1987).

[2] Sir Charles Oman, *Things I have seen* (1933), 77.

[3] For the Liberal politics, see 31 Jan. 90ff. For Fletcher's patronising recollections, see C. R. L. F[letcher], *Mr Gladstone at Oxford 1890* (1908). The Fellows of All Souls evidently seem to have thought they were being generous in allowing Gladstone, an Honorary Fellow of the College since 1858, to exercise his rights. Fletcher was, in fact, a Fellow of Magdalen College at the time of Gladstone's visit; but his tone is throughout proprietary.

Minister of the 1890s had been in office, as a Treasury whip and an under-secretary for war and the colonies, in those days of William IV. He could even recall the defining years of nineteenth-century Britain, for, as a four-year-old, he had heard the guns of Edinburgh Castle rattling the windows as they announced the abdication of Napoleon.[1] To be cogently pre-Victorian in the 1890s was a triumph in itself: '14 to dinner. I had to tell many old stories of politics.'[2]

Gladstone as an historical repository was a subject in itself. He wrote the history of his time in a variety of ways: through his huge output of articles on contemporary subjects; through his autobiography, begun in July 1892 and never completed;[3] through various memoirs of his friends and colleagues, written as obituaries or reminiscences, or as prefaces to biographies or reviews of them;[4] and behind the scenes through the availability (or sometimes unavailability) of his vast collection of private papers in the Octagon which he built to house them at Hawarden—he was probably the first Prime Minister to have a catalogued collection of private papers being used by researchers during his own lifetime[5]—and more discreetly by the advice and interviews he gave to biographers of his friends, most notably in the case of E. S. Purcell's preparation of his *Life of Manning*, in which Gladstone played a central role.[6]

We must beware of seeing Gladstone too much in his role of Victorian cultural remnant. It was certainly an important aspect of his activities in these

[1] *Autobiographica*, i. 14. Characteristically, Gladstone checked with D. Macgregor, the proprietor of the Royal Hotel in Princes Street, that his recollection was correct that there were five windows in the room.

[2] 9 Aug. 93.   [3] See Below, section VII.

[4] See Index volume under 'publications'. In these years he reviewed Wemyss Reid's *Forster* (6 Aug. 88) and his *Monckton Milnes* (14 Nov. 90), Smiles's *John Murray* (16 Apr. 91) and wrote recollections of O'Connell (26 Nov. 88) and notices of Dr. Döllinger (13 Jan. 90, 30 Aug. 90) and 'The great physician [Sir Andrew Clark, his doctor]', *Youth's Companion*, 27 June 1895; after the journal ends, he published 'Personal recollections of Arthur H. Hallam', *Daily Telegraph*, 5 January 1898. He was a prompt and assiduous contributor to the *Dictionary of National Biography*, writing a good deal of the entries on E. C. Hawtrey, Sir S. R. Glynne, G. W. Lyttelton, and his father.

[5] See Index Volume under 'biographies of G's friends and contemporaries'. In these years he was especially involved in the making of C. S. Parker's *Peel*, Wemyss Reid's *W. E. Forster* and *Monckton Milnes* (Houghton), Lane Poole's *Stratford de Redcliffe*, Davidson's *Tait*, Gordon's *Sidney Herbert*, Hallam Tennyson's biography of his father, and Purcell's *Manning*. In the case of Tennyson, Gladstone was unable easily to extract the letters, for they were filed by date rather than person; see to Hallam Tannyson, 7 Dec. 92. Gladstone's letters were also in the auction rooms. He was able to prevent the sale of his Eton letters to W. W. Farr; see 17 Mar. 92.

Gladstone was accommodating but careful: see 28 Mar. 93 for his refusal of permission to publish in Ricasoli's papers his account of his conversation with Piux IX in 1866.

He assisted Kotaro Mochizuki with his translation of a life of Gladstone into Japanese; see 21 Apr. 91n.

He does not seem to have been asked for help by A. F. Robbins whose careful study, *The early public life of William Ewart Gladstone* was published in 1894; it is based on published sources and there is no suggestion in the preface that Robbins had asked Gladstone for information.

[6] See 11 June 87, 29 May 93. Gladstone's conversations with Purcell were an important influence on this controversial biography, as Purcell's preface makes clear (though Purcell exaggerates the amount of attention Gladstone gave to him). Gladstone regarded Manning as a lost 'gem' of the Church of England and especially deplored his Ultramontanism. His copy of Purcell's *Life* (presently in my keeping) is one of the most heavily annotated of all Gladstone's books and has many *marginalia* rebuking Manning and correcting what Gladstone saw as his inaccuracies.

years, and a side of his character that he carefully developed: his beguiling of the Fellows of All Souls shows it at its most effective. His journal records the time and enthusiasm he spent in this way. He himself was aware that the 'excitement' that his presence often occasioned 'is capable of explanation on grounds less flattering than self love would suggest. For a very old man is in some sense like a commodity walking out of a Museum or menagerie into the haunts of men.'[1] But we must not allow this to distract us from the fact that Gladstone remained an extremely effective politician. He sometimes liked to give the impression that he was in some way removed from politics: but the years after 1886 were very different from those of the opposition years after 1874. Then he had talked of political retirement to literary and theological pursuits even when effectively leader of the opposition: now he was clearly committed to winning an election in order to lead another government. Amiable talk of literature might charm the literary classes—now in the main Unionist—but Gladstone's essential relationship was by this time with 'the masses'.

In all this outpouring of activity, there was an element of Dr. Johnson's female preacher: what was remarkable was not that it was done well, but that it was done at all. Much of it was done well, and especially in chosen areas of political action Gladstone still acted effectively and powerfully. Yet he knew that his physical system was maintained by will, and that his body was failing faster than his mind. Poor eyesight made him increasingly reliant on secretaries; neuralgia in his face—perhaps an early symptom of the cancer of the cheek which killed him—affected him and his sleeping from 1889.[2] Colds and influenza were serious setbacks. Deafness led to an end of regular theatre-going, such a feature of the 1870s and early 1880s: when he did go, he sat on the stage, but even then 'heard but ill'.[3] His memory, remarkably accurate with respect to the long-term past, began to fail him in the short-term. In 1887 he began to forget some of the names of his correspondents for the daily lists which form one of the standard components of the diary.[4] At the same time, he prepared for a political speech to Yorkshire M.P.s and Liberals: 'Thought over what to say tonight. I wrote even three sets of notes: but forgot to take any of them.'[5]

As long as the drive towards success in Irish policy was uninterrupted, bodily vigour was sufficiently sustained, and such difficulties were inconvenient but not seriously intrusive. Such an interruption came with the Parnell débâcle in 1890, and it aged Gladstone by the decade he thought he had saved.

In July 1892, in the face of his fourth Premiership, he candidly noted this remarkable judgment:

Frankly: for the condition (*now*) of my senses, I am no longer fit for public life: yet bidden to walk in it. "Lead thou me on".[6]

The bidding was the bidding of God, and the call was still 'Ireland, Ireland, Ireland'.[7]

---

[1] To Romanes, 18 Oct. 92.   [2] 8 Oct. 89.
[3] 11 May 92 (Irving and Terry in *Henry VIII*).
[4] 17, 19 Mar. 87.   [5] 17 Mar. 87.
[6] 15 July 92.   [7] 10 Apr. 87.

II

The dominance of 'Ireland' in this period of Gladstone's life is obvious enough. The circumstances of 1886 gave Gladstone, as he saw it, a clear role: the duty of leading a Liberal majority to pass a second and successful Government of Ireland Bill. The Home Rulers would show the genuineness of their commitment to a devolved Assembly, their moderation the more remarkable under the provocation of Unionist coercion; the purged Liberal Party would win the next general election outright with a significant majority, and would pass a Government of Ireland Bill (with the Home Rulers in support but at a distance) which the Lords would not dare reject; Gladstone would then retire. He underestimated the skill of Salisbury in forging the various groups of Unionists into what the Liberals liked after 1886 to refer to as the 'Unionist coalition' but what was by 1892 not far short of a Unionist party ('Toryism ... now includes what was once Liberalism, for shortness I call it all Toryism—there is no use beating about the bush in these matters and wasting time')[1] and he overestimated the capacity of Parnell as a political leader in the round.

'The speedy concession to Ireland of what she most justly desires'[2] was thus the objective of his prayers, and the statement of what was desired was that of the elected Home Rule party. If the Liberal Party could be reunited to achieve this goal quickly, so much the better. Gladstone was happy to go along with the Round Table talks about Liberal reunion in the early months of 1887, because they accorded well with his concept of politics as a process, so often deployed with Hartington and Chamberlain in the years 1880-6.[3] In 1886 he had succeeded at least in attracting Chamberlain and G. O. Trevelyan into his Cabinet. In 1887, a carefully arranged meeting over dinner with Gladstone provided the means of Trevelyan's return.[4] In so returning, Trevelyan admitted the principle of Home Rule (the concession was on the question of the inclusion of the Irish M.P.s at Westminster).[5] It was clear enough that an admission of this principle was the context within which Gladstone was working, as his speeches and literary productions showed. In this sense the process was teleological, not open-ended, and in this sense it differed basically from the early months of 1886, when the process was one of exploration of the *possibility* of Home Rule.[6] After 1886, the principle of Home Rule gave Gladstonianism a political rigidity matching the fiscal rigidity of free trade.

Was Joseph Chamberlain seriously considering what was in fact a required capitulation on this basic point? His behaviour was, as ever, erratic, with none of the sinuously developed fall-back positions of Gladstone in his pre-Home Rule days. Chamberlain's scathing public attack on the primacy of Home Rule in the Liberal programme, made in the midst of the private negotiations, seemed to

[1] Hutton and Cohen, *Speeches*, 408 (to conference of agricultural labourers, 11 December 1891).
[2] 1 Apr. 87.
[3] See above, x. cxlviiff.
[4] 8 March, 25-6 May 87, i.e. Gladstone's personal contacts with Trevelyan were before and after the third session of Round Table talks.
[5] 25-6 May 87.
[6] See above, x. cxlvii and 30 Jan. 86.

deny any serious intention of reunion.[1] Gladstone appeared to have nothing to lose: he half-turned his cheek and met Chamberlain twice at dinner. Both occasions went well, with 'Easy *general* conversation with Chamberlain' (easiness was not a usual feature of their always stiff relationship) at the first and 'very free conversation on the closure' at the second.[2] A few days later they met *tête à tête*: 'ambiguous result but some ground made'.[3] Gladstone tried to secure agreement on coercion, presumably as a first step, but nothing came of this. Chamberlain and his group of radical Unionists—Hartington kept well clear of Gladstone at this time—went their own way.[4]

The talks of 1887 confirmed the split of 1886 with respect to most of the Liberal Unionists: 1846 more than 1866 was the precedent.[5] This applied to the Liberal Party as much as to those who had left it. At least under Gladstone's leadership, and probably well beyond it given the political arrangements that that leadership implied, the Liberal Party was a party of Home Rule. Those who left it recognized this by their continued absence; those who stayed in, however much they might, like Sir William Harcourt, dislike Home Rule, recognized this by their presence.[6] This 'Home Rule' was therefore essentially that defined by the Government of Ireland Bill of 1886, in so far as it met the requirements of the Irish.

As Gladstone reminded the National Liberal Federation at the famous Newcastle meeting in 1891, whatever there was to be said about the various other items of policy with which a liberal government would wish to deal, there was no doubt about the priority of Home Rule:

> As to the title of Ireland to the precedence, there is no question at all about it—it is a matter fixed and settled and determined long ago, upon reasons which in my opinion—and what is much more, in the opinion of the people—cannot be refuted, cannot even be contested.[7]

There were therefore two elements to the case Gladstone so painstakingly elaborated after 1886: first, that Ireland had a legitimated and established grievance of such force as to demand priority; second, that 'Home Rule' was the natural constitutional development for the United Kingdom.

The background to the grievances and requirements of the Irish Gladstone investigated laboriously in his private reading. He reappraised his view of Daniel O'Connell (his first Cabinet meetings in 1843 had committed the Peel government to the prosecution of O'Connell for treason): O'Connell had been 'the missionary of an idea. The idea was the restoration of the public life of his country.'[8] Gladstone repented of his youthful views: 'In early life I shared the

---

[1] See 26 Feb. 87 and M. Hurst, *Joseph Chamberlain and Liberal Reunion. The Round Table Conference of 1887* (1967), ch. vii.

[2] 15 Mar., 2 Apr. 87.   [3] 5 Apr. 87.   [4] Ibid.

[5] The 1846 analogy was not absolute, for many more of those who opposed Home Rule in 1886 returned to the Liberal Party than those who went with Peel in 1846 returned to the Conservatives.

[6] Hurst, op. cit., 3, 58, rightly points out that, in the immediate context at least, Harcourt and the 'goodwill' Liberals were the real losers from the failure of the Round Table negotiations.

[7] Hutton and Cohen, *Speeches*, 382 (2 October 1891).

[8] 'Daniel O'Connell', a review of Fitzpatrick's 2v. edition of O'Connell's correspondence (1888), reprinted in W. E. Gladstone, *Special Aspects of the Irish Question* (1892), 263ff. Gladstone's reappraisal of O'Connell had begun as a result of a meeting with Rev. John O'Rourke during his visit to Maynooth in 1877, which led to Gladstone's memorandum of a conversation with O'Connell in 1834 being published in the 3rd ed. of O'Rourke's *Centenary life of O'Connell* (1877), see 4, 17 Nov. 77.

prejudices against him, which were established in me not by conviction, but by tradition and education'. Now, 'there cannot but be many, in whose eyes O'Connell stands clearly as the greatest Irishman that ever lived. . . . By the force of his own personality he led Ireland to Saint Stephen's, almost as much as Moses led the children of Israel to Mount Sinai.' O'Connell did this with support 'in the narrower rather than in the wider sense, [of] the masses only, not the masses with the classes'—a clear terminological analogy between Gladstone's view of O'Connell and Gladstone's view of himself.[1] Gladstone's repentance must become a national repentance. The policy of Home Rule was in part a recognition of an historical and therefore an empirically demonstrable grievance, not a deductivist case dependent upon abstract argument about a perfectible constitution. Winning this historical argument was therefore essential to the struggle. Unionist authors must be combated—and this involved Gladstone in sharp disputes with W. E. H. Lecky, J. Dunbar Ingram and others,[2] and, more constructively, in his own essay on Irish history in the eighteenth century, published in James Bryce's *Handbook of Home Rule* (1887).[3]

Winning this argument was important in part because to do so established the naturalness of Home Rule. The case against Home Rule in 1886 had been in part that it was unnatural—sudden, arbitrary, a break with the constitution—consequently leaving the British party which supported it as in some sense deviant and exotic. Gladstone, as we have seen in an earlier volume, insufficiently educated his party by public debate in 1885-6 on this point, and was aware of it.[4] Recognizing that 'the political education of a people is not to be effected in a moment, in a day, or in a year',[5] he set out to provide such an education. Home Rule was the established policy for the colonies:

> Sixty years ago we governed our own British Colonies from Downing Street. The result was controversy, discontent, sometimes rebellion. We gave them Home Rule, with the same reconciling results as have followed elsewhere; and with this result in particular, that what was denounced here beforehand as separation has produced an Union of hearts between us and the Colonies such as had never been known before.

The Imperial argument thus supported the policy, as did the military: 'we might at some period be involved in a great war', and the precedent of the French wars was that 140,000 men had been required in Ireland to subordinate the population: 'such, with an anti-Home-Rule policy, was the frightful demand of Ireland upon our military resources. . . . We must not then maintain, but alter the present state of things, if we wish to have our full strength available in war.' Home Rule, far from being a sudden invention of 1886, was a well-established European policy. States that declined it had done so at their peril: Holland had lost Belgium, Denmark Schleswig-Holstein, Turkey her European

---

[1] *Special Aspects*, pp. 267-8.

[2] See 6 Jan., 16 May, 8 July, 2 Sept., 8 and 20 Dec. 87, 30 Jan., 6 Aug., 26 Nov. 88, 23 May, 18 June 89, 20 Mar., 23 Aug. 90, 21 June, 27 July 92.

[3] 24 Sept. 87.   [4] See above, x. cxlviii–cxlix.

[5] 'Home Rule for Ireland. An appeal to the Tory Householder' (1890), reprinted in W. E. Gladstone, *Special Aspects*, from which subsequent quotations are taken. This article presents the same arguments as those used by Gladstone in his speech on the second reading of the Government of Ireland Bill, 1893.

provinces: 'such, with respect to the denial of Home Rule, are the teachings of experience'. Moreover, 'as the denial has in no case been attended with success, so the concession has in no case been attended with failure'. Norway and Sweden, Denmark and Iceland, Austria and Hungary, Turkey and Lebanon, all had improved and settled relations as a result of the same essential policy:

> Home Rule has everywhere appeared as in the nature of a cure, and the denial of it as a loss or a disgrace. It may be said, and said with truth, that in all those cases there are circumstantial differences from our case; but the essence has everywhere been the same.

Home Rule was thus neither strange nor unnatural, but commonsensical and successful, and especially so in the peculiar case of the British Empire. It was thus those who opposed it who should be seen as dangerous. The Unionists were the danger to the constitution, not those who agreed with the Irish in making a 'modest and temperate demand for a self-government complete indeed but purely local'. Gladstone made only 'one very simple' demand on the Tory householder: 'We only ask him to *think*.' If he did think, he would see the naturalness of the Home Rule solution; if he did not, the United Kingdom might go the way of the rest.

As an essay in prudential conservatism radically applied it was characteristically Gladstonian. Essential to it, of course, was the assumption that Home Rule would be consolidatory not separatist, the last step not the first. Gladstone believed this would be the case. His first draft of a Home Rule Bill had followed the receipt of Parnell's 'Proposed Constitution for Ireland' and had followed it quite closely. The behaviour of the Home Rule Party after the disappointment of 1886 confirmed his view. The revival of the land movement in the form of the Plan of Campaign, from October 1886 on, deliberately avoided the criminal aspects of the land war of 1880–2. Parnell went out of his way to distance himself even from the Plan. It was the Unionists and the Unionist press which practised dishonesty, defending forgery and unnecessary coercion. In the testing period of the Crimes Act, the Special Commission, and the Michelstown shootings, Parnell and his party confirmed the view Gladstone had formed of them in the period after the arrests of 1881: they were essentially sturdy constitutionalists. The difficulties were about details, not principles, and those details would be a re-run of the points of dispute in 1886: precise demarcation of powers, the financial bargain, and the role of Irish M.P.s (if any) at Westminster.

Gladstone discussed these matters at two meetings with Parnell, on 8 March 1888 in London and Hawarden on 18–19 December 1889 (i.e. five days before Captain O'Shea petitioned for divorce). On each occasion Parnell's demands were entirely within the accepted parameters of liberal thinking. After the first conversation, Gladstone noted: 'Undoubtedly his tone was very conservative'[1] and after the second, 'He is certainly one of the best people to deal with that I have ever known.'[2] The purpose of these meetings was partly tactical—at the

---

[1] 8 Mar. 88.

[2] 19 Dec. 89. See also 30 Apr. 88, a meeting at Armitstead's dinner table 'to meet Mr. Parnell. His coolness of head appeared at every turn.'

first Gladstone characteristically urged keeping the working of the Crimes Act 'before the eye of the country, and of Parliament by speeches, and by statistics'—and partly prospective, agreeing the terms of the future Government of Ireland Bill.

To the modern eye, the most curious feature of this period of liberal opposition is the absence of systematic 'forward-planning' on this Bill. It was clear there was to be a Bill, and that it would be the chief immediate business of the next Liberal Government in its first full Session. It was also clear from the experience of 1886 that there were many complex points of detail about such a measure, some of them involving major constitutional matters. Yet the Liberals re-entered government in 1892 with many of these points undecided or unconsidered.[1]

Gladstone's talks with Parnell in 1889 were clearly intended to make a start on such matters. For the second meeting, Gladstone prepared an elaborate memorandum setting out 'all the points of possible amendment or change in the Plan of Irish Government'. It pointed to a Government of Ireland Bill somewhat more confined than that of 1886, and, in its major departure from that Bill, it retained 'an Irish representation at Westminster . . . in *some* form—if the public opinion, at the proper time, shall require it'.[2] Gladstone had already, at Swansea in 1887, raised this probability.[3] It was not for him a major change, for in his initial draft of a Home Rule bill in November 1885, the Irish M.P.s had been 'in', and Parnell at that time had also taken an easy view of the matter.[4] The memorandum also took up the question of the financial bargain (of the importance of which Gladstone had reminded Parnell at their earlier meeting), and suggested a clause explicitly 'reserving the supremacy of Parliament over Ireland in common with the rest of the Empire'; it also dealt with some details of a land settlement, safeguards for contracts, and an imperial veto for seven or ten years on judicial matters.

After the first meeting, Gladstone noted: 'we had 2 hours of satisfactory conversation but he put off the *gros* of it'. The next day, there were two hours more of conversation *tête-à-tête*, following which Gladstone sent a memorandum round the members of the ex-Cabinet: he sensed no real difficulties: 'Nothing could be more satisfactory than his conversation; full as I thought of great sense from beginning to end . . . nothing like a crochet, or an irrational demand, from his side, was likely to interfere with the proper freedom of our deliberations when the proper time comes for practical steps.' The problematic area remained the Irish M.P.s at Westminster, but here Parnell had expressed 'no absolute or foregone conclusion'. Gladstone reported the conversations to the ex-Cabinet in more detail when it met: 'At 2.30 to 4.30 political meeting. I related my interview with Parnell. Sir W. H[arcourt] ran restive: but alone.'[5]

Parnell's conduct at these meetings thus suggested to Gladstone that, just as he had seen a Government of Ireland Bill in 1886 imposing responsibility on the Irish as well as satisfying their demands, so association with the Liberal

---

[1] Rosebery's complaints about this (see 7 July 89n) may have led to the notes printed at 8 Aug. 89 but, apart from the conversation with Parnell, these were not followed up.

[2] 18 Dec. 89.   [3] Speech on 4 June 87.

[4] See above, x. clvii and 14 Nov. 85.   [5] 8 Feb. 90.

Party in the preparation of the next Bill brought out the best qualities of Irish constitutionalism. The 'public life' of Ireland was being restored through unity of action on the Home Rule question. If the matters which Gladstone put to Parnell for discussion in 1889 amounted, as Parnell in the crisis of 1890 claimed, 'to a compromise of our [i.e. Irish] national rights by the acceptance of a measure which would not realise the aspirations of our race'[1] then Parnell certainly did not say so when they were put to him, either at the time or in subsequent months.[2]

It may be that Gladstone felt that the work done on the 1886 Bills, and in these conversations with Parnell, was sufficient preparation and that to attempt detailed decisions played into the hands of the Unionists. Certainly, it was wholly within the tradition of British government not to work out details of legislation before entering office. Yet the question of whether Irish M.P.s would be 'in' or 'out' of the House of Commons went to the heart of the difficulties raised about the 1886 Bill, and had important bearings on the 'home-rule-all-around' question. Gladstone several times in these years, including in his first conversation with Parnell, raised the question of whether the 'American Union' was 'a practical point of departure'. In seeming not to see the qualitative differences between devolution of power (which, as he frequently made plain, was a boon bestowed by Westminster and removable by it) and a federal system—in effect a new constitution—he seemed to share a common contemporary confusion;[3] but it was a serious confusion none the less.

There was, of course, an element of menace in the Irish M.P.s' position: that was inherent in their presence at Westminster as a party whose fundamental objective was to require the Crown in Parliament to pass a Government of Ireland Act. Gladstone recognized that the Irish should take what they could get, and if what they wanted could be got from the Tories, so much the better. He continued to think, privately and publicly, that Home Rule would be best settled by a Tory government.[4] But in the years after 1886 this could be no

---

[1] The concluding sentence of Parnell's manifesto 'To the Irish People', published on 29 November 1890; printed in O'Shea, *Parnell*, ii. 166.

[2] A point Gladstone made in his public response to Parnell's manifesto 'To the Irish People'; see 29 Nov. 90. As always in Parnell's dealings with British political leaders, there are no records on his side of these conversations. It may be said that Gladstone's denial of Parnell's statements—e.g. that he [Gladstone] made no statements whatever about County Court judges and resident magistrates (as opposed to judges)—seems entirely consistent with his memoranda preparing himself for the conversations: 'every suggestion made by me was from written memoranda' etc. Gladstone was of course exceptionally experienced at recalling the specific details of official discussions (in which category he clearly placed these) and in general his memory was accurate. Moreover, he had no reason to misrepresent the conversations of December 1889 to his ex-Cabinet colleagues. In those conversations he was recognizing Parnell as an equal, in the sense of party leader and Prime Minister of Ireland-in-waiting, and he presumed he would behave with the appropriate stiffness of honour he expected from such persons.

[3] Gladstone's idea that the 'American system' might 'in case of need supply at least a phrase to cover them [opponents of Home Rule] in point of consistency' greatly underestimated the implications; 8 Mar. 88. For an interesting discussion of the contemporary debate about federation, see John Kendle, *Ireland and the federal solution. The debate over the United Kingdom constitution, 1870-1921* (1989).

[4] See point 2 of his notes for conversation with Parnell, 8 Mar. 88, and *Special aspects*, 344: 'I for one have always declared my wish that this great measure should be carried by the Tories; because they can do it with our help (which they know they would have), more easily and rapidly than we can.'

more than a fancy. The menacing, disruptive edge of the Irish party could for the time being only cut the Liberals. That was why the securing of Parnell to the lines of discussion about the future Bill was so important. By the late 1880s a natural progress towards a fairly decisive Home Rule majority in each of the Kingdoms seemed a clear probability and Gladstone's goal since 1886 seemed within grasp. Indeed the conversion of the minority into a large majority seemed in the autumn of 1890 as certain as anything in politics could be certain.[1] But the cutting edge of Irish disruption sliced dramatically through the 'silken cords' at the end of 1890, when the O'Shea divorce case caused a political disruption greater than any achieved by a Fenian bomb.

On 17 November 1890 Katharine O'Shea did not appear in court, despite the pleadings of her counsel, Frank Lockwood (Liberal M.P. and soon to be Solicitor-General), and a decree *nisi* was given to Captain O'Shea, with Parnell as the co-respondent. Gladstone, at Hawarden, pursued his usual activities. On 20 November he held 'family conversations on the awful matter of Parnell'. Next day, with 'a bundle of letters daily about Parnell: all one way', he spent the morning 'drawing out my own view of the case', and writing it down. His conclusion was:

> I agree with a newspaper, supposed to convey the opinion of Davitt (*The Labour World*) that the dominant question, now properly before Mr. Parnell for his consideration, is what is the best course for him to adopt with a view to the furtherance of the interests of Home Rule in Great Britain. And with deep pain but without any doubt, I judge that those interests require his retirement at the present time from his leadership. For the reason indicated at the outset [i.e. that the decision rests in the first place with the Irish Parliamentary party and the Irish constituents generally], I have no right spontaneously to pronounce this opinion. But I should certainly give it if called upon from a quarter entitled to make the demand.[2]

This was a reasoned statement of his letter to Morley, two days earlier, that, whatever the qualifications and allowances to be made, 'I again and again say to myself, I say I mean in the interior and silent forum, "It'll na dee".'[3] As his notes show,[4] Gladstone at least half wished to say this in the public forum: that is, he wished to bring direct pressure to bear upon Parnell and his party, whose eve-of-session meeting was to be held on 25 November. Next day (a Sunday) after another 'cloud of letters', he decided 'I think the time has come'.[5] He travelled to London on the Monday, held a conclave with Granville, Harcourt, John Morley and Arnold Morley, the Chief Whip. Following this, he 'saw Mr. MacCarthy'.[6] His account of this meeting was stated in a letter to John Morley,[7] the gist of which was that, if Parnell looked like persisting with his leadership at the meeting on 25 November, McCarthy should disclose to the meeting that Gladstone's view was that Parnell's 'continuance at the present moment in the leadership would be productive of consequences disastrous in the highest degree to the cause of Ireland'. McCarthy probably did not know of a further point, added into the letter at John Morley's prompting, that this would 'render my [Gladstone's] retention of the leadership of the Liberal party . . . almost a nullity'.

---

[1] 29 Dec. 90.   [2] 21 Nov. 90.   [3] Morley, iii. 431.
[4] 22 Nov. 90.   [5] 23 Nov. 90.   [6] 24 Nov. 90.
[7] 24 Nov. 90.

Parnell, rather than McCarthy, was the objective of all this. Gladstone's interviews with Parnell in 1886, 1888 and 1889, had been aberrant. His normal means of communication with him was indirect, usually *via* Mrs. O'Shea. She could hardly be asked to play a part on this occasion, so the alternative indirectness of a letter to Morley was used. The strength of the O'Shea link in the 1882–6 period was that it was indirect but immediately efficient. Carefully avoiding inquiry into the details of Katharine O'Shea's domestic arrangements, Gladstone none the less knew that a letter to her was effectively a letter to Parnell. But on 24 November 1890 Morley, like many a Liberal in the past, could not find Parnell. Justin McCarthy, chosen presumably because of his journalistic connections with Gladstone, told Parnell of his interview with Gladstone, but when Parnell pressed ahead, did not tell the party meeting of Gladstone's letter, and Parnell was re-elected chairman. Gladstone published the letter two days later in the press, with sensational impact on Irish MPs and public opinion generally.[1]

As is well known, Parnell then published his manifesto 'To the Irish People' on 29 November, unprofessionally misrepresenting the conversations of 1889 on several points which Gladstone could and did correct from his memoranda;[2] Gladstone rejected requests to make specific assurances to the Irish party on particular points about a Home Rule bill;[3] and the party meeting of Home Rule M.P.s in Committee Room 15 disrupted on 5 December, McCarthy leading 45 M.P.s from the room leaving Parnell with 28.

As his birthday retrospect for 1890, Gladstone uniquely wrote a memorandum rather than an extended entry in his journal. It was, in personal terms, the most disappointing moment of his political career since the 1840s, as the 'master-violence of politics' tightened a grip which Gladstone had believed was shortly to be released. He recorded the full extent of the *débâcle*, triggered by 'the sin of Tristram with Isault'—and in that analogy he caught as well as any the mythic element of Parnell's tragedy and its private and public dimensions and, perhaps, his own forlorn and betrayed position as King Mark.

The task had been clear:

> In Ireland the Nationalists were to hold their ground; in Great Britain we were to convert on the first Dissolution our minority into a large majority and in the Autumn of 1890 we had established the certainty of that result so far as an event yet contingent could be capable of ascertainment.

The case was 'not hopeless', but 'the probable result of so scandalous an exhibition will be confusion and perplexity in the weaker minds, and doubt whether while this conflict continues Ireland can be considered to have reached a state capable of beneficial self-government' (thus wrote the former Colonial Secretary). The result was to

> introduce into our position a dangerous uncertainty . . . Home Rule *may* be postponed for another period of five or six years. The struggle in that case must survive me, cannot be survived by me. The dread life of Parliamentary contention reaches outwards to the grave.[4]

[1] 26 Nov. 90.   [2] See above, p. xxxviii.
[3] 30 Nov., 4, 5 Dec. 90.   [4] 29 Dec. 90.

Not surprisingly, 'this change of prospect hits me hard'. Gladstone's optimism had been 'based on pride and on blindness: He who sees all sees fit to quench it.' His duty was 'of course to preserve the brightness and freshness of our hopes as they stood a couple of months back'.[1]

Gladstone, despite his considerable public crusade at this time against divorce and in favour of marital fidelity, did not blame Parnell or Mrs. O'Shea. Though he never refers to it, he must have suspected that a liaison as close as theirs and one which he himself knew to be so established might have a sexual dimension. The affair was public from the day O'Shea filed his petition for divorce on 24 December 1889 (just after Parnell's visit to Hawarden). There was therefore almost a year to come to terms with its possible consequences (longer than initially expected).[2] The possibility that the case would require Parnell's withdrawal from public life had of course occurred both to Parnell and to Gladstone and the Liberal leadership. In March 1890, Gladstone's view had been that such a withdrawal would be 'a public calamity'[3] and he seems to have thought it an avoidable calamity. But he took no steps to avoid it. There were no meetings with Nonconformist or Roman Catholic leaders to limit the potential damage. Nor was there any discussion with Parnell as to how either of them might handle the political aspects of the case. The latter would have been a contradiction of the view that Parnell was a competent party and national leader.

It was not Parnell's morality that Gladstone deplored—he no doubt thought it no worse than Hartington's longstanding liaison with the Duchess of Manchester—but his inept management of its public consequences. It was Parnell's public handling of his position that he condemned, and his public handling of private political conversations which took place within very clearly accepted canons of political life. These showed Parnell to be less than the man Gladstone had taken him for.

Gladstone soon put Parnell behind him: he never had the nagging status of Disraeli. The journal entry on the receipt of the news of Parnell's death in 1891 has a cool edge to it:

> In 18 hours from six P.M. yesterday I have by telegram the deaths of Mr. W. H. Smith, Mr. Parnell—& Sir J. Pope Hennessy (not an inconsiderable man). So the Almighty bares his arm when he sees it meet: & there is here matter for thought, and in the very sad case of Mr. P. matter also of much public importance.[4]

III

Gladstone's years as leader of the Liberal Party in opposition—and the period 1886–1892 was the only sustained period when he was the opposition leader— were by no means solely concerned with the Irish question, important though the maintenance of its prominence was to him. Though he was an opposition

---

[1] Ibid.
[2] See 24 Dec. 89; in December 1889, it was expected that the case would be heard in June 1890.
[3] See 21 Mar. 90 for Hamilton's account of Gladstone's views.
[4] 7 Oct. 91.

leader in Britain, in many countries he was regarded as the prime British politician. This almost reached the level of actuality when he attended the centenary celebrations of the French Revolution,[1] celebrations that Salisbury's government declined to recognize officially. Fêted all over Paris, Gladstone ascended the Eiffel Tower ('I was persuaded to go up the tower & propose his [Eiffel's] health in a French oratiuncle [brief speech]'), visited the exhibitions, and made the speeches. When he entered the Paris Hippodrome, 'the performance was arrested and God save the Queen played';[2] when he attended the Opera, he sat in the President's box.[3]

If he had accepted any of the various invitations to visit the United States, his reception would have been even more lavish, despite the success of American protectionism. As Gladstone knew well, his Home Rule policy had gained him a world-wide reputation and, he believed, a consensus of support far greater than in England. In the areas of Irish-American settlement in this period the name of Gladstone rivalled that of Lincoln.

Gladstone throughout his life was well read on the United States. In his later years, he followed American politics and theological debate—obvious subjects for a Briton in public life—but he was also fascinated by the Shakers and he read on publication Jacob Riis's trail-blazing work on poverty in New York, *How the other half lives: studies among the poor* (1890).[4] It was a report of the state of marriage in the U.S.A. that prompted him to declare that, were he not so old, he would launch a Bulgarian-style campaign against birth-control.[5] His association with W. H. Rideing of the *North American Review* resembled to a lesser degree that with James Knowles of the *Nineteenth Century* and *Fortnightly Review*. His friendship with Andrew Carnegie, the greatest industrialist of the age, reflected—as did Carnegie's enthusiasm for his Scottish roots—the *rapprochement* taking place between the British governing class and East Coast wealth and politics. Gladstone energetically encouraged such links.

He enthusiastically welcomed the economic prominence of the American economy. He seems to have been unconcerned at the course of America 'boss' politics in this period, which so preoccupied most Tories and Liberals at this time. He saw it merely as a symptom of American protectionism, whose follies he went to some lengths to demonstrate in articles in the *North American Review*. His argument—in perhaps the most deductivist account of the free-trade case that he ever made—was the universalism of free trade and of its benefits: what had benefited Britain in her economic prime would benefit America in hers. All protection was monopolistic and corrupting: 'all protection is morally as well as economically bad'.[6] Gladstone's appeal to American universalism, as opposed to James Blaine's localist reply, anticipated the twentieth century dominance of the United States and sought to harness it for the cause of progress and international harmony based on free trade. In

---

[1] 3-9 Sept. 89.   [2] 5 Sept. 89.   [3] 6 Sept. 89.
[4] 29 Dec. 90.   [5] See 23, 28 Oct. 88.
[6] 'Free Trade', *North American Review*, cl. 1 (January 1890), 25; the article was planned over an extended period, being delayed in publication so as not to interfere with the American election (another example of Gladstone's quasi-primeministerial position abroad); see 10 Dec. 88, 23 July 89, 5 Oct. 89.

anticipating the danger of an America whose political arrangements were locally defined while her economic strength was hegemonic, Gladstone anticipated a vital failure of the world liberal system in the early decades of the twentieth century:

> How will the majestic figure, about to become the largest and most powerful on the stage of the world's history, make use of his power? Will it be instinct with moral life in proportion to its material strength? Will he uphold and propagate the Christian tradition with that surpassing energy which marks him in all the ordinary pursuits of life. . . . May Heaven avert every darker omen, and grant that the latest and largest of the great Christian civilization shall also be the brightest and the best![1]

This cosmopolitanism and Gladstone's defence of it was important in a world moving quickly into nationalistic protectionism. From the Liberal point of view, the cause of Irish nationalism in the form of Home Rule was a contribution to the maintenance of international right, because it recognized constitutional change in a free trade context: Home Rule was intended to show that recognition of national identity need not mean protection and cartelization.

By the time of the election of 1892, Gladstone stood as the world leader of a free-trade movement clearly in retreat, but still able to offer the world the best model of international harmony. It was an important consequence of the Home Rule preoccupation that British liberalism did not in these years play a more active role in advancing the sort of institutional development of internationalism implicit in Gladstone's campaigns during his previous if unofficial opposition years in the 1870s.[2] When Gladstone came to challenge British armament expansion, as he did in 1892–4, he was able to do so in the context of national politics only: the liberal movement had neither associated itself with the Second International (formed in 1889), nor provided an alternative international institutional structure. As the leader of world liberalism in its political form, this failure was a perhaps surprising blot on the British liberal record between the 1880s and 1914.

Free trade was to liberalism what class was to the International. Though 'free trade' was by definition an absence of impediments, it was not impossible to institutionalize it by treaty and international organization, though it would have seemed odd to most nineteenth-century Liberals to try to do so. By the 1890s it was a fiscal system clearly on the defensive: time was no longer on liberalism's side. What is curious is that British Liberals made no attempt to co-ordinate its international defence by co-operation with Liberals in other countries (except in a mild way in the Empire). The generation of British Liberals which played so prominent a part in the founding of the League of Nations was, for liberalism, really a generation or perhaps two generations too late. In his old age, we have seen Gladstone contemplate a campaign in the Bulgarian atrocities style against birth control,[3] which he saw as an attack on moral values in the private sphere. But the defence of free trade—the ordering principle of liberal internationalism—was seen in terms of articles for the *North American Review*.

---

[1] Ibid., 26–7.
[2] See above, ix. xxxviiiff. (Introduction, 1875–80, section IV).
[3] 28 Oct. 88n.; see also 23 Oct. 88, 4 Aug. 90.

The suggestion of a liberal association with the Second International is, in the context of European politics and ideologies, no doubt to point up its impossibility. Yet in domestic politics this was just what Gladstone achieved. Keir Hardie lost the by-election at Mid-Lanark in 1888 to a Liberal, but his slogan was: 'a vote for Hardie is a vote for Gladstone'.[1] Although Home Rule could be seen as demoting 'labour questions' in the order of precedence, it was also a question on which the parties of progress could unite, specially at a time when class questions were becoming more acute. All groups within the developing labour movement were enthusiastic Home Rulers, supporting the policy on the very Gladstonian argument that it was both right in itself, and an important means of clearing the legislative path in the Commons, and perhaps achieving reform of the Lords *en route*. It also associated the Gladstonian Liberals with an even wider argument. Gladstone argued that the Union was legal technically but not morally, because 'no law can possess moral authority in Great Britain, can be invested with that real sacredness which ought to attach to all law, except by the will of the community'.[2] This appeal to fairness and moral authority rather than law made by a process of government, fitted well with Gladstone's rhetoric of 'the masses against the classes', and also with the sort of arguments that the labour movement was developing as it moved into a phase of parliamentary activity. Home Rule and the constitutional question thus probably aided the Liberals in their attempt to continue as the hegemonic party of the left more than it disadvantaged them, at least in the short to medium term.

A plethora of political argument was seen by many Liberals as desirable in itself. For Gladstone, public discussion of issues was the life-blood of a healthy polity. He recognized that Christianity had, by its assertion of individualism, dethroned the Aristotelian ideal of an organic civil society. He also recognized that 'the modern movement of political ideas and forces' had afforced this Christian individualism, lowering 'in rank the political art by substituting in a considerable measure for the elaborated thought of the professional statesman the simple thought of the public into which emotion or affection enter more and computation less'.[3] How then were the desirable aspects of Greek civic life to be maintained in a society in which both Christian individualism and demotic emotion seemed to contrast with the concept of a good polity? The task of liberalism as the party of progress was to square this circle, to show that public debate could be adequately conducted within the enlarged franchise, that 'elaborated thought' could be understood by an extended electorate, and that individualism was not simply the assertion of an interest, through its participation in the rhetoric of self-government, but the basis of an organic society.

This implied a complex party ideology. Free trade and Home Rule (a settled fiscal and political constitution) might be its first-order determinants, but around them would cluster many related if lesser causes. Gladstone had always been good at developing second-order principles which groups within the

---

[1] Henry Pelling, *The Origins of the Labour Party* (1965), 65.
[2] 'Plain speaking on the Irish Union', *Special aspects*, 311; see 23 May, 18 June 89.
[3] 11 June 88.

Liberal Party might agree on for fundamentally different reasons. Irish disestablishment in the 1860s had been for Liberal Anglicans the pruning of the rotten branch, for Nonconformists the first step to a secular state. Home Rule in the late 1880s could be either the means of purifying the constitutional system and consequently leaving the British state with its natural harmony restored—as Gladstone saw it—or as the first, just step to a new system—as many labour leaders saw it. As he pointed out to the Queen, Home Rule might be in essence conservative, but the delay in implementing it might cause it to 'become very far from conservative' in a variety of directions, both Irish and British: 'the longer the struggle is continued, the more the Liberal Party will verge towards democratic opinion . . . indeed in the mouths of many the word democratic has already become a synonym and a substitute for the word Liberal'.[1]

Gladstone worked this vein carefully. During the opposition period, meetings were arranged, usually by a member of the Gladstone political circle such as Rendel or Armitstead, with most of the groups that made up the Liberal Party—the Scottish and Welsh M.P.s, the Wesleyans and others—and these included the 'Labour M.P.s'. Thus, 'dined with Mr. Armitstead to meet the Labour M.P.s—There was speaking'; and, 'to Greenwich with Rosebery: he entertained the Labour members, & a good lot they are'.[2] Two days later Gladstone 'devised a scheme for payment of members'[3] (the absence of which was held to be one major difficulty preventing an increase in the number of working-class M.P.s). Such meetings had a paternal element to them, but they would have been inconceivable in Germany.

At the Newcastle N.L.F. meeting in 1891, Gladstone included various items affecting 'labour' representation (amendment of registration, the lodger franchise, election expenses, payment of M.P.s) in the list, and he seemed to give them high priority: 'there ought to be a great effort of the Liberal Party to extend the labour representation in Parliament'.[4] But the Liberal Party was not as an institution capable of enforcing this intention. When it came to the point, with the Liberals in power in 1893, it was decided that Gladstone should not speak on the matter, and nothing happened. It was a clear chance lost.[5] Notoriously, as Gladstone's son Herbert found when, as Chief Whip after his father's death, he attempted a systematic improvement in labour representation, the local Liberal associations would only very rarely select working-class candidates and then usually in the few remaining two-member seats where a Liberal could run in tandem with a Labour candidate. Gladstone met the problem in principle, and the attention he paid to it was important in holding 'the party of progress' together. But it was attention that Gladstone provided, not a practical solution.

On fundamental questions of political economy, Gladstone remained, hardly surprisingly, a mid-century free-trade retrencher. The role of the State was that

---

[1] 28 Oct. 92. [2] 26 Apr. 87, 30 June 88.

[3] 2 July 88. Andrew Carnegie followed this up with a remarkable offer: 'Mr. Cecil Rhodes gave Parnell ten-thousand pounds to secure one point in Home Rule [the inclusion of Irish M.P.s at Westminster] which he thought vital to the unity of the Empire. I should like to give ten-thousand pounds for a bill paying members three-hundred pounds per annum; but we should talk this matter all over'; Carnegie to Gladstone, 28 March 1892, Add MS 44514, f. 156.

[4] Hutton and Cohen, *Speeches*, 382ff. [5] See 24 Mar. 93.

of an enabling agent in a society self-regulated by thrift, on the model of the Post Office Savings Bank he had set up in 1861:

> I rejoice to say that it has been in the power of the State to affect this [practice of thrift] by judicious legislation—not by what is called 'grandmotherly legislation' of which I for one have a great deal of suspicion—but by legislation thoroughly sound in principle, namely that legislation which, like your savings bank, helps the people by enabling the people to help themselves.[1]

The 'Newcastle Programme' contained no proposals, beyond an opaque passage on the 'eight hours' question, for any alterations to the mid-Victorian fiscal state in whose creation and definition Gladstone had played so large a part. On the other hand, Gladstone recognized that opinion was moving away (though perhaps less swiftly than is often thought) from a rigid distinction between politics and the economy, and his own view of the state had always recognized categories of 'interference',[2] including 'positive regulations ... for the sake of obviating social, moral or political evils'.[3] The identification of those evils came through the working of the representative system, and it was therefore for supporters of causes—whether political, religious, or economic—to work that system for the promotion of their cause. For Gladstone, injustice to Ireland was an 'evil' which required his prime attention in part because the Home Rule M.P.s represented that it was so. But he recognized that others of a different generation (or several generations) from himself would identify other such evils, and there was always a wishful, elegiac quality in his references to his own position in the traditional cause of retrenchment: economy was 'like an echo from the distant period of my youth';[4] Gladstone was in this area 'a dead man, one fundamentally a Peel-Cobden man'.[5] Hints might be given, but once again in office Gladstone's position—though not that of other members of his Cabinet—was in principle clear enough. Questioned on the unemployed by John Burns, one of those Labour M.P.s so carefully incorporated, Gladstone replied:

> questions of this kind, whatever be the intention of the questioner, have a tendency to produce in the minds of people, or to suggest to the people, that these fluctuations can be corrected by the action of Executive Government. Anything that contributes to such an impression inflicts an injury upon the labouring population.[6]

The association of Gladstone and the organized labour movement was based on a policy for constitutional change, on co-operative action on a wide front to achieve that change, and on an attempt to secure for labour a greater representation. On the underlying question of the future of the economy, Gladstone saw no need for significant change.

The case for constitutional development occurred, Gladstone believed, in a curious context. The nineteenth century had been one of substantial progress

---

[1] Speech to railway savings bank depositors, *T.T.*, 19 June 1890, 6e.
[2] See above v. xxxv.
[3] Ibid.
[4] Hutton and Cohen, *Speeches*, 377 (2 Oct. 91).
[5] Gladstone to Bryce, 5 December 1896, Bryce Papers 10, f. 167; see H. C. G. Matthew, *The Liberal Imperialists* (1973), vii.
[6] *4H* 16. 1734 (1 Sept. 93).

for 'the labouring man': 'instead of being controlled by others, he now principally, and from year to year increasingly, controls himself' and in so doing offered an example to the world.[1] Yet the political system within which this 'peaceful and happy, if not wholly fulfilled, revolution on behalf of the working man' was occurring was bizarre:

> the spectacle presented by this country at the present time is a remarkable one. The ultimate power resides in the hands of those who constitute our democracy. And yet, our institutions are not democratic. Their basis is popular; but upon that basis is built a hierarchy of classes and of establishments savouring in part of feudal times and principles; and this, not in despite of the democratic majority, but on the whole with their assent. I do not know whether history, or whether the present face of the world presents a similar case of the old resting on the new, of non-popular institutions sustained by popular free-will.[2]

The labouring class within this system, 'if they acted in union and with the same political efficiency as the classes above them', could 'uniformly be the prevailing sense of the country'. Yet the technicalities of politics and the lack on the part of working men of 'the means of constantly focusing current and fugitive opinion, such as are supplied by clubs and by social intercourse to the upper class, especially in the metropolis', left day-to-day political life in the hands of the wealthy. Acceptance of this situation presupposed agreement on fundamentals and the capacity of the political class to respond to changes 'on great and engrossing subjects', on which, once roused, 'the nation is omnipotent'.

The public articulation of such 'great and engrossing subjects' was, in Gladstone's view, the distinctive and pivotal role of the Liberal Party, the lens through which general objectives could be focused into political propositions and actions. The Liberal Party was thus the agent of political integration. That another party, with labour representation as its primary aim, could develop within the political system was not excluded from his analysis. But the difficulties would be formidable: 'notwithstanding his wide franchise, and though he were to widen it as he pleased, he [the working man] bears only a divided rule: and perhaps his share is the smaller one. It would be a great error, were he to overrate his strength through omitting to notice the causes which detract from it.' Consequently, Gladstone's message throughout his later years ran, the labouring man had a prudential as well as a principled interest in continuing to support the Liberal Party; once Home Rule—in itself a good—was achieved, the 'secret garden' of delights could be unlocked. It was a teasing prospect, whose realization depended on not losing the home-rule key.

Liberalism thus had a central role to play in the process of integration and representation. But it played it in the knowledge that virtual representation in a political system which claimed direct representation meant a constant squaring of a circle, and that required constant vigilance and ingenuity on the part of the Liberal leadership of the sort Gladstone was so adept at providing. Class was acknowledged but could be contained.

[1] W. E. Gladstone, 'The rights and responsibilities of labour', *Lloyd's Weekly Newspaper*, 4 May 1890, 8–9; see 28 Mar. 90 (this important article had not been hitherto noticed).
[2] Ibid.

This drive towards an increase of labour representation was intended to broaden yet further the still broad base of the Liberal Party. Many Whigs, some radical businessmen, a significant proportion of the press and of the intelligentsia might have left the party—some permanently, some temporarily—but the Gladstone Liberal Party appeared to retain—uniquely among the forces for progress in Europe—the capacity for class and national integration. The breakup of such a spectrum of progressive forces as the Liberal Party represented was a dangerous and formidable step, as the tentative founders of the various groups which eventually made up the Labour Party realized. But the very existence of those groups showed that the Gladstonian solution of constitutional change as the focal point of integration was not enough, however much one of its implications was a cleared road for labour legislation, if that was what the party of progress in the post-Home Rule period might wish to pursue.

The Gladstonian argument on grievance was widely applied. It was for the Scottish and the Welsh M.P.s to show that they represented significant demands for disestablishment: if they could, then disestablishment would take its place in the Liberal programme. Since there was no party mechanism outside the limited forum of the N.L.F., the character of this process was uncertain and often irritating for those taking part in it. It set up an open competition within the Liberal Party as well as between the Liberal Party and its opponents. Clearly it seemed to leave a decisive role for Gladstone and the Cabinet. However, this should not be overestimated. It is clear that Gladstone regarded Scottish disestablishment as a natural development which would in time ripen: his correspondence with Scottish disestablishers from 1885 is couched in these terms.[1] Welsh disestablishment he regarded as much less natural. The strength of the Church of England in Wales before the eighteenth century was a favourite theme (with Gladstone unsettling the young Lloyd George with a question on this point):[2] Gladstone saw Welsh nonconformity as a late and perhaps transitory phenomenon. None the less it was Welsh and not Scottish disestablishment which the 1892–4 government put forward as a bill.

Gladstone's leadership of the Liberal Party between 1886 and 1892 was thus arranged on terms suitable to him, though the consequences might not always be agreeable. His leadership and the primacy of Home Rule and free trade were the fixed points. All other aspects of domestic policy were open to competition and proof of support. This leadership then, despite the immediate block of Home Rule, encouraged a form of party debate which to many outside the party and some within it seemed factious. However, in the complex nether-land of British progressive politics in the period of the waning of the *laissez-faire* state, this pluralistic approach permitted a reformation of liberalism without serious schism and with eventual success.

[1] See above, x. cxxviii–ix.
[2] See 29 May 90 and B. B. Gilbert, *David Lloyd-George*, i. 79–80 (1987).

IV

On 15 August 1892, Gladstone went to Osborne House to receive the Queen's commission to form a government:[1] the only one of the four times on which she did not seriously attempt to find an alternative.[2] She did not need to: Gladstone's party position was unassailable, but his political position was broken by the results of the election. Early results were 'even too rosy',[3] but a gain of 80 British seats at least was expected. Soon this was seen to be clearly over-optimistic: 'The burden on me personally is serious: a small Liberal majority being the heaviest weight I can well be called to bear' ... 'an actual minority, while a personal relief to me would have been worse in a public view'.[4]

Not surprisingly, the result was an improvement on the catastrophe of 1886, when in England 105 Unionists were returned unopposed and the Liberals only won 47.2 per cent of the votes: a wretched performance for a party accustomed to winning clear majorities and to regarding 1874 as an aberration. The Liberals increased their vote in England from 1,087,065 (1886) to 1,685,283 (1892), but this was largely a measure of the increase of contested seats: the Liberal share of the vote in England in 1892 was 48 per cent—just short of the level necessary to make dramatic inroads on the Unionists (in the glory year of 1906 the Liberals won 49 per cent of the English votes). In Wales in 1892 the Liberals won 62.8 per cent of the vote and in Scotland 53.9 per cent. In Ireland the Unionists fielded many more candidates than in 1886, but there was no sign whatever that Home Rule had been killed by kindness: the Home Rulers, for all their problems over Parnell, took 78.1 per cent of the votes and 80 out of 103 seats. The effect of all this was to make the Liberals the largest party with 272 M.P.s, followed by the Conservatives with 268 (which with the 46 Liberal Unionists made 314) and the Home Rulers with 81: effectively a minority Liberal government sustained by Irish votes.

In view of the expectations at the start of the campaign of a clear Liberal majority this was a poor result.[5] It was, Gladstone reflected six months later, 'for me in some ways a tremendous year. A too bright vision dispelled. An increasing responsibility undertaken with diminished means.'[6] The general failure was compounded by a sharp fall in Gladstone's majority in Midlothian, where the poll was taken after the Liberals' setback in England was known: 'The "Church" has pulled down my majority much beyond expectation.'[7]

This political blow was reinforced by two serious physical accidents and the appearance of one symptom of decline. First, on 25 June Gladstone had been

---

[1] She had already invited him by letter to form a government; see 12–13 Aug. 92.

[2] She wished to send for Rosebery as a gesture, recognizing that 'she will have that dangerous old fanatic thrust down her throat' eventually; in 1880 she had sent 'for Ld Hartington & Ld Granville. Why not [in 1892] send for Ld Rosebery or some other person? She will resist taking him [Gladstone] to the *last*'; Ponsonby dissuaded her from this course; A. Ponsonby, *Henry Ponsonby, Queen Victoria's Private Secretary* (1942), 216–17.

[3] 4 July 92.   [4] 6, 9 July 92.

[5] Even so, the percentage of votes won by the Liberals in England was the third best of the eight general elections between 1885 and 1914.

[6] 31 Dec. 92.   [7] 13 July 92.

hit in Chester on 'the left & only serviceable eye' by a 'hardbaked little ginger-bread say 1½ inch across' flung by 'a middle aged bony woman ... with great force and skill about two yards off me'.[1] This required four days in bed, impeded his electioneering, and severely affected his reading powers for several weeks. After making his first speech in Midlothian, a week after the accident, Glad-stone realized there was 'a fluffy object floating in the fluid of my servicable eye',[2] i.e. that just recovering from the gingerbread attack. These developments marked the end of his ability to rely on his eyesight: though there was some recovery in October 1892, writing and especially reading were increasingly burdensome and by 1893 he saw the world through a 'fog'. Next, while still recovering and having just become Prime Minister, he

> walked and came unaware in the quietest corner of the park [at Hawarden] on a dangerous cow which knocked me down and might have done serious damage. I walked home with little difficulty & have to thank the Almighty.[3]

In fact, Gladstone was affected by the attack for about three weeks.[4] Both these incidents were reminders that a frail majority was to be led by a frail 82-year old. As always, however, we must be careful about the extent of that physical frailty. Unable to read, Gladstone instead wrote: 'I made today an actual begin-ning of that quasi Autobiography which Acton has so strongly urged upon me.'[5] It was also perhaps, for Gladstone began at the beginning, a deflection from the disappointments of 1892. He also began work on his translation of Horace's *Odes*,[6] wrote an article for the *North American Review*[7] attacking Argyll's views of Home Rule, and a little later began work on a paper for the Oriental Congress[8] and on his Romanes Lecture,[9] due to be delivered in Oxford in the autumn. Of these, only the Romanes was a commitment hard to avoid. In the gloom of the post-election period, Gladstone seemed driven to remind himself and others that he was, as he always claimed, 'a man in politics', not a mere politician. In politics he certainly was and moreover, he was by choice (most would say) or by God's calling (he felt) leader of a party with a mission, but now a mission almost impossible of fulfilment in the coming Parliament. While at Dalmeny, on the day after he began his autobiography, he 'also sketched a provisional plan of policy for the future'.[10]

Gladstone recognized that the small majority of about 40 (353 Liberals and Home Rulers combined over 314 Conservatives and Liberal Unionists) 'much reduces the scale of our immediate powers, as compared with our hopes ten days ago'.[11] It also threw the primacy of Ireland into question: 'if we had thrown British questions into the shade we should have had no majority at all'.[12] With a brutal realism, given all his hopes and claims since 1886, his first plan of action for the 1893 session accordingly demoted Ireland.

The context of the formation of the government perhaps in part justified Gladstone's view that it was unwise to plan far ahead, and better to wait for 'the

---

[1] 25 June 92.   [2] 2 July 92.
[3] 29 Aug. 92; the heifer was shot; its head can be seen in the Glynne Arms, Hawarden.
[4] See Magnus, 402–3.   [5] 8 July 92.   [6] 14 July 92.   [7] 27 July 92.
[8] 22 Aug. 92.   [9] 31 Aug. 92.   [10] 20 July 92 (begun 8 July 92).
[11] To Spencer, 13 July 92 (references to letters printed in these volumes are in this form).
[12] Ibid.

crisis' to act as a formative context for decision-making. For the context of Irish legislation could not but be gloomy. Gladstone aimed 'at obtaining a judgment upon the great Irish question without spending the bulk of the session upon its particulars (viewing the unlikelihood as far as can now be seen of their at once passing into law: and obtaining a good or fair sessional result for the various portions of the country) . . .'. He structured the various elements of Liberal intentions into three (later four) categories: government bills, bills initiated by private members and supported by the government, bills worked through Grand Committees, and reforms achievable by administrative action. It was the most systematic plan made for any of his four ministries. The main points of the 'Newcastle Programme' with respect to England, Scotland and Wales were to be translated into legislation.

In Gladstone's initial plan, Ireland was to be dealt with by Resolution—a return to a suggestion considered in 1885–6—which would have involved only a small amount either of preparation or of Parliamentary time, and also by the repeal of coercion and various minor measures. But 'stiff conversation' with Spencer and John Morley followed, with a long meeting 'on the course to be pursued as to Home Rule'.[1] As a result, in the second version of the 'provisional outline of work' for the 1893 session, Ireland came first in the form of a 'Bill for the Government of Ireland'.[2] This was a dramatic change. Gladstone had committed himself to the major task of drawing up the bill and to doing much of the work for it in the Commons, for the Viceroy would be in the Lords or in Dublin and the Chief Secretary often in Dublin also. The price of Irish support for the minority Liberal government was a full-scale Home Rule Bill.

This decision predicated much of Gladstone's work for the next eighteen months. It was a decision encouraged by most of the senior members of the incoming Cabinet except Harcourt, and, as we have seen, one taken against Gladstone's own preference which was, ironically, much the same as Harcourt's: both had initially felt that the election result implied giving priority to British bills. It was not surprising that as the Cabinet gathered in London Harcourt made a fuss. Gladstone archly noted: 'I am sorry to record that Harcourt has used me in such a way since my return to town that the addition of another Harcourt would have gone far to make my task impossible.'[3] Harcourt's manner was over-truculent, but his basic demand was only that Gladstone should remain true to his own best judgment.

Gladstone's fourth Cabinet contained four members of Palmerston's last administration, six who would be members of the 1905 government, and two who would be active in liberal politics after the First World War. It thus spanned the office-holding epoch of the British Liberal Party. Gladstone diminished the proportion of peers in the Cabinet (5 out of 17 as opposed to 6 out of 14 in 1880 and in 1886) and increased the number of non-Anglicans to 7, as opposed to 5 in 1886 and 4 in 1880. In certain respects, therefore,

---

[1] 27 and 28 July 92. Spencer was sent the first version (see 20, 23 July 92), replying that he was 'doubtful as to dealing with the Irish question next Session by Resolution'; the Liberals would 'be regarded as "faint-hearted", if we did not bring in a Bill, and send it up to the H. of Lords. We do not moreover know what the Irish will say'; *Spencer*, ii. 211.

[2] 1 Aug. 92.   [3] 14 Aug. 92.

Gladstone's Cabinet represented a changing party. In other respects, it represented the continued dominance of Oxford and Cambridge in progressive politics. All its members had been educated at Oxford or Cambridge[1] except one who had been at London University (Herschell), one who had been educated privately (Ripon), and two who had not been to university (Mundella and Fowler). Its largest profession was writing—it was probably the most literary Cabinet ever—with six of its members well-established and substantial authors in the area of history and allied subjects (Rosebery, John Morley, G. O. Trevelyan, Bryce, Shaw-Lefevre, Gladstone) and two more who had earned their early keep as journalists (Harcourt and Asquith). Several of the Cabinet had significant business interests on their estates, but only one, Mundella, had manufacturing experience. For all his years, Gladstone had much in common with the younger members of his Cabinet. Indeed, H. H. Asquith and A. H. D. Acland represented exactly the progressive, public-spirited generalists which his Oxford University Act of 1854 had been designed to nurture.[2] Gladstone had clearly identified Asquith's potential: 'He will rise', he noted in a comment rare of its sort in his diary.[3]

Important to Gladstone both personally and politically was John Morley. After a few months of office, Gladstone remarked of Morley: 'He is on the whole from great readiness, joined with other qualities, about the best stay I have'[4]—a slightly guarded encomium, but a strong one none the less. In dealing with Gladstone, Morley in fact kept himself on a tight rein. He sometimes found the old man with his 'monstrous glasses' physically repellent. He was put off by Gladstone's habit of putting his hand before his mouth when speaking and, recording Gladstone's conversation at Dalmeny, he 'felt something horrible and gruesome about it'. There was 'a horrid ⟨black⟩ pall of physical decline hanging over all, slowly immersing the scene and its great actor in ⟨dismal⟩ dreary night'.[5] Morley saw Gladstone at the most wretched political moments of his later years. He disliked Gladstone's political devices, referring in his description of his final Cabinet to 'that sham theatric accent of his'.[6] His descriptions in his diary of Gladstone in the waning months of his last premiership reflect impatience and horror as well as pity and admiration; they are far from the depiction of simple nobility found in the third volume of his biography.[7]

A notable missing minister was Lord Granville, who had sat in Cabinet with Gladstone since 1852. Granville died in 1891, his finances in as disastrous a state as those of the Duke of Newcastle twenty-seven years earlier. Gladstone had

[1] Trinity College, Cambridge led with 6, Christ Church, Oxford came second with 4.

[2] A. H. D. Acland was the son of T. D. Acland, Gladstone's Christ Church contemporary who had taken the same path to high-church liberalism; A. H. D. Acland had been Steward of Christ Church in the 1880s and had greatly improved Oxford's extra-mural activities—a particular interest of Gladstone in the 1840s and 1850s.

[3] Comment noted during Asquith's visit to Hawarden—also a very rare accolade for a young member of a Gladstonian Cabinet; 28 Oct. 93. Asquith had first come to Gladstone's notice to the extent of mentions in his diary in April 1887; see 2, 16, 19 Apr. 87.

[4] 6 Nov. 92.

[5] See the description of the scene at Dalmeny in July 1892 in Vol. xiii, Appendix I.

[6] Appendix I, p. 439.   [7] See below, vol. xiii, Appendix I.

toiled to straighten out the Clintons' affairs: now he spent part of the early
weeks of his government raising money among the aristocracy to prevent the
Granvilles going bankrupt. Rosebery and Hartington (now the Duke of Devonshire) especially stumped up: the Duke of Westminster would not help.
Gladstone paid the balance himself and public embarrassment was avoided.[1]
He thus benefited the family twice over, for he had already helped to save the
library of Granville's stepson, the historian Lord Acton, by similar behind-the-
scenes arrangements, in Acton's case *via* Andrew Carnegie.[2]

Gladstone missed Granville for his political skills: an 'infinite loss', he felt.[3] In
Rosebery he had a Whig successor with a sharper edge but a political personality which both beguiled and infuriated. Gladstone went to greater lengths than
he had with any colleague to persuade Rosebery into his Cabinet in 1892—
partly because he needed him to assuage the Queen and her circle and partly
because he had seen him as a possible successor and apparently still did. In his
efforts to hook Rosebery, he cast the fly of the premiership over him by
'glancing at the leadership'.[4] He soon regretted his persistence.

It would be wrong to go so far as to say Gladstone had planned the party's
future leadership and, with the exception of his energetic efforts to get
Rosebery into office in 1892, he so carefully avoided identifying his successor
that when he resigned and the Queen, as we shall see, did not consult him,
there was no person obviously supported by Gladstone and set aside by the
Queen. But, helped by the exodus of 1886, he had given some younger, fresher
Liberals their heads.

Gladstone thus led a Cabinet of sturdy Liberals, some ending their days in
politics, some in mid-career and anxious, some with the knowledge that they
were being given the best chance of their generation for the future. Their
liberalism was controlled and determined, with a certain ambivalence about the
metropolis. It was not clear whether the liberalism they represented was still
that of the governing classes, or whether they were an incursion of anti-
metropolitanism into what had become a Unionist-dominated political culture.
It had been an important objective of Salisbury's leadership since 1885 to
establish conservative unionism as the normative reference point of British
politics, with the Liberals seen as a dangerous and unpatriotic faction. It was an
important part of Gladstone's leadership of the Cabinet and of the party that he
presented himself as both the best product of the Christ Church tradition,
working self-consciously in the main-stream channelled by Canning and Peel,
and as the representative of 'the masses' against 'the classes' which constituted
a political establishment corrupted by imperialism and self-seeking Unionism.

As in his previous governments, he was Leader of the House as well as First

---

[1] A loan of about £60,000 was needed to stave off bankruptcy. B. W. Currie vetoed the first plan,
initiated by Devonshire; after the election F. Leveson-Gower visited Gladstone at Hawarden and it
fell to the latter to co-ordinate arrangements, which he did successfully at what was a highly inconvenient moment (see 3 June 92, 24–8 Sept. 92, and to Harcourt, 8 Oct. 92). He must have felt a
certain piquancy in co-ordinating the politically divided Whigs in their rescue operation.

[2] See 14 May, 9 June 90.

[3] 5 Nov. 92.

[4] 12 July 92. For the Rosebery episode—and for much on the 1892–4 government—see Peter
Stansky, *Ambitions and Strategies. The struggle for the leadership in the Liberal Party in the 1890s* (1964).

Lord,[1] a duty which involved him staying to the end of each day's sitting—often in the early hours of the next morning—and writing the daily report to the Queen. In 1893, Harcourt took on the late-hours watch on non-Irish nights (a minority).[2] Despite Gladstone's age, leading the House was a sensible tactical precaution as well as a characteristic maintenance of the tradition that the First Lord should lead the House if a member of it.

Gladstone still led the Cabinet, as he had done since 1868, as its most effective Parliamentary fighter. Even in his eighties he was always ready with an authoritative reply to a tory attack, almost always able to rally his forces in the Commons and give them cheer. In a government whose Commons' majority was made up from two parties, this was a vital attribute of his leadership, and one which his colleagues knew was very hard to replace. He retained the ability to command the attention of the Commons by a skilful combination of the general and the particular, the humorous aside, and the well-turned impromptu peroration. He could also, in this last Parliament, bring adequately to heel what H. W. Lucy called 'the malcontents in his own camp'[3] and maintain the loyalty of the Irish. Despite the awkward character of his government's majority, it lost no important divisions.

As the Cabinet huddled together in the sharp Unionist wind, Gladstone gave its members a degree of confidence and even enthusiasm. He protected them from both their enemies and their supporters. Even in the very last meeting of his Cabinet, he found himself, as we shall see, sent out to round an awkward corner, taking on both the Lords and the Radicals.

Gladstone linked the 1892 Cabinet with the great days of hegemonic liberalism, and he did so not sentimentally or nostalgically but positively and optimistically. In a political situation in which the Liberals could at best peg out claims for posterity, and at worst face considerable embarrassment if their majority fell apart, Gladstone offered dignity, resourcefulness, resiliance and a determination to see his party through. In the history of the party of progress, now so scorned by a Unionism confident even in the face of electoral defeat, these were happy qualities. The government of 1892 was a disappointment. But it could have been a great deal worse.

In the difficult political circumstances created by the 1892 election, Gladstone avoided risk in forming his Cabinet. He did not countenance Dilke,[4] and

---

[1] He was also Lord Privy Seal—effectively a frozen post.

[2] See to Harcourt, 27 Jan. 93.

[3] H. W. Lucy, *A diary of the Home Rule Parliament 1892–1895* (1896), 312.

[4] Gladstone was not initially hostile to finding a way to bring Dilke back to political respectability after the Crawford divorce case; various discussions occurred and a meeting was arranged which Dilke failed to attend (see 1 July 89). In the post-Parnell atmosphere of 1891, Gladstone wrote a memorandum distinguishing between the implications of the Parnell and Dilke scandals but concluding that, for the time being, the adoption of Dilke as a candidate would have 'a most prejudicial influence' because it would weaken the position of the anti-Parnellite Irish Parliamentary party. In 1892, Gladstone was irritated by Dilke's implication in 'a plaguy speech' that Gladstone supported his candidacy for the Forest of Dean seat; Gladstone took the high ground 'on the great subject of conjugal life' in a letter to W. T. Stead: 'You are right in supposing that my lately published letter is meant to show my entire and absolute disconnection from all matters associated with the Candidature of Sir Charles Dilke'; see 13 Mar. 91, 4 May 92.

he saw off Labouchere. A Home Rule Bill would not have failed until the Lords had actually rejected it; Gladstone went to considerable lengths to keep the Court as sweet as possible in the circumstances. Insulted by the Queen's extraordinary public announcement that she accepted Salisbury's resignation 'with regret', Gladstone accepted all the lectures and reprimands (fortunately for the Queen, Ponsonby's discretion prevented her most grotesque language reaching the Prime Minister).[1] He had incurred the irritation of much of his party (led by Labouchere) by his bipartisan approach to the Royal Grants question in 1889,[2] and he declined to press Labouchere on an unwilling Victoria.[3]

The fourth Gladstone Cabinet was thus chosen to reflect stability and continuity, with a nod to the future. As Gladstone liked to remind his colleagues, Melbourne's similarly placed government had lasted from 1835 to 1841. By continuity, Gladstone understood continuity in the preoccupations of the 1886 Cabinet: the 1892 Cabinet was formed after the strategic decision to press forward with a full-scale Home Rule Bill had been taken.

Given the difficulties of its political position, and the complications surrounding the negotiations which got Rosebery in and kept Labouchere out, the Cabinet worked better than might have been expected. It was an odd staging post in the history of the Liberal Party, and its members knew it. Everything about it was transitory: its leader, its majority, many of its legislative proposals.

It was primarily an emblem. Liberalism could still form a government, and govern well within the limits permitted by its majority. Home Rule could be passed by the House of Commons, and the Home Rule M.P.s consequently had a prospect of eventual success. The Unionists could be shown up as relying ultimately on an hereditary class to defend their interests regardless of the wishes of the majority of the representatives of the United Kingdom taken as a whole, and their willingness to corrupt the natural evolution of the constitution could be seen not merely on Home Rule but on other questions also. The self-contradiction of a Unionism which gave England a veto on constitutional questions could be exposed. Of course, this was a limited ground: it admitted the extent to which the Liberal Party, once the natural party of government,

---

[1] Ponsonby, op. cit., 214ff.

[2] See 9–25 July 92 and M. Barker, *Gladstone and Radicalism* (1975), 171ff.

[3] Of course, Labouchere had little of the substance of Dilke or Chamberlain, whose appointments Gladstone had insisted on and energetically defended in the 1880s; see Barker, op. cit., 173–4. It is unclear how seriously Gladstone took the campaign for the Cabinet of 'Mr Labbi M.P.' (see 19 July 92). It proved a major talking point from 3 July 92 onwards. Gladstone went through the motions, but without much drive. He must have known that the Queen would—as she did—object. When Labouchere published the correspondence between himself and Gladstone he referred to Gladstone's 'chivalry in covering the Royal action by assuming the constitutional responsibility of a proceeding' (22 Aug. 92n.) but the opposite may just as well have been the case: the Queen (for once) useful to Gladstone. It was important, with respect to keeping the Radicals in line for 1893, that Gladstone be seen to have tried and the Queen to have behaved prejudicially.

After an amazed initial reaction, Gladstone viewed more open-mindedly than might have been expected Labouchere's next request, for the Washington embassy: 'I am not at all sure that Labouchere would do the work of a mission badly. I had no idea he was so young at 60' (to Morley, 17 Oct. 92; see also 11 Nov. 92).

had become a party dispossessed. But the government of 1892 was a government for all that: if the Unionists cared to use the Lords to frustrate the Commons, then they would be seen in their true light.

The extent to which Salisbury would use the Peers was not apparent in August 1892. The Government of Ireland Bill was in question, but not the rest of the programme. Moreover, on all the previous major clashes with the Lords, the Commons had, rather quickly, triumphed. The Cabinet thus met for the first time on 19 August for 'an initiatory Cabinet', not seated formally by portfolio, but 'in looser order' for an informal discussion of priorities: 'To contemplate by preference (except Home Rule) subjects capable of the most concise treatment.' The 1893 session was to have a 'twin purpose': Ireland and British business.[1] The burden of Ireland was to fall to the Prime Minister. Gladstone's last Premiership was to be no dignified autumnal parade, like that of Churchill in 1951, but a full-scale battle with the Prime Minister at the head of his forces.

V

The Government of Ireland Bill 1893 was the last great statute prepared by Gladstone. It reflected all the strengths and weaknesses of the 1886 Bill and, unlike the 1886 Bill, it stood alone. The Land Bill, central and integral to the 1886 plan, was not repeated. Land legislation was mentioned in the conversations with Parnell before 1890, and a bill on evicted tenants was to be started from the backbenches, but of the bill which had occasioned Chamberlain and Trevelyan's exit from the Cabinet in 1886 there was no sign. That bill had had two objectives: to assist in the creation of a loyal peasant proprietorship, and to offer a way out of Ireland for the Anglo-Irish landowners. Unionist land purchase had done the second, albeit in a form Gladstone had disliked. The proposal of Home Rule and the Liberal Party's steady adherence to it had already secured the home rule movement for constitutionalism and consequently the social prudentialism of 1885–6 had to a significant extent become unnecessary.

The 1893 Bill was thus more limited in conception than that of the 1886 twin-bill plan: it was a straightforward proposal for constitutional amendment. The bill established as its central feature an Irish legislature with two houses and a British-style executive dependent upon it. Ireland would enter gradually into her full powers, with legislation on land, the judiciary, the police, and finance only permitted after a variety of intervals. There was, therefore, a deliberate element of the provisional about the initial character and powers of the Irish legislature. Since Irish representative government and politics would be starting from scratch, establishing its executive, its offices, its buildings and its parties, this was a common-sense approach, accepted as such by most of the Irish M.P.s and especially disliked by the Liberal Unionists because it was premised on the natural development of institutions rather than on the sort of schematic rigidity which Chamberlain favoured. It was also more limited in

[1] 19 Aug. 92.

another sense. The 1886 Bill had been seen as the precursor to a general restructuring of the constitution of the United Kingdom—much of the debate on the exclusion or inclusion of the Irish M.P.s had focused on this point. For if they were excluded, it could hardly be a precedent for extension of further measures for home rule (as Westminster would end up with no M.P.s at all). Save for the accompanying Parish Councils Bill, the 1893 Bill made no response to the 'home-rule-all-round' cry which the 1886 Bill had encouraged, and Gladstone attached to the preparation of the Bill—through the device of a Cabinet committee—those of his Cabinet especially committed to a simple Irish bill.[1] Terms of reference were discussed, but the Cabinet gave its committee no very clear direction.[2]

Gladstone now paid the penalty for his reluctance to get an agreed party position on the central problems. The Cabinet accepted the committee's recommendation that 80 Irish M.P.s be included at Westminster, but only for certain purposes: Irish and Imperial but not British questions. This was a distinction which for second-order matters could be drawn by compromise and experience. But on fundamental questions of power certainty was needed. The traditional means of forcing the expulsion of a ministry was a 'no confidence' motion in the Commons. As Gladstone himself pointed out, such motions would not mention details.[3] Would the Irish vote on them, or not? This was the basic problem raised by keeping the Irish M.P.s 'in', even if in a reduced number. As in 1886, dispute about this point led to a government amendment to the clause (clause 9) during the Committee stage in 1893 (Irish M.P.s were to attend the Commons at Westminster without any restrictions). Unlike 1886, however, the change was made without the Bill's majority being lost.

An agreement before the 'time of crisis' might have been reached in such a way as to tie the party to it, and it may have been Gladstone's intention to build on his conversations with Parnell in 1889, when this point was discussed, to achieve a quasi-public agreement. The split in the Irish party and its absence of an agreed leader made this impossible, from a Liberal point of view, after 1890.

Less easy to settle in advance was the question of finance. Gladstone had come to realize that the settlement proposed with Irish concurrence in 1886—a fixed cash contribution by Ireland to the Imperial exchequer, to be reviewed in 1916[4]—took no account of inflation or deflation of the currency.[5] The conversation with Parnell in 1889 pointed to Ireland paying 'a fixed percentage of the total *Imperial* charge, varying in amount only with the variation of that charge',[6] but this was not the proposal made in 1893. This was to retain some element of

[1] Its members were Gladstone, Spencer, Herschell, John Morley, Bryce and Campbell-Bannerman. See 21 Nov. 92. Gladstone considered including Asquith, who saw home rule in the context of the development of an Imperial constitution, but Spencer in a note preferred Campbell-Bannerman; ibid. See also J. Kendle, *Ireland and the federal solution* (1989), 74ff. for the 'home-rule-all-round' movement and the Bill. For meetings of the Committee, see 23, 24, 25 Nov. 92.

[2] 21 Nov. 92.

[3] To Kimberley, 12 Nov. 92.

[4] See above, x. clvii.

[5] See mem. at 18 Dec. 89. Parnell's manifesto 'To the People of Ireland' of November 1890 did not mention the financial settlement as one of the topics about which the 1889 meeting had disquieted him.

[6] Ibid.

the notion of a fixed sum, but not in a cash form. A financial settlement was approved by the Cabinet, but with a number of important questions left open for decision during the Committee stage and with Harcourt (as Chancellor of the Exchequer) trying to introduce major modifications after the Bill had been introduced and on the evening before its publication.[1] The British exchequer was to be credited with Ireland's customs duties (levied by Westminster) as her contribution, an arrangement to be reviewed after 15 years. The balance between that sum and the present Irish revenue would be the Irish government's income (which as it would control all taxes except customs and excise it could increase or decrease if it wished). The adequacy of this balance and the fairness of the solution rested on the financial expertise of the Treasury (Welby and the young Alfred Milner) and Dublin Castle in providing the figures. When they did provide them, they were wrong: the amount raised from excise duties in Ireland was badly exaggerated by a faulty calculation. Nobody spotted the mistake until after the Bill had been introduced.[2]

A complete restructuring of the financial clauses thus became necessary when the Bill was in Committee. The Bill was changed so that all Irish taxation would be aggregated as Irish revenue (instead of the Customs being transferred to the Imperial exchequer). Ireland would then contribute to the Imperial exchequer 'one third part of the general revenue of Ireland'. That is, there would be a calculation of what the general revenue of Ireland was—a highly contentious procedure; of this, one third would go to the Imperial exchequer as Ireland's payment for defence and all the governmental activities not devolved, and two-thirds would be available for expenditure on activities devolved to Ireland. Consequently, if the Irish revenue increased (through a higher yield from greater consumption or through higher taxes), one-third would go to the Imperial exchequer. Unlike the proposals of 1886, which as we have seen would have been highly favourable to the Irish,[3] and the initial proposals of 1893, this hastily produced recommendation would have been a serious political irritant, especially during the transitional period of six years.[4]

The error and the consequent amendments were humiliating for Gladstone: 'a very anxious & *rather* barren morning on Irish Finance. My present position as a whole certainly seems peculiar: but of this it is unheroic either to speak or think.'[5] The confusion compounded the Cabinet's change of front on the

[1] Harcourt's objective was to retain strategic financial control by the Treasury; his various proposals thus had the implication of sharply limiting the area of Irish financial autonomy. See 18 Jan. 93ff. and, for his last-minute attempt at amendment, 16 Feb. 93.

[2] The effect of the miscalculation in Excise receipts was to reduce the amount for government in Ireland by over £200,000 to a clearly inadequate level. Hamilton laid the blame for 'the blunder' clearly on Milner; Gladstone was less willing to apportion it; see 16 May 93. See also 25 May 93. The explanation of how the mistake in calculation occurred was given by Milner and Lacy Robinson in a letter published in *PP* 1893–4 l. 345. They remarked: 'On the basis of the revised figures, the contribution for Ireland for the year 1892–3 is £2,240,351, not £2,605,000, as estimated by Mr. Gladstone (relying upon the amount for the previous year given in the "Financial Relations" papers of 1891 and 1893) in his speech on the First Reading of the Home Rule Bill. We can only express our great regret for the occurrence of an error of such magnitude. . . .'

[3] See above, x. clvii–clviii.

[4] Gladstone tried, but failed, to hold onto the idea of a transfer of customs receipts; see 25 May 93ff.   [5] 30 May 93.

question of whether Irish M.P.s should be 'in' or 'out' of Westminster. In 1886, the Bill had been forged in the heat of a great political crisis. That of 1893 had been in the offing for seven years, yet there was still disagreement and muddle about the two central clauses of the Bill. To say that this simply reflected the inherent ambivalence of 'Home Rule' simply further reflected the short-term strength of the Unionists' case.

Despite this, the passing of the 1893 Government of Ireland Bill in the Commons was a remarkable exercise in representative politics. The Unionists appeared to take the bill at face value and fought it clause by clause, making most of the speeches. Backbench liberals and most of the Irish were almost silent, by the self-denying ordinance agreed at the 'excellent: most opportune' Liberal party meeting on 27 March. Only on 27 July as the guillotine fell on the Committee stage after sixty-three days did the mask slip. Chamberlain told the liberals that never since the days of Herod had there been such slaves to a dictator: he was answered by shouts of 'Judas'. In 'the sad scene never to be forgotten', fighting broke out on the floor of the House when the Unionists refused to clear for the division.[1]

The time-saving reticence of the Liberal-Irish backbenchers during the summer highlighted Gladstone's role on the Front Bench as he worked the bill seemingly single-handed and through a heatwave. He felt himself supported by some external force: 'It is fanatical to say I seemed to be held up by a strength not my own. . . .' 'Never have my needs been so heavy: but it seems as if God were lovingly minded to supply them only from day to day. "The fellowship of the Holy Ghost" is the continuing boon which seems the boon for me.'[2] Beginning a new volume of his daily journal, he made a list of biblical 'Texts for the present stress.'[3]

Gladstone was supported not only by such thoughts but also by the sense that the bill of 1893 was not the end of the matter. Once decided upon it—and as we have seen he was, in the light of the arithmetic of the election result, sceptical about going ahead—he saw it as a first step. The Lords would of course throw it out, but would they dare to do so again in 1894 if the Bill—or a Resolution on it—again passed the Commons? There must come a point when the Lords 'would not dare' (as he had put it in 1885). In thinking this, Gladstone probably underestimated Salisbury's resolute combination of short-term prag-matism and long-term constitutional sterility.

'This is a great step', Gladstone noted on the passing of the Third Reading by a majority of 34 on 1 September 1893 after eighty-two sittings and an extended Session. If he meant that it was a step to be followed by another great step, he soon found himself to be wrong. The Government of Ireland Bill of 1893 showed that a Home Rule Bill could pass the Commons, but it had not shown that it could do so conclusively.

This was a serious weakness, for it spoilt the thrust of Gladstone's second position, a dissolution on the House of Lords. If there was to be a dissolution on the wrecking powers of the Lords, it would have to be on a clear misuse of those powers. The events of the summer of 1893 played into the Unionists' hands. There was no overwhelming case for a dissolution on the Lords' rejection of the

[1] 27 July 93ff.   [2] 11, 23 May 93.   [3] 1 July 93.

Bill. On the day of their vote, 8 September, when the bill was rejected after a brief debate by 419 to 41, Gladstone was driving 'to the pass over Pitlochrie' and was translating Horace's *Odes* in the Scottish Highlands.[1] He made no comment on the Lords' actions in his journal. In the autumn he floated the idea of a return to home rule in 1894—perhaps by a bill or a Resolution—but his colleagues would not follow.[2] There was no Cabinet meeting to discuss the fate of the Bill, and Gladstone did not return to London until 1 November. When the Cabinet did meet, the Lords were not on the agenda, and neither was Ireland except for the position of the Evicted Tenants Bill in the usual Commons' log-jam.[3]

The great drive for the second Home Rule Bill which had begun in the aftermath of the election defeat in 1886 and which had reached a point of genuine optimism in the late 1880s, had ended with a stand-off. The Commons had passed a bill and the Lords had rejected it. The Liberal-Irish partnership was not strong enough to dissolve upon the Lords' actions. The 'cause' was not dead but it lacked the vitality and the urgency to take on and defeat Unionism. Such remained the case for the rest of Ireland's presence within the Union. Outrageous though the Lords' actions might be, Ireland by herself was not a sufficient battering ram to break them.

VI

The failure of the Government of Ireland Bill brought Gladstone close to a final reckoning with political life. His political presence since 1874 had been self-admittedly abnormal. He was in politics for the furtherance of specific causes, not for a political career of the usual sort. The last of those causes continued, but hardly in a way in which he could hope to assist: any further Irish initiative by the Liberals would require a fresh majority in the Commons, and Gladstone's hopes for a new Government of Ireland Bill in 1894 were, as we have seen, ignored by his colleagues.

Yet the resignation of a Prime Minister, however much it might be natural and expected, can never be a simple matter, and the sinuous complexities of Gladstone's life in politics would lead us to expect ambivalence. There were factors beyond his own preferences. He had spent 1893 largely absorbed in the Irish Bill, but his colleagues had not been similarly absorbed, as their absence from the government bench during its committee stage had made rather clear. The government was pursuing as full a legislative programme as the 82 days taken by the Irish bill permitted. It became clear that the willingness of the Lords to amend Liberal bills was not confined to Ireland: here was a possible opportunity for the furtherance of the Irish cause within a more general context. Instead of being seen as the impediment which blocked the way, Ireland might be linked to British measures obstructed by the Lords and thus the difficulty of the 'English' majority against Home Rule side-stepped. The

[1] 8–9 Sept. 93.
[2] See to Morley, 15 Sept. 93; to Asquith, 7 Oct. 93.
[3] 3 Nov. 93.

House of Lords and all it represented would become the chief focus of Liberal attention, with Irish Home Rule one aspect of it. Even on his own terms, therefore, there were reasons for Gladstone continuing in office, perhaps even fighting a final election on the basis of the Lords' disturbance of the balance of the constitution.

In addition to the question of the Lords, two other factors affected Gladstone's thinking about his retirement: his personal condition and the 'mad and mischievous'[1] matter of the defence estimates.

Gladstone ended the Irish marathon in fair shape. On his 84th birthday he noted:

> I record my 84th birthday with thanks and humiliation. My strength has been wonderfully maintained but digestive organs are I think beginning to fail: deafness is (at present) a greater difficulty, and sight the greatest.[2]

His eyesight recovered up to a point from the 'gingerbread' incident in Chester in 1892, but the cataract in his eye increasingly impeded sight.[3] Colleagues tried to help by having their letters to him typed, but he found this worse than their handwriting.[4] Moreover, the cataract was 'of the kind obstinately slow',[5] so an operation to remove it was not yet possible. His eyesight was thus a reason for retiring, but it was not sufficiently bad to make retirement imperative.

Gladstone's worries about his health were increased by the death of his physician, Andrew Clark,[6] on whom he had often relied at important political moments for advice as to how far his various illnesses and physical difficulties should determine his actions. Clark, with Mrs. Gladstone, had always encouraged continuing in politics. The domestic importance of Clark's death was compounded by the suicide of Zadok Outram, Gladstone's valet, whose alcoholism had been an increasing concern of the household. He had been replaced as valet in October 1892 'after what a course of years!',[7] subsequently disappearing and being found drowned in the Thames. Gladstone wanted 'to attend the Inquest, but at any rate I gave particular testimony by a letter'.[8] The episode considerably disquieted him. He noted after Zadok's disappearance:

> Outram's absconding really afflicts & somewhat alarms me. Ever since I began to feel I was growing old I have been his daily care & he has served me with daily intelligence and daily affection.[9]

The deaths of Clark and Outram were important disturbances in a routine of life in which Gladstone was, hardly surprisingly, increasingly dependent on his immediate circle:

> I have had a heavy loss in Sir A. Clark: & a touching one in Zadok Outram. The love & service of C[atherine] remains wonderful: that of all my children hardly less so.[10]

Personal difficulties such as these encouraged a review already required by the more general political situation. Moreover, Gladstone's handling of

[1] 9 Jan. 94.   [2] 29 Dec. 93.
[3] See e.g. 23 Apr. 93. He found it increasingly difficult to use notes when speaking in the Commons.
[4] See, e.g. to Rosebery, 19 May 93n., 24 May 93.   [5] 12 Jan. 94.   [6] 6 Nov. 93.
[7] 10 Oct. 93.   [8] 13 Dec. 93.   [9] 3 Dec. 93.   [10] 29 Dec. 93.

business began to show a want of proportion. Small items of business engaged his attention at the expense of more major matters. The career of West Ridgeway[1] (a Unionist civil servant), the question of a dukedom for the Marquis of Lansdowne on his retirement as Viceroy of India,[2] and the financial settlement for the Duke of Edinburgh on succeeding as Duke of Saxe-Coburg and Gotha[3] generated a considerable correspondence. But the Cabinet's move towards direct involvement in labour relations by appointing Rosebery as conciliator in the major mining lockout in the autumn of 1893[4]—a vital moment in the history of British corporatism—seemed hardly to engage Gladstone's attention at all, despite its implications for his view of political economy.

It was not that in earlier governments Gladstone would have fought the Queen any less stoutly over Lansdowne's title—Lansdowne would have been Gladstone's second duke and an important Liberal creation: the Queen was determined to block him—but that in earlier governments the Lansdowne affair would have been one item among a hundred. In 1893–4 the affair seemed to show Gladstone crotchety.

If the miners' settlement flitted by, the vacancy in the Poet Laureateship consequent on the death of Tennyson in October 1892 did not. This was a parlour game which all could play, including, of course, the Queen. Tennyson died on 6 October, babbling of Gladstone and trees.[5] Gladstone was at Hawarden and felt himself too busy with Uganda and the writing of his Romanes lecture to accept Hallam Tennyson's invitation to act as a pall-bearer at the funeral,[6] despite the significance of the Tennysonian link to the closest friend of his youth, Arthur Hallam. None the less, Gladstone was immediately in correspondence about a new Laureate, which he was keen to keep 'on the high moral plane where Wordsworth and Tennyson left it'.[7] His preferred solution was John Ruskin—a poet in prose—suggested by Acton. The appointment of Ruskin would have certainly represented the incarnation of the sage. The thought was magnanimous, for Gladstone had been denounced by Ruskin almost as vehemently as he had been by Tennyson, whose peerage he had secured: he had enjoyed with both an ambivalent *rapprochement* in old age. Henry Acland reported that Ruskin's mental illness ruled him out.[8] Swinburne and William Morris were inquired into, Gladstone being quite sympathetic to each (Morris had of course been a strong supporter of the Bulgarian atrocities campaign). He was already fairly well read in their works, more so in Swinburne than in Morris.[9] When he had read Swinburne's *Marino Faliero* in 1885 (at Laura Thistlethwayte's suggestion) he had thought it 'a work of great power: dramatic power, power of thought, and wonderful mastery over the English language'.[10] But both Swinburne and Morris were impossible candidates to

[1] See 30 Sept., 7 Nov. 92ff. [2] See 20 Sept., 2 Nov. 93, 8, 10 Jan. 94.
[3] See Sept. and Oct. 93. [4] See 13 Nov. 93.
[5] 6 Oct. 92n. [6] To Hallam Tennyson, 8 Oct. 92.
[7] To H. W. Acland, 10 Oct. 92. For the Laureateship, see also Alan Bell, 'Gladstone looks for a Poet Laureate', *T.L.S.*, 21 July 1972, p. 847. [8] To H. W. Acland, 10 Oct. 92n.
[9] For reading of Swinburne, see 17 Dec. 72, 2 Jan., 18 June 73, 29 Sept. 76, 6 June 81, 2 Oct. 84, 25 June 85; for William Morris, see 11 Aug. 68, 26 Mar. 70, 4 May 84; for the Laureateship Gladstone re-read 'Gudrun' from *The Earthly Paradise* (see 14 Oct. 93).
[10] 25 June 85.

propose to the Queen, Swinburne for his 'licentiousness', Morris for his 'Social-ism'.[1] Others were looked at—William Watson, Lewis Morris, Robert Bridges, Fred Henderson the I.L.P. poet, Alfred Austin the jingo versifier—but none was felt appointable.[2] With no candidate strong enough to be an adequate replace-ment for Wordsworth and Tennyson or to be worth a row with the Court, and with the detailed work on the Government of Ireland Bill predominating, Gladstone rather lost heart. The Laureateship was discussed at an audience with the Queen and it was agreed to leave it in abeyance.[3] After Kipling declined in 1895, Salisbury in 1896 successfully recommended Alfred Austin, the worst poet to hold the post in modern times, an appointment which emphasized the bathotic character of the 1890s and one which vindicated Gladstone's view (rather unusual for him) that it was sometimes best to do nothing.[4]

On the whole, ministers had a free run in the fourth Gladstone Cabinet. That overarching involvement of the Prime Minister in almost all his government's affairs had, hardly surprisingly, been lacking in the 1892 administration. Also hardly surprisingly, when Gladstone did attempt to assert his authority in a major way outside the area of Irish policy, it was in that other area of unsettled business of the 1880 government, Imperial policy. His fourth government began with a row about the extent of imperial commitments, and it and his premiership ended with one. On both questions, Gladstone was on the losing side. In the initial months of the government he led a majority of the Cabinet against Rosebery and the Foreign Office on the question of Uganda (which because there was no question of a formal colony came under the Foreign rather than the Colonial Office).

East Africa had been the single area of Africa where Gladstone had been able in the 1880–5 government to frustrate the 'forward movement'.[5] The Salisbury government in 1890 signed the Anglo-German Agreement by which the German government ceded British control of the areas later called Uganda and Kenya and recognized a British protectorate over Zanzibar in exchange for Heligoland. The Salisbury government had had recourse to imperialism by the back door in the area north and west of Lake Victoria, *via* the device of the Chartered Company, that curious but convenient half-way-house where venture capitalism and the British government could each have its separate room under the same roof. But when the roof began to fall down, the tenancy agreement was always found to be poorly drawn. Like other Chartered Companies, but quicker than most, the East African Company collapsed, leaving the Imperial government with undefined but implied residual respons-ibility. This responsibility was admitted by the Salisbury government only to the

[1] For Swinburne, see 7, 10, 17 Oct. 92; for Morris, see 17, 19 Oct. 93. Either would probably have produced a view of the Queen more recognizable to Gladstone than that found in Tennyson's 'On the Jubilee of Queen Victoria': 'She beloved for a kindliness Rare in Fable or History . . . All is gra-cious, gentle, great and Queenly.'

[2] See 10, 17, 28 Oct., 5 Nov. 93.

[3] 25 Nov. 92 and *L.Q.V.*, 3rd series, ii. 187.

[4] It was said that Salisbury justified the appointment by saying he had made it for the best reason in the world: Austin wanted it.

[5] See above, x. lxxxix.

extent of making preparations for the building of what became the Mombasa-Kampala railway. But there can be little doubt that Salisbury would have done whatever was necessary to maintain British control of the headwaters of the Nile against the French and the Belgians.

Somewhat to his surprise, almost immediately after persuading Rosebery to be Foreign Secretary, Gladstone found himself involved in a major row with the Secretary and the Foreign Office, which he saw as withholding information and misleading the Cabinet. As always in Imperial matters, disagreements about general principles were impossible to disentangle from the complex details of the historically given position. Thus Rosebery could argue with only partial disingenuity that what was at issue 'is not now the expediency of an East African Empire' but the fact that a company 'has been allowed to interfere, with a royal charter granted by the Executive for that purpose' and that if the Company could no longer administer the area, the British government had effective responsibility for the fate of 'the territory, the inhabitants and the missionaries'.[1] In addition to his usual objections to Imperial expansion—that 'prevailing earth-hunger'[2]—Gladstone not implausibly feared a repeat of the Gordon *débâcle*.[3] There were several common elements: the Company not the Cabinet was nominally in control; it would be difficult simply to retreat; communications made it almost impossible for the Cabinet to direct policy. On the other hand—unlike the case of the Sudan—there were missionaries of various denominations already in the area and there had already been deaths. An evacuation unaccompanied by the missionaries could lead to a disaster, as Rosebery pointed out.

Gladstone cunningly argued for a continuation of Salisbury's policy, by which, he told Rosebery, 'I saw clearly that they accepted the evacuation'.[4] This attempt to cast Rosebery as the radical disturber was only partly successful. Gladstone mounted the last of his full-scale campaigns, a blitz of letters and memoranda by which he hoped to close down Rosebery.[5] Much of the Cabinet was with him, or ahead of him. Gladstone rather assumed that having the Cabinet with him meant the success of his views. The object of much of his correspondence was to avoid defeating Rosebery in such a way as to provoke the latter's resignation.[6] But the steady drip-drip of Imperial expansion wore the Prime Minister down. Rosebery secured a Cabinet discussion[7]—against Gladstone's will—and extracted a delay: the Cabinets in November 1892 agreed to an inquiry, conducted by a Commissioner who would report 'on the actual state of affairs in Uganda, and the best means of dealing with the country'.[8] The possibility of indirect rule *via* a Zanzibari protectorate (a protectorate governed by a protectorate) was thrown in as a further softening of the pill.[9]

---

[1] Rosebery to Gladstone, 29 September 1892; see 27 Sept. 92n.

[2] To Rosebery, 6 Nov. 93.

[3] See to Asquith, and Harcourt, 23 Sept. 92.

[4] To Rosebery, 27 Sept. 92. [5] 24 Sept. 92.

[6] This was why he worked so hard—ultimately without success—to prevent Uganda coming to the Cabinet: he thought a Cabinet meeting would mean a public humiliation for Rosebery (for news of a defeat for Rosebery would immediately be leaked by the Court).

[7] 29 Sept. 92. [8] 3, 7, 11, 23 Nov. 92.

[9] See to Rosebery, 9, 11 Dec. 92.

Gerald Portal, the appointed Commissioner, was an old Cairo hand, formerly Cromer's secretary, and was already consul-general for British East Africa. He was a skilful propagandist, infuriating Gladstone with his public pronouncements.[1] In his report he did his duty.[2]

The remote town in Uganda named Fort Portal is placed at the meeting of the Ruwenzori Mountains and Lake Albert, which by the 1890s was the most vulnerable of the sources of the Nile to non-British European control. It symbolizes therefore the extent to which the question of Uganda was but an aspect of the larger dispute about Britain's role in the Near East. Gladstone had discussed precisely this region with Sir William McKinnon and H. M. Stanley, the explorer, at the time of the 1890 Heligoland–East Africa Agreement. The meeting was arranged by Dorothy Tennant, Stanley's *fiancée*, who advised Gladstone on aspects of his reading. Stanley produced a map of East Africa, hoping for an imperialistic discussion of its developmental potential, but Gladstone turned the conversation into a lecture on the folly of giving modern names to Crophi and Mophi, Herodotus's names for the highest peaks in the Ruwenzori Mountains. It is hard to tell which side of the conversation was the more surreal: Stanley's view that Uganda was the answer to the problems of the South Wales coalfield, or Gladstone's pedantic classicism.[3] The latter, at least, was probably a political ploy.

Uganda, because of its remoteness, was one of the last pieces in what was now a largely complete imperialist jigsaw puzzle. Its shape thus related to the general pattern of African demarcation. The row about Uganda consequently became interwoven with discussions with the French about Egypt.

All the old ambivalence continued. The British presence in Egypt was temporary, but how temporary? Could the collaboration of the early 1880s with the French on Egyptian policy be restored? Any progress towards developing a context within which a Liberal Cabinet might attempt a withdrawal was halted by the Egyptians themselves. In January 1893 the new Khedive, Abbas II, dismissed his Prime Minister, Cromer's puppet. Cromer demanded action from London in the form of extra troops and what Gladstone understood to be 'the putting down of treaty rights (such I believe they are) of the Khedive by British forces; the threat of it is the same thing'.[4] Sufficient troops were redirected to Egypt[5] to assuage the Egyptian lobby and the immediate crisis passed.

The Gladstonian occupation of Egypt in 1882 had had the objective of securing order, and order was understood to mean order on European terms. Only through demonstrated order could a context for withdrawal be achieved. But since this sort of order meant a harmony of European/Egyptian interests, with the Khedive's ministers effectively in the same position as the Residents at

---

[1] To Rosebery, 13 Oct. 92. Portal died of fever soon after his return to London in November 1893, but he had time to write an account for publication of his mission (*The British mission to Uganda* (1894)) which provided a useful base for protest should the government have rejected the report.

[2] The policy of withdrawal from Uganda was officially abandoned in March 1894 immediately after Gladstone's retiral and a Protectorate was declared on 19 June 1894; see K. Ingram, *The making of modern Uganda* (1958), 60–2.

[3] 23 June 90n.; to Mrs. H. M. Stanley, 7 Oct. 92.

[4] To Rosebery, 22 Jan. 93.

[5] To Rosebery, 22 Jan. 93.

the courts of the legally independent Indian Princes, a context for withdrawal could by definition never be achieved. The only likely change was a calling in of the European Powers. The Cabinet recognized this, however unwillingly:

> the general sentiment was that if the severance in spirit of Native and British Govt. became chronic, the situation in Egypt would be fundamentally changed, & the Powers would have to be called in.[1]

'Egypt for the Egyptians'[2] was further off than it had been in the aftermath of the occupation of 1882.

This was the basic weakness of the Gladstonians' attempt to avoid involvement in Uganda. The complex forces of capital investment, geography and British strategic interest which had sucked the Gladstone government into Egypt in 1882 made British occupation of the rest of the Nile hard to avoid. As Gladstone himself had put it in 1877:

> our first site in Egypt, be it by larceny or be it by emption will be the almost certain egg of a North African Empire, that will grow and grow until another Victoria and another Albert, titles of the Lake-sources of the White Nile, come within our borders.[3]

That Gladstone's 1880–5 government had taken the first two steps, in Egypt and the Sudan, had been ironic enough. That his last government had had to take the third showed how far beyond the control of individuals, however powerful, the forces behind imperial expansion lay.

Gladstone had resisted almost all of the many Imperial acquisitions of the Cabinets in which he had sat since 1843, but he had failed with almost all of them. His vision of a world economy progressing through free trade was frustrated by the territorial ambitions of some of his colleagues, the exigencies of the great departments of state and the historical forces of venture-capital expansion and strategic interest which conditioned the actions of British governments in the second half of the nineteenth century. Like the Liberal Imperialists, Gladstone had had no answer to the question: by what agency, if not European authority, was an infrastructure to be provided when venture-capitalism—the spearhead of that free trade which was the natural consequence of progress—spread to areas of the world hitherto outside the Atlantic economy and lacking a political structure which could maintain itself in the face of 'progress'?

The question was brutally posed by the actions of the British South Africa Company in Mashonaland and Matabeleland in 1893, as a manufactured war made those territories into Southern Rhodesia. Lost in the complexities of an administrative and legal structure obscure even by the standards of Chartered Companies, absorbed by the Government of Ireland Bill's passage in the Commons, obsessed and absented by the trivial case of the Duke of Edinburgh's settlement on accession to the dukedom of Coburg,[4] Gladstone,

---

[1] 23 Jan. 93.   [2] See above, x. lxviii.   [3] See above, x. lxxiv.

[4] For the Coburg affair, symbolic of the extent to which Gladstone had become mesmerized by the Court, see letters from Sept. to Dec. 93, especially 19 Sept. 93. The Coburg affair took precedence over Matabeleland at the Cabinet of 4 Nov. 93, and Ripon complained at the 'brief and unsatisfactory' discussion of the latter (see to Ripon, 4 Nov. 93n.). After the Cabinet, Gladstone took the Coburg affair further in great detail (see to Rosebery, 5 Nov. 93) but appears to have made little effort to meet his promise to Ripon for a thorough subsequent discussion about Matabeleland.

somewhat alarmed but disconnected, failed to stiffen Ripon, the Colonial Secretary, in his attempts to maintain Imperial control in the summer and autumn of 1893. Gladstone focused on the allocation of costs and the distribution of responsibility rather than on consequences.[1] 'Rhodes wants nothing' read Gladstone's note jotted down during the Cabinet on 31 August 1893—one of the most erroneous observations in the history of British imperialism—and Rhodes was effectively given a free hand.[2] This was not altogether surprising. Rhodes had contributed to Liberal Party funds and had energetically courted the party leadership. Meetings and dinners had shown him to be a good fellow: 'A notable man', Gladstone recorded on dining with him.[3] Morley—hardly a politician prone to imperial expansionism—thought Rhodes 'Evidently a man capable of wide imperial outlook and daring and decided views. I found nothing to dislike in him.'[4] Thus Gladstone's defence of Rhodes in the Commons—'that very able man'—and of the Company fitted an established context. Moreover, Gladstone thought race relations best sorted out locally between a responsible colonial government and the indigenous population, the Imperial factor being as likely to cause complications as to do good.[5] Though he recognized that the Company could not be regarded as a responsible colonial government, he effectively treated it as such.

Thus, Gladstone's last administration continued the process of mopping up what was left of sub-Saharan Africa. It did so in the face of Gladstone's own warnings about strategic and political involvements overstretching Britain's economic base, and it did so with no corporate commitment. None the less, act it did. For all the absence of real Imperial enthusiasm in the Colonial and Foreign Offices and for all the supposed power of the Prime Minister, Gladstone's will was frustrated. Uganda was an undoubted and obvious humiliation for Gladstone, and it turned him against Rosebery for the Premiership. It was ironic that Uganda, an area of significance to only the most determined Imperialist, was the focus of a major row and a powerful defeat for Gladstone and the anti-Imperialists, while, with Rhodes benefiting from Rosebery's victory over Uganda, Southern Rhodesia, which was eventually to come within an ace of being Britain's Algeria, was acquired in what was, as far as Gladstone was concerned, very nearly 'a fit of absence of mind'.

In what turned out to be the final months of his fourth government, Gladstone found himself more isolated and even impotent on another Imperial question: the size of the navy. He was more isolated because a strong navy was the centrepiece of the 'blue water school' of strategic thought, of which almost all Liberals were members. The increase of the French and Russian fleets and the *rapprochement* between those two nations (shortly to become an alliance), the pace of technical advance in shipbuilding, the questionable competence of

[1] To Ripon, 10 Oct. 93.

[2] See 3 Aug., 4 Nov. 93, and to Ripon, 7 Oct. 93ff., 4 Nov. 93ff.

[3] 19 Feb. 91.

[4] Morley's diary, 19 February 1891, reporting a dinner with Rhodes hosted by Rendel at which Gladstone was also present. Though Rhodes sat between Gladstone and Morley, his chief conversation was with the latter, for Morley noted: 'The African has a fine head; a bold full eye, and a strong chin. He talked to me during the whole of dinner, in favour of imperial customs union. . . .'

[5] 4H 18. 595ff.

the British fleet exemplified by the *Camperdown-Victoria* collision in June 1893 and the early stirrings of the Kaiser's navy programme, all pointed to increased expenditure on the navy. The question was linked to Egypt and to Imperial strategy by the fact that the immediate area of concern was not the strength of the home fleet but of that in the Mediterranean. This was precisely that area where the events of the government hitherto suggested that even Gladstone with Cabinet backing would find it difficult to stop the Imperial departments of state, and particularly the Foreign Office and the Admiralty, adept as they were at co-ordinating their tactics and at using the Queen and even the Opposition as auxiliaries.

From the summer of 1893, Spencer, the First Lord of the Admiralty, accepted strong advice from his Sea Lords and laid plans, keeping Rosebery and the Foreign Office informed.[1] Energetically working the Irish Bill, then out of London, then preoccupied by the deaths of Clark and Outram, Gladstone seems to have been unaware of the dramatic plan that was to be put to the Cabinet when the estimates were first considered in December 1893. His mind was focused on the matter by the Queen, who in a manoeuvre constitutionally extraordinary even by her standards instructed him to read to the Cabinet her letter on the condition of the navy—which he did[2]—and by Lord George Hamilton (Salisbury's First Lord in the 1886–92 government) who moved a motion on the navy in the Commons.

Gladstone persuaded the Cabinet to treat Hamilton's motion (intended to appear bipartisan while in fact embarrassing the Government) as a motion of no confidence. Gladstone moved an amendment to it:

> Moved my amendment. Majority 36. The situation almost hopeless when a large minority allows itself in panic and joining hands with the professional elements works on the susceptibilities of a portion of the people to alarm.[3]

He then went on to make the navy estimates a matter of the Cabinet's confidence in him. Nineteen years earlier he had dealt with an analogous situation, then to do with Cardwell's army estimates. The 1874 dissolution of Parliament had been, unbeknown to the public, a dissolution by Gladstone against the army expenditure of his own first government. In 1894 he threatened a resignation against the Liberal Cabinet which would be disastrous for it at the general election, whenever that came. The Admiralty's press campaign, accompanied by well-leaked threats of the Sea Lords' readiness to resign and Hamilton's motion, had made open a question which would normally have not been before the public at that stage. A problem which had in the past sometimes affected Gladstone's plans for a resignation of protest—that the matter was not one of public discussion—had thus been removed by his opponents. But as so often before, the Whigs would not let him go.

Spencer was as well-placed as anyone could be to keep the old man in line. Though he was First Lord of the Admiralty he was also, beside Gladstone himself, much the most effective and perhaps the most committed of the Home Rulers. Despite the row over the navy estimates, he was to be Gladstone's preference as his successor. They met, cordially, but made no progress. But 'we

---

[1] See *Spencer*, ii. 223, 225ff.   [2] 14 Dec. 93.   [3] 19 Dec. 94.

agreed that in any case I ought to wind up the present Session' (then due to end in mid-February 1894).[1] Spencer may not have picked up the point of this remark, which Gladstone probably expected would be passed on to other Cabinet colleagues.

Gladstone felt a rage of impotence against his failing powers and his weakening political position. John Morley saw him at the nadir, on 8 January 1894, when Gladstone returned from Brighton on a foggy day 'haunted by the Spectre in front'.[2] Morley 'roused him from a doze' and the old man rambled in his fury, as Morley recorded in his diary:

> not exactly an incoherent conversation, but there was no *suite* or continuity to it . . . [Gladstone told him] 'It is not a question of a million here or a million there. It is a question of a man resisting something wh. is a total denegation of his whole past self. More than that', he sd. with suppressed passion, 'I seem to hear, if I may say so, I seem to hear voices from the dead encouraging me.' With a gesture pointing to a distant corner of the darkened room. He soon came to what was, I verily believe, the real root of his vehemence, anger and exaltation. 'The fact is', he sd., 'I'm rapidly travelling the road that leads to total blindness. You are all complaining of fog. I live in fog that never lifts. . . .'
> This was perhaps the most painful thing about it—no piety, no noble resignation, but the resistance of a child or an animal to an incomprehensible & ⟨incredible⟩ torment. I never was more distressed. The scene was pure pain, neither redeemed nor elevated by any sense of majestic meekness before decrees that must be to him divine. Not the right end for a life of such power, & long and sweeping triumph.[3]

Gladstone no doubt sensed the same. He focused his fury into a long memorandum. With his usual powers of resilience he rallied himself and addressed the Cabinet next day for fifty minutes in a grave and dignified exposition of its follies in accepting the Admiralty's line on the navy estimates and on his personal position ('silent—and disgraced. A survival. $\frac{3}{4}$ of my life, a continuous effort for economy'), and he brought forward an alternative plan for gradual naval expansion.[4]

Following Gladstone's exposition, his retirement was overtly discussed in Cabinet in his presence, a remarkable and humiliating moment:

> Rosebery pressed for prompt decision; the govmt. wd be broken up either way: either Spencer & others wd. be obliged to go, or Mr. G. and others who thought with him wd. go; it was not a situation that permitted suspension until Feb. 15. For this was the question:- was Mr. G. to leave now, or at the end of the session. After some talk, I [Morley] made the suggestion that we should now adjourn, and then informally among ourselves consider whether there ought to be a Cabinet for definite decision this week or whether the retirement shd. be postponed until February. The wearied, dejected, and perplexed men flew to this solution, and off we went.[5]

It is clear from his journal that Gladstone was very close to resigning at this moment in early January 1894: 'My family, within *viva voce*, are made aware. . . . Fuller conversation with my children. It is hard for them to understand.'[6] A stop-gap compromise emerged on 10 January:

[1] 3 Jan. 94.   [2] 6 Jan. 94.
[3] Morley's diary, 8 January 1894.   [4] 9 Jan. 94.
[5] Morley's diary, 9 January 1894.   [6] 9, 10 Jan. 94.

> J. Morley with much activity, last night, & today after a long conversation with me prosecuted & brought into action the plan for time. I am to go to Biarritz on Saturday. The Estimates will be prepared departmentally as usual. The session will be wound up shortly after Feb. 12. No Cabinet at present.[1]

Next day he noted:

> I am now like the sea in swell after a storm, bodily affected, but mentally pretty well anchored. It is bad: but oh how infinitely better than to be implicated in that [navy] plan![2]

So Gladstone was sent to exile in France, and the Prime Minister spent a month in the country whose navy was the chief force against which the defence estimates were intended to guard.

Just before leaving for Biarritz, Gladstone had a further examination of his eyes by Granger, the Chester oculist who had treated him following the gingerbread assault. When Gladstone, in response to a report in the *Pall Mall Gazette* that his resignation was imminent, issued a statement from Biarritz *via* his secretary, Algernon West, that no decision had been made but that 'the condition of his sight and hearing have in his judgment, made relief from public cares desirable',[3] Granger was tricked by a reporter into making a public statement about his patient, giving his view that Gladstone's eyesight did not in itself require his resignation.[4] Hardly surprisingly, Gladstone was incensed at this intervention[5]—which seemed a further conspiracy against his arranging his retirement on his own terms.

With Gladstone removed to Biarritz, correspondents and emissaries—in particular Acton—tried to help him change his mind. He responded by setting down his thoughts in a memorandum remarkable in the annals of British radical writing:

The Plan

I deem it to be in excess of public expectation
I know it to be in excess of all precedent
It entails unjust taxation
It endangers sound finance
I shall not minister to the alarming aggression of the professional elements[?]
    to the weakness of alarmism
    to the unexampled manoeuvres of party
not lend a hand to dress Liberalism in Tory clothes.
I shall not break to pieces the continuous action of my political life, nor trample on the tradition received from every colleague who has ever been my teacher
Above all I cannot & will not add to the perils & the coming calamities of Europe by an act of militarism which will be found to involve a policy, and which excuses thus the militarism of Germany, France or Russia. England's providential part is to help peace, and liberty of which peace is the nurse; this policy is the foe of both. I am ready to see England dare[?] the world in arms: but not to see England help to set the world in arms.
My full intention is that of silence till the matter is settled in the regular course of sessional proceedings; when they are at an end, in the event of new circumstances and

---

[1] 10 Jan. 94.   [2] 11 Jan. 94.   [3] 31 Jan. 94.
[4] To Granger, 20 Feb. 94n. and Stansky, 36.   [5] To Granger, 20, 23 Feb. 94.

prolonged controversy, I may consider my duty afresh, upon the principle which guides me throughout, namely that of choosing the ultimate good and the smallest present evil. The smallest of all the present evils is the probable disparagement of myself (for surmise will arise, and probably will not be put down): great and certain evils are the danger to the party, and new uncertainties for Ireland. But these in my opinion are inherent in the plan itself, and would not be averted were it possible for me to say aye to it.[1]

To keep Gladstone from resigning, Acton was a good card to play, but he was not a trump. His lack of executive experience meant that he could count for little in Gladstone's mind on the particular point at issue. He could, and did, put the immediate question of the naval estimates in the wider context of the future of liberalism and the implication for that future if Gladstone resigned to oppose a policy which a Liberal Cabinet was prepared to execute. Gladstone was already aware of this aspect of the question and Acton's urgings probably gave him greater pause.

Two days after Acton's memorandum had been read to him in Biarritz by his daughter Mary, he began seriously to bring forward the quite different matter of the House of Lords, already adumbrated in correspondence.[2] A dissolution on the Lords—'whether the people of the U.K. are or are not to be self-governing people'—would unite the Cabinet and the party. Certainly the conduct of the Lords since 1892 had posed this as a major question for the future of liberalism. It was, however, one which would require a very careful selection of timing: in Gladstone's own terminology, the question did not yet seem 'ripe'. From Gladstone's own point of view, an immediate dissolution on the Lords had the great advantage of deferring decisions on the navy estimates until after the election.

Gladstone thus returned to London from Biarritz on 10 February 1894 with two routes to resignation open, and one to a further round of political activity. He had two reasons for retiring—his eyesight and the navy estimates—and the *ballon* of a dissolution at the end of the session on the question of the Lords. It was a flexible position for one whose political career most of his Cabinet assumed was over. He pressed the Lords dissolution to the fore just before his return, and it was at once clear that the Cabinet was uniformly hostile.[3]

It was obvious that Gladstone was not returning simply to chair the Cabinet in a routine way. He, and its members, expected a *dénouement*. He found the session not ended, but extended because of the Lords' amendments to the Employers Liability and Local Government Bills. Morley told him that if he (Gladstone) resigned on the navy plan, he (Morley) would resign also:[4] this was in effect a reminder that a resignation on the navy would harm the Irish cause. This probably was a trump card. More than anything, it is likely to have encouraged Gladstone to give several reasons rather than a single cause for his departure.

[1] 20 Jan. 94.
[2] Acton accompanied Gladstone to Biarritz, argued with him, returned to London, and then sent a detailed refutation of Gladstone's arguments to be read to him by his daughter and Acton's long-term friend, Mary Drew; 2 Feb. 94 and Stansky, 31–2.
[3] Stansky, 39.
[4] 11 Feb. 94.

At the Cabinet on 12 February, however, Gladstone chaired the meeting as if nothing had happened, or was expected to happen, and made no comment in his journal. Morley described the scene:

Cabinet met at noon. Everybody there, full of expectation. Mr G. easy and cheerful. In the most matter-of-fact way he opened the fateful sitting. Ripon, he sd., had something to say about N.S. Wales ... it was agreed to in a minute.... Next we passed to Employers' Liability. Asquith stated his point: with admirable clearness. Then to Parish Councils. About twenty minutes on this. That brought us to the end of the agenda. Now the moment had come. The declaration of his final purpose must now be made. ⟨The cruel suspense of all these weeks was now at an end⟩ We drew in our breaths. Mr G. moved in his seat—gathered up his notes—and in a dry voice with a touch of a sigh of relief in it sd., 'I suppose that brings us to an end for to-day.' Out we trooped, like schoolboys dismissed from their hour of class. Never was dramatic surprise more perfect.[1]

By the time of the Cabinet dinner on 17 February it had been made clear to him by colleagues *via* Sir Algernon West, his private secretary, that some sort of announcement was expected. Gladstone noted in his journal:

Cabinet dinner. All. I believe it was expected I should say something. But from my point of view there is nothing to be said.[2]

Next day Gladstone started work on an article on the Atonement, a clear sign that his mind had moved past the point of retirement. By this time it was apparent both that the Lords were pressing forward with their substantial amendments to the Employers' Liabilities Bill and the Local Government Bill and that there was no support for defiant action by the Cabinet.

As the session drifted to its end, Gladstone alerted Sir Henry Ponsonby, the Queen's Secretary who had worked so hard to contain the Queen's hostility, that it was 'probable' that when it ended 'I may have a communication to make to Her Majesty'—the first of several papers 'connected with the coming events'.[3] Gladstone's aim was to prepare the Queen for his resignation while trying to get her not to tell the Tories it was impending. He needed to be sure that what he said would not go 'beyond H.M.'.[4] The Queen refused to 'bind herself to preserve secrecy on a matter of which she knew nothing and asked for some hint ...'.[5] It required little imagination on the Queen's part as to what Gladstone had in mind, but she was determinedly and unpleasantly unhelpful throughout the process of the retirement for which she had so long wished and worked.

It would be easy to see these manoeuvres as an example of Gladstonian over-elaboration. Gladstone's request for an assurance of secrecy may have seemed offensive but Victoria's recent record suggested that it was necessary: vital

---

[1] Morley's diary, 12 February 1894.

[2] 17 Feb. 94. Morley noted in his diary on 12 February, further to his account of the non-resignation Cabinet that day: 'Three hours later, sitting on the bench between Mr G. and Asquith I recd. a card for a Cabinet dinner on Saturday. The others got theirs by & bye. Nobody had heard a word of this. What a curious ⟨silent⟩ move. Doubtless he means to make this an occasion for telling us he is off, and being a dinner, he will not have to report to the Queen. The delay for a week makes our position in respect of reconstruction, budget, and other business, almost impracticable.'

[3] 21 Feb. 94.   [4] 21 Feb. 94.   [5] 24 Feb. 94.

amendments by the Lords on various bills were still pending and tory tactics might be affected if Gladstone's resignation was known to be definite. Gladstone's need to ask for secrecy and Victoria's refusal of it was a sharp example of her marked political partisanship. It was an exceptional situation when the sovereign would not agree to accept a confidence from her Prime Minister.

Eventually, Gladstone cut the knot by writing to the Queen, on 27 February, of his intention to retire when the business of the Session was concluded. His resignation was 'on physical grounds'.[1] Next day during an audience of about half-an-hour—'doubtless my last in an official capacity'—he told her that 'if we had the Speech Council on Saturday my definitive letter might go to her on that day',[2] as indeed it did. Gladstone had done as he told Spencer in January he would do: resigned at the end of the Session.

His final Cabinet was on Thursday, 1 March 1894, the last of 556 he had chaired. It was not simply a formal farewell. The Cabinet gave in to the Lords' amendments to the Local Government Bill: '*Accept and protest? We adopt this*'[3] and the end-of-Session Queen's Speech was agreed to. Gladstone's 'words in the Commons today' were then discussed: he was urged to speak strongly against the Lords while announcing the capitulation, and he agreed to do so.

There then followed the moment anticipated for so long—at least since 1880—by his Liberal colleagues. They were too upset to manage it well, and the scene became known as 'the blubbering Cabinet'. Kimberley, the senior member of the Cabinet, began to speak but broke down. He managed to finish his few simple sentences. Harcourt, also weeping, read out a long letter which he had already sent to Gladstone and to which he had had a reply.[4] It spoilt the dignity of the occasion, but it reflected the character of the Cabinet. Gladstone, Morley noted, 'sat quite composed and still. The emotion of the Cabinet did not gain him for an instant.'[5] Gladstone noted:

Final Cabinet 12–1¾. A really moving scene.[6]

The Cabinet ended. Gladstone 'went slowly out of one door, while we with downcast looks and oppressed hearts filed out by the other; much as men walk away from the graveside'.[7]

In what can hardly have been an easy occasion for him, Gladstone went for the last time to the House of Commons and sat through his last question-time. He then spoke on the Lords' amendments to the Local Government Bill, withdrawing opposition to them 'under protest'. This was no formal epilogue. Gladstone was put up by the Cabinet to conduct an awkward retreat and in effect to announce the defeat of his own plan for a dissolution against the Lords. He did so, as so often before, by covering an immediate defeat by a call to action in a future crusade—it was 'a controversy which, when once raised, must go forward to an issue'[8]—and his speech helped to limit the radical vote against the Cabinet's decision to 37—a typically ambivalent conclusion to Gladstone's

---

[1] 27 Feb. 94n.　　　　　　　　　　[2] 28 Feb. 94.　　　　　　　　　　[3] 1 Mar. 94.
[4] 25 Feb. 94.　　　　　　　　　　　　　　　　　　　　[5] Morley's diary, 1 March 1894.
[6] 1 Mar. 94. For the final Cabinet, see also below, xiii, Appendix I and Lord Rosebery, 'Mr. Gladstone's last Cabinet', *History Today* (December 1951 and January 1952).
[7] Morley's diary, 1 March 1894.　　　　　　　　　[8] 4*H* 21. 1151 (1 March 1894).

relations with radicalism. As the House emptied, Gladstone with characteristic politeness stayed in his place to listen to the ramblings of Lord Randolph Churchill.

The House had sensed something unusual, but the Cabinet had not 'leaked' and Gladstone remained, of course, a stickler to the last for constitutional form:

> I tried to follow the wish of the Cabinet: with a good conscience. The House showed feeling: but of course I made no outward sign.[1]

VII

Gladstone never again entered the House of Commons, in which he had first set foot as an M.P. sixty-one years previously, in 1833. He again declined the Queen's offer of a peerage, and made it clear to his wife that in his view she should likewise decline a peerage for herself.[2] He thus died plain 'Mr.', an almost unique reticence for a Prime Minister.[3] To accept a title at the same time as declaring the House of Lords the central political question of the future would not, in the history of the British political élite's attempts to come to terms with constitutional change, have been an exceptional or even an unusual irony. But its refusal went beyond mere consistency. For all the many honours he had recommended for others, Gladstone always saw himself as a commoner. His veneration for hereditary land tenure and the social system that accompanied it was well-established. But despite the fact that he had at various times owned most of the Glynne family's lands in Flintshire, he always saw himself as outside the British tradition of aristocratic absorption. He was always a guest at Hawarden: it was not his home. It was entirely in character that, in encouraging his wife to resist the offer of a new peerage, he should in the same letter suggest she revive her claim to a dormant one. It was a thin line of distinction, but it was one which sharply illustrated Gladstone's curious relationship to the political class. To be both a leading executive politician—a man from the heart of the Oxford establishment with all the necessary credentials of experience and authority—and for several political generations the dominant voice in the party of progress, gave Gladstone a force unrivalled in the history of progressive politics. It was not the least ironic feature of Gladstone's long career that the last part of it was devoted to the promotion of a policy which he deemed and which from the perspective of a century later does seem conservative and conducive to the strength of the monarchy.

The Queen, of course, would have none of Gladstone's protestations. When he warned her in a huge memorandum that 'in the powerful social circles with which Your Majesty has ordinary personal intercourse' the views of her 'actual advisers' (i.e. the Liberal government) were barely represented, and that this could not but be dangerous to the monarchy, she only acknowledged receipt of

---

[1] 1 Mar. 94.   [2] To Mrs Gladstone, 21 Mar. 94.

[3] Henry Pelham, the younger Pitt, Spencer Perceval and Canning died in office. There have been three others (George Grenville, Bonar Law and Ramsay MacDonald) who had a period after holding the premiership during which they might have taken a title—in Bonar Law's case a very brief one.

it under pressure from her secretary, the long-suffering Henry Ponsonby. Gladstone and Ponsonby, a liberal, continued to shield the Queen. Her response was to assert her powers at least as energetically as in her dealings with earlier Gladstonian administrations. At the same time she expected—as Gladstone put it—'a party with whom she has publicly advertised her disgust at having anything to do'[1] to get a good settlement for her financially incompetent son, Alfred Duke of Edinburgh, when he decided to go to live in Germany as Duke of Saxe-Coburg. Gladstone sometimes referred to his relationship to her as a reason for leaving office. It is certainly the case that freedom from her constant importunities was the most pleasurable aspect of his retirement from the Premiership. His relations with the Prince of Wales, despite the scandal of the Tranby Croft affair, continued to be frequent and satisfactory[2] and he found the Duke of York—the future George V—'not only likeable but perhaps loveable'.[3]

Notoriously, the Queen did not ask her most experienced Prime Minister for his advice as to his successor. Ponsonby, perhaps with the Queen's knowledge, sounded out Gladstone on this before his final audience, but the latter refused to discuss the matter unless the inquiry was clearly 'from her and in her name . . . otherwise my lips must be sealed'.[4] Gladstone's stiffness was partly a matter of constitutional rectitude—precedent certainly suggested that he was right to expect formally to be asked—afforced throughout the episode by his sense that the crown was darkened by a dank Unionist shadow.[5] But the episode was also, as he realized, symptomatic of a more general malaise. Even discounting the Queen's hostility to Liberalism, Gladstone thought, there was in his relations with her 'something of mystery, which I have not been able to fathom, and probably never shall'.[6] In the fortnight after his resignation he was preoccupied in conversation and on paper with the Queen's behaviour towards him, for he felt he had been dismissed with the 'same brevity' used in 'settling a tradesman's bill'.[7] He was still worrying about the episode in 1896, dreaming about having breakfast with Victoria[8] and noting that his family was, after his death, 'to keep in the background the personal relations of the Queen and myself in these later years, down to 1894 when they died a kind of natural death'.[9] It was the Queen's personal discourtesy to him and to Catherine Gladstone which rankled, not her constitutional failure to ask his advice as to his successor.

---

[1] To Harcourt, 14 Sept. 93.   [2] See, e.g., 3 June 93.

[3] 16 Feb. 93.   [4] 3 Mar. 94.

[5] Gladstone's preference was Spencer, at first glance an ironic choice, for it was Spencer's naval programme that had caused the row leading up to Gladstone's resignation. But Spencer was of all the Cabinet, more so perhaps than Morley, the person most committed to Home Rule. Morley noted in his diary on 4 January 1894, when the navy row was at its height, Gladstone's 'extraordinary ejaculation, "Under certain circs., Kimberley."!'

[6] 10 Mar. 94.   [7] 10 Mar. 94.

[8] This dream—and Gladstone very seldom recorded having dreamt—was one of two in his lifetime involving people: the other was of Disraeli (see 3 July 64). His dream about having breakfast with Victoria may have had a sexual dimension, for he records having 'a small perturbation as to the how and where of access'. 'Reserved for access' was the phrase he had used in 1839 to describe his virginity on marriage (see 14 June 39). For sexual dreams about royalty, see W. Ronald D. Fairbairn, 'The effect of the king's death [George V] upon patients undergoing analysis' (1936) in his *Psychoanalytic studies of the personality* (1952).   [9] 2 Jan. 96.

Gladstone smarted at the Queen's handling of his retirement. If that was her intention, it was ignominious. If it was not, it showed a marked limitation in her capacity as a constitutional monarch.

The effort of his final government left Gladstone and his wife more exhausted than perhaps they first realized. Colds, coughs, diarrhoea, fatigue, deafness, the impending cataract operation, meant doctors were in constant attendance on them both: 'what a couple!'[1] Moreover, they were, outside Hawarden Castle, nomadic. None of the Gladstone children had a house in London, suitable for parental use. After the sale of the lease of 73 Harley Street in 1882, the Gladstones had no London base, except when entitled to live in 10 Downing Street (in 1894 Rosebery delayed moving in to take account of this). For accommodation in the south they thus relied on the 'Gladstonian court', that small group of rich relatives and friends who effectively looked after them through the period covered by these volumes (except when Gladstone was Prime Minister): the Aberdeens with their house at Dollis Hill, then regarded as north of London; Lucy Cavendish and the Rendels in central London; George Armitstead in London and Brighton. These arrangements cannot have been easy on either side—'Moving in and out of furnished houses is a serious affair after 80'[2]—but the alternative of a London house or flat—a return perhaps to Albany—was not sought on a permanent basis. Gladstone noted in 1887: 'to Dollis Hill: a refuge for my shrinking timidity, unwilling at 79 to begin a new London house'.[3] 10 St. James's Square—a vast and hardly suitable establishment, later Chatham House—was rented for six months in 1890, but the experiment was not repeated.[4]

Rendel and Armitstead, moreover, arranged and paid for most of the Gladstones' trips abroad which became a settled feature of the routine of their old age. Rendel hosted their visit to the south of France in 1887[5] and to Italy in 1888,[6] Armitstead their stays in Biarritz when for a time it replaced Cannes as their French wintering place in the 1890s, despite the fact that Gladstone was initially blackballed from the British club there.[7] One or other of them made the hotel arrangements. They booked the carriages for the Gladstones' day trips and sometimes for more extensive expeditions, including one to Lourdes in January 1892.[8] Sometimes both Rendel and Armitstead were in attendance together.

They were, from Gladstone's point of view, a convenient choice as companions. Neither had real political ambition or sharp intellectual power. But both were Liberal in politics, wealthy, interested in politics but largely outside the inner circle of active policy makers. Armitstead had been liberal M.P. for Dundee and Rendel, like Gladstone an Oxonian Anglican, was Liberal M.P. for Montgomeryshire until 1894. Each got on amiably with the Gladstones, genially advancing the old man's flow of conversation with a prompt or a question and happily taking their turns at the evening game of backgammon

---

[1] 14 Mar. 94.   [2] 5 Aug. 90.
[3] 5 Mar. 87. 16 St. James's Street was rented for a short period; see 8 Feb. 88.
[4] 13 Dec. 89, 29 Jan. 90.   [5] 3 June 87.   [6] 18 Nov. 88.
[7] 16 Dec. 91, 21 Dec. 92, 14 Jan. 94. For the blackballing incident, see 17 Dec. 91n.
[8] 12 Jan. 92.

which, almost as much as Church-going, was a regular part of Gladstone's daily round in his later years. They acted as companions almost in the professional, Victorian sense, except that they, not Gladstone, paid. Their relationship to him was thus easy. They were both 'old shoes'. Someone like Acton or Morley might be more stimulating for a day or so. But neither Acton nor Morley could become 'old shoes' in the way that Rendel and Armitstead did. Angry almost to the point of fury over the navy estimates in December 1893, Gladstone retired with Armitstead (a bachelor) to Lion Mansions, Brighton (Catherine Gladstone being ill at Hawarden) and the two of them spent Christmas week with Helen Gladstone at the seaside. Armitstead, particularly, seems to have been a calming crony. Like Catherine Gladstone they are frequently mentioned in the diary but no more than mentioned: like her, Gladstone took them for granted. Unusually among Gladstone's close friends, both were successful business men, Rendel in the armament and engineering firm of Armstrongs of Newcastle, Armitstead in the Baltic trade in his family's firm.

Various other friends attempted a similar role but were rather obviously using Gladstone to advance their interests. Andrew Carnegie offered 'as a Loan "any sum" needful to place me in a state of abundance, without interest, repayable at my death, if my estate would well bear it; if not, then to be cancelled altogether'. Gladstone considered the offer 'entirely disinterested' but 'of course, with gratitude, I declined it altogether' and tried to interest Carnegie in the Liberals' election fund.[1] For a man expecting to be Prime Minister this was clearly prudent, for to have been thus beholden to the world's most flamboyant capitalist could hardly have been seen as disinterested. Sir Edward Watkin's sponsorship of Gladstone's Paris visit in 1889[2] as part of his campaign for the Channel Tunnel and Sir Donald Currie's lending of his steamships for Gladstonian voyages are lesser examples. But Stuart Rendel and George Armitstead were not intrusive in this way. Both were capable of giving a political nudge—Rendel on Welsh affairs, keeping Gladstone in touch with Welsh M.P.s[3] and acting as a broker on the Welsh church question,[4] Armitstead introducing Gladstone to Labour M.P.s[5]—but their advantage was that they were political messengers rather than players. 'Attendant lords' was exactly their position, for Gladstone ennobled Rendel in his final honours list and Campbell-Bannerman saw to Armitstead in 1906.

A different sort of case was Lionel Tollemache, who saw himself as Gladstone's 'proxy-Boswell', though Gladstone hardly saw himself as Tollemache's Johnson. When in Biarritz he enjoyed an intellectual joust with Tollemache and noted of him: 'he in particular is a very interesting person'.[6] But talking to Tollemache was like talking in the All Souls Common Room: suitable for a literary show but not a confidence. Gladstone showed one side of his intellectual fascination to Tollemache, but he did so in such depth as to indicate a

---

[1] 12 June 87.   [2] 3 Sept. 89ff.

[3] 17 Mar. 86, 16 July 89, 7 June 90. He was consulted by Gladstone on his important speech at Swansea; see 3 June 87. Gladstone used him to contact the Welsh M.P.s during the Parnell crisis; see 26 Nov. 90.

[4] 18 Nov. 88, 5 July 93, 76 Nov. 93.

[5] 26 Apr. 87.   [6] 24 Jan. 94.

considerable compliment. Even so, Tollemache with his ready pen was a man to be watchful of.[1]

Parallel to the sustaining work of Rendel and Armitstead was the assistance of the Gladstone 'children', now in their 40s and 50s. They had what Gladstone aptly called (with respect to Hallam Tennyson) a 'filial career'.[2] The lives of seven of the eight living children were lived, whether by occupation or relationship, within a context largely of their parents' making: that is, their emotional focus remained parental. Several of them attempted non-filial careers or married, but in almost every case these were confirmations of their parents' interests rather than departures. William and Catherine Gladstone spread a long and subtle shadow.

Willy, the owner of Hawarden, and consequently the central figure of the familial support-network for his parents, died from a brain tumour in June 1891.[3] That he was seriously ill rather than cantankerous began to become clear from March 1889,[4] but the probability of his death does not seem to have been fully grasped by his parents. When his son's illness entered its final stage, Gladstone was with J. J. Colman at Lowestoft, recuperating from influenza. Catherine Gladstone left for London on 'her holy errand'.[5] The news of Willy's imminent death was kept from his father, who travelled next day to London only in time to see 'the dear remains'.[6] Gladstone's failure to see his son alive for a last time reflected their curious relationship. In terms of time spent together, Willy was probably the closest of the children to his father, yet there was always a sense of distance between them: that same unstated sense that the son had not come 'up-to-scratch' that had existed in the mind of Sir John Gladstone about *his* eldest son, Tom, William's brother, who died in 1889 just as the seriousness of Willy's condition first became apparent.[7]

Willy's unexpected death immediately caused confusion in the arrangements made for the succession to the Hawarden estates. In order for them to remain wholly within the Gladstone family, it was arranged that their ownership should revert to W. E. Gladstone,[8] who had very briefly owned them in 1875, so as to exclude Catherine Gladstone's niece, Gertrude Glynne, now wife of the choleric Lord Penrhyn, who disputed the reversion, eventually unsuccessfully.[9] For the second time in his life, William Gladstone was thus briefly laird of Hawarden. That he should own his wife's family estates as a result of the death of his son was a cruel irony.[10]

Gladstone enjoyed a cheerful relationship with his grandson William, who became the heir of Hawarden as a result of his father's death. The cross-

---

[1] For him, see Asa Briggs's introduction to *Gladstone's Boswell*, a reprint (1984) of the third edition of L. A. Tollemache, *Talks with Mr. Gladstone* (1903).

[2] To Hallam Tennyson, 8 Oct. 92.

[3] For him, see Michael Bentley, 'Gladstone's Heir', *E.H.R.* (October 1992).

[4] 2 Mar. 89ff.   [5] 30 June 91.   [6] 4 July 91.

[7] 2 Mar. 89.   [8] 11 Aug. 91, 12 Mar. 92.

[9] See 11, 18 Aug. 91n. The negotiations were initially handled by Lucy Cavendish.

[10] Changes were then made to the testamentary dispositions of Stephen Gladstone, the second son, lest the young W. G. C. Gladstone (the heir to Hawarden whose affairs were administered by his uncles as trustees), should die childless. This was prudent, as he was killed in the First World War, married but without an heir. See 4, 9 July, 5 Aug. 91.

generational link (and the discounting of W. H. Gladstone even before his death) was marked by the last of Millais's portraits of W. E. Gladstone, begun in 1889.[1] The least successful of the series, it shows Gladstone in a formal setting holding his top hat with his grandson by his side, the latter sporting a 'Little Lord Fauntleroy' suit (Gladstone had read the book and met Frances Hodgson Burnett in Italy).[2] The picture was finished, by odd coincidence, just as W. H. Gladstone died. 'Dossie' Drew (Mary's daughter) was the grandchild whose company the Prime Minister especially enjoyed; her disregard for convention was similar to Catherine Gladstone's and she is often described as being 'in great force'.

Increasingly Gladstone relied on his third son, Henry Neville Gladstone, now permanently returned from India, for business arrangements. Henry married Maud, daughter of Stuart Rendel, and thus the business links between the families were formalized.[3] Henry and Herbert both continued to take turns with their sisters Mary and Helen at supporting their parents and acting as their father's private secretary. Herbert and Helen remained unmarried. The decisive moment of Helen's career as a university teacher was her decision, strongly encouraged by her father, to decline the Principalship of Royal Holloway College[4] and to stay on at Newnham College, Cambridge. Newnham was rewarded by a visit from the former Prime Minister, a notable event for a young college.[5] Gladstone planted a tree, soon afterwards destroyed, probably by a tory undergraduate; he presented instead an oak reared in the grounds of Hawarden, which still flourishes.

Between them, Gladstone's children had made up for the clerical career for which he had sometimes yearned. Stephen was Rector of Hawarden and remained so, despite doubts about his calling which made him often restless and sometimes inclined to resign his valuable charge. His father's instinctive reaction was to try to link him to Hawarden in a different way—and one which would have put him much more directly under his control—by offering him at £300 p.a. the wardenship of the embryonic St. Deiniol's Library.[6] This came to nothing, but his advice seems to have played a part in persuading Stephen to continue during a period of severe doubt in 1893.[7] Agnes and Mary were both married to priests and Mary's unhealthy husband, Harry Drew, was wholly absorbed into the Gladstonian circle, becoming curate of Hawarden and acting Warden of St. Deiniol's Library. Of the children, only Agnes Wickham lived her life largely outside the context of her parents' activities. But she was not wholly outside them, for her father's patronage made her husband, Edward, dean of Lincoln in 1894, one of his last acts of ecclesiastical patronage.[8]

When out of office Gladstone did not employ a secretary. His correspondence increased as his capacity to deal with it diminished. His failing sight meant he had to have much of it read to him and though he continued to write most of his letters he no longer made his own copies of the important ones. His daily

[1] Reproduced below, vol. XIII. For its sittings, see 25 June 89ff., 29 July 91ff.
[2] See 12, 16 Nov. 87, 19 Jan. 88.   [3] 30 Jan. 90.
[4] 1, 22, 24 July 86.   [5] 31 Jan. 87.
[6] To S. E. Gladstone, 8 Apr. 93. Stephen took some time to recover from this crisis; see 17 June 93.
[7] 3 Apr., 20–6 May, 17 June 93.   [8] To Wickham, 23 Jan. 94.

routine required the processing of his vast post and he also needed the repose which reading gave him. Increasingly he depended for the latter on a reader. Without a secretary (though Spencer Lyttelton sometimes helped with the post) these duties fell largely on his 'children'—especially but not solely on Mary and Helen.

Gladstone and his wife thus created a set of extraordinarily powerful family ties, which, because he was Prime Minister, necessarily existed largely on Gladstone's terms. Those terms were generous. The children were well supported financially. The parents' company was scarcely dull or their life unexciting. The nature of obligation was understood and not stated. Overt requests for help never had to be made. The 'children' seem to have arranged their rotas willingly enough. But Henry, Herbert, Mary and Helen must sometimes have wondered how their lives would have developed if their father had employed a couple of secretaries.

Catherine Gladstone remains an enigmatic figure. Her illnesses and insomnia suggest a more complex character than the cheerful, slightly scatty chatterbox she is usually depicted as. What she knew of her husband's sexual temptations, we do not know. Had she seen the scars on his back when in the 1840s and 1850s he used the scourge after meeting prostitutes? What was her view of the regular letters to and fro to Laura Thistlethwayte and the visits to 15 Grosvenor Square and later to Laura's cottage in Hampstead? Certainly the view that the Gladstones' marriage was a matter of *simple* happiness is not one tenable by a systematic reader of these diaries. But, in these volumes at least, with Gladstone in his seventies and eighties and work with the prostitutes virtually ended[1]—the last recorded encounter was in the nervous days just before resignation as Prime Minister[2]—she had to deal with a less restless husband. Gladstone recorded much about himself and about most of his regular habits, including in his later years a good deal about his bowels. But for all its intimate detail, the diary is completely silent about his sexual relations with his wife. This is hardly surprising, but it means a central aspect of his life is unrecoverable.

In an age when the public position of women was fast changing, Catherine Gladstone was an important icon. She was the first woman to sit on the platform at political speeches. She energetically organized various homes and hostels. She was the first President of the Women's Liberal Federation, a role which led her into difficulties and finally to resignation in the face of demands from Lady Carlisle and others that the Federation be more active in demanding women's suffrage.[3] She always opposed her husband's suggestions of resignation and retirement from politics—and her illness and absence from him in December 1893 meant that she was not able to calm his fury at the naval expansion proposals.[4] Catherine Gladstone ran the Gladstone court with a firm

---

[1] 15 and 17 June 92 are the penultimate examples of encounters with prostitutes. Significantly Gladstone refers to being 'accosted', i.e. the initiative was the prostitutes', not, as in the past, his.

[2] 24 Feb. 94.

[3] See 22 May 89n., 17, 27 Apr. 92, 1 May 92. This episode merits further investigation. For it, see E. A. Pratt, *Catherine Gladstone* (1898), ch. xiii.

[4] Even so, Rosebery told Morley he was confident there would be no crisis, being 'sure that domestic influence wd. be too strong'; see Morley's diary, 9 January 1894, in vol. xiii below, Appendix I, p. 434.

but discreet hand. Like that of many political wives of the period, her influence in shaping the character of the political as well as the domestic *ménage* was as important as it is hard to document. Gladstone's comments in the diary usually present her as distanced from the political world, in accordance with his view of the proper sphere of femininity (as when he thought the Royal Commission on the Poor Laws was not the proper place for 'the first canter' of women on such bodies):[1] in fact, she was an integral part of his political world.

From the late 1860s to the mid-1880s, Laura Thistlethwayte and her *salon* had provided something of an antithesis to the Gladstonian circle. In the period covered by these volumes she no longer did. Though Gladstone would never have admitted it directly, her frequent importunities, her invitations to lunch and dinner, her presents and her requests for letters became something of a nuisance. He commented to his wife, she 'has cooked up a habit of much fuss about small things'.[2] In 1887 the indebted A. F. Thistlethwayte died through a revolver wound—perhaps a suicide but perhaps, as Gladstone and the world decided, an accident, for he was wont to summon his servants by firing his pistol at the ceiling of his bedroom.[3] For all that Gladstone had discussed with Laura the disappointments of her marriage, he may have felt ill at ease with her as a widow. She set up house in Woodbine Cottage in Hampstead with Melita Ponsonby, sister to the Queen's Secretary, as a quasi-companion. Catherine Gladstone was introduced to her for the first time in 1887[4] and subsequently often accompanied her husband on his not very frequent visits there. Gladstone guarded his flank with respect to possible developments as he and Laura Thistlethwayte aged. Gladstone twice examined with Lord Rothschild the correspondence of Disraeli with Mrs Brydges Willyams.[5] It cannot have escaped him that similar scenes would be played out after his death over his own papers. In 1893:

> Burned my box of Mrs Thistlethwayte's older letters. I had marked them to be returned: but I do not know what would become of them. They would lead to misapprehension: it was in the main a one-sided correspondence: not easy to understand.[6]

He did not, however, attempt to recover his letters to her, which could not but astonish those who read them and dismay members of his family. The early part of Gladstone's side of this correspondence was published in an Appendix to Volume VIII; the latter part, from 1870 to the last surviving letter from Gladstone in 1893, is in an Appendix to Volume XII. The correspondence confirms the cooling in their relationship, at any rate on his side. After the Thistlethwaytes became involved in a series of debt actions by Mr. Padwick, a well-known Paddington gambler and money-lender, Gladstone changed his salutation from 'Dear Spirit' to 'Dear Mrs Thistlethwayte' or, more often,

---

[1] To Fowler, 8 Dec. 92: 'I would rather give the ladies their first canter on some subject less arduous, & where there would be less danger of their being led astray by the emotional elements of the case.'

[2] To Mrs. Gladstone, 19 Dec. 93.

[3] 24 Aug. 87ff. His death certificate stated as 'Cause of death' after receipt of a Coroner's certificate: 'Pistol Shot Wound in Head Accidentally when carrying a loaded pistol[;] found in a helpless condition on the floor and died in 14 Hours.'

[4] 18 May 87.   [5] 17 Mar. 88, 28 Feb. 91.   [6] 25 Feb. 93.

opened the letter without any form of address. Laura Thistlethwayte had acquired anonymity. The likelihood—at one point acute—of Gladstone's name and letters being mentioned in the debt actions passed, and the possibility receded of Laura's lavish presents to him being publicly given as a cause of A. F. Thistlethwayte's inability to pay Padwick. But the old intimacy never really revived.

His trust in her discretion was, however, justified. Despite genteel poverty (though like many such she had in fact significant assets) and a life ultimately solitary and rather miserable, Laura Thistlethwayte never traded on her intimacy with the Prime Minister, even posthumously. When she died in 1894, she did not embarrass him with gifts left in her will, and there was no mention in it of his large correspondence with her, all of which she had preserved. She left her cottage to be a North London St. Deiniol's, 'a Retreat for Clergymen of all denominations true believers in my God and Saviour and literary men'.[1] Gladstone was not an executor, though he had advised her over her affairs after her husband's death. The correspondence was probably recovered by H. N. Gladstone from her chief executor, Lord Edward Pelham-Clinton, son of the Duke of Newcastle (who had with Arthur Kinnaird introduced Gladstone to Laura Thistlethwayte in the 1860s) and of Lady Susan Opdebeck, the former Lady Lincoln, whose life after she returned from exile on the Continent and until her death in 1889 seems to have become entwined with Laura Thistlethwayte's.[2] Thus did two of Gladstone's private preoccupations of the 1860s— the fate of the Newcastle Estates, of which he was a trustee, and the condition of Laura Thistlethwayte's moral being, of which he also saw himself as a trustee—come into a curious congruity.[3]

Gladstone's last recorded visit to Laura Thistlethwayte was with his wife in May 1894 just before Laura's death: 'We drove to Mrs T's to inquire. Bad account.'[4] She died three weeks later, just after the suspension of regular entries in the diaries. There is thus no Gladstonian epilogue to her life: he may have been relieved not to have to write one. He did not reopen his journal—as he did for some subsequent events—to record his views. Her death coincided with a miserable period of his own life and with 'Mrs Th.' his duty, as he saw it, was all-ended.[5] He did not attend her funeral.

[1] Will of Laura Thistlethwayte in Somerset House.

[2] The intertwined relationships of Newcastle, his divorced wife Susan, Laura Thistlethwayte and Gladstone merit further attention.

[3] Mrs. Jean Gilliland has discovered that the Thistlethwayte entry in Burke's *Landed Gentry* (1858 ed. only: the information is dropped in subsequent editions) shows Laura Thistlethwayte's mother, Laura Jane Seymour, to have been the illegitimate daughter of the third Marquis of Hertford, the notorious libertine. It has always been known that her father, Capt. R. H. Bell, was probably a bailiff on the Hertfords' estates in Co. Antrim, but this information makes much clearer the reason for the presence of Laura Thistlethwayte's portrait in the Wallace Collection (Wallace being another of Hertford's illegitimate descendants, inheriting Hertford's picture collection and his Irish estates). It is also better evidence than the unsubstantiated rumours that Laura Thistlethwayte was herself Hertford's daughter and it clarifies the various references to the Hertfords and the Wallaces in Gladstone's letters to her.

[4] 4 May 94. Her death certificate gave 'Acute Renal congestion' as the 'Cause of death', and gave her age as 62, though her date of birth is normally given as *c.* 1829.

[5] Her death occurred a week after Gladstone's operation on 24 May for cataract.

The wretched five months' period following his resignation in March 1894 showed the eighty-four year old Gladstone in marked physical decline, increasingly dependent on his Lear-like coterie as he moved from residence to residence in the south of England, not returning to Hawarden until August. He and his wife discussed arrangements for their funerals,[1] and Gladstone wrote verses on death.[2] In the midst of it, on 24 May, he had an only partially successful operation for the removal of cataract in his right eye.[3] The effect of the operation was 'disabling'.[4] Though there was some later revival in his eyesight, 1894 effectively saw the end of his ability for sustained reading, always a central part of his daily routine, however busy. His sight had, as we have seen, been for a considerable time in decline, but, though it had annoyed him, it had (except in 1892) not very seriously inconvenienced him, if the extraordinary level at which his reading and writing was maintained in the late 1880s and early 1890s is taken as a measure.

Throughout his life Gladstone used the Waverley novels as a base-point of departure for his reading, but he was none the less 'up' with the new style of best-seller which by its introduction of a new sexual tone moved sharply away from the Scottian framework of reference within which so much Victorian fiction had been written and read. Gladstone read Marie Corelli and met her to discuss her work (she hoped for a review).[5] He deplored Zola with a vehemence directed at no other author in the entire diary, but read a good deal of him: *La Terre* was 'the most loathsome of all books in the picture it presents',[6] *Nana* 'a dreadful and revolting delineation'[7] (rather curiously, 'a yellow-backed Zola' caught the eye of the visitor to the Humanities Room in St. Deiniol's Library).[8] A theme in Gladstone's comments on such works was the de-Christifying of morality: thus Zola's *La Bête Humaine* 'I think . . . shows what would be a world without Christ'[9] and Hardy's *Tess of the D'Urbervilles* was 'a deplorable anticipation of a world without a Gospel'.[10] Less violent in language, but similar in sentiment, was his reaction to Mrs. Humphry Ward's *Robert Elsmere* (1888); in this case, however, he marked respect for the author's motivation by reviewing the book, which was dedicated to the memory of T. H. Green and Laura Lyttelton, Catherine Gladstone's niece. His review, ironically, helped make it an improbable best-seller.[11]

He discovered some works hitherto surprisingly missed—at least since 1825—even by his catch-all approach (read 'Bunyan's *Pilgrim's Progress*: a clear cut objectivity reminding one of Dante')[12] and made acquaintance with what were then less obvious authors: 'Read . . . Kipling's *Light that failed* . . . read Kipling (bad)'[13] and 'O[live] Schreiner's *Dreams*—Mary kindly read aloud to me in evg—*but*.'[14]

---

[1] 28 Mar. 94.   [2] 13 July 94.   [3] See 19 July 94.
[4] 19 July 94.   [5] See 31 May, 4 June, 6 and 10 Aug. 89.
[6] 2 Apr. 88. For *Piping Hot*, 'That wretched book', see 1 July 88.   [7] 27 June 89.
[8] See *In the evening of his days. A study of Mr Gladstone in retirement. With some account of St Deiniol's Library and Hostel* (1896), 117 (anonymous, but probably by W. T. Stead).
[9] 13 Feb. 92.   [10] 8 May 92; see also 30 Apr. 92n.   [11] 16 Mar., 6–18 Apr. 88.
[12] 6 Apr. 90; in an autobiographical fragment, Gladstone records *The Pilgrim's Progress* as one of the books read or read to him as a boy, i.e. before he was 15, the age at which his surviving journal begins; *Autobiographica*, i. 19.   [13] 3 June 91.   [14] 30 Oct. 93.

Such works were just the tips of several very large icebergs. The volume of different works read by Gladstone in the late 1880s and early 1890s is as heavy as at any time in his life and his recording of them constitutes a considerable proportion of the journal's text. More perhaps tended to be pamphlets or light fiction and Gladstone's classical writings rested on critical reading in part out-of-date. But, just as his political life was fuller than his apparent preoccupation with Ireland might lead us to expect, so his reading and the correspondence which accompanied it kept him abreast of a wide range of subjects and authors. One example may suffice: his reading of Pareto and subsequent correspondence in Italian on free trade, protectionism and political economy, which looked forward to the debate on corporatism which has in its various forms constituted the focus of much twentieth-century politico-economic dispute.[1]

Final retirement from executive politics gave Gladstone at least a clear run for his writing. This he had maintained through the years of opposition, 1886–1892, at what was an astonishing rate. Books on the classics and the Bible, articles on current affairs, Egyptology, Ireland, the United States, Italy, the design of bookcases, and a wide range of other subjects—set out in Appendix II of Volume XIII—rushed from his pen. 'An Academic Sketch', his Romanes Lecture, the first of the series, gave him more trouble than anything else he published. The family was mobilized as research assistants; Acton was summoned; Oxford scholars such as Hastings Rashdall were alerted. Gladstone was determined to offer a scholastic piece worthy of the occasion.[2] It was as if he was again preparing for Schools. Scholarly work was maintained through the final government, with a translation of Horace worked on in odd moments. Work on the edition of Bishop Butler, the long-planned, chief objective of Gladstone's retirement, began immediately after his resignation as Prime Minister and was completed in 1896.[3]

For posterity, the most intriguing of Gladstone's later writings was his autobiography, begun at Dalmeny during the 1892 election campaign: 'Being almost shut out from reading [following the attack on him in Chester] . . . I turn to writing . . . and I made today an actual beginning of that quasi Autobiography which Acton has so strongly urged upon me.'[4] He continued at intervals until 1897 but it was never completed.[5] Though it might be thought that the keeping of this diary could be seen as anticipating an autobiography, the idea that Gladstone should write one seems to have been external, and to have come from three very different sources. First, and not surprisingly, publishers. In 1887 Cassell offered £5,000 for the copyright of Gladstone's autobiography and in 1891 the Century Company of Putnam New York offered a handsome sum for

[1] See 27, 30 Apr. 92.

[2] 24 Oct. 92. See Robert Blake, 'Gladstone, Disraeli, and Queen Victoria: the Centenary Romanes Lecture delivered . . . 10 November 1992' (1993).

[3] 4 Mar. 94, 11 Mar. 94ff.   [4] 8 July 92.

[5] Gladstone had stated his suggestive but ambivalent views about autobiography in the pamphlet written as a retrospect to his 'great and glaring change' with respect to church establishment, *A chapter of autobiography* (1868): 'Autobiography is commonly interesting; but there can, I suppose, be little doubt that, as a general rule, it should be posthumous. The close of an active career supplies an obvious exception: for this resembles the gentle death which, according to ancient fable, was rather imparted than inflicted by the tender arrows of Apollo and Artemis.'

serialization and what it anticipated would amount to two octave volumes. Gladstone was thus well-placed, with an international offer, to break another mould and become the first Prime Minister to make a large sum by writing about having been Prime Minister. He was encouraged in this by Andrew Carnegie, the Scottish-American steel magnate, with whom he forged quite close links in the 1880s. Carnegie, of course, liked money. He also energetically promoted Anglo-Americanism, and he probably saw the publication of Gladstone's autobiography as a further step in mutual understanding. That work was bound to be strongly attractive to Americans, for it would appear to tell a tale of escape from conservative, monarchic church-and-statism to liberal individualism. It was very probably Carnegie who in 1887 engineered an American offer of £100,000 (according to E. W. Hamilton) for Gladstone's political autobiography,[1] a gigantic sum by the standards of the day—Disraeli had been paid £10,000 in 1881 for his autobiographical novel, *Endymion*, and that was thought to be a record for a work of fiction.[2] The third, and least likely encouragement came from Acton. Like Carnegie, Acton was fascinated by Gladstone's capacity to maintain a sense of freedom of will and of destiny while at the same time being a supreme man of politics.

The autobiography was, as we have seen, begun at Dalmeny in a moment grabbed during the 1892 election campaign. This was to be its fate. Gladstone never allocated it a time for sustained writing. As far as can be discovered, it had no plan. Brief segments were written at odd moments, though when collected together they amount to a substantial body of writing. After he finished writing daily entries in his diary, Gladstone sometimes wrote autobiographical fragments as an alternative, but never very systematically. It cannot be said that he wrote 'an autobiography' but he did leave papers on a series of episodes, mostly dealing with early life, with religious development, and with political crises. Even so, their influence on Gladstonian biography has been pervasive. Morley started with them and most have subsequently followed. Though the diary provided help with dating, it is not the foundation document for the autobiography. Indeed, the autobiographical fragments are written in juxtaposition to the diary, as if Gladstone in old age regretted his decision to record in the diary a life seen as a routine and therefore wrote later accounts of dramatic episodes and political crises which he had not written about at the time.

VIII

On 23 May 1894 Gladstone wrote the last routine entry of his journal: from that day onwards the entries are episodic. The occasion was his cataract operation; but nonresumption when his sight partially recovered shows the cause to

---

[1] EHD, 22 July 1887; Hamilton, who advised against acceptance, noted that Gladstone was tempted by the sum, which would pay off the debts of the Hawarden estate. Unfortunately, there is no file for these various offers and references to them are widely scattered. There seem to be no copies of Gladstone's replies to them. It may be that he made no copies (unlikely given the sums involved) or that a file was lost, possibly during the writing of Morley's biography.

[2] Blake, *Disraeli*, 734. Gladstone was also offered £25,000 in March 1891, by the Century Co., New York, Carnegie again having been involved; see 3 Mar. 91.

have been deeper. For fifty years, Gladstone had discussed in his journal his impending retirement from politics. When at last it came, he was content to see the journal go with the politics: 'retirement from active business in the world . . . affords a good opportunity for breaking off the commonly dry daily Journal, or ledger as it might almost be called . . .'.[1] For Gladstone's diary had been chiefly a record not of reflection but of process—of the process of corresponding, reading and participating in public life broadly understood in the Victorian manner. It had of course also recorded what the twentieth century would see as 'private' religious observance and study, but which Gladstone saw as a natural part of a healthy society and of civic behaviour: the daily walk to church at Hawarden and participation in the services there was a public affirmation, and a good citizen read the literature of his or her day.

Physical decline and a sense of conclusion thus ended the daily diary entries. Gladstone enjoyed 'the relief from the small grind of the Daily Journal'.[2] Retirement—however late—brought at last the opportunity for sustained work on Joseph Butler. Gladstone took it energetically. He completed his edition of Butler and published it at the Clarendon Press together with his *Studies Subsidiary to Bishop Butler* (1896).[3] He thus kept true to his stated intentions. Given these objectives, in December 1894 he revived the journal for the limited purpose of recording the daily reading which sustained his intellectual interests.[4] But it was too much. After about two weeks and 'a fall over one of the drawers of my writing table, on my forehead, with the whole weight of my body', he noted pathetically (after beginning a short list of authors and books): 'Il male Occhio [the bad eye]. No. I *cannot* do it.'[5]

Short passages follow about his and Catherine's health, the Queen's rudeness to Catherine, the progress of the Butler edition, travel, the signing of the Trust Deed for St. Deiniol's, and a new will, made as he distributed most of his assets to his children or St. Deiniol's.

As his eighty-seventh birthday approached, Gladstone made an important move in the process of winding down the coil of life. On 7 December 1896 he made what became known in the family as the 'Declaration': a statement of his marital fidelity. In it—one of the most dramatic private documents in any Prime Minister's papers—Gladstone refers to 'rumours which I believe were at one time afloat' (probably a reference to those in the summer of 1886) and to 'the times when I shall not be here to answer for myself' as the reasons for making the 'Declaration'. Included inferentially in these must have been a decision not to destroy his daily journal. For the journal—already well-known to the family and the Gladstone circle but not yet read by any of its members—contained abundant evidence not merely of temptation but of acts variously interpretable. So also did the correspondence with Laura Thistlethwayte. When Gladstone

[1] Memorandum printed at 25 July 94; it is characteristic that Gladstone says more in a memorandum about breaking off the daily entries than he does in the journal itself.

[2] 17 Dec. 94.

[3] 23 Dec. 95, 2 Jan., 3 May 96. For it, see Jane Garnett, 'Bishop Butler and the *Zeitgeist*: Butler and the development of Christian moral philosophy in Victorian Britain' in C. Cunliffe, ed., *Joseph Butler's moral and religious thought: tercentenary essays* (1992).

[4] 17 Dec. 94.

[5] 24 Dec. 94.

stated in the 'Declaration' both that 'at no period of my life have I been guilty of the act which is known as that of infidelity to the marriage bed' and that 'I limit myself to this negation', he made a qualification whose force is apparent to any reader of his journal, especially for the years 1845 to 1875.

Having made the 'Declaration'—heavily enveloped, sealed and given to Stephen, his eldest son, and 'my pastor'[1]—Gladstone determined on his 87th birthday to write the last entry in the journal whose earliest extant record is for 16 July 1825,[2] for 'old age is appointed for the gradual loosening or successive snapping of the threads'.

'Retrospect' had been a theme of the birthday entries from 1826, since a birthday—especially for one of evangelical origins—was a moment of spiritual and temporal reckoning as well as a time for celebration. It was thus fitting that on 29 December 1896—sixteen months and one birthday before his death—Gladstone finished his diary.

Let us end with his conclusion:

> My long and tangled life this day concludes its 87th year. My Father died four days short of that term. I know of no other life so long in the Gladstone family, and my profession has been that of politicians, or more strictly Ministers of State, an extremely shortlived race, when their scene of action has been in the House of Commons: Lord Palmerston being the only complete exception.
>
> In the last twelvemonth, eyes and ears may have declined, but not materially. The occasional constriction of the chest is the only inconvenience that can be called new. I am not without hope that Cannes may have a mission to act upon it. Catherine is corporally better than she was twelve months ago.
>
> As to work I have finished my labours upon Butler, have made or rather remade my Will, have made progress with 'Olympian Religion' and good progress with a new Series of Gleanings, and have got St. Deiniol's very near its launch upon the really difficult and critical part of the undertaking.
>
> The blessings of family life continue to be poured in the largest measure upon my unworthy head. Even my temporal affairs have thriven.
>
> Still old age is appointed for the gradual loosening or successive snapping of the threads. I visited Ld Stratford at Froom Park(?) [sc. Frant Court] when he was 90 or 91 or thereabouts. He said to me 'It is not a blessing'.
>
> As to politics I think the basis of my mind is laid principally in finance and philanthropy. The prospects of the first are darker than I have ever known them. Those of the second are black also: but with more hope of some early dawn.
>
> I do not enter on interior matters. It is so easy to write, but to write honestly nearly impossible.
>
> Lady Grosvenor gave me today a delightful present of a small Crucifix. I am rather too independent of symbol.
>
> Adieu old year. Lord have mercy.
>
> WEG D. 29. 1896.

[1] It was, in the event of need, to be made known by Stephen Gladstone 'to his brothers'.
[2] There are therefore about 25,200 entries in the journal.

Sat. Jan. 1. 1887. Circumcision. [Hawarden]

Ch. 8½ A.M. Wrote to Sir W. Harcourt l. & tel.—King of the Belgians—Boller & Stewart tel.—Mr J. Greenwood—Rev. Johnston[1]—Mr Holmes Ivory—P[ost]master Hn—Archdeacon of Bristol—Mr Lefevre MP. Finished, under pressure, my annual statement of affairs,[2] to which I have of late found it so difficult to appropriate a couple of hours about the close of the year. Attended 7 PM the excellent ventriloquism, & dined with the W.H.Gs. Saw Mr MacColl.[3] Read Hurrish.[4] A little woodcraft to warm me.

2. 2 S. Xm.

Ch. 11 A.M. with H.C.—and 6½ P.M. Wrote to Sir W. Harcourt l.l.—Princess of Wales—Miss Tidall—Rev. Mr Johnstone—Rev. W. Thomas—Mr King—Mr Curry—Rev. G. Green[5]—Mr Robson—Canon MacColl (on Sir Chas Dilke's case for H.C.).[6] Saw Canon MacColl—Rev. E. Wickham. Read Treasury of the Covenant[7]—Battle of the Faith[8]—Norris on Butler[9]—Bp of Chesters Charge[10]—Thomas on Disestablt.[11]

3. M.

Ch. 8½ A.M. Wrote to Press Assocn Tel.—Mr Smart BP—Mr Labouchere—Archdn of Bristol—Rev. Mr Meade—Messrs Deakin—Mr E.A. Haed—Mayor of Limerick[12]—Ld Granville—Mr Morley—Ld Spencer—Miss O'Brien[13]—Mr Horsley—Mr Cramond. Worked hard upon the chaos of books papers & objects which has resulted from (estimate) 1300 postal arrivals in three days: but with no great apparent result. Conversation with Canon MacColl. Read MacColl on Dicey[14]—Dumaresq on Johnson[15]—[blank] on House Taxation—finished Hurrish.

---

[1] John C. Johnston, minister in Dunoon, had sent his 'Treasury of the Scottish covenant' (1887).
[2] Hawn P.   [3] See next day.
[4] E. Lawless, *Hurrish. A study*, 2v. (1886); see 23 Dec. 86. Discussed by Gladstone in *N.C.*, xxi. 180 (February 1887).
[5] Perhaps George Robert Green, headmaster of Eastbourne College 1887–8.
[6] MacColl was a member of a cttee. collecting fresh information on the Dilke case; see R. Jenkins, *Sir Charles Dilke* (1958), 330.
[7] See 1 Jan. 87.   [8] Untraced.
[9] J. P. Norris, *Lectures on Butler's 'Analogy'* (1887).   [10] By W. Stubbs (1886).
[11] W. Thomas of Whitland had sent his 'The disestablishment campaign in its bearings on established churches and unestablished nonconformity. Facts, figures and omens' (1886).
[12] Thanking F. A. O'Keefe for Limerick's good wishes, *T.T.*, 5 January 1887, 6c.
[13] Charlotte Grace O'Brien, 1845–1909; Irish poet and essayist; had sent a work, probably her *Lyrics* (1886). A strong Gladstonian (but also a Land Leaguer), her sonnets on him ('Oh, noble face marked deep by inward strife!') are collected in *Charlotte Grace O'Brien. Selections from her writings and correspondence with a memoir by Stephen Gwynn* (1909).
[14] M. MacColl, 'Professor Dicey on home rule', *C.R.*, li. 84 (January 1887).
[15] Untraced article by his relative; see 1 Jan. 87n.

4. Tu.

Ch. 8½ A.M. Wrote to Madam Novikoff—Ld Houghton—Sir Thos G.—Mr Jos. Howes—Mr Hayman—Messrs Murray (2)—John Gladstone (Fasque)—J.P. Hartley—C. O'Byrne—Rev. F. Barker—Rev. J. Ferguson[1]—Rev. J. O'Roorke—Mr E. Lever—Mr Loysdael—Mr Cook Smith—Eric Ross.[2] Saw Canon MacColl—A. Lyttelton—Prof. Stewart [sc. Stuart].[3] Read The Forgotten Nation—Hayward Letters[4]—and tracts.

5. Wed.

Ch. 8½ A.M. Wrote to Stewart & Douglas—Mrs Buckley PP—Mrs Ogilvie[5]—Gibb & Bruce—Rev. J. Anderson[6]—J.H. Tensenberg—Mr Saunders MP[7]—Sir Ch. Russell[8]—Bulgarian Delegates—J. Bell—W. Mackie—M. Furlong[9]—Mr Hamilton—Jas Knowles—Mr Holloway. Read Sir C. Russell's Speech—Hayward Letters. Twelve to dinner. Walk with party in the snow—as yesterday.

6. Epiph.

& dearest C's birthday. H.C. 8½ A.M. & H.C. Wrote to Ld Wolverton—J. Brady—Holmes Ivory—Mr Fitzhenry—Rev. Mr Lorimer—C.H. Strutt[10]—G. Snook—J. Cunliffe—A.A. Reade—G. Brooks—T.J. Brown—Sidney Kelland—Miss Prideaux—Serjeant Brophy[11]—Thos Wynne. Woodcraft with W.H.G. Read Cornwallis Correspondence[12]—Hayward's Letters (finished)—Dr E. Blackwell on Merchandise[13]—Account of Wordsworth.[14] Servant's Ball in evg. C.G., William of Wickham, and the Wilson girls, especially the elder, specially as I thought distinguished themselves. Worked on MS. Irish Article.[15]

7. Th.

Ch. 8½ A.M. H.J.G.s birthday. God bless him. Wrote to Messrs Cassell & Co—A. Morley MP—T. Aldreed BP—Mrs Hangham BP—Ld Northbourne B.P.—Mr

---

[1] John Ferguson, episcopalian clergyman in Elgin.

[2] Perhaps the s. of Cornwallis's editor (see 6 Jan. 87n.).

[3] i.e. James Stuart; see 26 Oct. 78.

[4] See 28 Jan. 85n.

[5] Miss C. Ogilvie of St. John's Wood, London, sent a book; Hawn P.

[6] John Farmworth Anderson, curate in Sefton Park 1886–90, in Toxteth 1891–4 (both Gladstone family livings).

[7] William Saunders, 1823–95; founded *Western Morning News*; favoured federal home rule; liberal M.P. E. Hull 1885–6, Walworth 1892–5.

[8] Sir Charles Arthur *Russell, 1832–1900, liberal M.P. Dundalk 1880–5, S. Hackney 1885–94; attorney general 1886; Parnell's Counsel 1888–9; lord chief justice 1894. Had sent his 'Speech . . . on November 23rd 1886, on the Irish question' (1887).

[9] Michael Furlong of Dublin wrote in admiration; Hawn P.

[10] Charles Hedley Strutt, 1849–1926; tory M.P. E. Essex 1883–5.

[11] Charles Albert Brophy; see Add MS 44499, f. 49.

[12] C. Cornwallis, Lord Cornwallis, *Correspondence*, ed. C. Ross, 3v. (1859).

[13] E. Blackwell, *Purchase of women: the great economic blunder* (1887).

[14] Perhaps *Literary celebrities* (1887); Wordsworth, Coleridge, etc.

[15] 'Notes and queries on the Irish demand', *N.C.*, xxi. 165 (February 1887); Add MS 44700, f. 1; reprinted in *The Irish question*.

Saunders MP—Jas Knowles—Canon McColl—Mayor of Kilkenny—Mr Heaps—
H. Taylor—Mr Macleod—Thos Smith—Mr Archer—Mr Borley—Mr Bath.
Worked on MS. for Irish article. 'Constitutional' in the snow. Read Ld Corn-
wallis—Hist. Reign Henry IV.[1]

8. Sat.

Ch. 8½ A.M. Wrote to Sir W. Harcourt—Central News Tel.—Heaton Chapel
Tel.—Messrs Murray—Mr Tattersall—C.H. Perkins—A.B. Todd[2]—G. Thorpe—
T. Elliot—W. Oakden—J. Parham—S. Greenway—Ld Herschell—Rev. H.S.
Fagan[3]—Stewart & Douglas[4]—Mr Fieldhouse—Rev. E. Bell—Mr Radford—J.
Beebe—J.D. Cooke. Worked on Ireland MS. Walk in the snow. Read Corn-
wallis—Jones, Atonement[5]—Ayrshire Martyrs.[6]

9. 1 S. Epiph.

Ch 11 AM & 6½ P.M. Wrote to Librarian B. Museum—Mr Knowles—Mr
Stawport—Mr Upton—J.H. Lewis[7]—Mr Tomkinson—Miss Davison—Prof. Charteris[8]—Mr Cudlepp. Read Salmon Introd.[9]—Colenso on Speakers Bible[10]—Todd
on the Covenanters[11]—Jeremy on the Williams Trust[12]—and [blank].

10. M.

Ch. 8½ A.M. Wrote to Mr R. Brown jun.—Professor Knight[13]—Mr Pollard[14]—Mr
Smithson—Messrs. Tillotson—Mr Ritchie—Mr Cobbe—Mr Stern. Wrote on
Olympian System[15]—MS for Irish Question. Read Tracts on 60 years since[16]—
Roscher on Hermes (un poco)[17]—Davies on the Dutch Waterways.[18] Dined at
Mr Johnsons: a pleasant party. I had today for the first time a singing in my
good ear.

[1] Perhaps A. Poirson, *Histoire du règne de Henri IV*, 2v. (1856).
[2] Adam Brown Todd, Scottish border poet and antiquarian; a strong Gladstonian (see his 'In
memoriam' (1898) in his *Poetical Works* (1906), 273). See 9 Jan. 87.
[3] Henry Stuart Fagan, d. 1888?; vicar of St. Just, Cornwall.
[4] London hatters.
[5] Perhaps J. Jones, *A token of Christian love* (1683).
[6] Probably Todd's book; see next day.
[7] Perhaps Sir (John) Herbert Lewis, 1858–1933; chairman Flintshire C.C. 1889–93; liberal M.P.
Flint boroughs 1892–1906; Kt. 1922.
[8] Archibald Hamilton Charteris, 1835–1908; professor of biblical criticism, Edinburgh, 1868–98.
[9] G. Salmon, *A historical introduction to the study of the . . . New Testament*, 2v. (1885-6).
[10] J. W. Colenso, *The new bible*, 6v. (1871-4).
[11] A. B. Todd, *Homes, haunts and battlefields of covenanters*, 2v. (1886-9).
[12] W. D. Jeremy, *The presbyterian fund and Mr. Daniel Williams's trust* (1885).
[13] William Angus Knight, 1836–1916; philosopher, literary critic and antiquarian; professor in
Aberdeen.
[14] Alfred William Pollard, 1859-1944; historian; then working in the printed books department of
the British Museum; an occasional correspondent; Hawn P.
[15] Renewal of work on 'Poseidon'; see 7 Dec. 86.
[16] Presumably tracts on Scott's *Waverley; or, sixty years since*.
[17] In W. H. Roscher, *Studien*, 4v. (1878-95). See 6 Apr. 91.
[18] G. C. Davies, *Old Dutch Waterways* (1887).

11. Tu.

On account of some giddiness in the head I lay in bed & had calomel. There was a sharp change of weather in the night. Wrote to Mrs Barclay Allardyce[1]—Sig. Parini[2]—Mr Mellor QC[3]—Mr Simson—Mr Pritchell—Lieut. Bathurst—Rev F. Meyrick—Ed. Baptist—C. Douglas. Read Waterways of Holland—Cornwallis Correspondence—Wright on Mushrooms.[4] Main work suspended.

12. Wed.

Ch. 8½ A.M. Wrote to Mr E. Russell MP l. & tel.[5]—Sir W. Harcourt—Miss Macintosh—Rev. T.M. Dickson[6]—Rev. C.C. Clarke[7]—A. Brownfield—Col. Laurie[8]—Miss F.A.D. Smith—A. Morley—J. Morley—Mr Wooller—Mr Burdett—Jas Grant—J.L. Thorn. Wrote on Irish Policy. Read Waterways of Holland—Brownfield's Pamphlet[9]—Cornwallis Correspondence. We received in the afternoon the news that Iddesleigh's gentle spirit had fled away from this world of strife.

13. Th.

Ch. 8½ A.M: but it brought back the giddiness. Wrote to Mrs Talbot—Ld Acton—Mrs Cater—Mr Moss—Mr Escott—Rev. H. Corden—Mr Henderson—T.J. Rauch—J. Lorimer—Sir Jas Bain.[10] Walk with C. Wrote on Irish Policy. Read Hibernia Pacata[11]—Cornwallis Correspondence.

14. Fr.

Kept my bed & alack no Ch. Saw Dr Doby.[12] Put under Sir A. Clark's restrictions of diet. Woodcraft with W.H.G. Wrote to Sir W. Harcourt—Ld Granville—A. Morley—J. Thorne—Mr Burdett—J. Moss—R. Taylor BP—E. Morton—C.J. Thynne[13]—Mr Sharples—E. Russell MP Tel.—Parl. Circular—Miss Phillimore—Messrs. Stoneham—J. Murray—J. MacOwens—W. Armstrong—Rev. J. Thomas. Read Dutch Waterways—Cornwallis Correspondence.

[1] Margaret Barclay-Allardice, 1816–1903; unsuccessful claimant of earldom of Strathearn.
[2] George Edward Parini of Genoa; occasional correspondent; Hawn P.
[3] John William Mellor, 1835–1911; liberal M.P. Grantham 1880–6, Sowerby 1892–1904; chairman of cttees. 1893–5.
[4] J. Wright, *Mushrooms for the million*, 2v. (1884–7).
[5] On Randolph Churchill; *précis* in *T.T.*, 15 January 1887, 7b.
[6] Thomas Miller Dickson, retired vicar and schoolmaster.
[7] Nonconformist minister.
[8] Robert Peter Laurie; business untraced.
[9] A. Brownfield, *What England owes to Ireland* (1887).
[10] Sir James Bain, 1817–98; lord provost of Glasgow 1877; tory M.P. Whitehaven 1891–2.
[11] *Hibernia Pacata* (1887).
[12] Of Chester; see 11 Apr. 82.
[13] Charles J. Thynne of the Church of England Working Men's Protestant Union asked leave to reprint 'The Vatican Decrees'; Hawn P. No reply or reprint traced.

15. Sat.

Ch. 8½ A.M. Wrote to Abp of Cashel—G. Thurlow—A. Morley—J. Wright—
Canon MacColl—Rev. J. Crompton—Lady Iddesleigh. Wrote to Lady Lothian—
Lady Russell—Lady Derby—W. Phillimore—Mrs Heywood—Sir A. Clark (all
B.P.). We finished felling our sycamore. Read Q.R. on Ld Shaftesbury—do on
Canadian Pacific R.R.[1]—Dutch Waterways—Cornwallis Corresp. Wrote Irish
'Notes & Queries'.

16. 2 S. Epiph.

Ch. 11 AM. 6½ P.M. Wrote to Sir W. Harcourt—Mr Morley—Mrs Th.—W. Walpole. Read Life of Rosmini[2]—Report of Dingwall Meeting[3]—Salmon on Apocry-
phal Gospels. Conversation with E. Wickham.

17. M.

Ch. 8½ A.M. Wrote to Professor Knight—J. Davidson—A. Brownfield—J.C. Haslam—F. C. Carr Gomm[4]—W.M. Sherriff—Rev. T.J. Leslie—W. Armstrong—W.M.
Brown—Sec. Club Buildings Co. Wrote on Irish Demand. Read Cornwallis Corresp.—Dutch Waterways. A pleasant visit from the two Eaton ladies.

18. Tu.

Ch. 8½ A.M. Wrote to Mr Labouchere MP—Mr Knowles—R. Salkeld—Mr
Cochrane[5]—E. Cameron[6]—Editor Life Ass. Journal—Rev. R. Nevill—S. Chap-
man—F. Robinson—F. Smyth. Finished and dispatched my MS. on Ireland.
Read Dutch Waterways—Cornwallis (Irish) Corresp. finished. Woodcraft with
W.H.G. Dined at the Rectory. Backgammon.

19. Wed.

Ch. 8½ A.M. Wrote to Messrs Macmillan—Ld Granville—Ld Spencer—Mr
Childers—Mr Knowles—Scotts—Mr Carlisle—Jas Kerr—G. Thompson—Dr.
Trimmer[7]—Ed. Bev[erle]y Recorder.[8] Walk with S.E.G. Finished Dutch Waterways. Read Leaves by an Extinguished Clergyman.[9] Corrected & sent off proofs
of Poseidon. (NB. 2%)

---

[1] Q.R., clxiv. 1, 119 (January 1887).
[2] W. Lockhart, ed., *Life of Antonio Rosmini*, 2v. (1886).
[3] Untraced.
[4] Francis Culling Carr-Gomm, barrister active in the militia; a liberal.
[5] Probably Robert Cochrane, correspondent in 1888; Hawn P.
[6] Ebenezer Cameron of Edinburgh, sent his verses, 'Auld Reekie's fair and the Grand Old Man';
Add MS 44500, f. 42.
[7] Robert Trimmer, retired anglican clergyman.
[8] Not found.
[9] H. Brinstead, *Leaves from the diary of an extinguished clergyman* (1886).

20. Th.

Ch. 8½ A.M. Wrote to Viceroy of India[1]–Mr Bryce MP–Mr Sprigg–Mr Goalen–Mr Hagerstom[2]–Messrs. Jarrold–Mr Stuart Rendel–Mr Carr Gomm–R. Brown jun.–J. Murray (2)–Mr Stanley Withers[3]–Ed. Dundee Courier–Mr Scott–Rev. Reynolds[4]–Prof. Creighton–J. Jones. Worked on 'The great [Olympian] Sedition'.[5] Read A Minister's Walk[6]–Bryce on Irish Question[7]–History of the Parks.[8] Felled a birch with W.H.G.

21. Fr.

Ch. 8½ A.M. Wrote to Sir W. Harcourt–Mr Morley MP–Rev. J. Crawford–Mr Aldridge–Ed. Glasgow Mail–T. Meakin–Scotts–Mr Sutton–Mr Sleath–Mr Norman. Woodcraft with WHG. Tea Mrs Toller's. Worked on & nearly finished 'The great Sedition'. Read Laveley's Austria[9]–'Beyond'[10]–Formation of Speech[11]–Grote Ch. 1.[12]–Thirlwall.[13]

22. Sat.

Ch. 8½ A.M. Wrote to E.W. Hamilton–A. Morley MP–Mr Lefevre MP–Mr Corbet MP–Bp of Oxford BP–Mr Dinard–Mr Quaritch–Lord Colin Campbell–Rev. N. Hall–Mr Unwin–Mr Holman–Mr Dobbyn–Mr Freeman–Mrs Doyle. Finished MS on the Great Sedition. Read Greville Memoirs[14]–Corbet on Ireland.[15] Nine to dinner. Ly Houghton most pleasing, granddaughter of Graham, Ld H. son of R.M. Milnes.[16]

23. 3 S. Epiph.

Ch 11 A.M. and 6½ PM. Wrote to Mr T.P. O'Connor–A. Morley MP–R. Yates–P. Stanhope MP.–Ed. PMG[17]–Sir Geo. Prevost–Rev. G. Brooks–Mrs Ingram–& Mr Ball.[18] Read Mr Ball's interesting history of Irish Ch. Walk with the Houghtons.

---

[1] i.e. Dufferin.　　　　　　　　　　　　　　　　　　　　　　　　[2] London publishers.
[3] W. Stanley Withers of Sale, corresponding on Homer; Hawn P.
[4] Agreeing to Creighton's request of 19 January that he review Greville for *E.H.R.*, 'whose continuance is at present somewhat precarious'; Add MS 44500, f. 50; see 3 Feb. 87.
[5] Returned to in May; see 12 May 87.
[6] Perhaps E. H. Hopkins, *Walk that pleases God* (1887).
[7] J. Bryce, *England and Ireland. An Introductory statement* (1884).
[8] Perhaps *The famous parks and gardens of the world* (1880).
[9] E. L. V. de Laveley, *La Péninsule des Balkans, Vienne, Croatie, Bosnia*, 2v. (1886), tr. by Mrs Thorpe with a letter by Gladstone (1887).
[10] Tract published by the Guild of Spiritual Healing.
[11] Untraced.　　　　　　　　　　　　　　　　　　　　　　　　　[12] See 19 Mar. 47.
[13] C. Thirlwall, *Remains, literary and theological*, 3v. (1877–8).
[14] Sent by Creighton; see 20 Jan., 3 Feb. 87.
[15] Untraced work, probably an article, sent by W. J. Corbet (see 22 July 84).
[16] Richard Offley Ashburton Crew-*Milnes, 1858–1945; 2nd Baron Houghton 1885; Irish viceroy 1892–5; cr. Earl of Crewe 1895; liberal cabinet minister and biographer of Rosebery; m. 1st Sibyl (grand-da. of Sir J. Graham, the Peelite) who d. 1887, 2nd 1899, Margaret da. of Rosebery.
[17] Not found published.
[18] J. T. Ball (see 13 May 69) had sent his *The reformed Church of Ireland 1537–1886* (1886).

24. M.

Ch. 8½ A.M. Corrected proofs of Irish Article. Wrote to Rev. Mr Middleton—Rev. Mr Lockhart—Ed. Young Man—H.S. Threlfall—G. Courthard—[W.J.] O'Neill Daunt—Rev. Mr Gradwell—Rev. E.S. Prout[1]—Earl Granville—Messrs Eggers—Sec. S. Wales Federation—Messrs Bailey—Watson & Smith—Scotts—Mr Knowles—J.H. Wylie—T. Hardy[2]—E.G. Brown—Mr Murphy—J.F. Cramp—W. Holder—Mr Alexander. Our guests went, also the Wickham group. A hard day of struggle to get things in order. Read Greville—Corbet on Ireland.

25. Tu. [London][3]

Ch. 8½ A.M. Wrote to Clergyman Campbelton—Miss Cully....... Arrangements for departure. Off at 10¾. Euston 3¾. A great and lively crowd. Dined with Sir A. West. Saw Mr Morley—Mr A. Morley—Sir W. Harcourt—Sir A. West—Mr Hamilton—Ld Granville. Struggled with the usual chaos. Read Greville.

26. Wed.

Alack, the Church. Wrote to Madame Loyson—Prof. G. Monti[4]—Mr Newson—Mr Gately—Mr Brand—Sig. P. Ellero[5]—Mr Dickinson. Saw Sir J. Carmichael—S. Lyttelton—A. Morley—E. Hamilton—Sir R. Hamilton—Ld Lyttelton—Ld Spencer—Sir R. Welby—Mr Digby. Conclave at Ld Granville's on the Speech 6-7½. Worked on papers. Read Greville—Stebbing's Cobbett.[6]

27. Th.

Wrote to Mr R. Holt—M. de Laveleye—Mr Rossiter—Mr Stebbing—T.M. Goalen. Saw Sir W. Harcourt—Ld Granville—Mr A. Morley—Mr S. Lyttelton. Finished Stebbing's Cobbett. Read Greville. Examined the Speech. H. of C. 4½-9¼. Spoke on Iddesleigh's character, and on the Speech: a little over an hour.[7]

28. Fr.

Wrote to Mr Stebbing[8]—Mr M'Gregor (Braemar). Saw Mr L. Lyttelton—Mr Morley (2)—Mr A. Morley—Ld Granville—Mr O. Morgan. Read Londoner Streifzuge[9]—Why Ireland wants Home Rule[10]—Greville Memoirs. House of C. 4¾-7.[11] Dined with Mr S. Rendell: I much like him & Mrs S.R.[12]

---

[1] Edward Stallybrass Prout, priest, translator and homiletician. See 20 Feb. 87n.
[2] If the novelist, letter untraced.
[3] Staying in 21 Carlton House Terrace.
[4] Giulio Monti of Tuscany; see Add MS 44505, f. 173b and 12 Oct. 87.
[5] Probably Pietro Ellero, published in Bologna on politics, including *Scritti politici* (1876).
[6] W. Stebbing, *Some verdicts of history reviewed* (1887); ch. v. on Cobbett.
[7] *H* 310. 74, 94.
[8] William Stebbing, d. 1926; journalist on *T.T.* and author. See 26 Jan. 87.
[9] See 8 June 87?
[10] J. A. Fox, *Why Ireland wants Home Rule* (1887).
[11] Queen's Speech; *H* 310. 170.
[12] Increasingly close ties between the Gladstones and the Rendels (see 20 Dec. 80); Ellen Sophy Rendel was niece of Gladstone's friend J. G. Hubbard.

29. Sat. [Sandringham]

Kept my bed until near three. Saw Mr A. Morley—Sir A. Clark—Bp of St Albans—Sir Ch. Wyke. Read Greville's Memoirs—Stebbings Vol. Wrote to Sir W. Harcourt—Ld Granville, and .... Off at 3.30 to Sandringham at 7. A large party. We were received with the usual delicacy and kindness: if possible more. Much conversation with the Prince of Wales.

30. 4 S. Epiph.

Parish Ch mg: missed Evg at W. Newton by an accident. Wrote to Mr A. Morley—and [blank.] Read Eichthal on Genesis[1]—Murray's Mag. on Ch. House—and on Shaftesbury[2]—Petrocchi on Manzoni[3]—[blank] on B.V.M. Walk with the Bp who charmed me much. Conversation with the Prince on his Institute.[4] Also with Princess and others. Sat to Mr Ber.[5]

31. M. [Cambridge][6]

Sat anew to Mr Ber. Photographed by Mr Ralph. Saw Wolferton Church. Off by 11.22 to Cambridge. Wrote to J.A. Lowson—J. Cochrane—Mess. Murray—A. Mackay—O. Morgan. Conversation with Mr Craven on horses. Dined with Master of Trinity[7] in Hall. Went over the Nuneham [sc. Newnham] Buildings. Greatly pleased: dear H. in her right place.[8] Saw Mr Sidgwick. Evening Service at King's. Read Greville Journals.

1 Feb. Tues.

Wrote to Mr A. Morley L.l.l. & tel.—F. Knollys—Mr Pardon—Mr Paterson—A.E. Owen—Mr Swift Macneill—Madame Loyson—Bp of St Alban's. We went over the College:[9] I spoke a few sentences to the young men at their luncheon.

2. Wed. [Hawarden]

Wrote to Miss Clowe—Sir W. Harcourt—Messrs Day & Sons—Miss Bourne—Mr Mead—A. Scott—Mr Dennie—Ld Rosebery. After prayers & breakfast off to London: my visit missed fire as no one appeared. Left Euston 12.10. Hn at 5.30.

---

[1] G. D'Eichthal, *Mélange de critique biblique* (1886); on the Pentateuch.

[2] *Murray's Magazine*, i. 173, 200 (February 1887).

[3] Probably an article by P. Petrocchi who ed. *I promessi sposi*, 2v. (1893–7).

[4] The Imperial (later Commonwealth) Institute in S. Kensington, opened 1893, but underfunded; see Magnus, *Edward VII*, 199 ff.

[5] Apparently *sic*; artist and picture both untraced.

[6] For this visit, see P. Gladstone, *Portrait of a family* (1989), ch. 25.

[7] Henry Montagu *Butler, 1833–1918; master of Trinity from 1886.

[8] i.e. his da. Helen was right to stay as a Fellow at Newnham College and not accept the headship of Royal Holloway College. During his visit, Gladstone planted a tree, which was shortly afterwards destroyed by tory undergraduates. He presented another, an oak from the grounds of Hawarden, which still flourishes. For the planting, see the photograph reproduced in this volume.

[9] i.e. Selwyn, where the Gladstones stayed with Arthur Lyttelton, the Principal, and his wife Kathleen.

Set to work on papers. Finished Greville Journals—read Lee's Introd. to Faust[1]—Lord E. Fitzmaurice on Ireland.[2]

3. Th.

Kept in bed until 11 A.M. but attended Mission Service 7–8½ A.M. Wrote to Sir W. Harcourt—Mr A. Morley—Mrs Ingram—Maison Quantin (Paris)[3]—Mrs Bolton. Dined with Willy: also walk with him. Wrote on the Greville Journals.[4] Read Stebbing.

4. Fr.

Ch. 8¼ A.M. and 7–8¾ P.M. Wrote to Dr Döllinger B.P.—Lady F.C., BP—Mary, l. & B.P.—Mr S. Lyttelton—Judge O'Hagan—Mr Richardson—Dr Zoupolides—Comtesse Jaunnes—Mr Macleod—Mr Hurlburt—Mr Burnett—Mr Imrie—Rev. Weldon.[5] Wrote on Greville (Crimean War). Woodcraft with W.H.G. Read O'Hagan on Sir S. Ferguson.[6]

5. Sat.

Ch. 8¼ A.M. with H.C. and 7 P.M. Wrote to Mr Andrews—Messrs Blackburn—Mr Macdonald—A. Macewan—Dr Ginsburg—Mr Haysman—A. Morley. Felled a Sp. Chestnut with Willy. Wrote on Greville (Crimean War). Read Stebbing—Poems of Ion[7]—OHagan on Sir S. Fergusson's Poems.

6. Septua S.

Ch. 11 AM & 6½ PM. Wrote to Miss M. A. Young—Rev. S. Warren—A. Morley—H. Stork—F. Brine. Read divers tracts—Ball, Church of Ireland—Ourtan[?] on Religion under Charles II.[8] Walk with C.

7. M.

Ch. 8¼ A.M. with Holy Commn and 7 P.M. Dined at the Rectory. Wrote to Mr Burne Jones BP—Mr Deverell BP—Lord Acton BP—Miss Waller BP—Mr Humphrey—Mr Feldman—A. Morley—S. Lyttelton—Miss Stearn—Mr Hickey—

---

[1] J. Lee, introduction to tr. of Goethe's *Faust* (1887).

[2] Lord Fitzmaurice, 'Ireland: 1782 and 1887', *C.R.*, li. 153 (February 1887).

[3] Parisian printers and publishers, specialising in bibliography.

[4] 'The history of 1852–1860, and Greville's latest Journals', *E.H.R.*, ii. 281 (April 1887); Add MS 44700, f. 95. Gladstone wrote to help the review financially and because he believed it should always have an article on 'quite modern history'; unfortunately his article 'made no appreciably difference in the sale'; *Life and Letters of Mandell Creighton by his wife* (1904), i. 342–3. See 20 Jan. 87n. Creighton thought Gladstone's review 'more valuable to most readers than the Memoirs on which it comments' and agreed that articles on modern history were essential, our 'ignorance of the last 60 years was colossal'—but no-one could be got to write them; Creighton to Gladstone, 11, 15 February 1887, Add MS 44500, ff. 101, 111.

[5] Perhaps George Warburton Weldon, 1825–89; author and vicar of Bickley from 1882.

[6] J. O'Hagan, *The poetry of Sir Samuel Ferguson* (1887).

[7] Perhaps the ed. by W. E. Weber, in *Die elegischen Dichter* (1826).

[8] Perhaps J. Stoughton, *The Church of the Restoration*, 2v. (1870).

Rev. J. Presland—and minutes. Woodcraft with WHG. Wrote on Greville. Read Stebbing—Deverell's (valueless) Hist.[1] Examined various books. The Mission[2] closed for me this evening; I do not face the early celebration. C. is braver. Saw Mr Linklater.

8. Tu.

Ch. 8½ A.M. Heard there were near 200 communicants. The whole process has I hope done all of us some little good. Wrote to Messrs Barrington and Saumarez[3]—Ld Granville—J. Tod—Mr Beaumont—Mr Haslam—Mr Brooks— Hon. S. Lyttelton—Mr Esslemont MP[4]—Canon M'Coll—Mr Fisher Unwin[5]—S. Austin—W. Petty—Adam Lee[6]—Miss Morgan. Woodcraft with W.H.G. Wrote on Greville: & Homeric Propositions. Read Brown, Dionysiak Myth[7]—Swift Macneill on the Union.[8] We dined with the WHGs. Saw Mr Mayhew.

9. Wed.

Ch. 8½ A.M. Wrote to Mr Shaw Lefevre—Mr Salkeld—Mrs E.M. Pike—Rev Mr Goalen—Mr Everett—Mr Wightman—Rev. Mr Stone—Messrs Blackburn—Rev. Mr Jarman. Wrote on Greville Papers. Woodcraft with W.H.G. Read Swift Macneill finished—Minchin on Balkan Pen.[9]—and [blank.]

10. Th.

Ch. 8½ A.M. Wrote to Sir W. Phillimore—Lady Chesterfield—Professor Creighton—Mr Matthews—Mr Chawnor—Mr Haslam—W. Fry—Mr Skipworth—W.B. Smith. Wrote on Greville & sent off chief part to Prof. C.[10] Woodcraft with S.E.G. Read Minchin—Perraud on Ireland.[11]

11. Fr.

Ch. 8½ A.M. Wrote to Sec. El. Comm. Burnley[12]—Ld Granville—Mr W.H. Carter—Mr Morley—Sir A. Clark Bt—Mr J. Nield—Sec. College of Physicians— Sir S. Scott & Co—Messrs Poulton. Finished Preface i.e. art. on Greville. Woodcraft with WHG. Read Minchin—Balls Irish Ch. History—Sayces Babylon &c.[13]

---

[1] W. T. Deverell, probably *The Norman Conquest* (1870).
[2] Mission to Hawarden, closing next day with early communion.
[3] To Eric Barrington and Arthur Saumarez; unable, following his general rule, to serve on cttee. for a memorial for Iddesleigh; Add MS 44500, ff. 93, 97.
[4] Peter Esslemont, 1834–94; liberal M.P. E. Aberdeenshire 1885–94.
[5] Thomas Fisher Unwin, 1848–1935; publisher and prominent liberal, though never an M.P.
[6] Of Oldham, on 'Rock of Ages'; Hawn P.
[7] See 24 Mar. 77.
[8] J. G. Swift MacNeill, *How the Union was carried* (1887).
[9] J. G. C. Minchin, *The growth of freedom in the Balkan peninsula* (1886).
[10] i.e. to M. Creighton, editor of *E.H.R.*
[11] See 20 Dec. 86.
[12] Letter of support for J. Slagg at a by-election, *T.T.*, 14 February 1887, 6f.
[13] A. H. Sayce, *The Hibbert Lectures* (1887); on Babylonian religion.

12. Sat.

Ch. 8½ A.M. Wrote to E.W. Hamilton—Messrs Murray—Mr Knowles—Rev. Mr Brierley—Mr Barnes—Messrs Cassell—Mr Noble. Woodcraft with WHG. Wrote on Homer. Read Minchin—Documents on Imp. Institute.[1] Dined with the W.H.G.s. Backgammon.

13. Sexa S.

Ch 11 AM (S. preached an admirable sermon, but with the matter of two in it) and 6½ PM also excellent. Wrote to Professor Knight—Mr Morley MP—Mr A. Morley MP—Canon M'Coll—Mr Flears. Read Memoirs of Mad. Guyon—Madame G.s Hymns (transl)[2]—The Christ & the Fathers[3]—Ball, Church of Ireland.

14. M.

Ch. 8½ A.M. Wrote to Professor Creighton—J. Russell[4]—Mr Rintoul[5]—Mr Annand[6]—Messrs Blackburn—J.T. Gresham—Mr Jeffery—Mr Fenelon—Rev. Mr Dyve. Felled an oak with W. Mary came on her way to Penmaenmawr: looked blooming.[7] Corrected Introd. to MS. on Greville. Wrote on Homer. Read Mahony on Glenbeigh[8]—Col Chichester on Irish Landlordism[9]—finished Ball's Ch. of Ireland.

15. Tu.

Ch. 8½ A.M. Wrote to Cashier Bank of E.—Ed. Lpool D. Post[10]—Rev. Mr Richardson—H. Duckworth—D.L. Duncan—S.B. Taylor—W.E. Sadler—Mr Knowles—Mr Corayn—W.H. Brown—M. Thomas—J.W. Hayes. Saw C.G. & S.E.G. on Jubilee.[11] Wrote on Homer. Read Odyssey—Minchin on Balkans and Sayce on Babylonia.

16. Wed.

Ch. 8½ A.M. Again at 11 A.M. for the Rowlands marriage.[12] Felled an Alder with W.H.G. Corrected Greville Proofs. Wrote to Ed. 'North & South'[13]—D. of

---

[1] See 30 Jan. 87.

[2] J. M. Guyon, *La vie . . . écrite par elle même*, 3v. (1792) and *Poésies et cantiques spirituels* (*de Mme. Guyon*) ed. P. Poiret, 4v. (1722).

[3] *The Christ and the Fathers: or, the reformers of the Roman Empire . . . by an historical scientist* (1887).

[4] James M. Russell of Portobello, Midlothian, on Scottish tenant farmers; Add MS 44500, f. 99.

[5] Charles Rintoul of E. Lothian; had written on tenant farmers, supporting R. B. Haldane's bill for simplifying land transfer; Add MS 44500, f. 91.

[6] To William Annand of Nova Scotia, on its relations with Canada; Add MS 44500, f. 105.

[7] After her severe illness.   [8] P. Mahony, *The Truth about Glenbeigh* (1887).

[9] Perhaps Charles Raleigh Chichester, 'The Irish question', *Dublin Review*, xiv. 243 (October 1885).   [10] *Liverpool Daily Post*, 18 February 1887, 5f.

[11] Plans for the Hawarden celebrations in June; the Gladstones were then in London.

[12] Gladstone signed the register as a witness to the marriage of Fred. Rowlands, Hawarden stationer and son of the vestry clerk, to Jane Elizabeth Forsyth.

[13] Congratulating Thomas Henry Webb, ed. of *North and South*, organ of the Protestant Home Rule Association, on his first number; *T.T.*, 19 February 1887, 7d.

Argyll—Jas Nield—J. Hawke—W. Rossiter—Mr Garratt—F. Stone—C. Beale—
Chairman Metrop. Dist. RR.—Supt. LNW Chester—W.D. Seymour—J.W.
Goalen—G.R. Bowden—P. Gabbitass[1]—E. Thomas—W. Brechin—Messrs Mur-
ray l.l. Read Minchin—and Odyssey.

17. Th.

Ch. 8½ A.M. Wrote to Editor Scotsman[2]—Mr Bryce M.P.—Rev. Mr Tucker—Ld
Granville—Mrs Ingram—Mrs Bolton—Ed. P.M.G.[3]—W.J. Smith—H. Culver—Mr
Rorison—Ed. D. News.[4] Wrote on Homer. Finished corr. sheets on Greville.
Read Odyssey—Minchin (finished)—Sayce on Babylon.

18. Fr.

Ch. 8½ A.M. Wrote to Mr J. de M. Brown—Messrs Murray (2)—Speaker's Sec.—
Messrs Scott—Mr J.H. Taylor—Mr Knowles—Mr H.B. Bare [sic]—Mr H.
Coynes—Rev. J. Kidson—Mr W. Robertson. Worked on books & papers in view
of departure. Read Odyssey—Laveleye on Balkan Countries. Worked on
Homer.

19. Sat. [Penmaenmawr]

Ch. 8½ A.M. Wrote to Mr Dawson Rogers[5]—Mr Strickland—Mr Franklin. Off to
Penmr. at 9.50–11.20. Forenoon devoted to the Shore. In afternoon walked up
the Gwdw Glas. Rather tired. Called on Dr Risk.[6] Read Sayce's Babylonia.

20. Quinq. S.

Ch. 11 AM. and H.C. Also 6½ P.M.—I am delighted with my Bell.[7] It only
requires to be hung higher. Called on the Ridgways:[8] & saw the Vicar[9] after
service. Read Huxley on Realism[10]—Anselm Cur Deus Homo[11]—Sayce on
Babylonia finished.

21. M. [London]

Wrote to Messrs Murray. 9.26–3.30. Journey to London. Saw Bangor Students—
Mr E. Lever and (in London) Ld Granville—Sir W. Harcourt—Mr Chamberlain.

---

[1] Perhaps the 'scholarly agency', Askin, Gabbitas and Killik.
[2] C. A. Cooper (see 18 Nov. 85) who had written on Home Rule; Hawn P.
[3] Not found published.
[4] On Ireland, D.N., 19 February 1887, 5d.
[5] Edmund Dawson *Rogers, 1823–1910; manager of the National Press Agency and a prominent
figure in the Hawarden 'Kite' in December 1885 (see above, xi, Appendix Id); also prominent in
Society for Psychical Research.
[6] James George Risk, of Irish origin; physician in Penmaenmawr.
[7] He joined in with the Penmaenmawr bell-ringers.
[8] The Misses Ridgway ran a ladies' school in Penmaenmawr.
[9] John Aneurin Howell, vicar of Penmaenmawr from 1881.
[10] T. H. Huxley, 'Scientific and pseudo-scientific realism', N.C., xxi. 191 (February 1887).
[11] St. Anselm, Cur Deus Homo? Why God became Man, tr. E. S. Prout (1886).

H of C. $4\frac{1}{2}$–$7\frac{1}{2}$. Spoke on procedure.[1] Dined with Canon M'Coll at the Devonshire Club. Much conversation with C[2]—who was very friendly. Read Rienzi.[3]

22. Tu.

Wrote to Mr Earp—Mrs Drew—Mr J. Taylor—Mr Deeth[?]. H. of C. 5–8.[4] Dined at Sir C. Forster's. Saw Sir R. Peel—Mr Smith. Drive with C. & shopping. Saw Mr Knowles—& wrote at his suggestion a Preface to Poseidon.[5] Wrote amended version of two passages for Greville. Saw Scotts—Mr Goschen—Mr A. Morley—Sir W. Harcourt—Mr Hamilton. Read Rienzi. Conclave on Procedure Resolutions.

23. Ash Wedy.

St James's 11 A.M. Wrote to Lady Iddesleigh—Mr A. Saumarez—Mr W.R. Thomas—Editor of The Baptist[6]—Mr J.M. Russell—Mr T. Thatcher—Mr R. Forrester—Mr Saumarez—Printer 19th C.—and Sir W. Harcourt. Conclave on the 'Round Table'.[7] Read Rienzi (finished)—Childers on Financial Qq.[8]—James, Modus Vivendi[9]—Roscher, Hermes.[10] Saw Mr. A. Morley—Ld Granville.

24. Th.

Wrote to W.H.G.—Mess. Murray—Mr Saumarez—Sig. E. de Huertas—Mrs Dewar—Professor Creighton. Luncheon at 15 G.S. Saw the A. Russells—Mr Bright—Sir A. West—Mr S. Lyttelton—Mr Sinclair MP—Mr B. Currie. Dined with Mr & Mrs Sands.[11] Saw the Agnew Water Colour Gallery. Read Life of Shaftesbury.[12] Worked on letters & papers.

25. Fr.

Wrote to M. Goldbecht—Mr Canny—Mr Cleghorn—G. Leach—Mr Hodge—Ed. Baptist[13]—Prov. St Ninians—Lord Spencer—W. Williams—Mr Saumarez. Saw Mr A. Morley—Mr S. Lyttelton—Mr Whitbread—Mr Illingworth—Mr Fowler. Conclave $5\frac{1}{2}$–$7\frac{1}{2}$ on Round Table. Wrote Mem.[14] H. of C. 5–$7\frac{3}{4}$ and after

---

[1] On proposals for new procedure rules; *H* 311. 190.

[2] i.e. Chamberlain; the meeting was set up by MacColl; see *MacColl*, 131.

[3] By E. Bulwer Lytton; see 4 Apr. 36.

[4] Procedure; *H* 311. 306.

[5] See 7 Dec. 86.

[6] Final version sent on 25 February, on *The Baptist*'s leader advocating Welsh disestablishment; Gladstone could not deal in 'abstract resolutions' and for the present saw no opportunity of time for a Bill; *T.T.*, 3 March 1887, 6a and Add MS 44500, f. 129.

[7] Preparations for the negotiations with liberal unionists; see M. Hurst, *Joseph Chamberlain and Liberal Reunion* (1967), ch. VII, and 26 Feb. 87.

[8] H. C. E. Childers, 'On some impending financial questions' (1887).

[9] Perhaps an untraced article by Sir H. James on the Round Table.

[10] W. H. Roscher, *Hermes der Windgott* (1886?).

[11] Mahlon and Mary Sands; she was American and a well-known beauty.

[12] E. Hodder, *The life and work of the 7th Earl of Shaftesbury*, 3v. (1886). See 27 Feb., 19 Mar. 87.

[13] First draft of next day's mem., with Harcourt's comments; Add MS 44773, f. 3.

[14] A response to Chamberlain's letter in *The Baptist* this day; *The Baptist*, 3 Mar. 1887. See Hurst, op. cit., 286n. and next day.

dinner.[1] Dined with the Wests. Read Land Commn Report[2]—Life of Shaftesbury.

26. Sat.

Wrote to Mr Westell—Rev. Mr Mackay l.l.—Sir W. Harcourt. l.l. and minutes. Read Shaftesbury Memoirs—Brabourne in N.C.[3]—and André Cornelis.[4] Rewrote Memorandum: difficult enough. Saw Mr S. Lyttelton—Mr G. Macmillan—Mr Godley—Ld Granville—Mr A. Morley. Luncheon in Brook St to see A. Lyttelton's fine motherless babe.[5] Tea with Mr Sturges (a good day of his.)

Private.   *Memorandum.*[6]

I am glad to find from the reports made to me that the recent conversations have been so promising. Perhaps, as regards the Government of Ireland, they have done everything which the time and circumstances would permit in ascertaining the existence of a real desire for union, & in showing that some supposed differences do not exist the points on which difficulty is felt are not such as to shut out the possibility of accommodation [*sic*].

It will at once be seen that I individually am not entitled on behalf of my late colleagues to deliver an Aye or No upon all particulars, or even all important particulars, on which alteration of their plans may be desired.

Nor do I feel certain that at this period, and in their present circumstances as representing a defeated party and a small minority, they can perform such a task. In a long experience of legislation I have never known a case where more was done than to agree upon broad principles and very general outlines, until a time had arrived when all the circumstances of the coming proposal, and the views and intentions of all the parties and sections concerned could be estimated with accuracy. General confidence has always supplied until their time came some kind of ground for conjuration.

It is a great advantage however to know, when such particulars have been brought into discussion, that on some or many of them ⟨there can be⟩ no apprehension need be entertained, and that none of them exclude the idea of further discussion, and of suggestions of a reconciling nature. Where however there is to be adjustment of detail, I think it is dangerous to attempt too much, for it is in regard to such detail that it is almost a necessity to forbear action except in full cognisance of the circumstances and needs of the moment when action is to take place.

I think that much has been done by the conversations, and I am not confident that a great deal more can be done now. At the same time if it is desired by Mr Chamberlain I am quite willing to call my late colleagues together, make known to them what has been reported to me, and learn their views upon the question whether and how far we can carry on any present communications with advantage *beyond* what has been already done. I think they would join me in thanking Mr Chamberlain for having promoted as well as shared in so much friendly intercourse.

[1] Complained at lateness of the Estimates; *H.* 311. 585.

[2] Report of Cowper's Royal Commission on the 1881 and 1885 Land Acts; *PP* 1887 xxvi. 1.

[3] E. H. Knatchbull-Hugessen, Lord Brabourne, 'Mr. Gladstone on the "Irish demand"', *N.C.*, xxi. 397 (March 1887).

[4] P. Bourget, *André Cornélis* (1887).

[5] Alfred Christopher Lyttelton, 1886-8.

[6] Undated holograph, Add MS 44773, f. 8. Docketed 'F.26.87. Mem. on upshot of Round Table Conversations. Suspended by reason of Mr Chamberlain's letter to "Baptist".' For Chamberlain's letter to *The Baptist*, published on 25 February and effectively ending the negotiations, see Garvin, ii. 292.

There is a point of the utmost importance also on the Land Question which seems to me to be nearly ripe for decision. I am of opinion, subject to some further sifting, that a good and effective scheme of Land Purchase and Sale may be framed without the use of Imperial Credit.[1]

27. 1 S. Lent

St James's mg: & Guards Chapel 6 P.M. Read Shaftesbury's Memoirs—Argyll (excellent) on Huxley[2]—And divers Tracts. The Shaftesbury book is an excellent discipline for me: it forces me to compare his nobleness with my vileness, his purity with my foulness. And this all through.[3] Saw Lady Farnborough.

28. M.

Wrote to Ld Spencer—Mr Drake—Sir Thos G.—Mr Gibson (Aberdeenshire). H. of C. $4\frac{3}{4}$-7.[4] Dined with the Oppenheims: much conversation. Saw Mr Macmillan—Ld Granville—Mr A. Morley. Read Shaftesbury's Life—André Cornelis. Worked on books & papers preparing for migration.

Tues. March One 1887.

Mr R. Brown—Mr Godley—Mr Holyoake—Mr Leveson—Dean of ChCh—Dean of Rochester—Provost of Kings—Provost of Oriel. Saw Mr A. Morley—Mr S. Lyttelton—Mr Morley—Sir W. Harcourt—Mr Childers. Ld Granville dined. Worked on papers &c. Visited Christie's. Attended Levee. Read Shaftesbury— Justin H. MacCarthy's Ireland.[5] H. of C. $5-7\frac{3}{4}$ and $10\frac{1}{4}-11\frac{1}{4}$.[6]

2. Wed.

Wrote to Sir C. Tennant. H. of C. $2\frac{1}{4}-5\frac{3}{4}$.[7] Read Shaftesbury—A. Cornelis—J.H. MacCarthy's Ireland—Walpole's Ireland.[8] Dined with the Speaker. Saw Mr Lyttelton—Mr J. Morley—Mr O. Morgan. Continued my preparations.

---

[1] Garvin, ii. 293, noted in 1933: 'Gladstone, returning to town, received the reports of his lieutenants upon the state of the Conference. He drew up a memorandum, which might assist our judgement of these transactions. Withheld in spite of Chamberlain's repeated request for disclosure, it has never seen the light.' Gladstone in fact wrote the memorandum on 25 February after a cursory perusal of Chamberlain's letter; on the 26th he 'read [Chamberlain's] letter carefully and it is denunciation of the "policy" and the "proposals" in a mass. I also find it has been widely noticed and has excited much not unjust indignation' (to Harcourt, 26 February 1887 in Hurst, op. cit., 291).

[2] G. D. Campbell, duke of Argyll, 'Professor Huxley: on Canon Liddon', N.C., xxi. 321 (March 1887).

[3] Hodder quotes passages from Shaftesbury's diary sharply critical of Gladstone's 'greed of place and salary and power'; he and Disraeli 'are two tigers over a carcass'; iii. 217.

[4] Estimates; H 311. 726.

[5] J. H. McCarthy, Ireland since the Union (1887), dedicated to Gladstone; see Add MS 44500, f. 140.

[6] Spoke on London corporation and on procedure; H 311. 910, 955.

[7] Procedure; H 311. 981.

[8] Sir C. G. Walpole, A short history of the Kingdom of Ireland (1882).

3. Th.

Wrote to Sir H. Dashwood—Mr Bridgman—Sir B. Samuelson[1]—Baron Tauchnitz—Mr J.H. MacCarthy MP—Mr J. Elliot—Mr Lloyd. Visited Collection of Old Masters. Saw S. Lyttelton—Mr A. Morley—Ld Spencer—Count Karolyi—Mr Knowles. H. of C. 5–7½.[2] Dined with Mr Knowles. Our journey to Dollis at night was cut short by fog. Read Shaftesbury—J.H. MacCarthy.

4. Fr.

Wrote to Ly S. Opdebeeck—Mr Wells RA—J.C. Brown—F. Milne—Mr Banes. Read Ld Ellenboroughs Journals[3]—Crozier on R. Churchill.[4] Saw Ld Kimberley —Sir W. Harcourt—Mr Morley—Mr Childers—Mr A. Morley. Dined with Mrs Peel. Again failed to get to Dollis by reason of the fog. H of C. 4¾–8. Spoke against proposed intervention of the Speaker in the Clôture.[5]

5. Sat. [Dollis Hill]

Wrote to Mr Blackwood—F.M.H. Jones[6]—Geo Russell—Canon Liddon—Mr Wells R.A.—W.H.G.—Mr Stead—Scott & Co. Off at 10.40 to Dollis Hill: a refuge for my shrinking timidity, unwilling at 77 to begin a new London House.—Walk with C. Read Shaftesbury's Life—André Cornelis.

6. 2 S. L.

Parish Ch mg & evg. Walk 3, drive 1–1¼ m. Read Shaftesbury—Life of Bp Fraser[7]—Tiele Religions Geschichte.[8] Wrote (little) on Olympians.[9]

7. M.[10]

Wrote to Mr T. Hughes QC—Mr A. Paterson—Mr W. Agnew—Rev. R. Macray. H of C. 5¼–8.[11] Worked on & read Odyssey (realien). Read Shaftesbury. Sat 2 hours to Mr Wells.[12] Went to London: saw Harcourt & Morley: dined with Northbourne: back 10¾.

---

[1] Sir Bernhard Samuelson.
[2] Estimates, *H* 311. 1090.
[3] See 18 June 81.
[4] J. B. Crozier, *Lord Randolph Churchill. A study of English democracy* (1887).
[5] *H* 311. 1281.
[6] Secretary of the Chelsea liberal association; letter read to meeting on 6 April; *T.T.*, 7 April 1887, 10b.
[7] T. Hughes, *James Fraser, bishop of Manchester* (1887); next day, Gladstone wrote to Hughes (*T.T.*, 11 March 1887, 10c) denying he had been a subscriber to the confederate loan, as the book claimed.
[8] C. P. Tiele, probably *Assyriologie und ihre Ergebnisse für die vergleichende Religionsgeschichte* (1887).
[9] 'The greater gods: part II: Apollo', *N.C.*, xxi 748 (May 1887).
[10] This day, *The Times* began publication of the series of articles, 'Parnellism and crime'.
[11] Spoke on business of the House; *H* 311. 1412.
[12] Probably Henry Tanworth Wells, 1828–1903; popular portrait painter with studio at Thorpe Lodge, Camden Hill; this portrait untraced.

8. Tu.

Wrote to Mr Anderton—T. Rogers—Mr Higgs—Lady Cork—G. Fuller—Lord Burton—Mr Marshall—Miss Ponsonby—Mrs Th.—Mr Catherall—and minutes. Also Mr Brown BP—Mrs Bolton BP. Read Odyssey (for realien)—Shaftesbury. Dined at Lucy's for a friendly conversation with Sir G. Trevelyan.[1] Church at 5 PM. Saw Rev. Mr Mills.

9. Wed. [Windsor]

Wrote to Mr Agnew—Mr Foote—Mr Wedlake—R. George—J.W. Goalen—T. Stoneman—Miss M. Holt BP—Mr M'Coll. Off to London 3 P.M. Wrote on Homer. Saw Mr Godley. Read Shaftesbury—Jebb on Homer[2]—Ellenborough's Diary. Off to Windsor 4¾. Conversation with Sir H. Ponsonby—Mr Morley—Sir J. Cowell—Lord [blank]—M. Falbe[3]—The Spanish Minister (fervent about Ireland)—Miss Ponsonby (very satisfactory)—Mr MacColl. The Queen courteous as always: somewhat embarrassed as I thought.

10. Th. [Dollis Hill]

St George's Chapel 10½ A.M. To London 11.40. Shopping. Saw Sir W. Harcourt(!!)—Ld Granville—Mr Morley—Mr A. Morley—S. Lyttelton—Lady S. Spencer—Mr Bryce. Dined at G. Russell's (saw Dr . . . . ., Mr Paul) and back to Dollis. Wrote to Rev. Mr Mackey[4]—Mr Mackay—Mad. Marlet[5]—and minutes. Read Ellenborough—Ld Shaftesbury's Memoirs.

11. Fr.

Ch 5 P.M. Wrote to Mr A.W.K. Wade—Mr Whorlow[6]—Mr Andrews—Jas M. Goalen—H.N.G.—Mr Guinness Rogers. Read Odyssey—Shaftesbury—Jebb's Introd. to Homer. Walk with C. S.E.G. came in evg.

12. Sat.

Ch. 5 P.M. Wrote to Mr A. Morley MP—Mr Annan—Mr Green—Sec. Trin. Ho.—Mr Simmons—Messrs Murray l.l.—Mr Bevan—Rev. Stewart—Mr Radford. Read Odyssey—Shaftesbury—M'Donnell[7]—Jebb's Introdn to Il. & Od.—Thring on the Irish Question[8]—Selborne on Radicalism.[9] Walk with S.E.G. Eight to dinner. Conversation with Cyril Flower.

---

[1] 'Trevelyan's Unionism now appeared to be Gladstonian Home Rule under another name'; Hurst, *Liberal reunion*, 324, 330. See 25–6 May 87.

[2] R. C. Jebb, *Homer; an introduction to the Iliad and Odyssey* (1887).

[3] Christian Frederick de Falbe, the Danish minister in London.

[4] Probably George MacKay, curate in Stepney.

[5] Perhaps wife of Everard Marlet, London importer of fancy goods.

[6] John Robert Wharlow, parliamentary agent; business untraced.

[7] Perhaps J. Macdonell, *The land question* (1873).

[8] Lord Thring, 'Home Rule and imperial unity', *C.R.*, li. 305 (March 1887).

[9] Lord Selborne, 'The radical programme', *C.R.*, li. 347 (March 1887).

13. 3 S. Lent

Willesden Ch mg & aft. Read Cur Deus Homo[1]—Memoirs of Bp Fraser—
Memoirs of Ld Shaftesbury.

14. M. [London]

Wrote to Sir W. B. Foster—Robn & Nichn—Sir F. Abel—Mr Leach—W. Boyd—
Mr Rhodes[2]—Mr Le Beau[3]—Mr Guiness Rogers—H.J. Gehlsen—Mess. Vevey &
Co—Rev. Mr Street—Mr Inderwick[4]—Keeper of the Vote Office and minutes.
2-7. To London & H. of C. Saw Bishop of Truro[5]—Ld Granville—Mr A. Morley
—Sir W. Harcourt *cum* Mr Morley. Read Odyssey—Ld Shaftesbury—Uncle
Tom's Cabin (*re*).[6]

15. Tu.

Wrote to Hales & Freeman—Miss A. Shore—R.G. Maxted—Miss Bergendahl—
Keeper of Vote Office—J.W. Maclaren—T. Breen—W.B. Adams—Sir W. Harcourt. Finished Odyssey. Worked a little on Homer. Read
Shaftesbury—Ellenborough's Journals. Dined at Sir C. Foster's. Easy *general*
conversation with Chamberlain. Saw Mr Inderwick—Mr Childers—Mr A.
Morley—W.H.G. H. of C. 5-7.[7] Six inches of snow: yesterday night 16 degrees of
frost.

16. Wed. [Dollis Hill]

Wrote to Ld Thring—Mr Illingworth—Mr Gwilt[8]—H.B. Murray—W.S. Bath—Dr
Buchholz BP.—Watsons. Midwinter in mid-March. Frost 16%, snow 6 inches.
Off to Dollis 10.30. Saw Mr A. Morley. Read Shaftesbury—Uncle Tom's Cabin—
Jebb's Introduction to Homer. Too lazy and remiss for "Apollo".

17. Th.

Wrote to ....—......... (both forgotten). Thought over what to say
tonight. I wrote even three sets of notes: but forgot to take any of them. Dined
with Mr Barran, & spoke 45 min.[9] Away 7-12. Conversation with Mr Stansfeld—Mr Barran. Read Shaftesbury—Jebb—Uncle Tom. Could hardly touch
Apollo.

---

[1] See 20 Feb. 87.
[2] Perhaps C. J. Rhodes, but letter untraced.
[3] J. Le Beau of Stoke Newington, sent a malacca cane; Hawn P.
[4] Frederick Andrew Inderwick, 1836–1904; barrister and historian; liberal M.P. Rye 1880–5.
[5] On Truro cathedral; see Add MS 44500, f. 154.
[6] See 23 Sept. 52.
[7] Procedure; *H* 312. 379.
[8] Charles Gwilt, London solicitor; Hawn P.
[9] Dinner for Gladstone held by Yorkshire liberal M.P.s. Gladstone's speech tried to entice dissentient liberals away from Chamberlain; *T.T.*, 18 March 1887, 10a and Hurst, *Liberal reunion*, 337–8.

18. Fr.

Wrote to Prof. Creighton—Mrs Drew—S.W. Norton—Scotts—J.L. Heaps—J. Godley—Canon MacColl—Mr Knowles—[J.]F. Moulton—Watsons—Captain Cole—H. Millwaters—Dawson Rogers. Worked on Apollo, well. Read Shaftesbury—Uncle Tom's Cabin—Jebb on Homer.

19. Sat.

Church at 5 PM. Wrote to (all forgotten). Saw Godley—walk with him. Drive with C. Wrote Mem. on Shaftesbury's Life, 'en ce que me concerne'. Worked a little on Apollo. Read as yesterday. Ten to dinner. Much conversation with Granville. Saw also Welby—Hamilton.

Memorandum.[1]

The large acquaintance with Lord Shaftesbury which this book imparts must I think raise him very high indeed in the estimation of all men. I knew him very long and on very friendly terms but our paths only touched at rare intervals, and the absorption of mind incident to political life, at least in my case left less than a due share of attention available for the great philanthropic purposes to which in the main he devoted his life. I never therefore was in conflict with him: and I greatly desired to avoid anything of the kind in relation to the matters on which during the last part of his life we differed. I knew and felt his philanthropy, his bravery, his self sacrifices, his deep and warm affection; though I saw from time to time indications that he was liable to influence from an *entourage* inferior to himself. The Biography has certainly elevated and deepened all my appreciations of this noble character. I felt myself soon after the commencement simply grovelling in the dust before him. Not until I made some progress was I aware that while thus down I was to be hit so frequently, may I say so violently, by his broad and unreserved condemnations. I could not have believed from the constantly kind relations between us that I could have presented to one sustaining those relations a picture of such unredeemed and universal blackness. It is true that I am not alone in the abyss. The mass of politicians is to be found there; and among them by name Lord Beaconsfield,[2] so far as that may be deemed a consolation, but with this difference that he impressed very forcibly on Lord Shaftesbury the idea of his greatness. I am now inclined to regret what I had used to reflect on with pleasure, that I had broken bread at Lord Shaftesbury's table for he must have been a reluctant host. It is evident indeed that his Diaries recorded the first and hasty impressions of the hour, and I think his Biographer is to be blamed for much reckless and painful publication rather marring as far as it goes than making the beauty of a splendid life. As respects myself what I would say on these passages is first that I must distinguish between statements of fact on one side & statements of opinion or views of character on the other. As to the first I cannot but observe not only that they are unverified, and incomplete, but as I could show in detail singularly inaccurate. As to the last, these are very humbling and will I hope help to teach me that biting the dust, that the attitude of

---

[1] Add MS 44773, f. 13. Pejorative extracts from Shaftesbury's diaries, as printed in Hodder's *Life*, were circulated later in the month in Hackney. On 27 April 1887 Gladstone wrote in a letter published in *The Standard* on 29 April that 'I entirely refuse to admit the accuracy of a number of statements concerning me which purport to be facts, and which have been published by his biographer, contrary, as it appears, to his intention.' Hodder offered to eliminate some of the passages in the popular edition if Gladstone pointed out the inaccuracies, but the latter declined to become involved in a detailed dispute; see exchange of letters, 29-30 April 1887, Add MS 44500, ff. 265-73.

[2] See 27 Feb. 87n.

inward prostration is that which alone befits me. Next they must be helps to improvement & some faint reaching forth to the qualities he would have approved. Thirdly that in my case the unjust clauses have never equalled the unjust eulogies. Lastly that it is a small and secondary thing, for there is an Eye that sees all. 'Let my sentence come forth from thy presence; and let thine eyes behold the thing that is equal.'[1]

20. 4 S. Lent

Willesden Ch 11 A.M. with Holy Commn & 6½ P.M. Sir C. Tennant & Wests in aftn. Read Shaftesbury—finished III.—Life of Bp Fraser—Anselm's Cur Deus Homo.

21. M.

Wrote to J.W. Goalen—Rev. Mr Backe—H.H. Johnson—Spanish Minr—J.D. De Lille—Mr Beckingsale—A.W. Laidlaw—Canon Creighton—J. Davidson—Mr W. Johnstone—G.F. Connor—Mr Irving—W.T. Westell—M. Drew—Mr Knollys—Mr P. Campbell—Sec. Royal Acad. Read Uncle Tom's Cabin. Worked 'some' on Apollo. 1.45–11.30. To London. Conclave on business 2½–4. H. of C. 5–6¼. Read Irish Land Evidence.[3] Saw A. Morley. Dined at Miss Ponsonbys. No rise to be had out of C. Villiers.[4]

22. Tu.

Wrote to Watsons—Manager of Central Press—J. Rollo—W. Macnight—W. Fleming—H. Whitaker—S. Scott—C.V. O'Donnell—R. Tangye—Rev. Gr. Roberts—H.V. Silver—E.P. Henderson—A. Kettle—F. Malthouse—W. Hands—Miss ab Ithel [sic]—R. Seaton—Rev. R.C. Jenkins—Mr W.H. Smith. Read divers tracts. Worked on Apollo. To London in aftn. H. of C. 5–7½.[5] Dined with the Roundells.

23. Wed.

Wrote Tel. to New York Meeting[6]—and minutes. Read Homeric Studies (Apollo & Athenè)—Froude English in Ireland[7]—Uncle Tom's Cabin. H. of C. 3½–6.[8] Went with Lucy to the entertainment at the Victoria & the Working Men's Club.[9] Then to Dollis. Saw Mr Freeman's daughter[10]—Sir W. Harcourt *cum* Mr Morley—Mr A. Morley—Herbert J.G.—Ld Granville.

[1] Rendering of Psalm xxvii. 2.
[2] Estimates; *H* 312. 861.
[3] See 25 Feb. 87.
[4] The M.P. for Wolverhampton and friend of Mrs. Thistlethwayte; a liberal unionist.
[5] Motion for urgency for treatment of Irish Coercion Bill; *H* 312. 1154.
[6] On a meeting held at the Cooper Institute, New York, against coercion in Ireland; a resolution was passed supporting Gladstone's policy; *D.N.*, 24 March 1887, 5h.
[7] See 25 Nov. 72.
[8] Spoke on urgency; *H* 312. 1278.
[9] The Victoria Coffee Palace, Waterloo-bridge-road; *T.T.*, 24 Mar. 1887, 9e.
[10] Margaret, da. of E. A. Freeman m. 1878 A. J. Evans, the archaeologist and d. 1893; she was a well-known indexer; see 9 Apr. 78n.

24. Th.

Wrote to Messrs Watson—Mr Maciver—Mr Connor—Draft Mrs Henderson to C.G.—and minutes. Worked on Apollo. Read Life of Marie Louise[1]—Uncle Tom's Cabin. Saw Mr Rathbone—Mr A. Morley. To London at 2¾. H of C. 5-8. Spoke 1 h. 20 m. on Urgency.[2]

25. Fr.

Wrote to Mr Tweedle—Mr Adcock—Jas Howard—A.M. Fraser—Mr Scott—Messrs Murray—Dr Biese[3]—Miss Goalen. Read as yesterday. Saw divers. Worked on Apollo. To London for debate & division. Well content with 260 to 348. Returned to Dollis before then[?]. Dined with W. James.

26. Sat.

Rose at 9.30. Some chill. Bed again at 3-7. Wrote to Watsons—Mr Scott—R. Bury—S. Hart—J.R. Monk—Mr Clancy More—Mr Quirk. Worked on Apollo. Read Life of Marie Louise. Eleven to dinner: a cheerful party.

27. 5 S. Lent

Kept my bed by order. Service alone. Saw Herbert. Finished Life of Bishop Fraser. Read G. Vos on Pentateuch.[4]

28. M.

Wrote to Mr W.T. Stead—Mr Smedley—Mr Campbell—Mr Hewlett—Mr May—Mr Simpson—Sec. Tabernacle—Mr Austin—Mr Bellingham—Rev. Whitlock—Rev. Durban—Mr Clutton Brock[5]—Messrs Murray. Read Pyecroft on Oxford[6]—Marie Louise. H of C. 5½-8. Heard Balfour's astonishing statement & plan.[7] Dined at Grillions. Home at 11 PM.

29. Tu.

Wrote to A. Morley—Ld Spencer—& minutes. Worked Apollo. Then turned to the Irish business & worked much with extreme difficulty in licking the question into shape. Went to House 5-8 and spoke 1½ h. as carefully & with as much measure as I could.[8] Saw A. Morley—Mr Stansfeld. Dined at Sir C. Forster's. H. of C. again 10½-11: & home. Read Memoirs of M. Louise.

---

[1] *Correspondence of Marie Louise, wife of Napoleon I* (1887).

[2] *H* 312. 1353.

[3] Dr. Alfred Biese of Kiel, classical scholar; corresponded on the Greeks; Hawn P. He was married to Mary Elinor, da. of Montgomerie Gladstone.

[4] G. Vos, *The Mosaic origin of the Pentateuchal Codes* (1886).

[5] John Allen Clutton Brock of Bickley; had sent verses; see Add MS 44500, f. 181.

[6] J. Pycroft, *Oxford memories. A retrospect after fifty years*, 2v. (1886).

[7] Balfour introduced the Coercion Bill, announcing that the govt. estimates of the need for coercion must go beyond the crime figures; *H* 312. 1626.

[8] Announcing support, if it were moved, for Parnell's amndt. to the Coercion Bill for a cttee. of the whole House; *H* 312. 1790.

30. Wed.

Wrote to Ld Spencer—Miss D. Tennant[1]—J. Rogers—Rev. Macanally[2]—and minutes. Worked on Apollo. Drive & walk with C. Eleven to dinner. Conversation with Ld Spencer—Ld Ripon—Mr P. Stanhope—Mr Godley. Read Marie Louise—Uncle Tom's Cabin.

31. Th.

Wrote minutes. To London 2–3. 3–4. Read Müller, M. Müller, Smith, at London Libr. Saw Mr Stead—Baron F. de Rothschild—Sir J. Lubbock—Ld Derby. Dined at Sir J. Lubbock's. Worked on Apollo: finishing, & correcting. Finished Marie Louise—read Uncle Tom's Cabin. H. of C. $5\frac{1}{2}$–8.[3] Conclave on coming course of business.

Frid. Ap. One. 1887.

Wrote to Messrs Hales & Freeman—Mr Knowles—Mr Kelly—T.A. Nash Esq[4]—E.W. Boles—Watsons—Ld Hampden—Mr Marshman—Mrs Webb—Mr de Lisle MP—& minutes. Finished & sent off Apollo. Read Uncle Tom's Cabin. Dined at Mr B. Currie's. Off to London 3.30. H. of C. $5\frac{1}{4}$–8 and $10\frac{1}{2}$–3 AM: with the mischievous Closure under the Speaker's authority.[5]

2. Sat.

Wrote to Mr Morley. Saw Mr Holl—W.H.G.—Ld Granville—Mr Norman[6]—H.J.G. Dined at Sir G. Hayter's: Mr Chamberlain, Mr Askwith,[7] & others. A very free conversation on the closure. Visited the fine portraits at Mr Holl's.[8] Misdirected: a four mile walk to Dollis. Worked on Apollo. Read Uncle Tom.

3. Palm S.

Willesden Ch & H.C. mg. At $4\frac{3}{4}$ drove over to Harrow for the striking service at 6. Supper after. Conversation with Mr Weldon[9] & some of his boys. Read Light

---

[1] Dorothy, da. of C. Tennant of Glamorganshire; she often sent Gladstone books, which he usually read; in 1890 she m. Sir H. M. Stanley (see 23 June, 12 July 90).

[2] Probably David Lancaster McAnally, Queen's chaplain at Hampton Court.

[3] Coercion Bill; *H* 313. 88.

[4] Thomas Arthur Nash, author, working on his *Life of Lord Westbury, . . . with selections from his correspondence,* 2v. (1888).

[5] Spoke on coercion; *H* 313. 320.

[6] (Sir) Henry Norman, 1858–1939 (liberal journalist, author and politician); interviewed Gladstone this day on the parliamentary situation for *New York Evening Post* and allied papers; copy of interview at Add MS 44500, f. 255.

[7] Presumably Herbert Henry Asquith, 1852–1928; liberal M.P. E. Fife 1886–1918; home secretary 1892–5 etc.; had recently made powerful maiden speech on Ireland. See 16 Apr. 87.

[8] A visit suggested by Dorothy Tennant to the studio of Frank Holl (see 25 Feb. 85 and Add MS 44500, f. 193); it bore fruit; see 31 Oct. 87, 24 Mar. 88.

[9] James Edward Cowell Welldon, 1854–1937; headmaster of Harrow 1885–98; later bp. of Calcutta, dean of Durham.

on the Path[1]—Life of Bp Hannington[2]—M'Kinney, Romanism[3]—Uncle Tom (finished). Saw Prof. Stuart. Wrote to Mr A. Morley—Mr Chamberlain (after reflection).[4]

4. M.

Ch. at 5 AM [*sic*]. Wrote to Mr Orme Blake(?)—Ld Hampden—Mr Willick—Watsons—Mr W.H. Thomas—J.H. Bell. Worked on Apollo. Read André Cornelis—Nineteenth Cent. Huxley (savage), A. Lang, Ld Cowper, Brett.[5]

5. Tu.

Wrote to Hales & Freeman—A. Spicer—T.A. Nash—J. Watt—E. Butler—Ld Rosebery—J.H. Shalcross—E.H. Bailey—A. Wilberforce—Mess. Murray—E. Gamlin. Conversation with Mr Chamberlain 12–1½: ambiguous result but some ground made. 2¼–11¼. To London. H. of C. 4–8¼.[6] Dined with Mr B. Currie. Saw Mr Morley—Mr A. Morley—S. Lyttelton—H.J.G. Wrote Mem. of Chamberlain conversation. Read André Cornelis: the quintessence of Frenchism.[7]

W.E.G. to J.C. mem[orandum][8]
  Avoid all retrospective discussion and regret.
  from whom should he and I have 'full powers'?
  between us and the two senior questions stands 'Coercion'.

  had always hoped we might find here a common ground.
  our line is taken.
  Coercion further complicated by *closure*.
  Glad to agree on the *new Rule*.
  Is the rule against alteration of it absolute? If not could not *its Ayes* promote change?
  As to arrangements the mischief lay in the announcement as to 2R *before Easter*.
  A conference *now* would be dangerous.
  Do our best from time to time—according to circumstances.
  Supposing Mr. C[hamberlain] were inclined to suggest the exclusion of the Speaker from the Closure Rule, would his doing it, or being known to desire & be ready to promote it, be well or ill taken by our friends?
  Randolph Churchill thought Parnell's demand wholly reasonable *except* for want of sufficient notice.

[Gladstone's memorandum of the conversation][9]
  Chamberlain
    has plenty of qualms on coercion
    finds John Bright has none
    agrees it is a good question for us, bad for them, with the country.

---

[1] M.C., *Light on the path* (1885); theosophy.
[2] E. C. Dawson, *James Hannington . . . first bishop of Eastern Equatorial Africa* (1887).
[3] Untraced.
[4] Suggesting the meeting on 5 April; Garvin, ii. 295.
[5] *N.C.*, xxi. 481–615 (April 1887).
[6] Coercion bill; *H* 313. 512.
[7] See 26 Feb. 87.
[8] Undated holograph; Add MS 44773, f. 36.
[9] Add MS 44773, f. 35.

his anxiety to bring Round Table to a result was because he saw coercion must greatly widen the breach.

a) Supposes (but asks if) I think coercion now occupies the ground and precludes further prosecution of the Home Rule & Land Purchase discussions.

He himself is very nearly of that opinion—not disposed to dispute it.

Sees that the bulk of his Wing will be destroyed at the next election.

Remains of opinion there *must* be a settlement and a large settlement of the question.

His course open in regard to particulars of coercion—and thinks the same of the Wing.

Dark anticipations for the future of the party wh. will have increased difficulty in holding up against the Tories.

Can never be a Tory, but the Wing on the Hartington side, will join the Tories.

Hartington has certainly been moving away from the Liberals.

He and James could readily agree upon a concession in the matter of Irish Govt. by formulating what they think might & ought to be given—fears Parnell wd. denounce it at once.

Hartington not desirous to give anything, might agree for a great purpose.

Agrees about *closure* that the present intervention of the Speaker is mischievous & ought to be got rid of.

b) Fears *his* mixing in the matter would be resented by our friends.

I said I would inquire on *a & b*.

WEG Ap. 5/87

I said I hoped the bill wd. be mitigated in its passage—though best for us, in a party sense, as it is.

He admitted coercion was a bad ground for them in the country.

He referred to his going out of Parliament as an alternative if Toryism dominates.

6. *Wed.*

Willesden Ch. 10½ AM. Wrote to Archbishop Walsh—Mr A. Morley—D.R. Edmunds—Watsons—J. Lee (Illinois)[1]—Mr Stead. The W.H.G.s dined. Read Th. Rogers on Bank.[2] Read André Cornelis—Société Française pendant la Revolution[3]—and Livland u. Irland.[4]

7. *Th.*

Ch. 5 P.M. Wrote to Mr Thorold Rogers—Mr Morley MP—Mr Luttrell—Mr A. Morley l.l. Worked on Athene.[5] Read Livland u. Ireland—Tuke on Ireland[6]— Archer on Old Testament[7]—finished André Cornelis. Saw Herbert J.G. Helen G. arrived.

---

[1] Corresponding on religion; Hawn P.

[2] J. E. T. Rogers, *The first nine years of the Bank of England* (1887).

[3] Many of this sort of title.

[4] *Livland und Irland. Ein Briefwechsel* (1883).

[5] 'The greater gods of Olympos: part III: Athenê', *N.C.*, xxii. 79 (July 1887); Add MS 44700, f. 256.

[6] J. H. Tuke, *Achill and the West of Ireland* (1886); on the seed potato fund.

[7] Perhaps W. Archer Butler, *Christ sought and found in the Old Testament* (1857).

8. Good Fr.

Ch. 11 AM and $3\frac{1}{2}$ P. M. Wrote to Mr Schnadhorst (& a packet of invitations)—Ed. N.E. Gazette Middlesb. (priv. and publ.)[1]—Central News—G.H. May—Press Assocn. Read Martineau on Church Federation[2]—Corn. a Lapide on St Luke[3]—G. Voss on Pentateuch—Life of Bp Hannington.

9. Sat.

Easter Eve. Ch 11 A.M. Wrote to Rev. Mr Hastings—Watsons—Mr Knowles—Mr Godley—Ld Rosebery—Mr Oldham—Mr A. Morley—and[4] L. Lady Waterford. Worked on Athenè. Saw W.H.G.—the F. Verneys. Read Livland u. Irland—Thorold Rogers on the Bank.

10. Easter Day.

Kingsbury Ch 11 A.M. with H.C.—Willesden Ch. evg. Read Life of Bp Hannington—Ditto Bp Bickersteth—G. Vos on the Pentateuch—Bellarmin, Selbstbiographie.[5]

On this great day what are my special prayers? They are three.

1. For the speedy concession to Ireland of what she most justly desires.

2. That the concession may be so timed and shaped as to be entirely severed from all temptations to self-glorifying so far as I am concerned.

3. That thereafter the tie between me and the contentious life may at once be snapped.

But now one prayer absorbs all others: Ireland, Ireland, Ireland.

Wrote to Mrs Th.[6] Saw Prof. Stuart.

M. 11.

Wrote to Lady A. Russell—Mr Godley—Ld Granville—H.G. Reid—Mr L.L. Gerhardi—R. Prentice—Sir P. Jennings[7]—Rev. C.J. Field—Mr Campbell—Alf. Lyttelton Tel.—Mr Moulton. Corr. proofsheets of Apollo. Read Livland u. Ireland—Rogers on the Bank—Infanticide in India.[8] Luncheon with the Ths. Saw Prof. Stuart.

12. Tu.

St Paul's 4. P.M. Wrote to Mr Armitstead—W. Wills—F. Finch—Mr Shield—F. Wright—G. Brownhill—Mr Bodkin—Mr Willis. Worked on Athenè. Off to London at $2\frac{1}{4}$ P.M. Visited the St Paul's reredos & Wellington Monument.

---

[1] Letter, dated 9 April, supporting meeting against the Crimes Bill, in *T.T.*, 11 April 1887, 4c.

[2] J. Martineau, *The national church as a federal union* (1887).

[3] Cornelius à Lapide, *St. Luke's gospel* (1887).

[4] Facsimile in Masterman, 368, starts here.

[5] *Die Selbstbiographie des Cardinals Bellarmin* (1887).

[6] This phrase obliterated for the facsimile by a slip of paper pasted onto the MS.

[7] Untraced.

[8] See 14 Apr. 87.

H of C. 5–8.[1] Saw Mr Broadhurst—Mr Morley—Mr B. Currie—Mr A. Morley. Dined at Mr Currie's: & home at 10¾. Read Livland u. Irland—Records of Wilmslow.[2]

13. Wed. [London]

Wrote to Ld Granville—Hon. Eli Taylor[3]—Mr Jackson—Professor Stuart[4]—Mr Fryer. No London till the Play: Sophia, clever & well acted.[5] Slept CHT. Worked on Athenè. Saw Mr Hastings. Read Livland u. Irland—O'Connell's Repeal Speech.[6]

14. Th. [Dollis Hill]

Wrote to Sir J.P. Hennessy—Mr Nisbet—Mr Reid—Mr Assiter—Mr Law—Mr Buchanan—Mr Officer—Mr Priest. Saw Mr Huxley—Sir [P.] Jennings[7]—Mr A. Morley—Ld Rosebery—W.H.G. H. of C. 5–7¼;[8] back to D. Read O'Connell (finished)—Lysons' Middlesex[9]—Ellenborough's Diary.[10]

15. Fr.

Wrote to Mr Knowles B.P.—Mr Newbigging—J.C. Rose—Mr Bedhook—H. Prince—Ed. D. News. To London at 3. Tea with Mrs Dugdale.[11] Dined with Childers. H. of C. 5–7¾.[12] Saw A. Morley. Worked on Athenè. Read on Infanticide—Physique of Irishmen[13]—finished Livland u. Irland.

16. Sat.

Wrote to Mr Henderson—Mr Robertson—Mr Stacy—R. Morris—R. Perkins—Messrs. Routledge. Finished Athenè. Fourteen to dinner. A happy party. Conversation with Mr Reid—Mr Askwith[14]—Mr Morley—Mr Fowler—Mr Maciver. Read Bp Hannington—Mulhall.[15]

---

[1] Interjected on Coercion Bill; *H* 313. 717.
[2] Sent by Alfred Fryre; Hawn P.
[3] Eli Thayer, 1819–99; U.S. congressman (republican) and colonizer.
[4] Letter supporting the demonstration in Hyde Park; *T.T.*, 16 April 1887, 11f.
[5] Robert Buchanan's 'Sophia' at the Vaudeville theatre. See Add MS 44500, f. 262.
[6] Unclear which; perhaps D. O'Connell, *Report to the Repeal Association, April 1840*.
[7] Sir Patrick Alfred *Jennings, 1831–97; premier of New South Wales 1886–Jan. 1887; in London for the colonial conference.
[8] Coercion bill; *H* 313. 892.
[9] In D. Lysons, *The environs of London*, 4v. (1792–6).
[10] See 18 June 81.
[11] Alice Frances, wife of W. Stratford Dugdale and da. of Sir C. P. Trevelyan.
[12] Interjected on Coercion bill; *H* 313.1029.
[13] Possibly W. Twamley, 'The cause of the Dublin poor' (1886).
[14] *Sc.* H. H. Asquith; note accepting invitation at Add MS 44500, f. 245.
[15] M. G. Mulhall, *Fifty years of national progress 1837–87* (1887).

17. *1 S. E.*

Kingsbury Ch & H.C. mg. Willesden Ch evg. Wrote to Mr A. Morley—Mrs Bolton—Mr Andrews—Mr Holgate. Saw Herbert. Read Life of Bp Hannington— of Bp Bickersteth[1]—of the Leslies[2]—St F. de Sales.[3]

18. *M.*

Working on materials for Irish Debate. To London at 1.30. H of C. $4\frac{1}{2}$–$8\frac{1}{4}$ and 10–2. Spoke $1\frac{1}{4}$ hour. My voice did its duty but with great effort.[4] Worked on papers. Finished Mulhall. Saw A. Morley—Sir C. Russell—Sir W. Harcourt. Conclave at Granville's on Irish Land Bill. 3–$4\frac{1}{4}$.

19. *Tu.*

Up late. Wrote to Mr Godley—Mr Egan—Mr Osborne—Mr Sanderson—Sir A. Hayter—Bp Woodlock—Watsons. H of C. $5\frac{1}{2}$–7.[5] Read Debates of 1870.—& work in Library H. of C. Worked on Irish papers. Saw Mr A. Morley—Sir W. Harcourt—The Speaker—Mr Bryce. Dined with the Eighty Club. Spoke 1 hour: without Tories to talk down my impaired voice.[6] Dollis Hill afterwards.

20. *Wed.*

Wrote to Mr Paterson—Mr Knowles BP—Sir R. Peel—Dr Buchholz BP.—Mr Davies—Stage Manager Vaudeville—Rev. Mr Barrett—Mr Woolacott—Mr W. Bardney—E. Austin—Mr W.C. Bennett. Kept my bed, by advice, to 11 AM. Read Q.R. on Nonjurors—on English History[7]—Contemp Rev., Geffcken on German Affairs—Laing, Plan of Campaign[8]—For better for worse.[9] Eleven to dinner.

21. *Th.*

Wrote to Mrs Bolton—Mr Callett—Mr Townsend—Mr Carpenter—Mr Stanwick—Rev. Dr Gordon—Dr. B. OConnor[10]—Mr W. Cope—'A correspondent'— Sir W. Harcourt—Mr W.H. Smith.[11] Worked on Homer (Herè). Dined with Mr Marjoribanks. Saw Mr Campbell White—Sir G. Trevelyan—Mrs Th.—Mr Martin. Read Ellenborough Diary—and Psychologus.[12]

---

[1] M. C. Bickersteth, *Life and episcopate of R. Bickersteth* (1887).
[2] R. J. Leslie, *Life . . . of John Leslie. With preliminary sketches . . . of the Leslie family* (1887).
[3] Perhaps H. L. Farrer, *S. Francis de Sales* (1871).
[4] Opposing Coercion Bill 2°R; *H* 313. 1186.
[5] Misc. business; *H* 313. 1241.
[6] H. H. Asquith in the chair; *T.T.*, 20 April 1887, 12a.
[7] *Q.R.*, clxiv. 322, 507 (April 1887).
[8] *C.R.*, li. 577, 586 (April 1887).
[9] By Diana Mulock in *C.R.*, li. 570 (April 1887).
[10] Bernard O'Connor, physician; see Add MS 44497, f. 129.
[11] And wrote to *P.M.G.* explaining that he did not fear a dissolution but did not desire one until England had had time to reflect on coercion; *T.T.*, 22 April 1887, 12a.
[12] J. B. Goddard, *Psychologus: the story of a soul* (1887).

22. *Fr.*

Wrote to Mr Manning—Mr Stuart Glennie—Dr Manners—E. Cooper—Dennies —Mr E. Cooper Solr—A. Morley (Resolutions). Worked on Homer 'Herè'. Read Ellenborough—Barry OBrien's Ireland.[1] Dinner party manqué. H of C. $4\frac{3}{4}$-7.[2] Worked on Criminal Statistics.

23. *Sat.*

Wrote to Mr Doggett—Mr Schnadhorst—Mr Barry OBrien—Mr Draper—Mr Reeves—Mr Abbott—W. Arnold—E. Owen. Worked on Homer's Herè. Read Ellenborough—Barry OBrien. 3-5. Hendon Sewage opening.[3] Well worth attention. Tea party 5-$6\frac{1}{2}$. Saw Granville.

24. *2 S. E.*

Kingsbury Ch mg with H.C. Willesden evg. Wrote to Mr Marjoribanks—Lady Holker—& .... Read Bp Hannington's Life—Bp Bickersteth do—Bellarmin, Autobiography—Voss on the Pentateuch. Saw Chas Lyttelton—Sir A. Clark. Six to dinner.

Without doubt, words of Scripture carry their commission. Today it was
I shall find trouble & heaviness, but I will call upon the name of the Lord: O Lord I beseech thee deliver my soul. Amen.[4]

25. *M.*

Wrote to Wms & Norgate—Ed. Northern D. Telegraph—Mr Tyndall—G. Bellis —Mr Howell—G. Potter—Mr Armstrong—L. Squire—Mr Moore (Supervisor)— Lord Hartington—Mrs Bolton—Messrs Wichart—Miss Goddard—Mr Cassidy— M. Brown—A. Gort.

Began work on Herè[5] but was interrupted by the arrival of Mr Marjoribanks with intelligence about finance. Made some financial notes. H of C. 5-8. Spoke (over an hour) upon the Budget.[6] R. Churchill excellent. Dined with Lady Farnborough: & interesting conversation with her on high matters. Conversation with Sir R. Welby.

26. *Tu.*

Wrote to Watsons—Messrs Southeran—Mr Turvill—Mr Sims—Mr Robins—Mr Agnew—Rev. T. Hall—Mrs Hancock. Conversation with Herbert. Worked on Herè. At 4.30 to London, driven by Miss M. Tennant. H of C. $5\frac{1}{2}$-8.[7] Dined with Mr Armitstead to meet the Labour M.P.s—There was speaking. Saw Lady Holker & back at 11.30. Read Ellenboroughs Journal.

[1] R. Barry O'Brien, *Irish wrongs and English remedies. With other essays* (1887).
[2] Misc. business; *H* 313. 1613.
[3] Opening new sewage works; *T.T.*, 25 April 1887, 11f.   [4] Psalm cxvi. 4.
[5] 'The Homeric Herè', intended as part iv of 'The greater gods of Olympos'; set in proof for *N.C.* but not published there; published in *C.R.*, liii. 181 (February 1888).
[6] Encouraging Churchill to speak after him; *H* 313. 1805.
[7] Spoke on Coercion bill; *H* 314.46.

27. Wed.

Wrote to Mrs Th.—Senator Lampertico[1]—Senator Palmer[2]—Earl of Aberdeen—Rev. G. Hessey(?)—Mr M'Kechnie—Mr Cox—Mr Verney—William Wickham (on his going to school).[3] Worked on Herè. $4\frac{1}{4}$-6. Drove to Hendon Hall and saw the objects there. Also to Brook St for dinner, by mistake![4] Read Ellenborough Diary Vol. I—Lysons' Middlesex.

28. Th.

Wrote to Ed. D. News[5]—Lady A. Campbell—Sir A. West—Rev. W.H. Shaw—Mr Osborne—Mr F.A. Russell[6]—A. Stevens—Dr Carpenter—Mr Hodgkinson—Press Assocn & Irish Times.[7] Worked on Ireland. Read Church's Poems[8] + and [blank.] To London at 11.30. American Exhibition: marvellous equitation: sumptuous luncheon: speech, on an easy subject.[9] Conclave at 4.30 on the forged letter.[10] Saw Sir A.E. West—T.P. O'Connor—A. Morley—Mr Knowles. Dined with Sir C. Forster. H of C. 5-8 and 10-1. Majority against us 101.[11]

29. Fr.

Wrote to Watsons (PP)—Mr A. Carnegie—Mr Osborne—Ld Aberdeen tel & l. Saw Ld Granville—Mr Brisbane. Read Ellenborough & [blank.] Academy $1\frac{1}{4}$ hour: saw half: it seemed *good*: sorely fagged: slept in afternoon. H of C. $4\frac{3}{4}$-$8\frac{3}{4}$: on Ch. 1 of Coercion Bill. We made rather a good beginning.[12]

30. Sat.

Wrote to Mr Hodder[13]—E. Benjamin—Rev. Langbridge—Rev. J.G. Deal—A.J. Church—R. Jackson—W.H.G.—J. Bell—S. Weil. Finished Herè. Saw Ld Northbourne—E. Hamilton—Mr Bancroft. Dined at Ld Breadalbane's. Visited the Grosvenor Gallery. Read Ellenborough Diary.

[1] Fedele Lampertico, 1833-1906; Italian economist and senator.
[2] Thomas Witherell Palmer, 1830-1913; Detroit merchant and U.S. senator 1883-9; minister in Spain 1889-91.
[3] His grandson; he was sent to Winchester.
[4] Perhaps with Lord Powerscourt, who lived there.
[5] Contesting its reporting of a speech; *D.N.*, 29 April 1887, 5e.
[6] Francis Albert Rollo Russell, 1849-1914; 3rd s. of 1st Earl Russell.
[7] *Irish Times*, 30 April 1887, 5e; communication acknowledged but not printed.
[8] A. J. Church, *The legend of St. Vitalis and other poems* (1887).
[9] Indian and Buffalo Bill horseback riding, Gladstone conversing with 'Red Shirt', a Sioux chief; speech on Anglo-American cordiality; *T.T.*, 29 April 1887, 10a.
[10] On 18 April, *The Times* published the facsimile of a letter purporting to be by Parnell (but in fact forged by Richard Pigott, 1828?-89, who had sold the letter and other papers to the Irish Loyal & Patriotic Union which sold them to *The Times*) condoning the Phoenix Park murders; Parnell at once gave details to the Commons showing that the handwriting could not be his. *The Times* continued its 'Parnellism and crime' series and was sued by F. H. O'Donnell; see O'Brien, *Parnell*, ii. 197 ff. See 5 May 87.
[11] On Reid's amndt. to the Coercion Bill; *H* 314.251.
[12] *H* 314. 357.
[13] See 19 Mar. 87n.

Sunday May One 87 SS. Phil. & J.

Kingsbury Ch. & H.C. mg. Willesden evg. Mr Leeman[1] has a power of preaching. Lucy & Herbert dined. Read Bp Hannington, finished—Bp Bickersteth—Church's Poems—Parker's Tyne Childe.[2]

2. M.

Wrote to Rev. Mr Suffield—G. Colley—W. Tebb[3]—W. Simon—Watsons—Mr Robertson MP—Mr Graham Spencer—N.W. Thomas. London. H. of C. $4\frac{3}{4}$–8 and 10–$12\frac{1}{2}$.[4] Dined at Grillion's. Read R. Brown's Poems.[5] Corrected MS of Herè for 19th Cent.[6] Saw A. Morley and others—Mrs Th.—Mr Mills[7]—E. Benjamin.

3. Tu.

Wrote to Mr Wodehouse—Mr Jenkins—Mr Nash—Mr Roberts—Mr R. Brown. Saw Ld Granville *cum* Ld Spencer—Mr A. Morley—Mr Grogan—S. Lyttelton—W.H.G. H of C. 5–8. Privilege.[8] Dined with Northbourne. Back to D[ollis]. Read Brown's Poems—Ld Ellenborough's Diary.

4. Wed.

Wrote to Vickers (I. Tax)—Sir W. Harcourt Tel.—Mr Garratt—Mr Palmer—Ld Breadalbane—Mr Rogers—E. Benjamin—Scotts—Dr Buchholz BP. Read Lecky Vol. V.[9] To London at 1.45. H. of C. $2\frac{1}{2}$–6.[10] Saw Sir W. Harcourt—Mr Childers—A. Morley—Lady Northbourne—Duchess of Bedford—Mr Marjoribanks. Dined with the Tweedmouths: & home. Read Lecky's Hist.

5. Th.

Wrote to Dean of Rochester—Ld Norton—Mr Davey—Mr Plowman—Mr Guinness Rogers. Read the earlier speeches of yesterday with care & worked up the subject of Privilege. H of C. 4–$8\frac{1}{2}$. Spoke $1\frac{1}{4}$ hour for Comm. & agt prosecn.[11] Saw

---

[1] W. L. Leeman, vicar of Louth, previously vicar of Gladstone's advowson of Seaforth; see 17 Feb. 79.

[2] J. Parker, *Tyne chylde; my life and teaching* (1886).

[3] William Tebb, president of Society for Abolition of Compulsory Vaccination; unable to attend its meeting because of the Crimes Bill; *T.T.*, 4 May 1887, 12e.

[4] Spoke on Coercion; *H* 314. 646.

[5] Robert Brown had sent his *A trilogy of the life to come, and other poems* (1887).

[6] See 25 Apr. 87n.

[7] Probably Charles William Mills, 1855–1919; Wolverton's partner in Glyn's; tory M.P. Sevenoaks 1885–92; 2nd Baron Hillingdon 1898.

[8] Gladstone read from Erskine May that in a breach of privilege (i.e. Dillon and *The Times*) a select cttee. was usual; *H* 314. 742.

[9] Vol. V of W. E. H. Lecky, *A history of England in the eighteenth century*, 8v. (1878–90). See 16 May 87.   [10] Privilege; *H* 314. 900.

[11] Arguing that there should be a select cttee., on *The Times*' charges against Dillon, rather than that he should prosecute the newspaper; Gladstone's advice was based on Freshfield's advice to him in 1859 when *The Times* accused him of helping the Ionian Assembly to commit treason; *H* 314. 993.

Mr Fowler—Mr Currie—Mr A. Morley. Dined with Mr B. Currie. Back to Dollis at 11 PM. Read Lecky Vol. V.—Varley on Priesthood.[1]

6. *Fr.* [*London*]

Long abed till 11.30. Wrote to Rev. R.C. Jenkins—Mr Salkeld—Mr Wood-house—Mr Isherwood—Miss C. Quinn—Rev. Mr Irwin—Mr Andrews. Also made dinner party for 18th & wrote the notes of invitation. Read Lecky Vol. V —Liszt[2]—Fitzpatrick on Falstaff.[3] To London 3.15. H. of C. $4\frac{3}{4}$–$7\frac{3}{4}$ and $10\frac{1}{2}$–1.[4] Saw Ld Rosebery—Mr Morley—Mr A. Morley—W.H.G. Dined at Lansdowne House.

7. *Sat.* [*Dollis Hill*]

Back to Dollis 11.15. Wrote to Baker & Symes—R. Brown—H. Hale BP—Amn Exhibn Comm.—W.L. Gladstone—J.A. Elliot—Mr Vickers. Corrected the press of Athenè. Garden tea party at 5. Fourteen to dinner at 8. Read Lecky's Hist.

8. *4 S. Easter.*

St Michael's Ch. mg and Willesden Ch. evg. Wrote to Mr Fitzpatrick—Lady Holker—Ld Acton—Rev Dr Parker. The Clarks came: & Lady Stepney with her dear child. Read Bp R. Bickersteth's Life—Restitution du pouvoir temporel[5]— Lenormant on the First Sin[6]—Cur Deus Homo, finished[7]—Congregational Mag. Fairbairn & Rogers.[8]

9. *M.*

Wrote to Mr Freshfield—Sir Jos Pease—Rev. Mr Meade—Mr Mayhew—Mr Appleton—L. Morris. Dined at Grillions. Worked on the Great Olympian Sedition. Read Lecky. H. of C. 5–8.[9] Went to Lady Holker's for tea. She told me much that was confidential.[10]

10. *Tu.*

Wrote to Miss Waller—Mr Dougall—Mr Hardman—Mr Holliday—Ed. Contemp. Review—Mr Dawson—Mr Collins—Mr Carlisle. Worked on the 'great Olympian Sedition'. To London at 2.30. H of C. 5–8.[11] Saw Mr A. Morley—Sir

---

[1] H. Varley, *père*, *Priesthood: the true and the false* (1887).
[2] B. Vogel, *F. Liszt als Lyriker* (1887).
[3] Probably one of the various theatrical writings of T. Fitzpatrick.
[4] Privilege; *H* 314. 1133.
[5] *Le Retablissement du Pouvoir Temporel du pape par le Prince de Bismarck* (1885).
[6] C. Lenormant, *The Book of Genesis* (1886).
[7] See 20 Feb. 87.
[8] *Congregational Review*, ed. J. G. Rogers (1887).
[9] Coercion Bill in cttee; *H* 314. 1278.
[10] She was the widow of Disraeli's attorney general, and was a Roman catholic; Gladstone became absorbed in conversations with her of a largely religious character. See 7 May 85.
[11] Coercion bill; *H* 314. 1470.

W. Harcourt. Dined at The Club: conversation with Ld Derby. Back at 11 PM.
Read Lecky's Hist.

11. Wed.

Wrote to Mr J. Chapman—Mr Marjoribanks—Rev. R. Jenkins—Mr Davey—Mrs
Bolton[1]—Mr Rossiter—Mr Hayman—Mr Macniel—Mr Mackay—Dr Simon.
Reflected on some aspects of the Irish question & the situation for the
luncheon. Off at 1.20 to Dr Parkers.[2] I spoke for an hour and our function lasted
till 5. I owe these good people a good deal which I cannot pay. Saw Lady
Holker, & renewed conversation. Various business. Dined with the Hothfields:
and home. Read Lecky.

12. Th.

Wrote to Mr Bunting—M. Saumarez—Mr Barlow—Rev. Mr Mathews—Mr
Wilson. With hard work finished 'The Great Sedition' & sent it.[3] Off at 4 to Mr
Holliday's interesting studio.[4] Mrs Th.s—Pever—and home. Read Lecky.—Wey-
mouth on πέλωρ &c.[5]—Autobiogr. of Mr Martyn.[6]

13. Fr.

Wrote to M. de St Mesmin—Dr. Weymouth—Miss O'Neill—Mr Oakshott—Mr
Goodhew—Mr Horne—Mr Wood—Mr Robbins—Mr Binder—Mr Dexter—Wat-
sons—Mr Dickson—Canon Farrer—Mr De Lisle. Arranging papers &c. Read
Lecky. Off at 3. Saw Mr Carlisle—Mr Morley—Mr A. Morley—Sir H. Vivian—Mr
Bryce—Mr Marjoribanks. H. of C. 5–11.30.[7] Dined there: well: an event.

14. Sat.

Wrote to Dr Weymouth BP—Rev. T. Vere Bayne—Mr Wilkinson—Rev. Gideon
Draper—J.C. Bull—Mr Gilbert—Mr Robson—Sir Thos G.—Mrs Th.—Mr
Barker—Mr Falvey—Mr Wolff. Garden party, Col. Delegates & others.[8] Dined
at Sir L. Playfair's. Interesting conversations; Lady Dalhousie, Lady Airlie, Lady
Playfair. Also saw Ld Spencer. Read Lecky.

---

[1] The quasi-rescue case whom Gladstone assisted; she was the niece of Sir John Simon (see
3 Feb. 82) to whom Gladstone also wrote this day. Gladstone's letters to her have been found in the
National Liberal Club.
   [2] Joseph Parker (1830–1902; congregational minister) who arranged lunch for Gladstone to meet
nonconformist church leaders; Gladstone's speech in *T.T.*, 12 May 1887, 10a.
   [3] Resuming writing (see 20 Jan. 87); 'The great Olympian sedition', *C.R.*, li. 757 (June 1887); Add
MS 44700, f. 203.
   [4] Henry Holiday, artist; studio on Hampstead Heath (see map at Add MS 44501, f. 1).
   [5] R. F. Weymouth, *The resultant Greek Testament* (1886).
   [6] H. J. Martyn, *The autobiography of an independent minister* (1887).
   [7] Coercion bill, *H* 314. 1818.
   [8] Party for delegates to the Colonial Conference given by the Gladstones at Dollis Hill; *T.T.*,
16 May 1887, 9e.

15. *5 S. Easter.*

Kingsbury Ch 11 A.M. Wrote to Ed. of Spectator[1]—Mr R. H. Hutton—Canon MacColl—Mr C. Miall. Read Ottley's Essays[2]—Autob. Indept Minister—Bp Bickersteth's Life (finished)—Smedley on F. Ignatius.[3]

16. *M.*

Wrote to Mr Jas Scott—Mr Rogers—L. Lewis—Lady Holker—Mr Bunting BP—Mrs Bolton—Ld Acton. Corrected proofs of 'The Great Sedition'. Began an article on Lecky's Hist. V & VI.[4] Settled with Mr Knowles for its publication in N.C. Read Lecky. Off to London at 6.30. Saw Lady Holker (2). Dined with Mr Knowles: & home. Saw Ld Hampden—Sir Jas Paget—Mr Lawson—Mr Robson? of Natal—Sir C. Forster. A hard day.

17. *Tu.*

Wrote to Mr Oakley—Mr OByrne—Mary Drew—Rev. E. Guthrie—R. Brown jun.—Mr Northy—Mr MacCarthy—Mr Wisdom. Wrote on Lecky. Saw the (W[illy] & G[erty]) children. To London at 3.30. H. of C. $4\frac{1}{2}$–$11\frac{1}{4}$.[5] Back home. Saw J. Morley—A. Morley—Sir H. Vivian. Read Lecky.

18. *Wed.*

Wrote to Mr Soper—Mr OByrne BP—Mr Grüninger[6]—Mr Malley—Mr Johnson. Twelve to dinner: chiefly MPs. Worked much on my MS. Read Lecky. Drive with C. At Pevers Cottage we fell in with Mrs Th. & C. was introduced to her.

19. *Th.*

Wrote to Mr Knowles—Mr Digby—Mr Salkeld—Mr Noble—Mr Bond—Mr Woolacott Tel.—N. York Press Assocn do. Worked on Lecky MS. Read Lecky: and went over the whole Pitt & Rutland Correspondence at the B.M. Saw Sir H. Vivian—Mr Acland—Mr Yeo—Mr A. Morley—Scotts—Mr Whitbread—Mr Morley. Another outburst from Harcourt. Dined at Mrs Tennant's. Conversation with Miss D.T. on Birt's Case.[7] Visited the Ladies' League meeting. Marylebone Church & H.C. at 11–$12\frac{1}{2}$. 30 to 40 received.

20. *Fr.*

Wrote to Sir W. Harcourt—Watsons—Mr Bunting—Lord Granville l.l.—Mr B. Binder BP—Mr Garaghty Tel. (abortive)—Mr Fry. Finished part of MS on Lecky

---

[1] Probably not printed; but *The Spectator*, 21 May 1887, has a letter from 'Y' defending Gladstone's Irish policy.

[2] E. Bickersteth Ottley, *Rational aspects of some revealed truths* (1887).

[3] J. L. Lyne, Fr. Ignatius, *Mission sermons and orations*, ed. J. V. Smedley (1886).

[4] Review of vols. v and vi of Lecky's *A history of England in the eighteenth century* (see 17 Apr. 78), in *N.C.*, xxi. 919 (June 1887); Add MS 44700, f. 170. See also 11 July 87.

[5] Spoke on Coercion bill; *H* 315. 292.

[6] Not further identified.

[7] i.e. with Dorothy Tennant; Birt's case untraced.

by hard work. To London at 3¾. H of C. 5–8.[1] Home at 10.30. Read Lecky. Early to bed for a slight cold. Conversation with J. Morley. Corrected and dispatched revise of the Great Sedition.

21. Sat [London]

Wrote to Mr Knowles—Mr Boielle—Mr Bruce—Mrs Lang—Mr Armstrong. Rather large; & interesting, garden party. To London evg. Dined in the beautiful house of Mr Wilson.[2] Corrected & dispatched MS of Lecky. Read Lecky: finished all necessary. Saw Ld Ripon—A. Morley.

22. S. aft Asc.

Breakfast at the Speaker's. Walked in the first Quartett of the procession.[3] The spectacle in Westminster Hall was beautiful: the service at St M[argaret's] impressive: the Sermon a very remarkable performance, & *most* Liberal.[4] The crowd too demonstrative: favourable with exceptions. Wrote birthday letter to the Queen & draft.[5] Willesden Ch. evg. Saw French Ambassador—WHG.—Mr Lawes—Sir [blank] Errington. Read Ignatius—Autobiogr. of Indept Minister.

23. M. [Dollis Hill]

Wrote to Sir W. Harcourt—Govr of Bank—Mr H. Hall—Mr Whitten—A. Smith—F. Wintle—Supt Euston Station—Dr Newman Kerr—Mr Washburn—Mr Graves—Geo. Arnold BP—Mr Hastings—Mr Trevelyan & drafts. To London at 2. Dined with the Northbournes. H. of C. 5–8 and 9½–11.[6] Back to Dollis before 12. Read Moritz on England.[7] Large conversation with Granville—J. Morley—Spencer—& Whitbread on the question & the form of a letter to Trevelyan which some think to be called for by his recent speeches. We agreed.[8]

24. Tu.

Wrote to Mr J. Morley L. & BP—Mr Noble—H. Peet—Messrs Watson—P.W. Bunting—W.H. Northy—W. Rossier—C.H. Andrews—Mr C. Townsend—Mrs Butler—Mr Noble—G.B. Andrews[9]—S.W. Norton—F. Johnston—W.R. Johnston—Mr Knowles—Mary Drew. Wrote Memorandum on the difficult subject of retaining Irish members: & sent it to J.M. A steady working day. Read Moritz—Dr Dale on Home Rule—Ferré, L'Irlande[10]—Bacon Society, No. 3.[11]

[1] Coercion bill; *H* 315. 731.
[2] Not further identified.
[3] Jubilee service in St. Margaret's; *T.T.*, 23 May 1887, 9e.
[4] Sermon by Boyd Carpenter, Gladstone's appt. as bp. of Ripon.
[5] Guedalla, *Q*, ii. 428.
[6] Coercion Bill; *H* 315. 907.
[7] C. P. Moritz, *Travels through various parts of England in 1782* (1798).
[8] See 25–6 May 87 and Whitbread's draft letter at Add MS 44501, f. 23.
[9] Birmingham unionist; in *T.T.*, 31 May 1887, 3f.
[10] E. Ferré, *L'Irlande. La crise agraire et politique* (1887).
[11] *Journal of the Bacon Society*, i. no. 3 (June 1887).

Secret. May 24. 87.

It is an entire mistake to suppose that I have ever set up the exclusion of Irish members from the Parliament at Westminster as a necessary condition of the measure of Home Rule for Ireland.

The 1886 provision was on the contrary made for their inclusion by the Irish Government Bill, and by the pledge of the Government, in three several modes: 1) on any occasion when the ⟨Bill⟩ Act itself was to undergo alteration 2) or when it was proposed to alter the taxation payable by Ireland. 3) We bound ourselves to recognise the claim of Ireland to a continued concern through her members in the treatment of Imperial subjects generally. Nor did we at all shut out the further and wider consideration of the subject; but we found, and I still find a difficulty in presenting to my own mind with any sort of clearness any definite or exact image of what the thing is which objectors severally desire, or in knowing whether they are in any way agreed among themselves.

For one, I have never referred to this subject with any further or other reserve than this; that I cannot & will not bind myself to any general proposition until I am convinced that there is some mode in which it can safely be carried into effect; and that I cannot adopt any proposal for the inclusion or retention of Irish members at Westminster which is to be made a ground for impairing the gift of a real and effective autonomy to Ireland in Irish concerns.

I should advise that any arrangement, extended beyond the limits of what Ireland through her members may ask under the head we are now considering, be not made a part of any compact of honour express or implied with Ireland, but that it be kept explicitly within the discretion of Parliament so that there may be no impediment to the removal of whatever inconvenience may arise.

I may be asked 'What would you do if, without impairing Irish self-government in Irish affairs, the prevailing sense of Parliament and of Great Britain should be found to require wider arrangements for the inclusion of Irish members at Westminster than you think expedient with reference to the proper conduct of business there?'

I will answer that question at once. As to becoming personally responsible for such a proposal, I must reserve my own discretion. But ⟨subject to the foregoing remarks⟩ I should not consider a blemish of this nature a sufficient ground for resisting, or for declining to promote on this ground a measure otherwise sound. For, if my opinion of the probable inconvenience should come to be supported by experience, the remedy would be in the hands of Parliament, and I should have full confidence in its disposition and capacity to meet that case.[1]

25. *Wed.*

Wrote to Abp Walsh—Central News—Press Assocn—Sir W. Harcourt—J.W. Turner—Mr Theobald—Lady Bath—Mr Knowles BP—H. Williams—Ld Aberdare—E.P. Watts—J. Wilson—W. Lewin—W. Pushney—A. Wilson—A.J. Wilson—Ly Northbourne—and minutes. Corrected my Lecky article for press. Saw S. Lyttelton. Fourteen to dinner. Conversation with Trevelyan—Lady Spencer—Lady Airlie—Sir A. West—Ld Hampden. Worked on books & papers in preparation for journey. Read Moritz.

[1] Holograph docketed 'May 24. Mem. sent to Mr.Morley'; Add MS 44773, f. 39. See 26 May 87.

26. *Th.* [*Hawarden*][1]

Wrote to [blank] & Keeper of Vote Office. Off at 9.45. Sandicroft at 3.15. Midland country more backward than Dollis & then Hawarden which is nearly the same. Journey quiet, the secret having been kept. Mary looked extremely well. S.s little Catherine[2] a singularly bright child. Went to work upon books parcels & letters. Fierce backgammon with S. in evg. Read Lefevre's Peel & O'Connell.[3]—Convict No 25.[4]

Secret.
Conversation with Trevelyan.[5]

Trevelyan dined here last night and we conversed on the subject of my letter.[6] He 'agreed with the whole of it' but would much prefer my speaking it, to its appearing as addressed to him, which he thought would diminish its effect. Especially he desired the concluding portion about Hartington to be known.

Strong on the necessity of speech at this time, and sanguine as to the disposition of the party to reunion, except as regards the mass of the Dissentients in the House of Commons who he thinks have no such desire, he also felt it was unreasonable to call on me at this juncture to propound methods of altering and improving the Bill of last year. He thinks however that the desire for the retention of Irish Members is very general. (Lady Spencer spoke in the same sense, West in the opposite.)

I told him of Macknight (Northern Whig) who expressed a very strong opinion the other way and of the utter insecurity, not to say more, of a committal to a plan without a clear idea of the mode for working it out; also I thought there was no uniform idea or plan even in the minds of those who called for the retention. He pleaded with justice that the average man was not well informed as to the scope of what had been already conceded, while he was perplexed or perverted by Chamberlain's unwarrantable assertions. He commented strongly on the Dissentient organisation.

I told him I had been thinking what I could contribute to the work of reunion outside (despairing within doors). Home Rule had really been put out of view for a length of time by coercion.

My opinion is as follows

The supremacy of Parliament being secure, there is but one essential point namely that a real and effective autonomy should be conceded to Ireland.

Can I safely say that, provided this condition be attained, I am of opinion that any plan for it ought to be accepted and promoted, or that it ought not to be set aside on account of its containing other faulty provisions for example provisions which might entail inconvenience (in my opinion) within the British Parliament, as that body would be sure to feel the mischief and would be free to apply a remedy.

If I said this I should reserve my own freedom as to proposing such a plan but should declare in favour of accepting and promoting it.

I understood him to say he thought this would cover everything. In fact he appeared to be greatly satisfied with the conversation. I said I would make up my mind before going

---

[1] Staying at the Rectory.
[2] Catherine, 1885–1947, first da. of S. E. Gladstone; she never married.
[3] G. J. Shaw Lefevre, *Peel and O'Connell* (1887).
[4] J. Murphy, *Convict no. 25; or, The clearances of Westmeath* (1886).
[5] Add MS 44773, f. 41; in *Autobiographica*, iv. 82.
[6] In *Autobiographica*, iv. 84.

to Wales[1] whether I would speak in the sense I had described: but my present inclination was that way.

WEG May 26.87

What I threw out to Trevelyan was in accordance with a Memorandum made on the 24th.[2]

27. Fr.

Ch. 8½ A.M. Sensible of a considerable loss of hearing since I was last at the service 3 months ago. Wrote to W.A. Greene Solr—S. Holman—J. Murphy—J.P. Ridley—C.J. Walls—C.H. Fox—N.W. Thomas—J.M. Hayes—Dr. Hine—Rev. Mr Bryant—Rev. J.M. Evans—Mr Davies, tel—R. Prentice—Miss M. Balder—A.C. Chesham—J. Henderson. Read Lefevre—Convict No 25 and went hardily to work with my Dict. & Grammar to help me on 'La Cuestion de Irlanda'.[3] I had tolerable success. Backgammon with S.E.G. Worked on books & papers.

28. Sat.

Ch. 8½ A.M. Wrote to Press Assocn Tel—Mr Morley L.l. & tel—Mr Carlisle—Rev. Dr. Hutton—Mr Wordsworth—Miss G. Latimer—Miss J. Martyn—Editor Austr. Trade World—Mr Quaritch BP—Mr Wright—Mr Inglis—Mr Pargett—Mr Geraghty—Mrs Jolly. Wrote Mema. for a pronouncement on Home Rule.[4] Read Nibelungenlied Tr.[5]—Lefevre's History. A little woodcraft in Rectory Garden.

29. Whits.

Ch 8 AM H.C. 11 AM and [blank.] Wrote to Sir G. Trevelyan—Ed. Southport Guardian[6]—Canon M'Coll—Mr D. Rees—Col. Young—Mr J.C. Wood—Mr Maitland Tel.—Padre Tondini—Ld Acton—Rivingtons. Wrote for C.G. draft of letter on the local Horticultural Controversy.[7] Read E. Ottley's Vol.[8]—Clergyman on Reformns[9]—Miss Cobbe & Dr Driver in Contemp. Review[10]—Autobiogr. Indept. Minister. Walk with W. & H.

30. Whitm.

Ch. 8½ A.M. Wrote to Sir J.E.E. Wilmot—Sir W. Harcourt—A. Morley—Mr Conachie Tel.—Rev. Th. Jones—Rev. E. Ottley—J. Jackson. Went to meet Ld

---

[1] i.e. for the speech at Swansea on 4 June, in which Gladstone followed the line adumbrated in his letter to Trevelyan. Trevelyan rejoined the liberals, successfully contesting a by-election at Bridgeton, Glasgow, in July; see G. M. Trevelyan, *Sir G. O. Trevelyan* (1932), ch. v.

[2] See 24 May 87.

[3] Untraced work in Spanish, unless Ferré (see 24 May 87) is intended.

[4] i.e. notes in preparation for the speech on 4 June.

[5] *The Nibelungen Lied*, tr. A. G. Foster Barham (1887).

[6] Not found published.

[7] Dispute between Mrs. Gladstone, who wished some of the proceeds to go to local parochial schools, and the Hawarden Horticultural Cttee.; S. E. Gladstone demanded an apology from the cttee. for notifying the press of the dispute. The cttee. declined, deciding to award the prizes and wind up the society; *T.T.*, 21 May 1887, 14f.

[8] See 15 May 87.   [9] Untraced tract.   [10] *C.R.*, li. 794, 894 (June 1887).

Acton in evg. Walk with him. Backgammon with SEG. Saw W.H.G. on plans. Read Nibelungenlied Tr.—Lefevre's Peel & OConnell—Murray's Mag. on S. Smiths Sermon.[1] Receptions in the Park began.

31. *Whit Tu.*

Ch. $8\frac{1}{2}$-$9\frac{1}{2}$ with H.C. Wrote to Archbishop Walsh—Sir A. Gordon—Ld Ripon L.l.l.—Mr Schnadhorst BP—Mr Macnaught—Miss Wheeler—Mr Monti—Mr Carlisle—Miss Bussell—Mr Francis—Mr Holden—Mr Folks. Receptions in the Park. Spoke, very shortly, to the Crewe party.[2] Read Lefevre—Nibelungenlied. Backgammon with S. Drive & walk with Acton: & divers conversations. Made some translations from Spanish & French.

Wed. June One 1887.

Ch. $8\frac{1}{2}$ A.M. Acton went. Full political conversation with him on H.R. & the position. Wrote to Archbishop Walsh—A. Morley BP—Mr Foster Barham[3]—Mr Schnadhorst—Mr Shaw Lefevre—S.T. Scrope—Dr Fenner—Mr Inderwick—Messrs Meyers—Mr Morley—Mr Ashby—Mr Martin—Mr Wills—M. Allan—Dr Tillie—Dr Collins—Mr Maclean—Speakers of the Quebec Houses.[4] Drive with C. Finished Lefevre: very good—finished Nibelungenlied: a great disappointment. Read Autobiogr. of Indept. Minister: not very favourably impressed. Backgammon with SEG.

2. *Th.* [*Swansea*]

Ch. $8\frac{1}{2}$ A.M. Wrote to Dr Buchholz BP—Mr Ferris—R. Milne—J. Fisher—Mr Dickson—Mr Graham—Mr Moon—Mons. Ferré[5]—Mr Redmayne—Mr Urquhart—R.H. Helmore—Rev. Mr Woolley—Miss Nellie Small—Mr M. Tennant. Saw the Nottingham gifts,[6] & addressed the people. Off at 11.40. A tumultuous but interesting journey to Swansea and Singleton where we were landed at 7.30.[7] Half a dozen speeches on the way, & saw divers friends. A *small* party to dinner. Read Baron Munchausen.[8]

3. *Fr.*

A 'quiet day'.[9] Wrote draft to the Associations on the road, as model: Tel. to Mr Schnadhorst. Spent the forenoon on settling plans, & discussing the lines of my meditated statement tomorrow with Sir H. V[ivian], Ld Aberdare, & Mr Stuart

---

[1] *Murray's Magazine*, i. 721 (June 1887).

[2] Attacking 'the present disastrous policy of coercion towards Ireland'; *T.T.*, 1 June 1887, 8c.

[3] Alfred G. Foster-Barham had sent his translation; see 28 May 87n.

[4] P. B. de La Bruère and J. S. C. Wurtele, respectively Speaker of the Quebec Legislative Council and Assembly.

[5] E. Ferré; wrote on Ireland; see 24 May 87.

[6] Gifts of Nottingham lace; for the day's progress and speeches, see *T.T.*, 3 June 1887, 6.

[7] He stayed at Park Wern with Sir H. Hussey Vivian, liberal M.P. for Swansea (see 13 Mar. 60).

[8] *Baron Munchausen, narrative of his marvellous travels*, by R. E. Raspe (1785 and later eds.).

[9] Mist caused the abandonment of the morning's programme; he visited Oystermouth and Mumbles after lunch; *T.T.*, 4 June 1887, 12c.

Rendell. In the afternoon we went to the Cliffs & the Mumbles and I gave some hours to writing preliminary notes on a business where all depends on the manner of handling. Small party to dinner. Conversation with Sir H.V.—Ld A—Lady V. Read Baron Munchausen—Cardiff & Swansea Guides.[1]

4. Sat.

Wrote to Sir J. Fergusson—Mr L.C. Martin[2]—& had S.E.G. at work. More study & notes. 12–4½. The astonishing procession. Sixty thousand? Then spoke for near an hour. Dinner at 8, near an hundred: arrangements perfect. Spoke for nearly another hour: got through a most difficult business as well as I could expect.[3] Read Baron Munchausen.

5. S.

Ch 11 A.M. Notable Sermon, and H.C. (Services long).[4] Again 6½ P.M. Good Sermon. Wrote to Sir W. Harcourt—Mr Morley—Mr Norton—Mr R.M. Lewis—Gloucester Dissentients—Cardiff Dissentients.[5] Conversation with Mr Talbot[6]—Canon Smith—Lady V.—Sir H.V.—Ld Aberdare. Walked in the beautiful pinetrees and the Garden. Read Lamennais's Société Premiere.[7] Considered the question of a non-political Address 'in Council': we all decided against it.

6. M.

Wrote to Sir W. Harcourt Tel.—Ld Hartington—J. Webster—A. Foley—Mad. Novikoff—Swindon Workmen Tel. Surveys in the House—then 12–4, to Swansea, for the freedom & opening the Town Library. I was rather jealous of a non-political affair at such a time: but could not do less than speak 30 or 35 min for the two occasions. 4–8. To Park Farm, the pedigree herd, beautiful vales, breezy common & the curious Chamered Cairn.[8] Small dinner party. Read Munchausen.

7. Tu. [London]

Wrote to Mr Richards—Mr A. Morley. Off at 8.15 & a hard day to London: succession of processions, hustles,[9] & speeches, that at Newport in the worst

[1] L. C. Martin, *Swansea and Gower ... a guide and handbook* (1879).

[2] Leopold Charles Martin, d. 1889, of Swansea; author of the local guide; in touch with diarist 1865. Add MS 44405, f. 270.

[3] Reviewing the proposed Irish legislation of 1886, emphasising his flexibility on the position of Irish members and the need for discussion; *T.T.*, 6 June 1887, 10c.

[4] At Sketty church, sermon by Canon James Allan Smith, vicar of Swansea, opposing disestablishment; *T.T.*, 6 June 1887, 10f.

[5] Letters to liberal unionists; *T.T.*, 8 June 1887, 12e.

[6] Christopher Rice Mansel Talbot, 1803–90; liberal M.P. mid-Glamorgan 1830–90; voted against home rule 1886 but did not act as a liberal unionist.

[7] F. de Lamennais, *De la Société Première et de ses lois* (various eds.).

[8] Reading uncertain.

[9] Proceedings and speeches in *T.T.*, 7 June 1887, 10f.

atmosphere known since the Black Hole.[1] Poor C. too was an invalid. Spoke near an hour to 3000 at Cardiff: about ¼ hour at Newport: more briefly at Gloucester and Swindon. Much enthusiasm even in the English part of the journey. Our party was reduced at Newport to the family, at Gloucester to our two selves. C.H. Terrace at 6.20. Wrote to get off the H. of C.

It has really been a 'progress', and an extraordinary one.

Finished Munchausen: mostly a heavy book. Read Robinson Crusoe:[2] that is alive. Saw Mr A. Morley, & Herbert as well as the Welsh friends. Dear Harry returned, perfectly well, quite unchanged.[3]

8. Wed. [Dollis Hill]

Wrote to S. Peters[4]—Hon. Mr Williams—Mrs Warner—D. Chadwick—P. MacCourt—T. Pengelly—Rev. R.H. Manley—Ld Hartington—J. Ransom—J. Irving—C. Dack—S. Shorter. Saw Lady Holker—Sir W. Harcourt—Mr Russell—Mr A. Morley—Lady Airlie—S.G. Lyttelton. Read Niebuhr on Ireland[5]—German on Life in London.[6] Dined at Ld Sherbrooks: & had a touching conversation with him. To Dollis at 11½.

9. Th. [London]

Wrote to Sir Thos Acland—Sir Thos G.—Mrs C. Maddock—Rev. S.E.G.—Dr Mackirmal(?)—Sir F. Abel—Mr Flint—Mr C. Gwilt—Mr A. Morley. Worked on books & papers. Read German (Brand) on London Life—Longfellow's Remains[7]—Gleanings from Morley.[8]

Long conversation with Harry on his commercial position and prospects which he explained with great ability & justice. Off to London at 7.15. Heard the fine Opera of Faust.[9] Saw Sig. Gavarre & Madam Albani behind. Then to H. of C. and Conference with Harcourt, Morley, and A. Morley.[10]

10. Fr. [Dollis Hill]

Off to Dollis at 10. Wrote to Edr of Notes & Queries[11]—Mrs Marks—Mrs Bolton—J. Parnell[12]—T.H. Jones—Mr Knowles—Mr Finch—Mr Brooks—Mr Hartley.

---

[1] Vast crowds impeded the progress of the train; reports and speeches in *T.T.*, 8 June 1887, 12a.
[2] By Defoe (1719).   [3] Back from India.
[4] Secretary of the Workmen's National Association, opposing sugar bounties, and coercion; *T.T.*, 10 June 1887, 5f.
[5] B. G. Niebuhr, *A letter upon the Roman Catholic emancipation question, and the state of Ireland in 1829* (1887).
[6] W. F. Brand, *London life seen with German eyes* (1887).
[7] S. Longfellow, ed., *Final memorials of H. W. Longfellow* (1887).
[8] Perhaps J. Morley, 'On the study of literature' (1887).
[9] At Covent Garden.
[10] Perhaps in preparation for a meeting between Harcourt and Hartington on 14 June, at Hartington's request: willing to meet Gladstone but no concessions on home rule; L. V. Harcourt's diary, 14 June 1887, MS Harcourt dep. 382, f. 12.
[11] Answering criticism of his Homeric articles; *Notes and Queries*, 18 June 1887, p. 489.
[12] Perhaps John Howard, C. S. Parnell's brother; then in America. But no letter found. More probably John Parnell, London barrister.

Further corrected Athenè & worked on Homer. Read Brooks on Coercion[1]—Brand on London Life. H. of C. 4¼–6½. Spoke. An *astounding* situation.[2] Dined at Pol. Ec. Club & spoke.[3] Saw Mr Morley—Mr Gwilt. 7–10½ Dined with the Polit. Econ. Club. Interesting discussion: in which I took a share.

11. Sat.

Wrote to Capt. L. Trotter[4]—Mr J. M'Carthy MP—Mr Edminston[5]—Sir Jos. Pease—Rev. C.T. Wilson—Mr Brand—Mr Bruce—Mr Jennings—Press Assocn.—G. Richmond—J.E. Jones—and minutes. Wrote on the Unity idea[6]—and on Tyndall's attack. Retrospective conversation with Lucy C. on political incidents.

4–5¾. Mr Purcell[7] by arrangement *tapped* me for information about Cardinal Manning: he *dropped* that the C. was unsympathetic, and narrow. Dined at Sir U. Shuttleworth's to meet the Lancashire Members. Saw Spencer, & had a very satisfactory conversation. Back to Dollis 11.30.

[The inside back cover contains:]

Mr Geo. Harris 94 Highbury New Park
Office from Feb. 10.

Goschen N.12; 22

95 Elm Park Gardens

Sympneumata L.O. Blackwoods 1 & c

Mrs Bolton Tower House Abervue Road Leicester

C. News Ludgate Circus

---

[1] Untraced.

[2] Business of the House; *H* 315. 1601.

[3] Paper by H. Sidgwick on relationship of assumptions about free trade to economic facts; *Political Economy Club* (1921), 113.

[4] Captain Lionel James Trotter, historian of India.

[5] Ernest Whalley Edminson of Merton College, Oxford, in correspondence on founding an honours school of English literature; Add MS 44501, f. 48.

[6] 'Universitas Hominum; or, the Unity of History', intended for *Youth's Companion* but published in *North American Review* (December 1887).

[7] E. S. Purcell (see 12 Feb. 80), Manning's biographer; Manning intended that the volume on his Anglican life should be published while he was alive, but this proved impossible. For this conversation, see Purcell, *Manning*, i. viii and Add MS 44501, ff. 29, 36.

[*12 June 1887 to 6 May 1889.*]

[The inside front cover contains:—]

[In pencil:—]

	T. Powell
	<u>13</u> Temple St Birmm.
Mem. send Leopardi	<u>fr.</u>100 + 100 + 20
Art. to Rescinati	£10.0.0
	Amalfi 100 + 50.

[in ink]   *Private.*

No 38.

June 12. 1887–May 6. 1889.

Yet have I more to say, which I have thought upon; for
I am filled as the moon at the full.

Eccl[esiastic]us XXXIX. [12]

Parran faville della sua virtute
In non curar d'argento nè d'affanni
Parad. XVII. 82.²

'Se io morissi, questa cosa sarà come l'idea de' poeti,
che, tagliato un capo, ne uscivano sette'.

Savonarola 1495. In Villari I. 387³

Wiclif Trialogus

[In pencil:—]

D.7. to Sidney
27. To Rice.

---

¹ Lambeth MS 1452.
² 'Sparks of his heroism shall appear in his disregard both of wealth and toil.'
³ P. Villari, *Storia di Savonarola*, 2v. (1859–61), i. 387.

12. Trin. S.

Kingsbury Ch mg & evg. W. and the two H.s here. Read Messianic Prophecy[1]—
Knox Little, The Broken Vow[2]—F. Ignatius, Sermons.[3]

13. M.

Wrote to Mr Allen—Mr Newton—Mr Blackie—Mr Meade—Mr Bunting—Ed. D.
News[4]—Mr Tattersall—Archdn of Natal—d[itt]o Montgomery—Sup. GWR
Chester—Hon Mr Williams—J.W. Williams—Rev. Knox Little—Mr O'Neill
Daunt—and minutes. Finished the Broken Vow. Read Wilson, Transl. from
Russ[ian][5]—Paper on Ld Salisbury[6]—Arthur Young, Tour in Ireland.[7] 3–8½. To
London & H. of C.[8] Saw Maharajah Holkea—Maharajah of Kutch—Sec. Trin.
House—Mr Carnegie & Mrs C[arnegie]—Mr Chamberlain (casual: we talked of
Manchr Ship Canal)—Mr Mundella—A. Morley—J. Morley—Sir H. Vivian—Sir
C. Russell.

Mr Carnegie offered me as a Loan 'any sum' needful to place me in a state of
abundance, without interest, repayable at my death, if my estate would bear it; if
not, then to be cancelled altogether. Such was my construction of his offer: so
large, & so entirely disinterested. Of course, with gratitude, I declined it
altogether. But I tried to turn him a little towards the election fund.

He said he should consider it disgraceful to die a rich man.

His income is £370000 p.ann.

I told A. Morley.[9]

14. Tu.

C. & I arranged two dinner parties. Wrote to W.H.G.—Mrs Th.—Mrs Watson—
Mr Murphy—Mr Stibbs—Mrs Bolton—W.H. Rogers—Mr Saunders—Mr Robins
—Mr Ambrose—Mary Drew. Wrote a little for 'Youth's Companion' (U.S.):
much puzzled about my title.[10] The W. children came. Off to London at 4.45.
H. of C. 5½–8 and after dinner.[11] Saw Sir W. Harcourt *cum* J. Morley—A. Mor-
ley.[12] Back at midnight. Two spoke to me.[13] All in the RR knew me. Finished
Brand on London Life. Read Rawlins on Ireland.[14]

---

[1] C. A. Briggs, *Messianic prophecy* (1887).

[2] W. J. Knox Little, *The broken vow. A story of here and hereafter* (1887).

[3] See 15 May 87.　　　　　　　　　　　　　　　　[4] Not found published.

[5] C. T. Wilson, *Russian lyrics in English verse* (1887).

[6] i.e. comments on Salisbury in a newspaper.

[7] See 28 Sept. 86.　　　　　　　　　　　　　　[8] Crimes Bill; *H* 315. 1745.

[9] Carnegie was on his honeymoon, having married Louise Whitfield; a version of this entry (misdated) was supplied to his biographer by H. N. Gladstone; see *Carnegie*, i. 318. For the upshot, see
18 July 87n.

[10] See 11 June 87n.　　　　　　　　　　　　[11] Coercion Bill; *H* 316.61.

[12] L. V. Harcourt noted in his diary, 16 June, MS Harcourt dep. 382: 'Gladstone and John Morley
will not come up to the scratch about conciliating Hartington because they cannot get hold of
Parnell and dare not or will not move without his consent.'

[13] i.e. he was approached by two prostitutes, but he did not approach them; he thus held to his
promise to Hamilton (see above, x. clxxxvii).

[14] C. A. Rawlins, *The famine in Ireland. A poem* (1847).

15. Wed.

Wrote to Mr Jenkins—Miss Rawlins—Mr Tuckerman—Siamese Chargé—Mr Bottom—Mr Bruce. Further long conversation with Harry on his affairs & prospects. His chief reward for nine years in Calcutta has been a great Education. Wrote 'some' for Youth's Companion. To London at 1.45. H of C. $2\frac{1}{2}$-6.[1] Grave conversation with Morley & Harcourt who has many excellent points but is a most uneasy travelling companion for a political journey along rough roads. Saw Sir C. Russell & Mr Morley on prospective amendments. Dined with the Maguires.[2] Conversation with Mr M.—Mrs M.—Lady Breadalbane—and Madlle La Claire. Read Young, Tour in Ireland—and [blank]'s History. Back 11.40.

16. Th.

Wrote to Mr Simon—Ed. Daily News[3]—M. Darwin Swift—Mary Drew—Mr Heathcote—Mr Hope Hume—Mr Bright[4]—Mr Eaton—Mr Nichols—Mr Tibbits —Mr Bunting. H. of C. $4\frac{3}{4}$-8.[5] Saw A. Morley—Ld Granville. Dined at Sir C. Forster's. Corrected & further wrote Paper for Youth's Companion.

17. Fr.

Wrote a *suit* of invitations to dinner. Also to Mr Henderson—Mr Hopkinson— C.W. Barker—Mr Smalley Tel.—Rev. S.E.G.—Mr Westell—Mr Ridgway—Mr Wolff. Luncheon with Mr & Mrs Thistlethwayte: they, C. & I, Miss Ponsonby, Mr Villiers! I had a long talk with him, which yielded something, not much.[6] Miss P. referred in her way to my relations with H.M: & showed that her brother[7] spoke of them with tact & prudence. H. of C. $4\frac{3}{4}$-$10\frac{1}{4}$. The close of the Committee. Violence upon violence.[8] Read Arthur Young's Ireland. Conversation with J. Morley, always so upright & calm.

18. Sat.

Wrote to Press Assocn Tel.—Ld Chamberlain—Mr Banerjea[9]—G Macmillan—T. Massey—Mary Drew—Mr Graham—Mr Rhodes—D. Curr—J. Foster. Garden party 4-7: large and animated. Conversation with Mr A. Carnegie—Gen. Sabuco[10]—Mr Newton—Mr N. Hall—Ld Acton—Ly W. Compton—& many more. Wrote notes on Ireland. And finished 'The Unity of History' for 'Youth's companion'.[11] Ten to dinner. Read Moritz 1782 finished[12]—A Young, Tour in Ireland, finished—The Amber Heart.[13]

---

[1] Coercion Bill; *H* 316. 157.
[2] Probably Thomas Miller Maguire, London barrister.
[3] On correspondence with Bright on Ireland; *D.N.*, 17 June 1887, 5e.
[4] Sharp exchange with Bright on Ulster; *T.T.*, 18 June 1887, 14c.
[5] Questioned Balfour on govt. timetable; *H* 316. 276.
[6] C. P. Villiers' persistent Unionism.
[7] Sir H. F. Ponsonby, the Queen's secretary.
[8] Spoke on concluding stage of Coercion Bill in cttee.; *H* 316. 427.
[9] J. K. Banerjea of the Middle Temple had written on Indian affairs; Hawn P.
[10] Unidentified.   [11] See 11 June 87n.   [12] See 23 May 87.
[13] A. C. Calmour, *The amber heart and other plays* (1888?).

19. 2 S. Trin.

Kingsbury Ch and Holy C.—Mr Mye,[1] an excellent preacher. Willesden Ch. evg. Also Lucy read to us a notable Sermon of E. Wickham. Saw H.J.G.—Sir C. Tennant. Wrote to Mrs Th.—Sir A. West—Mr Blackie—Mr . . . .

20. M. [London]

Wrote to Mary Drew—Mr Thos Dick—O. Morgan—Card. Manning—Ld Coleridge—B. Quaritch—W.H. Small—C.C. Davies—F. Cipriani[2]—Mr Stibbs. Corrected the later MS of The Unity of History. Read Kerr S. Africa.[3] H. of C. $5\frac{1}{4}$-$7\frac{1}{2}$. Dined at Ld Wolverton's. Saw Ld Wolverton—Mr Carnegie—Mr Blaine—Mr A. Morley—Mr Westell—Sir C. Forster—Mr Wertheimer.[5]

21. Tue. [Dollis Hill]

Wrote to W.C. Bull—Mr Stibbs—Scotts—Mr Lancaster—Mr Pettengell—T.J. Hughes.

To H. of C. at $9\frac{3}{4}$. In procession with the Speaker to the Abbey.[6] The sight was magnificent as we descended & caught the whole mass of human beings. Music good: vocalising admirable. Service, I thought, too courtly. We escaped Southwards from H. of C. & got to Dollis about 3. Ten to dinner. Read Bancroft's Hist U. States[7]—Brown's Kirké[8]—Kerr's South Africa.

22. Wed.

Wrote to Rev. R. Evans—Mr Newbigging—Mr Geo. Russell—Mrs Th. London Library for consultation of Books. Dined at Ld Ripon's. Political conversation with him. Conversation with Lady R. Worked on Pausanias. Read Newbigging, Speeches[9]—Kerr, South Africa. Worked on Pausanias. Visited Lady Holker on my drive back to Dollis. My hope was to have performed some office of real friendship, not yet fulfilled.

23. Th.

Wrote to Mr Errington—Mary Drew—Mr Morrison—Mr Crawford—Lord Acton. Reviewed again my paper in Mary's MS copy, & further added & corrected. Read over Dante's De Monarchiâ[10]—Mrs S.C. Hall, 'The White boy'[11]—

---

[1] Sic; but not in Crockford.
[2] Probably a relative of Cipriano, the Spanish ambassador in London.
[3] W. M. Kerr, Far interior: Cape of Good Hope to Lake regions, 2v. (1886).
[4] Misc. business; H 316. 632.
[5] Probably Julius Wertheimer, d. 1924; educationalist and author.
[6] Service of thanksgiving for the Queen's Jubilee; T.T., 21 June 1887, 6c.
[7] See 15 July 48.
[8] See 5 Nov. 83.
[9] Thomas Newbigging, president of the Gas Institute, had sent his Speeches and addresses, political, social, literary (1887).
[10] Perhaps in F. J. Church's ed. (1878).
[11] A. M. Hall, The Whiteboy; a story of Ireland in 1822, 2v. (1845).

Kerr on South Africa. Worked on Pausanias. Saw Mr Blackwell *cum* Mr Cobb to get Mr B. into the field for his division.[1] Walk with Helen.

24. St Joh. B[aptist]. Fr.

Wrote to Mr Moss–Ld Halifax Tel.–Mr Ambrose MP–Messrs Murray–Ld Breadalbane–Mr Carnegie–Ld Acton–Sig. [C.] Modena. Worked on Pausanias. And on correcting speech. Saw Brixton Deputation. Conversation with Lucy on the MS. Off to London at 4. Went over the building of the National Liberal Club.[2] Saw Ld Kimberley–Ld Granville–A. Morley–Lady F. Marjoribanks–Lady Houghton–Crown Prince of Sweden. Dined at Ld Breadalbane's, full dress: Buckingham Palace party afterwards. Read Jubilee of Geo. III[3]–'Is Ireland to obtain Home Rule' by J.O.E.[4]

25. Sat.

Wrote to Mr Cumberland–Sig. C. Modena–Mr Denneby–Mr Laurie–Mr Kegan Paul–Mr Wemyss Reid[5]–Rev. Dr. Parker–Mother Superior, Willesden–Rev G. Cunyer–Mrs Cathcart–C.W. Williams–H.J. Leech–J.O.E. Read Leech's Ansr to Jennings[6]–The Whiteboy–The Queen's Highway.[7] Garden party in aftn. Saw Ld Granville–Ld Spencer–Mr Lowell–Mrs Hancock–Sybella [Lady Lyttelton]. Worked on Pausanias. Finished correcting my poor Swansea Speech. Meditated on the case of Lady H[olker] & on my own position & its religious difficulties.[8]

26. 3 S. Trin.

Ch Willesden mg & Kingsbury aft. Wrote to Mr Rideing–Ld Acton. & [blank.] Read Kegan Paul, Hymns[9]–Jenkins on Jurisdiction[10]–Mathews on Ward Beecher[11]–T.F.B. on reunion[12]–'What is good?' & other tracts.

---

[1] Henry Peyton Cobb, 1835–1910; banker, solicitor and liberal M.P. Rugby 1885–95. Purpose of meeting obscure; perhaps to do with the 8 hour clause of the mines Bill.

[2] Of which he was President; see 2 May 83.

[3] T. Preston, *The jubilee of George III* (1887).

[4] J.O.E., 'Is Ireland to obtain Home Rule' (1887?).

[5] Untraced reply, presumably negative, to Reid's request for an interview to discuss Cassell's plan for an autobiography; Reid's initiative followed a conversation with Herbert Gladstone; Cassell's 'have authorised me to offer to you for the copyright of an autobiographical work ... (subject to certain stipulations as to length &c.) ... five thousand pounds.' Reid to Gladstone, 24 June 1887, Add MS 44501, f. 95. See 15 Aug. 87.

[6] H. J. Leech of Manchester had sent his untraced pamphlet replying to L. J. Jennings, *Mr. Gladstone: a study* (1887); Gladstone thanked Leech for his defence against 'wanton slander'; this day's letter in *T.T.*, 28 June 1887, 8d; Jennings replied, *T.T.*, 29 June 1887, 10e.

[7] Sent by its author, Stuart C. Cumberland.

[8] See 9 May 87.

[9] *Victorian Hymns*, sent by Kegan Paul; Add MS 44501, f. 94.

[10] Possibly D. Jenkins, *Pacis consultum; a directory to the publick peace* (1657).

[11] S. Mathews, *Men, places and things* (1887).

[12] T.B.F., *The reunion of Christendom with Rome* (1887).

27. M.

Wrote to Grogan & Boyd—Mr A. Morley l.l.—Ld Acton—Mr Marston—Mr Troughton—Mr Whitall—Miss Beckett—and minutes. H of C. 4¾–8.[1] Read Galton's Cromwell[2]—Hartington's Speech[3]—Queen's Highway. Dined at Grillions. Saw E. Talbot—Ld Acton—A. Morley—J. Morley.

28. Tu.

Helen's birthday. Requiescat. Wrote to T.G. Law—B. Currie—H. Lee—J. Dobbie—T. Inglis—Mr Stodart Walker—W.H. Rideing—Mr Humphry—Rev. C. Leach—E.H. Ennis—A. Reid. Further corrected, and dispatched, my *Universitas Hominum*. Finished Galton's Cromwell—read Queen's Highway. Dined at Wolverton's. Saw A. Morley—A.M. & J.M. *cum* Harcourt—Mr Stansfeld—Mr Childers—Lady Stanley [of] Ald[erley]—Sir Jos Pease. H of C. 6½–7¾.[4]

29. Wed. St P.

Wrote to A. Galton—E. Purcell—Mr Rintoul—Mr Vanderdroische[5]—Sec. Commn 1853—A. Morley—W.H. Palmer—Mr Story—Mr Willans. We went to the Queen's garden party. Disposed of eleven Royalties. Saw Abp. of Canterbury—and the Pope's Nuncio. Nine to dinner. Read Ital. Folk Lore.[6]

30. Th.

Wrote to H.G. Reid—Mr Hughes B.P.—Mr Sherlock—Mr Colthurst—Mr Marchmont—Archbp Walsh—Rev. Mr Mills—Mr Aubrey—Mr Carlisle—Mr Johns—Mr Tregise—Mr Barrow—Sir W. Harcourt—Central News Tel.—Press Assocn Tel. H. of C. 4½–7¼.[7] We all went to the Puritani.[8] *Suni la tromba* brought down the House. Saw A. Morley—J. Morley—Sec. Exhibition—Sir C. Russell—& o[thers.] Read Ingram's Hist. Union.[9]

Frid. Jul. One 1887.

Wrote to Mr Story Gofton—Mr Rain—Mr Carnegie—Mr Cobb MP. Read Ingram—Miss Busk. Worked on Pausanias. H. of C. 4¾–6¾.[10] Dined at Pol. Ec. Club & took part in the discussion on £1 notes.[11] Lady Holker's ¼ hour, and home. The short conversation might on my side have been better, though there was some effort.

[1] Spoke on Coercion bill amndts; *H* 316. 1057.
[2] Arthur Galton, historian and critic, sent his *The character and times of Thomas Cromwell* (1887).
[3] S. C. Cavendish, Lord Hartington, 'The Irish question' (1887); speech of 5 March 1886.
[4] Coercion Bill; *H* 316. 1167.
[5] Possibly D. Van Den Driessche, London manufacturer.
[6] R. H. Busk, *The folk songs of Italy* (1887).
[7] Spoke, mainly against, Lawson's motion that Parliament should ratify treaties; did not vote; *H* 316. 1325.
[8] At Covent Garden with Albani and di Spagni.
[9] T. D. Ingram, *A history of the legislative union of Great Britain and Ireland* (1887). For Gladstone's review, see 2 Sept. 87.
[10] Questioned Balfour on Coercion; *H* 316. 1501.
[11] Introduced by H. S. Foxwell; *Political Economy Club* (1921), 113.

2. Sat.

Wrote to Mr Carnegie—A. Symonds—T. Osborne—Mr Troughton—Rev. A. Beard—Mr Harvey—T. Potter—Mr Coates. Worked on Pausanias. Finished Ingram's so called History. Read Miss Busk. Worked on Pausanias. Dined with Sir J. Pease & spoke for an hour, mainly in reply to Hartington.[1] Home past midnight.

3. 4 S. Trin.

Kingsbury Ch & H.C. mg—Mr Mills gave a service for the haymakers aftn & 55 had tea & 25 quarterns of bread & butter. Wrote to Ld Acton. Read Father Ignatius—Times of John Leslie[2]—Barjonah[3]—&c.

4. M.

Wrote to Mr R. Cameron—J. Dodgson—P.W. Campbell—Hon Mrs Lawley—Miss Holiday[4]—Lady Holker—R. Thomson—J. Mills—Mr Richards MP—Ld E. Clinton. $11\frac{1}{2}$-$8\frac{1}{4}$. To London. Missed Lady Holker: saw Mrs Birks—Mr A. Morley—Mr Morley—Mr Childers. Spoke on Mr Smith's motion. H. of C. $4\frac{1}{4}$-$7\frac{1}{4}$.[5] Read Beust's Memoirs: heavy with egoism[6]—Burns's Poems[7]—Somnia[8]—and Our Lanes.[9]

5. Tu.

Wrote to Mr Fraser—Sir W. Harcourt l.l.—Ld Granville—Mr C. Villiers—W.H.G.—Mr Galton. 11.30-5. To London. Saw Lady Holker—Mrs Swinburne[10]—Lord Rosebery—A. Morley. Conclave at Ld Granville's $2\frac{1}{4}$-4 on Irish questions. All the late Cabinet summoned: two absent. Read Somnia—De Franqueville[11]—Burns's Poems.

6. Wed.

Wrote to Mr M'Coll—Ld Hartington[12]—M. Franqueville—Mr Ellinton—Mr Maxse—Mr Hughes—Mr Morris. Dined with Mr Bryce. Conversation with the fine old Lady his mother—Mr Gardner—Col. Hay—and others. Attended C.s concert 3-$4\frac{3}{4}$. Went with Mr Agnew to Christie's. Tea with Lady Derby. Saw Lady Airlie. Read Bancroft Hist U.S.—and . . . . Worked on Irish figures.

---

[1] *T.T.*, 4 July 1887, 11a.   [2] See 17 Apr. 87.
[3] Arthur Beard, rector of Southall, had sent his *Bar-Jonah, the son of the resurrection* (1887).
[4] Mary Holiday, on maps to illustrate Irish history; Add MS 44501, f. 129.
[5] Opposed Smith's motion for precedent for govt. bills; *H* 316. 1616.
[6] *Memoirs of Friedrich Ferdinand, Count von Beust*, ed. Baron de Worms, 2v. (1887).
[7] Robert Burns, probably in the new ed. of his *Works*.
[8] J. A. Goodchild, *Somnia Medici*, 2v. (1884-7).
[9] H. J. Foley, *Our lanes and meadow paths; rambles in Middlesex* (n.d.).
[10] Probably Constance M. Swinburne, wife of lieut. col. M. Swinburne of Forfarshire and Thurloe Square, London.
[11] A. C. E. Franquet de Franqueville, *Le gouvernement et le parlement britannique*, 3v. (1887). Correspondence in Hawn P.
[12] Published, dated next day, in *T.T.*, 7 July 1887, 8a, on statements on Ireland and local govt. 1880-5; reply in *T.T.*, 11 July 1887, 11b.

7. *Th.*

Kept my bed till one, the changes of temperature having brought on derangement. Looked over Irish papers & case. To London at 3¾. H. of C. 4½-8¼. Spoke 70 min. in moving rejection.[1] Dined at Sir C. Tennant's:[2] & home. Read Kerr on S. Africa[3]—Demetrius. Saw A. Morley—Mr J. A. Symonds.

8. *Fr.*

Wrote to Mr Parker—Lady Holker—Mr Coleman—Sir A. Clark—Mr Maclaren—A. Hardy—Mr Heaviside Tel.—Mr Cleaver—Mr Waring—Mr Huntley—Mr Jas Hogg—Dr Grece.[4] Wrote part of rejoinder to Lecky.[5] Read Demetrius—Ld Coleridge's Address[6]—Kerr's South Africa. 9¼-2 A.M. To London for Debate & Div. 262: 349.[7]

9. *Sat.*

Wrote to Mr Pease MP—Rev. Dr Parker—Mr S. Ramsay—Ld Coleridge—D. Smail. Wrote rejoinder to Lecky. 4-7. Receipt of N.Y. World Testimonial. Spoke 35 m?[8] Garden Party following. Saw Mr Agnew, Sir A. Clark—Miss Tennant—& others. Quiet evg. Read Kerr, South Africa—Queen's Highway[9]—The Whiteboy.[10]

10. *5 S. Trin.*

Kingsbury Ch. 11 A.M. Aftn service by the barn: haymakers exceeded 100. Rain after a month. Wrote to Ld Wolverton—Mr Routledge[11]—S.E.G.—Mr Schnadhorst. Saw Herbert J.G. Read Wilson's Essays[12]—Religion viewed by Philosophy[13]—Leslie's Life & Times.

---

[1] Of 3ᴿR of the Coercion Bill; *H* 317. 85: 'the new coercion . . . passes beyond the aim of crime, and it aims at association'.

[2] He sat next to J. A. Symonds, who next day wrote an excellent account of the conversation to his sister; see *The letters of John Addington Symonds*, ed. H. M. Schneller and R. L. Peters (1969), iii. 250.

[3] See 20 June 87.

[4] Clair James Grece, grammarian, living at Redhill; Hawn P.

[5] Lecky replied to Gladstone's review (see 16 May 87) in 'Mr. Gladstone and the income tax', *N.C.*, xxii. 52 (July 1887), defending his claim—attacked in Gladstone's review—that Gladstone had offered an electoral bribe in 1874 by offering to abolish income tax. Gladstone responded in 'Mr. Lecky and political morality', *N.C.*, xxii. 279 (August 1887), whose first version, amended as 'too sharp', is in Hawn P 1461.

[6] J. D., Lord Coleridge, 'Address delivered to the Glasgow Juridical Society' (1887).

[7] *H* 317. 316.

[8] A silver casket was presented by Joseph Pulitzer of the *New York World* and Perry Belmont, chairman of the House Cttee. on Foreign Relations; *T.T.*, 11 July 1887, 11a.

[9] See 25 June 87.

[10] See 23 June 87.

[11] Letter of sympathy to Edmund Routledge, defeated liberal candidate in N. Paddington; *T.T.*, 15 July 1887, 11f.

[12] James Maurice Wilson of Clifton school sent his *Essays and addresses* (1887).

[13] Perhaps R. S. Perrin, *Religion of philosophy* (1885).

11. M.

Wrote to Rev. J. M. Wilson—Canon Butler—W.A. Smith—Mr Burnard—W.H.G.—J. Kitson—Judge O'Hagan. Dined at Ld Rosebery's. Conversation with him: & with Sir P. Jennings?[1] H. of C. 4–8.[2] Saw Mr Morley—Mr Marjoribanks—Mr Childers—Mr J. Morley.—Mr Fottrell. Worked in the Library. Read Kerr's South Africa. Worked on arranging papers. Saw M. Drew respecting reply to Mr Lecky.

12. Tu.

Wrote to Mr Kirkham—Mr Grogan—Mr Knowles—R. Smith—W. Graham—F. Milner[3]—C.W. Stope—Ld E. Clinton—Rev. R.C. Jenkins—Miss Duthoit[4]—E. Alexander—Rev. A.H. Gilkes—Mr H.B. Price. To London $4\frac{1}{2}$–$11\frac{1}{2}$. Set about rewriting (nearly) the paper on Lecky, which is too sharp.[5] Saw Disestabl. Deputn from Scotland.[6] Dined at Sir W. Phillimore's. H. of C. $5\frac{1}{4}$–8.[7] Saw my friends on the situation. Also Mr Marjoribanks with a request from Ld R. Churchill. Read Northcote, Essays.[8]

13. Wed.

Wrote to Mr E. Bain—Ld Herschell—A. Morley—Mr Bond—Mr Mann—Cav. Martelli[9]—Mr Dornbusch[10]—Rev. A. Thomson.

Marjoribanks by appointment brought down R. Churchill to luncheon. At first he was not at his ease. He touched Ireland slightly but our long conversation was on public economy. The Archbishop of Canterbury came later to converse on Church Bills. Dined at Ld Vernons:[11] plenty of pleasant conversation. Read Scotch Union History.[12]

14. Th.

Wrote to Mr Armstrong—Mr Mason—Mr Irons—Mr Readwin[13]—Mr Knowles. Finished Lecky MS No 2. Called on Grogan & Boyd. Dined with Geo. Russell. Saw Sir W.H.—Mr Childers—Mr Morley—A. Morley. H. of C. $4\frac{3}{4}$–8 and $10\frac{1}{2}$–1. Spoke with prudent aim.[14] The situation critical and interesting.

---

[1] Sir Patrick Alfred Jennings, 1831–97; member of the legislative council of New South Wales.

[2] Irish Land Bill; *H* 317. 372.

[3] Sir Frederick George Milner, 1849–1931; tory M.P. for Yorks. and Notts. constituencies 1883–1903; on Trevelyan and Home Rule: Add MS 44501, ff. 169, 180.

[4] Minnie Duthoit of Chiswick; Hawn P.

[5] See 8 July 87.   [6] No report found.

[7] Irish Land Bill; *H* 317. 525.

[8] S. H. Northcote, Lord Iddesleigh, *Lectures and essays* (1887).

[9] Possibly Charles Francis Martell; London solicitor.

[10] K. Dornbusch of London; on grammar; Hawn P.

[11] George William Henry Venables-Vernon, 1854–98; 7th Baron Vernon 1883; household office 1892. See 20 Oct. 87.

[12] M. C. Taylor, *Historical account of the Union between Church and State in Scotland* (1886).

[13] Perhaps Thomas Readwin, who had corresponded in 1860 (see Add MS 44394, f. 18).

[14] On the Irish Land Bill, attempting to associate Chamberlain with the liberals' amndt.; *H* 317. 876.

15. Fr.

Wrote to Ld Rosebery—Mr R. Brown jun.—Rev. Dr. Hutton—Mr Lockhart A.S.A.[1]—Mr Aitken—Mr Pool—Mr Beale—Mr Stubbs—Mrs Fox. Worked on Pausanias. Ld Ch. & Mr G. Russell to Luncheon. Dined with the Buxtons in London.[2] Read The Whiteboy—Kerr on South Africa.

16. Sat.

Wrote to Ed. Leeds Express[3]—Mr Ashworth—A. Morley—Messrs Murray—Rev. Mr Fairbank—Mr G. Howell MP—Mr Maggs[4]—Mr Kibble—Mr Walker—Mr Roberts—Mr Leopold. Garden party 4-6½. The Sheikh[5] and some other interesting people. Off at 7¼ to London. Scottish Liberal MP.s dinner: very cordial spoke 50 m.[6] Saw Lady Holker afterwards. I am perplexed. Began to arrange papers in view of departure. Read Beust. Worked on Pausanias.

17. 6 S. Trin.

Kingsbury Ch with H.C. mg. Willesden evg. Tel to Central News—Press Assocn. Read Leslie Life & Times—Wilson's (very able) Essays[7]—Ignatius, Sermons. Worked on papers. Harry & Herbert dined.

18. M.

Wrote to Mr A. Morley MP—Mr Grogan—Mr Nicholls—Mr Tilley—C. King —Mr Trainer—Miss Backhouse—Mr S. Montagu MP—A. Carnegie[8]—Mr Williams—Mr Butterworth (B.P.)—R. Brown jun (B.P)—Dr Buchholz—C. News Tel.—Press Assn Do. Finished Pausanias, & partially summed up. Much packing. To London 3.45. H. of C. 5-7½.[9] Dined with the Miss Monks. Saw Abp of Canterbury. Read Isa.[10]

19. Tu.

Wrote to Capt. Richards—Mr Lewis—Mr Ingram—Mr Budger—Mr Cooksey— Mr Tranter—W.H.G.—H. Sharrock—Ld Acton—Hon. H. Hale BP—Mr Knowles—Press Assocn Tel.—A. Morley MP. Continued packing & arranging for removal. Distributed prizes for Mr M's school at 3 P.M.[11] To London at 7¼. Dined with the Miss Lefevres. Then attended the meeting at Mr Bryce's. Spoke

---

[1] William Ewart Lockhart, 1846–1900; painted a group portrait of the Jubilee Service 1887. See 18 June 89.

[2] Sydney Buxton (see 25 May 86) and his wife, Constance, née Lubbock; she d. 1892.

[3] On land reform; Leeds Evening Express, 18 July 1887, 3c.

[4] Probably Uriah Maggs, London bookseller.

[5] Unidentified; no report of the garden party found.

[6] Report in T.T., 18 July 1887, 12a.

[7] See 10 July 87.

[8] Asking Carnegie for money for the liberal party; he sent $25,000; Carnegie, i. 319 ff.

[9] Spoke on privilege (govt. proposed suspension of Dr. Tanner for swearing at W. H. Long in the lobby); H 317. 1183.

[10] Isa; a novel, 2v. (1887).

[11] No account found.

(25 m?).[1] Saw Mr Barry OBrien—Mr A. Acland—Mr Lefevre. Back at 11.40. Read The Whiteboy—Isa.

20. Wed. [London]

Wrote to Mr Hurlbert—A. to the American invitation[2]—Lord Aberdeen—Mr Rigg—Mr Blakey—Mr Douglas—Mr Dalston—Mr Sheeley—Mr Spond. Saw Mr Simson. Finished packing &c. To London at 4.15:[3] alack. Saw Mr J. Morley—Mr & Mrs Wilson. Dined at Mundella's. Afterwards went to Duchess of Bedford's party: lest we should seem huffed. Read Isa—The Whiteboy—Laing's Zoroastrianism.[4]

21. Th.

Wrote to Mr Whitehouse—Rev. N. Hall—Mrs. Murphy—J.B. Daly[5]—C.R. Brown—J.B. Black—Mr Pritchard—Mr Thomas—Miss D. Lynn. Read Isa. Saw Mr E. Hamilton—S. Lyttelton—Mr Davies—Ld Granville—Mr A. Morley—Mr Backhouse[6]—Mr Pease MP—Mr Richard MP—Mr Lane Poole.[7] H. of C. 4–8 and $9\frac{1}{4}$–$11\frac{3}{4}$. Spoke on Tanner case, &c. Harcourt wielded the scourge with tremendous force.[8]

22. Fr.

Wrote to Mr W.N. Rideing[9]—Mr Thomas—Ld Oxenbridge[10]—W.H.G.—Mr W. Hamilton—Miss M. Ronel—Ld Hampden—Abp Walsh—& minutes. H. of C. 3–$3\frac{1}{2}$.[11] Saw Mr Marjoribanks—Mr Schnadhorst—Mr Murray—Mr Agnew—Mr O. Morgan—Mr Dillwyn—Sir W. Foster. Dined at Sir C. Forster's. Read The Whiteboy—Q.R. on Lecky[12]—Isa—and divers tracts. Saw Phillips[?].

23. Sat.

Wrote to W. Woodall—E. Brown—Lady Holker—Mr Williams—Mr Macgowan —Mr Holl R.A.—J. Robb—B. Douglas—A. Francis—P. Bryce—A. Robbins—J. Simon—Hon R. Spencer[13]—Mr Higginbotham—Mr Baily Hn. Arranging & packing books &c. Am now tolerably in order here. Luncheon (with C.) at 15 G.S. Ten to dinner. Much conversation with Lady Russell. Read The Whiteboy—Isa—and [blank].

[1] Meeting of Marylebone Liberal Association; *T.T.*, 20 July 1887, 10d.

[2] Declining invitation to attend the centenary of the American constitution; *T.T.*, 7 September 1887, 10f.

[3] Staying with Lady F. Cavendish for the rest of the Session.

[4] S. Laing, *fils*, *A modern Zoroastrian* (1887).

[5] Of Holloway; had sent his *Ireland in the days of Dean Swift* (1887); Hawn P.

[6] Edmund Backhouse, 1824–1906; banker and liberal M.P. Darlington 1868–80.

[7] Reginald Lane *Poole, 1857–1939; historian; in 1887, assistant ed. of *E.H.R.* (see 3 Feb. 87).

[8] Under pressure from the Speaker, Smith withdrew his motion of suspension (see 18 July 88n); *H* 317. 1665.

[9] William Henry Rideing, 1853–1918; editor of the *North American Review* and author of *At Hawarden with Mr. Gladstone and other experiences* (1896). See Add MS 44285.

[10] i.e. Monson; see 18 June 45n.   [11] Spoke on Irish land; *H* 317. 1775.

[12] *Q.R.*, clxv.1 (July 1887).   [13] See 25 July 87.

24. 7 S. Trin.

St James's mg & aft. Saw Ld Tollemache—Sir C. Tennant. Wrote to Miss Chambers—Mr A. Morley—Miss Wright. Read Q.R. on C. Morrison[1]—Aveling on our Lord's character[2]—and divers tracts.

25. M. St James.

Wrote to Mr A. Carnegie—Ld Hampden (B.P.)—Mr Mayhew (B.P.)—T.W. Butler (B.P.)—J.D. Hill—Mr Johnstone—Sir Thos G.—& minutes. Saw Mr Dillwyn—Mr Smith—Sir W. Harcourt & Mr Morley: We decide to raise no grave controversy on the Land Bill. H. of C. $4\frac{3}{4}$–8.[3] Attended the R. Spencer marriage at St James's: and the breakfast afterwards.[4] Finished Isa—Read Curcio sul clima di Roma.[5]

26. Tu.

Wrote to Miss Lynn—Ld Granville l.l.—Archbp of Canterbury—Mr Loverdo—Mr Bath—Mr Wolff—G. Alexander—Rev. Mr Fletcher—Messrs Byrne—Miss Ross—Mr Strathern—Ed. Telegraph. Conversation with Ld Granville on matter of my speech for Friday. Saw C. & D. Dined with the Harcourts. H. of C. 5–$7\frac{3}{4}$.[6] Saw Ld Aberdeen—Mr A. Morley—Mr Brimmer (U.S.)[7]—Mr J. Knowles—Lady Hayter. Read Life of Liszt,[8] and [blank.]

27. Wed.

Wrote to Lady Holker—Mr Richardson—W. Hatton—A.L. Jones—Sir C. Watkin —T. Millward—Mr Causton[9]—Mr Warren—F. Bull—W.H.G. H. of C. $12\frac{3}{4}$–3.[10] Conversation with Mr MacColl on his great matter.[11] Saw Ld Kimberley—Ld Kilcoursie—Mr A. Morley—Ld Granville—Mr Morley—Mr W.H. Smith. Visited the Japanese Village.[12] Dined at Mr Flower's. Much conversation with Mrs Sandys, so pleasant. Read Abbé Liszt finished.

28. Th.

Wrote to Currie, also Dumas BP—Mrs Harvey BP—Mr Rideing—Mrs Dowling—Miss D. Lynn—Mr Robinson—J. Winter—H. Malcolm—W.H.G.—Mr Greyberg—

[1] Q.R., clxv. 218 (July 1887).
[2] F. W. Aveling, *Who was Jesus Christ?* (1878).
[3] Irish land; *H* 317. 1903.
[4] Charles Robert ('Bobbie') Spencer, 1857–1922; half-br. of 5th Earl; liberal M.P. N. Northants. 1880–5, Mid-Northants. 1885–95, 1900–5; household office; 6th Earl Spencer 1910. He m. Margaret, da. of Lord Revelstoke; she d. 1906.
[5] Untraced.
[6] Irish land; *H* 318. 53.
[7] Probably Martin Brimmer, American historian of ancient Egypt.
[8] See 6 May 87.
[9] Richard Knight Causton, chairman of the meeting on 29 July.
[10] Irish land; *H* 318. 198.
[11] Very probably his engagement to Miss Chambers; see 21 Aug. 87.
[12] At the Japanese Fine Art Exhibition.

Mr Lawrence—Mr Saunders. Saw S. Bernhardt in Adrienne.[1] Remarkable but painful. I heard very little. Saw Mr Holl R.A.—Mr Cope Whitehouse—Mr Carry *cum* Dr Awdrey—Sir W. Harcourt—Mr Morley—Mr Childers—Mr A. Morley—Mr T. Healy. H. of C. 5–6¾.[2] Read Ellenborough's Diary[3]—Mrs Birkicrosan on Japan.[4]

29. Fr.

Wrote to Sir W. Harcourt—Mr Gillespie—Mr Whiteford. Meditated much, & wrote & rewrote notes on the course of my speech for tonight.[5] Arranging papers. Breakfasted with Granville. Saw Ld Herschell—Ld Granville—Mr Harcourt—Mr A. Morley l.l.—Ld Acton. Read Ellenborough Diary—Cromwell in Ireland.[6]

30 Sat.

Wrote to Miss Chambers—Messrs Murray—Father Murphy—Mr Macartney—Mr Maugher—Mr Westell—Mr Strathern—Mr C.S. Loch[7]—Mr Holden—R. Davies & W. Matthews. Dined with the Aberdeens at Dollis Hill. My throat left tender by last night's work was smartly caught by the East wind returning to town. Call at Argyll Lodge; missed him. Read Ellenborough Diary–......... on Selenology[8]—Imlay & Wollstoncraft.[9] Academy at 10.15. Saw Miss Harvey.[10]

30. [sc. 31] 8 S. Trin.

St John's Evg. Saw E. Clinton. Kept my bed most of the day. Read Keble Poems[11]—Maclellan Hymns (U.S.)[12]—Articles in Reviews.

Monday Aug. One 1887.

Wrote to Dental Hospital for Mr Dexter—T. Fletcher—Mr Clark—T.W. Griffith—Mr Schnadhorst—Mr Morley. Saw Clark morng & evg. Up from 2 to 4½ P.M. Fighting hard against a tight cough. Saw Miss Harvie. Began correction of reported Speech: the most nauseous to me of all possible work. Read Articles in 19th Cent.

2 Tu.

Battle with cough continued: it gave way. Saw Sir A. Clark—Mr A. Morley. Finished my disagreeable task of correcting the report. Read Articles in N.C. & in Contemporary.

[1] 'Adrienne Lecouvreur' by Scribe at the Adelphi; one of Bernhardt's most famous roles.
[2] Irish land; *H* 318. 390.   [3] See 18 June 81.
[4] Perhaps her article on the Empress of Japan in *Girls' Own Annual*, xii (1882).
[5] At the National Liberal Club, on 'unlearned increments' of London landowners and on liberal unionists; *T.T.*, 30 July 1887, 12a.
[6] Probably Prendergast; see 11 July 67, 29 Aug. 87.
[7] (Sir) Charles Stewart *Loch, 1849–1923; secretary of the Charity Organisation Society 1875–1914.
[8] Perhaps J. Naysmith and J. Carpenter, *The moon* (1887).   [9] See 28 Nov. 83.
[10] Annie Harvey of Biggleswade had asked for an autograph; Hawn P.
[11] J. Keble, *Miscellaneous poems* (1869).   [12] I. Maclennan, *Hymns* (1834).

3. Wed.

Rose at one, by permission. Was weak enough, but worked on packing books. Wrote to Rivingtons. Read Ellenborough's Journal—Scotch Mixtures.[1] Saw Clark in evg. The Glasgow Election, confirming so many, produces a great sensation.[2]

4. Th.

Rose at 10 A.M. Wrote to Mr Gillespie—Mr Atkinson—D. of Argyll—W. Foster —Mr Powell—W. Stuart—T.P. Tomes—Mr Hepwell—Fr. Fox—Mr Duxbury— LNW Traffic Manager—Mr W. Murray—Ld Spencer—Mrs Harrison—Mrs Hartley—Miss Creeth—Mr Gaisley—Mr Richard MP—Mr Thompson. Dined with the Stanhopes. Much tired. Saw Ld Granville—Sir W. Harcourt—Mr Morley—Sir G. Trevelyan—Mr Bryce—Cook—respecting the Orient Line.[3] Read Ellenborough. Attended the Sarum marriage.[4]

5. Fr.

Wrote to Mr Carnegie—Mr Sime—H.H. Furness—Mr Sanderson. H. of C. 5–8. Short speech with a weak voice on a truly strange situation.[5] Worked on arranging papers & packing. Saw Sir W. Harcourt—Ld Granville—Ld Acton—Mr A. Morley. Read Ld Ellenborough's Diary.

6. Sat. [Hawarden]

Wrote to Armenian Gentleman—Keeper Vote Office—Mr King—Mr Duckham —Mr M. Gass. Carried another book to ... Clifton, absent.[6] Saw Cooks—Ld Granville. 5–10 (almost exactly) P.M. to Hawarden, door to door. Read Ld Ellenborough's Diary—how much more talent than weight. Residuary cold.

7. 9 S. Trin.

Hn Ch. mg (with H.C.) and evg. Wrote to Robertson & Nichn. Read Rodriguez on Perfection[7]—Canon Lucifer.[8] My cold rather hangs & drags in its retirement.

8. M.

Postponed resumption of my usual habits. Rose at 10.45. Wrote to Central News Tel.—Mr Pimblett—Mr Cherry—Editor of Chester Chronicle[9]—Editor of

---

[1] Untraced.

[2] G. O. Trevelyan, standing as a liberal, defeated the liberal unionist, A. E. M. Ashley, in a by-election in Glasgow, Bridgeton. See 16 Aug. 87 for start of 'Electoral facts'.

[3] i.e. Donald Currie's affairs.

[4] Rev. Lord Rupert William Ernest Cecil, 1863–1936, Salisbury's 2nd s., m. Lady Florence Mary, da. of Lord Lathom.

[5] On refusal of liberal unionists and the govt. to make reasonable concessions on Irish arrears in 1887; *H* 318. 1400.

[6] The rescue case; see 4 Dec. 84, 25 Aug. 87.

[7] A. Rodriguez, *The practice of Christian perfection*, 3v. (1861).

[8] J. D. Delille, *Canon Lucifer: a novel on an English social aspect* (1887).

[9] *Chester Chronicle*, 13 August 1887, 8g.

Baptist.[1]—Aalesund Postmaster. BP. Finished Ellenborough. Read Mackenzie's Hist.[2]—(Abandoned) Canon Lucifer—began Tom Jones.[3] Drive with C. 1½ hour. Bed early.

9. Tu.

Ch. 8½ A.M. Wrote to Mrs Thistlethwayte[4]—Miss Ponsonby—Mr Knowles—Sir E. Watkin—Mr Duglass[5] [*sic*]—Mr Darlington. Read Tom Jones.—Cromwell in Ireland—Greely on Alcohol[6]—The Alien Transvaal.[7] Long drive with C. by Connah's Quay & Wepre.

10. Wed.

Ch. 8½ A.M. Wrote to Mr Knowles (Tel.)—Rev. Mr Hodson—Mr F. Fox—Mr Kegan Paul—Mr Howe[8]—Mr Bousfield—Mr J.A. Fore—C. News & Press Assn Tel. Worked on books: my chaos is beyond all precedent. Read Currans Speeches[9]—Amours de Catherine II[10]—Tom Jones—and 'Coercion without Crime'.[11] Drive with C. Conversation with H. on his position.

11. Th. [*Royal Hotel, Hoylake*]

Ch. 8½ A.M. Wrote to Duke of Westminster—W. Digby—Mr Knowles—A. Morley—Town Clerk Chest—W. Digby—Messrs Philipp. Off at 2.30 to Hoylake (Royal Hotel) by Park Gate: for sea air. Read Catherine II.—Elisabeth Q. of Bohemia.[12] On the sands.

12. Fr.

Wrote to Mr S. Smith—Mr S. Hadfield—and minutes. Read Catherine II (What a portent!)—Queen Elis. of Bohemia. On the sands. Drive with Mr Wall.[13] A giro: saw the Kirby Church & ancient stones.

---

[1] *The Baptist*, 19 August 1887, 121a.
[2] J. Mackenzie, *The history of Scotland* (1867).
[3] H. Fielding, *The history of Tom Jones, a foundling*, 6v. (1749); see 29 Apr. 26.
[4] Her husband died on 7 August; Dr. Sibley of Harley Street wrote on 8 August to Mrs. Gladstone (Hawn P): 'Mrs. Thistlethwayte has asked me to write a few lines to inform you of the sad calamity which has befallen Mr. Thistlethwayte. Yesterday morning Mr. Thistlethwayte was found in his room with a wound in the head from a revolver. From the circumstances of the case there is very little doubt that this was the result of an accident. Mr. Thistlethwayte always kept a loaded revolver in his room. Mrs. Thistlethwayte is bearing this great blow with calmness and resignation.' Thistlethwayte was said to fire his revolver to summon servants. See also 24 Aug. 87.
[5] See 29 July 87.
[6] H. Greeley, *Alcohol, nature and effects* (1857).
[7] Annie Russel, *The alien Transvaal. A moral review* (1885).
[8] W. H. Howe, London publisher; Hawn P.
[9] J. P. Curran, *Speeches*, 2v. (1809); with those of Grattan, Erskine and Burke.
[10] *Histoire secrète des amours et des principaux amants de Catherine II*, 3v. (1799).
[11] J. A. Fore, 'Coercion without crime' (1887?); letter of approval by Gladstone in *T.T.*, 11 August 1887, 11f.
[12] Lady F. Erskine, *Memoirs relating to Elizabeth Stuart... Queen of Bohemia* (1770).
[13] George Wall, chairman of the liberal association; *D.N.*, 13 August 1887, 5d.

13. Sat. [Hawarden]

Off at 12.30: Hawarden at 4: without change of horse. All the better for the trip. Read Catherine II (finished)—Qu. Elis. of B.—Smith's Local History.[1] J. Morley came at 4. Conversation of 3 hours on the last Chamberlain overture. We were agreed.[2] Every time I see him I admire him more, especially the *morale*.

14. 10 S. Trin.

Ch. mg & evg. Wrote to Knowles—Grogan—Rivingtons. Read Wood on Natural Law[3]—Nathan the Wise[4]—Queen Elis.—&c.

15. M.

Ch. 8¼ A.M. Wrote to Rev Mr Armytage—Mr Knowles l.l.l.—W. Warden—W. Digby—W.T. Merry—W. Dodd—Mr J. Parnell—Mr Tattersall[5]—Messrs Cameron—Mr Brunner MP[6]—Mr Morley MP. Worked on books & papers. Saw J. Bailey on the various possibilities for a new muniment room.[7] Framed with care my l. to Mr Knowles on Copyright.[8] Read Elis. of Bavaria—History of a Foundling[9]—and Chez Paddy.[10]

16. Tu.

Ch. 8¼ A.M. Wrote to Duke of Westmr—Ld Acton[11]—Mr A. Morley—Mrs Agar—Mr Barry OBrien—Mr E. Moss. 12¼-4. Went to Initial Ceremony of the Dee Bridge, & made speeches.[12] Seventeen to dinner in evg. Began Electoral Facts.[13] Read Chez Paddy—Hist. of Tom Jones.

17. Wed.

Wrote to Mr T. Ashton[14]—Mr C.H. Andrews—Dr Cuthbertson—Mr R.G. Humphrey—Mrs Cooke Smith—& minutes. Spoke briefly to the Horticultural

---

[1] Perhaps J. Toulmin Smith, *Local self-government and centralization* (1851).

[2] Morley invited himself to Hawarden following a conciliatory talk with Chamberlain on 12 August. Gladstone, Morley told Chamberlain, was 'in an extremely friendly frame of mind towards anything that pointed towards effective accommodation', but awaited 'gradual removal' of 'irritation' (*via* parliamentary cooperation on questions such as the Land Bill) and the involvement of 'others of the group' (i.e. Hartington), before making a definite move; see Garvin, ii. 310ff.

[3] H. Wood, *Natural law in the business world* (1887).

[4] By Lessing; see 11 Apr. 82.

[5] Of Manchester; on Bright and Rochdale liberals; Add MS 44501, f. 220.

[6] Congratulating (Sir) John Tomlinson Brunner (1864-1919, chemical manufacturer and philanthropist, liberal M.P. Northwitch 1885-6; 1887-1910) on his election; *T.T.*, 18 August 1887, 9f.

[7] Plans for the building of the fire-proof, but not wholly damp-proof, Octagon (next to the Temple of Peace), where Gladstone's papers were housed until their dispersal. See Morley, ii. 526.

[8] Of his autobiography; letter untraced. See 16 Sept. 87.

[9] i.e. *Tom Jones*.   [10] Baron de Maudat-Grancey, *Chez Paddy* (1887).

[11] On the proposal that he should write his autobiography; *Autobiographica*, i. 2.

[12] New railway bridge built by Sir E. Watkin, linking N. Wales with Merseyside; *T.T.*, 17 August 1887, 8a.

[13] 'Electoral facts of 1887', *N.C.*, xxii. 435 (September 1887); Add MS 44700, f. 334; an early exercise in psephology.

[14] Thomas Ashton, liberal landowner in Cheshire and Lancashire; see 2 Dec. 89.

Meeting, wh was crowded.[1] Worked on Electoral Facts. Worked on books. Read Fermoy on Wolfe Tone[2]—Hist. of a Foundling—and Chez Paddy.

18. Th.

Worked much on 'Electoral Facts': much care needed with the figures. Began Plowden's Post Union Hist. of Ireland.[3] Began Autobiogr. of Nonagenarian.[4] Read Chez Paddy. Drive with C. Worked on books. Continue to nurse the cold.

19. Fr.

Wrote to Mr Knowles—Mr A. Morley MP—Sir Thos G.—and minutes. Read Autobiogr. of Nonagenarian, strange but I should think true (finished). Read Plowden's Post Union Hist. of Ireland—History of a Foundling. Drove with C. Nursing cold with some success: up only however on drive and 9.30. Worked on books. Finished and dispatched to London MS. on Electoral Facts.

20. Sat.

Wrote to Mr A. Morley l & tel.—Rev. Mr Kane[5]—Mr T. Elson[6]—Mr Griffin—Mr Morris—Mr R. Cameron BP—Mr Mullderson—Sir Jas. Paget. Drive & walk with C. Worked on books. Read Tom Jones—Plowden's History. Fourteen to dinner: but made a short evening.

21. 11 S. Trin.

Ch. mg & evg. Wrote to Sir W. Harcourt—Mr A. Morley—Mr Knowles. Wrote perforce
1. a draft of motion on Address
2. An addition to Electoral Facts.
Read Fremantle's Article[7]—Gore's Sermon & Appendix[8]—Le Normant on Genesis.[9] Conversation with Miss Chambers.[10]

22. M.

Ch. 8½ A.M. Wrote to Mrs Drummond—Ld Spencer—J. Scott—T. Hall—J. Braye—Mrs O'Shea—Mr Greening—L. Bierle[11]—C.H. Andrews—and minutes.

---

[1] *T.T.*, 19 August 1887, 8b.

[2] P. R. Fermoy (i.e. R. Johnson), *A commentary on the memoirs of T. Wolfe Tone* (1828).

[3] F. Plowden, *The history of Ireland, from its Union . . . in January 1801 to October 1810*, 3v. (1811).

[4] Probably *Recollections of old Liverpool, by a Nonagenarian* (1863).

[5] Richard Rutledge Kane, Grand master of the Belfast Orangemen; on Home Rule; *T.T.*, 10 September 1887, 8c.

[6] Liberal unionist in Manchester; on Ireland; *T.T.*, 9 September 1887, 10d.

[7] W. Fremantle, 'Theology under its changed conditions', *F.R.*, xlvii. 442 (March 1887).

[8] C. Gore, 'The clergy and the creeds' (1887); with an appendix on Fremantle's article.

[9] See 8 May 87.

[10] Miss Violet Chambers of North Berwick, staying at the Castle; H. V. B. She had been engaged to Malcolm MacColl; Hawn P.

[11] Had sent a lecture; not further identified.

Worked well on 'The Future of the English Speaking Races'.[1] Twelve to dinner. Walked with Mr Fergusson:[2] he is most pleasing. Conversation with Miss Chambers: certainly no common person. Read Plowden—Fielding's Hist. Foundling—Mr Bierle's Lecture.

23. Tu.

Ch. $8\frac{1}{2}$ AM. Wrote to Mrs Thistlethwayte—Mr E. Rideing—Mr H. Norman—Mr A. Gardner—Mr J.H. Quin—Rev. Page Roberts—Mr D. Salmond—Messrs Rivington. Worked on English speaking Races &c. & finished it in the rough. Worked on testing & correcting Electoral Facts. Read Plowden—History of a Foundling. Drove with C. to the fire at Wellhouse. It might have been very serious.

24. Wed. [London]

9.30-3.15 to London by Sandicroft. Corrected proofs of Electoral Facts. Read Oroonoko[3]—Hist of a Foundling. Wrote to C.J. Bailey Tel.—Mr Croxden Powell—Miss Baird—C.G.—Mr Knowles. Saw Harcourt, Spencer, A. Morley, Childers, Trevelyan, Cyril Flower: & settled form of Address. Dined with Mrs Th. who related to me the very sad story of her husband's death.[4] H. of C. $4\frac{1}{4}$-$5\frac{3}{4}$.[5]

25. Th.

Wrote to Mr Curtis—H.N.G.—Mr Millington—C.G.—Rev. Dr. Jessopp—Supt All Saints Sisters of Mercy—on behalf of Maud Clifton—Mr Kegan Paul. Saw Mr A. Morley—Mr Howell M.P.—A.M. Clifton. Worked on Irish Question & Address. Dined with Mrs Peel. H of C. $4\frac{1}{2}$-$7\frac{3}{4}$ and 10-11. Spoke (an hour & more) in moving the Address standing I think on sound ground.[6] Read Oroonoko—Hist. Foundling.

---

[1] 'The future of the English-speaking races', *Youth's Companion* (November 1888); Add MS 44700, f. 251.

[2] Ronald Craufurd Munro-Ferguson, 1860-1934; liberal M.P. Ross and Cromarty 1884-5, Leith Burghs (taking over Gladstone's seat) 1886-1914; Rosebery's secretary 1886, 1892-4; cr. Lord Novar 1914. Staying at the Castle with his sister Emma Valentine Munro-Ferguson, novelist, who jilted R. B. Haldane; H.V.B.

[3] Aphra Behn, *Oroonoko, or the history of the royal slave* (1678?).

[4] See 9 Aug. 87n. Gladstone described the dinner next day to his wife (Hawn P): 'I dined with Mrs Thistlethwayte alone. She gave me with much effort a long and painfully interesting account of the death. It fell *to her* to go in and find him weltering in his blood. After this she had to appear at the Inquest. I will give you all the details when we meet. . . . The feature of the narrative was that I am now really persuaded the death was by an accident.'

[5] Read out his motion for next day; *H* 319. 1775.

[6] Moved motion for an Address recognizing that there was no information offered to justify proclamation of the Irish National League; *H* 319. 1827.

26. Fr.

Wrote to Rev. R.R. Kane—Sir E.H. Currie[1]—Messrs Pitman—Mr Cutting—Dottore Renier[2]—Mr W. Smith—Rev. E. Piché—Mr Elson—Mr Edwards—Mr Aitken BP—C.G. Saw Mr Hamilton—Sir A. West—H.J.G.—Mr Woolacott[3]—Mrs Barrable. Worked at British Museum, and saw Mr Bullen.[4] Dined at Sir C. Forster's. H. of C. 5–8 and $10\frac{1}{4}$–2. Voted in 195:272 for Address.[5]

27. Sat. [Hawarden]

Wrote to Mr Algar[6]—Messrs Durmot—Dr Bernard—Mr J. Anderson—Mr G. Johnston[7]—Keeper of P.O. at H of C. Packed &c. and off by 10.30 train to Hawarden with H. and H. Attended C.s garden party at five. Read Hist Foundling—and [blank]. Ld Acton came: much conversation with him on a certain work.[8]

28. 12 S. Trin.

Ch mg & evg. Wrote to Ld Granville—and [blank.] Further conversation with Ld A and walk. Read a variety of Tracts & Sermons: also Wells on Heroes of Heathendom.[9]

29. M.

Wrote to Rev. N. Hughes—Countess Tolstoi B.P.[10]—Herr Stedman l. & B.P.[11]—Mr Camplin—Mr T.F. Bolton. Further conversation with Acton. $12\frac{1}{2}$–$4\frac{1}{4}$. Excursion to the top of Moel Famma: delightful. I made a walk of 6 miles or more without difficulty, in the mountain air. Read Hist. of a Foundling—Prendergast on Ireland of the Restoration.[12]

30. Tu.

Ch. $8\frac{1}{2}$ A.M. Wrote to Edr of Young Man—Sir A. West—Mr R.J. Evans—Mr G. Bowler—Mr J.D. Weston—Sir R. Owen, K.C.B. Corrected for Printer MS on English Speaking Races. Conversation with W. on the Muniment Room. Also with Bailey. $2\frac{1}{2}$–6. Gave the Jubilee entertainment to the old and the Estate

---

[1] Sir Edmund Harry Currie, 1834–1913; London distiller, active in education and charity; liberal candidate 1874; kt. 1876.

[2] Antonio D. Renier of Rome, had written on Anglo-Italian relations; Hawn P.

[3] Perhaps Hugh Woolacott of N. Kensington.

[4] George *Bullen, 1816–94; keeper of printed books at the British Museum.

[5] *H* 320. 148.

[6] H. Algar of Billericay, on Celts and Homer; Hawn P.

[7] Graydon Johnston or Johnstone, an American; visited Hawarden, see 5 Sept. 87.

[8] Presumably the proposal that Gladstone should write his autobiography; see 16 Aug. 87n.

[9] J. Wells, *Christ and the heroes of heathendom* (1886).

[10] Countess Ina Tolstoy had written to ask for a signature; she lived in London; Hawn P.

[11] A. de Barton Stedman wrote from Germany on classics and the scriptures; Hawn P.

[12] J. P. Prendergast, *Ireland from the Restoration to the Revolution 1660–1690* (1887).

Servants. All went very well. Spoke say 35 min.[1] Saw Mr Mrs Hales. Read Prendergast—Hist. Foundling—Bp of Derry on Irish History.[2]

31. Wed.

Ch. 8¼ A.M. Wrote to Mr Graydon Johnstone—A.W. Tait—Rev. Dr. Kane—J.H. Mackenzie—E. Lloyd Morris—and minutes. Read Prendergast (finished)—Hist. of a Foundling—Phelps on the Less True.[3] Drive with C. Worked on books. Saw the Baileys. W.H.G. Worked on 'English Speakers'.

Thurs. Sept 1. 1887.

Church 8¼ A. M. Wrote to Mr E. Rideing—Mr de Coverley—Mr Schnadhorst—Mr Harris Sanders—Mr Cadworth—Mr Harper—Messrs King—Messrs Murray—Mr Westell—Mr Preston—G. Tonge—W. Meynell. Revised and sent off to U.S. MS on English Speaking of 1887.[4] Saw Messrs Dexter (U.S.)[5] and an aged visitor from Edinburgh who said 'we're bairns o'ae year'. Read Hist. Foundling—Plowden's Hist. Ireland—Irish Stew[6]—The Sham Squire.[7]

2. Fr.

Ch. 8¼ AM. Wrote to Rev. Dr. Mackay[8]—Mrs Ross—Miss Marshall—Mr Taylor Innes—Miss Barclay. Began my article on Ingram's so called History.[9] Read Hist. Foundling—Green's Hist of England[10]—The Sham Squire—Plowden's History. We drove to Mold for tea with Mrs Pearson our old & valued housemaid.

3. Sat.

Ch. 8½ A.M. Wrote to Mr A. Morley—Lady G. Peel—Mr E.S. Lewis—Mr B. O'Brien BP—Mrs Kingwell—Messrs Whittingham[11]—Mrs Th.—Mr Bagnall—Rev. H. Roberts. Tea party, chiefly Cestrian[12] 4½–6. Worked on books. Read Plowden's Hist.—Stanhope's Pitt[13]—Ingram's Hist. Union—and Unclassed.[14]

4. 12 S. Trin.

Ch mg with H.C. and evg. Wrote to Mr P. Stanhope—Mr Bancroft—Mr Quaritch. Read Nelson's Address to Persons of Quality[15]—Unclassed—Fonseca

---

[1] *T.T.*, 31 August 1887, 10a; mainly on achievements during the reign, but concluding with 'a few words . . . on Her Majesty herself', who had understood and acted on 'the constitutional position' of the modern monarchy. See 10 Sept. 87.

[2] W. Alexander, probably 'Royalty and loyalty. A sermon' (1886). [3] Untraced.

[4] See 22 Aug. 87. [5] Unidentified. [6] *Irish Stew*, ed. 'J.R.' (1886).

[7] W. J. Fitzpatrick, *'The sham squire'; and the informers of 1798. With a view of their contemporaries* (1866).

[8] Perhaps Alexander *Mackay, 1815–95; free-churchman and educationalist.

[9] 'Ingram's *History of the Irish Union*', *N.C.*, xxii. 445 (October 1887), reprinted in *Special aspects*, 135. A powerful attack on a Unionist account. See 30 June 87.

[10] See 1 Dec. 75, 19 Feb. 78, 15 Feb. 82.

[11] Probably W. B. Whittingham, London stationers and booksellers.

[12] i.e. from Chester. [13] See 2 Apr. 61.

[14] G. Gissing, *The unclassed*, 3v. (1884).

[15] R. Nelson, *An address to persons of quality and estate* (1715).

on the Love of God[1]—Our Modern Philosophers[2]—Life of Bp Smyth.[3] Walk with C.

5. M.

Ch. 8½ A.M. Wrote to Miss Phillimore—Rev. B. Maturin[4]—Central Press—Press Assn—P.W. Campbell—Rev. Mr Ritchie—Rev. R.R. Kane—Rev. E.B. Birks[5]—Mr Busbridge—W.R. Clarke[6]—G. Holman[7]—Mr Stedman[8]—J. Nisbet Gl[asgow]—J. Nisbet Ed[inburgh]. Worked on books. Drive with C. Saw Mr G. Johnstone (U.S.). Read Plowden—The Sham Squire—Unclassed. Worked on Rev. of Ingram. Saw Bailey.

6. Tu.

Ch. 8½ A.M. Wrote to Sir W. Harcourt—Mr Quaritch—Mr R. Thornely.[9] Worked on MS. Worked on Books. Axe work towards clearing the Bridge. Read Unclassed—Plowden—Sham Squire—and other works on Ireland. Ly Stepney & Alice here.[10]

7. Wed.

Ch. 8½ A.M. Wrote to Editors (circ.)—Press Assn Tel.—Central N. Tel—Miss L.E. Goalen—Judge Smith[11]—Miss Harvie. Worked on books. Also further at the Bridge. Read Sham Squire—Plowden Post Union Hist.—Ingram—Prize Essays on Repeal.[12]

8. Th.

Ch. 8½ A.M. Wrote to Mr E.R. Martin—Mr Knowles—Mr Quaritch—Mr J. Read. Worked on books. Also at Bridge. Walk with C. A little on the MS. Read Plowden, Post Union—Boulter's Letters[13]—Life of the Sham Squire—Unclassed.

9. Fr.

Ch. 8½ A.M. Wrote to Mr J. Davidson—Mr Clark B.P.—Mr Galloway B.P.—W. Dallyn—F. Skinner—Rev. Dr. Geikie—J. Blane—T. Moore—Mr Macombe—

---

[1] C. de Fonseca, *Tratado del amor de Dios* (1592).

[2] 'Psychosis', *Our modern philosophers: Darwin, Bain and Spencer* [in verse] (1887).

[3] R. Churton, *Lives of William Smyth and Sir R. Sutton* (1800).

[4] Probably Benjamin Maturin, vicar of Lymington.

[5] Edward Bickersteth Birks, fellow of Trinity, Cambridge, in correspondence on Homer; Hawn P.   [6] Of Harrogate, corresponding on Latin hymns; Hawn P.

[7] George Holman of Lewes, sent a book; Hawn P.

[8] A. M. M. Stedman of Godalming, 'tho' a political opponent', sent his *Oxford: its life and schools* (1887); Hawn P.

[9] Robert Thornely of Birkenhead, wrote in support; Hawn P.

[10] Margaret and Alice Cowell Stepney.

[11] Presumably Sir Montague Edward Smith, judge in the Court of Appeal; business untraced.

[12] M. J. Barry, 'Ireland as she was, as she is, and as she shall be' (1845); Repeal Prize Essays, published by the Loyal National Repeal Association of Ireland.

[13] H. Boulter, *Letters written... to several Ministers of State... containing an account of... transactions which passed in Ireland from 1724 to 1738*, 2v. (1769-70).

B. Tillett[1]—& minutes. Mr P. Stanhope Tel. Read Sham Squire—Judge Fletcher's Charge[2]—Unclassed (finished II)—Redmond's Irish Tract[3]—Clancy's ditto.[4]

10. Sat.

Ch. 8½ A.M. Wrote to Sir W. Harcourt Tel.—Press Assocn Tel.—Corresp. N.Y. Sun Tel.—Ld Granville l.l.—Editor of Liberal & Radical[5]—Mr Theobald—Rev. S.E.G.—Ld Acton—Mr Morton—Mr J. Stevens. Worked a good deal on MS. The Sandicroft fire brigade came. Saw Mr O. Morgan & party. Harry & I had a practical interview *sub dio* with Bailey & the architect on the new Muniment Room. Yesterday I told C. I thought H.M. would not like my Jubilee speech, and *why*.[6] Read Plowden—The Unclassed—Fitzgerald, Sham Squire.

11. 13 S. Trin.

Ch mg & evg. Wrote to Ld Rosebery—Ld Acton—Sir W. Harcourt. Read Nelson's Address—Scientific Defence of Xty[7]—Leibniz Opuscules[8]—and [blank.]

12. M. [London]

Ch 8½ AM. Wrote to Mr F.L. Gower Tel.—Mr Green Tel.—Press Assn Tel.— Eastern Superintendent—Mr Cyril Flower. Read Plowden—The Unclassed. 10¾-4 Off to London on sudden call for Mitchellstown [*sic*]. H. of C. 4½ to past midnight. Spoke at 9½: it was well that I did not then know the whole horror.[9] Saw Cyril Flower—J. Morley—Sir W. Harcourt—& others.

13. Tu. [Hawarden]

Wrote to Mr Morley—Mr Checkley—Ld Granville. Shopping: and saw Scotts— Mrs Th—the Mother Superior of All Saints respecting Maud Clifton. Train at 1 P.M: reached Sandicroft at 6 P.M. Ten to dinner: conversation with Ld Acton. Read Plowden—The Unclassed (finished)—and tracts.

14. Wed.

Ch. 8½ A.M. Wrote to Sir G. Errington—Mr Cyril Flower—Mr Beeley—Mr W.H. Smith—Mr Stephens—Duke of Argyll. Worked on my Ingram MS. Conversation

---

[1] Perhaps Benjamin *Tillett, 1860-1943; founded dockers' union 1887; trade unionist and labour leader. But no correspondence traced.

[2] W. Fletcher, *An Irish judge on an Irish question; reprint of Mr. Baron Fletcher's charge to the County Wexford Grand Jury in 1814* (1886).

[3] J. E. Redmond, 'Irish protestants and Home Rule' (1887).

[4] J. J. Clancy, 'Six months of "Unionist" rule' (1887).

[5] Not found.   [6] See 30 Aug. 87.   [7] Untraced tract.

[8] G. W. von Leibnitz, *Lettres et opuscules inédits* (1854).

[9] On 9 September, troops fired on a crowd at a political meeting at Mitchelstown, killing two and wounding many. This day Harcourt opened for the liberals, Gladstone later tangling with Balfour and Gibson; govt. legislation aimed, Gladstone argued, not at crime but 'at the liberty of the press, at the liberty of the subject, and at the liberty of public meeting'; *H* 320. 345.

with P. Stanhope. Walk with Lord Acton. Saw J. Bailey with [blank] and settled further the particulars of the intended muniment room. Read Knox's Essays[1]— Plowden Post Union Hist. Whist (involuntary) in evg.

15. Th.

Ch. 8½ A.M. Wrote to Rev. C. Thornton Forster[2]—Mrs Austin—Mr M'Combe. Our guests went off. Examined the Trueman's Hill ground, which attracts me for the *Library*.[3] Read Plowden (finished)—Knox's Essays—Grattan's Life & Times[4]—Grace Bevan.[5] Worked on Ingram MS.

16. Fr.

Ch. 8½ A.M. Wrote to Mr Barry OBrien—Mr Morley MP—Mr Boardman—Mr Pearsall Smith[6]—Sec. G.P.O.—Mr Peters—Mr Watts R.A.—Gen. Gloag.[7] Walk with E. Wickham. Read Knox's Essays—Lecky, and many historical books— Grace Bevan. Worked hard on Ingram MS.

17. Sat.

Ch. 8½ A.M. Wrote to Mr Calmont MP[8]—Mr Knowles—Mr O'Connor—Sir E. Watkin—Mr Laurenson—Mr A. Morley MP. BP—Mr Quaritch—Mr Charlton— Mr W.H. Smith M.P.—Mr Barker Tel. Worked *hard* on MS: finished and revised. Sat to Mr Agnew's friend the young sculptor.[9] Read Grace Bevan—Life of Garrick.[10]

18. 15 S. Trin.

Ch. mg & evg. Wrote to Mr A. Morley BP.—Mr Knowles—Mr Purcell—Cardinal Manning. Read Blyden on Mohamn in America[11]—Nelson's Address, finished— Gray's Letters.[12] Did some closing work on the MS: and conversation with E. Wickham.

---

[1] A. Knox, *Essays on the political circumstances of Ireland* (1799).

[2] Charles Thornton Forster, author and vicar of Hinxton.

[3] Early plans for St. Deiniol's Library; Trueman's Hill (west of the present library) was unsatisfactory and the first library—an iron shed—was built on the site of the present building.

[4] See 18 Sept. 85.

[5] Untraced.

[6] Letter on international copyright for Pearsall Smith's article with twelve letters from various persons in *N.C.*; see 31 Oct. 87.

[7] Archibald Robertson Gloag; Indian army; retired 1884; business untraced.

[8] Apparently *sic*; probably James Martin McCalmont, 1847–1913; soldier and unionist M.P. E. Antrim from 1885.

[9] Albert Toft, 1862–1949; sculptor. Herbert Gladstone's marginal note on the typescript of the diary reads: 'Bust now in Australia' but this is probably the bust in the National Liberal Club, London. A marble bust of Gladstone by Toft, dated 1898, is in Hawarden Castle.

[10] P. H. Fitzgerald, *The life of David Garrick*, 2v. (1868).

[11] E. W. Blyden, *Christianity, Islam and the Negro race* (1887); collected articles by the Liberian politician whose education Gladstone had assisted (see 16 June 60).

[12] *The letters of Thomas Gray*, 2v. (1819).

19. M.

Ch. 8½ A.M. Wrote to Mr F.M.H. Jones—Mr Gwilt—Mr Meynell—Mr Willis Q.C.—Mr Bowron—Mr Rideing (U.S.) Tel.—Mr J. Hughes—Mr Purcell—Mr E. Wood. B.P. to: Mr Hyam, Mr Greene, Mrs Th., Miss Tennant, Miss D. Tennant. Worked on Books. Went over Sandicroft: tea with Messrs Taylor. Read Primate Boulter—and [blank.] Twelve to dinner, incl. Mr Knox Little. Sat 2% to Mr Toft.

20. Tu.

Ch. 8½ A.M. Wrote to Mr G. Leveson Gower—Mr Quaritch—T. Barker—O.E. Roberts—J. Simpson—G.J. Campbell[1]—Mr Conborough—H. Angst[2]—W. Rines— H. Hibbert—Messrs Anson & Scarborough Commn. Tel. Gallant old Margaret gave us a capital tea. Worked on books. Read Boulter's Letters—Mastiff Voyage in Ireland[3]—and [blank.]

21. Wed.

Ch. 8½ A.M. Wrote to Mr A. Macpherson—Mr Thorndike Rice l. & BP—Mr de Coverley—Mr Thorp—Dr. J.W. Potter—Rev. Mr Brinckman—W.E.A. Coxon—S. Williams—H. Holiday—A. Morley MP—J. Burns[4]—G. Graham—J. Tod—A. Reid. Drive with C. Worked on books. Read Boulter—Horse of the Sahara[5]—Cundall on Bookbinding[6]—Revolution in Tanner's Lane.[7]

22. Th.

Ch. 8½ A.M. Wrote to G. Leveson Gower—Mr Knowles B.P.—Ld Granville— Aldn Cropper—Mr Whitley—Mr Richard MP—S.W. Norton—Mr Barwick—Mr Pryer—Mr Carnegie—'Cassius'—Mrs Ellis—Mr Howe—J. Smyth—Mr Parry. Worked on books. Corrected & dispatched my Review of Ingram: seen by M.D. and E. Wickham.[8] Woodcraft, solitary. Read Boulter Vol II—Horse of the Sahara—Rev. in Tanner Lane. S. returned, also Harry.

23. Fr.

Ch. 8½ A.M. Wrote to Mad. Aminska[?] BP—Mr Ladell(?)[9]—Mr Schnadhorst— Lord Rosebery—Card. Manning—Mons. R. Motte[10]—Mr Channing MP—Rev. R. Thomas—Mr Bryce MP—Scott & Co—Mr Holl R.A.[11]—Mr Corsey—J. Ramsay— S. Shorter—H. Williams—Miss Constance Gladstone. Worked on books.

---

[1] Of Inverness; corresponded on religion; Hawn P.

[2] H. Angst of Worth, sent a gift; later British consul in Zurich, see 20 Dec. 88n.

[3] Perhaps *Journal de voyage en Grande Bretagne et en Irland 1784* (1784?).

[4] Probably John Elliot Burns, 1858–1943; labour leader and politician; arrested in 1887 and imprisoned; lib.-lab. M.P. Battersea 1892–1918.

[5] Untraced.

[6] J. Cundall, *Bookbinding* (1881).

[7] M. Rutherford [i.e. W. H. White], *The revolution in Tanner's lane* (1887).

[8] See 2 Sept. 87.

[9] H. R. Ladell of the London International College; on spelling; Hawn P.

[10] Remi Motte of Neuilly had written on Homer; Hawn P.

[11] Portrait painter; see 25 Feb. 85, 31 Oct. 87.

Worked on family accounts. Read Boulter's Correspondence—Horse of the Sahara—Revolution in T. Lane. Woodcraft with H.N.G. Conversation with Harry on the affair he has in hand. He seems to me a great merchant with a spirit at once bold and cautious.

24 Sat.

Ch. 8½ A.M. Wrote to Rev. Mr Edwards—Miss Groom—T.E. Gibb—J. Macveagh—J. Wilson—J. Tate—J. Davidson—D.H. Gordon—Mr Haynes (N.Y.)[1]—Morgan Jones—Rev. H. Delamere. Began my MS. for Mr Bryce's Volume.[2] Finished Boulter's Letters II. Read Rev. in Tanners' Lane and [blank.] Worked on books. Woodcraft with the two Harrys.

25. 16. S. Trin.

Ch mg & evg. Wrote to Ld Lyons. Read Rev. in Tanner's Lane—Boswell's Life[3]—Blyden's Islam &c.—and Chapters in Oxford Life.[4]

26. M.

Ch. 8½ A.M. Wrote to Sir J. Millais—Laura Thornitz[5]—Mr E.H. Bailey—Mr Schnadhorst—Cardinal Manning—Edinb. Dispatch (Tel.)—Mr Burns—Mr Bonsor—Mr Thorp. Read Romilly's Memoirs[6]—Adolphus Hist. Engl.[7]—Green do—Molesworth do[8]—Rev. in Tanner's Lane—Blyden's Islam &c.—Burnart[?] on Cunard Steamers.[9] Worked on books. Woodcraft with Harry.

27. Tu.

Ch. 8½ A.M. Wrote to Ed. B[irmingha]m Daily Mail[10]—Mr A. Morley BP—Sig. Ribetti—Mr Rideing BP—F. Comyn[11]—E. Davis—A. Reid—Jas Wood—and minutes. Walks with Arthur Lyttelton. Worked on books. Worked on Irish Hist. MS. Read Duffy's Birds Eye View[12]—Lecky's Hist.—Revol. in Tanner's Lane (finished)—Cooper's Letters on Ireland.[13] Eleven to dinner.

---

[1] W. H. Haynes of New York, on the Hittites; Hawn P.

[2] 'Lessons of Irish history in the eighteenth century' in J. Bryce, ed., *A handbook of Home Rule* (1887); Add MS 44700, f. 376. This volume was proposed by Gladstone in 1886; see to Bryce, 8, 17, 26 July 86.

[3] J. Boswell, *The Life of Samuel Johnson*; probably the ed. of this year by G. Birkbeck Hill.

[4] See 5 Sept. 87n.

[5] Unidentified.

[6] Sir S. Romilly, *Memoirs... written by himself*, 3v. (1840).

[7] See 14 Aug. 86.

[8] See 27 Feb. 72.

[9] Perhaps J. Burns on the Cunard Line in *Good Words*, xxviii (April 1887).

[10] Not found published.

[11] H. E. Fitzwilliam Comyn, not further identified.

[12] Sir C. G. Duffy, *A bird's eye view of Irish history* (1882).

[13] Perhaps C. P. Cooper, 'A letter to the solicitor-general upon the bill to simplify and improve the proceedings of the high court of ... Ireland' (1850, several editions).

28. Wed.

Ch. 8½ AM. Wrote to Mr G. Leveson Gower—Editor of Paddington Echo[1]—Press Assocn Tel.—Mr Newbow—Mr Morley MP—Mr Schnadhorst—Mr Macbean—Mr Haysman. Walk with A. Lyttelton. Worked on books. Worked on Irish Hist. MS. Read Grace Bevan[2]—Brown, Lecky, Duffy, Cooper's Letters, and others on Irish affairs.

29. St M. & all A.

Ch. 8½ AM. and 7¼ P.M. Wrote to Mr P.W. Campbell—Mr Dickson—E. Purcell —Messrs Blackwood—Mr Gourlay—Mr Etheridge—Mr Kirkaldy. Worked well on MS and finished it. Walk with A. Lyttelton. The Ripons came: conversation with him. Read Grace Bevan—finished Cooper's Letters—Irish authors as yesterday.

30. Fr.

Ch. 8½ A.M. Wrote to Mr Barry OBrien—Ld Acton—Mr C. Darke—Rev. H. Seymour—Rev. H. Lambert. Walk with Ld Ripon: also forenoon conversation. Revised & dispatched MS on 18th Cent. History of Ireland. Read Dicey on Unionism[3]—F. Hill Breakdown of Parlt[4]—Brabourne on Irish History &c (trashy)[5]—Grace Bevan finished.

Sat. Oct. One. 1887.

Church 8½ A.M. Company went off. Wrote to Mr Thorndike Rice—Mr Marjoribanks MP.—Rev. Mr Bellairs l. & BP.—Mr Etheridge—Mr Hoyle MP.—Mrs Wren BP—Mr W.H. Rideing—Mr Allen—Mr Edwards—Mr Willis Blunt—Mr Grealey—Mr Parry. Saw Mr Bailey on the new Building: examination of plans. Worked on letters. Reviewed & dispatched MS on Universitas.[6] Read Oxford Life—Westmr Rev. on Irish Union—do on Status of Women—do on Jubilee (Sherman)[7]—Horse of the Sahara.

2. 17 S. Trin.

Ch 11 AM with H.C. and 6½ PM. Wrote to Dean of Manchester—Mr Hutton (BP.)—A. Morley MP—Dean of Manchester—Mr Clarke—Mr Green. Read Life of Muthio[8]—The Three Manchester Sermons[9]—Willis on Milton[10]—and divers tracts.

[1] See 11 June 87.
[2] See 15 Sept. 87.
[3] A. V. Dicey, *Letters on Unionist delusions* (1887); republished from *The Spectator*.
[4] In *N.C.*, xxii. 552 (October 1887).
[5] Lord Brabourne, 'Mr Gladstone and the Irish question', *Blackwood's*, cxlii. 443 (October 1887).
[6] See 11 June 87.
[7] *Westminster Review*, cxxviii. 793, 818, 875 (October 1887).
[8] Reading uncertain; untraced.
[9] Probably W. J. Knox Little, *Sermons preached for the most part in Manchester* (1880).
[10] W. Willis, 'John Milton; an address' (published version dated 1909).

3. M.

Ch. 8¼ A.M. Wrote to Messrs Dusie Brown & Co—O. Clarke—T. Thorp—F. Wheeler—E.F. Knox[1]—J. Radcliffe—J. Hughes—R. Rowland—R.P. Davis—J. Geehan—R. Wynne—H. Angst—Mr M'Calmont MP—Mr Campbell Ross—Ed. Scottish Leader[2]—Rev. J.S. Jones—Mrs M.P. Lalor—Miss L.H. Thomas—Mr M'Lean Cable—Mr Colman Collins—E.W. Toye—M. Morris—Mr Grant—and minutes. Walk with H. and H. Read Nicolas's Letters[3]—Old Sussex[4]—Sahara Horse—Willis's Lecture on Milton—Life of Adam Smith.[5]

4. Tu.

Ch. 8½ AM. Wrote to Mr A. Symonds l.l.—J. Morley—J.M. Hodge—D. Gordon—Chester Surveyor—Mr Green—Mr Aitken—Sig. Guardione.[6] Worked on books. Woodcraft, under C.s orders. The Kidderminster people arrived, & presented their carpet. Gave them luncheon, a speech, & a little lionising.[7] Read Kingsley on Irish History[8]—Ridgway on Afghan Frontier[9]—Justice Stephen on Mivart[10]—Ismay's Children.[11]

5. Wed.

Ch. 8¼ A.M. Wrote to Rev. J.W. Pringle—A. Morley MP—T. Baker—Mrs Bolton[12]—Mr Whitehead—Mr Craig[13]—Mr Meehan—Rev. J. Tripp.[14] Walk with Meriel Talbot. Worked on books. Read Horse of the Sahara—C. Phillimore, 'Warrior Medici'[15]—Ismay's Children—Mr James's most interesting tract on the Welsh language.[16]

6. Th.

Ch. 8¼ A.M. Wrote to Miss Phillimore 1 & PP—Ld Wolverton—Mr Ivor James—E.W. Hamilton—Mr Spottiswoode—A. Morley—L. Lyons[17]—Hon Mr Blaine—

---

[1] Perhaps Edmund Francis Veysey Knox, d. 1921; home rule M.P. 1890–8.
[2] *Scottish Leader*, 5 October 1887, 56.   [3] Not found.
[4] J. C. Egerton, *Sussex folk and Sussex ways* (1884).   [5] R. B. Haldane, *Life of Adam Smith* (1887).
[6] Francesco Guardione of Palermo, asked permission to dedicate a work to Gladstone; Hawn P.
[7] On liberal unionists; *T.T.*, 5 October 1887, 10a.
[8] J. Kingsley, *Irish nationalism: its origin, growth and destiny* (1887).
[9] Probably R. T. I. Ridgway, *Notes on Pathans* (n.d.).
[10] J. F. Stephen, 'Mr. Mivart's modern Catholicism', *N.C.*, xx. 581 (October 1887).
[11] M. Laffan, later Harley, *Ismay's children. A novel*, 3v. (1887).
[12] The quasi-rescue case, whose nursing activities Gladstone was encouraging; letter in National Liberal Club.
[13] Edward Thomas Craig, journalist; present at Peterloo 1819; sent press cuttings on it and comments on comparisons with Mitchelstown; Add MS 44502, f. 1.
[14] John Tripp, rector of Sampford-Brett.
[15] C. M. Phillimore, *The Warrior Medici* (1887).
[16] Ivor James, registrar of the S. Wales College, Cardiff, had sent his *The Welsh language in the sixteenth and seventeenth centuries* (1887); letter of thanks for it in *T.T.*, 11 October 1887, 5e; Gladstone commented on the work in his speech to the National Eisteddfod on 4 Sept. 88, then mistakenly attributing it to Sir John Rhys.
[17] Lewis Lyons, London liberal, on police behaviour over a meeting on Tower Bridge; *T.T.*, 8 October 1887, 8b.

F. Edwards—Mr Ingram—Mr Wynents—Mr Tomes. Worked on books. Walk with H & H. Read 'Rosina'[1]—Ismay's Children—Horse of the Sahara (finished). Ten to dinner. Saw Mr Mayhew, also W.H.G. on the new Octagon.[2]

7. Fr.

Ch. $8\frac{1}{2}$ A.M. Wrote to Rev. L.P. Giurleo—Mr A. Morley MP—Chief Constable, Carlisle—Ed. Chester Chronicle[3]—Ld Mayor of Dublin—Conte Serristori B.P.[4]—Messrs Meehan—Mr Thorold Rogers—Sec. Grand Trunk Co BP. Saw WHG further on the Octagon. Worked on books. Woodcraft with W. & H. Read Ismay's Children—Rosina—Bp of Cloyne on Irish Church.[5]

8. Sat.

Ch. $8\frac{1}{2}$ A.M. Wrote to Mr Tyson—P. Wylde—Mr Brereton—R. Jones—Mr Bryce BP—W. Agnew—C.H. Allen—W.T. Stead—Mr Downing—Mr Edwards—Mr Heath—Messrs Kegan Paul & Co. Saw SEG on School Funds—J. Baillie on Octagon. Walk with Helen. Corr. proof on Irish History Lessons.[6] Read Rosina—finished Bp of Cloyne 1787—read Ismay's Children—Lecture on Trouvères.[7]

9. 18 S. Trin.

Ch 11 AM and $6\frac{1}{2}$ P.M. Wrote to Sir W. Harcourt—Sir E. Watkin—G.L. Gower—Mr A. Arnold. Read Heard on National Racn[8]—Stuart on O.T. Canon[9]—...... on the Cross—and ....

10. M.

Ch. $8\frac{1}{2}$ A.M. Wrote to Mr A. Morley l. & BP.—Mayor of Nottingham—Mr Westell—Mr Mackay—J.S. Thompson—Mr Scheibner—Mr Roxburgh—Mr M'Carthy—Mr E.S. Howard—Mr Barry O-Brien. Worked much on books. What a business! Friends came. Conversation with Stuart,[10] fresh from Ireland. Long conversation with Rosebery, Morley, Wolverton. Read Pike on Crime[11]—Vancenza.[12] Visited W.H.G.s Tent party.

[1] L. Devey, *Life of Rosina, Lady Lytton* (1887).
[2] See 15 Aug. 87.
[3] Not found published.
[4] Umberto Serristori, formerly diplomat at the Italian embassy in London; in Italian Chamber of Deputies 1892–1913; later a Senator.
[5] R. Woodward, *The present state of the Church of Ireland* (1787).
[6] See 2 Sept. 87.
[7] Not traced.
[8] J. B. Heard, *National Christianity; or, Caesarism and clericalism* (1877).
[9] A. M. Stuart, *Bible true to itself; the historical truth of the Old Testament* (1884).
[10] Professor James Stuart; see 26 Oct. 78.
[11] L. O. Pike, *A history of crime in England*, 2v. (1873–6).
[12] Mary Robinson, *Vancenza, or the dangers of credulity* (1792).

11. Tu.

Ch. 8½ A.M. Wrote to Mr Schnadhorst—Mr Montgomery—Mr Samuelson BP—Rev. J. Lascelles[1]—Mr Mundella—Mr Lancaster—Mr Kiddall—Mr Langford—Mr Cadder—Mr Ashmore. Walk with Morley & the party. A broken day: much useful conversation & worked up Stuart's information. Read Rosina—Shamrock on Sc. & Ir. Unions[2]—MacCarthy's Grattan.[3] Ten to dinner.

12. Wed.

Ch. 8¼ A.M. Wrote to Mr Douglas Gordon[4]—Mr J. Elliot—J. Heywood—Dr Tanner MP[5]—Mr Robinson Tel.—Mr J. Grant—Mr Irmson—J.K. Hodge. Woodcraft with Herbert. Conversation with Wolverton—do with Prof. Stuart. Read Rosina—Sig. Monti[6]—Macaulay on Irish Pensions[7]—Bullingbrook's Justice of the Peace[8]—O'Callaghan's Ireland 1827.[9]

13. Th.

Ch. 8¼ A.M. Wrote to Judge Pierrepont[10]—Lady Russell—Mr Piper—Mr Cuthbert—Messrs Robn Nichn & Co. Worked much on Books. Read Monti, Studj Critici—Rosina—Robinson's Vancenza. Woodcraft with WHG. Sat to Birmingham Photographers who undertake to sell at 3d and upwards.

14. Fr.

Ch. 8¼ AM. Wrote to Rev. J. Russell PP—O. Browning—J. Elliot—A.H. Millar—Mr Giltspur[11]—Mr Della Torre[12]—Mr Campkin—Mr Forrest—R.P. Newman—Miss Wyse—Mr Stanton—F. Cooper—J.F. Torr[13]—J.B. Watt—Mr Carter—W.S. Johns—Mrs Cox—and minutes. Worked on books. Felled oak with WHG. Sat again to photographers. Read Rosina Lady Lytton (finished)—Monti Studj—Lanigan on Home Rule[14]—and Vancenza.

15. Sat.

Ch. 8½ A.M. Wrote to Sir W. Harcourt—Mr A. Morley MP—Mayor of Nottingham—Press Assocn Tel.—Rev. Mr Tucker—Sig. Monti—Mr T.N. Carter—

---

[1] Probably James Walter Lascelles, 1831-1901; rector of Goldsborough from 1857.
[2] Untraced.
[3] J. G. MacCarthy, *Henry Grattan* (1886).
[4] Lived in Lancaster House, London.
[5] Charles Kearns Deane Tanner, 1849-1901; physician and home rule M.P. Cork 1885-1901.
[6] G. Monti, *Studi critici* (1887).
[7] See 7 Mar. 73?
[8] E. Bullingbrook, *The duty and authority of Justices of the Peace and Parish Officers for Ireland* (1766).
[9] A. O'Callaghan, *Observations on the state of political and religious feeling in Ireland* (1827).
[10] Edwards Pierrepont, 1817-92; U.S. judge 1857-60; attorney general 1875-6; minister in London 1876-8; strong bimetallist.
[11] C. Giltspur; not further identified.
[12] Manuel Garcia della Torre, London sherry merchant.
[13] James Fenning Torr, London barrister.
[14] S. M. Lanigan, *Home Rule: a study in social science* (1879).

Young & Sons—Mr C. Giltspur. Finished Vancenza—read the Bag of Gold[1]—
.... and [blank.] Drive with C. having had a little disturbance from the cold.
Worked on books.

16. 19 S. Trin.

Ch 11 A.M. & abstained in evg on CGs orders. Wrote to Mad. Novikoff l. &
BP—P. Campbell—Jas Cowan—Jas Pollard—A. Morley MP—F. Verney—Dr John
Lord[2]—Mr OCallaghan—T. Naylor—C. Marshall Tel.—Mr Hallifax Tel.—Messrs
Robn & Nichn—Mrs Th—Mr Grant—J.T. Gray—Dr Rainy—Mr Jas Greene—J.
Lloyd—W. Sharp. Read Blyden[3]—Simpson's Building Tract[4]—and [blank.]

17. M. [Manchester]

Off at 9.15. Manchester soon after eleven. Three & a half hours in the very fine
exhibition:[5] also luncheon & speech. Thence to Sir E. Watkin's House & party:
much conversation with the Bp[6] who seems a strong man. Read Thyrza[7]—
Through Green Glasses.[8] Tired, and could not face preparing materials for
tomorrow.

18. Tu. [Nottingham]

After addresses received & short speeches in reply, off at 10.45 with the recollection of a *very* kind hospitality. Crowds & little Speeches on the way. Nottingham at 2. Two miles of street procession to the kind Mayor's[9] House. Back
to the meeting at 4: spoke $1\frac{3}{4}$ hour. Home & down again to the Mayor's dinner
in the Town's Buildings.

19.

For once it has happened that here was left a blank which remained a blank
until Jan 3.88. I can only now note the principal facts: a speech to 6000 or 7000
for $1\frac{1}{2}$ hour in evg, and to the Students of the Congregational College in the
afternoon.[10] I was much pleased with them. We also drove to see the Corporation allotments.

I am not able to note my writings readings or interviews for the day: but we
were much pleased with the Mayor and his interior as well as this very pretty
situation.

[1] Anon., *The bag of gold* (1881).
[2] Physician in Barrowford; business untraced.
[3] See 18 Sept. 87.
[4] Mrs. A. R. S. Simpson, *Building for God* (1887).
[5] Royal Jubilee exhibition of manufactures, science and art.
[6] James *Moorhouse, 1826-1915; bp. of Melbourne 1876, of Manchester 1886-1903 (appt. by
Salisbury); Gladstone had withdrawn his recommendation of appt. to Southwell 1884 (see above, x.
clxx).
[7] G. Gissing, *Thyrza*, 3v. (1887).
[8] F. M. Allen (i.e. E. Downey), *Through green glasses* (1887).
[9] Alderman Turney; account of the day's proceedings in *T.T.*, 19 October 1887, 11a.
[10] *T.T.*, 20 October 1887, 6a.

20. Th. [Sudbury Hall, Derby]

Wrote to Mr Schnadhorst—Mr T. Baker—Messrs Robn & Nichn—Mrs Cowen—
Mr R. Hayward—Mr C. Brett—Thos Adams & Co—Mr Reddell & Mr Keith. Saw
Mr A. Morley—Sir W. Harcourt—Ld Wolverton—The Mayor. Received &
replied to Irish Deputation. Off at 11.45 for Derby: short reply at the Station to
a speech of the Mayor.[1] At Derby, visit to the Porcelain works: two miles (I
think) of procession with crowds through the streets. Meeting $1\frac{3}{4}$–$3\frac{1}{2}$. Spoke
three quarters of an hour & again briefly. The Vernons[2] then drove us off to
their beautiful House at Sudbury, 11 miles. A large party, & most kind hosts.
Read Thyrza.

21. Fr.

Wrote to Mr D.L. Winter[3]—T.A. Dickson—A. Acland MP—E.W. Hamilton—De
Hagen[4]—Mr Clyne—Mr Brownson. Drive with the V.s to the Vernon Oak &
other points. Read Q.R. on Conservatism[5]—Thyrza (finished I.)—Il Zibaldone &
La Cicccide [sic] in the bad Italian tour[6]—Q.R. on Ingram's Hist. Retired early
on account of throat and chest.

22. Sat.

Wrote Tel. to Central News—New York Sun. Kept my bed all day: ipec[acu-
anha] wine and linseed poultices.

23. 20 S. Trin.

Ch 11 AM. much better. Walk & conversation with Acton. Wrote to . . . . . Read
a little Thyrza—Q.R. on Cath. Counter Reformn.[7]—Giurleo Parole di un Credente[8]—The Imitation.

24. M.

Rose to luncheon but kept the house. Wrote to Rev. D. Robertson—Sir C.
Dilke—Mr Redfern—Ld Hamilton of Dalzell[9]—Mr Hargreaves—Mr Spielmann.[10]
Tried Sir C. Newton about the horse[11]—in vain. Read Thyrza—Novelle—
Aretino: a scandal and a puzzle.[12]

---

[1] *T.T.*, 21 October 1887, 10a.
[2] 7th Baron Vernon (see 13 July 87) and his wife Francis Margaret, an American.
[3] Letter of thanks to Secretary of the Rotherham Liberal Association; *T.T.*, 24 October 1887, 8b.
[4] Possibly Maria de Hagen, London dressmaker.
[5] *Q.R.*, clxv. 535 (October 1887).
[6] Perhaps D. Batacchi, *Il Zibaldone* (1805).
[7] *Q.R.*, clxv. 273 (October 1887).
[8] L. Prota Giurleo, *Pensieri di un credente sulla Italia dei plebisciti e cattolica in rapporto al Papato religioso e politico* (1887).
[9] See 23 Jan. 71.
[10] Marion Harry Spielman, ed. the *Magazine of Art*; see 28 July 88.
[11] i.e. the horse in Homer; for Newton, see 30 July 56.
[12] Again reading the works of the bawdy Pietro Aretino.

25. Tu. [*Studley Royal, Ripon*]

Went to see the Sudbury Factory for dairy produce: most interesting. This after tree-planting &c. Finished Thyrza. Read Tracts. Journey to Studley where we were met by the Ripons. Short speech at Leeds, & a longer one at Ripon, were dragged out of me.[1] We were received with an overflowing kindness.

Wed. 26.

Wrote to Sir R. Welby—Sir Thos Acland l. & B.P.—Mr R. Rice (Coroner)[2]—Mr Browne—Mr Schnadhorst—Mr Norman. Saw the grand ruins at Fountain's Abbey as well as the park & grounds with all their views & noble trees: almost too much for one afternoon. I must not forget to name the beautiful Elisabethan House: which has the back too close upon the hill.[3] The change to a bracing air here completely cleared my chest of cold.

27. Th.

Wrote to Dr Langenfeld—Col. Dopping[4]—Mr Jas Scott—Professor Stuart—Rev. P. Burd—Sec. Ch. House Fund—Khalil Khaggatt[5]—Lady Fl. Dixie[6]—Mr A. Goodier—Mrs Jos[ephin]e Butler—Mr Stuart Jones. Drove to the Minster, the beautiful Church in the Park, & round by a new valley with the dry bed of the Skell. All very full of interest. Read Memoirs of an Amn Lady[7]—and Irish Tracts. Saw the Museum & fine carving—Also much interested in the singing of the school children. Some tree measuring.

28. Fr. SS. Sim. and J. [*Hawarden*]

$9\frac{1}{2}$ A.M.—3. Journey to Hawarden by Leeds & Manchester. Wrote to Ripon Parish Clerk—Mr Rideing—Mr Pickering—F.M. Allen—Mr Finney—W. Smith (Morley)—W. Smith (Manchr)—Rev. Mr OKeefe—H. Vivian—C. Birchell—Mr Stuart Campbell—& minutes. Read Ismay's Children[8]—Q.R. on Beust[9]—Dairy Produce[10]—Ismay's Children.

---

[1] Speeches in *T.T.*, 26 October 1887, 8a; Gladstone's voice was 'scarcely audible', but he still filled a column.

[2] Perhaps the coroner in the inquest on A.F. Thistlethwayte; see 9 Aug. 87n.

[3] Fountains Hall, 1611.

[4] In his Nottingham speech, Gladstone accused Lt.-col. James Henry Dopping of pointing his rifle at a child during an eviction in Donegal. Faced with the start of a slander action by Dopping, Gladstone explained he had merely reported the statement of a gentleman 'of habitual accuracy', and later apologised (see 20 Nov. 87). See, for this letter, *T.T.*, 3 November 1887, 8b. Passage for insertion in brackets in pamphlet edition of the speech is at Add MS 44502, f. 114.

[5] Not further identified.

[6] Florence, wife of Sir Alexander Dixie (1851-1924, 11th bart.) and da. of Lord Queensberry; she d. 1905.

[7] Possibly C. Butler, *The American Lady* (1849).

[8] See 4 Oct. 87.

[9] *Q.R.*, clv. 327 (October 1887).

[10] Ibid. 298.

29. Sat.

Ch. 8½ A.M. Wrote to Dr Wilson (Toronto)—Ld Ripon BP.—A. Morley BP.—
Messrs Cassell—Mr W. Scott—Mr M'Ilwraith—Mr R.A. Jones—Rev. A. Fagan—
Mrs K. Chase[1]—Rev. G.H. Gotley[2]—Rev. R. Page Hopps. Mr Holl came.[3] Felling
an ash with sons. Read R. Reid in Cont. Rev.—D. Wells in Do[4]—Ismay's
Children. Saw Bailey on the Octagon.

30. 21 S. Trin.

Ch mg & evg. Walked 'some' with Mr Holl. Wrote to Messrs Trübner—Sir S.
Scott & Co. Read Loserth, Wiclif & Hus[5]—Wakeman, Ch. of E. & Puritans[6]—
Evans St Mark's 12 Verses.[7] Conversation with H.N.G. on his rather difficult
affair.

31. M.

Ch. 8½ A.M. Sat to Mr Holl (or rather stood) nearly all the forenoon.[8] Wrote to
Rev. Canon Hannah—Mr Knowles—A. Morley MP—Mrs Agar—E. Farley—Mr
Ridler—S.D. Neill—W. Yeats—R. Hanna DD—J. Dymock—Mr Schnadhorst—A.
Morrison—Mr Byron[9]—R. Stewart—Mess. Jarvis—& minutes. Began felling large
walnut. Read Ismay's Children—Nineteenth C. on Copyright[10]—Lytton's Prefa-
tory Memoir.[11]

Tues. Novr 1. 87. All Saints.

Church (& H.C.) 8½ A.M. Sat 2½ hours to Mr H. (*debout*). Woodcraft with
W.H.G. Wrote to . . . . Tel.—Messrs Trübner—Rev. A. Hall l & BP—T.H.
Allen—Mr Wakeman[12]—Capt. Courtenay—Herr Verrschagen—Mr Harcourt—
Mr Stibbs—Mr Downing—Mr Radcliffe—Mr D. Milne—Ld Rosebery. Read
Sophia Adelaide[13]—Dr Ismay's children.

---

[1] Of Woburn Square, London.

[2] On organic union of Anglican church in England and Wales, 'herein it differs from the Church
of Ireland'; *T.T.*, 2 November 1887, 9f.

[3] The artist; see 25 Feb. 78, 31 Oct. 87.

[4] Reid on Ulster, Wells on the fall in prices; *C.R.*, lii. 523, 605 (November 1887).

[5] J. Loserth, *Hus und Wiclif* (1884).

[6] H. O. Wakeman, *The Church and the Puritans 1570–1660* (1887); sent *via* E. S. Talbot, Add MS
44502, f. 68.

[7] H. H. Evans, *St Paul the author of the last twelve verses of the second gospel* (1886).

[8] Half-length portrait of Gladstone standing, holding a book in both hands; dated 1888. The
portrait, now in Hawarden Castle, was commissioned by Spencer and others, together with one of
Mrs Gladstone by Herkomer for their golden wedding, at first erroneously thought to be in 1888
(*recte* 1889); see P. Gladstone, *Portrait of a family* (1989), 171 and 25 July 88.

[9] James Byron, not further identified.

[10] R. Pearsall Smith and his own letter in *N.C.*, xxii. 602 (November 1887). See 16 Sept. 87.

[11] E. G. E. L. Bulwer Lytton, *Speeches of Edward, Lord Lytton. With a prefatory memoir by his son*
(1874).

[12] Henry Offley Wakeman, 1852–99; succeeded H. J. Gladstone as history tutor at Keble, Oxford;
historical author (see 30 Oct. 87).

[13] *Sophie-Adélaide. Histoire contemporaine* (1886).

2. Wed.

Ch. 8½ A.M. Wrote to Sir Salar Jung[1]—Mr Hampton Carson—Mrs Medline—Mr Ridler. Stood 2½ hours (with the aid of supports) to Mr Holl, whom it is a pleasure to assist, even to *extremity*. Woodcraft with WHG. The Granville party & Ld Spencer came. Finished Sophia Adelaide!!! Read Sir S. Jung in 19th C.

3. Th.

Ch. 8¼ A.M. Wrote to L.Ly Waterford BP—Mr A.C. Benson—Mess. Trübner—Mrs Dempster—J. Brierley—Mr Childers—Mr Hurlburt—C. Tylor—Mr Thatcher. Again stood 2½-3 hours: sleep comes on in afternoon & keeps me. But I delight to render all the aid I can to a great painter. We brought down the large walnut tree. Conversation with Granville & Spencer.[2] Also with Mr Agnew.[3] Read Dr Ismay's Children—Westmr Rev. on Hartington[4]—Causes occultes &c.[5]

4. Fr.

Ch. 8½ A.M. Wrote to Mr Capston U.S.—Mr Jas Gray—Mr Jas Byron—Miss Martin—Mr T.S. Wall—Rev. G. Lefevre—Mons. Magee—Queensf. Station Master. Final standings to Mr Holl: near 3 hours. The operation for me has been most exhausting: but the work is of a very high order indeed. The Agnews & Ld S. went. Walk & much conversation with G. Read Dr Ismay's Children, in the wreck of my day.

5. Sat.

Ch. 8¼ AM. Wrote to J.E. Gladstone—A. Morley B.P.—Lady Milbank—J. Pollard—Rev. Mr Malpas—E. Butler—Mr Jerries—J. Wild—J.D. Seel—P. Gorrie. Mr Holl went off. 10 m. to Saighton, interesting house; luncheon there.[6] Conversation with Granville. Mr Holl went: much liked. Finished Ismay's Children.

6. 22 S. Trin.

Ch 11 AM. with H.C. and 6½ P.M. Read Seybert Report[7]—Huxley in N.C. on the Bishops—also Arnold Forster on Irish Land[8]—Balfour's Speech (conversation with G. thereon)[9]—and [blank.] Clark examined me, & recommended Southern sun. He went off in aftn. Theol. conversation with him.

---

[1] Sir Salar Jung, 1863–89; prime minister of Hyderabad; published his experiences of the Jubilee in *N.C.*, xxii. 500 (October 1887).   [2] See *Spencer*, ii. 152.

[3] William Agnew (see 9 Apr. 74), involved in the painting of Holl's portrait.

[4] *Westminster Review*, cxxviii. 929 (November 1887).

[5] Perhaps P. I. Jacob, *Curiosités des sciences occultes* (1885).

[6] 3½ miles S.E. of Chester, seat of George Wyndham, 1863–1913; author; Balfour's secretary April 1887–92; tory M.P. Dover 1889–1913; Irish land reformer and chief secretary.

[7] Perhaps A. Sybert, *Statistical annals of the United States* (1818).

[8] *N.C.*, xxii. 625, 725 (November 1887).

[9] Balfour's speech on 4 November at Birmingham, attacking Gladstone's speeches as 'spiteful'; Gladstone sent notes to Spencer who discussed them with Morley and Granville, recommending Gladstone not to respond publicly; *Spencer*, ii. 152-3.

7. M.

Ch. 8½ A.M. Wrote to Lady West Tel.—Ld Spencer—Mr Morley—Ld Acton—Mr Godley—Mr Bryce MP—Ed. Press Directory—Mr J. Leach—Miss Hartley—Messrs Eaton—Messrs Murray—Messrs M'Gillivray—Mr Tomkinson. Granvilles & EWH went. Long walk & conversation with Sir R. Welby. Read Scottish Review on Sc. Union[1]—Causes Occultes &c.

A great grief came to us today in the death of our warm & generous friend Lord Wolverton. Peace be with him in the better land.

8. Tu.

Ch. 8½ A.M. Wrote to Lady Wolverton—Mr Thorndike Rice—Rev. Mr Douglas—Mr Osborne—Mr Gruenbaum—Watsons—Rev. Mr Thorely—Mr Wilkins—Mr R. Cameron. Conversation with S.E.G. on coming changes. Also with Welby. He went. Read Biese, Naturgefuhl[2]—Hindu Marriage Customs—G. Massey on Genesis[3]—Life of Miss Gilbert.[4] Worked on arranging letters for final deposit.[5] And on proofs for U.S.

9. Wed.

Ch. 8½ A.M. Wrote to Sec. Liby Pwlheli BP—Mr A. Morley—Miss Webb—Mr Thorndike Rice B.P.—Cardinal Manning—Mr H. Gardner[6]—Mr Waite—Mr Eddington—Mr Dexter—Mr Brennand—Mr Bryce MP—Warden of Keble—Dr A. Biese—Mrs Forster. Worked on papers. Felled a hornbeam with W. Conversation with Unitarian Minister. Read La Russia[7]—Question Bulgare,[8] causes occultes—Village Tragedy.[9] Finished & dispatched my proofs for N.A. Review.[10]

10. Th. [London]

Ch. 8½ AM. Wrote to Mr Godley Tel.—Rev. Dr Tulloch—Mr Baker—Mr J. Parnell—Mr Kelly—Rev. Mr Isaac. To London by Irish Mail. Kindly housed at 12 Portman St.[11] Saw Lucy Cavendish—Mr Bryce—Mrs Th—Ld Granville—Mr Godley. Finished Village Tragedy. Read Hutton (Carlyle).[12]

---

[1] *Scottish Review*, x. 213 (October 1887).

[2] C. J. A. A. Biese, *Die Entwicklung des Naturgefühls bei den Griechen und Römern* (1882).

[3] G. Massey, 'The Hebrew and other Creations fundamentally explained' (1887).

[4] F. Martin, *Elizabeth Gilbert and her life for the blind* (1887).

[5] i.e. in the Octagon.

[6] Herbert Coulstoun Gardner, 1846–1921; director of P. & O. Co.; liberal M.P. N. Essex 1885–95; cr. Baron Burghclere 1895.

[7] *La Russia. Studio storico sul progresso ed avvenire degli Slavi* (1887).

[8] *La Question Bulgare* (1888).

[9] *The village tragedy, or, murder upon murder* (1800?); a ballad.

[10] See 11 June 87.

[11] J. A. Godley's house.

[12] R. H. Hutton, 'Thomas Carlyle' in *Essays on some of the modern guides of English thought in matters of faith* (1887).

11. [*Hawarden*]

Wrote to Mrs Sands. Saw Mr Murray (on Copyright)—Mr A. Morley—Mr Hall. Went to Stratton St at 12. To the Kensington service 1–2. Then saw my good friend[1] laid in the grave at Ham at 3.15. Off by 5.30 and home before 10.30. Saw Lord Spencer.

12. *Sat.*

Ch. 8½ A.M. Wrote to Mr Taylor Innes—Mr R.H. Hutton—Mr Davenport Adams—Miss M. Maguire B.P.—Mr Thorndike Rice B.P.—Miss Taylor—Rev. A. Fagan—Mr Robinson—Mr Pulitzer Tel.—Mr Lundy—Mr Levy—Mr Shirley—Mr Clark—Mr Higham—Mr Salkeld. Read Cardinal M.s pamphlets on Education.[2] —Little Lord Fauntleroy[3]—Hutton's Reviews. We felled an oak. Worked on papers.

13. *23 S. Trin.*

Ch. 11 & [blank.] Wrote to Mr Hutton P.S.—Madlle Buchholz—Butler at Saighton—Rev. Page Hopps—Mr Goodall—Mr Burdett—Mr Beatty—Mr Gordon. Read Hutton—'For Further Consideration'—Wiclif and Huss[4]—T. May for Sun Worship!![5]—and Double Marriage.[6]

14. *M.*

Ch. 8½ A.M. Wrote to Mr A. Morley Tel.—Press Assocn Tel.—Central News Tel.—Sir C. Russell—Mr J. Morley—Mr Williamson MP—Mr Johnson[7]—Mr Schnadhorst B.P.—Rev. D. Milne. Corrected proofs of Speech delivered Oct. 18. Read Hutton—Little Lord Fauntleroy. Walk with S. & Harry. Worked on papers.

15. *Tu.*

Ch. 8½ A.M. Wrote to Mr Thorndike Rice—Mr Schnadhorst—Mr Pitkethlie—Mr Darlington—Rev. H. Meynell—Rev. A. Chaplin—Mr Stead—Mr Stone—Mr Burdett—Mr Tomes. Corrected proofs of speech delivered Oct. 19. Read & made extracts from Lecky's 'Clerical Influences'.[8] Read also O'Connor on Ireland[9]— Little Lord Fauntleroy—and [blank.] Felled a sycamore with WHG.

---

[1] i.e. Lord Wolverton.

[2] H. E. Manning's recent pamphlets included 'Is the Education Act of 1870 a just law?' (1886) and 'The working of the Education Act . . . unequal; therefore, unjust' (1886).

[3] F. E. H. Burnett, *Little Lord Fauntleroy* (1886); see 19 Jan. 88.   [4] See 30 Oct. 87.

[5] Untraced early version of T. May, *Solar-Life the desire of all* (1911); physical and moral exercises.

[6] C. Reade, *Double marriage or white lies* (1882).

[7] Telling J. R. Johnson, secretary of Bermondsey Gladstone Club, of the 'duty of every citizen to refrain from all resistance to the decision of the Executive government', i.e. not to demand by force a meeting in Trafalgar Square (where there were riots on 13 November); *T.T.*, 15 November 1887, 8a and leader.

[8] Notes untraced; [W. E. H. Lecky], 'Clerical influences', in *The leaders of public opinion in Ireland* (1861); the essay was omitted in later eds.; only 34 copies of the 1st ed. were sold (see W. E. G. Lloyd, ed. of *Clerical influences* (1911)).

[9] T. P. O'Connor, probably *The Parnell movement, with a sketch of Irish parties from 1843* (1886).

16. Wed.

Ch. 8½ A.M. Wrote to Sir Ch. Russell—Col. Dopping (dft)[1]—Mr Thorndike Rice—Rev. F. Langbridge[2]—Mr Cameron—Mr Elliot Stock—Mr Chaster. Read Langbridge's Poems—Chaster on the Executive[3]—Hutton's Essays—Hithersea Mere.[4] Finished the *delightful* 'Little Lord Fauntleroy'. Woodcraft with W. & Herbert. Worked in papers. The 'job' will be stiff and long. Conversation with Mr Mayhew in evg.

17. Th.

Ch. 8½ A.M. Wrote to Sir Lyon Playfair—A. Carroll—E. Hall—Mr Ridler—Mr Kempster—Mr Hadfield—C.F. Cooper[5]—and minutes. Sent out some presents. Worked on books & papers. Read Hutton's Essays—Smith's Cudine & Preface[6]—Bulgarie, Causes Occultes—Bibliomania in Middle Ages[7]—The Four Isles of Aran[8]—Hithersea Mere. Drive with C. Ten to dinner.

18. Fr.

Ch. 8½ A. M. Wrote to Sir Chas Russell—Mr Knowles—Earl of Elgin—Mr O.J. Burke[9]—Mr Schnadhorst—Mr Callimore. Woodcraft with my sons. Finished Isles of Aran—Read Conor's [*sic*] Hist. Ireland—La Russia—began The New Antigone.[10]

19. Sat.

Ch. 8½ A.M. Wrote to Mr Schnadhorst—Ld Granville—Rev. F. Rowden—Rev. A.O. Jay—Mr Gilbert Beith[11]—T. Milligan—Messrs Reeves—J.G. Hall—C. Marshall—T. Webster—Mr Heming—T. Baker—Messrs. Fawn—and minutes. We felled three sycamores. Read La Russia—Tracts on Ireland—The new Antigone.

20. Preadv. S.

Confined to bed. Went through mg & evg service. Wrote to Sir Ch. Russell—Col. Dopping—Sir H. Acland—Messrs Robins[12]—Mr Sheppard—Mr Petrie. Read Wiclif and Hus—Life of Miss Gilbert.

---

[1] See 27 Oct. 87n.
[2] Frederick Langbridge (1849–1922; rector of St John's Limerick) had sent his *Poor folks' lives: ballads and stories in verse* (1887).
[3] Albert William Chaster had sent his *The powers, duties and liabilities of executive officers as between these officers and the public* (1886).   [4] Lady A. Noel, *Hithersea Mere* (1887).
[5] Charles F. Cooper of New Cross; occasional political correspondent; Hawn P.
[6] Title scrawled; work untraced.
[7] F. S. Merryweather, *Bibliomania in the middle ages* (1849).
[8] O. J. Burke, *The south isles of Aran, County Galway* (1887).
[9] Oliver J. Burke, author and Irish land commissioner; see 17 Nov. 87n.
[10] [W. Barry], *The new Antigone. A romance*, 3v. (1887).
[11] Gilbert Beith, 1827–1904; Glasgow merchant and liberal M.P. 1885–6, 1892–5.
[12] Robins, Cameron and Kemm, acting for Dopping. Gladstone enclosed a letter of apology and Dopping dropped his slander action; *T.T.*, 23 November 1887, 10c. Gladstone altered the passage in the Liberal Publication Department's pamphlet of his speech, and added a note on the affair; *T.T.*, 28 November 1887, 9e. See 27 Oct. 87.

21. M.

Rose at 1. Wrote to Sir H. Davey—Ld Rosebery—Mrs Th.—Mr G. Beith—Mr Noble. Corrected speech at Congr. Coll. Nottm. Saw Harry on the Mines—Bailey on the Octagon. Read The New Antigone—'La Russia' (finished) —Davey's Law of Public Meetings[1]—La Mandragola: miserable stuff except the diction.[2]

22. Tu.

Rose at 10½. Wrote to Cardinal Manning—Sir Thos Acland—Mr W. Baker—Cawthorn & Hutt[3]—Sec. Metrop. Distr. R.R.—Mr G. Dudderidge[4]—Mr G.H. Dick—Editor N.E. Daily Gazette[5]—Mr Schnadhorst—Mr J.J. Healy—Mr Woolacott—Mr Edwards—Mr J.A. Murray—Rev. A.O. Jay—Messrs Rivington. 3-5. Conclave to discuss with Mr Mayhew the important question of the Mines. Read Dr Rünger Philosophy of Religion[6]—The new Antigone—The Maltese Question[7]—and Foggo on Ireland.[8] Worked on papers.

23. Wed.

Ch. 8¼ A.M. Wrote to Sir C. Russell—A. Petrie—W. Ridler l. & P.P.—A. Foggo—J.G. Keane—Sir H. Acland—Messrs Bull & Auvache[9]—P. Campbell—Messrs Deacon—Messrs Clark—Vicar of St Mark's Barrow[10]—Miss Morris—Mr Dudderidge—Mr A.M. Smith—Messrs Fawn—Mr Hogan—Col. Healy—W. Hall—and minutes. Read Newman on H. Wilberforce[11]—Dudderidge on Ireland—The New Antigone—Carlyle's Tour in Ireland.[12] Long conversation with Harry on mining & money arrangements in the family. Woodcraft with two sons.

24. Th.

Ch. 8¼ A.M. Wrote to Hn Postmistress—Mr Schnadhorst—Mr Pickering—T. Milligan—Secs Lanc. & Chesh. Hist. Soc.[13]—J.R. Johnson—Messrs Swann—Messrs Paterson. Worked on books. Felled & kibbled an ash with W. Read Carlyle Tour in Ireland—The New Antigone. Hawarden Concert &c. 8½-10.

25. Fr.

Ch. 8¼ A.M. Wrote to Sir Chas. Russell—S. Laing—T. Baker—Mr Salkeld—Mr Wilkins—C. Higham—Reeves & Turner—Mr Maclunivan—Mr Aitchison.[14]

---

[1] H. Davey, 'The law of public meeting' (1887).
[2] N. Machiavelli, *Mandragola* (new ed. 1887).
[3] London booksellers, including a lending library.
[4] Or Dodderidge; had sent an untraced work on Ireland; see 23 Nov. 87.
[5] *North Eastern Daily Gazette*, 23 November 1887, 4b.   [6] Not found.
[7] *Correspondence and remarks on the constitution of Malta from 'The Times' and other newspapers* (1887).
[8] Algernon Foggo, author of the second volume of T. P. O'Connor's *Disraeli* (see 30 July 81), had sent an untraced draft or article on Ireland.   [9] Booksellers in Bloomsbury.
[10] James Marshall Laycock, vicar of St. Mark's, Barrow, from 1878.
[11] H. W. Wilberforce, *The Church and the Empires. . . preceded with a memoir. . . by J. H. Newman* (1874).
[12] T. Carlyle, *Reminiscences of my Irish journey in 1849* (1882).
[13] No correspondence published.
[14] James Aitchison had sent his *The chronicle of mites: a satire: and other poems* (1887).

Woodcraft with W.H.G. Read Life of Wolfe Tone[1]—Carlyle's Ireland (finished) —The new Antigone. Read M.D.s Tract for Mothers[2] & suggested amendments.

26. Sat.

Ch. 8½ A.M. Wrote to Messrs Watson—Mr H. Robbins—Dr Potter—Messrs Bull & Auvache—Rev. Mr Carter—Mr C. Downes—Mr J.H. Boddy—Mr Carsey. Drive with C. Conversation with A. Morley. 12-2. Delivered to Mr Mayhew a lengthened narrative of Hawarden & O[ak] F[arm][3] Finance. Guests came in evg. Read Narrative of the Humbert Invasion[4]—The New Antigone (finished)—a book of much talent & a perpetual jar.

27. Adv. Sunday.

Ch. 11 AM. with H.C. and 6½ P.M. Walk with Lady L. Warner. Wrote to Ld Tankerville—Cawthorn & Hutt—Mr Kelly. Read Cobbett's Reformation[5]—The Chronicle of Mites[6]—Sibthorpe & Pretended Catholics.[7]

28. M.

Ch. 8½ A.M. Wrote to Mrs Bolton l. and P.P.—Ld E. Fitzmaurice[8]—Mr A. Morley—Mr C. Lacaita[9]—Mr Kennedy—Ld de Tabley—Mr Farnall—Mayor of Limerick—Rev. P. Burd—Messrs Robins B.P.—Mr Browning. Woodcraft with W.H.G. Conversation with A. Morley. Guests went: G.L. G[ower] came. Finished the interesting Humbert narrative—read Cobbett's Reformation—and Le Bouz on Ireland.[10]

29. Tu.

Ch. 8½ A.M. Wrote to Dr Schumbacher—Mr Macaulay BP—Mr Higgs—Ed. Forum N.Y.[11] Worked on papers. Walked with G.L.G. Finished Le Bouz. Read Dawson on Copyright[12]—Life of Wolfe Tone and David and Bathsheba.[13] Made Book notes.

[1] See 23 May 65, 17 Aug. 87.
[2] Not found published.
[3] The Staffordshire works which had nearly bankrupted the Glynnes in the 1840s; see above, iii. xliii.
[4] Not found.
[5] See 4 Mar. 39.
[6] See 25 Nov. 87n.
[7] Sir C. Sibthorpe, *A friendly advertisement to the pretended Catholics of Ireland*, 2v. (1622).
[8] Long letter on the whigs and Ireland; *T.T.*, 3 December 1887, 9e.
[9] Regretting Charles Carmichael Lacaita's resignation as a liberal M.P. ('a new impulse to Radicalism'); Add MS 44502, f. 143.
[10] Or Le Bourg; neither traced.
[11] Probably declining to write for it.
[12] S. E. Dawson, *Copyright on books* (1882).
[13] *The story of David and Bathsheba. A ballad*, 2v. (1662).

30. Wed. St Andrew.

Ch. 8¼ A.M. Wrote to Ed. 80 Club Circular[1]—Miss S.C. Hand[2]—Mr A. Morley—Mr Ebenezer Bain.[3] Worked on old letters. Read Contemp. on Scotch Ch.[4]—Nineteenth C. on Copyright[5]—Murray's Mag. on Mrs Goldschmid—Ireland—Jinisberg[6]—Bain on Aberdeen Guilds—David & Bathsheba—Petty's Reflections on Ireland.[7]

Thurs. Dec One 1887.

Ch. 8¼ A.M. with Mr Armitstead. Wrote to Mr Hildegard Werner[8]—Mr Jas Knowles & draft—J. Morley MP—J.B. Balfour MP—Rev. Laurence[9]—Dr Lewins[10]—H.G. Reid—W. Bowman—C. Tighe[11]—R. Scorcher.[12] Drive with Lady Aberdeen. Worked on papers. Read Argyll on Scotch Land[13]—David & Bathsheba—Wolfe Tone's Life—Ingram's Reply to WEG.[14]

2. Fr.

Ch. 8¼ A.M. Wrote to Chairman Distr. Co.—Mr Bradlaugh MP—W. Chadwick—Rev. Mr Cartwright—Mr Brown—W. Taylor. Worked on papers. Read Reading Diary—David & Bathsheba (finished)—Westmr Rev. on Darwin[15]—Dr Petty's Reflections on Ireland. Walk with Ld Aberdeen.

3. Sat.

Ch. 8¼ AM & H.C. Wrote to Mr Swift Macneill—Mr Routledge—Mr Hamer—Mr Schnadhorst—Mr Quaritch—Mr Kyle—Mr Henderson.[16] Read Lynch on Religion[17]—Plan of Campaign Vol. I.[18]—Daryl, Ireland's Disease[19]—and [blank.] Worked on papers. Woodcraft with Harry.

[1] Untraced; the Eighty Club was a liberal political dining and speech-publishing club.
[2] Of Regent's Park; business untraced.
[3] Ebenezer Bain had sent his *Merchant and craft guilds; a history of the Aberdeen incorporated trades* (1887).   [4] *C.R.*, lii. 867 (December 1887); Balfour of Burleigh.
[5] See 31 Oct. 87.   [6] Word scrawled.
[7] Sir W. Petty, *Reflections upon some persons and things in Ireland* (1660).
[8] *Sic*; in fact Miss Werner, a Swede living in Newcastle-upon-Tyne; wrote on her articles on Gladstone for the *Dageus Nyheten*, a liberal newspaper in Stockholm, and enclosed a letter from its editor, Rudolf Wall, on Gladstone, 'the Garibaldi of Peace', 'much more *universal* than what we in general find Englishmen to be, and it is in *this point*, that Mr Gladstone is so superior to Cavour and Bismarck'; Hawn P.
[9] Rev. F. Lawrence, on burial reform; *T.T.*, 3 December 1887, 13e.
[10] Dr Robert Lewins of London; corresponded on philosophy; Hawn P.
[11] Perhaps Charles Tighe, tailors in London.
[12] Perhaps Richard Ganney Scotcher, not further identified.
[13] Perhaps G. D. Campbell, duke of Argyll, 'Land reformers', *C.R.*, xlviii. 470 (October 1885).
[14] T. D. Ingram, 'Mr Gladstone and the Irish Union: a reply', *N.C.*, xx. 766 (December 1887), see 2 Sept. 87.   [15] *Westminster Review*, cxxxviii. 1136 (December 1887).
[16] To James Henderson, defeated liberal candidate in Dulwich; *T.T.*, 8 December 1887, 5f.
[17] Perhaps T. T. Lynch, 'Sermons for my curates' (1871).
[18] *The Plan of Campaign . . . extracts from the speeches and writings of the Parnellite party and press* (issued in various parts by T. W. Russell, M.P., 1887–9, for the I.L.P.U.).
[19] P. Daryl [i.e. P. Grousset], *Ireland's disease. Notes and impressions. The author's English version* (1888).

4. 2 S. Adv.

Ch. mg & evg. Wrote to Harpers f. Osgood[1]—Mr Knowles—Herbert J.G.—Sir A. Clark—Mr Leadam. Read Bp Ridding's Charge[2]—Mivart in 19th C.—Bp Goodwin in Do[3]—Foreign Church Chronicle[4]—Life of Miss Gilbert.[5]

5. M.

Ch. 8½ A.M. Wrote to The French Ambassador—Sir Thos. Acland—Mr Geo. Reid—Mr Thorndike Rice—Mr R.N. Hall—Ed. W. Daily Mercury.[6] Woodcraft with Harry. Read Ireland's Disease—'Forum' on Amn Nat. Debt[7]—on American Irish—The Plan of Campaign. Conclave with Mr Cochrane. Saw Sir J. Carmichael. Dined with Mr Mayhew. Worked on papers. Woodcraft in aft.

6. Tu.

Ch. 8½ A.M. Wrote to Mr Knowles—Mr Boydell—Mr Blew—Mr Vincent—Mr Brodie—J. Wild—Mr Broadhead—Rev. Mr Mackie l. & BP—Mrs Cropper—Mr Stuart Rendel—Mr Dunscombe—Mr Blachford—A.C. Kennedy[8]—Mr Fisher Unwin and Treas. Ed. Coll. Physicians.[9] Read Ireland's Disease—The Plan of Campaign—Blew's Medea &c.[10] Kibbling with W. and H.

7. Wed.

Ch. 8½ A.M. Wrote to Messrs Routledge l.l.—Rev. Prof. Stokes[11]—Rev. U.K. Thomas—Rev. J.N. Lloyd—Editor P.M. Gazette—Ed. Young Man—Judge O'Connor Morris[12]—Mr M'Kechnie—Rev. A. Thomas—Watsons. Worked on papers. Woodcraft with W. and H. Finished Ireland's Disease—read The Plan of Campaign—The Story of the Nations[13]—Life of Pickering.[14]

8. Th.

Ch. 8½ A.M. Wrote to Mr Thorndike Rice Tel. & copies—Mr Knowles—A. Wyon—W. Morris—H. Gardner MP—T. Holmes—Sir W. Fraser—F. Whitman—

---

[1] No correspondence published.
[2] G. Ridding, 'Primary charge' (1887).
[3] N.C., xxii. 850, 871 (December 1887).
[4] Probably articles on Old Catholics in *Foreign Church Chronicle*, xi (December 1887).
[5] See 8 Nov. 87.
[6] Not found published.
[7] *The Forum* (published in Philadelphia).
[8] Perhaps Alexander Clark Kennedy, F.R.G.S., of Dalry, Galloway.
[9] Declining an invitation to the Annual Dinner of the Royal College of Physicians, Edinburgh.
[10] William John Blew had sent his *Medea, from the tragedy of Euripides* (1887); Add MS 44502, f. 174.
[11] George Thomas Stokes, 1843–98; professor of ecclesiastical history at Trinity, Dublin, from 1883.
[12] William O'Connor Morris, 1824–1904; historian and Irish judge from 1872. See 8 Dec. 87.
[13] A. Gilman, *The story of the nations* (1885).
[14] *The life of Timothy Pickering. By his son [O. Pickering] and C. W. Upham*, 4v. (1867–73).

Mr Freshfield—Mr Shirlkeve. Began Letter to Ed. Westmr Review[1]—read Plan of Campaign—Judge Morris on Irish Land[2]—The Shetland Isles.[3]

9. Fr.

Ch. 8½ A.M. Wrote to Ed. Westmr Review—Mr Fitzpatrick—Wms & Norgate—Mr Pemblett—Mr Conbrough—Press Assocn Tel.—T. Baker—Mr Johnstone—Mr Stopford—Mr Pearce. Finished my rejoinder to Ingram: an irksome task. I feel like a thieftaker. Woodcraft with H. Drew. Read Plan of Campaign—[blank] on Shetland Isles.

10. Sat.

Ch. 8½ A.M. and Holy Communion. Wrote to Sir A. Clark Tel.—Mr Brisbane Tel.—Mr Rideing l. & BP.s—Messrs Watson—J. Mackenzie—Mad. Hyacinthe Loyson—Rev. Mr Fuller—Mr Knowles—S. Martin—T.P. Tomes—E. Russell. 12–2. Mr Mayhew on the Minerals & the Estate at large of the circumstances of which I have now to make the best estimate in my power. Woodcraft with sons. Read divers Tracts. Plan of Campaign (finished). Dined at the Rectory: Played Backgammon with the Rector.

11. 3 S. Advent.

Ch 11 A.M. and 6½ P.M. Wrote to Mr Minshull—Rev. Mr Jackson—Mr Gibson—Ed. Oban Times.[4] Read Benson's Laud[5]—Life of Miss Gilbert—Collinet on Alviella[6]—Luchman on AngloIsrael.[7]

12. M.

Ch. 8½ AM. Snow, frost (bad.) & fog. Wrote to Dr Ph. Collinet l & BP.[8]—Mr Davidson—Mr Butchard—Mr Luchman—Mr W. Jones—Mr Mills—Mr Bryce—Mr Gorset.[9] Made an examination (for Dec. 31) of my property and probable income for 1888, with a view to pending arrangements. Worked on papers.[10] Read Carlyle, Early Letters[11]—Philosophy of Art.[12]—and Fiske on Moral Destiny.[13]

---

[1] 'A reply to Dr Ingram' dated 9 December 1887, *Westminster Review* (January 1888), reprinted in *Special aspects*, 187.

[2] W. O'C. Morris, 'The land system of Ireland' (1888); reprinted from *Law Quarterly Review*.

[3] Perhaps C. Sinclair, *Shetland* (1840).

[4] *Oban Times*, 17 December 1887, 4g.

[5] A. C. Benson, *William Laud* (1887).

[6] Apparently *sic*. Probably one of the collaborative works on Ireland by Paul Collinet (see next day) and M. H. d'Arbois de Joubainville; perhaps *Essai d'un catalogue de la littérature épique de l'Irlande* (1883).

[7] May read 'Lachman'; work not traced to either author.

[8] See previous day.

[9] Pascal Grousset, French author; wrote as 'Philippe Daryl'; see 3 Dec. 87 and Add MS 44502, f. 196.

[10] And perhaps wrote the article on scarlet fever convalescents for *Hospital*, December 1887; see *T.T.*, 22 December 1887, 5e.

[11] T. Carlyle, ed. C. E. Norton, *Early letters*, 2v. (1886).

[12] Untraced.

[13] J. Fiske, *The destiny of man viewed in the light of his origin* (1884).

13. Tu.

Rose at 10.30. Wrote to Sir Thos Acland—Rivingtons—Murrays—Watsons—Sir S. Scott & Co—Dr Sigerson[1]—A. Stuart [*sc.* Stewart]—Ld Lyttelton—Mr Routledge—F.W. Cope—Mr Edwards—Miss Morris. Read Fiske on Man's Destiny—Reminiscences of Dunfermline[2]—Carlyle's Early Letters.

14. Wed.

Ch. $8\frac{1}{2}$ A.M. Wrote to Mr Thorndike Rice—Sir And. Clark—Mr Mathewson—J. Middleton—B. Hebditch—G. Unwin—Sir S. Scott & Co—J. Graham—F. O'Rourke—G. Higgins[3]—S. Webb[4]—Robertson & Nicholson. Woodcraft with sons. Read Carlyle's Letters—Reminiscences of Dunfermline—A. Sullivan on the Jubilee[5]—Parker on Dissent in England[6]—Greely's Narrative.[7]

15. Th.

Ch. $8\frac{1}{2}$ AM. Wrote to Wms & Norgate—Mr Joseph BP—Mr Murray—Mrs Agnew—Mr R.A. Brown—Mr Vanderbyl[?] BP. 12-$4\frac{1}{4}$ To Chester; saw Mr Bullen,[8] who gave me good advice & interesting professional talk. Read Carlyle's Letters—Bannatyne's Handbook U.S.[9]—Greely's Narrative—And Scartazzini's Dante.[10] Saw Mr Mayhew on our mineral plans.

16. Fr.

Ch. $8\frac{1}{2}$ A.M. Wrote to Mr Macmillan l.l.—Mr Gwilt—Rev. Mr Fuller—Scotts—Mr Mundella—Robertson & Nicholson—E.W. Hamilton. Woodcraft with sons. Worked on papers. Saw Mr Bailey & directed commencement [of the Octagon]. Read Oliphant's Venice[11]—Macaulay on Repeal[12]—Cornoldi's Dante[13]—Carlyle's Letters—Scartazzini on Dante.

[1] George Sigerson, physician and writer on Irish affairs.
[2] A. Stewart had sent his *Reminiscences of Dunfermline* (1886).
[3] To R. Hunt and G. Higgins of the Workmen's National Association for the Abolition of Sugar Bounties, supporting abolition; *T.T.*, 3 January 1888, 3e.
[4] Perhaps Sidney Webb, the Fabian; see 31 Aug. 88.
[5] Untraced article.
[6] Perhaps Joseph Parker, *Weaver Stephen: odds and evens in English religion* (1885).
[7] A. W. Greely, *Three years of Arctic Service: an account of the Lady Franklin Bay expedition of 1881–84 and the attainment of the Farthest North*, 2v. (1886).
[8] F. Bullen, Chester dentist.
[9] D. J. Bannatyne, *Handbook of republican institutions in the United States* (1887).
[10] G. A. Scartazzini, *A handbook to Dante* (1887), and his *Dante Alighieri; seine Zeit, sein Leben und seine Werke* (1879).
[11] M. O. Oliphant, *The makers of Venice* (1887).
[12] See 4 June 86.
[13] G. M. Cornoldi, *La divina Commedia* (1887); a commentary.

17. Sat.

Ch. 8½ A.M. and Holy Communion. Wrote to Sir E. Watkin MP—J. MacCarthy MP—A. Morley MP—Mr Chisholm[1]—Mr Halliwell Phillips—Mr Marples—Mr Tait—Mr Affleck[2]—Rev. J. Owen. Worked on papers. F. Leveson [Gower] came for the middle hours. Read Greely—Scartazzini on Dante—Cornoldi's Commentary—and Carlyle's Letters.

18. 4 S. Adv.

Ch. mg and evg. Wrote to Mr Whitfield—Mr Price—Rev. F. White—Mr Thorndike Rice. Read the Field-Ingersoll controversy in N.A. Review[3]—Dante & Cornoldi on him. Conversation on the coming journey.

19. M.

Ch. 8¼ A.M. Wrote to Sir E. Watkin—A. Morley—Master of Univy—Mr Thorndike Rice—J. Armstrong—Bull & Auvache—Rev. A. Thomson—A. Hargreaves—F. Bullen—Watsons—W. Glover—F. Statham—Mr Stevens—J. Crook—Mr Spielman—R. Ewen. Worked on papers. Read Greely—Carlyle's Letters. 1¼-3¼ To Chester: saw Mr Bullen. Woodcraft with S. Dined with S. Backgammon.

20. Tu.

Ch. 8½ A.M. Wrote to Ed. Westmr Review—Princ. Librarian Museum BP.—W.L. Gladstone—Mr C. Syon—Mr Macmillan—Mr G.S. Lefevre—and telegrams to Central News—Ly Phillimore—Press Assocn—A. Morley. Worked on papers. After much cons[ideratio]n, we cut down the only noticeable copperbeech (in the Rectory Garden). Read Greely—Carlyle—and O'Connell's Letter to Lord Shrewsbury.[4] Corrected proofs of letter to Ed. Westmr Review.[5]

21. Wed. St Thomas.

Ch. 8¼ AM. Wrote to Ld Northbourne—Mr Ellis Lever—Ld Granville—Mr J.H. Renton—Mr Leonard—Mr Childers—Sir J. Carmichael—Mr Waterton—Mr Macrone—Rev. Mr Fuller—Mr J.A. Baron—Ed. Westmr Review—W.H.G. (Private).[6] Woodcraft at the Rectory. Worked on papers. Saw Mr C. Acland—Mr Theed—Edw. Lyttelton.

22. Th.

Ch. 8¼ A.M. Wrote to Bull & Auvache—Prior Staples PP[7]—Mr Moscheles[8]—Mr P. Campbell—Mr Wilfrid Blunt—Messrs Talbot—Messrs Murray—Rev. G.

---

[1] Henry William Chisholm of the Exchequer; on secret service expenditure in Ireland 1799-1801; Add MS 44502, f. 209.

[2] Perhaps William Affleck of McCutcham and Affleck, merchants.

[3] *N.A.R.*, cxlv. 616 (December 1887). See 31 Dec. 87.

[4] Not traced.   [5] See 8 Dec. 87n.

[6] No letter traced.   [7] Not further identified.

[8] Felix Moscheles, artist; had sent an engraving of Rubinstein (whom Gladstone had wished to meet). See Add MS 44502, f. 221.

Williams—Mr Dowden[1]—T. Baker—Messrs Cook—Mr T. Henri—Mr Currey—
Mr Robertson—Mr Macquoil. Woodcraft at the Rectory. Worked hard on
papers. Much pleased with C. Acland.[2] Read Greely—Carlyle's Letters.

23. Fr.

Ch. 8½ A.M. Wrote to Sir W. Harcourt—Sir E. Watkin—J. Watson & S.—Miss D.
Harvey—Mr A. Morley MP—Rev. W.S.L. Szyrma[3]—Rev. Canon Curteis—Mr
Andrews—Mr Rogers—Mr Martin—Mr Purves—E.A. Judge. Read Greely, now
most absorbing—Carlyle's Letters—One man one Vote.[4] Drive with Lucy.
Worked on books & papers.

24. Sat.

Ch. 8½ A.M. Wrote to Messrs Freshfield—Sir C.A. Wood—Abp of Cashel—Col.
Kinnear—Ed. Kentish Express—Miss Ritter—Mr W. Donegan. Worked much
on books papers & packing for journey. A little woodcraft. Read Greely—
finished—Carlyle's Letters—Jacini on the Holy See.[5]

Xmas Day & S.

Ch 11 A.M. and H.C. Kept the house in evg. Wrote to Ld Northbourne—Mr
Illingworth—Rev. J.G. Rogers—Rev. B.J. Holmes[6]—Rev. Jos Parker—Mr Geo-
hegan—Mr Lund—Mr Keating—Mr Custance—Ld Tweedmouth. Final tidyings
& preparations continued. Read High Churchman on Future Punishment—
Church Army papers[7]—and [blank].

26. M. St Stephen. [Bettishanger, Kent]

Ch. 8½ A.M. So sorry to put by the books. Wrote to M. Waddington—Mrs
Ingram—Mr Vickers—P.A.—C.N. Finished packing. 10¾-7: Near 280 miles to
Bettishanger:[8] ending in 6 inches of snow. A party here. Saw Mr A. Morley—Ld
Spencer—Ld Granville. Read Ld Salisbury's Speech[9]—Le Alleanze d'Italia[10]—
Schley on the Greely Rescue.[11]

---

[1] Giving permission for Edward Dowden to publish his letter in his selection of Sir Henry
Taylor's correspondence; Add MS 44502, ff. 218, 234.
[2] C. T. D. Acland, liberal M.P. for Cornwall; see 18 Aug. 79.
[3] Wladislaw Somerville Lach-Szyrma, historian of Cornwall and vicar of Newlyn.
[4] Untraced.
[5] S. F. Jacini, L'Italia ed il Papato (1887).
[6] Baptist James Holmes, poet and vicar of New Mill, Huddersfield.
[7] Untraced tracts.
[8] House of Lord Northbourne, one of his oldest friends (see 15 Jan. 39).
[9] Salisbury at Derby, T.T., 20 December 1887, 7a, to which Gladstone replied on 27 Dec. 87.
[10] Una Alleanza possibile per un Italiano di Parigi con osservazioni di un Italiano d'Italie Torino (1885).
[11] W. S. Schley, Report . . . [on the] Greely relief expedition of 1884 (1887).

27. Tu. St Joh.

Worked on notes & extracts. Off at 12½ in 12 ins snow to Sandwich & Dover. Spoke 1¼ hour.[1] Back at six. Read the Greely Rescue. Saw Mr Godley—Ld Northbourne. Wrote to Mad. Hyacinthe Loyson—Mr Gennadios—Mr A.T. Rice—Ly Phillimore—Rev. Mr Cox—Mr A. Morley.

28. Wed. [Hotel Bristol, Paris]

9.40 to 6.50: by Sandwich & Folkestone to the Bristol at Paris. Very cold: in other respects a luxurious journey all provided by the S.E. Co. Read Surly Tim's troubles[2]—Mrs Oliphant's Makers of Florence.[3]

29. Th. [On train]

Entered my 79th year. When can I find a moment of sufficient withdrawal to *think*, or when even to say what I have thought.

Saw Capt. Gye (S.E. [Railway]) & M. Lemoinne ([Thomas] Cook) to make arrangements for journey. Wrote to Ld Hampden—Director of Theatre Francais—Ld Acton—Earl Lytton. Saw Dr Chapman (Ed. Westmr Rev.)[4]—M. Grousset—M. Léon Say—and at five P.M. had an interview with the President,[5] a frank straightforward courteous gentleman. Off by the train at 9.5 (nominal) with all the aids which Captain Gye (for S.E. Co), M. Le Moinne (for Cook) and Mr Mather could give us. Notwithstanding the bitter cold we were splendidly made up & slept 9 hours full.

30. Fr.

We breakfasted & had the small luggage at Modane where I remember sleeping, in strong cold, 56 years ago (or 55 y. 10 m.).[6] Then through the tunnel. 2½ hours late in Turin: could not go on till 8.15. Dined well in the Restaurant and walked with H[elen] in the town, which has been made a very fine one & seemed to show wealth and activity. Travelled all night. Read Henry IV.P.2.

31. Sat. [Florence]

Reached Florence by 8: friends met & helped us. The snow joined us S. of Paris & continued all the way. We find the apartment[7] very pleasant & shall soon

---

[1] The Gladstones were attacked with snowballs thrown by an angry tory crowd as they went from the station to the hall; *The Times'* leader denounced 'unmannerly rowdism'; *T.T.*, 28 December 1887, 4a, 7a.

[2] F. E. H. Burnett, *Surly Tim's troubles and other stories* (1877).

[3] M. O. Oliphant, *The makers of Florence* (1876).   [4] See 12 Feb. 52, 8 Dec. 87.

[5] Gladstone arrived in France just after a political crisis; Grévy resigned on 2 December after Clemenceau's defeat of the Rouvier ministry; on 3 December M. Sadi-Carnot, a 'moderate independent', was elected President by the Chamber, Tirard's ministry being formed on the 18th. Gladstone gave interviews to *Le Soleil* and *Le Temps*, in *T.T.*, 31 December 1887, 5b.

[6] See 29 Feb. 32.

[7] The Gladstones stayed in 34 Viale Principe Amedeo, in the apartment of Sir J. P. Lacaita (see 13 Nov. 50). Lacaita's son Charles had recently resigned as liberal M.P. for Dundee because of objections to Gladstone's Irish policies (see 28 Nov. 87n.); the *Daily News* claimed the offer of the apartment reflected J. P. Lacaita's disapproval of his son; see C. Lacaita, *An Italian Englishman* (1933), 263.

settle down into it. The weather however is much more northern than what we left at Hawarden. Helen & I went down to the Cathedral and the two Piazzas and for business. The interior is very disappointing & the dimensions hardly credible though true. Began to write on Ingersoll's reply in the N.A. Review.[1] Read Handbook—Henry IV finished & began Henry V.—Dante, Leben, Zeit, & Werke.[2] Tea at Miss Dickson's: conversation with Col. Denora.[3]

[1] 'Colonel Ingersoll on Christianity. Some remarks on his reply to Dr Field', *N.A.R.*, cxlvi. 481 (May 1888); Ingersoll replied to Gladstone in *N.A.R.*, cxlvi. 601 (June 1888), and there were many other contributions, e.g. in Manning, *N.A.R.*, cxlvi. 241 (September 1888).

[2] See 15 Dec. 87n.

[3] Unidentified; could read 'Denonu'.

Jan 1. S. & Circumcision 1888. [*Florence*]

The near Church at 11 AM with H.C. and 3.30. Luncheon at Miss Dickson's. Wrote to Archbishop Croke. On returning from morning Ch. encountered a body of 1000 or 1200 people come to salute me: & was compelled to see & make a sort of speech to a Commission from among them. Wrote on the Ingersoll reply. Read a good deal in H.S.—Newman, Grammar of Assent[1]—Butler's Analogy[2]—Dantes Leben &c.

2. M.

Tried Mr Tooth's[3] Ch. at 5 but there was no service. Saw the English Consul[4]—Prof. & Madame Villari.[5] Wrote to Sig. A. Parde—Carlo Cesare—Alisse Grifoni. Wrote on Ingersoll's Reply. Read Dante Leben &c.—Ricciardetto I.II.[6]—Handbook. Saw The Consul.

3. Tu.

The weather opened perceptibly. Wrote to Sir J. Lacaita—Sig. Birinna. Wrote on Ingersoll Reply. Saw Mr & Mrs Ross[7]—and [blank.] Another visit to the Cathedral: still impracticable. Read Dante's Leben &c.—Ricciardetto III—Mrs Ross on Italy.

4. Wed.

Weather again more genial. Wrote to King of the Belgians—Mr Temple Leader—Ld Brassey. Wrote on Ingersoll's Reply. Visited the Pitti Collection: we wind up with coffee at Doney's.[8] Read Dante's Leben &c.—Ricciardetto—Mrs Ross, Italian Sketches. Saw Mr Tuckermann.

5. Th.

Wrote to Mr Leader. Wrote on Ingersoll's Reply. Read Scartazzini Dante's Leben—Ricciardetto—Mrs Ross—Articles on Vincigliata & on Ld Carteret in Littell's well printed Periodical.[9] Saw Capt. Elliot

Prof. Villari	with their
The Prefect	ladies
Greek Consul	

---

[1] See 20 Mar. 70.

[2] See 8 Oct. 31.

[3] Charles Tooth, d. 1894; Anglican chaplain at St. Mark's, Florence, from 1884.

[4] (Sir) Dominic Ellis Colnaghi, 1838–1908; once Stratford de Redcliffe's secretary; consul at Florence 1881–96.

[5] The Dante scholar (see 11 July 65) and his wife.

[6] Perhaps N. Forteguerri, *Ricciardetto*, 2v. (1766).

[7] Henry James Ross and his wife Janet Ann Ross, author of *Italian sketches* (1887).

[8] Doney and Neveux, restaurant in Via Tornabuoni.

[9] *Littell's Living Age*, 175, 668, 695; published in Boston, U.S.A.

Visited the Academia—Santa Croce: has more effect of *space* than the Duomo. NB position of Morghen figure.[1] At One A.M. dear Harry arrived to pay us a flying visit on his way to India.

6. *Epiph. & C.s birthday.*

She is a marvel of help and energy. God be with her evermore.

Church at 11 and H.C. Saw Mr Leader[2] & revived old times. Wrote to Mr Vickers—Mr Steele—Sig. Benucci—Sig. Cortemiglia—H.H. Gordon—A.B. Wylde—President Constitl Association. Studied the work in the Piazza. Read Scartazzini—Ricciardetto—19th Cent. on Norway—Cremation—& other Articles.[3]

7. *Sat.*

Weather now mild but very dull. We went with Harry to the Uffizio & Santa Croce. Read Scartazzini on Dante—Ricciardetto—and Italian Sketches. Wrote to Comitato XX Settembre—Controller returned Letter Office—Mrs Robinson—Mary Drew—Sig. Catalani—Capt. Plowden—Sir J. Lacaita—M. Gaulin—Rev. V. Marshall—Mr Vickers.

8. *1 S. Epiph.*

Church mg & aftn. (Mr Tooth's). Tea with Miss Wimbush to see Miss Cobden.[4] Saw Mr Leader. Tel. to H.J.G. to authorize hiring house. Read Perowne on Pentateuch[5]—Beugnot Chute du Paganisme[6]—Deuteronomy—Stephen's answer to Mivart.[7]

9. *M.*

Wrote to Prof. de Marzo—Marchese A. di Gregorio—Sig. Malinverni—Sig. de Nino—Sig. Marcotti.[8] Read Ricciardetto—Scartazzini on Dante—Porciani on the Duomo[9]—Conestabile Chiesa e Patria.[10] Luncheon at Bello Sguardo:[11] in deep

---

[1] Monument by Fantacchiotti to Raphael Morghen, d. 1833, engraver, placed at the corner of the transept and left aisle of S. Croce.

[2] J. Temple Leader, his undergraduate friend; later a radical M.P.; retired to Florence (see 23 Oct. 29). On this visit, Leader acted as Gladstone's 'cicerone', surprised him by his vitality, and interested him in Tuscan philology (Leader's entry in *D.N.B.*). See also J. T. Leader, *Philological pastimes of an Englishman in Tuscany, with some letters of Gladstone to John Temple Leader (1898)*.

[3] *N.C.*, xxiii. 1, 54 (January 1888).

[4] The politician's daughter, with whom Gladstone, as literary executor, had dealings.

[5] T. T. Perowne, probably *The essential coherence of the old and new testaments* (1858).

[6] A. A. Beugnot, *Histoire de la destruction du paganisme en Occident*, 2v. (1835); Gladstone's notes at Add MS 44794, f. 177.

[7] J. F. Stephen on Mivart in *N.C.*, xxiii. 115 (January 1888).

[8] Giuseppe Marcotti, Leader's friend and co-author.

[9] G. Porciani, *In omaggio a S. Maria del Fiore, miracolo d'arte: ricordo artistico-letterario* (1887).

[10] Untraced work, probably by Count Carlo Conestabile, who published on socio-political questions.

[11] The Villa Bello Sguardo, near Monte Oliveto, with one of the finest views of Florence.

haze. She most kind. Saw Count Conestabile—Sig. Comandi. Made acquaintance with Francheschini.[1] Vale la pena.[2]

10. Tu.

Wrote to Mr A. Morley—Parliamentary Circular—Ed. D. News—Mr Colnaghi.
Out for business & bookbuying. Read Scartazzini on Dante—finished Chiesa &
Patria—Finished C.X. of Ricciardetto: there is much talent but I am weary and
shall leave off. Read Westmr Rev. on Dr Johnson[3]—finished [blank] on
Duomo—read Rucellai on the Jubilee.[4] Entrapped into a tea party at Miss Dick-
son's.

11. Wed.

Wrote to Mad. Wolfosclea (?)[5]—Pres. Council of Ministers[6]—British Consul.
Saw British Consul respecting intended Deputation. 12–5¼. Mr Leader took us
to Majano: we saw the Villa, Fattoria[7] in all its departments, the Church, & had
luncheon with much Italian & excellent *Vin Santo*.[8] Also I saw the Dome with
the setting sun behind it, and had never really seen it before, I thought. Read
Scartazzini on Dante[9]—Lecture on Hudson[10]—Berni (ed altri) Versi
Burleschi[11]—Vita Nuova & Fraticelli on it.[12]

12. Th.

Wrote to Mr E.E. Smith—Sig. Parini—W.H.G.—Scottish Leader—J.F. Murphy.
Did a good deal of work today in bookseller's shops & on their catalogues. With
H. to S. M[aria] Novella (an imposing Church with objects of great interest)
Baptistery & front of Dante's House. Read Berni—Scartazzini on Dante—Villari
Lettere Meridionali.[13]

13. Fr.

Wrote to The English Consul—Sig. Dotti (Librajo.) 12–5½. With Leader to
Fiesole (Etruscan Wall & Cathedral both very noteworthy) then by a delightful
drive to Vincigliata, a curious fabric with interesting & one or two very beautiful
objects.[14] He has been superlatively kind. Saw Sig. Corsi. Read Scartazzini—
Westm. Rev. on Isle of Man.[15]—Villari Lettere Meridionali.

[1] Probably Pietro Franceschini of Florence; wrote on Tuscan churches.
[2] 'Worth the trouble'.   [3] *Westminster Review*, cxxix. 12 (January 1888).
[4] G. Rucellai, *Il giubileo dell'anno 1450 con avvertenza di Giuseppe Marcotti* (1887).
[5] Gladstone's query; not further identified.
[6] i.e. Crispi, who had written a note of welcome; Add MS 44503, f. 3.
[7] 'Farm management'.
[8] Leader owned and restored two villas at Majano, near Florence, both named Villa Temple
Leader, one having a swimming pool (*D.N.B.*).   [9] See 15 Dec. 87.
[10] Not found; the deceased Sir J. Hudson (see 31 Jan. 59) was British envoy to Piedmont 1852–63.
[11] See 17 Jan. 52.
[12] P. Fraticelli, *Storia della vita di Dante* (1861); recommended by Villari; Add MS. 44503, f. 6.
[13] P. Villari, *Le lettere meridionali ed altri scritti sulla questione sociale in Italia* (1878).
[14] Castello di Vincigliata, a medieval castle by Majano, owned and restored by J. T. Leader.
[15] *Westminster Review*, cxxix. 29 (January 1888).

14. Sat.

Wrote to The English Consul—Sir J. Lacaita—Mr Leader—Sig. Addorio—Count Jacini.[1] Luncheon with Duchess of Sermoneta who was most kind. Bookhunting. Received the Constitutional Deputation: & made them a reply of about 20 min. the heads of which I had put down in English for publication.[2] Saw Mrs Ross (Tuscan friend)—March. della Staffetta, ditto. S. and his wife arrived. Revised a little of Ingersoll MS.[3] Read Scartazzini on Dante—Siga. Ruffino's Novellette[4]—and [blank.]

15.

Ch. 11 AM (with HC) and 5 P.M. Wrote to Rev. Mr [blank]. Revised more of Ingersoll MS. Read Beugnot Chute &c.—Scartazzini on Dante.

16. M.

Wrote to Mr Nicoll BP.—Col. Wilkinson—Siga. Ruffini—Mr W.H. Rideing—Mr A. Smith. Corrected & dispatched proofs of the Homeric Here.[5] Bookhunting. Saw Mad. French[6] (at Villa Rondinelli) very noteworthy—Countess Tolstoi[7]—Marchese Ricca. Read Scartazzini's Dante—Madame Ruffino.

17. Tu.

Wrote to Mr Tuckermann—Mad. de Vita—Count? Jacini—Miss Cunninghame—Ld Granville—Cav. Adriani—Mr Thorndike Rice. Revising & continuing Ingersoll MS. Saw Lady Hudson.[8] We visited the Villa Stibbort and its very remarkable collections. Read Scartazzini on Dante—Leader Simpatie di Majano[9]—Madame Ruffino.

18. Wed.

Wrote to Mr Morley—Mr Thorndike Rice—Mr Norton—The English Consul. 12–5. To Majano again, and the quarries, with Mr Leader. Book buying at Viviani's, and saw Isolina. Backgammon with S.E.G. on this (& also former) evenings. Read Scartazzini on Dante—Ingersoll's Letter: & other articles in N.A.R.[10]

19. Th.

Wrote to Mr Macquoil—Siga. de Vita BP—Mr W. Mercer—Mr H.C. Burdett. $11\frac{1}{4}$–$3\frac{1}{4}$. By the (wretched) road railway to Castagnole:[11] where we had excellent

---

[1] Stephano Jacini, Italian senator and writer on social questions; see Add MS 44503, f. 13.

[2] No report found; correspondence on the Deputation with Colnaghi, the consul, Add MS 44503, f. 8.   [3] See 31 Dec. 87.

[4] Untraced.   [5] See 25 Apr. 87.   [6] Not further identified.

[7] Probably Countess Ina Tolstoy; see 27 Aug. 87.

[8] Widow of Sir J. Hudson; see 11 Jan. 88.

[9] Probably J. T. Leader, *La Parrocchia di S. Martino a Majano. Cenni storici* (1875).

[10] R. G. Ingersoll, 'Another letter to Dr. Field', *N.A.R.*, cxlvi. 31 (January 1888).

[11] The Ross's villa about 8 miles outside Florence; the train broke down two miles short of the villa.

luncheon & excellent company: also good music, beautiful objects, & bird and plant collections. Saw Duchess of Sermoneta—Mrs Ross—Mrs Burnett[1]—The R. Spencers—The Consul. Then to dinner with Madame Tcheharcheff: small party but many interesting people. Read Scartazzini—Roundell on Ireland.[2]

20. Fr.

Wrote to Mr A.Th. Rice—Sig. S. Carlo—and draft for the Municipio. Went to the function in S. Sebastiano: & to Dottis. Finished off my article for the N.A.R.[3] and dispatched it: under the ridiculous rules of registration. Mr Leader took us to Pal[azzo] Pitti: an interior of extraordinary magnificence, with (I think) few faults of taste. Read Scartazzini's Dante—Siga. Ruffino, finished—Boissier on St Augustine[4]—Ld Hobart's Remains.[5]

21. Sat.

Wrote to Mr Leader[6]—Sig. Alessandro—Cav. Vircis—Sig. Cont. de Nino—Mons. Braun—Dott. Manzini—Mr Morgan—Sig. Cerreti—Messrs Cook—Mr Leader. Wrote in Italian a reply to the Municipio but am afraid & cannot decide whether to send it or my English draft.[7] Spent 1 to $1\frac{1}{2}$ hour in the perishing cold of St Mark's which has the freezing title of Museum.[8] The greatest gems I thought were the Crucifixion in the Chapter House, & the framed Madonna & Infant in the Cell No 43. We went to a luncheon party at Bello Sguardo: pleasant people, saw the digging in the garden, & planted a tree. Read Scartazzini's Dante—Hobart's Remains—Rev. 2. M. on St Augustine. In St Mark I must also record the wonderfully beautiful Coronation of BVM and the immense interest attaching to the banner & relics of Savonarola.[9]

---

[1] Frances Eliza Hodgson Burnett, 1849–1924, novelist; Gladstone had told her friend, Janet Ross, that he wished to meet her, having read her book (see 12 Nov. 87). For her account, see A. Thwaite, *Waiting for the party* (1974), 107 ff.: 'he told me he believed the book [*Little Lord Fauntleroy*] would have great effect in bringing about added good feeling between the two nations and making them understand each other. . . . Afterwards I took Mr and Mrs Gladstone home and it was a lovely drive. He was very much agitated because he thought they had taken possession of my carriage—and so was Mrs Gladstone. They were quite insubordinate at first and wanted to sit in the back seat, but I tucked myself into it and coaxed and beguiled them and related suitable anecdotes until they were soothed and resigned, and at the end of the drive he said, "I will no longer feel remorse, Mrs Burnett, I will only blush a little," and, of course, I replied, "Then you will be very wicked—to blush at having given a pleasure."'

[2] Not found.

[3] See 15 Dec. 87n.

[4] G. Boissier on St. Augustine in *Revue des Deux Mondes*, lxxxv. 43 (January 1888).

[5] V. H. Hobart, Lord Hobart, *Essays and miscellaneous writings*, 2v. (1885).

[6] Sending Leader a copy of his photograph taken in Paris; facsimile of letter in J. T. Leader, *Philological pastimes of an Englishman in Tuscany, with some letters of Gladstone to John Temple Leader* (1898), 7.

[7] Untraced.

[8] Museo di San Marco, with Fra Angelico's magnificent frescoes decorating the monks' cells.

[9] Once an inmate of the monastery, which preserved his crucifix and banner.

22 S. 3 Epiph.

Kept my bed from cold, the price of St Mark's yesterday. Read the prayers mg:
S.E.G. gave Service 7 P.M. Finished Saint Augustine. Read Beugnot—Scartazzini. The study of Dante is intensely sabbatical.

23. M.

Rose at 10.30. Wrote to Mr Grogan Tel.—The Direttore of Posts for Rosa—and
wrote out & delivered my Italian letter to March. Torrigiani the Sindaco.[1] Paid a
formal visit to the Palazzo Vecchio & was conducted over it. The true idea of
magnificence in decoration seems to have died out of the world in these our
days. Among the booksellers: some Churches: & had tea with Miss Lawley.[2]
Saw Baron Podastà—Countess A. Rasponi. Finished Scartazzini's really great
work.[3] Read Rev. 2 M. Souvenirs Diplomatiques.[4] Began Doyle's Reminiscences.[5] Backg[ammon] with SEG.

24. Tu.

Wrote to Cav. Fenzi—Mad. Tchhatchef [sic]—Mr J. Thaddeus[6]—Director of
Rass. Italiana—Sig. Domenico Luenze(?) Turin—Sig. B. Malatesta—Ed. Oswestry
Advertiser.[7] Read Beugnot—Doyle's Reminiscences—and Roman de Violette.[8]
Duchess of S[ermoneta] took me to the Torrigiani palace: a pleasing family. We
all saw the beautiful pictures. I was at a party there 50 years ago.[9] Went to
Franchi bookseller's.

25. Wed. St Paul.

But again I did not rise till 11. Wrote to The Barone Ricasoli[10]—Lord Acton—Mr
Spencer—Sig. B. Facceo. Orsi studio for drawing & singing: then to the book-
sellers. Saw The Consul—Professor Villari. Read Beugnot (& worked on it)—
Doyle's Reminiscences—Marzio's Crucifix[11]—& again looked into Roman de
Violette: a *bad* book.

---

[1] The mayor of Florence.

[2] Probably Alethea Jane Lawley, da. of 2nd Baron Wenlock; she m. 1890 Cav. Prof. Taddeo Wiel
of Venice.

[3] See 31 Dec. 87.

[4] *Revue des Deux Mondes*, lxxxv. 70 (January 1888).

[5] Sir F. H. C. Doyle, *Reminiscences and opinions 1813-1885* (1886), with much on Gladstone's
youth, and bitter comments on his recent career: 'it is extremely painful to me that I have to struggle
with a continually increasing dislike of Mr. Gladstone as a statesman, and a continually deepening
distrust of his character as a man'. The book ends with a verse tribute to Gordon (Doyle's son was
killed in the Sudan): '. . . a mighty life is marred By Babblers, without heart or shame, Who played it,
as men play a card, To win their worthless Party-game'. See 15 Oct. 86, 1 Feb. 88.

[6] Henry Jones Thaddeus, artist; see 27 Jan. 88.

[7] Supporting the resolution on Irish policy of the Shropshire/Welsh clergy; *T.T.*, 1 February
1888, 9f.

[8] Probably *Le roman de Violette. Oeuvre posthume d'une célébrité masquée* (1870).

[9] See 29 Sept. 38.

[10] Vicenzo Ricasoli, brother of Bettino Ricasoli, Italian statesman; see Add MS 44503, f. 23.

[11] A. G. di Marzo, *La Croce bianca in campo rosso vaticinata nella Divina Commedia nel risorgimento
d'Italia* (1885).

26. Th.

Stiff fighting off cold. Rose at 11. Wrote to Prefect of Messina—Mr Burrowes—Mr Mackaffie—Sig. Caprano—Sig. Rolandi. Again at the Booksellers', flying (for me) rather high. We went to the Bargello—the Opera del Duomo—the Palazzo Riccardi—& the Cathedral: under the instructed auspices of Leader. I have no hope of recollecting more than a very small part of what we saw & found well worthy of being remembered. Read Beugnot—Marzio's Crucifix—Doyle's Recollections.

27. Fr.

Wrote to Mr Thorndike Rice—Messrs Cook—Ed. Daily News—Mrs Ingram—Sir J. Lacaita—Sig. Brogi. Sat to Jones Thaddeus $11\frac{1}{2}$-$1\frac{1}{2}$.[1] Luncheon with the Miss Horners.[2] Saw Mr Childers. $2\frac{3}{4}$-6. With Mr Leader to the Certosa,[3] which we saw minutely, with a most kind reception. Read Beugnot—Doyle—Mazzio's [*sic*] Crucifix.

28. Sat.

The SEGs went off early. Wrote to The Barons Ricasoli—Siga. C. de Vita. We went to luncheon at the Villa Palmieri:[4] kind & pleasant company. Then some duty calls. Dined with the Duchess of Sermoneta[5] and went with her to the (junior) Torrigiani evening party. Much pleased with the interior of that family. The English tongue in great vogue. Finished Marzio's Crucifix. Read Beugnot—Doyle.

29. Septa S.

Ch mg with H.C. & Amn Ch. aft. Childers officiated; at 83 he has the voice of a man of 30.[6] Wrote to A. Morley—and Messrs. Cook. Read Beugnot—Rassegna Nazionale: divers articles, not very National—Bellarmini de Arte bene Moriendi[7]—Carducci's Dante.[8]

---

[1] Henry Jones Thaddeus, Irish portrait painter; portrait now in the Reform Club, London; engraving of it is in *Magazine of Art*, xii. 87 (January 1889).

[2] One of them was Susan Horner; they lived at 92 Viale Petrarca; Gladstone presented them with *The makers of modern Florence*; Hawn P.

[3] Certosa di Val d'Ema, monastery at the confluence of the Ema and the Greve, resembling a medieval fortress.

[4] Owned by James Ludovic Lindsay, 1847-1913, 26th Earl of Crawford and Balcarres, and his wife Emily Florence, *née* Wilbraham; he was a tory and an artistic patron. The Queen stayed at this villa shortly after Gladstone's visit.

[5] Of English birth; see 12 Nov. 66.

[6] Charles Childers, canon of Gibraltar and uncle of the politician; see 21 Feb. 29.

[7] St. Robert Bellarmino, *De arte bene moriendi. Libri duo* (1621).

[8] G. A. G. Carducci, *L'Opera di Dante. Discorso* (1888).

30. M.

Wrote to Sig. C. Corsi—A. Morley MP.—W.H.G.—Conn. Carotti—J.A. Godley—English Consul—Sig. Quaringhi—Ed. Chester Chronicle.[1] Sat again to Thaddeus ¾ hour. Saw studios of Hildebrand (Dr Döllinger) and Saul—Deserted Church with the beautiful monument (Levade Qu R.) Then the Salvador so justly called la mia bella villanella: in the simple beauty of its proportions[2]—and the San Miniato, a noble and beautiful interior: with its privileged burying ground, into which I regret to find that the obelisk has been creeping.[3] Read Beugnot—Doyle—and Bonghi's article on W.E.G. in the Antologia.[4] Wrote a little on Ireland.[5]

31. Tu.

Wrote to G. Brogi. Read Beugnot—Doyle. The cold seized me: but was beaten by 5 hours on my back. 12¼-2¼. With Villari to the Laurenziana. Ab. Anziani singularly courteous & pleasing. Delighted: especially with the Torelli Epistolario, and the building.[6] Dined with M. and Mad. Rasponi: greatly pleased with that interior. Sat to Alinari for my photograph—at Leader's special request.

Wed. Feb. 1. 88.

Wrote to Duca di Castellaneta—Sig. R. Fabris—Sir J. Lacaita—Sig. F. Scalera—Sig. Angeloni. Mr Leader took us to the Petraja a most attractive palace villa: but with the lowering association of Rosina.[7] Then to the neigh[b]our garden, the casino, and business. Read Beugnot. Finished Doyle. The silly parts might be cut out.[8] We dined at Prof. Villari's: an interesting party. I was obliged to reply after dinner to a complimentary speech from him.

2. Th. Purification.

Wrote to Ly Aberdeen Tel. Went (only) to the Annunziata: an imposing service and music. Finished Beugnot. Read the Rucellai Embassay to France (began).[9] Visited the Chapels. Saw The Consul—Sig. Dotti—March. Govoni. Dined at the Duchess of Sermoneta's. Made preparation of books for packing.

---

[1] Supporting resolution of Cheshire/Flintshire clergy on Irish policy; *T.T.*, 8 February 1888, 11 f.

[2] San Salvatore, the renaissance church of the Ognissanti, recently restored.

[3] The church and the whole hill of San Miniato, S.E. of Florence, were used as a burial ground in the late 19th century, with many examples of contemporary sculpture.

[4] Article by R. Bongi of Naples, later in correspondence; Hawn P.

[5] 'Further Notes and Queries on the Irish Demand', *C.R.*, liii, 321 (March 1888), reprinted in *Special aspects*.

[6] Biblioteca Laurenziana, the library of Cosimo the Elder and the Medici, the building designed by Michelangelo.

[7] Villa Petraia, once owned by the Brunelleschi, later by the Medici; in 1888 the royal palace in Florence; before 1870 it was much used by Victor Emmanuel II and his mistress, Rosina, Countess of Mirafiore.

[8] See 23 Jan. 88n.

[9] G. F. Rucellai, *Un Ambasciata. Diario . . . pubblicato da J. Temple Leader e G. Marcotti* (1884).

3. Fr.

Wrote to Rect. Univ. Perugia—Mr A. Morley—Siga. Molina—Rev. Mr Dakin[1]—
Contemp. Rev.—Sig. Dotti—Rev. E. Dakin. Calls & farewells with incessant stir:
Leader, Duchess of S., the Alfieri Serbagnos, the Rasponis, Pss. Corsini, De Nino &
others. Saw Agenzia Stefani—Photographer Alinari. Saw S. Salvi—also Madd. de'
Pazzi with the marvellously beautiful P. Perugino: & the Raphael Cenacolo.[2] Also
arranged matters with Dotti and at the Bank. Read Rucellai's Ambasciata—and
[blank.]

4. Sat. [Cannes]

Up at 6¼. Adieus at 7.30. Off from F[lorence] at 8: Ventimiglia say 6.30. Cannes
at 10. Most kindly received by the Actons.[3] Conversation with him. Read Guerrazzi's Isabella Orsini.[4] Many salutations by the way.

5. Sexa S.

St Paul's Ch 11 A.M. and H.C. Excellent sermon. A turbid Sunday. Luncheon at
Mrs Vyner's. Drive round Cannes. Dinner of 12: three very pleasant royalties,
and 6 others. Wrote to Sir E. Watkin and [blank.] Read Villari's (new)
Savonarola.[5] Saw D.N. Correspondent.[6]

6. M.

Wrote to Mr Jeaffreson—The Crown Princess—Sir Thos G. Made the journey
arrangements with the Cook representative. 11–12½. Conversation with the
Emperor of Brazil[7] in French. An effort. Saw also the very quiet Empress,[8] & the
Chamberlain or friend. A round of calls. Acton framed for me a sentiment for the
Grand Duchess's Book! Plague on all such books. Read Isabella Orsini—Sybel
on Burke & Ireland, (a pretentious poor affair)[9]—Scartazzini's Nachtrage.[10]

---

[1] Edward Dakin, nonconformist minister; Hawn P.
[2] Santa Maria Maddelena de' Pazzi with, in the adjacent house, a large fresco of Christ on the
cross by Perugino; the Raphael 'Cenacolo' in the refectory of the nearby S. Onofrio is now attributed to Perugino.
[3] Acton had arranged rooms for the Gladstones in the Hotel Montfleury.
[4] F. D. Guerrazzi, *Isabella Orsini, duchessa di Bracciano* (1844).
[5] P. Villari, *La Storia di Girolamo Savonarola e de' suoi tempi*, 2v. (1859–61, new ed. 1887–8); see
20 May 61.
[6] 'One interesting fact he particularly wished me to mention through the columns of the *Daily
News*. A report had been circulated that he occupied Sir J. Lacaita's villa at Florence as a sort of
political protest against the late member for Dundee [i.e. Lacaita's son]. This Mr Gladstone says is
utterly unfounded . . .'; 'Mr Gladstone at Cannes', *D.N.*, 6 February 1888, 5f.
[7] Pedro II, 1825–91; he was deposed next year and d. in Paris.
[8] Theresa of Naples, 1822–89.
[9] H. C. L. von Sybel, 'Edmund Burke und Irland', *Kleine Historische Schriften*, i (1863).
[10] Perhaps G. B. Scartazzini, *Zur Dante-Bibliographie* (1871).

Examined Göthe's Cinque Maggio[1] with A[cton]—curious results. Conversation with him on Salisbury's 'History'.[2]

7. Tu. [On train]

More picking of Acton's brains. Read Isabella Orsini—Villari's Savonarola. Saw Miss Lee: Amn of the older stamp.[3] Off by the 1.38 P.M: many kind farewells.

8. Wed. [London]

Prosperous journey. The passage scarcely over an hour! London soon after 7. Great kindness & help everywhere: I seemed to travel like a babe in arms: what I am now fit for. Pleasant first impressions of the new house 16 James St.[4] Not really a *street* here. Read Isabella Orsini—Villari's Savonarola. $9\frac{1}{2}$–11. Conclave (about 17) on the Speech. Saw Rosebery—Granville—A. Morley.

9. Th.

The process of settling down began. Studied the speech & relative papers. Saw A. Morley—Herbert G—Sir A. West—Sir C. Russell—and others. Dined with the Wests. H. of C. $4\frac{1}{2}$–8. Spoke 1 hour: with the object of clearing a little the work of the Session.[5] Wrote to [blank] Tel.

So I am planted once more in London, for a life of contention:[6] how hateful, but how deserved. Read Isabella Orsini.

10. Fr.

Read Guerrazzi and Villari. H. of C. $4\frac{1}{2}$–8.[7] Saw Mr Morley—Mr A. Morley—S. Lyttelton—G. Russell—Harry Drew—Mr Stuart Rendell—Scotts—Mr W.H. Smith—Mr Grogan—Mr Childers—Mr Macmillan. Wrote to Robertson & Nicholson—Mr Parnell (cancelled)[8]—Pres. Sydney National League—Mr Sec. Matthews[9]—Mr Dunphy—Mr Wilkinson. Further settling down.

---

[1] In 1822, Goethe translated Manzoni's ode 'In morte di Napoleone (il cinque Maggio)' as 'Der fünfte Mai. Ode von Alexander Manzoni' (Weimar ed. of his works, iii. 204); the poem leaves open the question of Napoleon's future fame, but pays homage to his 'mighty creativity'. Gladstone had himself tr. Manzoni's ode into English: *Translations by Lord Lyttelton and... W. E. Gladstone* (1861), 120.

[2] Perhaps a reference to Salisbury's speech on Ireland in Liverpool on 12 January 1888; Cecil, *Salisbury*, iv. 165–6.

[3] Probably the novelist; see 24 Nov. 88.

[4] The Gladstones rented 16 St James Street from Major John Scott Napier.

[5] *H* 322. 71.

[6] Particularly so at present; Salisbury's public remark that 'the great majority of Conservatives would rather not have a conversation with him [Gladstone]' was condemned by Granville and Kimberley in the Lords next day; Salisbury maintained he 'spoke as to a fact I observed with respect to others', but did not regret that this was the case; *H* 322. 133–8.

[7] Queen's speech; *H* 322. 158.

[8] To Parnell (cancelled): 'I forward you herewith a draft for five hundred pounds (now made payable to bearer) which has been sent to me by the President of the National League in Sydney with a request for its transmission to the proper quarters ...'; Add MS 44503, f. 38.

[9] i.e. Henry Matthews, home secretary; see 7 May 79.

11. Sat.

Wrote to W.H.G.—Mr A. Sidgwick[1]—Mr A. Morley—Lady Phillimore—Maharajah Holkar. Saw Mr Quaritch's notable Bibliographer—Ld Herschel—Mr Murray—Mr Stuart MP—The Aberdeens. Breakfasted at Grillions. Chamberlain blackballed! Herschell & I voting for: no other Home Ruler present. 2-5¼. Carried rather malgrè moi[2] to the great Circus.

12. Quinqua S.

Eaton Chapel mg and Guards Chapel 6 PM. Read Villari's Savonarola—Q.R. on R.C.s in England (pt)[3]—Bellarmini de Arte bene mor.—Sayce Hibbert Lecture.[4] Wrote to Mr P. Bunting.

13. M.

Wrote to Mr Carpenter—Mr Wilfrid Blunt[5]—Mr Firth—Mr Schnadhorst—& minutes. Read Q.R. on RC.s (finished)—Isabella Orsini finished. H of C. 4¼-8 and 10-11¾. Spoke on privilege.[6] Saw Sir W. Harcourt—Sir C. Russell—A. Morley—Mr Childers—Ld Kimberley—Ld Justice Bowen[7]—Ld Cavan—S. Lyttelton—Mr Godley. Dined at Grillions. Worked on Irish Notes & Queries.[8]

14. Tu.

Wrote to Messrs Bailey—Mr Carpenter—Mrs Crawfurd—Mr Vickers—Mr A. Winn—Mr W.H. Smith. H. of C. 4½-8.[9] Dined at Ld Aberdeen's. Saw S. Lyttelton—Lady A.—Sir W. Harcourt—Lady Spencer—Mr A. Morley. Read Q.R. on The Mammoth[10]—Villari's Savonarola (finished II). Wrote on Irish Notes & Queries.

15. Ash Wed.

Guards Chapel 11 AM. Wrote to Mr A. Morley—Mr Reader—Mr Bunting—Lord Acton—& minutes. Worked long & hard on Notes & Queries for Ireland. Saw Ld Granville—S.L. Read Savonarola.

---

[1] Arthur Sidgwick, d. 1920; classicist; fellow of Corpus, Oxford, from 1882; had sent a memorial of support signed by 74 resident graduates of Oxford University to counter the memorial to Hartington of 1887, which 'has given rise in many quarters to the idea that Oxford is all against Home Rule'. Sidgwick emphasised 'the number of *History* students & teachers who have signed'; Add MS 44503, f. 34.

[2] 'despite myself'.

[3] *Q.R.*, clxvi. 31 (January 1888).

[4] See 11 Feb. 87.

[5] Good wishes for a by-election; grateful reply from Lady Anne Blunt; Add MS 44503, f. 50.

[6] Wrongful arrest of P. O'Brien; *H* 322. 284.

[7] Charles Synge Christopher Bowen, 1835-94; assistant prosecutor in Tichborne case; H. H. Asquith's senior; judge 1879; lord of appeal 1893; became quite a close friend of Gladstone.

[8] See 30 Jan. 88.

[9] Queen's speech; *H* 322. 385.

[10] *Q.R.*, clxvi. 112 (January 1888).

16. Th.

Wrote to Ld Spencer—Mr Clancy MP—Mr Bryce—Ld Granville—& minutes. Worked long on Irish papers. Read Savonarola—[blank] on Engl. Monasteries. H. of C. $4\frac{1}{2}$–8.[1]

17. Fr.

Worked on Irish papers & arr. heads for Speech. H. of C. $4\frac{3}{4}$–$8\frac{3}{4}$ and 11–$1\frac{3}{4}$. Spoke over 2 hours & voted in 229 to 317: a satisfactory division under the circumstances.[2] Read Savonarola—Memoirs of Latude.[3] Saw Ld Spencer—S. Lyttelton.

18. Sat. [The Durdans, Epsom]

Rose at 12.30. Wrote to Canon MacColl—Mr A. Sutton—Mr A. Reader—and minutes. Dined at Mr Armitstead's. To the Durdans[4] afterwards. Worked in London Lib. & at home for Irish MS. Read Savonarola—Latude's Narrative—Macnevin's Hist. Volunteers.[5]

19. 1 S.L.

Snow & ill weather. Church 11 AM—prayers 7 PM in C.s room. Wrote to Mr Balfour. Read Sayce—Villari's Savonarola—Bellarmini de Arte &c.[6] Conversation with R[osebery] on characters of C., D., Dalhousie, Morley. And on the Continental outlook. With Mr Samson on O.T.

20. M. [London]

Wrote to Messrs. Franchi—Mr Guinness Rogers—and minutes. A quiet forenoon at the D. to push on my MS. Conversation with Rosebery on his plan for meetings.[7] Read Savonarola—Nevinson's [sc. MacNevin's] Hist. Volunteers. H. of C. $4\frac{3}{4}$–$7\frac{1}{2}$.[8] Saw A. Morley & S.L. Dined with the Northbournes.

21. Tu.

Wrote to Mr Arnold White[9]—Messrs Ballantyne Hansen & Co (BP)—and minutes. H. of C. $4\frac{3}{4}$–$6\frac{3}{4}$.[10] Bitter cold continues. Finished revised & sent off MS. Saw S.L.—Ld Granville—Mr Morley—Mr A. Morley—Mr Bryce—Mr Buchanan. Read Villari's Savonarola—Nevinson's [sc. MacNevin's] Hist. Volunteers. Finished Latude.

---

[1] Queen's Speech; H 322. 566.
[2] Queen's Speech: Parnell's amndt. on the Crimes Act and Land Act 1887; H 322. 746.
[3] J. H. Masers de Latude, Memoirs . . . during a confinement of thirty-five years in the State prisons of France (1787).
[4] Rosebery's house by the race course.
[5] T. MacNevin, The history of the volunteers of 1782 (1845).
[6] See 29 Jan. 88.
[7] i.e. for Midlothian.
[8] Queen's Speech: agricultural depression; H 322. 883.
[9] Exchange with him on the Plan of Campaign; T.T., 27 February 1888, 7c and Add MS 44503, f. 73.
[10] Queen's Speech: Scottish crofters; H 322. 1010.

22. Wed.

Wrote to Mr A. Morley—Sir H. Ponsonby—Mr Knowles—Rev. Aubrey Moore[1]—
Mr D.T. Smith—and minutes. H of C. $2\frac{1}{4}$-5: Scotch Farmers, & Foreign Affairs.[2]
Read L'Apôtre Bibliographique[3]—Villari's Savonarola—Bp Vaughan on the
Pope's sufferings.[4] Saw Mr Asher[5]—Mr A. Morley—Mr Reddington—Mr Hamil-
ton—A. Lyttelton—S. Lyttelton—Sir E. Watkin. Seven to dinner.

23. Th.

Wrote to Messrs. Ballantyne BP—Mr Allenson Winter—Mr J.O. Owen—Mr Wilkinson—Mr R. Brown jun.—Mr Quilter—Mr Head—Mr H. de Burgh—Mr Bunting B.P. Corrected proofs of MS on Ireland. Saw Sir H. Ponsonby (Florence)[6]—S.
Lyttelton—Mad. Novikoff—Mr Quaritch—Mr W.H. Smith—Mr. A. Morley—The
Speaker—S. Lady Lyttelton. Dined at Lucy's. H. of C. $4\frac{3}{4}$-$7\frac{3}{4}$.[7] Read Savonarola—Apôtre Bibliographique.

24. Fr. [The Durdans]

Wrote to Lady A. Blunt l.l.—Lord Acton—Mr Quaritch—H.N.G.—Mr Murray—
W.H.G.—Mr A. Morley—Mr Webster MP—Messrs. Cook—Cav. Cadorna—Mrs
Bolton—Madame Novikoff—Sir J. Fergusson (O) & minutes. H. of C. $4\frac{3}{4}$-$6\frac{1}{4}$.[8] Saw
S. Lyttelton—Mr Childers—Mr A. Morley—The Speaker. Read Villari—Letters
from Edinburgh.[9] To Durdans at 6.15.

25. Sat.

Prepared draft to Childers. Conversation with Rosebery. Drove to Mr Bryant's.
Read Ewald's Sir R. Walpole[10]—Villari's Savonarola—Letters from Edinburgh.

26. 2 S.L.

Ch mg. Afternoon prayers in C.s room. Wrote to Mrs Thistlethwayte—Mr
Childers—Mrs Bolton—Mr Smith. Read Sayce, Hibbert Lectures—Villari's
Savonarola—Salmon on Apocr. Books—Aubrey Moore on Darwinism.[11]

27. M. [London]

Return by 11.8 train. Wrote to Mr P.W. Campbell—Sig. Dotti—Mr Stevenson—
Sec. B.I.R.—Sig. Campanello—Sir F. Milner—Mr Mitchell—Mr Pyeman. H. of C.

---

[1] Aubrey Lackington Moore, canon of Christ Church, Oxford, had sent his book; see 26 Feb. 88.
[2] Spoke on foreign affairs; *H* 322. 1187.
[3] *Bibliographie clérico-galante, par L'Apôtre bibliographe*, 2v. (1884-6).
[4] H. A. Vaughan, *The sufferings of Leo XIII* (1888).
[5] Alexander Asher, 1835-1905; Scottish advocate; liberal M.P. Elgin district 1881-1905; Scottish
solicitor general 1881-5, 1886, 1892-4.
[6] The Queen visited Florence in April 1888.
[7] Made brief personal explanation on Irish Resident Magistrates; *H* 322. 1254.
[8] Questioned and spoke on business of the House; *H* 322. 1332.
[9] *Letters from Edinburgh, written in the years 1774 and 1775* [by E. Topham] (1776).
[10] A. C. Ewald, *Sir Robert Walpole: a political biography* (1878).
[11] A. L. Moore, *Evolution and Christianity* (1889).

$3\frac{1}{2}$–$4\frac{3}{4}$.[1] Read Darwin's Life[2]—Villari's Savonarola—Letters from Edinburgh. Dined at Mr Currie's. Unpacked box of books, bindings &c. from Florence. Saw Mr A. Morley—Mr Childers—Ld Advocate.

28. Tu.

Wrote to Mrs Bolton—Mr Hutton—Mr Chambers CCC[3]—Messrs .... & Willby—and minutes. H of C. $4\frac{3}{4}$–$6\frac{3}{4}$.[4] Saw Mr Guinness Rogers. 12–$1\frac{1}{2}$. Arr. for divers matters. Saw Mr Knowles—Mr Murray—The Swedish Minister—Sir Jas Paget—Mrs (May) Hardy. Read Villari's Sav.—Cashel Byron's Profession.[5]

29. Wed.

Wrote to Mr Childers—Mr Arnold White—Mr Stibbs—and minutes. H of C. 3–5.[6] Read Vineis on Sir R. Peel[7]—Villari's Savonarola—Shaw's Cashel Byron. Eight to dinner. Saw Mr Bryce—Mr Childers—Mr B. Currie—Sir J. Paget—Ld Wolverton.

Thurs. Mch One. 1888.

Wrote to Mr Arnold White—Ld Acton BP.—Cavv. Vineis—Marchese di Torre Arsa—Ed. Daily News. H. of C. 4–$8\frac{1}{2}$.[8] Saw Sir W. Gull—Mr A. Morley. Read Vineis on Peel—Villari's Savonarola—Cashel Byron.

2. Fr.

Wrote to Mr Lewis Hughes—Miss Alexander (O)—Mr Bannerman—Mr C.J. Webb[9]—Mr Mitchell—Dean of Winchester[10]—& minutes. Saw S. Lyttelton—Messrs Agnew—Ld Northbrook—Mr Stansfeld—Mr Bradlaugh—Sir C. Russell—Mr M'Donnell. Dined at Ld Northbrook's. H. of C. $3\frac{1}{2}$–8 and $9\frac{3}{4}$–$12\frac{3}{4}$. Voted in minorities of 115 and 88.[11] Read Giffen on Trade[12]—Villari's Savonarola—Meath's Vol. of Essays.[13]

---

[1] Supply; *H* 322. 1499.

[2] F. Darwin, *Life and letters of Charles Darwin*, 3v. (1887).

[3] (Sir) Edmund Kerchever Chambers, 1866-1954; an undergraduate studying classics at Corpus, Oxford; later a civil servant, publishing on English literature.

[4] Procedure; *H* 322. 1657.

[5] G. B. Shaw, *Cashel Byron's profession. A novel* (1886); sent by Dorothy Tennant with a note: 'I do not know who the author is, but I hear he is a socialist, with peculiar ideas about copyright . . . I cannot help thinking "Cashel Byron" will amuse you very much'; Add MS 44503, f. 77.

[6] Spoke on procedure; *H* 322. 1770.

[7] Nicolo Vineis, Italian advocate, sent his book on Sir R. Peel (no copy found); see Add MS 44503, f. 75.

[8] Spoke on expenditure in the Pacific; *H* 322. 1870.

[9] Of S. Antrim Constitutional Association; see *T.T.*, 3 March 1888, 15c, 6 March 1888, 10a.

[10] Thanks for resolution supporting Home Rule signed by Anglican clergy; *T.T.*, 5 March 1888, 10b.

[11] On Russell's resolution on public meeting in London; *Hansard* gives the minorities as 115 and 92; *H* 323. 134.

[12] R. Giffen, *Recent changes in prices and incomes compared* (1888).

[13] R. Brabazon, Lord Meath, *Social arrows* (2nd ed. 1887).

3. Sat.

Wrote to Mr W.H. George—Mr Rhys—Mr J. Page—Earl of Meath—Mr Stibbs—and minutes. Read Villari's Savonarola—Cashel Byron—Macdowall on Ireland.[1] We dined at Mrs Th's & were vexed with the large party (15) and the prominence given us. Conversation with Mr Innes—Lady Winchilsea.

4. 3 S. Lent.

Guards Chapel mg & evg. Saw Sir W. Phillimore. Read Savonarola—G. Russell on Maconochie &c.[2]—Visione d'un Piagnone[3]—and [blank.]

5. M.

Wrote to Mr Owen Lloyd[4]—Mrs Drew—Mr Macdowall[5]—Mr Stibbs—Sir E. Watkin MP.—Mr A. Morley—Mr Washn Moon—Lady Brownlow—& minutes. Saw Mr Mayhew cum WHG—Ld Armstrong—Mr Morley. Sir G. Trevelyan—Mr A. Morley. H. of C. 3½-5.[6] Dined at Mr Stuart Rendell's. Read Villari's Savonarola—Hist. of the Volunteers—Leech on the Continuity &c.[7]

6. Tu.

Wrote to Mr Downing—Mr D. Head—Mr F. Allen—Mr Stibbs—Mr Wolff—W.H.G. H. of C. 5-8 and again after dinner.[8] Dined at Sir A. West's. Saw S. Lyttelton—The Gilbys—Mr A. Morley—and others. Lady Sandhurst's party. All alive. Saw one who told me strange inventions.[9] Read Hist of the Volunteers—Villari, finished: a great book—finished Cashel Byron.

7. Wed.

Wrote to Mr Bunting—Mr Pritchard—Mr St Clair—Mr Macphilpin—& minutes. Attended the Prince of Wales's Levee. Saw S.L.—A. Morley—the G. Hamptons—The Speaker—Mr Waddington—Mr Balfour. Sent speech to press. Dined at the Speaker's. Read Letters from Edinburgh—Mad. Campan's Memoirs[10]—Agriculture of Lancashire.[11]

8. Th.

Wrote to Wms & Norgate—Mr Waddington—Mr Freeman—and minutes. Dined at Ld Spencer's. Visited Christie's. Saw Mr Thursfield (long conversation

---

[1] A. B. MacDowall, *Facts about Ireland. A curve-history of recent years* (1888).

[2] Untraced article.

[3] *Canzona d'un Piagnone. Ed. G. Dotti, with a preface by I. del Lungo* (1864).

[4] Perhaps Edward Owen Vaughan Lloyd of Berth near Ruthin.

[5] Alexander B. MacDowall, wrote on English and Irish social questions; see 3 Mar. 88.

[6] Imperial defence; *H* 323. 229.

[7] Probably H. J. Leech, *The Irish roll call; a record of the government of Ireland from 1685-1885* (1886).

[8] Spoke on Scottish business and procedure; *H* 323. 411.

[9] Probably to do with Lady Sandhurst's spiritualism; see above x. clxxxix. He also met Mrs. (later Lady) Thursfield who arranged the meeting with her husband (see 8 Mar. 88).

[10] J. L. H. Campan, *Memoirs of the private life of Marie Antoinette* (new ed. 1887).

[11] Untraced.

on Peel)[1]—Dean Lake—S. Lyttelton. Conclave 3–3¾ at H. of C. H. of C. 3¾–6.[2] 1½ hour with Mr Parnell: see Mem. Read Madame Campan. Visited Christie's.

Memorandum for March 8. 1888.[3]

1. To keep the administration of the Coercion Act in its details before the eye of the country, and of Parliament by speeches, and by statistics.
2. To remain detached and in a condition to accept a settlement from the Tories.
3. What course should be taken if the government offer measures good in themselves, but insufficient for a settlement? Accept without prejudice?
4. Non-Irish legislation to be promoted (but dissentients will not as a body dissent from the government).
5. Does the idea of the American Union afford a practical point of departure?

Private

I made the inclosed note of points[4] which I wished to include in my conversation with Mr. Parnell today.

He looked not ill, but far from strong. He gave a favourable account of his health.

I pressed the first point rather strongly. He did not appear to have considered it much, but to give weight to it and he made a note on the subject.

The second I merely set out before him *pour acquit de conscience*. He said he expected nothing from the Tories as long as they should feel that they could get on without concession.

On the third point, as indeed on all, he was extremely moderate and reasonable: and I was not entirely without an apprehension that the energies of his political pursuit were somewhat abated by his physical condition.

He thought the turning point lay in a Dublin Parliament. He did not see what could be given short of this that would be worth taking: whereas if this could be had, even with insufficient powers, it might be accepted. I understood him to mean might be accepted as a beginning.

I mentioned Sir E. Watkin's idea of Provincial Assemblies with a contingent power of election from themselves to constitute a body which should meet in Dublin for particular purposes. He thought it conceivable that this might resolve itself into a question of the mode of election.

He quite agreed as to no. 4.

Did not think the Irish people would be impatient even if Home Rule were not mooted this year in the House of Commons.

Believed crime, properly so called, was declining.

My chief point with him was that expressed in No 5. on this ground, that the opponents never so far as I know have condemned the American system as a possible basis of a plan of Home Rule: and I have always held the hope that it might in case of need supply at least a phrase to cover them in point of consistency. I said I was aware of no difficulty unless it should be found to lie in the incapacity to touch contrasts. On the practical working of which, I had not been able to obtain sufficient information.

---

[1] (Sir) James Richard Thursfield, 1840–1923; fellow of Jesus, Oxford, 1864–81; wrote leaders and naval comments for *T.T.* from 1881; published *Peel* (1891); a moderate home ruler.
[2] Imperial defence; *H* 323. 593.
[3] Add MS 44773, f. 48 ff.; in *Autobiographica*, iv. 87, where the conversation is wrongly dated as having occurred on 10 March. The account of the conversation was completed that day.
[4] i.e. those above.

He thought this idea might be made a groundwork. Did not wholly repel even the idea of parliamentary intervention to stop extreme and violent proceedings in Dublin. I said a Court would fix the lines of the respective provinces better than Parliamentary action.

Undoubtedly as a whole his tone was very conservative.

WEG Mch 10.88

He was much pleased to know I had declared the question of money required further investigation.

9. Fr.

Wrote to Bull & Auvache—Mary Drew—Mr P. Campbell—H.N.G.—Mr Blackie—Dr Chapman—Sir E. Watkin—and minutes. Saw S.L.—Mr F. Harrison—Mr Childers—Sir G. Trevelyan—M. Meyer—E. Hamilton. H. of C. 2½–5. Spoke briefly on Goschen's plan.[1] Dined at Mrs Tennant's. Read Mad. Campan —Letters from Edinburgh.

10. Sat.

Wrote to Rev. Mr Caudwell—Mr Watson[2]—and others. Wrote Mem. of conversation with Mr Parnell.[3] Dined at Ld Aberdeen's. Drive with C. Saw Abp of Canterbury—Mr Knowles, 1½ h. eclaircissement—Mr Blunt & Lady A. Blunt—S. Lyttelton. Read as yesterday.

11. 4 S. Lent.

Guards Chapel 11 A.M. St Andrews 7 P.M. Wrote to Lady Brownlow. Saw King of the Belgians. Read Mozley's Sermons[4]—Hettinger's Dante[5]—Rhys, Celtic Mythol.[6]—Henry VIII & the Monasteries[7]—Salmon on Ophites—& on Simon Magus.[8]

12. M.

Wrote to Ld Granville—Mr Bellis—Mr Downing—Miss Dickson—Mr Wyon— Mr Allen—& minutes. H. of C. 3½–5.[9] Dined with Lucy. Read Mad. Campan— Letters from Edinburgh (finished)—Vita di Pietro Aretino.[10] Saw S.L.—Lady Derby—Mr Morley—Mr A. Morley—Mrs Hamer X.—Herbert G.—Mr Stansfeld.

13. Tu.

Wrote to Mr E. Dolbie—Mr Gerahty—and minutes. H. of C. 3½–5.[11] Saw S.L.— Mr A. Morley—Mr Childers—Mr Hamilton—Mr G. Russell. Eight to dinner.

---

[1] Supporting Goschen's proposal for a partial conversion of the national debt; *H* 323. 731.

[2] Thomas Watson, Rochdale liberal unionist; on Home Rule and Bright; *T.T.*, 15 March 1888, 12c.

[3] See 8 Mar. 88.   [4] See 9 Nov. 79.

[5] F. L. Hettinger, *Dante's Divina Commedia: its scope and value* (1887).

[6] Sir J. Rhys, *Lectures on the origin and growth of religion as illustrated by Celtic heathendom* (1886).

[7] F. A. Gasquet, *Henry VIII and the English monasteries* (1888).

[8] See 26 July 85.   [9] Organization of the admiralty; *H* 323. 981.

[10] G. M. Mazzuchelli, *Vita di Pietro Aretino* (1830).

[11] Indian frontier; *H* 323. 1093.

A few friends afterwards. Read Mad. Campan—Vita di P. Aretino—Rogers's Recollections.[1]

14. Wed.

Wrote to Ld Granville—Mr Th. Hankey—Mr ONeill Daunt—Mr Macleod—C.S. Palmer—Mr H. Barton—Mr Lucas. Dined at Ld Rothschild's. Saw S.L.—Herbert J.G.—Ld Rothschild—Lady R.—Lady Harcourt[2]—Mr Poste—E.W.H.—Mrs Murray X. Read Campan—Life of P. Aretino—Rogers's Recollections. H. of C. $2\frac{1}{2}$–$5\frac{1}{2}$. Oaths Bill.[3]

15. Th.

Wrote to Mr P. Rathbone—Mr A. M'Gregor—& minutes. Visited Japanese Exhibition. Drive with C. Read Campan—Life of P.A.—Life of Ld Essex (Viceroy).[4] Saw S.L.—Mr Wemyss Reid—Mr Dillon MP. Dined at Mr Armitstead's.

16. Fr.

Wrote to Mr Blyth—Rev. J. Allan Smith—Mr W. Blunt—Mr Quilter—& minutes. H. of C. $2\frac{1}{2}$–$6\frac{3}{4}$ & $9\frac{1}{4}$–$12\frac{1}{2}$.[5] Saw Mr S.L.—Mr A. Morley—and others. Read Campan—Vita di P. Aretino—(began) Robert Elsmere.[6]

17. Sat.

Wrote to Mrs Preggin—Mary Drew—Mr E. Rimmel—S.E.G.—Mrs Th.—& minutes. Luncheon at Ld Rothschild's. He afterwards read aloud many of Ld Beaconsfield's Letters to Mrs Williams. Very characteristic.[7] Tea at Lady Stanley's. Conversation on Dante chiefly. Saw S.L.—Mr Knowles—Mr Meyer. Albert Hall Concert 8–11.[8] Sims Reeves was a marvel. Nikita a considerable fact at the other end of the scale. Read Campan—R. Elsmere—Aretino (finished): a life no less strange than repulsive.

---

[1] *Reminiscences of William Rogers . . . compiled by R. H. Hadden* (1888).

[2] Harcourt's second wife, Elizabeth (da. of J. L. Motley and widow of T. P. Ives) whom he m. 1876, with his son 'Lulu' as best man.

[3] *H* 323. 1182.

[4] Perhaps in H. B. Devereux, *Lives and letters of the Devereux, Earls of Essex* (1853).

[5] Supply; *H* 323. 1440.

[6] Mrs. Humphry Ward, *Robert Elsmere*, 3v., published in February 1888; dedicated to the memories of T. H. Green and Laura Lyttelton and depicting much of Oxford life and religious doubt. For Gladstone's review, see 6 Apr. 88.

[7] Mrs. Brydges Willyams' friendship with Disraeli lasted from 1851 until her death in 1863; some 250 letters of the correspondence survive; see Blake, 414 ff.

[8] Programme of Irish music for St. Patrick's day, though ending with 'Rule Britannia'.

18. 5 S. Trin.

Guards mg & Chapel Royal afternoon. Tea with the Sydneys. Read Rob. Els-mere—Life of Dr Dodd: Account of do.[1]—Barzelletto on David[2]—Mackworth on Occ. Conformity.[3]

19. M.

Wrote to Reeves & Turner—J. Seddon—H.W. Wolff—W. Blunt—Rev. W. Hughes—and minutes. Read Mad. Campan—R. Elsmere. Saw S.L.—Herbert J.G.—and others. H. of C. $3\frac{3}{4}$-7.[4] Dined at Mr S. Smith's.[5]

20. Tu.

Wrote to Mr Harman—Messrs Longbourne—Mr Jolly—Mr Maud—& minutes. Dined at Mr Morley's. Read Campan—R. Elsmere. H. of C. before dinner.[6] Saw S.L.—Mr L. Lawson—& others.

21. Wed.

Wrote to Prof. Villari—Mr Knowles—& minutes. H. of C. $12\frac{1}{2}$-2 and $2\frac{1}{2}$-6.[7] Dined at Lord Spencer's: a short run to the Speaker's Levee & back to the evening party. Read Mad. Campan—R. Ellesmere [sic]. Saw S.L.—Mr M'Carthy—& others.

22. Th.

Wrote to Reeves & Turner—Mr Stibbs—C. Palmer—Mr Knowles—Sister O'Connell[8]—Watson & Smith—Bull & Auvrache—Messrs. Trübner—Messrs. Longbourne—and minutes. H. of C. $3-4\frac{1}{2}$.[9] Saw Mr Morley—Mr S.L.—Mr A. Morley—Mr Childers—Mr C. Bannerman—Lady Stanley A. & two sons—Ly Harcourt—Ly Spencer. Read Mad. Campan—Robert Ellesmere—Rogers's Rem.

23. Fr.

Wrote to Reeves & Turner—Mr Arch. Grove[10]—Mr N. Palmer—Rev. Mr Elking-ton—& minutes. Read Mad. Campan—R. Elsmere. Saw Mr Longbourne—Mr

---

[1] *An account of the life, death and writings of the Rev. Dr. Dodd . . . by a citizen of London* (1777).

[2] G. Barzellotti, *David Lazzaretti di Arcidosso detto il santo* (1885).

[3] Sir H. Mackworth, *Peace at home* (1703); on the Occasional Conformity Bill.

[4] Ritchie introduced the England and Wales local govt. bill; Gladstone interjected on the role of the police; *H* 323. 1664.

[5] The liberal M.P. for Flintshire (see 12 Dec. 82n.); extensive account of 'the great event' in S. Smith, *My life work* (1902), app. xii.

[6] Spoke on national debt bill; *H* 323. 1820.

[7] Irish land; *H* 323. 1873.

[8] Of the Ursuline convent, Thurles, Ireland; had sent a shamrock; Hawn P.

[9] National debt bill; *H* 324. 55.

[10] (Thomas Newcomen) Archibald Grove, 1855-1920; liberal M.P. West Ham 1892-5; wrote from White's Club to propose 'starting a weekly paper, to take the place of the Spectator, which has so basely deserted Mr. Gladstone'; this became Grove's *New Review* (1889-97); Hawn P.

A.V. Peel—Ld Spencer—Mr Leveson—The Speaker—Mrs Th. St. James's 6. P.M. H. of C.[1]

24. Sat.

Wrote to Watsons—Mrs Warmisham[2]—Mr E. Morton—Messrs Sotheran—Mr Gillham—& minutes. Stood to Mr Holl $1\frac{3}{4}$ hours.[3] It was very exhausting. Dined at E. Hamilton's. An interesting party. Read Mad. Campan—Robert Elsmere.

25. Palm S. & Annuncn.

Chapel Royal 10 AM & St John's 7 PM. Wrote to Mr Tooley—Mr Maggs. Saw Mr West on H.M. & the Gordon letters[4]—Ld Herschel—and Sir A. Wood. Read Life of Col. Gardiner[5]—Boccaccio's Life of Dante[6]—Brinkman on Roman Methods[7]—Warmisham Leaves of the Tree—Memoir of Lady Watkin[8]—Carrière Weltanschauung.[9]

26. M.

Wrote to Mrs O'Shea—Mr P. Bunting—Sir A. Clark—Mr H. Bottoms—Mr Th. Rice—Archd. Farrar—Mr Allen—Ly Stanley of Alderley. Saw Mr Murray—Ar[thur] Lyttelton—Mr A. Morley. Read Rob. Ellesmere—Mad. Campan. H. of C. $4\frac{1}{4}$-$8\frac{1}{4}$ for the Budget.[10]

27. Tu. [Dollis Hill]

Saw Mr A. Lyttelton—Mr Godley—Mr Maggs—Mr A. Morley. Finished Mad. Campan's work—read Robert Elsmere—Foote's Trip to Calais.[11] Large conclave at Sp[encer] House 12-2. We all but decided on an important motion about the Death Duties.[12] H. of C. 4-$5\frac{1}{2}$[13] Off to Dollis at 6.

28. Wed.

Wrote to Mr Thorndike Rice 1. & packet—Sig. Salagno—Watsons—Ld Beauchamp—Mr G. Potter. Read Robert Elsmere—Foote's Capuchin. Corrected

---

[1] Supported W. H. Smith's modification to Bradlaugh's motion for revision of the pension system, and strongly defended the pension he gave to Lucien Bonaparte; *H* 324. 216.

[2] She had sent her *God's provision for the healing of the nations*; Hawn P.

[3] See 31 Oct. 87.

[4] General Gordon's sister was requesting permission to include three letters of the Queen to her in the 2nd ed. of C. G. Gordon, *Letters to his sister, M. A. Gordon* (1885, 2nd ed. 1888). The Queen, on Ponsonby's urging, referred the matter to Salisbury who approved two, recommending omitting the third, as it 'might give the impression that the Queen has less influence in the government of the country than is really the case' (RA Addl. MS A/12/1495 ff.).

[5] *The Life of Colonel James Gardiner* (1840).

[6] G. Boccaccio, *Vita de Dante Alighieri* (many eds).

[7] A. Brinckman, *The controversial methods of Romanism* (1888).

[8] *In loving memory of Mary Briggs, wife of Sir E. W. Watkin* (1888?).

[9] P. M. Carrière, *Die philosophische Weltanschauung der Reformationziel* (1847).

[10] Asking several questions in the course of Goschen's speech; *H* 324. 268.

[11] S. Foote, *A trip to Calais... to which is added The Capuchin* (1778).

[12] See 9, 23 Apr. 88.

[13] Irish land; *H* 324. 407.

with care & dispatched proofs of Article on the Ingersoll Controversy.[1] Saw W.H.G.

29. Th.

Ch. 10½ A.M. (& H.C.) Wrote to Mr T.B. Potter M.P.—Miss C. Croft—H.N.G. Read Robert Elsmere—Life of Drummond[2]—Foote's Maid of Bath.[3] Saw the Dumaresqs.

30. G. Friday.

Willesden Ch 3 PM. Read Service Scriptures at home. Wrote to Chancr of Exchr—E.W. Hamilton—Mary Drew. Read Rob. Elsmere—Bruno on R.C. Doctrine[4]—Life of Drummond.

31. E[aster] Eve. [Aston Clinton]

Ch. 10½ A.M. Wrote to Robn & Nicholson—E.A. Arnold—Mr Cotgrave—J.H. Allen—Rev. Mr Rees—Miss A. Brown—Mr A. Morley—and minutes. Wrote note to the Aberdeen letter.[5] Saw Lord Beauchamp—Messrs Grogan—Mr Quaritch—W.H.G. Went by 5 P.M. to Aston Clinton: the people as well as the place well worth visiting.[6]

Easter Day April One 88.

Wrote to Mr Miller Hockey—Lord Acton—Mr Knowles. Parish Ch. mg with H.C., and evg.—Excellent services & congregations. Conversation with the Rector,[7] Lady H. Read Vie d'une Parisienne[8]—Bellarmine de Arte &c.—Mansell on Child Marriage. It is a rich interior, not overdone like many R[othschild] houses.

2. M.

Ch. 11 A.M. Read, & finished Vie d'une Parisienne—Buckmshire Tale (Nell Grey)[9]—Burton Hist. Scotland.[10] Conversation with the Rector—Mr Russell—Mrs C. Flower—Mrs Brett. Drive among the beautiful beeches & visit to Halton. Attended the Village Concert.

3. Tu.

Wrote to Mr J.W. Spencer—W.H.G.—Messrs Watson—H.J.G.—C.J. Williams—Mr Carr Gomme—Mr S. Scott. Ch. 11 A.M. Conversation with Mr Russell—Ld

---

[1] See 31 Dec. 87.

[2] Perhaps J. F. M'Lennan, *Memoir of Thomas Drummond* (1867).

[3] S. Foote, *The Maid of Bath; a comedy* (1778).

[4] Probably one of the works of V. Bruno, seventeenth-century Jesuit.

[5] Obscure; *Gleanings*, iv has a note dated 1878 (unaltered in reprints) on the letters to Aberdeen of 1851.

[6] Seat near Tring of Louisa, dowager Lady de Rothschild.

[7] Thomas Williams, rector of Aston Clinton since 1881.

[8] Untraced.   [9] Untraced.   [10] See 19 Apr. 86.

Herschell—Mr C. Flower—Mr B. Wilberforce. Read Burton Hist Scotland—Sir H. Taylor's Correspondence[1]—and [blank.] Underwent photography. Planted a tree. The German sisters played. Wrote Mem. on Dee Navigation.[2]

4. Wed. [Oxford]

Magd. Chapel 6 P.M. At 11½ drove to Prince's Risborough: rail to Oxford—Keble. Read Dallinger, The Creator[3]—Sir H. Taylor, Correspondence—De Minut 'de la Beauté'.[4] Found the Warden [of Keble: E. S. Talbot] in good plight: much conversation with him. Saw Provost of Oriel. Wrote to Lady Phillimore—Mr Mrs Lanfeldt—Mr Weaver.[5]

5. Th.

Magd. Chapel 6 PM. Wrote to Rev. Mr Carter. Read Dallinger—De Minut—Letter to Aretino[6]—Mrs Ward on Amiel.[7] Visited the Bodleian & saw the Librarian.[8] Saw Mr Parker—Rob. Lyttelton—Mr Bramley,[9] and others. Much conversation on R. Elsmere.

6. Fr.

Service at Ch.Ch. 5 P.M. Wrote to C.G.—Watsons—Mrs Freeman—Mr Clifford. Saw Dr Bright—Dr Fairbairn—Mr Chursley. Read Dallinger—Letters to P. Aretino—Poole on Pentateuch[10]—Ratcliffe & James Letters.[11] Wrote on R. Elsmere—tentatively.[12]

7. Sat.

Magd Chapel 6. P.M. Wrote to Lady Phillimore—Mrs Cyril Flower—Bp of Western New York.[13] Wrote rather largely on Robert Elsmere. Saw Dr Roberts. Read Dallinger—Letters to P. Aretino.

[1] Sir Henry Taylor, *Correspondence* (1888); ed. E. Dowden.
[2] Not found; a dispute between the River Co. and the Hawarden Estate, resulting in clauses in the Dee Conservancy Act 1889.
[3] W. H. Dallinger, *The Creator, and what we may know of the method of creation* (1887).
[4] G. de Minut, *De la Beauté* (1587; new ed. 1865).
[5] A. E. Weaver of Birmingham had sent a drawing of Gladstone; Hawn P.
[6] *Lettere scritti a Pietro Aretino*, ed. T. Landoni and G. Vanzolini, 4v. (1873–5).
[7] H. F. Amiel, *Journal, translated with an introduction by Mrs Humphry Ward* (1885).
[8] It was on this occasion that Gladstone sketched out for E. B. Nicholson, Bodley's Librarian, a design for wheeled bookcases, pulled endways instead of forwards, which anticipated the 'rolling stack' method of book-storage first used on a large scale below the Radcliffe Camera and subsequently in many modern libraries; see E. Craster, *History of the Bodleian Library 1845–1945* (1952), 234 and E. B. Nicholson, *Mr Gladstone and the Bodleian* (1898), 10.
[9] Henry Ramsden Bramley, fellow of Magdalen; author and editor of carols.
[10] Probably M. Poole, *Annotations on the Holy Bible* (1852).
[11] *Letters of Richard Radcliffe and John James of Queen's College, Oxford, 1755–83*, ed. M. Evans (1888).
[12] '"Robert Elsmere" and the Battle of Belief', *N.C.*, xxiii. 766 (May 1888), reprinted in *Later gleanings*, 77. This review helped turn the book into a best seller. See also 8 Apr. 88 and W. S. Peterson, 'Gladstone's review of *Robert Elsmere*: some unpublished correspondence', *Review of English Studies*, NS xxi (1970).
[13] Arthur Cleveland Coxe; had sent his article, 'The decay of public morals'; Add MS 44503, f. 99.

8. 1 S.E.

ChCh mg—Magd. evening. Wrote on R. Elsmere. Wrote to Mr A. Morley—Ld Acton—Mrs Jolly—Mr Bunting Tel. Saw Rector of Lincoln:[1] his house & Mag. Chapel: conversation on Homeric questions. An hour's conversation with Mrs Humphry Ward.[2] Conversation with Miss Tasker[3] on Homeric questions &c.

9. M. [London]

Wrote to Mr W.B. Simson. Saw H. Gifford[4]—R.C. Jenkins. 12-2¼. Back to London. H. of C. 3-7. Spoke on Budget.[5] Saw Mr A. Morley—Sir W. Harcourt—Mr Childers. Dined at Grillions: only 3 but good company. Read Aretino letters: most singular.

10. Tu.

Wrote to Mr Gresham—A. Pepple—Mr Paterson—Mr Pringle Taylor[6]—Rev. Dr Pace L.l.l.—Rev. Mathews—Dean of Manchester—Mrs Bolton—Mrs Humphry Ward—Rev. J.G. Deed—A. Morley—Mrs Butler—Mr Godley—H.G. Reid—E.C. Perry. Saw W.H.G. (Dee Foreshore R[ailway])—Herbert J.G.—Quaritch—Ld Granville—Scotts—Mr A. Morley. Submitted my two new bindings to the Experts of the Br. Museum. Met C. at Euston. Club dinner. Saw Sir P. Howett, Sir C. Newton, Sir J. Hooker. Saw Ritso [R].

11. Wed.

Wrote to Mr Walker—Lady Gladstone—Sec. R. Academy—A. Carroll—Mrs Bayliffe—Mr Hobbs[7]—Mr Rideing—Mr Reader—Messrs Borthwick. Saw Sir E. Watkin—Mr Inglis—Mr A. Morley—Lady Sandhurst (Dowager)—W.H.G. H. of C. 2½-6.[8] Dined with the Liberal Federation: spoke on the situation & Smith's important reply.[9] Read Gibbon Ch. XV[10]—De Moleville.[11] Wrote a little on R. E[lsmere].

[1] William Walter Merry, 1835-1918; rector of Lincoln college, succeeding Pattison, from 1884; editor of Homer and Aristophanes.

[2] Mary Augusta Ward, née Arnold, 1851-1920; novelist and author of *Robert Elsmere* (see 6 Apr. 88n.). Gladstone requested this interview, which was continued next day (though unmentioned by Gladstone); see J. P. Trevelyan, *Life of Mrs Humphry Ward* (1923), 56 and Mrs. Ward's *Recollections*.

[3] Unidentified; apparently a visitor.

[4] Probably Edwin Hamilton Gifford, 1820-1905; wrote widely on the Bible; at Cambridge, but in 1880s had many Oxford connections.

[5] On death duties, announcing a proposition in the future to equalize duties on land and personal property; *H* 324. 730; see 23 Apr. 88.

[6] J. Pringle Taylor, sec. of the executive of the Midlothian Liberal Unionist Association, which had sent a public letter regretting Gladstone's policies. Gladstone's reply avoided detail 'to mitigate the estrangement of feeling'; *T.T.*, 16 April 1888, 7d.

[7] H.H. Hobbs, on the Suez Canal purchase; *T.T.*, 14 April 1888, 11e.

[8] Irish agriculture; *H* 324. 963.

[9] On Ireland, with comments on W. H. Smith's statement that there would be no Irish local govt. bill this session; *T.T.*, 12 April 1888, 7a.

[10] Of Gibbon's *Decline and Fall*; on Christianity and the Roman Empire; attacked with reference to the supernatural in Gladstone's review; *Later gleanings*, 93.

[11] B. de Moleville, *Histoire de la Révolution de France*, 14v. (1801-3).

12. Th.

Wrote to Mr Linder—Mrs Thistleth.—Messrs O[gilvie] G[illanders] & Co.—Mr Norton—Watsons—Treasurer King's Hospital. H. of C. 4–8.[1] Dined at Ld Northbourne's. Saw Sir R. Welby—Herbert J.G.—Mr Childers—W.H.G. Read de Moleville. Saw one [R].

13. Fr.

Wrote to Mr Walker—I. Donnelly—Mr Tighe Hopkins—J.E. Clegg—Mr Walker—Scotts. Saw E. Hamilton—WHG. Seven to dinner: conversation on R. Elsmere especially. H. of C. $3\frac{1}{4}$–$6\frac{1}{2}$.[2] Wrote on R.E. Read B. de Moleville.

14. Sat.

Wrote to Mr Sturge—Messrs O.G. & Co.—Mr Carlisle—Ld E. Fitzmaurice—P. Campbell—Mr Mitchell—Mr Walkerstone—E. Russell. Drive with C. Read B. de Moleville—Russell on Shylock[3]—Tacitus (at Lond. Libr.)[4] Wrote on R.E.

15. S.E.2.

Chapel Royal (and H.C.) 10 AM. St Andr. Evg. Wrote on R.E. Wrote to Rev. Newman Hall—Sotheron (Manchester). Read Livius on St Peter at Rome[5]—Shaker Sermons[6]—and [blank.]

16. M.

Wrote to Rev. Mr Muir—Mrs Humphrey Ward [sic]—Sir Jas. Fergusson—Rev. J.G. Rogers—Mr Baildon.[7] Busy correcting MS of R.E[lsmere]. H. of C. 4–$5\frac{3}{4}$.[8] Read B. de Moleville—Aretino Letters. Attended the Gilby gathering in evg: & made a speech.[9] Saw W.H.G.

17. Tu.

Wrote to Messrs Jewell—Mr Johnson Solr—Mr Ronayne—Halley Jones—Mrs Bolton—Mary Drew—Rev. Mr Pace—Mr Broad—Mr Brown—Mrs H. Ward. and .... Correcting & enlarging R.E. H. of C. 3–5.[10] Read B. de Moleville—Aretino Letters—Peg Woffington by Molloy.[11] Saw W.H.G.—Mr Childers.

[1] Spoke on disturbance at Ennis; *H* 324. 1096.
[2] Local govt. bill; *H* 324. 1199.
[3] Untraced piece sent by E. Russell.
[4] For the review; *Later gleanings*, 96.
[5] T. Livius, *St Peter, Bishop of Rome* (1888).
[6] H. L. Eads, *Shaker sermons* (4th ed. 1887); discussed in *Later gleanings*, 109.
[7] Henry Bellyse Baildon, Edinburgh poet, philosopher and secretary of the Edinburgh Philosophical Institution, of which Gladstone had become President; Baildon asked him, unsuccessfully, to address the Institution in November; Hawn P.
[8] Local govt. bill; *H* 324. 1331.
[9] *Soirée* of the Marylebone Women's Liberal Association, organized by Mrs. H. A. Blyth and Lady Sandhurst, its president; *T.T.*, 17 April 1888, 10d.
[10] Local govt. bill; *H* 324. 1499.
[11] J. F. Molloy, *The life and adventures of Peg Woffington*, 2v. (1884).

18. Wed.

Wrote to Mr Knowles—Mr J.G. Talbot—Messrs Alden—Mr Hill—Mr . . . . . . (Mid Lanark). Finished correcting MS. of R.E. and dispatched it.[1] Eight to dinner. Saw Sir J. Carmichael—Mr G. Russell—Sir J. Simon—Mrs Bolton. Drive with C. Read B. de Moleville—Shaw on Home Rule.[2]

19. Th.

Wrote to Mr S. Compston—Sec. K. Coll. Hosp.—M. Lalande (Paris)—Williams & N.—Duncan & Hepburn—Mr J. Talbot MP—Ld Acton—'H.R.C.'—Mr A. Reid— Mr Waddy MP—Sir A. West. Drive with C. H. of C. 3–8.[3] Saw Sir J. Carmichael —Ld Beauchamp—Mr Few—Ld Spencer—Mr Wickham—Mr Fowler—Sir W. Harcourt. Read B. de Moleville—Aretino Letters.

20. Fr.

Wrote to Bishop(!) Eads[4]—Sotheron & Co—H. Maggs—J.E. Clegg—Mr L. Bulgaris[5]—Rev. A. Abbott. H. of C. 4–5 and $10\frac{1}{4}$–12.[6] Visited the beautiful Niagara Panorama. Saw E. Talbot & Lavinia—Mr Knowles—Mr A. Morley—Mr Waddy & his party. Read De Moleville—Vizetelly Diamond Necklace.[7]

21. Sat.

Wrote to Mr Armstrong—Messrs Meynell & Pemberton—Ed. British Weekly.[8] Visited the Water Colour Institutions with E. Wickham. Worked on Death Duties: the subject is tough. Saw A. Lyttelton (River Dee)—Sir J. Carmichael. Drive with C. Dined with A.L.: interesting conversation with his lawyer guests on the Appeal sentences.[9]

22. 3 SE.

Chapel Royal mg. with H.C.—St Andrew evg. Read Green's Lay Sermons[10]— Hastings, Wonderful Law[11]—Livius Episcopate of St Peter. Fiveocloquai[12] with Lady Brownlow & Lady Lothian (C.) Some further work on Death Duties.

---

[1] See 6 Apr. 88.

[2] Untraced; probably an article by William Shaw, former Home Rule leader.

[3] Local govt. bill; *H* 324. 1746.

[4] H. L. Eads, bp. of South Union, Kentucky; see 15 Apr. 88 and *Later gleanings*, 109.

[5] Probably a relative of the Ionian; see 25 Nov. 58.

[6] Local govt. bill; *H* 325. 120.

[7] See 26 June 67.

[8] On disestablishment; *British Weekly*, 4 May 1888, 1b.

[9] See 24 Apr. 88. Notes made this day on the evidence of Col. Turner Freeman; Add MS 44773, f. 66. See 24 Apr. 88.

[10] T. H. Green, *Witness of God and faith: two lay sermons* (1883); Green, as Mr. Grey, the chief figure in *Robert Elsmere*, is the effective target of much of Gladstone's comment in the latter part of his review. See 7 Oct. 83.

[11] Possibly S. Hastings, *Short treatise on the law of fraud* (1888).

[12] Glynnese for five o'clock tea.

23. M.

Wrote to . . . . . . Began correction of proofs. Read De Moleville—Diamond Necklace. Worked finally on Death Duties. Saw Mr Fowler—Miss Tennant. H. of C. 4–7¾. Spoke 1½ hours on Death duties. Hartington's foot danced violently.[1]

24. Tu.

Wrote to Mr Knowles—Sir E. Watkin—Mr B. Potter—Messrs Longbourne.[2] H. of C. 4–8. Spoke upon the Appeal sentences.[3] Finished & dispatched the R. Elsmere proofs. Dined with the Miss Monks. Saw Mrs Murray. Saw W.H.G.—Mr Knowles—Mr A. Morley—Sir R. Welby. Read De Moleville—The Diamond Necklace.

25. Wed. St. M.

Wrote to Mr Maclaren[4]—Rev. J. Allen—Miss Dermott. Saw Neville Lyttelton—Ld Lamington—Mr Head—Mr A. Morley—Mr Morley—Mr [R.B.] Haldane—Ld Rosebery. Dined at Mr Maclagans[5] to meet Scots members. Read De Moleville—Vizetelly's D. Necklace. H of C. 2¼–6. Spoke on Irish Local Government.[6]

26. Th.

Wrote to Mr Knowles—Lady Milbank—Ld Lymington—T. Spencer—Mr Laurie—Mr Dalgleish—Mr Richardson. Read De Moleville. Saw Mr A. Morley—W.H.G.—Mr Scharf—Sir W. Harcourt—S. Lyttelton—Lady Hayter—The French Ambassador (9 PM)—Baron Ferdinand de R[othschild].

27. Fr.

Wrote to J. H. Paraden—F.B. Doveton—Mrs Sanford—Messrs Longbourne—A. Maggs—Messrs Murray—Mr Drennan—J. Macfarlane—J. Cloak—Mr Hodges—A. Spencer—W.J. Pool[7]—J. Hill—Mr Brown—A. Mills—Mr Bristow Tel. Saw S. Lyttelton—Sir Alg. West—Sir L. Playfair. H. of C. 2½–4.[8] Read De Moleville—Diamond Necklace—Zola's La terre.[9] Dined at Ld Hothfield's.

---

[1] Gladstone proposed an amndt. to the Customs and Inland Revenue bill to equalize death duties on real and personal property; Hartington had to explain his opposition to a proposal similar to that which the liberal cabinet had proposed in 1885; *H* 325. 190.

[2] Resigning as a Trustee of the Radcliffe Trust; letter of regret and thanks from the Trustees, Add MS 44503, f. 193.

[3] On increase of sentence by Irish courts, on appeal; Gladstone argued that the power of appeal was intended to be exercised for the advantage of the prisoner; *H* 325. 367.

[4] A brief history of Gladstone's conservatism to 1858; *T.T.*, 4 May 1888, 10a.

[5] P. MacLagan; see 4 Feb. 71.   [6] Supporting the Home Rulers' Irish local govt. bill; *H* 325. 489.

[7] William J. Pool of Heaton; later corresponded on hypnotism; Hawn P.

[8] Spoke on beer duty; *H* 325. 773.

[9] E. Zola, *La terre* (1887); naturalistic novel of rural life sent with a recommendation by Knowles (see Metcalf, *Knowles*, 362n.); see 2 May 88. For Gladstone's notes, see Add MS 44773, f. 60. On the urgings of S. Smith, liberal M.P. for Flintshire, H. Vizetelly, publisher of the English tr., was prosecuted later in 1888 for obscene libel and pleaded guilty; he was fined £100 and required to destroy his stock; see S. Smith, *My life work* (1902), 252 ff.

28. Sat.

Wrote to Mr E.C. Alison—Mr Grinfield—Mr Maggs—and minutes. Dined at [blank.] Saw Messrs. Longbourne—S. Lyttelton. Saw Brown [R.]. Drive with C. Visited Christie's—Agnew's. Read 19th Cent. on H of Lords—Ch. of Engl. & Tithe[1]—Zola's La Terre—The Diamond Necklace.

29. 4 S.E.

Chapel Royal 10 AM & 7 PM. Wrote to Rev. Mr Livius[2]—Ld Acton B.P. Read Livius on St Peter—Life of Bp Thomas Brown[3]—Zola's La Terre—Agortino's Sermons.[4]

30. M.

Wrote to Mrs Th.—Ld Spencer—Rev. Mr Hazzard—Mrs Grinfield—Mr O'Connor Morris. H. of C. 4–7½.[5] Drive with C. Saw A. Morley—S. Lyttelton. Dined at Mr Armitstead's to meet Mr Parnell. His coolness of head appeared at every turn. Read De Moleville—La Terre—Col. Maurice (a firebrand)[6]—Macaulay's Essays—La Nouvelle Cythère.[7]

Tues. May 1. St. Phil. & J.

Wrote to Mr J.M. Kirwan—Rev. J. Sinclair—Mr Downing—Mr Blagg—Mr P. Smith—& others. Drive with C. Dined at Mr Munro Seymour's. Saw S. Lyttelton—W.H.G.—Mr Thaddeus (at his studio)[8]—Mr Mundella—Mr A. Morley. H. of C. 4–5.[9] Read De Moleville—La Terre—Laveleye's new art. on Balkan Peninsula.[10]

2. Wed.

Wrote to W. Showring—Rev. H. Jopher—W. Taylor—S. Smith—Mr Salkeld. Drive with Constance: spoke of my Father. Saw Ld Granville—S. Lyttelton—Mr Stansfeld—Ld Rosebery. 8½–10¾. Attended the function at the N.L. Club & spoke for half an hour on the Library.[11] Read De Moleville—The Diamond Necklace—& La Terre, the most loathsome of all books in the picture it presents.

3. Th.

Wrote to Sir E. Watkin—Bp of Carlisle—Mr Vickers—Mr Dobbie—Mr Biggs—Rev. J.G. Rogers—Rev. R.R. Suffield—Mr Macpherson. Saw S. Lyttelton—

---

[1] N.C., xxiii. 716, 734 (May 1888), the number with his review of *Robert Elsmere*.

[2] Thomas Livius, Roman catholic priest, author and translator. See 15 Apr. 88.

[3] Perhaps J. C. Hedley, 'Sermon preached at the funeral of [bishop] T. J. Brown' (1880).

[4] *Sic*; perhaps *sc.* Aretino.   [5] Misc. business; *H* 325. 909.

[6] J. F. Maurice, *The balance of military power in Europe. An examination of the war resources of Great Britain and the Continental states* (1888).

[7] By M. Mativet (1888).   [8] See 27 Jan. 88.

[9] Scottish crofters; *H* 325. 1048.

[10] Untraced article.   [11] *T.T.*, 3 May 1888, 10a.

W.H.G.—Mr Mundella cum Mr [J.B.] Balfour—Mr Stansfeld—Ld Granville. Interview with Mr Parnell H. of C. Read De Moleville—D. Necklace—La Terre. Dinner of 8 at home. H. of C. 5–7 and 10½–11½.[1]

4. Fr.

Wrote to Miss F. Albert—Editor Cockburns Examinations[2]—A. M'Carthy—A. Pye Smith—Mrs O'Shea—Mr Romanes.[3] Saw S. Lyttelton—Mr Knowles—Lord Herschell—Mr Agnew—Mr [blank] from U.S. Dined with Mr Knowles. H. of C. 4–5, 6½–8½. Spoke on Railways—& on Tax Bill.[4] 10½–12½. Acad. Private View. Read De M.—D. Necklace finished.

5. Sat. [Dollis Hill]

Wrote to Ld Byron[5]—Mr Murphy—Mrs Th.—Mr Lahore—Rev. J.G. Rogers—Mr Downing—Rev. Mr Livius—Rev. W. Tarrine[6]—Sir S. Scott & Co. Royal Academy. 2½–4½. Saw S. Lyttelton—Sir A. Gordon—Mary D.—The Drews went. Read Hamer on Home Rule[7]—Myers on French Illusions[8]—De Moleville's Hist.—Cockburn on Scotch Trials. Dined at Sir R. Hayter's: off to Dollis in evg.

6. 5 S.E.

Kingsbury Ch (with H.C.) 11 AM. Willesden P.M. Read Life of Falconer[9]—Miller on the Romans[10]—Antiqua Mater[11]—Evangelical Review—Vance Smith's Sermon[12]—M'Coll on Islam.[13]

7. M.

Wrote to Rev. Mr Miller—Mr L. Hall. Drive with C. Read La Terre—Jack the Fisherman[14]—Gill in Contemp. Rev.—Dr Wright in do(!!)[15] Worked on Irish papers. A quiet day.

[1] Customs and inland revenue bill; *H* 325. 1253.
[2] Who had sent his ed. of H. T. Cockburn, *An examination of the trials for sedition . . . in Scotland*, 2v. (1888).
[3] George John Romanes, 1848–94; scientist and writer on evolution. See 24 Oct. 92.
[4] Opposing a royal commission on state purchase of railways, as despite his own provisions in the 1844 Act and a lingering predilection for freehold ownership by the State, public opinion was hostile and govt. already overstretched; also spoke on wine duties; *H* 325. 1399, 1421.
[5] George Frederick William Byron, 1855–1917; 9th Baron Byron 1870; had asked Gladstone for another contribution to the National Thrift Society; Hawn P. See 19 Oct. 88.
[6] Of Portsea; a Unitarian; had sent comments on Unitarianism; Hawn P.
[7] Untraced; an article?
[8] Perhaps F. W. H. Myer's comments in *Wordsworth* (1888).
[9] W. Falconer, *Poetical works . . . with a life by J. Mitford* (1854).
[10] J. Miller, *Commentary on Romans* (1887).
[11] Untraced.
[12] Perhaps G. V. Smith, 'Christians and Christians: a sermon' (1883).
[13] M. MacColl, 'Islam and civilization', *C.R.*, liii. 537 (April 1888).
[14] E. S. Phelps, *Jack the fisherman* (1887).
[15] T. P. Gill, 'A parliament or a congress' and W. Wright, 'The power behind the Pope' (Lasserre and the Gospels), *C.R.*, liii. 537, 748 (May 1888).

8. *Tu.* [*London*]

Wrote to Mr Gwilt—Rev. Mr Dickson—Mr Bunting—Messrs Grogan—Rev. Mr Scott—Mr ODonoghue—Treasurer H. of Charity—Central Press Tel. Luncheon at Woodbine Cottage[1] on our way back. H. of C. $3\frac{3}{4}$–$4\frac{3}{4}$.[2] Visited the new Gallery: a fine exhibition. Saw Mr Childers—Mr Halle[3]—Mr Morley—Lady A. Read De Moleville—La Terre. Worked on Irish papers.

9. *Wed.*

Wrote to Messrs Swan Sonnenschein & Co.[4] Worked on Irish papers. $2\frac{1}{2}$–4. Memorial Hall meeting. Spoke $1\frac{1}{4}$ hour.[5] $4\frac{1}{4}$–$5\frac{1}{2}$. Conclave at Mr Rigby's Chambers on the Dee Foreshores. Dined at Mr Maguire's. Conversation with Mrs M.—Miss Rhoda Broughton.[6] Read De Moleville—La Terre—Daly's Ireland in 1798.[7]

10. *Th. Ascension Day.*

Chapel Royal at 11 with H.C. Wrote to Williams & Norgate—H. Salmon—E.G.S. Browne—M.R. Williams—C. Reader—Mr Stibbs—Mr Marshall. Saw S. Lyttelton—Ld Granville—Mr Rathbone—Mr A. Morley. Nine to dinner. H of C. 4–$5\frac{1}{2}$.[8] Read as yesterday. Attended Lady Rosebery's Federation Party.[9]

11. *Fr.*

Wrote to Ld Salisbury—Mr Stibbs—Mr Salkeld—E. Russell BP—Lt. Col. Ross—C. Palmer. Read De Moleville—La Terre—Russell on R. Ellesmere.[10] Dined at Sir A. West's. H. of C. 4–$4\frac{3}{4}$.[11] Saw Sir A. West—Mr Morley.

12. *Sat.* [*Dollis Hill*]

Lumbago better: rose at 11.30. Wrote to Robn & Nicholson—Cawthorn & Hutt—Sir A. West—Mr Anderson MP.—Sir H. James—Rev. Dr. Hutton—Mr Palmer. Finished De Moleville—read Venetian Relation [*sic*] of England H. VIII.[12] Saw W.H.G.—S. Lyttelton—Mr Morley—Mr Stuart MP. Off to Dollis at 4 PM.

[1] Mrs. Thistlethwayte's cottage in Hampstead.
[2] Questions; London corporation; *H* 325. 1627.
[3] Perhaps (Sir) Charles Hallé, 1819–95; musician.
[4] London publishers, especially of progressive and left-wing material.
[5] Great meeting of nonconformist ministers, organized by Guinness Rogers, to support Home Rule; *T.T.*, 10 May 1888, 7e.
[6] Rhoda Broughton, 1840–1920; prolific novelist.
[7] J. B. Daly, *Ireland in 1798* (1888).
[8] Railway bill; *H* 325. 1831.
[9] No account found.
[10] Untraced review, perhaps by G. W. E. Russell.
[11] Row about the Bradlaugh affair; *H* 326. 52.
[12] Probably R. Brown, ed., *Four years at the court of Henry VIII*, 2v. (1854); despatches of Sebastian Giustinian.

13. S. aft Asc.

Kingsbury Ch mg and evg. Wrote to Ld Acton. Read Agortino's Sermons—Life of Bp Grant[1]—Harmony of Angl. & E. Doctrine[2]—and [blank.] Ld Ripon dined.

14. M. [London]

Wrote to Mr Collingwood[3]—Mrs Humphry Ward. Read Maimon Autobiographies[4]—Colnaghi's Report.[5] Saw Messrs Burnes & Oates[6]—Dr Wright—Mr A. Morley—Ld Hartington—Sir H. James—Conclave on Irish affairs—Conclave on Licensing. H. of C. $3\frac{1}{4}$-$7\frac{3}{4}$ and $10\frac{3}{4}$-12.[7] Saw Mr C. Bannerman.

15. Tu.

Wrote to J. Graham—Lady Napier—R. Hall—Mr Primrose—Mr Macewan—Sir D. Colnaghi. H. of C. $3\frac{3}{4}$-8.[8] Dined with the Ripons. Saw S. Lyttelton—Mr Leveson Gower—W.H.G. Much conversation on R.E. & kindred subjects with Mrs Flower & Lady Ripon. Read Life of Napier[9]—Autobiogr. of S. Maimon—Nature's Fairyland.[10]

16. Wed.

Wrote to Mr J. Stephen—Mr J. Donnelly—Mr A. Dodshon—London Stereoscopic Co—Mr A. Sutton—Mr Wilson MP. Dined at Ld Rosebery's. Read Napier—Maimon—Donnelly on Bacon-Shakespeare.[11] Saw S. Lyttelton—Mr Bryce. H. of C. $3\frac{1}{4}$-$4\frac{1}{4}$: for the Denning testimonial.[12] Drive with C.

17. Th.

Wrote to H.N.G.—Ogilvy Gillanders & Co.—Mr C. Palmer—Mr Lobley—Rev. Dr Field—Mr Knowles. Saw S. Lyttelton—W.H.G.—J. Morley—Scotts. Saw Murray [R]. Attended flowershow: piloted by Sir T. Lawrence. Read Maimon—Napier. Dined at Mr Basses[?]. Sat to Stereoscopic Co.[13] H. of C. 4-$5\frac{1}{4}$.[14]

18. Fr. [Hawarden]

Wrote to Mr H. Seymour—Traffic Manager—Rev. Mr Davies—Scotts—Mr Meynell—Mr Knowles. Read Napier's Life—Solomon Maimon (finished)—

---

[1] K. O'Meara, *Thomas Grant, first bishop of Southwark* (1886).

[2] Untraced.

[3] William Gershom Collingwood, 1854-1932; Ruskin's secretary and biographer.

[4] S. Maimon, tr. J. C. Murray, *An autobiography* (1888).

[5] Report on Italian agriculture sent by D. Colnaghi; Add MS 44503, f. 202.

[6] Who had sent a volume of Joseph Gillow's *Biographical Dictionary of the English Catholics*; Gladstone made inquiries about Lancashire; Add MS 44503, f. 253.

[7] Spoke on case of T. Hamilton, resident magistrate; *H* 326. 196.

[8] Spoke on business of the house; *H* 326. 348.

[9] Probably W. N. Bruce, *Life of General Sir C. Napier* (1885).

[10] H. W. S. Worsley-Benison, *Nature's fairyland* (1888).

[11] I. Donelly, *The great cryptogram: Francis Bacon's cypher in the so-called Shakespeare plays*, 2v. (1888).

[12] No account found in *H* or in the press.   [13] For his photograph.

[14] Questions; supply; *H* 326. 567.

Deremas's Serpent of Sin.[1] Off by 5.30: reached the Rectory about 10.5. All well there.

19. Sat.

Wrote to Mr Constable—Press Ass. & C. News Tel.—Letter to Editors[2]—Rev. T. Livius—Rev. G.S. Barrett—G.V. Morton—Sec. Etonian Club—Dr D'Eremas—Miss Lloyd—E. Purcell—J.S. Mackay[3]—Mr Buxton MP[4]—Mr St Clair—Mr Th. Fry MP—Mr Stuart Cumberland.[5] Read D'Eremas (finished)—Mann's Juanita[6]—Rolleston's Reply to Laing.[7] Worked on books & papers. Drive with C. The season is more forward here than in London. Church 8½ A.M.

20. Whits.

Ch 11 AM with H.C. and 6½ P.M. Wrote to Alfred Lyttelton—and J. Morley. Read Baxter's Life[8]—Lasserre's Preface to Gospels[9]—Sermons on C. Beard and M. Arnold.[10] Conversation on R. Elsmere. The children at the Rectory are charming.

21. Whitm.

Ch 8½ A.M. 6½ P.M. Wrote to S. Lyttelton—Mrs F. Evans—T. Mowbray—Miss A.J. Smith—J.R. Hughes—Ld C. Beresford[11]—J.R. Schofield—Rev. Mr Davies—J. Ogilvy—G.W. Barnes. Walk with Herbert: woodcraft. Got an account of the Staffordshire knot business from a Hanley artisan.[12] Backgammon with S. Read England & Napoleon in 1803[13]—Juanita—Lobley's Geology.[14] Attended a while the festivities on the Green.

22. Whit Tu.

Church 8½ AM and H.C. Wrote to G.B. Croucher—A. Morley MP—S. Worsley—Rev. Mr Lacey—Rev. Mr Gibson—Rev. Mr S. Du Lac—Jas Gray—A. Maclaren—F. Schnadhorst—Mr G. Coffey—Mr S. Price. Worked on Irish question & papers. Short speech to the Leeds company in the Park.[15] Walk & conversation with

---

[1] J. P. Val D'Eremas, D.D., had sent his *The serpent of Eden* (1888).

[2] Opposing extension on appeal of criminal sentences in Ireland; *T.T.*, 21 May 1888, 8a.

[3] Of Edinburgh; wrote to point out a 'very trifling inaccuracy' in *Gleanings*, i. 26; Hawn P.

[4] Who had sent his *Finance and politics*, 2v. (1888); see 20 Aug. 88.

[5] Stuart C. Cumberland; see 25 June 87.

[6] Mrs. H. Mann, *Juanita* (1887); romance in Cuba.

[7] Untraced article.

[8] J. H. Davis, *The life of Richard Baxter* (1887).

[9] H. Lasserre, *Les Saints Evangiles* (1888); see 7 May 88n.

[10] Memorial sermons by J. E. Odgers and T. W. M. Lund respectively on C. Beard and Matthew Arnold (1888).

[11] Lord Charles William De La Poer Beresford, 1846-1919; prominent in bombardment of Alexandria 1882; tory M.P. E. Marylebone 1885-9, York 1897-1900; a naval lord 1886-8.

[12] Not found; apparently documents on Hanley sent to Gladstone.

[13] O. Browning, ed., *England and Napoleon in 1803: being the despatches of Lord Whitworth and others* (1887).

[14] J. L. Lobley, *Geology for all* (1888).

[15] To liberals from Otley; *T.T.*, 23 May 1888, 7f.

Canon M[acColl]. Read Strype's Annals[1]—Döllinger on Mad. de Maintenon[2]—Browning's Engl. & Napoleon—Du Lac's La France[3]—Coffey on Home Rule.[4] Backgammon with S.

23. Wed.

Ch. 8½ A.M. Wrote to Messrs Ogilvy, G. & Co.—Ld Granville—Mr R. Maine—Mrs O'Reilly—Mr J.S. Skinner—Mr Digby Seymour. Walk & drive with Mr Herkomer; an accomplished man.[5] Read Döllinger—Napoleon & England—Strype's Annals—Juanita. Picnick under the beeches. Drafts with Rev. MacColl.

24. Th.

Ch. 8½ A.M. Wrote to Mr H. Ashworth—H. Jones—Mr Dowling—Rev. M.T. Eastwood—W.F. Whitehouse—Jas Williams—J. Wilson—H.D. Ellis—Rev. Dr Watts—H.W. Benison—T. Jones—C. Waddie. Read Döllinger on Mad. de Maintenon—Strype's Annals—England & Napoleon I (finished)—Juanita. Attended the Gymnastics. Drive with Lucy. Examined the new building with Bailey.[6]

25. Fr.

Ch. 8½ A.M. Wrote to Messrs Ogilvy G. & Co—A. Morley—J. Watson & Smith—S. Kelland—Miss Barrett—W. Irvine—F. Banfield. Read Döllinger—Strype's Annals—Collier's Hist.[7]—Palmer on the Church[8]—Juanita. Backgammon with S. Walk with Lucy.

26. Sat.

Ch. 8½ A.M. Wrote to Mr A. Mackenzie—Ld Spencer—Hygeine [sic] Food Co—Mr Benison—Rev. Mr Lathbury[9]—R. Cameron—D. Holdcroft—W. Holder—Florador Food Co.—W.J. Winter—Rev. J. Cuthbertson—Jos Staines—Mr Freeman Bell—Miss Howes B.P. Spoke 40 min. to the Rochdale party in the Park—by way of exception.[10] Read Juanita (finished)—Döllinger's Maintenon (finished)—Strype—Collier—Palmer—on 16th Cent. History. Backgammon with S.

---

[1] J. Strype, *Annals of the reign of Queen Mary* (1706); much quoted in his article; see 1 June 88.
[2] J. J. I. von Döllinger, *Die Einflussreichste Frau der französischen Geschichte* (1886).
[3] S. Du Lac, *France* (1888).
[4] G. Coffey, *Home Rule; answers to objections* (1888).
[5] (Sir) Hubert von Herkomer, 1849–1914, painter; at Hawarden to paint Mrs. Gladstone for her Golden Wedding; the picture is now in Hawarden Castle. See 31 Oct. 87n.
[6] i.e. the Octagon, built onto the Castle to accommodate Gladstone's MSS.
[7] See 4 Feb. 75.
[8] W. Palmer, *Treatise on the Church of Christ*, 2v. (1838).
[9] Perhaps Charles Edward Lathbury, vicar of Aldborough Hatch.
[10] On temperance; *T.T.*, 28 May 1888, 8a.

27. Trin. S.

Ch mg & evg. Wrote to Dr Döllinger l. & B.P.—and to [blank.] Read the remarkable Hanley Records[1]—Jews of Barnow[2]—Bertram on H. Eucharist[3]—Prize Essays on Xty. We dined at the Castle.

28. M.

Ch. 8½ A.M. Spoke a few words to the Hull excursionists.[4] Wrote to Sir W. Harcourt—R. M'Kay—W. Nield—F. Sparrow—J. Hodges—J. Ogilvy—J. Murdoch —Sir L. Playfair—Sir Thos Acland—Jas Rourke—C.G. Greer—L. Appleton—Wms & Norgate. Read L. Playfair on Trade[5]—Collier—Blunt[6]—Palmer—The Jews of Barnow. Twelve to dinner. Saw Mr Johnson—Mr Hurlbutt—Mr Mayhew— WHG.

29. Tu.

Ch. 8½ AM. Wrote to Sampson Low & Co—A. Morley—M.S. Elworth—R. Shaw—H. Martin—A. Sutton—Rev. Mr Howell—Rev. R.H. Harshaw—Rev. R. Bertram—Rev. Canon MacColl—W.G. Wellman—Mr Seymour Keay[7]—Rev. Mr OSullivan—Mr Thorndike Rice Tel.—Sir F. Milner—Mr Wilkinson. Visited the new Dee Bridge works. Saw the Rowleys. Worked on papers at the Castle. Read Lingard's Hist.[8]—Seymour Keay on Afghanistan—Jews of Barnow.

30. Wed.

Ch. 8½ A.M. Wrote to Messrs Lowery & Smith—Chairman of Vegetarians—W.H. Hewett—Sir E. Watkin MP—Fred. Kay—L. Collard—Rev. W. Hill—Rev. Sir G. Prevost—W. Fell—Miss E. Ramsden. Worked on Lingard—Wilkins[9]—Collier— Cardwell—read Jews of Barnow—Contemp. Rev. on France, Defence, & R. Elsmere: the *last* clever.[10]

31. Th.

Ch. 8½ A.M. Wrote to Ld A. Hill MP[11]—Mr Marky—Mr G.J. Holyoake—W. Nield—T.T. Willdridge—John Scott—H.J. Roberts—R. Cameron—H. Smith—G.J. Hudson—J. Pollard—J.J. Anderson—W. Mackenzie. Luncheon with Edith. Surveyed with S.E.G. five or six possible sites for my projected Library.[12] Read

[1] See 21 May 88.
[2] C. E. Franzos, *Die Juden von Barnow*, tr. M. W. Macdowall (1882).
[3] Robert Aitkin Bertram, b. 1836, congregational minister, had sent a sermon on the eucharist.
[4] Hull liberal club; *T.T.*, 29 May 1888, 12c.
[5] Sir L. Playfair in *C.R.*, liii. 358 (March 1888).
[6] See 11 Mar. 83.
[7] John Seymour Keay, 1839–1909, banker and liberal M.P. Elgin 1886–95, had sent his 'The great imperial danger. An impossible war in the near future' (1887).
[8] See 11 Jan. 34.
[9] D. Wilkins, *Concilia... 446–1717*, 4v. (1737).
[10] In *C.R.*, liii. 773 (June 1888); Andrew Lang reviewed *Robert Elsmere* in 'Theological romances'.
[11] Lord Arthur William Hill, 1846–1931; unionist M.P. Down 1880–98; a tory whip.
[12] See 15 Sept. 87.

Lingard—Wilkins—Collier—and others. Finished Jews of Barnow—read Caswall.[1] Backgammon with S. Read Ingersoll proofs.[2]

Rel[*igion*].[3]

The enormous contribution which positive religionism has made towards generating the present scepticism may perhaps be classed under the following heads
1. Exaggerations of statement & belief
2. Sins
3. Persecution—& intolerance
4. Offensive assumption of moral superiority.
5. Overvalue of positive as compared with moral commands.

Friday June One 1888.

Church 8½ A.M. Wrote to Chester Surveyor—Messrs Longbourne—S. Chatwood—Mr Thorndike Rice—T. Thomas—S.E. Thompson—S. Toncalier [?]. Worked hard on my Elisabethan paper.[4] Conferences with Bailey on the Octagon. Read Burnet[5]—Wilkins—Ingersoll proofs (finished)—Caswall. Backgammon with S.

2. Sat.

Ch. 8½ A.M. Wrote to Traffic Manager LNW—Mr Leech BP.—Canon Nisbet[6]—E. Dannatt—C. Rae Browne—S. Gallimore—J.E. Cracknell—W.L. Scott—J. Vaughan Hughes—C. Magrath—Rev. D. Marshall—J. Donnelly—C. Henderson—A.J. Dowling—Rev. R. Nightingale. Worked further on Elizabethan papers. Read Burnet—Wilkins—Caswall. Drove to see the Railway. Backgammon with S. Old Stanhope came over from Huddersfield to see me aet. 89. A fine hale old man.

3. 1 S. Trin.

H.C. 8 P.M. Service at 11 & at [blank]. Willy's birthday. God bless him: may I not say 'and he shall be blest'.

Wrote to Rev. Mr Beveridge—Mr Morley—Mr H. Quilter—Mr J. Williams. Read Dollinger on Dante[7]—Baxter's Life—Univ. Review on Zola—& on Martial.[8]

---

[1] *Caswell: a paradox*, 2v. (1887); anon. religious novel sent by Rev. Thomas Alexander Lacey with a note: 'It is not a *pleasant* book . . . it is an open secret that it was written by one of the ladies of Somerville Hall'; Add MS 44503, f. 266.
[2] See 31 Dec. 87.
[3] Dated 'May 88'; Add MS 44773, f. 68.
[4] Writing had evidently begun earlier on 'The Elizabethan settlement of religion', *F.R.*, xxiv. 1 (July 1888), reprinted in *Later gleanings*, 159.
[5] G. Burnet, *History of the Reformation of the Church of England* (new ed. in 7v. ed. N. Pocock, 1865).
[6] John Marjoribanks Nisbet, rector of St. Giles-in-the-fields and canon of Norwich.
[7] J. J. I. von Döllinger, *Umrisse zu Dantes Paradies* (1830).
[8] *Universal Review*, i. 27, 123 (May 1888); sent by the editor, H. Quilter; Add MS 44503, f. 250.

4. M. [London]

Wrote to Duke of Argyll—Rev. Mr [blank] U.P. Min of Stow—Mr Wm Robertson[1]—Messrs Horne. Packing & putting away. Off at 10.30. James St 4 PM. H. of C. 4¾–6½.[2] J. & Mary came to tea: on their way to Fasque. The voyage has answered. Finished Dante als Prophet. Read the Witches of Renfrewshire[3]—Ball on Legislation in Ireland.[4] Saw Bailey on the Octagon—Sir Alg. West—Lady West—Mr Marjoribanks—Mr Morley. Nine to dinner.

5. Tu.

Wrote to Canon MacColl—Mr Spielmann—Mrs Mackay—Mr Govan—Mr Calverhouse—& minutes. Dined at Mr Oppenheim's.[5] H. of C. 5–7½.[6] Saw Mr S.L.—Herbert J.G.—Mr Cracknell—Lady Cork—Duke of Argyll—Ld Granville—Ld Spencer. Saw the Exeter collection at Christie's. Read Hartmann on Religion[7]—Witches of Renfrewshire.

6. Wed.

Wrote to Mrs Sands—Sec. Trin. House—Rev. Duncan—Lord E. Clinton—Mr Ogilvy—Mr Seymour Keay—J. Murray—W. Griffith—Messrs Murray.—Mr H. Seymour—C.S. Palmer. Saw S. Lyttelton—Mr S. Walpole—Ld Aberdare—Stereoscopic Co. Dined at Lady Lyttelton's. Read Dollinger, Juden in Eur.[8]—Wakefield on Ireland[9]—Mlle. Girard ma Femme.[10]

7. Th.

Wrote to Rev. Dr Allon—Mr A. Lambert—Mrs Clark—Ld Acton—W.H.G. Nine to dinner. H. of C. 4¼–6 and 10¼–12.[11] Wrote further on Elisabethan settlement. Saw S. Lyttelton—Canon MacColl—Mr Anderson MP—Mr P. Campbell—J.E.G.—A. Morley—W.H.G.—Mr Chamberlain—Sir W. Harcourt. Read Döllinger's Vorträge.[12]

8. Fr.

Wrote to S.E. Thompson—Mr Knowles—Rev. Mr Wanstead—W.A. Brignal—H. Holiday. Saw S. Lyttelton—Mr Morley—Mr Anderson—Duchess of Marlborough

---

[1] Of the *Ayrshire Post*, on the by-election in Ayr burghs; *T.T.*, 9 June 1888, 15d. The liberals unexpectedly won.

[2] Imperial defence expenses; *H* 326. 1033.

[3] J. Miller, *A history of the witches of Renfrewshire* (1809, new ed. 1877).

[4] J. T. Ball, *Historical review of the legislative systems operative in Ireland, from the invasion of Henry II to the Union* (1888).

[5] Henry Maurice William Oppenheim, 1835–1912; banker and man-about-town; Gladstone already knew his wife, Isabella (see 22 July 86).

[6] Contagious diseases in India; *H* 326. 1187.

[7] C. R. E. von Hartmann, *The religion of the future* (1886).

[8] See 30 Aug. 57.

[9] E. Wakefield, *An account of Ireland, statistical and political*, 2v. (1812).

[10] A. Belot, *Mademoiselle Girard, ma femme* (1870).

[11] Questioned Balfour on his speech on Mitchelstown; *H* 326. 1401.

[12] J. J. I. von Döllinger, *Akademische Vorträge*, 3v. (1888–91).

(Dowr). Further corrected & sent off MS on Elisabethan settlement.[1] Read Ed. Rev. on Sir J. Moore[2]—Sir E. Watkin's Irish Scheme[3]—Lord Gower's dispatches.[4] Dined with Mr Marjoribanks.

9. Sat

Ch 10 AM. Wrote to Mr Milnes Gaskell—Messrs Reeves & Turner—Sir E. Watkin—Rev. Dr. Allon—Dined with Mr S. Williamson. Saw Mr A. Morley—Mr Rigby—Mr Knowles—Lady Stanley (Ald). Made calls. Read Ball on Irish Legislative[5]—Allon on Laud & the Puritans.[6] Tea at Lady Stanley's.

10. 2 S. Trin.

Guard's Chapel mg . . . . . . 7 P.M. Drive & walk with C. Wrote on position of Nonconformists Roman & other.[7] Wrote to Bp of Chester—Mr Hazel. Read Hartmann on the Religion of the Future—Guyau, Irreligion de l'Avenir[8]—Life of Bp Grant.[9]

11. M.

Wrote to S.E. Thompson—Mr Bayley—Reeves & Turner—H.G. Reid—Ld Halifax—Mr T.G. Law—Rev. Dr Allon—Mr G. Nash. Dined at [blank.] Wrote divers MSS.[10] Saw S. Lyttelton—H.J.G.—Mr H. Seymour (Col. Turner). H. of C. $4\frac{1}{2}$-8. Spoke on the question of 'selected members'.[11] Read . . . .

Pol[itics].[12]

The business of government, as an art and as a science, was in ancient times regarded as the highest among all the offices of man.

It was probably the power of Christianity which dethroned this idea and which set the culture of the individual man on a higher pedestal than the conduct of the State.

The modern movement of political ideas and forces has probably seconded the action of Christianity, and has further lowered in rank the political art by substituting in a considerable measure for the elaborated thought of the professional statesman the simple thought of the public into which emotion or affection enter more and computation less.

12. Tu.

Wrote to W.G. Roberts—Ld Hartington[13]—Mr Bullar—Rev. Guinness Rogers— Mr Knowles—Mr Thorndike Rice—M. Ragouet—Mrs Lacaita—Rev. Benham.

---

[1] See 1 June 88. [2] Untraced.
[3] Untraced speech or article. [4] See 30 Nov. 85. [5] See 4 June 88.
[6] H. Allon, *Laud and the Puritans* (1882). [7] Untraced.
[8] J. M. Guyau, *L'Irreligion de l'avenir. Étude sociologique* (1887). [9] See 13 May 88.
[10] Including a mem. of permission to quote as marked from his letters in Reid's *Life of Forster*, of which Reid had sent the proofs; Gladstone stated 'I cannot be a *party* to the publication, or in any way attest it, beyond the documents, often paragraphs against which I have placed a marginal mark . . . I say *this* because they contain some matter which my recollection does not bear out . . .'; Add MS 44504, f. 13. [11] Supporting election of all local councillors; *H* 326. 1740.
[12] Holograph dated 11 June 1888; Add MS 44773, f. 51.
[13] Long letter, replying to Hartington, on the position of 'Dissentient Liberals' and Irish local govt.; *T.T.*, 13 June 1888, 14a.

Dined with the P. Stanhopes. Saw M. Waddington—Sir E. Watkin—Lady Esher—E. Hamilton—S. Lyttelton (communication to Kathleen)—Ld Spencer—Mr T.G. Law—Mr Morley—Mr Hugessen—Mr A. Morley. H. of C. 2½-6½.[1] Read Döllinger. Saw Hayward X. Attended the (partial) funeral service at St George's (noon) for my dear old friend Sir F. Doyle.[2]

13. Wed.

Wrote to Miss Gale—J. Douglas Holms [*sic*]—Dr Collins—G.D. Bruce—G. St Clair—and [blank.] Conclave at H. of C. 4-5½ on L. Govt Bill. Expedition to B. Museum: saw Ld Acton—Mr Morley—Mr Law—Mr Bond—Mr Bullen. Exp. to Pembroke Lodge[3] for dinner. They are all most warm. Had to make a little speech. Read Döllinger—Allen on Disestablishment—Lingard's controversy with Allen[4]—&c.

14. Th.

Wrote to Mr S. Chaver—Mr Howell—Mr Finnimore—T.C. Martin. Dined at Sir C. Forster's. H. of C. 3½-7½ & after dinner.[5] Read Dollinger's Vorträge—Todhunter's Poems[6]—and Thiersch on Homer.[7] Worked on arranging books. Saw S. Lyttelton—Mr Smith.

15. Fr.

Wrote to Sir R. Welby—Mr Bullen—Mrs Th.—Rev. Dr Allon—Mr Thos Cook—E. Wastall—Mr Todhunter—W.G. Roberts.—Col. Gordon Cumming Tel.[8] H. of C. 4-7 and 9-12.30. Spoke on police controul.[9] Saw S. Lyttelton—HJG—Sir W. Harcourt—A. Morley—J. Morley. Read Dollinger—Wilkins. Worked in L. Lib. & Libr. H of C.

Th[*eology*].[10]

Granted that a Platonic monotheism had in some minds become through the influence of the Greek literature in Rome a preparation for Christianity.

Must it not on the other hand be conceded that antipathy to the Jews, the only great and defined monotheists of the age, must have operated in an opposite direction, and probably over a much wider sphere.

[1] Local govt. bill; *H* 326. 1834.
[2] In 1894 and 1895, Gladstone noted Doyle as one of those who had contemptuously or severely censured him; *Autobiographica*, i. 254.
[3] Lady Russell.
[4] J. Lingard, *A vindication of certain passages in the fourth and fifth volumes of the History of England* [*with*] *a postscript in answer to Dr. Allen's Reply* (1827).
[5] Custom's bill, Local govt. bill; *H* 327. 127.
[6] John Todhunter, 1839-1916; Irish physician, then a poet; had sent his *The Banshee, and other poems* (1888).
[7] H. W. J. Thiersch, *Griechenlands Schicksale* (1863).
[8] William Gordon Gordon-Cumming, 1829-1908; colonel in Indian army; D. L. Banff; uncle of the card cheat in the Tranby Croft affair. Business untraced.
[9] Need for county councils to be responsible for maintaining and controlling the police; *H* 327. 281. See above, x. c.
[10] Holograph dated 15 June 1888; Add MS 44773, f. 69.

And further that the ⟨dominion⟩ Stoic influence, largely prevalent at the time, was of very doubtful bearing in respect to monotheism, as the idea of a world-soul[1] has an innate tendency to diverge from the personality which is the base of monotheism.

16. Sat. [Dollis Hill]

Wrote to Ld Acton—Bp of Chester—Mr Knowles. Read Dollinger—Guillon, La France et l'Irlande.[2] Tea at Mrs T.s en route. Spent the morning 11-2 on my proofsheets (Elisabethan) and references about all which I am anxious to be strictly right. Reached Dollis Hill at 5¼, for a great Missionary gathering of which I did not know. Saw Dr Brown (Ab[erdee]n)[3]—Dr Underhill[4]—Mr Newman Hall, & several Americans indignant with Chamberlain, & others.

17. 3 S. Trin.

Rose at 4. PM. Willesden Church in evg. Saw Mr Lefevre—A. Morley—H.J.G. Read Logan, Great Social Evil[5]—Guyau, Irreligion de l'Avenir.

18. M. [London]

Back to London at 12. H. of C. 3½-7½. Eight to dinner. Spoke briefly on the Address of Condolence: with deep sincerity.[6] Read Guillon. Saw Mr Chancey—Sir W. Lawson cum Mr Illingworth.

19. Tu.

Wrote to Mr Crosfield—Mr T.G. Law—Sir W. Phillimore—W. Woodall—W.G. Roberts—Rev. Benham—J.J. Curtis—Messrs Murray—and minutes. Dined at Sir J. Paget's. Read & annotated Lingard in Dubl. Rev. on the Anglican Reformation.[7] Read True relation.[8] Saw Mr Bunting—Ld Granville—H.J.G.—A. Morley—Jacob Bright, from whom I find that his brother has diabetes & that as I fear, his public career is over. Saw M'Lachlan—M'Hugh—Murray [R]. Attended the Scott marriage in St Mark's. H. of C. 3-5¼.[9]

20. Wed.

Wrote to Mr Law BP.—Mr J.R. Hill—Mr H. Seymour—Rev. B. Martin—Mr Knowles—Mr Taylor Innes—Mr A. Morley—M. Le Blanc—Mr Thos Allen. Saw Mr Grogan—Sir W. Phillimore—Sir J. Lacaita who advised me carefully on each

---

[1] 'Döllinger Vorträge I. 166' (Gladstone's note); see 7 June 88.
[2] E. Guillon, La France et l'Irlande pendant la révolution (1888).
[3] David Brown, 1803-97; took part in the Disruption 1843; professor of apologetics, Aberdeen, from 1857; biblical critic and active in Balkan affairs.
[4] Edward Bean Underhill, 1813-1901; baptist missionary and propagandist.
[5] W. Logan, The great social evil (1871).
[6] Death of Frederick William, the German emperor; H 327. 459.
[7] [J. Lingard], 'Did the Anglican Church reform herself?', Dublin Review, viii. 334 (May 1840). Comment on this article is tacked onto the end of Gladstone's article; Later gleanings, 180.
[8] Untraced.
[9] Local govt. bill; H 327. 591.

of the old books lately bought. Dined at Mr Wilson's. Conversation with Lady Curzon. Read Suffield's Two Sermons[1]—Lockhart on Inquisition Decree (Rosmini)[2]—Wisbeach True Relation (finished)—Guillon La France et l'Irlande.

21. Th.

Wrote to Mr T.P. O'Connor l.l.—Mr A. Morley—Padre Tosti—and minutes. Dined at [blank.] Read Guillon. Saw Mr de Coverley—Mr A. Morley—Mr Hutton—Mr Knowles—Rev. Mr Martin—Sir W. Phillimore cum Dean of St Paul's on Bp King's grave matter.[3] Conclave 6–7¼ on the situation. Resolved on an Irish resolution: I do not anticipate any tactical advantage within the walls.[4]

22. Fr.

Wrote to Lady Taylor—Mr Manning—Mr A.W. Hutton—Rev. Dr Hutton—Mr Mann—Mr Digby. Saw Mr Knowles—Mr A. Morley l.l.—Mr Rideing—Mr E. Talbot l.l. (on Bp of Lincoln)—Sig. Bonghi—WHG—HJG.—Miss Swanwick. H. of C. $2\frac{1}{2}$–$5\frac{1}{4}$.[5] Read Guillon—Hutton on Angl. Orders[6]—Hassencamp Hist. Ireland.[7] Dined at Mr Bryce's.

23. Sat.

Wrote to Ld Carnarvon—Miss Blackburne—Mr S. Hawkins[8]—E.A. Robinson—M. Leon Say. Read Guillon—Hassencamp. Dined at 7: Opera, Lohengrin.[9] Saw Ld Granville—and others. A *dissipated* day: afternoon at the Tournament Agric. Hall.[10]

24. 4 S. Trin.

St Peter's & H.C. mg—Chapel Royal aft. Luncheon at Ld Magheramorne's.[11] Tea at 40 B. Square. Read Life of Grant—Warring on Genesis[12]—Döllinger, Greek in Middle Ages and [blank].

[1] Probably sermons sent by R. R. Suffield, Unitarian convert from Roman Catholicism (see 31 Dec. 74).

[2] A. Rosmini Serbati, *A short sketch of modern philosophies . . . with a few words of introduction by Fr.* [*W.*] *Lockhart* (1882).

[3] Prosecution by Church Association of E. King, bp. of Lincoln (see 21 Mar. 54) for ritualism; judgment in 1890 was substantially for King.

[4] See 25 June 88.

[5] Local govt. bill; *H* 327. 996.

[6] A. W. Hutton, *The Anglican ministry . . . in relation to the Catholic priesthood. An essay . . . with a preface by Cardinal Newman* (1879).

[7] R. Hassencamp, *The history of Ireland from the Reformation to the Union* (1888); sent by the translator, E. A. Robinson.

[8] Of Margate, on the Thanet by-election; *T.T.*, 26 June 1888, 10c.

[9] By the Royal Italian Opera, with Albani and de Reszke.

[10] Tournament held in the Agricultural Hall for benefit of soldiers' widows.

[11] See 17 Sept. 62.

[12] Charles B. Warring had sent his *'Strike, but hear me'. The Mosaic account of the Creation* (1875).

25. M.

Wrote to Rev. A. Mitchell—Warden of Keble—W. Macgange—Principal Warring U.S.—Harding & Willby. Dined at home: party of eight. H. of C. 4-7½ and
10¼-12. Morley's speech was excellent.[1] Read Hassencamp—Guillon. Saw S.
Lyttelton—A. Morley.

26. Tu.

Wrote to Mr Trotter—Sir E. Watkin—Sir J. Barrow—& minutes. Worked up the
Irish Question, esp. Killeagh. H. of C. 4-7¾ and 9¾-1¼. Voted in 274 to 367. Duty
done, at a small tactical expense.[2] Saw S. Lyttelton—Sir W. Harcourt. Read King
Lear—Guillon.

27. Wed.

Wrote to Mr Melvill—Mr Fagan—Mr . . . . . .—Mr Lloyd—& minutes. H. of C.
12¾-5½. Spoke 40 m on Channel Tunnel. Div. 307 to 165.[3] Home Rule will have
precedence of it. Saw S. Lyttelton—Ld Sydney—Mr Smith. Read Iddesleigh's
Trionfi[4]—Ld Gower's Dispatches[5]—Bridge's Hist. Ireland[6]—Channel Tunnel
MS.

28. Th.

Wrote to Mr A. Pryce—Sir E. Watkin—Mr Bryce MP—Mr Clancy MP.—Mr
Stead—Sir R. Welby—Mr Sands—and minutes. Dined at Sir C. Tennant's. Saw
Mrs Beckett—Lady H. Lennox! H. of C. 3¼-7¾, again after dinner.[7] Read Guillon.
Saw S.L.—Mr Woodall.

29. Fr.

Wrote to Rev. Kennedy Bell—Mr A. Ross l. & tel.—J.F. Wait—Mr Campbell
Bannerman—Mr A.P. Francis—Messrs Grogan—and minutes. 1¼-6. To 'Moses
in Egypt' at the Crystal Palace.[8] Saw S.L.—Sir C. Tennant—Abp of York—Mrs
White—Lady R. Read Berti's Cavour & the Autobiography[9]—Piping Hot, &
Moore's Introduction.[10] Dined at Lady Rothschild's.

30. Sat.

Wrote to Rev. S.E.G.—Mr R. Congreve—H.J.G.—J. Watson & Smith—and
minutes. Worked on Irish papers. 3¼-11¾ P.M. To Hampstead, Mr Holiday's:

[1] Resolution moved by Morley on the injurious effects of the Crimes Act; *H* 327. 1148.
[2] Spoke supporting Morley's resolution; *H* 327. 1325.
[3] Supported Walkin's bill for a Channel tunnel, which was heavily defeated; *H* 327. 1454.
[4] *Sic.* S. H. Northcote, Lord Iddesleigh, *Scraps, odds and ends*, ed. Lady Iddesleigh (1888).
[5] See 8 June 88.
[6] J. H. Bridges, *Two centuries of Irish history 1691-1870* (1888).
[7] Local govt. bill; *H* 327. 1574.
[8] As part of the Handel festival, with 4000 performers.
[9] D. Berti, *Diario medito con note autobiographiche del Conte di Cavour* (1888).
[10] E. Zola, *Piping hot* (1885); with a preface by George Moore.

spoke 1 hour on Ireland in his garden.[1] Then to B. Square & to Greenwich with Rosebery: he entertained the Labour members, & a good lot they are.[2] Conversation with R. Saw S. Lyttelton. Read Guillon—Paget[3]—Hutton's Sir Thomas More.[4]

1. July. 5 S. Trin.

St James's mg, & the near Church evg. Read Laing's Lay Sermons[5]—Gilliland, Future of Morality[6]—Paget's Pageant—Bp of Exeter Charge of 1887[7]—and looked into that wretched book 'Piping Hot'. Saw Mrs Sands 4–5½—Ld Granville—Sir C. Wood—Mr Irving.

2. M.

Wrote to Rev. H. Wakefield—Bp of Exeter—G.B. Smith—W. Robinson—T. Burgess—Earl of Iddesleigh—Mr Morley—& minutes. Dined at Mr Bunting's.[8] H of C. 4–6.[9] Read Guillon—L'Alliance Franco-Allemande.[10] Saw S. Lyttelton—Mr Smith—Sir E. Watkin—A. Morley—Sir G. Trevelyan—Sir H. Roscoe—J. Bryce—Mr Crawford—Mr Bunting—Lord Spencer cum Mr Morley—United States Exchange. Devised a scheme for payment of members.[11]

3. Tu.

Wrote to Card. Manning—Mr W.H. Rideing—Mr Hannay—Rev. Guinness Rogers—Mrs Sands—Mr Thorndike Rice—Rev. Mr Grove—The young Mathesons—Miss Clark—Mr F.E. Colenso—Miss Marsh—Mr Gillig [sic]—& minutes. Dined with Canon MacColl: NB Ld Weymouth—Miss Nisbet Hamilton[12]—Miss Geary. Read Guillon—John Ward the Preacher.[13] Saw S. Lyttelton—C. Acland—Editor of Secolo[14]—A. Morley—Burdett, & two others.

4. Wed.

Wrote to Rev. C. Voysey—Mr Bunting—J.B. Gibson—Major Ramsay—J. Page—Messrs O.G. & Co.—F. White—Rev. Prof. Reynolds—Sir W. Lawson—C.J.

---

[1] At the house of Henry Holiday, the artist; spoke on Ireland and the Thanet by-election, whose result had just been announced, the liberals just failing to capture the seat; *T.T.*, 2 July 1888, 7a. Gladstone had gone to see Holiday's mosaic of 'The Last Supper'; Add MS 44504, f. 1.

[2] No account found.

[3] F. E. Paget, *The Pageant; or, Pleasure and its price* (1843).

[4] A. W. Hutton, *Sir Thomas More, and his Utopia* (1885).

[5] Perhaps F. H. Laing, *The two evolutions, the real and the mock* (1888).

[6] M. S. Gilliland, *The future of morality as affected by the decay of prevalent religious beliefs* (1887?).

[7] E. H. Bickersteth, 'Some words of counsel' (1888), sent with other tracts; Add MS 44504, f. 52.

[8] (Sir) Percy William *Bunting, 1836–1911; methodist and social reformer; ed. *C.R.* 1882–1911; kt. 1908.

[9] Spoke on business of the house; *H* 328. 80.

[10] 'L'alliance franco-allemande. Par un Alsacien' (1888).

[11] See 6 July 88.

[12] Constance Nisbet-Hamilton of Bloxholm and Prestonkirk.

[13] M.W. Deland, *John Ward, Preacher* (1888).

[14] Periodical published in Milan; no copy found.

Dean—and minutes. Dined at Sir H. Vivian's. Saw S. Lyttelton—WHG—A. Morley—Mr Maguire—Lady Trevelyan—French [R]. Read Tolstoi's La Vie[1]—finished La France et l'Irlande. Read John Ward. Corrected part of Tunnel Speech.[2] Tea with Lady Derby & *friendly* conversation.

Pol[*itics*].[3]

O'Connor p. 10 on Home Rule. 'The movement was in existence centuries before Mr. Parnell's existence'.[4]

The growth of Irish nationalism has been singular & not quite easy to trace.

From Henry II down to 17th Cent. It subsisted *germinally* as race feeling & was warred & hunted down.

That it had the character of true nationalism was evinced strongly perhaps mainly[?] by its power of assimilation & of merging the English in the Irish element which however it largely modified.

As the Irish Parliament from the 17th Century onwards more and more felt the ground beneath its feet, a feeling of nationality grew up within its walls: but closely intertwined with & vitiated by, privilege.

There was simultaneously devised the system of the penal laws. They operated on the higher element in the nation which landlordism now developed & crushed the lower. The upshot was that nationalism lived feebly underground without air or light, in the Roman Catholic body before the Union: & O'Connell its prophet was almost solitary at that disastrous period while peers and bishops quailed around him. The nationalism of the Protestants was debased by corruption, yet it had both life and vigour.

The English influence was basely directed towards the purpose of stifling it by enlarging progressively the scope of that corruption.

But as only partial success was obtained the Union was devised to destroy the Protestant nationalism of Ireland. As regards the majority of Protestants, especially the upper class, it seems to have completely succeeded.

But the old spirit migrated into a larger and freer body namely that of what is after all the Irish nation. It became detached from all ideas of privilege and preference and it held and holds the large and open platform on which it was placed by the genuine liberalism of O'Connell.

The land-question so far from being its basis is an incidental, unhappy, and hampering accompaniment.

WEG Jul 4.88.

5. Th.

Wrote to Mr Pearson Tel.—Rev. F. Meyrick—Mr Knowles—Rev. J. Wright—Miss Beilby—R. Sanderson—J. Meynell—Sir E. Watkin BP—and minutes. Finished correcting Channel Tunnel Speech. Tea at Argyll Lodge: conversation with Duke, & Bp of St Albans. All very friendly. H. of C. $3\frac{1}{4}$-$4\frac{3}{4}$.[5] Saw S. Lyttelton—Sir W. Harcourt—French +. Finished Corr. C.T. Speech. Read Tolstoi—O'Connor on F. Hill[6]—John Ward—Mrs Green's Henry II.[7]

---

[1] Count L. N. Tolstoy, *La vie*, tr. E. Jardetzky (1888).
[2] See 27 June 88; reprinted as a pamphlet.
[3] Add MS 44773, f. 70.
[4] No relevant quotation from O'Connor traced; presumably an article.
[5] Misc. business; *H* 328. 518.   [6] Untraced.
[7] A. S. Green, *Henry the Second* (1888).

6. *Fr.*

Wrote to Mr Wemyss Reid—Baroni Ricasoli—Sig. Berti[1]—Mrs Menzies—C.E. Lea BP.—Maharajah Holkar—Under Sec. I.O.—and minutes. H. of C. $2\frac{1}{4}$–7 and $10\frac{1}{4}$–$12\frac{3}{4}$.[2] Saw Prof. Stuart—S. Lyttelton—J. Morley—A. Morley—Ld Granville—Mr Bradlaugh. Dined at A. Morley's. Conclave on Oaths' Bill.—Parnell Suit (disapproved)[3]—and [blank.]

7. *Sat.* [*Dollis Hill*]

Wrote to Gertrude G.—Messrs O.G. & Co.—Mr Ridler—Prof. Laughton—Rev J. Byles—A.L. Gladstone—Rev. B. Martin—Mrs Sands. Read Life of Forster Vol. I.[4]—Mrs Craven's Lady G. Fullerton.[5] Saw Mr Knowles—Mr Gillow *cum* Mr Meynell—Spencer Lyttelton—Mrs Th. Arr. Dollis 5 P.M. A most hearty, most exhausting, garden party. Saw Dr Parker—Mr Guinness Rogers—Sir J. Carmichael—Mr Agnew—&c.

8. *6 S. Trin.*

Willesden Ch mg & evg. Saw Granville—Lady Tavistock. Read Lady G.F.—Life of [blank.]—The Pageant (finished)—Byles, Wood, Voysey, on R. Elsmere.[6]

9. *M.* [*London*]

Wrote to Messrs Murray—Rev. Jas Smith—Jos. Ramke [*sic*]—Rev. Dr Geikie—Mr Westell—Mrs Bolton—Mr Knowles—Sec. Treasury. Returned to town at 12. Dined at Mr Stuart Rendell's. H. of C. $3\frac{1}{2}$–$5\frac{1}{4}$.[7] Saw S. Lyttelton—Murrays—Steresc. Co.—Mr Bryce—Lady Aberdeen—F. Harrison—Ld Rosebery—Ld Spencer. Read Life of Forster—Mrs Craven's Lady G. Fullerton—John Ward, Preacher.

10. *Tu.*

Wrote to Mrs Menzies—Father Coleridge[8]—R. Darlington—Lady Gladstone—Mr Knowles—Prof. Balfour—Ed. P.M.G. Dined with the Miss Monks. H. of C.

---

[1] Domenico Berti, editor of Cavour's *Autobiography* (see 29 June 88), published in Rome.

[2] Spoke unspecifically but sympathetically for Fenwick's motion for inquiry into payment of M.P.s; *H* 328. 672.

[3] F. H. O'Donnell had sued *The Times* for libel in publishing 'Parnellism and Crime' but the case collapsed, Sir R. Webster using the chance to add fresh anti-Parnell material. Parnell wished to sue *The Times* himself; Morley, advised by this conclave, dissuaded him; see Morley, iii. 394 ff. and Lyons, *Parnell*, chs. 12 and 13.

[4] T. Wemyss Reid, *Life of . . . W. E. Forster*, 2v. (1888); see 11 June 88n., 6 Aug. 88. Gladstone wrote to Wemyss Reid, 6 July 1888, Add MS 44504, f. 85: 'In reviewing my own relations with this most able & most genuine philanthropist, I find matters which do not lend themselves to a treatment satisfactory to myself, & on which I resort to my normal expedient, a suspension of final judgment. . . .' See 6 Aug. 88.

[5] P. M. A. A. Craven, tr. H. J. Coleridge, *Life of Lady Georgiana Fullerton* (1888). Granville's sister. The book criticizes Gladstone's review in 1844 of her *Ellen Middleton*, and contains various Gladstoniana.

[6] Reviews in periodicals.

[7] Local govt. bill; *H* 328. 745.

[8] Thanking him (see 11 Dec. 74) for his translation (see 7 July 88n.).

$3\frac{1}{4}$–$5\frac{1}{4}$.[1] Saw S. Lyttelton—Mr Ponsonby—Mr Waddington—A. Morley—Mr Phelps—J. Morley cum Sir W. Harcourt—Mr Childers. Read John Ward—Forster's Life—Pressensé's Speech.

11. Wed.

Wrote to R.T. Evans—Wms & Norgate—W. Ridler—Reeves & Turner—Rev. D. Mitchell—and minutes. Saw S. Lyttelton—Mrs Boryll [sic]—Messrs Agnew. Dined at [blank.] Read Memoirs of Trench[2]—John Ward—Forster's Life.

12. Th.

Wrote to R. Edwards—Sig. Moschini [sic]—Rev. Dr Samson—Mrs Bolton—Watsons—Rt. Hon. Mr Ball[3]—and minutes. Read Ball's Vol. finished—John Ward. Nine to dinner. H. of C. $3\frac{1}{4}$–5.[4] Saw S. Lyttelton—Scotts—J. Morley cum Sir C. Russell[5]—Mr Stansfeld—Mr Reid MP.

13. Fr.

Wrote to Mr W.H. Smith—Mr Carlisle—H.N.G.—and minutes. Dined with the Gaskells. Read John Ward—finished Green's Henry II. Saw S. Lyttelton—Mr Ph. Stanhope—Sir W. Harcourt cum Mr Morley on Parnell Inquiry & Land Purchase[6]—Mr A. Morley with them. Tea & long conversation with Mrs Sands. Shopping. H. of C. 3–$3\frac{3}{4}$.[7]

14. Sat. [The Coppice, Henley]

Wrote to Mr J. Morley—Bp of Winchester—Messrs. Watson—Messrs. Longman—Mr Oscar Wilde[8]—Mr T.G. Law—J.F. Finne—Jos Lawton—E.R. Shipton—Mr Meynell—J.K. Chalmers—J.H. Lloyd—J. O'Brien—T.H. Fox—and minutes. Visited the Egyptian Antiquities of 200 B.C. 4.45 PM. Off to the Coppice: it can hardly but be my last visit.[9] Read Mrs Green's Henry II—Story's Stephania[10]—Mrs Leeks & Mrs Aitchison (U.S.).[11] Saw S. Lyttelton.

---

[1] Spoke on business of the house; *H* 328. 908.
[2] *Richard Chenevix Trench . . . Letters and memorials*, ed. Miss M. Chenevix Trench, 2v. (1888).
[3] See 13 May 69, 4 June 88.
[4] Questioned Balfour on land purchase; *H* 328. 1103.
[5] Parnell's counsel at the Commission.
[6] Letter next day from John George MacCarthy, Irish land commissioner, requested Gladstone to 'kindly reconsider your opposition to a further grant under the Land Purchase Act . . . your opposition blights the hopes of thousands of Irish tenants who were just "taking heart" again. . . . It is only a development of your Land Purchase legislation of 1870 and 1881. It had its origin in a suggestion made by Mr Parnell to Lord Carnarvon in 1885 . . .'; Add MS 44504, f. 100.
[7] Local govt. bill; *H* 328. 1248.
[8] Wilde had sent a copy of *The Happy Prince* (1888); not noted as read.
[9] The Phillimores' house near Henley.
[10] Untraced.
[11] No work by these persons traced.

15. 7 S. Trin.

The new window for R. P[hillimore] first seen today, and preached on. Ch. mg & evg. H.C. and commendation of my dear old friend to God. Luncheon & the interval, at Shiplake. *Wrote* to Mr Morley. Read Watson on New Gospels[1]– Swanwick, Utopian Dream[2]–Manson's Council of Whitby.[3]

16. M. [London]

Wrote to Mr Train Gray–Mr Story–Mrs Hodgson–Mr Wallentine–Mr Mac-Carthy[4]–and minutes. H. of C. $3\frac{1}{4}$–$5\frac{1}{2}$.[5] Saw divers. Dined with the W. Jameses. Read Macdowall on Scots Minstrels[6]–Green's Henry II (finished). Conclave on the Parnell Bill. Saw S. Lyttelton–A. Morley–J. Morley.

Th[eology].[7]

1. Justification has always been sought for the Reformation of the Church in England by declaring that it followed the primitive pattern: the Church say of the four first General Councils, or of the first five centuries (Jewells challenge?)[8] or the Church before the schism in the time of Photius.
2. So that it was not an affair of private judgment exercised on the Christian Faith without any external test or standard.
   Nor with the one external standard of the Holy Scripture.
   But with the Hermeneusis,[9] or it may be said, the tradition of the earliest ages.
3. But then it remains obvious that we have still to deal with the argument on the Roman side that we do not accept the whole tradition of the Church–We sever one part from another: we embrace the first, we reject the last: and in making this severance the principle of 'private' judgment, the judgment of a particular Church as against the Roman church, is as much involved as if we likewise refused the authority of the early centuries. (The same applies also to those who admitted Trent & refused the Vatican Council in 1870.)
4. We are also open on the other side to the attacks of those who decline the authority of tradition altogether and accept as in lieu of it *geschichtliche entwickelung*,[10] historical development. It is doubtful whether these theologians, Rothe and others, would find themselves able wholly to verify their formula and draw a sharp line between their assumed opposites. Tradition is history and is historical development.
5. In like manner I think there is no broad standing ground for those who fix a certain number of centuries as marking the limit within which there is binding authority, & beyond it none.
6. But there is at least an approximation to a discrimination of this kind when we reach

---

[1] R. A. Watson, *Gospels of yesterday: Drummond, Spencer, Arnold* (1888).

[2] A. Swanwick, *An utopian dream* (1888).

[3] R. T. Manson, *The Synod of Strenonshall, or Council of Whitby; a parenthesis of Anglican church history* (1888).

[4] See 13 July 88n.

[5] Spoke on business of the house; *H* 328. 1411.

[6] W. MacDowall, *Among the old Scotch minstrels* (1888).

[7] Holograph dated 16 August 1888, Add MS 44773, f. 72.

[8] In his long controversy with Thomas Harding, John Jewel, 1522–71, recognised the legitimacy of an appeal to the authority of the first *six* centuries of Christian literature.

[9] i.e. scriptural interpretation.

[10] 'historical development'.

the point (if it can be fixed) of the first disruption of the Church into East and West. For it may not unfairly be said that the authority given to the Church in Holy Scripture is given to the United Church, and that the great Schism broke up the Sacrament of Unity.

17. Tu.

Wrote to Bp of Winchester—Mr W.H. Smith—Capt. Birkett—Mr de Wartegg—T.S. Cleary—Rev. Mr Bouverie—J. Hope—J. Kendrick—T. Eveleigh—Geo. Russell—Hon. Mrs A. Lyttelton—and minutes. Saw S. Lyttelton—Mr Schnadhorst—Mr Murray—Mr. A. Morley—Mr Gillig. H. of C. 3¼-5.[1] Read Ld Gower's Dispatches—Q.R. on Local Govt Bill &c.[2]—Memoirs of Duchesse de Tourzel[3]—Irish Tracts.

18. Wed.

Wrote to Mr Barlow—Mr Holms Ivory—Reeves & Turner—Mr Holyoake—and minutes. Christie's to see the Molesworth Collection.[4] Dined Sir W. Lawson's. Spoke 45 m.[5] Read Mad. de Tourzel—Torre Arsa, Sicilia[6]—Varigny on England (Rev. 2 M.)[7] Saw S. Lyttelton—D. of Sutherland—Sir H. Ponsonby—J. Murray—Mr Gillig. Staff[ord] H[ouse] Concert. Tea with Mrs Oppenheim. H. of C. 3¼.[8]

19. Th.

Wrote to Sig. M. Collalto[9]—Mr Vitalis—Wms & Norgate—M. Damala[10]—Mr Higham—Mr B. Field—& minutes. Dined with Mr Marjoribanks. Much conversation with Ld R. Churchill. H. of C. 3¼-6¼.[11] Saw S. Lyttelton—Mr Cunningham Graham—Herbert J.G.—Conclave on the Parnell Bill. Saw Burdett [R]. Read Mad. de Tourzel—Collalto, La Donna.

20. Fr.

Wrote to Rev. Mr Bridgett—Dr Döllinger—Mr Hutton—Mrs Rolffs—Mr J.G. Spencer—and minutes. Wrote on War Department &c.[12] Saw S. Lyttelton—E.W. Hamilton: War, & Ireland—Ld Spencer, Herbert G.: Ireland & Forster—Bp of

[1] Local govt. bill; *H* 328. 1535.
[2] *Q.R.*, clvii. 249 (July 1888).
[3] See 26 July 88.
[4] Collection of Lady Molesworth's silver, sold at Christie's 17–19 July.
[5] On, *inter alia*, the Parnell Commission; *T.T.*, 19 July 1888, 6a.
[6] V. Fardella, Marquis de Torrearsa, *Ricordi su la rivoluzione siciliana degli anni 1848 e 1849* (1887).
[7] M. C. de Varigny, 'Les grandes fortunes en Angleterre', *Revue des Deux Mondes*, lxxxvii. 872 (June 1888).
[8] Questions; *H* 328. 1645.
[9] Massimo di Collalto had sent his *La donna nella famiglia e nella società Conferenza* (1888); Hawn P.
[10] Emanuel Michael Damala, on the delivery of the marble bust and pillars sculpted by Vitalis (see 23 Oct. 83); Hawn P. Georgios Vitalis was commissioned to carve a statue of Gladstone after a competition; he completed it in 1886; it is in the courtyard of the University of Athens, with a plaster copy on the island of Tenos, from which Vitalis came. Another copy was sent to Britain, whereabouts unknown.
[11] Local govt. bill; *H* 328. 1784.
[12] See next day.

Albany, Mr Ledew, Lady Elcho, Mrs White, at dinner. Saw Phillips [R]. Read Tourzel. H. of C. 3¼–7¾. A Foolish affair.[1]

21. Sat.

Wrote to Sir Jos. Pease—A. Morley MP.—A. Galton—Dr Sterrett—E. Robson—E.W. Hamilton—and minutes. Finished writing my replies to Queries from the Commn on Departments.[2] Saw S. Lyttelton—Sir Chas Russell—do *cum* A. Morley. Six to dinner. Much conversation with Mr A. Hutton. Drive with C. 5–6½. Garden party at Lambeth & much interesting conversation.

22. 8 S. Trin.

St Margaret's 11 AM (Bp of Minnesota,[3] a striking figure & I believe a noble Sermon, but to me inaudible while loud) and Chapel Royal aft. Read Bridgett's Life of Fisher[4]—Life of Grant[5]—Döllinger, Vorträge on Reunion.[6]

23. M.

Wrote to Rivington's—Rev. Mr Barker—Robn & Nichn—Rev. Mr Bridgett—J. Gale—Professor Marino—Mr Bevan—Sig. Meale—Mr A.J. Bell—Mr M. Frewen—& minutes. Saw A. Morley—Sir C. Russell—S. Lyttelton. Dined at Ld Brassey's. H of C. 3¼–8¾. Spoke on the Parnell Bill.[7] Again 11–12. Read Life of Bp Grant—Meale, Moderna Inghilterra[8]—Mrs Burnett's Editha.[9]

24.

Wrote to Ld Spencer—Mrs Burdett, Mrs Bolton, Ld Brassey, BP—R. Lawley. Read Westr Rev. on Drunkards[10]—Blackie on Scotland[11]—Life of Bp Grant (finished)—and Sara at Miss Minchin's.[12] H. of C. 3½–7½.[13] Dined at Mr Cyril Flower's. Saw S. Lyttelton—Lady Windsor—and others. Repairing & packing books.

[1] Row about C. A. V. Conybeare's comments on the Speaker in a letter to *The Star*; *H* 329. 61.
[2] For the Ridley royal commission on civil establishments, not printed in its reports; see 23 Nov. 88.
[3] Henry B. Whipple, episcopalian bishop of Minnesota, 1859–1901.
[4] T. E. Bridgett had sent his *Life of Blessed John Fisher, bishop of Rochester* (1888).
[5] See 13 May 88.
[6] See 7 June 88.
[7] On the govt.'s bill setting up the Commission of Inquiry; Gladstone complained at the lack of specificity; *H* 329. 256.
[8] C. Meale, *Moderna Inghilterra: educazione alla vita politica* (1888).
[9] F. E. H. Burnett, *Edith's burglar. A story for children* (1888).
[10] *Westminster Review*, cxxix. 600 (May 1888).
[11] J. S. Blackie, 'A letter to the people of Scotland on the reform of their academical institutions' (1888).
[12] F. E. H. Burnett, *Sara Crewe; or, what happened to Miss Minchin* (1887).
[13] Parnell Commission bill; *H* 329. 333.

25. Wed. St James.

Holy Commn at St [blank] 8 A.M. with C. and Mary. At twelve we went to Spencer House to receive the Address and the Pictures.[1] To these were added unexpectedly three silver vases. Granville made an admirable prefatory speech. C. said a few words full of feeling. I bungled through little to my own satisfaction. The occasion hardly admits of speech. Nor can I in the *wirrwarr* put down the too abundant thoughts that come upon me. When will that leisure come? O when?

Saw Sir W. Harcourt—Ld Spencer—Sir C. Tennant.—Spencer Lyttelton—his last day of [secretarial] help. Finished Mrs Burnett's Sarah. Read Morley on French Models[2]—Westm. Rev. on International Copyright.[3] Dined at Mr Ponsonby's. Wrote to Mr Herkomer—Sir Thos Gladstone—J. Hunter—C. Palmer—Ld Hartington—& minutes. Completed & sent off my Memorandum on Military Departments. Saw Mr Cox & other Irish MPs, Mr T.P. O'Connor.

26. Th.

Wrote to Mr Hulse MP—Mr H. Hand—C. News & Press Association—and minutes. H of C. $3\frac{1}{2}$–5.[4] Drive with C. Saw S. Lyttelton—E.W. Hamilton—Herbert J.G.—Conclave on the place of Federation Meeting—Conclave on the Speaker's Imbroglio.[5] Saw Mr Quaritch. Read Mad. de Tourzel[6]—Our Country.[7]

27. Fr.

Wrote to S.W. Norton—Vestry Clerk St Marg.—J.B. Crosier—Watson Griffin—Mr Smith—Rev. S.E.G.—W.H. Robinson—Bp of Manr—F.L. Gower—Mrs Hamlyn—Mr Cowall. Read Genio di Lessing[8]—Westmr Rev on Copyright—Madame de Tourzel. Visited Mr Weigall's Studio to see his picture of C. which is promising well.[9] Irish Exhibition $11\frac{1}{4}$–$1\frac{1}{4}$: it is of great & varied interest.[10] Saw Sir W. Harcourt—Ld Sydney—Mr Grogan—Sir C. Forster. H. of C. 4–5.[11] Much packing. Read Mad. de Tourzel—Our Country. Dined with the Sydneys.

---

[1] Presentations arranged by Spencer on the misapprehension that this was the Gladstones' golden wedding day (see 25 July 89); the occasion was presented by Granville as being the start of 'the fiftieth year of their married life'; see P. Gladstone, *Portrait of a family* (1988), 171. The portraits by Holl and Herkomer (see 31 Oct. 87), donated by 116 subscribers, were presented; *T.T.*, 25 July 1888, 9f. In reply to a letter of thanks, Herkomer wrote, 27 July 1888, Add MS 44504, f. 155: 'There was so much necessarily unfinished that I felt a little nervous at its being seen by a large number of people. Its evident success will be a lasting pleasure to me....'

[2] J. Morley, 'A few words on French revolutionary models', *N.C.*, xxiii. 468 (March 1888).

[3] *W.R.*, cxxix. 405 (April 1888).

[4] Local govt. bill; *H* 329. 567.   [5] See 20 July 88.

[6] *Mémoires de Mme. la duchesse de Tourzel*, 2v. (1883); governess to Louis XVI's children.

[7] Many of this title; perhaps B. J. Lossing, *Our country. A household history...from the discovery of America [to 1876]*, 3v.l (1875–6).

[8] Untraced.

[9] Unknown portrait of Mrs. Gladstone by Henry Weigall, 1829–1925, well-known for presentation portraits.

[10] Large exhibition at Olympia of Irish products, amusements, etc.; it made a loss, an indemnity fund being started in 1891.

[11] Local govt. bill; *H* 329. 681.

28. Sat. [*Holmbury*]

Wrote to Mr H.W. Millar?—Mr J. Rosser—Mr Spielmann[1]—W.H.G.—Mr [blank.] Saw Mr Grogan. Packed another box of books. Off to Guildford and Holmbury[2] at 11. Conversation with Lord J. Bowen, and with Mr Lowell. Whist in evg. Read 'Twok'[3]—'Our Country'.

29. 9 S. Trin.

Ch mg & evg. Much conversation with F. Leveson—Lord J. Bowen—do cum Mr Lowell—Mr Stuart Rendell—Mrs S.R.—& my host. Read Life of Fisher—Our Country—Döllinger, Wiedervereinigung.

30. M. [*London*]

Wrote to Mrs Bolton BP—Mr G. White BP—A. Pryce—G. Arvanitojani—J.H. Smee—S.F. Milligan—Rev. Mr Tripp—Mr W.J. Taylor—W. Ballard. House of C. $4\frac{1}{4}$–8 and $9\frac{3}{4}$–12. $10\frac{3}{4}$–$1\frac{3}{4}$.[4] Back to J. Street. Conversation with F.L.G. on the affair of the Staffordshire Knot.[5] Read Twok—Intr. to Le Pape et l'Irlande.[6] Saw Ld Granville—Col. & Mrs Boscawen.[7]

31. Tu.

Wrote to Sir E. Watkin—Ld Methuen—Mr Donisthorpe[8]—Mr W. Grogan—Mr Gasterstein—Mlle Raffalovitch—Messrs Kellie—J.S. Curtius[9]—Sir A. Clark—E.W. Hamilton. Saw Mr Khambata—Scotts. H. of C. $3\frac{1}{2}$–$8\frac{1}{2}$ and $9\frac{1}{4}$–$12\frac{3}{4}$, on the shameful Bill.[10] Read 'In Opposition'[11]—and [blank.]

Wed. Aug. One. 88.

Wrote to Archdeacon Colley—Sir A. Clark—Mr Pryce—Mr Spiers—Mr Woodfield—Mr Macleod—Mr Lethby. Saw Mr Westell—Mr Healy—Ld Coleridge—Herbert J.G. H. of C. $2\frac{1}{2}$–$5\frac{3}{4}$ on the Bill.[12] Much packing & preparation. Conference on course to be taken about the Bill. Dined at Ld Coleridge's. Read Forster's Life[13]—'In Opposition'.

---

[1] M. H. Spielmann, editor of the *Magazine of Art*, on a forthcoming article on Gladstone's portraits by Wemyss Reid; see Add MSS 44504, f. 158, 44505, f. 232.

[2] E. F. Leveson Gower's house.

[3] Reading here and subsequently uncertain. Clearly a work of size—presumably the title of a novel—but untraced.

[4] Spoke on Parnell commission bill; *H* 329. 814.

[5] See 21 May 88.

[6] *Le Pape et l'Irlande. Documents relatifs au rescrit du Pape* (1888).

[7] Evelyn Edward Thomas Boscawen and his wife; he served in Egypt, Suakin 1885 etc.

[8] Wordsworth Donisthorpe, Individualist and anti-collectivist author; occasional correspondent; Hawn P.

[9] Julius S. Curtius had met Gladstone at Holiday's meeting on 30 June and presented him with *Das Kunstgesetz* (1888); Hawn P.

[10] i.e. the Parnell commission bill; *H* 329. 960.

[11] G. M. I. Blackburne, *In Opposition. A Novel* (1888).

[12] Spoke on the Parnell commission bill; *H* 329. 1161.

[13] See 7 July 88.

2. Th.

Wrote to Mr Theoph. Matthews—Rev. Mr Tripp—Mr Wilson—Mr Tilling—Mr Spiller—Messrs Scribner—Mr Garnham—Mr G. Dudson—Mr Galloway Weir[1]— Mr Thorndike Rice—Mr Clancy MP. Saw Ld Rosebery—Ld Granville—A. Morley MP—Mr Morley *cum* Sir W.H.—Rev. Dr. Liddon—Mr Illingworth. Dined at Sir C. Forster's [*sic*]. H. of C. 3½–8 and 10½–1½.[2] I should like to have 'renounced' after yesterday. But we could not without Mr P. & the Irish. Read Forster's Life. More packing.

3. Fr. [Berkhampstead House]

Clearing away from a London house is now to me a sort of harbinger of freedom: but I had a strained and busy morning. Off at 11½. Two hours at Watford. Visited Cashiobury Park.[3] Divers conversations: & the people rather lively. Reached Lady Sarah's[4] by road (a beautiful drive) soon after five. She is one who makes me very unwilling to part company with aristocracy. Wrote to Station Master Euston—Mr Carlisle . . . . List unhappily lost.[5] Read Twok—Forster's Life.

4. Sat. [Mentmore]

Wrote to Wms & Norgate—Mrs Ingram—H.C.W. Gibson—Mr English—Mr Rimonell—Mr Wallace—Mr T. Henri—Lady S. Opdebeck—Mr Molony—Mr R. Walker. Read Forster's Life—Carlisle—Montague Letters[6]—Twok. Drove 12 m to Mentmore:[7] parting company from the pretty country. Walk & conversation with Rosebery.

5. 10 S. Trin.

Ch mg (with H.C.) and evg. Wrote to Lord Camoys—Mr Campbell Bannerman. Walk with Rosebery. Conversation with Mr Ford on Spain & Greece. Read Cognel's Paris under Louis XVI[8]—Life of Card. Fisher—Döllinger's Vorträge (finished)—Bellarmine De Arte &c.

6. M. [Hawarden]

Off to Hawarden 11¼–3½. Read (largely) Forster's Life—Peggy Thornhill.[9] Crops as usual look better here than elsewhere: but the vegetation generally looks woe-begone. Began to write on Forster's Life for N.C.[10]

---

[1] James Galloway Weir, 1839–1911; member of L.C.C. and independent liberal candidate; liberal (crofter) M.P. Ross and Cromarty from 1892.
[2] Supported Goschen's motion to proceed with business of the day, thus setting aside Labouchere's motion that *The Times* was guilty of a breach of privilege for its comments this day on Gladstone and the liberal leadership; *H* 329. 1255.
[3] Lord Ebury's house.   [4] Lady Sarah Spencer (see 9 June 83), Spencer's sister.
[5] Phrase added later.   [6] Lady M. W. Montagu, *Letters and works* (1887).
[7] Rosebery's house near Leighton Buzzard.
[8] F. Cognel, *La Vie Parisienne sous Louis XVI* (1882).
[9] M. Damant, *Peggy Thornhill, an Irish tale* (new ed. 1888).
[10] 'Mr. Forster and Ireland', *N.C.*, xxiv. 451 (September 1888), reprinted in *Special aspects*; a review

7. Tu.

Ch. 8¼ AM. Wrote to Mrs Davenant—E. Evans—E. Morris—Mr Brophy—J. Weyman—Dr Freunkel—Messrs Grogan. Saw Bailey's—Herbert G—& examined the new Octagon.[1] Read Forster—Peggy Thornhill—Finished Twok. Walk with Lucy in park and woods.

8. Wed.

Ch. 8½ A.M. Wrote to Lady D. Neville B.P.—Mr Morley MP—Sig. G. Vedana— E.W. Hamilton—Rev. O. Shipley—Mr Holland—Mr Agnew—R. Cameron—E. Connal—A. Moffat. Attended the Rowley marriage[2] at 2.30, and signed [the register]. All but finished paper on the Life of Forster—Sinclair's Poems[3]— Stopes on Bacon-Shakespeare.[4] Drive with C. Gave my MS to Lucy[5] for perusal: her judgment is worth having.

9. Th.

Ch. 8¼ A.M. Wrote to Sec Art & Sc. Dept—Miss Clairmont—Mr Halliwell— H.C.W. Gibson—Jul. Sinclair—Mr Knowles—Mrs J. Thomas[6]—J. Curlill. Corrected & sent off the Forster MS: with Lucy's *imprimatur*. Drive with C. Saw Mr Mayhew. Read Harrison's Cromwell[7]—Peggy Thornhill—and [blank.]

10. Fr.

Ch. 8½ A.M. Wrote to Messrs Rivington—Prof. Stuart MP.—T.L. Wright—Rev. S.M. Carter—Rev. H. Algar—Messrs Heywood—Dr. Forshaw.[8] Worked on Basis of Homerology. Read Harrison's Cromwell—Peggy Thornhill—Danielo Cortis.[9] Drive with C. I have made a beginning on the very formidable business of arranging my papers wh I undertake boldly as a duty to my children whom it wd sorely perplex.

11. Sat.

Ch. 8¼ AM. Wrote to Rev. G. Jenkinson—Mr Morley MP—D. Martin—Mr T. Healy MP—Ld Aberdeen—Mr Arvanitojani. Saw Bailey & further considered arrangements for the Octagon. Drive with C. Read as yesterday.

of Reid's biography (see 7 July 88), especially controversial in its comments on Forster and the events of 1882; see R. Hawkins, 'Gladstone, Forster and the release of Parnell, 1882-8', *I.H.S.*, xvi. 417 (1969). A review for the *Contemporary Review* had been suggested in March by Bunting when Reid's book was expected to be published in May; Add MS 44503, f. 84.

  [1] The storage room for Gladstone's MSS built onto the Castle.
  [2] Ursula M. Dunstan, niece of Joseph Rowley of Queensferry, m. Thomas Henry Hancock, s. of W. Hancock; see 'Fashionable Wedding at Hawarden', *Chester Chronicle*, 11 August 1888, 5.
  [3] Julian Sinclair had sent his *Nakiketas, and other poems* (1887).
  [4] C. C. Stopes, *The Bacon-Shakespeare question* (1888).
  [5] i.e. Lucy Cavendish.
  [6] Thanking Mrs. J. Thomas of Woburn for her pamphlet on Irish leaders; see *T.T.*, 18 August 1888, 5f.   [7] F. Harrison, *Oliver Cromwell* (1888).
  [8] Thurston Forshaw, physician in Smalley, Derbyshire.
  [9] A Fogazzaro, *Daniele Cortis. Romanza* (1887).

12. 11 S. Trin.

Ch mg & evg. Wrote to Mr H. Gibson—Provost of Dalkeith[1]—P.S. to Mr Morley. Read Tschiraev[?], Fall des H.[2]—Vincenzi De Monarchiâ[3]—Report of Oxford Mission[4]—Bridgett's Fisher.

13. M.

Ch. 8½ A.M. Wrote to Mr A. Morley—Pres. *Philologi* of Bologna[5]—Lord Acton. Historical conversation with Herbert and H. Drew. Reviewed my 27 Propositions of 1842.[6] Wrote Notes on Ireland. Worked hard on the business of arranging my papers. It will seem small in my journal but must take much of my time for many weeks. Saw Bailey & Mr Douglas's assistant on the Octagon. Read Harrison's Cromwell—Emmanuel on Fusion of B. and S.[7]

14. Tu.

Ch. 8½ A.M. Wrote to Miss C. Marsh B.P.—Rev. Dr. Teape[8]—Mr Easterby—Mr Primrose—Dr Manfroni[9]—Mr Healy MP.—Mr Emmanuel—Mr D. Nutt—V.L. Cameron—J.H. Lloyd—Thos Aldred—G.C. Walton—F. Gell—A. Sutton—Mrs MacCray—Sig. Pellicione (Bologna).[10] Worked up Forster references. Worked 'some' on Homer. Drive with C. Read Cromwell—Peggy Thornhill—Laing on WEG & Ingersoll.[11]

15. Wed.[12]

Ch. 8½ A.M. Wrote to Sir E. Watkin MP—Mr Primrose—Scotts—Messrs Bailey. Yesterday & today busy in re-examining possible sites with WHG.[13] Spent 3 hours on private affairs & explained all to C. in the subject of the meditated Institute. A little Homeric work. Corrected proofs of art. on Forster's Life. Read

[1] For a meeting on Dillon's imprisonment: 'if Mr. Dillon broke the law he was driven to break it by the gross misconduct of the government and the Parliament of 1886'; *T.T.*, 15 August 1888, 7e.

[2] Author's name illegible; untraced.

[3] L. Vincenzi, *De Hebraeorum et Christianorum Sacra Monarchia et de infallibili in utraque magisterio* (1875).

[4] Probably of the Oxford Mission to Calcutta, in whose organisation S. E. Gladstone was involved.

[5] G. Pelliccioni; Gladstone had been awarded *in absentia* an honorary degree from the University of Bologna in June as part of its octocentennial celebrations; *T.T.*, 17 June 1888, 8d.

[6] 'Twenty-seven propositions relating to current questions in theology', 29 December 1842, with a note written this day finding 'nothing to demand change in what related to positive belief', but qualifying his comments on 'non-Anglican Protestants'; in *Autobiographica*, i. 236.

[7] Untraced tract on the bible and science sent by a Mr. Emmanuel (see next day).

[8] Charles Richard Teape, retired episcopalian clergyman living in Edinburgh; published on philosophy.

[9] Mario Manfroni, of Rome, a friend of Bonaventura Zumbini (whose *W. E. Gladstone* was published in 1914); he sent the good wishes of the University of Naples; Hawn P.

[10] See previous day's n.

[11] Proofs of article by S. Laing for the *Agnostic Annual*, sent by its ed., Charles A. Watts; Add MS 44504, ff. 182, 189.

[12] The dating and order of 15–16 Aug. 88 are uncertain.

[13] For what became St. Deiniol's Library.

Peggy Thornhill finished—Röthe on the Schenkel controversy[1]—. . . . . . . on Law of Tithes.

16. Thurs.

Wrote to . . . .
Worked on Homer. On books & papers. Conclave 1½ hour on River Dee Foreland Suit. Seven to dinner. Read P. Thornhill—D. Cortis—Life of Emmet. Worked on Theol. Examination of sites.

17. Frid.

Ch. 8½ A.M. Wrote to Tewfik Pasha[2]—Mr Mayhew—S. Laing—Mr Knowles—G.S. Hare—U. Sec. F.O.—Earl Selborne—Mr M'Nicoll. Worked on Homer. d[itt]o on Books & papers. Further examination of sites. Two decidedly preferred out of eight. Read Dan. Cortis and read Curtius, Kunstgesetz.[3]

18. Sat.

Wrote to Miss Canning[4]—Mr E.R. Russell—Mr Woodall, Mr Quaritch, J. Moore, R.M. Lewis, Miss Robertson BP., P. Master H of Commons. Worked on books & papers. Read Chalmers on Comparative Wealth & Strength[5]—Daniele Cortis.

19. 12 S. Trin.

Ch. mg & evg. Wrote to Mr Downing—Dr Macleod—Dr Wright—Dr Brown. Rothe—Dana & other papers in Biblioth. Sacra[6]—St Patrick's Works and Wright's Preface.[7]

20. M.

Ch. 8½ A.M. Wrote to Mrs Haverty—Mr Knowles BP—Jas Murray—Mr Buxton MP—Miss O'Byrne[8]—Mr Easton. Saw Mr Woodall MP[9]—Mr W. Bailey. 12-2. Function on receiving the beautiful vase from Burslem. Spoke 20 m indoors & an hour out.[10] Read Buxton Finance & Politics[11]—Daniele Cortis.

[1] R. Röthe, *Dogmatik . . . aus dessen handschriftlichem Nachlasse herausgegeben von Dr. D. Schenkel*, 2v. (1870).
[2] Thanking the Khedive for congratulations on his golden wedding; Add MS 44504, ff. 174, 185.
[3] See 31 July 88n.
[4] Louisa Canning had asked permission to include Gladstone's memorial letter in Poole's *Life of Stratford de Redcliffe*; Add MS 44504, f. 183; permission was granted, but the letter arrived too late for inclusion (Add MS 44505, f. 7).
[5] G. Chalmers, *An estimation of the comparative strength of Britain during the present and four preceding reigns* (1782).   [6] In *Bibliotheca Sacra and Theological Review*.
[7] *The writings of St. Patrick . . . with notes by G. Y. Stokes and C. H. H. Wright* (1887).
[8] *sc.* O'Brien; see 3 Jan. 87.
[9] William Woodall of Burslem, 1832-1901; pottery manufacturer; liberal M.P. Stoke 1800-5, Hanley 1885-1900; minor office 1892-5.
[10] On the Parnell Commission, and on the case of Manderville, imprisoned under the Crimes Act; Gladstone compared the Irish government with 'King Bomba' in 1851; *T.T.*, 21 August 1888, 10a.
[11] S. C. Buxton, *Finance and politics; an historical study 1783-1885*, 2v. (1888), with much material on Gladstonian finance. Still a standard work. See 19 May 88n.

21. Tu.

Ch. 8½ A.M. Wrote to Lady Rothschild—Mr Thorndike Rice—L.U. Reavis BP—F. Fitzsimons—W. Armstrong—Ld Ripon—B. Quaritch. Worked on Homeric Proposition. Also on Books & Papers. Saw Mr S. Halifax—Mr Webster. Whist in evg. Read Daniele Cortis—Chalmers, Compar. Wealth.

22. Wed.

Ch. 8½ A.M. Wrote to Mr E. Arnold—Mr Knowles BP—Mr Grenfell—Ld Houghton—Central News, Press Assocn, Tel.[1] Worked on letters & books. Worked on Homer. Drive with C. Read Daniele Cortis—Solon on English Pottery[2]—Chalmers—and [blank.] Dispatched Forster Revise.

23. Th.

Ch. 8½ A.M. Wrote to Lady F. Cavendish BP—Mr Walter—Earl of Selborne—Mr Edge—Mahomet . . . . . [sic]—Earl of Ashburnham—Earl Granville—E. Morton—J.J. Hughes—Mr Knowles Tel.—Mr Woodall Tel.—H.N.G.—Mr Stead—W.L. Scott—Mr Baldwin—Mr Tibbits. Read Rawson Prod. & Cons.—Daniele Cortis. Eleven to dinner. Visited the Horticultural Show, & spoke 45 m or more to the Assembly.[3] Worked on Hom. Geogr. Further work about site. Conversation with Mr E. Russell.[4]

24. Fr. St Bart.

Ch 8¼ A.M. Wrote to Mr H.R. Grenfell—Rev. E.R. Jones—Scotts—Rev. J.R. Mills—B. Quaritch—Mr J. Beauchamp—W. Thomas—T.W. Bunting. Conversation with Mr Russell. Walk with W. & Mr Bere. Worked on letter-sorting. On Homeric plots. Read Daniele Cortis—and Chalmers. Nine to dinner.

25. Sat.

Ch. 8½ A.M. Wrote to Sir E. Watkin MP—Mr Macmillan—Mr Morley—Editor of Tablet[5]—Mr J. Brown—Mr E. Spearman—Mr J.S. Vickers. Worked further on the question of site. On Homeric Propp.—on books and letters. Drive with Helen. Read Daniele Cortis and Mrs Caird's most repulsive article in Westmr Rev.[6]

26. 13 S. Trin.

Ch. mg & evg. Wrote to Mr A. Hutton—Mr Goadby—Mr Woolnott—Mr Tallach—Mr Lanihan?—Mr Fletcher—Miss Harvey PP. Read R.C. Reply in

---

[1] Defending his comparison of 1888 and Naples in 1851, though conceding some error of detail in his speech on 23 August: 'what have we come to when there is ground for such comparisons?'; *T.T.*, 23 August 1888, 3e.

[2] L. M. E. Solon, *The art of the old English potter* (1883), sent by J. Wilcox Edge; letter of thanks in *T.T.*, 25 August 1888, 5e.

[3] On land tenure and agriculture; *T.T.*, 24 August 1888, 5a.

[4] Good account in Sir E. Russell, *That reminds me . . .* (1900), 102ff.

[5] John George Snead Cox, who had sent 'The Elizabethan settlement of religion. A reply to Mr. Gladstone', *The Tablet*, 25 August 1888, 283; Add MS 44504, f. 216.

[6] Mona Caird, 'Marriage', *W.R.*, cxxx. 186 (August 1888).

Tablet[1]—Laing (Dr) on Evolution[2]—Dr Wright on Lassare[3]—Nippold on Rothe[4]—[blank] on St John.

27. M.

Ch. 8½ A.M. Wrote to Mr Reg. Brett—Mr S. Smith MP—Mr Rawson—Mr Burbridge—Lucy C.—Rev. Mr Manley—T. Judge—& minutes. Worked on Homer. On books & letters. Saw Mr Vickers & gave him instructions about the site on the spot. Read Daniele Cortis (finished)—Froude's Negrophobia.[5]

28. Tu.

Ch. 8½ A.M. Wrote to Mons. L. Mickiewicz[6]—Mr Westell—G. Ashdown—Messrs Hughes—J. Robertson Scott[7]—L. Biggs—G.J. Day—A. Thomson. Worked on books & letters: Helen assisting (Her birthday, God bless her)—Say four hours. Worked on Homer. Read Life of Mickiewicz—Macmillan on Doyle—on Coleridge[8]—Prince Crapotkin [sic] in NC—Mrs Priestley on Pasteur.[9]

29. Wed.

Ch. 8½ A.M. Wrote to Ld Coleridge—Mr Morley—S. Webb—J. Bullock—C. Morley—F. Read—Mr Crathurn—S. Hallifax—H.P. Ryland—A.N. Hutton—E. Hughes. Another four hours on books and letters. Drive afterwards. Worked on Homer. Read Mickiewicz—'I've been thinking'[10]—G. Smith on Amn Statesmen.[11]

30. Th.

Ch. 8¼ A.M. Wrote to Señorita Portelas[12] BP—Hon Rev. A. Lawley—C. Stratton—Mrs Haverley [sic]—H.J. Bale—Rev. Mr Bokkell—Tilston Tel.l.l. Four h. again on books & letters. Worked on Homer. Drive with C. Read Life of Mickiewicz—I've been thinking—Alexander on Aberdeenshire.[13]

31. Fr.

Ch. 8½ A.M. Wrote to Sir Charles Tennant—Dr Alexander—Mr Rawson—Rivingtons—Sir E. Watkin—Westell—T. Lowther—Baker (Soho Sq)[14]—Mr Vickers—Mr

[1] See 25 Aug. 88n.
[2] See 1 July 88 and notes at Add MS 44504, f. 204.
[3] Not traced.   [4] F. Nippold, *Richard Röthe*, 2v. (1873-4).
[5] J. A. Froude, *The English in the West Indies* (1888).
[6] L. Mickiewicz had sent his life of his father, *Adam Mickiewicz, sa vie et son oeuvre* (1888); Hawn P.
[7] John William Robertson Scott, 1866-1962; journalist on the *P.M.G.*, and much later its biographer.
[8] *Macmillan's Magazine*, lviii. 247, 285 (August 1888).
[9] P. A. Kropotkin, 'The coming reign of plenty', and Mrs. Priestley, 'Pasteur', *N.C.*, xxiii. 817, 838 (June 1888).
[10] A. S. Roe, *I've been thinking* (1853); a novel.
[11] *N.C.*, xxiv. 262 (August 1888).
[12] Amelia Portelas of Cadzada had written in admiration; Hawn P.
[13] W. Alexander, 'The making of Aberdeenshire' (1888).
[14] Perhaps in the House of Mercy on the corner of Soho Square.

Guinness Rogers—Mr S. Webb. Four hours on books & letters. Worked on Homer. Drive with C. Read Mickiewicz—Abp Walsh on Mr Wyndham[1]—Haddow on Miners of Scotland[2]—Webb on the Liberal Party.[3]

Sat. Sept. One. 1888.

Ch. 8½ A.M. Wrote to Rev. P.C. Clark—
Mr Tilston
Mr Roberts   at Wrexham where there is a row[4]
The Mayor
Mr L. Reynolds—F.E. Vales—Mr S. Jefferson—Press Assn Tel. 4½ hours on books & letters. Saw Warden Talbot—Mr Stevenson. Homer work stopped by the Wrexham messenger. Read I've been thinking—Merry Wives of Windsor—Robbery under Arms.[5]

2. 14 S. Trin.

Ch. mg (with H.C.) and evg. Wrote to Mr Tilston—Messrs Knowles. Read Life of Rhys Lewis[6]—West. Rev. on Forster[7]—Richmond, Xtn Economics[8]—Cristianismo e Scienza.[9]

3. M.

Ch. 8½ A.M. Wrote to Dr. Carpenter—Sir C.A. Wood—M. Kelly—S. Webb. Saw Mr Bailey—Mr Toller—Sir E. Watkin—Mr Johnstone. 4 h on books & letters. Examined Shakespeare[10] & other books about Wales. & Read . . . Twelve to dinner. Made very short notes in evg for my subjects tomorrow.

4. Tu.

Ch. 8½ A.M. The Psalms, as often, gave me a message: 'Send thee help from the sanctuary and strengthen thee out of Zion'.[11]
    Wrote to Lucy Cavendish—Mr Pryce—A.M. Palmer. Saw Bailey on the Octagon.
    9¾–4. Expedition over the new Railway to Wrexham. 10 or 12000 in the streets: 8 or 10 m[ille] in the two Buildings. Addressed the political meeting

[1] W. J. Walsh on G. Wyndham and Ireland, *C.R.*, liv. 447 (September 1888).

[2] R. Haddow in *N.C.*, xxiv. 360 (September 1888), the number contains his review of Forster.

[3] Presumably an article or pamphlet sent this day by Sidney Webb, 1858–1943; Fabian socialist and author; colonial office clerk 1881–91. See this day.

[4] About arrangements for the Eisteddfod; its organising cttee. objected to the local liberal association presenting an address of welcome; see *T.T.*, 31 August 1888, 8c and 4 Sept. 88. Gladstone's letter of this day attempting to defuse the row is in *T.T.*, 3 September 1888, 7e.

[5] R. G. Balderwood, *Robbery under arms*, 3v. (1888).

[6] D. Owen, ed., *Rhys Lewis, minister of Bethell: an autobiography* (1888).

[7] *W.R.*, cxxx. 310 (September 1888).

[8] W. J. Richmond, *Christian economics* (1888).

[9] Untraced.

[10] He discussed various quotations from *Henry V* on Welshmen in his speech next day.

[11] Psalm xx. 2.

first: then the Eisteddfodd.[1] Pretty well exhausted by the awful atmosphere of
the Hall. All was harmony. Luncheon at Mr Ellis's pleasant residence. Taken all
together, a day of much interest. A nap on returning set me up. Worked on
letters. Read Life of Rhys Lewis.

5. Wed.

Ch. $8\frac{1}{2}$ A.M. Wrote to Mr John Oakes BP—Mr Schnadhorst—W.L. Courtney[2]—
Mr Tilston Tel.—Mr Irvin—Mr Buckley. $4\frac{1}{2}$ h on books & letters. Attended in evg
the Lecture on Central Africa by Bishop Smithies,[3] & made a short speech of
acknowledgment.[4] Read Rhys Lewis. Drive with C.

6. Th.

Ch. $8\frac{1}{2}$ A.M. Wrote to Mr Ivor James[5]—E. Morris—Mr Morley MP—Mr Dillon—
Rev. Dr. Dike—J.E. Gladstone—Mr M'Closkey[6]—Mr Bryant—Mr Knowles.
　　We were photographed today with our ten grandchildren, all flourishing
thank God. Drive with C. Heard the beautiful music of the Wigan Choir. It has
not however the delicacy of the Welsh. 5 hours on books & letters. Read Rhys
Lewis.

7. Fr.

Ch. $8\frac{1}{2}$ A.M. Wrote to Mr Ricketts—Professor Rhys[7]—Mr Liversidge—Mr Naganowski[8]—Mr Footit BP—Mr Steuart—Mrs Th.—R. Hall—Mr Tague—Mr Garme-
son—Mr Dear. 5 hours on letters & papers. Went out with W. & Mr Mayhew to
prosecute further the examination of sites for St Deiniol's. Read Plutarch on
Isis[9]—Life of Rhys Lewis.

8. Sat.

Ch. $8\frac{1}{2}$ A.M. Wrote to Rev. Mr Mayow—Mr S. Lloyd—Mr L. Beale—R.A. Hudson[10]—Mr W. Livesay—Lord Cavan—Messrs Poole—D.C. Jones. Further investigation of sites for St Deiniol's. Four hours on letters &c. Read Plutarch on
Isis—Life of Rhys Lewis (finished)—Zamoisky's Russie-Pologne.[11]

---

[1] By separating the two occasions, the row (see 1 Sept. 88) was defused; *T.T.*, 5 September 1888, 6a.
[2] Replying to a series of questions on J. S. Mill; William Leonard Courtney was writing his biography (see 13 Apr. 89).
[3] Charles Alan Smythies, 1844–94; bp. of Zanzibar 1884.
[4] No account found.
[5] Apologizing to him for referring to him as 'Rhys' during his speech at the Eisteddfod, *T.T.*,
8 September 1888, 11f; see 5 Oct. 87n., 4 Sept. 88.
[6] Uriah McClinchy, president of the Protestant Home Rule Association of Banbridge; *T.T.*, 8
September 1888, 9e.
[7] John Rhys, Professor of Celtic in Oxford from 1877.
[8] Edmond S. Naganowski, secretary of the Friends of Poland, complained of inaccurate statements about Poland by Gladstone in his speeches at Hawarden and Wrexham; *T.T.*, 6 September
1888, 5f, 11 September 1888, 9c.　　　　　　　　　　　　　[9] Plutarch, *De Iside et Osiride*.
[10] Robert Arundell Hudson, 1864–1927; assistant secretary of the N.L.F. 1886–93; secretary from
1893; also secretary of Central Liberal Association; see Add MS 44504, f. 257.
[11] Probably L. Zamoyski, 'Poland' (1861); on Russo-Polish affairs.

9. 15 S. Trin.

Ch. mg & evg. Wrote to Mr Laing (belief)—Messrs Hughes—Mr J. Morgan—Rev. J.G. Rogers—Mr T. Graham—Rev. G. Dunnett—Rev. E. White. Read Hutton on Angl. Orders[1]—Rogers on present Religion[2]—[blank] on Pope's Rescript.[3] Examined into some of the Homeric Prayers.

10. M.

Ch. 8½ A.M. Wrote to Lady Sophia Palmer[4]—The Italian Consul—Mr Downing —J. Aldridge—Rev. Sir J. Philipps—Nawab Mohamed Mulk[5]—Rev. Mr Stark—Rev. H. Murphy—Mr Howell—T. Kemp—Dr. Flynn—Abp. Walsh. 9¼-7. Went to see the new Colliery & the Brickworks: then to see G. and her dear children. 3 h. on books & papers. Read Russie-Pologne (finished)—Chadwick on Sanitation[6]—and several articles in Contemp. Rev.

11. Tu.

Ch. 8½ AM. Wrote to Sir U. Shuttleworth—L. Morris—Mr Knowles—Mr Jas Eshelby—Rev. P. Tracey—Rev. E.T. Craig—T. Baker—T.H. Barker—A. Morris—T. Ashdown. 3 h on books & papers. The Cunliffes came bringing Mr & Mrs Humphry Ward[7] to tea & see the place. It was a pleasant visit. He is a great gentleman: & those who are outside have not drifted so far as the MPs. Read Pocock's remarkable tracts on Reformation[8]—read on Welsh Topography—'I've been thinking'—Marsden, & Mostara, on Mosaic Code.[9]

12.

Ch. 8½ A.M. Wrote to Ld Selborne & copy[10]—Miss Murray—Mr Primrose—Rev. Mr Felton. 12-7. To the top of Moel Famma, walking 7 miles, & C.G. walking

---

[1] See 22 June 88.

[2] J. G. Rogers, *Present-day religion and theology* (1888).

[3] See 30 July 88.

[4] Sophia Matilda Palmer, 1852-1915, da. of Lord Selborne; she m. 1903 Amable Count de Franqueville.   [5] See 15 Sept. 88.

[6] Sir E. Chadwick, 'The financial value of sanitary science' (1887).

[7] Sir Robert and Lady Cunliffe took Mrs. Ward and her husband (*inter alia* a leader-writer for *The Times*) over to Hawarden; she found that 'the G.O.M. was delightful. First of all he showed us the old Norman keep, skipping up the steps in a way to make a Tory positively ill to see, talking of every subject under the sun—Sir Edward Watkin and their new line of railway, border castles, executions in the sixteenth century, Villari's *Savonarola*, Damien and his tortures—"all for sticking half-an-inch of penknife into that beast Louis XV!"—modern poetry, Tupper, Lewis Morris, Lord Houghton and Heaven knows what besides, and all with a charm, a courtesy, an *élan*, an eagle glance of eye that sent regretful shivers down one's Unionist backbone. He showed us all his library—his literary table, and his political table, and his new toy, the strong fire-proof room he has just built to hold his 60,000 letters, the papers which will some day be handed over to his biographer. His vigour both of mind and body was astonishing—he may well talk, as he did of "the foolish dogmatism which refuses to believe in centenarians."' (Mrs. Ward to J. R. Thursfield, 14 September 1889, in J. P. Trevelyan, *The life of Mrs Humphry Ward* (1923), 71.)

[8] N. Pocock, *Records of the Reformation*, 2v. (1870).

[9] J. B. Marsden, *Influence of the Mosaic code upon subsequent legislation* (1862).

[10] See 21 Sept. 88.

six. Saw Mr Bailey on proximate & future operations. Read I've been thinking—and Sunny Memories.[1]

13. Th.

Ch. 8½ A.M. Wrote to Mr C. Allen l. & BP—Mr Brignal—R.A. Hudson—P.J. Stirling—J.C. Fowler—Mr Astley Cooper—W. Mull—A.M. Palmer—Mr Loverdo—E.J.C. Morton[2]—Ld Selborne. We entertained the band of the Welsh Fusiliers about 56 out of doors, in *hot* sun(!) and they gave a delightful concert to a mixed company. Mr Morley came: long conversation with him. Also with Mr S. Rendell. Read I've been thinking—and Sunny Memories—How on Welsh Laws.[3] Twelve to dinner.

14. Fr.

Ch. 8½ A.M. Wrote to Ed. Encycl. Dict.—Rev. R. Bulgarnie—Rev. J.W. Tristram[4]—Lord Houghton—Isaac Myer[5]—Revue de l'Orient[6]—Sir And. Clark—Mr Lorimer—C. Higham—Mr Trotman—G.J. Day—J. Hayward. Lady Grosvenor & Mr Wyndham came to tea. Visited the Bridge[7] with Mr Rendell. Long political conversation with Mr Morley. Read Plut. Isis & Osiris—Myer on the Cabbala—and the Canada Poet. Nine to dinner.

15. Sat.

Ch. 8½ A.M. Wrote to Miss O'Byrne—Ld Acton—Messrs Hughes—H. Algar—J.B. Jones—H. Summers—Ellis Hughes—J. Ouseley—J. Curtius. The Nizam's Indians came & seemed to be pleased.[8] Walk with W. for still further consideration of sites. Conversation with Mr Stuart Rendell who left us. Read Strype Annals[9]—Brewer[10]—& other Church Books.[11]—Hist. of West Kirby.[12]

---

[1] Probably A. R. Butler, *Little Kathleen; or, sunny memories of a child-worker* (1890).

[2] Edward John Chalmers Morton, 1856–1902; secretary of the Home Rule Union; liberal M.P. Devonport from 1892.

[3] Perhaps a slip of the pen for J. C. Fowler, 'Ancient laws and institutes of Wales attributed to Howel the Good' (1887).

[4] John William Tristram, episcopalian priest in Ireland and organiser of religious education in Dublin.

[5] Of Philadelphia; corresponded on 'Messianic Ideas'; had sent his work, probably his *Source of salvation: a catechism of the Jewish religion* (1879).

[6] Not found published.

[7] The new railway bridge over the Dee.

[8] Nawab Moolk Mahdi Ali, the Nizam of Hyderabad's representative, in England for the Deccan inquiry, visited Hawarden at Gladstone's invitation; their conversation ranged over the Crimean and Egyptian campaigns and Mahommedanism, Islam and the Indian Congress Party, and the education of Mahommedans at Oxford and Cambridge; account in *T.T.*, 21 September 1888, 6c.

[9] J. Strype, *Annals of the Reformation*, 4v. (1824).

[10] J. S. Brewer, *Endowment and establishment of the Church of England* (1885).

[11] Preparing for his article; see 18 Sept. 88.

[12] Untraced.

16. *16 S. Trin.*

Ch. 11 AM & 6½ P.M. Saw Herbert on Selborne. Read Cave on O.T.[1]—Thomson on the Supernatural[2]—and further works on Engl. Church History.

17. *M.*

Ch. 8½ A.M. Wrote to Archdn Denison—Mayor of Birmingham—Messrs Grogan—Mr Vickers—Mr J. Ogilvy. Again visited sites with W. Attended the Tea given to Mothers. Began stowage of letters. Read Cave on O. Testament—Collier & Strype—I've been thinking—Biogr. Dict. Cecil. Worked on storing letters.

18. *Tu.*

Ch. 8½ A.M. Wrote to Mrs Bolton B.P.—Mr Johnson—Mr Ohlson—Mr Herbert Rix[3]—C. Reid—A. Reid—Sec. Royal Soc.[4] Worked with H. on storing letters. Wrote on Q. Elisabeth.[5] Drove with C. Read 'I've been thinking'—Hume, Hallam, Collier, Froude—Finished [blank.]

19. *Wed.*

Ch. 8½ A.M. Wrote to Mr Atkinson—W.H. Gregory—F.J. Lynch—W.S. Ogilvy—J. Cameron—Mrs Butler—A. Godbolt—Jas Rankin—S. Sly. 2 h. on storing letters. Wrote on Q. Elisabeth. Read Collier—Strype—The Prayer Books—Ordinance of 1643—'Ive been thinking' finished—and Cave on O.T. Drive with C.

20. *Th.*

Ch. 8½ A.M. (and H.C.): also 7½ P.M. Wrote to N.M. M'Leod—W.H.G.—G. Brownen[?]—Mr Knowles—T. Greenwood—J. Trower—R. Shorach—Thos Wood. Drive with C. & calls. Worked on books & letters. Wrote on Elisabeth. Eight to dinner. Read Lingard[6] &c.—In Memoriam of Anderson.[7]

21. *Fr.*

Ch. 8½ A.M. Wrote to Ld Selborne l.l.—Press Assn Tel.l.l.—G. Stewart—Central News Tel.—C.G. Eames—Messrs Woodall—G. Abbott—Mr Barnes—Mr P.W. Campbell. Saw Mr Strong on his fine collection of Church Books. Walk with L. Harcourt whose manners are most winning. Sat to him.[8] I must now work

---

[1] A. Cave, *The inspiration of the old testament, inductively considered* (1888); an evangelical analysis.

[2] W. D. Thompson, *Christian miracles and the conclusions of science* (1888).

[3] Herbert Rix, assistant secretary and librarian to the Royal Society.

[4] Perhaps about Trinity House business; see Royal Society archives, MC. 14. 346–51.

[5] 'Queen Elizabeth and the Church of England', *N.C.*, xxiv. 764 (November 1888); *Later gleanings*, 181. The proofs were sent to Bp. Stubbs who did 'not think that, beyond a few clerical errors, there is anything that needs alteration. I suppose that the gainsayer of the period will say that you ascribe too much of the working of the period to the Queen, and too little to the Church, but you have your own answer to that'; 8 October 1888, Add MS 44505, f. 11.

[6] See 11 Jan. 34.

[7] Perhaps B. R. Anderson, of Edinburgh, *Broken lights; poems and reminiscences* (1888).

[8] i.e. for a photograph.

through this Selborne controversy, as he has set aside my warning.[1] Worked on books & letters. Read Cave on O.T.—Anderson's Poems—Salvador on Mosaism.[2] Hardly touched Elisabeth.

22. Sat.

Ch. 8½ A.M. Wrote draft of the reply to Selborne in anticipation & sent it to Spencer & Granville. Wrote to Messrs Agnew BP—Ld Granville—Rev. Mr Edwards—Ld Spencer—W.H. Chadwick[3]—P.H. James—Rev. H. Powell—J.H. Waters—T. Grainger—Sec. Nyassa Fund[4]—P. Mosley. Walk with Houghton & party. Worked on books. Read Cave on O.T.—Journal des Economistes[5]—Edwards on Welsh Church.[6]

23. 17 S. Trin.

Ch mg & evg. Wrote to Mr Burgess U.S.[7]—Mr Stancliff—Mr Evans—Mr Cobbold—Mr Hiller. Read Cave on O.T.—Rogers on Present Religion—Burgess on WEG & Ingersoll—and [blank.] Wrote a little on Elis. Walk with Houghton.

24. M.

Ch. 8½ A.M. Wrote to The Queen (under compn)[8]—Ld Selborne—Sir A. West—Mr P.W. Clayden—Mr Westell—Rev. M. Macaulay—S. Ranson—Rev. T. Davies—R. Reilly—Messrs Pickering—Mr Rees—Mr Leadbetter. Read Cave on O.T.—Volunteers & D. of Richmond[9]—Rees on Poverty & Wealth[10]—Much Wenlock Registers.[11] Worked on books. Visited the Railway Works.

[1] Letter by Selborne on Gladstone's review of Forster; Selborne sent *The Times* letters from Bright, Chamberlain, Hartington, Northbrook and Carlingford written in reply to his query to them on their recollections of the events of late April and early May 1882 and Forster's resignation. Gladstone had already pointed out to Selborne the inaccuracy of the latter's memory that H. J. Gladstone's mem. on his talk with F. H. O'Donnell had not been read to the Cabinet; *T.T.*, 21 September 1888, 6a; see also *T.T.*, 17 September 1888, 8a and, for confirmation that the mem. was read to the Cabinet, 22 Apr. 82: 'Herbert G.s mem. of conversation with [F. H.] O'Donnell was read'.

[2] J. Salvador, *Histoire des institutions de Moise et du peuple Hebreu*, 4v. (1829–30).

[3] An old Chartist and lecturer for the National Reform Union; on franchises; *T.T.*, 25 September 1888, 9f.

[4] Probably the Nyassa Anti-Slavery and Defence Fund, then requesting support to prevent Portuguese expansion up the Shiré River from the Zambesi.

[5] *Journal des Economistes*, xliii (September 1888); probably for its review of Buxton, *Finance and politics*.

[6] H. T. Edwards, *Wales and the Welsh Church* (1888).

[7] Had sent untraced work on the Gladstone/Ingersoll controversy (see 31 Dec. 87).

[8] Asking her permission to publish letters and a mem. of 29 April–2 May 1882 bearing on the dispute with Selborne about those events; the Queen agreed in principle, but to publication 'in Parliament, & not in any periodical or newspaper'; Gladstone knew of no such precedent for this and asked for permission to 'state the case in a tract or letter written for the purpose'; the Queen did not reply until prompted, and agreed to this on 12 October; Gladstone then let the affair drop and did not publish the material, which is in *L.Q.V.*, 2nd series iii. 272–6. For this correspondence, see Guedella, ii. 429 ff.

[9] Untraced.

[10] W. L. Rees, *From poverty to plenty; the labour question solved* (1888).

[11] Untraced.

25. Tu.

Ch. 8½ A.M. Wrote to Comm. Capellini[1]—C. Higham, B.P.—W.T. Hawkins, B.P.—J. Colgate, B.P.—C. Waddie—Mr Applegate. Worked on books. On Q. Elisabeth. Saw Deputn Saltney Library. Drive with C. Read Cave on O.T.—Hicks Geol. of North Wales[2]—Kingsley on Nationalism[3]—Robbery under Arms.[4] Eight to dinner.

26. Wed.

Ch. 8½ AM. Wrote to Ld Selborne—Mr Mitchell—Mr Kilburn—P.H. Davis—Mr Hillier[5]—Mr Quaritch. Worked 3 hours on books. We began the felling of a big ash. Read Berni Op. Burl. Alack X[6]—Robbery under Arms—Irish Country Gentleman of 1804 (most remarkable):[7] & Rev. Mr Brown on Ingersoll.[8]

27. Th.

Ch. 8½ A.M. Wrote to Messrs O.G. & Co—H.N. Gladstone l. & B.P.—Brooks & Webber—J.S. Jeans—Ed Daily News—J.C. Hart—AngloCol. L. Co.—R.T. Gaskin—Matthews & Brookes—Miss Kenny—G.J. Holyoake—Mr Schnadhorst. Read Jeanes, Develt of India[9]—Robbery under Arms—Reformatio Legum Eccl. Worked on papers. We finished felling a big ash. Worked on Q. Elis.

28. Fr.

Ch. 8½ A.M. Wrote to M. Bojusewskii[10]—C. Higham—J. Williams—E.A. Cherriton—W. Mitchell. Worked on books (1 h.) Worked on Q. Elis. Walk & conversation with Arthur L[yttelton]. Read Reformatio Legum—Hook's Parker[11]—Wilkins Concilia[12]—Robbery under Arms. Ten to dinner.

29. St Mich.

Ch. 8½ A.M. and H.C. Wrote to Messrs Watson l. & Tel.—Ogilvy Gillanders & Co.—Mr Schnadhorst—J. Edwards—Mr J.R. Sherman—T. Lowther—Sig. Mamoli—S.A. Cox—Mr C.E. Strong—Funk & Wagnalls.[13] Worked on papers. Worked on Q. Elis. Kibbling the Ash. Read Lamb on the Articles.[14]—Marshall on France

---

[1] Probably Giovanni Capellini, professor in Bologna; geologist and archaeologist.

[2] H. Hicks, *On the Col Gwyn cave, North Wales* (1888).

[3] Perhaps C. Kingsley, *Sermons on national subjects* (1852).

[4] See 1 Sept. 88.

[5] Of Dorchester; sent a press cutting; Hawn P.

[6] See 11 Jan. 88.

[7] W. Parnell, *An inquiry into the causes of popular discontents in Ireland. By an Irish country gentleman* (1804).

[8] Untraced article on the controversy; see 31 Dec. 87.

[9] James Stephen Jeans, 1846–1913, journalist and secretary of the British Iron Trade Association, sent an untraced article.

[10] Baron Nicholas de Boguschevsky, Russian scientist and an occasional correspondent.

[11] In W. F. Hook's *Lives of the archbishops*; see 23 Dec. 60.

[12] See 30 May 88.

[13] American publishers; business untraced.

[14] J. Lamb, *Historical account of the Thirty-Nine Articles* (1829).

(N.C.)[1]–Tirard French Finance (Cont)[2]–Robbery under Arms–Cromwell-Glyn Conference.[3]

30. 18 S. Trin.

Ch mg & evg. Wrote to The Queen–Lord Selborne–Scotts–Lord Spencer–Sir A. West–Rev Mr Dickson–G. Fraser–Rev. D. M'Leod–Watsons. Read Jamison's Sermons[4]–Freeman's Strossmayer Letter[5]–Laud's Thirty Nine Articles[6]–and Cave on O.T. Walk with Prof. Stuart.

· Monday Oct One 1888.

Wrote to Messrs Ogilvy G. & Co–Sir W. Foster–A. Ensor–F. Pape–Prof. Rogers. Walk with W. James[7] & Stuart. Worked on Q. Elisabeth. Read Historians–Robbery under Arms–Rogers Preface &c.[8]

2. Tu.

Ch. $8\frac{1}{2}$ A.M. Wrote to Mr Knowles–Mr Liversedge. A little work on books: but a good day's work in correcting my Q. Elis. Dined at Mr Johnson's. Saw Bp of Chester. Walk with S.E.G. and close talk on 'St Deiniol's'. Read Rebellion [sic] under Arms.

3. Wed.

Ch. $8\frac{1}{2}$ A.M. Wrote to Messrs O.G. & Co.–Mr Westell–R. Cameron–Mr Mac-Nicoll–Ld Norton–F. Bew–F. Hastings–Rev. Mr Hayden–R. Darlington–A.J. Symonds–Ld Selborne–Mrs Bolton–K. Marks. Worked on books. Worked a little on Homer.[9] Woodcraft with Herbert. Read Rebellion Under Arms–The Cromwell Conference.

4. Th.

Ch. $8\frac{1}{2}$ A.M. Wrote to Mr Thorndike Rice–Mr Schnadhorst–G. Lumsden–Mrs Brewster–A. Roberts–S. Hallifax. Worked well on Homer. Woodcraft with Herbert. Dined at the Rectory. Read Report on Education–Rebellion under Arms.

5. Fr.

Ch $8\frac{1}{2}$ A.M. Wrote to Mrs Macgregor–Mrs Robinson–Scotts–Prof. Barbier–Messrs Pratt–E. Hawes–C.F. Hursley. Woodcraft with Herbert. Worked on

---

[1] *N.C.*, xxiv. 455 (October 1888).   [2] Untraced.
[3] *Monarchy asserted to be the best, most ancient and legall form of government, in a conference . . . with Oliver, late Lord Protector, and a cttee. of Parliament* (1660); cttee. included John Glyn.
[4] Perhaps J. Jamieson, *Sermons on the heart*, 2v. (1789–90).
[5] Untraced; possibly an MS.
[6] i.e. in Lamb's book; see 29 Sept. 88.
[7] W. H. James; see 21 Nov. 76 and H.V.B.
[8] J. E. T. Rogers had sent his *The economic interpretation of history* (1888); Add MS 44504, f. 293.
[9] Article prepared and despatched for publication (see 6 Oct. 88), but not found published.

papers. Worked on Homer. Read Bp Nulty's Letter[1]—Home Rule for Wales[2]—Cromwell Conference—Rebellion under Arms.

6. Sat.

Ch. 8½ A.M. Wrote to Mr Thorndike Rice—Mr Westell—Scotts—Press Assocn—Mad. Brearey—Rev. Blackledge[3]—Reg. [sic] B.P.—W.M. Fuller—P.H. Pritchard—J. Rowans. Worked hard on Homer MS and dispatched it. Woodcraft with Harry Drew. Finished Cromwell Conference. Read Rebellion under Arms—Plumptre's Life of Ken.[4]

7. 19 S Trin.

Ch. 11 AM and H.C. 6½ P.M. Wrote to Rev. J.A. Macmullen—Mr Gill MP—Mr Schnadhorst—J.A. Bruce—Rev. G. Keogh—J. Martin—E.C. Evans. Read Plumptre's Ken—Divers Tracts—Rogers, Present Day Religion[5]—Cave on O.T.[6]

8. M.

Ch. 8½ A.M. Wrote to Mrs Macgregor—Mr Morley—Mr Harringan—H. Clark—Miss A. Shore—R. Barry—Miss Canning. Worked on Books & papers 3 h. Drive with C. Read Ld Stratford's Life[7]—Judd on Krakatoa[8]—Rebellion under Arms—Sir W. Hamilton's Phlegraei.[9]

9. Tu.

Ch. 8½ AM. Wrote to Dean of Wells—Mrs Bolton—W. Graham—W.T. Newman—Professor Judd—Wms & Norgate—J. Wyn. Worked on papers 2½ hours. Saw Mr E. Morris—W.H.G. Drove to the Man Hay. Read Cave on O.T.—Rebellion under Arms—Judd on Krakatoa finished—Life of Stratford de R.

10. Wed.

Ch. 8½ A.M. Wrote to Viceroy of India—G.H. Gladstone[10]—S.W. Hallam—A.W. Hutton—J. Holt—W.W. Caddell—G. Streetly—J.C. Roberton—W. Graham. Worked on papers. Drive with C. Corrected the proofsheets of article on Elizabeth. Read Hardwick on the Articles[11]—Cave on the O.T.—Rebellion under Arms.

---

[1] Perhaps T. Nulty, 'Letter to J. Cowen, M.P., on the state of public affairs in Ireland' (1881).

[2] 'Home Rule for Wales; what does it mean?', published by Cymru Fydd Soc. (1888).

[3] On difficulties of the Parliamentary timetable for Welsh disestablishment, to Rev. J. Ernest Blackledge; *T.T.*, 10 October 1888, 5c.

[4] E. H. Plumtre, *The life of Thomas Ken*, 2v. (1888).

[5] See 9 Sept. 88.   [6] See 16 Sept. 88.

[7] S. L. Poole, *The life of... Viscount Stratford de Redcliffe* (1888). See 18 Aug. 88n.

[8] John Wesley Judd, 1840–1916; professor of geology in London 1876–1905; specialist on volcanoes; had sent an untraced article or lecture on Krakatoa.

[9] Reading of title uncertain; probably Sir W. Hamilton, *Campi Phlegraei; volcanoes of the Two Sicilies* (1776).

[10] George Herbert Gladstone, b. 1860, s. of Rev. D. T. Gladstone (see 21 Oct. 47); lived in Rye.

[11] C. Hardwick, *A history of the Articles of Religion* (1851).

11. Th.

Ch. 8½ A.M. Wrote to Central News Tel.—Sir W.B. Gurdon—Rev. J.G. Rogers—Mr Schnadhorst—A. Gardner—Sec. Richard Memorial[1]—W.L. Williams—Messrs Murray—Ld Spencer—Mr H. White—A. Hanna—D. Milne—J.J. Black—The Queen. Mr Schnadhorst came to discuss & arrange about Birmingham. Drove with him. The Harcourts came: also Rosebery. Much conversation & a new view opened of the Selborne Parnell business.[2] Worked on papers & books 2 h.

12. Fr.

Ch. 8½ A.M. Wrote to Hon. J.J. O'Neill—Ld Selborne—O. Melton—R. Bithell—A. Strachan—P.W. Bunting—Rev. Lyall—E.H. Hall—W. Anderson—W. Brough—W.H. Buckland. 3 h. on papers. Conversation with Rosebery—Do with Harcourt—Do with A. Morley. Read Cave on O.T.—Robbery under Arms (finished). Walk with Harcourt.

13. Sat.

Ch. 8½ A.M. Wrote to Mr Agnew B.P. & l.—Mrs Pohlmann—Hon. A. Herbert—Rev. Mr Bowman—Rev. S.F. Smith—W.M. Fuller—Bp. of Chester—A. Hamyn[?]—W.H.G. Conversation with A. M[orley]—& the Harcourts. All went. West came. 2½h. on papers. Read Ld Stratford's Life—Cave on O.T.—Freethorne's Heritage.[3] Corrected report of my lame & confused speech at Spencer House.[4] Conversation with West.

14. 20 S. Trin.

Ch. 11 A.M. and 6½ P.M. Wrote to Mr Hebblethwaite—Mrs Th.—Mr Knowles—Mr Gilmour—Rivingtons—Rev. H.W. Clark. Walk & conversation with West. Read U.P. Report for 87[5]—Cave on O.T. finished—Smith's Reply to Selborne[6]—and [blank.]

15. M.

Ch. 8½ A.M. Wrote to Canon Luccock[7]—E.W. Hamilton—T.F. Unwin—Vicar of Mold—R. Martin—W.W. Cadell—J.P. Sharp—Messrs Sotheran—Rev. Mr Hughes.[8] Woodcraft. Sir R. Welby, Mr Holiday came. C.G. laid up with

---

[1] Monument for Henry Richard, who d. 20 August 1888.

[2] See 21 Sept. 88.

[3] W. C. Alvary, *Gilbert Freethorne's heritage. A romance of clerical life* (1888).

[4] See 25 July 88.

[5] Report for 1887 of the United Presbyterian church in Scotland.

[6] S. F. Smith sent his 'The alleged antiquity of Anglicanism. A reply to Lord Selborne' (1888).

[7] Henry Mortimer Luckock, canon of Ely, had sent his *After death: testimony of primitive times* (new ed. 1888).

[8] William Hughes, rector of Llanuwchyllyn, who had sent his *The Welsh bible and its editions* (1888) as part of the tercentenary celebrations (of which Hughes was secretary) of bp. Morgan's translation.

influenza. Efforts to begin on Ithaca.[1] Read Rev. Hughes on Bible in W.—Luccock on Future State—Gell on Ithaca:[2] Buchholz do[3]—Stratford's Life.

16. Th.

Ch. $8\frac{1}{2}$ A.M. Wrote to The Queen & draft—W.W. Caddell—Messrs George[4]—J.R. Hughes—F. Finch—Rev. T.E. Gibson. $1\frac{1}{2}$ h. walk with Welby. Worked on Ithaca. Read Gairdner, Preface to Henry VIII Vol VIII[5]—Life of Lord Stratford.

17. Wed.

Ch. $8\frac{1}{2}$ A.M. Wrote to Mr A. Hutton—A. Morley BP—D. Milne—E.T. Thomlinson—C. Turling—Bull & Auvache—E. Davies. Further corrected my Queen Elizabeth. Wrote on Ithaca. Woodcraft. Read The Last Hurdle.[6] Acton came & other company: Granville unhappily an invalid. C.G. better. Read Hallam—Green—on Henry VIII—Life of Ld Stratford—Letters to Morley.[7]

18. Th. St Luke.

Ch. $8\frac{1}{2}$ A.M. Wrote to Mr Schnadhorst Tel. & l.—Mr Knowles BP.—Mr Agnew—H. Macmichael—J.W. Brown—Sir J. Lambert—T. Whitwell—Professor Blaikie[8]—F. Hudson—Messrs Remington—Mr Stead—J.P. Gaffney. Walk $1\frac{1}{2}$ hour with the party. Dr Liddon came. Got a little work on Ithaca. Read Ld Stratford's Life—The Last Hurdle. Conversation with Ld Acton—with E. Hamilton—with two Irish Jesuit Priests.[9] Ten to dinner.

19. Fr.

Ch. $8\frac{1}{2}$ A.M. Wrote to Archbp Walsh—Mr Clancy MP[10]—Lewis & Co—Rev. Mr Wright—Sec. National Thrift Soc.—Sec. Charity Organisation Soc. Long conversation with Granville: on his coming speech &c.[11] Another $1\frac{1}{2}$ h. with the party over different ground but all within the walls. Worked on Ithaca. Saw Mr Scott Holland—Dr Liddon. Eleven to dinner. Read The Last Hurdle—Laurie's Prize Essay[12]—and Irish Pamphlets.

[1] 'Phoenician affinities of Ithaca', *N.C.*, xxvi. 280 (August 1889).
[2] Sir W. Gell, *The geography and antiquities of Ithaca* (1807).
[3] In E. Buchholz, *Die Homerischen Realien*, 3v. (1871–85); see 27 Apr. 74.
[4] Booksellers in Bristol.
[5] *Calendar of state papers . . . of the reign of Henry VIII*, vol. VIII (ed. J. Gairdner); quoted in *Later gleanings*, 183.
[6] F. Hudson, *The last hurdle, a story* (1888).
[7] *Irish issues; letters addressed to John Morley, M.P., by an Irish liberal* (1888).
[8] William Garden Blaikie, 1820–99; professor at New college, Edinburgh; wrote widely on religion and history. See 21 Oct. 88.
[9] Not further identified; they did not sign H.V.B.
[10] John Joseph Clancy, 1847–1928; wrote for *The Nation*; home rule M.P. N. Dublin 1885–1918.
[11] Granville's speech to the Liverpool Reform Club on 20 October; he discussed, *inter alia*, Hartington's position; *T.T.*, 22 October 1888, 6d.
[12] Not found; perhaps one of J. S. Laurie's model exercises for students.

20. Sat.

Ch. 8½ A.M. Wrote to W. George's Sons[1]—Mr Laing—Sir J. Lambert—Mr Westell—Mr Ridler—Mr Knowles BP.—Mr Cochrane—Mr R. Lovett—Ed D. Post Tel.—Tomkinson Tel. Woodcraft. Most of our friends went. Saw Mr Mayhew. Worked 3 h. on books. Read Last Hurdle—Baumann on the Session[2]—and [blank.] The Wentworths[3] remain. Mr MacColl came.

21. 21 S. Trin.

Ch. mg & evg. Wrote to Mr A.W. Hutton—Mr Knowles. Walk with Ld Wentworth. Read Life of Ken—Bradlaugh on Genesis[4]—Blaikie on Scotch Preachers[5]—and [blank.]

22. M.

Ch. 8½ AM. Wrote to E.B. Hatfield—Mr Jos. Gillow[6]—Ld Vernon—Col. Healy—Thos Wilson.[7] Walk with Mr W. Richmond: conversation on Bismarck.[8] Read Life of Ken—Teeling on 1798[9]—Laing on Coercion[10]—Gilbert Freethorne. Worked on Ithaca.

23. Tu.

Ch. 8¼ A.M. Wrote to Dr Pomeroy & copy[11]—C.H. Oldham[12]—Mr Eastman—Ed. Llangollen Advertiser—Mrs Bolton—Mr W. Wallis. Worked on Ithaca. Walk with the Tomkinsons and conversation on Ireland. Read Dr Pomeroy's awful book—Gilbert Freethorne—Teeling on 1798—Emperor Frederick's Journal:[13]

[1] See 16 Oct. 88.

[2] A. A. Baumann in *F.R.*, l. 313 (September 1888).

[3] Ralph Gordon Noel Milbanke, 1839-1906; Byron's grand-son; 13th Baron Wentworth 1862; he m. 1880 Mary, da. of J. S. Wortley.

[4] C. Bradlaugh, *Genesis. Its authorship and authenticity* (1882).

[5] W. G. Blaikie, *The preachers of Scotland from the sixth to the nineteenth century* (1888).

[6] Joseph Gillow, b. 1850; social historian of English Roman catholicism; see 24 Oct. 88n.

[7] Chairman of St. Rollox liberals; to support Carmichael's candidacy there; *T.T.*, 24 October 1888, 8a.

[8] W. B. Richmond noted that they did not discuss politics, but it was probably on this occasion that he told Gladstone of the message of Bismarck (whose portrait he had painted in 1887): "'*Tell him that while he is cutting down trees, I am busy planting them*'* . . . subsequently I delivered that message to Mr Gladstone who either did not see or did not desire to recognize the double meaning in it. Anyhow, the message fell quite flat'; *The Richmond papers*, 343, 371-2.

[9] C. H. Teeling, *Personal narrative of the 'Irish Rebellion' of 1798* (1828); sent by John P. Wright of Bridgnorth; Add MS 44505, f. 23. Quoted at some length to the Irish dpn. on 8 November 1888.

[10] S. Laing, *Coercion in Ireland* (1888).

[11] Henry Sterling Pomeroy, physician in Boston Mass.; had sent his *Ethics of Marriage* (1888) (written to combat birth control); with a request for a letter from Gladstone to preface his next book; see 28 Oct. 88. Gladstone was 'appalled' by the extent of birth control in America, but declined to write a letter for publication; Add MSS 44504, f. 275, 44505, f. 40.

[12] Secretary of the Protestant Home Rule Association; letter complaining at protestant behaviour during Hartington's visit to Belfast, and thanking the Association for supporting Home Rule; *T.T.*, 27 October 1888 11e.

[13] Frederick, Emperor of Germany, ed. H. W. Lucy, *The Emperor's diary of the Austro-German War of 1866 and the Franco-German War of 1870-71. To which is added Prince Bismarck's rejoinder* (1888).

he stood very high & I do not think it raises him. What a base creature was Louis Napoleon.

24. Wed.

Ch. 8½ A.M. Wrote to Messrs Logan—Mr Stansfeld—Mr Schnadhorst—A.J. Ogilvy—Shrimptons—Mr Evans—Mr Heatley—Mr Westell—Mr Robinson. Worked on Ithaca—and on books & papers. Drive with C. Finished Pomeroy's noteworthy & painful book. Read Q.R. for Octr—M. Arnold[1]—R.C. Debates of 1805[2]—Teeling on Rebellion of 98.

25. Th.

Ch. 8½ A.M. Wrote Tel. to Merthyr Assocn—Mr Caughey—Mr Hodson—Rev. Macdonnell—Mr Bennett—Mrs Glendinning. Finished Ithaca. Drive with C. Read 'Un crime d'Amour'[3]—Q.R. on O'Connell, and on Rogers.[4]—Teeling on 1798.

26. Fr.

Ch. 8½ A.M. Wrote to U. Sec. F.O.—M. de Giers—Mr Iverney—Mr Britnell[5]—J.W. Mellor—Rev. W.J.S. Smith—Mr Holms Ivory[6]—T.W. Russell—J. Bassiat—H. Davies—Mr Knowles. Worked on books. Drive with C. Finished Teeling. Read Debates of 1805—Un crime d'Amour—OConnell Correspondence.[7]

27. Sat.

Ch. 8½ A.M. Wrote to Lady Rothschild—Grogan & Boyd—Mr Spiller—E.W. Hamilton—E.C. Evans—Rev. Mr Wright BP.—G. Macmeach—Messrs Shrimpton. To Chester: saw the very curious Wall antiquities: then the Public Library. On to Saighton:[8] saw the Richmond pictures, Embryo Chapel, and Church. Saw Mr W. Richmond. Read Un Crime d'Amour—OConnell Correspondence—and [blank.]

28. 21 S. Trin.

Ch. 11, & 6½ P.M. A grandson born at the Rectory in the evening.[9] Deo Gratias. Wrote to Lady Rothschild and Mrs Bolton. Read Morris on W.E.G.[10]—Spencer

---

[1] *Q.R.*, clxvii. 273 (October 1888), opening with [H. Wace's] review of *Robert Elsmere*; and [M. Morris] on Matthew Arnold.

[2] In J. Gillow, *The Haydock Papers* (1888).   [3] Untraced.

[4] [J. L. Whittle] on O'Connell, [E. Eastlake] on S. Rogers, *Q.R.*, clxvii. 303, 504 (October 1888).

[5] John Britnell of Toronto; sent newspaper cuttings; Hawn P.

[6] Letters of support for Rosebery, speaking in Dalkeith; *T.T.*, 2 November 1888, 7f.

[7] *The correspondence of Daniel O'Connell*, ed. W. J. Fitzpatrick, 2v. (1888); see 26 Nov. 88.

[8] Saighton Grange, G. Wyndham's house near Chester, where W. B. Richmond was staying; see *The Richmond papers*, 370 and J. W. MacKail and G. Wyndham, *Life and letters of George Wyndham* (n.d.), i. 228.

[9] Charles Andrew, 1888–1968, Stephen Gladstone's second son; schoolmaster and 6th bart. (but did not use the title); assisted in the publication of vols. i and ii of these diaries.

[10] J. Morris, 'Mr Gladstone on the Elizabethan settlement of religion', *Dublin Review*, xx. 243 (October 1888).

de Legibus Hebræorum[1]—Un crime d'Amour finished. Conversation with Mary on the saddest & most sickening of subjects.[2]

29. M.

Ch. 8½ A.M. Wrote to Archbishop Walsh—Mr Schnadhorst—Mr Labouchere—J.M. Angus—Sir C.A. Wood—Mr Murray—R. Darlington—F. Moscheles—Mr Knox Little—C.A. Thompson—Robertson N.—L. Dillon—J.F. Knott—A. Linnys—C.H. Oldham. Two hours with Mr T.P. O'Connor: we walked in the woods.[3] Read OConnell Corresp.—Abp Walsh on Irish Land.[4] Worked on books. Dined at W.H.G.s: conversation with Mr Mayhew.

30. Tu.

Ch. 8½ A.M. Wrote to Douglas & Fordham—Mr Morley—A. Morley—J.A. Godley—Canon McColl—A. Hutton—H. Davies. Saw Mr Percy. Read Sigerson on Irish Hist.[5]—O'Connell Correspondence—Nineteenth Cent. on Examn[6]—Contemp. on Emperor's Diary[7]—La Tocnaye on Ireland.[8] Survey of trees with W. & H.

31. Wed.

Ch. 8½ A.M. Wrote to Mr W. H. Lambart—Director of La Bulgarie[9]—Mr Geo. Hutton—Mrs Bolton—J.E. Gladstone—J.M. Barrie.[10] Drive with C. Worked on books. Read Sigerson's Hist.—La Tocnaye on Ireland—Dewar on Ireland[11]—

[1] J. Spencer, *De legibus Hebraeorum ritualibus*, 3v. (1685).

[2] Perhaps the conversation recalled by Mary Drew as having taken place about 1894 (the reading of Pomeroy (see 23 Oct. 88) and this entry suggested she had misremembered the date): 'It was about the year 1894, after he laid down the Office of Prime Minister. I was at the time acting at Hawarden more or less as his Secretary; a volume was sent to him from America dealing with the complicated question of birth control. The daily postal arrivals were often to be counted in hundreds; it was my custom specially to look over the books that were sent to him. On this occasion after reading this treatise, I sent it down to him with a note of explanation, telling him that views generally held and practised in America were by no means confined to that continent, but were prevalent in Europe and in England. A message shortly after, reached me desiring my presence in the Temple of Peace. Never as long as I live shall I forget the sight that met my eyes as I entered the room. My Father was standing in an attitude of profound dejection by the fire, his head bowed, his face tragic—"Mazy dear," he said, "you have dealt me one of the greatest blows of my life." He then spoke most seriously and solemnly of the perils that beset the subject—"If I were only twenty years younger," he said (he was then eighty-four), his eyes flashing, his whole frame upright and alert—"I would fight. I would head a Crusade . . ." and words to that effect'; mem. by Mary Drew, 1 November 1925, Lambeth 1469, supporting H. J. Gladstone's comments of 3 September 1925.

[3] No record found in T. P. O'Connor's various reminiscences.

[4] Probably W. J. Walsh, *Interview . . . on the Home Rule and land questions* (1886).

[5] G. Sigerson, *From the establishment of legislative independence to the Act of Union, 1782-1800* (1888).

[6] *N.C.*, xxiv. 617 (November 1888).

[7] *C.R.*, liv. 609 (November 1888).

[8] De La Tocnaye, *Rambles through Ireland*, 2v. (1799).

[9] Thanking him for a copy of its recently published biography of him (no copy found); letter in *T.T.*, 13 November 1888, 5b.

[10] (Sir) James Matthew Barrie, 1860-1937; dramatist; had sent his book, see 1 Nov. 88.

[11] D. Dewar, *Observations on the character, customs, and superstitions of the Irish*, 2v. (1812).

Englishman on Ireland[1]—Marriage & Divorce, Ap Richard[2]—The Ghost of Dunboy Castle.[3]

Thurs. Nov. 1. 1888. All Saints.

Church 8½ A.M. Wrote to Mr E.W. Norfolk—Mr Oscar Wilde[4]—Mr Schnadhorst—Sir C.A. Wood—Mr Geo. Potter—E.S. Craig—B. Church—H. Grimshaw. Added to & revised Paper on Ithaca.[5] Read Bochart[6]—Sigerson on Union Period—O'Connor, Parnell Movement[7]—Auld Licht Idylls.[8] W., H., & I cut down two ash tr.

2. Fr.

Ch. 8½ A.M.

Wrote to		
A. Morley	Bp of Chester	
W. Ridler	Canon M'Coll	BP
Bull & Auvache	T.G. Law	
Mayor of Chester.	A.W. Hutton	

Conversation with Spencer: also walk. Worked much in reading up newspaper reports of speeches & on figures for B[irmingha]m. Read Merrymen[9]—Irish Tracts.

3. Sat.

Ch. 8½ A.M. Wrote to Mrs Bennett—Rev. E. Talbot—Rev. Dr. Hutton—Mr Croxden Powell—Mr Anastasios Berraios[10]—P.C. Cowley—Mr Downing—Mr D'Olive—Mr Westell. A hard day's work on putting material into order. Kibbled an ash. Read 'Merrymen'.

4. 22 S. Trin.

Ch. 11 A.M. with H.C.—& 3 P.M. with Baptism of dear S.s little Charles Andrew whose behaviour was perfect. Wrote to Mayor of Chester—Sir J. Simon—Prof. Stuart—A. Morley MP—Mr J. Galloway Weir. Read Divers Tracts—Knox Little,

---

[1] Perhaps *A few words about Ireland. By an Englishman* (1865).

[2] Tract by F. M. B. Richard, abp. of Paris.

[3] 'Huberto', *The ghost of Dunboy Castle* (1889).

[4] Declining to allow his name to be used for a memorial being prepared by Wilde (who replied, fully understanding: 'every one calls upon Achilles'); Add MS 44505, f. 87.

[5] See 15 Oct. 88.

[6] S. Bochart, *Sermons sur diverses textes*, 3v. (1714).

[7] T. P. O'Connor, *The Parnell movement, with a sketch of Irish parties from 1843* (1886).

[8] J. M. Barrie sent his *Auld Licht idylls* (1888) (tales of the Auld Licht Kirk at Kirriemuir, not far from Fasque) with a note, 30 October 1888, Add MS 44505, f. 73: 'Kirriemuir . . . is (I am confident) the most "Gladstonian" town in Scotland. Three years ago it was said to contain only one Conservative. I don't think it contains a dozen Unionists.'

[9] Tract by the 'Merrymen' on Irish rural violence, discussed in his Birmingham speech.

[10] Of Greece; sent good wishes; Hawn P.

Light of Life[1]—Mrs Bennett's Madonna del Buon Consiglio[2]—Blaikie, Scotch Preachers[3]—Poems.[4]

5. M. [*Lysways Hall, Rugeley*]

Ch. 8½ A.M. Wrote to Provost of Dalkeith—Mr Morley—Mr H.J. Wilson. Off at 10.30; Birmingham by Saltney at 1.15. Town hall meeting at two. Spoke 1 h. 40 m. with voice *lent* me, as heretofore, for the occasion.[5] Then to Sir W. Foster's[6] very hospitable & comfortable home. Large party at dinner. Read Dillon, Kinsella Case[7]—OConnell Correspondence—Lady Morgan, Absenteeism.[8]

6. Tu.

Wrote to Father Williams: Sir J. Carmichael[9] worked on letters for me. Drove to Hagley[10] & renewed old memories, most interesting. I felt the majesty of the place. Saw the younger, such very dear, children. Interesting conversation with Ld Compton. Small party at dinner. Spoke on Walsall Address in forenoon. Workmen's address & gifts 6½ P.M. Reply to Mayor 9.30 P.M. Perhaps 1½ hour in all.[11] Mr Wallis took us round the remarkable galleries & Exhibition. Read O'Connell Corr.—Lady Morgan's Absenteeism.

7. Wed.

Wrote to Mr J. Kenward—J. Brown—Jas Dempsey. Went over & made up my papers: my matter is too much to include in any speech. Saw Herbert J.G.—Mr Pierce Mahony[12]—Mr J. Morley—Rev. Father Neville: at the Oratory.[13] 7¼–10½. To the great meeting at Bingley Hall, 18000 to 20000 persons.[14] I believe all heard me. I was at once conscious of a great strain upon the chest: yet strength & voice were given me for a speech of 1¾ hours and I felt certainly less tired than

---

[1] W. J. Knox Little, *The light of life. Sermons* (1888).

[2] A. R. Bennett (Gladstone's cousin), *Our Lady of Good Counsel in Genazzano, compiled from the work of G. F. Dillon* (1888).

[3] See 21 Oct. 88.   [4] Author's name illegible.

[5] *T.T.*, 6 November 1888, 7a.

[6] Sir Charles Forster, the liberal M.P.; see 18 Mar. 58, 16 Apr. 78.

[7] P. Dillon, 'The murder of John Kinsella. A chapter from the history of law and order in Ireland'; discussed in his speech on 7 Nov. 88.

[8] S. Owenson, later Lady Morgan, *Absenteeism* (1825).

[9] Sir James Morse Carmichael, 1844–1902; 3rd bart. 1883; Childers' secretary 1882–5, Gladstone's 1885, 1886; liberal candidate St. Rollox, Glasgow 1888, M.P. there 1892–5. See above, x. clxxx.

[10] Seat of the Lytteltons much visited by Gladstone in the 1840s and 1850s.

[11] *T.T.*, 7 November 1888, 7c.

[12] Pierce Charles de Lacy Mahony, 1850–1930; Magdalen, Oxford; land commissioner 1881–4; home rule M.P. 1886–95.

[13] Newman had sent a note *via* William Neville, regretting his inability to see Gladstone: 'It is a great kindness and compliment your wishing to see me. I have known and admired you so long. But I cannot write nor talk nor walk and hope you will take my blessing which I give you from my heart' (Add MS 44505, f. 101). Gladstone called at the Oratory to deliver a reply; Purcell, i. 44n.

[14] Speech to N.L.F.; 'The hall is about an acre in extent. . . . Not a foot of standing room was left in the huge building, which was estimated to hold nearly 18,000 persons'; *T.T.*, 8 November 1888, 10 and 11.

on Monday. I am 'baculus in manu ambulantis: sed Ille magnus est qui ambu-lat'.[1] Read O'Connell Corresp.

8. Th. [*Wodehouse, Wombourne*][2]

Breakf. 9½. Speech of 20 m to Irish Deputation.[3] Then the photographing, the tree planting, the farewells. Off from N. Street at 11.50. Another speech at West Bromwich. Then two hours (14 miles) of rapid procession through the Black country, the road lined for much of the way with the teeming population. Con-versation with Mr Stanhope (on future movements & refusals)—Sir W. Lawson, & especially Rev. Mr Berry[4] of Wolverhampton from whom I obtained a great insight into the modern Nonconformity. A person seemingly of great and varied energies.

9. Fr.

Wrote to Lady Foster—Mr Childers—Mr Picton—Mr Dobbie. In the afternoon drove to Himley,[5] & walked with P. Stanhope. Conversation also with Ld Ash-burton, Lady Aberdeen, Sir W. Lawson. I woke without a voice: and in pouring rain, after the *four* days of fair weather while we wanted them. How He maketh all things in measure & in number. I think there have been since 1879 not less than fifty of these fair days: and not *one* has failed us. And I am asked to believe there is no Providence, or He is not 'Knowable'. Read O'Connell Correspon-dence—Memoirs of Falloux.[6]

10. Sat. [*Keble College, Oxford*]

Wrote to Rev. Dr. Cox—Rev. H.A. Hall—E.A. Mason—R.S. Kirk—Miss Lorimer. 1½-3½. to Wolverhampton & function there.[7] No speech: a vast concourse. Read O'Connell Correspondence—Memoirs of Falloux. We reached Keble Coll.[8] soon after six. Long conversation with Mr Gore on meditated Hawarden foundation & other matters.

---

[1] I am 'the stick in the hand of him who walks: but it is him who walks that is great'; quotation untraced: ecclesiastical latin, but not the Vulgate.

[2] House of Philip James Stanhope, 1847-1923; m. 1877 Alexandra, widow of Count Tolstoy; liberal M.P. Wednesbury 1886-92; Baron Weardale 1906.

[3] Printed account of this day's meetings, with Gladstone's proof corrections, is in the Bodleian Library.

[4] Charles A. Berry, congregational minister in Wolverhampton and a prominent ecumenist, much influenced by F. D. Maurice.

[5] Himley Hall, seat of Lady Dudley, who was out (see *T.T.*, 10 November 1888, 11f).

[6] Count F. A. P. de Falloux, ed. C. B. Pitman, *Memoirs*, 2v. (1888).

[7] Organized by H. H. Fowler; *T.T.*, 12 November 1888, 8c.

[8] Staying for the last time there with the Talbots, E. S. Talbot having been apptd. vicar of Leeds. On arrival at Oxford Station, Gladstone 'was hooted by a crowd on the platform, consisting for the most part of undergraduates'; *T.T.*, 12 November 1888, 8d. But he received an official welcome from the New College Home Rule Society; Add MS 44505, f. 114.

11. 23 S. Trin.

Keble service 9¾. Univ. Sermon 10½: a very fine sermon from Mr Eyton.[1] Cathedral service 5 P.M. Wrote to M. de Coubertin[2]—Bishop Bromby—Mr Edwards—Rev. Mr Bennett. Saw Dean of ChCh—Mr Acton—Archdn Palmer —& others. Read Gore on the Ministry[3]—Carpenter on Design[4]—Fairbairn in Contemp. Rev.[5]

12. M.

Slight sore throat. Rose at 12. Luncheon Sir H. Acland's. Visited All Souls at 4½. Tea at Mr Actons. Magd. Chapel at 6. Dined in Keble Hall. Full conversation with Warden & Mr Gore on Meditated foundation.[6] Made Mem. of heads. Saw Master of Balliol—President of Magdalen—Prof. Sayce—Mr Burdon Sanderson[7]—Mr Galton—and others. Read O'Connell Correspondence.

St Deiniol's.[8]

Town.
Liverpool the only possible town
An inhospitable atmosphere cuts off all idea of my personal agency.
An accommodation
To raise only temporary buildings & have Library placed & arranged in them: so as to allow of later[?] transmigration.
Purpose
(A. Higher, perhaps more difficult)
    a. Divine learning and worship.
2. Gradual formation of a body.
(B. Secondary & possible.)
1. Aid to the local Church—for a large & increasing parish—in the event of any great change.[9]
2. Home for retired clergy.
3. Holiday or temporary retirement for clergy.
4. Centre of occasional instruction by Lectures
5. Connection with the local study.
6. Study for holy orders.
7. Manual pursuits suited to the objects of the institution—e.g. printing—bookbinding—gardening.

           WEG N 11(?) [*sc.* 12] 88.

---

[1] Robert Eyton, rector of Upper Chelsea.

[2] Baron Pierre du Coubertin, 1863–1937; French educationalist; refounded Olympic Games 1894–6. Had probably sent his book; see 3 Dec. 88.

[3] C. Gore, *The ministry of the Christian church* (1888).

[4] W. B. Carpenter, *Nature and Man. Essays scientific and philosophical* (1888).

[5] *C.R.*, liv. 695 (November 1888); on puritanism.   [6] i.e. St. Deiniol's Library; see 15 Sept. 87.

[7] (Sir) John Scott Burdon-Sanderson, 1828–1905; professor of physiology at Oxford 1882–95; regius professor of medicine 1895–1903.

[8] Add MS 44773, f. 75. The first formulated statement of the aims of St. Deiniol's, Hawarden. A separate, undated, sheet reads: 'In giving so much power over the new foundation to my family, I am governed in no small degree by the hope that it may furnish, at any rate for some time, servants of true value to the Church.'

[9] i.e. anticipating disestablishment of the Church of England in Wales.

[St. Deiniol's][1]

The first and main purpose of this foundation, and of the Trust which has charge of it, is to promote

1. Devotion
2. Divine learning

in the Church of this land: the Church of the Monks who met Augustine at Bangor: the Church of Augustine himself: the Church of Stigand of Anselm and of Lanfranc: the Church of Grosseteste and of Bradwardine: the Church of Laud, of Wake, of Howley, and of Benson, with or without the accident of what is known as Establishment by the State.

But I by no means desire that the use of the institution should be confined to those who are in communion with that Church, or able to attend its services: provided only that they are set upon serious and solid studies of religion, and that in all other points they respect and conform to the rules necessary for the conduct of the foundation of which they accept the shelter and use.

The second purpose is the promotion of learning at large, especially of historical learning, by serious and solid studies intended for the benefit of the world.

The third is the promotion of social improvement in the parish or immediate neighbourhood.

To the first of these purposes I wish to give a wide construction. I wish it to include the advancement of the Pastoral work, in the following forms especially, if and so far as the extension of the establishment may permit.

1. Temporary rest for clergymen to recruit health strength & spirits.
2. Education of young men who have evident vocation and capacity for the Ministry.
3. Aid to the pastoral work of the church in the parish by harbouring any portion of the staff of clergy especially in the event of Welsh disestablishment; and next to the parish in the great city of Liverpool.

But under all these three heads the element of study and a true promotion of divine learning are to be prehended, although with variety according to the nature of the case.

[2]The principles by which I desire to be guided in the Foundation now if it please God to be carried into gradual effect are these

1. First and most, that alienation be during life and not *post mortem* with intention.
2. That large room be left for discretion as to the modes for attaining the objects of the foundation.
3. That this discretion remain with me until death incapacity or voluntary devolution.
4. That it then pass to the Trustees hereinafter designated.
5. That my descendants being in communion with the Church of England and otherwise competent shall while their line is continued whether by male or female be the principal part of the Trustees, inasmuch as I have a more direct claim upon their time and care than in the case of others.
6. That the Trust be perpetuated by co-optation, but that there be also always one Trustee appointed by the Bishop of the Diocese, or more than one if it shall seem good so to provide. The Bishop may appoint himself.
7. That after my ceasing to hold the controul the accounts and proceedings of the Trust be published.

---

[1] Undated holograph, placed with the dated memorandum printed above, though the mention of Trustees suggests a rather later formulation. The Trust Deed of St. Deiniol's was dated 23 December 1895, but the handwriting of this draft is much earlier than that.

[2] Undated holograph; Add MS 44773, f. 83.

8. That while the general aim of the Trust will have regard and be addressed to the purposes of the Church, its benefits shall also be made available, as far as may be without injury to the general aim, to fit persons independently of religious profession: that is to such as shall be eligible in respect of character, habits, devout purpose, and also companionable qualities.

9. That although the beginnings of the Trust may be small, it is established in the hope that the foundation may develop itself into a duly organised community under a Warden.

10. That as & when such a community shall be formed, the controul exercised by the Trustees be with due circumspection relaxed or diminished

Note on 1. Were it not for the urgency of other calls upon me I should devote myself forthwith to the completion of the present plan, in consideration of the uncertainties to which life is liable.

13. Tu. [London]

Keble Chapel mg. Wrote to Mr J.W. Blagg—Ld Acton—Mr W.H. Pearce.[1] Saw Dr Driver—Sir H. Acland. Off at 11.45. Whitehall Gardens[2] at 2.20. The *house* of great interest: the hospitality as refined as it is bounteous. H. of C. $3\frac{1}{4}$–$7\frac{3}{4}$.[3] Saw Mr Morley—Mr A. Morley—Mr Childers—Sir W. Harcourt—Mr Godley—Mr F. Leveson. Ten to dinner. Read OConnell Corresp.—Irish Letters of 1660.[4]

14. Wed.

Wrote to Prof. Sayce—Mr A. Nield—Sir J.P. Hennessy—H.W. Lucy[5]—Mrs Gregory—T. Adair—W.W. Garwood—Mr Rathbone—J. Davidson—and minutes. Saw Mrs Bolton—Sir J. Carmichael—Scotts—Ld Justice Bowen—The Speaker & Mrs Peel. Conclave at H. of C. 4–$5\frac{1}{4}$ on Land Purchase &c. Interesting dinner party: Ld Armstrong, Lady Bowen,[6] & others. Read OConnell Corr.—Peels Budget Sp. of 1842.[7]

15. Th.

Wrote to Mr T. Walker—Sig. Ipp. de' Riso[8]—C.M. Pulling[9]—R.C. Nightingale[10]— L'Abbé Paris—Ed. Worc. Chronicle[11]—and minutes. Saw Sir J. Carmichael—M. de Caubertin—Mr Broadhurst MP—Mr Morley—Mr A. Morley—The Speaker—

[1] Probably relative of Katie Pearce, in correspondence about John Hampden's house at Thame; Add MS 44505, f. 109.

[2] Staying with the Rendels, who lived in Whitehall Gardens for a short time; Rendel 'had rather a passion for fine homes'; *Rendel*, 9.

[3] Questions; supply; *H* 330. 1038.

[4] Not found.

[5] Unable to dine with the staff of *Punch*, but encouraging another invitation (see 7 May 89); H. W. Lucy, *Sixty years in the wilderness* (1909), 292.

[6] Emily Frances, wife of the judge (see 13 Feb. 88) and sister of S. Rendel.

[7] Sir R. Peel, 'Speech on the financial condition of the country . . .' (1842); see 11, 13 Mar. 42.

[8] Ippolito de Riso, Italian deputy.

[9] Mrs. Camilla Mary Pulling of London sent a prize essay by her nephew Theo. G. Soares of Minneapolis, 'Gladstone and Disraeli'; Add MS 44505, f. 123.

[10] Robert Cubitt Nightingale, curate in Hoxton (formerly a nonconformist); Hawn P.

[11] Good wishes to the new liberal paper.

E. Hamilton. H. of C. $3\frac{1}{4}$-$6\frac{3}{4}$.[1] Read OConnell Corresp.—Dr Salmon on Infallibility.[2] Dinner party of ten.

16. Fr.

Wrote to Ld Deramore—Warden of Keble—Rev. Macgillivray[3]—Rev. Toroud[4]—Mr Campbell Bannerman—Mr Leahy—Mr Bailes—and minutes. Saw Mr Knowles—Mr A. Morley—Mrs Th—Sir W. Gull Bt—Mrs Sandys—Mr Morley. More work on Ithacan article. H. of C. $3\frac{1}{2}$-$4\frac{3}{4}$. Gave notice.[5] Conversation with my attractive & accomplished host. Read OConnell Corresp.—Salmon on Infallibility.

17. Sat.

Wrote to Mr Tangye—Ld Granville—R.C. Bp of Minneth, U.S.[6]—Mr Jackson—Mr Sembrey—Mr Lucy—and minutes. Calls. Saw Messrs Cook—Mr S. Rendell—Mr Stuart. Went over the N[ational] L[iberal] Club Library. Read O'Connell Corresp.—Salmon on Infallibility—Belot, La Bouche de Mad. X.[7]

18. Preadvent S.

Whitehall Chapel mg. Chapel Royal evg. Dinner Tête a tête with my host. We talked of Welsh Ch. and other matters: he made his most kind proposal respecting Naples.[8] Read Balfours (*bad*) speech[9]—Salmon on Infallibility—France as it is (Eccl.)[10]—Life of [blank.]

19. M.

Wrote to Lady S. Opdebeck——& minutes. Worked much on Land purchase & arrear papers. H of C. $3\frac{1}{2}$-$7\frac{3}{4}$. Spoke about an hour in moving my amendment.[11] Poor broken reed. But the word sent me was 'Arm yourselves therefore with the same mind'. Dined at Sir C. Forster's. Saw Miss Tennant—Sir J.C. Read La Bouche de Mad. X.—O'Connell Correspondence.

20. Tu.

Wrote to Mr J. Romans—Lady Rothschild Tel.—Mr Macalister—Mr Smith—and minutes. Saw Mr Murray—Mr Waddy—Mr Macmillan—Mr Gill MP.—Messrs

---

[1] Supply; *H* 330. 1258.

[2] G. Salmon, *The infallibility of the Church* (1888); recommended by A. Galton of New College, Oxford (Add MS 44505, f. 115); Gladstone's notes are at Add MS 44773, f. 93.

[3] Archibald Macgillivray, episcopalian priest in Aberdeen.

[4] Apparently *sic*; untraced.

[5] Of amndt. to motion on land purchase; *H* 330. 1395. See 19 Nov. 88.

[6] Rupert Seidenbusch, d. 1895; bp. of Halia and vicar-apostolic of N. Minnesota 1875–88.

[7] A. Belot, *La bouche de Madame X* * * * (1882).

[8] Rendel organised the Gladstones' holiday; see 22 Dec. 88.

[9] At Leeds on 17 November: series of 'corrections' to Gladstone, Balfour acting as 'the patient schoolmistress'; *T.T.*, 18 November 1888, 16a.

[10] W. Playfair, *France as it is, not Lady Morgan's France* (1819); see 5 Nov. 88n.

[11] Moved amndt. to the govt.'s motion to introduce a bill to extend the 1885 Land Purchase Act, and proposed instead cancellation of arrears; *H* 330. 1531.

Agnew—Mr Hutton—Conclave on Mr Smith's Letter.[1] Read La Bouche &c.—
Corresp. of D. O'Connell—Inns of Court Report. Dined at Mr Armitstead's.
Much pleased with Mr O'Brien. H. of C. $5\frac{1}{4}$-$7\frac{3}{4}$ and 11-$12\frac{1}{2}$. Voted in 246:330.[2]

21. Wed.

Wrote to E. Hamilton—J.A. Godley—Mr Haldane MP—Mr Stuart MP—Mr
Thorndike Rice—E. Madeley—Archbishop Walsh—L. Lavenday—J.A. Lang-
ford—J.T. Knowles—A. Morley MP—J. Macdonald—S. Hayter—Murrays l.l.—
Rev. Dr. Driver—& minutes. Saw Rev. Dr. Hutton—Sir J. Carmichael—Mr
Bunting—Mr A. Morley—Mr Giffin—Ld Granville—& minutes. Wrote Box &
Cox. Saw Sir J.C.—Ld Granville—Mr Cashel Hoey—Mr Bret Harte[3]—Mr Mac-
Coll. We dined with Mr MacColl. H. of C. 3-5.[4] Read La Bouche &c. (fin-
ished)—Corresp. of O'Connell.

No 27. Grosvenor Square.[5]

1.

True many men know & all men say
That Box & Cox is a capital play
But no men have known, & none could say,
What I have only discovered today,
That Box and Cox has acted been
By the Earl & Countess of Aberdeen

2.

From earliest morn till the light grows faint
The carpenters hammer, and painters paint,
And nobody ever pretends to have seen
The Earl & Countess of Aberdeen

3.

But the evening falls, and lo they fly,
The carpenters painters & all their fry
So that the premises lodging afford
To the rightful lady & rightful lord

4.

Tis not so long since this curious plan
Of daily and nightly partition began,
Nor long will it be, as my hopes portend,
Before it shall come to a prosperous end.

5.

Ye painters ye carpenters greater & less
Have done with your clutter, have done with your mess

---

[1] Presumably from W. H. Smith on parliamentary procedure.

[2] His amndt. defeated; *H* 330. 1756.

[3] Francis Bret Harte, 1836-1902; American novelist; consul in Europe until 1885, after which he
lived in England.

[4] Land purchase bill; *H* 330. 1761.

[5] Holograph; Add MS 44773, f. 86.

Go make yourselves scarce, go yourselves & your (stuff?)
This Coxing & Boxing has lasted enough.
Go leave these premises clear & clean
For the Earl & Countess of Aberdeen.

W.E.G. N 21.88.

22. Th.

Wrote to Dr Pomeroy—Ld Compton—Sir M. Ridley[1]—Mr Mackay[2]—Scotts—
Mrs Lee—Mrs Bolton—and minutes. Saw Sir A. West—Chancr of Exr—Sir J.C.—
Mr A. Morley—Scotts—Lady Susan O.—Mad. Novikoff—Lord Meath—Mr
Knowles.

I dined with Mr Knowles & afterwards witnessed the astonishing performance of Mr Eddison's [*sic*] phonograph, and by desire made a brief address to
him which is to pass vocally across the Atlantic.[3] Staid to midnight.

23. Fr.

Wrote to Messrs Murray—Mr Geo. Offor—Mr Knowles—Mrs Halk—Ed. British
Weekly[4]—Mr Thos Hall—Prince of Wales—Miss Tennant—Cardinal Manning.
Corrected proofs of Ithaca.[5] Saw Mr Nicol—Mr Hamilton—Sir J.C.—Mr Stuart
Rendell—Mr A. Morley—Sir A. Clark. Read on the Revenue Boards amalgama-
tion. Finished O'Connell Corr. Gave evidence on Amalgamation of Revenue
Boards.[6] H. of C. 4¼–8. Spoke on Parnell's Instruction.[7] Dinner party at Mr S.R's.
Conversation with him on plans for journey.

24. Sat. [Hawarden]

Wrote to Mr A. Morley—Mrs Thackrey—Jos. Marghen—Treasurer Physic. Coll.
Edinb.—Mr J.R. Bailey—J.R. Jacob—Chas Ashton—Rev. D. Brown—E. Sted-
mond—Mr Bunting—W. Hilton—W.H. Garment—G.H. Baker. 3½–9. To
Hawarden (door to door). Read La Fin d'un Monde—Mrs Lee's 'Divorce'.[8] Saw
Ld Granville—Mr A. Morley—Grogans—Mr Stuart Rendell. Packing books etc.

---

[1] Sir Matthew White Ridley, 1842–1904; 5th bart. 1877; tory M.P. N. Northumberland 1868–85,
Blackpool 1886–1900; home secretary 1895–1900. Doubtless arranging his appearance next day.

[2] Probably N. McKay; see 10 Dec. 88.

[3] Recording of Gladstone made by Thomas Edison (beginning 'My dear Mr. Edison . . .'), later
issued commercially. There is a verbatim account of Gladstone's statement in *T.T.*, 11 January 1889,
5e, which shows it to have been rather longer than the recording extant in the B.B.C. Sound
Archives. There is an analysis of Gladstone's pronunciation by G. N. Clark and H. C. Wyld in *S.P.E.
Tracts* xxxiii and xxxix (1929, 1934).

[4] See 30 Nov. 88.

[5] See 15 Oct. 88; publication was deferred until August 1889.

[6] To Ridley's Royal commission on civil establishments; printed with its second report; *PP* 1889
xxi. 85. On balance he favoured amalgamating the customs and inland revenue boards, with the
I.R.B. dominant.

[7] Parnell proposed an Instruction to the land commission to abolish some arrears; *H* 331. 43.

[8] Margaret Lee, 1841–1914, American novelist, had sent her *Divorce* (1882), republished in U.K.
as *Faithful and unfaithful* (1889). Possibly met in Florence, see 7 Feb. 88.

25. *Preadvent S.*

Ch mg & evg. Read Letters &c. of Abp Trench[1]—Salmon on Infallibility—Zoological Mythol.[2]—Divorce.

26. *M.*

Ch. 8½ AM. Wrote to Sir Jas Carmichael—Bishop Blyth[3]—Rev. Mr Diggle—Rev. Rowland Hill—Mr D. Pinto—Prof. Blackie—Mr Willson—Lamont Scott—Mr Bamfeild—John Batty. Read Divorce—Brewer on Supremacy[4]—O'Rourke's O'Connell[5]—Cusack's O'Connell.[6] Began article for N.C. on the O'Connell Correspondence.[7] Drove to inquire for Mr Hurlbutt.

27. *Tu.*

Ch. 8½ A.M. Wrote to Mr J. A. Bright—Rev. S. Baring Gould—W. Morling—Miss K. Pearce—A. Chignell—Mr Reg. Wilberforce—A.W. Hutton—Sir W. Phillimore—Mr Ross Brown. Worked on O'Connell MS. Read Divorce (finished) Notable—Baring Gould, H. Eucharist[8]—Davidson's Book of Erin.[9] Walk with W.H.G.

28. *Wed.*

Ch. 8½ A.M. Wrote to Mr L. Dillon[10]—C.N. Tel.—Mr Knowles—P.A. Tel.—Mr R. Brown BP—Postmistress—Mr Jas Young—Mr D. Evans—Mr R. Nichols—The Speaker's Secretary—Mr W. Simons l. & B.P.—Mr J.M. Davidson.[11] Saw Mr Mayhew. Attended Mr Hall's ingenious entertainment. Wrote on O'Connell Corr. Read Gilbert Freethorne.[12] Walk with W.H.G. Wrote P.S. to Ithaca.

29. *Th.*

Ch. 8½ A.M. Wrote to Messrs Sotheran—Miss Harrop—W. Miller—Mr Sullivan —Sir C. Ward—H.M. Robinson—J.M. Cherrie—Warden of Trin. Coll—C. Hamon—Mrs Mackenzie—Jos Wilson—Messrs Freshfield—Geo. Brook—M. Serarty *cum* Broussali[13]—Mr Geo. Demster(?). Wrote on O'Connell. Woodcraft with W.H.G. Read Gilbert Freethorne—and [blank.]

---

[1] See 11 July 88.

[2] Untraced.

[3] George Francis Popham Blyth, d. 1914; Kimberley's chaplain 1863-6; bp. in Jerusalem from 1887.

[4] See 30 Apr. 84.

[5] J. O'Rourke, *The centenary life of O'Connell* (1875); see 17 Nov. 77.

[6] M. F. Cusack, *The Liberator. His life and times* (1872).

[7] 'Daniel O'Connell', *N.C.*, xxv. 148 (January 1889), reprinted in *Special aspects*.

[8] S. Baring Gould, *The death and resurrection of Jesus* (1888).

[9] J. M. Davidson, *The Book of Erin, or, Ireland's story told to the new democracy* (1888).

[10] Thanking him for a gift, and reiterating his wish that the tories would settle the Irish question; *T.T.*, 29 November 1888, 11f.

[11] John Morrison Davidson, Scottish radical author and organiser.

[12] See 13 Oct. 88.

[13] Jean Broussali of the Armenian Patriotic Association (office in Bayswater); Hawn P.

30. Fr. St Andrew.

Matins and H.C. 8½ A.M. Wrote to W.G. Henderson—Lord Acton—G.W. Smalley—R. Birkbeck—J.W. Glaister—Canon M'Coll—W. Tasker—Rev. W. Thomas—J. Whiteside—Mrs E. Cowen—J.W. Hall—J.H. Dingle—J. Ogilvy—F.T. Davies—Mr Skeffington—Sleson Thompson[1] (U.S.)—Ed. British Weekly.[2] Worked on O'Connell. Worked on papers. Read G. Freethorne—Tylers Speech to Grand Trunk[3] ....

Sat. Dec. One. 1888.

Wrote to Ld Granville—A. Morley—Miss Downer—Mr Tomes—W.S. Ryle. Chapel 8½ A.M. Woodcraft with W. & H. Worked much on O'Connell, & finished, in the rough. Read G. Freethorne—Rinuccini's Narrative[4]—Salvador.[5]

2. Advent Sunday.

Ch 11 AM with H.C. and [blank] P.M. Wrote to Rabbi M. Fluegel[6]—Mr Jas Knowles—A. Upward—Mr Stuart Rendell—Rev. J.H. Barrow—Mrs Bolton—W. Erskine. Read G. Freethorne finished—Demoiselle de bonne famille[7]—Salmon on Infallibility.

3. M. [London]

Ch. 8½ A.M. Wrote to Mr Shaw Lefevre—Mr Primrose—C.G.—Messrs Wheatley—Mr Downes—Mr Bill—and minutes. Packed. Off at 10.45, Whitehall Gardens at 3.50. Saw Herbert J.G.—Mr Morley—Mr Shaw Lefevre—Mr A. Morley—Mr Stuart Rendell. Saw Burdett [R?]. H of C. 4¼-8½. Spoke an hour on Irish Govt (Notes worked up in the Train).[8] Read Coubertin, Education en Angleterre.[9]

4. Tu.

Wrote to Mr A.N. Hutton—Mr E. Lane—W.J. Willaway—C.G.—Rev. W. Stephen—Euston Stationmaster—and minutes. Busy correcting proofs. Read Pedder on Historiography[10]—St Michons Antiseptic Vaults.[11] Saw Carmichael. H. of C. 3¼-7¾. Spoke on R. Churchill's point.[12] Dined at A. Morley's. Saw Spencer: a very touching conversation with Mr Healy.

---

[1] Editor in Chicago of *America*; requested (unsuccessfully) 'say 2500 to 3000 words on "George Washington"' to be published in February 1889; Gladstone's fee to be 'altogether your own decision'; Hawn P.

[2] On Parnell; *British Weekly*, 7 December 1888, 89b .   [3] Obscure.

[4] G. B. Rinuccini, tr. A. Hutton, *The embassy in Ireland* (1873).   [5] See 21 Sept. 88.

[6] M. Fluegel, Rabbi in Kentucky; sent a German work; Hawn P.   [7] Untraced.

[8] A general attack on Balfour's statements on outrages in Ireland; Balfour's salary was proposed to be reduced; *H* 331. 891.

[9] Baron P. de Coubertin, *L'Éducation en Angleterre* (1888).

[10] Perhaps H.C. Pedder, *Issues of the age* (1874).   [11] Untraced.

[12] Reserving judgment on Churchill's criticism of the govt.'s dispatch of an expedition to Suakin despite military advice; *H* 331. 1052.

5. *Wed.* [*Hawarden*]

Wrote to Sig. Monti—Mr Fiske—Mr Goadby—Mr Sutherland—Mr Downes—Sec. Italian Embassy—& minutes. Finished correcting proofs of Birmingham speeches. Saw Mr Morley—Mr A. Morley—Mr S. Rendell—Mr Foljambe. Read Fiske.[1] $3\frac{1}{2}$–$9\frac{1}{4}$. To Hawarden. H of C. $2\frac{1}{4}$–$3\frac{1}{4}$.[2]

Secret. Steps for consideration as alternatives or otherwise.[3]

1. Shall there be a motion on 'arrears'—a question now illustrated by a flood of light—early in 1889?
2. Shall it be in the shape of an amendment to the Address?
3. Shall there be, after this long interval, a motion on Home Rule?
4. Would it be wise to obtain from Ireland (at some expence) a national *petition* for Home Rule?
5. Would it be wise to bring in a Bill for shortening of Parliaments to 4 or 5 years? (On this intervening bye-elections may throw much light).

WEG Dec. 5/88.

6. *Th.*

Ch. $8\frac{1}{2}$ A.M. Wrote to Home Secretary[4]—Mr A. Morley—D.T. Loring—J. Leatham—C. Harrison—J.K. Bannerjea—Mr Knowles. Corrected & dispatched MS. on O'Connell. Woodcraft with W.H.G. Tea at Mrs Lindsay's. Read Hist. Hampton Court[5]—Fiske on American History.

7. *Frid.*

Ch. $8\frac{1}{4}$ AM. Wrote to Mr W.H. Rideing—Rev. Thatcher—R. Waters—Mr W.C. Angus[6]—W. Tasker—Ld Acton l. & BP—Rev. D. Smith—Major Ffoukes BP—A. Stewart—Rev. Blakiston—Geo. Parr—M. Broussali—W. Howell—Miss Rosinski—W. Crowther—H. Hindmarsh—T. Corry—T.H.B. Bamford—A. Morley. Wrote addition to O'Connell. Wrote on Free Trade.[7] Woodcraft with W.H.G. Read Fiske Amn History—Marcella Grace.[8]

8. *Sat.*

Ch. $8\frac{1}{4}$ A.M. Wrote to Sec. Agric Socy—President New England Socy—Mr Childers—C.S. Miall—Mr Hutchison—Miss A. de G. Stevens[9]—A. Tangye—

---

[1] J. Fiske, *The critical period of American history, 1783–1789* (1888).
[2] Supply; *H* 331. 1144.
[3] Add MS 44773, f. 87.
[4] Henry Matthews; business untraced.
[5] Perhaps *Guide to Hampton Court Palace and Gardens* (n.d.).
[6] One of the secretaries of the Scottish Home Rule Association; the Association had written suggesting that a Scottish local govt. bill would be harmful to achieving Home Rule; Gladstone's reply denied that, respecting Ireland, he regarded local govt. as compromising Home Rule and he observed: 'I have not yet witnessed the production of a serious plan of Home Rule in Scotland, approved by any large body of the people'; *T.T.*, 13 December 1888, 8b.
[7] Undated draft headed 'For Fair Play all round' (Add MS 44773, ff. 96–100), later used for article on protection in America (see 10 Dec. 88).
[8] R. Mulholland, *Marcella Grace* (1886).
[9] A. de Grasse Stevens had sent her novel *Miss Hildreth*, 3v. (1888); Hawn P.

J. Brown—Mr Purcell—Mr Collingwood. Luncheon & tea parties: 70 or 80 guests: went off very well. Read Fiske Amn History—Waters, Shakespeare delineated by himself.[1]

9. 2 S. Adv.

Ch 11 AM. 6 P.M. Wrote to Mr W. Mitchell—A. Morley—E. Waddie[2]—M. Broussali—Geo. Brooks. We dined with the WHGs. Read his Hymn Book[3]— Manning III[4]—many tracts—Salmon on Infallibility—Reeves Geschichte.[5]

10. M.

Ch. $8\frac{1}{4}$ A.M. Wrote to Nawab al Mulk[6]—J.A. Godley—Mr V.C. Cooke—Gen. Playfair[7]—Mr Earwaker—Jos. Lawley—A.G. Nichols—S.K. Hocking—M. Wilson —A.J. Pritchard—Rev. C. Gore. Worked on M'Kay letter.[8] Woodcraft with W.H.G. Read Fiske, Amn History—Waters on Shakespeare—Playfair in 19th Cent.—Greenwood in Do.[9]

11. Tu.

Ch. $8\frac{1}{2}$ A.M. Wrote to Rev. J.J. O'Carroll—Mr A. Beredin—Mr A. Morley—Mr Jas Latham—W. Erskine—Mrs Tyndale—Sam. Lowe—J. Hainsworth—Geo. Brooks—Sir W.B. Gurdon—L. Dillon—Miss L. Murphy—Mr Scott. Worked on M'Kay letter. Woodcraft with W. Saw Mayor of Chester—W. Bailey. Read Waters—Fiske on U.S. Hist.—and [blank.]

12. Wed.

Ch. $8\frac{1}{4}$ A.M. Wrote to S. Downing (dft)[10]—Miss Harding—J.B. Cooke—Messrs Reeve—C.H. Oldham—Mr W. Meynell—J. Davidson—Mr D. Pressly—Mr Knowles—Scotts—Barker Maidstone Tel. Corrected Ithaca Revise—O'Connell Corr. proofs. Worked on books & papers. Woodcraft with W.H.G. Read Miss Hildreth[11]—Fiske (finished)—and [blank.]

[1] R. Waters, *William Shakespeare portrayed by himself* (1888).
[2] Charles Waddie, the other secretary of the Scottish Home Rule Association; further exchange on Scottish Home Rule; *T.T.*, 13 December 1888, 8c. See 7 Dec. 88n.
[3] 'A selection of hymns and tunes made and arranged by W. H. Gladstone' (1882); copy at St. Deiniol's marked 'not for sale'; the book is hand-written. The preface states that the hymns are mainly selected to suit the tunes in Wesley's *European Psalmist*; some hymns were revised by Lady F. Cavendish, and some tunes written by W. H. Gladstone, a competent musicologist.
[4] Vol. iii of H. E. Manning, *Miscellanies*, 3v. (1877–88).
[5] Evidently a work sent by Reeves and Turner, the publishers; see 11 Dec. 88.
[6] See 15 Sept. 88.   [7] Elliot Minto Playfair, 1828–99; served in India.
[8] Eventually published as 'Free Trade', *N.A.R.*, cl. 1 (January 1890), a reply to the pamphlets, 'Free-Trade toilers. An open letter to workingmen. Which shall it be? The result of an American's tour among England's masses' (1888) and 'Starvation wages for men and women' (1888), by Nathaniel McKay, 1831–1902, of New York who wrote on 9 October 1888 requesting a public statement by Gladstone (Hawn P). Gladstone delayed his reply as 'it would have been impertinent of me . . . to accept the invitation of Mr. McKay whilst the Presidential contest was yet pending' (*N.A.R.*, cl. 2).
[9] L. Playfair and F. Greenwood in *N.C.*, xxiv. 785, 799 (December 1888).
[10] Samuel Downing of Birmingham, on the Selborne correspondence; Add MS 44505, ff. 190–2.
[11] See 8 Dec. 88n.

13. Th.

Ch. 8½ A.M. Wrote to J. Coldstream—C. Herbert—Mr Knowles—J.H. Spalding—Pr. Johnston—R. Hargreaves—Chas Hunter—D.W. Matthews—Mrs Kay—P.W. Campbell—Seva Ram[1]—G.J. Holyoake—J.C. White. Read Coldstream on Divorce[2]—Waldeck Rousseau, Discours[3]—Giffen, Financial Tracts[4]—Miss Hildreth. Much preparation, working on books & papers. Sat to Bolton Photographer.

14. Fr. [*London*]

10¾–4. Journey to London. Fog rather heavy from Rugby: 79 m to Willesden(?) 92 minutes. Then to the House & held conclave with Harcourt & the Morleys respecting Sessional Arrangements & Suakim. Saw E. Hamilton. Read Miss Hildreth—and [blank.] Wrote to Mad. Novikoff—Mrs Hulk—Mr Downing.

15. Sat.

Wrote to Messrs Grogan—Herbert—. . . & minutes. Set down my material for the Meeting. 2–6. To Limehouse Town-Hall. Spoke 1¼ hour.[5] Much enthusiasm. Near 2 h[ours] on the way there & back. A noble drive for near 3 miles. Dined at [blank.][6] Read Miss Hildreth. Saw A. Morley—Sir J. Carmichael—Mr Knowles—& others.

16. 3 S. Adv.

Whitehall Chapel mg. All Saints 4 P.M. Saw Ld Granville—Mrs Th.—Sir W. Harcourt—Mr S. Rendell. Saw one [R]. Wrote to Mr Drew—Mr Knowles. Read Par. Lost—The Spell of Ashtaroth[7]—Hügel's Gedanken.[8]

17. M.

Wrote to J.C. Hopkins—Rev. W. Forsyth—Rev. J. M'Connell—Rev. T.W. Perry—Rev. R.A. Armstrong—Gavin Hamilton[9]—Sir A.E. West—W.R. Stevens—W.J. Wright—S.W. Williams—Wms & Norgate—C. Herbert—& minutes. H of C. 3¼–7¾. Spoke on Suakim.[10] Dined at Sir C. Forster's. Saw Mr Cook (Murrays)—Sir J.C.—Lord Ronald Gower—Dr Liddon—Dr Quain[11]—Mr Birt MP. N.P. Gallery Meeting 3 P.M. Read Miss Hildreth, and [blank.]

[1] *Sic*; untraced.

[2] J. P. Coldstream, *On the increase of divorce in Scotland* (1881).

[3] P. M. R. Waldeck-Rousseau, *Discours prononcé au banquet du Cercle républicain de Lyon* (1888).

[4] One of R. Giffen's many works; perhaps *Essays in finance*, 2v. (1887, new ed. 1888).

[5] *T.T.*, 17 December 1888, 10a.

[6] Dorothy Tennant's; see Add MS 44505, f. 199.

[7] A. L. Gordon, *Ashtaroth; a dramatic lyric* (1867).

[8] Not found.

[9] Possibly Gavin George Hamilton, b. 1872; eldest s. of Baron Hamilton of Dalzell; entered Scots Guards 1892.

[10] *H* 332. 485.

[11] (Sir) Richard Quain, 1816–98; London physician; 1st bart. 1891.

18. Tu.

Wrote to Mr Walden[1]—General Greely[2]—Mr M. Fenton—Sir W. Stokes[3]—Watson & Smith,—Miss Waters—Miss E. Powell—Major .....—Mr Stead—A. White—F. Hawkins—W.L. Courtney—Messrs Matthews[4]—R. Hastings—Messrs Broughton—and minutes. Saw Sir J. Carmichael—Lady Rothschild—Mr A. Morley—Ld R. Gower—Col. Gouraud—Ld Granville—Mr Knowles—Mr B. Currie. H. of C. $3\frac{1}{4}$–5.[5] Conclave for Phonograph. Dined with Ld Justice Bowen. Packing & preparations. Read Miss Hildreth—Acts of Ld Dufferin's Govt.[6]

19. Wed. [On train]

Wrote to J.E. Gladstone—Mr Hilliard—Mr Knowles—Scotts—Mr Lee. Saw Sir J. Carmichael—Lady Stepney—& many friends at the Station. Good passage & prosperous journey.[7] Read T. AKempis and Marcella Grace. Made a few verses in the manner of the Presbeis of Aristoph.[8] The kindness of our Commander in Chief (Mr Rendell) is possibly more remarkable than his aptitudes.

20. Th. [Lucerne]

Lucerne 9.15 A.M. Schweizerhof: first rate. Wrote to Mr Knowles l.l.—Mr Macmillan. Traversed the town: saw the Cathedral: notable arrangement of seats. Read Marcella Grace—Aristoph. Acharn.—F. Harrisons very remarkable Appeal. Conversation with our Consul[9] who came from Zurich.

21. Fr. [On train]

Off at ten. The ascent to the great Tunnel thoroughly enjoyable, & grand: the descent milder air but not sunny. Luncheon Göschenen excellent: Tunnel 18 min. Dined at Milan & made up for the night in a fresh, comfortable, carriage. Much shaking. Read Marcella Grace—Aristoph Acharn.—Thos A Kempis.

22. Sat. [Naples]

Read T. AKempis—Marcella Grace finished—Virgil Æn. I. We skirted the sea for say 150 miles. Turned inwards from Gargano now bare of wood. The last hour into Naples was magnificent. The moon rose at nine from a glorious bed of

---

[1] G. Walden of Limehouse who had written on Gladstone's failure to mention unemployment in his Limehouse speech (see 15 Dec. 88); Gladstone replied: 'The cares of the House of Commons embrace the whole Empire, and I think it would be impossible to induce that assembly to take up seriously the case of local, even though acute, distress, unless it were upon the basis of some well considered proposal from the Government'; municipal self-government for London was the way forward; *T.T.*, 20 December 1888, 7b, Add MS 44505, f. 228.

[2] The explorer. See 17 Nov. 85 and Add MS 44505, f. 165.

[3] Sir William Stokes, 1839–1900; Irish physician; kt. 1886.

[4] George Matthews, London publishers.

[5] Supply; *H* 332. 651.

[6] Perhaps W. Leggo, *History of the administration of Lord Dufferin* (1878); on his Canadian years.

[7] Verses written in the train, at Add MS 44773, f. 92.

[8] Not traced.

[9] H. Angst, British consul in Zurich.

cloud, & on the other side Vesuvius shot his flames constantly recurring. At the station it was deeply touching: an eager & enthusiastic crowd, in great part students. After a drive & procession of over an hour, reached Rocca Bella[1] past 11. Replied shortly at the Station to various congratulations.

23. 4 S. Adv.

Angl. Church at 11 A.M. and H.C.—Prayers in evg. Dist. $2\frac{1}{2}$ miles. Read Barrow, Mary of Naz.[2]—Salvador, Mosaic Institns[3]—Döllinger & Reusch, Studigkeiten[4]— Thos A'Kempis.

24. M.

Drive in the City. Saw Press Repr. of Il Piccolo & a student. Conversation with Mr R[endel] on Scotts.[5] Read Exodus I–IX.—Salvador, Institutions—Bädecker on Amalfi District[6]—Flaxman's Letter on Italy[7]—and [blank.]

25. Xm. Day.

Ch 11 A.M. & H.C. Saw the Br. Consul. Visited the neighbour Villa in aftn. Conversation with Madame Rendell, a Roman. Conversation with Mr S.R. on sweating, and the morale of trade. He thinks ill of it. Read Thos A Kempis— Döllinger—Reusch—Nisco: death of Ferd. II. &c.[8]—Salvador, Institutions de Moïse.

26. Wed. St Steph.

Wrote to Mr Temple Leader—Sig. Bonghi—P.W. Campbell—H.J.J. Lavis[9]—Dr Vance Smith[10]—Dr Falcone[11]—Sig. Sorrentino—Barone N. Nisco.[12] Forenoon walk in the lovely Gardens of the Brother Rendel. Saw The Syndic (Sig. Amore) and the Editors of the Corriere, Tribuna, and [blank.] Read Salvador—Bryce on U.S.—La petite Fadette.[13] Wrote up Journal.[14] Settling down with my 'traps' about me.

---

[1] The villa of George, Stuart Rendel's brother, the latter being Gladstone's host.

[2] The first part of J. C. Barrow, *Mary of Nazareth: a legendary poem*, 3v. (1889-90).

[3] See 21 Sept. 88.

[4] The German version of J. J. I. von Döllinger, ed. F. H. Reusch, *Declarations and letters on the Vatican decrees, 1869-1887* (1891).

[5] Probably on S. Scott's, the bankers; Rendel may have allowed the Gladstones drawing rights on his account as part of the holiday in Naples which was his gift to them.

[6] Baedecker's *Southern Italy and Sicily* (1880).

[7] Perhaps J. Flaxman, *Lectures on sculpture* (1838), with addresses etc.

[8] A. Nisco, *Ferdinando II ed il suo regno* (1884).

[9] Classical scholar; see 7 Jan. 89.

[10] George Vance Smith, unitarian minister; see Add MS 44443, f. 319.

[11] Probably Giuseppe Falcone, liberal author and poet; published in Naples and Palermo.

[12] Niccola Nisco, 1816-1901; Neapolitan risorgimentist, historian, journalist and banker. See Add MS 44505, f. 236 and Hawn P.

[13] George Sand, *La petite Fadette* (1848); given him by Dorothy Tennant; Add MS 44505, f. 227.

[14] As did S. Rendel; extracts from his account of Gladstone in Naples from this day on are in *Rendel*, 52 ff.

27. Th. St Joh.

Wrote to Prefect Capitelli—Mr Rideing—Mr Thorndike Rice—Mr H. Wreford. Wrote on Protection in U.S.[1] Read Salvador—Bryce, Const. U. States[2]—La petite Fadette. Walked in Mr G.R's beautiful garden. Saw Mrs Wolfsohn[3]—Madam Meursikoffre.[4] Backgammon with Mr R.

28. Fr.

Wrote to Ipp. de Riso—Duca di Castellanita—Dr. T. Falcone—F. Powell—Ferd. Nappa. Saw Dr Vance Smith—Prof. Paladini (Riforma)—Mr G. Rendel. Trip in steam launch to Nisida, past Pozzuoli, & to bay of Baíae. Read Salvador—Bryce—La Petite Fadette. Backgammon with Mr S.R. San Carlo[5] in evg. Brilliant house: excellent orchestra: fine tenor (Spanish) and bass (Rapp, Sicilian).

29. Sat.

By launch to the Arsenal: saw the great iron ships and guns. C. shopped. We met the Dufferins.[6] Read Salvador—La Petite Fadette—received & began the important book of F. de Pressensé, L'Irlande et l'Angleterre.[7] Backgammon with Mr S.R.

Congratulations came in, & gifts. Never until the great change hoped for in my life occurs can I on this great day have proper recollection or detachment. All I can see is that I am kept in my present life of contention because I have not in the sight of God earned my dismissal. But with it there is a noble aim alike beyond my capacity & claim. Speaking generally I have the hope of improving a little: but improving upon what. *My* righteousness is assuredly filthy rags, though I do not think the same of others.

30. 1 S. aft Xmas.

Ch. mg. Prayers evg. Dufferins came to luncheon. Much conversation with him. Read Thos A. Kempis—Salvador—Döllinger & Reusch.

31. M.

Wrote to Mr Cowan l.l.[8]—Sec. Medical Faculty Univ.—L. Stucarani[9]—E. St J. Bruce—Eug. Gerdi—V. Vadura—R. Migliorini—N. Salvani—Dr Vance Smith—Mr Stead Tel. Read Salvador—Pressensé—La Petite Fadette.

[1] See 10 Dec. 88.

[2] J. Bryce, *The American Commonwealth*, 3v. (1888).

[3] Julius Wolffsohn acted from time to time as the British vice-consul at Naples.

[4] Wife of Sig. Meuricoffre, a leading Neapolitan banker; Gladstone became friendly with the family during this stay.

[5] The opera house in Naples.

[6] *En route* from India to Rome, where Dufferin was apptd. Ambassador; see 11 Jan., 8 Feb. 89.

[7] F. de Pressensé, *L'Irlande et l'Angleterre depuis l'acte d'union jusqu'à nos jours, 1800-1888* (1889); sent by the author; Add MS 44505, f. 234.

[8] In *T.T.*, 5 January 1889, 7b.

[9] Transcription of this and next five names uncertain; the ink has run.

From the steam launch we surveyed the formidable rockslip of last night, not yet known to have ended, & roughly estimated at 50,000 tons. It cuts off our neighbourhood from Naples by land. Backgammon with Mr S.R.

And so we ring out the year. In scenery and weather almost heavenly. Would that the spectacle I see within me corresponded with them. At any rate I learn more & more from year to year how deep & penetrating are the roots of selfishness: how subtle, sudden, untiring, manifold, the devices & assaults of the Evil One within the soul.

In evening a short but violent sickness & diarrhoea: hard to explain.

1 Tu. [1889] Circumc.

Wrote to Freshfields—Lady Aberdeen—Mr Grogan—Sir J. Barrow—J. Ogilvy—Ed. Daily News—S.W. Norton—W.H.G.—Mad. Meurikoffre—Roi des Belges—Sig. Taranto—Syndic of Naples—H. Ledward. Kept my bed in forenoon after a short but sharp attack last night. Drove with C. Read Salvador—F. Pressensé—La Petite Fadette.

2. Wed.

Wrote to Ed. Corriere di Nap.—Ed. Chester Chronicle[1]—Sindaco di Recanati—F. de Pressensé—Mr G. Brooks. 1–4¾. By steam to the Port: paid a public & formal visit to the Municipio & replied to the Sindaco's Address. Then drove to the Prefettura & saw the acting Prefect. Finished Salvador First Vol.—Read de Pressensé—La Petite Fadette. Backgammon with Mr R[endel].

In Naples we saw the Royal Palace. Vast scale: the finest of staircases: terrace excellent: wonderful bust called Bacchus, from Herculaneum.

3. Th.

Storm. Walk in Maraval Gardens. Saw Br. Consul and Mrs H.[2] Read de Pressensé—Bowes on Japan[3]—La Petite Fadette (finished). Wrote to Rector of University—Rev. Mr Lucas—J. Murray—Director of Scavi—Cav. de Simone—Ed. Tablet (Tel.)[4]

4. Fr.

Wrote to Miss Hurlbutt—Director of Royal Palaces—Editor P.M.G.[5] .... (that was all). Backgammon with Mr R. Drive to San Martino.[6] The view wonderful: Museo interesting: the void of the Church and buildings desolate enough. Saw Sig. Galletti & others. Read Salvador (II)—De Pressensé's Irelande—The Front Yard.[7]

5. Sat.

Wrote to the Syndic—Director of Scavi—Roman Corresp. of Tablet—Mr Reynolds Ball.[8] Saw Vice Prefect & Head of police—Mrs Wolfsohn—Sig. Nisco.

---

[1] Thanks for birthday congratulations; *T.T.*, 7 January 1889, 7b.
[2] Edward H. B. Hartwell and his wife.
[3] J. L. Bowles, *Keramic art of Japan* (1875).
[4] On the arbitration question (see next day); *The Tablet*, 5 January 1889, 10.
[5] On misunderstanding of his position on arbitration and the Roman question ('Still as much in the dark as ever' was the headline); *P.M.G.*, 8 January 1889, 4b.
[6] Suppressed Carthusian monastery with spectacular views and a fine museum.
[7] C. F. Woolson, *The Front Yard, and other Italian stories* (1889).
[8] Eustace Alfred Reynolds-Ball, d. 1928; travel writer; author of *Mediterranean winter resorts* (many eds.).

Read Salvador—F. de Pressensé—Coquelin on Actors.[1] Walk to see the Franco Inst. expected. Backgammon with Mr R.

6. Epiph. S.

Beloved C.s birthday. Ch 11 AM & Holy Comm. By the steamer. It took $3\frac{3}{4}$ hours.[2] Worked on Exodus. The form seems to have been much knocked about. Read Salvador—Thos A'Kempis—Balfour on Positivism[3]—Döllinger & Reusch.[4]

7. M.

Expedition to Berice: Piscina Mirabila etc. Read Lavis on Ischia[5]—Salvador—Pressensé on Ireland.

8. Tu.

Wrote to [blank]. Read Murray on Pompeii—Pressensé on Ireland. Expedition to Pompeii where the Director attended & gave us a Scavo[6] of the house of Emilius Celer. NB the serpent. It was most interesting. A break down on the hill returning. C. had to walk $2\frac{1}{2}$ m. Time $8\frac{3}{4}$-6.

9. Wed.

Wrote to Sig. [blank]—M. de Pressensé.[7] Read Salvador—De Pressensé (finished)—Contarella, Frederico III & Equilibrio Europeo.[8] Expedition to Pozzuoli: saw Amphith. & Serapium. Saw train of convicts: steam train.

10. Th.

Wrote to Mr J. Morley—Mr Knowles—Freshfields. And shops & calls in Naples. Tea at Bristol H. with Sir Ughtred:[9] they do not report well of the house. Read Salvador—Memoirs of Vicini.[10]

11. Fr.

Wrote to Ld Dufferin[11]—Baron Poerio[12]—Mr Gutteridge—Mr Thorndike Rice. Drive to the Studio: saw the sculptures. A noble collection which perhaps may

---

[1] C. Coquelin, *Les Comédiens par un comédien: réponse à Octave Mirbeau* (1882).

[2] This and previous phrase *sic*, though they probably refer to the next day.

[3] A. J. Balfour, 'The religion of humanity. An address' (1888).

[4] See 23 Dec. 88.

[5] H. J. J. Lavis, *Monograph of the earthquakes of Ischia* (1885).

[6] Literally, 'excavation'.

[7] Protesting at de Pressensé's claims that Gladstone had made a 'compromise' with the Lords in 1884 and had had negotiations with Parnell in 1885; *Rendel*, 60-1.

[8] Salvatore Contarella, *L'Equilibrio Europeo* (1887), *Federico III* (1888).

[9] i.e. Sir U. J. Kay-Shuttleworth.

[10] G. Vicini, *La Rivoluzione dell'anno 1831 nello Stato Romano. Memorie storiche e documenti* (1887).

[11] In A. Lyall, *The Life of... Dufferin* (1905), ii. 208. Abandoning the planned visit to Rome (where Dufferin was now Ambassador); Gladstone felt he could not go 'to Rome and see Crispi and the King without speaking out plainly [i.e. about the Italian-German alliance]', and that this would embarrass Dufferin; *Rendel*, 63-4.

[12] Probably a relative of Carlo Poerio, prisoner in 1850-1; see 4 Jan. 51.

compete for the place of the first in the world. Backgammon with Mr R. Read Salvador—19th Cent. on Jas. II.s remains—(F. Harrison) on Bryce.[1] Wrote (briefly) on Homer.

12. Sat.

Wrote to Ld Granville—Sig. Morlati—Miss Mulholland. Shopping expedition to Naples: & back by the Frana Ferry, after a short & curious interview in the Chiaja Gardens [R?]. Backgammon with Mr R. Read Salvador—Memoirs of Vicini (finished)—Miss Crawford's Tract.[2] Wrote on H. Scripture.

13. 1 S. Epiph.

Ch. 11 A.M. and V. Capella Service at 5¾. Wrote to Lady Aberdeen—Scotts—Ed. of Tablet[3]—Mr Birch (Hampstead)[4]—Mr J. Walcot. Read Thos a Kempis—Salvador—Leviticus.

14. M.

Wrote to Mrs Vyner—Sig. Marescalchi[5]—Sig. Bilia—Miss Crawford—Sig. Vicini[6]—Rev. Dr Brady—and Incognito Expedition to see the Neapolitan Exhibition of pictures and sculptures, greatly interested & struck with its merit. Read Salvador—Rosario Salve, I Siculi[7]—Serge Panini.[8] Sadly broken weather.

15. Tu.

Wrote to A. Sorrentino—Rosario Salvo—Mr Meurikoffre. 11–3¼. Luncheon at the Meurikoffre Villa:[9] most kind: saw the great magnolia [blank] feet round. Then went through the Capo di Monte Palace: some very interesting historical pictures. Read Salvador (finished)—Stephen on Divorce Extension[10]—Serge Panini—R. Salvo. Herbert came: rough passage.

16. Wed.

Wrote to Rev. Mr Jones—Prof. Paladini[11]—Miss Brough—Mr J.E. Bowen—Miss I.N. Gladstone[12]—Mr A.H. Gunn—Rev. Mr Armytage. Read Serge Panini—

---

[1] *N.C.*, xxv. 140 (January 1889).

[2] Mabel Sharman Crawford, novelist and travel writer, had sent an off-print of her article on Irish land, *C.R.*, lii. 263 (August 1887); Hawn P.

[3] On the Roman question; *T.T.*, 18 January 1889, 8b.

[4] To Thomas Birch, working-man candidate for Hampstead in the L.C.C. elections: 'It would give me great pleasure to see Liberal candidates elected to the County Councils. But I am not sure that it is wise for us to give a political colour to the elections . . .', *T.T.*, 21 January 1889, 9e.

[5] See 13 June 77.   [6] Gust. Vicini, published on Dante, and his memoirs (see 10 Jan. 89).

[7] R. Salvo di Pietraganzili, Sicilian author of *I siculi. Ricera di una civiltà italiana anteriore alla greca*, 2v. (1884–7).

[8] Georges Ohnet, *Serge Panine* (1811); unfinished review by Gladstone at Add MS 44702, f. 301.

[9] Villa of the banker (see 27 Dec. 88), near Capodimonte.   [10] Untraced.

[11] Prof. Carlo Paladini, scientist and author; closely associated with *Riforma* (see S. Smiles, *Autobiography* (1905), 409); wrote *Gladstone e Dufferin in Italia* (1889) (no copy found). Correspondence on *Riforma* and Gladstone's visit in Hawn P.

[12] Not traced as a relative.

R. Salvo, Civiltà Anteriore—Manfrin, Ebrei sotto Roma.[1] Backgammon with Mr R. Made an expedition to see Mr Silitze's great but rather strange erection.[2]

17. Th.

Wrote to A.G. Marshall—Sig. Siniscalco.[3] Read as yesterday. Tarantella dance entertainment at Mr G. Rendell's. *Touted* for information on Municipal Expenditure. Saw at the Museo the Pictures, the Pompeian objects, & above all the gems: wonderful. Also revisited the Belle Arti Exhibition.

18.

Vexed yesterday & today with gumboil. Wrote to Mr Thorndike Rice—Mr C.H. Rideing—Rev. C. Fletcher—Cav. Capobianco. Read Manfrin—R. Salvo—Serge Panini. Backgammon with Mr. R. Kept myself at home.

19. Sat.

Wrote to Mr Meurikoffre—Ld Rosebery (began).[4] Read Manfrin—Serge Panini—R. Salvo. To Naples. Visited Cathedral—S. Lorenco—Cloister & Tree at S. Severino—The paintings a sad sight.

20. S.

Ch. in Naples at 11. In returning waited to see the ineffectual firing at the Frana. Villa Capella evening prayers 5¾. Read Manfrin—Dollinger & Reusch—T.A. Kempis—Gen. Walker on Xty.[5]

21. M.

Wrote to Ld Rosebery (finished)—Sig. Raposardi—Mr F.W. Holls[6]—Canon Brosman[7]—Sig. N. de Nisco—A.B. Dunlop—Homersham Cox. Drive round to Naples: saw the Prefect (to whom I arranged what he may report in Rome)

[1] P. Manfrin, *Gli Ebrei sotto la dominazione romana*, 4v. (1888–97).

[2] The huge mausoleum in the Egyptian style erected on the Capo di Posilipo by Matteo Schilizzi, newspaper proprietor, with whom Gladstone became quite friendly later on this visit; see 31 Jan., 6–7 Feb. 89.

[3] Perhaps G. B. Sinisalchi, published on politics and banking.

[4] Rosebery had written, 15 January 1889: 'I am in truth rather dismayed at your idea of speaking your mind about the Italian alliance with Germany. Now is this really necessary? . . .'; Gladstone replied, 21 January 1889: '. . . The Italian business weighs upon me very much, and I do not think it has presented itself to you in those lights which make me so sensible of its gravity . . . [but] I shall not stir in it unless with a great deal of consideration . . . I am not appalled by the shadow of Bismarck, within which we all seem to stand; and I should have no fear of disturbing or dividing the Liberal party at home by anything I might say, but for want of a *locus standi* I may have to bottle up the turbid matter which surges within me . . .'; N.L.S. 10023 f. 242.

[5] J. T. Walker, *The Reasonableness in Christianity* (1888).   [6] Presumably the artist, F. Holl.

[7] Canon Timothy Brosnan, 1823–98, Roman Catholic priest in Cahirciveen (O'Connell's birthplace) asked Gladstone's assistance in building a 'great national monument to O'Connell here'; Hawn P. Gladstone's reply untraced; he is not mentioned as a subscriber in later fund-raising circulars, though Newman and the Lord Lieutenant each gave £5. A memorial church was built and is today the parish church.

and Mad. Meurikoffre. Read Manfrin—Shaw on Irish Trade[1]—Serge Panini (finished: how strong, & how strange!)—O.T. Book of Judges. Backgammon with Mr R.

22. Tu.

Wrote to Gen. Walker—Scotts—A.W. Shaw—Mr Knowles—Eug. Schuyler—Mr Lewis—Mr Cr. Powell. Drove to see the Armstrong works at Pozzuoli: very suggestive.[2] Read Manfrin—Shaw on Irish Trade (finished)—Book of Numbers—and [blank.]

23. Wed.

Wrote to Sir J. Lacaita—Ld Acton—Mr Henderson—Mr Sell. Change to sharp cold wind caught me with diarrhoea. Read Manfrin (finished)—Book of Numbers. Backgammon with Mr R. hearing delightful duets.

24.

(Bed all day) Thurs. Read Manfrin (finished)—Book of Numbers—finished Archarneses[3]—Fluëgel, Gebräüche.[4] Saw Mr A. Morley—and the Talbots.

25. Fr.

The attack though not violent is a little more obstinate than it has been. Saw Dr [B]arringer:[5] but when already improving. I go to arrowroot. Saw E. Talbot. Backgammon with Mr Rendel. Read The Equites[6]—Flugel—the Book of Numbers—Masters of the World.[7]

26. Sat.

Wrote to Siga V.L. Broli—Parliamentary Circular—Mr Waddington. Saw A. Morley who leaves. Read the Hippeis[8]—Book of Judges—Flügel, Gebräüche—Masters of the World—Ohnet, Maitre de Forges.[9] Backgammon with Mr R.

27. 3 S. Epiph.

Engl. Ch. 11 AM and Villa Capella evg. Tel. to Sig. De Dannis. Read Thos a Kempis—The Book of Joshua—Saalschütz Mosaische Recht[10]—Scene Italiche (Jones)[11]—and life of Mary Lamb.[12]

---

[1] William Shaw, 'Irish trade', sent by the author, a magistrate in Limerick; Gladstone's note of thanks in *T.T.*, 4 February 1889, 9f.

[2] The Cantiere Armstrong, a branch by Pozzuoli of Armstrong & Co, of Newcastle, actively supported by the Italian government.

[3] By Aristophanes.

[4] M. Fluegel, *Gedanken über religiöse Bräuche und Anschauungen* (1888).

[5] C. Wright Barringer, physician to the British community in Naples.

[6] By Aristophanes.   [7] M. A. M. Hoppus, *Masters of the World*, 3v. (1889).

[8] i.e. the *Equites* (see 25 Jan. 89).   [9] G. Ohnet, *Le Maître de Forges* (1884).

[10] J. L. Saalschuetz, *Das Mosaische Recht*, 2v. (1846-8).

[11] Thomas W. S. Jones, *Inni sacri per uso delle chiese, delle scuole e delle famiglie evangeliche italiane* (1881?).   [12] Mrs. Gilchrist, *Mary Lamb* (1883).

28. M.

Wrote to Sir Thos G.–Mr Campbell Bannerman–W. Cudworth–J.M. Buckley –Dr Antenori[1]–Cav. C. de Petris–Mr Childers–Rev. Dr. Cameron MP. We visited the Villa Delahante[2] and saw the superb view. Read Saalschütz–Antenori Studii Sociali[3]–....... Gebraüche–Masters of the World–Finished Hippeis. Backgammon with Mr R.

29. Tu.

$10\frac{1}{2}$–$5\frac{1}{4}$. To Ischia: saw Casamicciola.[4] Ascended the castle. View of Procida town. A delightful day. Conversation with two Priests whom we brought back–also with Dr Lavis. Read Antenori–Fluegel Gebrauche–Masters of the World.

30. Wed.

Wrote to Baron Nisco–Sig. Curati–N. Nicolaides–Rev. T.S.W. Jones.[5] Drove into Naples, calls & shops. Backgammon with Mr R. Read Antenori Studii–Profeta, Restitutzione[6]–Fluegel, Braüche–Masters of the World.

31. Th.

Wrote to Sig. de Riso–Mrs Vyner–Countess Carretto–Redattore Corriere di Napoli–Redattore Riforma–Mr Blackburn–Mr Gilder–Mr Macbride–Mr Stringley. Dined with Sig. Schilizzi and went to the Sannazzaro: Sig. Duse an actress of very considerable power.[7] Saw Sen. Scrumola. Conversation with my host. Read Antenori–Flügel (finished)–Book of Joshua. Home late.

Frid. Feb. One 1889.

Wrote to Newswoman–Mr Morley–Mrs Adams–Prince Filangieri[8]–Rev. V. Marchese.[9] Read Antenori–Book of Samuel II–Maitre des Forges–Speech of Dep. Baccarini. Wrote on Homer (Zeus). Attended the Casino Concert in Naples. Excellent.

---

[1] Giuseppe Antenori of Naples; 'a well-known and respected Neapolitan physician, who unites the characters of Liberal and believer' (Gladstone in *N.C.*, xxv. 768 (May 1889)).

[2] On the Capo di Posilipo.

[3] G. Antenori, *Studii Sociali* (1885); discussed in *N.C.*, xxv. 772 (May 1889).

[4] Destroyed by earthquake in 1883, and rebuilt under Governmental superintendence.

[5] Thomas W. S. Jones, methodist minister in Naples; published various works on evangelism in Italy (see 27 Jan. 89).

[6] Perhaps an early version of I. Profeta, *Riduzione dal poema di Moore di Italo Robin*, published in Naples (1897).

[7] Eleonora Duse, 1858–1924; Italian tragedienne; performed much in London in the 1890s. The Teatro Sannazaro theatre performed dramas and comedies.

[8] Prince Gaetano Filangieri, d. 1892; recently presented the Palazzo Cuonio (his museum) to the city (see 6–7 Feb. 89).

[9] Italian priest with whom Gladstone had been in touch when in Florence in 1888; Hawn P.

2. Sat.

Wrote to Mr A. Mee[1]–Prof. Moro–Mrs Jackson–Prof. Profeta. Read Antenori–II Samuel–Contemp. Rev. on Bismarck[2]–Maitre de Forges. To Naples, & saw. ...

3. S. Epiph.

Engl. Ch. mg & H.C.–Mr Bell's[3] service in evg. Herbert left us. Read I Kings–Life of Mary Lamb–...... agt Xty–Saalschütz Mos. Recht–and [blank.]

4. M.

Wrote to Grogan & Boyd–R. Darlington–L. Dillon–Canon Crossman–J.B. Law–Count Pirouti–Sig. Stolci–Sig. del Giudice–Sig. Paladini–M. Granini–Mr. Salazari–Pres. Acad. Scienz. Mor e Pol. Saw Mr Geo. Tendell. Rough weather. Backgammon with Mr R. Read Antenori–Saalschutz–Baccharini, Policy of Italy[4]–Le Maitre de Forges.

5. Tu.

Wrote to Sig. Schilizzi. Went to Naples, Antiquity shops: & left card for the Archbishop[5] in token of respect. The Bells dined. Backgammon with my host. Read Antenori (finished)–Italian Tracts–Maitre de Forges.

6. Wed.

Wrote to A. Gordon–Sir J. Lacaita–Mrs Webster–Cav. Cozzolini–Sig. Cichelli–Sig. Zaccharini. Visited Sig. Schilizzi. He took me to the Operaji: where I was put on a platform and compelled to make a speech. We then went to the Filangieri Museum.[6] And so home. Read Maitre des Forges–Life of Mary Lamb–Mosaische Recht–and [blank.] Backgammon with Mr R.

7. Th.

Off at $10\frac{1}{2}$. Went over the Aquarium. Then colazione with Schilizzi. I had much conversation with him. Then to the opening of the Filangieri Schools: here again a platform and a speech. Went over the schools. Then to Museo Nazionale: where we had the excellent aid both of Mr Rolfe[7] and of a Director. An active and interesting day. Back at $5\frac{1}{4}$. Backgammon with Mr R. Read Mary Lamb's Life–Maitre de forges–Zaccharini, rather trumpery[8]–Saalschütz Mos. Recht.

---

[1] Probably Arthur Mee, 1860–1926; journalist in Wales; ed. *Western Mail* 1892.
[2] *C.R.*, lv. 157 (February 1889).
[3] Possibly a mishearing of Barff; Henry Tootal Barff was Anglican chaplain in Naples from 1875.
[4] Untraced.
[5] Cardinal Gugliemo Sanfelice; for his reply, see Add MS 44506, f. 43.
[6] See 1 Feb. 89n.
[7] E. Neville Rolfe, worked in the Museo Nazionale and wrote its *Complete Handbook* with D. Monaco, the director.
[8] Untraced.

8. Fr.

Wrote to Card. Abp of N.—Mary Drew—Lord Dufferin—Geo. Potter—M. de Pressensé—S. Compston—Prof. Maldarelli—C.H. Turner—Sig. Nitopi—W. Moss—Sig. Montessori—E.J. Reid MP—March. Dragonetti—Signors Mancioni & Latheski—Prof. P. Fiore—The Prefect l.l.[1]—The Syndic l.l. Read Saalschutz—Dufferin's Banquet Speech[2]—Riforma on Dufferin—Life of Mary Lamb—Maitre de Forges. To Naples with Mr R. Saw Sig. Schilizzi—Monsignor Pacifico—Mr G. Rendel.

9. Sat. [Amalfi]

Wrote to Messrs Cook—Sig. F. Bruno—Mrs Rendel—Sig. Schilizzi. Packed up. Finished Maistre de Forges—Finished Mary Lamb—Read Lady W.W.s novel.[3] Farewells all round. Off between 2 & 3 from Station. A garden all the way to La Cava. Then a splendid 14 m drive in ill weather to Amalfi (Cappuccini).[4]

10. 5 S. Epiph.

Attended in the old Chapel of the Capuccini during mass. We then had the English service read in the Sala di Lettura 25 or 30 attending. And C. & I heard an Italian sermon in the Duomo in the afternoon. Read T. A Kempis; O.T.; Saalschütz; Il Papa by . . . .[5] and . . . .

11. M.

Wrote to Mr H.B. Stowe—Lady Watkin Williams—Mr M.Q. Holyoake.[6] In forenoon, received the Syndic and the Praetor. In afternoon visited the Municipio (ex-Benedictine Convent) also went over a paper-manufactory: where only rag is used. Saw Mr Bryce. Read Saalschütz—Lady W.W.s novel—Masters of the World—Marzella, Il Papa—Gravellona's Latin verses.[7] Backgammon with Mr R. At dinner the Padrone sang for us capitally: and after it there was a serenade on a large scale in the grotto with splendid lights.

---

[1] Letter on need for 'national regeneration' in Sicily; published by Codronchi in the Italian press; see *N.C.*, xxv. 774 (May 1889) and Add MS 44506, ff. 45, 50.

[2] Controversial speech in Calcutta on St. Andrew's Day, 1888, on the political situation as he left India; sympathetic in details and sceptical in general about 'democracy' in India; Dufferin told his wife on 10 February 1889: 'I have had a nice letter from Mr. Gladstone. He has read my (Calcutta) speech and he says it is a very able and comprehensive statement, and adds: "While your opponents as to their position require very little knocking down, I do not think any one who reads you equitably can question the sympathetic spirit in which you treat India and her people. I rejoice that the expression of opinion, even of native opinion, should be free . . ."'; Lyall, *Dufferin*, ii. 197 ff., 213.

[3] Lady Watkin Williams, *Even such is life. A novel*, 3v. (1888).

[4] The Gladstones and the Rendels stayed in the Cappuccini hotel, in the old Capuchin monastery above the town; 'the building, which stands in the hollow of a rock which rises abruptly from the sea to a height of 230 ft., contains fine cloisters, a charming verandah, and magnificent points of view'; Baedeker, *Southern Italy and Sicily* (1896), 169.

[5] By Marzella (see next day); but untraced.

[6] Malthus Questell Holyoake, active in liberal circles; presumably s. of G.J.

[7] F. Barbarara di Gravellona, *Leo XIII . . . Verses* (1888).

12. Tu.

Wrote to Sir W. Harcourt—Dott. E. Fazie—Scotts—and arranged with Pallini a reply to Sig. Crispi.[1] Read Saalschütz—Masters of the World. Fireworks & music in evg. We went to Ravello to see Mr Reid[2] whom I knew here in 1850. Mr R. & I walked up, but took to the carriage for our triumphal ingress. The drive down is splendid. The old Cathedral most curious and striking: also a cloister in Pal. Rufolo.

13. Wed.

Wrote to the Syndic—Marquis di S. Gregorio—Mad. Catalone Sgherzi—Mr F. Sabin—Mr H. Gray—Rev. Dr. Olliff—Rev. Orbanurichi. Walk with Mr R. along the half made road.[3] Read Saalschütz—Masters of the World—Aristoph. Ranae.[4]

14. Th. [On train]

Off at 10.15. Our journey was everywhere a public procession. The Municipio attended us to Amalfi & great crowds. The same at Maggiore. Envoys at La Cava. A crowd of friends at Naples. Crispi[5] and many more at Rome. Then came repose with the new line by the Maremma. Read Batrachoi—Masters of the World.

15. [Cannes]

Breakfast at Genoa. Our continuous journey ended at Cannes 6 P.M. Montfleury. Saw Ld Acton. Read Masters of the World (finished)—Batrachoi. The journey told a little on us both. The Sindaco came at San Remo. Began Giannetta.[6]

16. Sat.

Wrote to Sig. Dotti—Ctta. S. Stefano—Mr J.T. Gray.[7] Saw Ld Acton—Mrs Sands—Acton family—Sir A. West—Lady Ward—Lady Riddell—and others. Drive with Mrs Sands. *Sent* by Ld A. to Mr Fergus photographer: able but most exacting. Read Harris, Lent[8]. . . .—Ornithes[9]—Mes Pensées[10]—I Book of Kings.

---

[1] Interviewed with correspondent of *Riforma* on Irish agrarian reform and on Italian unification; *Daily News*, 15 February 1889, 5h.

[2] Francis Neville Reid, 1826-92 (mentioned but not further identified at 17 Dec. 50); settled in Ravello for health reasons; lived in Palazzo Rufoli.

[3] Road being built by F. N. Reid from Ravello to Amalfi.

[4] 'The Frogs' (also 'Batrachoi'), by Aristophanes.

[5] Reported as 'a brief interview' to which importance should not be attached; *Daily News*, 18 February 1889, 8g.

[6] Rosa Mulholland (later Gilbert), *Gianetta: a girl's story of herself* (1889).

[7] Edinburgh liberal, organizing meeting there; this letter, on Ireland, read out; *T.T.*, 20 February 1889, 9f.

[8] Perhaps G. C. Harris, *Lessons from St. Peter's life . . . a course of lectures* (1865).

[9] Aristophanes, 'The Birds'.

[10] Pascal; see 18 July 30.

17. Septa S.

St Paul's mg & aft. excellent service & Sermons. Luncheon with Mrs Vyner between. Dined with Lord Acton. Not a restful day. Saw The Prince of Wales—Duke of Cambridge—Mrs Vyner—Mr Vyner—Dr. Temple West[1]—& others. Saw Lady Acton—Ld Acton: most restful. Wrote to Dotti (Florence)—Horace Seymour. Read T. AKempis—Dio e l'Uomo[2]—Saalschutz—2 Kings.

18. M.

Wrote to A. Morley. Read 2 Kings—Giannetta—The Birds—Thos a Kempis. Saw Ld Dorchester—Mr Acland MP—Sir E. Watkin MP *cum* ....—Mr Stuart Rendel—Ld Acton—M. Roothem—and about six other French speakers and Americans. Luncheon at Ld Acton's—Dinner at do—Walk with him.

19. Tu. [*On train*]

Wrote to Miss Bentley. Saw Sir Chas Murray—Ld Acton—Mrs Sands—Mr Darlington—and others. Off about one. Read Saalschütz—Virgil Æn. II. Finished Ornithes: what a picture of the actual state of the ruling religion—Giannetta. Travelled all night.

20. Wed. [*London*]

Paris at 8 A.M. London $5\frac{3}{4}$ P.M. All well D.G. An enthusiastic crowd at Charing X, & at Folkestone. Read Virg. Æn. III.—Thomas a Kempis. Dined at Rosebery's. Accepted the general desire for an amendment on the Address. Conversation with Rosebery and Granville—Italy [and with] Sir Chas Russell: on the [Parnell] Commission.[3] Saw Burdett [R?].

21. Th.

Wrote to S.W. Stuckey—Mr H. White—E.W. Darby[4]—Jas Davidson—Mr W.H. Smith—W.H.G.—and minutes. Dined at 4 w[ith] the Meeting (noon) at Spencer House to determine amendment & consider plan of debate.[5] Also conclave in evg at H. of C. on Smith's letter.[6] H. of C. $4\frac{3}{4}$–8 and $10\frac{1}{2}$–$1\frac{3}{4}$.[7] Saw S. Lyttelton—Ld Hartington—Ld Ripon—Ld Granville—Jas Stuart—J. Morley—A. Morley—Mr W.H. Smith—and others. Read Giannetta.

---

[1] Richard Temple West; formerly Student of Christ Church, Oxford; vicar of Paddington from 1865.

[2] Untraced.

[3] Pigott this day began evidence as a witness for *The Times* at the Parnell Commission; Russell cross-questioned him next day and by that evening Pigott was a broken man. On 23 February Pigott called on Labouchere and signed a confession; on 25 February he attempted to revoke it by affidavit, and fled to France that evening. On 1 March he shot himself in Madrid as the police attempted to arrest him.

[4] Secretary of the Peace Society; a rather cautious reply to its memorial; *T.T.*, 26 February 1889, 10c, 27 February 1889, 4f.

[5] Morley gave immediate notice of an amendment on Ireland; *H* 333. 35.

[6] Presumably on Commons' arrangements; W. H. Smith was leader of the House.

[7] Opened debate on the Queen's Speech for the Opposition; *H* 333. 48.

22. Fr.

Wrote to F. Joseph—Miss L.J. Law—W.H.G.—Rev. G. Clements—H.N.G.—Mr Jas Stewart—Mr Mather—Mr J.A. Gunnill. H. of C. $4\frac{1}{2}$–$7\frac{3}{4}$.[1] Saw S. Lyttelton—Mr Hamilton—Mr Nicol (Good Words)—Sir A. Clark—Sir W. Harcourt—Sir L. Playfair—Mr S. Rendel—Mr Agnew jun.—Sir C. Russell—Mr Bartlett—Mr Lefevre—Mr Robinson—Mr Bartlett (U.S.)[2]—A. Morley—Mr Cook—Mr Woods. Read Life of Drummond.[3] Worked on books & papers.

23. Sat.

Wrote to W.H.G.—Ed. of Times & draft[4]—Mr Osborne. Attended the Circus at Covent Garden $2\frac{1}{2}$–4. Dinner party at No 4: & animated evening party. Saw Sir C. Russell—Scotts—Miss Ponsonby—Mr Reid MP—and others. Read Life of Drummond.

24. Sexa S.

Chapel Royal 10 A.M. & 5.30 PM. Saw the Sydneys—Mr S. Rendel. Read his corresp with Bp Hughes[5]—Thomas a Kempis—Kingsley on Puritanism[6]—Black on Ingersoll.[7] Wrote to Mrs Bolton.

25. M.

Wrote to Watsons . . . . . and minutes. Dined at Grillion's. H. of C. 5–8 and after dinner.[8] Read Life of Drummond—Rev. Clements on Conciliation.[9] Luncheon at 15 G.S: gave advice on the house. Visited Acad. Old M[asters] Exhn.

26. Tu.

Wrote minutes. Worked on Irish Question. Read Drummond largely—Morpeth's speech of 1839.[10] H. of C. 5–8.[11] Saw S. Lyttelton—A. Morley—J. Morley—and divers.

---

[1] Queen's Speech; *H* 333. 140.

[2] Perhaps John Bartlett of Cambridge, Mass., whose first ed. of *Familiar quotations* was published in 1888.

[3] R. Barry O'Brien, *Thomas Drummond* (1889); Irish undersecretary 1835–40. Discussed in his speech on 1 Mar. 89.

[4] Refuting allegations in leader of *T.T.*, 16 February 1889, 11f, of distraints on the estate; the tenants had held a meeting supporting W. H. Gladstone's record; this letter, with extracts from Liverpool *Daily Post*, in *T.T.*, 25 February 1889, 8c. Cuttings from various papers, with Gladstone's draft replies, in Add MS 44506, ff. 59–82. See also *T.T.*, 15 February 1889, 10f.

[5] S. Rendel, 'Disestablishment in Wales. A remonstrance address to the Bishop of St. Asaph [J. Hughes]' (1885).

[6] C. Kingsley, *Plays and Puritans* (1873).

[7] J. W. Black, 'Colonel Ingersoll's reply to W. E. Gladstone briefly considered' (1889).

[8] Queen's Speech; *H* 333. 269.

[9] Untraced.

[10] Perhaps that on Irish crime, 7 March 1839, *H* 46. 48.

[11] Queen's Speech; *H* 333. 389.

27. *Wed.*

Wrote to Watson & Smith—Mr Nield—Mr Meehan—& minutes. Attended Mr Mayhew's marriage.[1] H. of C. 2¾–5.[2] Worked much on Irish question & made extracts. Saw Mr Morley—Mr A. Morley—Mr W.H. Smith—Mr Childers—Sir W. Phillimore—& others. Read Rural Italy[3]—Began 'For the Right'.[4] Dined at Mr Glyn's.

28. *Th.*

Wrote to Scotts—Deputy V. Chancr of Cambridge[5]—Robertson & Nichn—and minutes. Worked on books & papers preparing for departure from No 22. Saw S. Lyttelton—A. Morley—Ld Northbourne—Lucy Cavendish—& others. H. of C. 4–8?[6] Read For the Right—finished Drummond.

Frid. Mch One 1889.

Wrote minutes. Saw S.L.—A. Morley—Read 'For the Right'—and [blank.] Worked hard on the Irish question again. Spoke 1¾ h. A poor scrannel pipe indeed unless He play on it.[7]

2. *Sat.*

Wrote to Mr H. Ward—G. Macmillan—H.C. Burdett—G. Bentley—C.T. Lusted—Miss J. Sutter—G. Hamilton—and minutes. Conclave on the Parnell explosion 12–2:[8] & other matters. Saw Mr Knowles 2½–3½—Lady Stanley 5¾–6½.

At noon C. went off to Hawarden with Herbert: having considerably kept back from me *yesterday* the news of Willy's seizure;[9] which indeed must have laid me (morally) on my back. I went to Sir A. C[lark']s in the late afternoon & perceived from his not having put off his return (Euston 8.20) that there could be nothing immediately urgent. But the occurrence is a grave one for the future.

Later came in a relieving telegram direct from Hawarden and an anxious one from Fasque.[10]

3. *Quinqua S.*

Chapel Royal 10 AM Guards [Chapel] 6 P.M. H.C. at C.R. Then went off to Sir A. Clark & drew even further on his unbounded kindness by a long & deeply

[1] Horace Mayhew of Broughton Hall, Flints., the Hawarden agent (see 22 Oct. 85), m. 2ndly Mabel Eleanor Joyce.   [2] Disappearance of Pigott; *H* 333. 485.
[3] W. N. Beauclerk, *Rural Italy* (1888); see *N.C.*, xxv. 773 (May 1889).
[4] C. E. Franzos, tr. J. Sutter, *For the Right* (1887); Gladstone reviewed it in *N.C.*, xxv. 615 (April 1889).
[5] Thanking James Porter, Master of Peterhouse, for a Dante commentary, just published by C.U.P.; Add MS 44506, f. 63.   [6] Queen's Speech; *H* 333. 603.
[7] *H* 333. 735; in fact the speech was a considerable success; later that day Gladstone (and all the Opposition front bench, save Hartington) joined in the standing ovation for Parnell when he rose to speak. The 'scrannel pipe' is a reference to Milton, *Lycidas*, 124.
[8] News of Pigott's suicide; see 20 Feb. 89n.
[9] See Introduction above, Section VII.
[10] Fatal illness of his brother, Sir T. Gladstone; see 20 Mar. 89.

interesting conversation. The sum as regards W. is excellent present progress—
sanguine hope of the level of the last 9 months, distant hope of an absolute
recovery & expulsion of the mischief.

Wrote a full report to C.G. Read Thomas a Kempis—Kingsley on Puritanism
—Bp Sandford's Address[1]—and [blank.]

4. M.

Wrote to C.G.—Mr Thorndike Rice—M. Drew. Dined at Ld Roseberys. Saw S.
Lyttelton—Sir W.H. cum A. Morley bis—E. Hamilton—Mr [E.T.] Cook
(P.M.G.)—Lucy Cavendish—Ld Rosebery—Mr G. Russell—Ly Rothschild. Con-
clave on Scottish H.R. Saw + & X.[2] Made special calls: Duc d'Aumale & French
Ambr—absent. H. of C. $3\frac{1}{2}$-7.[3] Read For the Right—Rural Italy.

5. Tu.

Wrote to Mr W. Keane[4]—H.J. Hillen—T.E. Young[5]—Dr Gladstone—Messrs
Meehan—and minutes. Read Rural Italy—For the right—and [blank.] H. of C. 5-
8?[6] Cold coming on. Early to bed. Saw Mr Murray—Lady Stanley Ald.

6. Ash Wed.

Forbidden [to attend] church. Read the Services[7]—Thomas a Kempis—For the
Right—Rural Italy. Wrote to Mr Smith—C.G. H. of C. $2\frac{1}{2}$-$4\frac{1}{2}$ on a necessity
which vanished:[8] went back to bed, but *paid* for the outing. Saw S. L[yttelton]
and A. M[orley].

7. Th.

Bed all day: cough stiff. Read For the Right (finished)—E.W.H. Mem. on Pensions[9]—Beauclerk's Rural Italy. Wrote to A. Morley. Saw S.L. but avoided all
conversations. Saw Lucy C?

8. Fr.

A repetition of yesterday with some improvement of the cough. Read Rural
Italy—Probyns Italy.[10] Saw S.L.—A.M.

---

[1] C. W. Sandford, 'A pastoral letter' (1889).
[2] i.e. rescue work.
[3] Queen's Speech; *H* 333. 851.
[4] William Keane of Holland Park, sent a cushion; Hawn P.
[5] Thomas Charles Young had sent his *Lectures on Scots Law* (1889); Hawn P.
[6] Spoke on Chiltern Hundreds; *H* 333. 986.
[7] i.e. read the Church services at home.
[8] Queen's Speech deb. this day was on the condition of the working classes; *H* 333. 1062.
[9] Mem. by Hamilton on political pensions; see E.H.D., 13 March 1889.
[10] J. W. Probyn, *Italy; from the fall of Napoleon I . . . to the death of Victor Emmanuel* (1884); see *N.C.*,
xxv. 777 (May 1889).

9. Sat.

Wrote minutes. Saw Sir A. Clark—J. Morley—Sir A. West—A. Morley—S.L. Seven to dinner: up, but weak. Read Rural Italy—Probyn's Italy—Chron. H. VIII.[1]

10. 1 S.L.

The weather kept me in bed. Read Service. Read Thos A'Kempis—Hengstenberg on the Pentateuch[2]—Wace's Reply to Huxley.[3] Downstairs in evg. Clark warned me much yesterday against bronchial catarrh.

11. M.

Wrote to Mr Stead—Sir J. Pauncefoot—and minutes. Cough now quite loose. Saw Scotts—A. Morley—S.L. Drive in aft. Dined with the Rothschilds. Conversation with Ld R—Ld R. Churchill[4]—Sir J. Pauncefote. Read Probyn's Italy—Q.R. on Gambling[5]—Farrer on Sugar Convention.[6]

12. Tu.

Wrote to G. Russell—D. Macgregor—Jas Pirie—Maj. Sharp Hume—Mr Maclaren—Rev. Mr Hitchcock—and minutes. Saw S.L.—A. Morley—E. Hamilton—Mr Labouchere. Dined at Sir C. Forster's. Read Farrer—Q.R. on Twelve Good men[7]—Probyn (finished)—began Motley's Corresp.[8] H. of C. $2\frac{1}{2}$–$4\frac{1}{2}$.[9]

13. Wed.

Wrote to Mr H. Davies—Mr Knowles l.l.—Mr Beaufoy[10]—& minutes. H. of C. $2\frac{1}{4}$–6. Voted in 193:259.[11] Read Motley's Corr.—Statesman's Year Book[12]—Farrer on Sugar Bounties. Saw Lady Stepney—Mr Childers—Mr A. Morley—S.L.

14. Th.

Wrote to Sig. Paladini—Riforma Newspaper—Mr S. OGrady—Mr Lusted—Ed Pall Mall G.[13]—Mr Smith—and minutes. Read Motley's Corr.—Orthodox[14]—

[1] F. A. Gasquet, *Henry VIII and the English monasteries*, 2v. (1888).

[2] E. W. Hengestenberg, *Dissertations on the genuineness of the Pentateuch*, 2v. (1847).

[3] H. Wace in *N.C.*, xxv. 351 (March 1889).

[4] Gladstone told Hamilton next day: 'He [Churchill] is certainly . . . a most extraordinary fellow. Unfortunately he has not, I fear, a single grain of conviction in him except in the abstract, even about economical subjects for which he has shewn such aptitude. He talked very little about Home politics. . . . He has become a Boulangist, believing that Boulanger is the coming man . . .'; E.H.D., 13 March 1889.   [5] *Q.R.*, clxviii. 136 (January 1889).

[6] T. H. Farrer, *The sugar convention* (1889); he told Hamilton 'the arguments in it [Farrer] were absolutely unanswerable'; E.H.D., 13 March 1889.

[7] *Q.R.*, clxviii. 167 (January 1889); [G. W. E. Russell] on Dean Burgon.

[8] *The correspondence of J. L. Motley*, ed. G. W. Curtis, 2v. (1889).

[9] Questions; supply; *H* 333. 1491.

[10] Mark Hanbury Beaufoy, 1854–1922; liberal candidate in Kennington, London; Gladstone sent a letter of encouragement; he was elected and sat until 1895.

[11] On Prisoners (Ireland) Bill; *H* 333. 1613.

[12] *The Statesman's Year Book* (1889).   [13] Not found published.

[14] D. Gerard, *Orthodox* (1888).

Defence of Bismarck.[1] Saw A. Morley. Saw Miss [Dorothy] Tennant's pictures. H. of C. $3\frac{1}{2}$–5.[2] Six to dinner.

15. Fr.

Wrote to Mr C.S. Miall–J. Charlton–C. Danby–W. Thorn–C. King–E.J. Peckover.[3] Saw A. Morley–S.L.–Sir W. Harcourt cum J. Morley–The Speaker–Mr Childers. H. of C. $3\frac{1}{2}$–5.[4] Tea at Lady Derbys. Conversation with her. and with Russian Ambassador. Read Motley–Divorce de Napoleon[5]–Orthodox. Saw Mr Harrison–S.L.

16. Sat.

Wrote to J. Hudson–Mr Gavan Duffy–M. Drew–Horace Seymour–W.H.G.– Sun Correspondent–and minutes. Dined at Ld Wentworth's. Saw Lady Taylor: A. Wortley: and others. Read Motley–Divorce de Napoleon–Orthodox–Bp Vaughan on Italian Qu.[6] Drive with C.

17. 2 S.L.

Chapel Royal mg & evg. Fiveocloquai with the Farquhars. Read Divorce de Napoleon–Thos a Kempis–Hengstenberg on Pentateuch–Foreshadowing of Christianity.[7]

18. M.

Wrote to Count C. Lozzo–Mrs Fitzroy–Mrs Drew–Mr Knowles–Mr S. Rendel–Mr Mather[8]–Rev. Bircham–& minutes. Dined at Mrs Th's. 15 G.S. Saw S.L.–A. Morley–Mr Bunting–F.L. Gower–Mr Trafford–Marq. de Breteuil– and *blank* [*sic*]. Read Motley–Divorce de Napoleon–19th Cent. on the Abbey.[9] H. of C. $3\frac{1}{2}$–$5\frac{1}{2}$.[10] Drive with C.

19. Tu.

Wrote to Dr Döllinger–Canon Liddon–Lady Taylor–Mr Kelly–and minutes. Saw S.L.–Ld Granville–Sir W.H. *cum* J. Morley–Mrs Paull. H of C. $3\frac{1}{2}$–$5\frac{1}{2}$.[11] Saw Mr Parnell: & proposed to him a public dinner, which he readily accepted.[12] Read Motley–Orthodox (finished)–Divorce de Napoleon finished.

[1] Perhaps C. Brumm, *Bismarck: his deeds and his aims* (1889); a reply to an article in *C.R.*
[2] Questions; *H* 333. 1625.
[3] Of Wisbech; had sent his *Foreshadowings of Christianity* (1888).
[4] Questions; cabinet salaries; *H* 333. 1819.
[5] H. Welschinger, *Le divorce de Napoléon* (1889).
[6] H. A. Vaughan, *The Roman question international and British, not purely Italian* (1889).
[7] See 15 Mar. 89.
[8] Letter of support to Mather in by-election in S.E. Lancs.; *T.T.*, 20 March 1889, 8b; (Sir) William Mather, 1838–1920; chairman of Mather and Platt; liberal M.P. S. Salford 1885–6, Gorton 1889–95.
[9] *N.C.*, xxv. 409. 415 (March 1889).
[10] Questioned Balfour on treatment of W. O'Brien; *H* 334. 46.
[11] Public business; *H* 334. 142.
[12] See 2 Apr. 89 for a well-publicised, though private dinner.

20. Wed.

Wrote to Gen. Greeley[1]–The Speaker–Mr Vickers–Mr Edminson–A.W. Hutton–Pickerings–Cawthorne & Hutt–Robn & Nichn–Westell–J.R.G. (Tel & L.)–Mr Lucy–H. Mayhew–Sig. Dotti–Scotts–Miles–Coverley–Quaritch–G. Bellis. At midday I received the news of my brother's peaceful death early this morning. I remain here without attending the House. Saw S.L.–A. Morley–Herbert J.G. Read Paper on Irish deposits[2]–Motley–Red Hugh's Captivity.[3]

21. Th.

Wrote to Ld Spencer–Mr Hunter MP–Mr Coppack–Christie & M. Unpacking & arranging papers: which I now find a more serious affair than formerly. Saw S.L.–Herbert J.G.–A. Morley–Mr S. Rendel. Read Motley–Red Hugh's Captivity–For Faith & freedom.[4]

22. Fr. [Dollis Hill]

Wrote to Ld Granville–Mr Rendel–Dr Murray–Mrs Bolton. Saw S.L.–Herbert J.G. In afternoon migrated to Dollis. Read Motley–For Faith & Freedom–Ed. Rev. on Ld Grenville.[5]

23. Sat.

Wrote to French Ambassr–Ld Rosebery. Saw F. Lawley–Herbert G–Mr Munro Fergusson.[6] Worked on Mackay MS.[7] Read Motley, finished.

24 3. S.L. [On train]

Willesden Ch: aft prayers read by C. Off at 8½ P.M. to Willesden for Fasque. Travelled all night. Wrote to Sir W. Harcourt–W.H. Pickering–Guy Logan[8]–Mr Fisher Unwin. Read Thomas a Kempis–Schurz Alt Testament Theologie[9]–The Digby Letters (remarkable)[10] and [blank].

25 M. [Fasque]

Joined by S. in the night. Fasque[11] at 12. Found all as ought to be. And all most kind. Dear Fasque: one of my three homes: the others are (or were) Seaforth and Hawarden. Walk with John:[12] I trust a worthy & loving successor. Read

---

[1] i.e. the explorer; see 17 Nov. 85.   [2] Not found.
[3] S. O'Grady, Red Hugh's captivity (1889).
[4] W. Besant, For faith and freedom, 3v. (1889).
[5] E.R., clxviii. 271 (October 1888).
[6] i.e. Ferguson, Gladstone's successor in Leith Burghs; see 22 Aug. 87.
[7] See 7 Dec. 88n.
[8] Of Wimbledon; asked for £10 assistance; Hawn P.
[9] By H. H. Schultz, tr. as Old testament theology (1892).
[10] Perhaps Sir E. Digby, The gunpowder treason (1679); with an appendix of letters.
[11] The house in Kincardineshire bought by Gladstone's father in 1830, and inherited by his elder brother, Tom.
[12] i.e. Sir John Robert Gladstone of Fasque and Balfour, 3rd baronet, inheriting his father Tom's title.

Thompson's Account of Cremation[1]—Grant's Recollections[2]—Seward's Anecdotes[3]—Novalis (Began).[4] Wrote to C.G. & Helen.

26. Tu.

Wrote to C.G. The funeral at 12¾. Abundant tokens of respect. St[ephen] read
his part admirably. The N.E. wind very bitter: but no damage. Walk with John.
Conversation with Louisa on a memoir of my Father. Perhaps *now* hardly possible.[5] Wrote a little on Motley. Read Novalis (finished)—Thomas a Kempis—
Duchillon, Travels[6]—Dio e l'Uomo.[7]

27. Wed. [On train]

Rel. at 10.30: Bright died at 10.30. A great orator: a good & most able man. A
loyal friend: a most pure politician. Peace be with him. Read T. A Kempis—
Duchillon's Travels—Tosca.[8] Service in the Chapel 11 A.M. Attended the reading of my Brother's will: a well considered instrument. Off at one after my last?
sight of Fasque. Travelled all night.

28. Th. [London]

Wrote to Madame Villari—M. Billard—Rev. Edmonson—Mr J. Wylie. Saw S.L.—
Mr A. Morley—Mr Cremer MP cum do—Mr Morley—Mr Childers. H. of C. 4½—
5¾.[9] Drive with C. Read Momerie[10]—For Fiath & Freedom—Gasquet, H[enry]
VIII & Monasteries.[11]

29. Fr.

Wrote to Mr Stibbs—H. Smith—Mr Maggs—R. Pullen. Mr Mansfeld & Mr
Brooks came & worked on their portraits of me.[12] Saw S.L.—F.R. Lawley—Ld
Rosebery—Mr Smith—Mr A. Morley—Mr Morley—Ld Granville—Lady Airlie—
Sir W. Harcourt *bis*—Mr Godley. Tea at Mrs Peels. H. of C. 3¾–5¾ Spoke on
Bright.[13] Godley and Lucy dined. Read Gasquet—For Faith and Freedom.

[1] Sir H. Thompson, *Cremation; treatment of the body after death* (1884).
[2] Probably U. S. Grant, *Personal memoirs*, 2v. (1885–6).
[3] W. W. Seward, *Anecdotes of some distinguished persons*, 4v. (1795); see 19 Dec. 61.
[4] 'Novalis' (i.e. F. L. von Hardenberg), *Schriften*, 2v. (1805).
[5] Samuel Smiles, at one time considered as a biographer (see Matthew, *Gladstone*, 3–4 and 19
Apr. 60), was still quite an active writer, but no memoir was written until Checkland's family
biography. For the *D.N.B.* entry on Sir John, see 22 July 89n.
[6] Perhaps L. Dutens, *Mémoires d'un voyageur* [*L. D. Duchillon*], *qui se repose*, 3v. (1806).
[7] Untraced.
[8] Perhaps V. Sardou's play (1887) on which Puccini's opera was based.
[9] Supply; *H* 334. 1047.
[10] A. W. Momerie, *Inspiration and other sermons* (1889); see 31 Mar., 5 Apr. 89.
[11] See 9 Mar. 89.
[12] Mansfeld or Mansfield untraced. Henry Jermyn Brooks, fl. 1884–1904, portrait painter; this
portrait's whereabouts now unknown; exhibited 1904 and said to be 'very small, but the sensitive
handling gives it a distinction lacking in some of the larger paintings'; C. Wood, *Dictionary of Victorian painters*, 2nd ed. (1978), 66, and *The Studio*, xxxi. 151 (March 1904).
[13] Tribute to Bright; *H* 333. 1169: '*Felix opportunitate mortis!*'

30. Sat.

Wrote to Mr F. Finch—Rev. J.G. Rogers—E. Casse—Mr E.R. Russell—Mr S. Rendel MP.—and minutes. Saw Sir William Gull—Scotts—S. Lyttelton. Read Coal Syndicate Tract[1]—Momerie on Inspiration—For Faith and Freedom—Gasquet.

31. 4 S. Lent.

Ch. Royal mg—St John's Westmr Evg. Wrote draft on Momerie case.[2] Wrote to Miss Fitzroy. Read Momerie on Inspiration &c.—Do on Agnosticism &c.—Luccock on H. Eucharist[3]—The Book of Ecclesiastes.

Monday April One 1889.

Wrote to M. Leon Say—Mr E. Law—Dhuleep Singh—F. Finch—H. Mayhew—L. Morris—Rev. C.M. Church[4]—Canon Luccock—Mr Godley—Mr Roundell—& minutes. Saw Sir C. Russell—Mr A. Morley—S.L. H of C. $3\frac{3}{4}$–$4\frac{3}{4}$. Visited A. Wortley's Studio.[5] Dined with Rosebery: long conversation with him. Read Life of Captain Rock[6]—For Faith and Freedom.

2. Tu.

Wrote to Mr Page Hopps—Sir W. Phillimore—Mr Nutt—Professor Hales[7]—Geo Freeman—and minutes. Attended the Levee. Read Fraser Volumes[8]—Villari Preface to Savonarola[9]—Hales on Chevy Chase—For F. and F. H. of C. $3\frac{3}{4}$–5.[10] Nine to dinner: a Parnell entertainment. Conversation with Mr P.—Mr Illingworth—Lady Stepney. Saw S.L.—A. Morley—J. Morley—Campbell Bannerman.

3. Wed.

Wrote to Bp of London—Rev. Dr. Parker—Mr Bancroft—Mr Cumberland—and minutes. Dined at Sir Alg. West's. At last, resumed the American Free Trade paper.[11] It is sadly behind. My motive power sensibly declines: thank God for what I have. Saw S.L.—A. Morley—J. Morley. Read Major Fraser—Hist. Captain Rock—For F. & F.

[1] Untraced.
[2] Add MS 44773, f. 173; Alfred Williams Momerie, 1848–1900, professor at King's, London, was forced to leave the college in 1891 after a long campaign against his Broad-churchmanship. Gladstone was a Life Governor of the college. See 5 Apr. 89.
[3] H. M. Luckock, *The divine liturgy* (1889).
[4] Charles Marcus Church, historian and canon of Wells.
[5] Archibald James Stuart Wortley, 1849–1905; son of G's friend; a pupil of Millais and a portrait painter; but no portrait of Gladstone traced.
[6] See 20 Apr. 68.
[7] John Wesley Hales, 1836–1914; professor of English at King's, London; editor of *Longer English poems* (1872).
[8] Maj. J. Fraser, *Major Fraser's MS... 1696–1737*, 2v. (1889).
[9] Preface to the 2v. tr. (1888) of Villari's *Savonarola* (see 20 May 61, 5 Feb. 87).
[10] Questions; supply; *H* 334. 1401.
[11] See 10 Dec. 88.

4. Th.

Wrote to Sir J.R. Gladstone—Mr Stephenson—Mr Hemingway[1]—Mr D. Nutt—Mr Theed—and minutes. Saw S.L.—Ld Rosebery—The Speaker—Mr Asquith—Mr Pease.[2] H. of C. $4\frac{1}{2}$–$7\frac{1}{2}$. Spoke on Navy Provision.[3] Dined with the 39 Club.[4] Worked on American paper. Read Major Fraser—For F. and F.—Memoirs of Capt. Rock.

5. Fr.

Wrote to J.S. Redmayne—W.H. Seymour—A. Gordon—Mahar Dhuleep Singh—and minutes. Worked on paper for America. Read Capt Rock's Memoirs—Major Fraser (finished)—For F. and F. H. of C. at 3.30.[5] King's Coll. 4–$6\frac{1}{2}$. $1\frac{1}{2}$ h. on the Momerie business.[6] Saw Dr Wace—Dean of Llandaff—Ld Chief Justice.

6. Sat.

Wrote to J.B.W. Riddell[7]—Mrs Fitzroy. Attended Bp of Ripon's Dante Lecture, & spoke briefly.[8] Saw Mr Westell—Ld Herschell—Mr Theed (worked from my head)[9]—Sir W. Harcourt *cum* A. Morley—Mr Robinson (Daily News)[10]—Mr & Mrs Paull. Dined at G. Russell's. Read An Author's Love[11]—Captain Rock finished. Saw E. Johnson.

7. 5 S. Lent.

Chapel Royal mg with H.C. and evg. Eight to dinner.[12] An innovation in our practice, caused by the duty of having Julia Neville: but I did not like the result of the experiment though I had useful conversations on Dr Momerie and (with C. Parker) on Sir R. Peel. Read Monier Williams on Buddhism[13]—An Author's

---

[1] F. Piercy Hemingway of Berlin; a supporter; Add MS 44506, f. 128.

[2] Probably Alfred Edward Pease, 1857–1939; liberal M.P. York 1885–92, 1897–1902.

[3] Opposing govt.'s means of financing its naval programme; *H* 334. 1622.

[4] i.e. the weekly Parliamentary dinner of the National Liberal Club; *D.N.*, 6 April 1889, 5c.

[5] Questions; vaccination: *H* 334. 1721.

[6] Momerie recorded: 'when I met him [Gladstone] shortly afterwards, he expressed the hope that some compromise might be arrived at between the Council and myself.... Nothing definite was decided at the first meeting; but the Bishop of London, as chairman, was requested to talk the matter over with me'; *Dr. Momerie: his life and work... by his wife* (1905), 160. Gladstone next day told Mrs. Fitzroy, Add MS 44506, f. 148 that 'it is plain to me under the circumstances that the evil may not be all on one side' and advised Momerie 'to take the advice of experienced and thoroughly dispassionate friends'.

[7] (Sir) John Walter Buchanan Riddell, 1849–1924; Eton and Christ Church, Oxford; barrister; 11th bart. 1892; had written successfully to ask for money for Pusey House Library in Oxford; Add MS 44506, f. 140, 182.

[8] At Grosvenor House; report in *D.N.*, 8 April 1889, 6d.

[9] Sculpture by W. Theed (see 2 Aug. 60); whereabouts unknown.

[10] Probably dictating his comments on Dante.

[11] *An author's love: the unpublished letters of P. Merimée's Inconnue*, by D.T.S. [*E. Balch*], 2v. (1889).

[12] Six guests was the usual number for dinner.

[13] M. Monier-Williams, *Buddhism in its connection with Brahmanism and Hinduism and in its contact with Christianity* (1889); sent at his request; Add MS 44506, f. 190.

Love—Life of Clowes[1]—Agnostic Faith[2]—Vinet on Pascal.[3] Wrote to Sir M. Williams—Author of Author's Love[4]—Williams & N.—T. Guttery.

8. M.

Wrote to Ld Queensberry—Mr W. Henderson—Mr Valieri & Mr Mellor—Mr Thorndike Rice. Dined at E. Hamilton's. Worked on paper for America. Saw S. Lyttelton—Mr Rigby—Mr Theed (working as before)—Sir E. Reed—Mr A. Morley—Mr Rathbone—Mr G. Lewis—Mr W.H. Smith (Momerie)—Lady Lister Kaye—Mr J. Talbot. H. of C. 4–7.[5] Read Merimée Letters &c. also M. Taine on M.[6]

9 Tu.

Wrote to Nath. McKay—Mr Thorndike Rice (packet)—Mrs Langdon Down—J. Knowles—Mrs Lawson—G.B. Smith—R.S. Hulbert—and minutes. Saw G.L. Gower (vice S.L.)—Ld Granville—Mr A. Morley—Mr Theed—Sir L. Playfair—Mr C. Bannerman MP. Finished revision & sent off my paper. Mr Lewis yesterday gave me some painful particulars about Mrs Th. in Money &c.[7] Dined with E. Hamilton. H. of C. 4–5 and $10\frac{1}{2}$–$12\frac{1}{4}$. Spoke on Scottish Home Rule.[8] Tea with Miss Tennant & Mrs M.

10. Wed.

Wrote to J. Beauchamp—Ed. Chatham Observer.[9] Saw Mr Sidgwick—Lady Ponsonby. Read Letters to Inconnue—Letter from do.—19th Cent. on I. Islands—do Gregory on O'Connell[10]—For F. and F. Long & interesting conversation with J. Morley. He is a prop. Dined with A. Lyttelton.

11. Th.

Wrote to Mr E. Morris—Author of Author's Love—Mr Thorndike Rice—Mrs Bolton—Mr A. Hutton—Mr A. Morley—Mr Sheridan Wood—and minutes. H of C. $3\frac{3}{4}$–$4\frac{3}{4}$ & $5\frac{1}{2}$–$7\frac{1}{4}$.[11] Wrote Supplement for paper on Amn Protection. Dined at Ld Sydney's. *Frvocloque* at Mrs Parker's. Saw G.L. Gower—Mr A. Theed—

---

[1] T. Compton, *The life and correspondence of the Rev. John Clowes* (1874).

[2] *Agnostic faith. Enlarged from a paper on 'Ethical Theism'* (1889).

[3] A. R. Vinet, *Studies on Pascal* (1859).

[4] [Elizabeth Balch], wrote as 'D.T.S.', author of the imaginary correspondence (see 6 Apr. 89), which she had probably sent anon. to Gladstone.

[5] Scottish local govt.; *H* 334. 1813.

[6] P. Merimée, *Lettres à une Inconnue, précedés par une étude sur Merimée par H. Taine*, 2v. (1874).

[7] Lewis not further identified.

[8] Cautious speech on Clark's Resolution for a Scottish 'National Parliament': 'I do not feel myself to be in a condition to deal with the question at the present moment definitely and on its merits', but if the Scots 'by a clearly preponderating voice' requested equal treatment with Ireland, he would not deny their title; Gladstone concluded with his usual cautions about abstract resolution; *H* 335. 99.

[9] *Chatham Observer*, 13 April 1889, 5c.

[10] *N.C.*, xxv. 558, 582 (April 1889).

[11] Questioned Smith on business of the House; *H* 335. 245.

A. Morley—Sir L. Playfair—Mr Childers. Read For F. and F.—19th Cent. on Monte Carlo: poor.[1]

12. Fr.

Chapel Royal at one. Wrote to J.J. Macbride Esq[2]—LNW Stationmaster—Mr Knowles—Mr Gilman—Mr Shirreff—and minutes. Dined at A. Morley's. H of C. $3\frac{1}{4}$–$7\frac{1}{2}$.[3] Saw G.L. Gower—Scotts—Mrs Th. (luncheon)—A. Morley. Read For F. and F.—and [blank.]

13. Sat. [Hawarden]

A busy morning putting up books & other preparations. Saw G.L. Gower. $11\frac{3}{4}$–5. To Hawarden. Read For F. and F. (finished)[4]—New Religio Medici[5]—Courtney's Mill[6]—Necklace of Liberty (U.S.)[7]—and Peveril of the Peak.[8] Wrote to Dr Robinson—A. Morley—& others.

14. Palm S.

Ch mg & evg. Wrote to W. Walker—J. Box—J. Leslie—J.H. Begg—Geo. Green—Mrs Bennett—Mr Casson.[9] Read Abbott on Romans[10]—Salmon on Infallibility[11]—Leonard Morris—School of the Eucharist—Bertrand's Treatise, with the (Protestant) Avertissement.[12]

15. M.

Ch. $8\frac{1}{2}$ A.M. Wrote to J. Morley—Mr Lyman Abbot[13]—S.N. Williams[14]—Mr Beecham. Read Salmon on Inf.—Peveril of the Peak—and [blank.] Saw Mr Hurlbutt. Went over the Railway line. Worked on my chaos; with little visible result.

16. Tu.

Ch. $8\frac{1}{2}$ A.M. Wrote to Lady Breadalbane—Sir C. Russell—Ten Invitations—Sec. Commn 1851—A.W. Brown—Mr Wardleworth—Mr Howell—A.J. Elliot—Mrs Th.—Mrs Morgan BP—Sig. Spadone—H. Haines & T. English—Mr Baillie.

[1] Article by H. Sidebotham, *N.S.*, xxv. 552 (April 1889).

[2] Of Washington, U.S.A.; sent a list of American Home Rulers; Hawn P.

[3] Ireland; supply; *H* 335. 344.

[4] See 21 Mar. 89.

[5] Frederick Robinson, physician, had sent his *The new Religio Medici. Chapters on present-day subjects* (1887).

[6] W. L. Courtney, *Life of J. S. Mill* (1889); written with Gladstone's assistance, see 5 Sept. 88.

[7] Untraced.

[8] By Scott (1822).

[9] Perhaps R. J. Casson of the *Dundee Courier*; in correspondence in 1887; Hawn P.

[10] L. Abbott, *The Epistle of Paul to the Romans* (1888).

[11] See 15 Nov. 88.

[12] Probably A. Bertrand, *La Psychologie de l'effort et les Doctrines contemporains* (1889).

[13] Lyman Abbott, 1835-1922; American congregational minister and author; friend of H. Ward Beecher; see previous day.

[14] Sympathetic letter to the leader of a deputation on the treatment of the Irish priest Fr. M'Fadden; *T.T.*, 19 April 1889, 7a.

Saw dear Willy.[1] He showed nothing but good symptoms. It was a good day. But at best it is piteous. Let us seek in prayer the restoration of his full vigour. Gerty has borne wonderfully. Drive with C.

Read Feydeau's Fanny, an evil but wholly unenticing book[2]—Peveril—Salmon on Infallibility. A little ordering work.

17. Wed.

Ch. 8½ A.M. Wrote to Mr & Mrs Slaughter—T.C. Robbins—Mr Morris—T. Wildridge—Mr A. Morley—Mrs Bolton—Messrs Brough—Mr L. Dillon—Mr Hugessen.[3] Worked on accounts. Read Salmon—Feydeau's Fanny (finished) *wretched*—Peveril—Byron's Heaven & earth.[4] Saw Mr Mayhew—Mr Powell MP.[5]

18. Th.

Ch. 8½ A.M. (& H.C.) 7 P.M. Wrote to Lord R. Gower—Rev. J.M. Jones—Mr H. Snowdon—G.F. Peabody—Khedive of Egypt—Mrs L. Murphy—J. Swan—J. Donaldson. Saw Willy: today I thought he shaped his words with a little effort. Wrote a beginning on Italy.[6] Read Salmon—Peveril—Byron's Heaven & Earth. A Titanic man.

19. Good Friday.

Church 10½ A.M. Three hours service 12¼–3. Sermon at [blank.] Wrote to M. Young—G. Hamilton—G.H. Gill—Mrs Stuart—J. Gemmall[7]—Rev. Pitchford—W.H. Brown—Rev. Page Hopps—G. Warmington—T.T. Wildridge—Mrs Bennett. Morning Service at 10.30. Then the Three Hours 12¼–3, a most valuable occasion. Sermon in evg. Read Salmon—Maguire's Proteus[8]—..... on Judaism —& other Tracts. Wrote on Italy.

20. Easter Eve.

Ch 8½ A.M. and [blank.] Wrote to Miss Townsend—Lady Mar—J. Franklin—Mr Bourne BP—Rev. Cooke—Press Assoc. Tel.—Mr Knowles Tel. Drive with C. Saw Willy decidedly somewhat advanced. A great concourse of people & obstreperous kindness. Worked on Italy. Read Salmon—Peveril.

21. Easter Sunday.

Holy Communion at 7 A.M. Service 11 A.M. 6½ P.M. Wrote to Rev. F. Cameron[9]— Sir A. West—Mr Westell—Mr J. Gill[10]—Mr J. Read. Theol. conversation with Mr

---

[1] See 2 Mar. 89.   [2] E. A. Feydeau, *Fanny* (1858).

[3] Congratulations on the liberal victory at Rochester; *T.T.*, 22 April 1889, 8b.

[4] Lord Byron, *Heaven and earth. A mystery* (1823).

[5] Walter Rice Howell Powell, 1819–June 1889; liberal M.P. Carmarthenshire from 1880.

[6] 'Italy in 1888–89', *N.C.*, xxv. 763 (May 1889); a largely enthusiastic review of Italy's progress since his visit to Naples in 1850–1.

[7] John Alexander Gemmill, Canadian author; Add MS 44506, f. 33.

[8] Possibly J. Maguire, *Alastor; an Irish story of today* (1888).

[9] Francis Marten Cameron; Christ Church, Oxford, rector of Bonnington from 1861.

[10] John Gill, liberal organiser in Sheffield; Hawn P.

Temple.[1] Walk with dear Stephy. Read Salmon—Ch. Quarterly on Coleridge, Gerson, & other articles.—Examining Thomas Aquinas & Trid. Can. & Cat. on the H. Eucharist.

22. E. Monday.

Ch (& H.C.) 8½ AM. Wrote to Mr W. Forbes—Mr Knowles—Mr Greenlees[2]—Mr Godley. Read Peveril—Salmon—Phallic Worship.[3] Worked much on Italy. Two exhibitions at the wall for large parties. Backgammon with the Rector.

23. Tu.

Ch. 8½ A.M. Wrote to Mrs Th.—Mr H. Gladstone—Rev. Richardson—Mr Knowles—G.W. Hambleton—Rev. Macguire Sloan. Worked hard: & sent off article on Italy. Walk & family conversation with Herbert. Dined with the Mayhews. We discussed mining matters & the subject of W.H.G.s will.[4] Read Salmon—Peveril.

24. Wed.

Ch. 8½ A.M. Wrote to Rev. Richardson—Canon Jones—A. Fergusson—A. Wilkinson—J. Beddols—G. Richardson—Rev. Penruddock[5]—Rev. Dr. Wace[6]—Rev. H.E. Thomas[7]—H. Llewellyn Davis—R. Nuttall—A.W. Hutton—Rev. J. MacDevett[8]—Lady Holker—Mr A. Morley. Read Kennedy's Report on Italian Finance[9]—Law &c. of Finland—Salmon—Peveril—Sardanapalus.[10] Walk with Herbert.

25. Th. St Mark.

Ch. 8½ A.M. Wrote to Lady Napier—Mr Knowles—Mrs Harrison—D. Evans—Mrs Pretiman—P.J. Cusack—Rev. C.J. Thompson—Mrs Glynn—Rev. Vaughan—J. Pickering—Mr Knowles—OConnell's daughter.[11] Walk with Herbert. Saw Mr Mayhew (on Estate). Read Salmon (finished)—Peveril. Corr. proofsheets on Italy: rewrote finance.

[1] Not further identified (not in H.V.B.).
[2] Gavin Greenlees; metal merchant in Glasgow; had sent his book on the Gifford lectures; see 28 Apr. 89 and Hawn P.
[3] *Phallic worship, a description of the mysteries of the sex worship of the ancients with the history of the masculine cross* (1886).
[4] A matter of general family concern, as Gertrude Glynne (now Pennant), da. of Henry Glynne, would share in the estate unless provision was made for a reversion to W. E. Gladstone; see Introduction above, section VII.
[5] Probably John Hungerford Penruddocke, vicar of South Newton, Salisbury.
[6] Henry Wace, 1836–1924; principal of King's College, London 1883–97; involved in the Momerie affair.
[7] Perhaps Henry Eaton Thomas, curate in Llangollen.
[8] See 28 Apr. 89.
[9] Report by Kennedy of the Rome embassy on Italian debts, incorporated at the last moment into Gladstone's article; *N.C.*, xxv. 777 (May 1889).
[10] [G. A'Beckett and M. Lemon], *Sardanapalus; or the 'Fast' King of Assyria* (1853).
[11] Elizabeth Mary Ffrench, née O'Connell; da. of 'the Liberator'; Add MS 44506, f. 93.

26. Fr.

Ch. 8½ AM. Wrote to Mr Wardrop—Mr Bowen—Mr Burdett—Mr Anderson—
Mrs Clarke—Messrs Brough—Jas Parker—Mr J. Grant. Saw Willy (advancing
well): Miss Davison: Miss Scott. Read Staniland Wake[1]—Peveril—and Q.R. on
Motley.[2] Backgammon with S.

27. Sat.

Ch. 8½ AM. Wrote to Mr Macbride U.S. BP.—R. Allerhead—E.J. Browne—S.H.
Stuckey—E.R. Russell—Mr E. Howell—Mr Rideing. Prosecuted & finished my
Motley paper. Canon MacColl came. Saw Sir A. Clark who paid Willy another
visit & reported hopefully but not of an *early* recovery. Read Q.R. on Goethe[3]—
Peveril—John Manners on Ireland.[4]

28. 1 S.E.

Ch. 8½ AM with H.C.—11 AM—6½ P.M. Wrote to Lord Acton. Conversation
with Canon M[acColl]. Read Harrison's Sermons[5]—Macdevett on H.S.[6]—Dore
on English Bibles[7]—Greenlees on Max Muller[8]—Slater Browne on Divorce.[9]
Worked a little at Salmon.[10]

29. M.

Ch. 8½ A.M. Wrote to H.C. Burdett[11]—A. Elliot—E. Capleton—A. Gardner—H.
Primrose—S. Chatwood—J. Marshall—Smith & Innes—J.K. Rowbotham—Canon
Slater Browne—Mr J.T. Dodd—Sir A. Robertson—Supt at Chester. 1½ h. with Mr
Mayhew: most satisfactory—Mr Shannon. Read Dale on Bright[12]—Sorbière on
England[13]—Playfair's Essays[14]—Peveril. Saw Willy: he was better than I have yet
seen him.

30. Tu.

Ch. 8½ A.M. Wrote to C. Spensley—R. Stone—Mr T. Groesart—Marquis
Dragonetti—Rev. Wiseman—Rev. J.W. Schofield—Rev. C. Bayley—Rev. W.T.

[1] C. Staniland Wake, *Serpent-Worship, and other essays* (1888).
[2] *Q.R.*, clxviii. 297 (April 1889).
[3] *Q.R.*, clxviii. 332 (April 1889).
[4] Lord J. Manners, *Notes of an Irish tour [in 1846]* (1849).
[5] Probably one of B. Harrison's many sermons.
[6] J. Macdevitt, *Introduction to the sacred scriptures* (1889).
[7] J. R. Dore, *Old Bibles, or an account of the various versions of the English Bible* (1876).
[8] G. Greenlees, *The Gifford Lectures and Max Müller; their religion considered in the light of philology and history* (1889).
[9] Edward Slater-Browne, canon of Salisbury, had sent an untraced work, probably a sermon.
[10] See 14 Apr. 89n.
[11] (Sir) Henry Charles Burdett, 1847-1920; physician, author and statistician; corresponded on Ireland; had sent his *Prince, Princess and People* (1889); Hawn P.
[12] R. W. Dale, 'Mr. Bright', *C.R.*, lv. 637 (May 1889).
[13] See 10 Sept. 44.
[14] L. Playfair, *Subjects of social welfare* (1889).

Taylor—Rev. J. Stark—Ed. Scott. Leader[1]—Mr A. Spurgeon—Mrs Morton. Bid goodbye at H[awarden] Hall.[2] He *looked* even brilliantly well. Read Roehn's MS.—do on Faust[3]—Gordon on Federation[4]—Peveril of the Peak. finished. Kibbled a thorn at Rectory. I bless God for the vacation. Tomorrow takes me back to slavery.

Wed. May 1. SS. Phil. & James. [*London*]

Ch. 8½ A.M. Wrote to H.C. Burdett—J. Hodson—J. Maddocks—J. Simkins—J. Alston—S. Brooks. Saw Bailey on the Octagon & on possible new Building. Off at 10.50. Drove from Euston to the New Gallery where M. & I had Mr Carr's[5] aid. Good. Then to the House. Saw A. Morley and friends. Read Maclaren's Memoirs I[6]—John Manners on Ireland.

2. Th.

Wrote to Spottiswoodes—Sig. Gallenga—I. Hoyle MP[7]—Sig. Fioretto[8]—J. Wilson. Saw A. Morley—G. Leveson—E. Hamilton—Sir W. Harcourt—Mr Childers. Visited Christie's. H. of C. 4¼-7½ on Budget.[9] Read A Daughter of Eve[10]—Maclaren's Memoirs II.

3. Fr.

Wrote to Mr O'Leary—Mr Murray—Ld Acton BP—Mr Figgis[11]—Ld Rosebery—Editor of Riforma—Mr Grogan—French Ambassador—D. San Denato, B. Nisco, Cav. Lacaita, Sig. Schilizzi, The Syndic, Count Codronchi, all BP.[12] Visited the Academy 10-12. Saw Mr Agnew, Ld Carlisle, Mr Leader and others. Shopping. Saw Mr A. Morley. Read A Daughter of Eve—and [blank.]

4.

Wrote to . . . . Saw A. Morley—Geo. Leveson—Ld Herschel—Ld Coleridge. 2-3¾. R. Academy, by appointment, with Mr Agnew. Breakfasted at Grillion's. Shopping. Drive with C. Read A Daughter of Eve.

---

[1] i.e. The *Scottish Leader*; not found published.
[2] Also known as the Red House, where Willy Gladstone and his family lived.
[3] Probably F. Roese, *Über die scenische Darstellung des Goethe'schen Faust* (1838); the reference to his MS is obscure.
[4] A. Gordon, *The future of the empire; or, a brief statement of the case against imperial federation* (1889).
[5] The New Gallery in 121 Regent Street; Carr not further identified.
[6] J. B. Mackie, *The life and works of Duncan McLaren*, 2v. (1888), much Gladstoniana.
[7] Isaac Hoyle, 1828-1911; Manchester merchant; liberal M.P. Heywood, Lancs. 1885-92.
[8] Professor G. Fioretto of Florence; sent a work on Dante; Hawn P.
[9] Spoke on succession duties; *H* 335. 1000.
[10] E. Kirk, *A daughter of Eve* (1889); a novel.
[11] Probably John Bradley Figgis, Huntingdon Connexion minister in Brighton and fa. of the historian and editor of Acton.
[12] Sending them copies of his article, on Italy (see 18 Apr. 89).

5. 2 S.E.

Chapel Royal at noon, with H.C.—Attended the service of 'Father Ignatius'[1] at
3½. Wrote to Messrs May—Dr Antenori BP. Read Life of Timothy Coop[2]—
Loughlin on St Patrick[3]—Sermons of Father Ignatius[4]—Report on Divorce in
U.S.[5]—and [blank.]

6. M.

Wrote to Mrs Bennett—Rev. Mr Evans—Mr Buchanan—D.J. O'Neill. H. of C.
3½–7¾. Spoke on the case of Harrison & others.[6] Saw Spencer Lyttelton *bis* on
the interesting question of the vacancy in Worcestershire.[7] Saw Mr A. Morley—
Mr Grogan—M. Drew (on 'Daughter of Eve')—Sir C. Russell—Sir W. Harcourt—
Mr Morley. Dined at Ld Northbourne's. Read Gordon's Hist.
Rebellion[8]—finished Daughter of Eve—Limits of Free Trade.[9]

Finis D.G.

[The back inside cover contains:]

⟨Oct 19. Speech at Nottingham:⟩   O G & Co   Saw Court
                                                         (67 *Cornhill.*

Daungellade compagnia & teaches Fr.It.
& Germ Chatillon Valdecosta Italia
⟨O.29. Mr Holl RA. / 36 Aldersgate St T. Henri⟩
Dr J. Chapman Avenue Kleber 46 Paris.
C. Neeve Dr M. Ferraris Via Milano 26 Rome
Ballantyne & Co Chandos St W.C.
Woodbine Cottage W. End Road, N.W. [Mrs. Thistlethwayte]
B 27 *Upper King St* Leicester. 1 Carlisle Pl. Victoria 12-
Commander Gye 4 Boulevard des It. Paris.[10]
Wands Glasgow
Mr Rideing.

Miss Salvater Inst de   Vol I

---

[1] i.e. J. L. Lyne; see 11 Dec. 68.
[2] W. T. Moore, *The life of Timothy Coop* (1889).
[3] Untraced.
[4] See 15 May 87.
[5] Probably C. D. Wright, *A report on marriage and divorce in the United States, 1867 to 1886* (1889).
[6] On action of the police at Falcarragh; *H* 335. 1286.
[7] Gladstone hoped but failed to persuade Spencer Lyttelton to stand in the E. Worcs. by-election; Add MS 44506, f. 228.
[8] J. B. Gordon, *History of the rebellion in Ireland . . . in 1798* (1801).
[9] *Limits of Free Trade, by a Liberal* (1889).
[10] Gye helped organise the Gladstones' Paris visit.

St Johns £5
Rigby   £1
         £1

                          Dr 1.13.9
                          1. 7.6
                          3. 1.3

Aug. £370

        275 copies M.2/ N 23/[1]

        [1] There is also some largely illegible pencil writing.

[The inside front cover contains]

Private.

No 39.

May 7. 1889–Feb. 28. 1891

16 James St S.W. May 7. 89.

Wrote to E.W. Hamilton—Edm. Sturge—W.P. Courtney²—J.F. Hogan—Jas Jackson—R. Morris—J. Mogford—W. Catchpool—P.J. Rumney—A. Dickson. Read Gordon Hist. Reb.—Parl. History 1800—and Lecky. Saw Mr Mayhew—Herbert J.G.—A. Morley—S. Lyttelton. Dined with Mr Lucy & the Punch camp.³

8. Wed.

Wrote to Mrs Swinny—W.H. Tilston—H. Riddell—J. Barratt—& minutes. Also drafted a letter for Alfred Lyttelton.⁴ Drive with Ca. Saw Mr & Mrs Oppenheim.⁵ Dined at Viscount Stern's. Read Gordon—Parl. Hist. 1790—and [blank.] Saw Scotts.

9. Th.

Wrote to Professor Ball⁶—J.B. George BP—Rev. Chisholm—Stuart Rendel—F. Tyndall—R. Buchanan—H. Wilson—Miss Parsons—J. Alston—W.S. Bartlett—R.A. Hardie—Mad. Meurikoffre B.P.—Rev. Griffiths—and minutes. Saw A. Morley—Lucy Cavendish—Herbert J.G.—Sir H. Davy—Mr Fowler. Drive with C.

---

¹ Lambeth MS 1453.

² William Prideaux Courtney, 1845–1913, ecclesiastical commissioner and author; had sent his *Parliamentary representation of Cornwall to 1832* (1889); Hawn P.

³ Present were H. W. Lucy, Burnand (the editor), Tenniel, Du Maurier, Linley Sambourne, Henry Furniss. Lucy's long description of the occasion includes: 'Another improvement he [Gladstone] noted in this connexion [i.e. over the past fifty years] is in respect of political cartoons. In his early days, when an artist was engaged to produce a caricature, he nearly always descended to gross personal caricature, sometimes to indecency. Today Mr. Gladstone observes in the humorous papers (he was speaking more particularly of *Punch*) a total absence of vulgarity, and a fairer treatment, which made this department of warfare always pleasing'; H. W. Lucy, *Sixty years in the wilderness* (1909), 300. A Furniss cartoon of Gladstone is reproduced in Vol. XIII.

⁴ Perhaps the E. Worcs. by-election; see 6 May 89.

⁵ See 5 June 88.

⁶ Sir Robert Stawell Ball, 1840–1913; professor in Dublin (1874–92), in Cambridge (from 1892); astronomer; had sent his *Story of the Heavens*, 2v. (1885–8); Add MS 44506, f. 222.

Read Gordon's History—Manning, Art. on Education[1]—Ball, Picture of the Heavens—Till Death us sever.[2]

10. Fr.

Wrote to Lady F. Cavendish—S. Lyttelton—Sir R. Ball—T. Sutcliffe—J. Canning —W.H.G.—W. Stapleford— & minutes. Saw Mr Schnadhorst—Mr Harrison—Mr A. Morley—Herbert J.G.—Lucy Cavendish—Cardinal Manning (on Edn and Donation scheme)—Mr Childers—Sir W. Harcourt—Mr Stansfeld. Read Gordon's Hist.—Till Death us Sever. Drive with C. H. of C. $2\frac{1}{2}$–$3\frac{3}{4}$.[3] Saw the new Irish scene[?]: much pleased.

11. Sat.

Wrote to T.N. Roberts—Watsons—Miss Latimer—Scotts—D.S. Cramby—C.J. Chase—J.C. Rodriguez—Jas Beddoes—W.A. Kelher—W.H.G.—J. Light (S.E.R.)— and minutes. Saw S. Lyttelton. Read Till Death &c.—Gordon's Hist. (finished). Visited American Exhibn:[4] 19th Cent. Art. Exhibition[5]—Concert at Grosvenor House.

12. 3 S.E.

Chapel Royal mg. All Saints Marg. St. aftn. Wrote to Sir B. Leighton—Mr Salkeld. Read Till Death &c.—Memoir of Theodore Talbot[6]—Science & Faith, A. Moore[7]—Life of [blank.] Saw The Sydneys—Sir A. Clark—Ld Spencer.

13. M.

Wrote to E. Hamilton—Mr Clancy MP—M. Drew—Rendel MP—S.E.G.—J. Beddoes (BP)—Ld Acton—J.A. Bruce—A. Morley—& minutes. Saw S.G.L.—A. Morley l.l.—Mr Stansfeld. Drive with C: & visit to Conduit St Exhibition.[8] Dined at Grillion's: a pleasant party. H. of C. $3\frac{1}{2}$–$5\frac{1}{2}$ again $7\frac{1}{2}$–$8\frac{1}{4}$.[9] Read Till Death &c— Sewards Collectanea [Hibernica][10]—The sad Indian case of Luckmen.[11]

14. Tu.

Wrote to Mr Stansfeld—Rev. Dr. Franklin[12]—Rev. D. Mitchell—M. Meletopoulos[13]—Rev. M. Roberts. Drive with C. H. of C. 3–5.[14] Worked on the Freeman

[1] H. E. Manning, 'The education commission and the school rate', *F.R.*, li. 732 (May 1889).
[2] J. L. Robson, *Till death us sever* (1888).   [3] Questions; estimates; *H* 335. 1699.
[4] Private view of exhibition of American decorative art and pictures at Johnstone and Norman in New Bond Street.
[5] At the Nineteenth Century Art Society in Conduit Street.
[6] Sir B. Leighton, *Recollections of Theodore Mansel Talbot* (1889).
[7] A. L. Moore, *Science and the faith* (1889).
[8] See 11 May 89n.   [9] Questioned Smith on sugar; *H* 335. 1855.
[10] See 27 Oct. 86.   [11] Untraced.
[12] Probably Edwin Lewis Franklin, Irish episcopalian scholar living in Southampton.
[13] C. Meletapoulas of Athens, vice president of the Anatolikes Omospondiae, had written with others of its officers about the plight of Orthodox Christians in Crete; Hawn P.
[14] Welsh disestablishment; *H* 336. 70.

business.[1] Saw Canon MacColl—A. Morley—J. Morley—Mr Clancy MP—Ld Granville. Six to dinner. Read Dodridge on Wales[2]—Till Death &c.—The Nun of Kenmare[3]—Timbs on Huxley (C.R.).[4]

15. *Wed.*

Wrote statement for press on the Freeman affair.[5] Also to Archbp Walsh—Mr Fergus—and minutes. Saw Mr Knowles—S.G.L. H. of C. 12½–2 and 4–5.[6] Dined with the Breadalbanes. Conversation with Mrs Singleton (+)—Ld R. Churchill, and John's friend. Read Till Death—Nun of Kenmare—Seward's Collectanea.

16. *Th.*

Wrote to Marchese Dragonetti BP—Mr E. Morris—Mr W.W. Law—and minutes. Visited Mr Field[7] for my ear with Sir A. Clark. Dined at Ld Burton's—*1 hour*: Busy at H. of C. 4–8¼ and 9¾–11½. Pensions & Finance.[8] Read Till Death us do sever. At Quaritch's. Looked into Rochester. Saw Mr Knowles—Mr A. Morley—S.G.L.

17. *Fr.*

Wrote to Mr Dunlop—Ld Revelstoke—Rev. D. Macleod—T. Russell—Rev. M.H. Peacock—T.E. May—and minutes. Finished Till Death &c. Read Collectanea Hibernica. A party of Nine to dinner, chiefly Dissentient: all kind & good.[9] H. of C. 2½–4½.[10]

18. *Sat.* [*Dollis Hill*]

Wrote to M.D. Anduaga—B. Dowden—J. Stuart—A.H. Beaven—C. Spensley—Mrs Drew—& minutes. Read West. Rev. on Shakespeare Bacon, & Home Politics.[11] 10–12½ Hawarden affairs &c. with Mr Mayhew, Mr Carrington, Mr Morris: & his partner Mr Jones. Saw also Mr S.G.L.—Mr Brodrick. Off to Dollis at four.

19. *4 S.E.*

Ch. mg (Willesden) and H.C.—cheated in afternoon. Read Nun of Kenmare—West Rev. on Rel. of the Future.[12] Conversation with Aberdeen.

---

[1] See next day.

[2] Sir J. Doddridge, *The history of the ancient and modern estate of the Principality of Wales, Cornwall and Chester* (1630).

[3] Sister Cusack, *The nun of Kenmare* (1889).

[4] T. V. Tymms in *C.R.*, lv. 692 (May 1889).

[5] On George Freeman, of Gorey, Wexford, and the murder of Kinsella; Add MS 44506, ff. 236–40; letter to unnamed correspondent in *T.T.*, 16 May 1889, 12d, reply from G. N. Curzon next day, *ibid.*, 8b.

[6] Spoke on Welsh Intermediate Education Bill; *H* 336. 134.

[7] George P. Field; leading London aurist; practised in Wimpole Street.

[8] Spoke on them; *H* 336. 289.   [9] Including Millais; Add MS 44506, f. 231.

[10] Questions; misc. business; *H* 336. 361.

[11] *W.R.*, cxxxi. 522 (May 1889).   [12] *W.R.*, cxxxi. 545 (May 1889).

20. M. [London]

Back at 11.30 to welcome dear Harry from Calcutta. Wrote to J.H. Hollowell[1]—Rev. Cheeseman[2]—Rev. Bradley—Rev. Canon M'Coll—Mrs Ellis—Mr Quaritch—O.P. Blair—T.N. Roberts—J. Williams—Mr Knowles—& minutes. Saw Mr Mayhew—do *cum* Mr Morris—Ld Spencer—Mr S.G.L.—Mr A. Morley—Mr Oppenheim. H. of C. 4–7.[3] Finished Collectanea III. Read Nun of Kenmare. Dined at Mr Oppenheim's. Gave 4/6 on my way home [R].

21. Tu.

Wrote to Mr A.G. Symonds—Mrs Ryley—Mrs Cribbes—and minutes. Dined with the Miss Knowles.[4] Lady Spencer's duty party afterwards. H. of C. 2–3.[5] Read Nun of Kenmare—Westgarth on Australia.[6]

22. Wed.

Wrote to A. Morley—Mr Rummals—J. Nutt—S.N. Williams—Ld Hampden—Ld Blachford—Bp of Meath. Saw Canon MacColl—Mr Morris *cum* Mr Mayhew—Mr A. Morley cum Mr Schnadhorst—Sir J. Fowler—Countess of Aberdeen—Sir W. Phillimore (Bp of L.)—Ld Aberdare—Mr Parnell—Sir E. Watkin. H. of C. at 1 and $4\frac{1}{2}$–$5\frac{1}{4}$.[7] Saw Mr Ritchie. Gave evidence against the LNWR Bill.[8] Saw Sir E. Watkin. Dined at Sir W.P.s. The Federation meeting after.[9]

23. Th.

Wrote to Mr Carnegie—A. Marcus—Ld Aberdare—Mr Sutherland. Wrote a little on Ireland.[10] H. of C. 4–$7\frac{1}{2}$.[11] Dined with Lucy Cavendish. Saw Sir C. Russell *cum* Mr Parnell—Ld Ribblesdale—Mr G. Lewis—Ld Granville—S.G.L.—Sir H. Robinson—Ld Lothian—Adm. Egerton. Attended the P[arnell] Commission Court $10\frac{3}{4}$–$12\frac{1}{2}$.[12]

24. Fr.

Wrote to Mr Luttrall—Mr S. Walpole jun.[13]—J. Murtagh [*sic*]—Mr C.H. Wilson MP[14]—Dr Hulton—Mr F. Turner—L. Dashwood—H.N.G.—and minutes. Dined

---

[1] James Hirst Hollowell, congregationalist minister and occasional correspondent; see Add MS 44461, f. 121.

[2] Henry Jordan Cheeseman, clergyman in Leeds. [3] Naval Defence Bill; *H* 336. 535.

[4] Lived by Regent's Park. [5] Questions; national debt; *H* 336. 651.

[6] W. Westgarth, *Half a century of Australian progress. A personal retrospect* (1889).

[7] Coal Duties Bill; *H* 336. 701.

[8] Opposing proposal to vest a portion of the Wirral Railway in the L.N.W.R.; *T.T.*, 23 May 1889, 10d.

[9] Women's Liberal Federation; Parnell, Gladstone and Mrs. Gladstone were the main speakers; *T.T.*, 23 May 1889, 10c.

[10] Start of 'Plain speaking on the Irish Union', *N.C.*, xxvi. 1 (July 1889), reprinted in *Special aspects*, 303; Add MS 44702, f. 66.

[11] Scottish local govt.; *H* 336. 836.

[12] Cross-examination of William O'Brien on role of *United Ireland*; *T.T.*, 24 May 1889, 3a.

[13] On use of Gladstone's letters for his *Life of Lord John Russell*; Add MS 44506, f. 147.

[14] Charles Henry Wilson, 1833–1907; Hull shipping owner; liberal M.P. Hull 1874–1905.

at Mr Lefevre's. Read Westgarth—Dunlop's Grattan.[1] H. of C. 3–4½.[2] Saw Inspectors of Police (on last night's accident)[3]—S.G.L.—Mr Knowles—F. Leveson—A. Morley. Saw M'Lachlan, suffering greatly [R].

25. Sat.

Wrote to Mrs Vyner—Mr Bullen—Rev. J. Hammond[4]—Mr Potter MP—Mr M. Dight[5]—Press Association. Drive with C. Saw Lucy Cavendish—E. Hamilton— L. Harcourt—F. Lawley—A. Morley. Visited Christie's—Agnew's—Miniature Exhibition. Dined at Lambeth. Conversation with Bp of L[ondon], Mrs Lathbury, & the Abp to whom I submitted the Bond plan.[6] Chapel at 7.30.

26. 5 S.E.

Ch mg & evg. Saw French Ambassador—Col. E. Smith. Conversation on Woman's rights. Read Ma Vocation[7]—Lindsay's Art.[8]—& Clewes Biography.[9]

27. M.

Back to J[ames's] St 11¾ AM. Wrote to Sir Thos Acland—Herr F. Kolb—Ld Coleridge—The G. Bruno Committee[10]—Mr Dight—and minutes. Saw S.G.L.— A. Morley—Mr Healy MP. H. of C. 4½–7¾. Spoke.[11] Dined at Sir C. Forster's. Read Cooke on The Union (at B. Museum).[12] Finished Dunlop's Grattan.

28. Tu.

Wrote to Mr W.T. Stead—Lady Aberdeen—J.S. Lupton—Ed. N.A. Review— H. Clews—J. Napier (U.S.)—C. May & Co[13]—Mr Westgarth[14]—& minutes. Dined at Sir C. Russell's.[15] Saw divers on business.—S.G.L.—Mr F.L. Gower—Miss Wyse—Lady A. Blunt—Mr Bryce—Mr F. Harrison. H. of C. 2½–7. Spoke on the

---

[1] R. Dunlop, *Life of Henry Grattan* (1889).

[2] Scottish local govt.; *H* 336. 956.

[3] On his way home the previous evening, Gladstone was knocked down by a cab which did not stop; though shaken, he chased it, apprehended the driver and waited with him until the police arrived, but without revealing his identity; *D.N.*, 25 May 1889, 4f, 5c.

[4] Joseph Hammond, vicar of St. Austell (appt. 1881 by Gladstone), assisted in the arrangements for the West country tour (see 8 June 89 ff.); Hawn P.

[5] M. L. Dight of Birmingham, sent gold spectacles; Hawn P.

[6] A means of financing St. Deiniol's Library?

[7] Possibly C. V. Varin, *Theophile, ou, Ma Vocation* (1834).

[8] Untraced.

[9] Henry Clews, a New York broker, had sent his *Twenty-eight years in Wall Street* (1888).

[10] One of the various cttees. celebrating the anniversary of Giordano Bruno (see B.L. Catalogue, xlv. 283).

[11] On Irish evictions; *H* 336. 1164.

[12] See 8 June 86.

[13] Gold and silversmiths.

[14] William Westgarth, 1815–89; of Leith; settled in Australia; politician, financier, free-trader; returned to U.K.; see 21 May 89.

[15] To meet Parnell; *T.T.*, 29 May 1889, 11e.

Lytton bêtise and on America.[1] Read Clews Hist. of Wall Street—Westgarth's Australia.

29. Wed.

Wrote to Mr A. Crump—Sir W. Harcourt—T.T. Kelly—and minutes. Attended the Dufferin celebration in the City:[2] then presided at a meeting of London Library.[3] Dined with the Hayters. Wrote a little on Ireland. Saw Agnes, here for medical purposes—Inspector of Police—Ld Rosebery—Lady Hayter—Sir E. Vincent. Read F. Lawley's Pamphlet[4]—Clews on Wall Street.

30. Th. Asc. Day.

Chapel Royal at 11: and H.C. Wrote to Mr Clews (New York)—Rev. W. Barker—Ld Acton—Mr Schnadhorst—A.T. Robbins—G. Harding. Luncheon at Mrs Tennant's to meet Coquelin.[5] H. of C. $3\frac{1}{2}$-$5\frac{1}{4}$ & 11-$12\frac{1}{4}$. Spoke on *Scotch* nationality.[6] Saw Agnes's Swede Doctor—E. Hamilton—Sir G. Trevelyan—Ly Compton—Ld Tweedmouth—Madam L. Rothschild—& the Belgian Minister. Read Clews.

31. Fr.

Wrote to Capt. Piry—Rev. Mr Evans—Rev. E.J. Philips—W.E. Heathfield—Sir J. Barrow—Rev. Mr Hannah—Mr A. Grove—Rev. Mr Dakin—and minutes. Saw French: doing well [R]. Saw Sir R. Welby—S.G.L.—E. Wickham respecting Agnes—A. Morley. Six to dinner. Sat to photographer. Wrote on Ireland. H. of C. $2\frac{1}{2}$-4.[7] Read *Romance of two worlds*.[8]

Sat June One. 89 [Combe Wood, Kingston]

Wrote much on Ireland: in letters, a blank. An 'intellectual' luncheon with Canon McColl.[9] Conversation with him—with Miss Schuster—Miss Schreiner. Saw John my nephew—A. Morley—S.G.L. Off at 4.15 to Combe Wood[10] with Harry: we conversed all the way on Hawarden affairs, on his, & on mine.

---

[1] On Lytton's absence from French revolutionary centenary celebrations, and on Disraeli's participation in the American centenary; *H* 336. 1288.

[2] Gladstone was 'warmly received' on arrival; *T.T.*, 30 May 1889, 10a.

[3] Taking the chair for Tennyson, who was ill, at its Annual General meeting.

[4] F. C. Lawley, *The bench and the jockey club* (1889).

[5] Constant-Benoît Coquelin, 1841-1909; French actor, at Comédie-Française until 1886, after which he toured.

[6] 'The Scotch are a dangerous people, and that majority so dolefully recited will be greatly aggravated unless the Scotch people are treated with prudence and consideration'; *H* 336. 1510.

[7] Questions; Scottish local govt.; *H* 336. 1570.

[8] Marie Corelli (i.e. Mary Mackay), *A romance of two worlds* (1886).

[9] MacColl arranged the lunch for Gladstone to meet Olive Emilie Albertina Schreiner, 1855-1920, whose *Story of an African Farm* he admired (see 17, 26 Apr. 85); she told Havelock Ellis: 'The lunch yesterday was lovely. I was quite unprepared to find Gladstone such a wonderful *child* of genius—nothing else. He's all genius'; she later remarked that he treated her 'as though I were his intellectual equal'; S. C. Cronwright-Schreiner, *The life of Olive Schreiner* (1924), 192-3.

[10] Wolverton's house in Kingston.

Found Lady W[olverton] very well. Read Bradley's Stanley[1]—Romance of two Worlds.

2. S. aft Asc.

Kingston Ch mg—Coombe evg. Read Romance &c: & Mackay.[2] Wrote to C.G.—Mr Drew. Conversation with Mr Harvey—A. Morley.

3. M. [London]

Wrote to M. Frère Orban—Canon MacColl—Miss Wyse—Mr Lockhart—Mr Walpole. Home at 11¾. Worked on Bimetallism[3]—and on papers. Finished Romance of two Worlds.[4] Read Contemp. on Johnson as Radical.[5] Dined with Mr Knowles: much conversation. Saw Shirley [R].

4. Tu.

Wrote to Grogan & Boyd—W.H.G.—Lady Maxwell[6]—Mr Grant—J.H. Adams Tel—and minutes. Saw S.G.L.—Mr Fowler—A. Morley—Mr Mather MP.—Jacob Bright—Sir L. Playfair—Ly Phillimore. An hour with Miss Corelli.[7] Dined with A. Morley. H. of C. 9¾-12¼ on Bimet[allis]m.[8] Read Contemp R. on Genesis—on Boulanger[9]—Parl. Hist Cornwall—Hist. Launceston. Worked on papers.

5. Wed. [Malwood, Lyndhurst]

Wrote to Mr. de Fontaine[10]—J. Morley—and minutes. Saw Scotts—S.G.L. Off at 12.30 to Sir W. Harcourt's at Malwood: a marvellous creation.[11] Carriage procession, meeting, & speech, at Southampton on the way.[12] Dinner party. Conversation with Mr Compton MP[13] and the Verderer. Read Life of Shelley[14] and . . . . .

6. Th.

Many hours of driving & walking in the New Forest: a tract without a rival in this country. A second Dinner party. Read Walpole's History[15]—Harcourt Papers Vol IX.[16]

---

[1] See 4 Mar. 83.   [2] Perhaps a reference to Corelli's real name.
[3] Notes in Add MS 44677, f. 53, 44773, f. 101.
[4] He this day called on Marie Corelli, calling again next day; Add MS 44507, f. 3.
[5] C.R., lv. 888 (June 1889).   [6] Probably Mary, wife of Sir H. E. Maxwell, 7th bart.
[7] Mary Mackay, 1855-1924, wrote novels as Marie Corelli; the story in her family was that Gladstone called eager to discuss her Ardath (1889), but it was in fact A romance of two worlds (just read, see 31 May 89); for the encounter, see B. Vyner, Memoirs of Marie Corelli (1930), 105-6 and Add MS 44507, ff. 3-7; she subsequently tried, unsuccessfully, to persuade Gladstone to review the 'Romance' and 'Ardath'. See 6, 10 Aug. 89.
[8] Chaplin's Resolution; but did not speak; H 336. 1869.
[9] C.R., lv. 900, 910 (June 1889).
[10] Perhaps Felix Gregory de Fontaine, American author; wrote on 'rapid writing'.
[11] Harcourt's house in the New Forest; for this visit, see Gardiner, ii. 134.
[12] T.T., 6 June 1889, 12a.
[13] Francis Compton, 1824-1915; tory M.P. S. Hampshire 1880-5, New Forest 1885-92.
[14] Perhaps W. Sharp, Life of P. B. Shelley (1887).   [15] See 7 Oct. 86.   [16] See 3 Sept. 81.

7. Fr.

Drove to Broadlands[1] for luncheon: most kindly received by E. Ashley. Then to
Romsey for Address and Speech.[2] Read Harcourt papers—finishing Vol IX.

8. Sat. [The 'Garland' at Dartmouth]

We started from this noteworthy & hospitable house at 11 to Brockenhurst and
Weymouth. Procession, address, and speech.[3] Then on to Portland. Amidst
much enthusiasm we embarked on the Garland & set off for Dartmouth arriving 8.30.[4] Read 'Steadfast'[5] & W.G. Ward.[6]

9. Whits.

St Saviour's 11 AM (with HC) and 6½ P.M. Luncheon at Mr Seale Hayne's 13th
Cent. Castle.[7] Read W.G. Ward. Wrote to English [sic].

10. M.

Rail to Torquay: long carriage processions, and speech over an hour to several
thousands, 12–8 PM.[8] Conversation with Lady Rothschild. Read Oxford & W.G.
Ward—Life of Shelley. Mapped out the work with A. Morley. Read 'Steadfast'—
Oxford & W.G. Ward—Pamphlet on Life Leases.

11. Tu. [The 'Garland' at Falmouth]

Processions & speeches at Falmouth & Redruth. I was extremely interested in
the population, truly British, & with so much beauty. At Redruth 15–20000
people.[9] Saw Mr Conybeare.[10] Finished Shelley—read Mines Pamphlet and
'Steadfast'.

12. Wed. [Lanhydrock House, Bodmin]

Start at 10.30. Arr. Llanhydrick[11] at 5.30. Speeches at Truro, St Austell, Bodmin.
F. Leveson joined us. Processions and enthusiasm as usual, everything at the
highest. I was *delighted* with Truro Cathedral. The clergy were most kind &
attentive. Read Standfast—W.G. Ward. Nothing could be kinder than our
reception by Ld & Lady R[obartes].

[1] Once the Palmerstons' house (see 22 July 68), now that of Evelyn Ashley (see 9 Mar. 58n.).
[2] *T.T.*, 8 June 1889, 10a.   [3] *T.T.*, 10 June 1889, 8a.
[4] The 'Garland' was the yacht of Mrs. Eliot C. Annie Yorke (da. of Sir A. de Rothschild and
widow of E. C. Yorke, s. of Lord Hardwicke) and was anchored in the harbour at Dartmouth.
[5] R. T. Cook, *Steadfast* (1889).
[6] W. P. Ward, *William George Ward and the Oxford Movement* (1889).
[7] Kingwear Castle, Dartmouth; seat of Charles Seale-Hayne, 1883–1903; liberal M.P. mid-Devon
from 1885.
[8] *T.T.*, 11 June 1889, 9a.   [9] *T.T.*, 12 June 1889, 10a.
[10] Charles Augustus Vansittart Conybeare, 1853–1919; barrister and liberal M.P. Camborne
1885–95; imprisoned under Corrupt Practices Act for 3 months 1889.
[11] Lanhydrock House, seat of Lord Robartes (see 24 Nov. 73) who had been at Christ Church and
was later a barrister and liberal M.P.; he m. Mary Dickinson 1878. The day's speeches are in *T.T.*, 13
June 1889, 7a.

13. Th. [Tintagel]

Saw the Church & place: then drove to Tintagel[1] or Trevines. Visited the Castle Rocks, then Boscastle: & spoke in answer to Address. Conversation with Rev. Mr. [blank]. Excellent hospitality from Lady Hayter. Looked up Memoranda for Plymouth tomorrow. Read W.G. Ward—Steadfast.

14. Fr. [On board the 'Garland']

Off at 11 to Launceston. Luncheon at the Mayor's, extremely well done. Met here my dear old friend Acland: so faithful! Off to Plymouth by rail. The enthusiasm there beyond all bounds. Dined at Hotel. Public meeting at 8. Spoke an hour & a little more.[2] Audience 7000. Fireworks afterwards: & returned on board the Garland. Night passage. Read Steadfast.

15. Sat. [Iwerne Minster]

Steamed all night. Outside Poole bar 11 A.M. Sympathy with a stranded brig. Conversation with the excellent Wesleyan Captain. Goodbye to kind Mrs Yorke. Landed at Poole at 4. Processions, great crowds, four speeches fired at me, spoke on Addresses at Poole, Wimborne, Hanford.[3] Driven by Mr Fuller four in hand to Ewerne:[4] large pleasant party. The enthusiasm was very great. Read Steadfast—W.G. Ward—De Vesigny, La Femme aux Etats Unis.[5] Conversation with Mrs St André, and others.

16. Trin. S.

Ch 11 AM & 6 PM. Read W.G. Ward—Barrington, Spiritual Life.[6] Conversation [with] Ly Camoys respecting Braborne. Wrote to Ld Tennyson.

17. M. [London]

Off at 10. H. of C. at 3. Four in hand drive to Gillingham. The people most enthusiastic. Speeches at Shaftesbury Gillingham & briefly at Salisbury: making 18 sp. in all.[7] H. of C. 3–5.[8] Drive in evg. Read W.G. Ward—(finished)—and Steadfast.

18. Tu.

Voice nearly gone. Wrote to Mr Macmillan—Messrs Trübner—Mrs Sykes—Sir John Phear[9]—and minutes. Drive with C. Saw Mr Lockhart (painter)[10]—Mr A.

[1] Seat of Sir A. V. Hayter (see 27 June 67) and his wife Henrietta, niece of Gladstone's old friend A. J. Beresford-Hope. As he drove through Wadebridge a pin-shot cartridge was thrown at him, but did not explode (Thomas, *Gladstone of Hawarden*, 140).

[2] *T.T.*, 15 June 1889, 9b.   [3] *T.T.*, 17 June 1889, 10c.
[4] Lord Wolverton's; see 22 Aug. 82.   [5] Untraced.
[6] J. S., Lord Barrington, *An essay on the teaching and witness of the holy spirit* (1785).
[7] *T.T.*, 18 June 1889, 12c.
[8] Questioned Smith on business of the House; *H* 337. 17, 18.
[9] Sir John Budd Phear, 1825–1905; judge in India; kt. 1877; contested West Country seats as a liberal 1885–93.
[10] Sittings for his portrait of the Jubilee service of 1887; see 15 July 87, 20 June 89 and Add MS 44507, f. 8.

Morley—S.G.L.—Mr Morley. Dined with Mr & Mrs Carnegie. A large American party: pleasant, effusive, courteous: manners generally different from ours. Worked on Irish Article.[1] Finished 'Steadfast'. Read Breitmann Ballads.[2] Began Giraldi.[3]

19. Wed.

From the state of my voice kept my bed till 11.30. Wrote to Mr Grenfell—J. Nicholson—Mr Lynam—Mr A. Morley—and minutes. Saw S.G.L.—A. Morley—E. Hamilton (long conversation on P. of Wales's family affairs)[4]—Ld Derby—Ly Brougham—M. Jusserand[5]—Ld Derby. Drive with C. Dined at French Embassy. Read Giraldi—A. Carnegie on Money.[6] Worked on Irish MS.

20. Th.

Wrote to Duke of Westmr—Mr H. Hoare—Rev. Dr Hutton—A. Morley—& minutes. Saw Mr Lockhart (sketch)—Mr Lloyd Bryce (N.A. Review)[7]—Mr Knowles—Mr A. Morley—Sir Drummond Wolff (Shah)—S.G.L.—H.J.G. Worked on Irish MS. Drive with C. Read Giraldi—Great Men at Play.[8]

21. Fr.

Wrote to Rev. N. Hall—Mrs Little—Ld Rosebery—Lady Marr—Rev. Costelloe—Lloyd Bryce—Mr Knowles—and minutes. Finished and revised MS on Irish Union.[9] Dined at Mr Bryce's. Read Geraldi—N.A.R. on U.S. Shipping—on Orthodoxy (Savage)[10]—and worked in Library on Grattan, Cornwallis &c. H. of C. $4\frac{1}{2}$-$5\frac{1}{2}$ and $10\frac{3}{4}$-$1\frac{3}{4}$.[11]

22. Sat. [Dollis Hill]

Wrote to Ed. D. News[12]—Ld E. Fitzmaurice—Mr M'Coll—Mrs Bolton l. & PP.—H.J.G.—Vicar of Truro—Mr Cowan[13]—Mr S. Edgecumbe—W. Findlay—Mr

[1] See 23 May 89.

[2] H. Breitmann, *Hans Breitmann's Party, with other ballads* (1868).

[3] R. G. Dering, *Giraldi; or, the curse of love*, 2v. (1889).

[4] Hamilton saw him at Knollys' request; Gladstone thought 'the Government grossly to blame for not having taken the matter (grants for Wales and his children) boldly in hand.... He thought that the Queen was behaving very badly towards the Prince of Wales ... she ought to have made over to him some £30,000 or £40,000 a year'; E.H.D., 20 June 1889. See 4 July 89.

[5] Jean Adrien Antoine Jules Jusserand, 1855–1932; historian and critic; French embassy councillor in London 1887–90.

[6] A. Carnegie, 'Wealth', *N.A.R.*, cxlviii. 653 (June 1889), sent in proof by Mrs. Carnegie (*Carnegie*, i. 339). See 25 Dec. 89n.

[7] Requesting permission to republish Carnegie's article in the U.K.; it appeared in *P.M.G.* as 'The gospel of Wealth', later as a pamphlet. Lloyd Stephens Bryce, 1851–1917; Christ Church, Oxford; American lawyer, politician and author; Thorndike Rice's will left him *N.A.R.*, which he ed. from Sept. 1889.

[8] J. F. T. Dyer, *Great men at play*, 2v. (1889); nothing on Gladstone. [9] See 23 May 89.

[10] N. Dingley and M. J. Savage, *N.A.R.*, cxlviii. 687, 711 (June 1889).

[11] Spoke on Irish evictions; *H* 337. 502.

[12] Forwarding for publication this day's letter to Fitzmaurice on Shelburne and 1800; *D.N.*, 24 June 1889, 5d. [13] Letter on state of politics; *T.T.*, 27 June 1889, 10e.

Stansfeld—W. Taylor—Messrs Baynes—W. Brown—Mr Thiselton Dyer[1]—J.B. Bryce—Mr Aubrey—Col. Healy—Mrs Th. BP.—Lady Holker B.P.—and minutes. Saw S.G.L.—W.H.G.—Lady Rothschild—Bp of Derry—Lady Playfair. Dined at Mrs Rathbone's. Off to Dollis at 10.30 PM. Read Giraldi—and [blank.]

23. 1 S. Trin.

Willesden Ch mg & evg. Mr Outram[2] excellent. Read Bryan Maurice[3]—Fuller's True anglicanism.[4] Saw Sir A. Clark. A cloud hangs over our dear Son: may God be pleased to disperse it.

24. M. [London]

Wrote to Sir D. Wolff—Ld E. Fitzmaurice—Sir E. Reid MP—Canon MacColl—W. Ridler—Mr Dwyer Gray—S. Hallifax—S.S. Martin—and minutes. Back to J[ames] St at 11¼. Saw Mr Godkin—Sir E. Reid—Sir J. Lacaita *cum* Count Vitelleschi—S.G.L.—Dr. Cameron—Mr Stansfeld cum Mr Morley—Mr Morley—Mr O'Morgan—Mr Böhme. Dined at Grillion's. Mrs Peel's for tea. Read Giraldi—Celtic Ireland.[5] Corrected Proofs of MS on the Union policy.

25. Tu.

Wrote to Mr Knowles—Mr Gray—Canon M'Coll—J. Smith—Mrs Bolton—W. Ridler—W. Browne—M. Kelly B.P. Sat to Millais 11 A.M.[6] Saw S.G.L.—A. Morley—J. Morley (so helpful). H. of C. 4¾-6¼.[7] Dined at Lincoln's Inn. A most kind reception.[8] Saw Payne—Phillips [R]. Read Celtic Ireland—Wordsworth's Emendations.[9]

26. Wed.

Wrote to A. Morley—Ld Northbourne—E. Hamilton sen. l. and BP—S. Smith & Co.—Jas Bohme—Mr A. Robertson—Mr Farquhar—and minutes. Went with Mr J[acob] Bright to examine the remarkable but ill named Linotype invention.[10] Saw S.G.L.—Mr Murray—Mr Macmillan—Ld Derby—Mr Quaritch—Ld Rosebery—Sir H. James—D of Argyll—French Ambassador—W.H.G.—and N. Dined with Sir H. James. Drive with C. Began Alan Thorne.[11]

---

[1] Thomas Firminger Thiselton-Dyer, folk-lorist and writer; had probably sent his book (see 20 June 89n.).

[2] Edmund Healy Outram, 1861-1929; curate of Willesden 1888-91.

[3] W. Mitchell, *Bryan Maurice. A novel* (1888).

[4] N. J. Fuller, *Pan-Anglicanism: what is it?* (1889).

[5] S. Bryant, *Celtic Ireland* (1889).

[6] Millais' third portrait of Gladstone (this time with his grandson, William Glynne Charles Gladstone, in a 'little Lord Fauntleroy' costume); the picture, a golden wedding gift from the women of England, Scotland, Wales and Ireland, is in Hawarden Castle and is reproduced in this volume.

[7] Misc. business; *H* 337. 714.

[8] His own Inn; no report found.

[9] Christopher Wordsworth, *Conjectural emendations of passages in ancient authors* (1883).

[10] Demonstration of the new American printing system using type matrices instead of type; an exhibition in London in July attracted much attention.

[11] M. L. Moodey, *Alan Thorne, a novel* (1889).

27. Th.

Wrote to Mrs Bolton—Miss Bryant—and minutes. Saw E.W. Hamilton—A. Morley—S.G.L. Drive with Agnes. Dined at Mr Fry's. Began Zola's Nana. A dreadful & revolting delineation.[1] Read Alan Thorne—The Fatal Phryne.[2] Called on Lady H. *out*.

28. Fr.

My sister Helen's birthday. How much *I* ought to feel for her. *Requiescat*.
   Wrote to the Prince of Wales—Mr J. Grant—T. Ashdowne—J. Ogilvy—F.J. Hughes—J. Clarke—A.S. Forbes—W.W. Law—and minutes. Read Macbeth—Nana. Sat to Millais at 2. H. of C. $3\frac{1}{4}$–5.[3] 5–$7\frac{1}{2}$. By river to Twickenham. Dined with Mr Labouchere. Conversation with Mrs L.,[4] Mrs Manwell (Miss Braddon),[5] Sir D. Wolff, Herbert G., Mr Lincoln, Mr Labouchere. Saw S.G.L.—H.N.G.—Mr Balfour *cum* Mr Bryce.

29. Sat. [Pembroke Lodge]

Wrote to Mr Morley—Mr Richardson—Mr Smith—Wrote Mem. on Royal Provision.[6] At noon waited on the Prince of Wales.[7] Saw Lady Holker—Mr Clinton. At $6\frac{1}{2}$ drove to Pembroke Lodge:[8] to stay till Monday. Read Nana—Balzac Seraphita[9]—19th Cent Dr Kidd on Ld B.[10] and [blank.]

30. 2 S. Trin.

Petersham Ch. mg & Combe evg. Saw Mr Wicksted—Mr Hamilton. Wrote to Mr Stead. Read Seraphita—Emans[?] on Swedenborg[11]—Walter Smith's [blank.]

Mond. Jul One. 89. [London]

Left our kind hostess $10\frac{1}{4}$ AM. Sat shortly to Millais with Will.[12] Called on Sir C. Dilke but he had not come.[13] Saw S.G.L.—Mr A. Morley—Mr W.H. Smith—Mr B. Currie. *Wrote to* Abp of Canterbury—C.S. Jackson—E. Evans—Mowbray Morris[14]—C.K. Cooke—and minutes. Read K. Blind on G. Bruno[15]—Nana—Ld Granville. H. of C. 4–7 and 10–$11\frac{1}{4}$.[16]

---

[1] E. Zola, *Nana* (1880).   [2] F. C. Philips and C. J. Wills, *Fatal Phryne*, 2v. (1889).
[3] Scottish universities; *H* 337. 1024.
[4] Henrietta Labouchere, *née* Hodgson, formerly an actress.
[5] Unidentified.
[6] Untraced.   [7] See 19 June, 4 July 89.
[8] Lady Russell's house at Richmond.
[9] H. de Balzac, *Séraphita*, tr. K. P. Wormeley (1885).
[10] J. Kidd, 'The last illness of Lord Beaconsfield', *N.C.*, xxvi. 65 (July 1889).
[11] Author's name scrawled; work untraced.
[12] i.e. his grandson; see 25 June 89.
[13] Meeting arranged by James to discuss Dilke's candidacy for Forest of Dean; see R. Jenkins, *Sir Charles Dilke* (1958), 377 and 10 Aug. 89.
[14] Presumably a relative of *The Times*' manager; see 24 Feb. 60.
[15] In *N.C.*, xxvi. 106 (July 1889).
[16] Arrest of O'Brien; *H* 337. 1169.

2. Tu.

Wrote to P.W. Campbell–Dr Döllinger BP–E.K. Connell–Mary Drew BP–
S.N. Williams–and minutes. Read Comte de Chambrun[1]–Nana: (enough of
such a congeries)–Kingsford's Illumination[2]–and Lyttle's Tale of 98.[3] H. of C.
4–7.[4] Saw S.G.L.–A. Morley–Mr Knowles–and others.

3. Wed.

Wrote to Scotts–W.H.G.–Mr Dight–H.N.G.–Mr W.H. Smith (and draft).
Conclave on Royal Provision 12¼–1¼. H. of C. 2½, and 4–5½.[5] Saw W.H.G.–
H.N.G.–H.J.G.–Mr W.H. Smith–Sir J. Gladstone. Dined with Ld Hamilton.
Saw Lu. French [R?]. Read Tale of 98–Celtic Ireland.

4. Th.

Wrote to Sig. Jacini–Mr W.C. Lyttle[6]–Mr F. Shad–and minutes. Read Celtic
Ireland–Jacini, Pensieri.[7] H. of C. 4–6. Debate on Royal Grants Committee:
minority of 125. Partly due I think to bad management: partly to the new
impulse to Radicalism. I did what I could. Marlb. House party. H.M. gracious in
the extreme. Saw The Prince–Sir F. Knollys–Abp of Canterb.–Dean of
Windsor. Attended the Shah's[8] reception at noon. He was most kind & fresh in
his memory. Saw Ld Derby. Selborne was something between ice & ink.

5. Fr.

Wrote to Messrs Watson–Mr R.L. Everett–E. Morris–Mr H. Mayhew–Dr
Cuyler[9]–Miss Corelli–& minutes. Read Jacini's Pensieri–Nineteenth Cent on
the Shah.[10] Saw S.G.L.–A. Morley–Sir H. Rawlinson (lit.)–Mr Parnell (Royal
Grants)–J. Morley–Ld Granville–Prince of Wales–Mr W. OBrien MP.
H. of C. 3–6. Spoke on Scotch Local Govt (Police).[11] Dined with Rosebery:
placed by the Shah, who was extremely kind & gracious.

6. Sat. [The Durdans]

Wrote to Mary Drew–Mr OBrien MP. BP.–Mr A. Morley–& minutes. To
Durdans by 5.30 train. Saw Mr Morris of Wrexham–Dr and Mrs Cuyler–
Rosebery cum E. Hamilton–Sir E. Reid [sc. Reed]. Function on receiving

[1] Comte de Chambrun, Ses études politiques et littéraires (1889).
[2] A. B. Kingsford, Clothed with the sun; illuminations (1889).
[3] W. G. Lyttle, Betsy Gray . . . a tale of ninety-eight (1894); no earlier ed. found.
[4] Spoke on arrest of W. O'Brien; H 337. 1197.
[5] Welsh education; H 337. 1388.
[6] Wesley Guard Lyttle of Bangor, Ireland; see 2 July 89.
[7] Count S. F. Jacini, Pensiere sulla politica italiana (1889).
[8] Nasr-ul-Deen, 1831-?; Shah of Persia; on a European tour.
[9] See 1 Aug. 85.
[10] N.C., xxvi. 160 (July 1889).
[11] Opposing the govt.'s proposal to exclude police from local govt. responsibility; H 337. 1619.

freedom of Cardiff. Two speeches of 20 min. each (or more). $1\frac{1}{2}-4\frac{1}{2}$.[1] To Durdans at 5. Read 'Divorced'[2]—'It is the Law'.[3]

7. 3 S. Trin.

Ch. with H.C. $11-1\frac{1}{4}$. Prayers with C. evg. Drive with Rosebery.[4] Read Thos a Kempis—and as yesterday. These books present a most strange picture. Much conversation with R.

8. M. [London]

Back to J. St at 12. Wrote to Ld Mountedgcumbe[5]—and minutes. Read Divorced (finished)—It is the Law (finished)—Clancy on Irish Land[6]—The Antijacobin of 1798.[7] H. of C. 3-6.[8] Saw Mr Smith—Mr A. Morley—Mr Childers—Mr Mason (U.S.)—The Speaker—Sir R. Welby—Mr Rhodes[9]—Mr Morley—S.G.L. Dined with Mr A. Morley.

9. Tu.

Wrote to Ld Aberdeen—and minutes. Also N.A. Review Tel. 12/-. H. of C. $3\frac{1}{2}-7\frac{1}{4}$. Anxious work, on the Grants.[10] Saw Ld Mountedgcumbe cum Mr Bolitho[11]—Mr Smith, pluries[12]—Mr Morley—Mr A. Morley—Sir W. Harcourt—Archbp of Canterbury. Luncheon at Mr Childers's: to admire Miss C.s pictures. Dined at Ld Aberdeens great party. Miss Simon sang.

9 July 1889.

1. I have communicated pretty fully with the ex-official portion of the Opposition.
2. They represent I think a shade of opinion rather more favourable to the intention of Govt than the general average of the body
3. I am unable to find, even among them, any indication⟨s⟩ of willingness to support new grants for younger members of the Royal Family in any case outside the family of the Prince of Wales

[1] *T.T.*, 8 July 1889, 7a; a deputation from Cardiff presented the Freedom in Sir E. J. Reed's house in Harrington Gardens, London.

[2] M. V. Dahlgren, *Divorced; a novel* (1887).

[3] T. R. Wilson, *It is the Law; a novel* (1888).

[4] 'In the course of a drive with Mr. G. this afternoon Rosebery raised again with him the question of a Committee to go through and criticise the Irish Bill of 1886. But as usual Mr. G. did not rise to the proposal: he could not see that much good would come of it. As regards any scheme of the future so much would depend upon the exigencies of the moment . . .'; E.H.D., 7 July 1889. See 8 Aug. 89.

[5] William Henry Edgcumbe, 1833-1917; Christ Church, Oxford; 4th earl of Mount-Edgcumbe 1861; lord steward of the Household 1885, 1886-92.

[6] J. J. Clancy, *Tracts on the Irish Question* (1886).

[7] *The Anti-Jacobin; or weekly examiner* (1798).

[8] Scottish local govt.; *H* 337. 1708.

[9] Probably C. J. Rhodes, but not confirmed.

[10] *H* 337. 1838.

[11] Probably Thomas Bedford Bolitho, 1835-1915; Cornish banker and industrialist; involved in the affairs of the Duchy; liberal (unionist) M.P. St. Ives 1887-1900.

[12] i.e. several times; see this day's mem.

4. As respects the family of the Prince of Wales, there is difference of opinion among them except as regards the eldest son
5. I do not abandon the hope however that something might be done in this direction, with a good deal of support from at least, a portion of them
I have of course had no communication up to the present time with the eight Liberal members of the Committee

WEG Jul. 9. 89[1]

10. Wed.

Wrote to E. Morris—Archbp of Cyprus—A. Morley—Sir J. Gladstone—J. Valentine—and minutes. Royal Grants Committee & H. of C. $2\frac{3}{4}$-4.[2] Sat to Millais at two. Eight to dinner. Saw Sir J. Lacaita—W.H.G.—Mr A. Morley—Mr J. Morley. Gave to the dear little man his reward—soldiers.[3] In bed till near noon, from diarrhoea: cares & fatigues of yesterday. Read Virginia[4]—Jacini Pensieri.

11. Th.

Wrote to Sir W. Butler[5]—Rev. R.C. Jenkins—and minutes. Saw S.G.L.—A. Morley—Mr E. Morris—Mr Mayhew—Ld Sydney (luncheon—R. grants)—Ld Rosebery. Read Virginia—Jacini's Pensieri & Ann. Reg[ister] 1797. 1798. H. of C. 3-5.[6] Evening at home.

12. Fr.

Wrote to Mrs Cotton—Sir J. Millais—Mr Hutt—Rev. B. Martin—and minutes. Finished Virginia. Read Jacini—Celtic Ireland. Gave evidence before Lords Committee on Railway Bill.[7] Saw A. Morley—J. Morley—Mr Smith—long conversation on Royal Grants—Ld Rosebery. Drive with C. Dined with the Vernons.

13. Sat.

Wrote to Mr C. Bannerman—Dr Dollinger—Mr W. Hutt—Mr T. Ashton—Subdean—and minutes. Saw Canon MacColl—Mr A. Morley—H.N.G. (Hn). Dined at Lord Norton's. Read Jacini (finished)—Celtic Ireland.

---

[1] Add MS 44773, f. 116. Docketed on the back: 'Shown to J. M[orley] and A. M[orley]. Spoken from memory to Mr Smith after the Divisions.' W. H. Smith, as Leader of the House, was responsible for obtaining passage of the royal grants.
[2] Misc. business; H 338.4.
[3] i.e. a present to his grandson as a reward for good behaviour during the sittings; see 25 June 89n.
[4] Perhaps [E. A. Towix], Virginia Tennant, 2v. (1888).
[5] General Sir William Francis Butler, 1838-1910; member of the Wolseley 'ring' in S. Africa, Egypt and Sudan; a strong liberal.
[6] Spoke on business of the House; H 338. 142.
[7] No report found; railway cttee.'s proceedings were not normally printed.

14. 4 S. Trin.

Chapel Royal mg & the near Church evg. Wrote to Mr B.M. Malabari[1]—Sir C. Russell[2]—Mr A. Morley—and [blank.] Saw Mr G.L. Gower—Sir A. Clark. Read T. A Kempis—Ma Vocation.[3]

15. M.

Wrote to Mr Morley—Abp of Canterbury—E. Hamilton. Saw Sir W. Harcourt—Mr Morley—Mr A. Morley—Ld Rosebery—Mr F.L. Gower. Read J. Morley's excellent chapter on the Cabinet.[4] Comm. on Royal Grants 12-2.[5] Conclave of the Eight Liberals 2-3½.[6] H. of C. to 5.[7] Dined with Ld Rosebery—Opera (Gounod's Romeo & Juliet)[8] after & walked home—through such a scene!

16. Tu.

Wrote minutes. Dined with Mr Stuart Rendell to meet the Welsh members. Saw Mr Dillwyn—Mr Bradlaugh—Mr Morley. Saw Harris, & one [R]. Committee on Royal Grants 12-3, H. of C. afterwards.[9] Read Quart. Rev. on Old Age[10]—Civil List Debates of 1837.[11]

17. Wed.

Wrote to Mr Smith—and minutes. Out of sorts & on my back most of the day. Lady Aberdeen's sculptress made such work as she could.[12] Sat to Sir John Millais. Read Celtic Ireland—Memoirs of Mrs Charles[13]—Letter to Prince of Wales 1794.[14] Long sleep & early to bed. Saw Mr Morley—Mr A. Morley—Sir A. Clark.

18. Th.

Wrote to Mr Smith l.l.l.—Messrs Cocks & Biddulph—Miss Banks—Mr Salkeld—and minutes. Dined with a party at Reform Club. Wrote Mem. on Royal Grants (sent to Mr S.) Committee 12-1½. Conclave of six. Read to them my MS and

---

[1] Bahramji Mehrbanji Malabari, a Parsi of Bombay, editor of the *Indian Spectator*, which published on 27 October 1889 Gladstone's long letter of this day on S. Laing and agnosticism (correspondence and off-print in Add MS 44507, ff. 69–81).
[2] On the Marylebone by-election; *T.T.*, 16 July 1889, 7f.
[3] See 26 May 89.
[4] Untraced.
[5] *PP* 1889 xi. 67.
[6] i.e. the liberals on the royal grants' select cttee.
[7] Scottish local govt.; *H* 338. 417.
[8] Royal Italian Opera at Covent Garden with Melba and the de Reszkes.
[9] Scottish local govt.; *H* 338. 533.
[10] *Q.R.*, clxix. 42 (July 1889).
[11] Various debs. in 1837; *H* 39. 137–1337.
[12] Bust for the Aberdeen family by Miss Redmond (see 19 July 89), an otherwise unknown sculptress.
[13] *Biographical memoirs and anecdotes of the celebrated Mary Anne Clark* (1809).
[14] Probably 'A letter to the Prince of Wales on an application to Parliament to discharge debts wantonly contracted since 1787' (1795).

made verbal changes. Saw Mr Morley (pluries)—Mr A. Morley—Sir J. Kitson—
Mr Routledge—Mr Perks—Mr Smith. Read Jannet, Etats[1]—finished Mrs Clarke.

19. Fr.

Wrote to Rev. J. Morgan—Sig. Sbarbaro—Dr Adler—Mr Rideing—Mrs Corbett—
Mr O. Tinker—Mr Morley—Mr A. Morley—Mrs Th.—and minutes. King's Coll.
4.15-5½ Momerie case. Saw Mr Morley, pluries—Mr A. Morley—S.G.L.—Miss
Redmond (sculptress)—Sir A. West—Mr Bryce—Sir R. Welby cum E.W.H. Most
kindly entertained by the corps of Private Secretaries & presented with a silver
inkstand of the old official type. Saw Murray. Read Jannet. Drive with C. Committee 12-3. Drew amendments.

20. Sat. [Dollis Hill]

Wrote to Mr Morley—Mr Noble—Mr Weston—Mr F.R. Burton—& minutes.
Luncheon with Mrs Th. on our way to Dollis Hill. Saw Mr Morley—S.G.L.—Mr
Quaritch—Mr Knowles. Read Jannet—Journal de M. Bashkirtseff.[2] Quiet evg.

21. 5 S. Trin.

Willesden Ch mg and evg. Saw Mrs Sands. Wrote to Mr W.H. Smith—Ferdinand Favre.[3] Read Ma Vocation—Missions of the Future[4]—Gore on Roman
Claims.[5]

22. M. [London]

Wrote to Jas Cassells—Sir Eardley Wilmot—Mr Parnell—Mr Knowles—Mr Sid-
ney Lee[6]—Sir E. Watkin—& minutes. Saw Scotts—Mr Morley—Sir H. Vivian—
Mr Smith. Corr. MS on Ithaca for press.[7] Committee 12-3½. H. of C. afterwards.[8]
Read Jannet—Baschkirtseff.

23. Tu.

Wrote to S.E. Odell—Mr C.C. Bonney—W. Singleton—C. M'Clury. Began the
required changes in MS on Free Trade about to appear in North Amn Review.[9]
H. of C. 4-5½.[10] Saw Mr Morley—Mr A. Morley—Sir W. Harcourt. Eleven to
dinner. Read as yesterday.

[1] C. Jannet, Les États-Unis contemporains, 2v. (new ed. 1889).
[2] Journal de Marie Bashkirtseff, 2v. (1887); see 9 Aug. 89 for Gladstone's review.
[3] Perhaps the French senator and mayor of Nantes; business untraced.
[4] Gen. W. Booth, The future of missions and the missions of the future (1889).
[5] C. Gore, Roman Catholic claims (1889).
[6] (Sir) Sidney Lee, 1859-1926, assistant editor of the D.N.B., had sent the notice of Sir John
Gladstone for approval; no author is given in D.N.B., xxi. 406, but the entry states that Gladstone
supplied notes (he probably rewrote the entry, as Lee sent it ignorant of Sir John's constituencies);
Add MS 44506, ff. 91, 98.
[7] See 15 Oct. 88.
[8] Spoke on royal grants; H 338. 995.
[9] In fact delayed until January 1890; see 10 Dec. 88n.
[10] Scottish local govt.; H 338. 1127.

24. *Wed.*

Wrote to Mr Wemyss—King of the Belgians—Speaker's Secretary—Rev. Husband—Mr Lloyd Bryce l. & B.P.—Rev. Dr. Hutton—Ld Monkbretton—& minutes. Ld Acton dined with us. Saw S.G.L.—Mr A. Morley—Ld Granville—Scotts—Miss Redmond—Ld Acton. Read Mlle Bashkirtseff. Visited R. Academy with C.

25. *Th. St James.*

H.C. at the near Church 8 AM.

Our 50th anniversary or golden wedding. For me it should have been a day of retreat & recollection, of mingled thankfulness & shame. But was one (after the service) of incessant calls outwards of every kind. Most loving visits, greetings, gifts, correspondence, business in its inevitable increasing round so that I am whirling round & round instead of being deeply still. I am indeed overwhelmed with undeserved kindnesses.

Wrote to the Queen & copy—Prince of Wales & copy—Mr W.H. Smith—W.L. Gladstone—Freeman & Marriott—Freeman's Journal[1]—Mr D. Nutt—Sir J.E. Millais—Mr Agnew—and minutes. Saw Archbishop of Cyprus—Bolton Deputation—Mr A. Morley & others. H. of C. 3.30–7.30. To H. of C. with a muddled & tired brain: but the kindness of the House helped me through a speech on the Royal Grants.[2] Dined at Mr S. Rendell's. Read Bashkirtseff.

26. *Fr.*

Afterwaves of yesterday in abundance. Wrote to Lady Aberdeen—Rev. J.S. Jones—Mrs Tennant—Miss Corelli—Lady L. Tighe[3]—Miss Tennant—Mr Jackson—Mrs S. Sinclair—Mr Smith—and minutes. H. of C. 3¼–7½ & 10½–12¼.[4] Worked on sorting & arranging papers. Saw Count Münster—Sir James Lacaita—Mr A. Morley—Mr Smith. Read as yesterday. Attended the demonstration at the Liberal Club & spoke in reply to the Address: but speech on such an occasion falls miserably short.[5]

27. *Sat.* [*Highcliffe Castle*]

Wrote to Ld Elgin—Ld Provost of Edinburgh—Darrell Lib. Club[6]—Dean of St Asaph—Capt. Blackwood[7]—and minutes. To the marriage at 11.30.[8] Then with long intervals luncheon & the party at Marlborough House. Off at 4.55 to High Cliff.[9] Most kindly received by H.M. the Prince & the Princess. Saw Sir H. Ponsonby—Ld Granville. Read Bashkirtseff—Original English.[10]

---

[1] *Freeman's Journal*, 29 July 1889, 5f, note of thanks from the Gladstones to well-wishers.

[2] *H* 338. 1310.

[3] Lady Louisa Madelina Tighe, da. of 4th duke of Richmond and widow of W. F. F. Tighe of Kilkenny. [4] Royal grants; *H* 338. 1436.

[5] *T.T.*, 27 July 1889, 12a. [6] *Sic*, though no such place.

[7] Perhaps Price Frederick Blackwood of the royal artillery; Northamptonshire landowner.

[8] At Buckingham Palace, of Princess Louise of Wales to the Earl of Fife.

[9] Seat 2 miles E. of Christchurch.

[10] H. J. Barker, *Original English, as written by our little ones at school* (1889).

28. *6 S. Trin.*

Ch. mg & evg: the whole party: now a rare sight. Read Alan Thorne[1]—Clifford's Father Damien[2]—Butler on the O.T.[3] Conversation with Lady W: now much poorer but without murmur. Had sight of the sea.

29. *M.* [*London*]

Wrote to Ld Carnarvon—Mr H. Mayhew—Mr Smith—Mr A.O. Butler—J. Westell—.......—& minutes. H. of C. 4–7 and $10\frac{3}{4}$–$12\frac{1}{2}$. Voted in 355 ag. 134 on Royal Grants.[4] Read Bashkirtseff—Original English. After another visit to the sea came up by express. Home at 2.15. Arranging books & papers.

30. *Tu.*

Wrote to D. of Rutland—Mr Thomson—Mr S.L. Lee—W. Coghlan—T. Snow—Bp of Bath & Wells—Dean of St Asaph—Sidney Hamilton[5]—& minutes. Saw Mr A. Morley—Mr Smith—Ld Carnarvon.[6] Read Brabourne on W.E.G.[7]—Bashkirtseff.

31. *Wed.*

Wrote to A.W. Tuer—Rev. Carruthers—I. Hoyle MP.—Miss Baillie—Mrs Bolton—Mr Creswick—Rev. Dr Preston[8]—N.Y. Mail & Express[9]—Mr Taylor Innes—and minutes. Dined at Ld Brassey's: circuit of introductions. Drive with C. H. of C. at 1.30 for the 2 R.[10] Read Baschkirtseff—From the Green Bag.[11] Much work on books & papers. Saw Mr A. Morley—F. de Lesseps.

Thurs. Aug One. 1889.

Wrote to Sec. Royal Soc.—Mr Westell—Mons. Fechner[12]—D.J. Smithson[13]—Prof. E.A. Grosvenor[14]—Sec. Dalbeattie Assocn—and minutes. H. of C. $4\frac{3}{4}$–8, and $9\frac{1}{2}$–$12\frac{1}{4}$ for the P. of Wales Bill.[15] Saw Mr E. Hamilton—Mr A. Morley—Mr Westell—Sir J. Carmichael. Another day of much slaving on books, papers, house arrangements. Read Bashkirtseff.

---

[1] See 26 June 89. [2] E. Clifford, *Father Damien* (1889).

[3] Joseph Butler; or A. R. Butler, *Stepping stones to bible history* (1889).

[4] i.e. opposing Labouchere's amndt.; *H* 338. 1684.

[5] Of the Isle of Wight; had sent congratulations; Hawn P.

[6] Carnarvon requested 'a few minutes conversation on a subject on which it is difficult to explain myself on paper' (to Gladstone, 28 July 1889, Add MS 44507, f. 118); no entry in Carnarvon's diary this day; he had had a long talk with Spencer on Ulster on 24 July, but his letter suggests a private matter; Add MS 60933, f. 12.

[7] 'Mr Gladstone's plain speaking', *N.C.*, xxvi. 257 (August 1889).

[8] William Preston, vicar of Runcorn; published on 'Romanism'.

[9] No correspondence traced.

[10] Of the Prince of Wales's Children Bill; *H* 338. 1795.

[11] Perhaps *The Green Bag: a new farce* (1807).

[12] Probably Hermann Fechner, historian of the Franco-Prussian war.

[13] David J. Smithson, author of *Elocution and the dramatic art* (1887).

[14] Edwin Augustus Grosvenor, historian of Constantinople; Hawn P.

[15] *H* 339. 133.

2. Frid.

Wrote to Dowr Lady Sandhurst l. & tel.—Lady Russell BP.—Mr Mundella—K. Hoffmann—Sir H. Rawlinson BP.—Khedive of Egypt. Saw Mr Leveson Gower—Count Münster—Sir J.C. Much work on books & papers. Dined at Sir C. Forster's. H. of C. $3\frac{1}{2}$-6.[1] At Murrays—Scotts—Macmillans—&c. Saw Lady Rosebery—Mr Leveson Gower. And had a full hours conversation with Mr (late Father) Matthews.[2]

3 Sat. [Hawarden]

Off at nine. Special train, & feast on board by Sheffield to Chester & Dee Bridge. Spoke at Grantham & twice at the Bridge. A very striking scene.[3] Then on to Hawarden: we were received with much affection & all possible display. Spoke, as well as I could; but it was very ill. The mercies of this time have indeed been overwhelming. Read Bashkirtseff. Conversation with Sir E. Watkin.

S. 7 Trin.

Ch. mg (with H.C.) and evg. Wrote to French Ambassador—Lord Acton—Mr Morley. Read Wiclif de Rege[4]—Hore, Hist Ch. of England[5]—Indian Tracts—Life of Grignon.[6]

5. M.

Church $8\frac{1}{2}$ A.M. Oh how amiable!

Wrote to Mr H.B. Baildon—Rev. J.B. Craven—Mr Jackson—Messrs Wheatley —J. Morgan. Lost in the chaos of books papers parcels &c. on which I laboured almost without visible result. Went out to the concourse of visitors at three: & spoke to them very briefly. Later we had Mr & Mrs Ellis Lever. He ought to be a *Candidate*.[7] Read Ardath—Marie Bashkirtseff.

6. Tu.

Wrote to Canon M'Coll—Dowager Lady Airlie—W.F. Dennaby—Sir W. Farquhar —E.H. Moss—Mr L. Knowles MP[8]—Mrs Sands—Sig. Rosario Saluso—Dowager Lady Sandhurst. Still struggling with Chaos. Saw Herbert (respecting Irish MP.s). Walk with Harry. Read Ardath[9]—M. Bashkirtseff—Songs of Innocence.[10]

---

[1] Supported grants for Wales's children; *H* 339. 191.

[2] (Count Arnold Jerome) Povoleri Matthews, formerly a Roman catholic priest; various letters about him from Lady Sandhurst in Add MS 44507.

[3] Opening of the swing bridge over the Dee, linking N. Wales with Merseyside; *T.T.*, 5 August 1889, 6a.

[4] J. Wyclif, *Tractatus de officio regis*, ed. Pollard and Sayle (1887).

[5] A. H. Hore, *The church in England from William III to Victoria*, 2v. (1886).

[6] Probably A. P. J. Cruikshank, *Life and select writings of ... L. M. Grignon de Montfort* (1870).

[7] The manufacturer (see 25 May 85); he was never a candidate.

[8] (Sir) Lees Knowles, 1857-1928; barrister and author on military affairs; tory M.P. W. Salford 1886-1906; 1st bart. 1903.

[9] Marie Corelli, *Ardath, story of a dead self* (1889); see 4 June, 10 Aug. 89n.

[10] By William Blake (new ed. 1888).

7. *Wed.*

Ch. 8½ A.M. Wrote to Rev. Mr Jenkins 1 & BP—R.P. Greg—R. Brown BP—Rev. H.E. Stone—Rev. A.G. Watson—A. Macdonald—Sig. Rondi—J.J. Macbride—J.L. Foulds—M.H. (Worcester)—E. Waugh—Watsons—Ld Rosebery. Continued labours in the direction of Order. Read Life of Mr Muir[1]—Sir J. Temple on Rebellion of 1641[2]—Ardath.

8. *Th.*

Ch. 8½ A.M. Wrote to Mr Parnell MP.[3]—B. Dobell—W. Goalen—G.G. Napier—G.D. Houghton—S. Rendell MP.—Rev. R.H. Smith—Rev. S.E.G.—Rev. J.P. Thompson—Miss Tennant—H.J.G. Tel.—and minutes. Walk with Harry to inspect sites.[4] A difficult choice. Read Miss Blind's articles on Bashkirtseff[5]—Ardath. Wrote Mema on Bill of 1886.

H.R.[6]

Prime points of difficulty
1. Shall Ireland be represented at Westminster by ⟨the same⟩ members also in Dublin or by others?
2. Constitution of the Irish Chamber or Chambers.
3. Shall the contribution to Imperial Expenditure be by a fixed sum or by a percentage.
4. Shall an adjustment be made upon portions of Excise or Customs Revenue levied in the one Island upon goods consumed in the other.
5. Shall the Title to legislate upon Land Contracts and Tenure be reserved say for 2 years and until the close of the actual or ensuing session?
6. Shall there be a provision against interference with contracts.
7. Can we have any safeguards for minorities. *Conflict of laws*.
8. Can we have a land law authorising landlords to sell (i.e. alienate) at . . . . years purchase of nett rental and tenants to buy at . . . . years' purchase (putting a difference of say 2 years between the two operations[ )].
9. Were there in Bill of 1886 any provisions likely to be obnoxious to Ireland.
10. As to the Receiver General.

9. *Frid.*

Ch. 8½ A.M. Wrote to Dr Sannervanni—Miss Robertson—Messrs Spink—Canon O'Hanlon—H. Owen—T. Adams—Jos Ferrit. Wrote on the Bashkirtseff Journal.[7] Read The Journal—Ardath—Divers Tracts. Walk with C.G.

[1] R. Smiles, *Brief memoir of William Muir* (1888).

[2] Sir J. Temple, *The Irish rebellion . . . 1641* (1646).

[3] No copy found; Parnell replied, 14 August 1889, Add MS 44507, f. 157, regretting various items of business prevented him immediately taking 'advantage of your kind invitation'.

[4] For St. Deiniol's Library; see 15 Sept. 87.

[5] In *Woman's World*; see Gladstone's comments in his review (9 Aug. 89).

[6] Add MS 44773, f. 239. These undated notes may be those referred to this day, and may result from the conversation with Rosebery on 7 July 89.

[7] Review of Journal of Marie Bashkirtseff (see 20 July 89) in *N.C.*, xxvi. 602 (October 1889). See also *The Gladstone Papers* (1930), 86 ff.

10 Sat.

Ch. $8\frac{1}{2}$ A.M. Wrote to Sir Chas Dilke[1]—Mr Labouchere—J. Romans—Mr Taylor Innes—Mr Morley—G.M. Sibbald BP & l.—A. Morley Tel—W. Wright BP—E. Perry & A. Hay—Mr & Mrs Gregson. Large return tea-party 5-6$\frac{1}{2}$. The presents are really dazzling.[2] Herbert told me of the slander against him.[3] Read Bashkirtseff—Ardach [*sic*] (a sag:[4] but I skim)—Lefevre on Irish members and English Gaolers.[5]

11. 8 S. Trin.

Ch mg & evg. Wrote to S.E.G.—Mr Hughes—T.E. Olivier. Read Ollivier on Bps[6]—.... on K. David—Sir M. Williams on Buddhism[7]—Fisher on Dogma[8]—New Aids to Reflections[9]—and divers Tracts.

12. M.

Ch. $8\frac{1}{2}$ A.M. Wrote to Mr Lefevre l.l.—Mr R. Brown jun.—Mrs Burgess—Miss Gonsales[10]—D. Macgregor—Walter Crane[11]—H.A. Hunt—Oswald Smith. Read Lefevre (finished)—R. Brown in Archaeol. Rev.—Cecil Smith in do.[12]—Ardach. Worked on books & papers.

13. Tu.

Ch. $8\frac{1}{2}$ A.M. Wrote to G.R. Gunmell—P.V. Valentine—Messrs Hagen—F. Perigal—W.H. Read—J.M. Miller—A. Allan—E. Dwyer Gray—G.F.R. Barker—Sir E. Watkin M.P. Read Bashkirtseff—Wicksteed on Ibsen[13]—Journals of 1800 —Ardach—Ch. Q.R. on O.T. Criticism.[14] Walk with C.

14. Wed.

Ch. $8\frac{1}{2}$ A.M. Wrote to U.S. Minister—E.W. Hamilton—Mr S. Montagu—Ld Rosebery l.l.—Mr Hitchman—Mr F.C. Philips—Mr Duffield. Worked on Mlle.

[1] Letter on Dilke's future consequent on the failed meeting of 1 July 89; in R. Jenkins, *Sir Charles Dilke* (1958), 378.

[2] Estate presents for the Gladstones' Golden Wedding.

[3] Matter apparently taken no further.

[4] Glynnese: dull.

[5] G. J. Shaw Lefevre, *Irish members and English gaolers* (1889).

[6] Probably O. E. Ollivier, *L'Église et l'État au concile du Vatican*, 2v. (1879).

[7] See 7 Apr. 89.

[8] G. P. Fisher, *The grounds of theistic and Christian belief* (1883).

[9] J. M. Sloan, *New aids to reflections* (1889).

[10] Miss Violet Elizabeth Gonsalez of Portobello had sent a Birthday-Book compiled from Pope's Greek translations, and asked permission to dedicate it to Gladstone; Hawn P.

[11] Walter Crane, 1845-1915, artist and socialist, who had illustrated with knightly motifs the album presented by the National Liberal Club for the golden wedding; Add MS 44507, f. 127.

[12] *Archaeological Review*, iii.297, 376 (July 1889).

[13] P. H. Wicksteed, 'Ibsen's Peer Gynt', *C.R.*, lvi. 274 (August 1889).

[14] *Church Quarterly Review*, xxviii. 112 (April 1889).

Bashkirtseff. I find it difficult. Read Philips, As in a Glass[1]—Hamilton on Salaries.[2] 1½ h. with Mr Mayhew on Estate affairs: good outlook but it tired me.

15. Th.

Ch. 8¼ A.M. Wrote to Ld Balfour of Burleigh[3]—Mrs Roundell—Mr J. Syme—Rev. J.M. Jones—W.H. Dawson—Rev. H. Kennedy—Mrs S. Rendel—Mr Macquoid. Saw W. Baillie (Octagon)—Mr Mayhew. Survey at Lane End. Read As in a Looking Glass—Histoire du Luxe[4]—Bashkirtseff. Worked on Notice of B.[5]

16. Fr.

Ch. 8½ AM. Wrote to Mr Taylor Innes—Messrs Watson l.l.—Mr J. Cowan—Mr Thurold—Mr A. Morley. Worked hard on & finished MS on Bashkirtseff. Saw Mr Baillie (Octagon)—Canon MacColl. Read As in a Looking Glass. Eight to dinner.

17. Sat.

Ch 8¼ AM. Wrote to Mr Howell—Miss D. Tennant—Mr H. Pink—J.M. Macleod—W.A. Bewes—Ronald Smith. Saw Mr Woolley (Quasi visit)—Mr Tomkinson (Bank & RR)—Conversation with Canon MacColl—Mr S. Rendel (came P.M.) Seven to dinner. Read As in a Looking Glass (finished). Preparation to write on Italy.[6]

18. 9 S. Trin.

Ch. mg & evg. Wrote to Mrs Newnham—Mrs Rich—Mr S. Gardson—Hon. F. Lawley—F. Slater. Read Newnham's Sermons[7]—MacColl's Lectures[8]—Anglic. on Dives & Lazarus[9]—and tracts.

19. M.

Ch. 8¼ A.M. Wrote to Rev. A.M. Jones—A. Stewart—F. Baum—Sir H. Ponsonby —Lady F. Dixie. Walk with Mr Rendel. Went over the competing sites,[10] & got his advice. Read Whitehead on Fruit culture,[11] & other kindred Tracts—Stewart on Deer Forests[12]—Mrs Roundell, Azores[13]—Histoire du Luxe.

[1] F. C. Philips, *As in a looking glass*, 2v. (new ed. 1889).

[2] Untraced article, probably by E. W. Hamilton.

[3] Start of sharp exchange on Scottish disestablishment; this and other letters in *T.T.*, 5 September 1889, 5b.

[4] Probably E. de Laveleye, *Le luxe* (1887).

[5] See 9 Aug. 89.

[6] Article signed 'Outidanos', 'The Triple Alliance and Italy's place in it', *C.R.*, lvi. 469 (October 1889).

[7] P. H. Newnham, '*Thy heart with my heart*' (1888).

[8] M. MacColl, *Christianity in relation to science and morals* (1889).

[9] A. C. Auchmuty, '*Dives and Pauper' and other sermons* (1887).

[10] For St. Deiniol's Library.

[11] See 24 Dec. 83; discussed in his speech on 22 August.

[12] Untraced tract, perhaps by Alexander Stewart, who wrote widely on the highlands (see this day).

[13] J. A. E. Roundell, *A visit to the Azores* (1889).

20.

Ch. 8½ A.M. Wrote to French Embassy—W.H.G.—M. Leon Say—Mr A. Morley —Mr Feldman—Prof. Freeman—J.B. Taylor—C. Greenlees—Mrs Malone—Press Assocn (Tel.). Worked on Library Plans. Mr Rendell went off—after inspecting the Octagon. Read Azores—Hardy's return of the native.[1] Drive & walk with C.

21. Wed.

Ch. 8½ A.M. Wrote to Mrs Bennett l. & tel.—Mr Howell l. & P.P.—J. Beale—Col. Liddell—Ld Spencer—Sig. Galliero—Dr Greenhill—E. Goodkind—Sir E. Watkin. Worked on Library plans. My ground floor is to be Theological & planned for 25000 volumes. Walk with Spencer. Read Mrs Roundell—Hardy's Novel.

22. Th.

Ch. 8½ AM. Wrote to Dowager Ly Sandhurst—A. Morley MP—HJG MP—Mr Dumbarton—Miss K. Rollins.[2] Again I puzzled long over the construction of the Library. And went over the tracts &c. respecting Horticultural matters. Examined the show in the tent: & addressed the meeting for 40 or 45 min.[3] Read The Return of the Native. Finished Mrs R.s Azores.

23. Fr.

Ch. 8½ AM. Wrote to Miss Conybeare—H.N.G.—Ld Balfour—Rev. S.E.G.— Messrs Meehan—Jas Corrie—F. Edwards—H.L. Wallenstein—Sir E. Watkin MP. Tel. More work on Library. I am rather turning to a temporary scheme. Sir E. Watkin came to dine & sleep. Agreed on the expedition to Paris.[4] Read Mr Leahy on O'Connell[5]—The Bownsham Puzzle.[6]

24. Sat. St Barth.

Ch 8½ AM. Wrote to Ld Balfour (copied out)[7]—Mr W.C. Vivian[8]—H.N.G.—Mr Morley—Mr Macquoid—Mr Hitchman—Rivingtons—Mr Lee Warner—Mr J.E. Thompson.—Sec. Anatoliké Omospondé.[9] Sir E. Watkin went: and Lady S. Drive with C. Worked on Galv. Iron plans.[10] And on MS Anon. Read Bownsham Puzzle—Hist. du Luxe—Flourens on Russia—Coleridge on Arnold II.[11]

[1] T. Hardy, *The Return of the Native*, 3v. (1878).

[2] Another name of the rescue case, Mrs. Scarsdale (see 20 Aug. 81, 2 Sept. 89); she used the name Kate Rollins when attached to the Convent of the Good Shepherd, Brislington, which Gladstone probably assisted her to leave in 1885, when she promised to 'lead an honest and respectable life'; see Add MS 44491, f. 175.

[3] *T.T.*, 23 August 1889, 8e.   [4] See 3 Sept. 89.

[5] D. Leahy, *The judgment of Lord Denman in the case of O'Connell and others* (1844).

[6] J. Habberton, *The Bowsham puzzle, and my friend Moses* (1884).

[7] On his statements on Scottish disestablishment; Add MS 44507, f. 187.

[8] On the imprisonment of Conybeare in Derry gaol; *T.T.*, 3 September 1889, 7f.

[9] See 14 May 89n.

[10] i.e. a temporary library built with galvanized iron, as was in fact done by the architect, Humphreys (see 27 Aug. 89).

[11] E. Flourens and J. D. Coleridge in *New Review*, i. 201, 217 (August 1889).

25. 10 S. Trin.

Ch HC. 8 AM. Service 11 AM and $6\frac{1}{2}$ PM. Wrote to Ed. Daily News[1]—Messrs Miller—J.H. Jones—H.N.G. Read MacColl's Lectures—Rawlinson on Chron.[2]—Black on O.T.—Wellhausen on do.[3]—Q. Elis. and the R.C. Hierarchy.[4]

26. M.

Ch. $8\frac{1}{2}$ A.M. Wrote to Sir Ch. Macgrigor[5]—Mr Lefevre[6]—Mr Reid—H.N.G. Worked further on Galv. Iron plans. Party given to the Tenants $4\frac{1}{2}$-8: the presents shown. Near a thousand came. I made a short speech:[7] C.G. led the dance. Read Hist. du Luxe—Bouillé's Memoirs[8]—New Review Arnold I—&c.

27. Tu.

Ch. $8\frac{1}{2}$ AM. Wrote to Mr Freeman B.P.—Mr O'Neill Daunt—Rev. D. Mitchell—Messrs Miller—J. Grant—J. Ogilvy—T. Baker—Mr Humphreys:[9] a substantive step towards the meditated Library: God prosper the design. Worked on Anon. MS. Read Reprints W.E.G. autore—1837 & Disraeli 38.—Bouillé's Memoirs—Hist. du Luxe—Bownsham Puzzle.

28. Wed.

Ch. $8\frac{1}{2}$ A.M. Wrote to Sir E. Watkin L. & Tel.—Watsons—Rev. M. Davies—K. Rollins—W.F. Denneby—Dr Bonwell—H. Wallenstein—S. Hallifax[10]—Creswicks—Scotts—Spiller—Th. Parker—Vote Office—Abp of Cyprus (BP). Arranged & put by my Journals: examined dates of the daily service here. Worked on Anon. MS 'The League of Peace'. Read Hist du Luxe—Bouillé's Memoirs—Contemp. Rev.

---

[1] Public letter urging govt. inquiry into *D.N.*'s reports of Turkish atrocities against Armenians, and forwarding an anon. statement 'which has just reached me' (presumably sent by the secretary of the Anatoliké society, see previous day); *D.N.*, 27 August 1885, 5d and leader.

[2] G. Rawlinson, *The Kings of Israel and Judah* (1889).

[3] Probably C. I. Black, *The proselytes of Israel* (1881) and J. Wellhausen, *Geschichte Israels* (1878).

[4] Probably the article, J. Morris, 'Mr. Gladstone on the Elizabethan settlement of religion', *Dublin Review*, xx. 243 (October 1888), to which Gladstone's next article (see 16 Sept. 89) is in effect a reply.

[5] Sir Charles Rhoderic McGrigor, 1811-90; 2nd bart. 1858; had written as 'a brother Etonian' on behalf of the Caledonian Asylum of London; Gladstone sent £10; Add MS 44507, ff. 188, 201.

[6] On his 'Irish members and English gaolers'; *T.T.*, 31 August 1889, 9f; see 10 Aug. 89.

[7] *T.T.*, 27 August 1889, 6e.

[8] F. C. A. de Bouillé du Chariol, *Memoirs relating to the French revolution* (1797).

[9] J. C. Humphreys, Albert Gate, Hyde Park, London, maker of corrugated buildings; involved in planning and construction of the temporary version of St. Deiniol's Library. For his plans, see Hawn P MS 2182.

[10] Sydney Hallifax of Cavendish House, Manchester, on his Irish visit; Add MS 44507, f. 195.

29. Th.

Ch. 8½ A.M. Wrote to .... Mr Pickles U.S.[1]—W.H.G.—Mr Power MP.[2] Tel. .... and [blank.] Lady Herbert came. Much conversation. Eight to dinner. Read Bouillé—Hist. du Luxe.

30. Fr.

Ch. 8½ A.M. Wrote to Ld Balfour (& draft)[3]—Mr Parnell MP[4]—Mr Channing MP[5]—E.W. Hamilton—Messrs Cook—Mr A. Morley MP—K. Rollins—Wms & Norgate—Watsons—H. Macmichael .... Seven to dinner. Worked on MS. Walk with Lady H. Read Bouillé—Hist. du Luxe.

31. Sat.

Ch. 8½ A.M. Wrote to Lucy Cavendish—Mr Godley—Mr Knowles—Mr Broom-head—Mr Bhamgara[6]—Mr Broussali—Press Assocn Tel.—Messrs Wheatley—Grogan & B.—W. Bailey—Dr Strahan—D. Patrick—Mr Morley—Mr Nisbet. Saw Mr Stansfeld (Irish Univ.)—Mr Carvell Williams (do)[7]—Lady Herbert (Biogr. of S.H.)[8]—S.E.G. Read Bouillé (finished)—New Review on Boulanger.[9] Worked on MS. A hard day, over 12 hours.

11 S. Trin. Sept 1. 89.

Ch 11 AM with H.C. and [blank.] Wrote to Herbert J.G.—Superior A.S. Sister-hood—Messrs Hubbard—K. Rollins—Miss Atkinson—E. Howell—Mr A. Grove—F. Baker. Finished my MS. Read Lilly in N.C.—Perry in do.[10]—divers tracts.

2. M. [London]

Wrote to Lady Rosslyn—Mr Doubleday—Mr Cox. Started at nine from Hawarden Station: King's Cross 3.5. Saw Mr Parnell: whose conversation was loyal and satisfactory. Saw Scotts—Grogan—& Mr Humphry with whom I arranged for the new structure at Hawarden: the nucleus I trust if it please God

[1] James Pickles of Jacoma, U.S.A., on religion; Hawn P.

[2] Either Patrick Joseph Power, 1850-1913, home rule M.P. E. Waterford from 1885 or Richard Power, 1851-91, home rule M.P. Waterford from 1874.

[3] Scottish disestablishment; Add MS 44507, f. 202.

[4] Further encouragement to Parnell to visit Hawarden, and discussion of tory policy and a Roman catholic university; in Hammond, 644. See 4 Oct., 18-19 Dec. 89.

[5] (Sir) Francis Allston Channing, 1841-1926; liberal M.P. E. Northants. 1885-1910; cr. bart. 1906; land reformer.

[6] P. Bhamgara of the Indian Palace at the Paris exhibition, arranging for Gladstone to visit it; Hawn P.

[7] John Carvell Williams, 1821-1907; congregationalist; liberal M.P. S. Notts. 1885-6, Mansfield 1892-1900; secretary of the Liberation Society. See 5 July 70.

[8] Gladstone and Lady Herbert agreed to approach Arthur Gordon, Lord Stanmore, then governing Ceylon; he accepted the invitation but, with his life of his father as his priority, did not publish his *Sidney Herbert* until 1906. See *T.A.P.S.*, n.s. li, part iv. 99.

[9] *New Review*, i. 111 (July 1889).

[10] *N.C.*, xxvi. 476, 500 (September 1889).

of something considerable. Saw Scarsdale (Rollins) [R]. Worked on Debates of 1868. Read Life of Hazlitt.[1]

3. [Paris]

Wrote to Mary Drew—Mr Knowles—Mr Th. Hankey. Saw Mr Stead (Irish Univ.)[2]—Dr Machale—Mr Logan. Reached Paris 6.30. We were received by the Railway Chieftains,[3] & lodged delightfully at the Bristol.[4] Read La Corruption de Paris[5]—Letters of the Duc'Orleans.[6] Ten to dinner. Much conversation with M. Josse.

4. Wed.

Wrote to . . . .—Col. Kornprobst.[7] Read Corruption de Paris. Out at Nine to the Trocadero, and some splendid collections there. The Ivories of Cent XIII much the deepest impression. Then to the *Chemin de fer glissant*: a circuit homewards by the challenging Church of St Augustin. Long drive in afternoon to make calls: 20 m. I think in streets & parks today. Saw heads of the Irish College. Worked on revising MS Triple All.[8]

5. Th.

Wrote to Mr Bunting l. & BP—Mr Knowles—Mr Stead. Forenoon again at the exposition, dejeuner at Saphiers. At night we went under the guidance of M. Josse to the Hippodrome. The performance was arrested and God save the Queen played. The cycling wonderful, said to be English. The Russian spectacle most interesting, received with an enthusiasm which I thought full of meaning. Finished M.S.

6.

Wrote to Mr Th. Hankey. Went early to the Indian Court, inspected, bought, received gifts & an address (*beautiful* & costly gifts) & I spoke in reply.[9] Then went to French Pictures & Sculpture (Machinery, & the Edison Department next, or today?)[10] the old coalmine & the new. At night we went to the Opera: in

---

[1] Alexander Ireland, journalist in Southport, had sent his *Selections from the writings of William Hazlitt with a memoir* (1889); Add MS 44507, f. 193.

[2] Meeting in the Paris train: 'Mr. Gladstone proceeded to take a seat in his carriage, where he at once became absorbed in an earnest discussion of the Irish University Bill'; *P.M.G.*, 3 September 1889, 5. For Stead's report, 'The proposed Catholic University: what Mr. Gladstone thinks', see *P.M.G.*, 4 September 1889, 1–2.

[3] The Gladstones were the guests of Sir E. W. Watkin, chairman of the S.E. Metropolitan and other railways, and promoter of the Channel Tunnel.

[4] In Place Vendôme.

[5] A. Coffignon, *Paris vivant. La corruption à Paris* (1889).

[6] F. d'Orléans, Duc d'Orléans, *Letters 1825–1842, publiées par le Comte de Paris et le Duc de Chartres* (1889).

[7] Wrote as aide to Madame Carnot to offer a box at the Opéra; see 6 Sept. 89 and Hawn P.

[8] See 17 Aug. 89.

[9] The Indian exhibit at the exhibition; see *T.T.*, 7 September 1889, 5b.

[10] i.e. the entry written up later.

the President's box: met the Directors; they took me behind where the spaces are vast. C. was overdone. Read O[rleans] Letters & Corr. de Paris.[1]

7 Sat.

Wrote to Ld Lytton—M.[2] After nine we went to the Exhibition.[3] We were received most kindly by M. Eiffel[4] & his coadjutors & I was persuaded to go up the tower & propose his health in a French oratiuncle. My poor weak brain was hardly at all disturbed. C. was unhappily prevented by indisposition. Dejeuner at Saphiers & passed several hours in the Exhibition: especially French pictures & sculpture, English procelain at the reproduced Bastille, and so forth. We went also to the Luxembourg and saw the two pictures by Marie Bashkirtseff. Read Orleans Letters—Corruption de Paris. Banquet at the Continental, 140 guests. Saw Mrs Crawford—M. Tirard, M. Leon Say, & others. After doubting to the last moment I attempted & made my speech (15 min?) in French: *all* its faults were drowned in kindness.[5] Saw M. Josse—Sir J. Carmichael.

8. 12 S. Trin.

Ch Rue d'Aguesseau mg and aft. In aft. we drove to the Bois, called on Sir R.W.[6] to inquire, & saw the beautiful Church near the Arc. At night we drove to see the illumination of the Tower. Read Elisabethan Ch. Hist.—Machale's Letters[7]—Crookleigh.[8]

9. M. [London]

Wrote to [blank.] Amid many kind farewells we went off by the 10 A.M. train and reached London at 6½. Dined at Mr Hankey's. Saw Miss Ponsonby. Saw MacLachlan—and . . . . [R]. Saw A. Morley. Read Orleans Letters—Le Crime et le Chatiment.[9]

10. [Hawarden]

Wrote to Mr Stead—Mr Leng. Worked at Br. Museum. Read as yesterday. Saw Mr Fitzgerald (N.Z.)[10]—Mr A. Morley—Mr Marjoribanks—Sir E. Watkin: fare-

---

[1] See 3 Sept. 89.

[2] Name erased, apparently with a pen-knife.

[3] The huge Universal Exhibition on the Champs de Mars (celebrating the centenary of the revolution), of which only the Eiffel Tower was preserved.

[4] Gustave Eiffel, 1832–1923; Watkin, Gladstone's host in Paris, began a similar tower at Wembley, but lack of funds prevented its completion.

[5] Banquet given by the Paris Society of Political Economy; *T.T.*, 9 September 1889, 3c. Gladstone also proposed the toast to the United States of America. Text in French in Hutton and Cohen, *Speeches*, x. 121.

[6] Not further identified.

[7] J. Machale, *Letters* (new ed. 1888).

[8] S. K. Hocking, *Crookleigh* (1887).

[9] F. M. Dostoevsky, *Le crime et le châtiment*, 2v. (1884).

[10] James Edward Fitzgerald, controller and auditor-general of New Zealand, who had requested a discussion; see his letter of 14 September on Imperial federation, which Gladstone had not discussed; Add MS 44507, f. 222.

well at Northenden after very great kindness. Off at two. Reached Hawarden before 8.30. D. Gratias.

11. Wed.

Ch. 8¼ A.M. Wrote to Mr Marjoribanks—Mr Humphrey—Mr Quaritch—Mr Nicol BP[1]—J.W. Laurie—Mr Grogan—Mr L. Bryce Tel.—Revised & dispatched MS. on Italy, with additions. Saw W. Bailey & fixed on the site [for St. Deiniol's library] which was pegged accordingly. Willy was there: we had tea with him afterwards, & were delighted with his great improvement. Saw Mr Adamson. Read Orleans Letters—Le Crime et le Chatiment.

12. Th.

Ch. 8¼ A.M. Wrote to Mr Knowles l. and B.P.—Mr Nicol—A. Grove—D. Patrick—Rev. Dr Webster—Mr Humphreys—Sister Eliza—Sir E. Watkin—Rev. H.S. Smith. Saw W. Bailey on the new Building. Tea at W.H.G.s after visiting the ground. Read as yesterday. Corrected & sent off proof of M. Bashkirtseff.[2]

13. Fr.

Ch. 8½ A.M. Wrote to Ed. Br. Trade Journal—Superior All S. Sisterhood—Lady Herbert—Mr Knowles—Mr Dick Peddie—Mr W. Macgeorge—Mr Bojanowski[3]—Editor of Science U.S.[4] Saw at much length, here & on the ground, Mr Humphreys, who dined here. Read Le Crime et le Chat.—Orleans Letters (finished).

14. Sat.

Ch. 8¼ A.M. Wrote to Mr Seymour May—Mr A. Morley—B. Quaritch—Mr M'Glashan—W. Ridler—A.B. Osborne—E. Brown—Rev. Mr Fitzroy—D.C. Thomson[5]—Dr Fitch. Long *sederunt* with Mr Humphreys on the new House. And in afternoon the ground was finally fixed. Mr Sharp gave a very reluctant assent. Wrote Mema. for Trust. Read Fitch on Endowments[6]—Le Crime et le Chatiment—and [blank.]

15. 13 S. Trin.

Ch mg & evg. Wrote to Ld Coleridge—Watsons—Mr Nicol. Read Crookleigh finished—Q. Elis. & the Hierarchy—Strype's Chch[7]—and Maimonides.[8]

[1] John Nichol, London printer and publisher; much correspondence, chiefly on *C.R.* and *Good Words*, in Hawn P.

[2] See 15 Aug. 89.

[3] Perhaps Paul Anton Stephan von Bojanowski, German authority on Shakespeare.

[4] In reply to a copy sent to him with an article on population; this letter is reproduced in facsimile in *Science* and printed in *T.T.*, 29 October 1889, 4f.

[5] David C. Thomson of the *Dundee Courier*, and founder of the publishing firm; Hawn P.

[6] J. G. Fitch, *Charity schools and the endowed schools commission* (1873).

[7] See 15 Sept. 89.

[8] Moses ben Maimun, *Maimonides Kiddusch Hachodesch* (1889).

16. M.

Ch. 8½ A.M. Wrote to Bp of Jerusalem—G. May—Mr Nicol—D. Curt—J. Cowan—Mad. Novikoff—A. Caddie. Saw WHG on Buildings. Walk with E. Wickham. Corr. Revise 'Outiadanos'.[1] Wrote on Elisabethan settlement.[2] Read Le Crime et le Chatiment—Hesper[3]—Monumenta Vaticana.[4]

17. Tu.

Wrote to Lady Herbert . . . . . Ch. 8½ AM as usual. Saw the Rector. Read Le Crime et le Chatiment—Hesper (Amn Drama)—American Pilgrimage.

18.

Ch. 8½ AM. Wrote to Mr Humphreys—Ed Daily Post—F.R. Darton—Mr Stead— Mr Knowles—Sec. Ld Mayor—Sir E. Watkin—Rivingtons—Mr Ridler. Walked with the Rendel cousins[5] in the Park. Worked on plans of new [library.] Worked on new MS of Elisabethan settlement. Reading at large for it. Also read Le Crime et le Chatiment—and [blank.]

19. Th.

Ch. 8½ A.M. and 7½ P.M. (Harvest Sermon). Wrote to Rev. Mr Johnson—Sig. Premi—G. Jack—J.R. Whitley—C.S. Miall—M. Dillon. Worked on Elisabethan settlement. Read Hist. Reb. of 1798[6]—Le Crime et le Chatiment. Mr Brown[7] here. He is striking and attractive.

20. Fr.

Ch. 8½ A.M. Wrote to A.E. Fletcher—F.W. Slater—Miss H.T. Mill[8]—C.S. Palmer—Mr Blyde. Saw Dr Cox[9]—Mr O. Morgan & Mr Hibbert—Lady Stapylton.[10] Worked on Elisab. Settlement. Finished Le Crime et le Chatiment—Read Kansas Campaign.[11]

---

[1] See 17 Aug. 89.

[2] Published as 'The English Church under Henry the Eighth', *N.C.*, xxvi. 882 (November 1889), reprinted in *Later gleanings*, 219. The proofs were sent to Bp. Stubbs for approval; Stubbs told Gladstone, 7 October 1889, Add MS 44508, f. 28 '. . . I may venture to say that I think you have knocked over your critics at every point touched & can thank you honestly for the Essay'.

[3] W. Roscoe Thayer, *Hesper: an American drama* (1888); civil war poetry.

[4] *Monumenta Vaticana*, ed. H. Lämmer (1861), quoted in *N.C.*, xxvi. 244.

[5] Maud Ernestine Rendel, part of a large Rendel visiting party; she m. H. N. Gladstone, see 30 Jan. 90.

[6] P. Harwood, *History of the Irish rebellion of 1798* (1844).

[7] Ernest Faulkner Brown, 1866–1938; curate in Liverpool; joined Oxford Mission to Calcutta 1880 (in which S. E. Gladstone was interested); H.V.B.

[8] Had written on a newspaper report; Hawn P.

[9] John Charles Cox, 1843–1919; historian and anglican (from 1917 Roman) priest; H.V.B.

[10] Mary Catherine, da. of A. S. Gladstone, m. 1878 Sir Francis George Stapleton, soldier and 8th bart.

[11] Untraced.

21. Sat.

Ch. 8¼ A.M. Wrote to Duke of Argyll l & BP.—Mr H. Mayhew—Mr B. Sharp—
Rev. Mr Howell—Mr Nicolls—Rev. J.H. Lloyd—A. Barrett—W.H. Harper—W.C.
Angus—S.E. Thomas—Mr Pattenson. Saw H.N.G.—W.H.G.—S.E.G. Drive with
C. & surveyed 'Lake Superior'. Worked on Elisab. Settlement. Read Kansas
Campaign—Dillon, Irish Banking[1]—Biograph. Magazine.

22. 14 S. Trin.

Ch 11 A.M. & 6½ P.M. Saw Canon Mason—Lady Sandhurst (from Ireland). Read
Life of Baxter[2]—Life of Bunyan[3]—P.P. Keller on Ponsonby Estate.[4] Walk with C.

23. M.

Ch. 8¼ A.M. Wrote to Richard Sleaford Tel.—Rev. J. Blaisdell—Rev. Goodall—
E.A. Fitzroy—Messrs Murray—Hon. J.B. Alley[5]—Rev. C. Ivens—Hon. S. Erskine
—Mr J. Wilson. Saw Lady Sandhurst—Mr W. Bailey. Inspected the new Building
now in progress. Looked up some points, and addressed Deputation from
Hyde: about 40 minutes.[6] Read Kansas Crusade (finished)—Revue Britannique
—Cowpers Tirocinium[7]—and divers works.

24. Tu.

Ch. 8¼ A.M. Wrote to Mrs Bennett—The Home Secy—Mrs Lomas—Rev. C.D.
Pater[8]—R.T. Burnett—C. Edmonds BP—J.W.S. Collie—Mr Hadwen. Spent most
of the day on the Henry VIII records, and Mr Gairdner's Prefaces.[9] Also read
Harwood's Hist. Rebellion 1798—Cowper's Adam,[10] & other Poems—and
[blank.] Saw WHG—HNG.

25. Wed.

Ch. 8¼ AM. Wrote to Sec. G.P.O.—Bull & Auvache—Mr W.R. Thafer—Mr
Malabari—Chas Roeder—Mr A.R. Palgrave—Rev. Strachan—Rev. Marshall—C.
Herbert. Another day mainly on Gairdner—the Records—Bridgett[11]—Dodd[12]—
Soames &c.[13] Read also Harwood. We commenced felling a large chestnut.

---

[1] J. J. Dillon, *Observations in explanation of the provident institutions, usually called savings banks* (1817).
[2] *Reliquiae Baxterianae, or Mr Richard Baxter's narrative of the most memorable passage of his life and times*, 3v. (1696).
[3] Probably E. Venables, *Life of John Bunyan* (1888).
[4] Probably a report brought by Lady Sandhurst.
[5] Perhaps J. H. Alley of the Royal Thames Yacht Club.
[6] *T.T.*, 24 September 1889, 10a.
[7] W. Cowper, 'Tirocinium; or, a Review of Schools'; Gladstone seems to have been using Cowper's *Poems* in the 2v. ed. (1794–5). See also 4 June 26.
[8] Charles Dudley Pater, perpetual curate of St. Anne's, Liverpool.
[9] J. Gairdner in *Calendar of letters and papers, foreign and domestic, of the reign of Henry VIII*, v. nos. 722–5, discussed in *N.C.*, xxvi. 229. See 16 Oct. 88.
[10] See previous day.   [11] See 22 July 88.
[12] See 8 Sept. 78.   [13] See 26 Aug. 60.

26. Th.

Ch 8½ AM. Wrote to Dean of Westmr—Vote Office—E.A. Judges—E. de Mattos. Worked hard on research & writing, chiefly about Fisher. Sat an hour with WHG and told him much of my Father. Read Poganuc folk.[1]

27. Fr.

Ch. 8½ AM. Wrote to Mr Weld Blundell—E. Brown—R. Darlington—W.L. Thomas—Ld Coleridge—Dr Tenison—Miss Hawkins—A.H. Hubbard—Rev. Mr Robinson. Worked again on research, writing, & rewriting. Assisted in felling a big Sp. Chesnut. The Bp[2] & other company came—Harry apparently near a crisis.[3] Read Poganuc folk—Coote's Hist. Irish Union.[4]

28. Sat.

Ch. 8½ A.M. The Bp & Mrs E. went: a good impression. The Rendells went: no crisis. Finished & revised my MS on H. VIII Church Legisl. We kibbled the Chestnut. Finished Poganuc People. Read also [blank.] Wrote to Rev. Sturrock —Mr Knowles—C. Herbert—Mr Whitewell—J. Miller.

29. St Mich. & 15 S. Trin.

Ch. 11 A.M. Cold sent me to bed in the evening. Examined Sander de Schism. & Lewis's Introduction.[5] Dispatched MS. to N.C. Read Beard, Sermons[6]—R. Buchanan's Letter[7]—M'Carthy on Irish College[8]—Hughes, Aspects of Humanity.[9]

30. M.

Bed the whole day. Conversation with H. and H. on Lane End Colliery partnership—With C.G. on H. and M.R.[10] Read many Chapters of Bryce on U.S. Vol. III.[11]

Tues. Oct. One. 89.

Bed all day again, as usual. Planned bookcases. Read more Chapters of Bryce's *great* book—Margot Tennant's extraordinary sketch of L.L. & herself[12]—M. Walsh, His Wife or His Widow.[13]

---

[1] H. B. Stowe, *Poganuc people, their loves and lives* (1878).   [2] Of St. Asaph; H.V.B.

[3] His relations with Maud Rendel (see 18 Sept. 89n.).

[4] C. Coote, *History of the Union of Great Britain and Ireland* (1802).

[5] See 10 Oct. 80 and Gladstone's comments in *Later gleanings*, 222.

[6] C. Beard, *The universal Christ and other sermons* (1888).

[7] R. W. Buchanan, 'On descending into hell, a letter concerning the proposed suppression of literature' (1889).

[8] J. McCarthy in *C.R.*, lvi. 622 (October 1889).

[9] E. Hughes, *Some aspects of humanity* (1888).

[10] i.e. Maud Rendel; see 18 Sept. 89n.   [11] See 27 Dec. 88.

[12] Memoir of Laura Lyttelton by her sister, Margot Tennant (later Asquith); there is a copy in the 'Notebook' in the Bonham Carter MSS in Nuffield College, Oxford. Mary Drew quoted the last two pages in her 'Memoirs of Laura Lyttelton'.

[13] Untraced.

2. *Wed.*

Rose at noon. Wrote to Nat. Bank (Phipps)—Sir J. Pease MP—J. Nicol—J.C. Humphreys—G.H.F. Nye—G.J. Campbell—J. Collings—Mrs Morris—S.H. Scott—J. Samuelson—A. Bradley—Dr Field 1. & BP.—Sec. G.P.O.—Messrs Worthington—Mrs Bennett—Higham—Downing. Finished His Wife or his Widow—read Fields *Irish* Confederates[1]—Delitzsch's Isis[2]—Bryce on America. Kept in my room—blow.

3. *Th.*

Rose at 11. Wrote to Princess of Wales—Mr Bryce MP—E. Sutherland—Rev. A. Cusin[3]—Mr W. Brough—Ld Rosebery—Rivingtons—Rev. Mr Webb—Miss Tennant BP—Hon. Sir H. Parkes—Mrs Smedes[4]—Vote Office—J.D. Dove—Mr S. Rendel BP—E. Tucker. Conversation with Godley—H.N.G. (Lane End Colliery)—and . . . . Read Confederate Irish—Delitzsch, the Iris—New Westmr Review[5]—Howard Collins Epitome.[6] Resumed place at dinner table: party of twelve.

4. *Fr.*

Ch. 8½ A.M. Wrote to Sig. Valery Tel.—Watsons—Capt. Verney—Scotts—Mr Parnell MP.[7]—Rev. A. Jack BP—W.M. Rush U.S.—W. Blair—H. Dickinson—J. Nicol—Earl of Cavan—H.J. Moore—F. Boydell—R. Carbeck—Lady Herbert—Baron Malortie—T.P. O'Connor MP. The Saighton party came over at five. Long conversation with Godley on S. Herbert.[8] Also walk with him. Mary, no doubt from sense of duty, made a conversation which much distressed me, but may do me good.[9] Conversation with Lucy on the subject in evg. Eleven to dinner. Irish conversation with Mrs E. L[yttelton]. I was much pleased. Read Irish Confederates—and Jesuit Letter.[10]

---

[1] H. M. Field, *The Irish Confederates and the rebellion of 1798* (1851).

[2] F. J. Delitzsch, *Isis: studies in colour and talks about flowers*, tr. Rev. A. Cusin (1889).

[3] Had sent his tr.; see previous day.

[4] Susan Dabney Smedes; had probably sent her book, see 7 Oct. 89n.

[5] *Westminster Review*, cxxxii (October 1889).

[6] F. H. Collins, *An epitome of the synthetic philosophy* [of Herbert Spencer], 2v. (1889–94).

[7] Copy at Add MS 44508, f. 10: hoping he can come to Hawarden in the next ten days: '. . . The subjects on which I desire to speak with you as fully as may be are / 1. Changes in the Home Rule plan of 1886. / 2. The Land question. / 3. Your & our position under the commission & the matters therewith immediately connected . . .'.

Parnell replied, 12 October, Add MS 44508, f. 62: 'I have not yet been able to go to Ireland, otherwise I should have arranged to go down to Hawarden some morning by an early train, returning in the evening, but I hope to write you again in a day or two. We expect to get the action tried before the end of the year, or early in the next. It cannot take more than a few days & should certainly be disposed of before the commencement of the Session.' See 18–19 Dec. 89.

[8] See 31 Aug. 89.

[9] No mention of this in Mary's diary; Add MS 46262, f. 114ᵛ.

[10] Sent by Robert Whitty, S.J.; Add MS 44507, f. 232.

5. Sat.

Ch. $8\frac{1}{2}$ A.M. Wrote to Ed. N.A. Review—Ld Granville—Mr Ridler—Messrs Ashworth—Miss Lynch—Mr E. Hubbard[1]—Miss Doyle—Mr A. Morley MP.—C.J. Trusted—T.A. Atkins. Corrected proofs (long delayed) of Free Trade Article for N.A.R.[2] Conversation with Mr Horner[3]—Lucy Cavendish. Directions for the new erection, some particulars. Read Jesuit Letter—Field, Irish Confederates. Tea with the WHGs.

6. 16 S. Trin.

Ch 11 AM with H.C. and $6\frac{1}{2}$ PM. Wrote to Lady Herbert—Mr Bunting—Bishop of Oxford. Corrected proofs of Art. on Henry VIII Church Legisln. Conversation with Lucy—H.N.G. (Mr Mayhew)—Prof. Stuart (Cornish Vacancy). Read Delitzsch on O.T.[4]—Huxley & Swedenborg[5]—Looking Backward.[6]

7. M.

Ch. $8\frac{1}{2}$ A.M. Wrote to Messrs Rothschild—Watsons—Reeves & T.—Scotts l.l.—Wms & Norgate—Westell—Miss B. Barr—Mr J. Ogilvy—Dr Bowles Daly—J.M. Russell[7]—H.E. Ivimey [*sic*?]—J. Johnston—Mr Higham—Messrs Brough. Eleven to dinner. Kibbling after the storm. Long conversation with H.N.G.—conversation with Lucy. Tea with the W.H.G.s. Read Looking Backward—Memoirs of Southern Planter[8]—Harwood, Rebellion of 1798—Field, Irish Confederates (finished).

8. Tu.

Ch. $8\frac{1}{2}$ A.M. Wrote to Hon. A. Hubbard—Mrs Hill—Ld Coleridge—Mrs Morgan—Mr Humphreys—A. Inland—Mr Conbrough—Rev. Beard—Mr A. Morley—Mr S. Laing—Rev. Whitty S.J.—Mr Weld Blundell. Saw H.N.G. (respecting Mayhew &c.)—Mr Mayhew—at much length. Kibbling at the Rectory. Face ache came on. Read Southern Planter—Wallace on Land Nationalisation[9]—Jacob on Education in India.[10] Arranging letters.

9. Wed.

My night was sleepless: but the pain was not severe. Church $8\frac{1}{2}$ A.M. Wrote to D. of Argyll l. & BP.—Mr Knowles BP. article with final corrections—Ld Gran-

---

[1] Evelyn Hubbard (s. of J. G. Hubbard), tory candidate in dispute on Gladstone's remarks about Irish representation; Add MS 44508, f. 22 and *T.T.*, 8 October 1889, 6b.

[2] See 10 Dec. 88.

[3] John Francis Fortescue Horner of Mells, 1842–1927; staying at the Castle with his wife Frances; a prominent liberal family; H.V.B.

[4] F. J. Delitzsch, *Old testament history of redemption* (1881).

[5] R. L. Tafel, *Huxley and Swedenborg. The claims of agnosticism critically examined* (1889).

[6] E. Bellamy, *Looking backward, 2000–1887* (1888).

[7] James M. Russell, farmer, of Portobello; on liberal affairs; Add MS 44508, f. 32.

[8] S. D. Smedes, *Memorials of a southern planter* [T. S. G. Dabney] (1887); for Gladstone's review, see 4 Nov. 89.

[9] A. R. Wallace, *The 'why' and the 'how' of land nationalization* (1883).

[10] Probably Sir G. Jacob, *English government of India* (1860).

ville—J. Westell—Messrs Ashworth—W. Michil [*sic*]—Rivingtons—Mrs H. Shaw—Mr Childers—Ld Cavan—Miss Woodall—Ld Houghton—Mr Hallamby. Conversation with Willy & Gerty. Read Southern Planter—Ld Houghton's verses[1]—Hervey on Federation[2]—Schutz on Welsh Tradition.[3] Drive with C.

10. Th.

Ch. 8¼ A.M. Wrote to Rev. Father Gasquet[4]—Mr C. Flower MP.—D. Lowe— Hon. A. Hubbard—Mr H. Hoare—Ld Brassey—C.H. Hazzard—C.H. Clayton— R.W. Montagu—Mr J. Knowles—Mr Fantoli—J.M. Russell. Proem to MS. on H.S. Kibbled at the Rectory. Read Houghton's Verses—Southern Planter—Schulz.

11. Fr.

Ch. 8½ AM. Wrote to Supt LNW Goods—Sec. G. Trunk—Mr Childers—Mr E. Hubbard—J.L. Miller—J.C. Humphreys—J. Nicol—Herr Fleischer—W. Lane. Read Southern Planter—Bismarck's Map of Europe[5]—Schultz (finished)— and [blank.] Kibbling. Tea with WHGs. Conversation with Lucy.

12. Sat.

Ch. 8¼ A.M. Wrote to Messrs Harrison—J. Ogilvy—Mr Wemyss Reid—Riving- tons—Prof. Freeman—Clay & Sons—Mrs Smedes—W.H.G.—Mr Timpany—Mr Knowles—Brisbane Tel. Finished the remarkable Biography of Dabney—read Munro on Canadian Constitution[6]—Ld Elphin (poor)[7]—Mids. Dream (good).[8] Tea with W.H.G.s. Again inspected the Building.

13. 17 S. Trin.

Ch. mg & evg. Wrote to Farnworth Local Bd—Mr Knowles—Mr Bickerdyke— Ld Acton—Rev. Mr Connell—A.C. Sheen. Read Aubry Moore Science & Faith[9]—Delitzsch on O.T.—Life of B.V.M. Conversation with Lucy on detach- ment, & my own case which I could not make good to her satisfaction.

14. M.

Ch. 8¼ A.M. Wrote to Dean of St Paul's—Sir R. Peel—R. Johnson—B. Quaritch— Messrs Ashworth—Mrs Beer—Bull & Auvache—W. Ridler—Mr Channing MP.

---

[1] R. O. A. Milnes, Lord Houghton, *Gleanings from Béranger* (1889); sent by Houghton, Add MS 44508, f. 30.

[2] Earlier version, untraced, of M. H. Hervey, *The trade policy of imperial federation from an economic point of view* (1892).

[3] A. Schulz, *An essay on the influence of Welsh tradition* (1841).

[4] Francis Aidan Gasquet, 1846–1929; prior of Downside 1878–85; an historian of considerable unreliability; haphazardly ed. Acton's letters (including some of Gladstone's) in *Lord Acton and his circle* (n.d.).

[5] Possibly *Bismarck's deeds and aims* (1889).

[6] J. E. C. Munro, *The constitution of Canada* (1889).

[7] Probably *Passages in the life of Sir L. Elphin of Castle Weary*, 2v. (1889); a novel.

[8] 'John Bickerdyke' (the pseudonym of Charles Henry Cook), of Donnington Newbury, sent his *Irish Midsummernight's Dream* (1889); a fairy-tale.

[9] See 12 May 89.

Saw Mr Henslow—S.E.G. Drive with C. A hard morning's work in establishing a sort of order in my room. Read Trussardi's Tracts[1]—Ly Lyttelton's Letters[2]—Life of Mad. Roland.[3]

15. *Tu.*

Ch. 8½ A.M. Wrote to S.L.—Br. Museum—A. Robertson—Ld Acton—C.E. Wilson—J. Pierson—Jas Knowles—W. Urwick. Long conversation with Harcourt on Ireland.[4] Walk with Marjoribanks and party.—Conversation with M. Twelve to dinner (8 yesty). Saw Lucy on her verses. Examining books. Read Life of Madame Roland. Conversation with Charles[5] on Hagley & Hawarden matters.

16. *Wed.*

Ch. 8½ A.M. Wrote to Mr Parnell—Miss M. Blind[6]—Mr Hulbert—J. Knowles—Mr Quaritch—W.H.G.—(Mr Lavis)—Grogan & Boyd—A. Ireland—Town Clerk of Nottm. Conversation with Mr Rendel on HNG[7]—with do & Charles on the Mayhew arrangements. Saw Lucy on her verses. Mr Mayhew, & W.H.G.s respecting him. Walk with Mary Cobham: she is a gem.

17. *Th.*

Ch. 8½ A.M. Wrote to Mr P.W. Campbell—Mr L. Tait—Dean of Durham—Rev. Collins—Messrs Sotheran—R. Russell—J.P. Hartley—Sidney Lee[8]—Messrs Harrison—J. Ogilvy—J. Serjeant—A.G. Symonds—Miss Tennant—Mr Melhuish—W. Henderson. Old party went—Ripons came: & Mr Stephenson.[9] Read Bute on Scots Home Rule[10]—Miss Blind's Mad. Roland—Robertson's Claverhouse.[11]

18. *Fr. St Luke.*

Ch. 8½ A.M. Wrote to Mr Weld Blundell—Mr Knowles—Rev. G.E. Mason—Hugh Lloyd—Messrs Methuen[12]—Press Assocn—Messrs Murray. Saw Mr Stevenson. Walk with Ld Ripon and much conversation. Eight to dinner. Ld Granville came: & Mr Morley. Read Mad. Roland—and [blank.]

---

[1] G. Trussardi, 'Gallofobia e monumento-mania' (1888); 'Lettera aperta a S S Leone XIII' (1888).

[2] MS version of *Correspondence of Sarah Spencer, Lady Lyttelton, 1787–1870*, ed. Mrs. H. Wyndham with an introduction by Lady F. Cavendish (1912).

[3] M. Blind, *Madame Roland* (1886).

[4] Harcourt favoured retention of all Irish M.P.s at Westminster and opposed public discussion of the details of a future Irish Government Bill; Gardiner, ii. 148–9.

[5] C. G. Lyttelton, Lord Cobham (see 27 Oct. 42), staying at the Castle with his wife Mary.

[6] Mathilde Blind, poet and writer; her writings interested Gladstone in Marie Bashkirtseff.

[7] His engagement; see 18 Sept. 89.

[8] Lee had sent the proof of the *D.N.B.* article on Sir Stephen Glynne; Add MS 44508, f. 70.

[9] Not further identified; did not sign H.V.B.

[10] Lord Bute, 'Parliament in Scotland', *Scottish Review*, xiv. 399 (October 1889).

[11] A. Robertson, *Lectures . . . on John Claverhouse and his times* (1889).

[12] London publishers of T. Raleigh's *Irish politics*, about whose p. 83 Gladstone complained; see Add MS 44508, f. 90.

19.

Ch. 8¼ A.M. Wrote to Archbishop Walsh—Ld Granville—G. Norway—Mrs Wickham—R.W. Davey—Ld Blachford—G. Antinori—Messrs Goodwin. Walk with the party. Irish conversation with G.R. & M.[1] Italian & French talk with G. Read Mad. Roland (finished)—Boutmy Etudes.[2] Eleven to dinner.

20. 18 S. Trin.

Ch mg & [blank.] Wrote to C.D. Stanniford—R. Mackinnon—F.M. Allen—H. Penn—Dowager Ly Sandhurst—E. Evans—C.W. Macminn—J. Knowles—Rev. Giddins—T. Burford—Messrs Humphreys. Took the party to the New Building & the Station. Saw Mr Morley. Read Driver on Isaiah[3]—Delitzsch O.T. on Redemption—Life of Alberti (Jenkins).[4]

21. M.

Ch. 8½ A.M. Wrote to Sir J. Lacaita l. & BP.—Ld Rosebery—Ld Kimberley—T.D. Dowson—Messrs Harrison—Abp Walsh—E.P.S. Greene—Wms & Norgate. Sharp testimonial. Saw Ld Granville (H.R. &c)—Mr Rendel—on domestic affairs—S.E.G. on arrangements. Read Alberti's Life (finished)—Boutmy on the Constitution—Miss Blind's Poems[5]—Lewin's Poems[6]—&c. Sat to Rev. Palmer (Photogr.) Kibbling at the Rectory. Tea with the W.H.G.s.

22. Tu. [Ince Blundell, Lancashire]

Ch. 8¼ A.M. Wrote to Mr Humphreys—Mr A. Morley—H.R. Clayton—Mr S. Walpole—Mrs Crawford—A. Stoneham—T. Baker—Miss Molyneux—Ed. Graphic.[7] At 2.45 off to Ince Blundell.[8] From Lime St we drove over near 7 miles of town. A most kind reception. Read Spencer's Life of Walpole[9]—Boutmy, Droit Constitut.—Thomas a Kempis.

23. Wed.

C. ill: a sharp attack. Saw Dr R. Notes & references for Southport. Procession through the streets. Spoke 1 h. 10 m.[10] Narrow escape from a bad chill. Saw old faces & new. Read Life of Ld J.R.—Cavalier's Note Book & Introdn[11] Saw the statuary.

---

[1] i.e. Granville, Ripon and Morley.

[2] E. G. Boutmy, *Etudes du droit constitutionnel* (1885); on France, Britain, U.S.A., sent by Dorothy Tennant; Add MS 44508, f. 71.

[3] *Biblical commentary on the prophecies of Isaiah by F. Delitzsch, with introduction by S. R. Driver* (1890).

[4] R. C. Jenkins, *The life of Valentin Alberti* (1889).

[5] M. Blind, *The ascent of Man* (1889).

[6] Perhaps H. Lewin, *Poema morale* (1881).   [7] Not found published.

[8] Seat of Charles Joseph Weld-Blundell, 1845–1927 (s. of Gladstone's colleague, see 16 Sept. 65); Roman catholic diplomat, connoisseur, journalist and liberal; contested Preston 1885.

[9] Slip of the pen for S. Walpole, *The life of Lord John Russell*, 2v. (1889), sent by the author; Gladstone had assisted in its preparation.

[10] *T.T.*, 24 October 1889, 12a.

[11] W. Blundell, *A cavalier's note book . . . with introductory chapters by . . . T. E. Gibson* (1880).

24. Th.

Wrote to Duke of Argyll—Mrs Drew—Arth. Gladstone—Mr Murray—Lady Derby—D.R. Aitken—Mr Lefevre Mp.—Mr A. Wildman tel. Read Life of Ld Russell—Cavalier's Note Book. Saw house, garden, water, wood: the trees here are for this country almost a prodigy. Southport Depn. Saw the school children. C. very decidedly better. Much conversation with Mrs Stourton.

[1] 25. Fr. [Courthey]

Wrote to Herbert G. Walks & conversations: tree planting &c. I left C. as a matter of prudence & went off to a pre-arranged dinner party at Courthey. Saw Mrs Stevenson—G. Melly—Mrs R.G.—Nurse. Read Walpole's Ld J.R.

26. Sat. [Hawarden]

Worked up my thoughts a little & delivered an hour's address at Saltney.[2] Courthey kind as ever: but there is a want of life. Read Walpole. Saw the buildings. Home at 6: C. also.

27. 19 S. Trin.

Ch. mg & evg. Wrote to Mr Blundell—and Mr Murray B.P. Read L'Evangeliste[3]—Wilkinson on E. Arnold (valuable on Buddhism)[4]—and N.T., Maldonatus, Wordsworth, Rigaud, &c. with a view to the N.A.R. questions on Divorce.[5]

28. M. SS. Simon & Jude.

Ch. 8½ A.M. Wrote to Mr Ll. Bryce l. & B.P.—Scotts—Messrs Methuen—C.W. Wilson—Hodgson Pratt—Dr Preston—Mrs Branson B.P.[6]—C.L. Lewis—Ld Kimberley B.P.—A.G. Bowie—Canon MacColl—G.E. Pozzi—H.C. Marshall—J.O. Bingham. Mlle. Janotti[7] came & played brilliantly for us. Saw Mr Mayhew—Also Humphreys foreman. Wrote paper on the Marriage Queries for N.A.R. & dispatched it.[8] Read Walpole's Ld Russell. Sir A. West came: conversation.

---

[1] Gladstone here turned two pages, but after filling Lambeth 1453, ff. 36–7, returned to fill ff. 34–5, before continuing on f. 38. Courthey was the home of his brother Robertson's family.

[2] On the progress of the working classes; *T.T.*, 28 October 1889, 8a.

[3] A. Daudet, *L'Evangeliste, roman parisien* (1883).

[4] W. C. Wilkinson, *Edwin Arnold as poetizer and as paganiser* (1884).

[5] J. Maldonatus, *Commentary on the Holy Gospels*, 2v. (1888); S. J. Rigaud, *The influence of Holy Scripture* (1856); see next day.

[6] Mrs. Juliet Branson, 'a fellow student of Marie Bastikirtseff' [*sic*]; Add MS 44508, f. 85.

[7] Natalie Janotti; signed herself in H.V.B. as 'Court pianist to Emperor of Germany'.

[8] 'The question of divorce', *N.A.R.*, cxlix. 641 (November 1889); a reply to four questions posed by the editor. Gladstone stated that 'remarriage is not admissible under any circumstances or conditions whatsoever'; he discussed the 1857 Divorce Act, arguing 'Unquestionably, since that time, the standard of conjugal morality has perceptibly declined among the higher classes of this country, and scandals in respect to it have become more frequent. Personally, I believe it to be due in part to this great innovation in our marriage laws; but in part only, for other disintegrating causes have been at work.'

29. Tu.

Ch. 8½ A.M. Wrote to Sir W. Harcourt—Sir A. Gordon—Mr Labouchere—Mr G. Potter—Mr W. Mitchell—Rev. Bainton—Dr Lewin—Mr Thos Hall—C. Adley—M. Superior of St Andrew's Midl.[1]—H. Frisby—D. Kaye—Watkinson tel. Nine to dinner. Saw Mr Armitstead—Sir A. West—A. Morley: all here. Walk with West. Copied out some Homeric bases. Read Life of Ld J.R.

30. Wed.

Ch. 8½ A.M. Wrote to The Rector—Watsons—Lady Russell—A. Arnold[2]—Mr S. Walpole—J.W. Wood[3]—Father Christie[4]—T.W. Wheeler—Mr P. Bunting—Princ. Librarian B.M.—Messrs Trübner[5]—Jas Johnstone. Walk with West & Mr Armitstead: New Library &c. Conversation with A. Morley on affairs. Read Walpole's Lord J.R. And 19th Cent. Jessop v. Perry.[6] Worked on Homeric MS.

31. Th.

Ch. 8½ A.M. Showed new Library (qy name it Monad)[7] to A.M. Wrote to Rev. D. Mitchell—V. Oger—Rev. C. Woodcock—F.W. Aveling—G.H.W. Cambry—W.H. Dawson[8]—T.B. Woodward—Miss A. Wright—Miss Thompson—Ed. N.A.R. Tel.—Rev. Dr Cox—Vote Office. Kibbling at the Rectory. Read Walpole—N.C. on Church of Rome[9]—City of Sarras.[10] Work on Homeric MS.

Frid. Nov One 89. All Saints.

Ch. 8½ A.M. Wrote to Sec. Saltney Library—Mr Murray—J. Nicol—W. Agnew—R. Hunt—E.L. Stanley—A. Sutton—S.A.K. Strahan—A.G. Symonds—A.E. Stanton—Davis Clancy. Worked on Homeric MS. Work at The Monad: and kibbling at Rectory. Read Ld J. Russell Vol II—The Resident Magistrate[11]—The New Review—Italy—on Bye Elections.[12]

2. Sat.

Ch. 8½ A.M. Wrote to Ld Granville—Mr T. Ashton—Editor Tablet[13]—J.F. Wilson—T.P. Crosland[14]—Mr Bunting—T.C. Collins—Messrs Robn & Nichn. Saw Mr Mayhew on the Estate Catastrophe of 1847.[15] Kibbling at the Rectory. Worked on Homeric MS. Read Walpole's Ld J.R.—and Reviews.

---

[1] Rescue work.
[2] On disestablishment; Add MS 44508, f. 102 and *T.T.*, 16 November 1889, 10f.
[3] On land reform; *T.T.*, 4 November 1889, 8a.
[4] See 5 Sept. 69. Correspondence 1889–90 in Hawn P.
[5] London booksellers.   [6] *N.C.*, xxvi. 825 (November 1889).
[7] The ultimate unity of being, a simple organism. See Introduction above, section I.
[8] Perhaps William Harbutt Dawson, 1860–1948; journalist and historian, specialising in German affairs.
[9] *N.C.*, xxvi. 801 (November 1889).   [10] U. A. Taylor, *City of Sarras* (1887).
[11] B. Marnan, *The resident magistrate* (1889?).   [12] *New Review*, i. 532, 561 (November 1889).
[13] Dispute with *The Tablet*'s comments on his remarks about Henry VIII and the Church; see 16 Sept. 89n. and Add MS 44508, f. 116.
[14] Of Birkby Grange, Huddersfield, on trade unions; *T.T.*, 12 November 1889, 8b.
[15] i.e. the Oak Farm bankruptcy; see above, iii. xliii.

3. 20 S. Trin.

Ch mg (with H.C.) and evg. Read Bp Goodwin, Foundations of Belief[1]—L'Evangeliste (Daudet)—Bp of Exeter's Address.[2] Visited Marg. Hughes:[3] my junior by 4½ months.

4. M.

Ch. 8½ A.M. Wrote to Dowager Ly Sandhurst—Bp of Carlisle—Bp of Exeter—Bp of Oxford BP.—W.E. Feldnish—J.S. Wood—Geo. Milne—Mr Beddard[4]—Mr Knowles—E.H. Nash[5]—Mr Bryce MP—W. Evans. Wrote Notice of Mrs Smede's remarkable book for N.C.[6] Wrote MS. on male succession for the Estate.[7] Read Walpoles Lord J.R.—L'Evangeliste.

5. Tu.

Ch. 8½ A.M. Wrote to Mr H.J. Bannerman—Mr A. Austin—Mrs Th.—Mr A. Morley MP—E. Gosse[8]—C. Lancaster—J. Murray—Homersham Cox—Robn & N.—Vedova Riccio[9]—Mrs Smedes. Worked on MS of Electoral Facts.[10] Worked on cutting a large peartree for S. Read Ld Russell—L'Evangeliste.

6. Wed.

Ch 8½ A.M. Wrote to Rev. C. Caverns[11]—Mr Downing—H. Coxon—J. Macveagh—Mr Dobell—Jas Baker—S.A.K. Strahan—Miss Wilson—R. Congreve—Sec. Anatol. Omospondias. Worked on Electoral Facts. Finished Walpole's Ld Russell: a weighty book. Read Comte's Appeal to Conservatives[12]—and L'Evangeliste. Drive with C.

7. Th.

Ch 8½ A.M. Wrote to A Morley MP. l.l.—Sotherans—Messrs Crowell—A. Sutton—Rev. W. Barker—Ellis & Elvey[13]—W.E.A. Coxon—J. Bennet—W.H. Prees—Editor of Wit & Wisdom.[14] Woodcraft with S.E.G. Worked through my MS on

---

[1] H. Goodwin, *The foundations of the creed* (1889).

[2] E. H. Bickersteth, 'The opening address at the Exeter diocesan conference' (1889).

[3] Of the village.

[4] Frank E. Beddard, London zoologist; about a book plate; Hawn P.

[5] Edward Henry Nash of Exeter college, Oxford, had inquired about forming a 'Gladstone Essay Society'; Hawn P. No such society seems to have been established.

[6] 'Memorials of a Southern Planter', *N.C.*, xxvi. 984 (December 1889). See 7 Oct. 89.

[7] Mem. untraced.

[8] (Sir) Edmund William Gosse, 1849-1928; man of letters; lecturer at Trinity, Cambridge 1885-90.

[9] *Sic*; unidentified.

[10] 'Electoral facts of today (No. II)', *N.C.*, xxvi. 1056 (December 1889).

[11] Of Colorado, had sent his work (probably a sermon); see 10 Nov. 89; Hawn P.

[12] I. A. M. F. X. Comte, *Appeal to conservatives* (1889).

[13] London booksellers.

[14] *Wit and Wisdom*, 9 November 1889, contained a long letter to Gladstone, dated 4 November, by 'Roderick Random'; but no reply found.

Electoral Facts. Read L'Evangeliste—Metzerott Shoemaker[1]—and Magyar Folk Lore.[2]

8. Fr.

Ch. 8½ A.M. Wrote to Jules Joissant—Scotts—Mr Rideing—Mr Smith (16)—Mrs Reancy—Rev. Mitchell—Ld Rosebery—A.W. Pollard[3]—J. Flint—C. Waddy—Rev. J. Morgan Jones.[4] 10½–12. With Humphreys & Bailey, settling particulars of the new Building. Walk with Mr Holiday[5] in the woods. Read L'Evangeliste—J. Morley's Walpole[6]—and Metzerott.

9. Sat.

Ch. 8½ A.M. Wrote to Mr P.W. Campbell—Ld Spencer—Mr Ridler—Mr J.W. Wood—C. Mackson—Messrs Duncan & Martin. Worked much on measuring books & planning bookcases: and saw W. Bailey thereupon & as to Octagon & so forth. Saw Ld Blantyre at tea with W.H.G.s. Willy came out with me to the door: I thought it marked a stage. Finished L'Evangéliste—read Mezzerott—Morley's Walpole.

10. 21 S. Trin.

Ch 11 AM & [blank] P.M. Wrote to Cardinal Manning—Mr A.W. Hutton—Mr J.C. Cox—Ld Rosebery—Mr A. Morley. Read Lyall's Poems[7]—Tablet Articles on W.E.G.[8]—Caverns on Marriage Laws[9]—'Whither' by Dr Briggs.[10] Visit to 'The Hall'.

11. M.

Ch. 8½ A.M. Wrote to Sig. G.B. Plini[11]—Mr Morley MP—Ellis & Elvey—Mrs Smedes—Messrs Clark—R. Gowring—Jas Knowles—Miss D. Tennant—Messrs Watson & Smith—Messrs W. & J. Bailey. Corrected proofs Horticultural Address—and of the Dabney Notice.[12] Read J. Morley's Walpole—Mezzerott—and [blank.] Walked with Lady E. Grey[13] in the Park &c.

---

[1] [K. P. Woods], *Metzerott, Shoemaker* (1889); a novel.
[2] *Folk tales of the Magyars* (1889).
[3] Pollard (see 10 Jan. 87) asked permission to use some of Gladstone's translations; Hawn P.
[4] On Welsh disestablishment; *T.T.*, 13 November 1889, 10f.
[5] The London artist whom he had met in 1887; see 12 May 87.
[6] J. Morley, *Walpole* (1888).
[7] A. C. Lyall, *Verses written in India* (1889); sent by Dorothy Tennant; Add MS 44508, f. 131.
[8] 'Mr. Gladstone's charge against Blessed John Fisher', and letters; *The Tablet*, 9 November 1889, 725, 740. See also 2 Nov. 89.
[9] Untraced; see 6 Nov. 89n.
[10] C. A. Briggs, *Whither? A theological question for the times* (1889).
[11] Of Naples; had sent a work on Italian politics; Add MS 44508, f. 134 and Hawn P.
[12] See 4 Nov. 89.
[13] Lady Elizabeth Anne Grey, wife of F. R. Grey, rector of Morpeth.

12. Tu.

Ch. 8½ A.M. Wrote to Mr Chewan 1. & BP.—A Morley MP.—G. Milne BP.[1]—Rev. Dr. Hutton—Lt Col. Ford—Mr Murray BP.—E.A. Kent—J.M. Skinner—H. Hadwen—J.R.W. Clark—M. Gemmell—Mr Wordsworth Donisthorpe[2]—Mr Willis Q.C.[3] Corrected proofs of Address at Saltney. Drive with C. Read Morley's Walpole—Geo. Eliot on Young.[4]

13. Wed.

Ch. 8½ A.M.

Wrote to		Rev. Mr Mitchell
Sir J.R.G.		T.G. Marshall
A.L.G.		H. Taylor
J.E.G.	BP	Sidney Lee[5]
Mrs Bennett		Miss Wilson
Mr T.G. Law		Messrs Forman
Rev. Walker		Mr Channing MP
Messrs Robertson & N.		H.N.G.

Tea with the W.H.G.s. Finished G. Eliot on Young—read G.E. on H. Heine—The Church & the Franchise[6]—and Mezzerot.

14. Th.

Ch. 8½ A.M. Wrote to Maud Rendel—J.A. Jones B.P.—Vote Office H. of C.—Scotts—Wms & Norgate—J.W. Woods—W. Fraser Rae[7]—J. Glennon—P.W. Clayden. Worked on Electoral Statistics. And on moving books. Read N.A.R. on Divorce—G. Eliot on H. Heine & Dr C.—The Resident Magistrate.

15. Fr.

Ch. 8½ A.M. Wrote to Dr Goulburn—Mr Knowles—Mr Robinson BP.—Mr Morley MP.—E.W. Fitcher—Miss [sc. Mrs.] Visger—J.F. Moulton—L. Appleton—D.F. Goddard—J. Ogilvy—W. Officer—Thos Gibson. Finished Ms. on Electoral Facts & sent it to press.[8] Walked with Mr Atkinson (U.S.).[9] Read G. Eliot on Dr Cumming—Miss Visger 'After Shipwreck'[10]—Willis on Burke.[11]

---

[1] George Milne of Upper Norwood, asked, apparently unsuccessfully, permission to reprint a speech; Hawn P.   [2] See 31 July 88.
[3] William Willis, 1835–1911; Q.C. and liberal M.P. Colchester 1880–5; contested seats 1885–6; his recreation was 'speaking to everybody he met' (W.W.W., i. 768).
[4] Start of reading of various pieces in George Eliot, *Essays and leaves from a notebook*, ed. C. T. Lewes (1884).
[5] Who had sent 'specially prepared copies' of the *D.N.B.* articles on Sir J. Gladstone and Sir S. Glynne which Gladstone had improved; Add MS 44508, ff. 138, 150.
[6] A. S. Lamb, *The church and the franchise* (1886).
[7] William Fraser Rae, 1835–1905; barrister and author; had sent his book (see 22 Nov. 89); Hawn P.
[8] See 5 Nov. 89.   [9] Not further identified; did not sign H.V.B.
[10] Mrs Jean A. Visger, *After shipwreck* (1889); probably sent by the author.
[11] W. Willis, *Edmund Burke; the story of his life* (1888).

16. Sat.

Ch. 8½ A.M. Wrote to Mr Macmillan—Ld Spencer—Robn & Nichn—J. Westell—Mr [W.] Seath 1 & BP.—A. Warren—Mr Haughton—Moderator of H. Constables. Worked on Homeric MS. And on books. Saw Mr Mayhew. Read G. Eliot on Lecky—Leger on AustroHungary[1] and Bury on E.R. Empire.[2]

17. 22 S. Trin.

Ch. mg & evg. Wrote to Mr Ashton—Ld Acton. Read Bleck-Wellhausen[3]—Homersham Cox's Review[4]—Bury on Chrysostom &c.—Rost on the Higher Criticism.[5]

18. M.

Ch. 8½ A.M. Wrote to Rev. Dr Goulburn—W. Ridler—Lady Milbank—Mr Clayden—Rev. J.T. Bramston—Mr Bunting—Mr Mackinnon[6]—Mr Cox (Tablet).[7] Wrote on H.S. Worked on planning book cases: & on books. Drive with C. Read G. Eliot on Riehl—Muir's History Vol. VIII.

19. Tues.

Ch. 8½ A.M. Wrote to Mr Watkin Lumley—W.H. Chadwick[8]—H. Scarlet—G.S. Alexander—Mr Potter MP—R.C. Richardson—S. Hallifax—Mr R. Anderson[9]—J.H. Harley—Col. McHardy.[10] Worked on proofs (Electoral Facts). Much bothered with the figures. 12–1½. Long conversation with Harry on his difficult position in his firm now further complicated.[11] Drive with C. Read G. Eliot Essays—City of Sarras[12]—Hume on Charles II 1678-80.[13]

20. Wed.

Ch. 8½ A.M. Wrote to Mr Hamilton Aidé[14]—Sir Thos. Acland—Dr J. Mairr—Mrs Engledew—P. Sheridan—D. Soteriades—J.S. Pigott—Duke of Argyll—Mrs Riley—Mr Knowles BP—Dr E. Leethon—Mr W. Seath BP.—Mr Rowlands MP.[15]

[1] L. P. M. Leger, *A history of Austro-Hungary from the earliest times to the year 1889* (1889).

[2] J. B. Bury, *A history of the later Roman Empire*, 2v. (1889).

[3] Untraced.   [4] See 24 Jan. 86?   [5] Untraced.

[6] Of Glasgow; on negotiations with Salisbury in 1885; *T.T.*, 20 November 1889, 11f.

[7] John George Snead Cox, editor of *The Tablet*; see 25 Aug. 88.

[8] Thanking W. H. Chadwick, old Chartist (see 22 Sept. 88) for a picture and a description of the Peterloo Massacre; Gladstone's reply compared Mitchelstown to Peterloo, and was published; Add MS 44508, f. 182.

[9] (Sir) Robert Anderson, 1841-1918; assistant commissioner of metropolitan police, and head of C.I.D.; on the 'Genesis' controversy with Huxley; Add MS 44508, f. 180. See 15 Dec. 89n.

[10] Lt. col. A. B. McHardy of Edinburgh, on records of toll-booths there; Hawn P.

[11] Presumably by his impending marriage.

[12] See 31 Oct. 89.

[13] In vol. ii of Hume's *History of England*; see 16 Apr. 25.

[14] Charles Hamilton Aidé, 1826-1907; author and musician; had sent his *Songs without music* (3rd ed. 1889); Add MS 44508, f. 179.

[15] Probably William Bowen Rowlands, 1837-1906; barrister and liberal M.P. Cardiganshire 1886-95.

Worked on books: on Homeric MS. Read Bury's Hist.—City of Sarras—L'Age des Etoiles[1]—Remarques sur l'Angleterre 1713.[2] Conversation with S.E.G. on *name* for the new Building. Woodcraft with Herbert. I play second fiddle.

21. Th.

Ch. 8½ A.M. Wrote to Mr Donisthorpe—Lady Taylor—Rivingtons—M. Janssen—Vote Office—J.H. Carter—Lady Lanerton—Mr T. Caldwell. Woodcraft with Herbert. Worked on books. Began MS. on the Melbourne ministry & Lord J. Russell.[3] Read Bury, Later R. Empire—W. Donisthorpe on Tithe &c.[4]—Maygrove.[5]

22. Fr.

Ch. 8½ A.M. Wrote to Mr Stuart Rendel—Mr Knowles—Rev. A. Thomson—A. Sutton—J.C.F. Stevenson—Mr Rolfe—Mr Bennett—Mr W. Evans—W.H. Hindley—Dr Grosart. Saw Bailey on the Building & Bookcases. Saw H.J.G. on the Malleson business.[6] Worked on books. Read Bury's Hist.—Pennell Tour in Scotland[7]—Maygrove.

23. Sat.

Ch. 8½ A.M. Wrote to Rivingtons—Mr J. Forrest—Mrs Bolton—Messrs Clowes. Deputation of workmen at 11½ from Manchester to present a Portmanteau: a small speech.[8] At 1½–3½ the Dee Bridge party came to luncheon & to present a clock to Mr Cochrane. Small speech again.[9] Saw Sir E. Watkin—Mr R. Meade—Ld Acton: walks & much conversation. Long conversation with Mr S. Rendel in evg on the Tithe, & the meditated tack. Read Melbourne Papers.[10] Fourteen to dinner.

24. Preadv. Sunday.

Ch 11 AM 6½ P.M. Saw WHGs. Walk & conversation with Acton. Wrote to Mr Knowles. Fourteen to dinner: too many for Sunday. Read Schrader[11]—The New Priest[12]—How we came by our Bible.[13]

---

[1] J. Janssen, *L'age des étoiles* (1887).
[2] L. F. Dubois de Saint-Gelais, *Remarques sur l'Angleterre faites en 1713* (1717).
[3] 'The Melbourne government: its acts and persons', *N.C.*, xxvii. 38 (January 1890).
[4] Untraced article or pamphlet by Wordsworth Donisthorpe, probably sent by him; see this day.
[5] W. Fraser Rae, *Maygrove, a family history*, 3v. (1889).
[6] Apparently estate business.
[7] J. Pennell, *Our journey to the Hebrides* (1889).
[8] *T.T.*, 25 November 1889, 6f.
[9] No report found.
[10] L. C. Sanders, with a preface by Lord Cowper, *Lord Melbourne's papers* (1889); for Gladstone's review, see 21 Nov. 89.
[11] Probably E. Schrader, *The cuneiform inscriptions and the old testament*, 2v. (1885–8).
[12] R. Lowell, *The new priest in Conception Bay* (1889).
[13] J. P. Smythe, *How we got our bible* (1886).

25. M.

Ch. 8½ A.M. Wrote to Rev. Dr Momerie—H. French—M.W. Borley—F.C. Lynch—Mrs M. Evans—W. Murray—Messrs Gill (Dubl.)—John Rae—Rev. Mr Suffield—Rivingtons. Full conversation with Mr Rendel on settlements & marriage arrangements: most satisfactory. Walk with R. Meade. Read Melbourne Papers—Maygrove.

26. Tu.

Ch. 8½ AM. Wrote to Mr Holms Ivory—Mrs Bolton—Sir R. Welby—A. Morley MP.—Mr Lloyd Bryce—Scotts—Dr Collins—Rev. Jas Hay—H.M. Oliver. Twelve to dinner. Saw Mr Mayhew—Also H.N.G. & H.J.G. on mine-arrangements (Lane End).[1] Read Melbourne Papers—Torrens's Lord Melbourne[2]—Maygrove. Worked on Melbourne Govt MS.[3]

27. Wed.

Ch. 8½ A.M. Wrote to Mr Norbury Williams—Mr Murray—A.K. Durham—Mr Godley—Rev. J.A. Smith—T. Moss—Mr Stringfellow—R. Fournet—Mr Banister —Mr Humphreys. Read Maygrove—Melbourne Papers—Laveleye on the Situation.[4] Worked 'some' on Melbourne MS.

28. Th.

Ch. 8½ AM. Wrote to Ld Granville—Mrs Bolton—T.W. Camn [*sic*]—Mr Cox— W.F. Tupper[5]—Vote Office—Mr Fox. Read Melbourne Papers—Torrens Melbourne—Maygrove—Fox Key to Irish question[6]—New Amazonia.[7] Saw H.J.G.

29. Fr.

Ch. 8½ A.M. and Holy Communion. Wrote to Lady Herbert—Mrs Th.—Sir A. Gordon—C. Bullock—W.H. Rideing—H. Buckley—Rev. J. Miller—D.B. Boyle— T.C. Horsfall—Earl Spencer KG. Saw Rev. S.E.G.—W.H.G.—H.J.G.—on business. Also long & full conversation with Harry on the complex question between him & his senior partner.[8] Read Howley on Prussian Education[9]—Captain Lobe[10]—Various Tracts—and . . . . .

---

[1] One of a series of negotiations about the Hawarden coal mines, leading to the replacement of Mayhew as mineral adviser by Mr. Tansley; see Thomas, *Gladstone of Hawarden*, 147–8.
[2] W. T. MacCullagh Torrens, *Memoirs of . . . Melbourne* (1878, new ed. 1890).
[3] See 21 Nov. 89.
[4] Untraced article.
[5] Son of M. F. Tupper; had reported his father's fatal illness; Add MS 44508, f. 193.
[6] J. A. Fox, *A key to the Irish question* (1890).
[7] Mrs. G. Corbett, *New Amazonia* (1889), probably sent by the author; (see 1 Dec. 89).
[8] Further difficulties with Wylie over the restructuring of the firm; see Thomas, *Gladstone of Hawarden*, 139, 146.
[9] Not found.
[10] J. Law, *Captain Lobe* (1889); of the Salvation Army.

30. St Andr. Saty.

Ch. 8½ A.M. Wrote to M. Opdebeeck[1]—Ld E. Clinton—Mr Murray—Mr McCarthy—F.J. Cross—Sir J. Carmichael—Canon McColl—U.S. Labour Commissioner[2]—U. Sec. Foreign Office. Woodcraft: Will[3] was much interested in seeing the axe and bruited it abroad. Worked on Irish and political papers: with sore reluctance. Read Captain Lobe—A Babe of Bohemia[4]—Roose on Leprosy.[5]

Advent S. Dec 1. 89.

Church 11 AM with H.C. and 6½ P.M. Wrote to Rev. Irwin Coates[6]—W.J. Lacey—Mr Waddy MP—Mrs Corbett[7]—Rivingtons. Saw H.J.G.—Mr Mayhew—W.H.G: now fit we hope to resume Church. Read Captain Lobe—Dawson on Genesis[8]—Wright on Protm in Russia[9]—Sayce Hibbert Lectures[10]—and [blank.]

2. M. [Ford Bank, Didsbury]

Ch. 8½ A.M. Wrote to [blank.] Off at 11.20 to Manchester by special train. Free Trade Hall at 1.15. Spoke nearly 1½ hour: very good audience.[11] Then drove processionally 6 or 7 miles to Mr Ashton's[12] refined & pleasant home at Didsbury. Large party at dinner. Saw Dr Ward—Mr Bryce—Mr Ashton. Read Law on Jesuits & Seculars[13]—Lambert on Franchise.[14]

3. Tu.

Mr Ashton gave me a drive to my old haunts (1828) at Wilmslow of which the salient points still remain.[15] Sat to photographers. Worked on Irish papers. Read Law on Seculars & Jesuits. We dined early & went into Manchester at 7.15. Spoke again in F.T. Hall 1 h. 20 m.[16] Returned at 10. The meeting satisfactory: but Radical.

---

[1] On the death of Lady Lincoln, reported by her son, Lord E. Clinton; Add MS 44508, f. 198.
[2] No business traced; perhaps on Gladstone's article on free trade, whose long delayed publication was now imminent (see 10 Dec. 88).
[3] i.e. his grandson.
[4] F. Danby, *A babe of Bohemia* (1889).
[5] E. C. R. Roose, *Leprosy and its prevention* (1889).
[6] James Irwin Coates, curate in Shepherd's Bush.
[7] Mrs. George Corbett, author; see 28 Nov. 89n.
[8] J. W. Dawson, *The origin of the world according to revelation and science* (1877).
[9] C. H. H. Wright, 'Stamping out protestantism in Russia', *N.C.*, xxvi. 912 (December 1889).
[10] See 11 Feb. 87.
[11] *T.T.*, 3 December 1889, 7a.
[12] Thomas Ashton (see 17 Aug. 87); lived at Ford Bank, Didsbury.
[13] T. G. Law, *Sketch of the conflicts between Jesuits and Seculars in relation to Elizabeth* (1889).
[14] J. Lambert in *N.C.*, xxvi. 942 (December 1889).
[15] In 1828, Gladstone was sent to study mathematics at Wilmslow with Rev. J. M. Turner, a moderate Evangelical; see 24 Jan.—11 Apr. 28 and Matthew, *Gladstone*, 19, 251.
[16] Addressing the National Liberal Federation; *T.T.*, 5 December 1889, 6a.

4. Wed. [Hawarden]

Wrote to Mr Lloyd Bryce—J.P. More—Hugh Ll. Jones—Dr Capon—J.W. Dunford—G.A. Macmillan. Read Law—Bagshaw—To Manchester before one. Saw the models of Thirlmere Works and of the Canal (Ship). Saw J. Morley—A. Morley. Spoke ½h at the Mayor's luncheon. Read Law on Seculars & J.—and Babe of Bohemia.[1]

5. Th.

Ch. 8½ A.M. Wrote to Mr Maclaren MP—Mr W. Tupper—Messrs Gibson—Mr T.G. Law—H.M. Robinson—Mr Bosanquet[2]—W. Downing—Vote Office—Watsons—Mr Macphail.[3] Eight to dinner. Saw Mr Sheepshank. Took Ld Aberdeen to the new Building, to be Saint Deiniol's. Read Law on Seculars and Jesuits (finished)—Melbourne Papers—Babe in Bohemia.

6. Fr.

Ch. 8¼ A.M. and 7–8 P.M. Wrote to M. Stambouloff[4]—Mr J.L. Bent—Mr Lefevre MP—P.M. Slater—Sir R.E. Welby—J. Coupland—J.M. Hamilton[5]—Ed. Lpool Daily Post.[6] Read Babe in Bohemia—Blaine's Reply on Protection[7]—Melbourne Papers (finished)—Delarive on the Social Position.[8] Worked on books & papers.

7. Sat.

Ch. 8½ A.M. Wrote to Mrs Bolton in P.P.—Ach. Apostolides[9]—J. Phipps—Rev. J.J.M. Perry[10]—H. Frowde[11]—Mr [W.] Probyn Nevins—F.A. Knight—Messrs Jerrold—J.P. Rylands—Mayor of Manchester—Ld Spencer. Wrote on Ld Melbourne.[12] Woodcraft. Read M. Delarive—Babe in Bohemia (finished)—Jonathan Merle[13]—and Bashkirtseff Article in Scribner.[14]

---

[1] See 30 Nov. 89.

[2] Robert Carr Bosanquet (1871–1935, archaeologist), then a boy at Eton, had unsuccessfully invited Gladstone to speak; Hawn P.

[3] A. Macphail; not further identified.

[4] Gladstone wrote to Stephen Stambouloff, archaeologist, at the request of James Theodore Bent to give the latter an introduction; Add MS 44508, f. 209.

[5] Perhaps John McLure Hamilton, 1853–1926, who drew several sketches of Gladstone at Hawarden in the 1890s; see 3 Sept. 90.

[6] *Liverpool Daily Post*, 9 December 1889, 5d.

[7] Printed with Gladstone's article in *N.A.R.*; see 10 Dec. 88.

[8] T. de la Rive, 'Le péril social et le devoir actuel. Le Mal. Le Remède. Discours prononcé à Genève le 17 et 24 mars 1889' (1889).

[9] Unidentified.

[10] Jevan James Muschamp Perry, vicar of Alnwick.

[11] Henry Frowde, 1841–1927; publisher to the University of Oxford and manager of the O.U.P.'s London office; had sent a prayer book printed by O.U.P.; Add MS 44508, f. 213.

[12] See 21 Nov. 89.

[13] E. B. Bayley, *Jonathan Merle* (1889).

[14] By J. Lazarus, *Scribner's Magazine*, vi. 633 (November 1889).

8. 2 S. Adv.

Ch. 11 AM 6½ PM. Wrote to Herbert J.G.—Williams & N.—C. Hotham—J.K. Hardie[1]—M. Delarive. Read 'The new Priest'[2]—De la Rive Social Question—De la Rive's Address—Collins, Genesis & Geology[3]—and . . . Visited W.H.G.s.

9. M.

Ch. 8¼ AM. Wrote to Messrs Freshfield—Rev. Dr. Angus[4]—Sir W. Harcourt—Ld Spencer BP—Mrs Bennett—W.H. Hughes[5]—E.E. Whitfield—J. Lightfoot—Dr Doudney.[6] Worked much on letters, papers, and books. Read The New Priest—Der Whig Bismarck u. Tory Windhorst[7]—Macfadden on Guerdon.[8] Drive with C.

10. Tu.

Ch. 8¼ AM. Wrote to Madame Novikoff—W.T. Stead—Rev. W.S. Wood—G.S. Pierce—Archdn Thomas—Messrs Scott—A.R. Gladstone—Rev. F.G. Scott—A. Macphail—W. Downing—Mr Whitfield BP.—Thos Baker—Mr Bryce. Saw Mr Pollard & Mr [blank.] Wrote on Melbourne Govt.[9] Read Stark's Letter[10]—The New Priest—Memoir of W.M. Praed[11]—Dal Lido Veneto &c.[12]

11. Wed.

Ch. 8¼ AM. Wrote to Mr P.W. Bunting—A. Morley MP.—Rev. Mr Mayow—J. Wilson—Messrs Wheatley—J.M. Brown—Mr J. Nicol—H. Robinson—J.W. Williams—Thos Baker—C.C. Byrne—J.W.H. Jockinson. Saw S.E.G. & Bailey on New Library (St Deiniol's). Worked on Melbourne MS. Read Wilson on Trees[13]—The New Priest—Le Secret de l'Empereur[14]—and . . .

12. Th.

Ch. 8¼ A.M. Wrote to Messrs Roberts, U.S.—Mrs Th.—Professor More—Rev. J. Harris—A. M'Kechnie—Alfree & Scudamore—Rev. Dr Symington—Messrs Murray. Worked on Melbourne Govt MS. And on Manchester MS. Read Mr Jack's Address[15]—The New Priest—M. Blind's George Eliot[16]—and historical books.

---

[1] Presumably James Keir Hardie, 1856–1915; founded Scottish labour party 1888, I.L.P. 1893; labour M.P. S.W. Ham 1892–5; socialist, but also fervent Gladstonian in international relations; business untraced. In his obituary of Gladstone, Hardie recalled 'a private deputation of colliers which met him in his hired house at 10 St James's Square to ask for his support for the Eight-Hours Bill . . . the whole of his reply centred round the need for maintaining the liberty of the collier'; see *Keir Hardie's speeches and writings*, ed. E. Hughes (1928), 79–80. For that meeting see 18 Feb. 90.

[2] See 24 Nov. 89.　　　　　　　　　　　　　　　　　　　　[3] Not found.
[4] See 15 Jan. 40.　　　　　　　　　　[5] William Huntley Hughes, London solicitor.
[6] See 16 Aug. 67.　　　　　　　[7] Untraced.　　　　　　　　[8] Untraced.
[9] See 26 Nov. 89.　　　　　　　　[10] Perhaps R. Stark, 'What is truth?' (1853).
[11] W. M. Praed, *Poems*, 2v. (1885); revised ed. by D. Coleridge; see 16 Feb. 65.
[12] Untraced.　　　　　　　　　　　　　　　　　　　　　　[13] Untraced.
[14] L. Thouvenel, *Le Secret de l'Empereur* (1889); correspondence with Grammont and Flahaut.
[15] Perhaps M. Jack, 'The religious difficulty in Ireland' (1870?).
[16] M. Blind, *George Eliot* (1883).

13. Fr.

Ch. 8½ A.M. Wrote to Miss Phillimore—Mr E. Goadby[1]—Mr Scharf Sec.—Thos Dawe—T.H. Brigg—Mr C. Brooks. Conversation with C.G. & H.J.G. on taking London house for 6 m[onths] in which I am entangled.[2] Worked on MS Melbourne Govt. And on Manchester proofs. Walk with Margo Tennant.[3] Read Tennyson's new Vol.[4]—M. Blind's George Eliot—The new Priest.

14. Sat.

Ch 8½ AM with MT. Wrote to Hodder & Stoughton—C. Higham—Bull & Auvache—Mr Barnum[5]—Ld Tennyson—W. Light—Rev. Prosser—W. Stokes—E. Robinson—E. Goadby BP—F. Coleclough—J.P. Whitney—HNG (Tel.). Walk with H.J.G. Saw M.G. on *caretaker*. Worked on Melb. Govt. Worked on Manchr proofs. Read The New Priest (finished)—Publisher's Circular Xmas No.—and [blank.]

15. 3 S. Adv.

Ch 11 A.M. and 6½ P.M. Wrote to Ed. Chambers Cycl.—E. Whitney—Rev. Dr. Preston—H. le Bas—Mr Dwyer Gray—E. Goadby BP.—Mr Liversedge. Read A Doubter's Doubts[6]—Beard's Luther[7]—Karl Blind in Fortnightly.[8] Walk with (Miss) M.T.

16. M.

Wrote to H. Tennyson Tel.[9]—W. Bailey—Mr Knowles—Mrs Smedes—A.R. Gladstone—Rev. J. Acton—Miss Tennant—Mr Cowan—Capt. Verney—F.J. Pooley—Rev. J.F. Cole—W. Kinsman.[10] Revised & sent off Melbourne Govt MS. Saw HJG—A. Lyttelton—C.G. Read Doubters Doubt (finished)—Home Rule by Steps[11]—Wiltshire Meeting of 1846[12]—M. Blind's Geo. Eliot.

17. Tu.

Ch. 8½ A.M. Wrote to Nicolaos Christodoulaki—Mr C. Lowe—Lord Salisbury[13]—E. Kay & Son—Mr Parnell Tel.—H. Barridge—G.H. Robinson—C. Downes—M. Jean Broussali—C.T. Knau—Miss Tennant. Walk with the party.

---

[1] Edwin Goadby of Westminster; an occasional correspondent; Hawn P.
[2] The Gladstones took 10 St. James's Square, later Chatham House, for 1890; see 29 Jan. 90.
[3] 'Margot' Tennant (later Asquith, see 28 Feb. 81) was staying at the Castle, her first visit; see her *Autobiography* (1920), i. 147 ff.
[4] Lord Tennyson, *The Throstle* (1889).
[5] See 30 Jan. 90.
[6] [R. Anderson], *A doubter's doubts about science and religion, by a criminal lawyer* (1889).
[7] C. Beard, *Martin Luther and the reformation in Germany* (1889).
[8] *F.R.*, lii. 789 (December 1889).
[9] Supporting Browning's burial in Westminster Abbey; Add MS 44508, f. 226.
[10] Of Cornwall; sent 'an old book'; Hawn P.
[11] *Home Rule step by step. By an Unionist Home Ruler* (1889).
[12] Presumably an account of a meeting on the corn laws.
[13] On Turkey; see Add MS 44508, f. 233.

Wrote on Books.[1] Read Blind's Geo. Eliot—Teetgen, The Blessed Hope[2]—The Lost Ring.[3] Wrote verses on Margot Tennant.[4]

18. Wed.

Ch. $8\frac{1}{2}$ A.M. Wrote to Cardinal Manning BP.—Author of 'a Doubter's Doubts'[5]—Rev. J.H. Bath—A.H.D. Acland MP—D.T. Carey—Mrs Elborough—E. Goadby—Hume Nisbett—T. Baker—A. Marshall—Dr Roose—Mr Parnell MP.— Mr Knowles—A. Teetgen. Read Blinds G. Eliot—Zimmer Assyriologia[6]—The Lost Ring.

Reviewed & threw into form all the points of possible amendment or change in the Plan of Irish Government &c. for my meeting with Mr Parnell.[7] He arrived at 5.30 and we had 2 hours of satisfactory conversation but he put off the *gros* of it.

Irish Government.[8]
Points prepared for Conversation. Dec. 18. 89.

1. *Land.* Irish guarantee.
   Irish guarantee. Secured as in 86.
   Russell's compulsory purchase. q[uer]y open to Dublin Parlt.?? (or *allow* this to be introduced?)
   Point out that the question of guarantee is a question of economy—of free choice—not of risk.
   Compulsion is twofold: a. from the State b. from the landlords OR tenants.
2. *Contracts.*
   Shall the Legislature be inhibited from voting a law against contracts, in the same manner as the American States are now restrained?
3. *Supremacy.*
   Shall there be a clause explicitly reserving the supremacy of Parliament over Ireland in common with the rest of the Empire?
4. *Mode of Legislature.*
   Shall the imperial questions be enumerated as in 1886?
   or
   Shall the delegated powers be fixed by enumeration
5. *Judicial appointments.*
   For *x* (*7 or 10*) years from the passing of the Act, no Judge of the Superior Courts of Ireland except under an instrument signed or countersigned by one of Her Majesty's Principal Secretaries of State.
   the present salaries & pensions of all persons being such Judges at the time of passing this Act, and the salaries and pensions which shall be appointed for all such other judges as above mentioned, to be charges upon the Consolidated Fund of Ireland and to be a lien on that Fund preferably to all voted charges.

---

[1] 'On books and the housing of them', *N.C.*, xxvii. 384 (March 1890).
[2] Alexander T. Teetgen, *Blessed hope* (1890); sent by the author.
[3] J. Crompton, *The lost ring* (1889).
[4] Sent this day; in her *Autobiography*, i. 147 and at Add MS 44773, f. 172.
[5] R. Anderson; see 19 Nov. 89.
[6] H. Zimmern, *Die Assyriologie* (1889).
[7] Version of this and next day's entry in Morley, iii. 420. See next day.
[8] Add MS 44773, f. 156.

6. *An Irish representation at Westminster.*
    1. To be retained—in *some* form—if the public opinion, at the proper time, shall require it.
    2. Cardinal conditions of a retention.
        a. Clause for their reappearance in full numbers to consider any alteration of the Act shall be retained.
        b. Outside of this, the question to be *British*, not *Irish*, in honour as well as in law. Parliament to retain a free hand.
        c. So much will depend upon experience that the first legislature should be marked as *tentative* (in the form supplied by the Bank Act of 1844).[1]

Practically perhaps the selection is to be made among three modes of proceeding.
    1. All Irish, voting on all questions
    2. All Irish, voting on some, i.e. Imperial, questions
    3. Some Irish, voting on all questions.

(A mode if full number retained)

Duplicate the Irish MPs. to form the Irish House.

Senior MPs to have seat in British Parlt.—and to vote on all questions *reserved* to that Parlt.

Speaker aided by a small Committee to decide in case of doubt.

So to continue for x years and thereafter until Parliament shall otherwise provide.

House of Lords. May decide upon notice given (or taken at the time) whether any particular question is or is not Imperial & if not may inhibit Irish Peers from voting, whether such Peers hold Peerages of the U.K. or not. But any Peer being also Peer of the U.K. may renounce his Irish Peerage if he think fit.

Peers.

1. Irish Peers at Westminster: to follow the analogy of the plan which may be adopted for the House of Commons.
2. If a *selection* has to be made, provision would be necessary to regulate the mode of voting, as Irish Peers are not necessarily connected with that country or any part of it.

Modes.

1. Election. Shall there be a separate *election* for Westminster? No
2. Numbers. Shall all Irish MPs have seats at Westminster? or a selection? If a selection, shall the Irish House choose them? under what conditions? (In provinces)
3. Voting powers. a. On all questions? or
                    b. on all Imperial questions? or
                    c. on all except *delegated* questions?
                    d. In case of doubt who decide?
4. Permutations and combinations of these.

7. *Finance.*
    1. Relative amount of burden in respect of Imperial charges to be considered by a Commission, and estimated with reference a. to capacity, b. to history, for the decision of Govt. & Parlt.
    2. When decided, shall it be embodied (as in 1886) in a fixed annual sum? or shall it be a fixed percentage of the total *Imperial* charge, varying in amount only with the variation of that charge?[2]

---

[1] Presumably a reference to the curious clause 29 of the 1844 Act, that 'this Act may be amended or repealed by any Act passed in the present Session of Parliament'.

[2] In 1886 the Gladstone–Parnell negotiations agreed on a proportion of the Imperial budget to be paid by the Irish, but this proportion ($\frac{1}{15}$) was expressed in the Government of Ireland Bill as a cash sum; see above, x. clvi ff.

3. Shall the sum, or percentage, thus fixed, be liable to reconsideration at Westminster, after a (sufficiently long) term of years?

4. The fixed proportion of Imperial expenditure would be a first charge on all Irish Receipts.

5. Shall the machinery of the Receivergeneralship[1] be retained? As matter of policy, for both sides of the water (i.e. for British opinion now and Irish *credit* hereafter) I attach to it the utmost value.

6. The Commission would have to consider
   a. what items of charge are Imperial
   b. how to deal with duties levied in one country for consumption in the other
   c. Whether Ireland has any financial claim in respect of bygone transactions

7. Imperial Parliament to tax Ireland only in Customs and Excise: direct and mixed taxation resting with the Irish Legislature.
   Q[uer]y can power of extending poor rate beyond counties (or Provinces?) be withheld.

[2]⟨ *Finance.*

1. Appoint a small Commission.
2. Determine what is Imperial Expenditure.
3. Fix a percentage of it for Ireland (to be lower than in 1886).
4. May be considered in Imperial Parliament after x years.
5. Duties levied in Ireland on goods (consumed in Great Britain would have to be taken into view).
6. As would the question whether the creation of 25m̄ Irish Debt in 1795–1800 and the subsequent financial arrangements give Ireland a claim for any compensation.
7. The fixed proportion of Imperial Expenditure to be a first charge upon Irish Customs & Excise receipts.
1. A Commission.
2. Substitute percentage for fixed sum.⟩

19.

Church 8¼ A.M. Wrote to Mr W. Meynell—Mad. Karostovetz B.P.[3]—C. Herbert—Sir R.S. Ball—Hon. R. Meade—J.M. Gray BP.—Vote Office—W.W.F. Synge[4]—W. Tickle—F.A. Atkins—W.R. Nicoll.[5]

Two hours more with Mr P. on points in Irish Govt plans. He is certainly one of the very best people to deal with that I have ever known. Took him [round] the Old Castle. He seems to notice and appreciate everything.[6]

Corrected proofs of the Melbourne paper. Finished Zimmern Assyriologia— read Stockmar Memoirs II[7]—Blind's Geo. Eliot—Ball, Starland.[8]

---

[1] In 1886 Gladstone attached great importance to the Receiver General as a means of encouraging Irish creditworthiness; see above x. cliff. and to Morley, 19 Apr. 86.

[2] This section (Add MS 44773, f. 167) is deleted; evidently a false start.

[3] Lydia Korostorely of St. Petersburg, had written in admiration.

[4] William Webb Follett Synge, d. 1891; author and former minor diplomat.

[5] (Sir) William Robertson Nicholl, 1851–1923; ed. *The British Weekly* 1886–1923; a strong liberal free churchman.

[6] For Gladstone's vital record of this controversial discussion, see 23 Dec. 89.

[7] *Memoirs of Baron Stockmar*, ed. F. Max Müller, 2v. (1872).

[8] See 9 May 89.

20. Fr.

Ch. 8½ A.M. Wrote to Rev. Exot. Illustria[1]—Mrs Smedes—Canon Floyd—Sidney Lee—Lady Ferguson—Jas Knowles—R.M. Theobald—J.D. Bryce—Dodd Mead & Co.[2]—L. Flood. Walk with K. Lyttelton. Worked on MS of Books. Read Blind's G. Eliot (finished)—Davies, Address at Regina[3]—The Lost Ring. Dispatched proofs of MS on the Melbourne Govt. Worked on the Books MS. Saw Mr Mayhew.

21. Sat.

Ch. 8¼ A.M. Wrote to Ed of Church & People[4]—Mrs Lunn—Messrs George—Mrs Laffan—Rev. W.J. Stracey—A. Moseley—Mr N.F. Davies—O. Browning—J.R. Russell. Finished MS on Books. Worked on books for the grand transfer: and sent off my first instalment to Saint Deiniol's. Read The Lost Ring—Rose & Shamrock[5]—Origines de la Civilisation Moderne.[6]

22. 4 S. Adv.

Ch. 11 AM and 6¼ P.M. Saw Dean of St Asaph. Wrote to Mr W. Richmond—Rev. Dr Hayman—J. Day—G.W. Moon—J.H. Dalziel. Read Hayman 'Why do we suffer?'[7]—Beard's Luther[8]—Norwich Report on Divorce—Origines &c.

23. M.

Ch 8¼ A.M. Wrote to Bull & Auvache—Ld Spencer—Watsons—Mrs Gamlin[9]—Mr M. Wells—Mr Mather MP—R. Williams—D. Cameron—Mrs. Lomas.

Having been led to entertain the subject of purchasing the important Liverpool Advowson,[10] from intelligence brought by H. Drew, I this day consulted severally my wife, Stephen, & then Willy. All were warmly for it. So I sent further questions about it. Worked with Harry on the question of family distribution. Also worked in St Deiniol's & placed 300 or 400 books. Luncheon at H. Hall. Saw Bailey. Read Shamrock & Rose—Histoire des Origines &c.

---

[1] *Sic*; obscure.

[2] New York publishers; unsuccessfully inviting Gladstone to write a 60,000 word biography of George Washington; Hawn P.

[3] Untraced.

[4] First of several letters denying the truth of an anecdote (in fact substantially correct) that he had voted against lay agents at a meeting of the evangelical Church Pastoral Aid Society in 1837 and, being defeated, had resigned from the cttee.; see *Church and People*, no. 4, p. 109 (January 1890) and no. 5, pp. 9–11 (April 1890). The incident had led to the founding of the Additional Curates Society. See also 16 Feb. 37 and P. A. Butler, *Gladstone: church, state and tractarianism* (1982), 67–8.

[5] Mrs. G. Lunn had sent her *Shamrock and rose*, 2v. (1888); see 24 Dec. 89.

[6] G. Kurth, *Les Origines de la civilisation moderne* (1886).

[7] H. Hayman, *'Why do we suffer' and other essays* (1889).

[8] See 15 Dec. 89.

[9] Hilda Gamlin of Birkenhead had sent a query on Lady Hamilton; Hawn P.

[10] Gladstone bought the advowson of the Rectory of Liverpool (deed signed 1 February 1890) from Robert Hornell of Lincoln's Inn and Rev. Robert Morey Weale of Byfield; he left it to his sons by his will and in 1902 they sold it to the Liverpool Cathedral Committee; Hawn P. See 31 Dec. 89.

Secret.[1] 1890.[2]

After a very long delay, of which I do not know the cause, Mr. Parnell's promised visit came off last[3] week. He appeared well and cheerful and proposed to accompany (without a gun) my younger sons who went out shooting.

Nothing could be more satisfactory than his conversation; full as I thought it of good sense from beginning to end.

I had prepared carefully all the points that I could think of, or recall from any suggestions of others, as possible improvements (as to essence or as to prudential policy) in the Irish Government Bill or Land Bill.

I did not press him to positive conclusions, but learnt pretty well the leaning of his mind; and ascertained that, so far as I could judge, nothing like a crotchet, or an irrational demand, from his side, was likely to interfere with the proper freedom of our deliberations when the proper time comes for practical steps.

The points were numerous, and I propose to reserve the recital of them until we meet in London, which, if (as I assume) the Judges have made their report, I think we ought to do not later than the Saturday, or perhaps the Friday, before Tuesday the 11th when the Session opens.[4]

I may say, however, that we were quite agreed in thinking the real difficulty lies in determining the particular form in which an Irish representation may have to be retained at Westminster. We conversed at large on the different modes. He has no absolute or foregone conclusion.

He emphatically agreed in the wisdom & necessity of reserving our judgment on this matter until a crisis is at hand.

Will those of my late colleagues who may see this paper kindly note the fact by their initials.   WEG D. 23. 89.

S[pencer] 24.12.89
R[osebery] 27.12.89
W. V. H[arcourt] 29.12.89
G[ranville] m[emorandu]m forwarded 30.12.89
H[erschell] 1.1.90
K[imberley] 2.1.90
J. M[orley] 3.1.90
R[ipon] 4.1.90
J. S[tansfeld] 7.1.90
A. J. M[undella] 8.1.90
H. C. B[annerman] 20.1.90
A. M[orley] 25.1.90

24. *Tu.*[5]

Ch. 8½ A.M. Wrote to the Baroni Ricasoli—Mr F. Barnes—Messrs J. Barker—Mrs Aitken—Abdulhah Bey—G. Halton—H.B.K. Charley—Author of A Doubters Doubts—T. Stanley—Messrs Bailey. Worked on *particulars* of book cases for a

---

[1] Holograph; Add MS 44773, f. 170.   [2] *recte* 1889; date added later by Gladstone.
[3] Originally 'next'; changed later by Gladstone.   [4] See 8 Feb. 90.
[5] Capt. O'Shea this day filed for a petition of divorce on the basis of his wife's adultery with Parnell since April 1886; it was thought this was a measure to be made public just before Parnell's libel action with *The Times*, but news of it broke quickly. The petition was not served on Mrs. O'Shea until early January, her solicitors having publicly requested its immediate service on 1 January; it was expected that the case would be heard in June; see *P.M.G.*, 1, 2 and 4 January. See 20 Nov. 90 ff.

fresh order. Met Mr Mayhew to define the the site of St Deiniol's. Worked on MS respecting Poets.[1] Read Origines &c.—'Cley' on Dr John Brown[2]—Rose & Shamrock: a disappointment.

25. Xmas Day.

Church 11 AM with H.C. and 6 P.M. A glorious day, bright, mild, and fresh: with a holy fitness. Wrote to Warden of All Souls[3]—Cardinal Manning—Mr Cook (*re* Carnegie).[4] Tea at W.H.G.s He D.G. was at Church & Communion. Read Carnegie Proofs—Calfhill—Davies—Rose & Shamrock—Gallway Apostol. Succession.[5]

26. Th. St Stephen.

Ch. 8½ AM. Wrote to Rev. D. Davies—Ld Granville—Messrs Murray—Mr Westell—Miss Hawkins—Ld J. Hervey—J. Macdonald—G. Anderson—Messrs Watson—B. Quaritch—Rev. Blakiston—J. Watts—C. Maynell—J.J. Green.[6] Saw Bailey & worked on books, & at St Deiniol's with Helen's capital aid. Saw H. Drew & H.N.G. on affairs. Worked on Poetry MS. Much work has to be done with the references. Read 'The Silver Whistle' (with difficulty).[7]

27. Fr. St John.

Ch. 8½ AM & H.C. Wrote to W. Davenport Adam—Scotts—Canon MacColl—C. Herbert—Mayor of Falmouth—E.W. Stibbs—G. Lakewood—J. Wright—H. Thompson—Jas Keith—Mr Westell—D. Milne. Spent time on (literary) table-drawers: failed to find my note of clergy-poets. Worked at St Deiniol's with Helen. Read 'With all my w. goods'[8]—U.S. Sec. of States Report.

28. Sat.

Ch. 8½ A.M. & service at the new Pentre School 3½ P.M. Wrote to Sec. Eccl. Commrs—Sir R. Welby—Judge O'Hagan—Ld Rosebery—Sydney Buxton—H.T.

[1] 'British poetry of the nineteenth century'; *The Speaker*, 11 January 1890; its ed. was T. Wemyss Reid.

[2] Untraced.

[3] Sir William Reynell Anson, 1843-1914; 3rd bart. 1873; warden of All Souls, Oxford, 1881-1914; lawyer and unionist M.P. Oxford University 1899-1914. Gladstone wrote to propose his visit (see 31 Jan. 90); in C. R. L. F[letcher], *Mr. Gladstone at Oxford 1890* (1908), 7. See 31 Dec. 89.

[4] Long letter to E. T. Cook on Carnegie's 'Gospel of Wealth': 'I follow Mr Carnegie in nearly everything he affirms and recommends. My main reservation is prompted by his language respecting the endowment of twenty millions (of dollars) granted with a splendid munificence to Stanford University. My mind is possessed with much misgiving . . . about the wholesale endowment of offices and places . . . I have doubts whether it does not raise the market price of the higher education, which it aims at lowering . . .'; letter in New York Public Library and *P.M.G.*, 1 January 1890, 1.

[5] P. Gallwey, *Apostolic succession* (1889).

[6] Of Stansted; on his birthday; Hawn P.

[7] *The silver whistle*, 2v. (1889).

[8] G. W. Moon, *With all my worldly goods I thee endow. A novel* (1899).

Pullan[1]—Messrs George—C.M. Bonnor—Hon. S.D. Horton—Mayor of Louis-ville[2]—Editor of Church & People[3]—Messrs Bailey—H. Taylor. Worked again upon arranging papers in drawers. And at St Deiniol's. Read Origines &c.—Child of the Ocean[4]—Towards Evening,[5] and [blank.]

29. S. aft Xmas.

Church 11 A.M. and [blank.] Wrote to Cardinal Manning—Mr Meynell Tel.[6]—W.T. Stead—W. Dav. Adams—Rev. Bristol—E.R. Garbett[7]—D. Milne—Mr Mur-ray—Tel. letter to the newspapers.[8] Read E. Talbot's Essay[9]—Ker on Psalms[10]—Asolanda[11]—Naden,[12] Myers, Kynaston—Methodist in search of a Church.[13]

Willy again at Church: I trust it is to continue. Excellent sermons. All things smile.

And so here I am, an eighty year old sinner. O for the time of recollection, detachment, and insight into the true measure of my relations to Him who has done such wonders for me, and yet Who mysteriously holds me on in a life of suspicion and contention, at a time when Nature which is the voice of God calls & sighs & yearns for repose. My physical conservation is indeed noteworthy. In the senses of sight and hearing and in power of locomotion there is decline, & memory is not quite consistent. But the trunk of the body is in all its ordinary vital operations, so far as I see, what it was ten years back: it seems to be sustained & upheld for the accomplishment of a work. In retrospect I trust the year indicates a slight relative improvement. I feel however that I never can get at the true measure of my sinfulness until I am permitted to pass into the condi-tion of a simply private person: a condition of which I never seem to taste for two hours together; or say a few hours. But *fiat voluntas Tua sicut in cœlo et in terrâ*.

---

[1] Of Leeds, on religion; Hawn P.

[2] Had presumably sent a congratulatory address.

[3] See 21 Dec. 89.

[4] R. Ross, *Child of the ocean* (1889).

[5] H. E. Manning, *Towards evening* (1889).

[6] Explaining that Meynell had, without authorisation, reprinted his (Gladstone's) review of Lady G. Fullerton's 'Ellen Middleton' in his Roman catholic periodical, *Merry England* (of which Ripon was a director); Meynell replied that Gladstone had given written permission on 12 December 1888; Add MS 44508, ff. 285–90. See 8, 24 May 44; the reprint is in *Merry England*, xiv. 159, 235 (January and February 1890).

[7] Of London; occasional correspondent on religion; Hawn P.

[8] Of thanks for birthday letters; *The Times'* leader, commenting on the celebrations, claimed he 'has toiled in the cause of anarchy as no one ever dreamed that a man of his years could have toiled'. Gladstone was eighty this day.

[9] E. S. Talbot, *Preparation in history for Christ* (1889).

[10] See 12 Dec. 86.

[11] Reading uncertain.

[12] Perhaps an obituary of Constance Naden, d. 24 December 1889, poet of science and evolution, 'whom Mr Gladstone's well-remembered reference helped to make famous'; see *The complete poetical works of Constance Naden* (1894), 20. See 21 Jan. 90.

[13] S. Y. MacMasters, *A Methodist in search of the church* (1862).

30. M.

Ch. 8½ A.M. Wrote Tel. to Liberal Assocns—Mr Knowles—Matthews & Co.—
Letter to the newspapers at large[1]—Prince of Wales—Mr Humphreys—Canon
MacColl—Macmillans—Duke of Westminster—J.N. Gladstone—E.T. Greavy—
Mayor of Chester—Mrs Corbould—Rev. Mansell.

Herbert spent with me two to three hours in simply going over a small selection of the letters telegrams books & other tokens. I only tasted of the rush
today: it is all the more humbling as I trust. My dear children yesterday
laboured hard themselves, & left me quiet. Worked at St Deiniol's with H.
Dined with W.H.G.s. Servants ball: Library sventrato[2] as they say at Naples. We
migrated. Read Mrs Corbould[3]—The Bronte Poems.[4] . . . . . .

31. Tu.

Ch. 8½ A.M. Wrote to King of the Belgians—Khedive of Egypt—U. Sec. F.O.—Sir
W. Harcourt—Parcels O. Chester—Warden of All Souls[5]—Mr Homersham
Cox—Messrs Bailey—Mayor of Falmouth—J. Elliot—Cox Biddulph & Co—
Archdn Taylor—Ed. Ch. Review. Finished MS on Poetry of the 19th Century.[6]
Worked at St Deiniol's. Had H.N.G. for my envoy to Liverpool today respecting
the Advowson. He steered his vessel admirably. Read Poems of V.[7]—Louis
Draycott.[8] After Harry had reported came the Tel. reporting acceptance of my
offer of £7200 for this great advowson.

And so the year has rolled into the great bosom of the Past. We had a grand
dinner of 12 at the Rectory: S. & I played backgammon. The Castle topsy
turvy, as usual at Xmas: but many are made innocently happy. Benedictus
benedicat.

---

[1] Birthday thanks; *T.T.*, 31 December 1889, 4e.
[2] 'Cleaned out' (literally, 'disembowelled').
[3] Perhaps D. M. Corbould, *Loyal hearts* (1883).
[4] In *Life and works of Charlotte Brontë and her sisters*, iv (1875).
[5] Anson (see 25 Dec. 89) encouraged Gladstone 'to avail yourself of your rights as an honorary
Fellow. . . . I assume from some expression in your letter that you would like to return for a while to
college life' (various details about accommodation follow); Add MS 44509, f. 1. See 31 Jan. 90.
[6] See 24 Dec. 89.
[7] See 20 Mar. 41.
[8] Mrs. R. S. De Courcy Laffan, *Louis Draycott; the story of his life*, 2v. (1889).

Circumcision, Wed. Jan 1. 90.

Ch 8½ A.M. and H.C. Wrote note for H. D[rew] to send to Mr Bell Cox.[1] Also to Mr Wemyss Reid—Mr Stibbs—Master Solomon—Mr Westell—Rev. Mr Halcombe—E. Walford—Rev. Lloyd Fowle—C.M. Bonnor[2]—Mr W. Meynell[3]—Ed. Mag. of Art[4]—Ed. Ch. & People:[5] work with H.J.G. as usual on the post. Then with Harry on my distribution (£43,000) among my beloved children. Then with H. & H. on Harry's very embarrassing position with his partners. Then polished a little my MS for Mr Wemyss Reid.[6] Amended also my MS on books & bookhousing.[7] Then worked with Helen on books at St Deiniol's. Then attended Xmas tree, beautiful! The children were all in fairy land. Saw WHG—S.E.G.—Helen G. Then scurried off to my post. Read Louis Draycott[8]—Walford's Pitt.[9]

2. Th.

Ch. 8½ A.M. Wrote to Mr P.W. Campbell—Mr F. Gregory—Hon. Sir H. Parkes—G.F. Bevan—E. Giles—Mr Dav. Adam—J.A. Wilson—Messrs Matthews—A. Collett—Alex. Robinson—H.C. Kirk[10]—Osborne Aldis. Worked on distribution business. And on Homeric MS. Worked on books at St Deiniol's. Read Ld Grey on Tithes[11]—Walford's Pitt—(N.C.) Huxley on Equality of Man (heavy?)—Lady Jersey on Woman: very clever—Ly Cowper ditto, Less so—Huish on British Art.[12]

3. Fr.

Ch. 8½ A.M. Wrote to Rev. Mr Thackeray—Rev. S.E.G.—A. Read—Mr Stibbs—Jas Knowles—J. Westell—T. Baker—J. Nicol. Worked much on the arrangement for my children. Wrote Memorandum respecting Provost Hawtrey.[13] Worked on books at St Deiniol's. Read Louis Draycott—Walford's Pitt.

---

[1] James Bell Cox, curate of St. Margaret's, Liverpool; involved in the negotiations of Gladstone's purchase of the Liverpool advowson (see 23 Dec. 89); Hawn P.

[2] Of the Addiscombe Beaconsfield Club; exchange of correspondence on Siberian exiles in *T.T.*, 4 January 1890, 6b.

[3] On the misunderstanding about his review of 'Ellen Middleton' (see 29 Dec. 89n.); reproduced in facsimile in *Merrie England*, xiv. 298.

[4] Not found published.   [5] See 21 Dec. 89.

[6] For *The Speaker*; see 24 Dec. 89.

[7] See 17 Dec. 89.   [8] See 31 Dec. 89.

[9] Edward Walford, historian and genealogist, had sent his *William Pitt: a biography* (1890) (dedicated to Gladstone); Gladstone's comments are in *T.T.*, 3 January 1890, 6a.

[10] Hyland C. Kirk of New York had sent essays; Hawn P.

[11] *N.C.*, xxvii. 150 (January 1890).

[12] All in *N.C.*, xxvii (January 1890), with his own article on Melbourne (see 26 Nov. 89).

[13] Recollections of Provost E. C. Hawtrey, assistant master at Eton during Gladstone's schooldays; Add MS 44790, ff. 1–3 and *Autobiographica*, i. 24; written at the request of Francis St John Thackeray and used for Hawtrey's *D.N.B.* notice.

4. Sat.

Ch. 8½ A.M. Wrote to Ld Granville (B.P.)—Lady Russell (B.P.)—Mr Buxton MP (B.P.)—Ld C. Russell (B.P.)—Gen. Ponsonby—Mr Campbell WS—Mr Showering—Hon. Hamilton Gordon—E.W. Hamilton—The Speaker—Mrs Th.—Mr Gregory—Watsons—Scotts l.l.—J.A. Berker—Rev. Mr Bernt. Worked on the Family Distribution of 43 m[ille] and took the different steps needful in order to set it going. Finished Walford's Pitt & examined various volumes of mediocre poetry.

5. S. after Circumcn.

Ch. 11 A.M. and H.C. 6½ P.M. Wrote to Mr Wemyss Reid BP—Mr Higham—H.T. Pullan—Abp of Canterbury. Read (moiety) article on Ellen Middleton[1]—Clodd, Hutton, Costelloe, Curtiss, Rawlinson, in Relig. of the World.[2]

6. M. Epiph. C.s birthday.

Ch 8½ A.M. and H.C. together. Wrote to Miss D. Tennant—Sir R. Welby—Messrs Matthews—Mr Noble—Sir J.D. Weston—Mr Knowles—Mr Quaritch—Sir T. Moss—Mr Baker—A.H. Curtis—Ed. Ch. & People[3]—Ld Coleridge—Mons. Tschirag—J. Teller—J.R.S. Harington[4]—Miss Kraeger. Wrote on O.T.[5] Finished the Distribution Statements & put them in circulation. Guests arrived. Rosebery and the Tennants.[6] Read B. Gould's new Vol.[7]

7. Tu.

Ch. 8½ AM (with the Tennants). Dear Herbert's birthday; God bless & keep him. Wrote to Watson & Smith—Scotts—Mr Atkinson—L. Tiller—W.W. Keyworth—Jas Mackie—J.W. Buckley—J.M.N. Keith—J.C.R. Marriott—W. Meynell—Rev. Dr. Cox. Worked on accounts of Property & Dedication Fund for the year. Saw H.N.G. on his affairs. Walk with the party. Showed the libraries: but got no work there. Read Baring Gould—Love & Unbelief.[8] Wrote on Homer (for Chambers Encyclop.)[9] Conversation with Rosebery.

---

[1] His review of 1844, whose reprint in *Merrie England* was the subject of controversy and misunderstanding; see 29 Dec. 89n.

[2] *Religious systems of the world: addresses at South Place Institute, 1888–9* (1890).

[3] See 21 Dec. 89.

[4] John Robert Strong Harington, nonconformist minister; had sent his articles on Gladstone's birthday, and defending him against pro-Roman charges; see Add MS 44509, f. 16.

[5] Start of preparation of what became seven articles on the bible in *Good Words* (April–November 1890), republished after revision as *The impregnable rock of Holy Scripture* (1890).

[6] Margot Tennant and her br., Charles Coombe Tennant (1852–1928), signed the Visitors' Book.

[7] S. Baring-Gould, probably *Historical oddities and strange events* (1889).

[8] Untraced.

[9] 'Homer' (unsigned), in *Chamber's Encyclopaedia* (1890), v. 754; also reprinted for private circulation.

8. *Wed.*

Ch. 8½ A.M. Wrote to Mrs B. Harrison—Mr D. Patrick—A.F. Winks—Roper & Drowley[1]—W.C. Blackett—Ald. Redmond—Jas. Fyfe—S. Pickering—W. Agnew—Bp. of Sodor & Man—H.G.B. Watkin—Mrs Ingram. Finished MS. on Homer. Gave it J. Talbot to read. Homeric conversation. Walk with the Breadalbanes and party. Read Miss Jay & Duke of W.[2]—Part of Miss Chapmans MS in reply to Milton.[3] Worked on books & letters. Twelve to dinner.

9. *Th.*

Ch. 8½ A.M. Wrote to Mr P.W. Campbell—S.E.G.—Mr Miller (Perth)—Mr Lowe—Messrs Watson—J. Allen—Miss Chapman—Mr Bridge?—Mr H. Seymour—B. Quaritch—J. Tabbenor—Mr Lloyd Bryce Tel. Wrote Queries on Miss Chapman's Paper—Worked on books & papers. Walk with W. Richmond.[4] He holds by Xty. Attended the Rent Dinner to *speak* only.[5] Conversation with Sir Jas Kitson. Read Duke of W. & Miss J.—Finished Chapman MS.

10. *Fr.*

Ch 8½ A.M. Wrote to Mad. Bashkirtseff[6] BP.—Sir C. Dilke—Mr P.W. Currie—Sir L. Bell[7]—Sig. E.G. Broya—Mr J. Nicol—M.Q. Holyoake—Mr W. Tarver—Rev. Jos Hammond. Walk with Ld Coleridge. Took him, also Mr W. Richmond, to St D.s—Both were interested & pleased. Saw Mr W. Bailey. Worked on papers. Worked a little on O.T. MS. Read Duke of W. & Miss J.:!!—Schaff's Toleration Act[8]—and . . . . .

11. *Sat.*

Ch. 8½ A.M. Wrote to Col. C. Chaillé Long—Mr A. Sutton BP.—W. Ridler—Messrs Remington—E. Wilson—C. De Botha—J. Henderson—Script Phonograph Co.[9] Lord C. went: most agreeable breakfast conversation. Worked at St Deiniol's. Worked on O.T. MS. Saw W.H.G.—Sir E. Watkin—H.J.G. (as usual). Finished D of W. and Miss J.—Read 'My Rectors'.[10]

---

[1] London publishers.

[2] Untraced.

[3] Elizabeth Rachel Chapman, author and member of the Moral Reform Union, had sent for Gladstone's comments her published MS, 'Why we should oppose divorce' (1980). See Add MS 44509, f. 25. See also 8 Dec. 90.

[4] i.e. William Blake Richmond, the artist.

[5] Spoke generally on agriculture; *T.T.*, 10 January 1890, 6a.

[6] Maria Bashkirtseff, mother of the artist; Add MS 44509, f. 39.

[7] Sir (Isaac) Lothian Bell, 1816–1904; coal-owner in North East; liberal M.P. 1875–80; cr. bart. 1885.

[8] P. Schaff, *Church and State in the United States; or, the American idea of religious liberty* (1888).

[9] Script Phonography Co. Ltd., shorthand teachers and publishers, in London, directed by Thomas S. Malone; business untraced.

[10] *My Rectors, by a quondam curate* (1890).

12. 1 S. Epiph.

Ch mg & evg. Wrote to Mr Wemyss Reid. Read Imago Christi[1]—H.S., O.T., respecting David &c.—Smith, Assyrian Discoveries[2]—Bp of Ripon B. Lecture.[3] We are much pleased with Lady B[readalbane]; she is earnest, has *character*.

13. M.

Ch. $8\frac{1}{2}$ A.M. Wrote to Ld Chief Justice—Ld Acton—Dr Leonard U.S.[4]—Mr Rigby Tel.—Wallace Bruce—Geo. Lewis—Rev. C.H. Irwin—Ed. Star (Tel)—R. M'Kinstry—Canon M'Coll. Worked hard on Döllinger MS.[5] An hour on books at St D.s Attended Herbert's Lecture on India: & spoke briefly.[6] Saw H.J.G. as usual with the letters: which he now handles, & extremely well. Read Origines de la Civ. Mod.[7]—and [blank.]

14. Tu.

Ch. $8\frac{1}{2}$ A.M. Wrote to Mr Wemyss Reid—Mr Lucy—Rev. A.W. Bates—Rev. E. Simons—R.W. Cameron—Mr J. Nicol—C.E. Girardot—A. Beecher—D.B. Anderson—Mrs Maury Corbin—F.B. Doveton. Saw H.J.G.—whom Mary is now to replace. Worked at St Deiniol's. Revised & dispatched Art. on Dr D. taking first the benefit of Mary's opinion. Read Freeman on Home Rule[8]—Professor Smith on Scripture and Science[9]—Life of Maury[10]—Life of Macdonell.[11]

15. Wed.

Ch $8\frac{1}{2}$ A.M. Wrote to W. Hamilton—Mr Leader—Prof. Haskell[12]—Mr Vickers—Mr O.J. Simon—Rev. S.E.G.—G. Gard Pye—Westell—Watsons—J. Sigerson—C. Lowe—C. Rintoul. Worked on O.T. MS. Worked on books—here & at St Deiniol's. Read Simon's Novel[13]—Macdonell's Life.

16. Th.

Ch. $8\frac{1}{2}$ A.M. Wrote to Watson & Smith—Dr Moir—Helen G.—F.C. Hutt—Mr Wemyss Reid—A.A. Harvey—Mr J. Nicol—E.F. Jacques—Mr Knowles—

---

[1] J. Stalker, *Imago Christi* (1889).

[2] George Smith, *Assyrian discoveries on the site of Nineveh* (1875).

[3] W. Boyd Carpenter, *The permanent elements of religion. Eight lectures* (1889).

[4] Charles H. Leonard of the U.S.A. had sent birthday congratulations; Hawn P.

[5] 'Dr Döllinger', *The Speaker*, 18 January 1890; a signed obituary, but also an account of Gladstone's dealings with him. Sent to T. Wemyss Reid next day; correspondence on the article is in the Montague Collection, New York Public Library.

[6] *T.T.*, 14 January 1890, 7d; Herbert Gladstone had visited India, as well as Henry Neville Gladstone who had worked there.   [7] See 21 Dec. 89.

[8] E. A. Freeman, 'Parallels to Irish Home Rule', *F.R.*, lii. 293 (September 1889).

[9] See 4 Dec. 76.

[10] D. F. Maury Corbin, *A life of Matthew Fontaine Maury . . . compiled by his daughter* (1888), who had sent the volume.

[11] Probably W. J. Macdonnell, *Reminiscences of the late Alexander Macdonnell, first Catholic Bishop of Upper Canada* (1888).

[12] Possibly B. D. Haskell, theologian in Massachussetts.

[13] Oswald John Simon had sent his novel, *The world and the cloister*, 2v. (1890).

A. Macleod—Mr P. Russell—Mr Holyoake. Much troubled for these few past nights with a sharp rheumatism in the right shoulder: quite *new*. Worked on books here and at St D.s. Corrected proofs on Books. Same on Dr Döllinger. Conversation with WHG on the great beech, & inspection. Read Life of Macdonell—and [blank.]

17. Fr.

Ch. 8½ A.M. Wrote to Lady Wolverton—Rev. R. Day—Rev. C.E. Stowe—J.A. Steven—Mr A.A. Marens—E. Mathews—Mr Temple Leader—Jas Knowles— J.E.M. Steele—D. Rees—S. Francis—Mr Nicol Tel. Read Life of Macdonell—Miss Nesbit's Poems[1]—Canon Cook on the Psalms[2]—Bp Wilberforce 'Heroes',[3] Thin! (inter alia, for O.T. MS.)

18. Sat.

Ch. 8½ A.M. Wrote to Warden of All Souls—Mr Maclaren MP,[4] also BP—Horace Seymour—Dean of St Paul's—W.S. Palmer—Dean of Westmr—Mrs Craw— Canon Liddon—Watsons—Rev. Manley—Helen G.—J. Macleod—Ld Acton— Funk & Wagnall—Lady Blennerhassett—and Fraülein Dollinger—Bishop Reinkens. Worked on MS 'Psalms'.[5] Drove with C. to tea at Mr Hurlbutt's. Worked on books. Read Macdonell's Life—Oration on J. Davis,[6] & divers other tracts.

19. 2 S. Epiph.

Ch 11 A.M. and P.M. Wrote to E.W. Hamilton—Sir R. Morier BP—Empress Victoria BP—Dean of Durham—Mr H. Anson—Rev. Mr. Matthew[7]—Mr Henderson—Sir Ch. Tennant—Messrs Garrett. Saw S. on Mr Matthew's[8] case. Read Bp of Ripon, B. Lectures—Abp of Cant. Christ & his Times[9]—Dean Lake's Sermon[10]—Bates on Ritualism[11]—Hammond Church or Chapel.[12]

20. M.

Ch. 8½ A.M. Wrote to Mr Stuart Rendel—Mrs Th.—Mr Jas Knowles—Scotts— J. Pembery—B.Boyle—R.H.B.Hutchinson—G.Melly—O. Browning—P. Crellin[13] —W.B. Richmond. Saw Harry (S.R. & Lp Adv[owso]n). Saw WHG: again going

---

[1] E. Nesbit, *Life's sunny side. Poems* (1890), sent by her friend J. E. Marshall Steele of Lewisham and Lee Liberal Club; Hawn P.

[2] F. C. Cook, *The Book of Psalms* (1880).

[3] See 20 Mar. 70.

[4] Walter Stowe Bright McLaren, 1853–1912, s. of Duncan; liberal M.P. Crewe 1886–95, 1910–12.

[5] See 6 Jan. 90.

[6] Probably on Jefferson Davis.

[7] i.e. A. J. P. Matthews, Add MS 44509, f. 68.

[8] Case of the convert from Rome; see Add MS 44509, f. 68 and 2 Aug. 89.

[9] E. W. Benson, 'Christ and His times' (1889).

[10] W. C. Lake, perhaps 'The religious movements of our time' (1881), or in M.S.

[11] See 18 Sept. 81.

[12] J. Hammond, 'Church or Chapel? An eirenicon' (1889).

[13] Of London; sent a copy of *The Rivulet*; Hawn P.

on well. Worked on MS of O.T. Worked on books at St D.s. Read Lynell's Poems[1]—Henderson's Poems[2]—Macdonell's Life. H.J.G. came back. I gave just praise to his manly straightforward evidence.[3]

21. Tu.

Ch. 8½ A.M. Wrote to Warden of All Souls—Mr A. Morley—R. Darlington—R.G. Tickle—Geo. Williamson—Rev. W. Moore—J. Savellariades[4]—A. Reid—R. Barry O'Brien—P. Wacksell—Watson & Smith—P. Mennell—Miss Pullan—Rev. Mr Allen. The Duckworths came to St D. & the Church—in sad weather. Worked on O.T. MS. Read Macdonell—Sigerson on Pol. Prisoners[5]—Miss Naden's Modern Apostle—powerful & painful.[6]

22. Wed.

Ch. 8½ A.M. Wrote to Rev. Williamson—Watsons—Mr Liversedge BP—E. Beavis—Eugene Field.[7] Worked on arranging papers. Looked up Irish papers &c. and made notes. Dined with the Tomkinsons at Old Bank Chester, & spoke 1 h. 20 m. in Music Hall.[8] Read Miss Naden—A new Continent.[9]

23. Th.

Ch. 8½ A.M. Wrote to Dr Talmage (Tel.)[10]—Ld Northbourne—Mr Rendel MP.—Grogan & Boyd—E. Hall—Sir Ch. Tennant—W. Caxton—Parl. Circular—A. Morley MP.—Rev. Dr Kerr—J.H. Hill—Dr W.F. Moore—T.J. Hughes. Worked on O.T. MS. Worked at St Deiniol's. Read Miss Naden, Elixir of Life—The New Continent—Angiles Temptations.[11]

24. Fr.

Ch. 8½ A.M. Wrote to Sig. Schilizzi—A. Sutton—Prov. of Oriel—A.H. Drake—W. Gregory p. HNG—W. Small—Lady Middleton—C. Maclean—Messrs Sinclair—C.E. Handford—H. Fox Bourne—J.A. Fox—Col. H. Vincent[12]—J. Wright—Rev. T.T. Shore—A. Sidgwick—C. Uppington. Dr Talmage[13] came: I walked with him in the Park: much talk: a good man. Also Ly Ailesbury & Ly H. Grosvenor.

[1] Apparently *sic*; but untraced.
[2] F. Henderson, *By the sea, and other poems* (1890).
[3] Obscure.
[4] Of Liverpool; had written on Greek affairs; Hawn P.
[5] G. Sigerson, *Political prisoners at home and abroad* (1890) sent by the author; Add MS 44509, f. 37.
[6] C. C. W. Naden, *A modern apostle, the elixir of life . . . and other poems* (1887); see 29 Dec. 89.
[7] Eugene Field, American poet; see Add MS 44509, f. 64.
[8] Meeting of Chester liberals; *T.T.*, 23 January 1890, 10a.
[9] Mrs. Worthley, *The new continent*, 2v. (1890).
[10] Thomas De Witt Talmage, 1832–1902; American evangelist, on a world tour. For later reminiscences of this visit, see L. A. Banks, *T. De Witt Talmage* (1902), 293.
[11] Reading uncertain.
[12] Col. (Sir) Charles Edward Howard Vincent, 1849–1908; in army and law; tory M.P. 1885–1908; a strong fair-trader and imperialist; kt. 1896.
[13] See previous day.

Worked on books. Examined Octagon with Harry. Read Q.R. on Welsh Church[1]—Canton's Poems[2]—Divers Tracts—Catherine von Bora.[3]

25. Sat.

Ch 8½ AM & H.C. Wrote to A.B. Farquhar—W. Ridler—G.E. Talbot—C. Lowe— S.G.B. Cook—C. Higham—Mr T. M'Crae—Rev. S. Lloyd—W. Kinmont—Murrays—J.G. MacSweeny[4]—J. Noble—J. Hetherington. Dined with the Mayhews. Worked on books: Castle and St Deiniol's. Worked on MS. of O.T. Read Q.R. on Poland[5]—Dana on Gen. I.[6]—and [blank.]

26. 2 S. Epiph.

Ch mg & evg. Wrote to Chester Station Master—Mrs Medge[7]—W.M.D. Bodkin[8]—Watsons—A.J.K. Trundell—Sir E. Malet—Miss Cotton—G. Dudron— T.C. Martin—A. Sidgwick[9]—J. Sparkes. Worked on O.T. MS. Copied extracts. Read Cath. von Bora (finished)—Coleridge, Confessions[10]—Plain Sermons[11]— and Divers Tracts.

27. M.

Ch. 8½ A.M. Wrote to Dean of Ch.Ch.—Miss Kenyon—Mr A. Peel—J.C. Humphreys—J.C. Moss—H.A. Carton—R. Wallace—Miss Chapman—Mr Medge. Saw Miss Scott—Mr W. Bailey (O. & St D.). Tea with W.H.G.s. Worked O.T. MS. Worked on books here & at St Deiniol's. Read Schrader on Cuneiform-Inscriptions[12]—Smith on do—Marlow's Faust[13]—Faust e Giobbe (Menza).[14]

28. Tues.

Ch. 8½ A.M. Wrote to Mr Lloyd Bryce—Mr D. Macpherson—Mr J. Nicol—Macmillans—Murrays—Clerk Parcels Office SER.—Ld E. Fitzmaurice—J. Walter— Messrs Garratt—W. Baker—Mr G.B. Gammoll. Worked hard on arranging my room, a chaos for 6 months: also at St D.s where I reckon there are now 5700 volumes. Worked on MS of O.T. Read Schrader—Smith—Delitzsch—Barnum's Autobiography[15]—finished Marlow's Faust.

---

[1] Q.R., clxx. 112 (January 1890).

[2] W. Canton, A lost epic and other poems (1887).

[3] H. F. Hofman, Katherina von Bora (1845).

[4] Of Dublin; sent songs; Hawn P.   [5] Q.R., clxx. 80 (January 1890).

[6] J. D. Dana, Creation or, the biblical cosmology in the light of modern science (1885); discussed in Impregnable Rock, 38.

[7] Eliza Medge, sister of O. B. Cole, in Hawarden school; Hawn P.

[8] Probably Mathias McDonnell Bodkin, 1850–1933, barrister and author; home rule M.P. N. Roscommon 1892–5.

[9] Declining his invitation, as president of the Oxford liberal association, to attend a political meeting during his visit; see also Add MS 44509, f. 77.

[10] See 31 Jan. 41.   [11] Probably those by Newman; see 9 Apr. 37.

[12] See 24 Nov. 89.   [13] See 11 Jan. 49.   [14] Untraced.

[15] P. T. Barnum, The life . . . written by himself (1855); see 30 Jan. 90.

29. *Wed.* [*London*]

Church 8½ AM: and so farewell to the loved daily service. Wrote to Professor Tyndall[1]—Mr A. Morley. Packing & preparing: off at 10.45. [10] St James's Square[2] 3.50: and chaos as usual. Dined at Mr Rendel's. The presents are a costly and wonderful show; with no trash. Maud was very affectionate and interesting. Read Dr Driver in Contemp. R.—Hill on the Monarchy—Green-wood on Fusion[3]—Wilson's Poets as Theologians[4]—Grey-Lieven Correspon-dence.[5]

30. *Th.*

Wrote to Macmillans—Mr D. Patrick[6]—Watsons—Rev. Morrah[7]—Mr Morton. Saw E. Hamilton—Sir H. Davy—Mr Knowles—Sir Alg. West—Mr Thompson—E. Talbot—Mrs Ward. Corrected Proofs Art. Homer for Chambers' Cyclop. Attended Barnum's Spectacle in evg. Worth seeing as a feature of the time. Conversation with him.[8] Read H.S. Books—Sack, Altjüdische Religion.[9] We went at two to the marriage.[10] With a few drawbacks in the service, it was beautiful. Both he & she spoke their parts in a perfect way. May every blessing be with them. Party at Mr Rendel's afterwards.

31. *Fr.* [*All Souls, Oxford*][11]

Wrote to Prov. of Oriel—Rev. G. Tidy—J. Dicks—J. Elliot—Mrs Bolton—Mr Warren—Mr Wemyss Reid—Dr Fairbairn.[12] 4.45—6.15. To All Souls.[13] Saw Sir Jas Carmichael—Rev. E. Talbot—Mrs Talbot—Lady Aberdeen—Scotts—Mrs B. Beere.[14] And at Oxford, the Warden,[15] Prof. Pelham,[16] Prof. M. Burrowes

---

[1] Start of dispute with John Tyndall about Pitt's Irish policy; *T.T.*, 10 March 1890, 4d.

[2] Now Chatham House; Gladstone took the house for the Session of 1890.

[3] All in *C.R.*, lvii (February 1890).

[4] H. S. Wilson, *Poets as theologians* (1888).

[5] *Correspondence of Princess Lieven and Earl Grey*, 3v. (1890).

[6] David Patrick, 1849-1914; ed. *Chamber's Encyclopaedia*; (see 7 Jan. 90n.).

[7] Probably Herbert Morrah; Hawn P.

[8] Phineas Taylor Barnum, 1810-91; began his great circus 1871 and toured with it.

[9] I. Sack, *Die Religion Altisraels nach den in der Bibel* (1885).

[10] Of H. N. Gladstone to Maud Rendel, at St. Margaret's, Westminster, S. E. Gladstone officiating, with Archdeacon Farrar and E. S. Talbot.

[11] Gladstone's time-table of meals, engagements etc. for his visit is at Add MS 44773, f. 176.

[12] Andrew Martin Fairbairn, 1838-1912; congregationalist and first principal of Mansfield College, Oxford, 1886-1909, where Gladstone dined, 5 Feb. 90.

[13] For this visit, see C. R. L. F[letcher], *Mr Gladstone at Oxford 1890* (1908) and Sir C. Oman, *Things I have seen* (1933), ch. iv. Gladstone was an Honorary Fellow of the College, which was staunchly liberal unionist or tory. Charles Robert Leslie Fletcher, 1857-1934, was fellow and modern history tutor at Magdalen, but returned to All Souls for Gladstone's visit; Gladstone confused him with H. F. Pelham, and does not mention his name in the diary.

[14] Fanny Mary Bernard Beere, actress.

[15] W. R. Anson; see 31 Dec. 89.

[16] Henry Francis Pelham, 1846-1907; Camden professor of ancient history from 1889; a leading University liberal.

[*sic*][1] and others. Read Gore's Masterly paper in *Lux Mundi*:[2] and The Bond-man.[3] Dinner in Hall—with the proper sequels.

Sat. Feb. One. Oxford.

Chapel 8½ A.M. Saw The Warden—Prof. Pelham—Dr Liddon—Mr [blank]—Sir H. Acland—Mr A. Peel[4]—Rector of Lincoln.[5] Made calls and mapped out time. Went over my particulars from Assyriology for the coming Lecture or conversation on Wednesday. Wrote to Mr Redmayne—Mr Creasey[6]—C.G.—Mr Rosse—Mr Morgan—Pres. Magdalen. Read The Bondman—et alia.

2. 4 S. Epiph. & Purifn.

A.S. Chapel 8¾. Univ. Sermon 10.30. Ch.Ch. evg. Wrote to Dean of Salisbury—C.G.—A.G.V. Peel—A. Morley—Miss Roberts—T. Baker—Sir R. Welby. Chief meals at A.S. Tea at the Dean's. Saw Dr [S.R.] Driver: long conversation on Genesis I. &c.—Saw Dr Paget. Read Altjüdische Religion (I. Sack) and divers books & Tracts.

3. M.

A.S. Chapel 8½ A.M. and Magdalen Chapel evg.

Wrote to J.S. Stevenson—Rivingtons—Pearson Hill—W.M. Adams—J. Cavenagh—R. Friend—A. Bayley—Miss Wild—L.K. Smith—C.G.—O. Der Neuwille. Breakfast at Oriel. Dinner at Ch.Ch. (Hall). Saw Warden of A.S. (on his book &c)[7]—Mr Robarts[8]—Dr Liddon—Mr Sampson[9]—Mayor of Oxford—Mr Carr (Senior Mag.)[10]—Dean of Ch.Ch.—SubLibr. and others.—Warden of Keble. Made calls. Visited A.S. Libr. Wrote on The Creation Story. Read The Bondman—Dana's Reply to Driver[11]—Hessor on the Cabinet.[12]

---

[1] Montagu Burrows, Chichele professor of modern history on Gladstone's recommendation to Palmerston (see 18 Mar. 61n.). 'M.B. had expressed in vigorous terms his conviction that he could not conscientiously meet Mr. Gladstone, but had been persuaded to join in the reception. Directly Mr. Gladstone heard his name he said, "Ah, Professor, it is one of the charms of Oxford that one meets at every moment some one with whose name in some branch of learning one has been long familiar." M.B. beamed with obvious pleasure, and at once surrendered to the spell. Soon after, I saw him trotting about after Mr. Gladstone with the sugar and cream-jug'; *Mr Gladstone at Oxford 1890*, 9.

[2] C. Gore, 'On Inspiration', in *Lux Mundi* (1889); a controversial and seminal contribution.

[3] Perhaps [Mrs. O'Neill], *The Bondman. A story of the time of Wat Tyler* (1833).

[4] Arthur George Villiers Peel, 1868–1956, grands. of the Prime Minister; as President of the Oxford Union organised Gladstone's visit on 5 February.

[5] William Walter Merry, 1835–1918; editor of Aristophanes; rector of Lincoln from 1884.

[6] Of Sidcup liberal association; *T.T.*, 6 February 1890, 6e.

[7] Anson was at work on the 2nd v. of *Law and custom of the constitution: on the Crown* (1892).

[8] Charles Henry Robarts, fellow of All Souls since 1865.

[9] Edward Frank Sampson, censor and mathematical tutor at Christ Church.

[10] J. R. Carr of 20 Beaumont Street.

[11] An article on J. D. Dana (see 25 Jan. 90) sent by Driver; Add MS 44509, f. 114.

[12] Untraced article.

4. Tu.

A.S. Chapel mg & Magdalen evg. Wrote to Mr Campbell—W. & T. Bailey—
T.J.W. Bennett[1]—D. Patrick l.l.—A. Galton—J.H. Hill—O.M. Tudor[2]—W. Down-
ing—A. Morley. Read Whewell, Bridgw. Treatise[3]—Morris on Religion &
Science (notable).[4] Breakfast at Balliol. Museum afternoon. St Frideswide &
Chapterhouse at 2.30. Saw Canon Fremantle—Master of Balliol[5]—Dr
Grueber[6]—Warden of Merton[7]—Dean of Ch.Ch.—Dr Tylor[8]—Mr Jacobs of
Wadham[9]—Pres. Magdalen—Mr Margoliouth[10]—Dr Driver. Dined with the
Dean of ChCh. Evening party followed. All most interesting.

5. Wed.

A.S. Chapel mg. Wrote to Mons. du Chaillu[11]—Mr Tyreman[12]—Rev. M. Williams—J.B. Oldham—Mr M. Morris—Rev. Mr Lucy—Mr A. Morley—Sir R.
Welby(?). Breakf. party of Fellows & Homeric conversation (A.S.) Saw Warden
of A.S.—Sir H. Acland—Mr Capell—Dr Birkbeck Hill—Dr Fairbairn[13]—Mr
Cheyne—Dr Murray—& many more. Read Shakespeare's True Life[14]—Acland,
Medical Studies.[15] After tea at the Warden's & seeing C.G.[16] I went to the Union
and made my lecture 75 min. on Homer & Assyria. All were too indulgent. It is
probably a farewell.[17]

---

[1] T. J. Wesley Bennett of Highgate, on *Ellen Middleton*; Hawn P.

[2] Not further identified.

[3] See 13 Nov. 34.

[4] H. W. Morris, *Work days of God; or, science and the bible* (1888).

[5] Jowett.

[6] Erwin Grueber, lecturer in Roman law at Balliol.

[7] G. C. Brodrick.

[8] (Sir) Edward Burnett Taylor, 1832–1917; anthropologist and Keeper of the University Museum; kt. 1912.

[9] Maurice Jacobs, a graduate of Wadham 1887 (later French consul in Brighton) with whom Gladstone had a conversation on Jews in the United Kingdom, reported by Jacobs to the press; Jacobs later wrote of its favourable reception by his 'coreligionists ... one and all expressed their gratitude & indebtedness to you for your generous and sympathetic opinions concerning us'; Add MS 44509, ff. 197, 207.

[10] David Samuel Margoliouth, 1858–1940; Laudian professor of Arabic and fellow of New College.

[11] Paul Belloni du Chaillu, the explorer, had sent cuttings on his book *The Viking Age*; Add MS 44509, f. 125.

[12] Had sent an essay; Hawn P.

[13] He dined this evening with Fairbairn in Mansfield College hall, meeting some of the Oxford liberal dons; *T.T.*, 6 February 1890, 6e.

[14] J. Walter, *Shakespeare's true life* (1889); sent (twice) by the author; Add MS 44509, ff. 79, 118.

[15] Sir H. W. Acland, 'Oxford and modern medicine' (1890).

[16] Somewhat to Gladstone's irritation, she had come to stay with Sir H. W. Acland to see that her husband was not over-exerting himself.

[17] *T.T.*, 6 February 1890, 6d; Archdeacon Palmer and Sir H. Acland spoke in thanks; Gladstone then made farewell remarks: 'To call a man a characteristically Oxford man is, in my opinion, to give him the highest compliment that can be paid to any human being.'

6. Th.

A.S. Chapel 8.30 A.M. Wrote to Oxf. Servants Society—Mr Blunt—S. Ball[1]—A.J. Butler—W. Stebbing—W. Woodford—G.H. Cooper—A. Connell—Thos Davies—T.E. Holland—Col. Lindsay—A. Ll. Roberts—Mr Cotton. 9–11¾. Breakfast at Magdalen: a gigantic dissipation. Luncheon at Exeter (Prof. Pelham). Dinner at the Vice Chancellor's (St John's) with the Club.[2] Read Shakespeare—Tracts on Oxford. Residue of time filled with conversations.

7. Fr.

Wrote to Mr Walter—Mr Binns—A. Higham—Mrs Bough—C.G.—Sir J. Barrow —Canon Driver—Canon Huntley—Mr Callisporis—Miss Ladner—Messrs Cassell—Mr Soulaby—Mr Charsley. Breakf. A.S.—Luncheon Sir H. Acland. Dinner The Warden. Walk with Master of Balliol. Visited Trinity—the 5½ acre Wadham Garden—& Dr Murray's Scriptorium.[3] Saw The Warden 11–12 Const. Hist.[4]— Dr Moore[5] on Dante—Mr Headlam[6]—Provost Munro—Mr Pelham—Mr Raper[7]—Mrs Green[8]—Mr Bertie[9]—and many more. Read Oxford Comic Verses[10]—Stebbing's Peterborough.[11]

8. Sat. [London]

No chapel! Off at 8¾. Home at 10¾. Worked hard in the direction of order. Wrote to Fraül. Döllinger—Sir R. Welby—Mrs Bursall—Sorabji Jehanger[12]—H. Wood—W.S. Bramington—W.S. Smart—S.A. Steinthal[13]—S.E. Odell—P.W. Bunting—Miss Buch—C.O. Weatherley. Saw A. Morley—M. Drew—Ld Granville—Mr Mundella. All the way to town I meditated: and well might! At 2.30 & to 4.30

---

[1] Sidney Ball, 1857–1918; fellow of St. John's from 1883; Fabian and reformer; he was secretary of The Club (different from that with which Gladstone dined this day), a body which encouraged university reform; Pelham was also a member. Ball may have invited Gladstone to a meeting; see *Sidney Ball. Memories and impressions* (1923), 192.

[2] James Bellamy, 1819–1900; president of St. John's from 1871; musician and conservative. The Club (an Oxford dining society not to be confused with The Club, of London, of which Gladstone was a member or that of which Ball and Pelham were members) dined in St. John's and celebrated Dean Liddell's 79th birthday; see F. Madan, *Records of 'The Club' at Oxford* (1917), 27 and Add MS 44773, f. 179.

[3] The iron shed in the garden of 'Sunnyside', 78 Banbury Road, where James Murray stored the materials for his *Dictionary*; at the insistence of A. V. Dicey, Murray's liberal unionist neighbour, the shed was sunk three feet into the ground, making it permanently cold and wet; see K. M. E. Murray, *Caught in the web of words* (1977), 242. Gladstone had secured a Civil List pension for Murray (see 1 Oct. 81) and his photograph hung on Murray's wall.   [4] See 3 Feb. 90.

[5] Edward Moore, principal of St Edmund Hall and linguist.

[6] Arthur Charles Headlam, 1862–1947; fellow of All Souls 1885; later a prominent Anglican.

[7] Robert William Raper, 1842–1915; fellow of Trinity 1871; founded Appointments Cttee.

[8] Charlotte, sister of J. A. Symonds and widow of T. H. Green, 1836–82, ethical philosopher, 'Mr. Gray' in *Robert Elsmere*. See Add MS 44773, f. 178 for H. W. Acland's notes for Gladstone on persons attending his luncheon.

[9] Henry Bertie, senior fellow of All Souls; he had been at Eton with Gladstone.

[10] Perhaps G. Nutt, *Greek comic iambics, recited in the Sheldonian Theatre, Oxford* (1866).

[11] W. Stebbing, *Peterborough* (1889).

[12] Parsee magistrate travelling in Europe; sent a copy of his book of Indian biographies; Hawn P.

[13] Of Manchester; apparently a Unitarian; Hawn P.

political meeting. I related my interview with Parnell.[1] Sir W.H. ran restive: but alone. We decided on a privilege motion for Tuesday: and a Bill to remove R.C. remaining disabilities for two great offices. Read Life of Peterborough—Fiske New England Settlement.[2]

9. Sexa S.

St James's mg (my Church in 1833-6), Chapel Royal aft. Worked on O.T. MS. Read Wiseman-Palmer Correspondence[3]—Liddon's Sermon on H.S.[4]—Fiske Puritans in New England—Free Theology. Saw the Farquhars.

10. M.

Wrote to Mons. N. Basile—Mr W.H. Smith—Watsons. Worked on O.T. MS. Saw Mr Bennett (Methodists)[5]—Ld Granville—Mr A. Morley l.l.—Ld Rosebery—Mr Bryce—and Sir A. Clark. Book buying. Dined at Ld Rosebery's. Read Articles of the New Review.[6]

11. Tu.

Wrote to Messrs Peacock—R.D. Roberts—Mr Mills B.P.—Jas Pollard—T. Wemyss Reid—Mr Downing—Ed. Independent (New York).[7] Meeting of political friends 12-1. Very harmonious. H. of C. 5-8¾. Spoke on privilege: and paired.[8] Saw Lucy Cavendish—Sir L. Playfair—A. Morley—and others. Worked on O.T. MS. Read Fiske on New England.

12. Wed.

Wrote to Miss Martyn—Sir C. Tennant—Ld Meath—M.K. Friend—Mr Knowles—Mr Roden Noel. H. of C. 12¾-2¾. Spoke fully on the Address.[9] Dined

---

[1] See 18–19 and 23 Dec. 90. Morley noted in his diary this day: 'I thought Mr. G. looking old and weary: he was rather deaf and a little confused. He described Parnell's views as to various points in H.R., the upshot of wh. was that P. wd. make no difficulties for us. Of course not: it is not his way to make difficulties before he is obliged. It soon came out, however, that plenty of difficulties existed in our own camp. Harct. showed that what he means is to give Ired. a big county council and no more. Poor Mr. G. shook his head, half sadly, half ironically, "Is that to be all after 4 years!!" He does not see that we are less and less able to force a strong scheme, as the years go on. When I thought of it all after, I felt la mort dans l'ame. 1) Half the [ex-]Cab[ine]t are for shelving H.R., and are only occupied in find[in]g how to do it without discrediting the party; they are for Joe's policy of 1885, and only wonder how they can steal it without being detected as Joe-ites. Harct. is the head of this section, and he frankly admitted that my view of the situation was quite right. 2) Real friends of a natnl. govmt. are Mr. G., Spencer, and me: Granville, Ripon, Kimberley, Stansf[el]d with us, but w. no particular grasp of the quest[ion]. 3) Rosebery, thinking first of A.R., and second of some vague notion of federalism: with him wd. be C[ampbell] B[annerman]. There are thus 3 sections: a. Home Rulers as in 1886. b. Federalists. c. Minimisers. . . .'

[2] J. Fiske, *The beginnings of New England* (1889).

[3] Correspondence between Wiseman and Palmer on Roman catholicism; see 10 Mar. 45.

[4] H. P. Liddon, 'The worth of the Old Testament' (1890).

[5] Joseph Bennett, 1829-1908; strong methodist; liberal M.P. W. Lindsey 1885-6, 1892-5.

[6] *New Review*, ii (February 1890).   [7] Not found published.

[8] Spoke on Harcourt's motion on privilege (the Parnell Commission and *The Times*' publication of Pigott's forged letters), which delayed discussion on the Queen's Speech; *H* 341. 63.

[9] On foreign affairs in 'language of congratulation rather than censure'; *H* 341. 136.

at Sir A. West's. Conversation on the Holfords:[1] also with Lady D. Neville[2] whom I asked to propose me for the Carlton!! Saw A. Morley. Worked on books & papers. Read Fiske on New England—The Bondman—Dyer's Great Senators.[3] Tea at Lady Derby's. Conversation with Ld & Lady St[anley] of Alderley.

13. Th.

Wrote to Mr Knowles—J. Elliot—J.W. Palmer—Mr Murray—Sig. Galiero—W.M. Fullerton—R.M. Millan—Sir L. Playfair—Rev. E.R. Young—Rev. J.M. Dawson—Rev. R.C. Jenkins—Miss Gonsalez. Worked on plan of Library for N.C.[4] Saw Mr Knowles—Sir J. Carmichael—A. Morley—Mr Stansfeld—Col. Bigge—Sir R. Blackwood. H. of C. $5\frac{1}{2}$–$7\frac{3}{4}$.[5] Dined with Mrs Neville: small & pleasant. Read Fiske—The Bondsman—Hansard (87).

14. Frid.

Wrote to Mr J. Nicol—Vote Office. Worked on MS. for Books. Dispatched O.T. MS No. I. Saw Sir C. Tennant—Ld Granville—A. Morley. Dined with [blank.] H. of C. till dinner. Read The Bondman—Fiske on New England—Began Parnell Commn Report.[6]

15. Sat.

Wrote to Rev. Mr Jenkins—Mr S.T. Evans—Messrs Charles. Worked on O.T. MS. Saw Mr Lushington (Guy's)—Mr Nicol—Sir L. Playfair—Mr Wemyss Reid—Ld Kimberley—Mrs Th.—Ld E. Fitzmaurice. Thirteen to dinner. Finished Fiske. Read Commission Report.

16. Quinqua S.

St James's mg (with H.C.) and evg. Read Ward (2nd Edn)[7]—Delitzsch on the Psalms—Laveleye Papauté[8]—Liverpool Churches[9]—Jenkins on the Succession.[10] Wrote O.T. MS.

17. M.

Wrote to Rev. Mr Sedgwick—Mr W. Meadows—Mr . . . .—H.M. Alden (NY).[11] H. of C. $4\frac{1}{4}$–$7\frac{1}{4}$.[12] Dined at Sir C. Foster's. Saw Mr A. Morley—Mr Knowles—Sir

---

[1] Probably R. S. Holford, former tory M.P. and owner of Dorchester House, and his wife Mary Anne; see 2 July 70.

[2] Lady Dorothy Fanny Nevill, 1826–1913; widow of R. H. Nevill; traveller and autobiographer.

[3] O. Dyer, *Great senators of the United States forty years ago* (1889).

[4] See 17 Dec. 89.   [5] Queen's Speech; *H* 341. 211.   [6] *PP* 1890 xxvii.

[7] Second ed. of W. G. Ward and the Oxford Movement; sent by Wilfrid Ward with a letter on its changes; Add MS 44509, f. 163. See 8 June 89.

[8] Untraced article by E. L. V. de Laveleye.

[9] D. Thom, *Liverpool churches and chapels* (1854).

[10] R. C. Jenkins, *The true apostolic succession* (1890).

[11] Henry Mills Alden, editor of *Harper's Magazine*; business untraced.

[12] Queen's Speech, Ireland; *H* 341. 445.

C. Russell—and after dinner with the conclave on the proper mode of meeting the Smith motion.[1] Read (largely) the Parnell Commn Report—The Bondman.

18. Tu.

Wrote to C. Moderna—Watsons BP.—Mr Pembery—M. Jacobs—L. Fagan. H. of C. $4\frac{3}{4}$-$7\frac{3}{4}$ and $10\frac{3}{4}$-$12\frac{1}{2}$. Voted for P.s Amn in 240:307.[2] Saw Sir J. Carmichael—Sir W. Harcourt—Do *cum* Ld Granville—Sir C. Russell—Mr Bannerman—Mr A. Morley. Miner's Deputation 3-4 PM.[3] Finished Parnell Report (Discussed methods of proceeding)—Lefevre on Ireland.[4]

19. Wed. (Ash).

Ch. 11 A.M. Wrote to Rev. E.K. Roberts—Mr W. Ward—Rev. Mr Jenkins—W.H.G.—Sir E. Watkin—Hugh Reid—A.B. Acworth—and minutes. Worked on O.T. MS. Saw Sir J. Carmichael. H. of C. $2\frac{3}{4}$-$5\frac{3}{4}$. Spoke on Scottish Home Rule.[5] Read Grey-Lieven correspondence and read Lefevre on Ireland.

20. Th.

Wrote to Sir W. Farquhar—M. Satouroff—Mrs Murchison—& minutes. Dined with Mr & Mrs Arbuthnot. Attended Ld Sydney's funeral at the dear old Church of Chiselhurst. Saw the Prince of Wales, Empress Eugenie, Ld Granville and others. Laid up with cold at night. H. of C. 4-$5\frac{3}{4}$ on P.C. motion.[6] Read Lefevre on Ireland—Ld Peterborough.

21. Fr.

In bed. Saw Sir J.C.—A.M. pluries, on form of motion. Wrote to Sir W. Harcourt. Read The Bondman—M. Williams Reminiscences.[7]

22. Sat.

In bed. Wrote to Mr Knowles—Lady Sydney. Finished Art. on Books for Press.[8] Read Williams—Life of Peterborough.

[1] Probably W. H. Smiths' resolution accepting the Parnell Commissioners' report moved on 3 March; *H* 341. 1670.

[2] Parnell's amndt. on coercion and land; *H* 341. 332, 675.

[3] Deputation on the Eight Hours question, led by Pickard, and including Keir Hardie; Gladstone agreed that 'the eight hours limit is a reasonable limit for underground labour', encouraged progress by non-statutory means, and stressed the difficulty of the worker who wished to work longer; *T.T.*, 19 February 1890, 8e. See also 8 Dec. 89n.

[4] G. J. S. Lefevre, *Combination and coercion* (1890).

[5] Arguing that 'sentiment in Scotland . . . though not yet articulate, is real and substantial' but that no definite commitment could be made until there was real promise of success; 'in my opinion, in the circumstances, this is a time of reserve'; *H* 341. 721.

[6] On Parochial Councils; *H* 341. 775.

[7] M. S. Williams, *Leaves of a life, being the reminiscences of Montagu Williams, Q.C.* (1890).

[8] See 17 Dec. 89.

23. 1 S. Lent.

In bed till dusk. Prayerbook and Bible alone. Wrote to Mr J. Nicol—Mr Becker. Read Delitzsch on the Psalms—Life of Hannah[1]—End of Ld Peterborough, sad enough. Saw Sir A. Clark.

24. M.

Rose at noon. Wrote to Sir B. Samuelson—Mr Nicol—W.H. Corfield—Mr Knowles—W. Heinemann[2]—W.H.G.—Archdn Farrar—A. Bekker—Col. M'Hardy —T. Sturrah—Rev. R.W. Dobbie[3]—Rev. Jenkins P.P.—Sec. Forth Bridge Co—Watsons—& minutes. Saw Sir J. Carmichael—Mr A. Morley—Mr Osgood.[4] Read Horace Ep. & Sat.—The Sutherland Democracy[5]—Williams, Reminiscences. Not quite off the sick list, but nearly. Tonics now in!

25. Tu.

Wrote to Rev. Mr Eyton—Madame Bashkirtseff—Dean of Durham—Mr Ridler— Watsons (Tel.)—Dean Lake—Archdn Farrar. Saw A. Morley—Ld Granville— Scotts—Macmillans. Drove out shopping. Read Northcote Memoir[6]—Antiquarian Jottings.[7]—Williams Reminisc. (finished).

26. Wed.

Wrote to Mr Hill—Mr Mont. Williams—Mr [blank]—Sir Dr. Wolff—A.W. Hutton—Bp of Ripon. Read Northcote Memoir & Notes—Antiqu. Jottings—and [blank.] Saw Sir J. Carmichael—A. Morley & others?

27. Th.

Wrote to Mr Bolton[8]—Mr Gilby—Robn & Nichn—Mr Nicol BP—J. Westell. H. of C.[9] Dined with Mr Knowles. Conversation with Mr K.—Gen. Ponsonby— Lord R. Churchill. Saw Sir C. Russell. Read Northcote Notes—Antiquarian Jottings. Wrote on O.T.

28. Fr.

Wrote to Mr A. Morley—Rev. F. Burnside—Mr Mayow—Mr Heinemann. Worked ineffectually on Parnell Report. Also on O.T. MS. Saw Sir J. Carmichael & others. Read From Cloister to Altar.[10]

---

[1] J. H. Overton, *John Hannah. A clerical study* (1890).

[2] William Heinemann, 1863-1920; founded his publishing house this year.

[3] Free Church minister in Glasgow, on Gladstone's Vatican Decree pamphlets; *D.N.*, 6 March 1890, 5g.

[4] James R. Osgood, *Harper*'s agent in London.

[5] D. W. Kemp, *The Sutherland democracy* (1890).

[6] A. Lang, *Life, letters and diaries of Sir Stafford Northcote*, 2v. (1890).

[7] G. Clinch, *Antiquarian jottings relating to Bromley, Hayes, Keston and West Wickham* (1889).

[8] Letter of support for St. Pancras by-election; *T.T.*, 1 March 1890, 11f.

[9] Misc. business; *H* 341. 1353.

[10] 'Claud', *From cloister to altar; or, woman in love* (1890).

Sat. March One 1890.

Wrote to Watsons—Mr E. Benjamin—Mr Moon. Read Wylie, Queen or Pope(!)[1]—Hallam Constit. Hist.[2]—From Cloister to Altar finished—Lefevre on Ireland. Worked on materials for Commission Speech.

2. 2 S.L.

Chapel Royal mg and H.C.—St James's evg. Saw Sir W. Harcourt—Lady G. & her daughter. Wrote to Mr Fullarton—Messrs Spottiswoode. Finished Vivien[3]— Read Carnegie No. II—Memoirs of Hannah—Delitzsch on the Psalms.

3. M.

Wrote to Lt Col. Gloag—Mr Nicol. Worked on material & order of Speech: say 4 hours. Saw Harcourt l.l.—A. Morley—Mr Rendel. H. of C. $3\frac{1}{2}$-$7\frac{3}{4}$. Spoke 1 hour 40 m on my amendment; with a deep sense of utter weakness but less to my dissatisfaction than usual.[4] Home for a quiet evening. Read Labouchere's Letter[5]— Davitt on the Commission[6]—Teague on Ken.[7]

4. Tu.

Wrote to Ld Acton 1 & BP—Bodley Librarian[8] BP—All Souls do BP—Mrs Downes—Mr Parnell MP—Mr Folkard—Mr Wagnall—Mr Mitchell—Ed. Bristol Mercury.[9] Saw Ld Granville—Mrs Peel—Mr A. Morley—Lady G. Read 'A Strange People'[10]—[blank] on Alsace. H. of C. 4-$7\frac{1}{4}$.[11] Worked on O.T. MS.

5. Wed.

Wrote to Ld Granville—Bp of Rochester—Mr Downing—Messrs Sotheran— Rev. Renham—W.H.G. Saw Mr Barry O'Brien—Ld Northbourne—Sir J. Carmichael—Mr Morley—The Speaker—Mr A. Morley. H. of C. 4-$5\frac{1}{2}$.[12] Mr Bryce. Worked on MS. of O.T. 3-4. Nachez[13] played on the violin: with extraordinary talent. Dined with the Speaker. Read Heimweh's Alsace.[14]

---

[1] J. A. Wylie, *Which sovereign? Queen Victoria or the Pope?* (1888).
[2] See 24 Sept. 27.
[3] M. Edgeworth, *Vivian and Almeria* (1856).
[4] Amndt. to Smith's motion accepting the Commissioners' report; Gladstone proposed that the House deplored the false charges and regretted wrong and suffering inflicted; *H* 341. 1670.
[5] Labouchere defended his attack on Salisbury for corruption in handling of Cleveland Street scandals; *D.N.*, 3 March 1890, 3c.
[6] M. Davitt, '"The Times"—Parnell Commission' (1890).
[7] *N.C.*, xxvii. 424 (March 1890).
[8] Sending off-prints of his article on housing of books; see 17 Dec. 89.
[9] Not found published.
[10] W. B. Westall, *A Queer Race: the story of a strange people* (1887).
[11] Parnell Commission report; *H* 341. 1783.
[12] Parnell Commission report; *H* 342. 3.
[13] Not further identified.
[14] J. Heimweh, *La régime des passeports en Alsace-Lorraine* (1890).

6. Th.

Wrote to Ed. Daily News[1]—Sotheran & Co.—Rev. Mr Hyett—V[ote] Office—M. Goadby?—Ambassador at Constantinople. Farewell visit to W.H.G. Attended the function for the May Bust at H. of C. and spoke.[2] Saw E. Hamilton—Agnews—H.J.G.—A. Morley—Alfred Lyttelton. H. of C. 5–7¾.[3] Sir C. Russell admirable. Dined at Lady S. Spencer's. Read Mons. de Camors.[4] Worked on O.T. MS.

7. Fr.

Wrote to Archbp Walsh—Canon Fremantle—Watsons—W. Downing—A.J. Levi[5]—W. Tyler BP.—J.B. Whieldon—Sir R. Lethbridge—J. Lewis Young for Phonogr. to N. York.[6] Read M. de Camors. Saw Sir J. Carmichael—Mr A. Morley—Mr Knowles—Mr Henderson—Ld Granville—Ld Herschel. Worked on MS of O.T. H. of C. 5–7½. Heard Asquith.[7] Dined at Ld Granville's.

8. Sat.

Wrote to Sir Edw. Malet—Pfarier Diestelkampf[8]—Sir Ph. Currie[9]—Prof. Tyndale[10]—Mr Percy Thornton[11]—Scotts—W. Leatham Bright[12]—Parsonses[13]—Ld Carrington—Mr Aubrey—Sec. D & F. Agric. Soc. *Phonographed* to Lord Carrington.[14] Saw J. Carmichael—A. Morley—Herbert G.—Lady Beauclerc[15] who pleased me much—Sarah Lyttelton. Dined at Lady Lyttelton's. Read M. de Camors.

9. 3 S. Lent.

Chapel Royal mg. St James's Evg. Worked much on O.T. MS Creation Story. Read Amn Ch. Review: on O.C. Movement—Eastern Church—Old Religions—

---

[1] Denying accuracy of transcription of letters published; *D.N.*, 7 March 1890, 5b.

[2] Unveiling of memorial bust of Sir T. E. May.

[3] Parnell Commission report; *H* 342. 138.   [4] O. Feuillet, *Monsieur de Camors* (1867).

[5] Of London; in correspondence on Jews and the Irish; Hawn P.

[6] J. Lewis Young, phonograph operator, made a recording of Gladstone this day; next day he sent an untraced transcript, adding: 'I have just heard the phonogram made this morning and truly it is marvellous. Not only did I hear your incomparable voice but your breathing'; letter of thanks from Carrington, 9 June 1890, Add MS 44510, f. 70: '. . . your phonographic message to me is the first ever sent from England to Australasia'. See 8 Mar. 90.

[7] Effective attack on James and the govt.'s handling of the Pigott affair by Asquith, who had been junior to Russell as Parnell's counsel; *H* 342. 296.

[8] Ludwig Diestel Kamp, German clergyman; see Add MS 44509, ff. 132, 166, 327.

[9] Sir Philip Henry Wodehouse Currie, 1834–1906; many diplomatic offices; undersecretary at F.O. 1889–93; ambassador at Constantinople 1893; assisted Armenians 1895.

[10] On Pitt and Ireland; *T.T.*, 10 March 1890, 6c.

[11] Percy Melville Thornton, 1841–1918; author and tory M.P. Battersea 1892–1910.

[12] William Leatham Bright, 1851–1910; liberal M.P. Stoke 1886–90, when took Chiltern Hundreds.

[13] Presumably 'various parsons'; but not a latinism used earlier.

[14] Carrington (see 27 Aug. 76) was presently governing New South Wales. The sending of phonograph messages was a fashion of the early 1890s. See previous day.

[15] Lady Frances Maria Beauclerc, in fact wife of Sir J. W. D'Oyly, but continued to use name of her first husband, Lord A. W. Beauclerc.

New Ed. St Bernard—Droits et torts du Pape.[1] Saw Sir W. Harcourt. Wrote to Mr Nicol.

10. M.

Wrote to Sir J. Carmichael—W.H. Howe—Prof. Tyndall—Mr Butterworth. Finished revising The Creation Story: sent it in.[2] Saw Mr Nicol—A. Morley—Sir J. Carmichael—S. Lyttelton—Sir [blank]. Herbert—Ld Derby. H. of C. $3\frac{1}{2}$-$7\frac{3}{4}$. $10\frac{1}{4}$-$1\frac{1}{2}$. Voted for amt in 268:339.[3] Book buying. Read Cath. Les Bas Souhaits.[4]

11. Tu.

Wrote to Mr de Cosson—Prof. Sylvester. (*See inf. 18*)[5] H. of C. $3\frac{3}{4}$-$7\frac{1}{2}$ and $10\frac{1}{4}$-$12\frac{1}{2}$. Voted in minority of 62.[6] This is only a beginning. Saw S. Lyttelton—Mr Power MP—A. Morley. Read Synods on R. Noel[7]—Conte de Camors. Nine to dinner. Again missed Parnell.

12. Wed.

Wrote to Rev. H. M. Baum—W. Ridler—R. Blackwood—Scotts—F. Gutekunst[8]—Jas D. Law—Gen. Sargent[9]—Hon. R. Noel—Herbert J.G.—J. Ashton—A.H. Gladstone. Visited Miller's studio to see picture of Robn G.[10] And Humphreys on additions at Hawarden. St James's Church 6 P.M. Dined with Mr Marjoribanks. Saw A. Morley MP.—Mr Power MP—Lady R. Churchill[11]—S.L. Addressed by divers l l l l l l.

13. Th.

Wrote to Sir Ph. Currie—W. Ridler—E.H. Wilkinson—P. Roscoe—P.D. Dupré[12]—A. Grove—Dr Langford. Saw S. Lyttelton—E. Hamilton—Ld Rosebery—Mr W.H. Smith. Read M. de Camors—Julien on M. Bashkirtseff[13]—Ierne[14]—Heimweh on Alsace.

---

[1] *American Church Review*, lvi (January 1890).

[2] See 6 Jan. 90.

[3] *H* 342. 460.

[4] Untraced.

[5] Reference in brackets added later; see 18 Mar. 90.

[6] Against Smith's motion on the Parnell Commission; *H* 342. 614.

[7] Untraced.

[8] Of Philadelphia, U.S.A.; sent a portrait of J. R. Lowell; Hawn P.

[9] John Neptune Sargent, minister of defence and education in Victoria, Australia; business untraced.

[10] Probably William E. Miller, *floruit* 1873–1903 as portrait painter in London; this was presumably a posthumous portrait of Robertson Gladstone; whereabouts unknown.

[11] Jennie Spencer-Churchill, *née* Jerome, wife of Lord R. Churchill; author, editor and society beauty.

[12] Theodore Dupree of Arlington Heights, U.S.A., had sent newspaper clippings.

[13] Nothing by Julien traced; perhaps *The journal of Marie Bashkirtseff*, tr. Mathilde Blind (1890).

[14] W. R. Trench, *Ierne, a tale*, 2 v. (1871).

14. Fr.

Wrote to Mr Howorth MP.[1]—Jas Gillies—Mrs Storell—Mrs Bolton—Mr Hodges. Read M. de Camors (finished)—Heimweh on Alsace. We dined at Mrs Th.s. Saw A. Morley—Mr Agnew—S. Lyttelton—Mr W.H. Smith. Saw Beer, and another in distress [R]. Twelve to Parl. dinner: good humour prevailed.

15. Sat.

Wrote to Sir H. Acland—W.B. Allen—Dr Warre—Mr W.H. Smith—Lady F. Dixie.[2] Read Ierne—M. de Camors—Usurpations of England.[3] Saw Sir Walter Phillimore—Sir J. Carmichael—Mr Murray—Mr A. Grove—S.R.L. Saw Ponsonby (Irish) [R].[4] Read Heimweh's Alsace (finished)—Ierne. Corrected proofs of O.T. No II.

16. 4 S.L.

Foundling with Rosebery mg. St James's aft. Luncheon at R.s. Dined with Lucy. Conversation on Lux Mundi &c. Read Lux Mundi[5]—Droits du Pape—Keble, Studies[6]—Elisabethan formularies.

17. M.

Wrote to Bull & Auvache—C.G. (Tel.)—W.M. Knox—Messrs Glen—Mr Gray—Mr Smith. Saw A. Morley—S.G.L.—Mr Roundell—Christies—Ld Granville. Conclave of Peers on the notice for Friday.[7] H. of C. $4\frac{1}{4}$-$5\frac{1}{2}$.[8] Saw The Speaker—Mr Courtney—Mr Robertson M.P. Read Ierne—Guyon on Creation.[9] Attended the Irish concert at Albert Hall in evg.[10]

18. Tu.

This day week we were happily awakened with the news that dearest Mary had a daughter born and that all was well: a most special cause for gratitude to God, after all that happened before. And down to this date all has gone smoothly. I saw her yesterday for the first time: wonderfully young and fresh.[11]
     Wrote to Mr T. Thorp—Mr Nicol—Messrs Haddan—Sir H. Acland—Mrs Josephine Butler—M. Broussali—A.E. Murray—Mr Jas Hogg. Saw A. Morley

---

[1] (Sir) Henry Hoyle Howorth, 1842-1923; geographer and tory M.P. S. Salford 1886-1900. On Madam Bashkirtseff; Add MS 44509, f. 261.
[2] Lady Florence Dixie, da. of 7th marquis of Queensberry; m. 1875 Sir A. B. C. Dixie, 11th bart.
[3] *The usurpations of England the chief source of the miseries of Ireland . . . by a native of Ireland* (1780).
[4] The rescue case; see 26 Jan. 82.
[5] See 31 Jan. 90.
[6] J. Keble, *Studia Sacra* (1877).
[7] To decide on liberal reaction in the Lords to the Parnell Commission report; *T.T.*, 18 March 1890, 9d.
[8] Naval affairs; *H* 342. 1013.
[9] A. H. Guyon, *The earth and the moon* (1850).
[10] 'Grand Irish Festival' with Simms Reeves, Irish Guards band etc.
[11] Dorothy ('Dossie') Mary Catherine Drew, later Parish; d. 1983.

cum J. Morley—H. Primrose—S.G.L.—Ld Rosebery—Sir C. Russell—Mr Labouchere *cum* J. Morley. Attended "Pair of Spectacles" at the Garrick Theatre.[1]
Read Guyon, Creation (finished)—Trench's Ierne.

19. Wed.

Lay up most of the day. Wrote to Vote Office—Archd. Farrar—A. Grove—W.D.
Smythe—Jas Haugh—Messrs Jarrold—Jas Knowles—Mr Lushington—W.H.G.
Read De Quincy Gk Literature[2]—Trench's Ierne—Cusack, Life inside Ch of
Rome[3]—and Lubbock's book.[4] Pleasant dinner at Baron Ferdinand's.[5] Drive
with C. Saw A. Morley—S.G.L. Worked on Proofs of No. II.

20. Th.

Wrote to Mr Howorth MP—Sir H. Acland—Rev. Urwick—Ed. Cabinet Portrait
Gall.[6]—Mr Cremer MP. H. of C. $3\frac{3}{4}$–$5\frac{1}{4}$.[7] Dined with Ld Northbourne. Saw
S.G.L.—Mr Emslie—Mr A. Morley—Mr Cremer—Mr Whitbread. Conclave on
question of a Parnell Inquiry by Committee. Negatived. Read Lubbock—
Cusack—Ierne. Doctored further my MS on O.T. Read & wrote a little on Pitt &
Rutland Correspondence.[8]

21. Fr.

Wrote to Sir Henry Acland—Mr W. Grenfell[9]—Josh. Tims—Sig. Galiero—W.
Downing—Mrs Bolton—J. Nicol. Read Upon the Rock[10]—Lubbock's Prehistoric

---

[1] With Hare, Cathcart and Blanche Horlock. Hamilton recorded: 'I took Mr G. to the Garrick
Theatre tonight by special request of John Hare who placed his box at our disposal. The Roseberys
joined us at the Play. The *Pair of Spectacles* is an excellent piece: and Mr G. enjoyed it much, following it with the greatest keenness. There was actually a slight cheer when he entered the house. He
talked a certain amount about Bismarck at dinner. He regarded the resignation [announced in this
day's papers] as a very grave event; though he had never been an admirer of the Chancellor's. There
were certainly never two men—the two most conspicuous men alive—who had so little in common.
In Mr. G.'s view of the man, the great failing of Bismarck was his utter want of sympathy with
liberty: but there was always one act of the Chancellor's which redounded splendidly to his honour.
It was on record at the Foreign Office that, when the Germans were approaching Paris towards the
end of 1870, Bismarck proposed to conclude peace involving the surrender of Strasburg only. Talking of the outlook at home, he said he was struck with the want of interest shewn in the House of
Commons: the fact being that people would think of nothing but Ireland'; E.H.D., 18 March 1890.
[2] 'Greece under the Romans' and other similar essays in T. de Quincey, *Collected writings*, ed. D.
Masson, 14v. (1889–90).
[3] M. F. Cusack, *Life inside the Church of Rome* (1889).
[4] See 6 July 66.
[5] Ferdinand de Rothschild.
[6] Possibly declining to be photographed for it; he was not included in the 1890 volume of W. and
D. Downey, *The Cabinet Portrait Gallery*.
[7] Civil service estimates; *H* 342. 1261.
[8] *Correspondence between William Pitt and Charles Duke of Rutland* (1890); signed review in *The
Speaker*, i. 363 (5 April 1890). See Add MS 44509, f. 285.
[9] Good wishes for Windsor by-election; *T.T.*, 26 March 1890, 10a.
[10] Probably G. T. Kingdon, *Upon this rock I will build my Church; or, Christ Himself, not Peter, the rock*
(1870?).

Times—and Russian Finance.[1] Saw Mr Parnell[2]—A. Morley—E. Hamilton[3]—Mary, going on beautifully—Sir W. Harcourt—J. Morley—Mr Whitbread. Tea at the Speaker's.

22. Sat.

Wrote to Sir H. Acland—Ly Londonderry—Robn & Nichn—Bp of Carlisle—Mr Jarvis—E. Burne Jones—Mrs Th.—Sig. Paronelli—D.B. Kitchin—Ed. Lloyd's Weekly[4]—R. Brathwayt—Duke of Argyll—Mr Milne. Saw S.G.L.—Sir J. Lubbock—Lady L.—Lady Coleridge. Worked on books. Dined at Sir J. Lubbock's. Read Louisiana Tales[5] X—Rawlinson's Phoenicia[6]—Miller, Unscientific Criticism.[7]

23. 5 S. Lent.

Chapel Royal mg and evg. Wrote to ...... Sat with M. All continuing well upstairs. Read Pritchard, Nature and Revelation[8]—Priestley's Invitation to the Jews, and the Reply[9]—Bp Alexander on the Psalms.[10]

24. M.

Wrote to Mr Peardon?[11]—Ld Coleridge—. ...... and minutes. Read De Quincy. Saw S.G.L.—A. Morley—Sir C. Russell—Mr Stuart MP. H. of C. $4\frac{1}{4}$-$6\frac{1}{4}$. Spoke

[1] Probably an article.
[2] The meeting arranged at Gladstone's request; see Add MS 44509, f. 263.
[3] Hamilton recorded: 'I went to St. James's Square early this morning with the object primarily of seeing at Lady Rosebery's request whether anything could be done towards ensuring R.'s speaking this evening. It was possible that Mr. G. might express some wish to Lord Granville on the subject. However he did not see his way to doing this. Anything like a *command* to speak would not be fair upon R. himself; because the only opportunity of getting up might be a bad one. Moreover R. did not want pushing to the front. He was already there, having done splendidly for himself. Indeed on such subjects as the House of Lords and Imperial Federation, he had gone a little too far ahead to please Mr. G. ⟨Mr. G. said (but said it without meaning anything harsh or unkind) that⟩ R. was the most ambitious man he had ever come across—(ambitious in the sense of being conscious that he had the power to lead and wishing to exercise it to the full.) He was also most difficult to understand—quite unintelligible at times; though Mr. G. admitted that this characteristic was common to almost all statesmen. Indeed out of the 60 or 70 Cabinet colleagues he had had, he believed that he had never really understood but one man and that was Lord Aberdeen. Mr. G. was expecting to be called upon this morning by Parnell; but I told him I would bet 2 to 1 Parnell never turned up. (I have not heard what happened.) Mr. G. is afraid that, from his not having asserted himself much lately, Parnell feels that matters may go so disagreeably for him in the impending divorce case that he may have to withdraw from public life and that he had better commence to prepare for this. His withdrawal would, in Mr. G.'s opinion, be a public calamity; it would be a great blow to this country as well as Ireland; and Ireland herself would be left leader-less: there being no one at all marked out to be Parnell's successor. Mr. G. thought that possibly it would be best for the Irishmen to take Davitt'; E.H.D., 21 March 1890.
[4] See 28 Mar. 90n.
[5] Perhaps A. Fortier, *Bits of Louisiana folk-lore* (1888), expanded in her *Louisiana folk-tales* (1895).
[6] G. Rawlinson, *History of Phoenicia* (1889).
[7] E. Miller, 'Unscientific criticism: a letter to Dr. Liddon' (1890).
[8] C. Pritchard, *Occasional thoughts of an astronomer; nature and revelation* (1889).
[9] J. Priestley, *Letters to the Jews* (1786).   [10] See 11 Apr. 79.
[11] *Sic.* Probably Karl Pearson, 1857–1936, mathematician and eugenicist; on 20 May, Mrs Daniell (see 27 May 90) had sent him a letter from Gladstone on 'the Matriarchate'; Hawn P. See 27 Apr. 90.

briefly on the daring Land Plan.[1] Worked up Irish papers on the Commission. Dined with the London MP.s & candidates at N.L. Club: spoke over an hour on the Commn.[2] Home at 11.30: tired.

25. Tu.

Rose late. Wrote to C.S. Palmer—F.T. Comerford[3]—C. Elflein—Miss Streatfield—J.L. Lobley—F. Paronelli—A. Ireland—J.C. Humphreys—A. M'Donald—Rev. T.M. Gorman—Mr Nicol BP—& minutes. Corrected revises of II O.T. Dined with Ld Northbourne. Saw S.G.L.—A. Morley—Mr Lushington *cum* Dr Perry—Sir C.A. Wood—Mr Scharf—Mr W.H. Smith—The Speaker—Sir W. Harcourt—Mr Fowler. 5-6. Tea with Lady Londonderry,[4] & conversation on Ireland. H. of C. $6\frac{1}{4}$-8.[5] Read De Quincy—Noel's Modern Faust.[6]

26. Wed.[7]

Wrote to R.J. Murray—Archbp of Canterbury—G. Lansbury[8]—Dean of Wells—T. Whitburn—R.J. Murray[9]—and minutes. Read De Quincy—Miss Sharp's Poems[10]—Tomline's Pitt Vol. II largely.[11] Saw A. Morley—Sir H. Robinson—Mr F. Harrison. We dined at Mr Mundella's. Saw Lady Belper. Read Parl. Hist. for Pitt-Rutland Correspondence.

27. Th.

Wrote to Mrs Daniell[12]—Mr Wemyss Reid—Mr H. Reade—Archdn Colley—Leggatts—Mr L.D. Roberts—Mr Wetherell—Lady Londonderry—and minutes. Saw S.G.L.—A. Morley—Sir W. Harcourt—J. Morley—Mr Spencer MP. Nine to dinner. Drive with C. Read Tomline's Pitt II.—Little St Elisabeth[13]—Kinling's Sketches.[14] Examined & sent off Revises of O.T. II.

---

[1] Balfour's congested areas in Ireland bill; *H* 342. 1720.

[2] *T.T.*, 25 March 1890, 10a.

[3] Thomas F. Comerford of Birmingham: on church affairs; Hawn P.

[4] Theresa Susey Helen, *née* Talbot, wife of Charles Vane Tempest Stewart, 1852–1905, 6th marquis of Londonderry and Irish viceroy 1886-9; she d. 1919. A Roman Catholic?

[5] Schools; Ireland; *H* 342. 1843.

[6] R. B. W. Noel, *A modern Faust and other poems* (1888).

[7] This day he also opened the new Medical College at Guy's Hospital, making a long speech; *T.T.*, 27 March 1890, 13a.

[8] George Lansbury, 1859-1940; left radicalism for socialism 1890, but continued as liberal agent for Bow and Bromley until 1892 campaign there won; active Anglican; later labour M.P. and party leader. See his *My Life* (1928), 71ff.

[9] Of Nottingham, on religion; Hawn P.

[10] E. A. Sharp, *Songs and poems of the sea* (1888).

[11] See 2 Dec. 52.

[12] Of Bryanston Square, London, in correspondence about her companion, the philosopher Constance Naden (see 29 Dec. 89n.); Hawn P.

[13] F. H. Burnett, *Little St. Elizabeth* (1890).

[14] Author's name scrawled; untraced.

28. Fr.

Wrote to W. Ellis—Rev. J. M'Lennan—A. Galton—Mr Montefiore[1]—E.B. Sargent—and minutes. Dined with Charles [Lyttelton]: a pleasant party. Worked on Labour Paper.[2] Saw S.G.L.—Mr Leadam—A. Morley—J. Morley. H. of C. 4-5¼.[3] Drive with C. The Speaker gave a critical judgment with great courage. I made bold to carry to him my concurrence, as it was against us. Read The Heriots[4]—De Quincey.

29. Sat.

Wrote to Mr Kearton—Mr Wemyss Reid—E. Dean—F.E. Thompson[5]—G. Joel—G. Johnston. Visited Exhibition of British Artists. Also Mr . . . . .s miniatures. Saw Mr Bayliss—Mrs Bolton. Haymarket Theatre 8.30-11¼ A Man's Shadow: well acted, ill planned.[6] Read A Modern Faust—The Heriots. Dictated Article for Scottish Liberal.[7]

30. Palm S.

St James's mg and Ch. Royal aft. Wrote to Mr Jenkins. Read Exegesis of Life[8]—Delitzsch on Psalms—A Modern Faust—Jenkins on Petrine Succession[9]—Cusack, Life in Ch of Rome—Liddon's Preface.[10]

31. M.

St Martin's 9 A.M. Wrote to Mr Beerbohm Tree—Mr Jarvis—Mr Hucks Gibbs[11]—Mr T. Thorp—Rev. Ugo Janni[12]—Mr C.S. Palmer—Mr Murray—J.P. Moss. H. of C. 4-6½.[13] Dined at Mr Rendell's. Saw S.G.L.—A. Morley—J. Morley—R. Spencer. Read The Heriots—Vesuvius: Review of Revs.[14]

Tues. Ap. One. 1890.

St Martins Ch. 9 A.M. Wrote to Col. Pilkington—Messrs Cassell[15]—C. Eason—Miss Simmonds—D. M'Laren—Mr D. Macgregor—C. Waddie—Mr H. Watt

---

[1] Claude Goldsmid Montefiore of Portman Square, sent an article; Hawn P.

[2] Published as 'The rights and responsibilities of labour', *Lloyd's Weekly Newspaper*, 4 May 1890, 8-9; an important examination of the historical lot of labour, its curious relationship to the British constitution and the (qualified) desirability of an increase in its representation and power.

[3] Parnell; *H* 343. 1811.

[4] Sir H. S. Cunningham, *The Heriots*, 3v. (1890).

[5] Francis Edward Thompson, master at Marlborough college; Add MS 44509, f. 278.

[6] The theatre was managed by Herbert Beerbohm Tree.

[7] Published in three parts as 'Early memories of Edinburgh and Dr. Chalmers. By the Right Hon. W. E. Gladstone, M.P.' in *The Scottish Leader*, 2, 9 and 16 May 1890. The recollections anticipate a number of the fragments on Gladstone's youth in Edinburgh in *Autobiographica*, i.

[8] Untraced.   [9] See 16 Feb. 90.

[10] H. P. Liddon, *Practical reflections on every verse of the psalter; with a preface* (1890).

[11] See 29 Mar. 90.

[12] Of San Remo; sent 1st no. of *Labaro*, organ of the Reforma Cattolica; Hawn P.

[13] Questions; customs dept.; *H* 343. 307.

[14] *Review of Reviews*, i. 255 (April 1890).

[15] London publishers.

MP[1]—C.J. Munich—Mr A. Acland MP.—Ld Coleridge—Printer of the Speaker. Saw S.G.L.—Ld Spencer—A. Morley—J. Morley. Tea at Lady Stanley's. Saw Ld Sherbrook, a wreck, very touching: with a worn wife, absorbed in him. Read Paterson Smyth on O.T.[2]—The Heriots—Sanctity of the Confessional[3]—Mrs Ward in N.C.—Also Sir R. Blenn[erhassett] on Bismarck.[4]

2. Wed.

St Martins 9 A.M. Wrote to Mrs B[olton?] (inclosing her two Licentious papers)—Mr Morley MP.—Jarrolds. Wrote MS on the Land Bill of the Govt.[5] Saw S.G.L.—Mr Morley—Canon MacColl. Read Paterson Smyth, O.T.—Review of Reviews: a great hit, of doubtful morality?[6] Read Paterson Smyth—MacColl on Döllinger—Mrs Aldis on Church Rate[7]—and [blank.]

3. Th.

St James's & H.C. 8 AM. Wrote to Dr Cameron MP—Scotts—Mr E.R. Russell—Watsons—Hon. Mr Pelham—Mr Dabling (Lloyds).[8] Saw Mrs Daniell—Scotts. Out bookbuying, for Guy's & otherwise. Read Chapman on Divorce[9]—Eyre's Union with I. Illegal[10]—Paterson Smyth on O.T.—Fairbairn Anglocatholicism.[11] Finished my paper on Labour for Lloyds.[12]

4. Good Friday.

Chapel Royal at 11 (No celebration). Then St Peters Eaton Square 1–3: Father Black,[13] very good, very full. Wrote to Mr Dabling (Lloyds W)—Mr Blackie—Mr O. Browning—Mr T. Baines—Sec. Academy—W.R. Melly—Mrs Bolton—Mr Howorth M.P. Read Paterson Smyth (finished)—A Modern Faust—and De Quincey.

5. Sat. [St. George's Hill, Weybridge]

Ch. 11 A.M. Wrote to Sir J. Colomb MP[14]—Mr Palgrave and [blank.][15] Saw Sir J. Carmichael. Shopping. Off by 2.15 train to Walton & St George's Hill. The

[1] Hugh Watt, 1848–1921; electrical manufacturer and liberal M.P. Camlachie 1885–92 (when he stood as Independent liberal). [2] See 24 Nov. 89.

[3] S. W. B. Coleridge, *The sanctity of confession* (1890).

[4] *N.C.*, xxvii. 651, 688 (April 1890).

[5] Perhaps a draft of his letter to Colomb; see 5 Apr. 90.

[6] W. T. Stead's *Review of Reviews* was a digest of articles in other periodicals, including, in its April number, most of Gladstone's 'Impregnable Rock' from *Good Words*.

[7] *C.R.*, lvii. 325, 421 (March 1890).

[8] Editor of *Lloyd's Weekly London Newspaper*; see 28 Mar. 90.

[9] E. R. Chapman, 'The decline of divorce', *Westminster Review*, cxxxiii. 417 (April 1890).

[10] J. R. Eyre, *Justice or coercion? Some leading English opinions upon Home rule in Ireland and elsewhere* (1886).

[11] A. M. Fairbairn, *The reformation and the revolution of 1688* (1889).

[12] See 28 Mar. 90.

[13] A visiting preacher; probably Raymond Charles Black, curate in Ealing.

[14] Sir John Charles Ready Colomb, 1838–1909, royal marine, imperialist and tory M.P. Tower Hamlets 1886–92, Yarmouth 1895–1906; kt. 1888. On Irish land; exchange in *T.T.*, 8 April 1890, 13f.

[15] Letter to J. Cowan on Midlothian affairs; *T.T.*, 8 April 1890, 9f.

THE GLADSTONE DIARIES

Admiral[1] met us. Place & weather lovely. Drive to Mr Wilson's Garden in aft. and walk with conversation on politics. Read Lucy's two articles[2]—Mrs Maguire's Diary[3]—and Memoir of Naden.[4]

6. Easter D.

Parish Ch. & H.C. mg. Worked on O.T. & read. Read The Latest Infidelity[5]— Gloag's Address[6]—Osgood[7]—Bunyan's Pilgrim's Progress:[8] a clear cut objectivity reminding one of Dante.

7. Easter M.

Wrote to Rev. Ld Forester—Mr D. Maxwell—Lady Wolverton—W.F. Forsyth— Archdn Norris—Scotts—Rev. Mr Duncan. Read Baccalaureate Sermon[9]— Speech on Marcus Dods[10]—Mr Maxwells Address[11]—Reviews & Articles—and Diary of a Refugee. Drive (Clairmont) & walk.

8. E. Tu. [Aston Clinton]

Off before ten. At 11¼ attended the Baptism of Mary's dear infant.[12] Searching in H. of C. Library. Wrote to Sec. Local Gov. Bd.—Sir E. Watkin MP.—W.H.G.—F.J. Hibjame—J.P. Moss—J.M. Davidson—A.B. Moss—Jas Stevens—D. Ross—Rev. Dr. Cox—B. Quaritch. Aston Clinton at 6.30. Made short addresses at Weybridge and at Tring.[13] Read Southern Refugee—Spedding, Elisabethan Demonology.[14] Much conversation with G. Russell & others especially on Lord R.

9. Wed.

Wrote to Sir J. Lambert—Lady Wolverton—Mr Colman MP. Visited Chequers[15] & walk in the beautiful park. Worked on MS for O.T. Read Edgeworth's Absentee[16]—Jewish Quarterly, 3 Articles[17]—How we got our Bibles[18]—Moss, anti-Bible[19]—James, Anc. Mariner.[20] Saw Sir P. Currie (Siberia &c.)—Miss Cobden.

---

[1] Admiral F. Egerton; see 6 Aug. 70.
[2] Perhaps H. W. Lucy's articles on parliamentary behaviour in *N.C.*, xviii. 58 (July 1885), xxv. 372 (March 1889).
[3] [Judith W. Macguire], *Diary of a Southern refugee, during the war, by a Lady of Virginia* (1868).
[4] W. R. Hughes, *Constance Naden: a memoir* (1890).
[5] Perhaps A. R. Grote, *The new infidelity* (1881).
[6] 'Closing address of Rev. P. J. Gloag as Moderator . . . of the Church of Scotland' (1889).
[7] Perhaps *Osgood's rebellion, and what became of it; or, Days at Westbrook College* (1877).
[8] See 3 Jan. 64.
[9] E. G. Robinson, *Baccalaureate sermons delivered at Brown University, 1872–1889* (1890?).
[10] D. Campbell, 'Speech on the case of Marcus Dods' (1890).
[11] Perhaps D. Maxwell, 'The vision of the world' (1890).
[12] See 18 Mar. 90.   [13] *T.T.*, 9 April 1890, 5e.
[14] J. Spedding, *Reviews and discussions* (1879).
[15] By Wendover, then owned by Rosalind, wife of Colonel Astley; the house became the Prime Minister's country residence in 1917 on the gift of Lord Lee of Fareham.
[16] M. Edgeworth, *The Absentee* in *Tales of fashionable life*, v–vi (1812); see 7 July 41.
[17] *Jewish Quarterly Review*, ii (April 1890).   [18] See 24 Nov. 89.
[19] A. B. Moss had sent his *The bible and evolution* (1890).
[20] I. James, *The source of "The Ancient Mariner"* (1890).

10. Th.

Wrote to Mr Noble—Mr W. Mitchell. Walk & conversation with Mr Birrell.[1]
Read The Absentee—Southern Refugee—Alison on Scots Law[2]—Canon Moore
on Agnostics.[3] Worked on O.T. MS.

11 Fr.

Kept my bed till evg: the bowels wrong. Read The Absentee largely (finished)—
How we got our Bible—Southern Refugee, conclusion—Reply to Bryce.[4]—Men
of the Time (G. Potter).[5] Drawing room in evg.

12. Sat.

Wrote to Geo. Potter—E.B. Steele—G. Griffith—T. Chippendale—Canon C.
Moore—Ed. Men of the Time. Saw Mr Hazell & party from Aylesbury Printing
Works.[6] Drive with G. Russell & Mrs Paull.[7] Read Emile de Coulanges[8]—How
we got out Bible? Conversation with Mrs Jebb—Mr Jebb—Mrs Paull—and
others: party enlarged. C. went to Hn.

13. Low S.

Parish Ch mg & evg. Striking sermon from the Rector. Wrote to C.G. and
Edwards. Worked on O.T. Read O.T.—Harris on St John[9]—finished 'How we got
our Bible'.

14. M.

Ill again. Could not go. Sir A. Clark came evg. & left me better. Kept my bed.
Wrote to Sir J. Carmichael l—Sir E. Saunders—Edwards—Mr Morley—Mrs
C.F.—C.G. The ladies visited me: levees. Read Castle Rack Rent[10]—
O.T.—Romance of a Station.[11]

15. Tu. [London]

Back to London 12–2¼, from a very edifying House. Wrote to Sir J. Colomb
MP—Watsons—A. Belasco—J. Noble—Mr Du Chaillu—Cusher—Mr Cook

[1] Augustine Birrell, 1850–1933; barrister, author and liberal M.P. W. Fife 1889–1900; later Irish
secretary.
[2] A. Alison, *Practice of the criminal law of Scotland* (1833).
[3] C. Moore, *Some practical issues of the weakness of contemporary agnosticism* (1890).
[4] Untraced.
[5] *The monthly record of eminent men*, ed. G. Potter (April 1890); Gladstone's note of approval
appeared in later numbers.
[6] From Hazell, Watson and Viney, printers in Aylesbury and London.
[7] Probably Henry John Paull, London barrister, and his wife.
[8] M. Edgeworth, *Emile de Coulanges* in *Tales of fashionable life*, v (1812).
[9] John Harris, a Cornish miner, *The strange preacher, John the Baptist* (1881).
[10] M. Edgeworth, *Castle Rackrent, an Hibernian tale. Taken from the facts, and from the manners of the
Irish squires, before the year 1782* (1800).
[11] R. C. Praed, *The romance of a station*, 2v. (1890?).

(PMG)—Mr Macfie[1]—Wms & Norgate—Hon. & Rev. S.R. Lawley. Saw the party—Lady Lindsay—Mr A. Morley—Mr C. Flower—Mr Westell. Read O.T.—Romance of a Station—The Heriots.

16. Wed.

Bed & room all day. Read O.T. (Leviticus)—The Heriots (nearly 2 vols). Saw Sir A. Clark—Mr Morley—Mr A. Morley—Herbert J.G.—H.N.G.

17. Th.

Rose at 1.30. Wrote to Messrs Macmillan—Treasurer Guy's—Mr Westell—Duke of Argyll—S.E.G. (BP.)—J.R. Godley—W. Gay—Sir W. Hunter. Saw Mr A. Morley—W.H.G.—Sir W. Harcourt—E. Wickham—Sir A. Clark. Read C.Q.R. Three Articles[2]—Cesaresco, Italian Characters[3]—Schulte Geschichte des A.R.[4]

18. Fr.

Rose at 11 AM. Wrote to Mr Knight Watson—Miss Knight—Mr Trumbull—Dr Rainy—Sig. Galliera—Mr Hillier—H.M. Jewett BP—V.O.—Mr Postgate—Countess Cesaresco[5]—Mrs Sands. Saw Archbishop Croke[6]—E. Hamilton—A. Morley—Mr Freshfield—S.G.L. Read The Century on Ohio Serpent[7]—Robertson Smith Lectures[8]—Iliowitzi, Jewish Dreams & Realities.[9]

19. Sat. [The Durdans, Epsom]

Rose normally. Wrote to Ld Granville—Sir P. Currie—Mary Drew—J.S.M. Crony—V.O.—and minutes. Saw Ld Granville—S.G.L. Off to Durdans at one. Walk with C.E. Hamilton. Worked on O.T. III. Read Hunter's Dalhousie[10]—and [blank.]

20. 2 S.E.

Church mg and evg. Walk with R[osebery] & much retrospective conversation on the Irish question. Worked well on O.T. No III. with O.T. Read Massey (Union)[11] and Ingraham on Bible.[12]

[1] On American copyright; T.T., 17 April 1890, 11f.
[2] Church Quarterly Review, xxx (April 1890); sent by C. K. Watson for its article on Gladstone's review of Ellen Middleton; Add MS 44509, f. 313.
[3] E. Martinengo-Cesaresco, Italian characters in the epoch of unification (1890).
[4] J. F. von Schulte, Der Altkatholicismus. Geschichte seiner Entwickelung... (1887).
[5] Countess Evelyn Martinengo-Cesaresco, d. 1931; da. of Dean Carrington and wife of Eugenio Martinengo-Cesaresco; historian of the Risorgimento and benefactress of St. Hugh's College, Oxford; had doubtless sent her book (see previous day).
[6] Thomas William Croke, 1824–1902; Roman Catholic Archbishop of Cashel.
[7] F. W. Putnam, 'The serpent mound of Ohio', Century Magazine, n.s. xvii. 871 (April 1890).
[8] W. Robertson Smith, Lectures on the religion of the Semites (1889).
[9] H. Iliowizi, Jewish dreams and realities contrasted with Islamic and Christian claims (1890).
[10] Sir W. W. Hunter, The marquis of Dalhousie (1890); in the 'Ruler of India' series.
[11] Probably in Massey's History (see 23 July 55).
[12] J. H. Ingraham, The Prince of the House of David (1890 ed.).

21. M. [London]

Back to London 3. PM. Wrote to Hon. Rev. S. Lawley—Miss Tennant—Mr Shaw—and minutes. Drive with Rosebery. Saw Mr Rogers. Back to town 3.30. Worked on O.T. No III. H. of C. $4\frac{1}{4}$-$7\frac{1}{2}$.[1] Dined at Grillion's. Read Dalhousie.

22. Tu.

Wrote to Mr Nicoll—Wms & Norgate—J. Westell—Sir E. Watkin—Mr W.H. Smith. Dined at F. Leveson's. Conversation with Lady Lascelles—Granville. Saw S.G.L.—Mr Morley—Mr A. Morley. Read Dalhousie: and B. Scott—Encycl. Brit. Stoics.[2] Finished & sent off No III. O.T.

23. Wed.

Wrote to T. Fielding—Cardinal Manning—B. Scott—Professor Damala[3]—J.H. Leonard—Mrs Thist. B.P.—H. Quilter—Lady Holker B.P.—H. Edwards—Mr Roden Noel—Mr Wakeman—Mr Dabling (Lloyd's Weekly)—Mr Bryant. Saw S.G.L.—Mr Nicol—Mr A. Morley. Corrected proofs of article for Lloyds Weekly. H. of C.[4] Drive with C.—Dined with Baron Stern: music. Read S. Keay on Land Bill[5]—Hunter's Dalhousie (finished)—Francesco Crispi.[6] Worked on books & papers.

24. Th.

Wrote minutes. Worked up Irish Land Purchase Bill: & spoke an hour: mild. H. of C. 4-$7\frac{3}{4}$.[7] Dined with the Granvilles. Saw the great Burne Joneses.[8] Saw S.G.L.—Ld Granville—Mr Agnew. Saw Mary. Read Jehovah—Francesco Crispi.

25. Fr.

Wrote to Mr Nicol—Mrs Flower B.P.—Mr Birkbeck—Judge O'Connor Morris—Mr Routledge—Mr Lloyd Bryce—Ld Breadalbane—and minutes. Saw S.G.L.—Mr Campbell Bannerman—Dowager Dss of Marlborough—Ld R. Churchill—Mr Childers. Photographed by Mrs Myers over an hour on the chair.[9] Read Lefroy

[1] Irish land purchase bill; *H* 342. 980.

[2] R. D. Hick's article on the Stoics in *Encyclopedia Britannica*.

[3] i.e. E. M. Damala (see 19 July 88) about Vitalis's statue of Gladstone for Athens; Hawn P.

[4] Misc. business; *H* 343. 1181.

[5] J. S. Keay, *The landlord, the tenant, and the tax-payer, an exposure of the Irish Land Purchase Bill of 1890* (1890).

[6] F. Narjoux, *Francesco Crispi* (1890).

[7] Spoke on Irish land purchase bill; *H* 343. 1288.

[8] No known series of Burne Joneses was commissioned by Granville; these might be studies for that commissioned by A. J. Balfour.

[9] Photographed by Eveleen Myers, wife of F. W. H. Myers of Trinity, Cambridge and the Society of Psychical Research, in which she was also active. She was the sister of Dorothy Tennant, who arranged the meeting; Add MS 44509, f. 335. These photographs are reproduced in this volume as Frontispiece and as a plate.

on the Church[1]—Coleman on the Stage[2]—Franc. Crispi. Certainly a *man*.
H. of C. 3¾.[3] Corrected proofs O.T. III.

26. Sat.

Wrote to Mary Drew—Archdn of Chester—Sotherans—Rev. Mr Riley—Mr H.
Tyson—Dr Rhomaides—Messrs Gray—G.H. Macmillan—Mrs Th.—H.J.
Cohen[4]—C. Nitzch[5]—Hon. R. Noel. Attended the Antigone in evg. Acting below
the mark: all else very good.[6] Read Crispi .... Saw S.G.L.—A. Morley.
Worked a little on O.T.

27. 3 S.E.

St James's mg. Chapel Royal aft. Worked on O.T. IV. 'Psalms'. Read K. Pearson,
Ethic &c.[7]—Bayley Sermons (New Church)[8]—Rev. [blank] on Altruism.

28. M.

Wrote to Ld Rosebery—Rev. S.E. Gladstone—Abp Walsh—Baron D. d'Amico—
A. Walls—W.D. Savage—R. Anderson—W.J. Cooper—J. Dobbie—and minutes.
H. of C. 4¼-8¼.[9] Dined at Sir C. Forster's, by fiasco.[10] Saw S.G.L.—Messrs Puttick
& Simpson[11]—Wms & Norgate. Worked on O.T. Psalms. Read Fr. Crispi.

29. Tu.

Wrote to Ld Acton—P.W. Campbell—Rev. J. Lamont—Mr Shone F.G.S.—Mr
Nicol—Rev. Page Hopps—Mr Dallas—Mr Carnegie—& minutes. Dined at Sir C.
Forster's. Read Shone's Lecture—Fr. Crispi—In a winter City.[12] Saw S.G.L.—
J. Morley. Worked a little on O.T. H. of C. 4¼.[13]

30. Wed.

Wrote to Ld Acton BP.—Mr W.M. Conway—Rev. Hugh Roberts—& minutes.
Saw S.G.L.—Mr A. Morley—Mr Parker (W. Australia)—Lady Holker—Mr

[1] T. E. P. Lefroy, *The Christian ministry* (1890).
[2] J. Coleman, 'Stage fright', *Temple Bar*, lxxxviii. 270 (February 1890).
[3] Electoral disabilities bill; *H* 343. 1426.
[4] H. J. Cohen, barrister of the Inner Temple. With A.W. Hutton, librarian of the National Liberal Club, he began work in 1890 on a 10 volume ed. of Gladstone's speeches, published by Methuen, working backwards from 1891; in 1892, vol. x (1888–91) was published with a preface by Gladstone and in 1894, vol. ix (1886–7); but the series was discontinued.
[5] Of Notting Hill; sent a book; Hawn P.
[6] Performance of Sophocles' 'Antigone', with Mendelssohn's music, in Westminster Town Hall; Lady Maidstone played Antigone; *T.T.*, 26 April 1890, 1e.
[7] K. Pearson, *The ethic of free thought* (1888).
[8] Sir J. R. L. E. Bayley, preface to *Sermons on the person and work of the Holy Spirit* (1860).
[9] Irish land purchase bill; *H* 343. 1541.
[10] i.e. he turned up a day early (see next day).
[11] Firm dealing with Acton's library; see 14 May 90.
[12] Ouida [L. de la Ramée], *In a winter city; a sketch* (1876).
[13] Irish land purchase bill; *H* 343. 1663.

[blank.] New Gallery Private View[1] with C.G. & drive. Nine to dinner. Finished Narjoux's Crispi—read Window in Thrums.[2]

Thurs May 1.

Wrote to H. Quilter—A.R. Gladstone—....... & minutes. H. of C. 5–8 & 10–12½. Voted in 268:348 on Land Purchase.[3] Worked on O.T. IV. Read Window in Thrums—Israel Sack[4]—Uebergang.[5] Saw S.G.L.—Sir W.H.—A.M.—J.M.—Parnell —O'Brien.

2. Frid.

Saw S.G.L.—Mr Bradlaugh—Mr Morley—Mr A. Morley—Mr Childers—Free Church Deputation—Dr Liddon—Mr Buchanan. Tea with Lady Salisbury. Worked on Scots Ch. question. H. of C. 5¾–6¾ and 9–1½. Spoke for Scots Disestabl. Voted in 218:256.[6] Read Window in Thrums. Attended Private View R.A.—Private View Grosvenor.[7]

3. Sat.

Wrote to Ly Phillimore—Mrs Bailie—Mr Elflin—and minutes. Royal Acad. 2½–4½. Drive with C. Evening at home. Read Window in Thrums—Caroline[8]—and [blank.] Saw Mr Humphreys—S.G.L.—A. Morley—W.H.G.—Star messenger— Mr Agnew.

4. 4 S.E.

Chapel Royal & H.C. mg—St James's evg. Wrote to M. Drew—Lady Holker BP— Saltney & Sandycroft R.Rs do. Saw the Farquhars—H.J.G. Read Missionary Bishop[9]—Bp Alexr on the Psalms[10]—New Truth & old Faith[11]—Dr Cave on O.T.[12] C. and I were swamped in a friendly crowd on its way home.

5. M.

Wrote to J. Nicol—F. Millar—Sir W. Farquhar—Bp of Derry—Mrs Daniells— Speaker's Secy—W.E.J. Leveson—J. Westell—Hawkins Simpson—Mrs Hogan— Messrs Murray—C. Dixon—R. Cameron. Saw S.G.L.—Rev. Mr Adams—Ld Granville—The Aberdeens—A. Morley—Mr. ....—and minutes. Worked in Lond. Library. Dined at Grillion's. Much Irish conversation with Bp Magee: & Church conversation with Mills.[13] Saw S.G.L.—A. Morley—Sir W. Harcourt—

---

[1] The New Gallery was the successor to the aestheticism of the Grosvenor Gallery; A. E. Emslie's 'Dinner party at the Earl of Aberdeen's', with Gladstone in its group portrait was on view; *P.M.G.*, 30 April 1890, 2.

[2] By J. M. Barrie (1889).   [3] *H* 343. 1940.

[4] See 30 Jan. 90.   [5] Untraced.

[6] Supporting Cameron's motion for disestablishment and disendowment; *H* 344. 89.

[7] See *T.T.*, 5 May 1890, 10a.

[8] Lady C. B. E. Lindsay, *Caroline. A Novel* (1888).   [9] Untraced.

[10] See 11 Apr. 79.   [11] A. B. Moss, *The old faith and the new* (1885).

[12] In *C.R.*, lvii. 537 (April 1890).

[13] Arthur Mills, secretary of Grillion's Club.

J. Morley—Rev. Adams—Mr [blank.] Drive with C. Read Caroline. Sent No IV. O.T. to Mr N. Saw . . .

6. Tu.

Wrote to Mr Fyffe[1]—Rev. Ugo Janni—A.J. Smith—Rev. Adams—W.D. Smyth—Rev. R.E. Nightingale—and minutes. Worked on O.T., V. Saw S.G.L.—A. Morley—Mr Lefevre—Mr Magniac . . . . . . Finished Caroline. Read Dixon on Birds[2] and G. Smith on Anglophobia.[3] Dined with the Breadalbanes. Conversation with Lady W. Gardner.[4] She is very clever.

7. Wed.

Wrote to Lady Lindsay[5]—A.H. Johnson—Rev. Dr. Moore—E. Woodhead—Watsons—and minutes. Read Mr Johnson's Poems[6]—Lady L. 'Robin' Literature—Dixon on Birds—A Miner's Rights (began).[7] Saw S.G.L.—A. Morley—Lady Derby (5 PM tea)—Mrs Ellice, Ld C. Russell & others. Worked on O.T. Dined at Mr Lefevre's. Saw Mr [blank] of Bradford.

8. Th.

Wrote to Rev. Wallis—Mr Richardson—Mr Kelly—and minutes. Read A Miner's Rights—Alexander on Opium[8]—and Wellhausen on the Hexateuch.[9] Saw S.G.L.—A. Morley—Bp of St Asaph. H. of C. $5\frac{1}{4}$-$7\frac{1}{2}$.[10]

9. Fr.

Wrote to Mr Leadam—Rev. G.H. Mann—D.T. King—H.T. Gowe—H.W. Lovett—& minutes. Saw S.G.L.—A. Morley—Ld Granville. Worked on O.T., V, Mosaic Legislation. Dined at Pol. Economy Club and delivered my sentiments.[11] Read a Miner's Right—and [blank.]

10. Sat. [Dollis Hill]

Wrote to Mr A. Morley—Ld Acton—Mr A. Arnold—Ld Hothfield—Rev. Mr Shamling—Mr J. Nicol—Baroness de Roque—Mr Duff—Mr R. Buchanan—

---

[1] To C. A. Fyffe, liberal candidate in E. Wiltshire, on allotments; *T.T.*, 14 May 1890, 5f.

[2] C. Dixon, *Annals of bird life: a year-book of British ornithology* (1890).

[3] Goldwin Smith, 'Hatred of England', *N.A.R.*, cl. 547 (May 1890).

[4] Lady Winifred Gardner, da. of Lord Carnarvon; m. 1890 H. C. Gardner (see 9 Nov. 87).

[5] Lady Caroline Blanche Elizabeth Lindsay, wife of Sir Coutts Lindsay (see 2 July 70) and author of *About robins* (1889), read this day, and *Caroline* (see 3 May 90).

[6] Perhaps D. M. Johnson, *Lethe and other poems* (1882); or verses sent by A. H. Johnson (see this day).

[7] R. Boldrewood (i.e. T. A. Browne), *The miner's right*, 3v. (1890).

[8] See 20 Dec. 56.

[9] J. Wellhausen, *Die Composition des Hexateuchs* (1889) and *Prolegomena zur Geschichte Israels* (1883).

[10] Finance bill; *H* 344. 483.

[11] Meeting to discuss use of Councils of Arbitration and Conciliation in labour disputes; Gladstone's comments not recorded.

G.H.F. Nye—Mr R.P. Ward—J.D. Young—Bp Bath & Wells. Saw S.G.L.—W.H.G. We went to Dollis: the Aberdeen hospitality embracing even the time of their absence. Read Miner's Right—and Clough's Poems.[1]

11. 5 S.E.

Willesden Ch mg & evg. Mr Outram excellent. Read Nye on Ch in Wales[2]— New truth & old Faith—and a good supply besides. The W.H.G.s came down.

12. M. [London]

Back to London at 11¾. Wrote to Mr Caine MP.—Mr . . . . & minutes. Saw S.G.L.—Dr Ginsburg—Ld Granville—Sir A. West—Miss Tennant. H. of C. 4½–7½.[3] Got up 'Free Trade' & Temperance. Presented the Address to Mr [T.B.] Potter (40 m.)[4] Dined with the Wests. Read The Miners Right—and Clough's Poems.

May 13 Tues.

Wrote to Dr Ginsburg—Mr J.L. Foulds—W. Ridler—Rivingtons—Mr Blackie— Sir T. Acland—Dean of Norwich—H.B.M. Watson[5]—W.H. Rideing—R. M'Car- rell—Mr Nicol—and minutes. Saw S.G.L.—Mr A. Morley—H.J.G. (Hawarden)—Mr Nicol—Ed. Hamilton. Dined at the Club: a good party. Read Miner's Right—Giffen, Growth of Capital[6]—Ryle on Old Test. Criticism.[7] Revised and sent to press No V. Mosaic Legislation.

14. Wed.

Wrote to Mr Nicol B.P.—Mr Stuart Rendel—L.W. Banes—W.H. Stewart—Mr Wemyss Reid—Col. Gascoigne—Mr Humphreys—Rev. Mr Bayne. Dined at Ld Burton's. Conversation Lady Curzon, Mrs Oppenheim, &c. Visited B. Museum & saw Dr Ginsburg on O.T. Ld Carnarvon on Acton Library.[8] The King of the Belgians: on Africa, Belgium in 1870 ("you saved it").[9] Saw Scotts. Saw Grassi, and another [R]. Read A Miner's Right—Horst, Beytrag zur Pent. Kritik.[10]

15. Th. Ascension Day.

Chapel Royal at 11 AM. & H.C. Wrote to Press Assn & Central News[11]—Messrs Chambers[12]—F.E. Healy—R. Crawfurd—Mrs Archer—R. Cameron—W. Ridler—

---

[1] A. H. Clough, *Poems* (1888 ed.).   [2] G. H. F. Nye, *The story of the Church in Wales* (1890).
[3] Caine's temperance amndt. to local taxation bill; *H* 344. 718.
[4] Speech on free trade; *T.T.*, 13 May 1890, 11a.
[5] Henry Brereton Marriott Watson, 1863–1921; novelist; see 16 May 90.
[6] R. Giffen, *The growth of capital* (1889).   [7] J. C. Ryle, *Is all scripture inspired?* (1890?).
[8] Acton, almost bankrupt, was auctioning his library through Puttick and Simpson on 16 July; Gladstone sought a solution, finding one in Carnegie; see Chadwick, *Acton and Gladstone*, 25 ff. and 9 June 90; Carnarvon noted next day: Gladstone 'is extremely interested in the matter, and threw him- self with the intense earnestness of his whole nature into it—as if he had nothing else to think of'; Hardinge, *Carnarvon*, iii. 315.
[9] i.e. Gladstone's statement on 10 Aug. 70 on Belgian neutrality and the Anglo-Prussian treaty.
[10] G. C. Horst, *Siona. Ein Beitrag zur Apologetik des Christenthums* (1826).
[11] Corrections on Chinese immigration to his speech on 12 May; *T.T.*, 16 May 1890, 9e.
[12] Facsimile in *W. E. Gladstone. A souvenir* (n.d., 1898?), 56.

and minutes. Much work on books & papers. Also on political notes. H. of C. 4¾–7¾. Spoke (¾ hour) on the Publicans' 'Endowment'.[1] Read Horst, Beytrag—A miner's Right: finished. Saw S.G.L.—A. Morley—J. Morley—Sir W. Harcourt—Mr Parnell.

16. Fr. [Stoke Holy Cross, Norfolk]

Wrote to Mayor of Hull—Mr Frowde & . . . . Off at 9.30. Reached Norwich at one. Procession through the streets. Read Lady Faintheart[2] and Bateman's Aphasia.[3] Spoke shortly at Ipswich. Made notes in afternoon for the evening's work. Spoke 1 h. 10 m. to 8000 people.[4] Then drove out 6 m. to Mr Birkbeck's at Stoke[5] for the night. Dined within the old Abbey of Carrow. The farewell to Smith[6] after his 8 years was sad enough.

17. Sat. [Corton, Norfolk][7]

Circuit in Norwich: then visit to the Cathedral conducted by the Dean and experts. Spoke at Lowestoft:[8] and reached Mr Colman's charming sea place to luncheon. Then slept 2½ hours. Walk afterwards: conversation with Rev. Mr Barrett[9]—Mr Cadge—Lord J. Hervey. Large party: the only complaint.

18. S. aft Asc.

Lowestoft Ch. mg. Corton evg. Drive round the town. Wrote to Miss D. Tennant. Read O.T.—Wellhausen's Prolegomena and [blank.] Conversation with Mr Barrett.

19. M.

Visit to Yarmouth. A remarkable manifestation: 20, or 25000 people.[10] Saw the noteworthy Church—School—&c. The clergy very kind. Much struck by the children in Infant School. Then went to Fritton[11] for tea & so home. Conversation with Ld J. Hervey[12]—Mr Barrett. Read Lady Faintheart—Bateman's Aphasia.

20. Tu. [Hawarden]

Wrote to Mr J.G. Cox—Rev. D. Henderson—H.N.G.—W. Robinson—Dr Bateman. Saw Prof. Stuart—Mr Follitt—Mr Shakespeare. Left Lowestoft soon after

---

[1] *H* 344. 992.
[2] H. B. M. Watson, *Lady Faintheart*, 3v. (1890).
[3] F. Bateman, *Aphasia: localisation of the faculty of articulate language* (1890); sent by the author, a physician in Norwich, Hawn P.
[4] *T.T.*, 17 May 1890, 14a.
[5] House of H. Birkbeck, who chaired this day's meeting; *D.N.*, 17 May 1890, 6.
[6] Presumably a servant.
[7] J. Colman's seaside house.
[8] On atrocities in Siberia; *T.T.*, 19 May 1890, 10c.
[9] George Willoughby Barrett, precentor of Norwich 1877.
[10] *T.T.*, 19 May 1890, 10c.
[11] Fritton Broad, Buxton's house, famous for its ducks.
[12] Lord John William Nicholas Hervey, 1841–1902; soldier; a whig.

11: 6¾ hours took us luxuriously 280 miles to Hawarden. Little speeches by the way. At Lincoln 5000 working men, so still that all must have heard.[1] The Rectory children *so* come on. Backgammon with S.E.G. Read Broads of Norfolk[2]—Bateman on Aphasia—Lady Faintheart Vol. I finished.

21. *Wed.*

Ch. 8¼ A.M. Wrote to Mr Williamson MP.—Rev. Mr Barker—Mr Nicol BP.—Dr Ginsburg—Dr Bateman—Herbert J.G.—Mr Curzon MP.[3]—D. Aitken—A. Castell—D.U. Preston—Thos Beet—Misses Northey—W. Lewis—Mons. A. Lyon—B. Barrett—Messrs Macmillan—C. Downes—Mr Williamson MP—M.F. Feldmann—Rev. S.A. Barnett[4]—J. Shanks—Sir B. Samuelson. Corrected revise on Psalms. Submitted the paper to S.E.G. Read Tolstoi's Sonate a Kreutzer[5]—Frazer Golden Bough[6]—Ov. Metamorph. I. Backgammon with S.

22. *Th.*

Ch. 8½ A.M. Wrote to Archbp Walsh—Dr Ginsburg—A. Morley MP.—Mr Nicol BP.—E. Foster—Miss Thompson—W.D. Weir—Messrs Hamilton—J.R. Cherry—Mr W. Toynbee[7]—H.E. Roy—J. Kempster—G. Beith—Canon Howell[8]—G.Y. Tickle—Rev. H.R. Baker[9]—Mr B. Sharp. Further corrected revise on Pss. in the light of Dr Ginsburg's remarks. Sent to press. Two hours work in St Deiniol's. Drive with C. The beauty! Read Tolstoi—Campbell, Phallic Worship.[10] Backgammon with S.

23. *Fr.*

Ch. 8¼ A.M. Wrote to Dr Ginsburg—Mr P. Hughes—Mr A.H. Smyth—S.G.L.—Mrs Lawrence—J. M'Gregor—Joshua Dyson—John Bair—H.B. Holding—W. Arnot—Sir A. West—Mr Spurge[11]—Mr Denneby. Worked on O.T. paper. Read Wellhausen & Black[12]—Tolstoi's La Sonate (finished)—Wellhausen, Israel.

24. *Sat.*

Ch. 8¼ A.M. Wrote to Mons. P. Meleagros[13]—G. Coleman—Lady F. Dixie—G.G. Gisdale—Sir T. Acland—J. Judd—Rev. H.V. White[14]—Mr Humphreys—Mr

---

[1] *T.T.*, 21 May 1890, 7f.
[2] Perhaps P. Dale, *Noah's ark: a tale of the Norfolk Broads* (1890).
[3] See 6 May 78; now tory M.P. Southport 1886–92.
[4] See 4 Oct. 77.   [5] L. V. Tolstoy, *La Sonate à Kreutzer* (1890).
[6] Sir J. G. Frazer, *The Golden Bough: a study in comparative religion*, 2v. (1890).
[7] William Toynbee, author and poet; see 30 May 90.
[8] Hinds Howell, rector of Drayton, Norfolk and canon of Norwich.
[9] Hugh Ryves Baker, vicar of Woolwich.
[10] Perhaps *Phallism: a description of the worship of lingam-yoni* (privately printed, 1889); no author given.
[11] Word smudged.
[12] Translation by J. Black of Wellhausen (see 8 May 90).
[13] Pericles Meleagros of Gladstone Street, Athens; Hawn P.
[14] H. Vere White, rector of Killesk; dispute on boycotting in Tipperary; *T.T.*, 28 May 1890, 5f.

Higginbottom—Canon [E.] Venables—Lpool Head Constable—Mr C. More-
land. Finished revising 'Mosaic Legislation'. Exp. with S. & tea at Dee Cottage.
Worked in St Deiniol's. Read Wellhausen's Israel—Ov. Metamorph. Backgammon with S.

25. Whits.

Holy Commn 8 A.M. Ch. 11 A.M. and [blank.] Wrote to Canon MacColl.—Col.
Gourod[1]—S.C. Hand—T.J. Hester—Mr Nicol—Mr T.P. Royle.[2] Read Wellhausen
Art. Israel and made relative references—Von Strauss, Allgemeine Religion's
Wissenschaft[3]—

Quin's letter[4]   } both of them
Howell's Sermon[5]   } remarkable.

26. Whitm.

Ch 8½ AM & H.C. Wrote to Mr Hazelhurst—Sir Thos Acland—Mr Officer—Mr
Taylor Innes—J. Westell—Mr Probyn Nevins—Sotherans—Sir E. Watkin MP.
Worked on Homeric Bases. 2-6¾. Expedition to Brin-y-Cluchin: reached the
top: view darkened by smoke. Tea on the Hill. Backgammon with the Rector.
Read Dowd on Limerick.[6]

27. Whit Tu.

Ch. 8½ A.M. Read Sieges of Limerick—Maurice of Statland.[7] Wrote to Bishop of
Derry—Warden of Ruthin—Owen Morgan—Cyril Flower MP.—G.W. Bailey—
Jas Tait.[8] Worked on Homeric Bases. Looked up my papers: met the Bristol
party at 1 and spoke to them an hour.[9] Afterwards a short speech to a vast
crowd in the park. Dined with the Mayhews. Conversation with Mr Weston
MP[10] and Mr Cochrane (Newcastle).[11]

28. Wed.

Ch. 8½ A.M. In the middle of the service the entire church was occupied by a
crowd of Excursionists, quiet & well behaved. Wrote to Head Const. Liver-

[1] Lt. col. G. E. Gouraud, Thomas Edison's agent in Europe; arranged Gladstone's recording on
22 Nov. 88.
[2] Thomas Richard Popplewell Royle of Magdalen college, Oxford; see Add MS 44510, f. 41.
[3] See 8 Sept. 86.
[4] Possibly W. T. Wyndham-Quin, 4th earl of Dunraven, 'The Irish question examined in a letter
to the *New York Herald*' (1890).
[5] Untraced sermon sent by H. Howell (see 22 May 90).
[6] J. Dowd, *Limerick and its sieges* (1890).
[7] *Prince Maurice of Statland* [a novel]. By H.R.H. (1890).
[8] Perhaps James Tait, 1863-1944; historian; on staff of Manchester university; professor there
1896.
[9] 'Never have so many thousands of excursionists flocked into Hawarden'; so that Gladstone
could be heard, visitors from Bristol were admitted, by ticket, to the courtyard of the Castle; Gladstone spoke standing on a table; *T.T.*, 28 May 1890, 6a.
[10] Sir Joseph Dodge Weston, 1822-95; iron manufacturer with extensive interests in Wales;
liberal M.P. Bristol 1885-6, 1890-5; kt. 1886. Organised this day's visit by the Bristolians.
[11] Not further identified.

pool—Ld Granville—Sister Zillah[1]—W. Hammond & others.—Sir J. Weston. Worked on Homeric Bases. Worked on Books & St D.s. Drove with C. Addressed briefly another crowd of some thousands.[2] Read Wales & its prospects[3]—Prince Maurice of Statland—Milman, Hist. Jews.[4]

29. Th.

Ch. 8¼ A.M. Wrote to Messrs Macmillan—Col. Sec. of State[5]—J. Coxbrough— Funk & Wagnall—F.A. Cooper—Rev. W. Benham—Mr W. Scott. Worked on Homeric Bases. Worked on Books, Castle & St D's. Made a short speech to the Carnarvon party.[6] Conversation with the heads on the Welsh 'situation' & proposed priority.[7] Read Vox on Astronomy & H.S.[8]—Prince Maurice &c. Saw Mr M'Coll—Mr Johnson—Mr Mayhew. Meeting of [Dee] Embankment Trustees (Chairman) 3½–5.

30. Fr.

Ch. 8¼ A.M. Wrote to Mr And. Carnegie[9]—J. Noble—Mr M'Kittrich—J.C. Durrell—Sir Thos Acland—R. Bird—Rev. C. Gregory—Jas Davis—Miss F.F. Miller— Mr Mayhew—E.T. Elliott. Worked on books & papers. Walk with Canon MacColl. Read Manning & Caine in Contemp. Rev. (June)—Rev. Haweis in do.[10]—Toynbee's Poems[11]—Prince Maurice finished—Dowd's Limerick. Backgammon with S.

31. Sat.

Ch. 8¼ A.M. Wrote to Messrs Isbister—Scotts—Provost of Oriel—D. Radigan—E. Mackenzie—Dr Manly—Mrs Daniell—Th. Buist—W. Lynel. Greetings with the Lancs. party—the last. Read Renouf's Hibbert Lectures[12]—Dowd's Limerick (finished)—and Remarks on Polygamy. Also Campbell on Phallism: not a sincere book. Backgammon with S. Walk with Alfred [Lyttelton].

---

[1] Untraced.

[2] *T.T.*, 29 May 1890, 12c.

[3] Henry Jones, 'Wales and its prospects' (1890), published in Wrexham by the N. Wales Liberal Federation; perhaps read in preparation for next day's meeting.

[4] See 13 May 30.

[5] Henry Thurstan Holland, 1825–1914; colonial secretary 1886–92; 1st baron Knutsford 1888. Business untraced.

[6] *T.T.*, 30 May 1890, 4e.

[7] Visit by the Engedi Calvinistic Methodist church. After Gladstone's speech, the 'heads' were shown the Castle; David Lloyd George (1863–1945), recently elected M.P. for Carnarvon Boroughs) pressed Gladstone on Welsh disestablishment, declining to accept Gladstone's usual prevarication. The confrontation concluded with Gladstone asking Lloyd George if he knew the number of nonconformist chapels in Wales in 1742 (105). The 'dialogue ended with Lloyd George being crushed for one of the few times in his life' (B. B. Gilbert, *David Lloyd George*, i. 79–80 (1987)). Gladstone's 'proposed priority' was between Scottish and Welsh disestablishment and, presumably, Irish home rule; see 2 July 90n.

[8] Vox [i.e. E. Parsloe], *Astronomy and the Bible reconciled* (1890?).

[9] See 9 June 90.

[10] *C.R.*, lvii. 769, 774, 900 (June 1890).

[11] W. Toynbee, *Lays of common life* (1890), sent by the author; Add MS 44510, f. 38.

[12] See 16 Nov. 84.

Trin. S. June One. 90.

Ch. 11 A.M. with H.C. & 6½ P.M. Walk with Mr M'C[oll] and S. Wrote to Ld Granville—Mr Dillon MP. & . . . . . . Read MacColl Science & Xty[1]—Bp Reichel SPG Sermon[2]—Miss Toozey's Mission[3]—Robn Smith on O.T.[4]—and [blank.]

2. M.

Ch. 8½ A.M. Wrote to Mr F.N. Charrington—Miss Shreve[5]—Mrs Gullifer—A.G. Tonkin—H.C. Marshall—Geo. Hine—Wms & Norgate—A. Ross—Lady Aberdeen. Worked on books papers & accts. at Octagon & St Deiniol's. Backg[ammon] with C. Read Campbell on Phallism—'With Essex in Ireland'.[6] Saw H.N.G. & H.J.G. on domestic matters.

3. Th.

Ch. 8½ A.M. Willy's birthday. In the last 12 ms. the advance has been great,[7] the change happy. Wrote to Mr Vickers B.P.—T.J.L. Brown—J. Stone—E. Playle—H. Lowe—M. Knight—S. Smith. Forenoon with Mr Dillon on Tipperary & Cashel meetings.[8] Conversation with S. on Intermediate School—Z.O.[9]—& other matters. Gave evidence before the Commrs 3½–4½ PM.[10]

Conversation with Zadok.[11] It went very well. The easiest of the four branches of the domestic trouble which illustrates 'Pride shall have a fall', for I fear that I had been proud of the long tranquillity in our establishment. Backgammon with S. Work at St Deiniol's. Read Harvey's With Essex—Tangye's Autobiography.[12]

4. Wed. [London]

Ch. 8½ A.M. Wrote to Mr Nicol—Mrs Th BP—M. Gust. Pellet—T. Cufett—Vicar of Barking. Dined at Sir U. Shuttleworth's. 10¾–3¾. To Euston. Calls on the way home. A busy morning: books papers & parcels. Read Enea in Biogr. Dict. Tangye's Autobiography. Much varied conversation at the Shuttleworth party.

---

[1] See 18 Aug. 89.

[2] C. P. Reichel, 'The earliest missionary organization of the Christian church' (1890).

[3] See 8 Feb. 80.

[4] See 18 Apr. 90.

[5] Miss V. Shreve of Philadelphia, sent poems; Hawn P.

[6] E. Lawless, *With Essex in Ireland* (1890).

[7] i.e. since his seizure (see 2 Mar. 89).

[8] Dillon was closely involved in attempting to prevent evictions by Smith-Barry in Tipperary; on 18 September 1890 he was arrested but slipped bail. See F. S. L. Lyons, *John Dillon* (1968), 109 ff and P. Curtis, *Coercion and conciliation* (1963), 252-4. Dillon's visit to Hawarden seems hitherto unrecorded. He had requested it so as 'to have a short interview with you in reference to the proceedings of the Magistrates and police in Tipperary'; Add MS 44510, f. 54.

[9] Zadok Outram; see end of entry.

[10] Inquiry in Hawarden's claims for a new school under the Welsh Intermediate Education Act; *T.T.*, 4 June 1890, 8c.

[11] His valet, whose alcoholism led eventually to his death.

[12] Sir R. Tangye, *The growth of a great industry. An autobiography* (1890).

5. Th.

Wrote to Mr F. Schnadhorst—The Speaker—E.C. Parsons—Mr T. Leeke—G. Harding—Sig. Rob. Stuart—Messrs Griffin—Rev. J.S. Cooke—Rev. W.W. Flemyng[1]—Prof. M. Burrows. Saw S.G.L.—Count Münster—Ld Granville—do *cum* Mr Renouf[2]—A. Morley—Mr Parnell. H. of C. 3¼–7. Spoke on Channel Tunnel:[3] and held conclave in my room on Irish Land Purchase & the Tipperary and Cashel business.[4] Dined at Ld Tweedmouth's. Conversation with Dowager Duchess of M[anchester?][5] Finished Tangye's Autobiography. Read [blank.]

6. Fr.

Wrote to Ly Londonderry—Mr Hucks Gibbs—T. Douglas—Sig. Lampertico—E. Johnson—Smith & Elder—W. M'George—H. Bawen (N.Y. Independent)[6]—Mr J. Nicol. Nine to dinner. Saw S.G.L.—A. Morley—Cross (for butler)—J. Morley—Mr Grogan—Mr Bryce—Sir A. West—Mr Godley. H. of C. at 4½.[7] Visited Christie's. Tea at Lady Derby's (Ld Acton's Library). Read Milman's Gibbon[8]—Burrows Collectanea[9]—Capt. Harrison.[10]

7. Sat.

Wrote to Mr G. Bentinck[11]—Press Ass. & C.N. (Telegrams)—Garter K[ing] at Arms—J. Williams 1 & BP—D. Howes—F. Freeland—Helen G. l. & Tel.—Mons. G. Pellet—Mr Trumbull—Mr J. Hooper—Sir S. Scott & Co.—Mr Fitch—Rev. Thomson—Mr C.R. Cooke MP[12]—Rev. H. M'Quaire[13]—Mr Cockerell. Saw S.G.L.—Press Ass. & C.N.—A. Morley—Rev. Mr Farquhar—Ld Aberdeen—Mr Stuart Rendel—Sir H. Vivian—Ld Cadogan. Dined at Mr Stuart Rendel's to meet the Welsh members.[14] Met with a singular case [R]. Tea at Holdernesse House. Read Capt. Harrison—and other works.

---

[1] William Westropp Flemyng, anglican priest in Waterford, had sent poems; Hawn P.

[2] (Sir) Peter Le Page Renouf, 1822–97; keeper of Egyptian antiquities at British Museum 1885–91; kt. 1896. Business with Granville untraced.

[3] Supporting the building of a Channel tunnel; *H* 345. 40.

[4] See 3, 9 June 90.

[5] Hartington's mistress. Her husband, the 7th duke, had just died; she married Hartington in 1892.

[6] Henry Chandler Bowen, 1813–96; New York silk trader and founder of the *Independent*.

[7] Education estimates; *H* 345. 162.

[8] H. H. Milman, *The life of Edward Gibbon* (1839).

[9] The first vol. in the 2nd series of M. Burrows, *Collectanea* (1890).

[10] Untraced.

[11] Exchange on Mitchelstown with G. A. F. Cavendish-Bentinck, M.P., *T.T.*, 9 June 1890, 9f.

[12] Charles Wallwyn Radcliffe Cooke, 1841–1911; barrister and agriculturalist; tory M.P. W. Newington 1885–92, Hereford 1893–1900. Had sent his *Four years in parliament with hard labour* (1890); see *T.T.*, 12 June 1890, 11d.

[13] Perhaps M'Queary; see 8 June 90.

[14] Lloyd George told his wife: 'All the Welsh M.P.'s had been invited to meet the G.O.M. I had a long talk with the old gentleman, mostly about compensation . . .'; K. O. Morgan, *Lloyd George family letters* (1973), 28.

8. 1 S. Trin.

Chapel Royal mg and St James's evg. We went at $4\frac{1}{4}$ to Argyll Lodge: the Duke has been three weeks in bed. Read Keble Studia Sacra[1]—Sayce Hibbert Lectures—Richardson on Gilbert[2]—Macquaire on Evolution.[3]

9. M.

Wrote to Miss E. Cowley—H. Lowe—Rev. W. Downe—J.B. Penel—Mr Bunting—W.H.B. Reid—Rev. S.E.G. Wrote Mem. on the Acton Library. Then saw Mr A. Carnegie: who outran all my expectations.[4] Saw S.G.L.—Mr Deverell—Mr Morley—Mr A. Morley—Ld Granville. H. of C. $3\frac{3}{4}$-$7\frac{3}{4}$. Spoke $\frac{1}{2}$ hour on the Tipperary & Cashel question.[5] Dined at Mr Rathbone's. Read Child on The Tudor Church[6]—The Gospel of Nature.[7]

Private.   *Memorandum*[8]

1. Lord Acton's Library, now about to be sold, is estimated to consist of from 70000 to 80000 volumes.

2. It is has [*sic*] been collected by himself, in a sense lying much deeper than that in which the phrase is commonly used. They have been purchased by him, purchased it may be said one by one, and there are few among them of which he is not believed to have a personal knowledge. They might be taken over in the lump with the certainty that no part or no appreciable part of the acquisition would be trash.

3. From what I have known and seen of them I conceive that their cost cannot have been less, and may have been more, than from £25000 to £30000; and that it is more likely to have exceeded than to have fallen short of the last-named sum.

4. The vast majority of the books are in foreign tongues; *mostly* French German and Italian: some in tongues less known.

5. The Library is in the strictest sense useful—the books may be termed the tools of an author and student—There is nothing in the collection to attract the bibliographer or *virtuoso.*

6. A deplorable necessity due to no dishonouring cause now compels the alienation of this remarkable library.

7. Not only is it apparently doomed to dispersion, but to dispersion (according to present appearances) by the ruinous method of auction.

8. I understood that (say) 10000 volumes are now being prepared for sale next month: and (say) 15000 more are designated for sale during the fall of the year.

(9. I mention only in passing that among these are a small parcel of about 500 volumes relating to America.)

[1] J. Keble, *Studia Sacra* (1877).
[2] Untraced.
[3] Probably H. Macqueary, *Evolution of man and christianity* (1890).
[4] To assist Acton's finances and to remove his library from the potential assets of his creditors in the event of bankruptcy, Carnegie bought it for £9000, the books being placed in the hands of Freshfield and Granville (Acton's father-in-law) as trustees, with a deed giving Acton possession for life. After Acton's death, Carnegie gave the library to Morley who arranged for it to go to Cambridge University; see *Carnegie,* i. ch. xviii and Chadwick, *Acton and Gladstone,* 25 ff.
[5] Conduct of the police in Tipperary and Cashel; *H* 345. 380.
[6] G. W. Child, *Church and state under the Tudors* (1890).
[7] *The gospel of nature. Being proofs of a creator, and of the recent origins of man, drawn from nature* (1875).
[8] Add MS 44773, f. 182. Docketed 'Memorandum prepared for Mr. Carnegie'.

The Gladstones planting a tree at Newnham College, Cambridge, 31 January 1887. The tree was stolen and replaced by an oak from Hawarden

The Gladstones at Hawarden, ca. 1895

Gladstone photographed by Eveleen Myers, 25 April 1890

Facsimile of 15–20 August
1888
Lambeth 1452, f.89

Facsimile of 3–4 July 1891
(death of W.H. Gladstone)
Lambeth 1454, f.23

(a)

(b)

Millais's portrait of W.E. and W.G.C. Gladstone (see 26 June 1889 ff)

10. With regard to these 25000 volumes I fear that their fate is sealed, and that they must go broadcast over this and many other countries.

11. Can the remaining mass (say 50,000) be saved and kept together?

12. If this were to be done it would be by transfer at a valuation.

13. I conceive that if the 50000 were taken over at 4/– a volume all round, the proceeds would be larger to Lord Acton than the nett result of an auction, and the purchase much more advantageous to the purchaser than an acquisition of the same kind in the ordinary way.

(14. I may mention by way of illustration that I sold a small political and historical library of about 2800 volumes in 1875 by valuation. The books were valued by Messrs. Sotheby and they yielded to me 5/– per volume or more. This was an *use*ful library without articles of rarity or show.)

15. All this is very rough: but there could be no difficulty, I apprehend, if the Scheme were entertained in sending down a valuer or skilled reporter on the part of an intending purchaser to Aldenham Lord Acton's place in Shropshire who would speedily test the conjectural statements on which I have ventured.

16. I take it for granted that any one making such a purchase would probably do it with a view to presentation of the books to some great public library.

17. With reference to the fear of duplicates I may quote some words from a private letter of Lord Acton's. 'One of my principles of selection was to avoid books that I was sure to find in every collection in the country.'

18. It might however be prudent on the part of the purchaser to reserve a limited power of exclusion on review, (at a valuation) of say from 2000 to 4000 volumes.

19. And in like manner I think it possible that the friends of Lord Acton might desire to present him with such of the books (to a limited and perhaps similar extent & on the like conditions) as might have for him personally from any cause a *pretium affectionis*.

20. Should this outline of a plan be, either in part or in whole, conditionally & without prejudice entertained, perhaps that result might be sufficiently set out in brief compass and I would submit it together with this memorandum to Lord Acton's legal adviser Mr Freshfield.

WEG June 9, 1890.

10. Tu.

Wrote to Warden of All Souls[1]—Mr Waddy MP—Rev. Mr Caldecott—Mr A. Acland MP—Mons. G. Pellet—C. Hunter—Rev. Mr Hobson—Lord Acton—Rev. H. Drew—Mr W.H. Smith. Saw S.G.L.—Ld Granville l.l.—A. Morley—Ld Derby—Lady Granville—Ly [Winifred] Gardner—Mr Whitbread *cum* Sir L. Playfair—Mr J.A. Bright. Dined at Mr H. Gardners:[2] wrote letter afterwards to A. at G.s and under his eye.[3] Read Blind on W.E.G.s Lecture[4]—Child, Church under Tudors. Worked on Homeric Bases.[5]

---

[1] On an honorary fellowship there for Acton, Add MS 44510, f. 87.

[2] H. C. Gardner (see 9 Nov. 87).

[3] i.e. Acton staying at Granville's and about to depart for Munich; his journey caused difficulties in finalising the agreement (see 9 June 90).

[4] C. Blind, 'Mr Gladstone's disestablishment of the Greek pantheon', *National Review*, xv. 452 (June 1890).

[5] Start of work on *Landmarks of Homeric study, together with an essay on the points of contact between the Assyrian tablets and the Homeric text* (1890).

11. Wed.

Wrote to Sheriff Grubb—Howarth Barnes[1]—Rev. Mr Langdon—Mr Williams MP—Dr Patton BP—and minutes. Worked on Homeric Bases. Read Child, Church und. Tudors—Giusti, Poemi Omerici.[2] Finished Capt. Harrison. Tea with Mrs Ellice. Saw Mrs Sands. Dined at Lambeth Palace. Saw S.G.L.: and in evg the Archbp, the Bp of Carlisle, Sir G. Stokes, and Dr Warre. Evening prayers at the palace.

12. Th.

Wrote to Duke of Argyll—Mrs Ellice BP.—Mr Edm. Dease—T. OBrien—J.F. Robertson—D. Milne—W. Hillier—and minutes. Saw S.G.L.—Mr Schnadhorst— Mr A. Morley—Sir W. Harcourt—Indian Deputation[3]—Lord Rothschild. Worked on Homeric 'bases' to be changed to 'Aids'.[4] Read Child—OConnor Morris on Dubl. Castle.[5] $\frac{3}{4}$ hour at the Opera, Romeo and Juliet.[6] H. of C. $4\frac{1}{4}$-$7\frac{1}{4}$ and $9\frac{1}{2}$-$11\frac{1}{4}$.[7]

13. Fr.

Wrote to Mr A. Carnegie—R. de Coverley—Lord Acton—Sec. Ch of Engl. Insurance Office—and minutes. Read Child, and [blank]. Saw S.G.L.—Mr Murray— Mr A. Morley—Lord Hampden—Ly Hampden. Luncheon at Lady Farnborough's. Dined at Mr Levesons. H. of C. $4\frac{1}{2}$-$7\frac{3}{4}$. Spoke on Public House Endowment Bill, and voted in good divisions.[8]

14. Sat.

Wrote to Rev. T. Walker—Mr Freshfield Tel.—Mr D. Nutt—Dean of Llandaff— E.H. Stout—Ld Carnarvon—C.J. Lupson—and minutes. Tea at Ld Tweedmouth's. Jehangier's evening party.[9] Saw S.G.L.—Ld Granville—Ld G. cum Freshfield's Clerk[10]—Sir E. Lyell—Ld Reay—Mr Knowles—Ld Ripon—Ld Tweedmouth. S. Kensington for Head Measurement &c.[11] Worked on Homeric Aids. Read Child—Tudor Ch.—A Royal Democrat.[12]

[1] Probably J. Howard Barnes, actuary to the Pelican Life Insurance Co.
[2] Untraced.
[3] No account found.
[4] Eventually 'Landmarks'; see 10 June 90.
[5] Untraced article by W. O'Connor Morris.
[6] Royal Italian Opera, at Covent Garden; with Melba and de Reszke.
[7] Questions; taxes on drink; *H* 345. 691.
[8] The bill was only carried in 275:243; *H* 345. 945.
[9] Reception on behalf of Indians resident in Britain given by Mr. and Mrs. Cowasjee Jehangier for Lord Reay on his return from Bombay; *D.N.*, 16 June 1890, 6c.
[10] Further negotiations about the Acton library.
[11] 'Mr. Gladstone was amusingly insistent about the size of his head, saying that hatters often told him that he had an Aberdeenshire head—"a fact which you may be sure I did not forget to tell my Scottish constituents". It was a beautifully shaped head, though rather low, but after all it was not so very large in circumference'; F. Galton, *Memories of my life* (1909), 249.
[12] Untraced.

15. 2 S. Trin.

Chapel Royal mg. St James's evg. Wrote to Mr Carnegie. Read Knobel Völker-tafel[1]—Sayce, Hibbert Lectures—finished Child.

16. M.

Wrote to Mr Freshfield—Mrs Drew—F. Verindor—G. Pellet—Mrs Thistl.—and minutes. Worked on Homeric Aids. Saw S.G.L.—Miss Tennant—Ld Acton—Sir W. Harcourt—Sir A. Lyall[2]—A. Morley—Mr Morley—Mr Stuart Rendell—Mr Summer[?]—Mr Bryce. Dined at Grillion's. Read A Royal Democrat—Watkins, Bampton Lectures[3]—La Venus Populaire.[4] H. of C. 5-8. Spoke on the Licensing Question.[5]

17. Tu.

Wrote to Messrs M'Millan—Mr W. Hind—Rev. A.G. Prichard—Rev. Mr Carter BP—Mr Witham—Mr J. Simmons—& minutes. Ten to dinner. Conclave 10-11½ Ld G. Mr F. & then also Ld Acton, on his affair.[6] Saw S.G.L.—A. Morley. H. of C. 2-7¾ and 10½-12. More speaking & good voting.[7] Read Blades on Enemies to Books.[8]

18. Wed.

Wrote to Williams & N.—Archdn of Bristol—Mr A. Ross—Rev. J.C. Cox—Mr E.W. Stibbs—Rev. J.M. Jones—Hugh Downe—H. Tiedemann—H.W. Cook—Rev. Mr Kemps—and minutes. Luncheon at Ly Brownlows. Read Ruby.[9] Saw Grogans—Scotts—M'Cust.—S.G.L.—Ld Herschell—Ly Lothian. Dined at the French Ambassador's. Saw Murray [R?]. 6-7½. S.E. [Railway] meeting at Cannon Street Hotel. Spoke ½ hour.[10]

19. Th.

Wrote to Mr Freshfield—Consul Zucchinelli—P. Witham—Rev. Dr. Damalas[11]—Paul Eaton[12]—D. Dudley Field—Watsons—Mr Whitbread—Mr W.H. Smith—and minutes. Saw Ld Rosebery—do *cum* Ld Reay—Ld Acton—Miss Kendall—S.G.L.—Ld Northbourne—A. Morley—Lady W. Gardner—Ly Ripon. Uproar on the Bench: Sir WH. in a storm of excitement about questions on

[1] A. Knobel, *Die Volkertafel des Genesis* (1850).
[2] Sir Alfred Comyn Lyall, 1835-1911; kt. 1881; member of Indian Council 1888-1902; poet, historian and liberal unionist.
[3] H. W. Watkins, *Modern criticism on the fourth gospel* (1890).
[4] *Vénus la populaire ou apologie des maisons de joye* (1727).
[5] *H* 345. 1059.
[6] See 9 June 90.
[7] Local taxation; *H* 345. 1377.
[8] W. Blades, *The enemies of books* (1880).
[9] C. Reade, *Ruby. A novel* (1889).
[10] On thrift, and on impact of railways on the century; *T.T.*, 19 June 1890, 6d.
[11] Nikolaos M. Damalas, scholar in Athens; published translation into Greek of an account of Gladstone's political golden jubilee, adding his own address (1883).
[12] Of Washington, U.S.A.; on free trade; Hawn P.

Heligoland. H. of C. $4\frac{1}{2}$-$7\frac{1}{2}$.[1] Dined at Mr Stuart Rendel's. Haymarket Theatre for Mrs Winslow's Reading.[2]

20.

Wrote to Messrs White—Ld Rosebery—J.F. Maguire—A. Wilcox—Mr H. Mayhew—Sir W. Harcourt & copy. Nine to dinner at home. Worked on the question of the Glebe land to be acquired at Hawarden. Saw S.G.L.—Mr Hutton—S.E.G.—Mr A. Morley—and others. Read Ruby—Venus La Populaire.

21. Sat.

Wrote to Mr Cramer MP—Mr Knowles Tel.—Mr Morley. Garden party 4–$6\frac{1}{2}$. Constant conversations, one on the heels of another. Confident rumours of dropping the 'Public H. Endowment Bill'.[3] Read Ruby (finished)—Miss Miles[4]—Sayce, H.L.—Gray, by Mr Gosse.[5]

22. 3. S. Trin.

Kingsbury Ch mg Willesden Evg. Read Sayce, Hibbert L.—Watkins Bampton L.[6]—Christ the pupil! of Buddha[7]—Christie on Scots Commn Office.[8]

23. M.

Wrote to Mr Foljambe—Miss Tennant—A.D. Castle—F.A. Ashmead—Mr F. Patey—Mr Carnegie—& minutes. Dined at Grillion's. Back to St J. Square 11.30. Saw S.G.L.—Sir W. Harcourt—H.N.G.—Mr A. Morley—Mr Black—Mr Morley—Ld Acton. Tea at Miss Tennant's: met Mr Stanley & Sir W. M'Kinnon[9] & discussed the map.[10] Read Daniel Cortis[11]—Gosse's Gray.

---

[1] Cession of Heligoland to Germany as part of the Anglo-German agreement; Harcourt did not himself ask a question; *H* 345. 1356.

[2] Mrs. Irving Winslow of Boston, Mass., gave an afternoon reading of Ibsen's 'An Enemy of the People' (1882).

[3] On 19 June the 1st clause had only been carried by 4 votes; but the bill was persevered with; see Lucy, *Salisbury parliament*, 282.

[4] Perhaps E. E. Miles, *Our home beyond the tide and kindred poems* (1878).

[5] E. W. Gosse, *Gray* (1882); biography.

[6] See 16 June 90.

[7] *Christ the pupil of Buddha. A comparative study* (1890).

[8] J. Christie, *The oblation and invocation in the Scottish Communion Office vindicated* (1844).

[9] Dorothy Tennant (see 30 Mar. 87) was engaged to Henry Morton Stanley, 1841–1904, explorer and writer, recently returned from an unsuccessful attempt to 'rescue' Emin Pasha during which he had explored the edge of the Rwenzori mountains and unknown areas of what became Uganda. Sir William McKinnon, 1823–93, had promoted Stanley's relief expedition; his British East Africa Co. had been chartered in 1888. The Anglo-German Agreement which settled the boundaries of East Africa, giving Britain Uganda, Kenya and Zanzibar, in exchange for Heligoland, was approved by the Cabinet on 10 June and formally concluded on 1 July; see *Africa and the Victorians*, 289–94.

[10] Stanley recalled this occasion (*The autobiography of Sir Henry Morton Stanley* (1909), 419):
'At the house of my dear wife-to-be, I met the ex-Premier, the Right Honourable Mr. W. E. Gladstone, who had come for a chat and a cup of tea, and to be instructed—as I had been duly warned—about one or two matters connected with the slave-trade. I had looked forward to the meeting with great interest, believing—deluded fool that I was!—that a great politician cares to be instructed about anything but the art of catching votes. I had brought with me the latest political map of East Africa,

[*See opposite page for n. 10 cont. and n. 11.*]

24. *Tu.*

Wrote to Mr Carnegie—Mr Freshfield—C.W. Duckworth—S. Simeon—Watsons—R.E. Smith—Reeves & Turner. H. of C. 4–7½.[1] Conclave of 17, 11–12¾. Attended County Council 3–4.[2] Dined at Sir B. Samuelson's. Saw S.G.L.—Italian

and, when the time had come, I spread it out conveniently on the table before the great man, at whose speaking face I gazed with the eyes of an African. "Mr. Gladstone," said I, intending to be brief and to the point, as he was an old man, "this is Mombasa, the chief port of British East Africa. It is an old city. It is mentioned in the Lusiads, and, no doubt, has been visited by the Phœnicians. It is most remarkable for its twin harbours, in which the whole British Navy might lie safely, and—"

"Pardon me," said Mr. Gladstone, "did you say it was a harbour?"

"Yes, sir," said I, "so large that a thousand vessels could be easily berthed in it."

"Oh, who made the harbour?" he asked, bending his imposing glance upon me.

"It is a natural harbour," I answered.

"You mean a port, or roadstead?"

"It is a port, certainly, but it is also a harbour, that, by straightening the bluffs, you—"

"But pardon me, a harbour is an artificial construction."

"Excuse me, sir, a dock is an artificial construction, but a harbour may be both artificial and natural, and—"

"Well, I never heard the word applied in that sense." And he continued, citing Malta and Alexandria, and so on.

This discussion occupied so much time that, fearing I should lose my opportunity of speaking about the slave-trade, I seized the first pause, and skipping about the region between Mombasa and Uganda, I landed him on the shores of the Nyanza, and begged him to look at the spacious inland sea, surrounded by populous countries, and I traced the circling lands. When I came to Ruwenzori, his eye caught a glimpse of two isolated peaks.

"Excuse me one minute," said he; "what are those two mountains called?"

"Those, sir," I answered, "are the Gordon Bennett and the Mackinnon peaks."

"Who called them by those absurd names?" he asked, with the corrugation of a frown on his brow.

"I called them, sir."

"By what right?" he asked.

"By the right of first discovery, and those two gentlemen were the patrons of the expedition."

"How can you say that, when Herodotus spoke of them twenty-six hundred years ago, and called them Crophi and Mophi? It is intolerable that classic names like those should be displaced by modern names, and—"

"I humbly beg your pardon, Mr. Gladstone, but Crophi and Mophi, if they ever existed at all, were situated over a thousand miles to the northward. Herodotus simply wrote from hearsay, and—"

"O, I can't stand that."

"Well, Mr. Gladstone," said I, "will you assist me in this project of a railway to Uganda, for the suppression of the slave-trade, if I can arrange that Crophi and Mophi shall be substituted in place of Gordon Bennett and Mackinnon?"

"O, that will not do; that is flat bribery and corruption"; and, smiling, he rose to his feet, buttoning his coat lest his virtue might yield to the temptation.

"Alas!" said I to myself, "when England is ruled by old men and children! My slave-trade discourse must be deferred, I see."'   [11] See 10 Aug. 88.

[1] Questioned Smith on Heligoland; *H* 345. 1797.

[2] Rosebery presided, Gladstone sitting by him; see *T.T.*, 25 June 1890, 10c. The *Daily News* reported the L.C.C. meeting on Gladstone's death: 'Many Councillors retain a vivid memory of the venerable figure seated in the recess of the dais. It is remembered, as a half whimsical incident of that occasion, how the visitor's patience suffered some strain at the hands of his courtesy. Greatly daring, many members presented themselves before him, hungry for recognition. But Mr. Gladstone was set on following the proceedings, as was abundantly made manifest by the eagerness with which, the word of personal recognition being spoken, he leant forward, hand to ear, and renewed close attention to what was going forward. So, even to the County Council, the national loss became also a personal loss.' See Sir H. Haward, *The London County Council from within* (1932), 50.

Ambassr—Lord Ripon—Sir W. Harcourt—Ld Rosebery—Mr A. Morley—Mr Mundella—Mr Hutton. Read Nicol, Pol. Spirit of our Times[1]—Case for New-foundland.[2] Conclave of peace M.P.s 4½-5.[3]

25. Wed.

Wrote to Mr Fyffe—Mr Scharf BP—W. Ridler BP—Jos King—Messrs Fresh-field—Mr Carnegie. Tea at Lady Farnborough's. To Soc. Antiquaries with Mr Foljambe for the Canterbury finds.[4] Saw S.G.L.—Arthur Lyttelton. Dined at Ld Rosebery's. Duchess of Edinburgh most winning. Conversation with Lady Airlie. Baron A. Rothschild—Ld Rosebery—Baron Staal. Read Lorna Doone[5]—Sayce, Hibbert Lectures.

26. Th.

Wrote to Rev. A. Robins—Ld Acton—C. Herbert—Ld Ripon—Mr P. Witham—A. Howell—Mr Schnadhorst—and minutes. Saw S.G.L.—Ld Granville—A. Morley—Mr W.H. Smith—Mr O. Morgan. H. of C. 4¾-7½.[6] Read Lorna Doone—Sayce H.L.—Venus Populaire (finished). Dined at J. Talbots.

27. Fr. [Dollis Hill]

Wrote to Reeves & Turner—J. Noble—H. Gardner—H. Lowe—Mad. Rebrey—A.W. Jephson—Mr J. Barr—and minutes. Saw Ld Rosebery—A. Morley—and others. H. of C. as usual to dinner time.[7] Off to Dollis at 9.30. Read Lorna Doone—Sayce Lectures—Gosse's Gray.

28. Sat. [London]

A reading day. Sayce, Lorna Doone, Schönhof, Industrial Situation,[8] Gosse's Gray. Three hours garden party, mostly indoors from rain. Dined with Mrs Th. on the way back to London.

29. St P. & 4 S. Trin.

St Margaret's mg: a grand sermon from Bp of Peterborough: Chapel Royal evg. Wrote to Lady W. Gardner—Bp of Peterborough. Read Watkins Bampton L.—Fisher on Revelation[9]—Huxley Science & Religion.[10]

---

[1] D. Nicol, *The political life of our time*, 2v. (1889).
[2] J. S. Winter, *French treaty rights in Newfoundland. The case for the colony* (1890).
[3] Preparations for peace conference in London in July; see 7 July 90n.
[4] Remnants found in the tomb of Hubert Walter; *Proceedings of the Society of Antiquaries* (1890), papers given on 17 April–19 June.
[5] By R. D. Blackmore, 3v. (1869).
[6] Questions; misc. business; *H* 346. 83.
[7] Police bill; *H* 346. 230.
[8] J. Schoenhof, *The industrial situation and the question of wages* (1885).
[9] G. P. Fisher, *Nature and method of revelation* (1890).
[10] T. H. Huxley, 'The lights of the Church and the light of science', *N.C.*, xxviii. 5 (July 1890).

30. M.

Wrote to Bp of St Asaph—Mr Duncan[1]—Rev. Mr Spooner[2]—Ld Ripon—Rev. Dr. Hayman—B. Fowler—Lady Holker—G. Parker—Temperance Comm. (cancelled)—W. Hutt—Mrs Rendel—and minutes. Dined at Mr Rendels. Procedure Committee 2–3.[3] Saw S.G.L.—Mr Knowles—Mr Chamberlain—Mr Morley—Sir W. Harcourt l.l.—Mr A. Morley—Ld Granville—Bp St Asaph l.l.—Mr Chamberlain—Mr S. Rendel MP.—Justice Mathew[4]—and others. Saw Jackson [R]. H. of C. $4\frac{1}{4}$–$6\frac{1}{4}$.[5] Read Lorna Doone.

Tues. July One 1890.

Wrote to W. Downing—Rev. Dr. Preston—Rev. Mr Anstiss[6]—and minutes. H. of C. 3–$4\frac{1}{2}$.[7] Dined at Mr K. Hugessen's. Saw S.G.L.—Sir W. Harcourt—Ld Granville—Ld Rosebery—Ld G. cum Ld Acton—A. Morley—Ld Spencer. Tea at Canon Rowsell's.[8] & long conversation. Read Lorna Doone—Sayce Hibbert Lectures.

2. Wed.

Wrote to Mr S. Rendel—Sir C. Forster—Rev. T. Graham—Mr Gee[9]—Rev. Canon Rowsell—Ld Rosebery—Mr W.S. Brown—Mr Casford—Rev. C.P. Hard—Mr Witham—Canon Barker—Mr W.H. Smith. Visited Sir A. Saunders (dental affairs)—Mr Ossani[10]—Saw S.G.L.—Sir W. Harcourt—Mr Agnew. Divers calls. Tea with Lady Sydney. Dined at Mr Buxtons. Read Sayce—Lorna Doone.

3. Th.

At one, attended the Memorial Service at the Savoy [Chapel] for Lord Carnarvon. Wrote few. Dined at Mr Acland's to see my old friend. Late. Comm. on Procedure and H. of C. 1–5 (except Savoy).[11] Tea with Lady Ribblesdale. Visited

---

[1] Letters of support for James Archibald Duncan, successful candidate in the by-election at Barrow where W. S. Caine was standing as an independent liberal, following his leaving the liberal unionists. *T.T.*, 2 July 1890, 10b. Caine explained away his subsequent complaint; Add MS 44510, f. 132. Draft letter encouraging orthodox liberals to withdraw in favour of Caine, marked 'Cancelled', is at Add MS 44773, f. 187.

[2] William Archibald Spooner, 1844–1930; fellow of New College, Oxford (warden 1903); active in C.O.S.; claimed never to have uttered 'Spoonerisms'.

[3] He was a member of the select cttee. on the business of the House; *PP* 1890 lvii. 129, xi. 1.

[4] (Sir) James Charles Mathew, 1830–1908; judge 1881; chaired commission on Irish evictions; strong Roman Catholic.

[5] Questions; W. Australia Constitution bill; *H* 346. 345.

[6] George William Antiss, vicar of Ivybridge.   [7] Questions; *H* 346. 450.

[8] See 3 May 50; Gladstone made him canon of Westminster 1881.

[9] To Thomas Gee, Welsh disestablishmentarian and ed. of *The Banner*: 'it is impossible at the present period to determine any question of priority [between Welsh and Scottish disestablishment]'; *T.T.*, 10 July 1890, 11f.

[10] Alessandro Ossani, portrait painter working in London in the 1880s (in 1884, at 45 Howland Street); See A. Graves, *The Royal Academy of Arts*, vi. 27 (1906) and 4–5 July 90. Ossani is the probable copier of a portrait at Hawarden of Gladstone's mother (see *The Gladstone-Glynne Collection* (1934), 12).

[11] India; army estimates; *H* 346. 699.

Sir C. Tennant's pictures.[1] Saw S.G.L.—Sir W. Harcourt—Mr Agnew *cum* Mr Sidney Cooper.[2] Read Lorna Doone—Sedgwick's Memoirs.[3]

4. *Fr.*

Wrote to Archdn Anson—Mr Caine—Archdn Palmer—Mr Crawford—Rev. Poynter—J.D. Cooper—Mr Schnadhorst. Commee & H. of C. 1–5.[4] Saw S.G.L.— Ld Granville—E. Benjamin—Mr A. Morley—W. Knowles[5]—Sir W. Harcourt— Lord Tennyson: well, but as C.G. observed, undoubtedly 'gruff'. Dined with Mr Knowles. Read Lorna Doone—Cooper's Eumenides.[6] Visited Mr Ossani's studio.

5. *Sat.*

Wrote to Ld Cobham—Ld Ripon—Wyllies BP—Ld Rosebery—W.H.G., B.P.— Rev. Benham—Ld Carnarvon[7]—Scotts. Saw Lord Rothschild (at 5 PM Tea): Froude[8] read aloud—S.G.L.—Ld Granville—Mr Ossani. Drive & calls with C. Read Lorna Doone (finished)—Paul Nugent[9]—Sayce Hibbert Lectures— Froude's Beaconsfield.

6. *5 S. Trin.*

St Edmund's 10.45 A.M. H.C.—An impressive sermon from Bp Ridding: and a *very* beautiful musical service. Chap. Royal in aft. Wrote to Bp of Newcastle— Archdn Watkins—Mrs Th.—Col. Macinroy.[10] Read Paul Nugent—Watkins Bampton Lect.—Norris of Bemerton on Soul's Immortality.[11]

7. *M.*

Wrote to Mr Cremer MP[12]—Mr W.D. Freshfield—A.B. Osborne—Bull & Auvache—Jas Wyllie—Mr W.H. Rideing—Macmillans. Read Paul Nugent— Digby on Conspiracy.[13] Saw S.G.L.—Sir J. Carmichael—Ld Rosebery. Worked on books. H. of C. $4\frac{1}{2}$.[14]

---

[1] The collection then included Millais' first portrait of Gladstone, which Tennant bought from the duke of Westminster (the latter disgusted with Home Rule); it is now in the National Gallery.

[2] (Thomas) Sidney Cooper, 1803–1902; painter, chiefly of animals.

[3] J. W. Clark and T. M. Hughes, *The life and letters of Adam Sedgwick*, 2v. (1890).

[4] Questions; W. Australia bill; *H* 346. 805.

[5] Walter Frank Knowles, priest in New Zealand; occasional correspondent; Hawn P.

[6] In J. D. Cooper, *Aeschylus* (1890).

[7] George Edward Stanhope Molyneux Herbert, 1866–1923, 5th earl of Carnarvon 1890. See 3 July 90.

[8] J. A. Froude, *Lord Beaconsfield* (1890).

[9] H. F. Hetherington and H. D. Burton, *Paul Nugent, materialist*, 2v. (1890?).

[10] See 17 Oct. 46.

[11] J. Norris, *A philosophical discourse concerning the natural immortality of the soul*, 2v. (1708).

[12] Unable, despite request of the 'peace M.Ps.' to take part in the conference in London; *T.T.*, 10 July 1890, 10f, Add MS 44510, f. 134.

[13] Untraced.

[14] Civil service estimates; *H* 346. 941.

8. *Tu.*

Wrote to Sir C. Dilke. Saw S.G.L.—Canon Rowsell—Mr Morley—Sir W. Harcourt—Mr A. Morley—Mr Howorth MP. Saw Clark—Collins—& another [R]. Ten to dinner. Conversation on Heligoland: Mr Winterbotham & Mr Summers.[1] Commee & H. of C. 12–6¾.[2] Read Paul Nugent—Sedgwick's Memoirs. Westminster Abbey service 3 PM.

9. *Wed.*

Wrote to Mr J. Nicol—Mr Hutt—Mr Downing—.......—Macmillans BP—........ Went to Church Insurance Office about St Deiniol's. Dined at Sir G. Trevelyan's. Saw Lord Granville—Lord Reay—Mr Dillon. Saw Jackson—Hel [R]. Read Paul Nugent—and Senate Speeches U.S. Dined at Sir G.T.s. Corrected proofsheets.

10. *Th.*

Wrote to Mr Freshfield—Canon Rowsell—Messrs Cook—Mr Oppenheim—Miss Hetherington. H. of C. 12–5¼[3] (with Committee). Read Paul Nugent (finished) —Sedgwick's Memoirs. Saw S.G.L.—Sir W. Harcourt—M. Staal—Mad. Staal—Ld Spencer—Mr Humphreys (cl.) Dined at the Russian Embassy.

11. *Fr.*

Wrote to W.W. Lucas—J. Walcot—Sir B. Leighton—Warden of Bradfield[4]—Thos Wager[5]—Lady Sydney—G.W. Mingley?—Rev. J. Stark—Rev. H. Wright—Rev. T. Foston—Mrs Bolton PP. Saw S.G.L.—A. Morley—Ld Rosebery. Dined at Sir C. Tennants. Read Dublin Review[6]—Rawlinson's Phoenicia.[7]

12. *Sat.*

Westminster Abbey 2 PM marriage of Miss D. Tennant.[8] Saw Sir E. Saunders. Wrote to Messrs Bull & Auvache—Sig. Arena[9]—Mr C. Herbert—Messrs Bailey—D. of Edinburgh's Controller. Saw Mr A. Morley. Drive with C. Read Rawlinson's Phoenicia—Downe's Innocent Victims, all.[10] Worked on Homeric papers.

---

[1] Arthur Brend Winterbotham, 1838–92; cloth manufacturer; liberal M.P. Cirencester 1885–92 (voted against Home Rule 1886 but returned to the party) and W. Summers (see 9 Oct. 84).

[2] L.C.C. bill; *H* 346. 1051.

[3] Questions; *H* 346. 1307.

[4] H. B. Gray; Gladstone had been a member of the Council of Bradfield School 1859–88 (never attending a meeting), but this business is untraced.

[5] Perhaps Thomas Wager, London saddlemaker.

[6] *Dublin Review*, xxiv (July 1890).

[7] See 22 Mar. 90.

[8] To H. M. Stanley; see 23 June 90. Gladstone was invited by Dorothy Tennant to sign the register; Add MS 44520, f. 160.

[9] G. Arena of Malta, concerned about English replacing Italian there; Hawn P.

[10] H. Downe, *Innocent victims* (1890).

13. 6 S. Trin.

Chapel Royal mg. St James's evg. Wrote O.T. paper.[1] Read Life of Mrs Chisholm[2]—Watkins Bampton Lectures—Lambert on Downside Educn[3]—Insignia Vitae.[4] Wrote to Sir J. Lambert.

14. M.

Wrote to W. Mitchell—Mrs Von Neergaard—Mr W.H. Smith—Card. Manning BP—Ld Coleridge—Macmillans BP—Mr Hankey—E. Barrett—Mr J. Nicol—Mr A. Morley—Mr Downe—Mrs Fairfax. Corr. 3 sheets Hom. Proofs. Saw S.G.L.— Sir W. Harcourt—Mr Morley—Mr A. Morley—Mr Knowles—Sir E. Saunders— Mrs Henderson—Card. Manning. At Marlborough House party. Read M. Arnold[5]—Ld Holland[6]—Ld Coleridge.[7]

15. Tu.

Wrote to A. Chopin—Watsons—Mrs Th.—Provost of St Ninian's—Mr L.H. Wilkins—Mr Sidney Cooper RA—Subdean Chapel Royal—Rev. J.S. Brooks—Mr E. Nimmo—Mr Stanford—Mr Fulcher—Mrs Bolton—Rev. S.E.G.—A. Sutton—J. Letztengroschen. Saw S.G.L.—A. Morley—Mr Bigland[8]—E. Hamilton—Mr Robinson—Mr M'Donnell—Mr Oppenheimer—..... An attack after 2 PM. kept me from the House: but I dined with Mr Oppenheimer.[9] Saw Rosebery—Sir W. Harcourt. Read Ld Holland—Q.R. on Walpole—do on Eton.[10] Weather turned to fine.

16. Wed.

Wrote to Mr Campbell—E.G. Bartlett—Med. Officer Guy's—Dean of Windsor— Miss Hetherington. Garden party Montagu House:[11] D. & Duchess very courteous. Worked on Hom. Assyr.[12] Saw S.G.L.—Mr Nicol—Lady Londonderry (tea 5 PM)—Lady Ormond. Dined at Alford House, Mr Williamson's.[13] Read Ld Holland, Notes—and. . . .

---

[1] Paper on 'Biblical exaggeration', Add MS 44773, f. 189.
[2] Perhaps *The story of the life of Mrs. Caroline Chisholm, the emigrants' friend* (1852).
[3] Untraced article, probably by Sir J. Lambert.
[4] C. H. Waterhouse, *Insignia Vitae; or, Broad principles and practical conclusions* (1890).
[5] Probably the 1890 ed. of M. Arnold's *Poetical works*.
[6] See 9 Mar. 52.
[7] J. D. Coleridge, 'The law in 1847 and the law in 1889', *C.R.*, lvii. 797 (June 1890).
[8] Probably Ernest Bigland, London merchant.
[9] William Oppenheimer of Cornwall Terrace, Regent's Park, art dealer and Dresden china importer.
[10] *Q.R.*, clxxi. 1, 172 (July 1890).
[11] In Portman Square, then occupied by several tenants; the duke and duchess were evidently also guests.
[12] See 10 June 90 and 7 Sept. 92.
[13] James Williamson, 1842-1930; manufacturer; liberal M.P. Lancaster 1886-95; cr. Baron Ashton 1895; lived in Alford House, Princes Gate.

17. Th.

Wrote to Mr Tragaski—Scotts?—Rev. Mr Pudley—Remingtons. Worked on Hom. Ass. paper. Dined at Ld Herschells—saw Lady Jersey[1]—Mrs Benson—Abp of Canterbury. Saw S.G.L.—A. Morley—Mr Smith—Mr Fowler. Attended Burlington School Anniv. and spoke.[2] H. of C. $4\frac{1}{4}$–$5\frac{1}{4}$.[3] Read Ld Holland—Memoirs of Reynolds.[4]

18. Fr.

Wrote to Rev. Urquhart—Mr R. Tangye—Mr Ramsbottom—Mr P. Bunting—Mr Hogg. Dined with Lucy. Drive with C. Saw Sir W. White—S.G.L.—Sir J. Lacaita—Mrs Bolton. Worked on Hom. Assyr. Read Life of Reynolds—Jonathan Merle.[5]

19. Sat.

Wrote to Colin Allan—J. Maggs—Messrs Remington—H. Parratt—W.M. Wixley. Read Jon. Merle—Life of Reynolds. St Michael's for the Vyner marriage at 11.30 AM.[6] Luncheon party: M. & Mad. Meurikoffre[7]—Sir J. Lacaita—Mr G. Russell. Dined at Mr Schwann's.[8] Saw S.G.L.—Mr G. Russell—Mr A. Morley—Miss Colenso[9]—Mr W. OBrien MP[10]—Mrs Schwann.

20. 7 S. Trin.

Willesden Ch mg with H.C.—Prayers read evg. Read Jonathan Merle—Jenkins on Ignatian Epistles[11]—Urwick on Isaiah[12]—Answer to Colenso[13]—Binley on Genesis[14] &c. Prof. & Mad. Villari[15]—Dr Maclagan[16]—Mr Robertson (Austr.)[17]—came.

---

[1] Margaret Villiers, 1849–1945; wife of 7th earl of Jersey; author, traveller and political hostess.

[2] Distributed prizes and spoke on women's education; *T.T.*, 18 July 1890, 10f.

[3] End of questions; civil service estimates; *H* 347. 103.

[4] J. Northcote, *Memoirs of Sir Joshua Reynolds*, 2v. (1813–15).

[5] See 7 Dec. 89.

[6] Violet Aline, da. of Gladstone's friend from Cannes, Mrs Vyner (see 30 Jan. 83) m. James Francis Harry St. Claire-Erskine, 5th earl of Rosslyn, divorcing him 1902.

[7] i.e. the Meuricoffes from the Continent (see 27 Dec. 88) where they knew Mrs. Vyner.

[8] (Sir) Charles Ernest Schwann, 1844–1929; Manchester merchant; liberal M.P. N. Manchester 1886–1918; m. 1876 Elizabeth Duncan who d. 1914. Cr. bart. 1906.

[9] Da. of the bp.; had sent pamphlets on him.

[10] See 17 Oct. 77.

[11] R. C. Jenkins, 'Ignatian difficulties and historic doubts' (1890).

[12] W. Urwick, *The servant of Jehovah. A commentary . . . upon Isaiah* (1877).

[13] Perhaps T. H. Candy, 'Antediluviana; or answer to . . . Colenso' (1864).

[14] Untraced.

[15] Pasquale Villari, Italian historian much read and admired by Gladstone, and his wife.

[16] William Dalrymple MacLagan, 1826–1910; high-church ecumenist; bp. of Lichfield 1878; abp. of York 1891–1908.

[17] Presumably of Australia; not further identified.

21. M.

Wrote to C. A. Fellowes—G. Walpole—T.S. Townend—W.T. Sharp—Messrs Jarrold—Rev. C. Baker—Rev. J.P. Hopps—Rev. W. Urwick—Ed. Daily News. Dined at Ld R. Churchill's: a more perfectly worked entertainment I never attended. Saw P. of Wales—Princess—M. de Staal—Ld R.C.—Mrs Depens. Worked on Hom. Assyr. Read Watson on Austin[1]—Life of Reynolds. H. of C. 4–6$\frac{1}{2}$ and 11$\frac{1}{4}$–2.[2]

22. Tu.

Wrote to Mr Tregassis—Mr J. Nicol—Mr U. Maggs—Mr Wilkins—H.J.G.—The Russian Ambassador—Ld Rosebery. Dined at Lady Hayter's. Saw S.G.L.—Mr Harrison—Dean of Windsor (Abp T. & Carnegie)[3]—Sir W. Harcourt—A. Morley. Saw Mrs R. Mills—Mrs Henderson. Worked on Hom. Ass. Read Reynolds. H. of C. 3$\frac{3}{4}$–5$\frac{1}{4}$.[4] Drive with C.

23. Wed.

Wrote to Dr Warre (BP)—Dr Weldon (BP)—E. Wickham (BP)—J. Westell—Mr Dods Shaw—Mrs R. Mills—A.H. Mynor. Corrected Hom. Ass. proofsheets. Saw S.G.L.—De Coverley—Zähndorff—Macmillans—J. Nicol—Ly Aberdeen—Ly Wood. Dined at Mr C. Wilson's. Read Life of Reynolds—Life of De Quincey.[5] Worked on Heligoland.

24. Th.

Wrote to Mr Turnbull—Rev. Trevor Owen[6]—Mrs Lynch—P. Witham, Solr. Dined at Sir J. Paget's. Saw Mr Parks—Miss Swanwick.[7] Packed a hamper with papers &c. Saw S.G.L.—Mr A. Morley—Sir W. Harcourt—Mr Godley. 3.30, Presentation of phonograph.[8] 4–7$\frac{1}{2}$. H. of C.—Spoke an hour on Agreement & Right of Cession.[9] Read Life of Reynolds.

---

[1] Untraced.

[2] Questions; housing; savings banks; spoke on adjournment; *H* 347. 442.

[3] Davidson had requested an interview to discuss the use of Gladstone's letters in his life of A. C. Tait, then in preparation; Add MS 44510, f. 166.

[4] End of questions; census; *H* 347. 514.

[5] A. H. Japp, *Thomas de Quincey: his life and writings* (1890).

[6] Richard Trevor Owen, vicar of Oswestry; archaeologist.

[7] See 30 May 78.

[8] Presentation at Edison House, Northumberland Avenue, of a phonograph, with cylinders of messages from Gen. Sherman, Sen. Evarts and A. Carnegie; *D.N.*, 25 July 1890, 3a. Prothero's account is amusing but probably *ben trovato*: 'After dinner I found, to my horror, that we were all expected to speak into the phonograph, and that the record of our speeches was to tour the country. Gladstone led the way with an eloquent and lengthy speech on the new link between England and America, delivered with such fire that no one noticed that the cylinder was exhausted half-way, and that the needle was rotating in mid-air. The calamity was discovered after he had left and the next morning he gave a totally different and even more eloquent record to Edison's enterprising representative, Colonel Gouraud'; *Whippingham to Westminster. The reminiscences of Lord Ernle* (1938), 140.

[9] Generally favourable to the Anglo-German Agreement, with observations on the powers of the Commons with respect to treaties; *H* 347. 753.

25. *Fr. St James,* [*Wedding*] *Anniversary.* [*Colwood Park, Sussex*]

Wrote to A. Macdonald—Mr A. Morley—Rev. Gardner—J. Westell—Scotts. At
$4\frac{1}{4}$ off to Colwood.[1] Saw S.G.L.—Ld Granville—Mr A. Morley. Read Life of Reynolds—Dawkins on Early Man in Engl.[2]—Northanger Abbey.[3] H. of C. $3\frac{1}{4}$–$4\frac{1}{4}$.[4]

26. *Sat.*

Drive to Worth Church. Saw Ld Albemarle[5] at 92. Read Northanger Abbey—
Dawson, Science in Bible Lands.[6] Wrote for No VI O.T.[7] Much conversation
with the Lord Justice[8]—Bp of Peterborough—Mr Wright.

27.

Parish Ch. mg & evg. Went to see Ld Albemarle again at Mr Noel's.[9] Read
(much) Dawson—Pattison's Memoirs.[10]

28. *M.* [*London*]

Wrote to Ed. Mid Sussex Directory—Mr Taylor Innes—H. Humphrey—Sir Jas
Fergusson—Messrs Wyllie—Mr Freshfield—Ly Sydney. Saw S.G.L.—Sir W. Harcourt—Mr Morley—Sir H. James[11]—Mrs Sands—Sir C. Russell. Back to town ($2\frac{1}{2}$
h. journey) $1\frac{1}{4}$. H. of C. $3\frac{3}{4}$–5 and 11–12.[12] Seventeen to dinner. Read Northanger
Abbey—Dawson, Science in Bible Lands, and Vaccination Report.

29. *Tu.*

Wrote to Sir R. Lethbridge[13]—Mr T. Sidney Cooper—Mr W. Evans—Col. Bryan.
H. of C. 4–$7\frac{1}{2}$. Worked on Dawson for O.T. VI. Worked much on books. Saw
S.G.L.—Mr A. Morley—Mr G. Russell—Miss Schuster[14]—Lady D. Neville—Lady
Aberdeen. Worked on O.T. VI. Dined with Mr M'Coll: rather a grand party of
14. Read Smith Debates 1834[15]—Sinclair N. of Scotland.[16] Saw Howard & two
more [R].

[1] By Cuckfield, Sussex; rented by Lord Justice Bowen (see 13 Feb. 88) from Martin Seth Smith,
landowner.
[2] W. B. Dawkins, *Early man in Britain and his place in the tertiary period* (1880).
[3] By Jane Austen (1818); read for the first time.
[4] Questions; *H* 347. 884.
[5] George Thomas Keppel, 1799–1891; once Russell's secretary and a whig M.P.; 6th earl of
Albemarle 1851; traveller and historian.
[6] J. W. Dawson, *Modern science in bible lands* (1888).
[7] See 6 Jan. 90.   [8] i.e. his host, C. S. C. Bowen.
[9] R. B. W. Noel of Livingstone House, Burgess Hill.   [10] See 12 Mar. 85.
[11] James's country house, Shoreham Place, was not far off.
[12] Questions; end of temperance deb.; *H* 347. 1041, 1141.
[13] Sir Roper Lethbridge, 1840–1919; tariff reformer and imperial federationalist; kt. 1890; tory
M.P. N. Kensington 1885-92.
[14] Adela Schuster (probably a sister of Sir F. O. Schuster, the banker), in correspondence on
portraits; Hawn P.
[15] Obscure.
[16] J. Sinclair, *Scenes and stories of the north of Scotland*, 2v. (1890-1).

30. Wed.

Wrote to Rev. T.B. Knight—Dr Ginsburg—Capt. Douglas—Mrs Bolton—Mr A.W. Hutton—C. Higham—Mr Chilson MP[1]—Mr Westell. Tea at Argyll Lodge. Saw S.G.L.—Count Campello—Mr Westell—Mr A. Morley—Mr Perks—Mr Fowler—Lady [blank]. Campbell.—Messrs Puttick & Simpson. Dined with Mr Perks[2] and the Wesleyans. Spoke some 50 min. on Malta & Judge Harrison.[3] Read Sinclair N. of Scotland. Worked on books.

31. Th.

Wrote to Mr G. Anderson—Mr W.W. Wood—Sir E. Watkin—Sir J. Millais—C.M. Robins—Mr L. Morris—A.E. Skeen. Saw S.G.L.—Sir J. Carmichael—Mr Howell MP—Mr A. Morley MP.—Sir W. Harcourt—Sir A. West. Sir A. Gordon came to breakfast: long & diversified conversation on the events of many years. St Peter's Eaton Square for the West marriage.[4] Under orders, I proposed the health. Henry VIIs Chapel at 6.15 to hear Mr Hamilton's Vocalion.[5] Dined at Mr Hankey's. H. of C. 4–6.[6] Read The Hymn Lover[7]—Gambia Papers[8]—Huxley in N.C.[9]

Frid. Aug. One. 1890.

Wrote to Mrs Gostwick—Messrs Watson—L.S. Myers—Mr Bryce—Rev. R.C. Jenkins—Rev. W.W. Smith—Rev. R.M. Spence—Mr T.W. Russell MP.[10] Dined with Mr A. Morley. Saw S.G.L.—F. Lawley—Sir G. Baden Powell(?)[11]—A. Morley MP.—Mr Howell MP—Sir C. Russell—Mr Humphreys—Lady F. Marjoribanks.[12] Luncheon at the Miss Ponsonbys. Tea on the Terrace where was Lady H. Duncombe.[13] A day of dissipation. H. of C. 3–5¼ and 5¾–7¾.[14] Worked on Books & papers. Read Life of De Quincey—Stolen America.[15]

---

[1] Apparently *sic*; but none of this name.

[2] (Sir) Robert William Perks, 1849–1934; H. H. Fowler's legal partner; strong methodist and increasingly imperialist ('Imperial Perks'); liberal M.P. Louth 1892–1910; 1st bart. 1908.

[3] *T.T.*, 31 July 1890, 4a.

[4] August William, s. of Gladstone's secretary Sir A. E. West, m. Edith, da. of Lord Trevor.

[5] In Westminster Abbey; a vocalion was a harmonium or free-reed organ with three manuals made by James Baillie Hamilton.

[6] End of questions; business of the house; *H* 347. 1380.

[7] W. G. Horder, *The hymn lover* (1889).

[8] *PP* 1890 xlviii. 235.

[9] See 29 June 90.

[10] Thomas Wallace Russell, 1841–1920; liberal unionist M.P. S. Tyrone 1886–1910 (rejoined liberals 1904).

[11] Sir George Smyth Baden-Powell, 1847–98; br. of the scout; tory M.P. Kirkdale 1885–98; social commentator; kt. 1888.

[12] Lady Fanny Octavia Louisa, Lord R. Churchill's sister, m. 1873 Edward Marjoribanks, 1849–1909; liberal M.P. Berwickshire 1880–94; chief whip 1892–4; 2nd Baron Tweedmouth 1894; lord privy seal 1894–5. She was a prominent hostess and d. 1904.

[13] Lady Harriet Christian Duncombe, da. of Lord Queensberry and widow of Dean A. Duncombe.

[14] Questions; drink duties bill; *H* 347. 1547.

[15] Isobel H. Floyd, *Stolen America* (1890); a novel.

2. Sat.

Wrote to Dr Hayman BP.—Mr Carvell Williams—Dr Pomeroy—Miss Colenso—
Mr Witham—Rev. Mr Rodwell—Mr J. Nicol—Mad. Säuger BP.[1] Worked on O.T.
VII. Dined at Mrs S. Rendel's. Worked on books. Saw S.G.L.—E. Hamilton—
H.N.G. (plans)—Mr Haldane MP—Mr Hankey. Read Owen's Gerald[2]—'In
exchange for a Soul'.[3]

3. 8 S. Trin.

Chapel Royal and H.C. at noon. St James's Evg. Dined with Lucy C. Saw Ld
Granville. Read Owen's Gerald (finished)—In Exchange &c. Worked on O.T.
VI.

4. M.

Wrote to Mr A. Brown MP—Watsons—H.V. Handlon—E. Parker—Messrs Stanford—Mr Westell—Sir A. Clark—C. Higham—Euston Station. Worked much on
books. Dined at Grillion's. Saw Jackson [R]. Saw A. Morley—Mr Bryce MP—Mr
Howell MP—Mr Bennett MP.—Dr Pomeroy—Sir W. Gregory—Mr Böhme.
Read 'In exchange for a Soul'—Ld Carnarvon's Ld Chesterfield.[4] Dr Pomeroy's
conversation disclosed a state of things absolutely appalling.[5]

5. Tu.

Wrote to Mr E. Hayworth—Mr Brocklehurst—Mrs Ingram—Macmillans—
Messrs Allen. Completed my laborious preparations for departure. Luncheon at
the Macewan's. Read 'In Exchange' &c. (finished)—Whewell's Astronomy.[6]
Dined at Sir C. Forster's. Saw S.G.L.—Mr A. Morley—Lady W. Gardner.
Animated discussion on Irish Land after dinner. Moving into & out of furnished
houses is a serious affair after 80!

6. Wed. [Hawarden]

Wrote to Ld Aberdeen—Chester Station Master—Mr Routledge. Read
Howorth's Mammoth[7]—Atkinson Martineau Correspondence[8]—Molière. $8\frac{1}{2}$–$3\frac{1}{4}$.
Journey to Hawarden: much delayed.

7. Th.

Ch. $8\frac{1}{2}$ A.M. Saw Mr Redington—W.H.G.—Rev. Mr Owen—S.E.G. Worked on
O.T. VI. Read Howorth—M. de Pourceaugnac.[9] A little unpacking. 8 to dinner.

---

[1] Not further identified; name scrawled.
[2] H. Owen, *Gerald the Welshman* (1889).
[3] S. Yorke [i.e. M. Linskill], *In exchange for a soul* (1889?).
[4] H. H. M. Herbert, Lord Carnarvon, ed., *Letters of . . . 4th earl of Chesterfield* (1890).
[5] H. S. Pomeroy was the American whose revelations of the state of marriage and of birth control in America had so shocked Gladstone; see 23 Oct. 88.
[6] See 11 Oct. 85.
[7] H. H. Howorth, *The mammoth and the flood* (1887).
[8] *Letters on the law of man's nature and development. By H. G. Atkinson and Harriet Martineau* (1851).
[9] By Molière.

8. Fr.

Ch. 8¼ A.M. Wrote to Mr Henderson—Mrs Simms BP.—J.R. Jackson—Mr F.L. Gower—W. Short—Rev. R.H. Boles[1]—A. Morley MP.—J.D. Richardson—Rev. Macleod—Adm. Alexander[2]—Mr Humphrey. Read Howorth—Lenormant Origines[3]—M. de Pourceaugnac. Divers family conversations. Visited St Deiniol's: where the doubling has begun.[4]

9. Sat.

Ch. 8½ A.M. Wrote to Macmillans BP—Rev. Kerfoot—Watsons BP—H.B. Wicker—Mrs Sandford—Benj. Yeates—H. Ridelle—Rev. Hoskins—G. Goodwin. Read Howorth—Lenormant—Molière L'Avare.[5] Corrected Homeric sheets (last) with enlargement.

10. 10 S. Trin.

Ch. mg & evg. Read Unitarian's Conversion[6]—Döllinger's Briefe[7]—Bp Brown Commentary on Genesis[8]—and [blank.]

11. M.

Ch. 8½ A.M. Wrote to Lucy Cavendish—A. Morley—Rev. Mr Bury BP—Mrs Th.—J.S. Markham. Worked on O.T. VI, Section respecting Genesis X. Read Döllinger, Briefe—Knobel, Volkertafel[9]—Memoir of Childs[10]—L'Avare. Worked at St Deiniol's.

12. Tu.

Ch. 8¼ A.M. Wrote to Mr Clancy MP.—J. Noble—Bp of St Asaph—S. Mann—C.V. Apperson—J. Romany—J.D. Richards—Mr Bunting—Rev. G. Nelson—Mr Knowles Tel. Read Völkertafel—all the morning—English Rogue[11]—Molière, Bourgeois Gent.[12]—Childs's Memoirs. Worked on O.T. &c.

13. Wed.

Ch. 8½ A.M. Wrote to Herr Ag. Meyer[13]—Mr Nicol—Miss Mearns—Mr Long MP.[14]—C.H. Perkins. Worked hard & finished No VI for O.T. Drive with C.

---

[1] Richard Henry Boles, vicar of Bodmin; business untraced.
[2] Henry McClintock Alexander, retired rear-admiral; an Irish landowner.
[3] See 28 Dec. 84.
[4] i.e. doubling up the books, the hut being already almost full.
[5] See 24 Feb. 26.
[6] Perhaps *The converted Unitarian* (1852?).
[7] J.J.I. von Döllinger, ed. Dr. Reusch, *Briefe und Erklärungen... über die Vaticanischen Decrete, 1869-1887* (1890); for Gladstone's review, see 26 Aug. 90.
[8] Perhaps R. H. N. Browne, *Christ in Genesis* (1870).   [9] See 15 June 90.
[10] G. W. Childs, *Recollections*, ed. M. Philips (1890); including accounts of English visits.
[11] [R. Head and F. Kirkman], *The life and death of the English rogue* (1700?).
[12] First read 3 Oct. 25.   [13] Not further identified.
[14] Walter Hume Long, 1854-1924; Christ Church, Oxford; tory M.P. Wilts. 1880-92, Liverpool (Derby) 1893-1900 and other seats; parlt. sec. to L.G.B. 1886-92.

Read Memoirs of Childs—Bourgeois Gentilhomme—Manzoni, Schiller, Ld Derby, W.E.G.,[1] aloud to C. Lyttelton in evg.

14. Th.

Ch. 8½ AM. Wrote to Dow. Ly Aberdeen—Mrs Cooper—Sir J. Fergusson—D. Macgregor—Mr Humphreys—Mr T. Wemyss Reid—Mr Hernbrook—M.H. Roberts—Canon M'Coll. Drove to Chester & saw the proposed Memorial & the works of Mr Griffiths.[2] Worked on No VII O.T. Read Grossman on Maimonides[3]—Molière Fourberies de Scapin[4]—Grossi and Leopardi aloud to Caroline.

15. Fr.

Ch. 8½ A.M. Wrote to Mr Marjoribanks MP—Herr Copecky B.P.—Mr J. Duncan—A.E. Wright BP.—H.D. Pierce—Mr G.W. Childs[5]—M. Mull—C.W. Robinson—J. Cameron—W.H. Tilston—Helen G.—Mr A.E. Taylor. Worked at St Deiniol's. Conversation with foreman on his health. Read Molière finished F. de Scapin—Memoir of Childs finished. Read Dryden Hind & Panther[6] aloud to C.L. Worked on O.T. No VII.

In my youth, the quality and habit of reverence made men Conservatives.
So far as I see there is no such tendency, no such association, now.
Reverence is not in fashion on either side of politics. It is largely at a discount with both. But the offence of forgetting it is very different, and much aggravated in the Conservative: just as a Liberal would be the more guilty when caught out in an indifference to Liberty.
These two are I think the great poles on which a sound creed revolves and is secure.[7]

16. Sat.

Kept my bed till 11 A.M., after slight disturbance. Wrote to Mr J.W. de Caux[8]—Mr W. Bailey—H. Nicholson—W.O. Boot—T.T. Wildridge—Mrs Dunlop. Drive with C. Worked on O.T. No VII. Worked on arranging papers. Read Scott's Introduction Vol I[9]—De Caux—and Hind and Panther.

17. 11 S. Trin.

Ch 11 AM 6½ PM. Wrote to Mr H. Taylor—Mr Pearson—Mr Irwin. Read Döllinger Briefe—T.C. on Song of Solomon—'Strangely Led'—'What is the Soul'—Thyself and others.[10]

[1] Extracts from translations by Derby and Gladstone.
[2] The Gladstone Memorial Fountain being made by Edward Griffin of Chester for Hawarden; see 29 Dec. 90.
[3] L. Grossman, 'Maimonides. A paper' (1890).
[4] *Les Fourberies de Scapin*, by Molière (1671); set in Naples; see 7 Oct. 61.
[5] George W. Childs, American publisher and friend of President Grant; see 11 Aug. 90.
[6] Being read in Scott's ed., 18v. (1828); see 7 May 70; quoted in conclusion of *Impregnable rock*, 283.
[7] Holograph dated 15 August 1890; Add MS 44773, f. 195.
[8] J. W. De Caux had sent a work, perhaps his *The herring and the herring fishery* (1881).
[9] The 1st v. of Scott's ed. (see 15 Aug. 90) is a life of Dryden.   [10] Untraced tracts.

18. M.

Ch. 8½ A.M. Wrote to Mr Marjoribanks MP.—Mrs A. Kemp—Sir T. Acland—Dean of St Paul's—Mr C. Rowlands. Worked up & wrote on the case of Gadara & the Swine.[1] Also worked on Revising and altering VII. O.T. Conversation with Mr Mayhew. Read Lettres de Ninon de l'Enclos.[2]

19. Tu.

Ch. 8½ A.M. Wrote to Mr J. Robertson—Mr J. Nicol—Rev. J. Mackie—W.J.H. Yates[3]—W.B. Orton—Mr D. Curr. Corrected Proofs of vi and dispatched them with MS. of VII. Saw Mr Parrot. Spoke to WHG on the conversation with Mr Mayhew. Inspected work at St D's. Worked on packages. Read Robertson on [blank]—Ninon de l'Enclos Autobiogr.—Hind & Panther Part III.

20. Wed.

Ch 8½ A.M. Wrote to Dean of St Paul's—W.G. Parrish—F. Hudson—A. Tranter—R.H. Edwards—Mr A. Grove—Mr Bernard—Vote Office (a batch)—Master Cutler of Sheffield. Drive with C. Worked *some* on books. Read Ninon de l'Enclos Autobiography. Genuine?—Clifton's Broadlands.[4]

21. Th.

Wrote to Mrs Sherriff—Mr Campbell Bannerman—Mr Clifton—Ld Norton—Rev. R.D. Hope—W. Quartier—Rev. H.E. Stone—Watson & Smith—Macmillans. Worked on books. Went through papers, saw Mr Taylor, & spoke ½ hour for the Horticultural folk.[5] Read Broadlands &c (finished)—Balls Starry Land[6]—and [blank].

22. Fr.

Ch. 8½ A.M. Wrote to Rev. Mr Smethwick—Wms & N.—Mr Humphreys—Robn & N.—Mr J. Nicol—B. Quaritch—Jos. Smith U.S.—J.D. Darley—P. Macalister—L. Dillon—J. Gillespie—J. Robertson—Mr D.C. Thomson—Rev. F. Bingham—J.C. Markley.[7] Worked here & at St D. on books: also on papers. Read Sir R. Ball's Star Land—Roundell's Lecture[8]—Du Pontet[9]—and Priesthood & Penitence.[10]

23. Sat.

Ch. 8½ A.M. Wrote to Seaman & Smith BP & l.—Mrs Pearson BP—W.J. Lees—Mr Roundell BP—Rev. C. Mackie—Mr Schwann MP.—W. Hall—Mr Rathbone

---

[1] Attack on Huxley on this question; see *Impregnable rock*, conclusion, especially 294 ff.
[2] See 11 Apr. 85.
[3] London liberal and occasional correspondent; Hawn P.
[4] E. Clifford, *Broadlands as it was* (1890); church army.
[5] On cottage gardening and fruit farming; *T.T.*, 22 August 1890, 5a.
[6] Sir R. S. Ball, *Starland* (1889); long letter of appreciation in *T.T.*, 16 September 1890, 5d.
[7] John T. Markley had sent his *Songs of humanity and progress* (1882); Hawn P.
[8] C. S. Roundell, 'The progress of the working classes during the reign of the Queen' (1890).
[9] R. L. A. Du Pontet, *Alaricus. Carmen Latinum* (1890).
[10] Untraced.

MP.—Mr J. Nicol—B.M. Malabari—Messrs Hudson—Mr Raffles Moore—Mr Littlewoods—Sec. Band of Hope. Worked on Routledge Paper.[1] At St Deiniol's with Edith, also at home, on papers. Read Ball's Star Land—Mr Bryant's Mistake[2]—Memoir of Warwick Brooks.[3]

24. St Barth. & 12 S. Trin.

Ch 11 A.M. and [blank.] Wrote to Bp of Moosonee—Mr Trumbull—Hugh Bow—Mr W. Meynell—L. Dillon—Ed. Cosmopolitan Mag.[4]—Sec. Scots Home Rule Assn[5]—Rev. H. Forrester BP. Read Toland's Hypatia[6] &c.—Innocent III on Mass & H.E.[7]—Forrester on Reunion—Phelps, Struggle for Immortality[8]—and [blank.]

25. M.

Ch. 8½ A.M. Wrote to Card. Manning—Sir J.R.G.—Mr Wemyss Reid—Editors—Press Assocn—Mr Cockshort—Mr Dawson—Mr Turnerelli—Mr Jas Baker—Mr Humphreys—Sir T. Acland. Worked on Döllinger.[9] A slight disturbance kept me at home. Read Baker on Payne[10]—Ball on Star Land—Mr Bryant's Mistake.

26. Tu.

Ch. 8½ A.M. Wrote to Mr Schnadhorst—Mr Reid—Mr Wemyss Reid—Jas Hogg—Rev. Mr Sadler—F. Bailey—Miss Wiseman—Dr. Reusch—F.W. Bromwich—W.H.H. Rogers. Finished & dispatched paper on Döllinger. Finished & corrected proofs of No VII. OT.[11] Drove with C. Read Star Land—Mr Bryant's Mistake—Döllinger, Briefe.

27. Wed.

Ch. 8½ AM. Wrote to Macmillans—Sir John R. G[ladstone]—R. Duckett—Sir R.S. Ball[12]—T.C. Martin—A.W. Hutton—Mr Marjoribanks MP.—A.M. Grant—W.M. Adams—A. Morley M.P.—G. Harding—E.A. Phipson—Mr A. Hutton. Worked a little on O.T. Also at St. Deiniol's. Finished Ball's Lectures—Reread M. Janssen[13]—Bourgets[14] [blank]—Chinese in S. Francisco.[15]

---

[1] 'Home Rule for Ireland (an appeal to the tory householder)', *Subjects of the Day*, iii. 1 (November 1890), ed. James Samuelson, published by George Routledge and Sons.

[2] K. Wylde, *Mr Bryant's mistake*, 3v. (1890).

[3] T. Leatherbrow, *Warwick Brookes' pencil pictures of child life* (1889).

[4] Not found published.   [5] See 7, 9 Dec. 88n.

[6] J. Toland, *Hypatia* (1753).

[7] Innocent III, *Mysterorum Evangelicae legis et sacramenti Eucharistiae libri* (1860 ed.).

[8] E. S. Phelps, *The struggle for immortality* (1889).

[9] 'Dr. Döllinger's posthumous remains', *Speaker*, 30 August 1890; see 10 Aug. 90.

[10] Earlier ed. of J. Baker, *A forgotten Great Englishman . . . Peter Payne, the Wycliffite* (1894).

[11] See 6 Jan. 90.

[12] In *T.T.*, 16 September 1890, 5d; interesting explanation of Gladstone's use of numerical abbreviations: m = 1000, ⋔ = 1,000,000, Ⓜ = thousand million.

[13] Probably J. Janussen, *Geschichte des deutschen Volkes* (new ed. 1890); not noted previously.

[14] P. C. J. Bourget, *Le disciple* (1889).

[15] *The Chinese in California. Descriptions of Chinese life in San Francisco* (1880).

28. Th.

Ch. 8½ A.M. Wrote to Printer of Speaker—C.G.—Mr Wrigglesworth[1]—W.R. Duncan—Mr Smith (Edinb.)—Mr Sherwell—H.G. Warner—J. Darrell—Digby & Long—J. Westell—Mrs Roundell—J.E. Chapman—Mrs Nelson—Swan & Sonnenschein. Worked on books. D[itt]o at St. Deiniol's. Tea with W.H.G. Conversation with Edw. Lyttelton. Ten to dinner. Read Wrigglesworth—Lawrence on Peace[2]—Address on Gen. Lee[3]—Bourget Le Disciple—& other tracts.

29. Fr.

Ch. 8½ AM. Wrote to Ed. Greenwich Observer[4]—Sec. Treasury l. and BP.—Mr Nicol—Mr Walker QC.—C.G.—H.G. Reid—President of Magdalen. Worked on Books & papers. Do at St Deiniol's. Read Oliver on Ireland[5]—Bourget Le Disciple—Irwin Hist. Presbytm.[6]

30. Sat.

Ch. 8½ AM. Wrote to Mr Hutchison—Mr Howell—Mr Dawson—Mr Walker. Worked much on books. Read Bourget, Le Disciple—Oliver on Ireland—Irwin Hist. of Presbm—Kegan Paul on Newman.[7]

31. 12 S. Trin.

Ch. 11 AM & [blank.] Wrote to Mr Mayow jun.[8]—Watsons BP—Mr Wemyss Reid—Sir R. Ball BP—Dr Pomeroy. Read Irwin, Presbm—Life of Vinet[9]—Phelps Struggle for Immy[10]—and [blank.]

Mond. Sep 1.

Church 8½ A.M. Wrote to Ld Granville—Dr Pomeroy—Ld Acton—Mr Hutton—W. Mitchell. Drive with C. The Roundell[11] party came to luncheon. Walk & conversation with him. Worked on H.R. for Mr Routledge.[12] Worked on letters. Read Le Disciple—Senior in 19th Century.[13]

---

[1] E. Wigglesworth had sent his *Illustrated guide to Hull* (1889).
[2] Perhaps J. Laurence, *Christian prudence; or, Christianity a gospel of peace* (1720).
[3] Perhaps T. Sweeney, 'A vindication from the Northern standpoint of Gen. R. E. Lee . . . from the Northern charge of treason and perjury' (1890).
[4] Plea for support, in facsimile in *Greenwich Observer*, 5 September, 5b–e.
[5] R. Oliver, *Unnoticed analogies; a talk on the Irish question* (1888).
[6] C. H. Irwin, *A history of presbyterianism in Dublin and the south and west of Ireland* (1890).
[7] C. Kegan Paul, 'Newman', *New Review*, iii. 208 (September 1890).
[8] S. S. W. Mayow, s. of M. W.; had sent a book; Hawn P.
[9] L. M. Lane, *The life and writings of A. Vinet* (1890).
[10] See 24 Aug. 90.
[11] Presumably C. S. Roundell (see 13 June 68), then between seats.
[12] See 23 Aug. 90.
[13] N. W. Senior, 'Behind the scenes in English politics', *N.C.*, xxviii. 369 (September 1890).

2. Tu.

Ch. 8½ A.M. Wrote to Mr Marjoribanks—Dr Reusch BP.—Mr Bennet—Mr S. Mayow—W.E. Allan—Mr or Dr Greenhill.[1] Worked on Routledge paper. Worked at St Deiniol's. E.L.s went. Wickhams came. Read Le Disciple: to the end a book of extraordinary power, & upright intention: the fibre not fine. Read Irwin's Presb. Ch. History.

3. Wed.

Ch. 8½ A.M. Wrote to Messrs Macmillan—Mr Nicol BP—Mrs M'Kenzie—J.S. Jenkins—J.R.S. Harington—Jas Whitehead. Worked on Routledge paper. On Proof Sheets O.T. VII & Hom. Landmarks. On books at St Deiniol's. Tea at Branch Bank. Read Ball on Time & Tide[2]—Life of Vinet—A Knight of [blank.][3] Mr Griffiths,[4] also Mr Hamilton:[5] quasi sittings.

4. Th.

Ch. 8½ A.M. Wrote to Wms & Norgate—Ld Provost of Dundee—Grogan & Boyd—J. Ross—W.H. Wilkins—Bp of London. Mr Hamilton came again. Walk with E. Wickham. Worked on Routledge H.R. paper, finished. Worked a little on books. Read Ball, Time & Tide—A Knight of Faith—Foreign Church Review[6]—Ld Russells Don Carlos.[7]

5. Fr.

Ch. 8½ A.M. Wrote to Mrs L.H. Fenmore—Mr Routledge—Mr W. Young—Mr A. Hutton—J.R. Stewart—D. Donworth—H. Swift—M. Meupes. Mr Hamilton came 3°. He is very clever. Finished my Routledge paper & dispatched it. Walk with E. Wickham. Read Ball (finished)—Knight of Faith—Woffington's Memoirs[8]— Sullivan's Irishmen.[9]

---

[1] W. A. Greenhill of Hastings, in correspondence on the psalms; Hawn P.

[2] Sir R. S. Ball, 'Time and tide, a romance of the moon. Two lectures' (1889).

[3] *A knight of faith* (see next day); untraced; Gladstone probably noted the sub-title.

[4] Perhaps Tom Griffiths, *fl.* late 19th century; mainly a painter of rural scenes.

[5] John McLure Hamilton, 1853–1936; American artist, in London from 1878. Hamilton was introduced to Gladstone by the daughters of Joseph Rowley, who were staying nearby and with whom Hamilton lodged. It was agreed that rather than have formal sittings he should draw and paint in the Temple of Peace, thus depicting Gladstone in a series of natural poses. His series of drawings and three portraits (1890 in the Luxembourg, now the Louvre, Paris), 1892 (in the Pennsylvania Academy of Fine Arts), and c.a. 1896) thus show Gladstone reading and writing. See J. MacLure Hamilton, *Men I have painted* (1921), 41 ff., with foreword by Mary Drew. He wrote to Gladstone 17 June 1892: 'One of the small portraits which you were kind enough to allow me to paint in your library at Hawarden has been selected from the "Salon" by the French Government for the National Museum in France. I cannot express to you the great pleasure which this distinction has given me'; Add MS 44515, f. 53.

[6] *Foreign Church Review*, xiv (September 1890).

[7] Lord John Russell, *Don Carlos; or persecution. A tragedy in five acts* (1822).

[8] See 17 Apr. 88.

[9] See, probably, 3 Nov. 77.

6. Sat.

Ch. 8½ A.M. Wrote to Ld Hartington—Ld Acton l. & B.P.—D. Clark—R. de Coverley—C.A. Martin—C.H. Daniel—B. Quaritch—Messrs Tillotson. Worked on papers in Octagon. Also at St Deiniol's. Read P. Woffington (finished II)—A Knight of Faith (finished)—Life of Vinet.

7. 14 S. Trin.

Ch 11 AM with H.C., and 6½ PM. Wrote to Wms & Norgate—Mr Nicol—Rev. Mr Carrick[1]—Mr H. Owen—H.W. Lovett—Scotts. Read Carnegie's Speech. Fie![2]—Articles in Amn magazines—Life of Vinet, and examined divers works.

8. M.

Ch. 8½ AM. Wrote to Miss Hemingsley—Rev. Mr Harrower BP.[3]—Watsons—J.T. Leighton—Rev. W. Chaplin[4]—W. Bailey. Tea with Gerty G. & conversation. Read Jupiter Lights[5]—Blackwell, NeoMalthusians[6]—Pigeon on Vaccination[7]—Life of Vinet.

9. Tu.

Ch. 8½ A.M. Wrote to Miss O'Sullivan BP—Rev. Tyndall BP[8]—J. Durden—Mr Young BP—H.W. Lovett—P.H. Johnstone. Tea with the Rowleys.[9] Worked on Books & Papers. Read Life of Vinet—Jupiter Lights—O'Sullivan, Chalemont[10]—Le Misanthrope.[11]

10. Wed.

Ch. 8½ A.M.: heard the sad news of Canon Liddon's death. Wrote to Contemp. Rev. Tel.[12]—Ld Rosebery—Editor P.M.G.[13]—Mr Nicol—Greenwich & D. Obsr—Thos Smith—M.Q. Holyoake—S. Topley—G.W. Balfour—Ed. Kentish Mercury[14]—W. Donaldson. Worked on O.T. Worked in Octagon & on papers. Read Four Years in Rebel Capitals[15]—Jupiter Lights—Life of A. Vinet (finished)—Misanthrope.

---

[1] Robert Mallabar Carrick, priest living in Durham.

[2] A. Carnegie, 'Some facts about the American Republic' (1890); address at Dundee. Gladstone commented in his article: 'the address was not an assault merely, but an onslaught on all which accompanies and qualifies, or as some of us would say, mellows, consolidates, and secures the principles of popular government in this country. He evidently does not stop short of the opinion that rank, as it exists among us, is a widely demoralizing power'; see 18–19 Sept. 90.

[3] Gordon Harrower of Liverpool; Hawn P.

[4] William Chaplin, curate in Everton.   [5] C. F. Woolson, *Jupiter lights* (1889).

[6] F. W. Newman, *The corruption now called Neo-Malthusianism . . . with notes by E. Blackwell* (1889).

[7] Author's name scrawled.

[8] Henry Annesley Tyndale, rector of Holton, Oxfordshire.

[9] See 3 Sept. 90n.

[10] Apparently sent by Miss O'Sullivan, presumably its author (see this day); untraced, possibly by Sister Alice O'Sullivan.   [11] By Molière.

[12] Not published.   [13] Not found published.

[14] *Kentish Mercury*, 12 September 1890, 5c.

[15] T. C. De Leon, *Four years in rebel capitals* (1890).

11. Th.

Ch. 8½ A.M. Wrote to Ld Hartington—Vote Office—W. Brough—Count Zuboff[1]—Mr E. Davis—Mr Dedson—A.T. Storey. Worked on books & papers. Read Jupiter Lights (finished)—Four Years in Rebel Capitals—Gilfillan, Bards of the Bible (flatulent?)[2]—Ahearne's Address[3]—The Louisiana Purchase.[4] Ly Grosvenor came. Astronom. conversation with Mr Wyndham.[5]

12. Fr.

Ch. 8½ A.M. Wrote to Lady Harcourt B.P.—Rev. H.Y. Hind—Mr Stanford—D. Nutt—Mr Quaritch—D. Tregaskis—Mons. Tscheraz—E. Howell—J.A. Elliot—W. Ridler—J.M. Russell. More guests came. Worked in Octagon. Read [blank] on Geo. Eliot—Peg Woffington Vol. I.[6] Visited the Anchor Works at Saltney: & spoke to the members of the Institute.[7]

13. Sat.

Ch. 8½ A.M. 7¼ PM. Wrote to Mr Weld Blundell—Dr Reusch—R.M. Sillard[8]—A.H. Hutton—Mr Routledge—Mr J.G. Cox—Messrs Young—Messrs Chatto & Windus. Walk with Mr Weldon[9] and a party. Corrected proofsheets of Homerick Article for Mr Routledge.[10] Read Peg Woffington—The Primitive Family.[11] Heard Mr Lloyds very touching Sermon in evg. B.O. Flower—C. Shaw.

14. 15 S. Trin.

Ch 11 A.M: a noble Sermon from Archdeacon Howell—and 6½ P.M. Wrote to Mr Storey MP[12]—Mr Hall—Mr J. Nicol. Read Mr Gore's Preface[13]—Barber's Science & Religion[14]—Hutton's papers on Newman.[15]

[1] Count Roman Zubof, of Boston, Mass., sent his *The nationalists*, 'collected during four year's residence in England and Ireland'; Hawn P.

[2] G. Gilfillan, *The bards of the bible* (1852).

[3] Untraced; author's name smudged.

[4] Perhaps C. F. Robertson, *The Louisiana Purchase in its influence on the American system* (1885).

[5] See 5 Nov. 87.

[6] Probably vol. i of Charles Reade, *Peg Woffington* (1857); see also 5 Sept. 90.

[7] Speech on industrial progress to the workers of the Dee Iron Works, also known as Wood's Chain and Anchor Works, and to members of the Saltney Literary Society; *T.T.*, 13 September 1890, 11e.

[8] Of Dublin; on Homer; Hawn P.

[9] J. E. C. Welldon, headmaster of Harrow (see 3 Apr. 87); H.V.B.

[10] See 23 Aug. 90.

[11] C. N. Starke, *The primitive family* (1889).

[12] Samuel Storey, 1840–1925; manufacturer; liberal M.P. Sunderland 1881–95, 1910; spasmodic tariff reformer.

[13] Charles Gore's preface to the 10th ed. of *Lux Mundi* (1890).

[14] T. Barber, *Scientific theology* (1884).

[15] R. H. Hutton collected his various papers on Newman for his *Cardinal Newman* (1891) (who d. 11 August 1890).

15. M.

Ch. 8½ AM. Wrote to Mrs Crawford—Messrs Young—Mr Sheridan—Messrs Brough. Worked in Octagon. And at St Deiniol's. Read Mirage or Life[1]—Peg Woffington—Hist. of Astronomy.[2] Drive & walk with Ld N[orthbourne].

16. Tues.

Ch. 8½ A.M. & 7½ P.M. Wrote to Mr G. Hagopian[3]—W.L. Gladstone—Mr Morley—and Mr De Leon.[4] Worked in Octagon & on books. Twelve to dinner after the Harvest Service: great congregation. Read Hist. of Astronomy—Unrest[5]—Sheppard Essays & Pictures.[6]

17. Wed.

Ch. 8½ A.M. Wrote to Mr Nicol—Sir E. Watkin MP—Sir A. Clark—Mr Jas Carter—T.E. Young. Garden Tea party. Worked on books here & St Deiniol's. Walked *some* with Northbourne. Read Gore, Preface, & on Sin—Tylor on Winged Figures &c.[7]—Toscanelli Religione e Patria[8]—Sheppard Essays &c.

18. Th.

Ch. 8½ A.M. Wrote to Messrs Macmillan—Rev. W. Sadler—Mr Westell. We worked hard on books—here and at St Deiniol's. Began article on Carnegie's "Wealth".[9] Ld Northbourne went: a delightful inmate. Drive with C. Read Le Misanthrope (I think a very poor play)—Unrest: an apology for a novel?—Toscanelli: remarkable.

19. Fr.

Ch. 8½ A.M. Wrote to Mrs Crawford—Mr Agnew—Mr O. Morgan—Mr Rankin—Chev. Norchi[10]—B. Quaritch—E.R. Mullins—A. Stewart Gray.[11] Worked hard at St Deiniol's: where I hope we approach 10000 volumes. The Carnegies called. I took them about the old Castle & grounds: & talked of the Dundee speech & the coming article.[12] Read Le Tartuffe—Toscanelli.

---

[1] *The mirage of life* (1883); a tract.
[2] Sent by George Wyndham following his visit; Add MS 44510, f. 266. Perhaps R. A. Proctor, *Astronomy old and new* (1888).
[3] G. Hagopian, Armenian living in Fulham; activist for the Armenian cause; Hawn P.
[4] Thomas Cooper De Leon, American author, had presumably sent his book (see 10 Sept. 90).
[5] W. E. Hodgson, *Unrest, or the newer republic* (1887).
[6] Perhaps J. Sheppard, *Essays designed to afford Christian encouragement and consolation* (1833).
[7] E. B. Taylor, *The winged figures of the Assyrian and other ancient monuments* (1890).
[8] G. Toscanelli, *Religione e Patria* (1890).
[9] 'Mr. Carnegie's "Gospel of Wealth": a review and a recommendation', *N.C.*, xxviii. 677 (November 1890): a commendation of part of Carnegie's argument, but also a defence, against him, of hereditary wealth. Gladstone proposed a movement, voluntary but natural, for 'proportionate giving'.
[10] C. E. Norchi wrote from the Italian section of the International Exhibition in Edinburgh; Hawn P.
[11] Edmund Archibald Stuart-Gray, 1840–1901; of Kinfauns, Perth; 15th earl of Moray 1895.
[12] See 7 Sept. 90n and previous day.

20. Sat.

Ch. 8½ A.M. Wrote to Lady Harcourt l. & BP.—Rev. D. Mitchell—Dr Hine—
J.W.C. Haldane—Mr J.C. Cox—Rev. Davenport—J.D. Dunham—Mr W.J. Davis.
Worked on books here & at St Deiniol's. Afternoon tea party. Wrote on Wealth.
Read Toscanelli—Street's Jesus the Prophet[1]—Le Tartuffe: a poor ending.

21. St Matt. & 16 S. Trin.

Ch. 11 A.M. and 6½ P.M. Wrote to Mr Curtis l. & B.P.—Mr Morley MP.—Rev.
Street—Mr Carmichael. Read Street's Jesus the Prophet—Macleod on Scottish
Office[2]—Foster on Ruskin & others[3]—Abbott on Agnosticism[4]—Dr [blank]'s
Sermons. Conversation with C. on Clark's important letter respecting the slow-
ness of W.s progress towards recovery.

22. M.

Ch. 8½ A.M. Wrote to Mr Trumbull—Mr B. Quaritch—Mr J. Nicol—Sir A.
Clark—Miss M. Evans—Sec. Wrexham Library—Dr Abbott—Rev. C.C. James—
J. Forster. Worked on books here & at St Deiniol's. Drive with C. Wrote on
Carnegie & Wealth. Read Toscanelli—and Miss Montizambart.[5]

23. Tu.

Ch. 8½ A.M. Wrote to Miss K.P. Lorne—Mrs Sands BP—Jas Matthews—Ld
Rosebery—Percy Harrison—Sir A. West—T.C. Martin—G.B. Wood—C.H. Collette[6]—R.R. Rae—W.F. Denneby—J. Westell—Mr E. Walford.[7] At St Deiniol's
fixing book-cases in the second room. Worked on Carnegie Article. The Phillimores came. Read Gibbins on Industrial History[8]—Miss Montizambart—Collette's Queen Elisabeth.

24. Wed.

Ch. 8½ A.M. Wrote to Mr G. Wyndham l & BP—Rev. Dodwell l. & B.P.—Mr De
Coverley—J.H. Rawlins—Mr E. Hart—Scotts—Bp of St Asaph—Mr Gibbins.
Visited Mr Hamilton at Queensferry.[9] Worked at St Deiniol's. Worked on
Carnegie article. Read Gibbins—Collette—Miss Montizambart. Conversation
with Lady Phillimore.

---

[1] C. J. Street had sent his *On the nature and character of Jesus* (1889); Hawn P.

[2] Untraced.

[3] J. Foster, *Four great teachers* (1890); including Ruskin.

[4] F. E. Abbot, *The way out of agnosticism; or, the philosophy of free religion* (1890).

[5] M. A. M. Hoppus, *Miss Montizambart*, 2v. (1885).

[6] Charles Hastings Collette, anti-Romanist author, had sent his *Queen Elizabeth and the penal laws* (1890).

[7] Ernest Leopold Walford, stockbroker, in correspondence on the advantages to health of strict application of the 'Mosaic Laws', especially circumcision; Add MS 44511, f. 5.

[8] H. de B. Gibbins, *The industrial history of England* (1890).

[9] i.e. the artist, staying with the Rowleys; Lady Phillimore had peremptorily interrupted Hamilton's authorised work in the Temple of Peace; see J. M. Hamilton, *Men I have painted* (1921), 41 ff.

25. Th.

Ch. 8½ A.M. Wrote to Mr Scribner USA Tel.—C. Herbert—A. Morley MP.—A.W. Hutton—Rev. Hutchins—Col. Gouraud—J. Morley MP.—Rev. R. Hardie—H.S.H. Pegler—Rev. M.C. Richards. Worked at St Deiniol's. Finished Carnegie Article. Read Hindoo Marriage[1]—Gibbins Industr. History—Miss Montizambart: &c. Backgammon with Lady Ph.

26. Fr.

Ch. 8½ A.M. Wrote to Lady F. Cavendish—Mr Knowles—Mr J.S. M'Gregor—Mr J.B. Greig—Bp of St Asaph. Walk with L. Harcourt. Read Lady Hamilton in Biogr. Dict.—Miss Montizambart—Xty & Spiritualism &c.[2] Backgammon with Lady Ph. Revised & sent off Article on Wealth.

27. Sat.

Ch. 8½ AM. Wrote to Mr Geo. Allen—Dr Parker—T.C. Martin—Mr Mawer—Messrs Grogan—Dr Flemyng—Mr Morley MP.—Dr Butcher—J.A. Robertson—Rev. Badworth—R. Hopton—A. M'Kechnie—S.F. Van Oss—Rev. T. Mills[3]—A. Galton—Secy Liddon Memorial. Worked at St Deiniol's. Most of the friends went. Read [blank] on Jews—Germany 14th Cent.—Machin Xty & Modern Spiritualism—and Catullus, beautiful and vile!

28. 17 S. Trin.

Ch. 8½ A.M. and 6½ P.M. Wrote to Mr Melville—Miss Clark—& . . . . . . Worked on Revising. Read Scientific Theology[4]—Fiske, Idea of God[5]—Suffield's Sermon[6]—Account of Jerusalem[7]—Pierre and Jean.[8]

29. S. Michael.

Ch & HC. 8½ A.M. Wrote to Sec. Home Rule Assn—Sir A.E. West—Rev. Dr. Hutton—Digby & Long—J. Ogilvy—T.W. Barber—J.S. Macgregor—Jas Goring. Worked on revision O.T. II.[9] Worked at St Deiniol's. Consultation on changes in the approach & the yard. All this troubles my Conservatism. Read Pierre et Jean—and [blank.] Fourteen to dinner.

---

[1] Madhurdas Rugnathdar, a Hindu living in Bombay who had, against the law of his caste, remarried a widow, sent his 'Story of a Widow Remarriage'; Add MS 44510, f. 250.

[2] Perhaps *Primitive Christianity and modern Spiritualism*, no. 25 of *Information for the Thoughtful*, published in Melbourne; but see 27 Sept. 90.

[3] Thomas Mills, vicar of St. Jude's, Dublin, on clerical disabilities; *T.T.*, 2 October 1890, 7c.

[4] See 14 Sept. 90.

[5] J. Fiske, *The idea of God as affected by modern knowledge* (1885).

[6] Untraced sermon by the Unitarian R. R. Suffield.

[7] Perhaps *An account of the siege and destruction of Jerusalem* (1822).

[8] G. de Maupassant, *Pierre et Jean* (1888), with a famous preface on Flaubert's influence.

[9] Revision of his articles (see 6 Jan. 90) for reprinting in the *Impregnable Rock*.

30. Tu.

Ch. 8½ A.M. Wrote to Mr P.W. Campbell—Mr Knowles—W.A. Harris—J.P. Coldstream—Miss A. Jones—Rev. Dr. Parker—T. Davies—Editor of Star.[1] Party grows & grows. [Blank] to dinner. Walk with the gentlemen. Conversations with Morley. Revised O.T. No III. Read Pierre et Jean—Milton Paradise Lost—Globe Rev. (U.S.) on Carnegie[2]—Pater Noster on Newman and on Liddon.[3]

Wed. Oct One. 90.

Ch. 8½ A.M. Wrote to Sir Wilfrid Lawson—Dr. Parker—J. Macintosh—Dr. Behrens[4]—V. Gadesden—J. Tomkinson—Rev. J. Parker. Worked on revising O.T. IV. Saw Morley & studied & discussed his speech. High water mark with visitors. Worked in new Library and showed it. Read Pierre et Jean—Lockhart on Newman.[5] Much conversation with Mr [T.G.] Law and Mr [A.W.] Hutton.[6]

2. Th.

Ch. 8½ A.M. Wrote to Mr Humphreys—Mrs Sands—R.M. Sillard—Sir A. West—Mrs Hutchison—R. Bird—R.A. Shibley—R. Roberts—Mr A. Morley MP. Showed library here & St Deiniol's to Messrs L. & H: walk & drive & very much conversation aft & evening. Worked further on O.T. IV. Read N.C. on Newman—Pierre et Jean (finished)—and [blank.]

3. Fr.

Ch. 8½ A.M. Wrote to Duke of Argyll—Ld Rosebery—Rev. Mr Stark[7]—Mr Howell—A.L. Gladstone—P.A. Hurd—J. Russell Smith—G.C. Carley—Ed. Book Review[8]—J.C. Collison—T.C. Melville—P. OByrne Cooke—V[ote] O[ffice]. Farewell conversation with Mr Law & Mr Hutton. I tried to do a very little good. Worked on Books here & at St D.s. Saw S. on Glebe questions. Worked on O.T., V. Read Hutton (R.H. on Newman).[9] Dinner party every day this week!

4. Sat.

Ch. 8½ A.M. Wrote to Messrs Walton—R.W. Johnson—A.J. Myers—Mrs Grayson—F. Bucher—J.M. Leahy—A. Scott—J.H. Raymond. Conversation with Parker (Peel letters).[10] Walk & conversation A. Gordon (Ld Abn & S.H.)[11]

---

[1] Not found published.
[2] No copy found.
[3] Not found.
[4] Dr Henry Behrend, London physician, on laws of the Jewish faith; Hawn P.
[5] W. Lockhart, *Cardinal Newman* (1891).
[6] T. G. Law, the Scottish librarian whom Gladstone had helped (see 17 Dec. 78) and A. W. Hutton, librarian of the National Liberal Club and ed. of Gladstone's speeches (see 26 Apr. 90n.).
[7] Perhaps Alfred Stark, anglican missionary in Bengal.
[8] Unclear what is intended; the *Book Review* was first published June 1892.
[9] See 14 Sept. 90.
[10] i.e. C. S. Parker, to whom Gladstone made available books and letters for his *Peel*; see above, 4 Dec. 86 and x. clxxv.
[11] i.e. Lord Aberdeen and Sidney Herbert, about whom Gordon was to write.

Worked on books at St D.s. Read Hutton on N.—Mrs Grayson's well meant tale on the Sonata[1]—and divers tracts.

5. 18 S. Trin.

Confined to bed with the menace of a cold. Rose in evg. Read Hutton, finished—Lea, Keynotes from Rome—do on Indulgences—do on Martyr St (Mr Lea, U.S.)[2]—Conversation with Sybella [Lyttelton]—A. Gordon.

6. M.

Ch. 8½ A.M. Wrote to Cardinal Manning—Mr Knowles—Mr R.H. Hutton—Ld Acton—Mr J.M. Miller—E. Seward—J.G. M'Sweeny—A. Bennett. Corrected & enlarged, & dispatched, my Carnegie MS. Worked at St Deiniol's: where Helen gave us a tea. I have now *in situ* bookcases for 22 ... 24000 volumes: & full 12000 carried up. Read Chief Baron's Charge, articles and tracts. Conversation with Mrs Dugdale[3] who rises in proportion as she is seen. Walk with Sir A. Gordon who also comes out well.

7. Tu.

Ch. 8½ A.M. Wrote to Rev. Jas Gammack—A. Morley MP.—Mr Roby—Mr T. Fletcher—C. Hill—W.M. Mackeane—E. English—Mr H. Seymour—Miss Albut—Miss Jessie Weston[4]—Rev. Mitchell. Axe work on walnut. Saw Mr Lloyd. Party thinned. Read Scott Holland on Liddell—O'Hagan on Davis[5]—Roh's What is Christ?[6]—Miss Weston's [blank.] Worked on O.T. papers.

8. Wed.

Ch. 8½ A.M. Wrote to Mr A. Mackenzie—Ld Rosebery—Ld Spencer—Mr Knowles—Mr T.G. Law—Mr J. Nicol—Mr Aitchison. Added to Carnegie article. Worked on O.T. papers VII. Worked on books. Walk with N. Lyttelton. Read Zincke's Egypt[7]—Gifford Lecture—Miss Weston's N.Z. tale—and [blank.]

9. Th.

Ch. 8½ A.M. Wrote to Mr D. Ainsworth—Rev. Salmond—Mr Ridler—Rev. D. Mitchell—Mr Waddie—Ld Iddesleigh—Mr Bridgett—Mrs Cyril Flower—Mr Harington—Mr Haldane MP—Mr Zähnsdorff[8]—A.R. Gladstone—J. Nicoll. Worked on O.T. papers for revised Edition & sent the remainder to London.

---

[1] Untraced; evidently sent by the author.

[2] Various papers by H. C. Lea, later collected as *A history of auricular confession and indulgences in the Latin church*, 3v. (1896).

[3] Alice Dugdale; see 15 Apr. 87.

[4] Had sent her *Ko Meri, or 'A cycle of Cathay'. A story of New Zealand life* (1890).

[5] Both in *C.R.*, lviii. 473 (October 1890).

[6] P. Roh, *Was ist Christus?* (1887).

[7] See 29 Dec. 71.

[8] London bookbinder; sent his recent book on bookbinding; Hawn P.

H. & I felled the walnut tree. Conversation with N. Lyttelton. Read KO. Meri (Weston)—Gorman on Canada[1]—Steuart's Kilgroom.[2] Backgammon with Miss West.[3]

10. Fr.

Ch. 8½ A.M. Wrote to Mr Marjoribanks MP—Consul Bowes[4]—Funk & Wagnall —Messrs Brough—Lucy Cavendish—J. Westell—J.A. Steuart—J.M.A. Brown?[5]— Rev. G. Gladstone—Dr. C.P. Taylor—Rev. C.H. Irwin.[6] Saw Mr Tomlinson. Kibbled the Walnut Tree. Worked on public questions for Midlothian. Worked on Bills. Read Kildrum [*sc.* Kilgroom]—Lewin on Robert Owen[7]—Dr Cameron Creation Story[8]—Ginsburg on Cabbala.[9]

11. Sat.

Ch. 8½ A.M. Wrote to Mr Marjoribanks—Lord Rosebery—J.R. Allen—W.E. Doubleday—M. Catton—Father Kennedy—R.A. Macfie—Mr Lloyd Bryce NAR. Tel. Worked on *Homerics*. Worked at St Deiniol's. Much pleased with WHG's recent progress. Read Kildrum [*sc.* Kilgroom] (finished)—Ginsburg on Cabbala —and [blank.] Dined at the Rectory. Much conversation with Captain Bigge.[10]

12. 20 S. Trin.

Ch. 11 AM & [blank.] Wrote to Rev. W.C. Bowie—Mr Blackie BP.—Mr Schnad-horst—Mr Knowles BP—Mr A.C. Yates—Mr J. Cowan—Mr OBrien—Rev. Wil-liamson—G.E. Farran—Rev. Woodward—R. Holmes.[11] Corr. Carnegie Revise.[12] Worked on Hom. Theol. Read Connell Amn Church[13]—Carpenter on Synop-tics.[14]

[1] Untraced.
[2] *Kilgroom, a story of Ireland* (1890), sent by the author, John Alexander Stuart, d. 1932, traveller and novelist.
[3] Mary, daughter of Sir A. E. West.
[4] J. L. Bowes, Japanese consul in Liverpool, had sent his book on Japanese art for the library; *T.T.*, 17 October 1890, 5f, Add MS 44511, f. 87.
[5] Obscure.
[6] Clarke Huston Irwin, 1858-1934; presbyterian minister in Bray, Wicklow 1881-92; went to Australia 1892-6; theologian and historian. See 29 Aug. 90.
[7] Presumably on the socialist; but no work by Lewin (or Leurin, another possible transcription) traced.
[8] Possibly C. R. Cameron, *The mystical sense of the binding of Satan* (1850).
[9] Untraced article by the British Museum's classicist.
[10] Arthur Bigge, the Queen's assistant secretary (see 29 Sept. 83), staying at the Castle.
[11] Draft of replies to questions on God by Richard Holmes of Christ's college, Cambridge; Add MS 44511, f. 78.
[12] See 18 Sept. 90.
[13] Not found.
[14] J. E. Carpenter, *The first three Gospels* (1890); sent this day by W. Copeland Bowie, secretary of the Sunday School Association; letter in *T.T.*, 16 October 1890, 4e.

13. M.

Ch. 8½ A.M. Wrote to Mr J.B. Balfour MP—Scottish Leader Tel.—Ld Cowan—
P.W. Campbell—D M'Gregor—G.G. Macleod—C. Waddie[1]—J.M. Macintosh—E.
Johnson—Rev. Geo. Hill[2]—H.W. Lucy. Worked on prints &c. here and on books
at St D.s. Worked on papers for Midlothian. Read Haldane on Eight Hours
Bill[3]—E. Hugessen, dramatic effect[4]—The lost Explorer.[5]

14. Tu.

Ch. 8½ A.M. Wrote to Japanese Consul Lpool[6]—A. Taylor Innes—Mr T. Healy
MP—Messrs Scribner—G. Ballingall—E.S. Payne—G. M'Crewe—C. Aitchison—
Sir A. West—Miss Harriman—A. Pearce—Mrs Morgan—R.A. Macfie. Worked
on Midlothian papers. Also on O.T. proofs. Also on books at St D.s. Read The
lost Explorer—O'C. Morris on Irish Land.[7]

15. Wed.

Ch. 8½ A.M. Wrote to Sir W. Harcourt—F.W. Hindley—Mrs Ingram—Mr Brown
MP—Mr Jackson—Mr Balfour MP.—Stanfords—Mr Haldane MP.—Mr J.
Cooke—P.W. Campbell—Mrs Ingram [sic]—Ed. Jewish Chronicle.[8] Worked on
books here & St D. Worked on papers for Midl. Also on O.T. Proof Sheets. Read
Hogan, Lost Explorer—and Spottiswoode Wilson on W.E.G.s Creation Story.[9]
Wrote on O.T.

16. Th.

Ch. 8½ A.M. And 3 P.M. for Miss Scott's Funeral.[10] Wrote to Mr Marjoribanks—
E. Nicoll. & P.P.—J.A. Clyde—Rev. Thomson—J. Davies—Mr Murray—T.F.
Myers—Rev. Mitchell—J. Caverhill. Worked hard on O.T. proofs. Read Reeve's
Poems[11]—Bodley on R.C. Ch in U.S.[12]—and Hogan.

17. Fr.

Ch. 8½ A.M. Wrote to Mr P.W. Campbell—Mr Nicol—Mr Hogan—Mr Ridler—
Mr Howell—Ld Rosebery—A. Maxwell—W.F. Deevey—Mr Knowles—

[1] On Scottish home rule; *T.T.*, 15 October 1890, 9f.

[2] George Hill, octogenarian priest in Co. Down, told Gladstone: 'Your glorious policy is only opposed here now by a few Orange preachers and two or three platform haunting old women'; Hawn P.

[3] R. B. Haldane, 'The eight hours question', *C.R.*, lvii. 240 (February 1890).

[4] E. Knatchbull-Hugessen, 'A dramatic effect', *Blackwoods*, cxlii. 753 (December 1887).

[5] J. F. Hogan, *The lost explorer. An Australian story* (1890).

[6] See 10 Oct. 90n.   [7] See 8 Dec. 87.

[8] On his 'pain and horror' on reading of Jewish sufferings in Russia; if the reports are established, the 'conscience of Russia and Europe' to be raised; *T.T.*, 17 October 1890, 4d.

[9] J. Spottiswoode Wilson, *The creation story and nebular theory* [*in the Impregnable Rock*] *by W. E. Gladstone, investigated* (1890).

[10] Funeral of Elizabeth Susan Scott of Hawarden, formerly governess at the Castle.

[11] Perhaps A. Reeve, *Euterpe Montana and other poems* (1885).

[12] J. E. C. Bodley, *Roman catholicism in America. The catholic discovery of America* (1890), sent by the author; Add MS 44511, f. 85.

B. Reeve—J.G. M'Cann—Messrs Brough—R. Friend—Mr Cropper[1]—T.C. Melville—C. Herbert—J. Westell—Mrs Schlüter[2]—Mons. Broussali—F.W. Hindley—Mrs Chetwynd—J.E.C. Bodley[3]—Dr Rhomaides[4]—Mr M'Kechnie—J.H. Norman—Mr Murray. Worked again on O.T. proofs. And on Midlothian papers. Saw Mrs Holmes. Finished Hogan.

> Fret not, haste not, droop not, fear not
> When the Siren warbles fear not.
>
> Fear not, fret not, haste not, droop not
> Climb the heights of faith and stoop not.
>
> Droop not, fear not, fret not, haste not
> Heed thy store of time, and waste not.
>
> Waste not, droop not, fear not, fret not
> I have taught thee; thou, forget not.[5]

18. Sat. St Luke. [Courthey, Liverpool]

Agnes's birthday. God bless and aid her. Church with H.C. at $8\frac{1}{2}$ A.M. Wrote to Mr Nicol l. & PP—Mr Morley BP—Mr Anketell—Mr Birkwyn—L. Canard—Mrs Robinson—Miss Holdsworth—Sir W. Fraser—Mr M'Niven—Mr Aitchison—Pr. Ass. & C.N.—Garcia & Co[6]—Mr Cropper. Read Lowell 'Among my books' and 'In the Valley'.[7] Finished proofs O.T. Off at 3. Courthey at five. A family party dined. Much conversation with Mr & Mrs Robert G.

19. 20 S. Trin.

Drove to St Thos Toxteth mg (much & happily changed) and walked to Childwall evg. Saw Mr Stephenson evg. Wrote to Mr Nicol. Read Introd to Vampires of Ch. of Engl.[8]—and O.T.

[1] James Cropper, 1823–1900, Kendal manufacturer; liberal M.P. Kendal 1880–5; chaired Westmorland C.C. from 1889.

[2] Auguste Schlüter, a German who joined the Gladstones in 1867, originally to look after Mary and Helen; on Mary's marriage, she replaced Stüme as Mrs Gladstone's personal maid; from 1890, she lived mainly in Hanover caring for her parents, but returned occasionally to Hawarden; she d. 1917. See her *A Lady's Maid in Downing Street* (1922) and P. Gladstone, *Portrait of a family* (1989), ch. xv. Gladstone, like many Victorians, often referred to established spinsters as 'Mrs.'.

[3] John Edward Courtney Bodley, 1853–1925; Dilke's secretary 1882–5; sec. to housing R.C. 1884–5; wrote widely on French affairs; involved with Manning in his last days. See previous day.

[4] Dr. C. B. Rhomaides of Athens; in correspondence on dedicating his *Praxiteles* to Gladstone; Hawn P.

[5] Holograph dated 17 October 1890; Add MS 44773, f. 196.

[6] Probably Jacob Garcia, Covent Garden fruit dealers.

[7] J. R. Lowell, *Among my books*, 2v. (1870–6).

[8] A. Gemariah, *Vampires of the Church of England* (1890).

20. M. [*Edinburgh*]

Wrote to The Chief Constable. Off at 11: reached Edinb. at 6 warmly received by my kind host the Dean of Faculty.[1] Dinner party. Saw Mr Campbell—Mr A. Morley—Mr Marjoribanks—& others. Read In the Valley.

21. Tu.

Saw Mr Campbell—Herbert J.G.—Mr A. Morley—Ld Rosebery. Worked all the morning on Irish papers. Meeting at 3.30.[2] Spoke 1½ hour: voice came as usual, dropping as it were from the skies. Concert 8–10. Saw Madame Patti[3] between the acts. She sent me a beautiful little box with her lozenges. Read In the Valley.

22. Wed.

Wrote to Mad. Patti—Mrs Childers[4]—W. Curteyne. Drove to the Forth Bridge:[5] a marvellous, & not an ugly, structure. Saw Mr Campbell—Herbert G.—Mr Childers. 12–1½. Conclave on Scottish questions. Dinner party of 20. Drove also to Dalmeny: the prospect sadly clouded there.[6] Read 'In the Valley'. We sat late for Eccles Election.[7]

23. Th.

Wrote to Mr J. Pollard—Rev. Dr Hayman. Finished 'In the Valley'. Read Lowell on Dante. Worked up points of Irish case: & especially of Labour case. 2½–7¼. Expedition to West Calder. Great enthusiasm. 2000 people: a manageable audience, *much* better than 5000. Spoke 1 h. 20 m.[8] Large dinner party. Saw Mr Long—Mr Macfarlane—Mr Campbell—Mr Marjoribanks—Herbert G.

24. Fr.

Wrote to E. of Iddesleigh—Mr Menzies—Baroness de Royan—J. Sheridan—J. Maclauchlan—Messrs A. Brown. Visited St Giles's—three Public Libraries—& divers other points. Saw Herbert J.G.—Mr Marjoribanks—Sir A. Mitchell—Mr T.G. Law—Dr Rainy—Dr Dods.[9] Worked on Scotch papers. Luncheon at Mrs Buchanan's. Large dinner party at home. Tea at St Leonard's: & *noble view* of

---

[1] Because of the fatal illness of Lady Rosebery (see 22 Oct. 90), Gladstone stayed with J. B. Balfour at 6 Rothesay Terrace, Edinburgh.

[2] *T.T.*, 22 October 1890, 6a.

[3] Adelina Patti, 1843–1919; the leading soprano of her time; various letters to Gladstone in Add MSS 44511–3.

[4] As president of the Edinburgh Women's Liberal Association; *T.T.*, 23 October 1890, 5c.

[5] Just opened. For Gladstone's assistance to the Forth Bridge workers on a visit during its construction, see 28 Aug. 84.

[6] Lady Rosebery was dying from Bright's Disease, compounded by typhoid. See 25 Nov. 90.

[7] H. J. Roby gained the Eccles seat for the liberals, defeating A. F. Egerton at the by-election.

[8] *T.T.*, 24 October 1890, 4a.

[9] Marcus Dods, 1834–1909; free church minister in Glasgow 1864–89; professor of New Testament criticism at New College, Edinburgh, 1889; his views on inspiration libelled by General Assembly 1890, but not prosecuted; succeeded Rainy as Principal 1907.

Arthur's seat & the Crags. Conversation with bevy of lawyers on judges great & small. Read Life of Freytag.[1]

25. Sat. [Beeslack, Penicuik]

Wrote to Mr Law BP—Mr Henderson. Alarming accounts of Lady Rosebery. 2–$6\frac{3}{4}$. To Dalkeith and Beeslack.[2] Spoke 1 h. 25 m.[3] Saw friends as usual. Read Froude's Beaconsfield[4]—Lang's Lord Iddesleigh.[5]

26. 21 S. Trin.

Mr Cowan had morning & evening prayer of the old Scottish fashion. He is truly excellent. Much conversation with him. Also with Rev. Mr Crockett (Free).[6] Read Woolman's Journal[7]—Booth's Darkest England.[8]

27. M. [Edinburgh]

Wrote to . . . . Left Beeslack 11.20 for Edinb. Music Hall 3.30–6. Spoke 1 h. 40 m. & most thankful ought I to be for having been brought through these labours.[9] Dined at the Esher's.[10] Read Life of Iddesleigh. Worked up papers & notes on the procedure & the performances. Great & delightful change in the reports from Dalmeny.[11]

28. Tu.

Wrote to W. Graham—Mr de Coverley—F. Thomson—Rev. Dr. Fergusson—J. Paterson—Rev. G.S. Muir—R. Grant—Mr J.C. Dunlop. Dined at Mr Campbell's.[12] Saw Sir J. Carmichael—Mr Mill—Mr Maclagan—Mr Guthrie. $12\frac{1}{2}$–$6\frac{3}{4}$. Drive to luncheon at Mr M's & then to the Pumpherston shale works.[13] Saw the works. Spoke 35 min. Then to another work. Short speech, and home.[14] Read Life of Iddesleigh.

29. Wed. [Fasque]

Wrote to Mr R. Beard. Off at $9\frac{3}{4}$ Dundee $11\frac{1}{4}$. Processions through the streets. Have [not] known any more enthusiastic or better ordered. Received the

---

[1] C. Alberti, *Gustav Freytag* (1886).

[2] Seat of Sir J. Cowan, chairman of the Midlothian Liberal Association; see 30 Jan. 79.

[3] *T.T.*, 27 October 1890, 7a.

[4] See 5 July 90.   [5] See 25 Feb. 90.

[6] Samuel Rutherford Crockett, 1860–1914; novelist, Scott scholar, and minister of the Free church in Penicuik 1886; in 1895 he resigned from the ministry.

[7] J. Woolman, *A journal of the life, gospel labours and Christian experience of J. Woolman* (1776); notes on it at Add MS 44773, f. 198.

[8] W. Booth, *In darkest England and the way out* (1890), sent by the author, Add MS 44511, f. 100.

[9] *T.T.*, 28 October 1890, 9f.

[10] Presumably in a rented house; no Edinburgh family of this name.

[11] False hopes for Lady Rosebery's recovery; see R. R. James, *Rosebery* (1963), 225.

[12] P. W. Campbell, his agent in Midlothian.

[13] By East Calder; *T.T.*, 29 October 1890, 10d.

[14] Ibid.

freedom at Kinnaird Hall. Spoke 40 m. M'K. Tariff.[1] Then Exhibition. Spoke 35 m. Then luncheon. Spoke say 12 m. Off at 5¼ to Fasque.[2] Arrived at 7. Most warmly received. Party in the house. The incidents of this tour ought to overwhelm me with gratitude and humiliation before God. Read Life of Iddesleigh.

30. Th.

Wrote to Mr Baildon—Mr Nicol—Mr Kennedy. Read Iddesleigh's Life.— Froude's Beaconsfield—M'Carthy on Lecky's Volumes.[3] Whist in evg. Drove to Fettercairn Hall & the Burn. Col. Macinroy[4] most kindly gave me his wife's drawing of my Father: at about 85 ... 6. Here they are all Tories & all most kind. Much pleased with Lady Alice Stewart[5] & the F[ettercairn] Ladies.

31. Fr.

Wrote to Jas Hastings—Sir C. Tennant Tel.—Mrs Th. B.P.—Ed. Dundee Courier—Mr Petrie—Ed. Dundee Advertiser—Dr Warre—Barret, Scott, & others.—J. Grant. Walk with John. He, & they, are all most kind. Inspected the new Distillery. Whist in evg. Read Fell's Fox[6]—Froude's Lord Beaconsfield— Lang's Iddesleigh: not well done.

Sat. Nov 1. 1890. All Saints.

Wrote to W. A. Dennelly—Mr Lang—W. Marwick—J. Kerr—Mr E.C. Phillips— Mr Carton. Ch. 11 A.M. Drove to Drumtochtie Chapel an excellent fabric. The glen looked most beautiful. Backgammon with M.G. Read Froude's B. Finished Lang's Iddesleigh—ill done, except the Preface.

2. 22 S. Trin.

Chapel 11 A.M. and H.C.—also 3 P.M. Wrote to Mr Mackey—W.H.G. Visited the Jollies—Anderson—Hepburn—Mrs Duncan (an excellent specimen). Read Mrs Butler on Mrs Booth[7]—Burgh, Dignity of Human Nature[8]—Woolman's Journal. Walk in the Den: loved and yearned.

Th[eology].[9]

Observe on the sealing of the twelve tribes in the Apocalypse:
1. The omission of Dan: does not this show that the tribe had in the main, & not merely a section of it, gone into idolatry.

---

[1] Referred to his visit to Macclesfield (see 28 Jan. 28) as his first contemplation of free trade; *T.T.*, 30 October 1890, 4b. The 'M'K Tariff' is the American McKinley tariff, just introduced.

[2] The family home in the Mearns, now owned by his nephew, Sir John Robert Gladstone, 3rd bart.

[3] J. H. McCarthy, 'Mr. Lecky's last volumes', *C.R.*, lviii. 673 (November 1890).

[4] William Macinroy of the Burn, Fettercairn (see 10 Nov. 36n., 17 Oct. 46); the drawing is no longer extant.

[5] Alice Emma, da. of 4th Lord Bath and wife of Michael Hugh Shaw-Stewart, 1854–1942, tory M.P. E. Renfrew 1886–1903.

[6] M. Fell, *The testimony of Margaret Fell concerning her late husband George Fox* (1694).

[7] Josephine Butler, 'Catherine Booth', *C.R.*, lviii. 639 (November 1890).

[8] J. Burgh, *The dignity of human nature* (1754).

[9] Holograph dated 2 November 1890; Add MS 44773, f. 197.

2. But the schism of Jeroboam does not prevent the recognition of the ten tribes: it is as with our Saviour 'on twelve thrones, judging the twelve tribes of Israel'.
3. And the number twelve is made up by the bisection of Joseph's descendants.

3. M. [*The Glen, Innerleithen*]

Off at 10 to L[aurence]kirk. Arrived at the Glen[1] ab. 4.30. Short speech to 2 . . . 3000 at Peebles. Great warmth of the people all the way. C. went to Erskine.[2] Charmed with the beauty of the Glen. Saw Pictures[3] prints &c. Read Clues[4]— Froude's Beaconsfield (finished)—Letters on Religion.[5]

4. Tu.

Wrote to Mr J. Grant—A. Morley MP.—S. Brown—T. Wemyss Reid—Jas. Bendle[6]—Mrs Royston—A.F. White—Mr Lefevre—Mr Nicol—Dr Ginsburg—Mr S. Wood—Hon. F. Lawley. Drive, walk, & view of the place in Departments. Conversation with Mr Steele. Our host's birthday. He overbubbles with contentment, even beyond 'his ordnar'. Read Henderson's Clues.

5. Wed.

Wrote to D. Tillies—Lord Provost of Dundee—J. Morley MP. l.l.—Mr H. Clay Trumbull[7]—Ld Rosebery—Mrs Ingram—Stuart J. Reid—Mrs Helmore. Saw Rev. Mitchell—Mr . . . . . .—Mrs J. Tennant[8]—Mr J.T.—Sir C.T. Finished off the cutting of a Scotch elm. Drive to Innerleithen & Walkerburn. Friendly gift & greetings. Read Clues (finished)—Letters on the Religion essential to Man (interesting on acct of Burns).

6. Th. [*Hawarden*]

$9\frac{1}{2}$–$12\frac{1}{4}$ To Carlisle. Spoke $\frac{1}{2}$ hour to 10,000.[9] $1\frac{1}{2}$–$5\frac{3}{4}$ to Hawarden. Margot [Tennant] left us at Warrington. Read Freytag—Gasquet on Edward VI.[10]—Grey on Parlt (N.C.)—Davitt on Ireland (do).[11]

7. Fr.

Ch. $8\frac{1}{2}$ A.M. Great storm: much damage in the night. Wrote to Mr Nicol l. & tel.—Sir E. Watkin—Mr Humphreys—Vote Office—C. Hooper—Ed. Banker's

---

[1] Sir Charles Tennant's great house between Peebles and Innerleithen.
[2] Erskine House near Paisley; she rejoined her husband at The Glen.
[3] Including Millais' first portrait of Gladstone, which Sir C. Tennant now owned.
[4] W. Henderson, *Clues; or leaves from a chief constable's notebook* (1891).
[5] M. Huber, *Letters containing the religion essential to man*, translated from the French (1738).
[6] Secretary of the N. Cumberland liberal association.
[7] H. Clay Trumbell, publisher in Philadelphia; dealt with American sales of *The Impregnable Rock*; Hawn P.
[8] Harold John, 1865–1935, youngest s. of Sir C. Tennant; Asquith's assistant secretary 1892–5; liberal M.P. Berwickshire 1894–1918; he m. 1889 Helen Gordon Duff, who d. 1892.
[9] *T.T.*, 7 November 1890, 4c.
[10] F. A. Gasquet, *Edward VI and the Book of Common Prayer* (1890).
[11] *N.C.*, xxviii. 694, 854 (November 1890); the number included Gladstone's article on Carnegie (see 18 Sept. 90).

Magazine[1]—Sec. Scottish Corporation—Geo. Gregory—Rev. Melville Scott. Lost in a chaos of accumulated papers. Read (for many hours) Wemyss Reid's Lord Houghton.[2] Saw Herbert respecting the damage at St Deiniol's.

8. Sat.

Ch. 8½ A.M. Wrote to Ed. Mark Lane Express[3]—Ld Selborne—Vote Office—Miss Marsh—Mons. Schwande[4]—L.H. Moore—A.H. Pollen—E. Stanford—W.G. Bowen—Rev. J. Carter. Conversation with Herbert on Estate matters. Read Life of Houghton (much)—Monist on the Sexual relation.[5] C. still an invalid.

9. 23 S. Trin.

Ch. 11 AM & 6½ PM. Wrote to Mr C.H. Robarts—J. Morley MP.—W.M. Marshal—Rev. W. Lock—Duke of Argyll—J. Nicol—Col. Turner—W. Douglas— A. Webster. Read Webster on Burns[6]—Woolman's Journal (finished)—Swift, Spiritual Law.[7]

10. M.

Ch. 8½ A.M. Wrote to Mr Wemyss Reid—Mr Carnegie BP.—Mr Patten—Ld Granville—Mr A. Morley. Worked hard on Houghton and finished Vol I. Read also Scott's Journal.[8] Cath. much better.

11. Tu.

Ch. 8½ A.M. Wrote to Cardinal Manning—Mr D. Douglas—H.G. Reid[9]—General Booth[10]—J. Nicol—Messrs Williams—A. Gould—J.H. Davidson—Mr Stuart MP.— Professor Guppa—Mr Greensmith. Threat of cold—early bed. Read Houghton (hard)—Scotts Journal.

12. Wed.

Kept my bed till evening. Wrote to Sir F. Mappin MP.[11]—B. Quaritch—T.F. Waddington—W. Holt—Rev. R.R. Rogers—T. Dewhurst. Read Ld Houghton— Scott's Journal.

---

[1] Declining an invitation to contribute on the currency question; letter reproduced in facsimile in *The Bankers' Magazine*, l. 1997 (December 1890). The Baring banking crisis broke next day.

[2] Proof sheets sent by T. Wemyss Reid of his *The life and friendships of Richard Monckton Milnes, first Lord Houghton*, 2v. (1890), Add MS 44511, f. 112; much Gladstoniana; Gladstone is thanked in the preface for the use of letters. For his review, see 14 Nov. 90.

[3] Not found published.

[4] Unidentified.

[5] *The Monist*, i. 38 (October 1890); article by E. D. Cope.

[6] Rev. Alexander Webster of Aberdeen had sent his *Burns and the Kirk* (1888).

[7] E. Swift, *Spiritual law in the natural world* (1890); *T.T.*, 11 November 1890, 9f.

[8] D. D. [i.e. David Douglas], ed., *The journal of Sir Walter Scott*, 2v. (1890).

[9] Liberal candidate for Handsworth; letter in *T.T.*, 17 November 1890, 10b.

[10] William Booth, 1829-1912; founder of the Salvation Army 1878; see 26 Oct. 90.

[11] Sir Frederick Thorpe Mappin, 1821-1910; Sheffield manufacturer; liberal M.P. E. Retford 1880-85, Hallamshire 1885-1906; cr. bart. 1886.

13. Th.

Ch. 8½ A.M. Arranged letters. Drive with C. Wrote to Rev. Mr Williamson—Watsons—Madam Patti—Scotts—Mr R. Brown jun.—R. Lowe[1]—Matthew Drohan—Miss Weston—Macmillans. Cold thrown off—by *early* care. Read Williamsons Poems[2]—Life of Houghton (finished)—Scott's Journal.

14. Fr.

Ch. 8½ A.M. Wrote to Sir W. Harcourt—A. Morley—J. Morley—Mrs Hicklinson —J. Nicol—Lady Lindsay—Col. Turner—Rev. Williamson. Worked on a short paper about Milnes: difficult enough.[3] A little woodcraft. Read Scott's Journal— Life & Times of Bp Morgan.[4] Saw the Humphreys foreman.[5]

15. Sat.

Ch. 8½ A.M. Wrote to Mr Stuart Rendel MP—Mr Humphreys—E.A. Beaumont —Mr Angerstein—C. Menken—Ld Selborne—Clem. Wise[6]—Mr Henderson—E. Thompson—Mons. Debidour[7]—W. Armstrong—Ed. Literary Churchman[8]—Ed. Everlasting Nation[9]—Card. Manning. Saw W. Bailey—Mr Mayhew. Small woodcraft. Revised & finished paper on Milnes: submitted to Mary for her judgment.[10] Read Scott's Journal—and [blank.]

16. 24 S. Trin.

Ch. mg & evg. Wrote to Mr Mundella MP—Mrs Th. l. & BP.—J. Morley MP.— Mrs Bolton .... Read Alexander's Confucius[11]—Oxley's [blank][12]—Booth's Darkest London.[13] Saw S.E.G.

17. M.[14]

Ch. 8½ AM. Wrote to Mark Lane Express—Ld Acton—Cawthorne & Hutt—Ld Monkswell—Messrs Saxon—J.A. Steuart—W. Oxley—A. Fraser—J.E. Crump—

---

[1] Probably Robert William Lowe, theatrical historian and bibliographer.

[2] Rev. David R. Williamson had sent his *Poems of nature and life* (1888); Hawn P.

[3] Signed review of T. Wemyss Reid's *Life of Houghton* (see 7 Nov. 90) for *The Speaker*, ii. 596 (29 November 1890).

[4] T. E. Jacob, *The life and times of Bishop Morgan* (1890).

[5] i.e. foreman of the men working on St Deiniol's library, damaged in the storm.

[6] Clement Wise, author of *Puritanism in power* (1890).

[7] Probably Antonin Debidour, inspector general of public education in France; historian and biographer.

[8] Not found published.

[9] A. A. Isaacs, ed., *The everlasting nation . . . relating to the Jewish people* (no copy of the first series found).

[10] See previous day.

[11] G. G. Alexander, *Confucius, the great teacher* (1890).

[12] W. Oxley had sent his *Modern messiahs and wonder workers* (1889).

[13] See 26 Oct. 90.

[14] This day Mrs. O'Shea did not appear in court to contest the divorce petition of Captain O'Shea, and a decree *nisi* was given.

C. Lowe—Rev. D.R. Thomas. Worked on books & papers. Woodcraft. Read Col. Long on Gordon[1]—Haine on Gordon[2]—Scott's Journal—and Q.R. on do.[3]

18. Tu.

Ch. 8½ A.M. Wrote to Mr Macgregor jun.[4]—Ld Rosebery—Dr Robinson—Mr Morley MP—Sir W. Fraser—W. Ridler—S. Broadbent—J.A. Storry—Mr Seligman[5]—J.A. Aynscough—M. Morifalcone—T.G. Aspward—Miss Nichol—Moderator Edinb. H. Constables—Mr Bram Stoker.[6] Read Scott's Journal—Paladin's Glances[7]—The Snake's Pass. Twelve to dinner. Conversation in evg with Mr Mayhew on Manor & Estate history.

19. Wed.

Ch. 8½ A.M. Wrote to M'Leod of M'Leod[8]—Mr A. Mild—S. Buxton MP—Mr Morley MP.—Appleton & Co—H.M. Doughty—J.T. M'Cleary—Rev. J. Bickford—A. Riley—J.W.S. Caller—J. Nicol—A. Carpenter—A. Mozely—Genl Alexander—D. Milne—S. Hughes. Worked at St Deiniol's. Read Scott's Journal—Q.R. on Chesterfield[9]—The Snake's Pass.

20. Th.

Ch. 8½ A.M. Wrote to Card. Manning—L. Ly Waterford—A. Morley MP—Ly W. Gardner—W.T. Stead—Ld Kinnaird—The "Speaker"—Rev. Crosdaile Harris[10]—H.M. Wallis—Macmillans—A.W. Hutton—Messrs Wheatley—Jas Knowles—Ld Selborne—Central News Tel. Good work at St Deiniol's. Family conversations on the awful matter of Parnell.[11] Saw Mr Mayhew. Read The Snake's Pass—Manning Gospel of Wealth (proofs)[12]—and Wilson on Giving.[13] Corr. proofs of Milnes article.[14]

21. Fr.

Ch. 8½ A.M. Wrote to H.C. Trumbull—L. Morris—Mr Brunner MP.—Mr Colman MP.—Jas Knowles—Mr Childers MP.—D. Nicoll—Lucy Cavendish—A. Ireland[15]

---

[1] Untraced; probably an article.
[2] Probably an article by C. R. Haines; see his *General Gordon* (1902).
[3] *Q.R.*, clxxi. 386 (October 1890).
[4] Of Lords' cricket ground, evidently the son of the Edinburgh hotelier with whom Gladstone sometimes stayed. Macgregor was a wicket keeper; Gladstone's letter is in M.C.C. archives.
[5] De Witt J. Seligman of New York sent a copy of *The Epoch*; Hawn P.
[6] Bram Stoker, 1847–1912, historian, journalist, and novelist; inventor of 'Dracula'; had sent his Irish novel, *The Snake's Pass* (1890), read this day. Stoker was also Henry Irving's stage manager, and discussed the book with Gladstone on the latter's visit to the Lyceum on 2 Dec. 90.
[7] *Glances at great and little men*. By Paladin (1890).
[8] Norman Macleod of Macleod, 1812–95; 22nd chief of the clan.
[9] *Q.R.*, clxxi. 287 (October 1890).
[10] Croasdaile Harris, British chaplain at Weimar 1888–93.
[11] See next day.
[12] Proofs of H. E. Manning, 'Irresponsible wealth', *N.C.*, xxviii. 876 (December 1890).
[13] Untraced.   [14] See 14 Nov. 90.
[15] Alexander Ireland, journalist, sent reminiscences of Scott; Add MS 44511, f. 166.

—Wilfrid Ward.[1] A bundle of letters daily about Parnell: all one way. Spent the forenoon chiefly in drawing out my own view of the case.

Dined with the Mayhews. Worked at St Deiniol's. Fivocloquer at the Orphanage. Read The Snake's Pass—Sir J. Dawson on Huxley[2]—Scott's Journal.

Secret.   *The O'Shea Suit.*[3]

The political situation, brought about by the O'Shea suit in the Divorce Court, is one without example, both for its character and for the commanding interest it creates: and the duty of every one concerned in that situation is to form, in the first place, an accurate conception for himself as to his own proper office in regard to it.

For myself, then, I have to say that there have been and there are questions, on which I have done, and do, my best towards the formation of a public opinion; but this is not one of them. It is no part of my duty, as the leader of a party in Parliament, to form a personal judgment on the moral conduct of any other leader or fellow-member.

But it is my duty, and it is almost inevitable, that I should estimate in my own mind the probable results, where they are serious, which any given course of conduct, no matter whose, is likely to produce upon the public interests with which a party has to deal.

No man ought to suffer prejudice in his public capacity for any conduct, except such as is known: and the first question that arises is, what ought in such a case to be held to constitute knowledge. A line has to be drawn for practical purposes; and in my opinion knowledge, in a subject of this kind, is cognisance of what has been judicially established, and can rarely if ever go beyond it. All the matter then, which was put in proof in the O'Shea case, is to be taken as known.

It is plain that the question arises upon these facts whether Mr. Parnell can, in view of them, continue to discharge with advantage to the Irish party and people his duties as their leader: since leadership ought always to begin or cease according to the public, and not the personal, considerations involved.

It is also plain that the decision of this question rests in the first place with the Irish Parliamentary party, and with the constituents of Mr. Parnell and the Irish constituencies generally. Let us take it for granted that they have decided it for themselves.

In passing let me say that I for one honour the profound gratitude of the Irish party and people for the inestimable services, which, by his sagacity integrity and persistence, Mr. Parnell has done them: and that I can well understand their reluctance to take out of his hands the office which he holds.

But the great cause of constitutional Home Rule has to be decided by the free assent of the people also of Great Britain; and the Irish demand has to be pleaded in the House of Commons.

The main question, then, appears to be this: will the desire or resolution of the Irish to continue their confidence to Mr. Parnell enable him to exercise in Parliament the weight and influence necessary for the progress of his cause: and will the Liberal constituencies of England continue, in unimpaired strength, to support that cause, represented in Parliament by Mr. Parnell as the spokesman of Ireland, after the disclosures in the O'Shea suit?

Up to what point the judgment of Ireland ought to be respected, in such a case, is a question of interest: but it would not be decisive of the issue, if it still remained true that Mr. Parnell's weight and moral force in Parliament were likely to be impaired or lost by the continuance of his leadership, and that the Liberal constituencies would not, as

---

[1] Wilfrid Philip Ward, 1856–1916; Roman catholic and biographer.
[2] Sir J. W. Dawson, *Modern ideas of evolution* (1890).
[3] Holograph; Add MS 56448, f. 45.

matter of fact, be available in their unimpaired strength, under that condition, for returning to Parliament friends of the national cause of Ireland.

It is necessary here to observe, adhering strictly to the issues judicially established without going back upon particulars at any single point, that the criminal act is complicated, in this instance, with the prolonged abuse of hospitality, and with the uncontradicted assertion of deception and untruth. I do not here indicate any personal opinion; for justice requires me to state that I should continue with full confidence to anticipate from Mr. Parnell all that exact integrity and veracity, by which, in our rare but important communications he has been uniformly guided.

But, in the affair of the scandalous Parnell commission, he was charged with having deliberately deceived the House of Commons: and though, in my opinion, the charge was unjust and untrue, yet it has been revived, and will be urged in the present sensitive state of the public mind, with a certain effect, as combined with portions of the recent evidence, to cast a doubt upon good faith, not so as to carry away the best-informed, yet so as to influence a certain number of minds.

I must also notice, as a thing partially though not more than partially relevant, that Mr. O'Brien and other members did some years back insist, in one or more cases of atrocious criminality, real or supposed, that it ought to be a disqualification for civil employment. They did this in their places, with much persistency and effect; and references to it, which will probably be made, would, whether justly or unjustly, be found in some degree to operate.

I think it may also be worthwhile to observe that if there be no voice in Ireland dissenting from the public unanimity, this appears by no means to be the case with the Irish race in America who form no unimportant factor in the question.

I agree with a newspaper, supposed to convey the opinion of Davitt (*The Labour World*),[1] that the dominant question, now properly before Mr. Parnell for his consideration, is what is the best course for him to adopt with a view to the furtherance of the interests of Home Rule in Great Britain. And, with deep pain but without any doubt, I judge that those interests require his retirement at the present time from his leadership. For the reason intimated at the outset, I have no right spontaneously to pronounce this opinion. But I should certainly give it if called upon from a quarter entitled to make the demand.

WEG Nov. 21. 1890.

22. Sat.

Ch. 8½ A.M. Wrote to Bp of Edinburgh—Warden Trin. Coll. NB,[2] BP.—W. Ridler—Rev. S.S. Walker—J.D.O. Hyme—Herr Brentano—Rev. H. Fyfe—Robn & Nichn—Mr Menken—Rev. W.M. Lewis—A. Neild—Mr H.F. Fox. Corrected proofs Midl. Speeches. A mass of Parnell reading again: made Mema. Read The Snake's Pass—Scott's Journal.

---

[1] Davitt was then editor of the *Labour World*; Parnell had assured him that there would be nothing disreputable in the divorce case; his editorial of 20 November declared that both British and Irish home rulers had a right to expect him to deliver their cause from 'the deadliest peril by which it has yet been assailed ... [Parnell] is urged by the highest considerations that could appeal to a leader to efface himself, for a brief period, from public life, until the time which the law requires to elapse before a divorced woman can marry enables him to come back, having paid the penalty which the public sentiment rightly inflicts on such transgressions as his'; see Lyons, *Fall of Parnell*, 78–9.

[2] i.e. Trinity College, Glenalmond.

The conduct of Mr. Parnell in certain instances, of which I was personally cognisant, during the period when he was acting in opposition to the Liberal Government, impressed with a sense of his scrupulousness in matters of veracity, and have likewise left upon my mind the belief that in considering his course at the present juncture, with regard to his retention or surrender of the duties of political leadership, he will be guided principally by the question what is most for the interests of the national cause of Ireland, and will include in his grounds of judgment the views of the present situation which may be taken by Liberals in the constituencies of Great Britain.   N.22.

There may be contingencies which would justify or require my giving an opinion on Mr. Parnell's continuance in the Leadership of the Irish party: but it is no part of my duty to bring about, or to take a share in bringing about, those contingencies.   N.22.[1]

23. Pre Adv. S.

Ch 11 A. [blank]-PM. Wrote to Sir W. Harcourt—Card. Manning—E.R. Russell —J. Morley MP—J. Westell—A. Morley MP—C. Lowe—Mr A. Galton—W.C. Angus—Mr Newman Hall—Mr Smith. Another cloud of Parnell letters: I think the time has come. Read Booth's Darkest London—Smith's The World Lighted[2]—Döllinger, Addresses.[3]

Qu[estion] now[4]

1. Not *whether*,
2. But how,
       to convey &c.
3. Convey what
          my judgment
          not on the merits
          but on the facts
4. have waited, in order to collect them fully, to the last moment
5. It is that
    the present force of the Lib. party for carrying H.R. would be practically broken up were it to approve the continuance under the actual circs. of Mr P.

24. M. [London]

Ch. 8½ A.M. Righting papers &c. Wrote to Mr M'Carthy MP—Mr Morley MP—Ld Acton—Elliot & Stock. Off at 10¾. In Carlton Gardens[5] at four. We find the house as if our own. Conclave Ld Gr., Sir W.H., J. Morley, A. Morley.

---

[1] Both these notes are holographs; Add MS 56448, ff. 58, 60.
[2] C. E. Smith of Fredonia, N.Yk., *The World Lighted; a study of the Apocalypse* (1890).
[3] J. J. I. von Döllinger, *Studies in European history*, tr. M. Warre (1890).
[4] Docketed by Gladstone: 'Parnell N. 1890'; Add MS 44773, f. 199; otherwise undated, but appears to refer to this day's decision.
[5] 1 Carlton Gardens, Rendel's house.

Saw Mr. MacCarthy.[1] Dined at A. Morley's: consultations. Read Scott's Journals.

To J. MORLEY, M.P., 24 November 1890.[2] *The Times*, 26 November 1890, 10a.[3]

Having arrived at a certain conclusion with regard to the continuance at the present moment of Mr. Parnell's leadership of the Irish party, I have seen Mr. M'Carthy on my arrival in town, and have inquired from him whether I was likely to receive from Mr. Parnell himself any communication on the subject. Mr. M'Carthy replied that he was unable to give me any information on the subject.

I mentioned to him that in 1882, after the terrible murder in the Phœnix Park, Mr. Parnell, although totally removed from any idea of responsibility, had spontaneously written to me, and offered to take the Chiltern Hundreds, an offer much to his honour, but one which I thought it my duty to decline.

While clinging to the hope of communication from Mr. Parnell, to whomsoever addressed, I thought it necessary, viewing the arrangements for the commencement of the Session to-morrow, to acquaint Mr. M'Carthy with the conclusion at which, after using all the means of observation and reflection in my power, I had myself arrived. It was that, notwithstanding the splendid services rendered by Mr. Parnell to his country, his continuance at the present moment in the leadership would be productive of consequences disastrous in the highest degree to the cause of Ireland. I think I may be warranted in asking you so far to expand the conclusion I have given above as to add that the continuance I speak of would not only place many hearty and effective friends of the Irish cause in a position of great embarrassment, but would render my retention of the leadership of the Liberal party, based as it has been mainly upon the prosecution of the Irish cause, almost a nullity. This expansion of my views I begged Mr. M'Carthy to regard as confidential, and not intended for his colleagues generally if he found that Mr. Parnell contemplated spontaneous action; but I also begged that he would make known to the Irish party, at their meeting to-morrow afternoon, that such was my conclusion, if he should find that Mr. Parnell had not in contemplation any step of the nature indicated.

I now write to you, in case Mr. M'Carthy should be unable to communicate with Mr. Parnell, as I understand you may possibly have an opening to-morrow through another channel. Should you have such an opening, I beg you to make known to Mr. Parnell the conclusion itself, which I have stated in the earlier part of this letter. I have thought it

---

[1] An interview arranged by Harcourt and Morley *via* Labouchere to enable Gladstone's views to be made known to Parnell. McCarthy noted that night that Gladstone told him that Parnell's remaining in the leadership meant the loss of the next elections; Gladstone 'said he would not write this to Parnell himself, because it might seem harsh and dictatorial and might hurt Irish feeling; but he authorised me to convey his views to Parnell when I see him. This will not be until to-morrow . . .' (J. McCarthy and Mrs Campbell Praed, *Our book of memories* (1912), 258). After McCarthy left 1 Carlton Gardens, Gladstone wrote him a short letter to show to Parnell; it is not clear that Parnell received it or, if he did receive it, at what time. No copy of the letter has been found but this day's entry confirms that it was written. See also Lyons, *Fall of Parnell*, 85 ff.

[2] After the meeting with McCarthy, it was agreed that Gladstone should write to Morley a letter which he could show to Parnell next morning. Gladstone showed the draft letter to J. Morley, Granville and Harcourt at dinner at A. Morley's this evening, Morley then persuading Gladstone to add the sentence about the retention of the liberal leadership. Next day, Morley was unable to find Parnell until after the meeting at 2 p.m. at which Parnell was re-elected Chairman. After Morley's interview with Parnell, the liberal leadership agreed, with Gladstone enthusiastic and Morley hesitant, to release this letter to the press. See Morley, *Recollections*, i. 260 and Lyons, *Fall of Parnell*, 86 ff. See 20 Aug. 91n. and Introduction above, Section II.

[3] Printed under the heading 'Ultimatum from Mr. Gladstone'.

best to put it in terms simple and direct, much as I should have desired, had it lain within my power, to alleviate the personal nature of the situation. As respects the manner of conveying what my public duty has made it an obligation to say, I rely entirely on your good feeling, tact, and judgment.

25. Tu.

Wrote to Mr Smith—Card. Manning—Mr Irvine—. . . . . . . Saw Mr Morley—Mr A. Morley—Mr Bryce—The Speaker—E. Hamilton—E. Marj[oribanks]. H. of C. 3¾–8. Spoke on the Address.[1] But all minds were absorbed in the Parnell business which was full of sad incidents. Dinner party at Mr R.s.[2] Read Scott's Journal. 10–1¼. Lady Rosebery's funeral. Saw R. and his boys. The service at Willesden is dignified and touching, wanting to be filled up with our Lord's name.[3]

26. Wed.

Wrote to Rev. Dr Warre. H. of C. 3½–4½.[4] Mr Rendell on my suggestion moved the Welsh M.P.s.[5] Saw J. & A. Morley, repeatedly—Sir W. Harcourt—Ld Granville—Mr Childers—Prof. Stuart—Mr Lefevre—Sir F. Mappin—Mr Mills—Ld Justice Bowen. Read Scott's Journal—Stead's Tract on Parnell[6]—Bride of Lammermoor.[7]

27. Th.

Wrote to Ld Hampden—Lady Galway—E. Routledge—Mr Wemyss Reid—C. Lowe—Mr Ernest Noel[8]—Rev. C.H. Cope[9]—Earl of Meath[10]—J. Nicol—Ed. Newbery House Mag.[11] Corrected Milnes article. Luncheon at 15 Gr. Square.[12] Saw Mr Rendel—Mr A. Morley—Mr Wemyss Reid—Ld Spencer—Prof. Stuart—Sir W. Harcourt—Scotts—Sir J. Carmichael—H.N.G.—Mr Rendel—Mr Fergusson Munro[13]—Mr Trafford. H. of C. 3½–6.[14] Dinner party. Read Bride of Lammermoor.

[1] *H* 349. 52.

[2] i.e. Rendel.

[3] Gladstone's comment on the Jewish funeral at the United Synagogue of Lady Rosebery, a Rothschild. He attended the service at Rosebery's house and at the cemetery; *T.T.*, 26 November 1890, 10d.

[4] Series of bills given 1°R; *H* 349. 101.

[5] Presumably deferring an arranged meeting.

[6] W. T. Stead, *The discrowned King of Ireland* (n.d.); a summary of press comments and argument requiring Parnell's resignation as party leader.

[7] By Scott; see 8 Aug. 26.

[8] Ernest Noel, 1831–?; s. of Baptist Noel; liberal M.P. Dumfries 1874–86 (defeated as a liberal unionist).

[9] Charles Henry Cope, anglican priest living in Bruges.

[10] See 19 Oct. 77.

[11] Not published.

[12] i.e. Mrs. Thistlethwayte's.

[13] i.e. R. C. Munro-Ferguson, the liberal M.P., see 22 Aug. 87.

[14] Irish land bill; *H* 349. 137.

28. Fr.

Wrote Mem. on my course of proceeding. Wrote to Cardinal Manning—Rev. Dr Warre—Sig. Brentano—Mr Hilken—F.F. Stone—H. Powell. Saw Mr Childers—Sir J. Carmichael—Conclave: A.M., J.M., and Lord Spencer—Mr B. Currie—Mr MacCarthy (bis)[1]—Mr Whitbread—and others. Dinner party. Read Bride of L.

The continuance of Mr. Parnell's leadership means the cessation of relations and of common action between the Irish party and the Liberal party.

I should not finally abandon the hope of some change which might revive that common action: but it could not be on the side of the Liberals of Great Britain.

Until such change arrived, my position as the Leader of the Liberal Party could not continue as it is.   WEG N. 28. 90.[2]

29. Sat.

All Saints 5 P.M. Astonished by Parnell's reckless and suicidal manifesto.[3] Set to work after breakfast and wrote *my* reply. Wrote also to Mr Mellor—Cardinal Manning. Sixteen to dinner. Saw Mr C. Morley[4]—A. Morley—J. Morley—Mr Stuart MP.—Mr Cook (P.M.G.)—Mr Stuart (Star)[5]—Lucy C.—Spencer L.—Mr S.R.—Herbert—Sir J. Carmichael—Sir W. Harcourt—Ld Granville. Read The Bride—Scott's Journal.

To THE EDITOR OF [blank], 29 November 1890.[6]   Add MS 56449, f. 18.

It is no part of my duty to canvass the manifesto of Mr. Parnell which I have read this morning, and I shall not apply to it a single epithet. For I am not his judge in any matter, and I believe myself to have shown, in the matter of the Pigott Commission, that I had no indisposition to do him justice.

But the first portion of the document consists of a recital of propositions stated to have been made by me to him, and of objections entertained by him to those propositions. The Irish as well as the British public has a right to know whether I admit or deny the accuracy of that recital. And in regard to every one of the four points stated by Mr. Parnell, I at once deny it.

1. The purpose of the conversation was not to make known 'intended proposals'. No single suggestion was offered by me to Mr. Parnell as formal, or as unanimous, or as final. It was a statement perfectly free and without prejudice, of points on which either I myself or such of my colleagues as I had been able to commit, inclined generally to believe that the plan of 1886 for Home Rule in Ireland might be improved, and as to which I was desirous to learn whether they raised any serious objection in the mind of Mr. Parnell.

---

[1] i.e. twice.

[2] Add MS 56449, f. 30; docketed; 'N.28. Mem. made but not used'. Another version with deletions is at ibid., f. 31.

[3] In the press this day, giving Parnell's recollections of the Hawarden conversation, arguing that Gladstone had given it as the 'unanimous opinion' of his colleagues and himself that 'it would be necessary to reduce the Irish representation from 103 to 32', that the Irish legislature would not be given the power of making a land settlement and that pressure would not be put on the liberal party to do so, and that the police would remain under imperial authority but paid for by the Irish; see Lyons, *Fall of Parnell*, appendix I. For Gladstone's notes for and record of the talks, see 18 and 23 Dec. 89.   [4] See 21 Aug. 86n.

[5] E. T. Cook of the *Pall Mall Gazette* and James Stuart, M.P., of the *Star*; see S. Koss, *The rise and fall of the political press in Britain* (1981), i. 309.   [6] Released to the press.

2. To no one of my suggestions did Mr. Parnell offer serious objection: much less did he signify in whole or in part that they augured the proposal of a 'measure which would not satisfy the aspirations of the Irish race.' According to his present account, he received from me in the autumn of 1889 information of vital change, adverse to Ireland, in our plans for Home Rule; and kept this information secret until, in the end of November 1890, and in connection with a totally independent and personal matter, he produces it to the world.

3. I deny, then, that I made the statements which his memory ascribes to me or any thing substantially resembling them, either on the retention of the Irish members or on the settlement of the land or agrarian difficulty, or on the controul of the Constabulary, or on the appointment of the Judiciary. As to land in particular I am not conscious of having added any thing to my public declarations: while as to County Court judges and resident magistrates I made no suggestion what[ever].

4. The conversation between us was strictly confidential: and in my judgment, and as I understood in that of Mr. Parnell, to publish even a true account of it is to break the seal of confidence, which alone renders political cooperation possible.

5. Every suggestion made by me was from written memoranda. The whole purport of my conference was made known by me in the strictest confidence, when it had just taken place, to my colleagues in the Cabinet of 1886; and I assured them that in regard to none of them had Mr. Parnell raised any serious difficulty whatever.

6. Neither Mr. Parnell, nor I myself[,] was bound by this conversation to absolute and final acceptance of the propositions then canvassed: but, during the year which has since elapsed, I have never received from Mr. Parnell any intimation that he had altered his views regarding any of them.

I have now done with the Hawarden conversation and I conclude with the following simple statements.

1. I have always held, in public as private, that the National party of Ireland ought to remain entirely independent of the front bench party of Great Britain.

2. It is our duty, and my duty in particular, conformably to the spirit of Grattan and O'Connell, to study all adjustments in the great matter of Home Rule which may tend to draw to our side moderate and equitable opponents: but for me to propose any measure, except such as Ireland could approve on the lines already laid down, would be fatuity as regards myself, and treachery to the Irish nation in whom even by the side of Mr. Parnell I may claim to take an interest.

30. *Adv. S.*

St James & H.C. 11 A.M. St Thomas 7 P.M. Read Aubrey Moore's Hist. Lect.[1]— Persecution of the Jews in Russia.[2] Wrote to Mr McCarthy. Saw Sir W. Harcourt. Saw Mr McCarthy $2\frac{1}{2}$–$3\frac{1}{2}$ and declined an impossible proposition. Sir A. Clark came for C.

Proposal of Nov. 30.

'Will Mr. Gladstone, Sir W. Harcourt and Mr. Morley entrust Mr. Justin MacCarthy with letters promising that in the event of the return of the Liberal party to power they will introduce a Bill under which

1. The control of the constabulary shall be given to an Irish Executive responsible to an Irish Parliament.

---

[1] A. L. Moore, *Lectures and papers on the history of the Reformation in England* (1890).
[2] J. Jacobs, *The persecution of the Jews in Russia* (1890).

2. Such Parliament shall have power to deal with the Land Question.

3. These shall be *vital* conditions of the Bill which is not to pass without them.'

This was the purport of the written proposal of Mr. M[cCarthy] as written down by me on Mr. M[cCarthy']s quitting us—not a copy.

Mr. M[cCarthy] added two assurances

1. That this was confidential, and under no circumstances to be divulged

2. That power over the Land question meant only in so far as it should not have been disposed of by the Imperial Parliament.

My answer was, with some collateral observations, that I could deal in relation to the Home Rule question only with the Irish Parliamentary party through its leader or those whom it authorised to approach me, whereas Mr. P[arnell] had renounced this party and going from it had assumed a right of appeal to the Irish nation. I therefore had no 'full powers'.

Sir W. Harcourt came in half way & gave a reply arriving at the same point.[1]

Monday December One 1890.

Wrote to Mr Evans (Spital O.H.)—J. Westell—Mr Schnadhorst—J. Ornstein [*sic*]—Messrs Watson—Scotts—Mr E. Evans—The Speaker. Saw Sec. to Mr Cook of P.M.G.—Ld Granville—A. Morley MP—Lucy Cavendish—Mr Smith—Sir W. Harcourt. H. of C. 4–5¼.[2] Dined at Sir C. Forster's. Finished the Bride: loftiest of romances. Read Pommaris on Greece.[3]

2. Tu.

Wrote to M. Pommaris—Archbp Croke—Brough & Sons—Judge O'C. Morris. H. of C. 3½–6¼.[4] Saw J. Westell—Sir C. Russell[5]—Sir C. Russell [*sic*]—A. Morley MP.—Ld Granville. Conclave 12–1 on Irish land: (no J. Morley). Saw Ravenswood at the Lyceum. A striking piece: Miss Terry fine in the great scene. But the Book, the Book![6] Read Scott's Journal. Spoke ½ hour on Land Purchase.

3. Wed.

Wrote to Demetrio Zanini[7]—Mr J. Nicol—Mr Richardson—J. Douglas—Rev. G.A. Crossle. Saw Ld Granville—J. Morley—A. Morley—Prof. Stuart—G.S. Lefevre—& others on Irish matters. H. of C. 2½–6.[8] Dined at Grillion's: saw Ld Derby, Böhme, Ld J. Bowen. Read Scott's Journals—Duffy's Davis.[9]

---

[1] Holograph note, docketed, 'November 30. Memorandum of Conversation with Mr. McCarthy; at 2.30 p.m.'; Add MS 56449, f. 28.

[2] Tithe bill; *H* 349. 241.

[3] Untraced; evidently sent by the author (see next day).

[4] Spoke on Irish land bill; *H* 349. 358.

[5] Parnell's counsel during the Commission 1888–9.

[6] Merivale's dramatisation at the Lyceum of *The Bride of Lammermoor*, with Ellen Terry as Lucy Ashton; she agreed with Gladstone that the adaptation was unsatisfactory, but added: 'I had to lose my poor wits, as in Ophelia, in the last act, and with hardly a word to say I was able to make an effect' (Ellen Terry, *The story of my life* (n.d.), 310).

[7] Demetrio Zanini of Barcelona; see Add MS 44223, ff. 129, 133.

[8] Made interventions on Irish land bill; *H* 349. 484.

[9] C. G. Duffy, *Thomas Davis; the memoirs of an Irish patriot* (1890).

4. *Th.*

Wrote to Card. Manning—Rev. J. Adam—Sir G. Saunders—J.R. Haig[1]—Messrs Power & Deasy.[2] Wrote Mema on the situation. Saw Prof. Stuart—Sir G. Trevelyan—A. Morley—Mr Rendel—Mr Morley—Sir W. Harcourt—Lady Aberdeen—Mr Stansfeld—Mr Bryce—Mr J. Murray. Wrote Mema &c. H. of C. $3\frac{1}{2}$–$5\frac{1}{4}$.[3] Read Scott—Dem[etrios] Bikelas.[4]

The new state of facts.[5]

1. Disclosures in the Divorce Court
   In part *directly* connected with leadership
2. Strong action in the Liberal party
3. My intervention: not as judge, but as witness.
4. Present attitude of Liberal party.
5. No harm to Home Rule in Britain by what has occurred
6. But it may come from Ireland—by reflex action

It is an established and legitimate custom ⟨in matters⟩ when measures of importance and difficulty are in course of being considered, reconsidered and matured for the leader of a party if he sees cause to take counsel confidentially with persons of ability and influence, in order to test the suggestions which are before him, and to be assured that their general tendency is not likely to be disapproved.

Such was the position in which I have stood and ought hereafter to stand relatively to the leader of the Irish party.

I speak now of suggestions for developing and improving on an acknowledged basis, which was a. management of Irish affairs by an Irish Parliament b. subject to the supremacy of the Imperial Parlt.

  { a. secured by British strength
  { b. by declaration, and obvious need.[6]

   1. Pledge to Ireland.
    a. In the words
    b. In the facts.

2. MY answer of last Sunday.
   (H. and M.)
⟨2⟩ 3 The Hawarden interview.
4. The Morley letter
5. Unity and independence of the Irish party.
6. For Great Britain the matter is settled. *No* damage.
     Unless reflex.

 The question rests with Ireland.[7]

And pass[?] to my own expressions of opinion upon these communications which represent my views *then and now.*'

---

[1] James Richard Haig of Blairhill, Perthshire; F.S.A. and J.P.

[2] J. Deasy and Richard Power were two of the Irish whips; Deasy left Parnell the previous day, Power remaining with him.

[3] Questions; supplementary estimate for Irish distress; *H* 349. 543.

[4] D. Bikelas, *Seven essays on Christian Greece* (1890).

[5] Holograph dated 'D4'; Add MS 44773, f. 200.

[6] Holograph dated 'D.4'; Add MS 44773, f. 201.

[7] Undated holograph; ibid., f. 202. Docketed: '*Manifesto.*'

[To Irish Whips:] So far as I comprehend the tenor of the letter I have just had the honour to receive, I understand that it is proposed by you to constitute a body consisting of Sir William Harcourt, Mr. John Morley, and myself, which is to deliver to you assurances as to the course which the Liberal Party if in power would take in a future Parliament with regard to two of the many important particulars connected with any plan of Home Rule.

I would on no account attempt to fetter in any way your liberty of communication in any quarter to which you may think proper to address yourselves. But I regret to be unable to enter upon the joint consideration of any matter submitted to me in combination with a selection of my friends and former colleagues which has been made neither by me nor by the Liberal Party of this country. I leave it to you to consider how far this leaves it open to you to prosecute further your request, and I think it best at the present moment to abstain from touching on any point except the one I have just raised.[1]

5. *Fr.*

Wrote to A. Morley .... and in evg to the Irish Whips. Saw A. Morley—Mr Whitbread—Mr Childers—Mr Morley—Sir W. Harcourt—Mr [E.T.] Cook's Sec. Conclave at $11\frac{3}{4}$ in preparation for Irish Dep. who came at $12\frac{1}{2}$ & staid $1\frac{1}{4}$ hour. They went away with *some* hope—but not much. Wrote Mem. & read to them. Wrote subsequent Mem. Conclave of colleagues &c. at 6: a hesitating letter I had prepared was approved with some changes of expression. H. of C. $3\frac{3}{4}$–7.[2] Read as yesterday.

1. I agree with Sir William Harcourt (see his letter of the 2nd) in holding the opinion that the present time, when the Irish party is so far as I know without a head is ⟨not a convenient time⟩ wholly unsuitable for discussing the particulars of a plan of Home Rule. I consider that such discussion of particulars at such a time could not but be injurious to the Irish cause.
2. Much less could it in my opinion be advantageous to discuss two particular points selected from a number of others equally ⟨important⟩ vital which it is not proposed now to elucidate.
3. The grounds alleged for the selection is a difference of recollection as to the interview at Hawarden. I recognise no such difference. I can say or do nothing which implies that the general purpose of that interview is in doubt. Besides my own recollections and written notes, and the recollections of my former colleagues founded thereon, I rely on the recollections of Mr. Parnell himself conveyed in conversations with one or more individuals, and in public speeches both immediately after the visit and again when several months had elapsed.
⟨4. If any word or act of mine can be cited to show that I have receded in any way from any of the principles heretofore laid down by me and accepted on behalf of Ireland by her representatives: above all if it could be shown that I was chargeable with the guilt and folly of forgetting my duty never to be a party to proposing any measure of Home Rule except such as Ireland could accept on the principles already laid down, then indeed I should gladly offer any explanation in my power to the Irish party even in the present anomalous and exceptional circumstances.⟩
5. In my view compliance with the request made to me would strike a blow at the sacred-

---

[1] Secretary's copy, docketed in Gladstone's hand 'D.4. To Irish Whips'; Add MS 56449, f. 67.
[2] Spoke on death of the Speaker's wife; *H* 349. 665.

ness of confidential communications which alone renders political cooperation possible, and at the vital interests of Ireland in connection with the question of self-government.

It is with deep regret that I decline a request proceeding from a large meeting of the Irish members but they will be the first to feel that I cannot transfer to them any trust which I hold from the Liberal Party of Great Britain.[1]

To Irish Whips: I have the honour to acknowledge the receipt of your letter transmitting to me two Resolutions of the Irish Parliamentary party.

By the first of these Resolutions, the subject of our correspondence is entirely detached from connection with the conversation at Hawarden.

In the second I am requested to receive a deputation which besides stating the views of the party is to request an intimation of my views and those of my colleagues as to certain details connected with the subject of the settlement of the Irish Land Question, and with the controul of the Irish Constabulary forces in the event of the establishment of an Irish Legislature.

As your letter reached me during the early hours of the sitting of the House, I have had the opportunity of learning the views of my colleagues in regard to such a declaration of intention on two out of the many points which may be regarded as vital to the construction of a good measure of Home Rule.

I may be permitted to remind you as I mentioned to the deputation this morning that the question raised by the publication of my letter to Mr. Morley was a question of leadership, and that it is separate from and has no proper connection with the subject of Home Rule.

We have arrived at the conclusion that I cannot undertake to make any statement of our joint intentions on these or any other provisions of a Home Rule Bill in connection with the question of the leadership of the Irish party. When the Irish party shall have disposed of this question which belongs entirely to their own competence in such a manner as will enable me to resume the former relations it will be my desire to enter without prejudice into confidential communication such as has heretofore taken place, as occasion may serve, upon all amendment of particulars and suggestion of improvement in any plan for a measure of Home Rule.

I may venture to assure you that no change has taken place in my desire to press forward on the first favourable opportunity a just and effective measure of Home Rule. I recognise and earnestly seek to uphold the independence of the Irish Parliamentary party no less than that of the Liberal party. I acknowledge with satisfaction the harmony which since 1886 has prevailed between them and when the present difficulty is resolved I am aware of no reason to anticipate its interruption. From what has taken place on both

---

[1] Undated holograph, Add MS 56449, f. 33. The Home Rule M.P.s meeting in Committee Room 15 this day passed Clancy's amndt. (proposed the previous day) that, in the light of the 'difference of opinion . . . as to the accuracy of Mr. Parnell's recollection' of the Hawarden conversation, the Irish whips should obtain from Gladstone, Morley and Harcourt their views on control of the constabulary and the settlement of the land question; Sexton, T. M. Healy, J. Redmond and Leamy were chosen as delegates. Harcourt and Morley both replied to the Irish invitation that any interview should be with Gladstone alone, as their party leader; see Lyons, *Fall of Parnell*, 135 ff.

This mem. appears to be that used by Gladstone as the basis of his comments to the deputation, for it is clear that, rather than discuss the police and land, he argued that discussion about recollections of the Hawarden conversations was unacceptable. The deputation retired and this afternoon Clancy's amndt. was replaced by one omitting reference to the conversations. The whips wrote again to Gladstone but in the meantime his discussions with the other liberal leaders led to the views incorporated in the letter to the Irish whips printed next; see Lyons, *Fall of Parnell*, 143.

sides [of] the Channel in the last four years I look forward with confidence as do my colleagues to the formation of and prosecution of a measure which in meeting all the just desires of Ireland will likewise obtain the approval of the people of Great Britain. I shall at all suitable times prize the principle of free communication with the Irish National party. And I will finally remind you of my declaration this evening that apart from personal confidence there is but one guarantee which can be of real value to Ireland. It is that recently pointed out by Sir William Harcourt in his letter of Dec. 2 when he called attention to 'the unquestionable political fact that no party and no leader could even propose or hope to carry any scheme of Home Rule which had not the cordial concurrence and support of the Irish nation as declared by their representatives in Parliament.'

After this statement of my views and those of my colleagues I anticipate that you will concur with me in the opinion that there would be no advantage in a further personal interview.[1]

6. Sat.

Wrote to Mr Gardner—Mr A. Morley. Went in evg to Princess's Theatre for Antony & Cleopatra.[2] Saw Mr A. Morley's Sec.—Mr Rendel—Miss Childers—Mr A. Morley—Ld Granville—Mr Stuart l.l.—Mr [blank]—Mrs Langtry—Mr Peel. Read Bikelas[3]—Antony & Cleopatra (all). Received in evg the accounts of the great Denouement in the Irish party.[4]

Written tentatively after the Deputation of Dec. 5 to see whether it was possible to 'do something' in aid of the *44* majority.

Not liked by Harcourt, Morley, Childers.

Superseded by the communication from the Irish received between 5 and ½ past 5 which desired to be informed of the intentions of myself and my colleagues on the specified points.[5]

7. 2 S. Adv.

Chapel Royal at noon with H.C. Smatterings of cold have been upon me & I went out no more. Saw Mr A. Morley—Mr Stuart—Ld Granville—H.J.G. Read Hosea & Amos[6]—Aubrey Moore, 16th Cent.

8. M.

Wrote to Mr J. Cowan—Mr Peel[7]—Miss Wallis—J.T. Knowles—G. Russell. H. of C. 3½–7.[8] Except this, I kept the house. Saw Mr Peel—H.J.G.—A. Mor-

[1] Holograph draft, dated 5 December 1890; Add MS 56449, f. 93. Docketed 'Sent off 7¾ PM'.

[2] Lillie Langtry as Cleopatra; attacked by the critics for being too long.

[3] See 4 Dec. 90.

[4] At about 4.30 p.m., McCarthy closed the debate in Committee Room Fifteen by suggesting 'that all who think with me at this grave crisis should withdraw with me from this room'; forty-four M.P.s followed him out; Lyons, *Fall of Parnell*, 148.

[5] Holograph; Add MS 56449, f. 97. This note evidently refers to a lost mem. Its reference to the '44' relates it to this day.

[6] i.e. the books of the Old Testament.

[7] Letter of support to R. Peel on adoption as liberal candidate for Marylebone; *T.T.*, 22 December 1890, 11b.

[8] Questions; Irish land; *H* 349. 710.

ley—Mr Stuart—Ld Granville—J. Morley. Read Bikelas—Miss Chapman on Divorce.[1]

9. Tu.

Wrote to Miss Chapman—C. Gregory—D. Francoudi—Sir W. Marling—Rev. G. Curry. Read Pompery, La Morale[2]—Bikelas (finished)—Paul Wentworth's Repentance.[3] Saw Mr A. Morley—Mr Godley—Mr Knowles—Herbert—Mr L. Harcourt—Sir A. Clark—Mrs Sands—Mrs Th.—Canon Scott Holland.

10. Wed.

St Marg. 1¼ PM. Special. Wrote to M. de Pompery—Rev. Aitchison—A. Morley —Mad. Novikoff—Miss Edwards—Mrs Chambers—Dr Luccock. Dined at Sir A. West's. Saw H.N.G. (house plans R.)—Mr Wilfrid Ward—Mr A. Morley—Divers [persons]—L. Harcourt—Mr M'Coll—Herbert—Mr B. Currie. Read Scott—Wentworth's Repentance.

11. Th. [Hawarden]

Off at 9.30 in dense fog. Hawarden 4½ by Retford say 230 m. Spoke at Retford—with total absence of order—and at Worksop to a large & most orderly meeting, for Bassetlaw.[4] Saw J. Morley—A. Morley—Mr Pollet. Read Paul Thornton:[5] and at Hawarden a lot of tracts of various kinds.

12. Fr.

Wrote to Mr Bunting Tel.—Mr Lawrence[6]—C.H. Sharp[7]—H.E. Tregellas[8]—Mrs Cockle[9]—J. Gilfillan—J.S. Keltie[10]—A.S. Gladstone—Rev. Fisher. Ch. 8½ A.M. Saw WHG—S.E.G. Read Lawrence on Tobacco—Cockle's Poems—Sharp's Poems—Tregellas, plays—Keltie, Geography—The Princess's Secret[11]—&c.

13. Sat.

Ch. 8½ A.M. Still bitter cold. Wrote to Wms & Norgate—J. Westell—H.C. Trumbull—J. Nicol—C.A.G. Bridge[12]—Scotts—J.H. Mitchell—J. Haywood—Herbert

---

[1] The Moral Reform Union pamphlet whose preparation Gladstone had assisted; see 8 Jan. 90.

[2] E. de Pomery had sent his *La morale naturelle et la religion de l'humanité* (1891).

[3] C. Smith, *The repentance of Paul Wentworth. A novel*, 3v. (1889).

[4] Where there was a by-election; *T.T.*, 12 December 1890, 7e. This personal appearance by Gladstone (rather than the usual letter) was unprecedented. See 16 Dec. 90.

[5] Untraced.

[6] Had sent a work on tobacco (see this day); untraced.

[7] Possibly Charles Henry Sharpe, Roman catholic and sender of poems (see this day); but the work untraced.

[8] A. E. Tregelles, *King James I. A drama* (1890) and *Queen Elizabeth. A drama* (1890).

[9] Mrs Rita F. Moss Cockle had sent her *The Golden guest and other poems* (1890).

[10] (Sir) John Scott Keltie, 1840-1927, geographer and ed. *The Statesman's Year Book*, had sent his *Applied geography* (1890).

[11] Mrs. H. Sutherland Edwards, *The secret of the princess; a tale of life in Russia*, 2v. (1890-1).

[12] (Sir) Cyprian Arthur George Bridge, 1839-1924, sailor; director of Admiralty intelligence 1889-94; had sent Mahan's *Sea power*; Hawn P. See this day.

J.G.—D.F. Howorth. Read Huxley's Art. in N.C.[1]—The Secret of the Princess—Influence of Sea Power.[2] Cold gathering force.

14.

Kept my bed all day. Private Readings. Also read Milman's Hist. Jews (largely).[3]—God in His World (pretentious)[4]—and . . . .

15. M.

Bed until evg. Carried on my readings & searchings about Josephus and the Palaestinian geography. Also read all Vol II of the Secret of the Princess.
How sad the picture which Ireland presents.[5]

16. Tu.

Rose at 11: cold better. Wrote to Mr J. Nicol l. & P.P.—Abp. Canterbury—A. Morley MP—Sec. Treasury—E.W. Hamilton—Mr Mundella—G. Harding BP—P.H. Patterson—Watsons BP—Canon MacColl—A.H. Hutton.
Bassetlaw defeat. A lesson: but the reading of it not yet clear.[6] Read Old Edinburgh[7]—Searching Josephus, Eusebius, Calmat Palestinian Maps, & other sources. Also worked in Josephus, not easy to follow the Gadara case.

17. Wed.

Rose at 10. Walk in aftn. Wrote to Lady Aberdeen—D. of Argyll—Sir J. Carmichael—Mrs Nichol—Mr Allison MP.[8]—T.E. Young. J. Morley spent some hours here. The case in Ireland is very dark & uncertain: as it is also strange & unexampled. But God reigneth. Read (Friends) Examiner on the Gothenburg system[9]—Argyll on Huxley[10]—Guy Mannering[11]—Josephus.

---

[1] T. H. Huxley, 'The keepers of the herd of swine', *N.C.*, xxviii. 967 (December 1890); a strong attack on Gladstone's biblical criticism.

[2] A. T. Mahan, *The influence of sea power upon history 1660-1783* (1889).

[3] See 13 May 30.

[4] H. M. Alden, *God in his world. An interpretation* (1890).

[5] In the Kilkenny by-election Parnell had persuaded Barry O'Brien to stand against the previously agreed Home Rule candidate, Sir J. Pope-Hennessy; Vincent Scully eventually took O'Brien's place. The election speeches confirmed the bitter split in the Home Rule party; see Lyons, *Fall of Parnell*, 154 ff.

[6] The liberals failed to gain Bassetlaw at the by-election on 15 December; in 1886 the tory had been unopposed; in 1885 he had won by 295 votes.

[7] A. H. Dunlop, *Anent old Edinburgh* (1889).

[8] (Sir) Robert Andrew Allison, 1838-1926; classicist, railway director and temperance advocate; liberal M.P. N. Cumberland 1885-1900.

[9] Not found; on drink control; probably sent by Allison.

[10] See 27 Feb. 87.

[11] By Scott; see 5 Dec. 48.

18. Th.

Ch. 8½ A.M. May I be permitted to keep it up. Wrote to Mad. Novikoff—Dr Ginsburg—J.W. R[obertson] Scott. Began a Reply to Huxley.[1]—Read Josephus—Guy Mannering—Lady Lindsay's Poems.[2]

19. Fr.

Ch. 8½ AM. (Snow). Wrote to Mr J. W. Mellor—Mr A. Morley—W. Abbots—H. Patterson—Mr Knowles—G. Farquharson. Wrote on Gadara & the swine. Read Josephus—Guy Mannering—Grellet's Memoirs[3] Divers tracts.

20. Sat.

Ch. 8½ A.M. 18 degr. frost. Day cold & fine. Wrote to Mr E.N. Buxton[4]—Sir A. Gordon—Rev. Dr. Whyte—Mr George's Sons. Worked on anti-Huxley paper. Read Grellet's Memoirs—Guy Mannering—Josephus, further—Robinson, Holy Land.[5]

21. 4 S. Adv.

Frost 28°: the coldest I remember here. Ch 11 A.M. only. Worked on Gadara. Read Grellet—Aubrey Moore Reformn[6]—Shipley Euch. Devotions[7]—Poems of V——, new Edn[8]—Momerie Sermons on Evil.[9]

22. M.

Ch. 8½ A.M. Wrote to Mr Gardner. Wrote on Gadara; & worked at Strabo, Robinson, Williams, Milman, & others. Read Marq. Brady papers[10]—Guy Mannering. 12 to dinner & Backgammon with Mr Banks.

23. Tu.

Ch. 8½ AM. Wrote to Cardinal Manning—Mr Schnadhorst—Mr Morley—A.E. Cropper[11]—Mr Nicol—W.E. Hodgson—J.H. Frank—Canon Lonsdale[12]—F. Wills[13]

[1] 'Professor Huxley and the swine-miracle', *N.C.*, xxix. 339 (February 1891).

[2] Lady C. B. E. Lindsay, *Lyrics and other poems* (1890).

[3] *Memoirs of the life and gospel labours of S. Grellet*, ed. B. Seebohm, 2v. (1860).

[4] Edward North Buxton, 1840-1924; sportsman and educationalist; also writing for the *N.C.* February number.

[5] W. C. Robinson, *Pilgrim's Jerusalem* (1890).

[6] See 30 Nov. 90.

[7] O. Shipley, *Eucharistic litanies from ancient sources* (1860).

[8] See 17 Oct. 85.

[9] A. W. Momerie, *The origin of evil and other sermons* (1881).

[10] W. M. Brady, *Anglo-Roman papers* (1890).

[11] Probably a member of the liberal family in Westmorland.

[12] John Gylby Lonsdale, 1818-1907; canon of Lichfield from 1855.

[13] Probably (Sir) Frederick Wills, 1838-1909; tobacco merchant; contested seats as liberal unionist in 1890s; M.P. N. Bristol 1900-6; cr. bart. 1897.

—Miss Emerton—K. Moore. Worked on Gadara. Read S. Grellet—Guy Mainwaring [*sic!*]—Memoirs of Erskine.[1]

24.

Ch. 8½ A.M. Wrote to Rev. E.S. Hilliard[2]—J. Westell—Messrs Wheatley—G.R.
Read—Rev. J. Hastings—W.S. Dalgleish. Worked on Gadara. Read Grellet—Guy
Mannering—Memoirs of Erskine.

25. *Th. Xmas.*

Church with H.C. 11 AM. Again 7 PM. Worked on Gadara.[3] I think I am
emerging from the puzzle: and it is for the honour of our Lord. Read Milman—
Josephus—Grellet—Syme on Organisms (very able?)[4]

26. *Fr. St. Stephen*

Ch. 8½ AM. Wrote to Wms & Norgate—Ld Coleridge—T.H. Elliot—A. Morley
MP—Rev. W. Benham—J. Nicol—S. Criglington—J.P. Rafter—J. Todhunter—Ed.
Astrolog. Magazine[5]—J. Truslove. Worked on Gadara. *Began* reducing my room
to a little order. Read Guy Mannering—Cardinal Erskine—and S. Grellet Vol. II.

27. *Sat. St John.*

Church A.M. Holy Comm. A great season, amidst the grave exterior trials.
Wrote to Secy of Treasury—Ld Acton—Messrs Powell—Mr Blaik—Edr Xtn
Union—W. Naismith—W. Mitchell—S. Lloyd—Mrs Dugdale—A. Reid—Rev.
Kavanagh.[6] Worked on Gadara. Finished delightful Guy Mannering. Read
Grellet—Question d'Irlande.[7]

28. *H. Inn. & 1 S. Xm.*

Ch. 11 A.M. and [blank] P.M. Wrote to Dr Ginsburg—Mr Knowles—Mrs Th.
Read Schürer Geschichte[8]—Grellet—Fiske, Idea of God.[9]

29. *M.*

Ch. 8½ A.M. Wrote to Prince of Wales—Ld Ripon—Abp of Cashel—The Mentmore Children[10]—Mad. Novikoff BP—J. Cornish—Rev. Dr Kinns—Mr Hayman.

---

[1] 'Memoirs of Cardinal Erskine, Papal envoy to ... George III, part 3 of Brady's *Anglo-Roman papers* (see 22 Dec. 90n.).

[2] Ernest Stafford Hilliard, secretary of East London Church Fund 1887–91; on conditions in the East End; Hawn P.

[3] See 18 Dec. 90.

[4] D. Syme, *On the modification of organisms* (1891).

[5] Not found published; it carried a monthly horoscope of the famous but does not seem to have included Gladstone.

[6] James Daniel Kavanagh, chaplain of Exeter hospital.

[7] Perhaps T. Fortin d'Ivry, *Question d'Irlande. O'Connell* (1843).

[8] E. Schürer, *Geschichte des Jüdischen Volke im Zeitalter Jesu Christi*, 2v. (1890).

[9] See 28 Sept. 90.

[10] i.e. the motherless Rosebery children, who had probably sent birthday good-wishes.

Went at 12.40 to the 'Inauguration'. There were I suppose 2000 there, in this wild season. I made a short speech.[1] At 7 to the Concert. Worked on Gadara. Read S. Grellet—How half the World lives.[2] Wrote a Mem. on the altered outlook. But the Lord God Omnipotent reigneth.

The feelings which the return of my birthday brings in connection with the last solemn account, are hardly fit to be projected into written words, and if I sometimes put down anything of the kind it is with a sense that it must seem and may be unreal, not a transcript of what is in the heart but so to speak a work of art and man's desire.

However, apart from that innermost circle of thought, the present birthday has brought with it a great and at first view a severe change in the prospects of my remaining life.

All my life long I have cherished from day to day the idea of
    'Some space between the theatre and the grave[']'[3]
substituting for theatre the far more formidable detention of the contentious life of Parliament such as I have known it. In 1874, 5, 6, until in the fall of that last year the Eastern Question became inexorable in its calls upon me, I thought my object had been gained. On the back of this the urgency of the Irish Question and of the franchise. When that last was settled in 1885 and the Government dismissed, the Irish Question again came up in a new and advanced form, and seeming to see my way to a settlement after the present Parliament I devoted myself to the pursuit of it. From eighty five to ninety we have fought that battle with two fully organised parties, each of them compact and determined, allied together yet independent of each other. In Ireland the Nationalists were to hold their ground; in Great Britain we were to convert on the first Dissolution our minority into a large majority and in the Autumn of 1890 we had established the certainty of that result so far as an event yet contingent could be capable of ascertainment.

Then came the sin of Tristram with Isault[4] and the discovery with this of much that they did not wot of. Then came the precipitate re-acceptance of Mr. Parnell in Ireland: the Liberal resistance in England: my announcement that if Mr. Parnell continued to be leader, our army would be no longer available for carrying Home Rule: the retreat of the Irish from their false position, hampered by the skill and immeasurable immorality of the Parnell tactics; his violent resistance: and the picture of a divided Ireland, the two sections in fierce conflict together before a deriding foe.

The case is not hopeless: but the probable result of so scandalous an

---

[1] Inauguration of the Gladstone Memorial Fountain in the centre of Hawarden (still there today); *T.T.*, 30 December 1890, 5e.

[2] J. A. Riis, *How the Other Half lives: studies among the poor* (1890); trail-blazing commentary on New York life, with remarkable photographs.

[3] 'Between the cradle and the grave', from John Dyer, *Grongar Hill* (1726).

[4] Gladstone had not seen Wagner's opera. His knowledge of the legend came from reading A. C. Swinburne, *Queen Yseult* (1858) (see 18 June 73) and Tennyson's 'The last tournament' (1872) in *Idylls of the King* (frequently read). He was also probably familiar with Matthew Arnold's *Tristram and Iseult* (1852), though he does not record reading it.

exhibition will be confusion and perplexity in the weaker minds, and doubt whether while this conflict continues Ireland can be considered to have reached a state capable of beneficial self-government. The case is not that of Parnell as the accepted leader: he has been deposed. But his desperate struggles to regain the post and his pretended appeal to the people have received countenance sufficient to make him at the moment a formidable rebel against Parliamentary Government, supported by about as many members as he led in 1880. This is enough to introduce into our position a dangerous uncertain[ty]. We may if things do not go decisively well in Ireland lose hold of that margin which in the constituencies spans the space between victory and defeat. Home Rule *may* be postponed for another period of five or six years. The struggle in that case must survive me, cannot be survived by me. The dread life of Parliamentary contention reaches outwards to the grave.

This change of prospect hits me hard. I was desiring from 1885 onwards to hope to see this battle fought, and yet have a moment of repose to draw my robe around me shall I say, nay but to detach and adjust my soul after it has been for nearly sixty years under the master-violence of politics. Lord Byron with the insight of genius described them as one of the two superlative pursuits that enchain and engross the minds of men. Shakespeare with a yet deeper insight wrote:

'O 'tis a burden, Cromwell, tis a burden
Too heavy for the soul that hopes for heaven'[1]

Undoubtedly it is a new and aggravated condition of my life if I am finally to resign all hope of anything resembling a brief rest on this side the grave.

I can well understand, indeed an inward voice makes reply, that that rest is a privilege and 'thou hast not earned it: hast not reached the condition which qualified you to rise to a higher spiritual level with the aid of recollection and detachment: could at best be suitable for nothing but to struggle onwards in the "lower room"'.

Yet both the duty of submission and the place for faith are clear. It may not be so, but if it be so, then it is rightly so. My hope to emerge from contentious life was based on pride and on blindness: He who sees all sees fit to quench it. There is indeed even yet more place for humility. This change has come about without my agency. It is my duty of course to preserve the brightness and freshness of our hopes as they stood a couple of months back. It is lawful to pray for success in this endeavour: but it is obligatory to pray also for meekness so as to be prepared for failure—fiat, laudetur, superexaltetur κτλ.[2]

WEG D. 29. 90.

[P.S.] This is a paper of reflex and solitary views. It does not represent but neither does it exclude the consciousness that this question affects millions, and that millions are more than one.   WEG D. 90.[3]

---

[1] Shakespeare, *Henry VIII*, iii. 2; a repeated quotation, see 24 July 80 (fly leaf) etc.

[2] 'May He come to be, may He be praised, may He be glorified etc.'.

[3] Holograph; the *post script* was apparently written at the same time as the text; Add MS 56447, f. 105.

30. Tu.

Ch. 8½ A.M. Wrote Circular letter to the Press.[1] Also to J. Morley l.l.—Wms & Norgate. Busy on revision of reply to Huxley. Arranged letters. Conversation on question of a move for C.G. Read S. Grellet—How half the World &c.—Erskine's Memoirs.

31. Wed.

Ch. 8½ A.M. Wrote to Duke of Argyll—Marq. of Bute—Rev. T.T. Carter—Dean of Wells—Mr A. Morley—Mr Knowles—Mr Edgar. Worked to finish Gadara, and dispatched it.[2] Read Quaker Home[3]—Card. Erskine's Memoirs.

[1] The usual public thanks for birthday greetings; *T.T.*, 31 December 1890, 5d.
[2] See 18 Dec. 90.
[3] C. E. Stephen, *Quaker strongholds* (1890).

Thurs. Circumcision Jan. 1. 91.

Church 8½ A.M. with H.C. Wrote to Mr J. Morley l.l.—Postmistress Hn—J. Simpson—Prov. of Oriel—Mr J.H. Bell—Mr Labouchere—Mr Byles[1]—Sir J. Lambert—Dr Angus—King of the Belgians—Mr Wemyss Reid. Read Beeton Xtn Relig.[2]—Schloss on Jewish Workmen[3]—Quaker Home[4]—Schreiner Dreams[5]—Madlle Ixe[6]—and Art. on Odyssey.

2. Fr.

Ch. 8½ A.M. Wrote to Sir W. Harcourt—Mr R. Brett—Prof. J. J. Johnson—Mrs Stumes—Mr J.M. Miller—Mr J. Grant—Gerald Massey—G.R. Reid—Mr G. Hagopian. Worked on arr. books & papers. Went to meet Fasque party[7] at Sandycroft. Read Madlle Ixe—Quaker Home—Present position (Lib. Diss.).[8] Backgammon with Lady G.

3. Sat.

Ch. 8½ A.M. Wrote to The Lord Mayor—Greek Minister—Mr J.H. Bell—Sir W. Gregory—Mrs Th.—Mr H. Rathbone. Worked on letters papers & accounts. Read Quaker Home—Finlayson on Koheleth.[9] Worked in New Library.

4. 2 S. Xm.

Ch 11 AM and H.C.: also 6.30 P.M. Wrote to Madame Schliemann—Bishop of Cork—Mr Pitman. Read Grellet[10]—Bp of Cork's Sermon—Dean of Lincoln's do[11]—Ballard (Wesleyan)[12]—Mitchell, Testimonies on Xty[13]—various other Tracts—Miss Small on Zenana Life.[14]

5. M.

Ch. 8½ A.M. Wrote to Ld Carrington—Mr Furness l.l. (& *drafts*)[15]—Ld Granville—Miss Tennant—Geo. Butler—Sig. Riccioni—M. Bourdache—W. Macdou-

---

[1] (Sir) William Pollard Byles, 1839–1917; journalist and liberal M.P. Shipley 1892–5; kt. 1911.
[2] S. O. Beeton, *Illustrated dictionary of religion* (1886).
[3] D. F. Schloss, 'The Jew as workman', *N.C.*, xxix. 96 (January 1891).
[4] See 31 Dec. 90.   [5] Olive Schreiner, *Dreams* (1891).
[6] [M. E. Hawker], *Mademoiselle Ixe: a novel* (1891).   [7] Gladstone relatives visiting the Castle.
[8] Possibly C. MacKay, 'The liberal party, its present position and future work' (1880).
[9] T. C. Finlayson, *The meditations and maxims of Koheleth* (1887).   [10] See 19 Dec. 90.
[11] W. J. Butler, 'What is our present danger? A sermon'.
[12] F. Ballard, *What are Churches for? A modern religious inquiry*, 2v. (1890–1).
[13] Probably W. Mitchell, *Story of the crucifixion* (1890).
[14] A. H. Small, *Light and shade in Zenana missionary life* (1890).
[15] Christopher Furness, 1852–1912; shipping owner and liberal M.P. Hartlepool Jan. 1891–5, 1900–10. Draft of letter of support and on Parnell at Add MS 44773, f. 211; printed version in *T.T.*, 12 January 1891, 7f. See also this day's letter denying Capt. Price's charge in Devonport that Gladstone offered Parnell, during the divorce case, a Cabinet seat in the next liberal government; *T.T.*, 9 January 1891, 7f; drafts at Add MS 44773, f. 211 and 44512, f. 25ff.

gal—Dr Conolly. Much thought & conversation about letter to Hartlepool. Worked on books: also at St Deiniol's. Read S. Grellet—Quaker Home. Saw Mr Mayhew.

6. *Epiph. Tu.*

Ch. 8½ A.M. and H.C. My dearest wife's birthday. How safe she is with her pure true noble character. Wrote to Sir W. Harcourt—Mr Morley—Mr Bunting—M. Léon Séché[1]—Mr Murray—Principal Cirenc. Coll.[2]—Miss Cardwell (U.S.) Saw the Rector on the Interm. School question. Read Derniers Jansénistes—Quaker Home—Butler Translations[3]—S. Grellet (finished).

7. *Wed.*

Ch. 8½ A.M. Wrote to Mr Mayhew—Mr Stansfeld—Mr Lefevre—Master of Trinity. Worked at St Deiniol's. Read L. Séché (Jansenistes)—A Quaker Home—Histoire Diplomatique.[4]

8. *Th.*

Ch. 8½ A.M. Wrote to Mr Labouchere MP—Mr Vickers—Mr Furness Tel.—Rev. M'Lellan—S.G. Reid—C.G. Banks—J. Edgar—Vote Office—Mr Morley. Correcting Gadara.[5] Worked at St Deiniol's. Read Derniers Jensénistes—Dunckley's Melbourne.

9. *Fr.*

Ch. 8½ A.M. Wrote to Mr Davenport Adams—Ld Acton—Mr Storey MP—Mr Morley—Chairman Lpool Jun. Ref. Club.[6] Worked at St Deiniol's. A little Josephus—read Séché—Dunckley's Melbourne.[7] Sir A. West came. Conversation.

10 *Sat.*

Ch. 8½ A.M. Wrote to Mr Stansfeld MP—Gen. Cesnola—Hon. A. Brand—Mr Leake MP. Drive walk conversation with West. Further work on proofs. Read McCarthy's Peel[8]—Derniers Jansenistes—Lecky on Ireland (NAR)[9]—Dunckley's Melbourne.

[1] See 29 Aug. 77; had sent his *Les derniers Jansénistes* (1891).
[2] Rev. J. B. McClennan, principal of Royal Agricultural College, Cirencester.
[3] *'Crossing the Bar' and a few other translations. By H.M.B.* [*G. M. Butler*] (1890).
[4] A. Debidour, *Histoire diplomatique de l'Europe . . . 1814-1878*, 2v. (1891).
[5] See 18 Dec. 90.
[6] Untraced.
[7] H. Dunckley, *Lord Melbourne* (1890); recommended by Margot Tennant, Add MS 44512, f. 6.
[8] J. McCarthy, *Sir Robert Peel* (1890).
[9] W. E. H. Lecky, 'Ireland in the light of history', *North American Review*, clii. 11 (January 1891).

11. *1 S. Epiph.*

Ch 11 AM 6½ PM. Wrote to A.W. Hutton—Mr Knowles. Wrote a few notes on the [St. Deiniol's] Trust. Some more revision of Gadara. Read Lawson Pulpit Oratory[1]—Rev. [blank] on Inspiration[2]—Derniers Jansénistes—Tracts.

12. *M.*

Ch. 8¼ A.M. Wrote to Vicar St Martin's—J. Morley—Capt. Price MP[3]—W.T. Stead—J.R. Adams—W.A. Gray—H.M. Sherriff—J.J. Spencer—P.M.G. Telegr. Worked at St Deiniol's. Read Wesley Orig. Sin[4]—Dunckley's Melbourne— Derniers Jansénistes. Mr Temple dined.

13. *Tu.*

Ch. 8¼ A.M. Wrote to Miss Balfour—Mr Morley MP—Mr Williamson—J.A. Barclay—Mr Buzzard—A.S. Thomson—C.P. Dykes. Worked at St Deiniol's. A real? break in the frost. Read Wesley, Orig. Sin—Borlase, Reduction of Ireland[5]— Dunckley's Melbourne (finished)—Stoppani on Genesis (in the Rassegna).[6]

14. *Wed.*

Ch. 8¼ A.M. Wrote to Mr Robertson MP—Mr Morley MP—Jas Wilson— M. d'Eichthal—Edm. Kelly—Lucy Cavendish—Th. Hankey—Mrs Brewster— Rev. Barrow—Rev. Mr Jenkins. Worked at St Deiniol's. Conversation with Herbert before his expedition.[7] Read D'Eichthal on Free Trade[8]—Hist. Dipl. de l'Europe—Rev. Gough on the Incarnation.

15. *Th.*

Ch. 8¼ A.M. 7–8 P.M. Rent dinner & speech.[9] Wrote to Sir J. Lacaita—S. Scho-field—P. Witburn—J.C. Collins—V[ote] Office—E. Phillips—E. Parry—Sir W. Fos-ter MP. Saw Herbert further. Walk with F. Leveson. Read Robroy[10]—Hist. Diplomatique—and [blank.]

16. *Fr.*

Ch. 8½ A.M. Wrote to Rev. J.H. Kennedy—A. Morley MP.—J. Grant—Mr A. Mills—G. Harding—W. Ridler—R. Walker—Mr J.H. Hughes—J.G. Graden.

---

[1] J. Lawson, *Lectures concerning oratory* (1758).
[2] Probably E. Gough, *A defence and definition of verbal inspiration* (1890).
[3] Capt. George Edward Price, 1842–1926; tory M.P. Devonport 1874–92. See 5 Jan. 91n.
[4] J. Wesley, 'A sermon on original sin' (1771).
[5] E. Borlase, *The reduction of Ireland to the Crown of England* (1675).
[6] Probably A. Stoppani, *Sulla Cosmogonia Mosaica* (1887).
[7] Destination untraced.
[8] A. d'Eichthal had sent his *Liberté des échanges et protectionisme* (1890).
[9] Spoke on 'Fifty years of progress'; *T.T.*, 16 January 1891, 8b.
[10] By Scott; see 23 Sept. 57.

Worked on books &c. Read Robroy—Hist. Diplomatique—Memoir of Constance Naden[1]—Edersheim, Life & Times of Christ.[2]

17. Sat.

Ch. 8½ A.M. Wrote to Ed. Figaro[3]—Mons. Angot[4]—J.G. Greig—Capt. Petrie—Mr Cotgreave. Wrote annual statement of property for Jan. 1. Worked at St D's. Read Robroy—Debidour's Hist. Diplom.—and Sermon on Distary [sic] Laws.

18. 2 S. Epiph.

Ch. 11 AM 6½ PM. Wrote to J. Morley—A. Morley. Read Memoir of C. Naden—Newman's Letters[5]—Modificn of Organisms.[6] Corrected revise of Art. on Swine Miracle.[7]

19. M.

Ch. 8½ A.M. Wrote to Sir W. Harcourt—Ld Granville—Mr Knowles—Mr F. Harrison—Rev. Mr Howell—W.A. Hargreaves—U. Maggs—Rev. Page Hopps—T.C. Horsfall—Mrs Daniell. Worked at St Deiniol's. Saw W. Bailey—E. Wickham (from L[incol]n). Read Robroy—Debidour's Hist. Dipl.—Newman's Letters.

20. Tu.

Ch. 8½ A.M. Wrote to Miss Fitzgerald 1 & BP[8]—J. Morley MP—O.T. Bilkeley—A. Morley MP—Sir T. Acland—Mr Storey MP—J. Westell—Mr Bryce MP—W. Griffin—Dr H.M. Jones[9]—Mr Horniman Tel. Walk with Canon M'Coll & E. Wickham. Conversation on Gadara. Worked on books. Read Robroy—Newman's letters—Ruskin-Horsfall on Beauty.[10] Backgammon with S. Wrote notes on the situation.

1. as I have already stated I can give no pledges in the matter before us on behalf of the Liberal party.
2. Least of all could I give any such pledge, where the particulars of Home Rule are treated with reference to any prospective arrangement with reference to the leadership of the Irish party.
4. [sic] As to my own opinions, I hold them on particular points with reference to their respective merits, but I hold them subject to the consideration of what the general interests of the questions may require.

[1] *Further reliques of Constance Naden*, ed. G. M. McCrie (1891).
[2] A. Edersheim, *The life and times of Jesus the Messiah*, 2v. (1883).
[3] Not found published.　　　　　　　　　　　　　　　　　　[4] Name scrawled.
[5] *Letters and correspondence of J. H. Newman, during his life in the English Church*, ed. Anne Mozley, 2v. (1891).
[6] D. Syme, *On the modification of organisms* (1890).　　　　[7] See 18 Dec. 90.
[8] Perhaps Geraldine Penrose Fitzgerald, novelist and writer on Ireland.
[9] Henry Macnaughton Jones, physician in Harley Street; involved in W. H. Gladstone's treatment.
[10] T. C. Horsfall, *The study of beauty and art in large towns . . . with an introduction by John Ruskin* (1883).

5. Subject to these considerations, I am of opinion
a. that the charge of the entire Police of Ireland should be placed under Irish authority at the earliest moment which considerations of practical convenience will permit.
b. As is plain from my speeches in Parliament, that the Land question cannot be closed by the provisions of the present Bill, and that when the Imperial Parliament has had the opportunity of taking such precautions as it deems requisite in respect of the operation of old antipathies between class and class Ireland ought not to be precluded from giving to the measure if her Parliament shall think fit an enlarged extent.
c. That it is both impracticable and unwise to attempt to lay down at the present time particular propositions which are to be declared incapable of any modification.
6. That when the Irish party shall have determined upon its new leader, it will be my desire to enter without prejudice into free and confidential communication with him as occasion may require upon any particulars heretofore proposed which may be thought to require amendment or any suggestions which may appear likely to improve the character of a measure for Home Rule.
7. That I cannot proceed even so far as I have gone under No. 5 of this paper, without saying that I think any discussion of these matters at the present time far from convenient and that the true ultimate course[?][1] for Ireland is that which Sir W. Harcourt has pointed out.[2]

21. Wed.

Ch. 8½ A.M. Wrote to Mr McCarthy MP—Mr Dillon MP.—Mr Mayhew—Ld Granville—W. Mitchell—Mr Fowler MP—Rev. W.H. Brown[3]—Rev. Girdlestone—G. Massey—Mr Horniman Tel.—Dr Wace. Worked on books. Read Robroy—Newman's Letters—A Humble Romance.[4]

22. Th.

Ch. 8½ A.M. Wrote to Central News Tel.[5]—Ld Granville Tel.—G. Spencer—Estate Office—H.N.G.—A.C. Fletcher—Jas Wilson—Rev. S.G. Law—Jas Dodds—Rev. J.H.N. Nevill[6]—Macmillans BP. Saw Mr Mayhew. Worked at St Deiniol's. Read Robroy—Newman's Letters—Virgil Æn ii. Trouble in evg about a quasi-summons to London.[7]

23. Fr.

Ch. 8½ A.M. Wrote to Marquis of Bute—Mr Morley—Ld Granville—Mr A. Morley—Mrs Blyband[?]—Jas Hart—and tel.—J. Noble—Thos Rogers—H.N.G. Tel.—S. Young—Hodgson Pratt—W. Smith jun. Worked at St Deiniol's, & on preparation of all kinds. Read Robroy—Newman's letters—Bickford Autobiogr.[8]

---

[1] Reading of this word uncertain.
[2] Undated holograph; Add MS 56449, f. 98; the basis for the liberal position on 28 Jan. 91.
[3] William Haig Brown, headmaster of Charterhouse.
[4] M. E. Wilkins, *A humble romance and other stories* (1890).
[5] Celebrating the liberal gain in the Hartlepool by-election; *T.T.*, 23 January 1891, 7e.
[6] John Henry Napper Nevill, vicar of Stoke Gabriel, Totnes.
[7] To consider the 'Boulogne negotiations' of early January (between Parnell and O'Brien) and their aftermath; see Lyons, *Fall of Parnell*, 232 and 28 Jan. 91.
[8] *James Bickford: an autobiography of Christian labour* (1890).

24. Sat.

Ch. 8½ A.M. Wrote to Miss A. Mozley[1]—Ld Hampden—Rev. Dr Rigg—J. Lloyd—
T. Mackay[2]—J. Vivian. Packing & setting in order. Read Robroy finished—Newman's Letters I (finished)—and [blank.] Saw Mr Roth. Backgammon with S.E.G.

25. Septua S.

Ch 11 AM 6½ PM. Wrote to Chester Stat. Master—Sig. Monti—E.T. Cook—G.B.
Reed—R. Ahmael [*sic*]—A. Morley. Read Bell's Why &c. a remarkable book[3]—
Puritanism in Power a silly book[4]—Ginsburg on the Essenes[5]—Aubrey Moore
on the Reformation—on Wiclif.[6]

26. M. [*London*]

Ch. 8½ A.M. Saw S.E.G. (St D.). Packing &c. 10¾ Off to Crewe: luncheon. Saw Ld
C. Ld H. & the ladies. London 1 CG at 7. Saw A. Morley—Ld Justice Bowen.
Read Finlayson's Koheleth[7]—Morley Studies in Literature[8]—Lang on Oxford.[9]

27.

Wrote to H. Moore—Mr Mayhew. Saw J. Morley—A. Morley—H.N.G.—Ld Granville—E. Lyttelton—Sir W. Harcourt—Sir G. Trevelyan *cum* Mr Fowler—Mr Whitbread. H of C. 3½–5½. Spoke on the (Bradlaugh) Expunction.[10] Read Morley on
Wordsworth[11]—Wordsworth's Excursion[12]—F. Newman on Cardinal N.[13]

28. Wed.

Wrote to Mr Hankey—Mr [J.] Carvell Williams—C. West. H. of C. 3½–7¼.[14]
Conclave on assurances for the Irish party &c. We shaped a plan.[15] Read

---

[1] Anne Mozley, 1809–91; poet and editor (see 18 Jan. 91n.).

[2] Perhaps Thomas Mackay, 'individualist' writer on social policy.

[3] A. J. Bell, *Why does Man exist?* (1890).

[4] C. Wise [i.e. J. M. Robertson], *Puritanism in power; an argument* (1890).

[5] C. D. Ginsburg, *The Essenes* (1864).

[6] See 30 Nov. 90.

[7] See 3 Jan. 91.

[8] J. Morley, *Studies in literature* (1891); Wordsworth, etc.

[9] A. Lang, *Oxford* (1882).

[10] Successfully supporting the motion that the Resolution of 22 June 1880 recording the refusal to
allow him to take the oath or affirm, be expunged from the Journals of the House; *H* 349. 1166.

[11] See 26 Jan. 90.

[12] See 15 Nov. 33.

[13] F. W. Newman, *Contributions chiefly to the early history of Cardinal Newman* (1891).

[14] Conspiracy Law Amndt. Bill; *H* 349. 1239.

[15] Terms sent to O'Brien in France: Irish land to be settled by the imperial parliament at the time
of home rule, or within a specified subsequent period, or power to be given to the devolved legislature; Royal Irish Constabulary to be replaced with a civil force. Parnell raised various questions
about the details and about Irish M.P.s in the Commons; the liberal leaders declined to alter the
terms further and thus ended 'the last chance Parnell and his opponents were to have for a negotiated settlement which might have preserved the unity of the party, ended the strife in Ireland, left
the Liberal alliance intact, and prepared the way for the next Home Rule Campaign'; see Lyons,
Parnell, ch. 19 and *Fall of Parnell*, 236 ff.

F. Newman (finished)—Mrs Snyder, U.S. Civil War[1]—Morley on Aphorisms.[2] Saw H.N.G. (house)—A. Morley—J. Morley—Stansfeld.

29. Th.

Wrote to Mrs Robertson—Archbp Walsh—Rev. Dr. Paton[3]—Rev. H.D. Brown. Troubled with pain in right hand which impeded work. H. of C. $3\frac{1}{2}$–$6\frac{1}{2}$.[4] Saw A. Morley—L. Harcourt—H.N.G.—Sir J. Carmichael—J. Morley—Mr Fitzgerald.[5] Lyceum for 'Much ado about Nothing'. Saw Mr I. & Miss T.[6] Read Mrs Snyder— Vindex on Gen. Gordon[7]—Consequences.[8]

30. Fr.

Wrote to Mr B. Currie—Mr Stead l.l.—Mr J. Knowles—Mr Bennett. Read Con- sequences—Mrs Snyder & Appx. Luncheon at the Courts with Ld Justice Bowen & very good company. H. of C. 4–$7\frac{1}{4}$.[9] Dined at Mr Hankey's. Conversation with Mr Lidderdale.[10] Saw Mr A. Morley (Irish funds)—Mr Bryce—& others.

31. Sat. [Dollis Hill]

Wrote to Mr A. Grove—Provost of North Berwick—Rev. G. Bainton. Wrote also Jan. 31 to J. Gorsham—Miss Balls [sic]—C. Cheston—Miss Marsh—Rev. Mr Campbell.[11] Breakfast at Grillion's. Saw Ld Norton—Mr Stuart—Herbert J.G.— the two Morleys. Read Kenyon's Preface to the new treatise[12]—'Conse- quences'—and Jay on H. Trinity Shoreditch.[13] Off to Dollis at 3 for Sunday.

Sexa S. Feb. One 1891.

Willesden Ch. mg 11 AM and H.C. Evg $6\frac{1}{2}$ PM. Wrote to Spottiswoode's. Read Gasquet, Origins of the Prayer Book[14]—Newbery Mag. O.T. Criticism & Bever- ley Minster[15]—Jay on H. Trin. Shoreditch finished.

---

[1] A. E. Snyder, *The Civil War from a Southern standpoint* (1890).

[2] See 26 Jan. 90.

[3] John Brown Paton, 1830–1911; congregationalist minister, social reformer and editor; see 15 May 79.

[4] Questions; tithes; *H* 349. 1299.

[5] James Gubbins Fitzgerald, b. 1855; Parnellite M.P. 1888–92.

[6] i.e. Irving and Ellen Terry.

[7] 'Vindex' [G. W. Rusden], *The great refusal. . . An account of the events which led to the death of General Gordon* (1890).

[8] E. Castle, *Consequences. A novel* (1891).

[9] Irish land; *H* 349. 1404.

[10] William Lidderdale, 1832–1902; governor of the Bank of England 1888–92.

[11] This sentence added later.

[12] F. G. Kenyon, ed., *Aristotle on the constitution of Athens* (1891).

[13] Presumably an article by A. O. Jay, later author of *A story of Shoreditch* (1896).

[14] See 6 Nov. 90.

[15] *Newbery House Magazine*, iv. 129, 181 (February 1891).

2. M. [London]

Back to London 12–1. Wrote to Sir M. Mackenzie[1]–Duke of Fife–Rev. A.O. Jay–M. Drew–Rev. Mr. Mayow. H. of C. 4–7¼.[2] Worked on the curious subject of the Disabilities.[3] Dined at Grillion's. Conversation with Sir R. Buller[4]–Mr F. Leveson. Saw Scotts–Ed. Hamilton. Saw Douglas [R]. Read Mr Williams Recollections[5]–and [blank.]

3. Tu.

Wrote to Mr Leader–Mr M. Williams–Mr Day[6]–Mr Fisher Unwin–Mr Stead. Interesting conversation with Harry on Chandernagore.[7] Dined at Mr A. Morley's. Saw Sir J. Carmichael–Lady F. Marjoribanks. Saw K. May [R]. Read Mr Williams–and the new Aristotle. H. of C. 3½–5.[8]

4. Wed.

Worked on Disabilities. H. of C. 12–5¼. Spoke 70 m.; *most* kindly received in all quarters.[9] Saw A. Morley–Sir W. Harcourt–Mr B. Currie. Read Williams. Walk, & much tired.

5. Th.

Wrote to Miss Döllinger–Mr Thaddeus–Mr Nicol–Wms & Norgate–Mr Stead–Editor P.M.G.–Mr A. Hutton–Mr Nutt. Shopping. 12½–2. National Gallery with Mr Burton[10] & Mr S.R. A glorious collection. Saw Mr Morley cum Mr A.M.–Mr Paull–Mr Bond (Br. Museum). Read the Hotten Lord Byron[11]– Williams Recollections–Drama of Empire.[12]

6. Fr.

Wrote to Ayowo Hattori[13]–Homersham Cox–Father Lockhart[14]–D. Macgregor–Sig. Lion.[15] Read Williams–Adams, Drama of Empire. Saw Mr Bond at

---

[1] Sir Morell Mackenzie, 1837–92; throat specialist; controversially treated Frederick III; perhaps assisting W. H. Gladstone.   [2] Tithes; *H* 349. 1534.

[3] Memorandum on religious disabilities, with annotations by H. H. Asquith, Add MS 44635, f. 56.

[4] Sir Redvers Henry Buller, 1839–1908; part of the 'Wolseley ring'; in South Africa 1881, Egypt 1882, Sudan 1884; adjutant-general 1890–7.

[5] Probably M. S. Williams, *Later leaves . . . being further reminiscences* (1891).

[6] S. H. Day, barrister; on religious disabilities; Add MS 44635, f. 80.

[7] H. N. Gladstone negotiated with the French government a manufacturing monopoly in Chandernagore, Pondicherry (i.e. in French India) for his firm, Gillanders, Arbuthnot and Co.; see Thomas, *Gladstone of Hawarden*, 144.   [8] Rifles; *H* 349. 1631.

[9] Unsuccessfully moved 2°R of Religious Disabilities [of Roman Catholics] Removal Bill; *H* 349. 1733.

[10] Sir Frederick William Burton, 1816–1900; director of the National Gallery 1874–94.

[11] Obscure: reading of 'Hotten' uncertain.

[12] W. M. Adams had sent his *The drama of Empire* (1891).

[13] Sent Gladstone a Japanese translation of the Bible; staying in Y.M.C.A., San Francisco: 'I am a young Japanese, who has received and is receiving unspeakable benefits from your life and works'; Hawn P.

[14] William Lockhart, rector of St. Etheldreda's, London, Add MS 44512, ff. 17, 98, 123.

[15] Diodato Lion of Naples had sent his 'The philosophy of right'; Hawn P.

B.M.—Mr Hutton—do *cum* Mr Cohen[1]—Mr Morley *cum* Mr A.M. on the Irish complications: & Mr M. 2° & 3°[2]—Mr Foljambe—Mr Marjorib.—Mr Rendel. Saw Bernard X & another.

7. Sat. [*Dollis Hill*]

Wrote to Mr Adams—A. Hutton—J. Powis J.P.—T.P. Allen—F.J. Stone—Jas Orton—Mr Corrall—J.T. Leader. Saw Sir A. Clark. Shopping. Off at 2 to Dollis Hill. Read Mrs Butler's Memoirs[3]—Consequences: a waste of time?—Ascertained K.Ms return to business [R?]

8. Quinqua S.

Willesden Ch. mg. Evg prayers at home. Wrote to Mr Brasill. Read Gaskett [*sc.* Gasquet] Prayerbook—Sainte Beuve, Port Royal[4]—Girdlestone, Old Test.[5]

9. M. [*London*]

Wrote to Helen G.—Ed. Guardian[6]—H.P. Palmer—E.A.C. Belcher—J.F. Foulds—Jas Hart—W.C. Angus—U. Maggs—Mrs Bolton. H. of C. $3\frac{3}{4}$-$4\frac{3}{4}$.[7] Off to Ln. $12\frac{3}{4}$. Saw P. of Wales. Saw Mr Morley—D. of Fife—The French Ambassador—Ld Rothschild—Mr H. Farquhar—S.Ln. Read Butler's Memoirs—London as it is[8]—Sainte Beuve Port Royal. Dined at Duke of Fife's. Saw Corna—Bentley X.

10. Tu.

Wrote to Mr Harwood—Mr C.S. Loch—H. Wootton—Dollis Footman—Mrs Bolton—Sir P. Currie—Ld Acton. H. of C. $4\frac{1}{4}$-$7\frac{1}{2}$.[9] Saw S.Ln—Mr Hutton—Ld Kinnaird—A. Morley l.l.l.—Rev. Mr Kitto[?]—Mad. Novikoff—J. Morley l.l.—do *cum* Sir W.H. Saw Mrs Bolton: suffering.[10] Read Waddie, Scottish Union[11]—Hotten's Byron Colln (finished). Cards with Miss R.

11. Wed. [*Dollis Hill*]

Willesden Church at 10.30. Off at 9.30 to Dollis. Wrote to C.G.—Dr Ginsburg B.P.—H.G. Barker—M. Gilliland—E. Lyneham—G.M. Boissevain[12]—T.P. Allen.

---

[1] Hutton and Cohen were editing Gladstone's speeches.

[2] The liberals decided not to accept any changes proposed by Parnell to their statement of 28 Jan. 91.

[3] *Sic*; but further reading suggests Charles Butler, *Historical memoirs respecting the English, Irish and Scottish Catholics from the reformation to the present time*, 4v., probably the 1822 ed. which included further letters etc. See 26 Nov. 74.

[4] C. A. Sainte-Beuve, *Port-Royal*, 5v. (1840–61).

[5] R. B. Girdlestone, *The foundations of the bible* (1891).

[6] Not found published.

[7] Tithes; *H* 350. 227.

[8] Perhaps *London as it is today* (1851).

[9] Questions; tithes; *H* 350. 312.

[10] The former rescue case.

[11] C. Waddie, *How Scotland lost her parliament and what became of it* (1891).

[12] Gideon Maria Boissevain, Dutch economist; wrote *The money question* (1891).

Read Butlers Letters—London of today—Thompson on Libraries[1]—Consequences. A solitary & calm day.

12. Th.

Wrote to Mr Stead—Rev. Mr Husband—R. Friend—Mad. Novikoff—Robn N. & Co—C.A. Salmond—Vote Office. Worked on Library information & off at 12.25: returning 4.45 from London. Luncheon at St Martin's Vicarage: spoke 35 m at meeting afterwards.[2] Saw Mr Rendell—Mr Morley *cum* Mr A. Morley. Read Butler's Records—Consequences. Sketched a beginning for my 'Olympian religion' to be denoted here O.R.[3]

13. Fr.

Wrote to Ld Queensberry—Mr Corbally[4]—Mr Sturrock—Mr H.W. Campbell—Mr Noble—Mr Heathcote B.P. Breakf. in bed after a disturbance. Read Butler Records finished.—Consequences. Sir A. Clark came to dinner, physics, & metaphysics. A little O[lympian] R[eligion]. Saw Lucy Cavendish.

14. Sat.

Wrote to Rev. Dr Warre—Sir A. Clark—Messrs Isbister—Rev. Mr Stead[5]—Vote Office—Mr T.G. Law—Mrs Bolton. Worked on O.R. Read Butler's Further Records—Consequences.

15. 1 S. Lent.

Willesden Ch mg. Willy came to luncheon. In aft. a rather sharp bout with the bowels: & the usual castor Oil. Bed at 5½. Read Macneil's Sermons[6]—Gasquet Prayerbook Origins—Sainte Beuve Port Royal.

16. M.

Bed till 2¾. Then to London & H. of C. 4–8. Spoke on Morley's Charges agt the Irish Executive.[7] Dollis at 9. Read Sainte Beuve—finished Consequences, a bad novel.

17. Tues.

Drive with C. Wrote to Dr Warre—Vote Office—Mr G. Melly—and [blank.] Worked on O.R. Read Butler—Sainte Beuve—and 'The Wages of Sin'.[8]

[1] Untraced.

[2] Speech on Free Libraries, opening the Free Public Library in St. Martin's Lane; *T.T.*, 13 February 1891, 12a.

[3] Never completed; drafts in Add MSS 44711–3.

[4] J. H. Corbally of Nairn; spasmodic correspondent on Catholic and Irish affairs; Hawn P.

[5] Probably Walter Benjamin Vere Stead, rector of Huntshaw.

[6] J. McNeil, *Sermons*, 3v. (1890–1).

[7] H 350. 726.

[8] L. Malet [Mrs St. L. Harrison], *The wages of sin* (1892?).

18. Wed.

Wrote to A. Wright—W.J. Cooksley—J.V. Hagart—Rev. Buchanan—J. Ogilvy—C.A. Salmond—Jas Wylie—Swan Sonnenschein & Co. Worked on O.R. Read Sainte Beuve—Mrs Butler—The Wages of Sin. A. Gordon dined (with L.C., J. Morley *manqué*). I told him much private matter: he some to me. Made notes on the Balfour speech.[1]

19. Th.

Wrote to Rev. R. Jenkins—Mr Bellis—Miss Kellie—Mrs Bolton—A. Ireland—G.J. Rawson. To town at 2.45. Shopping. Saw Mr A. Morley—Mr Morley—Mr Cecil Rhodes, a notable man[2]—Sir W. Harcourt—Ld Spencer—Mr Rendel. Dinner party at Mr Rendel's. H. of C. 4–5.[3] Read Sainte Beuve. Worked on O.R. Tea at Lady Stanley Ald.'s.

20. Fr.

Wrote to Ld Acton L & BP.—Mr Stibbs—Mr J. Hawkins—Mr May—A.B. Griffiths—R.M. Leonard—Mr H.G. Dickson—Mr Wm May—Rev. F. Mann—J.W. Martin—Rev. Williamson—Rev. S.E.G.—Rev. Gregory—Sig. Petroni—Mons. L. Seché—D. of Norfolk—Mr Oswald Smith.[4] Read Sainte Beuve—The Wages of Sin—Bryce's Review of Lecky[5]—Q.C. on Private Bill Legisln.[6] Saw H.N.G.—S.L.—Dean of St Asaph—Mr Bryce—Mr Whitbread. H. of C. 4–7½. Spoke & paired on Welsh Church.[7] Back to Dollis Hill at 11½.

---

[1] Balfour's speech on 16 February, replying rumbustiously to Morley and Gladstone; *H* 350. 769. Notes untraced.

[2] Cecil John Rhodes, 1853–1902; imperialist and benefactor; prime minister of the Cape 1890–6; the Trust established by his will has paid for most of the research costs of this edition. Shortly after this meeting, Rhodes sent Schnadhorst a cheque for £5000 for liberal funds, to be kept secret and to be returned if the next home rule bill did not provide for Irish representation at Westminster; see G. P. Taylor, 'Cecil Rhodes and the Second Home Rule Bill', *Historical Journal*, xiv. 777 (1971). This is his first established meeting with Gladstone, but see 14 Mar. 87, 8 July 89. Morley recorded: 'A downright pleasant evening: the party just the right size, a round table, and the dinner recherché and not too long, and the wine famous. I thought Mr. G looked sadly white and old. Rhodes sat between him and me, and I between Rhodes and my host. The African has a fine head; a bold full eye, and a strong chin. He talked to me during the whole of dinner, in favour of imperial customs union, and when we parted, hoped I would give him another chance of resuming the subject: evidently a man capable of wide imperial outlook, and daring and decided views. I found nothing to dislike in him ... Rhodes told Mr. G. that Parnell had promised him he wd. never assent to exclus[io]n of the Irish mem[ber]s. Yet he left Mr. G. to suppose t[ha]t it was indifferent to him.'

[3] Questions; *H* 350. 1069.

[4] Oswald A. Smith, poet; see 23 Feb. 91.

[5] Perhaps Bryce's review of Lecky's *European morals* in *Q.R.*, cxxviii. 49 (January 1870).

[6] Untraced.

[7] On Pritchard Morgan's motion for Welsh disestablishment; Gladstone stressed the increased vitality of the Church in Wales, while admitting it represented only the few and the rich, and effectively admitting the disestablishment case, but not explicitly; *H* 350. 1257.

21. Sat.

Wrote to . . . . Ed. of Truth in B. Columbia[1]–. . . . . Worked on O.R. Read
Sainte Beuve—Wages of Sin—Mrs Butler (finished). Made choice provisionally
of Artemis for Eton Lecture.[2] Walk—in heavy fog.

22. 2 S. Lent.

Willesden Church mg and evg. Read Gasquet Prayerbook—Sainte Beuve, Port
Royal—Heathcote, Salvation Army[3]—Field, The Better World[4]—Mowat Evid-
ences of Xty.[5]

J. Morley dined here, alone. Thoughtless but selfishly & most wrongly, I
talked him down.[6]

23. M.

Wrote to Hon. Mr Mowat[7]—A. Morley—Messrs Stanford—Jas Knowles—Mr
Oswald Smith—Ly Aberdeen—J. Darlington—Mr S. Rendel—Rev. McNeill.
Visited with C. Mr Tadema's studio: in the fog.[8] Worked further on material of a
Lecture on Artemis. Read O. Smith's Auburnia[9]—Poems in Shetland Dialect[10]—
Sainte Beuve's Port Royal—The Wages of Sin. Exema [sic] which in 1887 this
place cured, now bothers me a good deal.

24. Tu.

Wrote to Mr S. Walker—Lady Rothschild—Miss Helen G.—Mr A.W. Hutton—
Chancr of Exr—Mr A. Morley—Rev. Ld Forester. Worked on O.R. Dense fog
prevented me from going into London for the Income Tax motion. Read The
Wages of Sin—Sainte Beuve's Port Royal—Flower de Hundred.[11] C. went (mid
day) to Leeds.

25. Wed.

Wrote to C.G.—Ed Lpool Post[12]—Vote Office—Lady Stepney. Worked on O.R.
Read Lady Abns very interesting social papers.[13] Read also Sainte Beuve—
Wages of Sin. Drive with Helen. Sad tidings from Ly Stepney.[14]

---

[1] On 25 November 1890, *The Daily Truth* (New Westminster, British Columbia) published a
leader on 'The duty of the well-to-do', which the editor sent to Gladstone; his letter of thanks was
published in *The Morning Ledger* (which incorporated *The Daily Truth*), 13 March 1891, with the
comment: 'Pity that such a man as Gladstone should ever grow old!'

[2] See 14 Mar. 91.   [3] W. S. Heathcote, *My Salvation Army experience* (1891).

[4] Probably a further article by H. M. Field in his dispute with R.G. Ingersoll.

[5] Untraced.   [6] No comment in Morley's diary.

[7] Perhaps Hon. Robert Anderson Mowat, barrister and colonial judge. See previous day.

[8] A social call; Alma-Tadema (see 10 Mar. 74) did not paint Gladstone.

[9] Oswald A. Smith had sent his *Auburnia* (privately printed by Swan Sonnerschein 1891), using a
quotation from Gladstone's and Lyttelton's *Translations*; Hawn P.

[10] J. J. H. Burgess, *Shetland sketches and poems* (1886).

[11] Constance C. Harrison, *Flower De Hundred. The story of a Virginia plantation* (1890).

[12] On Religious Disability Bill; *Liverpool Daily Post*, 7 March 1891, 4j.

[13] Papers on social reform by Lady Aberdeen (see 17 Dec. 83n.); see her *D.N.B.* entry.

[14] See next day.

26. Th.

Wrote to Cardinal Manning—Mr Stead—S.H. Vickers—J.W. Jaques—Mr Knowles—Rev. D. Jones—W. Gardner—Rev. N. Hall—Ld Granville. 11–2¾. To London. Saw Lady Stepney & her Lawyer & wrote substance of an affidavit.[1] Saw E. Hamilton—A. Morley—Ld Aberdeen. Read The Wages of Sin: finished —a remarkable & singular book[2]—Read Port Royal.

Fr. 27.

Wrote to C.G. Tel. & l.—A. Morley. Worked on O.R. To town at 12. Saw S.L.— Mr Ducane *cum* Mr Gamlin—Ld & Lady Aberdeen—Mr Campbell Banner- man—Sir H. James. Visited Old Masters. R.Ac. H. of C. 4–7¾:[3] spoke on land taxation. Dollis at 9 PM. Read Port Royal—Prince of the Glades.[4]

28. Sat. [Tring Park]

Wrote to Scotts—V.O.—Ed. Baptist[5]—Mr A. Morley—Mr Drumgole [*sic*]. Worked on O.R. Off to Tring Hall[6] at 2¾. Charming house, very kind hosts. Saw J. Morley—B. Currie—Lady R. Read Port Royal—Disraeli & Mrs W. Corresp.[7]— Port Royal.

---

[1] Lady Stepney requested Gladstone to write an *affidavit* that her husband ('again suffering under painful and quite insane delusions') should not have charge of their daughter; see Lady Stepney to Gladstone, n.d., Add MS 44512, f. 124.

[2] See 17 Feb. 91.

[3] *H* 350. 1878.

[4] H. Lynch, *The Prince of the Glades*, 2v. (1891).

[5] On Religious Disability Bill; *Baptist*, 6 March 1891, 153a.

[6] Rothschild's seat in Hertfordshire.

[7] Correspondence between Disraeli and Mrs Brydges Willyams, in Rothschild's possession and shown by him to Gladstone earlier, in London; see 17 Mar. 88.

[*1 March 1891 to 30 June 1893*]

Private.

No 40.

March 1. 91–June 30. 93.

Le propre d'une raison faible
et basse est de méconnaître
tout ce qui ne la flatte point.²
(Remusat, Passé et present,
Du choix d'une opinion.)

"Take away the filthy garments
from him; and clothe him with a
change of raiment."
Dying words of William Law. (See
Whyte xlvii).³ O si sic.⁴

[Also, in pencil, now faint:—]

1.30.20.

£1.—Bailey

Mary 9.11. AM 1 CG Mr Grant

Brown Testl £2 + 2 of 2.

[On the flyleaf is pasted a newspaper cutting:—]

In a letter to the author of "St Michael's Eve",⁵ a new novel, Mr Gladstone writes:
"It seems to me that with us at the present day talent is running overmuch into the field of invention, and that, setting apart the few cases where an author is conscious of strong creative power, other fields of history and research,

---

¹ Lambeth 1454.
² From 'Du choix d'une opinion' in Charles de Rémusat, *Critiques et Etudes littéraires, ou Passé et Présent* (1859), i. 163.
³ See *Characters and characteristics of William Law, nonjuror and mystic. Selected and arranged with an introduction by Alexander Whyte, D.D.* (1893), xlvii. Whyte was a Free Church minister in Edinburgh.
⁴ 'Would it were so'.
⁵ W. H. De Winton, pseud. of William Henry Wilkins, author of *St. Michael's Eve*, 2v. (1892); novel of aristocratic life and religious doubt. See 2 June 91n.

especially perhaps of history, are more fruitful. Forgive this intrusion of the irrelevant, and let me have the pleasure of acknowledging what is so soon obvious, the high aim and purpose of your work.—I remain, yours very faithfully, W. E. GLADSTONE.—1, Carlton-gardens, May 21, 1892."

1. 3 S. Lent.

Tring Ch 11 A.M. 6½ PM. Wrote to Rev. Dr Warre—Mr Garratt—Mr Horsfall. Extreme kindness here; but it is very unsabbatical. Read Disraeli-Withycome[1] correspondence—Sainte Beuve's Port Royal—Kennedy, Nat. Theol. & Modern Thought.[2]

2. M. [Dollis Hill]

10-12. Back to Dollis. Wrote to Bp of Ripon—W. Andrews—W. Collins—Rev. Miller. Saw Mr White. Worked on O[lympian] R[eligion]. Read Andrews, Old Time Punishments[3]—Sainte Beuve.

Will is the faculty of internal self-determination, never to be over-ruled by the action of any power from without, whether belonging to the visible or to the invisible world. If it be a force, it is one incommensurable with any other force.

If the being possessed of will gives way under temptation, it is, in the last resort, from the want of will to resist, and not because the will being placed in one of two scales, and (so to speak) the temptation in the other, the temptation proves to be the heavier & will kicks the beam.

It is incorrect to say God cannot do wrong. It is not power which prevents Him but self-determining will. It is not a question of can—can is no more capable of stating the case truly than of stating futurition.[4]

3. Tu. [London]

Wrote to Ld Rosebery—Ed. Baptist—and Rev. Dr Warre. Worked on O.R. Off to London at 1. Literary proposals from America, promising from 100 gs to £25000!![5] Saw Card. Manning—Lady Granville—Mary D.—Mr Morley—S.L.

---

[1] Sc. Willyams; see 28 Feb. 91n.

[2] J. H. Kennedy, *Natural theology and modern thought* (1891).

[3] W. Andrews, *Old-time punishments* (1890).

[4] Holograph dated 2 March 1891; Add MS 44773, f. 217. A further illegible sentence at the end is not transcribed.

[5] Proposal by the Century Co. 'for the publication of autobiographical papers and personal memoirs by him [Gladstone] ... The Century would be glad to print a portion of the work in the Magazine, beginning in November of 1891 or November 1892, and continuing monthly for at least a year. The Century Co. would like to bring out the complete work in two octavo volumes'. The magazine claimed a circulation of 'nearly 200,000 copies' per month. Typed memorandum, 'Memorandum in the matter of a proposed autobiography of Mr Gladstone', in the Century Collection, New York Public Library. See also Carnegie's letter of 12 January 1891 (thought by Carnegie's biographer not to have been received, but in Add MS 44512, f. 200), suggesting he dictate his autobiography; *Carnegie*, i. 415.

H. of C. 4–12½: a long bout for me *now*.[1] Read Smith's Dict.[2]—Began Lecky's Hist.[3]—Nansen's Greenland.[4] Saw Murray [R?].

4. *Wed.*

Wrote to C.S. Palmer—Sec. Irish Land Commn—Mr Brown—Mr Maitland—Lady Rothschild—Mr Terrell—Bp of St Asaph—Rev. Mr Hogg—Messrs Putnam—Rev. Hodson. Dined with Lord J. Bowen at the Athenaeum. Worked on books and papers. Saw Lady Stepney—Mr A. Hutton—Miss Cobden. Read Huxley 19th Cent.[5]—Argyll Letter to Presbyterians![6]—And Sainte Beuve. Saw Dashwood [R].

5. *Th.*

Wrote to Mr Morton[7]—Mr Aspden—Mr[?] Meyer—Mr Seale Hayne MP. Endeavouring to settle down and arrange my books & papers. Saw Mr A. Morley—Mr Marjoribanks *cum* Mr Campbell Bannerman—Ld Herschell—S.L.—H.N.G. (Chandernagore)[8]—Lady F. Marjoribanks . . . . . Read Port Royal (II)—Cruise of Dunottar Castle.[9] Drive with C. Worked at London Library.

6. *Fr.* [*Dollis Hill*]

Wrote to Sir D. Currie—Mr P. Russell—Dr O.W. Holmes[10]—Mr L. Tollemache—Ld Vernon—Messrs Johnson—Messrs Funk & Wagnalls. Off to Dollis in afternoon. Saw S.L.—Mr Godley—Mr A. Morley. Read Sainte Beuve—Verga, Novelle[11]—Old Time Punishments. Worked on Artemis.[12]

7. *Sat.*

Wrote Lady Stepney (Deo Gratias)—Mr Godley—Mr Morton. Worked long & hard on Artemis for my Lecture. She is hard to disentangle. Also began an article or Chapter on her.[13] Read as yesterday—Ld Vernon in 19th Cent.[14] I now try to meet Exema by steeping in hot vapour: I think with benefit.

[1] Supporting Stansfeld's resolution on plural voting; *H* 351. 62.
[2] W. Smith's *Dictionary of the Bible*.
[3] Vols. vii and viii of Lecky's history (1890); see 26 July 82.
[4] F. Nansen, *The first crossing of Greenland*, 2v. (1890).
[5] T. H. Huxley, 'Illustrations of Mr Gladstone's controversial method', *N.C.*, xxix. 455 (March 1891).
[6] Duke of Argyll, 'Some words of warning to the Presbyterians of Ireland' (1890).
[7] E. J. C. Morton, on Dilke's candidacy; Add MS 44512, f. 151.
[8] See 3 Feb. 91.
[9] W. S. Dalgleish, 'The cruise of the "Dunottar Castle" on her trial trip' (1890).
[10] Oliver Wendell Holmes, 1809–94; American author and professor.
[11] G. Verga, *Nouvelle Rusticane* (1883).
[12] See 14 Mar. 91.
[13] Given as his lecture at Eton (see 14 Mar. 91) and published as 'Mr. Gladstone on Artemis', *Eton College Chronicle*, no. 550, pp. 619–24 (19 March 1891).
[14] G. W. H. V. Vernon, 'Overmortgaging the land', *N.C.*, xxix. 415 (March 1891).

8. 4 S. Lent.

Willesden Ch mg (excellent Sermon). Evg service at home (rain). Mr G. Russell dined. Wrote to Mrs Mitchell—Bull and Auvache—Mr Hardinge. Read Sainte Beuve—Simon on the Bible[1]—and [blank.]

9. M.

Wrote to Mr A. Morley—Mr Papucci—Mr Stead—Mr Hutton—Mr James. 12–5. To London. Attended the Levee. Saw S.L.—A. Morley—Ld Ripon. Worked on O.R. (Artemis). Read Sainte Beuve—Old Time Punishments (finished)—Knowles in N.C. on Elgin Marbles—Dunraven's article,—what nonsense.[2]

10. Tu.

H. of C. $3\frac{1}{2}$–$4\frac{3}{4}$.[3] Then to tea with Lady Derby: an hour's conversation. Worked freely on Artemis. Off at 2.45: *shift* over[?] for good, as they say. Saw Mr A. Morley—Sir H. James—Mr Mundella—Sir W. Harcourt—Ld Herschell—Mr Godley. Thirteen to dinner. Read Sainte Beuve—Johnson's Ionica.[4]

11. Wed.

Wrote to Mr D. Nutt—Bull & Auvache—Garratts—Mr W. Rideing—Mr Bentley—H.J. Burdett—T.A.W. Bell—Rev. Mr Lloyd. Dined at Mr Gardener's.[5] Conversation Lady W.G., Ly Carrington. Conversation with Harry on the Hawarden Coal Pits. Fivocloquai[6] with Lady Londonderry: long conversation some of it even stiff. Read Sainte Beuve—Manchr Ship Canal.[7] Worked on O.R.

12. Th.

Wrote to Mr J.H. Pease—Mr C. Watson—Miss Leake—P.W. Claydon—Mr Tollemache—P. Russell—W. Garig. Read Sainte Beuve—Verga—Preller[8]—Welcker[9]—Nägelsbuch.[10] Saw Ld Northbourne—Mr A. Morley—Mr S. Rendel—Prof. Pelham. Conclave on Finance at 5 PM. Saw Harcourt & Morley on the Dilke business.[11] H. of C. 4–6.[12] Dined at Mr Buchanan's.

13. Fr.

Wrote to Bp of St Asaph—Canon M'Coll BP.—Mr Knowles—A.H. Maldock—J.F. Hunt—Messrs Clark—M. Swan—Mr Mackechnie—Mr Cohen—S. Halstead—Rev. S.E.G.—C.S. Palmer. Wrote Mem. on Dilke case for communication to him. Saw A. Morley—J. Morley—Mr F.L. Gower—Mr Stuart. Worked on

---

[1] Probably R. Simon, *A critical history of the Old Testament*, 4v. (1682).

[2] J. T. Knowles, 'The joke about the Elgin Marbles' and Lord Dunraven, 'Commercial union within the Empire', *N.C.*, xxix. 495, 507 (March 1891); Dunraven was an early supporter of differential tariffs.

[3] Questions; *H* 351. 583.

[4] W. Johnson Cory, *Ionica* (1891).

[5] H. C. and Lady Gardner; see 9 Nov. 87, 6 May 90.

[6] Glynnese for five o'clock tea.

[7] Not found.

[8] E. C. J. F. Preller, *Homer's Iliad* (1879).

[9] See 1 Nov. 67.

[10] Untraced.

[11] See next day.

[12] Questions; Irish estimates; *H* 351. 778.

Artemis. H. of C. $4\frac{1}{2}$–6.[1] Read Sainte Beuve—Verga—and [blank.] Saw Depn on Hastings Visit.[2]

I am as far as possible from assuming any title to advise in such a case as that of Sir C. Dilke; and it is my opinion that the Liberal party in Great Britain will *generally* recognise the broad and vital differences between a case which lies wholly between a given person and a constituency, and a case like that of Mr. Parnell, which has nothing to do with his seat in Parliament, and which is not confined even to the fact of its involving the leadership at Westminster, but which also would have involved, through a Home Rule Bill, the virtual gift to him, by the Liberal Party at large, of the constitutional headship of his own country.

At the same time, it is my duty to receive and take note of all evidence which comes before me as to facts likely to exercise a prejudicial influence on a great public cause: and unquestionably evidence has been presented to me, which convinces me that, in *Ireland*, at the present juncture, and in the highly acute stage of the Parnell controversy, which must require a little time for its settlement, the assumption of a candidature by Sir Charles Dilke, although a matter in which the Liberal party at large should have taken no part whatever, yet would exercise a most prejudicial influence upon the course of that struggle, and would greatly weaken the ground occupied by the Irish Parliamentary party in their assertion of their claims and their position, as alone entitled to represent Irish Nationalism in the face of Great Britain. I should be greatly obliged to [blank] if as a friend of Sir Charles he were able to apprise him of the state which has been made known to me, and which I think he ought to know.
W.E.G. Mch. 13. 1891[3]

14. Sat. [Eton College]

Wrote to Mary Drew—Lady Londonderry—Mr Gent Davies [*sic*]. Off to Eton 3.40. Worked on Artemis for Lecture. Saw S. Lyttelton—Central News—Mr Cohen. Read Sainte Beuve—Fantasia.[4] Eton sent up Verses. Large dinner party & much conversation with Mrs Davison[5] and others. 7–$8\frac{3}{4}$. Lecture & proceedings thereon.[6] The audience were very kind.

15. 5 S. Lent.

Eton Chapel 10.40 a moving sight. St George's 5. P.M. Then 'audience' of Empress Frederick. A much broken day. Luncheon with the Provost. Tea at the Deanery. Visited the new Chapel—new Buildings—the Library—the portraits—the rooms of the collegers. Large dinner party & much conversation with the elder boys. Read Roberts (Chas II)[7]—Bligh[8]—Cunningham[9]—Tomlinson on Lambeth Judgment.[10]

---

[1] Question; local taxation; *H* 351. 912.   [2] See 17 Mar. 91.

[3] Add MS 44773, f. 218. See also R. Jenkins, *Sir Charles Dilke* (1958), 383–4.

[4] Probably B. Benvenuti, *Fantasia e realtà. Novelle* (1886).

[5] Edith Murdoch Davidson, da. of abp. Tait, whose life her husband R. T. Davidson, dean of Windsor, was completing.

[6] Spoke on the Homeric Artemis; *T.T.*, 16 March 1891, 7f.

[7] Possibly M. A. Roberts, *In Memoriam. Charles Edward Stuart* (1881?).

[8] E. V. Bligh, *Prophetical signs of the Second Coming* (1891).

[9] Probably W. Cunningham, *The path towards knowledge* (1891).

[10] J. Tomlinson, *The 'historical' grounds of the Lambeth Judgment examined* (1891).

16. M. [London]

Ch. 9.25 A.M. Off at 10.15 to London. Wrote to Rev. J.O. Johnston[1]—Mrs Lazarus—Mrs Beere—Mr E. Howell. Read Sainte Beuve—Farrar on Finance. Worked freely on the political subject for tomorrow. Dined at Ld Aberdeen's. Saw S.L.—A. Morley—J. Morley—Dr Warre. H. of C. $3\frac{1}{4}$-$5\frac{1}{4}$.[2]

17. Tu.

$11\frac{3}{4}$-$7\frac{1}{4}$. The Hastings Expedition. All went well, even the weather. Spoke 10 m at Tunbridge, 1 h. 20 m. at Hastings.[3] Worked on Pol. Mema. Read Sainte Beuve—Fantasia.

18. Wed.

Wrote to Mr Knowles—Ed. 19th Cent (and draft)[4]—Rev. Dr Warre—Miss Wyse—Mr Schnadhorst—E. Howell—Sir C. Forster—J. Oldfield—Chancr of the Exchequer[5]—Mr Goschen. Saw S.L.—Mr A. Morley—Mr James MP—Ladies Deputn on eligibility to C. Councils[6]—Mrs Oppenheim—Austrian Ambassador —Countess Deym[7]—J. Morley—Sir L. Playfair—Sir And. Clark—Ld Herschell. Dined at Marlborough Ho. Read Carnegie in 19th C.[8]

19. Th.

Wrote to Mr J. Balton—Jas Miles—Mr Picton MP—Mr Bunting Tel.—T. Bayliss— Mrs Bennett—Rev. H. Richards—Rev. J. Morris—Rev. J.M. Rodwell—H.G. Barker—Rev. T. Wright—Chancr of Exchequer. Saw S.L.—A. Godley—Mr Cohen—Mr Talbot—Mr Morley—Mr A. Morley—Mr Mundella—Mr Bunting. Conclave on Irish Land & on Labour Commission. Read Rosebery Preface & Vol.[9]—'Continental Statesman' on Italy.[10] Went to Mad. Novikoff's music. Dined at Ld Aberdeen's.

20. Fr.

Wrote to Lord Reay—Mr Bunting—J. Fisher—Mr Lanin—Mr W.H. Smith MP. l.l.—Mrs Bennett BP—Miss A. Curtis—Rev. Mr Thackeray—Rev. Dr. Allon—Rev. Dr. Kirkpatrick. Made a statement of my (part) estimated literary earnings.[11]

---

[1] John Octavius Johnston, chaplain of Merton, Oxford; completing Liddon's *Life of Pusey*.

[2] Spoke on business of the House; *H* 351. 1078.

[3] Speeches at Tunbridge Wells station and the Gaiety Theatre, Hastings, with extensive comments on 'the remarkable career of Mr. Parnell'; *T.T.*, 18 March 1891, 11a.

[4] Published as 'Letter explaining a sentence in the article in the February number', *N.C.*, xxix. 690 (April 1891); on his article on Huxley (see 18 Dec. 90n.).

[5] Exchange with Goschen on Exchequer matters raised in his Hastings speech; *T.T.*, 20 March 1891, 11c.   [6] No account found.

[7] Count and Countess Deym, the Austrian ambassador and his wife.

[8] A. Carnegie, 'The advantage of poverty', *N.C.*, xxix. 367 (March 1891).

[9] Lord Rosebery, *Pitt* (1891).

[10] *C.R.*, lix. 465 (April 1891); perhaps a proof.

[11] In Hawn P, Account Book 1878–97: literary earnings for 1890: £1915–8–7 (making a total to 1890 inclusive of £14,862).

Saw A. Morley–S.L.–F.L. Gower–Mr Lefevre–The Speaker–Mr Caulton MP [*sc.* Causton]–Mr Reid MP.–Ld Rosebery. Read Sainte Beuve–and [blank.]

21. Sat.

Wrote to Ld Knutsford–Rev. Dr. Warre–Mr H. Fowler–Mr Knowles–Mr R. Brown jun. B.P. Worked on O.R: but the impediments & distractions are hard. C. went off at 11 A.M. Saw A. Morley–S.L. Read Sainte Beuve–Fantasia– Verga, Novelle.[1]

22. Palm S.

Ch. Ch (Dover St) 11 AM with H.C. & 6½ P.M. Read Sainte Beuve–Fantasia– Thackeray's Prudentius[2]–Hutton on The Word[3]–The rhythmic 'Imitation'.[4]

23. M.

Westm. Abbey 3 P.M. Wrote to Mr Smith–Sir F. Milner BP. Saw S.L.–A. Morley–Mr Fowler MP–Scotts–Mr Bryce MP–Sir E. Watkin. Feeble attempt at O.R. H. of C. 4-6¼.[5] Read Sainte Beuve–Fantasia (finished)–Life of J. Murray.[6]

24. Tu.

Wrote to Rev. Mr Dunckerley–Rev. Mr E.B. Finlay–Mr Mayhew–W.M. David–Jas White–Messrs Murrell–Vote Office–A.F. Robbins[7]–Robinson–Mr Tomkinson. Saw S.L.–Rev. Dr Kinns–Mr Murray?–Mr Armitstead. Saw Mr Murray–S.L. Curzon St Chapel 5. P.M. Read Sainte Beuve–Murray's Memoirs–Verga, finished I. A very little O.R.

25. Wed. Annunciation. [Hastings]

Wrote to Canon Scott Holland–Ed. Kings Own[8]–Rev. Dr Hutton–L. Gilbert– Mr Geo. Russell–J. Burton–Mr Murray–Lady Aberdeen. Worked on O.R. Off to Hastings at 3¼ i.e. St Leonard's Vict. Hotel: our most kind host Mr Armitstead.[9] Mr Wemyss Reid dined. Much conversation. Read Collis Visit to Alaska[10]–Memoir of Murray.

26. Th.

St John's Church and H.C. at noon. Wrote to A.C. Simpson–Ld Acton–H. Linton. Worked on O.R. Exploratory walk with Mr Armitstead. A kind anonymous

---

[1] See 6 Mar. 91.

[2] *Translations from Prudentius... by F. St. J. Thackeray* (1890).

[3] G. C. Hutton, *The Word and the Book* (1891).

[4] *Musica Ecclesiastica. The Imitation of Christ ... now for the first time set forth in rhythmic sentences* (1891).

[5] Misc. business; *H* 351. 1682.

[6] S. Smiles, *A publisher and his friends. Memoir and correspondence of the late John Murray* (1891). See 16 Apr. 91.

[7] See 22 July 75.   [8] Not found published.

[9] George Armitstead; see 20 Dec. 80.

[10] Not found; M. M. Ballon's *Summer journey to Alaska* was just published.

Tory showed me the public garden. Saw Sir G. Trevelyan. Read Sainte Beuve—
Memoirs of J. Murray—Visit to Alaska. In our *host* (at this hotel) we have a
prize: he is of rare modesty, courtesy and generosity: rare in his class, or in any
class.

27. Good Friday.

The Hours at Ch.Ch. 1–3¼. Evg service at St Pauls. Wrote to J. Murray—and
[blank.] Read Sainte Beuve—Miss [blank] Holy Week. Began Church's Hist. of
the Oxford Movement.[1]

28. Easter Eve.

Church mg. Too lazy for writing. Drive to Bexhill. Loud Oxford conversations
with Dean Lake & Dr Greenhill.[2] Also saw Mr Mundella. Read Sainte Beuve—J.
Murray—Collis's Alaska.

29. Easter Day.

Celebration Ch.Ch. at 9¼—Ch of this parish at 6.30. (Bp Beccles!).[3] Read
Church—*admirable*—Sainte Beuve—Braithwaite on Geo. Fox[4]—The Holy
Gospels—& ....'s 'Holy Week'.

30. Easter M.

St Paul's 11 A.M. Two dark shadows overcast the day. A Tel. from Clark
announced that Granville is sinking. A letter from E. Hamilton told of fresh
swelling in the other leg: which I construe as of the very worst omen. Conversation with the Mayor of Hastings. Wrote to Boning & Small—F.J. Sawyer—
Messrs Scribner—E. Durham—Wms & Norgate—A. Burrell—W.H.
Pearson—Frau Nylander. Read Sainte Beuve—J. Murray's Memoirs—Constable's do.[5]

31. Easter Tu.

A little rheumatism. Drive in afternoon. Wrote to Hon F.L. Gower—F.J. Parsons—Mr Murray—C. Caffin—Sec. Eisteddfod.

Before 6 PM I learned with grief the death of my dear & fast friend Lord
Granville. Peace be with him.

Read Constable—Murray's Memoirs. G. Russell here & Sir G. Trevelyan with
his sons.[6] Worked on O.R.

---

[1] R. W. Church, *The Oxford Movement. Twelve years, 1833–1845* (1891).

[2] Probably William Ridge Greenhill, rector of Newenden, Kent; formerly of Magdalen Hall,
Oxford.

[3] Edward Hyndman Beckles, d. 1902; retired colonial bp. living in St. Leonard's.

[4] Untraced.

[5] T. Constable, *Archibald Constable and his literary correspondents*, 3v. (1873).

[6] (Sir) Charles Philips Trevelyan, 1870–1958, later liberal and labour M.P. and minister; Robert
Calverley Trevelyan, 1872–1951, poet; George Macaulay Trevelyan, 1876–1962, historian.

Wed Ap. One 1891.

Missed Church by misinformation. Pier—Castle—and drive. Wrote to T. Gilderson—Mr Knowles Tel.—C. Spicer—Adams Acton do.—W. Digby—Rev. R. Owen—J. Huggett—G.H. Elridge—A.H. Stow. Worked on O.R. Read Murray—Constable's Mem. Drive, & visited the Castle.

2. Th.

Wrote to Sir W. Harcourt—and . . . . . Worked on O.R. Saw Mr G. Russell—Sir A. West—& Pier projector. Went on Pier. Read Constable—Church's admirable book.

3. Fr.

Ch. $10\frac{1}{2}$ A.M. Wrote to Archbp of Canterbury—Dr Weymouth—Mr Corbally—Rev. H.D. Jones—M.F. Cotton—H. Avery—T.J. Thompson—C. Chambers—R.D. Whyte—D. Gillies—F. Smyth. Worked on O.R. Saw Dean of Durham. Drive to Fairlight. Read Dean Church—& Constable.

4. Sat. [Brighton]

Wrote to Mr Caffyn—Mr Schnadhorst—W. Hawthorn—Sir E. Watkin—H.G. Baily—Mr Macer Wright—C.J. Murphy—Mr J. Murray—G.J. Murray—Mr C.J. Humphrey—D. Talmage—O.O. Williams—& others.—Rev. F.E. Warren—Mr A. Morley. Off at 10 to London for the Memorial Service.[1] Then to Metropole Hotel Brighton (what an abode of luxurious comfort) at $5\frac{1}{4}$ P.M. Saw Sir W. Harcourt—E. Hamilton—Duke of Argyll—Agnes & E.W. Read Arch. Constable—Dean Church's History—"What will Mrs Grundy say?"[2]

5. 1 S.E.

St Paul's morning (with H.C.) & evening. Saw E. Hamilton. Wrote to A. Morley. Read Protest agt Agnostm[3]—Dean Church's great book (finished).

6. M.

Wrote to Dean of St Paul's—Mrs Church—Wms & Norgate. Explored the shops. Read Murray—Roscher's Hermes.[4] Worked on O.R. Dined with Duchess of Marlborough. Conversation with Ld Randolph. Saw E. Hamilton.

7. Tu.

Wrote to M. Bratiano—Card. Manning—J. M'Veagh—A.E. Hollingworth—Sir W. Harcourt. Worked on O.R. Read Roscher's Hermes—Murray's Memoirs.

---

[1] Granville's memorial service in the Chapel Royal, held at the same time as the funeral in Staffordshire; *T.T.*, 6 April 1891, 8a.

[2] M. Rustoff, *What will Mrs. Grundy say? or, a calamity on two legs* (1891); a romance.

[3] P. F. Fitzgerald, *Protest against agnosticism* (1890).

[4] W. H. Roscher, *Hermes*, the 1st part of *Studien zur griechischen Mythologie und Kulturgeschichte* (1878 ff.); see 10 Jan. 87.

8. Wed.

Wrote to Ld Leveson—Lady Holker—Mr Greening—Mr Bevan. Worked on O.R. Duchess of Marlborough took us to Devil's Dyke.[1] Air, luncheon, photographing, & fortune telling (not mine). She is extremely kind. Read Murray's Memoirs—Constable's Memoirs III. Saw E. Hamilton.

9. Thurs. [London]

Wrote to Mr A. Farrier—T.G. Bishop—L.J. Richardson—Dr Irving[2]—L. Melitopoulo—Mr A. Grove—W. Stanforth—C.E. Ford—Ld Oxenbridge[3]—Ld Rosebery—Mrs Bolton. 1-3¾: return to London. Saw Dowager Duchess of Marlb.—Sir W. Harcourt—Mr A. Morley—Mr Armitstead—Mr Morley—Mr MacCarthy MP. H. of C. 4-8.[4] Dined at Mr Armitstead's. Saw three [R]. Read Constable Vol. III—Murray's Memoirs.

10. Frid.

Wrote to Abp Manning—Mr A. Carnegie[5]—C.G.—Ed. Greater Britain.[6] H. of C. 4-8.[7] Ten to dinner. Saw Lady Holker—Rev. Mr Tucker—Mr Knowles—Mr A. Morley—H.N.G.—Mr McCarthy. Read Murray's Memoirs.

11 Sat.

Wrote to Mr Thaddeus—Carrington & Barker—Mr Darlington—C.G.—A. Cooper. Saw Ld Oxenbridge. Visited the Guelph Exhibition with Helen.[8] Read D. of A. on Huxley—Ld Acton on Talleyrand.[9] Finished Murray's Memoirs. Dined at Sir L. Playfair's. Conversation [with] Ly Cork—Ld F. Marjoribanks & others.

12. 2 S.E.

Curson St Chapel mg—St Paul's Kn. evg. Read Sainte Beuve—Sharp on Personality[10]—Luccock Intermediate State[11]—Rivett Ch. in S. Africa.[12]

13. M.

Wrote to E.J. Curtis—Sig. Schilizzi—A. Chisholm—M. Martin-Laya—Mr Sulherst—Rev. H. Friend—Mr Otto. H. of C. 4¼-5½.[13] Dined at Grillions. Saw

---

[1] Escarpment N. of Brighton.
[2] Alexander Irving, science master at Wellington; Hawn P.
[3] See 18 June 45n.   [4] Irish land purchase bill; H 352. 168.
[5] Presumably declining Carnegie's renewed invitation of 12 January—this time for the *Century*—to write his autobiography; Add MS 44512, f. 200.
[6] Not found published.   [7] Irish land; H 352. 256.
[8] Exhibition, 'The royal house of Guelph', in the New Gallery, Regent Street.
[9] Argyll, 'Professor Huxley and the duke of Argyll'; Acton, 'Talleyrand's *Memoirs*', *N.C.*, xxix. 670, 685 (April 1891).
[10] Possibly S. Sharp, *Idolatry: from scripture and profane history* (1891).
[11] H. M. Luccock, *The intermediate state between death and judgment* (1890).
[12] A. W. L. Rivett, *Ten years' church work in Natal* (1890).
[13] Questions; H 352. 365.

Gravett [R]. 12–1½ Conclave of Peers. We settled on the *status quo* as to Leadership in the Lords and I framed a paragraph to announce it.[1] Saw D. Robertson—A. Morley.

14. Tu.

Wrote to Ld Spencer—J. Barton—W. Taylor—J. Stibbs—W.S. Jones—Ld Rosebery—Miss Murray—Rev. H. Drew—Rev. J.S. Gray—D. Tolmer—Mr Hawkins Simpson[2]—President Buckham[3]—Vote Office. Dined with the Misses Monk. H. of C. 4–6.[4] Worked on arranging papers. Saw Ld Spencer—M. Rodd—A. Morley. Read Goldbeck's Report[5]—Momerie in Contemp. Rev.[6]

15. Wed.

Wrote to Mr Dobbie—Mr Mapleson—Mr W.H. Smith—Mr Goldbeck—Rev. Atkinson—G. Allen—Miss H. M'Kenzie. H. of C. 2–6. The Parnell Healy scene.[7] Dined at Sir W. Harcourt's. Saw Ld Kimberley—Sir J. Carmichael—A. Morley—Mr Seward U.S.[8] Read on the Roumans of Transylvania.[9] 2–3½ Saw Mr McCarthy & Mr Sexton. Home rule confidences.

16. Th.

Wrote to Mr Murray—Baron F. Rothschild—Mr Vickers—Mrs Grandt B.P.[10]—H.W. Lovett—Rev. W.J. Wintle—Sec. R. Acad.—J.C. Chisholm—G. Martinelli—S.R. Gardiner.[11] Saw A. Morley & others. Began article on J. Murray.[12] H. of C. 4–8.[13] Read Hamley on Crimean War[14]—Finished tract on Roumans.

---

[1] 'It is not intended to appoint at present a successor to Lord Granville as leader of his political friends in the House of Lords. On the occasions of Lord Granville's absences from his place, Lord Kimberley has habitually conducted any communications with the Government which were required by the course of business, and he will continue to discharge this duty with a view to the general convenience'; *T.T.*, 15 April 1891, 5e.

[2] John Hawkins Simpson, author; wrote on France and Ireland.

[3] *Sic* but obscure.

[4] Irish land; *H* 352. 498.

[5] Possibly J. C. Goldbeck, *The metaphysic of man* (1806).

[6] *C.R.*, lx. 570 (April 1891).

[7] M. Healy humiliated Parnell for his failure to resign and fight Cork; *H* 352. 635.

[8] Probably Frederick William Seward, 1830–1915; journalist and retired diplomat.

[9] Perhaps *The Roumanian question in Transylvania and in Hungary* (1891?).

[10] Probably a rescue case; see 21 Apr. 91.

[11] Samuel Rawson Gardiner, 1829–1902; historian of the commonwealth and protectorate; unsuccessfully requested Gladstone to begin Gardiner's editorship of the *English Historical Review* 'with an article . . . on the early ministerial career of Sir Robert Peel', i.e. a review of Thursfield's *Peel*; Add MS 44512, f. 224.

[12] 'Memoir of John Murray', a review of Smiles (see 23 Mar. 91), *Murray's Magazine*, ix. 577 (May 1891).

[13] Questions; arrest of Abdul Rasoul; *H* 352. 696.

[14] E. B. Hamley, *The war in the Crimea* (1891).

17. Fr.

Wrote to Mrs Stuart BP—Mr Stuart Rendel—Ly Londy—and long letter to Mr [blank] for the coming Elections.[1] Worked on Murray. Saw Mr Hutton—Mr Acton—Mr Morley—Mr A. Morley. H. of C. $2\frac{3}{4}$-7. Read Life of Mr Gilchrist Thomas,[2] and [blank.]

18. Sat.

Wrote to Baron F. de Rothschild—Mr Murray—Mrs Th.—E.W. Hamilton—Mr Hardwick. Worked on J. Murray. Mr Darlington came: conclave on the Hn Collieries. Dined at Mr Armitsteads. Saw Verne [R]. Saw A. Morley—Mr Hardwick. Drive with C. Walk. Read Gilchrist Thomas.

19. 3 S.E.

Curzon Chapel 11.30 AM & H.C.—$6\frac{1}{2}$ PM. Wrote to Mrs Gilchrist Thomas[3]— Mr Murray—Rev. Mr Lilley. Visited the Argylls. Read S.G. Thomas (finished)— Rivett, South Africa[4]—Gk Church Offices (Lechmere)[5]—Lilley on the Sabbath.[6]

20. M.

Wrote to Mr Shee—Mr J. Kennedy. Twelve to dinner: & evening party. H. of C. 4-7.[7] Finished & sent in residue of paper on Murray. Saw Sir W. Harcourt, Nfdd[8] and Granville's affairs—Mr Rendel on Granville's affairs[9]—Sir A. West—A. Morley—Mr Mather—Alf. Lyttelton.

21. Tu.

Wrote to V. Office—M. Cotaro Muchizuki[10]—Lady Lechmere[11]—T. Turnerelli— Mrs Richardson—H.L. Robinson—D. of Argyll. Corrected proofs of 'Murray', and sent to press. Saw The Speaker (re Courtenay). Saw Grandt—Clarke [R?]. Saw A. Morley—J. Morley—Sir W. Harcourt. H. of C. 3-$5\frac{1}{2}$.[12] Dined at Mr Murrays. Read Thursfield's Peel.[13]

[1] To G. R. Benson, liberal candidate for Woodstock; *T.T.*, 20 April 1891, 7b.

[2] S. Gilchrist Thomas, *Memoir and letters*, ed. R. W. Burnie (1891). For Gladstone's intended review, see 5 May 91.

[3] Had sent her husband's biography.

[4] See 12 Apr. 91.

[5] J. Lechmere, *Synopsis, or a synoptical collection of the daily prayers of the Greek Orthodox Church* (1891).

[6] J. P. Lilley had sent his tract.

[7] Questions; Irish land; *H* 352. 937.

[8] Newfoundland.

[9] Granville died leaving substantial debts; Gladstone and others worked to pay them off by donations.

[10] Kotaro Mochizuki, Japanese author; of Keiogijuku University; had translated a *Life of Gladstone* into Japanese. See Add MS 44512, f. 225 and 23 Apr. 91.

[11] Louisa Katharine, wife of Sir Edmund Lechmere, 3rd bart., doubtless relative of the author (see 19 Apr. 91).

[12] Spoke on Irish land; *H* 352. 1048.

[13] J. R. Thursfield, *Peel* (1891); see 16 Apr. 91n.

22. Wed.

Wrote to Ld Acton BP—Mr T.M. Healy MP.—V. Office—Hon. Sir A. Gordon—Sir A. West—Mr P.W. Campbell—Rev M'Gent—G. Washington Moon—A. Morley. 8–12. Mr Seale Hayne's Eton dinner of 20. Read Thursfield—Newfoundland Papers[1]—Report on French Budget. Saw Ld Kimberley—Ld Coleridge—C. Parker. Saw Grant X strange case.

23. Th.

Wrote to Mr Kempe—Mr B. Currie. Saw Muchizaki with Mr Mugford[2]—A. Morley—Mr Fowler. Helen left us. Read Parker's Peel[3]—19th Cent (Feb) on Japan[4]—Dicey on the Council.[5] H. of C. $4\frac{1}{2}$ to dinner.[6]

24. Fr.

Wrote to Ld Acton—Mad. Nylander BP.—C.O.—Mrs Tyndale—J. Macdonald—J.M. Miller—J. Davies—J.E. Mathison—Sir A. West. H. of C. 3–$4\frac{1}{2}$.[7] Tea with Lady Londonderry. Dined with Mr Knowles. Saw Sir W. Harcourt—A. Morley—J. Morley—Mr Dillwyn. Read Thursfield. Pondered & wrote a little on Woman Suffrage.[8]

25. Sat.

Wrote to J.E. Palmer—Maharajah Holkar—Abp of Canterbury—Mr Wemyss Reid—Mr Knowles. Saw Lady Stepney—Mr James—Ld Herschel (Clerks Bill)[9]—Mr Morley *cum* Sir W.H.—12–1. Conclave on Newfoundland. Shopping: friendly mob. Dined at A. Lyttelton's: *small*, pleasant. Read Thursfield.

26. 4 S.E.

Down St Ch mg, & Chapel Royal evg. Tea with the Farquhars: &c. Saw Canon Rowsell. Read Major's In the Gods' Shadow[10]—& Background of Mystery[11]—Rivett, Ch in S. Africa[12]—Emily Shore's Journal[13]—Brinckman's Dr Pusey.[14] Wrote to Mr Brinckman.

[1] *PP* 1890-1, xcvi. 21.

[2] Mugford, otherwise unidentified, was probably assisting Mochizuki with the translation into Japanese of the *Life of Gladstone*; see 21 Apr. 91.

[3] C. S. Parker, *Sir Robert Peel. From his private correspondence*, 3v. (1891). Parker had read Gladstone's Peel MSS and library, see above, x. clxxv and 4 Dec. 86.

[4] *N.C.*, xxix. 267 (February 1891).

[5] A. V. Dicey, *The Privy Council* (1887); the Arnold Prize for 1860.

[6] Goschen's budget; *H* 352. 117, 1214 (missing the first quarter hour).

[7] Misc. business; *H* 352. 1320.

[8] Not published (see 30 Apr. 91), but used in his public letter to S. Smith; see 9 Apr. 92.

[9] Perhaps the government's Stamp Duties Bill, referred to the Standing Cttee. on law; *H* 353. 945.   [10] Untraced.

[11] Perhaps also by Major; also untraced.

[12] See 12 Apr. 91.

[13] M. E. Shore, *Journal of Emily Shore* (1891).

[14] Probably an untraced article on Pusey by Arthur Brinckman, author of several works on ritualism.

27. M.

Wrote to Mr C. Lavis—Mr Thursfield—Dr Major—Editor of E. Shore's Journal—Rev. Chisholm—Central News (Tel.) Tried Woman Suffr. a little. H. of C. 4–7$\frac{1}{2}$.[1] Dined at Mr S. Rendel's. Saw Mr Evans MP[2]—S.L.—Mr A. Morley—H.N.G.—Mr S. Rendel—Canon Rowsell. Read Webb on Ireland[3]—Parker's Peel.

28. Tu.

Wrote to Ld Hardinge—Lady Aberdeen—Mr Roberts—Miss F. Robertson—V. Office—Bull & Auvache—Dr Currie U.S.—Rev. Mr Carrier—Ld E. Clinton. Dined at Mr Warner's. A little more Woman's Suffr. Saw Mr A. Hutton—S.L.—Ld Northbourne. Read Parker's Peel—Hamlyn's Crimean War. H. of C. 3$\frac{1}{4}$–6$\frac{1}{4}$.[4]

29. Wed.

Wrote to V. Office—Ld Kimberley—A. Gregory—Rev. Lloyd—J.A. Fisher—Rev. Martins—W. Gibbings—J. Ogilvy—J.D. Phillips—H.J. Testy—Mr Fisher Unwin. 10$\frac{3}{4}$–1. Attended General Robertson's funeral.[5] Saw Walter Larkins—A. Morley—J. Bryce—Lady Hayter—S.L. Read Parker's Peel—Memoir of Lady Hamilton.[6] Dined at Sir A. Hayter's. Tea with Lady Salisbury.

30. Th.

Wrote to Canon Rowsell—Mrs Th. BP.—W. Laycock—Mr J.D. Balfour—Messrs Blunson. H. of C. 4$\frac{1}{4}$–7.[7] Dined at Ld Northbourne's. Read Parker's Peel—Lady Hamilton's Memoirs. Saw A. Morley—S.G.L.—Bp of St Asaph. Wrote on Woman Suffrage. But the question is now interred for the year.[8]

Frid. May 1. SS Phil. & J.

Wrote to Mr Taylor Innes—Mr Courtney (Editor)—Mr Petrie—Mr F. Turner. R. Acad. Private view 2$\frac{1}{4}$–3$\frac{1}{4}$. H. of C. 6$\frac{1}{4}$–7$\frac{1}{4}$.[9] Read Taylor Innes in C.R.[10]—Parker's Peel—Lady Hamilton. Dined at Ld Reay's. Saw A. Morley—Mr Gilbert—Lady D. Neville [sc. Nevill].

2. Sat.

Wrote to W. Roberts—Lady F. Dixie—E.M. Littlejohns—Pres. of Magdalen—Rev. J. Stephenson. Dined with Mr Evans.[11] Much interesting conversation with

---

[1] Spoke on the budget; *H* 352. 1508.

[2] (Sir) Francis Henry Evans, 1840–1905; partner of D. Currie; liberal M.P. Southampton 1888–95, 1896–1900; kt. 1893. See 2 May 91.

[3] Probably an untraced pamphlet or article by A. J. Webb; see 6 May 91.

[4] Irish land; *H* 352. 1626.

[5] Henry Larkins Robertson, late of the Bengal Staff Corps; probably a distant relative on his mother's side; *T.T.*, 27 April 1891, 1a.

[6] *Memoirs of Emma, Lady Hamilton*, ed. W. H. Long (1891).

[7] Spoke on business of the House; *H* 352. 1775.

[8] See 24 Apr. 91.

[9] Irish land; *H* 352. 1875.

[10] *C.R.*, lix. 750 (May 1891).

[11] See 27 Apr. 91.

the Delegates from Newfoundland. Read Hatton & Harvey's Hist. Newfoundland[1]–Parker's Peel. Royal Acad. $2\frac{1}{4}$–$3\frac{1}{4}$. Hardly an average? Saw S.G.L.–A. Morley–J. Morley.

3. 5 S.E.

Down St Ch. 11 AM. with H.C. Curzon St evg. Dined with the Cobhams. Wrote to Mr H.J. Barker.[2] Read Nemo 'What is Truth?'[3]–Cave on the Standpoints[4]–Dr Kirkpatrick on the Psalms[5]–Barker's Poems.

4. M.

Wrote to Ed. Printing Rev.[6]–Rev. N. Hall–Rev. Dr Lee–Rev. R.C. Jenkins–Bull & Auvache–H.J.G. Watkins–J.L. Thomas–J. Westell–Jon. Nield. H. of C. $5\frac{1}{4}$–$7\frac{1}{4}$.[7] Saw S.G.L.–Ly Stepney–Mr Cohen–A. Morley–Ld Northbourne–Mr Fowler–Mr Rogers *cum* Ld Londonderry–Mr Meade, on the affairs of the Granville Family. Dined with J. Morley: met Mr Jusserand[8] & a capital party. Read Lady Hamilton. Finished Parker's Peel.

5. Tu.

Wrote to G.F. Munro–Ld Kimberley–Miss A. Cox–M. Waring–D.M. Rose–Ed. Northern D. News[9]–Mrs Robertson P.P.–Sotheran & Co. H. of C. 5–7.[10] Saw Mr Forbes (Canada Artist)[11]–Mr Cohen–S.G.L.–Mr Morley–Ly Compton–Sir U. Shuttleworth–Ld Spencer. Finished Lady Hamilton. Made a beginning for S.G. Thomas.[12] Dined at Ld Tweedmouth's.

6. Wed.

Wrote to Mr W.H. Rideing–D.R. Williamson–Sir W. Gregory–Mr Sonnenschein–Mr Schenkhäuser. Barraud Photogr. at 2.30.[13] H. of C. 3–5.[14] Read

[1] J. Hatton and M. Harvey, *Newfoundland, its history and prospects* (1883).
[2] Henry Ross Barker sent his poems, *Looking back* (1891).
[3] *What is Truth? A consideration of the doubts as to the efficacy of prayer raised by evolutionists. By 'Nemo'* (1890).
[4] A. Cave, *The battle of the standpoints* (1890); on the Old Testament.
[5] A. F. Kirkpatrick had sent his *The divine library of the Old Testament* (1891).
[6] Unpublished.
[7] Irish land; *H* 353. 79.
[8] The French author and diplomatist; see 19 June 89.
[9] Not found published.
[10] Irish land; *H* 353. 154.
[11] John Colin Forbes, b. 1846; Canadian artist working in London, known for portraits of politicians. This portrait is in the National Liberal Club, London. It initially included Gladstone's missing index finger, but, following public criticism, Forbes painted it out; *D.N.*, 14 January 1892, 5c. See 30 July 91.
[12] Start of a review (see 17 Apr. 91), apparently abandoned as a result of influenza. See also 25 May 92.
[13] Herbert Rose Barraud, photographer in Oxford Street.
[14] Irish land; *H* 353. 328.

Bertha's Earl.[1] Saw Ld Northbourne—Mr Webb MP.[2]—Mr A. Morley. Worked on S.G. Thomas. Dined at Sir C. Russell's: evg party.

7. Th. Ascension Day.

Curzon St Ch. $11\frac{1}{2}$–$1\frac{1}{2}$. Worked on S.G. Thomas. Wrote to Miss Forbes. Dined at Mr Munro Fergusson's. H. of C. 3–$7\frac{1}{2}$.[3] Read Goldwin Smith's Canada[4]—Ly Lindsay's Bertha's Earl. $2\frac{1}{2}$ PM meeting on Granville Commemoration. Saw Mr Smith *cum* C. of E.—Ld Herschell *cum* Ld Kimberley—Ld Hartington (G.s affairs)—Ld Spencer—Mr Darlington (Aston Colliery)—Sir E. Watkin—Mr Mayhew.

8. Fr.

Wrote to C.B.R. Kent—T. Harley—J.R. Clarke—W. Gwyn—T.A. Tallack—W. Robb—A. Ross.[5] Dined with the Jameses. H. of C. $5\frac{1}{2}$–8.[6] H. of C. Commn at 12 to give evidence on Railway.[7] Saw Mr Currie jun.—E. Wickham—Ld Hardinge—Mr Lefevre—A. Morley—S.G.L. Read Bertha's Earl—G. Smith's Canada—Jusserand, Engl. Novel.[8] Worked on S.G. Thomas.

9. Sat.

Wrote to Mr Rathbone—Lady Lindsay—Callender—Mr Murray. We had a dinner party of 17: small evening company. Read Bertha's Earl—Jusserand. Worked on S.G. Thomas. Visited H. Hunt's Picture.[9]

10. S. aft Ascension.

Down Street Ch. mg. After luncheon very conscious of the influenza I went to bed. I return to my writing table now for the first time on Wednesday the 20th. The fever departed after nine days. Weakness & cough remain: no appetite: much physic. Wrote nothing except a note to Mr Smith (Verney case)[10] & one to Mary for the Hawarden Gymnasium. Saw Sir A. Clark twice daily. Saw occasionally Mr A. Morley—Mr Marjoribanks—Canon MacColl. Made a good deal of way in reading—Bertha's Earl 3 v.—Sir George 1 v.[11]Jerome. 3 v.[12]—Ld

---

[1] C. B. E. Lindsay, Lady Lindsay, *Bertha's Earl. A novel*, 3v. (1891).

[2] Alfred John Webb, 1834–1908; protestant Nationalist M.P. (anti-Parnellite) W. Waterford 1890–5.

[3] Questions; Irish land; *H* 353. 288.

[4] Goldwin Smith, *Canada and the Canadian question* (1891).

[5] Of Edinburgh; on copyright; *T.T.*, 11 May 1891, 6e.

[6] Irish land; *H* 353. 378.

[7] No account found.

[8] J. A. A. J. Jusserand, *The English novel in the time of Shakespeare* (1890).

[9] Holman Hunt's 'May Morning on Magdalen Tower, Oxford', on display in Bond Street; Hunt invited Gladstone to the private view; Add MS 44512, f. 263.

[10] On 12 May, Smith, as Leader of the House, moved the expulsion of E. H. Verney, M.P., consequent on his imprisonment; *H* 353. 573.

[11] Mrs. F. Henniker, *Sir George*, 2v. (1891–3).

[12] A. Gray, *Jerome, a novel*, 3v. (1891).

Houghton's Poems[1]—Anderson Oration on Lee[2]—C.Q. Neo Paganism & Lincoln Case[3]—Ld Hardinge by his Son[4]—Count Campello & his work[5]—Nemo's What is Truth—Delbert Social Evolution[6]—Jusserand English Novel—Mrs Hort's Tahiti[7]—A Girl in the Carpathians.[8] And now as a first effort towards a regularity I recite for today. Wrote to Hon. Mrs Henniker[9]—Card. Manning—Mrs Th.—Mons. P. Delbert. Resumed Sainte Beuve's Port Royal.[10] Downstairs for 6 hours or more.

21. [May] Th.

Wrote to Mr Stanley—Mr Rideing l. & BP—Messrs Stanley—Sotherans—Robn & Nichn—Mr Stanford. Fair progress, of course not like 20 or 30 years ago. Saw Sir A. Clark—S.G.L.—W.H.G.—Ld Rosebery—Mr A. Morley—Mr Marjoribanks. Read Manipuri papers[11]—Sainte Beuve—Jerome.

22. Fr. [Hawarden]

Off at 9.45. Hawarden Rectory 4.10. Day ungenial: but journey excellent, ending at a perfect home. Read Jerome—Dr Phillips. Backgammon with S.

23. Sat.

Rose at one. Read Jerome finished—Dr Phillips—Eurip. Κύκλωψ—the whole. Backgammon with C.

24. Trin. S.

Intimidated into keeping the house. Services alone. Read Spurgeon on the Psalms[12]—Gesetze ü d. Juden in Russland[13]—Report on Divorce Reform in U.S.—poor.[14]—Grätz, Hist. of the Jews.[15] Wrote to J. Morley.

25. M.

Wrote to Ld Acton—Mrs Baker—Mr Farmer. Read Eurip. Helena—Dr Phillips—Grätz Hist. of the Jews. Weather still cold: but even in the house I make progress. Backgammon with the Rector.

[1] R. M. Milnes, Lord Houghton, *Selections [of poems]*, ed. H. J. Gibbs (1891).
[2] Untraced.
[3] *Church Quarterly Review*, xxxii. 29 (April 1891).
[4] C. S. Hardinge, Lord Hardinge, *Viscount Hardinge. By his son* (1891).
[5] A. Robertson, *Count Campello and Catholic reform in Italy* (1891).
[6] P. Delbert had sent his *Social evolution* (1891).
[7] D. Hort, *Tahiti, the garden of the Pacific* (1891).
[8] M. M. Downie, *A girl in the Carpathians* (1891).
[9] Florence Henniker, author of the novel read this entry.
[10] See 8 Feb. 91.
[11] On state of affairs in Manipur; PP 1890–1, lix.
[12] C. H. Spurgeon, *My sermon notes. Old Testament* (1885).
[13] Untraced.
[14] Perhaps D. Convers, *Marriage and divorce in the United States* (1889).
[15] H. Graetz, *History of the Jews*, 5v. (1891–5).

26. Tu.

Wrote to E.L. Walford—Sir W. Harcourt—C.C. Domvile—Mrs Meredith—Sotherans—F. Henderson—Gilbert & Fowler. Read Grätz—Dr Phillips—Eurip. Helena—Genesis in advance of Science.[1] Backgammon with S.

27. Wed.

Wrote to Gen. Grant—C.G. (for meeting)—Mr Waldstein—Guernsey Tel.—P.W. Bunting—Miner's Dep. Tel.[2]—J.W. Laurie—Mr Montagu MP.[3]—Ed. Jewish Chronicle.[4] Read Grätz—Dr Phillips finished: what a book.—Crispi Art. in Contemp. Rev.[5]—Elmslie on Gen. I.[6]—Eurip. Heraclidae &c.—Memoirs of Jenny Lind.[7]

28. Th.

Continuing wet. Wrote to C.G.—Rev. Mr Davies—Mr Dana—Sir H. Verney—H.N.G.—Rev. Canon Lowe—W. Nield. Read Grätz's History—In God's Way[8]—Juvenal Sat. 1.—Schliemann Ausgrabungen.[9] Backgammon with S. Wrote on O.T.

29. Fr.

Weather changed. I went to meet C. at the Station & walked a mile. Wrote to Sir D. Wolff—Prince L.L. Bonaparte—Hon. Rev. Glyn—W.D. Wilcox. Read Grätz V. I and II.—Juvenal Sat. II.—In God's Way. Backgammon with S.

30. Sat.

Ch 8½ AM: first time for three weeks. Wrote to Ld Ronald Gower—Barkers—Barclay Bevan & Co—W. Nield—Mrs Duckworth—Ld Lorne—W.P. Nevins—Ed. Musical Standard[10]—Mr G.J. Stone. Read Grätz—Milner Hist. Jews[11]—Juv. Sat III.—In God's Way—Stephen on Divorce.[12] Drive with C.—Backgammon with S.

---

[1] Untraced.

[2] Perhaps a message for the Miners' Federation meeting in Chester on internationalism; *D.N.*, 29 May 1891.

[3] (Sir) Samuel Montagu, 1832–1911; banker; liberal M.P. Whitechapel 1885–1900; cr. bart. 1894, Baron Swaythling 1907. Montagu wrote on 5 May on the condition on Russian Jews; his letter and Gladstone's long reply on the difficulties of the case concluded 'I view with warm and friendly interest any plan for the large introduction of Jews into Palestine, and shall be very glad if the Sultan gives his support to such a measure'; *T.T.*, 29 May 1891, 12c.

[4] Sending a copy of his letter to Montagu, which it published on 29 May 1891, 7a.

[5] F. Crispi, 'Italy and France', *C.R.*, lix. 777 (June 1891).

[6] W. G. Elmslie, *Memoir and sermons* (1890); p. 302 on Genesis.

[7] H. Scott Holland, *Memoir of Madame Jenny Lind Goldschmidt*, 2v. (1891).

[8] B. Björnson, *In God's way* (1891).

[9] See 15 Jan. 84.

[10] Declining to comment on the current controversy of choral *versus* congregational singing; *Musical Standard*, 13 June 1891, 490a.

[11] See 13 May 30.

[12] A. Stephen, 'The law of divorce. A reply to Mr. Gladstone', *C.R.*, lix. 803 (June 1891).

31. 1 S. Trin.

Ch. mg & evg. Read Skrine's Memory of Thring[1]—Grätz Hist. of Jews—Isaiah (2)—Milman Hist. Jews.

Mond. June 1. 91. Hn.

Ch 8½ A.M. Wrote to Miss Byrom—Watsons—H.H. Millar—A. Morley—Ed. Lyceum[2]—J.W. Butler[3]—D.S. Salmond—Jas Knowles. Read Grätz—Milman—Huxley on Hasisadra[4]—In God's Way—Juvenal. Drive with C.—Backgammon with S.

2. Tu.

Ch. 8½ A.M. Wrote to Ed. Xtn Commonwealth[5]—W.H.G.—R. Barclay—Mr Dunn MP.[6]—H. Mayhew—D. Nutt. Read Milman—Grätz—In God's Way (but qy?) finished—Juvenal—The Light that failed.[7] Worked on O.T. Drive with C & M.—Backgammon with S.

3. Wed.

Ch 8½ A.M. Wrote to Bp of Rochester—Sir W. Harcourt—S. Coit—Mr Montagu MP—P.M. Newton—Messrs Osgood—Rev. OHanlon—Mr R.M. Lewis[8]—Rev. W. Thomas. Read Grätz—Milman—Juvenal—Kipling's 'Light that failed'. Backgammon with S.

4. Th.

Ch. 8½ A.M. Wrote to Warden Trin. Coll.—Mrs Rylands—H.N.G.—Mr F.L. Gower—W.K. Tupper—Rev. Dr. Ginsburg—Mr R. Hutton—Sir A. Gordon—Mr B. Currie—Dean of Westmr—Rev. Sime—Station Master Chester. Conversation with C. on the operation meditated for W. It is sad: but we are in God's hands.[9] Read on this baccarat business: deplorable *all round*.[10] Read Kipling (bad)—Grätz—Juvenal—and . . . . Backgammon with S. Saw Mr Mayhew.

5. Fr.

Ch. 8½ A.M. Wrote to Barker & Rogerson—Mr Morley—Ld Houghton—Mr A. Morley—Rev. Dr Hutton—G. Gregory—Mr Swift Macneill—W. Fraser—P.W.

---

[1] J. H. Skrine, *A memory of Edward Thring* (1889).

[2] Not found published.

[3] James W. Butler of Blackheath sent a gift; Hawn P.

[4] T. H. Huxley, 'Hasisadra's adventure', *N.C.*, xxix. 904 (June 1891).

[5] Comments on *St Michael's Eve* (see 1 Mar. 91 ff.); *The Christian Commonwealth*, 9 June 1892, 578e.

[6] Letter of congratulation to (Sir) William Dunn, 1833–1912; South African banker; liberal M.P. Paisley 1 June 1891–1906; cr. bart 1895.

[7] R. Kipling, *The light that failed* (1890); see 4 June 91.

[8] R. Morris Lewis, corresponded on Homeric questions; Hawn P.   [9] See 2 July 91.

[10] The Tranby Croft case; an action for slander unsuccessfully brought by Sir W. Gordon-Cumming, accused of cheating at baccarat; the Prince of Wales, one of those who had been cheated, was subpoenaed by Cumming at the sensational trial 1–9 June 1891; see Magnus, *Edward VII*, ch. 12.

Campbell—J.B. Paul[1]—T.F.A. Agnew—A.M. Smith. Saw S.E.G. on St D[einiol's] &c.—Bailie on fresh bookcases—Mrs Holms (aet. 95). Read Grätz—Juvenal—and . . . . .

6. Sat. [Holmbury]

Wrote to A.G. Symonds—Messrs Freshfield . . . . . Packing & preparing. $10\frac{3}{4}$-4. To 18 Park Lane. Saw Willy & G.—A. Morley—S.G.L. 4.50-$7\frac{1}{4}$. To Holmbury:[2] our farewell visit. Conversation with J. Morley. Read Demidoff on the Jews[3]— Life of Archbp Tait.[4]

7. 2 S. Trin.

Church 11-$1\frac{1}{4}$ (with H.C.) Prayers with C. at night. Read Archbishop Tait (largely). Conversation with Mr Rendel (G. affairs)—Mr Morley(Abp Tait— κτλ.[5])—The kind host—on parting with Holmbury.

8. M. [Hatchlands]

Wrote to Mr Acton.[6] Read Abp Tait—Baron Hübner[7]—Shakespeare Henry V. & Oxf. Dict.[8] Long drive to Mr Rendel's new place and fine trees at Hatchlands.[9]

9. Tu. [London]

Wrote to Mr Carnegie—Rev. Mr Atkinson—Sig. Stuart [sic]—Mr W. Bailey. Walked my farewell with the kind host. $3\frac{3}{4}$. Off to London. $6\frac{1}{2}$-$8\frac{1}{2}$ H. of C.[10] Saw Sir W. Harcourt—A. Morley. Read Life of Abp Tait.

10. Wed.

Wrote to V.O.—M. Léon Séché—Rev. Denny—Sir E. Saunders—F.E. Tirbutt[11]— Macmillans—Bp of St Andrews. Saw Sir W. Harcourt $11\frac{1}{2}$-1 (Baccarat—Irish Land—Manipuri—Free Educn)—Mr A. Morley—S.G.L.—Dr Ginsburg—Ld Rosebery—Mrs Oppenheim. Kept away from H. of C. Eight to dinner. Read Demidoff—Life of Abp Tait.

---

[1] Sir James Balfour Paul, 1846-1931; Edinburgh author and Lyon King of Arms.

[2] Leveson-Gower's house in Surrey. Rendel was also present; his account of the visit is in *Rendel*, 76.

[3] P. P. Demidov, *The Jewish question in Russia* (1884).

[4] R. T. Davidson, *Life of A. C. Tait, Archbishop of Canterbury*, 2v. (1891); much Gladstoniana.

[5] Greek for 'etc.'.

[6] Richard Maximilian Acton, s. of the historian; 2nd Baron Acton 1902; wrote to Gladstone on his wish to enter the foreign office; Add MS 44512, f. 292.

[7] J. A. von Hübner, *Ein Jahr meines Lebens* (1891).

[8] James Murray's *Oxford English Dictionary* which had then completed 'B'.

[9] Rendel's house near Guildford.

[10] Spoke briefly on Irish land; *H* 354. 59.

[11] Francis E. Tirbutt of Crewe; on religion; Hawn P.

11. *Th.*

Wrote to Bp of Rochester—Mr Heffermann. Signs of cold in evg. Read Life of Tait—and [blank.] Saw Sir E. Saunders 11 AM—Sir W. Harcourt—S.G.L.—Mr A. Morley—W.H.G.—E. Wickham. H. of C. 4–7.[1]

12. *Fr.*

Wrote to Warden of Trin. Coll.—and .... Conclave 3 PM on Education—Tranby Croft—and [blank]

[No entry for 13 June 1891]

14. *S. Trin. 3.*

Bed until evg. Morning service with C. Saw Lucy—Mary Drew. Read largely Abp Tait: no slight exercise, tho' the book is most attractive. Saw Sir A. Clark.

15. *M.*

Rose at 11.45. Wrote to Abp of Canterbury—Mr W.H. Smith—M'Millans—Col. Gascoyne[2]—Mr Holyoake. Relieved by the kindness of friends from the House. Much thought on the P. of W. Saw Ld Spencer—Mr A. Morley—Mr Morley—H.N.G. (back)—S.G.L.—Sir W. Harcourt—H.J.G.—Lady Londonderry—Duc d'Aumale. Read Life of Tait—Red Letter Stories.[3]

16. *Tu.*

Rose at 11 AM. Wrote to Mr Shirreff—Sir A. Gordon—F.N. Jackson—J.W. Johnson—& minutes. H. of C. 3¾–7.[4] Saw Sir F. Knollys—Mr A. Morley—S.G.L.—H.N.G. (Collieries plan). Read Life of Tait—OHanlon's Monck Mason[5]—A. Gordon's Preface[6]—From King to King.[7]

17. *Wed.*

Wrote to Mr Reid MP—Rev. J.C. Grant—Mrs Th.—Mr Taylor Innes—Mr H. New—G.L. Dickinson.[8] Dined at Baron Stein's. Drive with C. Saw S.G.L.—A. Morley—Ld Spencer—Sir A. Clark—Mr Percy Bunting. Read Abp Tait (finished)—From King to King (finished)—Unity of Isaiah[9]—Westmr Review on Gambling.[10]

[1] Questions; Irish land; *H* 354. 174.
[2] Probably William Julius Gascoigne, colonel in the Scots Guards; business untraced.
[3] R. H. Davis, *Gallagher and other stories* (1891), 'Red letter stories' series.
[4] Harcourt's motion on Manipur; *H* 354. 541.
[5] Untraced.
[6] The introductory chapter of his biography of his father, Lord Aberdeen, not yet sent to press; see *T.A.P.S.*, n.s. li. 100.
[7] G. Lowes Dickinson, *From King to King. The tragedy of the Puritan revolution* (1891).
[8] Goldsworthy Lowes Dickinson, 1862–1932; fellow of King's, Cambridge; author and liberal humanist. See previous day.
[9] J. Kennedy, *Popular arguments for the unity of Isaiah* (1891).
[10] *Westminster Review*, cxxxv. 648 (June 1891).

18. Th.

Wrote to Mr Watts—Sir F. Knollys l.l.—Rev. A. Caldecott—Mr Fairweather. Tea with Lady Derby. H. of C. 4–4¾.[1] Saw Sir W. Harcourt—J. Morley—A. Morley—S.G.L. Read Tracts on Col. Bprics—Life of Dana[2]—and [blank.]

19. Fr.

Wrote to Mr Stead—Treasurers C.O. Fund—Sir W. Phillimore—Sir F. Knollys (P. of W.).[3] Saw S.G.L.—A. Morley—Mr Carnegie—Mr Cohen—Bp of London—Bp of Chichester. Attended Col. Bprics meeting & spoke 40 m. the voice seeming to come at command.[4] H. of C. afterwards—saw Mr Montagu MP—Mr A. Morley. Read Life of Dana—Accounts of D. of Bedford.[5]

20. Sat. [Dollis Hill]

An hour of bad cough in the morning. Nature's revenge for the speech of yesterday. Unable to see Sir W. Phillimore, I had communication with him on the Clergy Bill by written Mema. Rose at 11½. Wrote to Rev. Dr Momerie. Read Florine (all)[6]—Life of Dana. Off at 4½ to Dollis Hill. Felt sensibly stronger on arriving in that air.

21. 4 S. Trin.

Forbidden to go to Church. Morning Service alone. Saw Mr Findlay. Read Bp Bickersteth's Charge—Adams on Isaiah[7]—Kennedy on do—Cheyne in Indian Ch. Quarterly.[8]

22–4. M.–Wed.[9]

Three days of bed & battles with the cough. Daily visits from kind Sir Andrew.[10] The morning bout continuous from Saturday. Wrote Tu.—Cardinal Manning—Bp of Exeter. Wed.—A. Morley. Read The Ridout volume on Upper Canada[11]—[author and title illegible]—Kennedy on Isaiah—Ch. I.Q. on Indian

---

[1] End of questions; *H* 354. 785.

[2] C. F. Adams, *Richard Henry Dana. A biography* (1890).

[3] Gladstone supported the Queen's view that the reluctant Prince of Wales should write for publication a letter to the Abp. of Canterbury condemning gambling; Knollys next day was about to arrange this with the Abp. when Salisbury wrote to Wales that such a public statement would be 'injudicious'; on 31 August, Wales, having replaced baccarat with bridge, did write to the Abp. for publication; see Magnus, *Edward VII*, 230 and 4 June 91.

[4] In Hutton and Cohen, *Speeches*, x. 364 and *T.T.*, 20 June 1891, 14a.

[5] 'The late Duke of Bedford' (1891).

[6] See 16 July 58; pornography.

[7] Perhaps M. Adams, *Creation of the bible* (1891?).

[8] T. K. Cheyne, 'Biblical doctrine of immortality', *Indian Church Quarterly Review*, iv. 127 (April 1891). See 20 Aug. 91.

[9] This entry written in a weak and barely legible hand.

[10] Sir Andrew Clark, his doctor.

[11] T. Ridout, *The years of Upper Canada in peace and war, 1805–1815* (1891).

Philosophies[1]—Wilkins American Studies.[2] I long to be up & at full work: yet the work in bed may be full too. (Thus far on Wedy).

25. Th.

Wrote to A.W. Hutton—Rev. F. Meyrick—Rev. Mr Tucker—Rev. Dr Kennedy—Miss Marshall. Made advance today and rose at noon. Read Kennedy—Ridout Corresp. (finished)—M. Bashkirtseff Lettres.[3] Saw Sir A. Clark who brought Dr Habershon.[4] The air here has given me strength but despite it & much physic the cough continues.

26. Fr. [The Clyffe, Corton, Lowestoft]

Back to London & on to Corton, Lowestoft[5] at 6¾. Wrote to Lady Aberdeen—Sir B. Powell—Scotts—Mr Rideing—Mr Childers—Ernest Rhys—Watsons BP—Rev. E.G. Wood—F. Reynolds. Here I am closely & skilfully looked after by Dr Habershon: and am allowed to pursue a recluse life. Read Wood's Petland[6]—Pilgrim's Progress[7]—Simon, Theocratic Literature.[8]

27. Sat.

In my room all day. The doctor most assiduous: & baby Dorothy[9] a delight. Did some paper-work, revising: to writing I am hardly equal. Read Fortnightly Review—Mehler on Humes—Von Egidy, Serious Thoughts[10]—Henry & Clarkes Commentaries[11]—Drage on Eton.[12]

28. 5 S. Trin.

Church absolutely forbidden: services at home. Read Theocr. Literature—Pilgrim's Progress, largely—Throne of Canterbury[13]—Sainte Beuve P. Royal VI.[14]—and Stead's Article.[15] Cough much lightened after this morning. Went out a little. Wrote to Mr Suffield—Mr Stead (P. of Wales)—D. Nutt.

[1] *Indian Church Quarterly Review*, iv. 139 (April 1891).
[2] Possibly M. E. Wilkins, *New England nun, and other stories* (1891).
[3] M. K. Bashkirtsev, *Letters* (1891).
[4] Samuel Herbert Habershon, 1857–1915; London chest specialist.
[5] J. J. Colman's house.
[6] J. G. Wood, *Petland revisited* (1890).
[7] See 3 Jan. 64.
[8] D. M. Simon, *The Bible an outgrowth of theocratic life* (1886).
[9] His grand-daughter, Dorothy Drew.
[10] C. M. von Egidy, *Serious thoughts on the doctrine of the church* (1891).
[11] M. Henry, *The family bible, or complete commentary* (1838).
[12] G. Drage, 'Eton and the Empire. An Address' (1890).
[13] M. Fuller, *Throne of Canterbury; or, the archbishop's jurisdiction* (1891).
[14] See 8 Feb. 91.
[15] [W. T. Stead], 'Character sketch: the Prince of Wales', *Review of Reviews*, iv. 19 (July 1891), on the Tranby Croft affair. Proofs were widely circulated and revised; see F. Whyte, *Life of Stead*, ii. 14 ff., 103 ff. (1925). Stead's remedy was to 'Sandringhamise Marlborough House'. On 2 July 1891, Gladstone wrote to his wife: 'Stead has revised his article and is thought very much to have taken out the sting'; Hawn P.

29. M.

A longer walk. Saw Rev. Mr Barrett—Mr Colman. Read Pilgr. Progress—Sainte Beuve—Debidour Hist. Dipl.[1] Surfeited with kindness.

30. Tu.

Wrote to Sir A. West—Mr Stead—Rev. Dr. West—A. Fortis—J. Macveagh—E. Rhys—J.J. Hedges—Mr Stead. Tea in the open. Read Debidour—Pilgrim's Progress—Stoughton on the First Ages.[2] J. Morley came: much conversation.

Jun 30 1891. Tues.

C. went off early on her holy errand.[3] Wrote to her—and to A. Morley. Read Stoughton—Debidour—Pilgrim's Progress—T. Mozley Letters from Rome[4]—Caine on Isle of Man.[5] Walk with Mary.

1. [July] Wed.

Wrote to C.G. and Sir W. Harcourt. Read Pilgrim: finished. It has a real genius & is essentially good. Read also Debidour—and Hall Caine. Drive with Mary. Renewed conversations with J. Morley: most useful.

2. Th.

Wrote to Mr Carnegie—Mr Stead—H.N.G.—C.G. Yesterday was a day of deep anxiety, but all is anchored in God.[6] What we hoped has not been given: but there is a little gift as the result. He knows what is best: assuredly Willy is in His love. Drive with M. Long final conversation with J.M. on the Irish question. Read Debidour—Hall Caine—Dr [blank].[7]

3. Fr.

Wrote to C.G.—Mr Stead—J. Morley went early. Drive with M. Backgammon with Mrs C[olman]. For it was a day of illusion. Read Debidour—Hall Caine (finished)—Mozley's L. from Rome—and [blank.] The sad news of the turn in the evening was too kindly kept from me.[8]

---

[1] A. Debidour, *Histoire diplomatique de l'Europe 1814-1878* (1891).
[2] J. Stoughton, *Lights and shadows of primitive Christendom* (1891).
[3] See 2 July 91.
[4] T. Mozley, *Letters from Rome on the occasion of the Oecumenical Council*, 2v. (1891).
[5] T. H. Hall Caine, *The little Manx nation* (1891).
[6] Exploratory operation on 1 July on Willy Gladstone; the tumour found in his brain was inoperable.
[7] Name scrawled.
[8] 'At dinner received a telegram with less good account of Willy, and at 10 a very much more serious and alarming one. Consulted first with Harry ... and settled that Father should be strengthened by an undisturbed night'; *Mary Gladstone*, 415.

Sat. Jul. 4. [*London*]

The day of dear dear Willy's entry into rest, at 5.30 A.M.

I was called at six.[1] The telegrams when read suggested only death though not in terms. On reaching Liverpool Street it was confirmed. And we met in P[ark] Lane, still eight living members of the family, who were ten in all.[2] At 3 we went to see for the last time the dear remains & we prayed by him & for him.[3] Saw the dear heroic widow for a moment. A heavy day for her and the children!

Wrote to Sir A. Gordon—V. Office—Mr Heinemann—Mr Osborne. Read as yesterday.

5. 6 S. Trin.

Ch Ch mg with H.C.—Curzon St Evg. The services spoke to us at so many points.

Wrote to A. Morley—Prince of Wales—Rev. Newnham—C.A. Walker—Lady Breadalbane—Mr D. Fortescue. Read Newnham's Essays[4]—The Agnostic Island.[5] We had a long and interesting conversation with Sir A. Clark. Among ourselves we spoke much of the beloved, not lost, only hidden for a time. C. & I went to a solitary tea kindly devised for us at Argyll Lodge. Praised be God for all His goodness: The God of the widow and the fatherless.

6. M.

Wrote to A. Morley—Archbp of Canterbury l.l.—J. Westell—Mr English—Sec. K. Coll.—Mr Cameron—Sec. Royal Soc. Saw A. Morley—S.G.L. Read Debidour—&c. Worked hard & long on arranging, distributing, and packing, books and papers for the year's clearing out. A short drive with C. Conversation on household arrangements.

7. Tu. [*Hawarden*]

Wrote to Mr W.H. Smith—Mr T.P. O'Connor—Ld Ripon—Mr Mather MP.—Mrs Kay—Duc d'Aumale—Rev. Lilly—Khedive of Egypt—Mr Childers—Ld Norton—Empress Eugenie—Scotts. Saw S.G.L.—Mr Westell—Sir W. Harcourt—Mr A. Morley. After a laborious morning off at $\frac{1}{4}$ to 4: home soon after nine. Read Gavin Carlyle[6]—Bickersteth—Greek Euchologion.[7] We found the Castle Porch

---

[1] 'At 6 I went in to Papa and told him gradually of the alarming news, tho' keeping the worst from him till we were within half an hour of London. He was terribly shocked and broken down, and at Liverpool Street [station] the little note from Helen reached us telling us of the end at 5.30'; *Mary Gladstone*, 416.

[2] i.e. including Jessy, who d. 1850, and Willy.

[3] At W. H. Gladstone's house, 41 Berkeley Square. As a result of his death, the Hawarden estate passed, *via* a reversion to W. E. Gladstone, to Willy's six year old son, W. G. C. Gladstone, with his wife (Gertrude), H. N. and H. J. Gladstone as trustees. See 11 Aug. 91n.

[4] W. O. Newnham had sent his *Alresford essay for the times* (1891).

[5] F. J. Gould, *The agnostic island* (1891).

[6] G. Carlyle, *Moses and the prophets* (1890).

[7] The Greek liturgy.

prepared with most beautiful white flowers. Harry and Herbert brought the precious remains from Chester after midnight.

8. Wed.

Our son in the prime of middle life was followed to the grave, with its wide and inspiring outlook, between twelve and one, by his mother in her 80th, and his unworthy Father in his 82d year.

We had all attended a Celebration in the Orphanage at nine.

The devoted widow went to the service & the grave. It was more than she could bear. All besides in the procession its reception and the entire service was harmonious and soothing: what he would have wished it to be. The family on his side was affectionately and thoroughly represented.

I wrote no letters but gave my disposable time to a paper of recollections, which I thought it well to put down.[1]

Read Euchologion, & Bell.

9. Th.

Wrote to Mr Cook—Sir E. Watkin—Lord Leigh—Mr de Coverley—Mr Godley—Mrs Bampfylde[2]—F.B.O. Cole—Lord Tennyson—Archdn Denison.

Drive with C. & Agnes & a remarkable conversation with the nurse which went to show more & more cause for thankfulness.

I examined the Will yesterday & today had further conversation with Harry: also with Stephen on his position, which he had never dreamt of.[3]

Also I was much pressed to take Catherine *at once* to the sea, which causes me extreme embarrassment.

The problem of conflicting duties is frequent & perplexing. Perhaps it is a good *general* rule to prefer the one we are disinclined to. There are however serious affairs here on which I had a long conversation in evg with the two H.s. [4]Read The Jew.[5]

10. Fr.

Ch. 8½ A.M. Wrote to Lady Aberdeen—Mr Morley—Mr A. Morley—D. of Argyll—Ld Stalbridge—Mrs Worke—Rev. D. Robertson—Mrs Robertson—Canon Venables—Mr Henniker Heaton. Read The Jew—Bashkirtseff's Letters. Further conversation with C.G. Lucy C. and the H.s on the Mayhew case. Drove with C.

---

[1] Memoir headed 'For the sacred memory of William Henry Gladstone'; copy, in Mary Gladstone's hand, dated 8–9 July 1891; Add MS 46269, f. 144.

[2] Perhaps Lady Marcia Bamfylde, novelist.

[3] Presumably his and his childrens' position as prospective heirs to Hawarden if (as he did) W.G.C. Gladstone died childless. See 5 Aug. 91.

[4] Next phrase written at right angle to rest of entry.

[5] J. I. Kraszewski, *The Jew: a novel* (1890); tr. from Polish.

11. Sat.

Wrote to W. Richmond—Prince Louis Lucien B.—King of the Belgians—(U. Sec. of State)—J. Mellor—Madame Bashkirtseff—Bp of Carlisle—Rev. Carlyle[1]—Mr Labouchere[2]—W. Meynell. Ch. 8½ A.M.

Visited Gerty for the first time. It was touching, almost heartbreaking but she was admirable. Anxious conversations with H. and H. respecting Mr Mayhew & future arrangements. Also one with Mr M. himself. Read The Jew—Bashkirtseff Letters.

12. 7 S. Trin.

Ch. 11 A.M. & 7 A.M. Edw. Wickham preached a sermon on the dear departed which was absolutely perfect.

Wrote to Ld Rosebery l.l.—Gertrude G.—Rev Mr Scott—Sir W. Harcourt—Rev J.G. Rogers—Abp of Canterbury—Mayor of Chester. Conversation with S.E.G. on prayer for the departed. Read Paradisus Animae[3]—Gasquet on Prayerbook[4]—The Christ that is to be[5]—and [blank.]

13. M.

Ch. 8¼ A.M. Wrote to Rev. F. Meyrick l. & BP.—Archdn Colley—Miss Norbury —Bp of Exeter—A. Rickett—Mad. Loyson—A. Andrew—Mr Gilbert—Mrs Th.— Sir Jas Farquhar. Conversation with H. & H.[6] afterwards with Mr Mayhew also when we settled the questions with him to our general satisfaction. Read The Jew—Nero and Actaea.[7] Spent much time on arranging small things. Drive with C. Backgammon with S.

14. Tu.

Ch. 8½ A.M. Wrote to Dean of Durham—Mr Mayhew—Ld Coleridge—E. Menken[8]—Sir E. Watkin—T. Townsend—Mr Heinemann—A. Hassard—Robn & Nichn—W.H. Rideing—Prof. Waldstein[9]—Mrs Hutton—F.T. Palgrave BP—Rev. W. Miller. Conversation with Stephy. Read 'The Jew'—Nero and Actea—Bashkirtseff Letters: &c. A little Kosmos.

15. Wed.

Ch. 8¼ A.M. Wrote to Rev. Canon Scott l & PP—Sir W. Harcourt—Mayor of Windsor—Sir W. Barthelot[10]—Ld Just. Bowen—S. Van Campen[11]—Messrs Dodd

---

[1] Gavin Carlyle, author of old testament studies and editor of Edward Irving; see 7 July 91.

[2] On the Triple Alliance; in Thorold, *Labouchere*, 372.

[3] See 25 Feb. 46.   [4] See 6 Nov. 90.

[5] [J. Compton-Rickett], *The Christ that is to be: a latter-day romance* (1891).

[6] i.e. Harry and Herbert Gladstone.   [7] E. Mackay, *Nero and Actea* (1891).

[8] Bookseller; a copy of his 'Catalogue of second hand books' (1890) with Gladstone's annotations is in British Library c. 60. 1. 6.

[9] (Sir) Charles Waldstein (later Walston), 1856–1927; reader in classical archaeology at Cambridge 1883–1907; excavated tomb of Aristotle 1891.

[10] *Sc.* Barttelot; see 20 Feb. 63.

[11] Samuel Richard Van Campen, Dutch historian.

N.Y.[1]—Ed. Expository Times.[2] Worked Kosmos (i.e. ordering & arranging).
Read The Jew (finished)—Bashk. Letters—Dr Kinns.[3] Backgammon with the
Rector. Saw dear Gerty: & had a most interesting conversation on little Will[4] &
prayer for the departed.

16. Th. [*The Clyffe, Corton, Lowestoft*]

Wrote to R. de Coverly—Mr Rutherford—Mr A. Brand[5]—Mrs Spurgeon. 10-6¼.
Journey to Corton:[6] received with overflowing kindness. Read Cic. de Officiis—
The Canadians of Old.[7]—Q.R. on Sir R. Peel—On J. Murray[8]—&c. &c.

17. Fr.

Wrote to Mr Childers—Mr R.S. Archer—Mr Astley [*sic*] Cooper. Read Canadians of Old—Langen Romische Kirche[9]—Cic. de Senect.—Alexander's Confucius.[10] Walk with Mr Colman.

18. Sat.

Wrote to Mr Stead—Rev. Ventris BP—Mr Appleton—Mr Joseph[11]—Mrs Ireland.[12] Read Cic. de Senectute (finished)—Langen Geschichte—The Canadians
of Old. Saw Mr Shakespeare.[13]

19. 8 S. Trin.

Lowestoft Ch mg, & Corton evening. Wrote to Sir W. Harcourt—A. Morley—
Mr Story. Read Parad. Animae[14]—Langen Geschichte—Cic. De Officiis—Q.R. on
Séché's Later Jansenistes.[15]

20. M.

Wrote to A. Morley—Rev. J. White[16]—T. Vearey—Rev. J. Monckton—O. Brown-
ing—Mr Pritchard. Drive & walk with Mr Stuart. Long conversation with Mr
Shakespeare. Wrote on O.R. Read Langen—Cicero de Offic.—Mrs Carlyle's
Life.[17] Backgammon with Mr Colman. Looked into Guatemala case.[18]

---

[1] See 20 Dec. 89.   [2] Not published.
[3] S. Kinns, *Graven in the rock; or, the historical accuracy of the bible* (1891).
[4] i.e. W. G. C. Gladstone, his grand-son.
[5] Best wishes to Arthur Brand, liberal candidate in by-election at Wisbech; *T.T.*, 20 July 1891, 7c.
[6] See 26 June 91; for this visit, see H. C. Colman, *J. J. Colman* (1905), 406.
[7] See 22 June 91.   [8] *Q.R.*, clxxiii. 1, 173 (July 1891).
[9] See 16 Oct. 81.   [10] See 16 Nov. 90.
[11] Thanking N. S. Joseph for sending the first number of *Darkest Russia*, journal published by the
Russo-Jewish Committee; *T.T.*, 13 August 1891, 7f.
[12] Mrs Alexander Ireland, author; see 20 July 91.
[13] Perhaps a visiting friend of Colman; no 'Shakespeare' listed in local directories.
[14] See 12 July 91.
[15] *Q.R.*, clxxiii. 211 (July 1891).
[16] Joseph Neville White, vicar of Stalham, Norwich.
[17] Mrs A. E. Ireland, *The life of Jane Welsh Carlyle* (1891), sent by the author, Add MS 44513, f. 65.
[18] Further problems of boundary demarcation; see 24 Oct. 61, 5 June 63.

21. *Tu.*

Wrote to Sir W. Harcourt—Freshfields—H.N.G.—Sir J.E. Wilmot—T. Lloyd—Harvey Beales & Co. Read Langen—Cic. de Off.—Mrs Carlyle's Life—Canadians of Old. Shore-walk.

22. *Wed.*

Wrote to Roffinddin Ahmed[1]—Mr Illingworth MP—Ld Kimberley. Read Langen—Cicero—Canadians of Old (finished)—Mrs Carlyle's Life. Shore walk.

23. *Th.*

Wrote to R. Brown—T.J. Woodrow—T.C. Eldon—Messrs Sotheran—E. Evans—Peter Terry. Read Langen—Cic. de Off. III—Mrs Carlyle. Saw Mr Birkbeck. Backgammon with him.

24. *Fr.*

Wrote to A. Morley—and Lucy Cavendish. Sailed in Mr C.s yacht. Read as yesterday & A Russian Priest[2]—finished Cic. Off. Backgammon with Mr C[olman].

25. *Sat.*

Wrote to Mr Brand—Mr Bunting[3]—H. Baverstock—G. Petrie—A.W. Hutton—T.D. Keighley—Mr Butterworth. Read Langen—Mrs Carlyle—A Russian Priest. Conversation with H.N.G. on the Will, & Estate affairs. Saw Mr Judd—Mr Guinness Rogers.

26. *9 S. Trin.*

Lowestoft Ch. 11 A.M. Corton 6½ PM. Wrote to A. Morley. Read Langen—Homes &c. of Wesley[4]—Morden on Agnosticism[5]—Mors Janua Vitae.[6] Conversation with Mr Rogers.

27. *M.*

Wrote to Ld Spencer—Ld Herschell—Sir A. Clark—Rev. Wilkinson—Mr Bryce. J. Morley came over: we traversed the Irish field together. Read Langen Geschichte—Life of Mrs Carlyle.

28. *Tu.* [*London*]

Wrote to C. Higham. Farewell conversations with Mr Rogers & our host. 12.40–4¼ to London. Saw Ld Spencer—A. Morley—Mr Rendel—did shopping. Saw Sir A. Clark—Mr Agnew. Read Langen—Mrs Carlyle's Life.

---

[1] Rofinndin Ahmed of Bournemouth; Hawn P.   [2] N. Potapenko, *A Russian priest* (1891).
[3] To P. W. Bunting on Anglican-nonconformist reunion, published in facsimile in *Review of the Churches*, i. 1 (1891).
[4] *The homes, haunts and friends of John Wesley . . . the centenary number of 'The Methodist Recorder'* (1891).   [5] J. W. Morden, *Agnosticism found wanting* (1891).
[6] W. J. Hocking, *Mors Janua Vitae; a contribution to the problem of immortality* (1891).

29. Wed.

Wrote to W. Tudor Johns—J. Knowles—Messrs M'Caw—J. Sinclair—Editor Walsall Free Press[1]—Ly Cunliffe Owen—Sir W. Harcourt—W.H. Holland. Sat to Millais 11-12.[2] Saw three South African Chiefs: interesting.[3] Saw Mr A. Hutton —Ld Herschell—Sir W. Harcourt—Sir J. Lacaita—Mr A. Morley—S. Lyttelton— H.N.G.—Scotts—and E. Hamilton, a marvellous recovery. Read Langen.

30. Th.

Wrote to Rev. Smith—Mr W.M. Adams L. & BP.—Scotts—Mr Beaumont—Mr Judd—Mrs Gunn. Packing books. Sat to Millais 11-12. Also Mr Forbes came & worked on pictures.[4] Saw S.G.L.—Sir A. West—Sir W. Harcourt—Miss Tennant —Mr Childers—A. Morley—Mr Armitstead (re Carnegie). Dined at Mr Armitstead's. Read Langen—Waddy on Electoral Facts[5]—WEG on do (N.C., D. 1889)[6]—Dicey on the situation.[7]

31. Fr. [Hawarden]

Wrote to Mr J. Knowles—Miss E. Pigott—Ld Rosebery—Miss James. Final sitting to Millais. Visited Royal Academy. Saw A. Morley—F.L. Gower—Mr Armitstead—Sir J. Lacaita. 3.45-9.45. To Hawarden. Train heavy and late. Read Langen—Mrs Carlyle finished.

Sat. Aug. One. 1891.

Wrote to Bp of Gibraltar—Wms & Norgate—Rev. Lester—Capt. Douglas—Rev. Falconer. Forenoon with Mr Barker & the H.s[8] on Estate matters. Conversation with Gerty. Read Langen Geschichte—Cornish Jeux[9]—and Folks of Carglen.[10]

2. 10 S. Trin.

Ch 11 A.M. and H.C.—also 6½ P.M. Wrote to Cardinal Manning—Mr J. Morley —Sir A. Clark—Mr Knowles. Read Langen—Manning on Leo XIII[11]—Two Sermons of Spurgeon—Gasquet on the Prayerbook.[12]

---

[1] Walsall Free Press, 1 August 1891, 5d.
[2] Presumably a retouching of Millais' fourth portrait of Gladstone (with W.G.C. Gladstone); see 25 June 89.
[3] Perhaps attached to the 'African Native Choir', performing to raise funds for a technical college, and recently received at court; The Graphic, 1 August 1891, 146.
[4] See 5 May 91.
[5] Untraced article, presumably by the secretary of the Scottish Home Rule Association.
[6] See 5 Nov. 89; see 5 Aug. 91.
[7] Unclear which work; Dicey unusually refrained from controversy in 1891; see R. A. Cosgrove, The rule of law: A. V. Dicey (1980), 152.
[8] H. J. and H. N. Gladstone and H. Mayhew, the Hawarden agent.
[9] Untraced.
[10] A. Gordon, Folks o'Carglen; or, life in the North (1891).
[11] H. E. Manning, Leo XIII and the condition of labour (1891).
[12] See 6 Nov. 90.

3. M.

Ch 8½ AM. Found my heart a little weak for the hill. Worked at St Deiniol's. Wrote to Father Gasquet l. & BP.—A. Morley MP.—H. Mayhew BP.—Rev. Clarendon(?)—H. Lewis—W.E. Willcox—M. Minissy—N.S. Ivanovitch:[1] and sent off over 40 copies of E. Wickham's Sermon,[2] with inscriptions for each. Read Gasquet—Langen—B. & F.s Valentinian.[3] Saw Father Ryan[4]—H.N.G. on affairs.

4. Tu.

Ch. 8½ A.M. Wrote to Mr J.C. Deverell[5]—Rev. Dr Ginsburg—Ld Acton—Rev. Macdonald—S. Wentworth—A.W. Marchmont. Worked at St Deiniol's. Read Langen—Gasquet—finished Valentinian (a play with fine poetry) & examined dear Willy's Iambics.

5. Wed.

Wrote to Mr Fordham—Mr Rowlands l.l.—J. Noble—Miss Ponsonby—R. Call—J. Mainwaring—Rev. Tucker. Saw Gerty—and Lucy C. Read Langen—Gasquet—& Cooks Business of Travel.[6] Began a new Electoral Facts[7]—at the special desire of Mr Knowles. Dined at the Rectory: backgammon. Conversation with Stephy on his Testamentary dispositions. Ch. 8½ A.M.

6. Th.

Ch. 8½ A.M. Wrote to M. Waddington—D. of Argyll BP.—H.N.G.—Keeper of V.O.—A. du Plat—Mast. Cutler El.—Messrs Jack—T. Aldred—J. Brick. Worked on Electoral Facts. Worked at St Deiniol's. Read Langen—Gasquet—and Locusta.[8]

7. Fr.

Ch. 8½ AM. Wrote to J.R. Miller—J.M. Cook—Mr Morley MP.—Sir A. Clark—L.S. Blair BP.—Canon Knox Little BP.—Jas Knowles—Sir H. Oakeley—F. Burar [*sic*] —Austin Short. Saw Gerty. Work at St Deiniol's. Worked on El. Facts. Read Langen—Locusta. Conversation with Herbert on his troubles about the Irish Exhibition.[9] He behaves admirably.

---

[1] See 10 Aug. 91.
[2] Preached at W. H. Gladstone's funeral.
[3] F. Beaumont and J. Fletcher, *The tragedy of Valentinian* (many eds.).
[4] Not further identified.
[5] John Croft Deverell, barrister at Lincoln's Inn.
[6] W. F. Rae, *The business of travel* (1891): on Thomas Cook.
[7] 'Electoral Facts, No. 3', *N.C.*, xxx. 329 (September 1891) and correction at ibid., 676; offering four methods of calculating on basis of 1885-6 election results and subsequent by-elections, and expecting a liberal majority in 1892 of between 46 and 97 (excluding Home Rule support). Correspondence with Knowles on this is in the Montague Collection, New York Public Library.
[8] W. O. Tristram, *Locusta* (1890).
[9] The Irish Exhibition at Olympia in 1889 was a financial failure, and in July 1891 an indemnity fund was started.

8. Sat.

Ch. 8½ A.M. Wrote to Mr H.R. Williams—Messrs Murray—W.J. Heppell—Rev. H. Worsley—Miss Nairn. Wrote inscription for the Shaftesbury Monument.[1] Read Langen—Population Returns[2]—Locusta. Worked at St Deiniol's. Drive with C. & visit to a *senior*. Backgammon with S.

9. 11 S.Trin.

Ch mg & [blank.] Wrote to Canon Knox Little—Rev. Roberts—Mr A. Hutton—Rev. Davies. Read Langen—Worsley on Engl. Reformn.[3]

10. M.

Ch. 8¼ A.M. Wrote to Mr Ivanovitch—A. Morley—Rev. Gasquet—Miss Ogilvie—F. Williams—Messrs Isbister—Mr A. Sutton. Conversation with G[ertrude] G[ladstone] on the inheritance. Worked at St Deiniol's. Read Langen—Ivanovitch on Servia[4]—Locusta—and Cathedra Petri.[5] Backgammon with S.

11. Tu.

Ch. 8½ A.M. Wrote to Canon M'Coll BP—Sir J. Lacaita BP.—W.H. White—Rev. E.T. Vaughan—Mr Hodges—Messrs Warne[6]—Miss Murray—Mr Rosenfeld—Dean of St Paul's—Miss Negroponte. Worked & read at St Deiniol's. Reviewed Lucy's letter to Ld Penrhyn.[7] Worked on Ol. Rel. Finished Langen's remarkable work Vol. I.[8] Read Acton's Intr. to Macchia.[9]—Gasquet Pref. to Edn 2.—Locusta (finished).

12. Wed.

Ch. 8¼ A.M. Wrote to M. Alhan. Vucaré—Sir P. Currie—Mr E. Brown—Mr W. Andrews—E. Menken—A. Stapleton—J. Walter—Dowager Lady Sandhurst—Sampson Morgan. Saw S.E.G. respecting Father Matthews. Worked & read at St Deiniol's. Read Lowe's Ch. Reformn[10]—Dickens Tale of two Cities[11]—Higgins Morals & Geol.[12]—Andrews Old Church Lore.[13] Worked on Olympian Religion.

---

[1] Inscription provided for the 'Eros' statue (a memorial to Shaftesbury) in the centre of Piccadilly Circus; inscription requested by H. R. Williams, secretary to the memorial; drafts at Add MS 44773, f. 237 and 44513, f. 90.   [2] The 1891 census returns.
 [3] Henry Worsley had sent his *The dawn of the English Reformation* (1890).   [4] Untraced.
 [5] C. F. B. Allnatt, *Cathedra Petri: a brief summary of the chief titles and prerogatives ascribed to St. Peter and his see* (1878 and later eds.).
 [6] Frederick Warne, London publishers.
 [7] In Hawn P, MS 2354; on the reversion of the Hawarden estate, as a result of W. H. Gladstone's death, to W. E. Gladstone, necessary so that Penrhyn's wife Gertrude (daughter of Henry Glynne) did not inherit an interest. Penrhyn was shown Gladstone's letter of 3 October 1885 (part in Morley, i. 347), and another document, giving the history of the estate; Penrhyn replied in a choleric exchange; matters were put in the hands of solicitors and agreement on Gladstone's terms was reached in 1892.
 [8] See 16 Oct. 81.
 [9] Acton's introduction to L. A. Bird's ed. of Machiavelli, *Il Principe* (1891).
 [10] Untraced.   [11] (1859); first time of reading.
 [12] See 9 Oct. 85.   [13] W. Andrews, *Old Church lore* (1891).

13. Th.

Ch. 8½ A.M. Wrote to Warden of Trin. Coll.—Mr Schnadhorst—Mrs Ingram—Mrs Coghill—Rev. Little—Lady Derby BP—Ld Crewe BP. Worked at St Deiniol's. Worked on O.R. Also on Electoral Facts. Read Dickens Two Cities—Rinck Relig. der Hellenen.[1] Backgammon with S.E.G.

14. Fr.

Ch. 8½ A.M. Wrote to Miss O. Scunn BP.—Miss M. Tennant l. & BP.—Mrs Brock Hollinshed—Mr Murray—Mr Schnadhorst—A. Dyson—A.J. Cuthbert—Mr Romanes—Mrs Beaumont—Treas. Liddon Memorial. Worked at St Deiniol's. Worked on El. Facts. Sat (in part) to Mr Forbes.[2] Read Tale of Two Cities—Rinck (little; valueless). Family conversation on our household plans. Consequent conversation with Zadok on his place:[3] he is to go out of livery.

15. Sat.

Ch. 8½ A.M. Wrote to Rev. Dr M'Leod—Mrs Ingram—J. Westell—R. Cameron—C. Higham—W. Ridler—W.R. Bogle—E. Arnold—R. Morris. Tea at G.G.s. Worked at St D.s. Worked on El. Facts. Read Tale of Two Cities—MacColl on the Wages of Sin.[4]

16. 12 S. Trin.

Ch mg & evg. Wrote to Spottiswoode's—Ld Acton—Mr Knowles—and [blank.] Read Vaughan's Hulsean Lectures[5]—St Martin of Tours by Scullard[6]—Baldwin on Prehistory.[7]

17. M.

Ch. 8½ A.M. Wrote to Canon McColl—Mr Colman MP—Mr Morley MP. Worked on O.R. Worked at St D.s. Read Tale of Two Cities—Baldwin on Prehistory (much).

18. Tu.

Ch. 8¼ A.M. Wrote to Mr Schnadhorst—W. Stevenson—W.T. Stead—Messrs Gallagher. Tea with G.G.: conversation on Will & the Estate. Worked on books & at St Deiniol's. Read Tale &c. (finished)—Baldwin as yest.—Diana of the Crossways.[8] Wrote MS. Wrote Estate Mem. for Lucy to see with Ld Penrhyn.

---

[1] W. F. Rinck, *Die Religion der Hellenen*, 2v. (1855).   [2] See 5 May 91.

[3] Zadok Outram, Gladstone's valet, was increasingly alcoholic; he continued with the family as a footman.

[4] Untraced.

[5] E. T. Vaughan, *Some reasons of our Christian hope* (1876).

[6] H. H. Scullard, *Martin of Tours, Apostle of Gaul* (1891).

[7] J. D. Baldwin, *Pre-historic nations* (1869).

[8] G. Meredith, *Diana of the Crossways* (1885); political novel, the hero said to be drawn from Sidney Herbert. See 20 Aug. 91.

19. Wed.

Ch. 8½ A.M. Wrote to Dowager Lady Sandhurst—Mr Warmington—C. Carter—Mr Schnadhorst—A. Sanderson—Messrs Isbister—J.M. Laurie. Worked at St Deiniol's. Wrote on O.R. Read Pichler, Treasury[1]—Hesiod, Theogony[2]—Diana of the Crossways—St. Ellicott's Daughter.[3]

20.

Ch. 8¼ A.M. Wrote to Mad. Novikoff—Central News Tel.[4]—R. Williams—Contemp. Rev. Tel.—A. Upward—Jos. Mann Tel.—E. Barker—R.H. Sutton—L.A. Wheatley—L. Nicolson—E. Atkinson—Mohammed Hassan Sultan.[5] Worked on El. Facts. Worked at St Deiniol's. Read Ind. Ch. Rev.[6]—S. Ellicott's Daughter—Diana of the Crossways (I can get no further).

21.

Ch. 8¼ A.M. Wrote to Spottiswoode's—F. Schnadhorst—J. Whyte—Dr G.S. Sommer—L.J. Binks—Rev. Dr Owen—T. Dowson—Bp. of St Asaph. Worked at St Deiniol's. An hour with G.G. Read Pichler—S. Ellicott's Daughter—Letters to Authors.[7] Backgammon with S.E.G.

22. Sat.

Ch 8½ A.M. (I now drive up but I am not well satisfied with my breathing.) Wrote to Lady Sandhurst—Rev. E. Jenkins—N. Smith—Sir J. Lacaita—J. Noble. Worked on O.R. Worked at St Deiniol's. Read Gow on Scotch Home Rule[8]—Sybel, Mythol. des Ilias[9]—Ellicott's Daughter. Backgammon with S.E.G.

23. 13 S. Trin.

Ch mg & 6½ P.M. Obliged to work a little on El. Facts for N.C. Wrote to Messrs Spottiswoode—Mr Hudson—H. Waters—Mr Slade Butler. Read Vaughan Hulsean Lect.—Lockhart on Newman—on Pusey[10]—Bp B. & Wells Charge—Bp Jerusalem Charge. Tea with G.G. & conversation on the Penrhyn letter.

[1] Perhaps an untraced work by Louisa Pichler.
[2] Probably C. A. Elton's ed. (1891).
[3] Mrs. J. H. Needell, *Stephen Ellicott's daughter*, 3v. (1891).
[4] In *T.T.*, 21 August 1891, 10a: 'The letter of Mr Parnell in the *Pall Mall Gazette* of yesterday states that I have possessed means of communication which I have frequently employed on behalf of Mr. Morley. On very rare occasions I have been so fortunate as to see Mr Parnell in the House of Commons. Otherwise his address and residence have been totally unknown to me. He told me his best address was at the House of Commons, but I could not count on any period within which a letter so directed would reach him. Hence I addressed my letter of last November to Mr M'Carthy, for I had no other means of getting anything into the hands of Mr Parnell before the meeting of the Irish members'.   [5] Not further identified.
[6] Article by Prof. Cheyne in *Indian Church Quarterly Review*, ii. 127 (April 1891), discussed in his article (see 12 Sept. 91). See 21 June 91.
[7] J. A. Steuart, *Letters to living authors* (1890).   [8] Untraced article.
[9] L. von Sybel, *Die Mythologie der Ilias* (1877).
[10] W. Lockhart, *Cardinal Newman . . . to which is added an Essay [on Pusey's 'Eirenicon']* (1891). See 1 Oct. 90.

24. M.

St Marth. Ch 8½ AM. Wrote to Lady Londonderry—Mr Schnadhorst—W. Rid-
ler—A.C. Jones—E. Keenan. Worked on O.R. Worked at St Deiniol's. Sir J.
Lacaita came. Read Sybel on Iliad—Steuart's L. to Authors—Ellicott's Daughter.
Backgammon with S.

25. Tu.

Ch. 8½ A.M. Wrote to Bp of Lincoln—Ly Sandhurst—Mr Stewart—U.S. Minister—B. Findlay—Abp of Canterbury—W.T. Stead—Rev. C. Primrose[1]—E. Turnbull—Cawthorn & Hutt—J. Hitchin—Spottiswoodes—Sig. Guccia—Mr
Creechman[?]. Worked on O.R. Took Sir J. L[acaita] to St Deiniol's: also to
tomb. Read Sybel: valueless.—Lauer, Mythologie[2]—S. Ellicott's Daughter.

26. Wed.

Ch. 8½ A.M. Wrote to Spottiswoodes—T. Wilson—J.C. Cummins—A. Cargill—
W.R. Bogle—J.A. Jones—W. Buttress—Mr de Coverley. Corrected revises of
Electoral Facts.[3] Worked at St Deiniol's. Read Lauer Mythologie—S. Ellicott's
Daughter. Backgammon with S.

27. Th.

Ch. 8½ A.M. Wrote to Wms & Norgate—W. Hyam—Rev. D.G. Wylie—J.G.
Low—W.H. Rideing. Worked on O.R. Drive & walk with Mr Colman & showed
him St D. & the Rectory. Read Lauer Mythologie—S. Ellicott's Daughter—Wilcox on Divorce.[4] Backgammon with Mr Colman.

28. Fr.

Ch. 8½ AM. Wrote to Duchess of Cleveland—Ld Rosebery—E. Nesbit[5]—Sir A.
Gordon—W. Coote—Bruce Findlay—Dr Wilcox—J. Templeton. Worked on O.R.
Worked at St Deiniol's. Read Lauer, Mythol Gr.—Von Sybel Mythol. Ilias—S.
Ellicott's Daughter—and Divers Tracts.

29. Sat.

Ch. 8½ AM. Wrote to R.B. Oakley—V. Office—M. Evans. Worked much on
books, here & at St Deiniol's. Tea with G.G. Read 'Sir A.W.' on James I[6]—Steph.
Ellicott's Daughter—Lodge (Physical) Address[7]—Du Chaillu Vikings.[8]

---

[1] Charles Primrose, curate of Heigham, Norfolk.
[2] Probably J. F. Lauer, *Quaestiones Homericae* (1843).
[3] See 5 Aug. 91.
[4] Untraced.
[5] Edith Nesbit (Mrs. Hubert Bland), 1858–1924; author and Fabian.
[6] Sir A. W[eldon], *The court and character of King James* (1650).
[7] O. J. Lodge, *Papers circulated by Sir O. J. Lodge in connection with an address to be presented to J. Ruskin*
(1885).
[8] P. B. du Chaillu, *The Viking age*, 2v. (1889).

30. [14] S Trin.

Ch mg & [blank.] Wrote to Rev. Dr. Matheson—Mrs Bolton—M.J. Kavanagh—Scotts—A.O. May—Watsons—J. Squibb BP. Read Matheson on Paul[1]—Howorth on Columban Monk[2]—Maclagan's Sermons[3]—and Lewis, Life of Bp Fisher.[4]

31. M.

Ch. $8\frac{1}{4}$ A.M. Wrote to Jones Rhyl Tel.—J. Hickman—W.L. Dash—Thos Wilson—Rev. C. Pixell[5]—J. Standing—D.T. Fish—Watsons. Worked on O.R. Worked on books here & at St Deiniols. Read S. Ellicott's Daughter—Ingersoll on Walt Whitman[6]—Low on Montrose Church[7]—Gardner [sic] on Bangor College.[8]

Tues. Sept 1. 1891.

Ch. $8\frac{1}{2}$ A.M. Wrote to Sec. Saltney Libr.—T. Whitburne—C.A. White—H. de Burgh—J. Fraser—A. M'Kenzie—Ogilvy Gillanders & Co. Worked on O.R. Worked on books here & at St Deiniol's. Read S.E.s Daughter (finished)—Leighton on Leighton Family[9]—Lady Verney's Grey Pool.[10]

2. Wed.

Ch. $8\frac{1}{4}$ A.M. Wrote to Sir B. Leighton—J.R. Thomas—Watsons—J.A. Parsons—J. Ogilvy—Rev. Barton—Mr Dobson. Worked hard on books at home: also at St Deiniol's. Read Lady Verney—Rawlinson Ancient Religions.[11]

3. Th.

Ch $8\frac{1}{4}$ A.M. Wrote to Gordon Teale[12]—Mr Arney—G.H. Saunders—H.N.G.—Messrs Stanford—H. Riddle—W.H. Rideing—Mrs Blight—Mr de Burgh—W. Edwards—Ed. Star Tel.[13] Worked on books here & at St D.s. Read Rawlinson—Nägelsbach on H. Theol.[14]—Lady Verney. Worked on O.R.

4. Fr.

Ch $8\frac{1}{4}$ A.M. Wrote to Editor of the Times[15]—Editor of Star—J.G. Kitchen—Rev. Dr. Hayman—Mr Cohen. Worked on books here, also at St Deiniol's. Worked

---

[1] George Matheson, 1842-1906, blind presbyterian divine, had sent his *Spiritual development of St. Paul* (1891).

[2] H. H. Howorth, *The Columban clergy of North Britain* (1879).

[3] W. D. Maclagan, probably *The Church and the age*, 2v. (1870-2).

[4] J. Lewis, *The life of John Fisher, bishop of Rochester*, 2v. (1855).

[5] Charles Henry Vincent Pixell, vicar of Stoke Newington.

[6] R. G. Ingersoll, 'Liberty in literature. Testimonial to Walt Whitman' (1890).

[7] J. G. Low had sent his *Memorials of the Church of St. John . . . the parish church of Montrose* (1891).

[8] Probably an address by S. R. Gardiner (not found published) delivered at Bangor; see J. G. Williams, *The University College of North Wales* (1985), 121.

[9] Untraced work sent by Sir B. Leighton (see next day).

[10] F. P. Verney, Lady Verney, *The grey pool and other stories* (1891).

[11] G. Rawlinson, *The religions of the ancient world* (1882).

[12] A schoolboy in York learning Greek; Gladstone sent him a book; Hawn P.

[13] i.e. Massingham, see 5 Oct. 91; not found published.

[14] See 5 Jan. 57.

[15] On the calculations in 'Electoral Facts'; *T.T.*, 7 September 1891, 7f.

on Electoral Facts in reply. Read Cheyne on Psalms[1]—Rawlinson Anct Relig.—
Nägelsbach Hom. Theol.—Hungarian reply to Rouman students.[2] Saw Mr
Spencer.

5. Sat.

Ch. 8½ A.M. Wrote to Mr L. de Panterich—Mrs Gattie—J. Marchant—A. Hayes—
D. Cumming—Chairman Flintsh Co. C.[3]—J. Davidson. Worked on O.R. Saw
Harry on W.s affairs. Worked at St Deiniol's. Read Rawlinson—Hungarian Reply
(finished)—Lady Verney's Tales. Backgammon with Albert [Lyttelton].

6. 15 S. Trin.

Ch. 11 AM. with H.C. and 6½ P.M. Wrote to Rev. Mr Belcher—Mr Foster—Messrs
Warne—Bp of Moosonee B.P. Read R.C. on Abps Judgt[4]—Wilkinson on Israel[5]—
Belcher on Miracles[6]—Cheyne on the Psalms—Campbell on the Hittites.[7]

7. M.

Ch. 8½ A.M. Wrote to Ld Northbourne—Hon. W. James—Mrs Bolton—Editor of
the Star[8]—Jas Knowles—H.C. Robinson—Sir H. Verney—S.R. Crockett—H.J.
Snell—Mr E. Weston—J.H. Shorter—Herr Fleischer—A. Lowe. Worked at St
Deiniol's. Tea with G.G. Devoted the morning to examining books in arrear:
among them Wilkinson on Theol—Crockett's Poems[9]—Aur. Martin's Poems[10]—
. . . . &c. &c. Also Read Rawlinson on A.R.—Lady Verney.

8. Tu.

Ch. 8½ A.M. Wrote to Rev. Dr. Linklater—Hon. W. James—Messrs Cassell—W.T.
Miles—Messrs Machin[11]—G.H. Palmer—Rev. Dr. Barrow—G.J. Bowden—Miss
Sinclair—J. Baron. Worked on O.R. Worked at St Deiniol's. Read Rawlinson—
Potter's Antiq.[12]—Browning's Life[13]—Lady V.s tales. Saw Mr Spencer.

9. Wed.

Ch. 8½ A.M. Wrote to Sir A. Clark Tel.—Mr Ainsworth—Sec. N.P.G.—Sir H.
Verney l. and BP.—Messrs Stanford[14]—Mrs Bolton—Mr R.B. Johnston—Mr
Rideing. Worked on O.R. Worked at St Deiniol's. Read Müllers Mythology[15]—
Life of Browning—Lady Verney's Tales.

---

[1] See 20 Aug. 91n.   [2] Untraced.   [3] Business untraced.
[4] Untraced.   [5] J. Wilkinson, *Israel my glory* (1889).
[6] Thomas Waugh Belcher, rector of Frampton-Cotterell, Bristol, sent the 2nd ed. (1890) of his
Our Lord's miracles of healing; for the first, see 2 June 72.
[7] J. Campbell, *The Hittites* (1891).   [8] Not found published.
[9] S. R. Crockett, perhaps *Dulce Cor. Poems* (1886).
[10] Author's name uncertain; perhaps E. S. Martin, *A little brother of the rich and other poems* (1888).
[11] London bookbinders.
[12] J. Potter, *Archaeologicae Graecae or the antiquities of Greece*, 2v. (1697).
[13] W. Sharp, *Life of Robert Browning* (1891).
[14] Edward Stanford, London booksellers.
[15] F. Max Müller, *Lectures on the origin and growth of religion* (1891).

10. Th.

Ch. 8½ A.M. Wrote to Vote Office—J.D. Machan—Jos Hatton—Rev. Canon Lowe—F. Prout—Rev. Dr Mitchell—J. Baron—S.F. Pells—G. Turner. Read as yesterday. Worked on O.R. & at St D's.

11. Fr.

Ch. 8¼ A.M. Wrote to Sir W. Harcourt—Mr Sketchley BP—F.A. White—Mr O. Morgan MP—Dr Belcher—J.S. Symington—Dr Hine—H.G. Henderson—J. Blackie—Sir A. Gordon. Worked, feebly, on O.R. And at St Deiniol's. Spent much time on reducing my room to a sort of order. Mr Armitstead came. Read as yesterday. *Summer began Sep. 9.*

12. Sat.

Ch. 8½ A.M. Wrote to Rev. Mr Forrester—Rev. Père Hyacinthe—L.M. Fothering-ham—Messrs Macphail—J.H. Mitchell—Stanfords. Worked on Future State among the Jews.[1] Worked on books, here. Walk with Mr Armitstead. Saw Mr Vickers. Conclave on Trust affairs. Read Browning's Life—"By order of the Czar".[2]

13. 16 S. Trin.

Ch mg & evg. Wrote to Pres. of Magdalen—Ridler—Rev. Mr Rutherford—Salkeld—Sir H. Verney—Sec. Stanley Hospital—Messrs Mallett. Read Clodd on Creation[3]—Relig. Review of Reviews[4]—Maclaren's Sermons.[5]

14. M.

Ch. 8¼ AM. and H.C. at 9 A.M. Wrote to Fasque Tel.[6]—Mr Hudson—Mr Morley—Central News Tel.—Isbisters—Sir W. Harcourt—Ld Rosebery—Warden of Trin. Coll.—Mayor of Newcastle—Mr Rideing. Worked on Books at St D's. And on Hebrew paper. After careful examination and much conversation Sir A. C[lark] agreed to my going to Newcastle on conditions.[7] My laziness regrets, but I think duty calls. Read Rawlinson Herod.—Browning's Life—Herodotos on Eg. Relig.[8]—Juvenal Sat. XV. Worked on books. Worked on Hebrew Article.

15. Tu.

Ch. 8½ A.M. Wrote to Mr Wemyss Reid—Mr R. Stuart—Messrs Stanford—Mr Fox Davies—J.R. Guthrie—Mr C. Booth[9]—Rev. G. Robertson—J. Marchant—

---

[1] 'On the ancient beliefs in a future state', *N.C.*, xxx. 658 (October 1891); a critique of T. K. Cheyne's article (see 20 Aug. 91); for Cheyne's reply, see ibid., 951.

[2] Joseph Hatton had sent his *By order of the Czar*, 3v. (1891).

[3] E. Clodd, *The story of creation* (1888).

[4] *Review of the Churches*; an ecumenical journal beginning publication; specimen sheet sent to Gladstone and circulated with facsimile of Gladstone's letter to Bunting, 25 July 1891; Add MS 44513, f. 77.   [5] A. Maclaren, *The God of the Amen and other sermons* (1891).

[6] See 25 Sept. 91.   [7] See 1-2 Oct. 91.   [8] In Herodotus's history, book 2.

[9] Responding to a question from C. Booth as to whether discussion of theosophy should be allowed in the working men's club in London that he founded; Gladstone thought it would 'be the precursor both of strife and of conflict'; *T.T.*, 17 September 1891, 10c; Booth's letter is in Hawn P. It is unclear whether this is Charles Booth, 1840-1916, the social observer.

W. Paul—H.M. Beckett. Sir A. Clark went at noon. Worked on books. Worked on Art. for N.C. Read Life of Browning—Haug on the Parsees[1]—Wilkinson on Egypt.[2] Tea with G.G. Backgammon with Mr A.

16. Wed.
Ch. 8½ A.M. Wrote to Mr de Coverley P.P.—

Macmillans ⎫
Isbisters   ⎬ (for)[3]   Mr Bayne
Murrays   ⎭   Hon. R. Acton
Murrays (for) Rev. Webb
Mr Douglas Cooper.
Keeper of Printed Books BM.

Mr Armitstead in the morning opened the subject of his giant treat to us.[4] Conversation with H. on Trust matters. Walk with Mr A. Worked on N.C. Article. Read Browning's Life—Haug on the Parsees—and divers. Backgammon with S.E.G.

17. Th.
Ch. 8½ A.M. Wrote to Mr Schnadhorst—Messrs Watson—H.M. Neville—G.J. Bowden—A. Morley—Rev. Mitchell—Dr. Greer[5]—Rev. Monaghan—Jas Knowles—Rev. Warden Trin. Coll. [Glenalmond]—Rev. Mr Cobb. Worked at St Deiniol's. Saw Mr Temple. Worked on art. for N.C. Read Browning's Life. Backgammon with S.E.G.

18. Fr.
Ch. 8½ A.M. Wrote to Keeper of Pr. Books—F.A. Coleridge—Mr Knowles—Mr Rideing—Scotts—P. Morris. Worked on Books. Saw Mr Guinness Rogers—Canon Furse[6]—Mr Temple—ride & walk. Worked on MS for N.C. Read Browning's Life—F. Tennyson's Poems.[7]

19. Sat.
Ch. 8½ A.M. Wrote to H.N.G. (to aid)—Rev. Martin—C. Cratten—Messrs White—A. Morris—Dr Macintyre—Hugh Lloyd. Saw Mr Redington. Worked on books here & at St Deiniol's. Finished paper for N.C. & began correction.[8] Read Duncker's Hist.[9]—Dr Driver on O.T.[10]—Haug on Parsees—Memorials of Hurstwood[11]—F. Tennyson's Poems.

[1] M. Haug, *Essays on the sacred language, writings and religion of the Parsees* (1890); discussed in his article (see 12 Sept. 91).
[2] J. Gardner Wilkinson, *Manners and customs of the ancient Egyptians*, 3v. (1837–41); discussed in his article, see 12 Sept. 91.   [3] New abbreviation, apparently meaning 'materials sent'.
[4] The holiday in Biarritz; see 15 Dec. 91.
[5] Probably William Benjamin Greer, rector of Woldingham; classical scholar.
[6] See 12 Dec. 79; he was canon of Christ Church, Oxford 1873–94, and of Westminster 1883–94.
[7] F. Tennyson, *Daphne and other poems* (1891).   [8] See 12 Sept. 91.
[9] M. W. Duncker, *History of Greece* (1883).   [10] S. R. Driver, *The Book of Daniel* (1877).
[11] J. F. Tattersall, *Memories of Hurstwood* (1889).

20. 17 S. Trin.

Ch mg & evg. Wrote to Messrs Spottiswoodes—Mr [blank.] Corrected MS. and dispatched it to London. Read Maclarens Sermon—Mackey on Scots Episc Ch.[1]—On a future state 1700[2]—Dr Driver on Daniel—and Reader on Russia.[3]

21. St Matthew

Ch 8½ A.M. Wrote to Rev. F.D. Perrott[4]—Mr W.S. Cairne [sc. Caine]—J. Westell—Sir W. Lawson—Jas Miles—Rev. Ch. Gore—C.T. Thomas—H.C. Shelley—J. Prentice—W. McIlwraith.[5] Worked much on books. Read Wellwords Poem[6]—Tattersall's do[7]—H.J. Brown on Spiritism[8]—Hill on Condn of the Poor[9]—McIlwraith on Theosophy—and [blank.]

22. Tu.

Ch. 8½ A.M. with Holy Commn: also 7½ P.M. Wrote to Rev. Dr Sullivan—Mr Stern MP[10]—J. Symington—Mr G. Gray jun.—D. M'Gregor—A.L. Gladstone—T. Wardle—Mr Williamson—Mr Harding. Tea & farewell with G.G. Saw Rev. Mr Stephenson—Mr Adams Acton (Statuette).[11] Worked much on books. Worked on Parl. papers. Read Williamson's Poems[12]—Reader on Russia—and Tregellis on Daniel.[13]

23. Wed.

Ch 8½ A.M. Wrote to Mr Schnadhorst—Spottiswoode's—R. Morris—Mr Tattersall[14]—R. Rhode—Warden of Trin. Coll. NB.—Keeper of Printed Books B.M.—Rev. A. Robertson—A. Reader. Corrected proofs & sent off for Press. Saw S.E.G. Worked further on Books. Mr Rideing 12½-2½. Read Tregelles—Condemnation of Spiritualism[15]—and [blank.]

24. Th. [On train]

Ch. 8½ A.M. Wrote to Cawthorn & Hutt—C. Lowe—Mr Guinness Rogers BP—Mr Smith MP.—R.H. Sutton—A.B. Wylie BP—Vote Office—W. Ridler—Dr

---

[1] Perhaps an article by Donald John Mackey.
[2] R. Day, *Free thoughts in defence of a future state* (1700).
[3] A. Reader, *Russia and the Jews. A brief sketch of Russian history* (1890).
[4] Frank Duerdin Perrott of University Hall, London.
[5] Had sent his untraced work on theosophy; see this day.
[6] A. Wellwood, *Snatches of world-song* (1891).
[7] J. F. Tattersall, *The baptism of the Viking and other verses* (1890).
[8] H. J. Browne, *The grand reality, being experiences in spirit life* (1888).
[9] Octavia Hill, *Homes of the London poor* (1875).
[10] Sydney James Stern, 1844–1912; liberal M.P. N.W. Suffolk May 1891–5; cr. Baron Wandsworth 1895.
[11] The sculptor (see 7 Nov. 64); probably executing another of his several busts (now at Hawarden) of Mr. and Mrs. Gladstone.
[12] D. R. Williamson had sent his *Poems of nature and life* (1888); Hawn P.
[13] S. P. Tregelles, *Remarks on the Prophetic Visions in the Book of Daniel* (1852).
[14] Poet and author; see 19, 21 Sept. 91.
[15] Untraced.

Mitchell—Warden T.C. [Glenalmond]—J. Salkeld—Hon. Sir A. Gordon—Mr
Morrison—M. Evans—Hon. R. Acton—Stanfords—Spottiswoodes—A.H. Ince[1]—
Jas Torrie—J. Hitchman. Worked on books & preparations. Also on political
notes. Read Jane Cameron[2] and Driver, Introd. to O.T. Off at 9¾. Travelled all
night, swift and rough.

25. Fr. [Fasque]

L[aurence]kirk 7½ Fasque 8¼.[3] Most kind reception. Wrote to Mr Hare
FRCS[4]—and .... Began a new perusal of the Iliad, noting particulars. Whist in
evg. Also read Jane Cameron and .... Prince Dammerong of Siam[5] & his party
came in afternoon: We were much pleased with his straight forward simple
intelligence.

26. Sat.

Wrote to Mr Greig—Read Iliad. Also Jane Cameron—Kurios in Blackwood.[6]
Four mile walk to & on the Garrol with Mary G. Backgammon with L[ouisa].

27. 18 S. Trin.

Ch 11 A. 3 P.M. Read Eccl[esiastic]us, Manning, Unity of the Church,[7] Savage,
State of the Departed,[8] Jane Cameron. Walk up the Delala den. Catherine since
arriving has been touched with deafness. Better thank God today than yesterday.

28. M.

Wrote to Mr Waddie[9]—Bp of Newcastle—G. Colburn—A. Morley tel.—J.B.
Scott—Messrs Blackwood—P. Pullar—Miss R. Seaton—F. Brown. Read &
worked on Iliad. Read Jane Cameron—Ecclus. C.s hearing again improved.
Drove to the Dalhousie Arch.[10] It is dreadful: &, with the dear names on it, sad.
Whist in evg.

29. Tu.

St Mich. Ch 11 AM. Wrote to Mr MacCulloch—V. Rev. Dean Harrison—Rev.
Dr Hutton—Miss S. Robertson. Long drive to the Esk fishing. That road gives a
capital approach. Saw the Jollies. Backgammon with Louisa. Worked on Iliad.
Finished Jane Cameron.

---

[1] Probably Henry Alexander Ince of Thurloe Square, London.
[2] *Memoirs of Jane Cameron, female convict*, 2v. (1864).
[3] The family house in Kincardineshire, now owned by his nephew, Sir J. R. Gladstone.
[4] Arthur William Hare, surgeon in Manchester and authority on cranial tumours; doubtless in
correspondence on W. H. Gladstone's condition and death.
[5] Prince Damrong, King of Siam's half-brother, staying at Balmoral during his European mission.
[6] 'Kurios' [E. F. Law], 'Current influences on foreign politics', *Blackwood's*, cl. 461 (October 1891).
[7] See 27 Feb. 42.
[8] Perhaps Minot J. Savage, *The signs of the times* (1889).
[9] On Scottish home rule (misdated); *T.T.*, 30 September 1891, 3f.
[10] Memorial to the Earl of Dalhousie as viceroy of India.

30. Wed. [Trinity College, Glenalmond]

Off at nine: arrived Glenalmond[1] at one. Wrote to Sir W. Phillimore—S.P. Jopson—E.F. Strange—C.W. Roberts. Worked on Iliad: got to VIII. Walk & survey with the Warden. Quiet evening. Conversation with several of the Masters—Mrs Smith—also [blank.] Read divers Tracts.

Thurs. October One 1891. [Newcastle]

A long busy day. Holy Communion at 8.30. Morning prayers at 10¾. Musical performance noon. Public luncheon at one. Speeches at 2–3½. Mine usurped 35 or 40 m.[2] Saw Mrs P. Campbell—R. M'Caig—Mr Miller—Ld Lothian—& others. Off at 4.30 to Perth and thence to Newcastle. Arrived there 10.30. Great enthusiasm. Read Iliad.

2. Fr.

Worked up the points of my subject: very many and needing compression. Saw Mr Morley—The Mayor—The Bp of Newcastle—Sir W. Harcourt—Sir A. Clark. Read the Iliad. Drive with C. Meeting 7–9. Spoke 1 h. 20 min.[3] Dr Sp. Watson[4] excellent.

3. Sat. [Hawarden]

Meeting at 10.30. Received the freedom & spoke about 25 m. to 2500.[5] Saw divers—and off at 12.40. Hawarden at 5.5. Wrote to Mr Scott (at Manchester).[6] Read Iliad. Deo gratias for having finished a work heavy at near 82.

4. S. 19 S. Trin.

Ch. 11 AM with H.C. and 6½ P.M. Wrote to Bp of St Andrews—Scotts—Sir E. Watkin MP—V. Office—Isbisters BP.—H.G. Bridge—Messrs Murray—W. Stuart —Madame Patti—J.D. O'Flynn. Read Wordsworth (Bp. L.)[7]—and Poems of Romanes.[8]

---

[1] For the Jubilee of Trinity College, Glenalmond, the episcopalian boys' school which Gladstone and his father had helped to found in 1841; he still owned a significant proportion of its property through mortgage. For the proceedings, during which Gladstone laid the foundation stone for 'New Wing' (his father having laid the stone for the original building in 1846), see G. St. Quintin, *The history of Glenalmond* (1956), 130 ff.

[2] The Glenalmond jubilee celebrations; *T.T.*, 2 October 1891, 10d.

[3] The so-called 'Newcastle programme'; *T.T.*, 3 October 1891, 10b.

[4] Robert Spence Watson, 1837–1911; solicitor, social reformer and alpinist; president of National Liberal Federation 1890–1902.

[5] *T.T.*, 5 October 1891, 12a.

[6] Supporting Charles Prestwich Scott (1846–1932; ed. *Manchester Guardian* 1872–1929) as liberal candidate in by-election N.E. Manchester; *T.T.*, 5 October 1891, 6e. Scott failed there three times, being elected for Leigh 1895–1906.

[7] J. Wordsworth, *The one religion. The Bampton Lectures* (1881).

[8] G. J. Romanes, *Poems 1879–1889* (1889).

5. M.

Ch. 8½ A.M. Wrote to Dr Ginsburg BP.—Mr Menken—Rev. Harrison—Mr Fraser—G. Greenfield—J. Salkeld—Mr Seymour Keay—W. Fraser—Prof. Romanes—J.F. Avery—Mr Massingham[1]—A. Gooden—S.T. Francis—S. Shaw—Edr Education.[2] Worked on Homer, Iliad. And at St Deiniol's. Read Bp J. Wordsworth—Iliad B. XII II.—and Hanging in Chains.[3]

6. Tu.

Ch. 8½ A.M. Wrote to Press Assocn. Tel.—Central News Tel.—E. Friend—Mr L.H. Mills—S. Cohen—Rev. C.C. Rowley—W. Naismith[4]—Ld Mayor Lond.—J. Davidson—Mr Hartshorne—J. Gibbon—Abp of Canterbury—A.J. D'Orsay—W. Wright. Worked on Homer. Worked at St Deiniol's. Read Mills on Zendavesta[5]—Hanging in Chains (finished)—Iliad, and By order of the Czar.[6]

7. Wed.

Ch. 8½ A.M. Wrote to Mr Hebblethwaite—A. Morley MP.—W. Ridler—Mr Paterson Pr. Sec.—Rev. C. Cook—Consul Fröhlich[7]—Messrs Reid—Edr of Education—Rev. Mr Deane.

In 18 hours from six P.M. yesterday I have by telegram the deaths of Mr W.H. Smith—Mr Parnell—& Sir J. Pope Hennessy (not an inconsiderable man). So the Almighty bares His arm when he sees it meet: & there is here matter for thought, and in the very sad case of Mr P. matter also of much public importance.

Worked on Homer. And on books here & at St Ds. Drive with C. Read Homer (XIV, XV)—and 'By order of the Czar'.

8. Th.

Ch. 8½ A.M. Wrote to Rev. Dr Ginsburg—Mr L.H. Mills BP—Watsons—Lord Acton BP.—W.J.H. Isles—Sec. of Treasury—Jas Watt—Gilbert & Fowler—J. Taylor—Eugene Mason[8]—J.B. Massey. Worked at St Deiniol's. Drive with C. Worked on Homer. Read Iliad—By Order of the Czar. Saw Arthur Lyttelton.

9. Fr.

Ch. 8½ A.M. Wrote to Mrs Richards BP—J. Westell—Mr Morley l. & BP—Murrays—Mr Boscawen—Thos Wilson—Hon. R. Meade. Woodcraft with S.E.G. Read Iliad—By Order of the Czar—Missy. Priest on Missouri.[9]

---

[1] Henry William Massingham, 1860–1924; radical journalist; ed. *The Star* 1890, *Labour World* 1891; on *Daily Chronicle* 1892–5, editor 1895–9.

[2] Not found published.

[3] A. Hartshorne, *Hanging in chains* (1891).

[4] Of Paisley; occasional correspondent on religion; Hawn P.

[5] L. H. Mills had sent his *Avesta* (1880).   [6] See 12 Sept. 91.

[7] R. Frölich, Italian consul in Manchester.

[8] Of Highbury; sent poems.

[9] *Life and scenery in Missouri. Reminiscences of a missionary priest* (1890).

10. Sat.

Ch. 8½ A.M. Wrote to Mayor of Pwlheli—Rev. C.A. Cooke—F. Longman—Rev. Dr. Lunes—G. Mitchell—Rev. A. Leslie. Read Grey's Newcastle 1649[1]—Hom. Iliad—By Order of the Czar. Worked on Ol[ympian] Religion.[2] Woodcraft with S. & H. Worked on books.

11. S. 20 Trin.

H.C. at Sandycroft School 8 A.M. (52 communicants, the fruit given to H. Drew's labour)—Parish Ch. 11 AM & [blank.] Wrote to Lady F. Cavendish— J. Grant—Canon Luccock—Sec. S.P.G.—Rev. W. Blissard[3]—Mr Seymour Keay MP. Read Dr Huggins's Addr.[4]—Luccock on Wesley[5]—W. Lyttelton on Future[6]—Howell on Prayer.[7]

12. M.

Ch. 8¼ A.M. Wrote to P.M. Chaudry[8] B.P.—V. Office—Rev. Dr Spalding—S. Smith MP.—J.S. Stephen—G. Colburn—Ed. of Bookman.[9] Worked on books here & at St Deiniol's. Worked on MS. Ol. Rel. Read Iliad—By order of the Czar finished.

13. Tu.

Ch. 8½ A.M. Wrote to Messrs Bull & Auvache—Mr Marsh—Ly F. Cavendish—J.J. Smith—J. McCulloch—Jos. Hughes. Walk with R. Acton[10] and A. Lyttelton. 3 m. Worked on Ol. Religion. Read Iliad—H. Spencer's last Vol.[11]—Andrée Hope in Murray.[12]

14. Wed.

Ch. 8¼ A.M. Wrote to Canon Venables—Hon. R. Meade—J.S. Brownrigg—Mad. Patti BP.—J. Taylor—E.A. Robinson—Messrs Bailey—W.F. Denneby. Long & anxious conversation with Mr Rendel on Granville's affairs. Walk with him & Acton 1¼ h.—4 miles? Worked on Ol. Rel. Read Iliad—Hall Caine.[13] Ten to dinner + 1.

---

[1] W. Gray, 'Chorographia; or, a survey of Newcastle upon Tine' (1649).
[2] Two articles, each in two parts, 'The Olympian Religion. I. Its sources and authorship. II. Outline of its particulars', *N.A.R.*, cliv. 231, 365, 489, 613 (February–May 1892).
[3] William Blissard, vicar of Seasalter, Canterbury; formerly headmaster of King's, Canterbury.
[4] Probably an address by (Sir) William Higgins, astronomer.
[5] H. M. Luccock, *John Wesley's churchmanship* (1891).
[6] Untraced.
[7] Perhaps W. Howell, 'The word of God . . .' (1730).
[8] Of Chittagong, India, had written in admiration; Hawn P.
[9] Acknowledging receipt of the first number of *The Bookman*; his letter was used as a puff in the second, p. 47.
[10] Visit of Acton's son (see 8 June 91), encouraged by President Warren of Magdalen college, Oxford, where he was an undergraduate; see Add MS 44513, ff. 144, 168.
[11] Unclear which; perhaps *Justice* (1891), reprinted from *Principles of Ethics*.
[12] A. Hope, 'Scenes in Russia. I', *Murray's Magazine*, x. 554 (October 1891).
[13] T. H. Hall Caine, *The scapegoat*, 2v. (1891).

15. Th.

Ch. 8¼ A.M. Wrote to J.C. Humphreys—A.W. Hutton—Messrs A. Reed—Ernest Rhys—F. Penna[1]—J. Alexander—J.B. Massey. Read Iliad—Hall Caine. Worked on Ol. Rel. Walk with R. Acton. Long conversations with R. Acton—A. Morley—and Sir A. Gordon: *all* satisfactory. Ten to dinner.

16. Fr.

Ch. 8¼ A.M. Wrote to Mr F. Schnadhorst—V. Office—Miss Kortright—T.E. Young—Mr Bruce Findley—E. Hewitt—Rev. Mr Crockett—H.J. Cousins—Messrs. Cornish[2]—Mr Montefiore—Mr Symington. Acton & A. Morley went off. Walk with A. Gordon 4 m. Corrected Newcastle (Theatre) Speech.[3] Read Iliad—Memoirs of Miss Hutton[4]—Hall Caine.

17. Sat.

Ch. 8½ A.M. Wrote to Agnes Wickham l.l.—Watsons—Wms & Norgate—E.A. Arnold—G.P. Rayne—Thos Reid—R.S. Holmes. Worked on books. Walk with Sir A.G. Worked on Ol. Rel. Read Miss Hutton—Hall Caine—Q. Rev. Backgammon with S.E.G. Ten to dinner. Saw H.N.G.

18. St Luke.

Ch. 11 A.M. and 6½ P.M. Wrote to Gertrude G.—Ld Blantyre—Mr T. Baker—W. Hutcheson—Rev. R.L. Douglas[5]—M. Cotton—W. Russell. Walk with Sir A. Gordon. Read Fothergill's Essays[6]—Bible as described by itself[7]—Zalmoxis[8]—Mason's Motherhood in the God Man.[9]

19. M.

Ch. 8¼ AM. Wrote to Sir E. Watkin MP.—Mr Bramwell Booth[10]—Rev. J. Gall—Rev. Mr Molesworth—Mr E. Mann—S. Fothergill—J. Knowles—T.L. Greenwood[11]—J. Wilson—Rev. T.H. Guest.[12] Worked on books here & St D. Worked on Ol. Religion. Read Scapegoat, Hall Caine—Memoirs of Miss Hutton.

20. Tu.

Ch. 8½ A.M. Wrote to Keeper Printed Books [British Museum]—Mr Leader BP.—E. Turnbull—Mr Morley—J. Marchant—J.B. Massey—Gertrude G.—

---

[1] See 29 Mar. 78.
[2] James Cornish and Sons, London booksellers.
[3] See 2 Oct. 91.　　　　　　　　　　　　　[4] C. Hutton, *Reminiscences* (1891).
[5] Robert Langton Douglas, unbeneficed priest living in Beaumont Street, Oxford.
[6] S. F. Fothergill, *Essays on popular subjects* (1888).　　　　　[7] Untraced.
[8] Probably a privately printed ed. of J. H. Wilson, *Zalmoxis* (1892); poems.
[9] E. Mason, *Womanhood in the God Man* (1891).
[10] William Bramwell Booth, 1856-1929, chief of staff of the Salvation Army.
[11] Perhaps Thomas Greenwood, 1851-1908, promoter of public libraries; occasional correspondent; Hawn P.
[12] Thomas Hill Guest, vicar of Poulton-le-Fylde, Preston.

P. Maxwell—Josiah Hughes—T.P. O'Connor MP. Saw Mrs Benson—Mr O. Morgan—Mr Rendel: walk & conversation. Worked on books at St D.s. Worked on Ol. Rel. Read The Scapegoat—O'Connor's Life of Parnell.[1]

21. Wed.

Ch. 8½ A.M. Wrote to Sig. G.E. Parini BP.—Mrs Th. BP.—Mr W.H. Rideing—J. Westell—Wms & Norgate—Sig. Ricci—J. Haysman—Vicar of St Mary's Peckham. Worked much on books here & at St D.s. Saw Mr S. Rendel. Tea at Mr Mayhew's. Read O'Connor's Parnell—The Scapegoat—Prof. Jones on Barbaric Greece and Italy.[2]

22. Th.

Ch. 8½ A.M. Wrote to Mr E. R. Russell—G.F. Millin—Mr Hall Caine[3]—D.C. Doig—Dr Mackenzie—E. Knowles—Messrs Fawn. Visited Aston coll[iery] & brickwork. Worked at St Deiniol's. Worked on Ol. Rel. & prepared Art. for dispatch. Read Hall Caine (finished)—Began Gerard (Mrs Braddon)[4]—and [blank.]

23. Fr.

Ch. 8½ A.M. Wrote to Keeper of Printed Books—Mr W. Rideing—J. Grant—Sir A. Gordon—J.F. Hogan—Miss Marshall—J. Macrae. Worked on letters & papers. Read Boucher The Book[5]—Dr [blank] on Colour Sense—Mrs Maxwell's Gerard. Mr Cohen[6] came. Two hours with him on the list of Speeches.

24. Sat.

Ch. 8½ A.M. Wrote to Mrs de Tatton Egerton—Sir E. Watkin—Mrs Maxwell—Mr E. Brown—W.H. Warton—Mr Salkeld—T. Anderton—A. Lewis—W. Cramond—Miss M. Powell. Three hours on Speeches with Mr C[ohen]. Worked at St Deiniol's. Witnessed the Fire Engine operations. Read Mrs Maxwell's Gerard
. . . .

25. 21 S. Trin.

Ch mg & evg. Wrote to Bp of Ripon—Sotherans—Rev. Jenkins L. & BP.—Mr Godley—Mrs Melville—Sig. R. Stuart [sic]—Mrs Daniell—J.G. Hill—W. Eames. Read C. Naden Remains[7]—Seaver on Christ's quotations from O.T.[8]—Mason Womanhood in the Godman.—Maclaren's Sermons.

---

[1] T. P. O'Connor, *Charles Stewart Parnell. A memory* (1891).
[2] G. H. Jones, 'Barbaric Greece and Italy' (1891); paper read to British Association.
[3] (Sir) Thomas Henry Hall Caine, 1853-1931; romantic novelist, whose *The Scapegoat* Gladstone had been reading; lived with Rossetti.
[4] M. E. Braddon (Mrs Maxwell), *Gerald*, 3v. (1891).
[5] Perhaps J. S. Boucher, *Doctrine and practical notes* (1891).
[6] H.J. Cohen, editor with A. W. Hutton of the planned series of Gladstone's speeches; see 26 Apr. 90.
[7] See 16 Jan. 91.
[8] J. Seaver, *The authority of Christ in the criticism of the Old Testament* (1891).

26. M.

Ch. 8½ A.M. Wrote to Baron de Volkaerslake[1]—Mr Rich. Mason—Dr O. Holmes—Rev. E. Griffith—Mrs Harvey—Mr de Coverley—Mr Dobson. Worked much on books, here and at St D.s. Read Gerard—Renan on "Share of Semites"[2] —Elisabethan Society.[3] Saw Canon Scott Holland.

27. Tu.

Ch. 8½ A.M. Wrote to Bp of E. Africa[4]—J. Grant—Rev. Dr. Ginsburg—W. Ridler—Sir E. Watkin MP—Mr F. Wright—Messrs Wyllie. Work on books here & St D. Walk &c. with Canon S.H. Read Gerard Vol. II—Memoir of Robertson[5]— Renan, Judme et Xtme—Sutherland's Wordsworth.[6]

28. Wed.

Ch. 8½ A.M. & H.C. Wrote to Messrs Bull & Auvache—E. Evans—T. Wilson—J. Baker—Reeves & Turner—A. Morley MP—Dr Mackenzie—Jas Wilson—W. Canton—Rev. F.A. Elliot[7]—Brook & Chrystal. Effected the restoration of the tall case to its old place. Much on my legs here & with books at St Deiniols. Canon Holland *most* worthy. Much conversation with him. Read Gerard—Sutherland's Wordsworth.

29. Th.

Ch. 8½ A.M. Wrote to Messrs Merryweather[8]—A. Smith—Rev. R. Jenkins—R. Banks—Geo. Potter—A.W. Marks—S. Webb. Worked on books here & at St D. Walk with Rosebery.[9] Read Gerard—Knight on Beauty[10]—Sutherland's Wordsworth—Cheshire Report on Licensing.[11] Rosebery's dear boys came.[12]

30. Fr.

Ch. 8½ A.M. Wrote to Professor Knight—Ld Kimberley—Mr A. Hutton—Mr Cuthbertson—Th. Wilson—Mr Symington—Pres. Coll. Surgeons Edinb. Walk with Rosebery. Worked on books. Read Gerard III—Sutherland's Wordsworth— N.C. on Pepys—Xtn Hell—Psychical Society.[13]

[1] Not further identified.
[2] J. E. Renan, *Le Judaism et le Christianisme* (1883).
[3] H. Hall, *Society in the Elizabethan age* (1886).
[4] C. A. Smythies.
[5] W. Robertson, *Essays and sermons with memoir and portrait* (1891).
[6] J. M. Sutherland, *William Wordsworth* (1887).
[7] Frank Albert Stringer Elliot, curate in Chelsea.
[8] Fire equipment suppliers; for St. Deiniol's?
[9] Sir A. West, also staying at Hawarden, suggested to Rosebery that in the next liberal government Gladstone 'should be in the Cabinet, without office'; Crewe, *Rosebery*, ii. 375.
[10] W. Knight, *Philosophy of the beautiful: outlines of aesthetics* (1891).
[11] Untraced.
[12] The future 6th earl of Rosebery (see 21 Feb. 82) and his brother Neil James Archibald Primrose, 1882-1917.
[13] *N.C.*, xxx. 699, 712, 764 (November 1891).

31. Sat.

Ch. 8½ A.M. Our guests went off early. Wrote to Professor Londini[1]—Ld Acton—Rev. S. Blackwood—Mr E. Evans—Mr E.F. Benson[2]—Lady Simon. Worked on books here & St D. Read Contemp. Rev.—Branch of Cain—and Irish Local Govt (de Vere)[3]—Sutherland's Wordsworth—Gerard (finished).

All Saints. Sund. Nov 1.

Church 11 A.M. and H.C. also P.M. Wrote to Ld Acton—Mr Nye—A. Neale—Mr Kinsman—R.L. Chrystal[4]—A. Spurgeon—Rev. Turberville—W.L. Williams—J. Grant. Read Acct of Douay Transln[5]—The Church & her Doctrines[6]—Turberville, Saintly Life[7]—Lady Simon, O.T. Texts[8]—Colquhoun's Wilberforce.[9]

2. M.

Ch. 8¼ A.M. Wrote to Rev. E.B. Hewett[10]—Tregaskis—W. Cramond—T. Ismay[11]—W. Blair jun.—E.V. Jones—H.S. Moberly—J.A.H. Smith—H.C. Edmunds—Ld Kimberley. Saw Mr Mayhew, on the Coal. Worked on books at St D.s. Worked on Homer: on a telegr. message from America. Read Sutherland's Wordsworth—Finland's Union with Russia.[12] Dined at the Rectory. Backgammon with S.

3. Tu.

Ch. 8½ A.M. Wrote to Father Lockhart—Salkeld—Rev. T. Stephens—Sotherans—Mr Picton MP.—D. Wyllies—Rev. Dr. Ginsburg—E. Stanford—Ld Acton—Mr E. Ling—Worked on Ol. Rel. Worked on books at St D.s. Read Finland's Union with R.—Moral teachings of Science[13]—Life of Sir J.A. Picton[14]—and 'Tim'.[15]

4. Wed.

Ch. 8½ A.M. Wrote to Mr G.J. Holyoake—Messrs Cassell—J. Smith—Robn & Nichn—Mr F. Weber[16]—C.H. Perkins—W. Small. Worked on O.R. for U.S.

---

[1] Sending E. Londini, of University college, Liverpool, a small sum to assist endowment of a chair in Italian there; *T.T.*, 7 November 1891, 10b.

[2] Edward Frederic Benson, 1867–1940; author; his *As We Were* (1930) has interesting reminiscences of Gladstone. [3] *C.R.*, lx. 760, 729 (November 1891).

[4] Of Munich; a visitor to the Castle; see 7 Nov. 91.

[5] Untraced. [6] Untraced.

[7] A. C. Turberville had sent his *Types of the saintly life* (1891).

[8] Untraced article by Rachel, Lady Simon; see her *Records and reflections* (1894).

[9] J. C. Colquhoun, *William Wilberforce; his friends and his times* (1866).

[10] Edward Balvaird Hewett, chaplain at Clewer House of Mercy 1881–2; in charge of St Margaret's Mission in Glasgow 1882–95.

[11] Probably Thomas H. Ismay of Liverpool; Hawn P.

[12] J. R. Danielson, *Finland's union with Russia* (1891).

[13] Arabella B. Buckley, *Moral teachings of science* (1891).

[14] J. A. Picton, *Sir James Allanson Picton* (1891).

[15] [H. O. Sturgis], *Tim. A story* (1891).

[16] Friedrich Weber, organist of the Royal German chapel, staying at St. James's Palace; had sent his book (see 6 Nov. 91); Hawn P.

Worked on books at St D.s. Read Tim—Life of Picton—Mr Rendall on Education.[1]

5. Th.

Ch 8½ A.M. Wrote to Mr Rideing l. & B.P.—V. Office—Lady Harcourt—Mr Godley—Messrs Nisbet—Rev. H. Lunn—Prof. Londini—J.W. Reader—Rev. V. Morgan—C. Walkden—E. Litchfield. Finished & dispatched paper on Ol. Religion.[2] Worked on books at St D.s. Walk with Margot [Tennant]. Read Tim (finished)—Life of Picton.

6. Fr.

Ch. 8½ A.M. Wrote to Mr Lambert (Canad.)—A. Morley MP—Mrs Melville—J. Morley MP—G. Fitzgerald—Mr Pascoe Glyn[3]—J. Westell—J.C. Campbell—Mr Dobson. Worked on books here & at St. D.s. Read Life of Picton—Educational Review[4]—Proposed Irish Union 1751[5]—Weber's Hist Music[6]—Letter on the Rundle case.[7]

7. Sat.

Ch. 8½ A.M. Wrote to Mr Stuart l. & Tel.[8]—Sig. Schilizzi—J. Kinsman—Mrs Bella Cooke—J.W. Reader—Ed. Fin. Reform—Jas Cross—Messrs Fawn—A. Sutton. Saw Mr Chrystal from Munich. Worked on books at St D.s. Read Cross Hom. Transl.[9]—Barabbas &c. Poems[10]—Cecilia de Noel (finished)[11]—Life of Picton.

8. S.

Ch 11 AM and PM. Wrote to Mr P.W. Campbell—Mr W. Wren—W. Downing—W. Ridler. Read Rifted Clouds[12]—Wright Biblical Essays[13]—W. Stalher on Preaching[14]—Memorials of Oxford[15]—and divers Tracts.

9. M.

Ch. 8½ A.M. Wrote to Mr Dowden BP.—Mr Daniel—Sir E. Watkin—H. Harbour—E. Litchfield—E. Swift—C.A. Mitchell—Bp of E. Eq. Africa. Worked on

---

[1] Perhaps F. Rendell, 'School leaving examinations v. University inspection' (1872).
[2] See 10 Oct. 91.
[3] Pascoe Charles Glyn, 1833–1904; banker and liberal M.P. E. Dorset 1885–6.
[4] *Educational Review*, n.s. i. 1 (November 1891).
[5] 'A proposal for uniting the Kingdoms of Great Britain and Ireland' (1751).
[6] F. Weber, *Popular history of music* (1891).
[7] Untraced.
[8] On the Boulogne negotiations between the home rulers; *T.T.*, 9 November 1891, 10c.
[9] J. Cross, *Daughter of the gods. Ballad from the Iliad* (1891).
[10] [J. J. Brown], *The vision of Barabbas and other poems* (1891).
[11] L. Falconer, *Cecilia de Noel* (1891).
[12] Perhaps Catherine Marsh, *The rift in the clouds* (1871).
[13] See 30 May 86.
[14] Untraced.
[15] Sent by C. H. O. Daniel of Worcester college, Oxford; Add MS 44513, f. 194.

books & papers, here & at St Deiniol's. Saw Dean of St Asaph: & advised him to be stiff on the school controversy. Read Life of Picton—A Little Minister[1]—Chillingworth Novissima[2]—Nottingham Ministers' Correspondence.[3] Mr Smithwick[4] came.

10. Tu.

Ch. 8½ A.M. Wrote to Reeves & Turner—Mr Morley MP.—Mrs Th—A.T.Phythian—A. Neale—J.R. Robinson—Jas Nicol—Messrs Murray—J. Westell —Col. Luard—E.V. Jones—T. Wemyss Reid—E. Howell—C.S. Lee. Worked on 'the Rock'.[5] And on books at St D's. Read Life of Picton—The Little Minister—Memories of Madden.[6]

11. Wed.

Ch. 8½ A.M. Wrote to H.A. Salmond—G.G.—Bull & Auvache—J. Harding—Miss Leighton—Dean. St Asaph—H.W. Lovett—Town Clerk of Newcastle. Worked on Rock—and on books, at home. Saw Mr Smithwick—Miss A. Balfour. Read Little Minister—Picton's Life & Headlam's Athens.[7]

12. Th.

Ch. 8½ A.M. Wrote to Bp of Dunedin[8]—Rev. A. Duncan—J. Grant—J. Salkeld—Edgar Fell—Mad. Novikoff—M. Downing—Robn & Nichn—Rev. Dr Ginsburg. Read Westmr Rev. on Sir J. Macdonald; & on Ireland[9]—Little Minister—Picton's Life. Saw Mr Bickersteth—S.E.G. Worked on Rock—And on books δίχως.[10] Backgammon with S. Dined at Rectory.

13. Fr.

Ch. 8½ A.M. Wrote to Sir W. Harcourt—Midland Educ. Co.—C.C. Robertson—Jas Wilson—E. Anthony—J.C. Forbes—Rev. D. Smith—Mr N. Walsh. Saw Mr & Miss Benson. Worked on Rock. And on books at St D.s. Read Picton—Little Minister.

14. Sat.

Ch. 8½ A.M. Wrote to Rev. D. Macrae[11]—Wyllie & Co—Sir T. Acland—Mr Canton—Mr E. Menken—F.E. Steele—Mr Holmes (Tel.) Read Flint Borough

---

[1] J. M. Barrie, *The little minister*, 3v. (1891).
[2] See 18 Apr. 86.   [3] Untraced.
[4] Richard Fitzgerald Smithwick (see 7 Dec. 81), had become vicar of Gladstone's living of Seaforth, Liverpool, 1882.
[5] Further work on *The Impregnable Rock of Holy Scripture* (see 6 Jan. 90) for the 'revised and enlarged' second edition (1892).
[6] R. R. Madden, *Memoirs—chiefly autobiographical—from 1798 to 1886* (1891).
[7] J. W. Headlam, *Election by lot at Athens* (1891).
[8] Samuel Tarratt Neville, bp. of Dunedin 1871.
[9] *Westminster Review*, cxxxvi. 476. 497 (November 1891).
[10] 'doubly, in two ways'.
[11] Had sent his book; see next day.

Hist.—Little Minister (finished). Worked on Rock. Worked on Books. Back-gammon with S.

15. S. 25 Trin.

Ch. mg & 6½ PM. Wrote to Treas. Edinb. Physns—Rev. T.V. Bayne—Dr Gillies—Mr O'Malley. Finished making up my books for Mold Library. Read Macraes Gilfillan[1]—Warring, Miracle of Today[2]—Kerieff, Briefwechsel[3]—Gillies on Pain[4]—and . . . .

16. M.

Ch. 8¼ A.M. Wrote to D. Davidson (& made up parcel)—Mr H. Frowde—Mrs Bolton BP.—Messrs Virtue[5]—Mrs Rendel—Mr Blathwayt—J.M. Russell. Worked on 'Rock'. Worked at St D.s. Saw Dr Ginsburg.[6] Walk with him & Acton. Read Headlam Lot at Athens—Lady of Balmerino[7]—Prince L.L.B. on S. Italian Languages.[8]

17. Tu.

Ch. 8½ A.M. Wrote to Mr A. Morley MP—E.V. Jones—W.T. Fearings—Rev. T.E. Clark. Long & interesting conversations, also walk, with Dr G. and Lord A: also bibliographical information. Other guests came. Worked at St D.s Whist in evg. Read The Convict King[9] and Canning Religious Thought.[10]

18. Wed.

Ch. 8¼ A.M. Wrote to Sir W. Harcourt—Mr Morley—Mr Hartley—Mr Channing MP[11]—Isbister & Co.[12]—E. Howell—C.S. Harding—G.E. Waller. Saw Dr Ginsburg—Mr Marjoribanks—Lord Acton. Walk & drive—Mr Marjoribanks. Worked on Rock. Read Jorgenson (Convict King)—Times on the Massorabi.[13]

19. Th.

Ch. 8¼ A.M. Wrote to Mrs Th.—Mr Lloyd Bryce Tel.—V. Office—Mr Channing Tel.—Scotts—J.W. Russell—Mr J. Owen—Rev. W. Sadler—Rev. T.F. Carter. Worked on Books here & at St D.s—12½–2. The M[arjoribank]s went. Yesterday a sad trouble about Edwards the Coachman, today about Zadok: both from

[1] D. Macrae, *George Gilfillan. Anecdotes and reminiscences* (1891).
[2] Untraced.
[3] Not found.
[4] H. C. Gillies of Brockley had sent his *The meaning of pain* (1891?); Hawn P.
[5] J. S. Virtue & Co., London booksellers.
[6] C. D. Ginsburg, Hebrew scholar (see 15 July 83); visiting the Castle.
[7] Marie C. Leighton, *The Lady of Balmerino* (1891).
[8] Prince L. L. Bonaparte, *On the dialects of eleven southern and south-western counties* (1877).
[9] J. Jorgenson, *The Convict King* (1881).
[10] A. G. S. Canning, *Thoughts on religious history* (1891).
[11] On the 1868–74 govt.'s rates policy and Goschen; *T.T.*, 20 November 1891, 10e.
[12] Publishers of *The impregnable rock*.
[13] No obvious entry found in *T.T.*

that subtle enemy drink. Worked on Rock. Read Jorgensen's Life—Miss Montefiore's Concession[1]—Miss Fitzroy's 'Dogma'.[2] Conversation with Ld Acton.

20. Fr.

Ch. 8½ A.M. Wrote to Mr Labouchere (long)[3]—Mr Channing—Mr Pollitt—A.W. Hanwell—Est. Begbie[4]—Miss Fitzroy[5]—Jas. Shaw. Worked on Rock. Conversation with Acton & saw him off. Stepneys—R. Lytteltons came. Worked at St Deiniol's 2½–3. Read Jorgensen—Miss Fitzroy—and Owen on the Cymry.[6]

21. Sat.

Ch. 8½ A.M. Wrote to Lloyd Bryce Tel.—Rev. Mr Owen—Rev. Mr Scrivener—Moderator of Edinb. Constables—Mrs Salmonè—Mr Massingham—R. Thompson—Mr Officer—Chas Rowe. Saw Herbert on Irish Corr[espondence]. H. & H. on Estate matters. Concert 5–6¼ P.M. Worked on books at St D.s. Worked on proofs of O.R.[7] Read Jorgensen (finished)—Miss Blind's Poems[8]—Miss Fitzroy on Dogma—Dipsomaniac[9]—Eternal Peace.[10] Fourteen to dinner.

22. Preadv. S.

Ch. 11 A.M. and 6½ P.M. Wrote to Miss M. Blind—Mr Rideing—Miss Fitzroy. Finished correcting Proofs on O.R. & dispatched them. Read Fitzroy on Dogma—Dipsomaniac—Evans, Examen of Barclay.[11]

23. M.

Ch. 8½ A.M. Wrote to Rev. R.C. Jenkins—J. Westell—Mr Rideing—J. Grant—Jas Fergusson—F.E. Garrett—Mr Morley MP—W. Ridler—Messrs Isbister—Dr Pomeroy—Sir W. Harcourt—H.N.G. (on his Trust). Saw H.N.G. on the Trust—Mr Mayhew. Worked on books at St D's. Read 'In afrikander land'[12]—Dipsomaniac—Collins Study of Engl. Literature[13]—Pomeroy on Man.[14] Worked on 'Rock'.

---

[1] Untraced.
[2] A. I. Fitzroy, *Dogma and the Church of England* (1891).
[3] Untraced.
[4] E. H. Begbie, vegetarian in London; an occasional correspondent; Hawn P.
[5] Miss A. I. Fitzroy, authoress; see previous day.
[6] Robert Owen, minister and author, had sent *The Kymry*; Add MS 44513, f. 259.
[7] See 10 Oct. 91.
[8] M. Blind, *Selected poems* (1892); probably sent in proof.
[9] Untraced.
[10] Perhaps [A. A. Sykes], *The eternal peace of the Church* (1716).
[11] C. Evans, *An examen of parts . . . in a recent book by R. Barclay* (1878).
[12] F. E. Garnett had sent his *In Afrikanderland and the Land of Ophir* (1891).
[13] J. C. Collins, *Study of English literature at the Universities* (1891).
[14] H. S. Pomeroy, 'Is man too prolific? The so-called Malthusian idea . . . with a letter from . . . W. E. Gladstone' (1891); reprint from *Andover Review*.

24. Tu.

Ch. 8½ A.M. Wrote to A.R. Gladstone—Fawn & Son l.l.—Mr Pascoe Glyn—F. Impey—Dr Rhomaides—Rafereddin Ahmed[1]—A. Mudge—Messrs Jones—E. Tripe—John Fox. Worked on Rock. Worked on books at St D.s. Read Dipsomaniac (finished)—Rosebery's Pitt.[2]

25. Wed.

Ch. 8½ A.M. Wrote to Swan Sonnenschein—Ld Rosebery—Mr Fergusson—W. Ridler—Mr Patterson—Mr H. Magniac.[3] Saw Mr Stark & Mr Young—Mr Williamson M.P.[4]—Mr Tomkinson. Worked at St Deiniol's. Read Mr Godard Poverty &c.[5]—Ld Rosebery's Pitt.

26. Th.

Ch. 8½ A.M. Wrote to Mr Lyttelton Gell[6]—Mr Hart Tel.—Mr Morley MP.—Vote Office—Mrs Clifford—Sir E. Watkin M.P.—W.G. Wickham: for the dear boy's confirmation. Worked on Rock—And on books at St D.s. Read Rosebery—(the second half—with sighs at important parts)[7]—Mrs Clifford's 'Love Letters'.[8]

27. Fr.

Ch. 8½ A.M. Wrote to Lady Crawford—Mr Colman MP[9]—Mr Hodley—Mr Patterson—Rev W. Hunt—L.H. Moore—Mr Trumbull—Messrs Fawn—Card. Manning—L. Lewis—Dr Ginsburg. Walk & conversation with F. Lawley. Worked on books at St D.s. Read Rosebery, finished—Ld Salisbury's Speech[10]—Dawson's [blank.][11]

28. Sat.

Ch. 8½ A.M. Wrote to Gibraltar Ansr Tel.—F.A. Atkins—J.R. Bailey—W.L. Thomas—Dowager Ly Sandhurst. Worked on newsp. & materials. 11¾–5. To Port Sunlight. Political speech, & Labour Speech, together perhaps an hour.[12]

---

[1] See 22 July 91.

[2] See 19 Mar. 91.

[3] On death of his father, C. Magniac, liberal M.P.; Hawn P.

[4] See 16 July 90.

[5] J. G. Godard, *Poverty, its genesis and exodus* (1891).

[6] Philip Lyttelton Gell, 1852–1926; assistant publisher to Hart and Frowde at Oxford University Press; imperialist and friend of Milner.

[7] Probably Pitt's commitment to the war with France (which Gladstone saw as a great error) and the consequent Act of Union; see above, 19 Sept. 85 and *Spencer*, ii. 176.

[8] L. Clifford, *Love letters of a worldly woman* (1891).

[9] In H. C. Colman, *J. J. Colman* (1905), 406.

[10] Salisbury's Guildhall speech of 9 November, replying to Gladstone's remarks on Egypt on 2 October; see Cecil, *Salisbury*, iv. 393.

[11] Noted on 30 November as 'Dawson's Inconsequent Lives'. In fact J. H. Pearce, *Inconsequent lives: a village chronicle* (1891).

[12] Speeches on politics at Spital Old-Hall to the liberals of the Wirral and on labour at Lever's Port Sunlight; *T.T.*, 30 November 1891, 12a.

Saw Mr Ismay, Mr Lever,[1] Mr Evans[2] & others. Saw F. Lawley. Read Dawson's [blank]—and [blank.] Worked on 'Rock'.

29. Advent Sunday.

Ch 11 AM with H.C. and 6½ P.M. Wrote to Prof. Cheyne—Reeves and Turner. My nephew Sir J.G. went. Read Russell on Abp Tait (C.R.)[3]—Cheyne's Reply to W.E.G.[4]—The Soul and Money[5]—Mrs Benson's Vol.[6]—Well pleased with the position *quoad* Mr Cheyne.

30. M. St Andrew.

Ch. 8¼ A.M. with H.C. Worked on old W.E.G. letters for S.E.G. Wrote to Countess of Crawford—Capt. Gregory—E. Howell—Mr J.W. Wright—J. Grant—S. Bright Lucal—W. Hampson—Mr Marsden Howie—Sir W. Lawson. Worked on Books at St D.s. Saw F. Lawley—who went. Read Ld Crawford, Creed of Japhet[7]—Dawson's Inconsequent Lives. Dined at the Rectory. Backgammon with S. Worked on 'Rock'.[8]

Tues. Dec. One. 1891.

Ch. 8¼ A.M. Wrote to Mavernohose Ghosa—Mr Mayhew—T. Woodock [*sic*]—Mrs Benson—F.H. Groome—Talookdar of Majeddimpur—R.W. Perkins[9]—Abdool Lutief—Ed. Cosmopolitan[10]—Vice Chancellor of Oxford. I went to meet dear Gerty and her children at the Station, on their mournful return from Scotland. Worked on 'Rock'—And on Books &c. Read Dawson's Inconsequent Lives (finished)—Articles in N.C. and New Review.[11]

2. Wed.

Ch. 8¼ A.M. Wrote to Messrs Fawn BP.—H.J.G.—Mr A. Morley MP.—Ld Spencer—Wms & Norgate—Ld Acton—D. Rowley Soper—G. Beith—H.G. Rawson—J.D. Cooper—S.K. Hocking. Worked on 'Rock' (Swine miracle &c.) Worked on books & papers. A touch of axe-work.[12] Read Contemp. & New Rev.—Hocking's Tale[13]—Deacon Phelp's Selfish Nature[14]—and [blank.]

---

[1] William Hesketh Lever, 1851–1925; founded Port Sunlight for soap manufacturing 1888; later a liberal M.P., peer and benefactor.

[2] Edward Evans, chairman of the Wirral liberal association.

[3] G. W. F. Russell, 'Archbishop Tait', *C.R.*, lx. 840 (November 1891).

[4] T. K. Cheyne, 'Ancient beliefs in immortality: a reply to Mr Gladstone', *N.C.*, xxx. 951 (December 1891).

[5] Possibly P. Carus, *The soul of man* (1891).

[6] Mary E. Benson, *At sundry times and in divers manners*, 2v. (1891).

[7] A. W. C. Lindsay, Lord Crawford, *The creed of Japhet* (1891).

[8] See 10 Nov. 91.

[9] Perhaps a slip of the pen for R. W. Perks (see 30 July 90).

[10] Not found published.

[11] *New Review*, v (December 1891).

[12] The last recorded in the journal.

[13] Perhaps J. Hocking, *Jabez Easterbrook; a religious novel* (1890).

[14] Untraced.

3. Th.

Ch. 8¼ A.M. Wrote to Mr Lloyd Bryce–Sir W. Lawson–Ed. Recorder N.Y. (Tel.)–Rev. Birch Jones–Mr A. Morley–Mr D. Nutt–Ch. Enright–Mons. Viarol–Mr Menken–Fred. Rogers–Messrs Stanford. Worked on books here & St Ds. Corrected & dispatched proofs Hom Article 'Sources'.[1] Finished work on Rock. Read Letters from Heaven[2]–Bowden on Creation[3]–19th Cent. Ld Meath & Miss Bigg[4]–Weatherley & Maskelyne.[5] Saw S.E.G.

4. Fr.

Ch. 8½ A.M. Wrote to Mr Pascoe Glyn–Mrs Ingram–Hon. G.G.–Lp. Ref. Club Tel.–Mr Marchant–Rev. Mr Owen–Rev. Dr. Kinns–Miss Robertson–C.F. Forshaw–F. Hammill–Mr Miles–Mr Weatherley–A. Morley MP–Halley Stewart MP.[6]–Mr Pascoe Glyn–Major Martin Hume.[7] Worked at home in preparations & at St D.s on books. Called on Mr & Mrs Sykes.[8] Attended Volunteer Prize Meeting and spoke.[9] Put in order my additions &c. to the 'Rock'. Read 'Don Juan'[10] through–E.W.H. on Private Secretaries[11]–Ld de Vesci Hibernia Pacata.[12]

5. Sat. [Courthey, Liverpool]

Ch. 8¼ A.M. Many farewells & other business after Church: & a morning of many-sided occupations. Wrote to Mr Labouchere–Mr A. Morley–Mr Mayhew–Lord Spencer–Rev. Smethwick–Mr L. Durasso–Mr Dobson– *Recommendation* for Cross & Edwards. Conversation with the latter, a little moving. Saw S.E.G.: Mrs Jones (The Lodge) & others. Off at 2.40. Courthey at 5. I write my accounts of them to C.G. Saw Robert G.–Mr Smithwick on St Th. Seaforth. Read The Redemption of Strahan.[13]

6. 2 S. Adv.

10.15-1¾. To St Thomas Toxteth[14], most interesting: & I hope not without promise. Wrote to Mr Smithwick–C.G.–Ed. S. Wales Press.[15] Childwell Ch after: crowd again. Read Ecclesiasticus–Redemption of Strahan.

---

[1] See 10 Oct. 91.   [2] *Letters from Heaven* (1886); tr. from German.

[3] See 22 June 45.

[4] Meath on Norwegian drunkenness, Heather Bigg on women glove makers, *N.C.*, xxx. 933, 939 (December 1891).

[5] L. A. Weatherby, *The supernatural... with a chapter on oriental magic, spiritualism and theosophy by J. N. Maskelyne* (1891).

[6] Halley Stewart, 1838-1937; cement manufacturer; liberal M.P. Spalding 1887-95, Greenock 1906-10.

[7] Major Martin Sharp Hume, liberal candidate at Stockport; see *T.T.*, 28 December 1891, 4d.

[8] Probably Mr and Mrs John Thorley Sykes, Liverpool cotton broker living at Croes Howell, 6 miles from Hawarden.

[9] *T.T.*, 5 December 1891, 6d.   [10] By Byron (1818-24).

[11] E. W. Hamilton, 'The private secretary', *New Review*, v. 443 (November 1891).

[12] Lord de Vesci, 'Hibernia pacata', *N.C.*, xxx. 872 (December 1891).

[13] W. J. Dawson, *Redemption of Edward Strahan: a social story* (1891).

[14] The church in Liverpool of which Gladstone owned the advowson.

[15] Not found published.

7. M. [*Althorp Park, Northamptonshire*]

Wrote to Mr Barclay—C.G.—Mary Drew. Serious conversation with Arthur respecting his brother's health. 11¼-3¾. To Mossley Hill & thence to Althorp.[1] Harcourts, Morley, Rosebery, here or came. Read Redemption &c.—Rodd on Modern Greece.[2]

8. Tu.

Wrote to C.G.—Duke of Clarence—Ld Ripon—Dr Collins—C.J. Rowe—C. News & Press Assn Tell.—Bp of Ripon. 11½-2. Political confabulation & survey: good.[3] Walk with Morley and much conversation. Read Rodd on the Greeks— Monceau, Langue Populaire des Latins.[4]

9. Wed. [*Mentmore*]

Wrote to Mr A. Morley—W. Perry—Rev. Mr Oldroyd—Mr T. Law—Courthey Coachman—W. Barringer. Journey to Mentmore. Spoke at Northampton on the way. Saw Ld Spencer—Ld Rosebery—Ld Carrington—Ld Stafford. Rejoined C. Read Rodd.

10. Th.

Worked on Rural papers: driven late & worked 11¼-12½ P.M. Bad night followed. Read Rodd—C. Rothschild on Judaism.[5] Saw E. Hamilton—Ld C.— A. Godley—Mr Benn—Ld Rosebery (on his intention).[6]

11. Fr. [*London*]

Wrote to M.G. Bath—Mr Middleton—Dr Ginsburg—Miss Robertson—Abp of Canterb.—Mr de Coverley—Mrs Th.—Sir A. Gordon—Scotts. Saw Scotts—A. Morley—H.N.G.—Rosebery—A. Godley—Mr Armitstead—E. Ha—[*sic*]. Read Rodd—Althorp Trees.[7] Spoke 1 h. at the remarkable rural meeting: much fatigued in aftn.[8] Luxuriously lodged by the Harries at No 1. C.G.[9] Small & nice dinner party.

---

[1] Gladstone's fourth visit to Spencer's great house. For Lady Spencer's diary of the visit, see *Spencer*, ii. 176.

[2] J. Rennell Rodd, *The customs and lore of modern Greece* (1892).

[3] The purpose of the meeting was a general discussion of future liberal policy; see Crewe, *Rosebery*, ii. 376.

[4] Probably an untraced article by Paul Monceaux, French historian of Africa and the Mediterranean.

[5] C. de Rothschild, *Letters to a Christian friend on the fundamental truths of Judaism* (1869).

[6] Rosebery's intention not to return to public life; Gladstone 'was emphatic on the point that when one had attained to a certain point in politics it was not possible to retire'; Crewe, *Rosebery*, ii. 376.

[7] Untraced.

[8] At the Holborn restaurant, on the condition of the rural population; in Hutton and Cohen, *Speeches*, x. 397 and *T.T.*, 12 December 1891, 7a.

[9] i.e. Stuart Rendel's house, 1 Carlton Gardens; the Harries were presumably Rendel's servants.

12. Sat.

Wrote to Mr Tragaskis—Mr Lloyd Bryce—Mr Pennington—Mr Rennell Rodd[1]—Rev. E.A. Watson—Mr Wright—Midland Educ. Instn—Mr Zahnsdorff—Reeves & Turner—M. Drew—H. Mayhew—Rev. S.E.G.—W. Collis—E.A. Walford—E. Menken—Jas Miles—C. News & Pr. Assocn. Saw Princess of Wales—Sir A. West—Sir R. Welby—Mr A. Morley—Messrs Graves—Mr Mundella—Miss Ponsonby—Sir Jas Paget—Sir F. Knollys—Mr Asquith—S. Lawley & Trust Lawyers l.l. Nothing could be kinder than the Prince, or so winning as the Princess. Dined at Sir A. West's. Read Rodd's Modern Greece—Adye on Military Forces.[2]

13. 3 S. Adv.

Chapel Royal mg & afternoon. Saw Lady Ailesbury—A. Morley. Wrote to Wms & Norgate. Read Ednor Whitlock[3]—Häckel Hist. Creation[4]—Ecclesiasticus.

14. M.

Wrote to Countess Lytton—Lady Phillimore—Bull & Auvache—Rev. Mr Muir—Mr Chaster—Mrs Vanne—Mr A. Grove—Mr H. Frowde—Prov. Trin Coll Dublin—Mr Rendall—Mr Stebbing—Rev. Mr Tucker—M. Drew—Wms & N.—Mr Phillips. Saw H.N.G.—Mr Hutton—Mr Schnadhorst—E. Wickham. 12–1½ B[ritish] Museum with Dr C.D. Ginsburg: hard at work on collations—Wellhausen—& Häckel. Saw Mr Schnadhorst—Sir A. Clark—Mr G. Russell.

15. Tu. [Paris]

Wrote to Prof. Goodhart[5]—Arthur R.G.—Sir A. Gordon—D. Young. Left by 10 A.M. train. Paris (H. Bristol) at 6¼. Went to the Embassy. Read Haliburton on the Atlas Dwarfs:[6] but little on the R.R. Saw Dr Ginsburg—Sir E. Watkin—M. Josse—M. Jusserand. Everything most comfortable: but too sumptuous. We are three G.s[7] with J. Morley as guests: Mr Armitstead our host.

16. Wed. [Grand Hotel, Biarritz]

Off at 8.30. Biarritz at 11.20 PM. Reading much disturbed by motion of the carriage. We drove through an immense tract of the small culture in Central France. It looked most cheery. Read H. Heine[8]—The Soul &c.[9] Saw Mr Condy Stephens.[10]

---

[1] James Rennell Rodd, 1858–1941; diplomatist and author; had sent his book, see 7 Dec. 91 and Add MS 44513, f. 298.

[2] Sir J. Adye, 'Military forces of the crown', *N.C.*, xxx. 628 (October 1891).

[3] H. MacColl, *Ednor Whitlock* (1891).   [4] See 21 May 82.

[5] Harry Chester Goodhart, professor of humanity at Edinburgh University and married to Rose, Rendel's daughter.

[6] R. G. Haliburton, *The dwarfs of Mount Atlas* (1891).

[7] William, Catherine and Helen Gladstone. Also present was Sir Algernon West, whose letters to his wife reporting Gladstone's conversation are in West, *P.D.*, 23–31.

[8] Work unspecified; a collection of Heine's poems and prose was edited in Paris in 1891 by A. Lévy.

[9] Untraced.   [10] See 7 May 85.

17. Th.

Walk & drive. Saw The Consul—Sir A. Fairbairn.[1] As usual much conversation with J.M.[2] Read Butcher's Greece[3]—The Soul & Money—The Anglican Magazine +.[4] Backgammon with Mr A.

18. Fr.

Wrote to A. Morley—Prof. Romanes[5]—H.N.G.—J.B. Taylor. Visited the Tollemaches.[6] Also had a long conversation with the Mayor. And with Morley on politics: as well as much general. Read Heinrich Heine—The Soul and Money—Butcher on Greece—Mrs Tollemache's Poems.[7] Backgammon with Mr A.

19. Sat.

Walk to the Imperial Villa, now rotting: and to the Russian Church, a good fabric. Read Heine—Butcher—Soul and Money—as yest: and Climatologie:[8] also guide books.

20. 4 S. Adv.

Ch. 11 A.M: & H.C. also 3.30 P.M. The Chaplain (Mr Broade)[9] good. Wrote to C.S. Palmer. Read Soul & Money (finished)—Tollemache Stories of Stumbling[10]—Didon, Jesus Christ.[11]

21. M.

Kept the house for a slight diarrhoea. Read Marbot[12] (which delights me)—Mrs Oliphant's Jerusalem[13]—Butcher's Greece. Conversation with Morley.

---

[1] Sir Andrew Fairbairn, 1828–1901; machinery manufacturer; liberal M.P. W. Riding 1880–6; opposed Home Rule. Resigned as President of the British Club at Biarritz on 19 December on the Club's refusal to elect Gladstone an hon. member; on the affair becoming public, the members changed their votes and Gladstone accepted membership; *T.T.*, 28 December 1891, 3e.

[2] Morley's notes on Gladstone's conversation in Biarritz are in Morley, iii. 463–89.

[3] S. H. Butcher, *Some aspects of the Greek genius* (1891).

[4] *Anglican Church Magazine*, xi (December 1891).

[5] Agreeing to give the first Romanes Lecture at Oxford; planned for Trinity term 1892, it was postponed until 24 Oct. 92; see *Life of G. J. Romanes* (1895), ch. 4.

[6] L. A. Tollemache (see 28 Jan. 57); for Gladstone's conversations with him at Biarritz, see L. A. Tollemache, *Talks with Mr Gladstone* (various eds.), part II.

[7] Beatrix Tollemache, *Engelberg and other verses* (1890).

[8] Untraced.

[9] George Edgar Broade, 1838–98; chaplain of St. Andrew's, Biarritz 1879–92 and continued living there.

[10] L. A. Tollemache, *Stories of stumbling* (1891 ed., with appendices).

[11] H. L. Didon, *Jesus Christ*, 2v. (1891).

[12] J. B. A. M. de Marbot, *Mémoires*, 3v. (1891).

[13] M. O. Oliphant, *Jerusalem, its history and hope* (1891).

22. Tu.

Wrote to Mr Sheldon—Mayor of Biarritz—Mrs Harold Browne—Ed. Albemarle Journal[1]—Rev. J. Parker. Conversation with J.M.: & with Mr A[rmitstead]. Backgammon with Mr A. Read Marbot—Butcher—and Life of Raleigh.[2]

23. Wed.

Wrote to Gerty G.—Mr Macintosh B.P. (Edinb.). Drove to Bayonne. Read Marbot—Webster's Notes Archeologiques.[3] Mr A. had a dinner party. Conversation with the Mayor—Miss Wallace[4]—Mr Tollemache—Mr Broad (the Chaplain)—Also saw Mr Justice Hawkins.[5]

24. Th.

Ch. 10 A.M. Wrote to Ld Hartington—Mr Pennington—Mr Granville—G.E. Thompson—Mardwick [sic]. Read Marbot (most valuable)—Butcher, Gk Genius. Outings daily.

25. Xmas Day.

Ch. 11 A.M. with H.C. and 3 P.M. Mr Broad preached admirably: with a great command of his art. Read 'A wasted Life'[6]—Moberley, Bampton Lectures,[7]—and [blank.] We are very happy, in our host and otherwise.

26. Sat.

$9\frac{1}{2}$–$5\frac{1}{2}$. Expedition to S. Jean de Luz and Fuentarabia.[8] Saw the two Cathedrals: both noteworthy: St J. for internal arrangement, F. very popish: but both had a certain association with grandeur. The walls & streets of Fuentarabia very curious. The people ugly, very different from Biarritz Basques. The Rhune[9] beautifully seen on the drive home. Read Marbot—and 'A wasted Life'.

27. 1 S. Xm.

Ch mg & aft. Sea in increasing grandeur. Read Pere Didon[10]—Moberly Bampton L.—Ly G. Stock 'A wasted Life'—Mrs Oliphant's O.T.

---

[1] The liberal Albemarle. A monthly review, ed. W. H. Wilkins and H. Crackanthorpe, first appeared in January 1892 but soon failed.

[2] W. Stebbing, Sir Walter Raleigh (1891).

[3] Probably an untraced pamphlet on the archaeology of Biarritz by W. W. Webster.

[4] Presumably the 'young lady' who, Tollemache noted, 'sprung a mine by saying Scott was dull, and adding that she got more pleasure from Thackeray and George Eliot'; Tollemache, Talks with Mr. Gladstone, 44.

[5] Sir Henry Hawkins, 1817–1907; defended the Tichborne claimant; supreme court judge, known as 'Hanging Hawkins'; 1st Baron Brampton 1899.

[6] Lady G. G. Stock, A wasted life, 3v. (1891).

[7] G. Moberly, The administration of the holy spirit (1868).

[8] Small town just across the Spanish border.

[9] The mountain buttressing the western end of the Pyrenees.

[10] See 20 Dec. 91.

28. M.

Wrote to Messrs Brown—Rev. Mr Manley—Mr M. Theobald—Rev. A. Kennion —J. Stuart MP.—Mrs Oliphant.[1] Worked on proofs of O.R. No 2.[2] Read Marbot— Butcher, Greek genius. Sea glorious. Saw Dr Machagh[3]—Sir A. Fairbairn. Long morning conversation on Locke[4] & on the Univv. C. better. Conversation with W[est] & Morley on the M.P. ship.

29. Tu.

I struck 82. In my *trunk* there seems still to be much life. I have the inconvenience of old age: but not such as to stop my work. It is a singular lot: I am not permitted the rest I long for: Amen. But I am called to walk as Abraham walked, not knowing whither he went. What an honour. Yet I long, long, long, to be out of contention: I hope it is not sin.

It could not be a quiet day. Formal visit from the Mayor. Ditto from a deputation of the Club.[5] This M[orley] and I visited in the afternoon. Then we walked to admire & glorify the sea.

Finished & dispatched proofs of O[lympian] R[eligion]. Wrote to Mr Rideing—Mr Trumbull. Read Marbot (II)—Goitia, Cuestion de Irlanda[6]—Butcher. Backgammon with West.

30. Wed.

Wrote to Editor of Record[7]—Señor Goitia—The Herschells[8] came. Conversation with him. The sea continued grand and terrible. Read Marbot—Butcher—A wasted Life. Backgammon with West.

31. Th.

Drove to see Bayonne Cathedral. Also on the sea pier. Read Marbot & Wasted Life pretty largely. Also Butcher. Conversation with Herschell. Conversation after dinner on payment of members.[9] Backgammon with Mr A[rmitstead].

So ends the year: not rung but roared out by this magnificent sea, great alike for ear and eye.

---

[1] Margaret Oliphant Oliphant, 1828–97; novelist and historian; see 21 Dec. 91.

[2] See 10 Oct. 91.

[3] Probably S. Mackew, physician to the English community in Biarritz.

[4] In dispute with Morley: 'a tremendous tussle, for Mr G. was of the same mind, and perhaps for the same sort of reason, as Joseph de Maistre, that contempt for Locke is the beginning of knowledge. All very well for De Maistre, but not for a man in line with European liberalism'; Morley, iii. 476.

[5] i.e. the Biarritz club's climb-down; see 17 Dec. 91n.

[6] Francesco Goita of Villafranca, Spain; had sent his 'poor tract in Spanish' (no copy found); Hawn P.

[7] Responding to its editorials on biblical criticism with a cautious letter; *The Record*, 8 January 1892, 30a.

[8] Gladstone's lord chancellor in 1886 and 1892; see 20 Apr. 80.

[9] Gladstone repeated his view that M.P.s with incomes of less than £400 p.a. should receive a salary.

Where days pass unworthily it is hard to imprint on the mind the significance of the passage from year to year. To one like St Paul I suppose it was hardly significant. Would that our days might be passed one and all if not so near to God, yet as truly by Him & for Him.

APPENDIX

Gladstone's Letters to Laura Thistlethwayte, 1870–1893

This selection of letters continues the series in the Appendix in Volume VIII. It is taken from the collection of Gladstoniana in Lambeth MSS. Information on Mrs. Thistlethwayte will be found in the Introductions, especially those to Volumes V, VII, IX, X and to this volume.

The letters are printed in full, including the superscription and the subscription. Up to the Padwick debt action against the Thistlethwaytes in 1878, the superscription is normally: 'Dear Spirit'. After the letter of 30 August 1878 ('Dear "Broken Spirit"') the superscription is either 'Dear Mrs Thistlethwayte', or none. In later years almost all the letters open without a salutation. Mrs. Thistlethwayte's letters—mostly undated and many barely legible—have not been included.

It may be helpful to note that the frequently mentioned 'Miss Ponsonby' or 'Miss P.' is Melita Ponsonby, sister of Sir Henry Ponsonby, the Queen's Secretary; that 'K.' is Arthur Kinnaird, Gladstone's life-long friend, and that 'C.P.' or 'C.P.V.' is C. P. Villiers, the whig M.P. for Wolverhampton who frequented Laura Thistlethwayte's salon. 'Lady S' is Lady Susan Opdebeck, daughter of the duke of Hamilton and the divorced wife of the 5th duke of Newcastle who as Lord Lincoln had been Gladstone's undergraduate friend and was later colonial secretary. Lady Susan's elopement and divorce figured prominently in Volumes III and IV. In later years as a Trustee of the Newcastle Trust Gladstone spent much time on the affairs of the variously aberrant Newcastle children and on trying to salvage a small income for Lady Susan. Gladstone had met Laura Thistlethwayte in the context of the Newcastle family (see Introduction to Volume V) and she maintained links with a number of its members, especially Lady Susan and Lord Edward Pelham-Clinton who was one of her executors and to whom she left her personal possessions and the residue of her estate.

4 Carlton House Terrace.
4 May 1870.

Dear Spirit

There is no likelihood I fear of my being free to dine on Friday. But I am much struck by your inclosures. Although they name no one it is plain to whom they refer. If such a person as the writer can think he knows enough to put you on your defence, & impose on you the burden of defending me, others nearer or more considerable may with more reason or less unreason be critical. It is plain that in the case of persons each of whom though from disparate causes is likely to be made the subject of remark any unusual amount of intercourse, the justifying causes remaining unknown, is likely to be critical & to bear unjust construction.

I was in hopes that the last letter I wrote you from Hawarden[1] had satisfied you that what you sometimes & now once more call cold was not cold but the

---

[1] That of 22 April; see above, viii. 585.

reverse. However willing you in a generous ardour may be to me risks in point of appearances such as I have above referred to, your willingness cannot before God or man acquit *me*, who have the burden of so many more years to bear, in whom folly or want of reflection would be much more justly & more severely condemned; & whose occupied time & overcharged mind ought to be in no condition to give space & occasion for what does not befit his grown and fast growing age. The friendship cannot keep in honour, unless its workings aim steadily at what you sometimes say you will not allow me to talk of. Pray consider *this K.*[1] and the meaning of such things as he speaks from *such* a mouth.

I was struck by his manner as I found him at the head of the stair & made a kind of bow which did not seem to be returned.

Ever yrs   WEG

11 Carlton House Terrace.
7 May 1870.

I hope to call on Wednesday not earlier than five nor later than 6 or thereabouts. Pray do not refuse yourself to others—it would not be wise. Do not withdraw your forgiveness from that strange K. but try to be of use to him: make him cautious in what he says & at the same time let us not decline the lesson derivable from the proceedings of the incautious, or uncharitable. It is odd that he should mention the Burlington Arcade for I pass through it more rarely perhaps than any well known thoroughfare in this part of London: say twice a year.

I am grieved at the death of Sir J. Simpson[2] for what he was in himself and to the world: I am also deeply grieved at the loss to you, for I think you could hardly have had a greater loss.

Also I had been accustomed to look to *him* to consult and aid in my little plans about relieving you from injustice so strange and so unparalleled. But the Almighty has ordered otherwise. Had I wilfully neglected an opportunity of seeing him, I should have felt very guilty. But it was necessary to wait for oral communication in such a matter.

Ever yours dear Spirit.   WEG

I am half confined to bed & half out with cold & cough which however are passing away.

11 Carlton House Terrace.
9 May 1870.

Dear Spirit

I am concerned that your letter for Lady Simpson which was sent over to Downing Street immediately came too late for the private Govt Sunday post, which goes out early.

[1] Presumably A. K. Kinnaird, another of Mrs. Thistlethwayte's confidants.
[2] The physician.

I do not know whether you see the Daily Telegraph and so I have cut out an article on the remarkable & admirable man in whom the world has had a great loss and you a very special one.

The last time I met him was at your table—Had I then known all I know, I should not have been so slack as to let pass the possible moment & should have made him my co-conspirator in matters relating to you.

Thanks for inquiries. I am up & to be out, again today.

Return my letters? No! But I think I should like to have the one, that very egotistical one, which I wrote from Hawarden before you left Boveridge,[1] that when time serves I may even further develop the egotistical part of it

Ever yours   WEG

Private
Miss Cortwright's [sc. Kortright's] pamphlet has pleased the Queen.[2]

11 Carlton House Terrace.
20 June 1870.

Dear Spirit

There *can* be no forgiveness where there is no offence. There *can* be no offence, from you to me. I think you will find my letter referred rather to sending than to writing—I believe & hope my words were words of prudence, not inconsistent with sympathy & friendship. There is not any change in me. In things personal I am little given to change, so far as I know

God bless you   In dire haste   WEG

By 7.15 on Friday I hope to be with you

11 Carlton House Terrace.
August 11. 1870.

Dear Spirit

Pray keep the little book returned herewith: which I hope awakened your interest.

I have read your letters. I cannot plead guilty, as to writing, or as to visits. In sincerity and truth I must assure you, that it is too much, & not too little, that I have to answer for to my own conscience—What does this show? That you expect more than is your due? Certainly not. But that you have spent a prodigal attachment on a mind, a heart, a life, so absorbing and pre-occupied that it is smitten with barrenness in almost all voluntary relations a barrenness which I know & painfully feel must cause misgiving & revulsion. But be assured the little I can give, will be given faithfully.

[1] Of 16 December 1869; see above, viii. 579.
[2] See 31 Jan. 70.

You will have the first notice I can send about my movements. But as in regard to them I obey & do not command I *cannot* justly ask you to alter your plans in the least degree for purposes which even at the last may fail.

All blessings go with you. Ever yours WEG

[P.S.] I put in two speeches, which you may like to have.

Walmer, Deal.
Aug. 13. 70.

Dear Spirit

I do not see that my remarks were hard, and if they were so this makes them all the worse, for they were meant otherwise, and if, meaning to be considerate, I was unkind, this makes it all the worse as it shows (& it may be so) that I do not know what is kind or what is not. I am afraid I may now displease you again but I promised to write to you if there was any change, & I have just found it is quite uncertain whether I shall be in town Wed. Thurs. or Friday. On one of the last days of the week I ought to be on my way to Balmoral where I am ordered to arrive on the 22d: but even this journey is uncertain, as affairs on the Continent *may* require me to break the command to Balmoral & stay hereabouts instead of going ⟨to⟩ the North. All I know is 1. if I can be in town on one of the days I have named & if you are there I shall call as agreed. 2. you shall have the first intelligence of my movements. But, always a slave about them, for I know not when the mapping of my time has depended on my own choice—I am now, from the state of affairs, bound with more and harder chains than usual.

Near you (I think) at Ballachulish will be an illustrious sufferer—Lady Lothian, she has lived, and will live a noble life. Her whole thought now is, to devote herself to the care & relief of suffering.

God bless you—Ever yours WEG

For[?] North, as I hope, my day & yours must be very near.

P.S. I am sure you did not really think there was one word of laughter in my letter.

Indeed I have laughed but little for weeks past.

Walmer.
18 August 1870.

Dear Spirit

Tomorrow, I mean to come up & call as agreed. About 'preoccupation' I do not think you wholly understand me—I am obliged to plead it to others as well as to you. It does not refer merely to a particular sentiment. As regards *that* sentiment, what just relation has the frustration of it to my time of life? Such frustration is a grace & glory to its own proper period—is it not folly and almost ignominy to the time when life treads downhill? Is it not then against that order & proposition of nature, which is the fixed Divine Law also?

I mean to bring you a book, a novel, called Longleat;[1] it has come into my hands by one of those accidents which I always interpret as being a purpose & here the purpose I think was that it should pass on to you
Ever yours   WEG

Walmer Castle, Deal.
Aug. 24. 70.

Dear Spirit

I rec[eive]d your letter from Glasgow when in London with no indifferent feeling: and I shall await with much expectation your further account of the impressions you receive, & the opinion you form, about 'Longleat'[2] which is certainly a work of considerable power as well as high principle & aim.

Meantime I have a question to put to you, or indeed a request to make. You know that I am about communicating with Ld Bathurst in conformity with a little plan of my own touching your fair fame. May I tell him that I know from yourself that the rumours which obtained currency about you, & which I need not specify, were utterly groundless?

We continue to look with awe for the accounts of the war almost from hour to hour. Nothing seems likely to avert the final defeat of the French, but the struggle may still have many stages. Paris according to my son's[?] account does not *look* unquiet. Ever yours   WEG

I am obliged to address to Grosvenor Square, memory failing me a little as to your direction in Scotland.

11 Carlton House Terrace.
31 August 1870.

Dear Spirit

I thank you very much for your permission to make the statement to Lord Bathurst as I had asked it: and I have without delay made use of this permission.[3] Treat indulgently (as you do) my curiosity on this subject; I am sure every friend of yours would understand it.

And now, in a lower sphere, let me also thank you for so kindly sending grouse.

What you ask were my reasons for giving you 'Longleat'[4] and urging you to read it? They are not far to seek. I wished much to have your opinion upon it: to

[1] Novel by E. Lake [Mrs. D. Armstrong]; see 12 Aug. 70.
[2] See previous letter.
[3] See previous letter.
[4] See 12, 19 Aug. 70.

know what you thought of the manner in which the author has handled an imperfect but very interesting character, an abnormal marriage, a great transgression, and a noble repentance. Divers weaknesses and flaws are easy to discern: the aim is high, and as I felt the lessons taught, not didactically but all the more forcibly, to be strong and pungent, I desired in sympathy to know how they struck you.

About the great restitution I am sure I misread or misunderstood you. You cannot but think Helena was right in cutting herself sharply away from a state of enjoyment based in wrong, and in giving her whole self to a great and noble act of penitence. She inflicted by this no wrong upon Glen, but took him too, though by force, out of an unblessed condition.

What I had next to say was that there was much in your letters that I should like to speak of & hear you speak of: but I must assure you my aim in giving you the book, which I have described above, in no way included what you suppose. On that most inward subject of your domestic life I said last autumn and winter all I had to say. You proved to me by your recital that in such a case the measure of married life could not be filled up. I never thought it right to return to the subject. Had I done so, it would have been done openly. That on which I *have* since spoken or written, and might again, assumes & takes for granted the impossibility ⟨of⟩ which you name. It flows from my doubts whether you can in *justice* to yourself rely upon any substitute for the thing wanting. Did I not refer in a letter to your 'hunger of the heart'. Do I not feel for it? Must not every one, made of flesh & not of stone, feel for it & that deeply upon learning it? It is indeed hard in sound [*sic*] to say 'bear that hunger'. Perhaps weakness or worse than weakness dims my view and prevents my being able to rest in a solid conviction on a matter I would give much to clear: but I cannot arrive at a persuasion that you are safe, or that you may not be inflicting new wounds upon yourself, in seeking for your soul elsewhere the satisfaction denied you in its proper home. Are these words cruel? I hope not. I can say with truth, that to me it would be a lively gratification to minister to your weal: but you must not forget the hard conditions of my life, & my exhausted mind time & powers, even as they revive drunk up again by the constant succession of demands.

Now I must pass over various things, the Sonnet, Lady L.; the Address (surely it has been changed? or my memory is even a greater wreck than I supposed) to say how much I have thought & felt for you since the woful [*sic*] death of Lord Hertford.[1] I knew it would be a great blow to you and I feel for & with you under it. Some part of what you say about him, is to me, as you would anticipate, enigma. So is your reference to the visit at Boveridge. Some day you will explain. Meantime God bless you   Ever yours   WEG

---

[1] i.e. the 4th marquis. He was the half-brother of Laura's mother. The entry for Thistlethwayte in Burke's *Landed Gentry* (1858 ed. only) shows Laura Jane Seymour, Laura Thistlethwayte's mother, to have been the illegitimate daughter of the 3rd marquis of Hertford, the notorious libertine. The relationship is confirmed by labels on the back of portraits belonging in the early 20th century to Lady Sackville and noted in the archives of the Walace Collection. The portrait of Laura Thistlethwayte by Girard (reproduced in Volume VI) hung in the billiard room of Hertford House, now the Wallace Collection. Laura Thistlethwayte's father, Capt. R. H. Bell, of Glenconway, near Glenavy, was bailiff in the Hertfords' Irish estates in Antrim.

11 Carlton House Terrace.
Sept. 16. 70.

Dear Spirit

Your letter of the 10th was most kind. I wish I could answer you in letters at all equivalent to yours. But the table is not rich, & the crumbs that fall from it are very poor. However I send you herewith a photograph, the best I think which ever has been done of me.

The questions concerned with the war have detained me here from day to day—tomorrow I hope & expect to move away to Hawarden until Tuesday.

There is no real progress made towards peace. We do not indeed yet know whether the Germans will receive an Envoy from the present French Government. It is a sad & horrible business.

I fear you find your life lonely but there is a great secret for those who have it of turning loneliness into a wealth of enjoyment ⟨for⟩ of nature & of the mind.

Did you not thrill at the disaster to the 'Captain'[1]—I had a godchild on board, Reginald Herbert, and sons of other friends. Think of that great iron coffin for one & all. But their death has a voice—like the other great events that are thundering in our ears. May God incline the hearts of men to mercy & to peace   Ever yours   WEG

11 Carlton House Terrace.
Sept 24. 70.

Dear Spirit

I am so glad that the Photograph pleased you, & the sending it. But believe me when I tell you, it was done in the same spirit ⟨of⟩ as when I sent Longleat, the spirit of sympathy and good will. I think you will find no difficulty in attaching a good sense to that gift. I had derived benefit, I had found the book open subjects that it was well to think on, & that were of much interest—Is not this reason enough? If (unconsciously) I use rude & hard words, is not this a security against covert insinuation & for my telling you plainly what I have to say.

I hope you are better permanently and not only on the day of your victory over Col. Napier Sturt of which I was so glad to hear from him as well as from you.

Here I am the slave of events. I do not clearly gather from your letter when you will come. October is my best indeed for the present only hope of home and holiday. Our last Telegram about the war reports that yesterday there was violent cannonading and rifle-firing in Paris itself. We have been now nearly a week without any direct news from the City. There does not seem to be any immediate hope of peace but I *trust* there will be no more *rivers* of bloodshed.

I have been & am likely to be hard at work but always pleased to hear of your wellbeing and welldoing. When I have a little time I hope to write more. Ever yours   WEG

[1] Capsized off Finisterre with over 450 drowned on 7 September; see 9 Sept. 70.

Hawarden.
Oct. 9. 70.

Dear Spirit

I feel as much as you could with the truth of what you say that you have been tried hard in directions quite opposite, by petting and flattering on one side, by the fires of sorrow and suffering in a yet higher degree on the other. Believe me whatever else you may find wanting in me you will not find a disposition to run hastily into narrow or uncharitable judgments or where perchance I may have been betrayed into them a spirit of tenacity in holding fast to them.

Many thanks for the copies of Little Nelly. Two of them go into the orphanage here & my wife will read aloud to the children. The old one I retain.

If you ask me about your desire to go to the theatre, I should say go. Of Amy Robsart I know nothing, but it ought to be interesting. I recommend much Dick's Darling as a play of good aim.[1] Also Mr. Pennington's Hamlet at Sadler's Wells.[2] That drama is indeed a marvellous work. I do not recommend the 'Two Roses': a poor thing, it tries to make up for its poverty by sneers at Dissenting Religion which are unpardonable.[3]

God bless you now & always   Ever yours   WEG

(Did I forget?)
The watercolour is very pretty—Where is the scene? are you the artist?

11 Carlton House Terrace.
Nov. 7. 70.

Dear Spirit

Even a hard word if such there be comes soft from you, & if it did not it would be lost in so many other words of far other nature: It is these last which if you would permit I ought to check you for using: the first-named kind will never do me any harm or be out of place.

What a beautiful little ring. But will it go on any finger that I own? You shall try—but I fear not.[4] To your kind conditions of keeping it, in any case, I shall be able to accede, if I cannot persuade you to let it abide in the place where it is most becoming.

I have not made & cannot make a single country engagement for myself this year, however kindly they may be pressed—and I hope you will contrive to do with London opportunities of speech. These are threatening to close for the present—but I will not leave town without seeing you. I think the Cabinet will probably disperse after Thursday. God bless you. Ever yours   WEG.

[1] Not recorded as seen.
[2] See 23 Sept. 70.
[3] See 16 Sept. 70.
[4] A second ring, apparently not worn. The first ring (see above, viii. 575-6) can be seen in a number of Gladstone's portraits.

10 Downing Street.
Dec. 1. 70.

Dear Spirit

I send the mutilated ring and am very sorry it will not be in my power to bring it; you are too ethereal to feel the limitations of time, but they weigh upon me & all gross mortals.

It was stupid of me, too, not to speak to you about Major Collier. Unfortunately I have no acquaintance with Sir P. Fitzgerald except as an old political opponent & this would not form, you will see, a proper ground for a private introduction.

Farewell until you come up again. I am waiting and hoping to flit.
Ever yours WEG

11 Carlton House Terrace.
Dec. 18. 70.

Dear Spirit

I received, & thankfully keep, the second sketch: besides the difference of the hair, the likeness is stronger.

You will allow I had a very good reason for not informing you beforehand of my plans, when I tell you that my summons, to go to London Thursday morning, came to me on Wedy evening after post. And so, or nearly so, it has been on almost every occasion in this year. Rarely have I known that I was to remain in a place for 48 hours ahead.

And very selfish it would be in me to complain of this when it is recollected what horrors are abroad, and how mercifully we are spared from them. It is said, by no biassed witnesses, that there is now much harshness and cruelty on the part of the Germans; and, stranger to say, especially of the Bavarians. Many talk of peace through the exhaustion of France: I am sceptical, though there are one or two indications of it.

I am afraid your time on the 30th will be between two of mine. At least my ambition & many duties would lead me to remain at Hawarden till between 15 & 18 Jan

Thank Mrs Morton warmly for her kindness & believe me
Ever yours   WEG

Divinus vobiscum: a happy Xmas

Hawarden Castle.
Jan. 1. 71.

Dear Spirit

Though my day's work even on Sunday is commonly such as to leave me good for little at its close, and I am now writing late in the evening, I must not longer delay thanking you for the birthday letter, and saying how very glad I was to find by the one of Wedy which followed it that I had not made you misunderstand me.

Warm & sincere congratulations & good wishes are indeed pleasant gifts, but a birthday becomes more & more a solemn thing when so many of them have been counted.

The 'tale' was full of interest but you have seen that it had reference to something which I had in no way conveyed. Unfortunately the process of writing on my memory & rubbing out from it goes on with such portentous rapidity from day to day that I do not sufficiently bear my last letter in mind to understand fully all you say of it. Nevertheless I will answer your question—I told you I would trust you until I learned from you it was no longer safe—Would it be painful to me, you ask, to be so informed? My answer is twofold: first I do not think any thing you told me would excite any feelings except those of sympathy, & how far they partake of pain you can judge: secondly, it would be indeed painful to me if I knew that you thought the time had come for so telling me and yet you forbore to do it.

Remember I am always waiting for the 'many things' and if I cannot bear them now when can I.

My boy continues thank God to improve much but will not be fit to move for some time. His dear mother is nursing him in London.

God send you this & many happy new years. Ever yours   WEG

10 Downing Street.
Jan. 18. 71.

Dear Spirit

I thank you for your kind letter. The change of place was sudden & one acceptable with reference to my breaking the engagement to you: yet I did not feel that dependent as I am on other bonds & calls I should be justified in coming up simply to keep it. I am a slave & so must continue, nor is it to be complained of: nor am I, it seems, enough a slave, as the Times of today complains that the members of the Govt. have taken four months holiday! For my part if I have had it I must have had it in my sleep. The two days I spent at Boveridge have been I believe the only days I have passed without public business since I was sent for to the Queen in Dec. 1868.

How is the foot, & how are you generally? And do you think you are likely to come up again? I inquired in G[rosvenor] S[quare] on Sunday for the chance of finding you and learned that you had gone on Thursday according to your plan and Mr. T.s desire. What you had told me of him & his feelings was very touching.

The sad sad war you see goes on—the Prussians say they hardly expect to take Paris before some day late in February—I think it very difficult indeed to say either when it will end or how.

God bless you   Ever yours   WEG

All accounts of your friends are acceptable. Kinnaird & I shall I think quite agree.

Feb. 26. 71.

Dear Spirit

I thought you would like to know that I saw Lord Bathurst at the Levee yesterday as young & sprightly as possible—he made the backward evolution required after passing the Prince and the Royalties as if he had just come of age.

The times are dark and anxious. Peace is not made. It is most doubtful whether if made, it will be stable: it is doubtful even whether it will be made at all. There is an account today which I hope & think may be true, of 48 hours added to the armistice. Bismarck doles out time by the second.

I hope you are well & surrounded by good friends. For my own part I am thankful to say our boy continues to make progress but it is not rapid: and though the times are hard my health is good thank God.

I read the verses in your last with much interest and I return the Photograph as you desired.

As I am writing a Telegram comes in saying peace has been made as far as M. Thiers is concerned—Alsace & Lorraine with Metz taken, & an indemnity of £200,000,000. Will they pay the last? Will they let Germany keep the first? I am not sure about this news.

God bless you   Ever yours   WEG

A noble sermon from Bishop Temple this morning.

10 Downing Street.
March 16. 71.

Dear Spirit

Welcome to town. Welcome on paper, & in my thoughts. But I am at present chained to the wheel—Cabinets in the morning, long & grave House of Commons debates in the evening: and on Saturday, the first time for many weeks I go out of town till Monday, & on Sunday again to Windsor!

So go the stars! Nevertheless I have an idea that on Saturday if we have just a Cabinet I may get to G. Square either at two when you will probably have luncheon or else at five for a half hour

God bless you
Ever yours   WEG.

I return the Petrarchs. You ought not lightly to flirt with them.

Susceptible was meant to be general, not special as you suppose, &, as general, it is true.

[*Mrs. Thistlethwayte docketed this letter:*]
These first words of welcome being the only kindness received by *me* for nearly a *year*[.] oh! what I have suffered[.] Thank God I can never again suffer *as I have done*. Will he bear with my weakness—God willing I hope to get strong.

He can *care* for *nothing* of mine. or nothing from me. oh how madly I love   March 16th

11 Carlton House Terrace.
Mch. 20. 71.

Dear Spirit

I should have liked to ask for luncheon, without 'people', on Wed. [22 March] at 2: but there is a Levee; and I have at 3.30 a Deputation of U[nited] P[resbyterian]s (one-legged, for which none allow me to substitute as being from me less invidious three-fingered) but I hope to call at five. And next week I may perchance have a little more leisure. I will *bring* my note back: how vilely it is written—no wonder you could not read it well: it was very creditable to you to keep your temper.

Do not take too seriously a miserable joke. Christianity is in deed & truth union with Christ. They are the most perfectly shaped Christians, who are most united. This is your creed, and it is mine. But there are all manner of means to this end: although it happens too often that those who have most & best means, not using them best, fall short of those who have fewer and poorer. Nevertheless depend upon it the Church, not as an aggregate ideally conceived above[?], but as the polity and society founded by Christ to gather His elect, is one and a mighty, and above all an *appointed* means: & those who do not recognise this, if it be the truth, are *in that respect* defective or if you like deprived.

Now I have given you a tough morsel to digest. Pray make due note of it. If I have any convictions, this lies, & has lain for 40 years, near the root of them. God bless you
Ever yours   WEG

11 Carlton House Terrace.
March 26. 1871.

Dear Spirit

From your written language, plaintive but uncomplaining, I cannot but see that you have suffered, and that in some way I have made you suffer. Here is a double ground, which leads me to turn my thoughts, in my first & fleeting moments of peace, to you & to this suffering of yours.

Its cause seems to have a date. I know not whether that date was a conversation which took place in your sittingroom, where I have seen you a few times. However this may be, if I did not write or speak, if I did not try to remove that for which I may be responsible, it would be wrong, it would be unnatural. For all forms, & all degrees, of attachment between human beings, in that attachment friendship, love, loyalty, or what it may, have this common and indispensible basis, that there must be a sincere interest, and a desire coming from the heart, for the welfare, and the best welfare, for the peace & calm & joy, of the person who is the object of it. How then can I promote them ever so little? It is this which I would wish, in every way, & every degree, open to me. And first I must ask myself how it can best be done?

Now in honesty and honour I cannot doubt what would be, what is, best for you. You have an incomplete life—A life incomplete in its basis—in marriage, which is the basis of married life. After all you have generously, trustfully, & I am sure truly told me (for great indeed in such a case would be the guilt of untruth), after all that most sad & tragic history, I cannot but reflect now on the years that have rolled by, on the confidence & admiration you have won, upon the good acts of which you have been and are the object; and I ⟨say⟩ now repeat what I said when I knew much less; the truest steps towards completeness of life for you would be any step that could be made *towards* a fuller communion in your married life. I do not say all could be done, but could not something? Could not some ties be drawn closer? If they could I am persuaded it would be greatly for your peace. Completeness of life, which alone satisfies, cannot be fully had out of the sphere in which the life is cast. It would be a comfort to me, and I should feel inwardly that I had done something for you, had I been able to move you in this direction: & next to this to encourage you in that steady painstaking cultivation of your native gifts of mind, which is the most notable, and the most noble—characteristic of your friends the Germans.

Lest this letter too should wear an aspect of unkindness—for who can tell what aspect his words will wear?—let me say that every sentiment on my part of interest, confidence, and trust, remains unaltered. Tomorrow I must be at the H of C. till past midnight. Sunday probably the same: but on Wednesday I should probably be free from a dinner at Grillion's Club by ten?[1] God bless you. Do not feel bound to reply.

Ever yours   WEG

Hawarden Castle.
Ap. 11. 71.

Dear Spirit

My petition about an undress dinner, where I can only come in & out, was one of such freedom as at least showed great trust, and this always implies sympathy.

I am glad to have your note of yesterday. It shows me that the letter of Saturday, which I read with amazement, was written in a dream. I am certain it was a painful dream, as it was one in which, it seems, I told a lie to you; & this in order to conceal my going out of town to Walmer! *Such* a liar ought to be in Bedlam. What strange fancy can have suggested such an idea? You might as rationally suppose me now in Kamschatka[?]. Had the thing really happened, surely (at least so I hope) you would not, as you do, have been ready to see me, so kindly, at dinner; or to let me come within your door. I am truly sorry for the pain this imagination gave you, and for its driving you forth as you describe at night (like Lancelot into the wilderness) and for its forcing you also to write a letter of that kind at such a time as on Easter Eve, when it could have no answer before the great Easter Day. However I hope you have dismissed all this from your mind. If not, pray explain to me clearly how you received this most false impression & what it is, that I may undeceive you, as you would wish.

Would it not be better that you should keep the Duke of N[ewcastle]'s letters

[1] Gladstone saw her that evening, after dining with Glyn; see 29 Mar. 71.

until you can collect them?[1] I notice something in this one which I will explain when we meet.

Ever yours   God bless you   WEG

11 Carlton House Terrace.
May 2. 71.

Dear Spirit

Thanks for your good wishes about H of C. You see that affairs went well last night. But the pressure on time is very great, & on brain greater still.

So *she* is dead: & I should like to hear more of her, whom you call a wonderful woman.[2] She is an object of interest to me through you, & some day perhaps you will let me know more about her.

I am glad to see your confidence that she has departed into that rest for which we all should long.

When time permits, I hope to come up and see you but I cannot yet see my way to time for a visit. Indeed I have found it difficult to secure even my minimum of daily walk.

When we last met, we did not speak about the picture. It is not even well placed, being too far from the eye. I say it must have gone there without your leave.

Look at a bust of me by Burnand—I never SAT for it & yet he has done much—a very clever man, with few advantages.

May all blessings attend you.   Ever yours   WEG

11 Carlton House Terrace.
Aug. 20. 71.

Dear Spirit

Certainly you shall not leave London without a word from me though I am exhausted in mind so as to shrink from almost every voluntary effort. And the matters of necessity not choice coming pretty thickly prevent the recovery of any free movements. But to talk or write about this is no better than selfish egotism.

Recollect I beseech you about forgiveness that it can only exist where there is something to be forgiven; and it must be difficult for forgiveness to pass from me to you because you have never done to me anything but what was conceived in the spirit of kindness & goodness; and it is only the overflow of them, if any think [*sic*], that I have to 'forgive'. More strength indeed I can ask for you, as we can all most well and truly ask for one another, for which of us has enough? and though I do not think your defect is as great as mine yet from the ardour of your nature, which the history, the singular history of your life has so tended to

[1] For Mrs. Thistlethwayte's link with Newcastle before she met Gladstone, see above, v. ciii.
[2] Unidentified.

quicken, no doubt your mind too is great—and you will I doubt not as you live on have a great work of self-repression to perform in the strength of the most high. Not the self-repression of those who have simply ignoble and evil parts of nature to contend: you will I think, have to fight with much that is tender and true and yet that threatens you but I feel confident that in the strength of Him who cares for you, and who gave Himself for you, and for us all, you will conquer everything that goes beyond, and will bring up & bring out everything that falls short of the will of God concerning you. This is your vocation: it is the vocation of us all, and to live up to our vocation is the only life worth living.

If all this be a riddle, or if any of it be a riddle, the key to the lock will be found when I write to you about myself and the future that lies before me. There is one deep and irremovable difference between your condition and mine. In the main, *I have lived*. In the main you *have yet to live*. In speaking thus I do not forget your strange & varied, your most touching & most moving experience. I speak by the years counted and to be counted, according to the laws of nature, those laws written with a pen of iron, graven upon the rock for ever. My future is every day taking shape before me, in a definite and narrow form. The present life of over-action and excess cannot & must not long continue—and I see or seem to see plainly before me what is the remainder of my vocation & what kind of life it will require, that I may hear securely those solemn words, which ought also be sweet words

'Prepare to meet thy God'.

Meantime believe that you will not and cannot be forgotten by me—I have taken measures to provide that you shall not, but no measures are needed. The trust you have given me—to say no more—renders that an impossibility. And I appreciate and honour the generosity of your letter now before me. That generosity more than anything else convinces me that Love better than any here on earth has you ever in its eye, & will bear you on above the waves into the tranquil haven.

May it ever so bless you, & keep you, & pour upon you, in whatever forms, more than you can ask or think.

yours ever   WEG

You will be surprised at my date. I gave up moving late yesterday: & I spend this day here with two of my sons.

I am a little rebellious about that ring—the last.

No. 2.   11 Carlton House Terrace.
Au 20. 71.

Dear Spirit

I return Ld. Carysfort's letters. There are things in them that I admire—especially "at what time of life will men cease to be idiots"?

I am not surprised that you were too transparent, and that you have had a hard battle to fight but without doubt you have fought it well.

You will I am sure by the instincts of your nature be kind to him, and the more you find yourself able to give them scope without incurring inconvenience the better

May you have a pleasant journey—I mean to spend the evening quietly at home with my sons. It is better. On Tuesday I hope to go to Whitby.

God bless you   WEG

I send a copy of a *good* little tract—worth reading.[1] Let A. K[innaird] also read it.

Whitby.
Aug 24. 71.

Dear Spirit

I am so glad my letter (which I return) was kind—and I do not think my *act* was unkind. First because I had other occupations on Sunday afternoon, when I got your letter—two of them, which were special, took $4\frac{1}{2}$ hours—and I had my sons to look to, whom I see so little of. Secondly, even if this had not been so, I think it would scarcely have been wise in me again to go to G. St [*sc.* Square]. When I speak of your vocation, I speak for the future. I am deeply interested about your happiness, your lot. It pains me much when you suffer for me; pains me more to think you may suffer more; and that my vocation, as I sink into the vale of years, may bring that suffering, and make such high and exacting calls upon you.

I follow with interest as always the whole of your letter but I do not attempt to comment. Only understand that you never have anything to explain or apologise for as before me. That is all on my side.

Surely I will keep the ring if you do not like to let me return it. Though I do not like to have all these pretty things as property it pleases me to keep them together and to look upon them as memorials.

I trust the White Heather will please and soothe you.

God bless you   WEG

Thornes House.
Wakefield.
Sept 6. 71.

Dear Spirit

Your letter addressed to Balmoral came round to me at Whitby. As a general rule where you are *uncertain* about my whereabouts the quickest access to me is through London—where your packet would not be opened though common letters are. A perfect security is a double envelope—but I do not think you need take this trouble. I destroyed Lord Carysfort's letter as you desired me, as it

---

[1] Probably D. MacClausland, *The builders of Babel* (1871), just read; see 17 Aug. 71.

seems to have struck you, that there was in its language any thing strange or requiring to be specially accounted for—You had made a deep impression upon him and an⟨d⟩ enduring one but he seemed to me, in my hasty judgment, to write with as much regard & respect as warmth.

I am mindful that you are doing a great act of duty by your present sojourn in an air that does not agree with you,[1] and I shall be anxious and glad to learn that you have not suffered; as well as interested in learning how you pass your days in your mountain solitude. One sentence you shall have of preachment, which I continually repeat to myself: remember that our whole life is school for the purposes of culture as well as for those of the higher discipline. And how *full* it is! "good measure, pressed down, and running over."

I return to Ld. C. to say that I am grieved to hear of the dark letter which I have not seen: and that I do not remember why the word 'follow' which if I did use it was a careless one. The meaning was that my memory was not clear as to the pecuniary means by which the removal was effected and I thought he or any one interested in you might have had to do with supplying them in the same way as happened afterwards with one when you were in Wilton Place. But my memory revived when you reminded me of what was stated in your narration.

I hope to arrive at Hawarden tonight and to remain 10 days or a fortnight if not more. Our visit to Whitby was full of interest, though it had not *quite* the repose I desired and needed, and find difficult to get. It is however one of the more retired as well as of the most striking watering places.

I really believe "no thought sees light within me that puts you in a false form before me"—but why should I, or rather how could I, have to forgive a disclosure which you say was a great wrong 'to your own nature'? You are at all times often in my thoughts, for I feel a debt & a burden towards you, not merely in the sense of so much kindness received and not requited, but on account of that deep unbounded trust (to say no more) which you have reposed in me, of which I should like to prove myself worthy but feel that I have not found the way. I should like to make you my debtor; or even (in homely phrase) to balance the account. God bless you ever more   WEG

Hawarden Castle.
Sept. 15. 1871.

Dear Spirit

A magnificent present of grouse from Kinloch Lodge just missed us at Whitby but how kind it was of you to send & send in such bounteous measure. And now has come the wine! Would I were a better judge of such objects. But it seems to me fine and I shall try to obtain some better judgment on it. Meantime, your gifts multiply, and while I have pleasure in seeing & using them, I look upon myself as a kind of Banker, and them as a store which in the course of nature you will allow to go back into your hands.

[1] i.e. the Scottish highlands; see next letter.

I am struck with the verses headed 'Songtide'—From what, & whose, are they?

Your going to Kinloch Lodge did please me for it was an act of duty and self-sacrifice which could not fail to carry its reward.

That is a sad and touching story of Garcia.

Do the words in that conversation at Boveridge[1] seem to you as if they stand alone, as in a wilderness of the past? Have you read Tennyson lately, I mean the Idylls of the King? If not shall I send you my copy of the Book? There is so much in them that is noble, pure, lofty and broadly true—Read Lancelot's words at p. 215

'Not at my years, however it hold in youth'

But he also said p. 192

> 'and loved her with all love except the love
> Of men & women when they love their best,
> Closest, & sweetest, & had died the death
> In any knightly fashion for her sake'.

It is a wonderful book and the man who wrote it a great man.

My plans form themselves a little—what are yours?

I am to start for Balmoral on the 25th—to leave it probably on the 3rd October. I *think* perhaps then of crossing the hills from Braemar to Aviemore sleeping the night at the Inn there[2] and coming back by the Highland railroad to Perth, & Edinburgh &, there to visit my dear old friend Dean Ramsay
and now God bless you
Ever yours   WEG

Hawarden Castle.
21 September 1871.

Dear Spirit

My plan now is to go across by Glen Tilt to Blair Athol & sleep there, Oct 4—go on to Edinburgh Oct. 5. I do not know what your route would exactly be. What is your hotel in Edinbro'? I shall offer myself on a visit to my old friend Dean Ramsay. I should probably return to Liverpool and Hawarden Oct 7. And go on to London 10 to 12 days later. It is just possible, but not likely, that I might be kept a little longer at Balmoral than Oct 4.

I send you my Tennyson. The marks on it were made in reading for myself. Keep it if you like, and read it all over again. It touches much of woman's nature, and I think nobly & well.

Much too is opened by your letter. Lord C[arysfort?] is I think kind upon my Whitby speech:[3] did you think it egotistical? That epithet touches me. On the other hand the personal one he uses is most just. His style in this letter to you is

---

[1] For Gladstone's visit to Mrs. Thistlethwayte at Boveridge, see 11–13 Dec. 69.
[2] A walk in fact delayed until 1873; see 1 Sept. 73.
[3] On the ballot, and London wealth and the press; see 2 Sept. 71.

unfamiliar, he approaches nearer, and I do not quite understand him about quiet visiting—The letter is destroyed, and I cannot refer. So it was only 2 years ago that you 'became at last a woman'? I thought but a small part of the experience contained in your narration had made you fully one long long years before. But this will do to talk of. I am so glad you discussed with A. K[innaird]. I did not read much of his speech. Some one told me it was not kind to the Government about religious matters—he is perhaps a little suspicious but I am always glad of your cultivating his friendship.

I hope you have thanked Mr T. for me or shall I write. Why has Lord Otho left his place in Dorsetshire? Have you heard? I am in the dark.

God bless you.   Ever yours   WEG

p. 192 in Tennyson.

Balmoral.
S. 27. 71.

Dear Spirit

Before leaving Hawarden on Monday I received a most kind letter from you.

Since that time I have been busy, especially at Aberdeen but you will see enough probably too much about me & my doings in the newspapers which now-a-days leave one no secrets even for a moment.

In some way I had got into a mistaken [view] of your route which I supposed to be from some point on the Highland Route by Perth to Edinburgh—where I expect to be in the latter part of next week but my dates are not absolutely fixed yet.

Further on, my time is likely to be mapped out as follows[:]

My wife goes to London in the earliest days of October to watch over a niece's first confinement, and look after the East End schemes. I expect to go there about Oct 18 or 20 and remain for almost the first ten days of November when I should probably follow her to Hawarden.

I should then expect to be in London again for a short visit early in Decr.

All this is liable to be overset by any public want or motion.

Nothing could be so kind or clear as the explanation you have given me about the conversations with Ld. Carysfort & your account of me to him. But though it began about the Duke of Newcastle (whose print is on the wall before my eyes as I write) I hope & am sure you know it did not end there. I feel, & feel every day as if I ought to do something for & to you, which I had not done, & could not discover. Take this as a true good wish, for the little, the very little, it is worth & with a true A-Dieu believe me ever yours   WEG

[P.S.] I saw Ld Kintore yesterday at Aberdeen. He spoke of some fireworks in his family, I did not know what.

Hawarden Castle.
Nov. 17. 71.

Dear Spirit

Nothing could be more fair & considerate than your words about Mr Mackenzie. I reply separately.

As regards the Book,[1] it appears to me that all or nearly all your criticisms are well founded, and there is in it a great deal to be misliked or blamed. It seems full of crude hot and hearty youth with a zeal which supposes itself omniscient or supreme. But I think there is more in it than this and that it should be considered as a sign of the times. The man has shown pluck and perseverance, which in religious matters are faith & constancy; power of laying hold on the masses, & on some ardent spirits of a higher class. Also this complete abnegation of the world is remarkable in our Church & society: much of what passes for this is very incomplete indeed, I mean in the 'religious world'. So I think you do not do full justice? And are you not struck with the writer's full unquestioning adoption of the favourites[?] high 'Evangelical' phraseology?

Lady A. Ewing has been here and was most grateful for your (forgive me for saying) most handsome gift. God bless you.

Yours ever   WEG

Hawarden Castle.
Nov. 29. 71.

Dear Spirit

Thanks upon thanks. The Daily News was kind, and true—I have to thank you for two books: I have read most of Dr. Macduff,[2] and do not wonder at your being interested. The Mr P— whom he mentions is Mr J. H. Parker a friend of ours who has found out all which has yet been discovered around in and about the house of Puchus[?]. He has spent more in Roman exploration than he can well afford, but is now forming a Company to pursue the work. He has been made C.B. as a public honour.

For days I have not known, & do not now know, whether I may not be called to town suddenly before the week is over. But if all goes smoothly it will not be till the 11th. Shall I propose myself for dinner on that day? and at what hour?

Will you say to Mr Thistlethwayte, if he is still with you, that I am still paying attention to the matter of the Paddington Estate, which seems to me to involve questions of great public importance.

All must be thankful for the improved accounts of the Prince of Wales. He has had a really alarming illness and of course the danger is not yet over though much mitigated.

God bless you   Ever yours   WEG

---

[1] *The secular hymn book* (1871); Gladstone's quotation from it in his speech at Greenwich led to controversy; see 28 Oct., 16 Nov. 71.
[2] J. R. Macduff, *St Paul in Rome* (1871): see 26 Nov. 71.

On the way to Hawarden   11 Carlton House Terrace.
                                                             Dec. 22. 71.

Dear Spirit

Your letter of yesterday morning was a great relief to me; for I feel sure you did not continue to think I had inflicted on you an 'insult'—No mere mistake or error can amount to *this*. To inflict it on any one would be extremely wrong: on you, it would be cruel, unseemly[?], and ungrateful. Believe me in this; whatever I have said—and it may well have been wrong—I have said with no other thought than the thought of you: of you, not in the present, but in the future: of the long years which in the *course of nature* are before you, and with respect to which I must truly say my only wish & my fervent wish is that they may be happy ones.

My note of yesterday would not adequately convey to you the feeling with which I had read yours, just before received. It filled me with a deep sense that you are capable in an uncommon degree of the spirit of self-sacrifice; the noblest spirit that can possess a human creature. I will not on that account hastily rush in with peremptory words. When I told you the feeling that had been in my own mind, it was far from my thought to aim at pressing or over-persuading you. Still further is it now, when you, with a rare generosity, open the door. I think it is not good to write on. The ground is too tender and too sacred. Whether it can be made the subject of speech I cannot tell. Be assured it shall not be so made by violence or with abruptness on my part. Circumstances have separated me from you locally at this juncture. It may be from three to four weeks before I am in London again. I have done enough or too much in speaking freely. Respect is due to you as well as trust acknowledgement & sympathy: and I hope you will not find a want of it. Meantime God bless and guide you & cover you with all blessings at this coming time & at all seasons.   Ever yours   WEG.

Hawarden Castle.
2 January 1872.

Dear Spirit

It would have been more kind had I answered earlier your letter of the 14th, and wished you in good time a happy New Year. It was on my mind to do it but my ordinary & rather heavy work has been a little aggravated during a few days by an accidental attack of lumbago or rheumatism, which is now passing away.

So let me in the first instance reply to the question about plans which indeed I had meant to put myself. You are without doubt quite right in going to Bover-idge and the date you name falls in very well—I expect to come to town on the 16th and to have no evening engagement for two or three days, unless my only sister returns from Cologne, which she says she will do but I fear she will not, for she has lived I think $3\frac{1}{2}$ years in an hotel there, always intending to depart in a few days, & having a courier ready.

Reverting to the former letters, I hope I have made clear the distinction between a wish or a conviction in my own mind, and the desire to force or even press it upon others—I hope I have a strong desire to respect their liberty, their judgment, their conscience: to remember their—in several at least—superior knowledge, & higher responsibility, in what relates to themselves; and all this is not least where there prevails a disposition to yield—and again more still in a case like yours where since you admitted me to confidential knowledge of it, I have recognised so much not of peculiar & separate, not to say marvellous & mysterious, nature—I see how God has built up the will through the ordinance of the family itself a great mystery; but I can understand how in certain circumstances that ordinance may not attain to its entireness. To yourself & to God over & for you it belongs to judge; for me, I often feel, & here feel, it would be not only inexpedient but let me say profane to intrude—Every blessing attend you   WEG

11 Carlton House Terrace.
15 February 1872.

Dear Spirit[1]

As the Paris violets came with all their odour wonderfully preserved, so I can assure you that your letters are fragrant to me in another sense, for they satisfied me that you saw I at least meant no ill in going off to Church on Sunday evening though the act seemed rather abrupt. I think you can hardly tell what the necessity of church-going is to me; how much greater & more stringent than it is to other & better people. It is almost the only thing which seems to lay a strong hand upon me from without and it does me great and needful good, nor can I afford to intermit it at all without for it does me mischief. Be assured this is true of *me*. My own case, viewed impartially, reminds me of an old saying which I remember hearing from an Oxfordshire farmer in 1830 (before some baby was borne) 'I wants my church as bad as any man' though he had given up going to it. I went away home from you with many internal twinges, and therefore it was an act of true humanity in you to let me have the assurance that you understood my conduct. Well I have travelled with you on each of your days journies, though of course I made the mistake of supposing you at Dijon on Tuesday evening. Then I went on with you to Turin where there are multitudes of beautiful things to see but you would have no time. After this we go on together to Ancona, a sticking point of land and sea, where in 1866 for some reason or other my party & I slept in a saloon carriage at the station (perhaps the same one you have travelled in): I think it was to avoid a very short night at the Inn some way off. But here I part from you. You went to Brindisi without me for I have never travelled that road. I wonder whether you will get sight of Corfu, and of Cephalonia. The San Salvador in the first is near 3000 feet high & I have seen Italy from it. The Black Mountain of Cefalonia (so it might be spelt) is 7000. At Zante I leave you altogether for I have never been further southwards.

[1] Laura Thistlethwayte left for Egypt on 11 February; Gladstone noted: 'It is as well for me that she goes.'

Today I sent to Mr Thistlethwayte the letter to the Consul at Cairo procured from the Foreign Office but I think you will be very independent of him. You will be immensely interested in Egypt. Some think it the grandest and most solemn thing to be seen anywhere. There is every reason to believe it may represent the very earliest product of material civilisation. Now remember we are all pursuing our education & turn this great opportunity to the best account.

We are all much put about with American difficulties & party attacks, the result of which will overtake you by telegraph quicker than by post. Never mind: be of good cheer O ye of little faith I say to myself—I add once more God bless & guide you & give your journey all the fruit you desire & design from it. (You must write small or you will be ruined in postage)
Ever yours   WEG

House of Commons.
1 March 1872.

Dear Spirit

Already two miscarriages seem to have befallen this short correspondence.

On this Yesterday fortnight I wrote to you from this place, believing my letter could be delivered to you at Brindisi on Sunday: and then your letter informing me that it had not arrived, and giving me your address in Egypt reached me late on Friday night, last week, just after what as I supposed was the proper time for the Egyptian mail. I hope you have got long ago the letter to which I refer but I am sorry to have seemed neglectful.

Your account of your journey through Italy interested me much and I shall be desirous to hear of the other points & places which strike you—I have not been through the Mont Cenis Tunnel, or beyond Ancona on the East Coast: all the rest of your line so far was familiar to me and I rejoiced to travel it once more, but at Cefalonia or Zante if you see it but it is low in comparison I leave you, or rather you leave me.

The times continue very unfavourable to careful correspondence and I have no choice but to snatch a few minutes when I can. But this week has become of great interest & I am very sorry you could not claim your ticket for St Paul's. Every thing was very grand within the building & the service most touching & impressive. The Prince suffered a good deal from attending, but was resolved not to give way, and it must have done him good. The reception which he had with the Queen & Princess all over the long line of the procession which must have been from six to seven miles was enthusiastic beyond all precedent & the people present are stated at a million & a half. It was certainly a wonderful manifestation & I am very thankful that we have had it. Then there came yesterday evening the strangest contrast. A crack-brained stripling got to the Queen's carriage as she was returning from her drive with a greasy parchment in one hand purporting to be a document for her to sign and in the other an old crazy pistol wh was not loaded & could not have been fired if loaded but of course it availed to give serious alarm. The document was in two parts, the first releasing the Fenian prisoners, as he calls them & the second a promise that he the stripling should for his offence not be strangled but shot by the soldiers & his body given over for Christian burial to his friends. It is a painful proceeding mixed up between guilt folly & fanaticism. He will probably be whipped & imprisoned. I have seen the Queen today & she had quite recovered her serenity.

We are assailed with all manner of votes of censure & other weapons & the adversary especially hopes to turn even the American difficulty to account—but we shall see. When the day of rest arrives it will be a welcome day to me.

I went past No 15 [Grosvenor Square] but saw no sign as yet of workmen in it.

I do not wonder at your becoming enthusiastically Italian—everyone should be so in going through that beautiful (and to me dear country). You must not let Egypt banish Italy from your heart—but you have great wonders to see there. Only why are you still troubled about my wrong views of your whole nature? Imperfect they may be but in what way are they wrong? Why do you repeat (in terms I observe which might be misunderstood) assurances which I have always received from you without hesitation? I believe that one of my faults, in intercourse with others, is credulity not misbelief. Let me tell you what I do not understand—the growth of the eyelashes: but it is a harmless vagary which kind Nature has played on you. The whiteness of the skin is not surprising: it is because of the stronger contrast with the Italian than with the English.

Well now good bye & God bless you & prosper your going out & bye and bye your coming in
Yours ever　　WEG

London.
9 April, 1872.

Dear Spirit

The last few days have brought me abundant intelligence of you: from Jerusalem March 14–19—from Cairo March 27 & this morning from Brindisi April 5. All these have come I think between Thursday or Friday and Tuesday. I am glad they report so well of you as to exemption from sea sickness which when really it deserves the name is a visitation serious enough although one is ashamed it should have such power over the immortal spirit of a man. Your last letter encourages me to write to Rome if by return of post, and business in the H of C happily allows me half an hour to do this. I ought to tell you that from the thinness of the paper or otherwise there is here & there a word that I do not make out: they are very few, but somehow they always seem to be important words. I am sorry, and surprised that you did not find my letter at Brindisi. If it had been sent back here it would have been returned to me from what is called the dead letter office. You will have found at Rome as I trust one written some ten or twelve days ago to you there addressed Poste Restante.

And now I come to the matter of your letters which is full of interest. What a new Chapter of Life and of the interests of life this tour, brief as it is, must have been to you, especially in the Holy Land. I have never seen it and know not without seeing how it would impress me but I always feel that it ought to be so much the most interesting place on earth. For me however this feeling is founded on the past because this was the land trodden by

> Those blessed feet once nailed
> For our advantage to the bitter cross.

If I read you aright you found yourself very much in the future. But do you really think we know much from prophecy and its intentionally dark sayings of what is to happen there.

And now thank you for the photographs and especially the book of flowers. My wife is most thankful for the kind present and delighted to be the possessor of it. I had previously been amazed at the preservation of these little and tender objects in so fresh a seeming life after death. And I see that the contents of the envelope marked Garden of Gethsemane bear the same kind of preservation.

In such a life all your experiences must have been most interesting & I shall expect to see the mark of them upon you. Though I hardly expect that you will fulfil your threat to arrange your worldly affairs here and then go back for good. I gladly release you from your promise to give out a higher promotion in Egypt, than Joseph got from Pharoah—for your own people & country will not part with you. Your next letter I expect will probably tell me the probable date of your return especially as I see from what you say that the House in G.S. has not been delivered over to the tender mercies of the upholsterer.

But your rough passage to Brindisi is quite eclipsed by the storm at Jaffa from which you had so merciful an escape. Was the idea of danger really present to your mind? and how did it affect you? I am sure you were brave. Luxury and delight from nature's bounty are the lot of those who travel in Italy, and these innocent enjoyments which relived in thankfulness I hope you will largely drink in. The very sight of Naples & the bay is worth a long journey. When you go to those well known scenes I seem to go with you and reproduce the impressions they have made—I have spent I suppose six months in Naples though 21 years have passed since I last saw it and I did not then consider myself young. What am I now? As Dizzy says an exhausted volcano[1] or as an Irishman has improved the joke an used up *cratur*: just trying to discharge the remains of a cough which came on very sharply some time back & threatened to be a stiff bronchial attack. Two nights at Brighton have I think materially helped me.

And now may your remaining journey prosper as all has thus far prospered: and all blessings attend your going out & your coming in
Ever yours   WEG

Thanks for the photographs so still so calm.

From the time when I got your letter desiring me to restrain communications of your whereabouts, in the spirit of obedience I was stingy of news to A.K. who had been liberal to me. Kind as you have been in writing I shall have so much to ask you about new places & all else.

[1] Disraeli's famous description in his speech on 3 April at the Manchester Free Trade Hall of the Cabinet as 'a range of exhausted volcanoes'.

11 Carlton House Terrace.
24 April 1872.

My dear Mrs Thistlethwayte[1]

I have been puzzled as to your address: but yesterday night I got your announcement that you expected to be in Paris tomorrow. I therefore fearlessly address to the Hotel Bristol, though you do not mention it: as you were there before.

I am utterly puzzled at the non-arrival of two of my letters to you. But I think you are probably right in supposing that they may have come back to the dead letter office here and not been sent to me for the double reason that I think I merely signed with initials only and have also lazily given my address (it being familiar to you) in initials only. *Still* I am surprised they have not come back. The better way would have been *always* to put my name on the envelope—as I do today. I am doubtful about making any efforts to recover the missing epistles.

Even at a distance you will perceive that we have had a rough time and in truth I have been rather hard driven & have scarcely pith enough left in me to write anything or do anything except what necessity requires of me—and that is a good deal. You will be back among us in a few days and I hope not many will pass after your return without my having an opportunity of talking fairly on all the experiences of your travel, which must have been deeply interesting even to a person less capable of fresh & lively impressions. Mind this is a compliment and not a criticism. It does not mean to imply changefulness but unexhausted stores of nature

You did not I suppose fall in with the Prince & Princess of Wales as I should much wish to have known how you were impressed. He will be back here I suppose in six or seven weeks—& it [is] a great, perhaps the great, crisis in his life.

It is marvellous to think what you have seen in so short a time, Jerusalem, Rome, Florence, Naples & ever so much more. You will I hope pour out liberally your treasures of recollection.

May all blessings attend alike your going out & your coming in: & many thanks for telling me so vividly your experience of the storm.

I fell in with Mr Thistlethwayte last week in Bond Street. He told me you were expected soon: & (I am sorry to add) that the Ecclesiastical Commissioners had not ceased to vex him. Ever yours   WEG

Rely upon it that whatever I have said of myself has been said in sober seriousness, to use mild words.

---

[1] The formal form of address is to be explained by the fact that Gladstone had put his full name on the outside of the envelope, which might be opened if undelivered.

10 Downing Street.
29 April 1872.

Dear Spirit

I have been out of touch since Saturday afternoon—and I hope this may find you arrived safely, freed from your cold, & in all respects satisfied with your travel.

Let me have no gift or else the poorest of what you have brought for I never [word deleted] receive a gift from you without feeling what a barren friend I have been; making no returns in things material or otherwise. Do not row me for these words but accept them as my humble petition.

We are just in the crisis of this great American business and I never know when I may be free from it but I hope to come to G.S. not later in any case than Wednesday about five   Ever yours   WEG

Deus vobiscum
I should be able to come at 2 on Wedy I hope to do it

Hawarden Castle.
24 May 1872.

Dear Spirit

I read with much concern two of the inclosures in your letter, and burnt them according to order immediately after perusal. But I hope & believe that when your friend, please God, should hold a little new comer in her arms, her mind will greatly change and she will welcome as a precious gift what she now views with apprehension. I hope she will be able to nurse her own baby. Much mischief arises from the opposite practice, so contrary to Nature, when Nature has given the strength needful for the proper process. But what impertinence for me to have an opinion about it.

You speak of what your feelings would have been in given circumstances. Even without your assurance, I feel quite certain about *them*. Except in what [word deleted] is referred as above to another, I read your letter of Wednesday with much pleasure & entered into its cheerful tone. I have not forgotten the Egyptian dress: Probably the only one I shall ever see worn, and no one could wear it with more skill and becoming appropriation.

My wife is full of gratitude for your received munificent contribution. How kind Lady C.'s letter is—I did not know before that there was any family grief there. If you go to Rome again, beware of fever.

I heard with grief through the newspapers of Lord Carysfort's death. Need I say how much I shall be interested in the question & answer of which you speak? But somehow I think you are much in my debt as to things you have got to say to me but which remain unsaid? There is never time! On Monday I must be in town for the House of Commons but I never go away from it, unless upon a command i.e. Royalty's invitation, even then if business is not kind enough to allow me to do it without risk of mischief. But on Tuesday I hope to come to luncheon at 2 and if prevented then, at any rate not later than Wednesday.

God be with you   Ever yours WEG

Hawarden Castle.
21 August 1872.

Dear Spirit

I will tell you when we meet the reason, a very simple one, why I did not in my last notice the memorandum or note you put into my hands. I read it with a mixture of feeling, but all on one side. It was a wondering pleasure. You have not spoiled your palate, when so little contents it, as I have been able to supply. Indeed your letters are too full as ever of kindness, & of attachment which I would fain appreciate & yet feel that I do not as I ought. Your strain raises many questions—for instance about appearances: is there not a right and a wrong—a wrong, to use them for the purpose of covering evil with a semblance of good—a right, to avoid giving rise to surmises which may cause good to be evil spoken of. Your friend Lady Elizabeth wrote me a most kind & gracious answer to which I returned my best answer yet not a very good one—our plans are quite unfixed but I am very sensible of her goodness & anxious to profit by it as indeed she must be well worth knowing.

Did I say 'wisest' or was it a misreading of bad writing?

I send you cut out from the Standard a strange tale of human love: one of the cases in which the crime is greater than the guilt. What do you think of it? It is much better than if the revenge had been taken on the rival.

God bless & guide you   Ever yours   WEG

Hawarden Castle.
29 August 1872.

Dear Spirit

I really do not know how to thank you for the Naples Gallery, which arrived last night by Rail, in the *most* beautiful binding I ever saw—But alack there are four volumes. I thought it would be only one. Do not be angry with me for feeling rather ashamed, while a great deal obliged.

Another most kind note to me from Lady E. M. P[ringle]—as well as that to you: which I return. I had no idea that the Corsican story was a hoax—is it really so? I should not have troubled you with it. It is certainly very French. You cannot sincerely mean that the woman ought to have killed herself. There are cases—you can guess them—in which I think the great Saint Augustine discusses the question whether a woman could rightly kill herself. It is difficult to conceive any others, under the Christian law.

I follow with a deep interest what you say on the subject: but the part in which you speak of an intention twice formed I *must* take as a mental delusion. It is impossible that your kind & moral being could work so fearfully. There is another mental delusion signified by the word *rival*. If I know the meaning of it, it is connected with the No 17: and a more perfect phantom never since Eden passed before the human mind. In general I find my memory too weak & too charged to recognise any expression quoted *sole* from my letters. In "wisest" however I can see a true meaning. Remember a letter of your own lately inculcated on me words of the truest wisdom—the other citation I cannot recollect or realise. What I wish & hope you will generally believe is the truth and I might even say depth of my regret that I am to you such a poor & barren friend.

But you have I trust a Friend the best of all. May He bless & keep you.
Ever yours   WEG

I know *nothing* of my plans except that I expect to be here for ten days or more at any rate.
Did I give you Tischendorft's Tract on the Gospels? It is really valuable. Did you read the Mirror of Monks?

Hawarden Castle.
6 September 1872.

Dear Spirit

I will not conceal from you my trouble. It was a great pain to me to find once more from the two letters you wrote me on the 31st that I am always doing the thing I least wish to do—hurting you, wounding you, forgetting my former self to you, presenting strange, inexplicable (I think even cruel) contrasts: all this when God knows I have never taken up my pen to write to you with any but one & the same intention, ever since you distinguished me by that never-forgotten confidence & trust; and that has been to testify as well as I could my sense, inadequate I know, of that confidence & trust, of the friendship, & the attachment, you had so freely lavished—it is a great pain, also a perplexity, to me, that I should thus defeat & frustrate all my own wishes, & should, when I have frankly desired only to interest you, seem or be thought almost to insult you. What am I to do & how to escape this? I do not think ⟨you would wish me to do it by silence & that would perhaps be a real unkindness done to escape the appearance of one. But I am pained & angry with myself because there must be something very wrong in me to allow of my seeming to manifest myself in so odious a light. If I were intending to speak & act as you think I speak & act, there are no words that would be too strong to condemn me whether in point of truth, honour, manliness, gratitude, or kindness; all of which have as towards you strong ties upon me⟩

And now I turn to more pleasant matters. I am extremely pleased to find that Sir R Wallace[1] has broken ground with you, and that in the thoroughly kind & gentlemanlike manner which was to be expected from him. So also am I interested in your young adventurer: take good care of him. I send back the first of Lady E.L. [*sic*] P[ringle]—The second which arrived this morning I shall keep with your leave for I am sure you will recollect the advice contained in it. How I wish I could put mine as "sweetly". You use the word with proper justice. It is something in the *grain* that provides such a perfection: mere good intention will not do. Besides in her it is all founded in Christian Charity.

But what she says so well I have often tried to say badly. I think you were bound in 'wisdom' to take account of what the world said, however untruly, because it spoke according as you frankly avow to appearances, and only by

---

[1] Distantly related to Laura as an illegitimate son of Lord Hertford.

appearances can it judge & speak at all. What she says of your present self is eminently true.

My wife wishes me to go, & please God I shall go, to Scotland, between the 16th & 20th: to be absent probably about three weeks.

Besides not remembering, I am deficient in comprehension as to the enclosed morsel—except the last part of it.

And now above, apart from & despite of, all troubles such as I have described, I heartily wish you God speed in all you think say & do & am ever yours WEG

Have you seen Père Hyacinth's marriage letter?

11 Carlton House Terrace.
18 November 1872.

Dear Spirit

I walked home[1] ruminating on many things; and even in bare justice to you, but also as a satisfaction to myself, I must put down two or three.

I think that you were last evening noble—and wise—as also you were most kind and that only the Grace of God directed you, as I hope it ever will direct you.

If there has been any fault—in the circumstances, and relations, between us, every equitable (not to say generous) mind would perceive that that fault is not yours but mine.

I wish that my prayers were less unworthy—they will always be offered for you. On the other side, I copy the remarkable words of your letter of July 14.[2] They enhanced the apprehension ever hanging over me lest I should be, or should have been, to you an instrument of harm.

Your going out & coming in will always be of true interest for me; especially with reference to an occasion like that which now impends. Still I feel it due to you, that I should not call on Thursday[3] without a note from you, before that day to warrant it.

Lastly, I did not see, though I guessed, something which I believe you hastily put inside my coat or waistcoat. But on reaching home I found nothing & fear it may have been lost.

Every blessing be with you. Ever yours   WEG

[Extract from Mrs. Thistlethwayte's letter of 14 July 1872:] 'Forgive my weakness. I ought to have talked to you on many subjects, instead of showing its depth. Where you are inclined to judge, remember you ever[?] burn these first feelings, you must do all in your power to quench them']

---

[1] i.e. on night of 17 Nov. 72: 'Saw Mrs. Th. It was distressing: & left me much to ruminate upon: but it was good.'

[2] See the end of this letter.

[3] Gladstone records no visit to her on Thursday, 21 November 1872; his next recorded visit was on 25 November.

11 Carlton House Terrace.
19 November 1872.

Dear Spirit

You ask me with great justice why I did not notice or act upon the letter of July 14 at the time. Receive my answer. Partly perhaps for the reason I mentioned, & lamented, on Sunday; that with an overburdened mind I seem incapable of *due* reflection, for ⟨the⟩ absorption in public affairs. But this was not the main cause. I was struck with the letter, but did not feel sure that you had written with full sense and intention as to the meaning of the words. In short I waited to see what followed. On Aug 18 & Aug 23 you wrote two letters which seemed to me to follow up that of July 14. I felt that I ought to take notice of these expressions: and I meant to consider them carefully before coming to London. I left the letters locked up at Hawarden, and went to Scotland. From there I was summoned unexpectedly to town *direct*; and I had not opportunity, therefore, of referring to the letters before leaving. But you may remember an allusion of mine to my doubt whether I was to call again. This is the simple history of the case. And your saying I was not to mind what you wrote put me off the subject again, till in the country on referring to the letters I thought more of it. Pray understand this is not an argument but a recital. I am very conscious that I never have given you all the thought & care that you were entitled to, although probably I have not thought so much about the matters affecting any other human being during the last three years, as about yours, which came before me in a manner so peculiar, touching, never to be forgotten. I wish I could feel quite certain what was best, but I am in many things a poor fluctuating creature; on the whole (please God) I will come on Thursday to say how much pleased I am at the good report you give me. All blessings be yours   WEG

I am afraid there was a mistake about what you *thought* was a pocket.

10 Downing Street.
20 November 1872.

Your letter of today is good, is holy, & is kind. But you say in it you are afraid of me now. "Now" I hope, means you will not always be so. But it would not be kind in me I think to come, until this has gone by—until I know that fear has passed, or will not make my coming an untoward thing. By this impression I shall govern myself tomorrow.

Osborne House.
5 February 1873.

Dear Spirit

I have not yet been able to read the MS book you were so kind as to send me. The truth is that this which precedes & follows the first meeting of Parliament is one of the worst & most closely packed periods of my year, and I have no chance of improvement until I have been able to introduce into Parliament our measure on the Irish University question. This will be fixed for Thursday the 13th when I shall have to make what I hope will be my last very long speech in Parliament.

I write from Osborne whither I am come for the Council at which the Speech from the Throne for tomorrow is to receive formal sanction. But I am to be back in London in the evening when I have to give a large dinner with a party to follow it.

This change of weather will I hope be good for you & enable you to get out. With much benefit & comfort.

It is strange that in your neighbourhood, within 300 or 400 yards of your house, besides Dr Bence Jones whom I have only known in recent years, I have three very old friends, all of them of dates between 36 or 38 & 50 years—i.e. from before your birth, all lying on what is likely to be their death bed. Mr Hope Scott, Mr Milnes Gaskell, & Mrs Mildmay granddaughter of Archbishop Harcourt: besides these I have *lost* three other friends, one of them about my oldest, in the last six weeks; and yet, through the mercy of God, the hand of death has not come nigh my own dwelling.

May your friends be long spared to you, as indeed mine have been
God bless you   Ever yours   WEG

11 Carlton House Terrace.
7 May 1873.

Dear Spirit

Here are the two notes. I had them ready to deliver on Monday: but did not like to do it in the eye of Lady E. M. Pringle the writer.

They impressed me much.

If not before Monday, *on* Monday at the same hour I hope to present myself: without breaking faith as I have today here and that I did on Monday last by going up to G.S. & remaining over the time when I had an appointment here— you are not responsible.

Perhaps I may then find an opportunity to tell you the subject of my conversation with your excellent & most valuable friend.

Also I shall like to hear further your view of Kenelm Chillingly.[1]

You are "at a loss to understand"—so am I. I have not an idea to what you can regret in my unfortunate note: but unhappily there are so many of them unfortunate I have a mental clumsiness not I fear to be got rid of.

God bless you ever   WEG

[1] By Lord Lytton (1873), sent Gladstone by the Earl of Lytton and read from 27 Mar. 73.

Balmoral Castle.
22 August 1873.

Dear Spirit

I arrived here two days back and found your kind note with the inclosures which I return. Since then I have had a touch from my old enemy and I write from my bed but I am about to get up & I hope be all right again.

I have often told you how many of my friends and my oldest friends the great reaper Death has since last Christmas gathered in. Also events continually tend to bring at least my own political death into view, not perhaps as immediate, but as proximate. Even amidst the crush of affairs, this makes me a little meditative. How great are the purposes of life, and how greatly do they soar above the mere business of presuming or trying to govern men. How can we best and most certainly help one another to fulfil them? You will answer by prayer. And that is the true answer. Blessed is he, whose whole life prays. And next blessed he, who has much time & much collectedness to pray.

From what you say of Mrs Agar I hope the baby is *well* again. I am sorry your visit to Lord Bathurst was cut short: it would be such a pleasure to that *fine* old *English gentleman*: You will soon I daresay be going to the Isle of Wight: which I trust you will enjoy. I remain here a week. May you ever be in Holy Keeping.

Always yours   WEG

Balmoral Castle.
30 August 1873.

Dear Spirit

I now have a piece of family news, which indeed I would have sent earlier except that I have been so heavily charged with writing of all kinds. My eldest daughter Agnes is going to be married to Mr Wickham the headmaster of Wellington College. He is a man of high religious character as well as of intellectual culture & distinction and I believe that on both sides there are qualities which promise under God a happy union. There will be no great store of wealth but my daughter is not greedy.

I know you are in a beautiful spot but it is difficult to compete with the beauties of Deeside. I have just bid good bye to Her Majesty & I am going to Invercauld further up among the hills till Monday morning when I am to start for a grand hill-walk down upon Aviemore,[1] from then to turn southwards and to reach Hawarden I hope sometime on Thursday next to think & arrange a little about the marriage arrangements.

I was much struck with your estimate of Mr Vernon Harcourt,[2] because he has evidently tried to make himself agreeable & because you could have no prejudice to impede the real acuteness of your vision. I wish I could greatly dispute on his behalf what you say. I may not be a fair judge as he has upon the whole (what is called) made himself troublesome in the House of Commons. It

---

[1] In fact to Kingussie; see 1 Sept. 73.
[2] i.e. the future cabinet minister.

is a pity that vanity should inflate & even pervert a character which I understand is otherwise by no means difficult in parts really good.

I wish you heartily all enjoyment of the sea & sky & scenery with which you
are begirt & every other & higher blessing which God can give you.

Ever yours   WEG

11 Carlton House Terrace.
21 November 1873.

Dear Spirit

Many thanks for the intimation of the Kinnaird engagement & may it be
happy in its results. I made due note of Mrs K.s wish about the Assessed Taxes.
You would have heard of me, spontaneously, before this time, had I not been
engaged in another sadness. For the seventh, or ninth time in the last eleven
months, I have been among the dying or the dead. After a short, painful, fluctuating illness, Lord Richard Cavendish, a very dear old friend of nearly forty
years, died in our sight on Wednesday evening. Tomorrow or Monday I am to
go to his funeral at Chatsworth. It has indeed been an extraordinary year outside the small but vital circle of the family, and another such would leave me
desolated.

I was sorry you did not keep the Life of S[chleiermacher][1]—you would have
been welcome to my copy but it had lists of references which I had made on it.
You perhaps did not know or I did not properly explain the light in which I
wished to present Henrietta Von Millich to you. It was not as an ideal, heroic, or
perfect character: but as one presenting many points of nature, truth and
beauty. Within these limits I should be glad that you thought her worthy of
appreciation. The parents of Dr S. too are interesting. He was a man of great
powers, & great merits but somehow does not kindle my feelings violently.

The books you have sent me I hope to read in due course: meantime many
thanks. I have been employed in the most singular of all books the Autobiography of John Mill, a book most saddening, yet full of useful lessons. I would
not recommend your reading it. In some points it resembles the Life of Grote:
both I think rejected Christianity and yet had qualities which they would hardly
have acquired but from Christian associations. I think you might like the
Memoir & Letters of Sara Coleridge which perhaps you have seen.

Heartily wishing you the blessings of the Almighty I remain always your
faithful friend   WEG

Mrs Thistlethwayte

Hawarden Castle.
1 January 1874.

Dear Spirit

I have divined your kind thought about my daughter's marriage, and was
afraid lest you would execute it: You will say, why afraid? I give two reasons in

[1] See 22 Sept. 73.

answer. First you know I am always endeavouring to restrain the activity of your *giving* propensities in a certain direction—a very rare case I may say, as the world is constituted! Secondly she already has a beautiful little memorial from you: a small diamond ring in blue enamel which was a thought too small for my least finger, and (I think with your sanction) I made it over to her.

Please to understand that I did not speak for the public what you hear in the newspapers; but only for neighbours, and from neighbours: how a reporter got in one cannot imagine.[1]

The sum you have put aside will do for some good purpose—but I have not yet bestowed what you gave me a little time ago.

I think I could dine in G. Square on the 15th or 16th if it be convenient.[2]

On this new year, & through all its course may the Eternal Eye be over you & keep you & may you never take harm from   WEG

Hawarden Castle.
6 January 1874.

Dear Spirit

Your kind & truthful letter of Jan 3 contained these words—"if you are likely to receive harm from me, you must *decide* that *we* never meet alone." These were words to cause me thought.

That you do me harm I have never thought. Whether I do my self harm is another question. If there is a doubt, a fear, of it, would it not be wise, would it not be what you so well call Christlike, to make that decision? But I do not like to proceed imperiously to any one, certainly not to you—I would gladly consider it with you, in all freedom & frankness—and, if I had your free & willing *assent*, I would make that decision.

Say the 15th if you please (at 8?) and invite or not according as you would like to have the talk to which I have referred—I am *not* so trustworthy as you.

Inclosed is a letter from Miss Marsh—keep it for me—I inclose it on account of the statement about Ld. Kintore's son, wh I think you would like to see.

I am hard pressed with work. But Mr Herbert (R.A.) is here making a head of me. He began to talk to me about you & Landseer, and I will report to you his conversation which I have not time to write.

May the Almighty be with you   WEG

11 Carlton House Terrace.
13 February 1874.

Dear Spirit

I received this morning your letter of yesterday and I must frankly say as I said once before I cannot reply to it.

---

[1] Gladstone's comments on Victoria's kindness to Agnes were published without permission; see 27 Dec. 73.
[2] See 16 Jan. 74.

There can be *no* advantage however in any private conversation when words meant to be words of kindness prove to be words of deep offence.

To your conversation of yesterday I meant to have replied, or rather to your statement, by praising its courage, & its kindness, & by a few words more, which I will now put down.

There are many matters in which we poor human creatures see before us clear lines of right & wrong to save us from vacillation. There are others to be determined on consideration of the wisest & the safest, which are by no means so precise. When these touch more than one, they cannot be considered just as if they touched one only. Sympathy, gratitude, confidence, a feeling of equity enter into them. Let them excuse me a little, if I have not been consistent. They ought not to prevent me from saying that what you said yesterday, & what you wrote after, was the wisest & the safest, & that it will be well to act upon it.

May God keep & bless you   Ever yrs   WEG

                                                              2 April 1874.

Dear Spirit

I am sorry to say the magnificent box you have sent would not hold nearly what is required & it would attract so much attention that I hope you will not ask me to keep it—I am afraid the matter must therefore stand over *unless* I can find my key in which case I shall have all that is necessary—I shall have the splendid box addressed to you,

God bless you   Ever Yrs   WEG

                                                        Hawarden Castle.
                                                           9 April 1874.

Dear Spirit

Who told you that you had done wrong in sending that superb box? Never I. If wrong was done it was to your own purse! But all my repositories and implements are plain even to Quakerism, without the slightest touch of ornament. This by its contrast would have excited constant remark & that was not desirable.

I return the inclosures you kindly sent me. That account of the Neston's[?] bequest is most curious. Why was it set aside? I should much like to know where I could read or find the history of the proceeding. I also inclose a hymn with music of which an anonymous writer sent me two copies. What do you think of it?

I hope you have & enjoy the fine spring weather which has blessed us here.

My hands are very full. My own affairs require my attention, which while in office I could not give—and my volunteer correspondents are I am sorry to say so many & importunate that if I let them they would utterly absorb my time and reduce me to another slavery. I have now a great ambition to fulfil: the application of my days and hours to work which, according to my means and scale, may be of service to my kind. You will agree with me this is the aim with which we should live, for thus God is glorified.

My tenant I think leaves my house today.

God be with you & bless WEG

Thanks also for the "Rights of women".[1]

Hawarden Castle.
10 May 1874.

Dear Spirit

I am bound for town again this week & shall be happy to have luncheon with you on Thursday, Ascension Day at two.

I was shocked to go to you when I was last in town (as you no doubt observed) without the Mizpah ring, your last kind gift, on my finger—I was glad you did not ask me for I had actually mislaid it and though I fully expected to find it I was ashamed as well as disturbed about it. On returning here I found it, only a little too carefully put away. I am writing with it on. My rustic life agrees with soul and body. It is not an idle one but it is free from the wearing excitement. I need it much, believe me, and much of it. We have sometimes spoken of books of devotion: *one* is at the head of them all, the Psalms. From this ancient storehouse God seems to bring forth treasures of consolation, guidance, and utterance for us, according to our needs. And one that as I feel well suits me is 'Bring my soul *out of prison*, that I may give thanks unto thy Name'. I do not think you have so much need: I doubt whether any one has

But may He keep you & feed & heed you WEG

I daresay Miss Kortwright has sent you her new book.[2]

Hawarden Castle.
14 June 1874.

Dear Spirit

I have postponed answering your note again from uncertainty of plans; but I thought much both last Sunday and today.

Your sentiments about Church Order are not mine, for to me the Church is the Body of Christ, and its order a portion of this Legacy or Testament: but I know well your generous & upright intention, and freedom from all spirit of narrowness and schism, and I earnestly hope that whatsoever you do may be blessed in your deed.

[1] Apparently unread.
[2] F. A. Kortright, *A little lower than the angels* (1874); see 2 May 74.

Probably I may come to London by the 23rd and on the 25th I shall be glad to present myself at luncheon if you can have me.

There is the old frustrated engagement with Mr Herbert who live [*sic*] at the Chimes Kilburn. If it suited you to ask him for July 3 (Friday) I should be happy to dine.

Do you see that three pieces of Sèvres China at Christies have just brought 10000 Guineas? What are we made of, & what shall we come to.

God be with you now & ever   Yours   WEG

Penmaenmawr.
14 August 1874.

Dear Spirit

I have been troubled since coming here with giddiness physic and work but I had observed the death of Ld Annesley and was about to write to you on it when your letter came this morning. I can well understand that it may or must have brought up on you a tide of mingled feelings in the vivid recollections of the past which you have *elsewhere* so well described. I also see from your letter that his departure was attended by that feature of suddenness which, except in happy cases, always adds an element of awe to death. I never (I believe) had any personal acquaintance with him however slight but now knowing all I have learned I have naturally regarded this event with much interest & sympathy.

I asked the Bookseller to send you Mr Williams's Sermon on Confession[1] because I thought it apart from this or that point of opinion an able honest and striking exposition of the view he takes, and one very fit to be submitted to an upright and liberal mind, such as I consider yours to be, in order to know how it appeared to you. But if you suspect in it a more personal appeal, which was not intended & which I have no title to make to any one, pray hand it over to Lady Elizabeth [Pringle] (through whom I send you this) and I think she may find some interest in reading it, since it comes from a man who, as I understand, is performing a more marked work than any other man among the wealthy and luxurious classes of the West End.

It was most kind of you to move her to write to me & a very interesting letter she wrote.

I expect to pass the afternoon & evening of Sept 7 (Monday) in London at my own house on my way with two of my sons to Munich and to return some 15 or 16 days afterwards then to pass the remainder of the year at Hawarden.

God be with you   WEG

Hawarden Castle.
30 September 1874.

Dear Spirit

I well know Sir James Simpson's feelings of interest and attachment towards you. It is a great regret with me that I did not talk more to him about you and

[1] By G. H. Wilkinson (1874); see 9 Aug. 74.

(what is called) pick his brains. The book is curious—Shall I send it back to you?

So likewise I am much interested in Mr Paget's letter. I entirely agree with him in his great principle that the Christian Ministry is only to be exercised by those who are sent. (This is not meant as a hit at you for I know the distinction you honestly draw.) But surely it is extravagant to hold what he seems to hold that no other person may open his mouth on a religious question—Not so thought the early Christians, or the late: not even the R.Cs. Why does he so summarily smite me for speaking about theology? I wonder in all good humour whether he has laboured at it—to say nothing of anything else—as much as I have. But I like the earnest purpose of the letter, & the principle I have named.

I wrote 29 letters on Monday, & working all yesterday & today am not yet out of my arrear.

Your observation that my paper was heavy is confirmed by Mr Paget—I thought it a very *fair* & *useful* remark, very kindly as well as frankly made. All such I like—& hope you will always make them.

I shall soon hope to hear what you think of Bp Patteson (the publisher tells me he duly sent you a copy).[1] Woe be to you if you do not like *him*!

Pray send me what you wrote on Sunday: & may He the Holy One be with you.

Ever yours   WEG

Hawarden Castle.
5 October 1874.

I return your verses—They have in my opinion spirit, feeling, and promise. So also was I struck with 'seem hard'. But that *ladder* can only be ascended by steps. Hard work & plenty of it is wanted. You cannot fly to excellence: it is not given to man of woman born unless in the rarest instances. That is the reason why I am always boring you to work hard at the lifelong business, for such it is, of education. I will say for my wretched self that I am always about this work.

Well, you have conquered—*we* keep, & therefore gratefully though shame-facedly keep your gift. My petition for time, you see, ends in yielding. But I want to make a condition, or truce of peace between us. It is that you promise faithfully for the future never to give me anything exceeding 10/– in value without previous notice & the consent of both parties. If you agree to this I will promise to make known to you every really good case for aid in money to which I think you would like to contribute.

You see the Romans and Irish appear to be very angry with me.[2] The passage which has made the *hulluhbaloo* was much shorter in the proof that [I] sent you. I put the rest in, with deliberation, when I was at Munich: partly moved thereto perhaps by seeing Dr Döllinger and remembering that he is *excommunicated*.[3]

---

[1] i.e. Gladstone's review article of Yonge's *Life of J. C. Patteson*, 2v. (1874); see 2 July 74n.
[2] Gladstone's article 'Ritualism and ritual'; see 2 Aug. 74.
[3] For the notorious inserted passage, see 13 Sept. 74.

I suppose you meant me to send back the verses.

What more of the Syrian Patriarch? Mr Pugin has not even yet done persecuting Mr Herbert but he has had a lesson.

God be with you   Ever yours   WEG

11 Carlton House Terrace.
21 November 1874.

Dear Spirit

Thank you so much for the Punch; which is an indication of the same public feeling that has forced the Times & Pall Mall Gazette to accord with the purpose of the Pamphlet.[1] But Punch is straightforward & true.

I am indeed thankful to have been brought to know that. Watching & sharing in the correspondence of course finds me much work. What I am immediately anxious for is that the truly gallant man, Lord Camoys and his few companions, should be gallantly supported; for this is the cause of truth, reason, human happiness, & the Glory of God. Could you not bring Mr Herbert to write *in the same sense* either to a public journal, or if not then to Archbishop Manning? Pray consider this & try what you can do. I am afraid that if I were to write to him, he might think I was only doing it selfishly in support of my own polemic.

We go to Hawarden on Monday. I mean to post this so that it may reach you on that morning.

God be with you   Always yours   WEG

Hawarden Castle.
23 January 1875.

Dear Spirit

I am afraid that you again broke your covenant in sending the prairie hens—and that your givingness is not to be restrained without a very severe bit. But I am bound to admit that they were most excellent, and extremely popular. But now pray hold your hand and remember the limit of 10/– and in consideration of having twice overpassed it, you should fine yourself say 3 or 6 months, during which to maintain a total abstinence from giving me any thing.

Well I am hard at work preparing materials and parts of my answer to the Papal antagonists who have risen up in such numbers. I do not know whether to recommend you to read Dr Newman. I should say certainly not Manning, whose book is about to appear. But on the other hand I think you will be interested in reading the Article in the Quarterly Review, on account of the very singular picture it presents of the declarations of the Pope.

I trust in God Prince Leopold may recover. He is really as to [?] the flower of the flock & in the summer of 73 he seemed as if he had outlived his ailments.

---

[1] i.e. reactions to *Vaticanism*.

Our housekeeper of 34 years has just lost by consumption a son of 23—an excellently conducted youth, beautiful, almost angelic, in appearance. So runs on this world of shifting shadows.

And the bustle of a new Session is at hand. I do not expect to be present at the opening. I shall be glad to hear in due time how you get on with your bust & of Mr Herbert, & all friends.

Does Mr H. agree with Newman?

May the Almighty be with you & keep you   Always yours   WEG

22 March 1875.

Dear Spirit

A sad time since I saw you. When I got home full of showing my wife the photographs from your bust,[1] I found she had just been rudely summoned away by telegram from Hagley, to witness, & to soothe as she best might, renewed pain and struggle.

The sad and sore fight is over. That bright and noble young creature finally gave way yesterday forenoon after a few hours of blessed calm and peace.[2]

She was the flower of her generation: very dear to us all. I expect to go on Wedy. for the funeral. Tomorrow I could come at two, if you like it, & if you have no party—I do not call that kind Lord B[athurst] 'party', any more than Lady E. Pringle.

God be with you   WEG

11 Carlton House Terrace.
31 March 1875.

Dear Spirit

I have returned from the house of mourning to the whirl of petty business.

In breaking up the house it will be a comfort to leave some trifles in the hands of friends and with or after this I will send you a few coffee cups (with a sugar basin) which I hope you may like.

Tomorrow I offer myself for luncheon: silence is consent.

May the Almighty be with you   WEG

11 Carlton House Terrace.
6 April 1875.

Received your most kind letter. My wife is greatly pleased with the photographs and will write, the moment she emerges from this Chaos, to thank you for your goodness. You ought not to pass by such an offer for the bust.[3]

God be ever with you   WEG

[1] i.e. the bust of Gladstone made by Mrs. Thistlethwayte.
[2] Death of May Lyttelton, Catherine Gladstone's niece.
[3] Mrs. Thistlethwayte's bust of Gladstone, unfortunately untraced.

The George, Nottingham.
11 May 1875.

Dear Spirit

I did not fail, of course, to destroy the letter of Saturday according to your wish. But it was impossible to read it without strong sympathy nor is it easy to forget. I am indeed fearful lest it should have portended trouble to your peace. You know how much apprehension I have always had upon that subject. 'What shadows we are' said a great man (Mr Burke) 'and what shadows we pursue!' I am a shadow gradually fading from your view, for I must by the law of nature now waste with the years, and the will of God, which seems to lead me into retirement will leave me, it is probable, less and less within the reach of your bodily eye: but I earnestly hope, & offer my unworthy prayer, that with the eye of your heart and mind even more and more upon the realities of the world invisible you may acquire progressively a greater mastery over what ever would bind you, and a greater freedom to devote yourself to the actual performance of the will of God. Him you truly love, and in time you will find the only lasting satisfaction. Though I know you will also & thankfully drink of the wells in the way, which He has planted for our refreshment.

My business[1] is done here and with Mr Ouvry I go over to Clumber this afternoon. Be assured I was right in saying that Mrs Hope or any one authorised by her is alone in strictness entitled to give access there. I have no *power* whatever and am now going to the house by Mrs Hope's permission only. It would have been a great impertinence in me to assume any right in the matter, and I felt it my duty to abstain from giving any advice or expressing any wish, as it would have been like a plot if I had done so; I go there on business & should travel out of my province if I took any thing else upon myself although if you came there & sent your name to me I should of course ask then & there that you might see everything and have no doubt you would be treated with every courtesy as the old & valued friend of the Duke, & would experience no difficulty. The place is extensive, & therefore has a kind of grandeur, with great woods, but can hardly be called beautiful in scenery—nothing like Chatsworth for instance.

I hope to be at Mr Aitken's[2] Church in Liverpool on Sunday & at Hawarden on Whit Monday—to remain for a week.

God be ever with you   WEG

18 May 1875.

Dear Spirit

The note I sent from Clumber was opened by me rather clumsily and I had not time duly to seal it over before dispatching it. On the day you kindly name for dinner I am engaged to be out of town with my wife—and all my days here will be full and hold me until I return to town on Monday.

---

[1] Newcastle Trust business. Mrs. Thistlethwayte had had a long-standing relationship with the deceased duke, and one of his children was her executor.

[2] The revivalist; see 29 Apr., 16 May 75.

You will I hope hear of me soon after, not later at any rate than luncheon on Thursday 27th.

I was greatly pleased with Clumber, on the whole a noble place and well managed property—But the associations connected with it are deeply melancholy, while the many prospects for the future are brilliant. I regretted much that you could not see it.

May the Almighty be with you   WEG

I went to Mr Aitken's church in Liverpool on Sunday *morning*, when he said he would be here but he was absent.

Every one seems to have the notion that he is rather too much away. The congregation was good not crowded.

His character is high in Liverpool.

Hawarden Castle.
9 August 1875.

Dear Spirit

We were detained in London until Saturday by my wife being unwell. She had a menace of erysipelas, the consequence of her relentless work and knocking herself about. I am thankful to say it did not become severe and she is now almost well.

I shall be anxious to hear how you made out your journey, and how Ems and its waters agree with you. In hot weather it is rather a trying place: but this year the trying place is more likely to be flooded. They do not gamble there now I believe? When I was there the general company went at it every week day, and began about noon on Sunday.

After ample consideration, though I have strong sympathy with my dear friend Dr Döllinger, I made up my mind that I ought not to appear at Bonn[1]—it is too pronounced a part for one who is still in the political world though (thank God) he has retreated to the verge of it—I think if you could run over there as one of the public you would be much interested in hearing one of the debates; and you would certainly be struck & pleased, unless I much mistake you, with Dr D. It is a great & holy work which he has in hand—a work of faith, truth, order, freedom. What a sisterhood! and I hope he will have the prayers of many.

I have much to do here in executorship, and have now also to look to my son's marriage settlements. I am also about writing a paper about the state of the religious question in Italy,[2] which is full of deep interest. The villagers of various parishes, unable to bear papal oppression, are demanding & apparently obtaining, the right to elect their own priests.

Is there an English Church at Ems? There used to be a small Roman one where the man preached well, and a large Italian one, with a rather cold service. Tell me if it has still the crucifix on the Altar? and candlesticks?

[1] At the Bonn Conference of Old Catholics, Orthodox and Anglicans; see above, v. xxi ff.
[2] 'Italy and her church'; see 16 July 75.

Dr Andrew Clark convicted me before I left town of having the gout! in very slight manifestations, but still the gout!

Tauchnitz of Leipzic is printing my Vatican Tracts in one of his portable volumes.

And now may God be with you, & lift up the light of his countenance evermore upon you   Always yours   WEG

Having stupidly forgotten your hotel I send this to Grosvenor Square.

Hawarden Castle.
26 August 1875.

Dear Spirit

The whirl of life in its varied forms continues about us—We are now deep in the arrangements of another family marriage, next to that of a child—our orphan niece, Gertrude Glynne, is to marry the Pennant of Penrhyn Castle in October, and it will be from under this roof.

But you see the [black] border on my paper: & while we have been thus buried in joyful troubles, an excellent & much respected Cousin of mine, Mr Murray Gladstone, has been called away in a moment, to a world indeed which we believe he was well prepared to enter, but with a suddenness, & violence of circumstances, which is a shock to our poor humanity. He went out with his children to fish in the sea—did not come home—all went out at night to search for him: and the calamity was announced by a shreik from his youngest daughter who found him, face downwards, floating on the rising tide.

Did you read the accounts of the proceedings at Bonn—I think you would be interested in them, especially in that brave, wise, learned, & truly Christian old man, Dr Döllinger. Thanks for giving me your judgment as to my not going—I am glad to find you approved—I was much tempted.

I shall be glad to hear of your plans and earnestly hope Ems may, please God, give you the perfect restoration which Sir W. Gull desired. For me there is one fixed point alone at present, viz. London for two or three nights at least on or about the 27th of Septr.

I am very glad to hear particulars of Ems but hope you will find something there better than the hotel charges.

Lady E.P.s letter (returned herewith) is as usual interesting

What do [you] say to the sad accident in the Solent?

God be with you in all abundance of His blessings.   WEG

Much truth[?] is there in your remarks about clergy abroad: but if you had known them as they were, & as I did, forty years ago you would perceive a vast improvement.

I am exceeding glad of your having found a subject to direct your gift upon.

Hawarden Castle.
6 October 1875.

Dear Spirit

Accommodated, through your courageous kindness beyond my wishes, I had a prolonged journey of almost unbroken beauty along the valley of the Severn to Shrewsbury where I became familiar with the road onwards.[1] It was a most interesting day. I cannot help thinking of that gorgeous Church. If you see the Contemporary Review, you will find some curious remarks by Bishop Thirlwall on the ritual of heaven. Will the worship in that Cathedral rise, in proportion to the glories of the structure and embellishments? If not, the worse, I fear, for the worshippers. I hope you got home well and made amends to Mr Herbert for the loss of the raptures of the previous evening, when he sat between the two Cirencester beauties.

Well: will you accept my acknowledgement of the rare truthfulness of spirit and courage which you have shown.

There was one word of yours to which I took and take exception: the word 'humbling'. There may be something humbling when that is withheld, which it is optional to give, but not when there is, in honour and faith, no option.

This however makes no deduction from the admiring acknowledgement I make—I feel that you achieved a greater triumph. Most earnestly do I hope that the gracious Father may enable to keep that which He has enabled you to gain, & may cover you with every good gift. In this thought & prayer be assured I can never 'change'.

Oakley Park will be remembered by me, for itself, & for more than itself.
Ever yours   WEG

Hawarden Castle.
9 October 1875.

Dear Spirit

I thought the words which I ventured to commend were severe, indeed, as towards yourself, most mild and equitable towards me, but wise, brave and Christian words. What drew them forth were words of mine not new but spoken oftentimes before, sometimes much noticed by you, sometimes not, but *then* they seemed to convey of a fuller light; not wanton words, not spoken without pain, or without the true sympathy, which yours in return could only deepen.

The subject does not well bear discussion upon paper and I *wait* & the pen often misleads where the voice does not, for the voice is sustained and *piloted* in its work by the eye and ear. God be with you—you have high and wide opportunities, a deep heart, quick observations, a spirit intensely generous, a desire to realise the life of God in the soul—with neck or stock which I glance at rather than describe, all will go well: I do not say easily, heroism was nursed in or with care, but well.

[1] Letter written following Gladstone's three 'visits' to Laura Thistlethwayte during their stay at Lord Bathurst's home at Cirencester; see 1 Oct. 75 f.

I am indeed sorry for the Dean of Gloucester. It seems to be a narrow fanaticism; but on his principle, I do not say he was not right in avoiding me; though I am afraid he lost the morning prayers. I am so glad to have introduced Mr Herbert to the circle of your friends.

Miss Bathurst wrote kindly to thank me for sending her the verses respecting my brother-in-law.

After next week, we shall have two weeks, necessary weeks, of festive disturbances, & general rumpus. I have not *pluck* to meet these things well, as quiet is the desire of my inmost soul—but they are in their way right and they give joy to many loyal hearts.

And now goodbye. There are words, a few, in your letter which I must either contend against, or pass—I pass, and end with expressing my gratitude for your exhaustless feelings & many acts of further kindness.

Ever yours   WEG

I shall hope, and be glad, to hear that Sir W. Gull makes a good report of you.

Hawarden Castle.
18 October 1875.

Dear Spirit

It is possible or even probable that I may be in London about Nov 10 to discharge an engagement at Greenwich but this week, as I thought you knew we have the reception for my son & his bride to look to and the marriage of my niece, and next week there will be four more days of festivity.

The heroism to which I meant to pay a just acknowledgement (I should be sorry if you really thought me capable of flattery, which you do not) was in the sentiment you expound. I have not changed my mind about it. What will you say if I proceed to wish you many happy returns of this day and all the richness of Divine blessing? assuring you that on this day, & on every day you are remembered. Why do you say you feel it will be your last on earth? How do you, can you, know? I should flatter you if I called that language heroism—I would flatly persuade you out of it.

The place is full of triumphal arches preparation for fireworks & illuminations & I know not what: but we are in some dread about the weather.

Ever yours   WEG

You may have seen it stated that I have been invited to Constantinople to doctor the Turkish finances. No such invitation, I can assure you, has reached me.

Hawarden Castle.
12 November 1875.

The Speech at Greenwich shall be sent you or to A.K.

Dear Spirit

After three days of hurry and hard work in London I left it this forenoon to return home and before starting I received the inclosed Telegram (which I interpret as from you)—interesting but through the fault of some Telegraphist imperfectly instructed or half asleep, somewhat obscure. What in the world is 'the speech'? Surely the wires to Bologna were made for some worthier purpose than to talk to you of my pratings at Greenwich last night—I think it *must* after all be Dizzy at the Guildhall two nights before which you through your representation and signatory are anxious to get! On the whole I am pleased for I interpret this telegraphic activity after your day's journey and its fatigues as a sign of your general well doing and well being. May these continue to your journey's end & home again, and may the return be with all objects gained.

I was very sorry to hear of Mr T.s inability to proceed with you & be commander in chief of the party but you are in excellent hands with A.K. who has so much experience & all the knack of travelling—say all kind things for me to him: say also that I expect it will be found that he is *really* gone in order to set right the finance of Egypt if not of Turkey himself and that I hope he will bring back with him that perfect solution which the Prime Minister (after dinner) seemed to guarantee.

Yesterday at Greenwich I dined with the good Vicar & had the Bishop for a fellow-guest. Admiral Hamilton was there. He is quite impervious to the access or assault of age—and looked as well and active as ever.

At No 4 C. Gardens I found the cast and this morning have seen Mr Edwards. A dull and slow judge of all works of art I am a particularly bad one of any representation of myself—You know my impression generally and I really could add nothing. But I told him what is the fact that my wife is a very acute observer of likeness indeed and he will leave the cast in its present place for some considerable time with the hope that she may have to make some excursion to London and may see it

Tell A.K. that I think the Government have been uncommonly busy in blundering or going wrong—the Share circular followed by the Vanguard minute; and capping both the proceedings of the Fund in Africa which quite apart from the policy of competition[?] seem to me open to the greatest objection.

Our marriage festivities are now nearly over: nothing but a dinner remains, which we are to receive on Monday. They have been at least in amount respectable. Of 900 diners on two days not one was in the slightest debauched by liquor.

God be with you   Ever yours   WEG

Hawarden Castle.
6 December 1875.

Dear Spirit

Again I have to address you in a far distant land—but I have a tie in one further yet, for my Third Son Harry is in India, from whence I trust he may return in January or February. I wrote to you as you flew through Paris—Receiving with astonishment a telegram, which shewed you had heard of my speaking at Greenwich almost before the words had left my mouth, I sent off one or two papers with a report. I am going to republish & enlarge the Address. Since then I have had a letter kindly written by Kinnaird under your not less kind instruction, which gives me a most excellent account of your progress to Cairo, and very cheerful expectations as to your health. He tells me all except your address so that I am obliged to direct to the Poste Restante.

We have had great commotion here with compound marriage rejoicings among a population really enthusiastic: all is now quiet, and we look to a tranquil Christmas time, though with me it must be a very busy one as I happen to be singularly laden with private affairs of my family and relations. Of these I hope that a very few months will substantially dispose.

The great excitement of the last fortnight has come from your quarter—who would have thought that you would have sent us such an echo or rebound of your journey as the purchase of the shares of the Khedive in the Suez Canal. It was received with general approval, nay enthusiasm, in this country, and, I am sorry to add, for bad and discreditable reasons. We were going to manage the Canal—we were going to control Egypt and if needful annex it—we were showing that we were not to be trifled with—in that we were to do all manner of things that if done by another would be intolerable but if done by us righteous.

It now appears that it was the acquisition of ten votes in a body of many thousand shareholders by a payment of five millions. The transaction is rather stripped of its glory and its perils—it has to be judged on rather dry grounds, and I am far from sure that it will bear the judgment.

Tell me all you hear about this purchase & about Egyptian politics.

I hear of old Lord Bathurst through my nephew. Not readily or soon can I forget his courtesy & kindness, much of it for your sake, but much also ingrained in himself.

We have just had the Jubilee singers to see this place, and sing. Their "John Brown" is really noble, almost sublime. Do not miss hearing it when you have an opportunity.

You must enjoy your climate. As years creep on I find the summer decidedly preferable to the winter with its cold & colds. You will get groups of passing English from time to time. Heartily do I wish you a happy Christmas, & may God be with you in all His goodness & His Grace at that & at all times

Ever yours   WEG

Hawarden Castle.
Xmas Day 1875.

Dear Spirit

I cannot pass this anniversary without addressing you in a distant land my earnest wishes & the assurance of my poor prayers for your happiness. May it be a blessed Christmas for you, and may it be followed by many & many another. And yet I think though I write today I had better not send to post for two or three more days. Your last letter told me what perhaps I ought already to have known that there was but one weekly post to Brindisi leaving London on Friday, and my last had gone to post just before yours arrived. I have heard also of you through Mr Herbert who kindly sent me your letter but I am sorry to say I have not answered him nor some scores more who sit at my left hand noted as requiring reply but not yet having got it. The Post brings me 150–200 letters & packets a week & my compulsory & most frivolous correspondence exhausts the time I would wish freely to give to what would be more acceptable & profitable. I send you by book Post a letter of my son's to his parishioners. If you look it over you will find that his life is not an idle one.

This winter has brought me a correspondence of a most unexpected kind. My third son [Henry Neville] has for six or seven years, since 17 years of age, been preparing himself for a place in the mercantile house & business originally established by my Father: this at the suggestion and under the auspices of my Brother the Senior Partner. It pleased God to remove him suddenly three months ago, and his successor in the headship of the House seems inclined to repudiate, & put my son into the street. Please let this be strictly private at present, for the matter is not quite over, but it has been a grave anxiety to me, & I could not keep it from you, kind as you are in all things. Whatever comes I do not doubt it will work out for good.

I shall be anxious to hear the Egyptian version of the Suez Canal business. My information is that first & last there will be much trouble about it here; but perhaps not much at first.

We are looking for a humble abode somewhere in London—I know not where it will be—but we finally move out of the old quarter before Easter. Our address will be there 4 Carlton Gardens. But we shall be here 3 or four more weeks.

Within that time I hope to have good, very good, accounts of your health and doings.

May the Almighty be with you now & ever   WEG

[Gladstone's surviving correspondence with Mrs. Thistlethwayte for 1876 consists of three postcards]

Hawarden Castle.
12 January 1877.

Dear Spirit

I have now (somewhat) reduced in height my heap of unanswered letters, and I have just been able to write to my dear son in India my first letter since his departure from this country now two months or more ago, so I feel myself able to take up my pen to express my hope that you have been well and have had much satisfaction in dealing with your poor people at Christmas.

In your last letter there was one passage to which you know I can make no answer as it would only be a repetition of what I have said so many times. Let me thank you for the verses inclosed in a wire[?] yesterday. They seem very good but the type is extremely small & the light has been too scanty to allow of my reading them thoroughly yet.

On Tuesday I am going to give our villagers a 'reading' from the very interesting Mackenzie & Irby book; and on Wednesday we go to Longleat to meet some like minded people, & then probably to one or two other visits in the West. The proceedings at Constantinople fill me with astonishment. I would not have believed that assembled Europe would have undergone such a loss of dignity and self-respect in the face of the Turk. The conference may rally ere it dies, God grant it. But at present I am in a state of entire bewilderment. I believe in the honour of the Emperor of Russia, and of Lord Salisbury: and then I come nearly to a standstill.

May the Almighty & all good always bless you   Ever yours   WEG

Dunster Castle, Dunster.
26 January 1877.

I am very sorry it has not been in my power to return the printed verses. They are in their small slip of paper in my drawer at Hawarden amid much beside and could not I fear be got out except by myself. We have been paying visits in the West and I find everywhere new indications of the unabated interest of the country in the Eastern Question. It exhibits itself in continued efforts to bring me out at all the places near which I pass and though I have avoided much of this I have been obliged to accede to one or two requests and I am to hold forth at Taunton tomorrow morning on my way westward. On Monday we visit our nieces in Wiltshire at Bowden Park Chippenham & by Saturday we expect to reach London.

This country, North Somerset is very beautiful with hill wood and sea, as well as genial and mild in climate. I do not know whether you have ever seen it.

I am not sure if I have recommended to you the book of the Misses Mackenzie and Irby on the Slavonic Provinces.[1] If not let me do it now.

God bless & keep you   Always yours   WEG

Harley Street.
14 February 1877.
Ash Wednesday.

Dear Spirit

It is very kind of you to take me & all I said in good part: nor was it pleasant to me to have to speak, under a sense of what comes with the lapse of time & other circumstances, of increasing difficulties & lengthening intervals. But no difficulty & no interval will or can ever make me indifferent to whatsoever

[1] To which Gladstone wrote a preface for a new edition; see 14 Dec. 76.

concerns your happiness or otherwise than deeply wishful to promote it. For me, for you, for us all, it remains to feel the value of the one, broad, ever open way of access by which we may, in & by one better than ourselves, seek & obtain what is good on behalf & to the profit of one another.

Never I hope when I am breaching or trying to breach that way shall I forget what I have just said in its application to you: amidst the pressure of my own great, indeed great need for pardon & for grace. May this time of Lent—for there is force in times & seasons—do something for us both.

I think your verses inclosed are beautiful. There is a great spirit of reality about them & this does not lose its force from their not being the representation of an actual state of things.

May the all merciful crown you richly with His truth & grace   Ever yours
      WEG

If a note in my hand reached you *today* it was a blunder of mine: forgive it.

31 March 1877.

I am very sorry to have lost my patience today[1] for a moment when I said 'For God's sake do not begin again with that['.] I was wrong, wrong on any day, especially on a day which commemorates our Lord's rest in the Grave, and when I ought to be learning to die to all sin and all infirmity.

I had however had a particularly annoying matter, of quite another kind, this morning: & it left my heart-strings very sore & sensitive. I ought not to have inflicted this on you.

Let me however assure you, I hope without harshness, that I have done all, the very outside, of what I could.

God be with you   WEG

Hawarden Castle.
18 May 1877.

Dear Spirit

Your gift to Miss Irby came this morning in a letter by post. I do not know if you are aware that it is penal to send money nor am I certain whether this extends to Bank Notes, but it is dangerous: however it is safe. I will send it to Miss Irby's Bankers when I get back to London—and in the meantime I do *not* thank you for it—in obedience to your express order.

The new & enlarged edition of her book has just come out, published by Isbister.[2] I think you will find it very interesting.

It was rumoured on Monday that the Irish would prolong the debate over that night but as it ended I was too happy to come off the next day and set to

---

[1] Easter Eve.
[2] And with a preface by Gladstone; see 14 Dec. 76.

work (afresh) here in a new air and amidst the opening green of our very late spring.

We got here on Tuesday evening and I hope to remain until the morning of the 31st when I am to appear at Birmingham and make another pleading before a great meeting there for the cause of the East.

Were we but right minded, I mean us as a State not as a people, we might I am confident bring this war to a close in a very few weeks. But the people are one way and the Parliament another.

I hope you will enjoy the opening spring in your little drives & I should be glad to think also that Mr Thistlethwayte would profit by it in his uncertain and tantalising illness.

The proceedings of Lady S. have been very strange and the best I can hope for you in connection with her is that she may be kind enough to let you alone.

May the Almighty bless and guide all your ways   Ever yours   WEG

Hawarden Castle.
19 August 1877.

Dear Spirit

I send you a copy of my article on Egypt[1] in which I think you will be interested from your knowing the country.

I did not expect when I left town that these three weeks would have passed without my being recalled thither. But the Government as well as the leader of the Opposition wished to be quiet on the Eastern Question, and I think both were right.

I have myself made no manifestation except in a summary way yesterday when I expressed the hope that Govt. would at any rate keep the neutrality they have announced, & said that if they did not there would be men to try again the operations of last year.

So this bud of the Stafford House blanket scheme has unblushingly burst into the support of the wounded Turks and the Archbishop of Canterbury!! is among the leading promoters if the newspapers are to be trusted. A Russian Fund has been started which will serve to test in some degree the question between humanity and partisanship.

For my part I shall confine myself to the case of the simply suffering and non-fighting inhabitants. Have you been brave enough to try Mr Th. again?

I hope you enjoyed your visit to Lord Bathurst now probably over—as I am sure he would. You are a great prop and comfort to that fine and good old gentleman. To judge from appearances, I think he has yet many, I mean relatively many years to live.

Pray give my love to Lady E. Pringle if she is still with you.

God be with you   Ever yours   WEGladstone

[1] 'Aggression on Egypt'; see 21 July 77.

Hawarden Castle.
10 September 1877.

Dear and kind Spirit

My plans are still unsettled and I have little to say but I think it possible that I may be in London for a night or two before the end of the month. Some of my octogenarian friends are always there especially for Sir A. Panizzi to whom a visit is always a great boon. I may also have to go to Nottingham on business connected with the affairs of our common friend [i.e. Newcastle].

The last of the large executive parties has now been here and I am relieved from the further apprehension of what I have found an awkward and inconvenient necessity, which came upon me unawares. I was not sorry however for the opportunity of speaking about the recent course of outrage in the East.

We watch with extreme interest as indeed all must the course of the tremendous operations in the East. God grant that they may work out their end, & obviate the necessity or occasion for weak things hereafter. I am truly delighted with the capture of Niksich by the Montenegrins.

The inclosure seems to show a great precipitation on our side, unless there had been encouragement on the other.

I trust you have kept well and followed what my excellent doctor calls the laws of health—I should like to know it, and also that our friends Ld Bathurst & Lady Elizabeth are thriving. Kinnaird too if you know anything of him though I am sorry to hear he has had some displeasure at some of my proceedings

Perhaps Mr T. will be better disposed towards the Russian sick & wounded Fund than towards the Bosnians: I have however not meddled with it.

May the Almighty graciously keep and guide you   Yours ever   WEG

Woodlands, Clonsilla.
11 November 1877.

Dear Spirit

I came to Ireland expecting libraries with books which I have not read and with papers which I have not moved from their reports: and I thought I should before this time have written to you from the land of your birth, which you have not seen for long, but which I believe you love right well. However I must not quit the green shores without sending you a letter.

Our departure is fixed for tomorrow and indeed I have promised to make a short speech to the people at Holyhead though the wind which is piping loud in the chimney reminds me that I may be in a sorry condition for redemption of the pledge. My days and hours have been filled full of interests of every kind and Ireland much surpasses my anticipations. The country is more beautiful, the capital finer and ever improving, the antiquities more venerable & profoundly interesting, the people more kind & indulgent to me, than I could have reckoned on finding them respectively.

The members & clergy of the disestablished Church shew no resentment and I have been dining with the Provost of Trinity College and staying in the house of the Archbishop of Dublin. Both these are men of very high stamp.

Cardinal Cullen on whom I went to call received me with great civility but said they could have given me a warmer welcome had it not been for certain pamphlets which I had written & which were not liked in Ireland. But I must say that the only other (R.C.) Bishop whom I have seen, and the Priests in general, have given me the warmest welcome possible, and have appeared to thrust themselves in my way for the purpose of doing it. I greatly doubt whether they like the servitude to which it is the purpose of the Vatican to reduce them.

I do not know whether you have seen the County Wicklow much. We have been pretty well over it and have greatly enjoyed its beauties. We have not been in more than about five counties and I leave a great deal to stand over for another visit which I hope soon to pay. It is among the pleasures of the visit that I find so many worthy and excellent people of station in this part at least of the country who love Ireland and reside on their estates looking carefully after the people. My estimate of the disestablished Church is not very sanguine. I cannot but think the level of religious life in general is lower than in the Church of England: and I do not see the smallest likelihood at present of its becoming formidable in any way to its Roman sister or rival. You have seen a portion of Ireland that I have not but I wish you had also seen or could see the part in which I have moved about.

The worst of the case I think is that few of them seem to care much about the poor Christians of the East. God however I trust will be their friend and indeed He seems to have stretched out His arm for their deliverance.

All I hope goes well with you in health comfort friends & every higher matter—May it so continue. I hope to be at Hawarden tomorrow night   Ever yours   WEG.

Hawarden Castle.
22 December 1877.

Dear Spirit

So we are all thrown afresh into a pucker by the recent action of our Earl-Premier.[1] It is not pleasant to live under a succession of these alarms: and each of his proceedings is a fresh effort at mischief. He means war, or if he cannot get that then the thing nearest to it that he can get. But I hope the country will resist & overthrow his schemes. Certainly we who have been counteracting him for 18 months shall kick vigorously.

I return you the Duke's little memorandum and I cannot carry on a controversy with his mother's son. Instead of thinking of him and the Turks, I will think of him and Italy. The book is a collection of all the Turkish forgeries and figments together with certain statements of the newspaper[?] products. Of them some are not without importance but it is rather against the Bulgarians— who are such as the Turks have made them—than against the Russians. I had sometime before examined it with care. Count B. had a fair subject and his effort is *bold*. 'None but the bold' it is said, 'deserve the fair'.

[1] British fleet sent to Constantinople following the fall of Plevna to Russia.

The Grindleys[?] were extremely kind to us, and I think people think well of those they have been kind to, as men are supposed to hate those they have injured.

I cannot but hope you have had some enjoyment from this fortnight of beautiful December weather.

God send the Russians the gift of moderation, and the Turks a prudent mind and to you a happy Christmas with all other good   Ever yours   WEG

Harley Street.
7 April 1878.

I have not been able to call, nor shall I *tomorrow*, for it is a very special day of work, but I have indeed been deeply concerned at what has happened.[1] It was to me quite unexpected. Had I had the least idea of anything of the kind, I would have suggested, nay begged, that the matter in difference should be referred to a friend—especially to such a person as Sir Fitzroy Kelly if he could be got to act.

I fear much mischief has been done while on the other hand I hope that a speedy accommodation may follow.

No one, or hardly any one, can judge better than I can how large a proportion of your alleged debts is simply the expression of what your bounty has conveyed to others in every variety of shape & almost without limit in amount. But all this makes the occurrence more sad—I can regret that you were out anywhere yesterday after it, and as one to whom you have done so much kindness I earnestly hope that you will find the means by which, if it please God, the best provision may be made for the future, and nothing done to [?] the traces of the event. With a particular emphasis let me give my usual ending   God be with you

WEG

Hawarden Castle.
30 August 1878.

Dear "Broken Spirit"

(Your letter carries me back to the days when you used the phrase—I have taken many days to think of it before replying.)

Let me in the first place put by what is of little consequence. Do not trouble yourself, either much or little, about the Duke of Sutherland on my account. It is idle to pay attention, at least for me to pay attention, to what he may utter or write. Nothing I could say would alter him at all—but should be very sorry to

---

[1] Henry Padwick, a well-known gambler and money-lender, summoned A. F. Thistlethwayte to the debtors' court, Laura Thistlethwayte's possessions being also involved. A. F. Thistlethwayte contested Padwick's claims in court; it seemed likely there would be a further action in 1879. See subsequent letters and above, ix. lxxxviii.

interfere with any of his friendships or acquaintances, both on general grounds
& for his mother's sake. He calls me a coward about you—but how, from whom,
& in what, does he know? I cannot reply to such imputations.

Much more seriously do I take the general strain of your letter. It brings
home to me how much I have failed, though not all in intention, yet in giving
effect to my duty, towards you. Out of the bounty and activity of your mind, you
have framed a kind of ideal, and invested it with high qualities: have in the same
sort called it by my name, & have bestowed upon it feelings so far beyond what
it can [overwritten] duly merit or meet. Then I look at the facts of the case—
who & what I am—my time of life—my growing disposition to retire from
London & its life—my duty to contemplate the evening of my days and to
impart to them a tone of calm and recollection, very different from the kind of
tumult in which they have been passed—I cannot reproach myself with not
having pointed out how all this must come, & must grow. The trust & confidence, & all else, which you bestowed, made it alike my duty and my desire to
minister, in the small measure in which I could to your happiness and welfare. A
sad light flowed in upon me when you said, as you may recollect, in answer to
something from me about married life 'I am married, and I am not.' All this you
unfolded in that remarkable written detail, which of course I preserve and
cannot forget. I could not attempt any violence to your feelings: but, within the
limit thus marked, it was my duty, as that of any other friend according to the
manner of his or her knowledge (I am thinking of that dear Lady E. P[ringle]),
to build up if ever so little, to cause approximation if ever so little, knowing well
as I do that the family, with or without offspring, is God's ordinance, upon
which this great framework of the human world is built: and that nothing can
be a substitute for it. Yet, this year, I seem to have seen that, in lieu of approximation, your married life was further (so to speak) decomposed. I have heard
you say words of it this year, that I had not heard before; I mean when you
alluded to the idea of "separation".

Then again, I am deeply concerned at what you tell me of Lady P. and your
husband. You will recollect something similar many years ago about Lady K.,
who was your guest. But in this instance there are indications, which would lead
to placing little confidence in the person named, & which did not exist in the
other one.

I hope you will study to make things more in the right direction, and that
God will reward your efforts, and that I may at least do nothing to mar them.
May He be with you, & keep & bless, now & evermore   WEG

                                                          Harley Street.
                                                          28 February 1879.
My dear Mrs Th.

I was impressed, deeply impressed with what you told me last night[1]—So
much so that what I said might seem incoherent. Certainly I never should have

---

[1] 'Mrs. Th. gave me intelligence which touched me and moved me'; 27 Feb. 79.

dared to guess it. But it seemed to me to do you great honour. I could not but recognise in it the hand of God: the hand of God, signally and solely. May He reward and bless it.

> Praise to the Highest in the Height—
> And in the Depth be praise.
> In all His works most wonderful,
> Most just in all his ways.

I could not refrain from sending you this word of cheering and benediction
Ever yours   W. E. Gladstone.

Inclosed are what I think you will like—sent me (a plurality of copies) by the author.[1]

Harley Street.
1 March 1879.

My dear Mrs Th.
   This question you name was inexcusable—I meant to allude to it in saying my language might seem 'incoherent'. I deeply regret it: but it really was due to confusion; and perhaps this was not unnatural when I learnt that to be fact, which you had I think ordinarily regarded & described as impossible. But that does not alter my regret. Deus tecum
   Always yours   W. E. Gladstone

Your letter just received.
1. I think I had better not name to anyone the circumstances told by you. There is no call for it, & especially no call for it to come from me.
2. Let me have a little time to think about a Trustee. At first sight I should say ought not Mr T. to take a connection of his family.
Ever Yours   W. E. Gladstone

Hawarden Castle.
10 April 1879.

My dear Mrs Th.
   I have reflected on Mr Padwick['s] actions and I feel constrained to lay before you what I most sincerely think
1. I proceed on the *supposition* that Mr Padwick has really lent you money & that Mr Thistlethwayte intends to refuse the acknowledgement of this debt.
2. If so, I presume that the scene of last year will be repeated: & I cannot but state my conviction that everyone who feels an interest in him or in you, or who remembers your hospitalities, must ably deprecate such a repetition, &

---

[1] Perhaps the duke of Argyll's *The eastern question from 1856*, just published; see 4 June 78, 20 Feb. 79.

anticipate from it consequences most mischievous to you & to him: mischievous to a degree which it would be difficult to describe.

3. The witnesses under sub poena will or may be compelled to stand before the world as parties in a domestic controversy, for it must be Padwick's intention to make them show Mr T's liability for the debt. If so they will appear his adversaries. Some of them will refer to his declarations of last year about them having been received in his house without his approval

3. [sic] They will probably be asked *whom* they met at your table—& will be taken either for informers against others (under the circ.) or for persons desirous to the truth.

4. ⟨1. The witnesses would probably be asked whether they had partaken of your hospitality. I should have to reply yes, especially at luncheons from time to time where I used to meet some greatly esteemed friends; but this was before the trial of last year, when I learned from the newspapers that Mr Thistlethwayte seemed to disclaim having been a party to the visits of these guests— since then of course my practice has been altered.

2. I would probably be asked who were the guests I had met at your table. It would be most offensive to me to detail their names as if charging them with something discreditable. But the Court might require answers.⟩

3. You have repeatedly sent me presents, ⟨and of a value proportional to your generosity but far exceeding my merits or wishes: you⟩ have refused to let me decline them & have insisted that they were trifles. After what happened last year, when it appeared you were under some money obligation disowned by your husband, I pressed anew to be allowed to return them. They have principally been kept untouched. But if you are to be ⟨arraigned⟩ sued in Court ⟨as a debtor⟩ for unpaid monies, you will at once see that I have no option, ⟨on being made aware of such a state of facts⟩ but to return them all ⟨under⟩ (or an equivalent)* even at the risk of your displeasure

⟨I think⟩ I ought not to close without begging you and if I may Mr T. through you to consider this matter well to consult friends in whom you can confide some two points especially in connection with it. First that if money is really owing, a claim for it is not answered by saying it is quite safe & will be paid at some future time. There is a right to have it *now*. Secondly that I doubt whether either you or Mr T. is at all aware of the amount & kind of mischief done by the trial of last year: It was exceedingly great; and rely on it that by any similar trial now repeated it would be aggravated tenfold

Most sinc. yours   WEG

*as will the donations you have repeatedly given me for private purposes of charity.

Worksop.
13 April 1879.

I return the Duke of Sutherland's note: entirely concurring in his opinion about Mr T.—What sort of solicitors can they be who after the affair of last year are leading him into such a scrape again! But I do not agree with what the Duke says about the world. ⟨And⟩ In some cases, and in this case, the world is really the champion of family peace and virtue, and has *right* on its side though it may uphold that right with an unjust uncharitable severity.

I am glad to infer from your note that you acquiesce in my returning the presents should the matter not be settled. That which would always have been (as I thought) desirable is thus made necessary, and I am thankful for your acquiescence which is all I could expect.

I could not do less than speak strongly of the mischief I foresee. Having spoken I will not worry you any more. But I hope your efforts may prove successful. If they do not, the future will bear the marks of these so sadly false steps

God be with you this Eastertide.

I remain at and about Worksop till Wednesday—then probably to Mentmore
Ever yours   WEG

Easter Day
I suppose your Padwick loan was *before* the proceedings of last year?

Harley Street.
25 April 1879.
My dear Mrs Th.

I had not heard the rumour you have explained.

I am sorry to say Mr Thistlewayte's conduct remains to me a perfect enigma. I have done all I could & have been summarily silenced. Without meaning it, he last year drove men from his table. Without meaning it, he will probably this year drive them from his door. If he acted by the advice of his solicitors, in whom he has 'perfect confidence', what solicitors they must be!

But I have only one duty remaining at present—to put together and return as soon as I can find them—those tokens of your exuberant bounty, which under the present circumstances it is not possible to retain in my house.

All this I write on the supposition
1. That Mr Padwick has a rent claim on you—
2. That Mr T. intends again to contend in Court that a claim on you is not a claim on him. And this he thinks, I suppose to be for his well understood interest! Against such an opinion it is vain to argue

May all good attend you   Yours always   WEG

Harley Street.
3 May 1879.
My dear Mrs Thistlethwayte

I was truly sorry to receive your last letter. If I inclose it herewith it is only that you may have the power to peruse it again, after you have read this reply: and again send it to me, or not, as you may think fit.

I confine myself to facts, & avoid, I hope, every disturbing word.

I have never proposed or meant to return your gifts *of a class* such as may ordinarily pass between friend & friend.

But you have also from time to time sent me presents *which go beyond that scale, & which in the aggregate must have cost hundreds*.

As you know, I have expostulated again & again: and only because my words have seemed to annoy & disturb you, I have submitted to keeping them by me. They have, however, remained, generally speaking, laid aside, & unused. Two or three objects have disappeared: for these, under the circumstances, I must roughly endeavour to make up.

This I consider will be not, in substance, to *you* but *to Mr Thistlethwayte*. I cannot, at my time of life, carry my submission to your judgment up to such a point as you desire, & think yourself entitled to require of me[?]. You have lately apprised me that you have borrowed money a good while back, which Mr Thistlethwayte refuses to pay, and which he will even refuse in Court to pay, at least for the time, if & when it is demanded there by the man to whom it is owed.

What I may think of this conduct, as between you & him, is not for me to say. What I think of it on general grounds, he has in writing desired me not to say.

Honour will not permit me to retain in my house gifts on the scale I have described, under the circumstances I have described. I consider this, however, to be a matter between him & me, rather than between you & me. (If you think fit, I will return the articles to *him*.)

I have made known this intention in the gentlest terms I could: and if I have erred in these terms, I lament it.

In answer to this, you have (within the inclosed) not reassured but denounced.

If you ask me to do *more* than I have said, the first question would be as to the ring and studs, & smaller things, that I had thought to retain as memorials of your kindness.

As to these, I must certainly obey at once your wish whatever it may be. Any thing beyond this I must maturely consider.

I shall not, until I hear more abandon the hope that, on a perusal of this note, and with reflection, you may attach some weight to what I say. You blamed Mr Rainsford for not telling you his mind. This is just what I have the right to do. With your honour and well-being, estimated to the best of my judgment, for my main object. God be with you, & keep you

Harley Street.
4 May 1879.

The assurances you give me are welcome and will enable me to hold my hand until I hear again. Many thanks.

It is difficult for me to understand the inclosed without knowing to what it was an answer.

I saw Mr Hayward yesterday afternoon—after writing to you
Heartily wishing you all good   Yours   WEG

Harley Street.
27 June 1879.

I am concerned and touched at what you report to have happened. It seems a strange fancy to discuss your medical advice of such old standing, most of all at such a time. It cannot have been by Sir Wm Gull's advice, or you would have known it. You do not mention what was the result of the consultation on Monday. I hope good. I am sorry to read what Mr Sibley says at the bottom of his second page about your 'present feelings'. Had it been the will of Him who wills all for the best I should have rejoiced to hear that they indicated a reality and the approach of an event which it seems to me would have promised to be the happiest in your life. Mr S's letter will be kept as you bid, and will be forthcoming here if you should wish for it.

I do not agree with the critic in the Morning Post but I hope that in another week we shall have reasonably full details from responsible firms and shall be in a better condition to form a judgment.

I continue to be very hard pressed by work. Indeed as the only method of escape I am thinking with my wife of a short continental trip about September.

You have I suppose no news about the Chief Baron & the wretched trial—it is said not only that Padwick is ill, but that his quarrel with the Duke of Hamilton is of the most serious kind, not involving any thing less than the supposition of very large misappropriation of the Duke's money.

May the Almighty be with you   WEG.

Harley Street.
3 July 1879.

I am so sorry to miss you—I called, as you may suppose, to offer my best and heartiest congratulations. Alls well that ends well!

So now Padwick abandons the idea of getting more than his due, while his due will be offered to him. Good.

I have actually got a pound, or a guinea, of the poor man's money! by this affair. As a record of matter into which he had dragged me, I should much like a copy of Mr Lewis's very clear letter—if you will kindly let me have one.[1]

---

[1] Letter from Lewis & Lewis, London solicitors, 1 July 1879: '. . . you have gained a complete victory over Mr Padwick. He has, by consent, obtained a decree for an enquiry into your separate estate but it is not proposed by his Solicitor to proceed with such enquiry and I do not think you will be further troubled in the matter. Mr Thistlethwayte has, by consent, obtained a decree in his favour with costs which he does not propose to ask for so long as Mr Padwick does not further trouble you. . . .'

Thanks for your invitation but I am compelled to keep in & near the H. of Commons tomorrow night as we have a motion on Agricultural Distress.

I am anxious for a good account of your health.

God be with you   WEGladstone

I hope all will go well with the Chief Baron.

Hawarden Castle.

15 August 1879.

Beyond or against my expectation I have escaped this far a call to London & the Session is now virtually dead.

I thought I might have seen you and I could not but think often of you & of the circumstances which have made this year a marked one in your life. I am quite sure you understand and excuse the interest I felt in the intelligence made known to me by you, beyond all my expectation as it was, on that evening when we had dined with the kind Miss Ponsonby and you helped me on my way home by a seat in your carriage. Marriage is the foundation stone of Christian Society, the primary ordinance of God and the conversion of a half marriage into a full marriage makes the union worthy of the venerable name. I mourned sincerely over the change of prospect which shortly after ensued—as your friend & one who has so much reason to recollect your trust & kindness I am constrained to hope that prospect may yet be secured, with a great gain to your happiness in a more distant future.

It is a descent from this theme to go back upon the subject of the Padwick suit: but I am rejoiced from the bottom of my heart that controversy with the relations it suggested never was brought into court. It would have been a deplorable business and could not have done otherwise than operate disadvantageously to a serious extent on your life & on your relations to your friends, and to the world, whose judgment it is sometimes right to disregard, but not I think in a case like this. I do earnestly hope that now when the appearance of menace is withdrawn Mr T. will make speedy and effectual arrangements for clearing off the whole of the true and real debt. I am sure you feel that nothing less than this can suffice. Debt is an unpleasant incident of any life but the anomaly is glaring & even more than glaring in conjunction with a certain scale of living & of establishment.

As it annoys you that I should press any thing about the presents, I will only say I should take it as not the least among your many kindnesses if by a spontaneous act you would allow me to return them: retaining by your permission two or three memorials.

I hope you have profited by the changes of weather, & the almost beginning of summer with which we have been blessed.

You are spared agricultural cares. We have them here, although I thank God with less darkly coloured prospects for the immediate future than in many districts. We have 1200 acres thrown on our hands and I have just authorised accepting a rather bad offer as a smaller evil than having 1200 or 1500 more thrown up.

The young Duke of Newcastle and his brother were here last week—and were much liked.

Wishing you all health & every other blessing & bounty   Ever yours
   WEG

Taymouth Castle, Aberfeldy.
4 December 1879.

I am sure your kindness will have supplied the reason why I have not sooner thanked you for your note, your 'mindfu' note as the Scotch would say. I am glad you see the Duke of Sutherland—perhaps you will mollify his politics. He must now surely be sick of the state of matters in the East.

The pressure here had been and continues to be very great[1]—tomorrow I have a fearful day before me. We hope to get to Hawarden on Monday evening & then I hope for a period of something like repose. The two last days however at this splendid place have only been days of hard not of unquiet work.

The enthusiasm shown here has certainly exceeded everything that I have seen in a political life which began in 1832. It is not to be described; with the illuminations, the bonfires, the bands, the crowds, even in remote places: also all the hearts & the voices expressing them. It cannot be exaggerated.

It takes an ulterior effect in all sorts of gifts. I have had to purvey a great box to hold them—but they still multiply—People will soon begin to cry out "Corruption—"

I earnestly hope that you can in all things make the best reports of yourself & every thing around you—I have not forgotten that bright & every way curious sight you showed me of the locket & the ear-rings: though we both wish I believe that the cost or the bulk of it had gone another way. The kind & noteworthy host & hostess here,[2] so earnest in their politics, are most loyal in their devotion to the memory of Lady Elizabeth [Pringle] your dear & valued friend.

Believe me, while wishing you every blessing from on high   Ever yours
   WEG

Hawarden Castle.
21 December 1879.

Many thanks for the Embryo Play. There seems to be material, and life, in it. But I have always ventured to tell you what a work it would be to compose a real play. One of the most arduous to which the mind can be given; to most people, to me for example, impossible: to the most apt very difficult. For any readers of the print as it now stands I think you want a list of 'Dramatis

---

[1] The first Midlothian campaign.
[2] Lord and Lady Breadalbane.

Personae' and a clear statement of the argument[.] Have you had Mr Hayward's opinion. None would be more useful.

I was so glad to receive your account of Mr T. Let me add also that of the Duke of Sutherland. I have been told the Duchess has had a good influence on him, since her own life became more solid and firm.

I understand Padwick so minds the Duke of Hamilton's affairs as to run his debt up to £1,400,000, with an income of £140,000 a year.

What is to be done about the great Paddington offer.

It is just possible I may have to run up to London about the 30th for a night or two, on Newcastle Trust affairs.

Pray for a good result at Sheffield.

Scotland was wonderful, indescribable. The 'presents' have not yet done coming in.

Skating unbroken for three weeks

God be with you in all things   Ever yours   WEGladstone

Look into the question of the Irish Distress.

Hawarden Castle.
1 January 1880.

I must not let *another* day pass as I have allowed several, but must send you the heartiest good wishes for the New Year. May every first of January bring you increase of blessings for long long years to come.

It seems unkind not to have said this before but for the last week my letters & packets by post & telegram have been running between seventy & a hundred and twenty, and though it is all an influx of kindness that causes the difficulty I have scarcely known how I should get on & am still drowned in arrear.

Please give all my best wishes to Mr T. with our thanks for an excellent salmon. My wife was ill and confined to her room for a fortnight & this prevented an earlier acknowledgement so that I hope the delay will be forgiven.

I did not well understand your kind offer of dinner 'on Monday or Tuesday'—I had a vision of London this week on Trust business but it passed away. Indeed I am not in a condition to stir anywhere until the flood I have described shall a little diminish.

I have been writing to the Duke of Sutherland! about the refugees in Eastern Roumania. He referred me to Baroness B. Coutts to whom I have sent a contribution.

Do you see in the papers the Paragraph about placing an Inspector at Windsor to look after the Queen's safety? How does it strike you?

I may come up for a night or two before the Service but am quite uncertain.

God be with you   Ever yours   WEG

Hawarden Castle.
5 February 1880.

It is comparatively long since I have written to or seen you: my life has been both actively and passively marked through the interval. I could not find time to call on you during my stay of one full day only in London, between the deathbed at Cologne,[1] and the deposition in the last home far North—I have bridged over too that broad streak which seems to divide the time lying within "the year of our age" from the time lying beyond it—and on this day, considering what is now passing in London, my date will show my strong desire to avail myself soon, if it be permitted me, of some retirement.

You will easily conceive how broad was the contrast between my first journey to Scotland and my second, and yet the time between the return, and the setting out again under a peremptory summons from Germany did not exceed a month. The visit to Cologne was even more full of touching interest than those would suppose who heard of it simply as the death of an only sister, who has left my brother & me, both older than herself, the sole survivors of our generation. There was a profound religious interest attaching to it. For apart from sentiments of proselytism, which I do not much love or harbour, it was a question of real interest to know whether she would be laid in one and the same grave with her own people without any wall of separation between them in point of faith or ecclesiastical communion.

This question was cleared and settled as Nature and Religion alike prompted me to wish. She had for years past, perhaps for as many as ten years, been thoroughly estranged from the Roman Church, to which she had attached herself about thirty eight years ago. On this fact I had long been substantially informed for a long time, but the closing scenes supplied me under various forms with more definite knowledge.

Coming home last week I found this large Parish engrossed with the proceedings of a Mission which had been planned by my son. It was conducted by two clergymen of great ability. For fourteen days, the daily services, prolonged and varied, have been crowded. They ended with Holy Communion at 4 am today: and there is really I trust reason to believe that God has blessed the work.

This is however an egotistical letter—I ask then to hear, when it may be convenient, of you, your health, your occupations, your drama (on which I dare not speak until I see it completed & in form), your husband, & your friends. I should much like to hear of Mr Herbert & Mr Hayward. I fear you do not know about Lord Kinnaird, and I am also afraid that his state of health is a sad one & that his tenure of his title may not be long.

God prosper the Liverpool Election tomorrow.

And may He in all things & in all ways prosper you   Ever yours   WEG

---

[1] Death of Gladstone's sister Helen, a convert to Roman Catholicism.

Hawarden Castle.
9 April 1880.

I must not delay in answering however hastily to your most kind invitation. But why do you spoil or propose to spoil the Duke's agreeable dinner by the intrusion of at least one disagreeable face?

I am very sorry to say we cannot come—We remain here as long as possible, I cannot say how long as I am not altogether my own master but I hope it will be beyond next week.

If I come up to town, I shall hope to make an early call.

The proposed public reception on arrival troubles me, as I fear it might be misunderstood and I am trying to escape from it quietly.

What a wonderful time it has been, what an unexampled crash! From my point of view I cannot but see in it the hand of the Almighty, working out His great design through this poor and frail creature.

I wonder whether Mr T. voted in Middlesex.

God be with you, in all times & places   Always yours   W. E. Gladstone

10 Downing Street.
9 September 1880.

I kept your kind note in hope but amidst all my arrears, and with the intention of leaving London tomorrow, a visit out of town is impossible.

Another opportunity for seeing your new abode,[1] which must be so pretty, may arise, as I expect to come up from time to time in the rather unsettled condition of affairs.

I should much like, and I hope I may be in town to see Mr Herbert's picture. There is *in the air* a sort of idea that possibly this unhappy B.C[2] marriage may after all not take place. Heartily do I wish it for every reason, especially for the sake of one who may have made mistakes but who has done very good deeds & has earned a most honourable name by them.

I expect to reach Hawarden on Saturday.

God be with you   Ever yours   WEG

10 Downing Street.
15 November 1880.

Your hospitality is ever wakeful in its kindness but I am sorry to report myself engaged every day this week, together with my wife: & indeed, were it not so, I could not well dine out and leave her alone.

I have in mind your amiable suggestion about Mr Herbert's picture[3] & if I can

---

[1] Her cottage in Hampstead.

[2] Marriage of A. Burdett-Coutts to W. Ashmead-Bartlett, which Gladstone was working, unsuccessfully, to prevent.

[3] Herbert's 'Susannah'; see 23 Nov. 80.

find or make an opportunity you will hear from me without fail. Work is hard and anxiety is great—I am much absorbed and I fear likely to remain so.

Take care of yourself in the cold which has now I believe returned

And may all things attend you   Always yours   WEG

It reaches me, but not *certainly*, that the B Coutts marriage stands over until January & that *he* is thought not keen for it.

10 Downing Street.
24 January 1881.

What weather! How are you. As for me I am in bed & out of it, and maintain a struggle with my duties in Parlt. partly to do & partly to shirk them.

I send you back some letters. I cannot be sure but do not think I have any offers from Lady S[eabright] to you. The letter in which she gave you the narrative about the other Lady S.[1] was very sad. She ought to look upon the gambling table as poison, pestilence, and worse.

Some time I hope will come when I may get as far as G[rosvenor] Square—but I have not for a fortnight been further than the H. of C.: not even to visit an invalid.

God be with you   WEG

10 Downing Street.
1 February 1881.

1. I think there is not likely to be any *great* delay about the arrangement for an annual payment to Lady S.—But I would not wonder if something be tacked to it about gaming. For indeed that is rather a formidable subject as appeared in the letter about Lady Seabright.

2. I return you the letter's [*sic*] last sent me—one part of one among them I read with sadness and some surprise—you will easily know which.

3. I return the letter about Mr Tyrell. I have found since receiving it that the rich appointment to the Provostship rests with the *Irish* Govt. not with me.

4. Sittings day & night—much confusion, much wrath—we shall probably be worse before we are better.

God be with you, & more peace than we have   WEG

---

[1] Lady Susan Opdebeck, the former Lady Lincoln and divorced wife of the duke of Newcastle; Gladstone, though no longer a trustee of the Newcastle estate, was attempting to arrange a better settlement for her; see letter of 19 February 1881.

10 Downing Street.
19 February 1881.

I return Lady S.s letter—I regret that she has had no positive intimation, but there is really no connection whatever between the agreement subscribed & the proposed grant from the Newcastle Funds.

There is no *hitch* that I know of as to this grant and no cause for anxiety, as I believe. For I do not think Mrs Hope is a woman to recede from her word.

I am glad to think the soldiers wound is not serious.

God grant that business may soon be over. It is serious, but *ought* speedily to end.

I groan over the accomplishment of the horrid marriage.

Glad to hear that you have no difficulties as to cottage expenditure.

Off to Brighton today. God be with you   WEG

Hawarden Castle.
13 September 1881.

Both your notes have arrived this morning, and I must not lose any time in answering about H. Clinton. I cannot doubt you will see it would be useless, were it possible, for me to interfere between him and his brother.[1] Had I some sources of knowledge open to me which were not open to his brother the case would be different. But I have none—all or mainly all that I have heard about him has been learned from Mr Ouvry and Lord E.C. is now in the position I formerly held,[2] & something more. The case would be that of an ignorant person undertaking to advise one more instructed.

As to Friday night I hope you will tell me the joke, that I may share the amusement: I was going to add 'and *then* I will tell you what I did after dinner'. But I will be more generous and without waiting for the joke tell you that I went about the business for which you kindly gave me a Bank note, and that I *hope* it will be satisfactorily disposed of.

The troubles in Egypt are perplexing enough.

I hope you will take the best advice about your ailments, and reap the profit of it in restoration to full strength

All good be with you. Ever your faithful   WEG

10 Downing Street.
9 November 1881.

I came to town yesterday afternoon and was so sorry to find on going to G. Square that you had been tediously and painfully ill—Mr Thistlethwayte however gave me an improved account for the day, and as soon as I may be able

---

[1] Further difficulties among Newcastle's children.
[2] As trustee of the Newcastle Estate.

I hope to receive personally in confirmation of this at your door or perhaps from your mouth.

Things have gone better in Ireland than when I was last here I ventured to expect—And in most quarters they are easier—thank God.

My wife, who suffered much in the summer from loss of sleep, has I am glad to say recovered the faculty. She is going with me today to the Lord Mayor's dinner. I have some idea I may get away on Saturday.

When we meet you will tell me all you heard of the case in S. Kensington[1] as to which you are curious—I think it will probably prove to have reference to the case for which you kindly gave me £5. I am not yet able to report to you the upshot.

All blessings to you & speedy recovery   WEG

Hawarden Castle.
4 January 1882.

It was a great pleasure to receive the letter which Lady Susan wrote assuring me of your great improvement. Tomorrow evening I go up to London and I hope that I may find & see for myself that the improvement has continued, & has ended in convalescence.

Lady Susan told me she was not to stay into January, and I dare say you will miss her much. I should think she must be a most available & kind nurse.

You have undergone long privation in the stoppage of your usual habits, & the cottage will scarcely know you again.

Your friends were I think much concerned to see once more a case in the newspapers about furniture: I am sure you will understand my hoping it will be the last. ⟨These things attract much, & much ill-natured attention⟩ I wonder if you have read the account of this horrible and loathsome assault in Derbyshire—Irish crime is nothing to it.

And I am glad & thankful to say that Irish crime is somewhat diminishing.

I hope to call on Saturday, before or after Cabinet.

God be with you   Yours ever   WEGladstone

Hawarden Castle.
14 April 1882.

Indeed I was glad to see your handwriting, the sign of progress at least towards recovery, from your long and I fear painful ailments. May further progress be rapid and uninterrupted.

From what you say I fear you are rather forced out of Grosvenor Square. Perhaps the change of air may be very good for you, and in that case it is not to be regretted. Where do you go? If I am able to call soon after my return—which stands for Monday shall I have a chance of seeing you?

---

[1] Rescue work.

If you happen to write to Mr Villiers pray tell him how gallant I thought he was in coming down to vote for us on that late night before we adjourned.

You have lost much of a delightful season: the only really delightful early months of the year, thus far, that I distinctly remember.

I hope, and feel sure, that your 'deep thought' on Lander's life was not on the whole displeasing.

Thanks for Arnold—I have read his Essays[1]—those on Ireland are strange, and not very helpful.

The sky beyond the water is still dark, but the Land Act is working powerfully for good. The session has been stormy thus far, and very laborious—I think it will thus continue, but the Almighty will I trust vouchsafe to prosper our handiwork.

May he be with you in all things   WEG

10 Downing Street.
21 April 1882.

I am truly glad you are relieved from compulsory migration now to the Cottage.

But it has chanced at an odd moment—I am under a continued prohibition & permission which never came upon me before—Dr Clark allows me to go out but forbids me to speak—unless under necessity. He says I may be free by Monday. But next week is a very busy one with the marriage festivities at Windsor in the midst.

Many thanks for the Merimée letters—he was a finished literary man; but he does not so much command my liking now that I read him in full, as he did in the lighter intercourse of society.

Have you read Miss Fox's Journal.[2] It is very interesting & she was a good woman, a Quakeress, refined, & not extreme.

Outrages continue sad in Ireland: but the No Rent movement as such, is in a great degree defeated.

I hope air & exercise will now bring & keep you in full health.

All blessings   Yours   WEG

It may be a week before I can call. Thanks for the account of the family with its fine old Norse name.

10 Downing Street.
3 May 1882.

I am drowned in affairs and hardly know which way to turn: but you know I always receive advice with thankfulness.

---

[1] Matthew Arnold, *Irish essays and others* (1882); see 5 Apr. 82.
[2] See 24 Mar. 82.

The Irish affair, what is done, or what is left undone, is & must be hazardous.[1] But there are more and more genial days on the horizon than I have seen for a good while.

We cannot at present make known all we know: a few weeks, say May & June, will probably make all clear, for us or against us. I am extremely glad to hear about Kinnaird: pray remember me kindly to him & say that only want of time prevents my going to see him. Reconciliations are delightful, before God & man.

Ever yours   WEG

10 Downing Street.
9 May 1882.

Again I have to thank you for your kind & warm sympathy.

I return Mr Villiers' inclosure. His interpretation is not I think the true one. He had perhaps read the article in the Times of yesterday,[2] which I not only think most perverse, but I am tempted to call fiendish or diabolical. I believe the crime to have been the act of men who say their craft was in danger from the work of reconciliation, and were resolved to stop it by stirring up such vindictive passions against the people of Ireland as found vent in the Times.

We go down tomorrow to the funeral—to be back probably on Friday.

You can hardly conceive how pure & noble a life has fallen in F. Cavendish. His wife was worthy of him and 'in the great waterflood they shall not come nigh her'.

I hope you keep your recovered strength and have recovered more, and are now in full enjoyment of this delicious year which God has so far vouchsafed to us.

May he have you, as the French say, in His holy keeping   WEG

10 Downing Street.
22 July 1882.

Thanks for your kind notification & offer of hospitality—But I am tied fast hand & foot & my wife's solicitude carries me off into country on each Saturday as it comes round. I had hoped to present myself for luncheon day [*sic*] but every prospect gradually melted away. We are in the very thickest of the Egyptian question and are taking all the most decisive resolutions.

It is always sad to use or contemplate force but in this case there is every consolation which the case admits of.

When matters are a little easier rely on hearing from me—I do not feel sure whether you have really recovered and wholly: & I shall be glad to know Benedictus benedicat   Yours   WEG

---

[1] The 'Kilmainham Treaty' episode; Forster resigned on 2 May as British Secretary.
[2] On the Phoenix Park murders.

10 Downing Street.
4 August 1882.

So glad you have had a good journey—thanks for letting me know. I hope that what remains may be equally propitious.

And your letter is as always kind—But there are parts of it that are, as it were, Hebrew & Sanscrit to me—your pain at not being remembered when all alone 'at the end of last season' What does it mean?

I have no doubt that I am very deficient, & much to be found fault with, for not exhibiting towards you sufficient *marks* of remembrance: but unfortunately, mark my words, I have hardly a friend, or relative, or member of my own family, who could not show that towards each of them I am ten times as bad.

I do not think I have been able to convey to your mind the belief that I am really an absorbed & occupied man and that as two blades of grass cannot grow in the place made for one so it is not possible for a man in my position to be like one who has not its duties & cares—I am concerned at all this because I feel (& have often said) that it must become aggravated as I grow older, less able for work, & more irresistibly inclined to seek the rest which befits old age and its relation to the unseen future.

Interpret all this kindly & indulgently, & may all good & all joy be with you
    WEG

10 Downing Street.
14 August 1882.

I am so glad to hear that you have arrived safely and your reception—I do not wonder that the people remember your kind deeds & words.

You take my gruff (a Lancashire word) expostulation and compare me with that most note-worthy person Mr C. Villiers. I do not & cannot hope to have at his time of life his marvellous life, animation, quickness & general as well as sarcastic turn. But what I have not yet made sufficiently clear to you is that, as he had laid out his future for himself, so have I mine. What he looks to is (I think) continuance as & where he is, for the remaining fraction of life. What I look to is withdrawal, detachment, recollection. So soon as the special calls that chain me to the oar of public duty, are sufficiently relaxed, I look to removal not from office only but from London, & to a new or renewed set of employments wholly different from those I now pursue.

Not all this change at once, but by two stages.

See what is written in the Book—if I live.

Wherever & whenever, there is one think [*sc.* thing] I cannot move away from, the remembrance of your reliance & all your kindness. But on the other hand I ask myself what have I been to you? I am obliged to answer that as a friend I have been to you poor, barren, valueless.

Perhaps some day when you return we may find an opportunity to talk this out.

May a little Friend, the best of Friends, be always with you to teach & train & bless   WEG

Thanks once & again about the grouse. Movements absolutely uncertain after Thursday for say 10 or 12 days when I hope the anchorage will be at Hawarden.

Hawarden Castle.
9 September 1882.

I am shocked to find that the kind gift of grouse had never been acknowledged. It arrived duly & we ate it. There was a misapprehension between my wife & me: I thought she would charge one of the P. Secretaries, & she thought I was to write. Pray accept thanks even though late.

I have read Lady Susan's letter with great interest & I sympathize with her entirely about the Hamilton Tale. Poor soul she takes an indulgent view, I am afraid over-indulgent, of her son Albert's trouble.[1]

I cannot be surprised at your lengthening your stay in the Highlands and I hope you will profit much by the change and find it conducive to the solid & complete re-establishment of your health.

On Wednesday I must be in town for a cabinet but I hope to get back here Thursday or Friday.

In Ireland things pretty steadily improve. The harvest weather supplies another cause for thankfulness. A third is to be found in the success thus far of every operation in Egypt and in the admirable manner in which they have been conducted. We ought I think to have had a prayer in the Churches, but the Archbishop's illness has been an impediment. We must not presume on the future: but we have every ground for buoyant hope. And our ends are good: peace, justice, freedom.

I think it is easy to give a good & appropriate meaning to the words of your waking & may God prosper you   WEG

Hawarden Castle.
20 September 1882.

Thanks for your letter of the 18th. I do not know who is meant by Mr V. You certainly do not mean the only Mr V.[2] who occurs to my mind. You may be assured that so far as I am concerned my effort will be to work the Egyptian question for Egypt and in an Egyptian sense eschewing on the right & left the multitude of selfish schemes that are in the air.

You will have seen the accounts of the deaths in the papers, but you will not have known how near one of these comes home to me. The Dean of Windsor was one of my very oldest and dearest friends. Near sixty years! and the last twenty years of the very closest intercourse. He was also one of the Queen's dearest friends; and in my public capacity I suffer with his death an

---

[1] A transvestite.   [2] i.e. C. P. Villiers.

incomparable loss. I leave home early tomorrow to attend Dr Pusey's funeral at Oxford, and on Saturday the Dean's at Strathfieldsaye.

Everyone seems, over Dr Pusey's grave, laudably to forget the controversies with which his name has been associated.

I hope to return home in the course of Saturday night—and I am sorry that this time also I shall have no opportunity of seeing with my own eyes that re-establishment of your health which I trust the Scotch visit has completed.

God be with you   WEG

House of Commons.
Friday 27 October 1882.

Many thanks for the interesting letter of Lady Susan. Especially I read with interest the part about the Newcastle children. I return it and together with it an old one which I have kept by some mistake.

You have evidently been most kind to her and she is grateful in proportion.

Yes, last Friday, this day week, I was without engagement after dinner & on a sign from you I could have staid longer—But I am now almost drowned in business, the weight of the H. of Commons engagements being particularly great under the present plans of business.

However I hope to call upon you either tomorrow at any rate not later than Monday.

All good & joy be with you   WEG

Cannes.
23 February 1883.

I am very much concerned to hear of the illness of your Husband, and while I hope that your natural anxiety may have contributed somewhat to darken the colour of your report, I earnestly trust that what appears to be so grave an attack may soon be overcome, and may leave no trace behind it, either upon him, or upon you.

The time has come when duty calls me away from this very remarkable place, which at once restored my shattered sleeping power, and removed the sense of brain-weakness that I had felt so much in England—I have never at any time when in office, perhaps hardly when out of it, had a period of such indulgence, but it seemed to be called for by the case, for I could not go on.

Next week I hope to arrive in London and again try my recovered strength.

On Tuesday & Wednesday I expect to be at the British Embassy, Paris.

Your note about Lady Susan O[pdebeck] was recovered from Nice; but I have not thought it desirable to go to Monte Carlo for reasons which I will explain when we meet.

You observe that you have not heard from me: this reminds me of many offences some of them worse—I have five children in England and until yesterday had only written to one of them, and that on business. Such is my life—Let

me end by repeating the earnest wish with which I began: & may all good be
with you   WEG

10 Downing Street.
9 June 1883.

I am heartily glad to hear that your wishes are fully accomplished about
your Cottage through the kindness of Mr Thistlethwayte, & it is pleasant too
that this should have happened at the season of the year when you will most
enjoy it.

I hope some day to become better acquainted with its attractions—as you
have so kindly wished, but my work is very heavy & naturally I feel it more.

You will have seen in the papers an account of my doings at Stafford House.[1]
The Duke [of Sutherland] is very kind to me, and I think some barrier, that had
got in the way between us, seems to be removed.

God be with you now & ever   WEG

10 Downing Street.
19 August 1883.

For one that breathes metropolitan and Parliamentary air it is still refreshing
to hear that his friends are better off and I can well believe you are enjoying, &
hope you ⟨you⟩ will heartily & fully enjoy, hill lake & wood in your beautiful
country.

The House of Commons has sat near 70 hours in the last six days. Think of
that, if indeed you can realise such a horrible conception.

However I hope to escape on Saturday—my wife is already gone.

I fear there is no likelihood while the yoke of office continues to be upon me,
of my visiting the Forest, as you so kindly invite me.

We are very desirous to make a trip this year into Eastern Scotland but I am
not sure that it will be accomplished as the time will be so short before we may
have to meet in Cabinet again.

Better I hope is the chance of seeing you in G. Square or in the Cottage. This
week might have afforded one but you have taken wing.

The Irish are wofully ferocious. Much allowance should be made for them;
but after making it there is I fear a great deal to lament & condemn.

Pray remember me kindly to Miss Ponsonby and Mr T.; and try to understand (I admit it is difficult) my position & appearances of unkindness, nay in
many cases the lack of duty which it entails.

God be with you   WEG

[1] See 2 June 83: Gladstone's speech there at the Garibaldian Commemoration.

Hawarden Castle.
6 September 1883.

Thanks upon thanks for your most beautiful gift of grouse. Some we hope to eat here and some on board the 'Pembroke Castle' Steamer, in which we hope to start for a week's trip on Saturday next. The weather has not been all we could wish but the glass at present moves upwards.

How very awful are the physical convulsions passing over the globe; storm, earthquakes and volcano, seven plagues sent to work mysteriously the purposes of the Almighty. I suppose the calamity in Java and Sumatra to pass almost any thing upon record. And how foolish are the French adding to these natural convulsions troubles made at the hand of man. Their enemies must rejoice to look at Madagascar and Tonkin. It begins to look as if Mr Shaw[1] had been very harshly & unjustly treated but I am of course specially bound to suspend my judgment until full information arrives.

Was not Miss Ponsonby right in going to the Consecration? Were not Timothy and Titus, and even Samuel and Barnabas, made by man in addition to their inward call.

I hope you are enjoying hills & breezes & if I am called to town I shall also find you there. Meantime may all good be with you & please carry on my hearty thanks to Mr T. and give kind remembrances to Miss Ponsonby

Ever yours   WEG

Hawarden Castle.
6 October 1883.

I thank you for announcing your arrival and hope I may congratulate you both on a good journey, and upon a new access of health and vigour from your stay in the North.

Let me also thank you for a new arrival here of a haunch of red-deer venison, the best of all when skilfully handled as it is by Mr Thistlethwayte. I have no doubt my acknowledgements are due to both.

Under the rather ambiguous title of "only a girl"[2] I have been reading a book which seems to me beautiful. It is adapted from the French. The character of the girl is one which through faith courage and love exhibits in a singular degree the Image of our Lord.

Pray read it & let me know what you think of it. A copy will I hope reach you from me in a day or two.

God be with you   WEG

From Monday to Friday I expect to be about, at Knowsley. I may be in town for a day soon—but am quite uncertain.

[1] British missionary arrested by the French; see 22 Oct. 83n.
[2] By C. Clayton (1883); see 29 Sept. 83.

Hawarden Castle.
30 December 1883.

As your kind congratulations reach me, I am on the point of starting for London, when I may thank you *vocally*, and where I should have been happy to dine with you in G. Square had you been there.

I expect to be at Euston 2.45 PM and in D. St 3.15.

Be assured that I value truly and highly the many prayers which have ascended and do ascend for me, and rejoice that you think of me in that happy form, in which we all, poor mortals can do nothing but good to one another.

If you liked to have me to dinner I should ask you to drive down to my garden door in the Park (close by Treasury passage) at 7.30, and carry me. But I shall not expect it.[1]

God be with you   WEG

10 Downing Street.
7 May 1884.

These are interesting letters, so I think it best to return them, & with them many thanks for your renewed offer of hospitality at the Cottage, which rely on it I shall bear in mind, but as to the time I fear I can say nothing for the pressure of business on me is extreme, especially at my age, and I am for the present a slave, hardly able to find a moment to write these hurried lines.

God be with you in all things   WEG

Hawarden Castle.
17 August 1884.

Your bounteous boon of birds has arrived in due course, all I believe in good condition & they are in process of being rapidly devoured with much appreciation—

You are I hope enjoying to the full both weather and scenery.

What hearty heartiest thanksgivings ought this year to be offered up.

I have also to be thankful for deliverance from I think the most worrying session of Parliament I have known.

Two months appear and are a Liberal holiday: but it is formidably broken by the manifestation I have to make a fortnight hence in Midlothian. We start on Wednesday week.

Beyond that anything I do in Scotland must be very brief, and for health only, almost exclusively in that wonderful health-giving country on Deeside.

Your invitation is most kind but we must not think of going to the West: indeed open doors in the East will have to be churlishly passed by. I do not expect to go to Taymouth.

[1] Gladstone dined 'with Mr & Mrs Thistlethwayte at their "Cottage"' on 1 Jan. 84.

Be assured your counsels, or rebukes as they may be, about Egypt are always welcome; but you do not seem to me aware of all the difficulties of the case.

May all good attend you   WEG

Hawarden Castle.
29 September 1884.

Now I have finished my noisy journey—Is your quiet trip to Scotland also at an end and have you resumed your place in Grosvenor Square, all the better and stronger I hope for the fresh air

I had fresh and wonderful experience of the depth and fervour of the Scottish character—exceeding even what I have seen before.

It is not improbable that I may have a forced run to London this week or next. But I know nothing yet, except that Fate chains me to London in the week beginning Oct 19.

Have you seen the Biography of a remarkable woman, Eliza Fletcher, attached though of English birth to the Free Church of Scotland.[1] If not may I send it you.

I am hoarse as a crow but in other respects thank God wonderfully well.

I saw Kinnaird at his beautiful place:[2] he was in no way ill, but he looked and moved as an old man.

Wishing you all blessings   Ever yours   WEG

Hawarden Castle.
20 December 1884.

Do you remember my obtaining a £5 note from your kindness some few years back, to help an effort for reclaiming a damsel gone astray? I gave it, with other money from myself, and I believe it was chiefly employed in redeeming articles of dress from pawn, but, as to the main object it appeared to fail. However I have this morning received the inclosed letter,[3] which I think you will read with pleasure. It had sometimes seemed to me that I ought to return the £5, but I thought you would not take it back, and now I think you will regard it as well spent.

I remember she described herself as a Roman Catholic, & that matter I did not attempt to touch.

Many thanks for the fish, announced in your last, & found here.

And all good wishes for the coming Xmas and New Year   WEG

---

[1] E. Fletcher, *Autobiography of Mrs. Fletcher of Edinburgh* (1874); see 7 Sept. 84.
[2] See 23 Sept. 84.
[3] From Mrs. K. Hollins, the redeemed rescue case; see 20 Dec. 84n.

Hawarden Castle.
10 January 1885.

Your most kind note arrived this morning.

I entirely understood your silence. The birthday work was somewhat over-whelming—a thousand *extra* letters telegrams & packets: yet all so kind, some very touching.

I expect to be in town tomorrow for the House on Tuesday at two.

Should all go off easily I might be able to call for a cup of tea at five: if not, I hope to try Wednesday at two, or failing this at five, as I may find myself free.

May God be with you (nor was the need ever greater for us all)   WEG

10 Downing Street.
26 February 1885.

Do not I live in a glass house?

Am I to give an account of my dining with Mrs L. Ellis?[1]

I have dined with her *twice* in my life.

The invitation was sent 2 months before!

Accepted when I expected easy times, before Fagnay[?] came upon the stage.

At her table I had met persons useful for me to see, & whom I had little chance of seeing elsewhere.

Such is my case.

Finally, my wife was away.

Parlt. & business absorb my time & I must think of the evenings. But should I see a vacant opportunity I will use the freedom you give.

Many thanks for Rawlinson. He is a sound able learned man, & his subject of deep interest.

I return the account you sent me.

Those who would purge the Govt. wish above all (see P.M. Gazette) to purge *me* out of it.

What a favour they would do my 75 years!

All good be with you   WEG

10 Downing Street.
20 June 1885.

Be assured that I will not fail to try and see you when first there shall appear to be an opening. At present it is an incessant whirl and so it has been all week. Now I am going to change the air for Sunday but I may be dragged back here even tomorrow.

---

[1] Apparently a protest from Mrs. Thistlethwayte at Gladstone's dining with Mrs. L. Ellis (see 16 Feb. 85: Mrs. Gladstone had gone to Hawarden that day) rather than herself. It was probably at Mrs. Ellis's that he met Lillie Langtry.

I was so glad to hear of your having settled matters with Mr Geflowski. They looked very disagreeable at the time when you reported them to me.

Thanks for your kind words about the title. I speak not for others but undoubtedly I am much better without it. No coronet will ever grace my head.

And again for your offer of quarters. But we have accepted a friendly proposal to go to the house of Mr Currie close by in Richmond Terrace as a situation most convenient for Parliament.

God be with you   WEG

                                        Dollis Hill, Kilburn.
                                        1 July 1885.

Both the books which I owe to your thoughtful kindness have arrived, and I have read through Marino Faliero.[1] It is I think a work of great power: dramatic power, power of thought, and wonderful mastery over the English language, not to mention the hymnody in Latin which is memorable. I did not fail to notice your marks. One could wish the book were more clear on the great matter of belief.

I received the question raised by your previous note about Ld Breadalbane, as one easier to speak than write about. What you say must evidently refer to some matters unknown to me as I could [not?]in any way interpret it.

The advancement to a marquisate was given, after the usual consultation with political friends for political service, and so far as I know that grand old Lady E. Pringle would have been likely to approve it.

The singularly changeful weather has I fear tried you in point of health but you are as I trust enjoying this beautiful day. May you enjoy with it all other blessings   WEG

                                        1 Richmond Terrace, Whitehall.
                                        15 July 1885.

I had been looking forward to a visit to G. Square but yesterday a little blow fell upon me. My voice has long been ailing, and my throat was carefully examined. The result was that I am forbidden public speech, and conjoined to confine any private conversation within the limits of absolute necessity. This rule observed, there comes regular treatment of the throat: and when this has been gone through it is hoped that a sea-voyage may restore me to the full or at least moderate use of my voice.

This is an inconvenience which I ought patiently and thankfully to bear, for how little of trial of this kind has been laid upon me. It is merely local and in no degree interferes with the general health. And now I have done with this egotism; but you will see that it stops me from visiting for conversation.

The trip to the cottage was you will remember completely unfortunately

[1] Swinburne's tragedy, sent by Mrs. Thistlethwayte on 25 June 85.

thrown out—now I dare not project anything of this kind. I can only hope you are well, & that you may have the society of friends not like me dumb for the time. Even the marriage at Osborne next week I have been obliged to excuse myself from attending.

I have been reading the memoirs of Beau Brummel,[1] a most humbling and therefore most edifying book: it teaches well 'to lift up our eyes unto the hills, from whence cometh our help'.

All blessings be with you   WEG

1 Richmond Terrace, Whitehall.
21 July 1885.

Last Wednesday I wrote a letter to you to explain that I was put under orders not only not to speak in the House of Commons but to avoid even in private all conversation that can be avoided—on this account I have not called. The affection of my throat and voice is entirely local, without pain, & having no connection with general health: but it has from necessity been much too long neglected and the matter has become urgent if I am to look to the recovery of the organ. My needs go much I believe beyond the aureoniophone which Mr T. so kindly presented to me. I am now under daily treatment by medicine & by interior applications to the vocal chords as well as by galvanism outside.

What a long story, some of it repetition, but a kind note received from you gave me the idea that perhaps you had not received my prior letter. Let me repeat my hope that you have quite recovered & that all your friends as well as yourself are well though I dare not speak about calling for my visitings are for the time at an end except in case of necessary business & that confined within the narrowest limits.

All good in all ways be with you.   WEG

1 Richmond Terrace, Whitehall.
24 July 1885.

The memoirs of Beau Brummel were written by Captain Jesse and published by Saunders & Otley in 1844 [overwritten]

I hope you will not be disappointed in the book. You may find it not easy to procure. The copy I read was not my own. I suppose it can only be had second hand. You might try Westell in New Oxford Street who has a very large stock.

You have spoken out right honestly when you say that I never had true and manly courage. I believe this is not the common opinion: but I think there is a great deal of truth in it. As to physical courage in particular I have always thought it. You would however please me still better, if you would take the pains to set out the particulars of speech and conduct on which your opinion is founded.

[1] See 24 May 44, 27 June 85.

The genial airs will I hope bring you all that may yet be needed for your health.

The doctors have made some progress with my throat and I am studying how best to dispose of the remainder of the summer with a view to a cure. All blessings be with you. Miss Ponsonby most kindly invited me to dine on Monday but a party had already been made to take me to the 'Inventions' on that evening. Yours always WEG

London.
31 July 1885.

Your remark about 20 years reminds me of much. How little have I used those 20 years in friendly office. They have been marked by your confidences & kindness, on my side how near are they to a blank so far as regards any return that might have been worth remembering for good. I am old & the old have a great responsibility in all their intercourse with others. When we meet I do not so much recollect this as I ought and the minutes pass in conversation that does not leave a mark behind. I had always hoped to be of some use, but I am afraid even your charity & kindness can hardly think the hope has been fulfilled.

I visit the throat doctor daily and this is to continue without change for another week (the third) when I expect probably to go to sea in Thomas Brassey's yacht and to try the Norwegian coast—I have been acting on the idea that the recovery of my voice is now my prime duty; for I have the prospect of abundant sea-sickness unless the weather prove very fine.

And it is a blessing to see every thing at present looking so well for the harvest.

After I leave London say 7th or 8th any correspondence will pretty well stop and as to 99/100 of it this will be a great relief.

Forgive an egotistical letter & let it close with wishing you all manner of good in & from your northward trip. I address this to Grosvenor Square for certainty. Ever yours WEG

1 Richmond Terrace, Whitehall.
3 August 1885.

I have had the most afflicting letter from Lady S. Opdeboerk [sc. Opdebeck] who describes her own pecuniary distress, & that of her husband (combined with his long illness) as extreme. She asks me to appeal to any rich friends on her behalf. She speaks of having written to you, whose kindness she remembers, but of not yet having had a reply.

Can you tell me any thing which can throw light upon this sad case.

I cannot dismiss the recollection of her as she was 50 years back one of the brightest among stars of youthful grace & beauty.

In much haste Ever yours WEG

Hawarden Castle.
17 September 1885.

This morning I had asked myself 'can I write to Kinloch Lodge today' when lo your letter appeared. I return the inclosure: and will begin with Lady Susan. She is just come: & is at Holloways Hotel. I wrote to her yesterday to tell her I should be most ready to do my best, if invited, & had made this known. But I dare not yet act uninvited. It might possibly or probably, be most injurious to her interests with the young Duke, on whom *everything* will now absolutely depend.

The Norway cruise was, in many points delightful, and certainly interesting. It has materially helped my voice and throat: but I still have to be very reserved in the use of them.

Since my return home last week I have been absorbed in the difficult and anxious business of writing an Address, which amounts to a short pamphlet.

Now I hope for a little remission and must turn for a few days to personal & domestic affairs which, for five or six years, have been of necessity utterly neglected.

I had an interesting note from you before leaving England. You and I have each a favourite or usual phrase. You do not admit mine—I have not yet got at the sense of yours nor can I understand in any way 'made me a woman'. You will take pity & some day tell me. Nor can I think my wife has in any way been open to blame regarding you, though I may have cause to blame myself for being so barren towards you after all your confidence.

I think I can understand what you said of spirit & courage, and find no fault. I note your expectation of return. Should I come to London for medical advice, you will hear of me. Meantime 'good bye' that is as you know God be with you
                                                                    WEG

Hawarden Castle.
23 October 1885.

I postponed my reply to your hospitable note because I had written to Sir A. Clark to know whether he advised me to run up to London for the purpose of having my throat & voice examined, and I expected by each post an answer. It has not come.

So I will not any longer delay sending a line to thank you & to say you shall hear forthwith in case I come.

The expectation is that we shall go to Scotland *about* the 6th for the Election & that Parliament will be dissolved about the 17th. All our people expect a large Liberal majority. The other side limit themselves to a hope that by steady aid from the Parnellites they may possibly have strength enough to get in. Not a very honourable prospect.

My throat and voice are certainly much better & should be equal to a little speaking when the time comes.

It is a sad disappointment to me not *now* to make a total, and final retirement after my 53 years of labour.

How did you speed in Scotland?

Your health? your employments? What are you about in London? What intelligence do you hear? How are the town-keeping friends? How is the cottage?

Any progress about your Church there?

All blessings be with you WEG

The answer has come: I may perhaps come up for a night on Wednesday: shall if so be heard of at Lady F. Cavendish's Carlton H. Terrace.

Hawarden Castle.
8 November 1885.

The walnuts have been fully tested, and are unanimously declared by all the consumers to be superlative.

I had sight of Caroline Bauer's book, I think in your house—If you send Vol III, it will be very kind: let it be when you have done with it. The work has not been confuted as it concerns King Leopold—It is probably right that it should be published.

Tomorrow morning early we start for Midlothian, that I may take another plunge, my last plunge, into the billows.

My address is Dalmeny Park Edinburgh.

I am sorry for Lady Susan but you have done all you can.

God be with you WEG

Hawarden Castle.
5 December 1885.

How kind of Mr T. to offer the present. I cannot refuse.

Thanks for your tidings about Mr Villiers.

The course of the Elections has been wonderful—It seems that if we do not top the combined army, we must come near it.

I trust you are well & pray God bless you.

London.
29 January 1886.

Your most kind letter & the parcels have reached me in the midst of the most absorbing anxieties from which I cannot divert my mind for a moment: you will therefore I am sure give me a little time & I will either write or call as soon as I can obtain the least freedom. But pray recollect that the overflow of bounty does constitute a real difficulty to the most grateful.

God be with you WEG

Hawarden Castle.
28 April 1886.

As friend and visitor I am indeed very bad, as others beside you could tell, and must grow worse, for old age has brought me mercy and discipline in the shape not of rest and of care, but of augmented care & labour with diminishing strength for them.

What I covet now is the prayer of all for the work placed in my unworthy hands.

I remember your kind promise about helping my wife's work. Next quarter will I have no doubt do very well.

I have got & read the book you name & kindly offer.[1] It seemed to me to be a pure romance ⟨of⟩ for which occasion was taken from certain facts. The character of the lady is commonly stated & estimated in a very different way.

Redesdale's fine contribution makes a Good fight so does that of my brother Sir Thomas, who was next above him in the school at Eton.

But we all march in one way, and we three must be near the march's end.

A sad tragedy, in which we have a deep interest happened in Brook Street last Friday: the death of Mrs Alfred Lyttelton, a noteworthy person, at 23.

I have been reading an admirable & delightful book, the Life of Mr Bazely[2] which I hope to send you in a few days. Pray read & inwardly digest it. It is very lofty & makes me sorely ashamed.

All good attend you   WEG

10 Downing Street.
21 July 1886.

A thousand thanks from my wife for your most handsome donation.

Were I to tell you a little of the establishments it will help to support I think you would be interested.

I wish you had told me at the time of the words reported to have been used—I should have liked, & should even more like, to be authorised to ask her about them. I have a strong belief it was a fiction or a *great* exaggeration.

The parcel which you would have me take has come with the money.

Well as to authentic news? We have resigned.

Salisbury has been sent for.

And is expected in London on Friday.

Do not yet believe any thing else.

And may all good be with you   WEG

21 Carlton House Terrace.
21 August 1886.

The grouse came in good order, & was excellent. Very many thanks.

I return your inclosures.

[1] Perhaps 'Connie', Edith Coppleston (1886); see 21 Apr. 86.
[2] See 23 Apr. 86.

On or about Wednesday I hope to go abroad, with my friend Lord Acton, for a short time.

Your account of Mr B. Hamilton's intentions pleases me. I hope he will find it practicable to execute them. But I have some fear that he has to deal with help from a variety of quarters.

I regret also to be under the impression that poor [J. R.] Herbert's circumstances are *bad*. I do not know any particulars.

Have you heard that C. Villiers has declared himself against us on the Irish question? So I am informed, & am much concerned at it. There is but one end to that matter. If what we ask is refused, more will have to be given.

I have the paper to which you refer carefully stored away & I have no doubt it can be got at when required.

I hope you enjoy your Highlands, & pray all good may be with you WEG

Hawarden Castle.
5 October 1886.[1]

Again Mr Thistlethwayte's kindness sent us a superlative haunch, and its arrival was most opportune. It was served up yesterday at a luncheon to the Irish deputations of which you will find an account in the papers. There were between fifty & sixty at luncheon, and the haunch was a great circumstance.

You were if my memory (too often treacherous) does not deceive me to be in London before this time and I address you there, sincerely hoping that you have had much good from the Highland air and climate. When I was in London at your door they could not tell me anything.

My short excursion to Germany was of great use. It broke the flood of correspondence, and it took me for a time entirely out of the atmosphere of contention and suspicion, for which I got in exchange free & harmonious conversation with friends on subjects of deep interest.

We have had however a great anxiety in the illness of my daughter Mrs Drew. Just during the last days of my trip to Germany and the journey home, it was a great alarm & a case of extreme danger connected with a miscarriage and requiring the presence of a highly skilled expert from London. Thanks to the mercy of God, we are bidden no longer to fear any fatal issue, but are also warned that a good deal of time may yet elapse before her restoration to health & strength.

I should be very glad if you could tell me any thing of the political intentions of Mr [C. P.] Villiers. He is one of those whom I should expect to look well into the future, though like me he cannot expect to make much of it. May all blessings, all good, be with you   WEG

---

[1] Letter wrongly placed in Lambeth MS 2764, f. 178.

Hawarden Castle.
18 October 1886.

I should have been glad to meet your kind wish but it was impossible. My daughter's case which at one time when I was abroad in Germany was of extreme danger continues to be one of gravity entailing anxiety though thank God we are assured that danger is not now in view. I should not think it right to leave my wife and house even for one evening's absence except for some very strong reason. We are still given to understand that some weeks may elapse without a great change. Sir A. Clark has been here twice and his kind interest in us may bring him yet again.

But you will gather around your hospitable table guests more suitable for the occasion than I at my age can well think myself to be. My birthdays are I hope acquiring, certainly they ought to acquire, a most sober hue. After a life of pressure and excitement such as mine I feel that much time is required for me to do the real work of my life, to acquire a true sense of sin in all its forms, and of the subtlety of its poison, and to follow with something like earnestness after the attainment of the image of Christ. Then I might hope with God's help to be an instrument of good to others also. The mere lifting off of the weight of public cares would be an immense thing for me for these & not private cares are what have habitually kept me down.

But this has become a most egotistical letter. I change my strain and wish you heartily every blessing which (say) St Paul would have wished for you, or which our Lord Himself can give. May your bounties return into your own bosom & may they be crowned and circled with every other gift   WEG

Hawarden Castle.
21 November 1886.

Indeed I have but little to say on the subject of Madame Novikoff. First that she is a very clever writer is beyond dispute. Secondly she makes a certain amount of impression in society, and is considered by some persons handsome, or fascinating, or both—I am not conscious of her being either. Whether she is kind & good all round I cannot say. But I have seen her perhaps a score of times and I never heard her say any thing rude, and I am astonished at her having said to you anything which could be taken to mean that you were the enemy of my wife, to whom you have always (I believe so lately as last July) been particularly kind: or the enemy of any one as I believe you live 'in charity with all men'.

Turning to a pleasant subject I send you the inclosed excellent letter which reached me this morning. I believe it is anonymous—Perhaps the writer did not know it would meet with my hearty acknowledgements.

You have not told me any thing about Mr Villiers: I take an interest in him & should like to know what is his tone. I am afraid you may not have any thing very favourable to report of Mr Herbert?

We have enjoyed a really beautiful November.

This is a day of blessing: may it & all blessings be yours   WEG

Hawarden Castle.
25 November 1886.

I am glad to hear of your expedition to Paris, & hope it will do you good.

The Hotel Bedford, two minutes from the Madeleine, is or was a few years back, excellent: quiet, clean, excellent kitchen, moderate charge.

Perhaps you will go to hear Pere Hyacinthe Loyson who is very eloquent, honest, poor.

I have heard no more of Madame N[ovikoff] nor am I likely. Sorry to read Miss Ponsonby's account of her behaviour.

I have nothing to ask you to undertake (at your kindly offer) but I should really like to hear about Mr Villiers views. He is an old & attached Liberal. He cannot view with satisfaction the present breach, & no attempt made to improve the state of things. Does not he agree that the Govt. ought at any rate to produce their plans?

When that is done, who knows but they may contain at any rate something useful & good.

Very likely you will let me know any thing learned tonight—or hereafter if he dine with you again, before he goes.

May all blessings go with you   WEG

Hawarden Castle.
16 January 1887.

I am glad you have been struck with that remarkable book Mehalah.[1] Not that I like the marriage or what follows: but it is a grand conception of a character.

I have read another tale, a short Irish one called Hurrish[2] which I think you would find very interesting.

We may perhaps talk of these in London whither I am once more, at any rate, to report for Parliamentary work, probably in nine or ten days.

I return Mr Grant's note. The purport of it does not surprise me: but I wish it were a little more definite upon the facts in Egypt where I really hope much has been done for the people, though in an irregular & most embarrassing & costly way.

Be assured I will understand you about my birthday. In truth the kindnesses I then receive have become extremely embarrassing—I am not out of the confusion it entailed. Many friends show their special friendship by their silence. Had I time & eyesight & brain, many of the manifestations are extremely touching.

I was rather waiting for you about your friend in Paris for I did not remember your naming her on any earlier occasion (perhaps my memory is at fault) & I did not happen to know anything of her. You have escaped probably cold more

[1] See 6 Dec. 86.
[2] See 23 Dec. 86.

severe than ours by not returning. I trust both you & Mr T. are well. Lieut. Bathurst has been writing to me recently about the Estate.

Wishing you every blessing   WEG

I had seen Rev Mr C.s tract

Dollis Hill.
21 May 1887.

Pressure this week beyond the common (in preparing an article on Mr Lecky's book) with attendance in H of C. & all the rest has kept me from answering.

My wife thanks you as I do for your kind proposal about luncheon: next week we break up but, after returning when Whitsun recess is over, we hope that you will give us a day for the purpose.

Pray do not speak or think about bequests. We shall have what God sends us.

He has sent a good deal of anxiety in the various branches of our family. Mrs Drew's was an anxious illness, of the most critical nature for near six months. Next came an equally critical illness of a nephew for three months—and now, a fortnight back, my eldest brother's only son, an officer in the Guards, is lying in his barracks at Windsor, with his life hanging on a thread. His mother attends him & his father at 82 remaining with one daughter in Scotland.

I greatly doubt the accuracy of the recital made to you, if it implies that my daughter said of you, or of anyone, what she ought not. I have noticed at various times that you have lent an ear (forgive me) to reports insufficiently attested & indirect. Do you know the game called Russian scandal? which shows convincingly how things get twisted in transmission.

I hope Mr Villiers is well: am glad that he has had no part in this wretched Bill, should have been much more glad had he joined in actively resisting it.

I thought that our Mrs Pever[1] had what seemed a Bible. You have been very kind. I gave Mr [Pever] Thomas à Kempis.

All good & blessings   WEG

The inclosed should have gone back before.

Dollis Hill, NW.
18 June 1887.

Since receiving your kind note I have wanted to propose something: and I now ask whether my wife and I may come to luncheon at your Cottage on Friday (2 PM)?

If you should be so good as to ask Mr Villiers I should be very glad.

It has occurred to me whether in your bounty you would think of purchasing

---

[1] A family in whose welfare Gladstone had become interested.

the two drawings of the young man of the roadside cottage? He would not want much for them I imagine.[1]

21 Carlton House Terrace.
5 August 1887.

We are I can assure you impressed with your cause for thankfulness and we join in it heartily. May all continue to go as you would wish.

I infer from your letter that there has been some altered and improved verdict from Sir W. Gull & your other medical advisers.

Pray let me know at Hawarden whether the good report remains fully sustained.

We go there tomorrow evening.

The elections in their present course are most significant. Not yet demonstrative but constantly coming near it.

All blessings go with you   WEG

Hawarden Castle.
9 Aug 1887.

My dear Mrs Thistlethwayte

Remembering the tone of anxiety in which you last wrote, I feel that there ought not, perhaps, to have been deep surprise, so mingled with pain in receiving the sad intelligence which we received this morning from Miss Ponsonby on your behalf.[2]

I knew there had been uneasiness, in one shape or another before, and it had passed by. I had not known any incident which pointed particularly to danger. And the escape from London, with the arrangements for companionship on the journey, all looked so bright and hopeful.

To his own Master each of us stands or falls, and assuredly he lived at all times, as it seemed, in the fullest consciousness beneath that Master's eye, Who is so loving and so wise, and Whose hand can alone support us in this dangerous life, or in the death valley beyond it, in the hour of death or in the day of judgment. Peace be with him, the peace of God & of Christ. To me his kindness & courtesy were extreme; he imagined I had done him service but I had done nothing beyond what the plainest duty required. And now he comparatively young is taken, while a piece of my pilgrimage yet remains, & with a heavy burden on it.

But I ought only to think of you, and of this great transition, of the transformation of life that must be before you. I have hope that some of your

---

[1] No signature. With this letter is a receipt in Gladstone's hand for £5 paid to G. Pever for his son's instruction in art.

[2] Death of A. F. Thistlethwayte on 7 August while cleaning his revolver; death notice in *The Times*, 10 August 1887, but no obituary or coroner's report found.

younger friends may gather around you, for in an hour when the smitten spirit cries out for rest, you will have much to do and to see done.

My anticipation, as well as wish for you is that so far as temporal affairs are concerned he will have left behind him everything straight—well adjusted and easy. He always seemed to be one who so well understood his concerns.

But in other respects it is a great unmooring of the vessel of your life to go forth upon an unknown sea—may its waves be ever calm, or its storms controuled and chained.

My view into the land beyond has but a short space to traverse, yours a long one—may all the vigilance, the prayer, the faith, the love, which at my age it seems so unnatural to come short in, be yours at once in abundance, and for us all may the great Physician

> Be of sin the double cure
> Cleanse us from its guilt and power.

My wife joins in all my feelings

I need not say how much any advice or aid of mine are now at your command, if there be occasion.

We are going to a *near* sea in Cheshire to get rid if possible of the remains of a sharp cold I had in London. Only a short delay by post. I will send the address

And once more may all things be with you, and the Presence which makes all griefs into blessings   Yours ever   WEG

Hawarden Castle.
3 September 1887.

My dear Mrs Th.

I left you yesterday week in your new & sorrowing state and I have not failed since to remember you at the times when friends can be best remembered. I feel you will have been much pressed and I sincerely wish it had been practicable for you to effect a change of air and scene: but I do not doubt you have constantly sought for strength where it is to be found; where I & those like me in age should have our minds perpetually fastened on the quest of it, but where all do so well to search and draw even when a long life's course still remains probably before them.

I need not say I was disappointed with Mr Villiers'[1] letter which I return. It completely dissipates every idea of his having leanings or even qualms in our favour. But I am glad you sent it as it enables me to say that there is not a shadow of foundation for his belief that anything has been done against him from London. It so happens that I had spoken about him to Mr A. Morley (in terms which I should not now be qualified in using) a few hours before your letter reached me, and had found him absolutely ignorant of any intended movement or disturbance at Wolverhampton.

---

[1] C. P. Villiers was in difficulty in his Wolverhampton constituency, which he was said not to have visited since 1846.

All accounts of you will be very welcome but I should not like to ask you for them as I am sure you have much on your hands. May they be held up from on high now & ever   WEG

I was very well pleased with the Huntingdonshire Election.

16 St James Street,
Buckingham Gate.
15 February 1888.

Are you obliged to conclude that those who do not write do not think of their friends?

If this be true I am indeed unhappy for I have scarcely a friend in the world to whom I am able to write.

I am altogether overwhelmed with work & must continue so for nearly a week but next week I hope you will hear of me. Meantime I will show your letter to my wife.

I had supposed you were abroad.

When we meet I shall be greatly interested to learn your progress—& most glad if I can in the least thing be useful.

Ever yours   WEG

The Durdans,
Epsom.
26 February 1888.

I think I can advise you about the investment which through my wife you have mentioned to me: but I should wish one of your relatives whom you trust to hear my recommendation & the reason of it. With this view, would you like us to dine with you on Saturday next, Mar. 3 at 8? If this be inconvenient, I could come (at one perhaps) to luncheon on Thursday. You will perhaps tell me then about the House, and all that concerns you. What I have to say on the invest-ment might require a quarter of an hour.

We return to J. St tomorrow forenoon. All good be with you.

I am sure you feel with & for the Crown Prince & his family

Ever yours   WEG

16 James Street.
12 April 1888.

I am very much vexed about your Rosslyn troubles, after you had virtually made them a present of from three to five hundred pounds.

The first time I had a house to let I did it myself and I lost many hundred pounds. The burnt child dreads the fire.

Let me advise you to act through a house agent even now and if you do not approve of mine (Grogan & Boyd) no doubt there are plenty of others.

The name of Lord Aberdeen's bailiff (so to call him) is Simson. My impression is that he is very good for anything about farm or garden. I suppose it is not for work about No 15 [Grosvenor Square] that you want him.

I do not know his precise relation to Lord Aberdeen, i.e. how far it is that of a servant. I advise that if you write to him you should say that as to anything you propose you rely upon *him* to be sure that it will cause Lord Aberdeen no inconvenience.

Pray consider what I said about the House Agent. If you have a good one it will save you much in money or trouble, probably in both.

We are well pleased with our little snuggery here but I do not enjoy the freedom which I had at Dollis Hill.

Wishing I could be of more use, & also heartily wishing you every blessing
Ever yours   WEG

Hawarden Castle.
Easter Tuesday, 23 April 1889.

I am very glad you have arranged the letting. I hope it is to your mind. I reckon the real cost of a house like No 15 [Grosvenor Square] at £2500 to £3000 a year: independently of any addition it may require to what would otherwise be your establishment.

I remember perfectly your making known to me your surmises and suspicions about the writer of the letters I had hoped to see: but I do not remember to have seen a confirmation of them by evidence. As you had spoken of sending them for perusal and destruction, and as I was here in Passion Week, I thought that those days when one's own sins come or ought to come especially into the mind's view would be the best time for my learning what has to be learned about the sins of another, or the appearances or suspicions of sin, as I should then be more on my guard against hasty and uncharitable judgment, well knowing that appearances are not always a safe guide, and also believing that acquaintance with the errors of others ought to have a humbling effect, and to throw one's self more & more into the mood of Saint Paul (with how much greater reason) who believed himself the chief of sinners.

The longer I live the more I am impressed with the idea that shallow & deficient *sense of sin* is the greatest danger of our time; it prevails of course in all ages among the careless and obstinate; it is the great snare, so far as I can see, of the sceptics of the present age: but it prevails also I fear among believing people and those who believe themselves to be endowed with high spiritual privilege. And I cannot but wish that sermons, and cutting sermons too, on this subject, were more frequent. At all events, without judging others I am very sure of this shallowness and deficiency in myself. Many thanks for your interesting account of Mr Villiers. I trust it may be more than verified. Wishing you All blessings of this season   Yours always   WEG

I find much beauty in the verses. Of course they are outside the subject of which I have written.

Hawarden Castle.
5 November 1889.

In truth I am indebted to hundreds, I might say thousands, & some of them
very near ones, for unanswered letters, but I do not think I have any such from
you.

I too feel an interest about the young Lord Russell[1] for his grandfather's sake
though I have never known him personally. I am told he is with the Liberals in
Politics, as I am certain the first Lord R. would have been.

Neither do I know Miss Scott.

You are I think most wise in wishing to sell your House. It is a capital one but
it requires a large fortune.

I sincerely hope you will make the Cottage healthy.

You say nothing of the plan you had formed of going abroad?

In the course of this month I hope to send you a copy of a most interesting
book which has a title not very interesting, 'Memoirs of a Southern Planter'.[2] It
is American & Murray is going to publish it here.

Do you know anything of Sir Wm. Gull? Of C. Villiers? Of poor Herbert
whose case I fear becomes a very sad one?

May the best blessings attend you   WEG

Hawarden Castle.
29 November 1889.

It was indeed most kind of you to forward to me the inclosed which is to me
matter of deep and touching interest.[3] Will you thank Mr Opdebeck on my
behalf if you are writing to him & say I have a lively remembrance which can
never be effaced of her great and uniform kindness from a very early date.

You have nothing to look back upon but a series of most kind acts done to
one who stood in need. There are few lives more suggestive in retrospect, more
charged with honour[?]. Do you not think she had acquired a great humility
that rare & precious gift.

I wonder how the poor man will now live out the residue of his days

Do not be hasty to blame the Duke. He made a considerable voluntary gift. If
there was an unfulfilled obligation it was more upon the part of the brother,
who is I should think as rich or richer.

I wonder whether the Russell marriage can have anything not agreeable to
the family. We have heard nothing of it through them, although I had a letter
from Lady R. not very long ago.

All blessings to you   WEG

[1] J. F. S. Russell, 2nd Earl Russell and brother of the philosopher.
[2] See 7 Oct. 89; Gladstone reviewed the book, see 4 Nov. 89.
[3] Death of Lady Susan Opdebeck, formerly Lady Lincoln.

Hawarden Castle.
12 December 1889.

Our poor friend then is laid peacefully to sleep. So passes beauty, glory, charm. None had more. There was a worm at the root. It is the same worm with us all. Peace be with her.

I wonder what will become of Mr O. It strikes me he may turn up as a petitioner. It was most kind and generous in you to offer to defray expence. It would have been wrong, even scandalous, had the offer been accepted.

Should you hear more about the Russell marriage I should so much like to know. I have not yet learned whether it has the full sanction of the mother & widow.

Unless I have blundered by omission you ought to have received a copy of the Memoirs of a Southern Planter, which pray read—I think it will interest you much. If you have not had one please send the accompanying note to Murrays, and they will send one by bearer.

All Christmas joy to you   WEG

St James Street.
22 March 1890.

In haste.

Many thanks for the inclosed.

Herbert[1] was a sincere and devout Christian and has gone to his rest—God grant it be deep and sweet. You were kind to him as to many. There is some melancholy in the retrospect of his later life: he was made perhaps to suffer more than to enjoy.

We are glad you are in the full enjoyment of this spring weather, and hope you have a good tenant in G.S.

Do you observe Gull's very large fortune—£34000 besides land. The Doctors are looking up.

Ever yours   WEG

Hawarden Castle.
16 November 1890.

Since you heard from me I have travelled much, talked much, and worked much, but I trust you have been well & are now in your warm winter quarters: How much I hope (forgive me) that they may not prove inconveniently expensive.

It is dreadful news which you will read in the papers tomorrow about Mr Parnell. He has undoubtedly great and rare gifts; & his country which I suppose will have to dispense with his services, will sadly miss him. How sad too it all is in itself, and how humbling.

[1] J. R. Herbert, the artist.

In a few days you will receive a copy of my papers on the Old Testament revised and enlarged in a small volume. I will not ask you to plough your way through them. But I will ask you to read another small volume which I am going to send you, the product of John Woolman the American Quaker.[1] It is a book of much interest in connection with the history of slavery, and is the exhibition of a life singularly pure, and near to God. It is good to look up to him.

Any word of Miss P., Mr V., or other friends, will be acceptable and I sincerely trust you can speak well of yourself.

Ever yours   WEG

Hawarden Castle.
3 January 1891.

Indeed I am very sorry for the delays caused by the weather. The boxes had to be sent over iced roads to the new building for the Library. Today I have got them unpacked and I now return the keys with thanks. On Monday or at furthest Tuesday we shall, I hope send them off by rail addressed to Woodbine Cottage. As they are what the Rail calls 'Empties', I am afraid to pay carriage beforehand as they might go astray.

Now I want you to do me a favour. Let me for once share in your ticket charities this year. I feel so sure you will not refuse that I inclose a cheque for the purpose.

I do not clearly gather your plan for the circular you kindly sent. I have no doubt you have considered the case of Naples & the Orient Steamers. If you care to inquire all information could be had at Cook's office in Piccadilly. I daresay your plan is a wise one for relief & change & I heartily hope that it will do you good, & that wheresoever you go blessing may attend you.

I find the burden of my work grow much with the years but how good is God to me when I think of my desserts.

All good be with you   WEG

Hotel Metropole, Brighton.
6 April 1891.

I saw Mr Trafford yesterday, & heard from him of your illness, and of your having recovered from near peril of death so far at least that you were to be in Paris today. There I hope this note will find you tomorrow morning: and if it please God that you continue to renewal I have no doubt that you will soon be back at your own house. There I hope shortly to find you.

The last eighteen months have been for me packed as it were with the deaths of friends; the last of them, Lord Granville, the most intimate of them all. His is a loss that can never be replaced. And it always seems to me, when persons

[1] See 26 Oct. 90.

sensibly younger than myself are taken away, as if my surviving them were a kind of fraud.

The prospect of relief from public business and its incessant contentions is as remote as ever. I know myself to be quite unworthy of that anticipation of the final peace which is offered by old age devoted to peaceful and congenial pursuits.

Lord Rosebery goes abroad again today. When I saw him he seemed well but he has suffered a greater blow than some would have supposed.

We have a serious anxiety in the rather mysterious illness of an old & dear friend though a young man, E. Hamilton for a good while my private secretary & now a distinguished public servant. He is confined to bed in this (admirable) Hotel, his recovery, though to be hoped, remote and not very certain. Ought we not all to long for the great Advent which is to clear away the clouds overhanging on all sides this strangely checquered [*sic*] world. What manner of persons, ought we all to be and when can there be enough of self-reproach.

I return to 18 Park Lane on Wednesday but do not take the trouble to write. I will send shortly to your housekeeper at Hampstead or to Miss Ponsonby for the last account of you.

May you remain in the Divine keeping. Always yours   WEG

18 Park Lane.
20 May 1891.

You have been very good in inviting me and if I have seemed slack it has not been from neglect. A fortnight ago I was musing on what day we could propose for luncheon—when on the 10th I was laid down with influenza and this is the first time I have got to my table for a portion of the day. Fever, thank God, is gone, cough & weakness remain: appetite which disappeared for a week slowly reviving. We hope to get away to Hawarden on Friday. Recovery in the eighties is not what it used to be in other days and I ought to be very thankful that the subtle disease has dealt leniently with me.

I am sorry to learn that you have been suffering too, of which I had not heard—I am glad to think that at your time of life convalescence & recovery ought to come more easily.

I think that in the House of Commons one fourth of the members in town have been laid prostrate.

It was most kind of you to send me E. Clinton's letter. I have read it with deep interest: the melancholy close to a melancholy chapter. E. Clinton was reared in the midst of beauty, rank, prosperity & splendour—& now for 40 years he has had poor Mr Opdebeck for a step-father! Certainly if we do not learn lessons it is not because the world is not full enough of them.

Sir A. Clark will not yet venture on making an estimate of the time when I may get back to work.

With warmest thanks & wishes.   Ever yours   WEG

Hawarden Castle.
13 July 1891.

We thank you much for your kind letter. Only indisposition prevented our coming to the Cottage before the time of trial arrived. But *ten* days ago, I had no idea that it was the will of God to take our dearly loved son[1] to Himself. And now he sleeps in the Hawarden Churchyard; and rests in the peace of God, to which we commend him until the last day comes. Looking back we recognise in him the features of the Lord he loved.

A funeral sermon was preached yesterday of which when printed I will send you a copy.

Would God that my account were clean as his. But there is a gospel even for me, the publican's gospel.

The Almighty has been indescribably good to us. Had he lived he must have lived in agony or mental decay which only his powerful constitution warded off so long.

In two or three days we shall probably return to Corton, Lowestoft, for my wife's health. To me all needful strength came back with the crisis.

I sincerely hope you have returned to good health—and that you continue to find the Cottage suit & soothe you.

If you see Miss or Mr Ponsonby, or Mr Villiers, pray remember me kindly to them.

Wishing you all blessings. Ever yours in truth   WEG

1 Carlton Gardens.
5 March 1892.

I was sadly vexed in Paris when Miss Ponsonby having made an appointment to come to our hotel was unable from some cause to keep it, and we thus missed hearing about you so that I do not know whether you are at home or have fulfilled your plan of going abroad.

If at home I hope to come and call on an early day next week.

Since coming back on Monday evening I have been in a whirlpool of business and have not at all escaped from it, and do not well know when I shall. Two months & a half of truancy heap up a great arrear.

I shall be so glad to hear that you are well.

We had an excellent time: excellent climate, mild weather, beautiful scenery & other objects, and interesting intercourse with French people more than I had ever had before.

I think it *most* probably that a general election will come upon us by the time we are two months older [rest of letter missing.]

[1] W. H. Gladstone.

Hatchlands, Guildford.
11 August 1892.

Your kind note reached me here yesterday evening.

You are outside the world? It is the night of the division—then follows Labour almost without bounds.

Be assured you will have something of me when I get out into anything like smooth water—when that will be, who can say?

All blessings be with you & with us all according to our needs   WEG

Hawarden Castle.
7 September 1892.

It is always interesting to hear of you: but voluntary writing, i.e. writing which does not grow out of business, has long been for me a growing difficulty, & is rapidly becoming an impossibility. It is hard for you, in very different circumstances to understand this.

So sorry you have been prevented from taking your trip, a change would I daresay be of great advantage to your health.

I do not remember whether you stand the sea well. If you do, it might be worth your while to consider, before the equinox, whether it might suit you to go to Naples in a steamer of the Orient Line (*first rate* service) and from thence by a short trajet to the Convent Hotel at Amalfi on the face of the rock, a delicious place, & as unlikely to invite Cholera as any in the world.

I will readily look into any book you recommend: but do not like giving you the trouble to send.

The fête here did wonders, organised by my son Herbert: 25000 people, 6000 went through the House to see portraits &c., £2000 taken, £1500 nett to pay the expence of an Institute for Hawarden.

All depended on the lottery of the weather. All good & all best wishes
WEG

Biarritz might be worth your thinking of—fine climate, glorious sea, no English at *this* season. Kindest remembrances to Miss P.

The Chalet, Hafod-y-Llan, Beddgelert, North Wales.
14 September 1892.

I have finished the 'Penitent Soul'[1]—shall I send it back to you?

It is not a commonplace book, and there is a great deal to say upon it: to say in a letter, or with the tongue when we meet. I will give you all my criticisms, if you will give me all yours.

It reads to me as if it were not absolute fiction but had grains, perhaps veins, of truth in it.

---

[1] See 11 Sept. 92.

It also seems to me to be written with pure and pious intention, and yet not to be of a tendency likely to strengthen belief. Some infirmity appears to lurk in the writer's hold on the elementary truths of religion: the great world with Christian tradition seems to be little or nothing to him.

The characters of Aunt Grace and Mary Fleming are done I think with more skill and truthfulness than that of the Penitent Soul himself.

Supposing it to be not simply a work of art but the transcript of a man, the history is a very curious one. He is better and worse than some other men: better inasmuch as he nowhere appears to have been a mere sensualist: worse from the lamentable lack of will and self-government in his last relapse when he has no tempter, indeed he never had—and becomes a tempter again himself. Fleming's character is hardly natural? He murders the *whole* of his *dramatis personae* except Alison and her husband!

I agree that he is laudable and skilful in suppressing what would be justly thought offensive. All good be yours.

I hope you are better   WEG

My address is Barmouth until 19th from London: afterwards Hawarden.

10 Downing Street.
20 February 1893.

The Kinnairds invited us to their house and I was so sorry that the fates were against our going: the fates in a shape in which we may all believe in them, the shape of a prior invitation. I believe they are excellent people.

We would certainly come to luncheon or tea when time permits: but it is at present most difficult, indeed I have not been out to luncheon this year. What my wife & I should most like is that you should interpose the barrier of absence for a time; inasmuch as I have knowledge enough of cold & coughs to be aware that in a case like yours prudence and high duty impose upon you the obligation to take some decided measure of relief, or change so as to prevent the evil from becoming *Chronic* and immovable. To be a little better in this mild weather is so far well but ought not to satisfy you.

I hear other excellent accounts of Irving in Becket. All good words and wishes: and pray take to heart my medical advice. Yours ever   WEG

10 Downing Street.
26 February 1893.

How kind of you to send me in your P.S. a gratifying report: perhaps over-coloured by good nature in the channels of conveyance

I thought I had given you my explanation as to your MS.[1] Viewing my years I think it is evidently better lodged with you than with me.

All blessings   WEG

---

[1] Mrs. Thistlethwayte's MS autobiography, read by Gladstone in the early 1870s and now returned to her.

10 Downing Street.
14 November 1893.

Conditions have combined with labours to delay our making any visit to you after your recovery (as I hope) from that grave illness.

Would it be agreeable to you to receive us at luncheon Thursday the 16th *at two*? which we could manage? All blessings   WEG[1]

---

[1] This is Gladstone's last extant letter to Laura Thistlethwayte; she died on 30 May 1894, just after Gladstone's journal ceased to be written regularly, so there is no notice of her death. Her will, dated 29 July 1892, named Lord Edward Clinton (son of her friend the Duke of Newcastle), Charles Innes of Inverness and G. E. Lake of Lincoln's Inn as her executors, Lake being struck out by codicil on 13 March 1893. She left Woodbine Cottage in Hampstead to be a mini-St. Deiniol's: it was to be a 'Retreat for Clergymen of all denominations, true believers in my God and Saviour, and literary men'.

WHERE WAS HE?
1887–1891

The following list shows where the diarist was each night; he continued at each place named until he moved on to the next. Names of the owners of great houses have been given in brackets on the first mention of the house.

1 January 1887	Hawarden	25 October	Studley Royal, Ripon (Lord Ripon)
25 January	London		
29 January	Sandringham House (Prince of Wales)	28 October	Hawarden
		10 November	London
31 January	Cambridge	11 November	Hawarden
2 February	Hawarden	26 December	Bettishanger, Kent (Lord Northbourne)
19 February	Penmaenmawr		
21 February	London	28 December	Hotel Bristol, Paris
5 March	Dollis Hill (Lord Aberdeen)	29 December	On train
		31 December	Florence
9 March	Windsor		
10 March	Dollis Hill	4 February 1888	Cannes
14 March	London	7 February	On train
16 March	Dollis Hill	8 February	London
13 April	London	18 February	The Durdans, Epsom (Lord Rosebery)
14 April	Dollis Hill		
6 May	London	20 February	London
7 May	Dollis Hill	24 February	The Durdans, Epsom
21 May	London	27 February	London
23 May	Dollis Hill	27 March	Dollis Hill
26 May	Hawarden	31 March	Aston Clinton (Lord Rothschild)
2 June	Swansea		
7 June	London	4 April	Keble College, Oxford
8 June	Dollis Hill	9 April	London
9 June	London	5 May	Dollis Hill
10 June	Dollis Hill	8 May	London
20 June	London	12 May	Dollis Hill
21 June	Dollis Hill	14 May	London
6 August	Hawarden	18 May	Hawarden
11 August	Royal Hotel, Hoylake	4 June	London
13 August	Hawarden	16 June	Dollis Hill
24 August	London	18 June	London
27 August	Hawarden	7 July	Dollis Hill
12 September	London	9 July	London
13 September	Hawarden	14 July	The Coppice, Henley (Lady Phillimore)
17 October	Manchester		
18 October	Nottingham	16 July	London
20 October	Sudbury Hall, Derbyshire (Lord Vernon)	28 July	Holmbury (E.F. Leveson-Gower)

30 July	London
3 August	Berkhampstead House (Lady Sarah Spencer)
4 August	Mentmore Towers (Lord Rosebery)
6 August	Hawarden
8 November	Wodehouse, Wombourne (P. J. Stanhope)
10 November	Keble College, Oxford
13 November	Hawarden
3 December	London
5 December	Hawarden
14 December	London
19 December	On train
20 December	Lucerne
21 December	On train
22 December	Naples
9 February 1889	Amalfi
14 February	On train
15 February	Cannes
19 February	On train
20 February	London
22 February	Dollis Hill
24 February	On train
25 February	Fasque
27 February	On train
28 February	London
13 April	Hawarden
1 May	London
18 May	Dollis Hill
20 May	London
1 June	Combe Wood, Kingston (Lord Wolverton)
3 June	London
5 June	Malwood, Lyndhurst (Sir W. Harcourt)
7 June	On board 'The Garland' (Mrs. Eliot Yorke)
12 June	Lanhydrock House, Bodmin (Lord Robartes)
13 June	Tintagel (Lord Hayter)
14 June	On board 'The Garland'
15 June	Iwerne Minster (Sir A. V. Hayter)
17 June	London
22 June	Dollis Hill
24 June	London
29 June	Pembroke Lodge (Lady Russell)

1 July	London
6 July	The Durdans, Epsom
8 July	London
20 July	Dollis Hill
22 July	London
27 July	Highcliffe Castle
29 July	London
3 August	Hawarden
2 September	London
3 September	Paris
9 September	London
10 September	Hawarden
22 October	Ince Blundell, Lancashire (C. J. Weld-Blundell)
25 October	Hawarden
26 October	Ford Bank, Didsbury (T. Ashton)
4 December	Hawarden
29 January 1890	London
31 January	All Souls College, Oxford
8 February	London
5 April	St. George's Hill, Weybridge (F. Egerton)
8 April	Aston Clinton (Rothschild)
15 April	London
19 April	The Durdans, Epsom
21 April	London
10 May	Dollis Hill
12 May	London
16 May	Stoke Holy Cross, Norfolk
17 May	Corton, Norfolk (J. Colman)
20 May	Hawarden
4 June	London
27 June	Dollis Hill
28 June	London
25 July	Colwood Park, Sussex (C. Bowen)
28 July	London
6 August	Hawarden
18 October	Courthey
20 October	Edinburgh
25 October	Beeslack, Penicuik (J. Cowan)
27 October	Edinburgh
29 October	Fasque

1 November	The Glen, Innerleithen (Sir C. Tennant)	22 May	Hawarden
		6 June	Holmbury
6 November	Hawarden	8 June	Hatchlands
24 November	London	9 June	London
11 December	Hawarden	20 June	Dollis Hill
		26 June	The Clyffe, Corton, Lowestoft
26 January 1891	London	4 July	London
31 January	Dollis Hill	7 July	Hawarden
2 February	London	16 July	The Clyffe, Corton, Lowestoft
7 February	Dollis Hill		
9 February	London	28 July	London
11 February	Dollis Hill	31 July	Hawarden
28 February	Tring Park	25 September	Fasque
2 March	Dollis Hill	1 October	Newcastle
3 March	London	3 October	Hawarden
6 March	Dollis Hill	5 December	Courthey, Liverpool
10 March	London	7 December	Althorp Park, Northamptonshire
14 March	Eton College		
16 March	London	9 December	Mentmore Towers
25 March	Hastings	11 December	London
4 April	Brighton	15 December	On train
9 April	London	16 December	Biarritz